ASP.NET

IN A NUTSHELL

Other Microsoft .NET resources from O'Reilly

Related titles	Programming C# C# in a Nutshell Programming Visual Basic .NET Programming ASP.NET ADO.NET in a Nutshell	.NET Windows Forms in a Nutshell .NET Framework Essentials Mastering Visual Studio .NET

.NET Books Resource Center *dotnet.oreilly.com* is a complete catalog of O'Reilly's books on .NET and related technologies, including sample chapters and code examples.

ONDotnet.com provides independent coverage of fundamental, interoperable, and emerging Microsoft .NET programming and web services technologies.

Conferences O'Reilly & Associates brings diverse innovators together to nurture the ideas that spark revolutionary industries. We specialize in documenting the latest tools and systems, translating the innovator's knowledge into useful skills for those in the trenches. Visit *conferences.oreilly.com* for our upcoming events.

Safari Bookshelf (*safari.oreilly.com*) is the premier online reference library for programmers and IT professionals. Conduct searches across more than 1,000 books. Subscribers can zero in on answers to time-critical questions in a matter of seconds. Read the books on your Bookshelf from cover to cover or simply flip to the page you need. Try it today with a free trial.

ASP.NET

IN A NUTSHELL

Second Edition

G. Andrew Duthie and Matthew MacDonald

O'REILLY®

Beijing • Cambridge • Farnham • Köln • Paris • Sebastopol • Taipei • Tokyo

ASP.NET in a Nutshell, Second Edition

by G. Andrew Duthie and Matthew MacDonald

Published by O'Reilly Media, Inc., 1005 Gravenstein Highway North, Sebastopol, CA 95472.

O'Reilly Media, Inc. books may be purchased for educational, business, or sales promotional use. Online editions are also available for most titles (*safari.oreilly.com*). For more information, contact our corporate/institutional sales department: 800-998-9938 or *corporate@oreilly.com*.

Editor:	Tatiana Apandi Diaz
Production Editor:	Jane Ellin
Cover Designer:	Emma Colby
Interior Designer:	David Futato

Printing History:

June 2002:	First Edition.
August 2003:	Second Edition.

 This book uses RepKover™, a durable and flexible lay-flat binding.

ISBN: 0-596-00520-2

[M]   [9/04]

Table of Contents

Part II. Intrinsic Class Reference

Part III. Namespace Reference

Preface

ASP.NET is the web development technology of Microsoft's .NET development platform. While it has a lot in common with its predecessor, Active Server Pages, ASP.NET is a quantum leap over classic ASP; it adds such new features as rich server controls, a much more powerful programming model, and built-in support for XML web services.

ASP.NET also allows you to access the full richness of the .NET Framework Class Library, which provides classes for everything from sending mail via SMTP to performing multithreaded operations. ASP.NET also brings object-oriented programming to the Web. Object orientation is at the very heart of the .NET Framework, and ASP.NET takes full advantage of it—particularly in the area of its robust server control model.

This second edition of *ASP.NET in a Nutshell* also includes information about new features and settings introduced in Version 1.1 of the .NET Framework.

ASP.NET has many new features and aspects, but with the help of this reference, you'll be up and running before you know it.

Who Is This Book for?

This book is intended primarily as a reference and learning tool for developers who have experience in web development. Both professional and amateur developers will find this book helpful in making the transition from classic ASP (or other web development technologies) to ASP.NET.

This book is not intended for beginners or those with no experience with web development. While the tutorial section that begins the book is intended to bring you up to speed on ASP.NET quickly, it does not teach basic web development skills. Beginners or those with no experience with classic ASP would do well to find a good introductory web development book and then return to this book once they understand the fundamentals of web development.

How to Use This Book

This book consists of an introductory tutorial section, two reference sections, and an appendix. If you're new to ASP.NET, you may want to read through the entire tutorial section from start to finish. This will give you a good exposure to all of the features of ASP.NET as well as experience writing ASP.NET code.

Once you've become comfortable with the concepts introduced in the tutorial section, the remaining reference sections will help you work through everyday ASP.NET development tasks.

How This Book Is Structured

ASP.NET in a Nutshell, Second Edition, consists of four parts. Part I, *Introduction to ASP.NET*, provides an introductory tutorial to ASP.NET consisting of the following 11 chapters:

Introduction
Provides an overview of the .NET Framework and the features of ASP.NET.

ASP.NET Applications
Describes the types of applications that can be written with ASP.NET and discusses the file types used by ASP.NET and the structure of an ASP.NET application.

Web Forms
Describes the structure of ASP.NET Web Forms, including page directives, coding styles, event handling, and page output caching.

Web Services
Describes the web services architecture provided by ASP.NET and shows how to create and consume web services in ASP.NET. It also shows how to publish and locate web services.

ASP.NET Server Controls
Describes the HTML controls and web controls built into ASP.NET and shows how to use them in your ASP.NET pages.

User Controls and Custom Server Controls
Describes two of the reuse techniques available in ASP.NET—user controls and custom server controls—and shows when and how to take advantage of each to enable code reuse in your applications.

Data Access and Data Binding
Describes ADO.NET, the new technology for data access in the .NET Framework, and shows you how to use ADO.NET and the new data binding framework of ASP.NET to quickly build robust data-driven pages.

ASP.NET Configuration
Describes the new configuration system in ASP.NET and shows you how to configure your application for several common scenarios.

ASP.NET Security
Describes the new authentication and authorization features in ASP.NET and shows you how to take advantage of them in your applications.

Error Handling, Debugging, and Tracing
Describes the new structured exception handling features of the Visual Basic .NET language and the tracing feature of ASP.NET. It also shows you how to use these new features, along with the .NET Framework SDK Debugger and/ or Visual Studio .NET, to troubleshoot and debug your applications.

ASP.NET Deployment
Describes the options available for deploying ASP.NET applications and shows you how to take advantage of them.

Like classic ASP, ASP.NET exposes a number of intrinsic objects to every page. These objects provide information on requests, allow sending of or manipulation of responses, and provide useful utility functions. Part II, *Intrinsic Class Reference*, documents each of the classes that provide the functionality for the Application, Context, Request, Response, Server, and Session intrinsics, as well as for the HttpException class and the Page class, which forms the basis for each ASP.NET page. Part II also includes a reference of the most common elements of the *web.config* configuration file.

The first reference section provides detailed information on the classes that replace classic ASP intrinsic objects, on the Page class, and on the elements found in the *web.config* file. Each chapter is divided into the following sections to help you locate the information you're looking for quickly:

Introduction
This section introduces the class and describes its purpose and common uses.

Summary
This section lists the most commonly used properties, methods, collections, and events of the class. Members that are inherited from a base class or not typically used may be omitted.

Comments/Troubleshooting
This section provides information about gotchas to watch out for when using the class, as well as other important things to be aware of.

Properties
This section describes the properties for the class and provides examples of their use.

Collections
This section describes the collections for the class and provides examples of their use.

Methods
This section describes the methods for the class and provides examples of their use.

Events
This section describes the events for the class, and provides examples of their use. Note that not all classes expose events, so not every chapter will have an "Events" section.

Because ASP.NET is considerably broader in the scope of its APIs than classic ASP, Part III, *Namespace Reference*, provides a high-level reference of the namespaces that are most relevant to ASP.NET development. These namespaces include:

System.Web
System.Web.Caching
System.Web.Configuration
System.Web.Hosting
System.Web.Mail
System.Web.Mobile
System.Web.Security
System.Web.Services
System.Web.Services.Configuration
System.Web.Services.Description
System.Web.Services.Discovery
System.Web.Services.Protocols
System.Web.SessionState
System.Web.UI
System.Web.UI.Design
System.Web.UI.Design.WebControls
System.Web.UI.HtmlControls
System.Web.Mobile.UI.MobileControls
System.Web.Mobile.UI.MobileControls.Adapters
System.Web.UI.WebControls

The chapter covering each namespace describes each of the types contained in the namespace, and lists all members of each type.

Finally, the book includes one appendix, *Type, Method, Property, and Field Index*, which contains an alphabetical listing of the types and members found in Part III. You can use it to determine the namespace to which a particular type or member in which you're interested belongs.

Conventions Used in This Book

The following font conventions are used in this book:

Italic

Used for pathnames, filenames, program names, Internet addresses such as domain names and URLs, and new terms where they are defined.

Constant Width

Used for command lines and options that should be typed verbatim, and names and keywords in program examples. Also used for parameters, attributes, configuration file elements, expressions, statements, and values.

Constant-Width Italic

Used for replaceable terms, such as variables or optional elements, within syntax lines.

How to Contact Us

Please address comments and questions concerning this book to the publisher:

O'Reilly & Associates, Inc.
1005 Gravenstein Highway North
Sebastopol, CA 95472
(800) 998-9938 (in the United States or Canada)
(707) 829-0515 (international/local)
(707) 829-0104 (fax)

To comment or ask technical questions about this book, send email to:

bookquestions@oreilly.com

There is a web site for this book, which lists errata, examples, or any additional information. You can access this page at:

http://www.oreilly.com/catalog/aspdotnetnut2

For more information about our books, conferences, resource centers, and the O'Reilly Network, see the O'Reilly web site at:

http://www.oreilly.com

Acknowledgments

I'd like to start by thanking my editor Ron Petrusha for his patience, skills, and technical savvy. It is a pleasure working with an editor who is not only good with words, but sharp with technology. Thanks also to Val Quercia for helping me to sound good and make sense, and to Daniel Creeron, for making sure the book was technically sound. My thanks also to Tatiana Diaz, John Osborn, Phil Winstanley, and Joseph Croney for their work on the second edition of this book.

Thanks to both Doug Reilly and Raja Mani for their contributions to the book. I truly appreciate your efforts. Thanks also to Matthew MacDonald, for his work on the namespace reference, which will hopefully make my work that much more comprehensible.

A big thank you to the ASP.NET team at Microsoft, without whose efforts we would not have this fabulous new technology, and without whose willingness to explain and answer questions, this book would not be nearly as useful. Rob Howard, Susan Warren, and Erik Olson in particular have provided me with much insight and information into how ASP.NET works. I thank you all.

Thanks to Stacey Giard and all the folks at Microsoft who make sure that authors get both the information and the software necessary to do their jobs. It might be possible without their efforts, but it would sure be a lot harder.

Thanks to my mom, for believing in me, encouraging me, and listening to me kvetch when I'm close to a deadline.

As always, I'd like to thank my wife, Jennifer, whose cheerful support and tolerance for late nights and long weekends made it possible to finish this book, and whose love makes it all worthwhile.

And finally, I want to dedicate this book to my new son, Joseph Andrew Duthie, who was born during the writing of the second edition. He is a joy and an inspiration, and Jennifer and I are delighted that he has come into our life.

Introduction to ASP.NET

This part is an introduction to ASP.NET, Microsoft's next-generation technology for developing server-side web applications and web services that work with Internet Information Server. Part I consists of the following chapters:

Introduction

ASP.NET is Microsoft's latest technology for building web-based applications and services, a successor to Active Server Pages (ASP) that draws on the power of the .NET Framework development platform and the Visual Studio .NET developer toolset. To better understand ASP.NET, it is important to understand some key concepts of the .NET development platform. It is also helpful to grasp object-oriented development (OOD), which is at the very heart of the .NET Framework that provides the foundation for ASP.NET development. In this chapter, we'll review these concepts, look at what's new in ASP.NET (versus classic ASP), review new features in ASP.NET 1.1, and discuss choosing a language to suit your needs.

.NET Platform Fundamentals

At the core of Microsoft's .NET platform initiative is a new set of technologies known collectively as the *.NET Framework*, which we'll refer to commonly as the Framework. The Framework provides a platform for simplified rapid development of both web-based and Windows-based applications. The Framework has two primary components, the *Common Language Runtime* (CLR) and the *Framework Class Library* (FCL).

As with many new technologies, there are a host of new terms and acronyms to understand, so we'll introduce and explain the most important ones in the Framework over the next several sections.

The Common Language Runtime (CLR)

The CLR is the execution environment for code written for the .NET Framework. The CLR manages the execution of .NET code, including memory allocation and garbage collection (which helps avoid memory leaks), security (including applying differing trust levels to code from different sources), thread management, enforcing type-safety, and many other tasks.

The CLR works with every language available for the .NET Framework, so there is no need to have a separate runtime for each language. Code developed in a .NET language is compiled by the individual language compiler (such as the Visual Basic .NET compiler) into an intermediate format called (appropriately enough) Intermediate Language (IL). At runtime, this IL code generated by the compiler is just-in-time (JIT) compiled by the CLR into native code for the processor type the CLR is running on. This compilation provides the flexibility of being able to develop with multiple languages and target multiple processor types while still retaining the performance of native code at execution time.

 While there is some up-front cost on first execution to the JIT compilation model, the Framework also offers the ability to pregenerate native code at install time through a utility called *NGen.exe*. This utility eliminates the startup cost of JIT compiling the code, at the expense of some of the optimizations that are available with JIT compiling.

The .NET Framework Class Library (FCL)

The FCL is a set of reusable object-oriented classes that provide basic platform functionality, from the data access classes of ADO.NET, to filesystem utility classes (including file, directory, and stream classes), to networking classes that allow easy implementation of DNS resolution, WHOIS lookups, and other network-related functionality. Developers can use the base classes directly or derive from these classes to provide customized functionality.

The FCL also contains all classes that make up ASP.NET. These include classes that implement all of the functionality of the ASP intrinsic objects, as well as classes that provide additional functionality, from a rich engine for caching output and data to the ASP.NET Server Control model. This functionality brings to ASP.NET the simplicity of control-based development that has long been available to Visual Basic developers.

In addition to classes that support Web application development, the FCL provides classes for developing console applications, Windows applications, and Windows NT or Windows 2000 Services.

The Common Type System (CTS)

The CTS describes the set of types that are supported by the CLR. This includes both value types, which include primitive data types such as Byte, Int16, Double, and Boolean, and reference types, which include arrays, classes, and the Object and String types.

Value types are types that store their values directly in memory and are accessed directly by name, as shown in the following code fragment:

```
'VB.NET
Dim myFloat As Single
```

```
myFloat = 3.1415

// C#
float myFloat;
myFloat = 3.1415;
```

In addition to these built-in data types, value types also include user-defined value types (types derived from the System.ValueType class) as well as enumerations.

Reference types are types that store a reference to the location of their values, rather than storing the value directly. Frequently, the value is stored as part of a defined class and is referenced through a class member on an instance of the class, as shown here:

```
'VB.NET
'Define class
Class myFloatClass
    Public myFloat As Single
End Class

'Create class instance and assign value
Dim myInstance As New myFloatClass()
myInstance.myFloat = 3.1415

// C#
// Define class
class myFloatClass
{
    float myFloat;
}

// Create class instance and assign value
myFloatClass myInstance = new myFloatClass();
myFloatClass.myFloat = 3.1415;
```

Individual language compilers may implement types using their own terminology. For example, while the .NET representation of a 32-bit integer is referred to as *Int32*, in Visual Basic .NET it is referred to as *Integer* and in C# as *int*. Internally, however, both Visual Basic's Integer and C#'s int are implemented as the .NET Int32 type.

Boxing and unboxing

Converting to and from value and reference types is accomplished through a process called boxing and unboxing. *Boxing* refers to the implicit conversion of a value type, such as a C# int, to a reference type (usually *Object*). For this conversion to take place, an instance of type Object is created and the value type's value and type is copied into it—in this case, int. *Unboxing* refers to the explicit conversion of an Object type into a specific value type. The code example shown here demonstrates boxing and unboxing:

```
// C#
int myInt = 123; // declare an int and set its value to 123
object myObject = myInt; // value of myInt is boxed into myObject
int myOtherInt = (int)myObject; // unbox myObject into myOtherInt
```

The Common Language Infrastructure (CLI)

The CLI is a subset of the .NET Framework that has been submitted for standardization through the ECMA standards body. The CLI includes the functionality of the Common Language Runtime, as well as specifications for the Common Type System, type safety rules, Metadata, and Intermediate Language. It also includes a subset of the Framework Class Library that includes a Base Class Library (for built-in types and basic runtime functionality), a Network Library (for simple networking services and access to network ports), a Reflection Library (for examining types and retrieving information about types at runtime), an XML Library (for parsing XML), and Floating Point and Extended Array Libraries.

Microsoft has also committed to providing what they refer to as a "shared-source" implementation of the CLI, which will be available for both the FreeBSD and Windows operating systems. You can find out more about the shared-source CLI implementation at *http://msdn.microsoft.com/library/en-us/dndotnet/html/mssharsourcecli2.asp*.

There is also a group working on an open source implementation of the CLI, based on the ECMA specifications, called Mono. You can find out more about Mono at *http://www.go-mono.org/*.

Information on the ECMA standardization process, including documentation of the proposed standards, is available at *http://msdn.microsoft.com/net/ecma/*.

The Common Language Specification (CLS)

The CLS is a subset of the types supported by the CLR, as well as a set of rules that language and compiler designers must follow. The purpose of the CLS is to provide robust interoperability between .NET languages, including the ability to inherit classes written in one .NET language in any other .NET language and cross-language debugging.

The rules defined by the CLS apply only to publicly exposed features of a class. For example, the internal implementation of a class can use non-CLS–compliant types (such as the unsigned integer types), but as long as only CLS-compliant members are exposed publicly, the class can still take full advantage of the interoperability features enabled by the CLS.

Classes

While not a term specific to the .NET platform, the term *class* may be new to many ASP developers. A class is essentially the blueprint for an object. It contains the definition for how a particular object will be instantiated at runtime, such as the properties and methods that will be exposed publicly by the object and any internal storage structures.

Developers work with classes by creating instances of the class at runtime using the new keyword, as shown here:

```
// Instantiate the .NET StreamReader class in C#
System.IO.StreamReader sr;
sr = new System.IO.StreamReader("C:\\Test.txt");
```

```
string Line;

while(sr.Peek( ) != -1)
{
    Line = sr.ReadLine( );
    Response.Write(Server.HtmlEncode(Line) + "<br/>");
}
```

We preface the name of the class, StreamReader, with its namespace name, System.IO, to prevent naming collisions with other classes in different assemblies that might have the same name and to ensure that we get the StreamReader class we expect. We'll discuss namespaces and assemblies later in this section.

 In C#, the lowercase new keyword is used to instantiate classes. In Visual Basic .NET, the New keyword is uppercase, but since the Visual Basic language is not case-sensitive, this is a standard practice, rather than a requirement enforced by the compiler. C#, on the other hand, is case-sensitive, so keep this in mind when switching between C# and VB.NET.

Namespaces

Namespaces, a key part of the .NET Framework, provide scope to both preinstalled framework classes and custom-developed classes. Namespaces are declared for a given set of classes (types) by enclosing those classes in one of the following declarations:

```
// C#
namespace myNamespace
{
    class myClass
    {
        // class implementation code
    }
}

' VB.NET
Namespace myNamespace
    Class myCls
        ' class implementation code
    End Class
End Namespace
```

Namespaces may also be nested, as shown here:

```
' VB.NET
Namespace myFirstNamespace
    Public Class myCls
        ' class implementation code
    End Class
    Namespace mySecondNamespace
        Public Class myCls
            ' class implementation code
        End Class
```

```
    Public Class myCls2
        ' class implementation code
    End Class
  End Namespace
End Namespace
```

This code is perfectly valid because we've declared the second myCls in the nested namespace mySecondNamespace. If we tried to declare two identically named classes within the same namespace, we would get a compiler error informing us that there was a naming conflict, because each class name must be unique within its namespace. To use the classes we just declared, we can do something like the following:

```
' VB.NET
Imports System
Imports myFirstNamespace
Imports myFirstNamespace.mySecondNamespace

Module namespaces_client_vb

    Sub Main( )
        Dim newClass As New myFirstNamespace.myCls
        Dim newClass2 As New myCls2
        Console.WriteLine("Object creation succeeded!")
    End Sub

End Module
```

We use the Imports keyword in Visual Basic .NET to enable the use of member names from these namespaces without explicitly using the namespace name. However, because we used the class name myCls in both the myFirstNamespace and mySecondNamespace namespaces, we need to use the fully qualified name for this class, while we are able to instantiate myCls2 with only the class name. We can just as easily use these classes from C#, as shown here:

```
using System;
using myFirstNamespace;
using myFirstNamespace.mySecondNamespace;

class namespaces_client
{
    public static void Main( )
    {
        myFirstNamespace.myCls newClass = new myFirstNamespace.myCls( );
        myCls2 newClass2 = new myCls2( );
        Console.WriteLine("Object creation succeeded!");
    }
}
```

C# uses the using keyword for importing namespaces. Notice that in both cases, in addition to importing the namespaces we defined, we've also imported the System namespace. This is what allows us to use the Console class defined in the System namespace to write to a console window without referring explicitly to System.Console.

Classes that are part of the .NET Framework are organized by functionality into namespaces that make them easier to locate and use. All classes that are a part of the .NET Framework begin with either "System" or "Microsoft." Examples include:

System
> Contains all the .NET primitive data types as well as utility classes such as Console and Math that are apt to be widely used in .NET applications.

System.Collections
> Contains classes used to implement various kinds of collections in .NET, including ArrayList, Dictionary, and Hashtable.

System.Data
> Contains classes used to access and manipulate data, as well as child namespaces such as System.Data.SqlClient, which contain data access classes specific to a particular data provider.

System.Web
> Contains classes used to process web requests, as well as child namespaces such as System.Web.UI, which contains such classes as the Page class, the basis for all ASP.NET pages.

Assemblies

Also known as Managed DLLs, *assemblies* are the fundamental unit of deployment for the .NET platform. The .NET Framework itself is made up of a number of assemblies, including *mscorlib.dll*, among others. The assembly boundary is also where versioning and security are applied.

An assembly contains Intermediate Language generated by a specific language compiler, an assembly manifest (containing information about the assembly), type metadata, and resources. We'll discuss IL, manifests, and metadata later in this section.

Assemblies can be either private, residing in the directory of the client application from which they are used (or, in the case of ASP.NET, in the / bin subdirectory of the Web application), or shared. Shared assemblies are stored in a common location called the *Global Assembly Cache* (GAC). Assemblies that are to be installed in the GAC must be strongly named, which means that they must have a cryptographic key associated with them. Strong naming can be accomplished either through Visual Studio .NET, or you can use the *sn.exe* tool supplied with the .NET Framework SDK to generate a key pair for signing the assembly, and then use the *al.exe* tool to create the signed assembly based on the generated key. We'll demonstrate creating and sharing strongly named assemblies in Chapter 6.

Assemblies are self-describing, thanks to the manifest contained within them. One advantage of their self-describing nature is that it makes it possible for different versions of the same assembly to be run side by side. Clients can then specify the version of the assembly that they require, and the CLR will make sure that the correct version of the assembly is loaded for that client at runtime.

Intermediate Language (IL)

IL, also known as MSIL (for Microsoft Intermediate Language), is a processor-independent representation of executable code. IL is similar in some ways to assembly code, but it is not specific to a particular CPU; rather, it is specific to the CLR. IL is generated by each of the language compilers that target the CLR. As mentioned above, .NET assemblies contain IL that is to be executed by the CLR.

At runtime, the CLR just-in-time (JIT) compiles the IL to native code, which is then executed. There is also a tool called *ngen.exe*, which is supplied with the .NET Framework SDK and allows you to precompile assemblies to native code at install time and cache the precompiled code to disk. However, while precompiling an assembly to native code will improve the startup time of an assembly, the JIT process used by the CLR performs optimizations that may allow JITed code to perform better than precompiled code, the difference in performance will depend on the code being executed, and how subject to these optimizations it is.

Managed Execution

Managed execution refers to code whose execution is managed by the CLR. This execution includes memory management, access security, cross-language integration for debugging and/or exception handling, and many other features. Managed assemblies are required to supply metadata that describes the types and members of the code contained within the assembly. This information allows the CLR to manage the execution of the code.

 Note that not all languages in Visual Studio .NET are managed. While Visual C++ offers what are called the "Managed Extensions for Visual C++," it is still possible to write unmanaged code in Visual C++.

Manifests, Metadata, and Attributes

Metadata and manifests are key pieces of the managed execution world. *Manifests* are the portion of an assembly that contains descriptive information about the types contained in the assembly, the members exposed by the assembly, and the resources required by the assembly. The manifest contains *metadata*, which, simply put, is data that describes the assembly. Some metadata is generated by the language compiler at compile time. The developer may add other metadata at design time through the use of attributes. *Attributes* are declarations added to code that describe some aspect of the code or modify the code's behavior at runtime.

Attributes are stored with an assembly as metadata and are used for many purposes in the .NET Framework—from the <webMethod( )> attribute used to turn a normal method into a web service to attributes used to define how custom controls interact with the Visual Studio .NET environment.

Object Orientation in the .NET Platform

The .NET Framework was built to be object oriented from the ground up. What does this mean? For those of you who are unfamiliar with object-oriented programming, here's a quick review.

We've already discussed classes. Classes are the blueprints or templates from which objects are created. Objects, the heart of object-oriented programming, are usable instances of a class. Objects expose properties, which contain data related to or about the object, and/or methods, which allow actions to be performed on the object.

In object-oriented programming, objects need to support three important qualities: encapsulation, inheritance, and polymorphism.

Encapsulation refers to the ability of an object to hide its internal data from outside view and allow access to only that data through publicly available methods. This helps prevent clients from accidentally or purposefully leaving object data in a corrupt state and makes it easier for the developer of the class on which the object is based to change the internal implementation of these data members without breaking its clients.

Inheritance refers to the ability to derive one class from another. This allows developers to create a new class based on an existing class. The new class inherits all methods and properties of the existing class. The developer can then add new methods or properties or override existing methods. Inheritance allows you to develop specialized versions of objects that are customized to meet your precise needs. We'll discuss this type of scenario more in Chapter 6.

 The .NET Framework offers only single inheritance—that is, a class may only derive from a single base class. This is different from languages such as C++, which allow classes to be derived from multiple base classes.

Polymorphism refers to the ability of multiple classes derived from the same base class to expose methods with the same name—all of which clients can call in exactly the same way, regardless of the underlying implementation. Thus, a Car class could expose a Start method and a derived class SportsCar could override that Start method to provide a different implementation. From the client's perspective, however, both methods are used the same way.

This is a very high-level overview of object-oriented programming. While we'll discuss object-oriented techniques in more depth throughout the book, if you are unfamiliar with the topic you may want to pick up a book that specifically addresses object-oriented programming.

Why Is It Important? Rapid Development and Reuse!

What's important about the object-oriented nature of the .NET platform is that it allows much faster development than did previous generations of Windows development technologies and offers much greater opportunities for reuse.

Because the functionality of the .NET Framework is exposed as a set of object-oriented classes rather than a set of obscure and finicky API calls, many operations that were difficult or downright impossible in classic ASP are simple in ASP.NET. For example, about ten lines of code can perform a DNS lookup on a domain name using the classes in the System.Net and System.Net.Sockets namespaces. This task wasn't even possible in classic ASP, without the use of external components.

What's more, because many classes in the .NET framework can be used as base classes, it is easy to reuse them in your own applications by deriving from a class to provide common functionality and then extending the derived class to add functionality specific to your application. In fact, much of the .NET Framework is built this way. For example, all classes that make up the ASP.NET Server Controls are ultimately derived from the Control class of the System.Web.UI namespace, which provides properties and methods common to all server controls.

OO Is at the Heart of Every ASP.NET Page

One of the coolest things about object orientation in ASP.NET is that you don't have to know much about how to use it since most of it is under the covers for basic page development. Every ASP.NET page implicitly inherits from the Page class of the System.Web.UI namespace, which provides access to all ASP.NET implementations of the intrinsic objects that were introduced in classic ASP, such as Request, Response, Session, and Application, and to a number of new properties and methods. One advantage of this is that each page is compiled into an assembly based on the Page class, providing substantial performance improvements over classic ASP, in which code was interpreted at runtime.

Object orientation is also the key to another important new feature of ASP.NET: code-behind. *Code-behind* allows developers to separate executable code from the HTML markup that makes up the user interface. Executable code is placed in a module called a code-behind file, which is associated with the ASP.NET page via an attribute in the page. The code-behind file contains a class that inherits from the Page class. The ASP.NET page then inherits from the code-behind class, and at runtime, the two are compiled into a single executable assembly. This compilation allows a combination of easy separation of UI and executable code at design time with high performance at runtime.

Choosing a Language

Choosing which language to use when developing ASP.NET applications is both easier and harder than choosing a language for classic ASP development. It is harder because it may be intimidating for some to choose between a substantially revised Visual Basic and a completely new language, C#. It is easier because the choice of language no longer requires giving up substantial amounts of functionality for your preferred language.

As in many other cases, including language choice in classic ASP, a lot of the decision is determined by where you're coming from. If you're:

An experienced ASP developer who has used VBScript
You'll probably prefer Visual Basic.NET.

An experienced ASP developer who's used JScript
You'll want to look at C# or JScript.NET (keeping in mind that finding code examples in C# is easier, since the novelty of the language makes it more interesting for many).

An experienced Visual Basic developer
Visual Basic.NET is the obvious choice, but you may also find it worthwhile to check out C#, which offers a lot of the power of C++ without such a steep learning curve.

An experienced C, C++, or Java developer
You'll probably feel right at home with C#, which, as a C-derived language, shares a lot of syntax with these languages.

New to ASP.NET development, with no prior ASP experience
Visual Basic.NET will probably be easiest to learn, although C# runs a close second.

Because of the level of cross-language interoperability in .NET, your choice needn't be an either/or. You can feel free to create applications and classes in Visual Basic.NET, C#, JScript.NET, or any .NET-enabled language, knowing that they will be able to work together smoothly and easily, thanks to the CLR.

Why and When Would I Use ASP.NET?

You should use ASP.NET for any new projects you are about to start for the following reasons:

- Reduced development time
- Increased performance
- Increased application stability
- Increased scalability
- New ASP.NET features (see the discussion later in this chapter)

 Some of these benefits, such as reduction in development time, assume familiarity with the .NET development platform. If you are starting your first ASP.NET development project, you should allow some time for getting up to speed on the new platform. Subsequent projects should see reduced development time over classic ASP, as developers become more familiar with the platform.

In addition to these factors, ASP.NET, like ASP, is available for free. The only costs associated with ASP.NET development are the costs of the operating system on which you wish to run your application (Windows 2000, Windows XP, or

Windows Server 2003) and the cost of the development environment you choose to use. Of course, as with classic ASP, you can use free or inexpensive text editors to create your applications. Given that the .NET Framework is a free add-on to Windows (and is integrated with the Windows Server 2003 line), it is possible to create ASP.NET applications without spending a penny beyond the cost of the operating system and hardware on which it will run. Integrated development environments, such as Microsoft Visual Studio .NET 2003, are also available at an additional cost and greatly simplify ASP .NET development.

Why and When Would I Port an Existing Application to ASP.NET?

A trickier question is, "When will it be worthwhile to make the effort to migrate an existing application from ASP to ASP.NET?" The reality is that while classic ASP and ASP.NET have many common features, for most applications, it will not be a trivial task to migrate an application from one to the other. Changes in languages, as well as some changes in the way that ASP.NET operates compared to classic ASP, mean that depending on how your classic ASP application is structured, migration could require a significant amount of effort.

How do you decide whether a migration is worthwhile? If your application is in production, meets your needs functionally and in terms of performance and scalability, and you do not anticipate further development on the application, it's probably best to simply run it as a classic ASP application. One big plus of the ASP.NET architecture is that it runs side by side with classic ASP, so you don't have to migrate applications. Keep in mind, however, that while classic ASP and ASP.NET applications can run side by side, even in the same directory, they do not share Session and Application context. Thus, you will need to devise your own means of transferring any information you store in the Session or Application collections to and from ASP and ASP.NET, if you want to share that information between classic ASP and ASP.NET pages.

If your application is due for a new development cycle or revision, it's worth examining the types of functionality that your application uses and examining whether ASP.NET would be helpful in meeting the needs of the application. For example, if you have an application that struggles to meet your needs in terms of performance and scalability, the improved performance of the compiled-code model of ASP.NET and its new out-of-process Session State support may enable you to meet these goals easily.

What's important to consider is balancing the cost of migration against the benefits offered by migration. In this book, we will discuss the improvements and benefits offered by ASP.NET. It is left as an exercise for the reader to weigh these improvements against one another and determine whether to migrate a particular application.

New Features in ASP.NET

We'll close our introductory look at the .NET platform with a list of new features that are unique to ASP.NET and the chapter in which each will be discussed.

Web Forms
> A new feature that, in combination with an editor such as Visual Studio .NET, provides the ASP.NET developer the same drag and drop development convenience enjoyed by Visual Basic developers for years. Web Forms improve the speed of development by encapsulating frequently used features into server controls, which are declared using a tag-based syntax similar to HTML and XML. We'll discuss Web Forms in Chapters 3 and 12.

Web services
> Web services allow developers to expose the functionality of their applications via HTTP and XML so that any client who understands these protocols can call them. Web services can make the task of application integration easier, particularly in situations in which application-to-application integration is made difficult by firewalls and/or differing platforms. We'll discuss web services in Chapter 4.

Server controls
> Server controls are declared using an HTML-like syntax, making them easier to work with for page UI designers. They are executed on the server, returning HTML to the browser. Server controls may be manipulated on the server programmatically and provide power and flexibility for applications that must support a variety of browsers. We'll discuss using server controls in Chapter 5 and custom server control development in Chapter 6.

Validation
> One group of server controls is designed to simplify the task of validating user input. It includes controls to validate required fields, to compare one field to another or to a specific value for validation, and to validate user input using regular expressions, which allow you to specify a format that user input must follow to be valid. Validation controls will be discussed in Chapter 5.

Improved security
> ASP.NET offers tighter integration with Windows-based authentication, as well as two new authentication modes: forms-based authentication (which allows users to enter authentication credentials in a standard HTML form, with the credentials validated against your choice of backend credential store) and Passport authentication (which makes use of Microsoft's Passport authentication service). We'll discuss these improvements and new techniques in Chapter 9.

New Features in ASP.NET v1.1

In Version 1.1 of the .NET Framework, several features have been added that are of interest to ASP.NET developers. These include:

Request Validation
> Request Validation, when enabled (the default), checks all forms of posted input (form fields, querystring, etc.) and raises an exception if any HTML or

script code is found. This can help prevent cross-site scripting attacks in your applications. We'll discuss Request Validation further in Chapter 9.

Side by side execution

Starting with ASP.NET 1.1, you can choose which version of the .NET Framework your application will run against. Assuming you have both Version 1.0 and Version 1.1 installed, you can configure individual applications to run against either version. We'll discuss how to do this in Chapter 8.

Built-in mobile control support

In Version 1.0, support for targeting mobile devices such as cell phones and PDAs was provided via a set of controls available as a separate download. In Version 1.1, these controls have been fully integrated into the .NET Framework, and a new application type has been added to Visual Studio .NET 2003 to support development of ASP.NET applications for mobile devices. We'll discuss mobile development in Chapter 5.

ADO.NET enhancements

In Version 1.0, developers wishing to access data from Oracle and/or ODBC data sources had to download and install a separate data provider for these data sources. In Version 1.1, the ODBC and Oracle data providers have been integrated into the .NET Framework.

2

ASP.NET Applications

In Chapter 1, we introduced the .NET platform, some of its most important concepts, and new features available in ASP.NET. In this chapter, we'll look at the types of applications you can create with ASP.NET, discuss when you might want to use one type over another, explore the structure of ASP.NET applications, and look at the various file types that make up an ASP.NET application.

Application Types

In classic ASP, there was really only one type of application—one in which a client accessed a page with the *.asp* extension and in which that page, either through embedded VBScript or JScript or through script in combination with components built on Microsoft's COM standard, returned HTML to the browser to form the user interface with which the client would interact. Clients typically interacted with the application only through this user interface and did not have the option of creating their own alternative interface to the functionality exposed by the application.

ASP.NET provides an enhanced version of this type of application, which we'll discuss in the next section. ASP.NET also introduces a new type of application, called a web service, which provides clients the ability to use functionality exposed by an application without being tied into that application's user interface implementation.

ASP.NET Web Applications

The ASP.NET Web Application is the type of application most developers will work with on a regular basis. The terminology comes from the description used in the Visual Studio .NET environment to describe the project type used to create this type of application. You may also hear this type of application described as an ASP.NET Web Forms Application. For reasons we'll explore in the next chapter, we prefer the former term.

An ASP.NET Web Application, in its simplest form, consists of a directory made available via HTTP using the IIS administration tool or through the Web Sharing tab of a folder's Properties dialog (or by creating a web application project in Visual Studio .NET) and at least one ASP.NET page, designated by the *.aspx* file extension. This file (or files), whose structure we'll discuss in detail in the next chapter, typically contains a mix of HTML and server-side code. This HTML and server-side code combine to create the final output of the page, typically consisting of HTML markup that is sent to the client browser. A simple ASP.NET page is shown in Example 2-1.

Example 2-1. A simple ASP.NET page

```
<%@ Page Language="VB" %>
<html>
<head>
   <title>Simple ASP.NET Page</title>
   <script runat="server">

      Sub Page_Load( )

         Message.Text = "Hello, world!"

      End Sub

   </script>
</head>
<body>

<asp:Label id="Message" Runat="server"/>

</body>
</html>
```

The page shown in Example 2-1 simply executes the code appearing in the <script runat="server">, which uses an ASP.NET Label control to display some text, along with the standard HTML tags that are contained in the file. Figure 2-1 shows the output of the page as viewed in Notepad by using the View Source option in Internet Explorer. In this case, the Page_Load method (actually an event handler, which we'll discuss more in later chapters) sets the Text property of an ASP.NET Label control to "Hello, world!". Because the Label control will render its Text property to the browser automatically, "Hello, world!" will appear in the output that is sent to the browser, as shown in Figure 2-1.

The key to understanding how ASP.NET Web Applications work is understanding that the code in a <script runat="server"> block (or a <% %> render block) is executed on the server—after the client requests the page, but before the output of the page request is sent to the client browser. This allows developers to decide, based on the code they write and the input received from the user, just what output actually is sent to the browser, either directly (such as by calling the Write method of the Response object) or by manipulating controls, as shown in Example 2-1. It also allows additional functionality, such as server-side state management, to be provided to these applications.

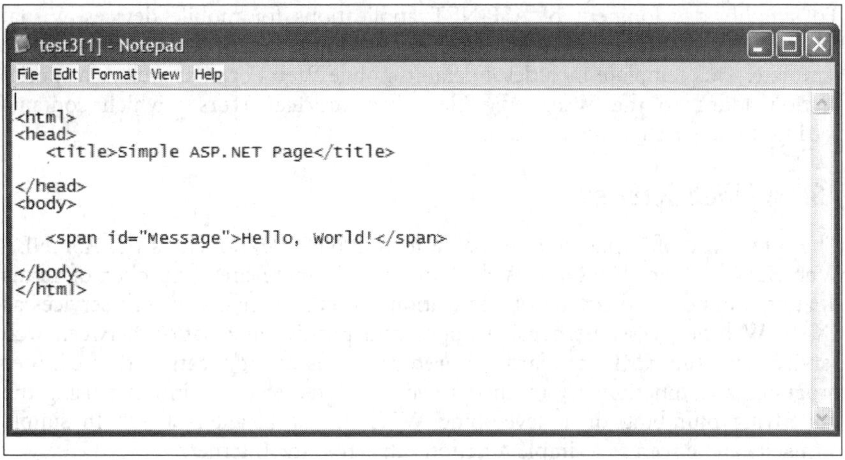

Figure 2-1. Output of a simple ASP.NET page (source view)

Web Forms and Web Controls

Example 2-1 uses a control called the Label control to output text to the browser. This control is an example of what are referred to as Web Controls. Web Controls (also referred to as Server Controls), which are discussed in detail in Chapter 5, are compiled classes that run on the server and provide functionality similar to that of Windows controls such as textboxes, dropdown lists, etc. The key is that these controls run at the server, and so can be manipulated programmatically in server-side code.

Web Form is a term used to describe an *.aspx* file that makes use of Web Controls.

Besides the containing directory and ASP.NET file(s), an ASP.NET Web Application may also contain configuration files (*web.config*), User Control files (*.ascx*), and an application settings file (*Global.asax*), as well as code-behind, assembly, and class files that provide additional functionality to the application. We'll discuss each of these file types later in this chapter.

ASP.NET Mobile Web Applications

The ASP.NET Mobile Web Application is a subtype of Web Application specific to developing for mobile devices such as cell phones and PDAs. The primary thing that distinguishes a mobile web application from a standard web application in ASP.NET is the use of the ASP.NET mobile controls, which are built into the .NET Framework as of Version 1.1. These include the mobile Form control and standard controls such as labels, textboxes, and panels, as well as mobile-specific controls such as the TextView, PhoneCall, and SelectionList controls. Note that both mobile Web Forms pages (those that use the mobile controls) and standard Web Forms pages can coexist within the same application, if desired.

To simplify development of ASP.NET applications for mobile devices, Visual Studio .NET 2003 provides an ASP.NET Mobile Web Application project template. This template includes a default mobile Web Form, as well as a special section added to the *Web.config* file called <deviceFilters>, which contains settings for device-specific rendering.

ASP.NET Web Services

The other type of application available to ASP.NET developers is the ASP.NET Web Service. Like ASP.NET Web Applications, there are a number of terms floating around for this type of application. (Microsoft refers to web services as "XML Web Services," perhaps in hopes of a positive association between web services and the XML standard.) A *web service* is an application that exposes programmatic functionality to clients over the Internet or an intranet using the underlying plumbing of a developing W3C standard called SOAP. In simple terms, it can be seen as a simple function call across the Internet.

What Is SOAP?

The proposed SOAP standard, which at the time of this writing was a W3C Candidate Recommendation (see *http://www.w3.org/Consortium/Process-20010719/tr.html#RecsCR* for information on where this fits in the standardization process) and versioned at 1.2, describes a protocol that may be used within the framework of HTTP (other transport protocols are possible, but the SOAP specification does not define how to use them) to send and receive requests and responses consisting of either specific data or remote procedure calls and responses, or both. The SOAP specification defines the format for messages sent via SOAP, methods for communicating how a message should be processed, and encoding rules for communicating data types across heterogeneous platforms.

Assuming that the proposed SOAP standard is adopted as a W3C Recommendation (*recommendation* is the term used by the W3C to describe stable standards such as HTML 4.01; see *http://www.w3.org* for more information on current recommendations), application developers on a given platform can expose their functionality to others on different platforms in a fashion that makes the differences in platform transparent. As long as both the server and the client follow the SOAP specification, the applications can communicate, regardless of the platform differences.

Since SOAP has not yet been adopted as a recommendation and is still under development, current implementations from Microsoft and other vendors have not yet achieved the level of cross-platform interoperability that is promised once SOAP is adopted as a recommendation. As such, you should take the time to test and evaluate the interoperability of your chosen platform(s) before committing substantial resources to web services, if you are planning to use web services to facilitate cross-platform interoperability.

The simplest form of an ASP.NET Web Service consists of a directory made available via HTTP using the IIS administration tool or through the Web Sharing tab of a folder's Properties dialog (or by creating a Web Application project in Visual Studio .NET) and at least one web service file, designated by the *.asmx* file extension. Unlike an ASP.NET page, this file (or files), whose structure we'll discuss in detail in Chapter 4, typically does not contain HTML, but consists solely of server-side code. The methods to be exposed by the web service carry the WebMethod attribute (note that the syntax of the WebMethod attribute varies depending on the language used). A simple web service is shown in Example 2-2.

Example 2-2. A simple web service

```
<%@ WebService Language="VB" Class="Hello" %>

Imports System
Imports System.Web.Services

Public Class Hello : Inherits WebService
    <WebMethod()> Public Function SayHello( ) As String
        Return("Hello, World!")
    End Function
End Class
```

If the *.asmx* file that makes up this web service is called from a browser, ASP.NET will output a page that documents how the web service should be called, and also provides the ability to test the invocation of the web service. This page is shown in Figure 2-2.

When invoked, the web service shown in Example 2-2 will return "Hello, World!" as an XML-formatted response, according to the SOAP 1.1 specification, as shown here:

```
<?xml version="1.0" encoding="utf-8" ?>
<string xmlns="http://tempuri.org/">Hello, World!</string>
```

The documentation page provided by ASP.NET also allows you to review the Web Service Description Language (WSDL) description of your web service. WSDL, which we'll discuss further in Chapter 4, is an XML-based format for describing the functionality exposed by a web service, including the format and data type of input and output parameters, and can be considered a contract for how clients interact with the web service. In this way, WSDL plays a role similar to that of Interface Description Language (IDL) in Microsoft's COM component specification.

 Besides providing a detailed discussion of how to create a web service, Chapter 4 shows you how to consume a web service.

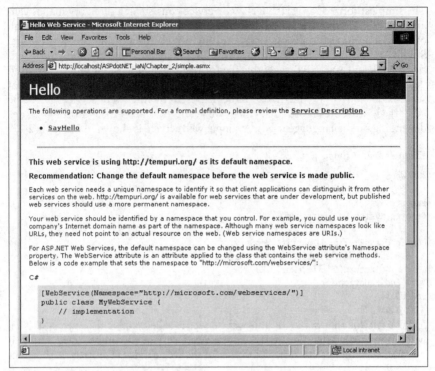

Figure 2-2. Output of a simple web service

Application Structure and Boundaries

Although it is convenient, for the sake of discussing application types, to divide ASP.NET applications into web applications and web services, the truth is that from a practical standpoint, ASP.NET applications can be comprised of both types; an ASP.NET Web Application may contain *.asmx* files that implement web services, and a web service application may contain *.aspx* files that implement user interfaces for web services or functionality contained in .NET assemblies. Thus, from the standpoint of application structure, ASP.NET Web Applications and ASP.NET Web Services are quite similar.

Application Structure

The structure of an ASP.NET application consists of a site or virtual directory in IIS and at least one ASP.NET page or web service. Optionally, each ASP.NET application may have:

- A single *global.asax* file, located in the root of the application.
- One or more *web.config* files. There can be only one *web.config* file per directory or subdirectory in the application.
- One or more User Control files bearing the *.ascx* extension.

- One or more class files, either for ASP.NET code-behinds or for assemblies used in your application.

- A */bin* directory containing .NET assemblies you wish to use in your application. Assemblies in the */bin* directory are automatically made available to your application.

- ASP.NET Web Applications created in Visual Studio .NET contain Solution and Project-related files (*.sln*, *.suo*, *.vbproj*, and *.csproj*, for example), and an optional default cascading style sheets file (*.css*). These applications may also optionally contain resource files (*.resx*), dataset and/or XML schema definitions (*.xsd*), and other file types.

- Any other type of file (*.htm*, *.asp*, images, etc.) that you'd expect a classic web application to contain. Note, however, that *.asp* pages within an ASP.NET application will not share an Application and Session state with the ASP.NET application.

Figure 2-3 provides a visual explanation of how an ASP.NET application is structured.

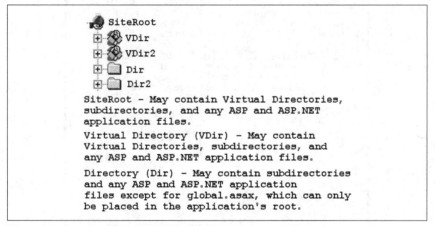

Figure 2-3. Structure of an ASP.NET application

Application Boundaries

In ASP.NET, as in classic ASP, the boundary of an application is determined primarily by the site or virtual directory defined for that application in IIS. Requests for ASP.NET pages or web services that reside within that site or virtual directory and its subdirectories are treated as part of the application and have access to application-specific items such as the Application and Session intrinsic objects (provided, respectively, by the HttpApplicationState and HttpSessionState classes). They also share resources with other requests to the application.

Request Lifecycle and Handling

When a request comes in from a client for a file within the purview of IIS (i.e., an HTTP request for a file within one of the sites or virtual directories set up in IIS),

IIS checks the file extension of the file being requested and then checks its mapping of file types to handler programs to determine which program should be used to process the request. In the case of a classic ASP application, a request for a file with the *.asp* extension is handled by the *asp.dll* ISAPI application. The App Mappings tab of the Application Configuration dialog for IIS, shown in Figure 2-4, allows you to view and modify the mappings of file extensions to the executables used to handle those extensions, as well as to determine the HTTP verbs (GET, POST, etc.) that qualify the mapping.

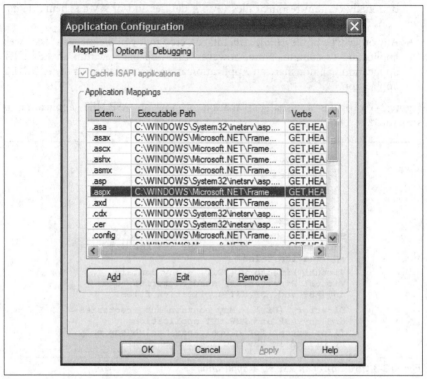

Figure 2-4. The IIS Application Configuration dialog

Requests for files with the *.aspx* and *.asmx* extensions and for other ASP.NET-related files are handled by the *aspnet_wp.dll* ISAPI application. This application, in turn, hands the requests off to the *aspnet_wp.exe* worker process. Once the request is handed off to the ASP.NET worker process, it handles the rest of the processing by:

- JIT (just in time)-compiling the code in the page (and in any code-behind page identified with the src attribute) if no cached compiled version of the requested resource exists.

- Executing the compiled assembly associated with the page or web service, including refreshing any control or page state from a previous request, handling events raised by the request, and rendering the appropriate output to the client.

- Releasing used resources and discarding any transient state information (information not stored in either the Application or Session state collections).

With the exception of the Application state collection, which is available to all clients within a given ASP.NET application, and the Session state collection, which is associated with a specific client by a value either stored in an HTTP cookie on the client or munged into the URL for the application, each individual request to the application is independent from any other, even for that client.

The practical effect is that each request must contain sufficient information to successfully process the request—whether that information comes from form fields passed from the client, information stored in the Application or Session collections, or even information from cookies or a database.

Application File Types

A number of different file types are associated with an ASP.NET application, and it's important to understand the purpose of each type, even if you aren't using all of them in your current applications. In this section, we'll look at the major file types associated with ASP.NET Web Applications and web services and what each of them does.

web.config Files

web.config is the file type used for configuration of various settings within an ASP.NET application. Applications may contain more than one *web.config* file (though there may be only one per directory or subdirectory), and the *web. config* files are applied in an hierarchical fashion. What this means is that if you have defined a particular setting (such as the user accounts permitted to access that directory) in the *web.config* file at the root of your application, this setting applies to the application and all of its subdirectories, if it has any. You can override that setting for a particular subdirectory by using a *web.config* file in a subdirectory of the application. The *web.config* files use an XML-based syntax, and both the tag names and their attributes are case-sensitive.

web.config provides configuration settings for:

- Application-specific settings, such as connection string information (since the *web.config* file resides within the web application's file space, it is probably best to avoid storing sensitive information such as passwords in plain text in a configuration file, or at all, if that's feasible).
- Authentication and authorization.
- Browser capabilities (mapping specific functionality to the information retrieved from a User Agent string).
- Compilation settings, including whether an application should be run in debug or release mode.
- Custom error handling information.
- Globalization settings.
- HttpHandlers and HttpModules associated with the application.

- HttpRuntime settings.
- Application Identity and encryption/decryption key settings.
- ASP.NET Page defaults (for the @ Page directive).
- ASP.NET Process settings, including settings for Web Gardens, and proactive restart of applications based on memory used or number of requests received.
- Code-access security settings, including mappings of trust levels to security policy files, and trust setting for an application.
- Session state settings, including whether to run Session state in process, out of process, or in SQL Server.
- Application Trace settings. Tracing is a useful new feature for debugging and troubleshooting that we'll discuss in Chapter 10.
- Web service settings.

Note that *web.config* is an optional file. Any configuration settings not set in a *web.config* file within the application will be inherited from the server-level configuration file, *machine.config*. A sample *web.config* file is shown in Example 2-3.

Example 2-3. Sample web.config file

```
<?xml version="1.0" encoding="utf-8" ?>
<configuration>

   <system.web>

      <compilation
         defaultLanguage="c#"
         debug="true"/>

      <trace
         enabled="true"
         requestLimit="10"
         pageOutput="false"
         traceMode="SortByTime"
         localOnly="true"/>

      <sessionState
         mode="InProc"
         stateConnectionString="tcpip=127.0.0.1:42424"
         sqlConnectionString="data source=127.0.0.1;user id=sa;password="
         cookieless="false"
         timeout="20"/>
   </system.web>

</configuration>
```

We'll discuss how to make changes to *web.config*, and the syntax of the various configuration sections, in Chapter 8.

global.asax Files

global.asax performs a similar function in ASP.NET that *global.asa* performs in classic ASP. That is, it is an optional file that may contain code to respond to Application- or Session-level events. Like *global.asa* in classic ASP, there can be only one *global.asax* file per ASP.NET application. Unlike the *global.asa* file in classic ASP, which was parsed, the *global.asax* application file is compiled at runtime into a .NET managed assembly ultimately derived from the HttpApplication class. In addition to handling Application- and Session-level events, such as Session_OnStart, *global.asax* also allows you to handle events raised by HttpModules associated with your application (in fact, the Session state in ASP.NET is implemented as an HttpModule, so its events are already handled this way).

The *global.asax* file can be constructed one of two ways. The file can contain the event handlers and other code you want associated with your application directly, or it can reference a code-behind class file that contains the event handlers and code to associate with the application. Note that the code-behind used, if any, must inherit from the HttpApplication class in the System.Web namespace. The latter is the way that the *global.asax* files in ASP.NET applications created with Visual Studio .NET are constructed. Example 2-4 shows a typical *global.asax* file that uses code-behind, while Example 2-5 shows the code-behind file it uses.

Example 2-4. global.asax using code-behind

```
<% -- Global.asax file-- %>
<%@ Application Codebehind="Global.asax.vb" Inherits="<namespacename>. Global" %>
```

Example 2-5. Code-behind file for global.asax in Example 2-4

```
'Global.asax.vb codebehind file

Imports System.Web
Imports System.Web.SessionState

Public Class Global
   Inherits System.Web.HttpApplication

   Sub Application_BeginRequest(ByVal sender As Object, _
      ByVal e As EventArgs)
      ' Fires at the beginning of each request
   End Sub

   Sub Application_AuthenticateRequest(ByVal sender As Object, _
      ByVal e As EventArgs)
      ' Fires upon attempting to authenticate the user
   End Sub

   Sub Application_Error(ByVal sender As Object, ByVal e As EventArgs)
      ' Fires when an error occurs
   End Sub

End Class
```

We'll discuss the uses of the *global.asax* file in more detail in Chapters 13 and 19.

.aspx Files

.aspx files, also known as ASP.NET pages or Web Forms, are the meat and potatoes of an ASP.NET Web Application. These files contain the HTML tags, server controls, and code that present a user interface to your users, and process their requests (or call helper functions in business-tier components to do so). Like the *global.asax* file, *.aspx* files may either contain code directly or refer to a code-behind class that contains the code for that page. Note that the code-behind used, if any, must inherit from the Page class in the System.Web.UI namespace. We'll discuss *.aspx* files in detail in Chapter 3.

.asmx Files

.asmx files are the files used to implement ASP.NET Web Services. These files contain the methods, marked with the WebMethod attribute, that will be exposed by your application as web services. Like *global.asax* and *.aspx* files, *.asmx* files may either contain code directly or refer to a code-behind class that implements the methods to be exposed as web services. Note that the code-behind used, if any, must inherit from the WebService class in the System.Web.Services namespace We'll discuss *.asmx* files in detail in Chapter 4.

.ascx Files

.ascx files are used to implement what are known as ASP.NET user controls. User controls are a technique for code reuse that lies somewhere between the function of the #Include directive in classic ASP (which you can still use in ASP.NET, if you choose) and the function of custom ASP.NET Server Controls. User controls are made up of HTML tags, server controls, and code (or any combination of the above), and can be reused through a simple tag-based syntax. They have the advantages of being simpler to develop than custom server controls, as well as offering greater functionality than includes (such as the ability to expose properties and methods). We'll discuss user controls further in Chapters 3 and 6.

Code-Behind and Class Files

In addition to the file types mentioned here, you'll also frequently deal with code-behind and/or class files. A code-behind file, also known as a code-behind class file, is a file containing .NET managed code (such as VB.NET or C#) that defines a class from which an ASP.NET page file, web service file, or application file inherits. This inherited relationship is indicated by the codebehind or src attribute, which indicates the file containing the code-behind class, and the inherits attribute, which indicates the namespace name (if any) and the class name of the class to inherit. Example 2-4 shows these attributes in action. At runtime, when the page, the web service, or the application is initialized for the first time, the ASP.NET runtime locates the code-behind file and either executes the compiled assembly associated with it (in the case of the codebehind attribute, which is used when the class will be precompiled) or compiles the class into an assembly dynamically (in the case of the src attribute). We'll discuss the use of code-behind classes and the choice of which attribute to use in greater detail in Chapters 3 and 4.

Class files are simply source code files containing .NET managed code that is organized into namespaces and classes and that has been compiled before deployment, using either the Visual Studio .NET environment or the appropriate command-line compiler, into a .NET managed assembly. Class files are typically kept separate from the web application in which their assemblies are used, just as the source code for COM components used in classic ASP applications is typically kept separate from the web tree.

.vb extension

The *.vb* extension indicates source code files written in Visual Basic .NET. By default, code-behind classes created by the Visual Studio .NET environment use the naming convention *filename.parentfileextension.languageextension*. Thus, a VB.NET code-behind file for an ASP.NET page might have the name *WebForm1.aspx.vb*. This naming convention clearly conveys the relationship between the code-behind file and the page that inherits from it, as well as the language used in the code-behind file, so you can adopt this naming convention or use a similar one, even when not developing in the Visual Studio .NET environment.

.cs extension

The *.cs* extension indicates source code files written in Microsoft's new C# (pronounced "C Sharp") language. These files, when created by Visual Studio .NET, use the same naming convention as the one just described.

3

Web Forms

Web Forms are an ASP.NET technology used to create programmable web pages. They are the primary building block of ASP.NET Web Applications. The main goal of Web Forms is to bring the same productivity to web applications that Visual Basic brought to Windows applications. Web Forms consist of the user interface (UI) and the UI logic written on the server side. The UI and UI logic can reside either in the same file or in separate files.

Web Forms in ASP.NET offer a number of advantages over ASP and other technologies for generating web applications. ASP.NET Web Forms:

- Provide support for any HTML 3.2–compliant browser. Even ASP.NET Server Controls that provide advanced client-side functionality will gracefully degrade for browsers that do not support DHTML or script. These controls will, however, take advantage of such support in browsers such as Internet Explorer 5.0 or later.

- Are built on the Common Language Runtime and provide all the benefits of the runtime, such as managed execution, type safety, and inheritance.

- Can be built with any Common Language Runtime language, including C#, Visual Basic .NET, and JScript .NET.

- Can be created using rapid application development tools such as Visual Studio .NET. You can build a Web Forms page simply by dragging and dropping controls from the VS.NET toolbox onto the page.

- Provide a rich set of server controls that provide almost all the functionality required for a web application. ASP.NET ships with a broad array of built-in server controls.

- Offer a flexible programming model, in which code may be included in the same file as the Web Form, as in the classic ASP model or in separate module files, referred to as code-behind files. Code-behind promotes the separation of code and content, which can improve your code's readability, maintainability, and reusability.

- Preserve the state of the page and its controls between requests with the inclusion of state management features. This facility is explained in detail in the "State Management" section later in this chapter.

- Provide an extensible model that allows you to develop your own controls or purchase third-party controls to add functionality to your application.

Structuring an ASP.NET Page

An ASP.NET page is a declarative text file with the extension *.aspx*. A page consists of structural elements that can perform various operations—ultimately resulting in output of HTML or other MIME-type output that can be handled by the browser. An ASP.NET page can contain any or all of the following elements:

Page directives
> Start with the @ symbol, followed by attribute/value pairs, and are used to specify page-level settings, such as the language used in the page or namespaces to be imported. For example, the following code specifies the C# programming language:
> ```
> <%@ Page Language="C#" %>
> ```

Code declaration blocks
> Consist of variable and member declarations within <script>...</script> tags, as follows:
> ```
> <script language="C#" runat="server">
> // code goes here
> </script>
> ```
> Note that there are limitations on what code you can place in <script> blocks in ASP.NET. In classic ASP, you can write executable code in a <script> block without wrapping that code in a subroutine. In ASP.NET, only variable declarations can be placed outside of a subroutine. Any other executable code not contained in a subroutine will result in an error.

Render code blocks
> Used to write inline code and inline expressions within HTML elements. For example:
> ```
> <% int i; %>
> <H1><%=Heading%> </H1>
> ```
> There are limitations on what code you can place in render blocks in ASP.NET. In classic ASP, you can define subroutines in render blocks. In ASP.NET, this is not permitted and results in an error.

 Render blocks, while quite common in classic ASP, are less frequently used in ASP.NET, since they don't fit very well with the control-based, event-driven model introduced in ASP.NET. Support for render blocks is included for backward compatibility, but you should consider other alternatives carefully before using them in new development work, since extensive use of render blocks can make your pages difficult to debug.

Server-side comments

As always, comments are used for documentation and testing purposes. You can use them to prevent any code from executing, as in the following example:

```
<%-- Debugging Code To Be Removed --%>
```

Server controls

HTML and web controls declared with the `runat="server"` attribute/value pair. For example, the following code declares an HTML input server control and an ASP TextBox control:

```
<input type="text" id="MyText" runat="server">
<asp:TextBox id="Mytext" runat="server"/>
```

Server-side object tags

Used to declare and instantiate classic COM components and .NET classes. For example:

```
<object id="MyDataSet" class="System.Data.DataSet" runat="server">
```

Server-side include directives

Used to include any text file into your page. This was the primary code reuse mechanism in classic ASP. For example:

```
<!-- #Include file="TopNavigation.inc" -- >
<!-- #Include virtual="Menus.inc" -- >
```

In ASP.NET, the preferred means of sharing code is to create a shared class or server control that contains the functionality to be reused.

Server-side <form> element

Many server controls, including the TextBox control, must be contained within a server-side <form> tag pair with the `runat="server"` attribute:

```
<form runat="server">
    <asp:TextBox id="Mytext" runat="server"/>
    <asp:Button id="submit" runat="server"/>
</form>
```

Literal text

Any text that is not one of the elements listed previously is literal text and appears as it is in the output. This text also includes standard HTML tags. In the following example, "Name" is the literal text:

```
Name: <input type="text" id="txtName">
```

Using @ Directives

ASP.NET provides a number of @ directives—processing instructions that give the runtime and compiler additional information about how you want your code to run. These directives let you enable certain features, specify whether you want your pages to be based on the `System.Web.UI.Page` class (the default) or on a custom class that you name, etc. Under ASP.NET, @ directives can also have attributes that further enhance the configuration ability of the directive.

The list of @ directives in ASP.NET is greatly expanded from classic ASP, which provides only five directives (whose functionality is now provided by attributes of the @ Page directive). The following @ directives are available in ASP.NET:

@ Page

Arguably the most important directive, @ Page is included at the top of each ASP.NET page and allows you to set the page language and enable or disable such features as buffering, session state, and debugging. The @ Page directive has the following attributes:

AspCompat
`<%@ Page AspCompat="True|False" %>`

Specifies that the page should be executed in a single-threaded apartment (STA) to provide compatibility with COM components written in Visual Basic 6.0 (or other development tools that create only STA components). This attribute also provides access to unmanaged wrappers of the ASP intrinsic objects (Request, Response, etc.) for components that need access to these objects through ObjectContext or the OnStartPage method. By default, ASP.NET pages run in a multi-threaded apartment, so enabling this feature by setting AspCompat to True can have a negative impact on the performance of your pages. The default value of this setting is False.

AutoEventWireup
`<%@ Page AutoEventWireup="True|False" %>`

Specifies that standard events (Page_Load, Page_PreRender, etc.) will be automatically wired to any handlers you provide. The default for this attribute (set in the *machine.config* configuration file) is True. Pages created with Visual Studio .NET have this attribute set to False, since Visual Studio creates the code to wire up events in a code-behind file for you. As such, turning on AutoEventWireup in a page created with Visual Studio .NET results in event handlers firing multiple times.

Buffer
`<%@ Page Buffer="True|False" %>`

Specifies whether or not ASP.NET page output should be buffered in memory and sent to the client when the entire page has been rendered, or until the End or Flush method of the HttpResponse class is called. (See Chapter 17 for more information on the HttpResponse class.) The default value is set to True.

ClassName
`<%@ Page ClassName="classname" %>`

Specifies the class name to be used for a dynamically compiled page. The default is the filename of the page, with the dot between the filename and the *.aspx* file extension replaced by an underscore (_). This class name appears as the top-level object in the Control Tree when ASP.NET tracing is enabled. See Chapter 10 for more information on tracing in ASP.NET pages and applications.

ClientTarget
`<%@ Page ClientTarget="UserAgent/Alias" %>`

Specifies that the page should be rendered using the defined capabilities of one of the browsers defined in the <clientTarget> section of the *web.config* or *machine.config* configuration files. Use of this attribute substitutes the user agent string defined in the <clientTarget> section for the one sent by the actual client browser, causing server controls that query browser capabilities to render for the browser type specified in the `ClientTarget` attribute. Note that setting this attribute to a value other than those defined in the `<clientTarget>` configuration section results in an exception.

Codebehind
`<%@ Page Codebehind="path" %>`

Specifies the code-behind class file that contains code for the page. This attribute is used by the Visual Studio .NET environment when building a project and is ignored by the ASP.NET runtime. Pages using the Codebehind attribute must compile their code-behind classes manually.

CodePage
`<%@ Page CodePage="codepage" %>`

Specifies the code page (a definition of how characters are mapped to the available bit patterns in each byte—code pages are used to define different character sets for different languages or regions) to be used for the page output.

CompilerOptions
`<%@ Page CompilerOptions="options" %>`

Specifies one or more command-line switches to be passed to the compiler for the language specified in the `Language` attribute. Behavior and availability of this attribute may vary depending on the language used for the page.

ContentType
`<%@ Page ContentType="MIMEtype" %>`

Specifies the HTTP content type sent as part of the HTTP headers for the response generated by the page. Can be set to any standard MIME type. This attribute is especially useful when returning types other than text/html—such as when using an ASP.NET page to generate binary image output. In this case, you would set the `ContentType` attribute to the appropriate MIME type, such as image/jpeg. This attribute performs the same function as the ContentType property of the `HttpResponse` class. (See Chapter 17 for more information on the `HttpResponse` class.)

Culture
`<%@ Page Culture="culturename" %>`

Specifies the name of the culture to use for formatting numbers, dates, etc. For example, the culture name for United States English is en-US, which is also the default. Setting the `Culture` attribute to another culture name will result in alternate values, such as the date returned by the Visual Basic Now function being formatted for the specified culture.

Debug
`<%@ Page Debug="True|False" %>`

Specifies whether the page will be compiled with debug symbols. Enabling debugging allows the use of debuggers to step through code and provides more detailed information in the event of an exception, but also entails a performance penalty. For this reason, the Debug attribute should always be set to False in production applications. Note that the default value, which is False, is set in the `<compilation>` section of the *machine.config* configuration file.

Description
```
<%@ Page Description="textdescription" %>
```
Specifies a text description of the page. This attribute is ignored by the ASP.NET runtime.

EnableSessionState
```
<%@ Page EnableSessionState="True|False|ReadOnly" %>
```
Specifies whether the page supports session state. This attribute can be used to disable or delay the creation of sessions, which are used for state management. Setting this attribute to False when session state is not utilized can improve the performance of your application. If set to True, code within the page may read or write session values, and if no current session exists for the user, a new Session is created. If set to False, attempts to read or write session values result in an exception, browsing the page will not result in the creation of a new session, and if a session exists for the user, it will be unaffected. If set to ReadOnly, an existing session may be read from, but not written to, and browsing the page will not result in the creation of a new session. The default value, which is set in the <pages> section of the *machine.config* configuration file, is True.

EnableViewState
```
<%@ Page EnableViewState="True|False" %>
```
Specifies whether ViewState is supported for the page. ViewState is a new feature of ASP.NET that allows server control state (as well as developer-specified values) to be persisted across multiple requests to the page. ViewState is stored as a hidden form field containing an encoded text string representing the state of all controls for which ViewState is enabled; thus, any controls for which you want ASP.NET to manage state should be placed inside a server-side <form> tag pair. When ViewState is enabled for a page, individual controls can disable their own ViewState for better performance. Because ViewState is round-tripped between the server and client, you should be cognizant of the size of the ViewState field for the page. Disabling ViewState where it is not necessary (either at the page or control level) may improve performance. The default value, which is set in the <pages> section of the *machine.config* configuration file, is True.

EnableViewStateMac
```
<%@ Page EnableViewStateMAC="True|False" %>
```
Specifies whether ASP.NET should run a machine authentication check (MAC) on the ViewState contents to ensure that the ViewState was not tampered with on the client. This can make your page more secure, but may carry a performance penalty. The default value, which is set in the <pages> section of the *machine.config* configuration file, is False.

ErrorPage
```
<%@ Page ErrorPage="URL" %>
```
Specifies the URL of a page to which the user will be redirected if an unhandled exception occurs. This attribute should be considered a last line of defense in error handling and not a substitute for proper error/exception handling. See Chapter 10 for more information on handling exceptions.

Explicit

```
<%@ Page Explicit="True|False" %>
```

Specifies whether pages written in Visual Basic .NET will be compiled using Option Explicit mode. This mode requires that all variables be explicitly declared before use. The default value, which is set in the <compilation> section of the *machine.config* configuration file, is True. Note that the documentation for the @ Page directive indicates that the default for this attribute is False (while also indicating that the value is set to True in *machine.config*). This may refer to the *vbc.exe* compiler having Option Explicit turned off by default. Since the explicit attribute in the <compilation> element of *machine.config* is set to True, however, the default for ASP.NET pages is effectively True.

Inherits

```
<%@ Page Src="path" Inherits="namespace.class" %>
```

Specifies the namespace (optional) and class name of a class from which the page will inherit. This attribute is used with the Src or Codebehind attribute to specify a code-behind file from which the page should inherit, thus making any properties and/or methods of that class available to the page.

Language

```
<%@ Page Language="languagealias" %>
```

Specifies the language that will be used for server-side <script> blocks and render blocks on the page. Typical values are VB (for Visual Basic .NET) and C#. You can also use the Language attribute of a server-side <script> tag to specify the desired language for individual <script> blocks. Unlike classic ASP, ASP.NET only supports one language per page.

LCID

```
<%@ Page LCID="localeidentifier" %>
```

Specifies the locale identifier (LCID) for the page. The locale identifier is used by functions such as the Visual Basic .NET FormatCurrency function to determine the desired format. For example, setting the LCID attribute to 1041 results in FormatCurrency returning values formatted as Japanese yen (¥).

ResponseEncoding

```
<%@ Page ResponseEncoding="encodingname" %>
```

Specifies the encoding to be used for the page response. This attribute can be set to any valid encoding supported by System.Text.Encoding. The default is Unicode (UTF-8).

Src

```
<%@ Page Src="path" Inherits="namespace.class" %>
```

Specifies the path to a code-behind class to compile dynamically. This attribute is used in conjunction with the Inherits attribute to specify a code-behind class for the page that will be compiled when the page is requested (unless a cached version of the compiled assembly for the page already exists). Unlike the Codebehind attribute, which is only used by Visual Studio .NET (and is ignored by the ASP.NET runtime), the class file specified by the Src attribute is compiled dynamically at runtime.

SmartNavigation

```
<%@ Page SmartNavigation="True|False" %>
```

Specifies whether ASP.NET's SmartNavigation feature is enabled. SmartNavigation, which is supported only by IE 5.x and later, uses IFrame elements to allow only portions of the page to be refreshed when an ASP.NET page containing a form is posted to the server. This can eliminate the flicker associated with page refresh, and also prevents multiple entries in the browser history from postbacks. The default value, which is set in the `<pages>` section of the *machine.config* configuration file, is False.

Strict

```
<%@ Page Strict="True|False" %>
```

Specifies whether pages written in Visual Basic .NET will be compiled using Option Strict mode. This mode does not permit any implicit data type conversion that would result in data loss (also known as narrowing conversions) and does not allow late binding. Option Strict also includes the restrictions of Option Explicit, so setting the Strict attribute to True also requires that all variables be explicitly declared before use. The default value, which is set in the `<compilation>` section of the *machine.config* configuration file, is False.

Trace

```
<%@ Page Trace="True|False" %>
```

Specifies whether the ASP.NET tracing feature is enabled for the page. Enabling tracing at the page level results in information about the current request—including request time, HTTP status code, cookie information, page control tree, and HTTP header information—being appended to the page output. Tracing can provide a great deal of information useful for debugging or understanding what is happening with a given page. For performance and security reasons, tracing should not be enabled for production applications. The default value, which is set in the `<trace>` section of the *machine.config* configuration file, is False.

TraceMode

```
<%@ Page TraceMode="tracemode" %>
```

Specifies the sort order of entries in the Trace Information section of the page trace. Valid values include SortByTime, which sorts entries in the order in which they are processed, and SortByCategory, which sorts entries based on the category assigned to the entry. Developers can write custom entries to the trace output using the Trace.Write method and assign categories to these entries. In the SortByCategory trace mode, all custom entries using the same category would appear together. The default value, which is set in the `<trace>` section of the *machine.config* configuration file, is SortByTime.

Transaction

```
<%@ Page Transaction="transactionmode" %>
```

Specifies the transaction mode of the page. Valid values are Disabled, NotSupported, Required, RequiresNew, and Supported. Default is Disabled.

Web Forms

UICulture
```
<%@ Page UICulture="culturename" %>
```
Specifies the culture that should be used when loading language-specific resources for pages that use resource files.

ValidateRequest
```
<%@ Page ValidateRequest="True|False" %>
```
Specifies whether request validation should be performed. Request validation, a new feature in ASP.NET v1.1, checks all posted input data for potentially dangerous values, such as HTML and script. If such input is found, an exception of type HttpRequestValidationException is thrown. The default value, which is set in the `<pages>` section of the *machine.config* configuration file, is True.

 You should always leave Request Validation enabled, unless your application must accept HTML input. If this is the case, you should filter your input (using regular expressions or similar techniques) for the specific input you wish to allow (such as <b>, <i>, etc.) and disallow everything else. If instead you attempt to filter out invalid input, you are almost certain to miss some form of dangerous input, leaving your application vulnerable to exploit. Once you are confident that your filtering is working, you can disable Request Validation at the page level. While it's possible to disable Request Validation at the application and machine level, doing so exposes your application to higher risk, since this makes it too easy to add a new page that accepts input, forgetting to include filtering logic. Without Request Validation enabled, such a page could pose a security risk.

WarningLevel
```
<%@ Page WarningLevel="warninglevel" %>
```
Specifies the compiler warning level at which ASP.NET should abort compilation of the page and display the warning. The available values for this attribute depend on the language in use. See the documentation for the appropriate compiler for more information.

@ Control

Provides much the same functionality as the @ Page directive, only for ASP.NET user controls. The attributes available for the @ Control directive, which are a subset of those for the @ Page directive, include the following:

```
AutoEventWireup
ClassName
Codebehind (Visual Studio .NET only)
CompilerOptions
Debug
Description
EnableViewState
Explicit
Inherits
Language
```

```
Strict
Src
WarningLevel
```

@ Import

> Allows access to members of a namespace without using the fully qualified (namespace and member name) name. The @ Import directive has a single attribute, Namespace, which specifies the namespace to import. Multiple @ Import directives must be used to import multiple namespaces, with one @ Import directive for each desired namespace.

@ Implements

> Specifies an interface that the page or control implements in which the directive appears. By implementing an interface, the page developer agrees to provide implementations of all methods and/or properties defined by the interface. Failure to implement any of the members defined by the interface results in a compiler error. The @ Implements directive has a single attribute, Interface, that specifies the .NET interface to be implemented.

@ Register

> Allows the instantiation and use of user controls and custom server controls in ASP.NET pages and user controls through an HTML-like tag-based syntax. The @ Register directive is used to specify the tag prefix (similar to the asp: prefix for built-in ASP.NET Server Controls) and the information necessary to locate the user control or custom server control. The @ Register directive supports the following attributes:

> TagPrefix
>> Specifies the prefix to be used to differentiate the tag used to create an instance of the user control or custom server control.

> TagName (user controls only)
>> Specifies the tag name (the portion of the tag immediately following the tag prefix, which is separated from the tag name by a colon) used to create an instance of a user control. For custom server controls, the class name of the class that defines the server control is used for the tag name, so this attribute is not necessary.

> Namespace (custom server controls only)
>> Specifies the namespace of the custom server control.

> Src (user controls only)
>> Specifies the path to the *.ascx* file containing the desired user control.

> Assembly (custom server controls only)
>> Specifies the assembly containing the custom server control class.

> A complete @ Register directive for a custom server control is:

>> ```
>> <%@ Register TagPrefix="foo" Namespace="foo" Assembly="bar" %>
>> ```

> Assuming a class name of "bar" for the custom server control, the corresponding tag for an instance of the control is shown here:

>> ```
>> <foo:baz id="myBar" runat="server"/>
>> ```

> See Chapter 6 for additional examples.

@ Assembly

Specifies the name or path to an assembly to be linked in with the current page. This specification makes any classes or interfaces in the assembly available to the page. Note that the following assemblies are linked into pages by default based on the `<assemblies>` child element of the `<compilation>` element in the *machine.config* configuration file (see Chapters 8 and 20 for more information on configuration files):

mscorlib
System
System.Data
System.Drawing
System.EnterpriseServices
System.Web
System.Web.Services
System.Xml

Note that the `<assemblies>` element of *machine.config* also contains a wildcard reference (*) that tells it to link any assemblies residing in the *bin* subdirectory of the application. Any custom assemblies you place in this directory (including custom control assemblies) will be available to your application automatically. Unlike the @ Import directive, this directive does not make it possible to access members of an assembly without using the fully qualified name. The @ Import directive is still required for that. The @ Assembly directive supports two attributes, which are exclusive of one another:

Name

Specifies the name of the assembly to link. This is typically the same as the filename of the assembly, without the file extension (i.e., the assembly name for System.Web.dll would be System.Web).

Src

Specifies the path to a class module that is to be dynamically compiled and linked into the current page.

@ OutputCache

Enables and specifies settings for caching the output of ASP.NET pages or user controls. Caching can significantly improve the performance of ASP.NET applications. Output may be cached on the server, on the client, or on intermediate machines, depending on the value of the Location attribute. The @ OutputCache directive supports the following attributes:

Duration

Specifies the time in seconds for the output of the page to be cached. Note that for output cached by the ASP.NET cache engine on the server, cached output may be evicted from the cache before this duration has elapsed if the page is requested infrequently or if there is a shortage of available memory on the web server. This attribute is required.

Location (pages only)

Specifies where page output should be cached. Valid values include Any, Client, Downstream, None, or Server. The default is Any. This attribute is supported only for output caching with ASP.NET pages. Attempting to use this attribute for caching user controls results in a parser error.

VaryByCustom

Specifies a custom caching variation scheme. Setting the value to browser varies the cache based on the name and major version number of the client's browser. To use this attribute for any other custom value, you must override the GetVaryByCustomString method of the HttpApplication class in the *global.asax* file.

VaryByHeader (pages only)

Specifies a list of one or more HTTP headers, delimited by semicolons, to be used to vary the output cache. Requests with identical values for the specified headers will be served a cached version of the page (if one exists). If no matching page exists in the cache, the page is processed and the resulting output is cached. This attribute is supported only for output caching with ASP.NET pages. Attempting to use this attribute for caching user controls will result in a parser error.

VaryByParam

Specifies a list of one or more HTTP GET or POST parameters, delimited by semicolons, to be used to vary the output cache. Requests with identical values for the specified parameters will receive a cached version of the page (if one exists). If no matching page exists in the cache, the page is processed and the resulting output is cached. This attribute is required. To disable varying the cache by parameter, set the value to none. To vary by all parameters, set the value to the * wildcard.

VaryByControl (user controls only)

Specifies a list of one or more properties of a user control, delimited by semicolons, to be used to vary the output cache. Requests with identical values for the specified parameters will receive a cached version of the user control (if one exists). If no matching user control exists in the cache, the user control is processed and the resulting output is cached. This attribute is required unless a VaryByParam attribute has been specified for the user control's @ OutputCache directive.

@ Reference

Specifies the path to an ASP.NET page or user control that will be compiled dynamically and linked into the current page. The @ Reference directive supports the following attributes:

Page

Specifies the path to a page to be dynamically compiled and linked.

Control

Specifies the path to a user control to be dynamically compiled and linked.

Combining User Interface and Code

Although ASP.NET makes it possible to create much more complex, structured web applications, you can continue to use the simple coding style characteristic of ASP in which code and HTML are combined. This is illustrated in Example 3-1, a simple form that displays the message "Hello World" in the browser window.

Example 3-1. A simple Web Form (HelloWorld.aspx)

```
<%@ Page Language="VB" %>
<html>
<head>
<title>My First Web Form</title>
<script runat="server">
   Sub Page_Load(Sender As Object , e As EventArgs )
      Message.Text = "Hello World!"
   End Sub
</script>
</head>
<body>
   <form runat="server">
      <asp:Label id="Message" runat="server" />
   </form>
</body>
</html>
```

This Web Form uses a server control, <asp:Label>, to output the text "Hello World". The server control is declared using a tag with the prefix asp: followed by the attribute runat="server". The attribute runat="server" indicates that the code will run on the server and the output will be sent to the browser. The Label control is used to display static text and can be changed using the control's Text property. The entry point into the executable code in Example 3-1 is the event handler for the Page object's Load event, which is called automatically when the page loads.

The tag prefix asp: denotes the namespace. Namespaces define the scope of the controls. Namespaces allow the existence of multiple controls with the same name. Using namespaces, the .NET Framework classes are neatly grouped under hierarchies based on their functionality.

When the page is requested from the browser for the first time, it is compiled and cached. The compiled code is then used to generate the content dynamically. You may notice a delay when you request any ASP.NET page for the first time because of the compilation. Subsequent requests will execute much faster.

To understand how an ASP.NET page is rendered on the browser, you should look at the generated HTML content from within the browser, which is accessible by selecting Internet Explorer's View → Source menu option. The generated HTML from Example 3-1 is shown in Example 3-2.

Example 3-2. Generated HTML from an ASP.NET page

```
<html>
<head>
<title>My First Web Form</title>

</head>
<body>
   <form name="_ctl0" method="post" action="HelloWorld.aspx" id="_ctl0">
```

Example 3-2. Generated HTML from an ASP.NET page (continued)

```
<input type="hidden" name="__VIEWSTATE"
value="dDw4MDEONzIOMDA7dDw7bDxpPDI+Oz47bDxoPDtsPGk8MT47PjtsPHQ8cDxwPGw8VG
V4dDs+O2w8SGVsbG8gV29ybGGQhOz4+Oz47Oz47Pj47Pj47Pg==" />
```

```
    <span id="Message">Hello World!</span>
  </form>
</body>
</html>
```

As you can see by comparing Examples 3-1 and 3-2, the Label server control has been modified to become the HTML <span> tag. Also notice that a hidden form field stores the state of the Label server control.

Code-Behind Files

ASP.NET promotes the separation of code and content. The use of *code-behind files* is one of the mechanisms that aides the separation of the UI and the UI logic. Developing an ASP.NET page using code-behind files requires two steps:

1. Developing the page's UI using HTML and web controls.
2. Developing the UI logic (code-behind) using any of the .NET languages.

A code-behind file consists of a class inherited from the Page class. It provides an object-oriented way of developing the UI logic of an ASP.NET page. The code-behind file has member variables, event handlers, and helper methods that are called from the event handlers specific to an ASP. NET page. The ASP.NET page and the code-behind file are tightly coupled, meaning that changes in one usually often require the other to be changed in order for both to function correctly. Fortunately, when developing pages using code-behind in Visual Studio .NET, most of this is taken care of for you.

The extension of the code-behind file varies depending upon the .NET programming language you choose to develop the code. Typically, it will be *.cs* for C#, *.vb* for Visual Basic, or *.js* for JScript. You can decide to either precompile the code-behind file or let ASP.NET compile the code-behind file for you.

The Page directive provides the glue between an ASP.NET page and a code-behind file at the beginning of your ASP.NET page. The Inherits attribute of the Page directive specifies the name of the .NET class that encapsulates the UI logic. The Src or Codebehind attribute specifies the path to the filename that contains the .NET class itself. Use the Codebehind attribute if the code-behind file is precompiled; otherwise, use the Src attribute. Note that the Codebehind attribute is used only by Visual Studio .NET; it is ignored by the ASP.NET parser. By contrast, the ASP.NET parser uses the Src attribute to locate and compile the code-behind class.

One of the most commonly used pages in any web application is a sign-in page. Example 3-3 shows the HTML source for a simple ASP.NET sign-in page that uses a code-behind file. Note that this example is not designed to show a secure login procedure, but rather to demonstrate the use of code-behind with a Web Forms page. We'll look at creating a login page in Chapter 9. Also note that this example requires that either the page and code-behind class belong to a Visual

Studio .NET project, which Visual Studio would need to build before the page is browsed, or the code-behind class be manually compiled and placed in the application's *bin* subdirectory before the page is browsed.

Example 3-3. ASP.NET page using a code-behind file (CodeBehind.aspx)

```
<%@ Page language="vb" Codebehind="Codebehind.vb"
   Inherits="aspnetian.CodeBehind" %>
<html>
<head></head>
<body>
   <form runat="server">
      <h1>Code-behind demonstration</h1>
      <p>
         <asp:label id="Message" runat="server">
         Enter your name to sign in:
         </asp:label>
      </p>
      <p>
         <table id="SignInTable" cellpadding="5"
           cellspacing="1" bgcolor="Silver" runat="server">
           <tr>
           <td align="right">Name:</td>
              <td align="left">
                 <asp:textbox id="SignInBox" width="200" runat="server"/ >
              </td>
           </tr>
           <tr>
              <td colspan="2" align="middle">
                 <asp:button id="SignInButton" runat="server"
                   text="Sign in"/>
              </td>
           </tr>
         </table>
      </p>
   </form>
</body>
</html>
```

The first line of the page is a Page directive that has the Codebehind and Inherits attributes set to appropriate values. Note that when declaring server controls, we have the option of using both an opening and closing tag (as exemplified by the Message Label control) when the tags contain text to be applied to one of the control's properties (in this case, the Text property), or using a single tag with a closing slash (/). This follows the standard for XML/XHTML syntax.

The source code for the code-behind file is given in Example 3-4. If you look at the member variables of the code-behind class, they have a one-to-one mapping with the IDs of the controls in the ASP.NET page. This mapping is very important because these member variables are the *programmatic accessors* to the controls in the page. You should also note that they are declared as Protected, which means that they are accessible only within the code-behind class and the Web Form that inherits from the code-behind class.

Example 3-4. Code-behind file (CodeBehind.vb)

```
Imports System
Imports System.Web
Imports System.Web.UI
Imports System.Web.UI.WebControls
Imports System.Web.UI.HtmlControls
Namespace aspnetian

Public Class CodeBehind : Inherits System.Web.UI.Page
    Protected Message As Label
    Protected SignInTable As HtmlTable
    Protected WithEvents SignInButton As Button
    Protected SignInBox As TextBox

    Protected Sub Page_Load(sender As Object, e As EventArgs)
        If Page.IsPostBack Then
            Message.Text = "Time is: " & DateTime.Now( ) & "<br />" & _
                Message.Text
        End If
    End Sub

    Protected Sub SignInButton_Click(obj As Object, e As EventArgs ) _
        Handles SignInButton.Click
        Message.Text = "Congratulations, " & SignInBox.Text & _
            "!!! You have successfully signed in."
        SignInTable.Visible = false
    End Sub

End Class
End Namespace
```

 If you are using Visual Studio .NET to test the preceding example, you should note that Visual Studio automatically inserts the AutoEventWireUp attribute of the @ Page directive in each new *.aspx* file created with the IDE, and sets its value to False. If AutoEventWireUp is set to False, the Page_Load event handler shown in Example 3-4 will not fire. Fortunately, Visual Studio .NET also automatically adds a Handles clause (Handles Page.Load) to wire up the event handler automatically as well, so you shouldn't have to worry about it.

All code for the page has been removed from the Web Forms page into the code-behind class.

Because the Codebehind attribute is specified in the Page directive, the code-behind file needs to be compiled into a *.dll* file and deployed into the */bin* folder of your application. Since the code-behind file shown in Example 3-4 uses Visual Basic, you will typically invoke the VB compiler with the options shown here:

```
vbc.exe /out:bin\Codebehind.dll /r:System.dll,System.web.dll /t:library
Codebehind.vb
```

For convenience, it's usually a good idea to set up a DOS batch file (.*bat* extension) with the compilation instructions. Then you can double-click the batch file in Windows Explorer to recompile the code-behind class. Example 3-5 adds the pause command to allow you to view any warnings or errors returned by the compiler before the command-line window is closed.

Example 3-5. Batch compilation file (MakeCodebehind.bat)

```
vbc.exe /t:library /r:System.dll,System.web.dll /out:bin\Codebehind.dll
Codebehind.vb

pause
```

Because the .NET Framework SDK setup program does not register the path to the command-line compilers, the command in Example 3-5 will work only if you add the path to the compilers to the PATH environment variable. Otherwise, you will need to use the full path to *vbc.exe* in your batch file. To add the path to *vbc.exe* to the PATH environment variable, do the following:

1. Right-click the My Computer icon on the desktop and select Properties from the menu.
2. Select the Advanced tab and then click the Environment Variables... button.
3. Under System Variables, scroll to the Path variable, select it, then click Edit...
4. Add a semicolon, followed by the path to *vbc.exe* (typically %windir%\ Microsoft.NET\Framework\%version%\, replacing %windir% with the path to your Windows directory and %version% with the version number of the framework install you want to target) and click OK.
5. Click OK on the Environment Variables and System Properties dialogs to close them. You may need to reboot for this change to take effect.

In Visual Studio .NET, the compilation of a code-behind class is taken care of automatically when you build the project containing the Web Form that uses it. This is tracked by the Codebehind attribute of the @ Page directive.

Stages of Page Processing

During Web Forms processing, the page goes through distinct stages, which are illustrated in Figure 3-1. The Web Forms processor calls a corresponding page processing event at each stage.

In ASP pages other than *global.asa*, you have to write your program logic sequentially because your code is executed in the order in which it appears (termed *procedural programming*). ASP.NET, on the other hand, features *event-driven programming*, in which the order of execution of a particular code block is not predetermined. You write a block of code called an *event handler* that is executed whenever that event occurs.

If you've developed client-side code or have programmed using Visual Basic, you're already familiar with event-driven programming. ASP.NET takes event-driven programming to the server side, encouraging you to structure your

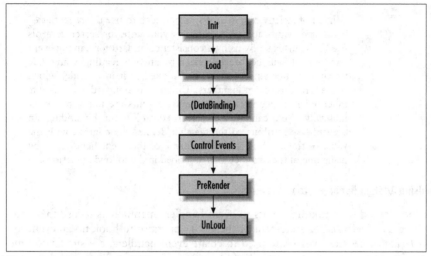

Figure 3-1. The stages of Web Forms page processing

programming logic into event handlers. In ASP.NET, the *Page* object is the representation of your ASP.NET page, and you can write handlers at the page level. ASP, on the other hand, supports only events at the application and session levels.

The Page class inherits all of its important events from the System.Web. UI.Control class, which is the ultimate parent of all server controls. This means that all events described below also apply to both built-in and custom server controls because all of these controls ultimately derive from System.Web.UI.Control.

We'll examine these events in detail. First, however, we'll examine how an event is associated with a particular event handler in Visual Basic .NET and C#.

Handling Events

There are three main techniques for handling events in ASP.NET, one of which takes advantage of ASP.NET's ability to wire up standard event handlers automatically and two of which rely on wiring up event handlers manually.

Automatic event wiring

When handling events in a page that consists of a single *.aspx* page, it is often simplest to create event handlers in the standard *objectname_eventname* syntax familiar to most Visual Basic programmers. By default, ASP.NET will automatically look for handlers such as Page_Init, Page_Load, Page_PreRender, and Page_ UnLoad, and will call them automatically at the appropriate time during page processing.

While not strictly required, it's a good idea to use the *objectname_ eventname* syntax for event handlers you write for server controls used in your page. By using a consistent standard for naming event handlers, it will be much clearer to anyone reading your code (including yourself, if you haven't looked at it in a while) which procedures are event handlers. Unlike the standard page events inherited from Control, server control events are not wired automatically. You can wire a server control event by adding an OnEventName attribute to the tag that defines the control, with the value of the attribute set to the name of the event handler, or by using one of the two methods described in the following sections.

Using AddHandler or += to wire events

One method of wiring up events to event handlers manually is to use the Visual Basic .NET AddHandler statement or the C# += operator to hook up an event to a *delegate*. Delegates, which are used to create event handlers, are similar to function pointers, but are type-safe. The following code snippets illustrate hooking up an event handler for the Click event of an ASP.NET Button server control named Button1:

```
// C#
Button1.Click += new System.EventHandler(Button1_Click);

' Visual Basic .NET
AddHandler Button1.Click AddressOf Button1_Click
```

In both cases, the code tells ASP.NET where to find the procedure to execute when the Click event (namely, Button1.Click) is fired. If, for some reason, you want to unwire an event handler, you can use the Visual Basic .NET RemoveHandler statement or the C# -= operator to accomplish the reverse of AddHandler and +=.

Using the WithEvents and Handles keywords to wire events

Visual Basic .NET developers have a third option for wiring up events: the WithEvents and Handles keywords. The WithEvents keyword precedes the name of a declared control (usually in a code-behind class) and tells ASP.NET that you want to be able to handle the control's events using the Handles keyword. The Handles keyword is appended to the first line of the event handler procedure and is followed by the object name and the name of the event it handles. The syntax of these keywords is shown in the following code snippet. Note the use of the VB line continuation character, which indicates that both the Sub declaration and the Handles keyword should be interpreted as a single line of code:

```
Protected WithEvents MyButton As New Button

Private Sub MyButton_Click(sender As Object, e As EventArgs) _
    Handles MyButton.Click
    'Event handling code
End Sub
```

When using the `AddHandler`, `+=`, or `WithEvents`/`Handles` techniques for wiring up the standard events (Init, Load, etc.) manually, you should add the `AutoEventWireup` attribute to your page's @ Page directive, with the value set to `False`. Otherwise, the event handlers will be called more than once. Fortunately, new pages added to a web project in Visual Studio .NET have this attribute set to `False` by default.

ASP.NET Page and Control Events

Each stage of Web Forms processing shown in Figure 3-1 exposes particular events that can be handled in your code. In this section, we'll examine those events in detail.

Init

The Init event, which is fired with each request, is used to initialize the page. If variables need to be declared and initialized before the majority of page processing begins, the event handler for the Init event is the place to do it. A good example of this is that for C# web projects in Visual Studio .NET, the Page_Init event handler is used to wire up other events handled by a page's code-behind class. The Page_Init handler, in turn, is wired up in the constructor for the code-behind class.

It's important to ensure that the logic performed in the Init event handler is the same for each request to the page, particularly with respect to adding controls to the control tree. Not following this recommendation can lead to problems when posting back to the page.

Load

The Load event is fired on every request to the page, immediately after all the controls on the page have been initialized. Since this event is fired every time the page is loaded, and if your page is posted to itself (known as a *postback*), you can use the IsPostBack property of the Page object to write logic that executes only once. For instance, in the code in Example 3-6, you will see the label "Before Post-Back" the first time you load the page because, since the page has not been submitted to itself yet, the IsPostBack property is `False`. When the page is posted back, you will see the label "Posted Back" because the IsPostBack property has become `True`.

Example 3-6. An ASP.NET page using the PostBack property

```
<%@ Page Language="vb" %>
<html>
<head>
<title>IsPostBack Demonstration</title>
<script runat="server" >
    Sub Page_Load(Sender As Object, e As EventArgs)
        If Not IsPostBack Then
            lblMessage.Text = "Before PostBack"
```

Example 3-6. An ASP.NET page using the PostBack property (continued)

```
      Else
          lblMessage.Text = "Posted Back"
      End If
   End Sub
</script>
</head>
<body>
   <h1>Demonstration of IsPostBack property</h1>
   <form id="frmPostBack" runat="server">
      <asp:label id="lblMessage" runat="server"/>
      <asp:Button type="Submit" text="Post Back" runat="server"/>
   </form>
</body>
</html>
```

DataBinding

The DataBinding event is fired when the page (or a control) is bound to a data source. This will usually occur when the DataBind method of the Page object is called, generally from the Page_Load event handler. The DataBinding event handler can be used to do any special processing related to the data-binding portion of page processing. Databinding is covered in greater detail in Chapter 7.

Control events

Server control events are used primarily in an ASP.NET page to write the UI and programming logic of that page. Control events can be categorized broadly as either change events or action events.

The control event handlers are identified by an attribute of the control's tag. For example, in the following tag:

```
<asp:Button id="MyButton" onClick="MyButton_Clicked" runat="server">
```

the attribute/value pair onClick="MyButton_Clicked" connects the control event (the Click event) with its event handler (the MyButton_ Clicked procedure).

Change events execute only on the next request to the server. For example, if you have written an event handler for the TextBox_Changed event, only when the page is submitted to the server will the code inside the handler be executed. Server-side change events are not the same as the client-side change events that execute instantly.

The most commonly used Change events and the controls that raise these events are listed in Table 3-1.

Table 3-1. Change events

Event	Description	Controls
OnAdCreated	Raised after creation of the control and immediately before the page is rendered. If an Advertisement file is provided, OnAdCreated is raised after an ad has been selected from the file.	AdRotator
OnDayRender	Raised as each cell is created.	Calendar

Table 3-1. Change events (continued)

Event	Description	Controls
OnVisibleMonthChanged	Raised when the user clicks a button for the next or previous month in the Calendar's title.	Calendar
OnSelectionChanged	Raised when the user selects a day, week, or month selector.	Calendar, List
OnSelectedIndexChanged	Raised when the user changes the selection.	CheckBoxList, DropDownList, ListBox, RadioButtonList
OnCheckedChanged	Raised when the user clicks the control.	CheckBox, RadioButton
OnPageIndexChanged	Raised when the user clicks a page selection element.	DataGrid

Action events, unlike Change events, immediately cause the page to be posted back to the server. For example, if you have an event handler for the Command_Click event, the logic inside the handler will be executed as soon as you click that command button (after the page is posted back to the server, of course).

The most commonly used Action events and the controls that raise them are listed in Table 3-2.

Table 3-2. Action events

Event	Description	Controls
OnClick	Raised when the user clicks the control.	Button, ImageButton, LinkButton
OnCommand	Used to pass the CommandEventArgs argument which allows data about which command should be executed, based on the CommandArgument and/or CommandName properties of the control.	Button, ImageButton, LinkButton
OnCancelCommand	Raised by a control whose Command property is Cancel. Typically, this Button or LinkButton control is declared in the EditItemTemplate.	DataGrid, DataList
OnDeleteCommand	Raised by a control whose Command property is Delete. Typically, this Button or LinkButton control is declared in the ItemTemplate.	DataGrid, DataList
OnEditCommand	Raised by a control whose Command property is Edit. Typically, this Button or LinkButton control is declared in the ItemTemplate.	DataGrid, DataList
OnItemCommand	Raised in the control when an embedded control raises an event that is not already covered by Edit, Cancel, Delete, or Update.	DataGrid, DataList
OnUpdateCommand	Raised by a control whose Command property is Update. Typically, this Button or LinkButton control is declared in the EditItemTemplate.	DataGrid, DataList
OnItemCreated	Raised on the server each time a control is created.	DataGrid, DataList
OnSortCommand	Raised when a column is sorted.	DataGrid

Web Forms

PreRender

The PreRender event is fired just before the page (or control) is rendered and sent to the client. The PreRender event is the last chance for page output to be modified before it is sent to the browser. It is also the last event that fires before the ViewState of the controls on the page is saved, so any control changes you wish to have saved to ViewState should be made either before or during this event. ViewState is discussed more fully in the "State Management" section in this chapter. The PreRender event is also the last opportunity for registering client-side script blocks using the helper methods of the Page class (such as Page.RegisterClientScriptBlock).

Unload

The Page_Unload event is fired after the page is rendered. You can use the Page_Unload event handler to write cleanup code.

For example, in the following snippet, the database connection objConnection is closed:

```
Sub Page_Unload(sender As Object, e As EventArgs )
    ' Close the database connection
    objConnection.Close( )
End Sub
```

State Management

In a typical web page, it is very common for data entry forms to retain their values after the form has been posted and the same page is returned to the client (that is, to retain the values from a posted form in the postback). To implement this feature in classic ASP, you need to determine whether or not the page is requested by a client for the first time. You also need to write code that will display the submitted value in the controls. In contrast, ASP.NET performs state management automatically in postbacks.

ASP.NET uses a simple hidden HTML form field to retain the values automatically during postbacks. There are no ActiveX controls or applets or client-side scripts used to maintain state. Thus, you need not write code to retain values explicitly.

 ASP.NET maintains only the state of server controls—i.e., the controls declared with the runat="server" attribute/value pair. State management can be enabled or disabled for individual controls or an entire page by setting the MaintainState property to True (its default value) or False.

Now let's revisit the concept of ViewState, which was introduced earlier in this chapter. ViewState is a collection of information about the properties of an ASP.NET page and its controls (maintained in a hidden form field named _VIEWSTATE). Since control state on the server does not exist once the page has been rendered to the client, ViewState exists to store the value of properties of controls on the page. As the name itself implies, ViewState preserves the state associated with a particular view of a page. It is used by the noninput controls (such as Label and DataGrid) to store their ambient state across requests. Thus, when a page is posted back to the server, and the result of the postback is rendered to the browser, controls such as textboxes and listboxes will automatically retain their state, unless the control's EnableViewState property has been set to False or the state of the control was modified programmatically on the server.

 Only base properties are persisted in the ViewState. Any change in these properties before rendering the page will be persisted.

If your page is not posted back to itself, you can set the property EnableViewState to False at the page level (via the @ Page directive) to avoid the extra processing and storage space required for maintaining ViewState. You can also disable/ enable view state on a per control basis.

Caching Page Output

Another new feature of ASP.NET that should not be overlooked is its support for caching—in particular, output caching. Output caching provides the ability to have the rendered output of a page cached for a specified duration simply and easily. By caching the rendered output in memory, subsequent requests for the page can be delivered substantially faster and with considerably less processor utilization than if the page needs to be re-rendered for each request, which can lead to substantial performance increases. The ASP.NET team has reported page delivery two to three times faster when using output caching. Output caching is available for both ASP.NET pages and ASP.NET user controls.

Not every page can be cached in its entirety. Some pages contain too much dynamic information to be cached as a whole, but even these pages may have portions that seldom change. By moving these static portions into user controls (which also provides the possibility of reuse) and then output caching the user controls, at least some performance benefit can be realized—even for very dynamic pages.

The best part about output caching is its simplicity. In its most basic state, caching the output of a page requires a directive like the following (which you should add directly below the @ Page or @ Control directive):

```
<%@ OutputCache Duration="20" VaryByParam="None" %>
```

This directive tells ASP.NET to cache the output of the page for 20 seconds and to return the same cached version of the page for all requests. Example 3-7 demonstrates how to cache the output of a page for 60 seconds and to cache a different version of the page for each different value of the name parameter, when sent as part of the query string of a GET request (for example, *http://localhost/aspnetian/ OutCache.aspx?name=John*). The cache can be varied by form fields in a POST request as well, if desired, by setting the value of the VaryByParam attribute to the name of the form field to vary by.

Example 3-7. Output caching in ASP.NET

```
<%@ Page Language="vb" %>
<%@ OutputCache Duration="60" VaryByParam="name" %>
<html>
<head>
<title>Output Cache Demonstration</title>
<script runat="server" >
   Sub Page_Load(Sender As Object, e As EventArgs)
      lblMessage.Text = "Current time is: " & _
         DateTime.Now( )
   End Sub
</script>
</head>
<body>
   <h1>Demonstration of Output Caching</h1>
   <form id="frmPostBack" runat="server">
      <asp:label id="lblMessage" runat="server"/>
   </form>
</body>
</html>
```

As explained in the "Using @ Directives" section earlier in this chapter, you can also have ASP.NET cache multiple versions of a page on the basis of specific HTTP headers by using the VaryByHeader attribute, or you can cache multiple versions of a user control on the basis of some of its properties by using the VaryByControl attribute. Caching the output of a user control is essentially the same process as that shown in Example 3-7, except that you may not use the VaryByHeader attribute in a user control.

Additional Resources

The following sites provide more information on topics discussed in this chapter:

http://www.gotdotnet.com/QuickStart/aspplus/
   The ASP.NET QuickStart samples, which can also be installed locally, provide a wide range of examples and sample code and explanations that can be very useful when starting out. The GotDotNet.com site also has sample code available from other users.

http://www.asp.net/forums/
   The ASP.NET forums includes forums specific to a wide variety of ASP.NET programming topics, including Web Forms, Caching, State Management, and many more. Questions are answered by experts within the ASP.NET developer community, and even sometimes by members of the ASP.NET development team themselves.

4

Web Services

The primary purpose of ASP.NET web services is to provide access to application functionality through standard web protocols (including HTTP and XML), regardless of the application's location or the platform on which it is built. When your application exposes functionality as a web service, that functionality can be consumed by clients on any platform, presuming the clients understand XML and SOAP and can communicate via the HTTP protocol. More plainly, a web service is a function that is called over the Internet.

An ASP.NET web service can be very simple or it can provide complex functionality. It can return a variety of data types—from simple strings and integer values to complex data types such as classes and datasets. Web services are traditionally thought of as providing only business services (e.g., you call a method, perhaps passing in some parameters, and you receive a return value), but there's no reason why you can't create a web service that returns a chunk of HTML. Doing so would allow you to provide cross-platform access to functionality similar to that provided by ASP.NET Server Controls, albeit with some performance overhead.

Standards and Specifications

The ability of web services to fulfill their mission of providing cross-platform interoperability and application integration depends on a number of existing and emerging standards and specifications. The following list describes the most important standards, including their current standardization status. Note that the W3C term for a stable standard is *Recommendation*.

HTTP (Current version 1.1, Recommendation; http://www.w3.org/Protocols)
> HTTP is the standard protocol of the World Wide Web. HTTP is essential to web services because most organizations allow communication over TCP port 80 (the default HTTP port) to traverse their firewalls. This contrasts with protocols such as DCOM, which use ports that are routinely blocked—making them virtually useless for the Internet.

XML (Current version 1.0, Recommendation; http://www.w3.org/XML)
> eXtensible Markup Language (XML) provides a standardized way of structuring and communicating data via a tag-based text syntax. Combined with the XML Schema standard, XML allows simple and complex data types to be serialized and deserialized to text for transmission over an HTTP connection.

SOAP (Current version 1.1, Submission; http://www.w3.org/2000/xp)
> Simple Object Access Protocol (SOAP) is an emerging standard that specifies how to format RPC-style requests and responses using XML and communicating over HTTP. SOAP is essential to web services. See "What Is SOAP?" in Chapter 2 for more information on the SOAP protocol status and its impact on developing web services. Note that SOAP Version 1.2 is a Candidate Recommendation at the time of this writing, so it will soon replace Version 1.1.

WSDL (Current version 1.1, Submission; http://www.w3.org/TR/wsdl)
> Web Services Description Language (WSDL) is a specification for creating XML schemas that describe a web service. This description is analogous to a COM type library in the sense that a WSDL file provides a contract of the publicly exposed members of a web service, just as a type library does for a COM object. By reading the WSDL contract for a web service, clients can learn what methods are exposed by the web service and how to call them.

UDDI (http://www.uddi.org)
> Universal Description, Discovery, and Integration (UDDI) is an open platform-neutral framework being developed by Microsoft, IBM, and other vendors to address the need for a way to publish, locate, and integrate web services simply and robustly. Web service developers can register their web services with one of the UDDI directories, and potential clients can search the UDDI directory for web services appropriate to their needs.

WS Specifications
> The WS specifications, which were originally introduced by Microsoft as the Global XML Web Services Architecture (GXA) specification, are intended to address some of the issues not covered by the HTTP, XML, and SOAP specifications. These include security, transactions, message routing, and more. You can read more about these specifications at *http://msdn.microsoft.com/library/en-us/dnglobspec/html/wsspecsover.asp*. You can find information about all of Microsoft's efforts in the Web Services area at *http://msdn.microsoft.com/webservices/*.

SOAP, WSDL, UDDI, and the WS specification are not settled standards. Thus, incompatibilities between different implementations of SOAP and web services are possible if those implementations use different drafts of a given standard or specification. A good example of this possibility is WSDL, which is a successor to an earlier draft specification called SDL. Because of incompatibilities between SDL and WSDL, communicating between a client using SDL and a web service using WSDL (or vice-versa) will probably require some tweaking to achieve interoperability. As specifications such as SOAP and WSDL work their way through the standards process (or in the case of vendor specifications, as they gain acceptance), instances of incompatibility should become rarer.

Web Services Architecture

In ASP.NET, a web service is essentially a listener that monitors a particular URL exposed via HTTP, looking for requests packaged as SOAP messages. When a request arrives, the ASP.NET runtime unpackages the request and calls the method for which the request is intended, passing in any parameters included with the request. If the request has a return value (which is not required), the ASP.NET runtime packages up the return value (based on the XML schema datatype specifications) and sends it to the client as a SOAP message. What this means to developers is that your application doesn't need to know anything about the client that will consume it, other than the fact that it can understand XML and SOAP. Thus, developers can essentially write methods that will be called as web services just as though they were writing methods that would be called locally.

This functionality is provided by the runtime largely for free. Developers expose their functionality as web services by marking their methods with a specific metadata attribute, the WebService attribute. The Common Language Runtime (CLR) takes care of the rest—from packaging and unpackaging SOAP requests to automatically providing HTML documentation of the web service—if it is called from a web browser (rather than by a SOAP request).

Figure 4-1 illustrates how an ASP.NET web service works.

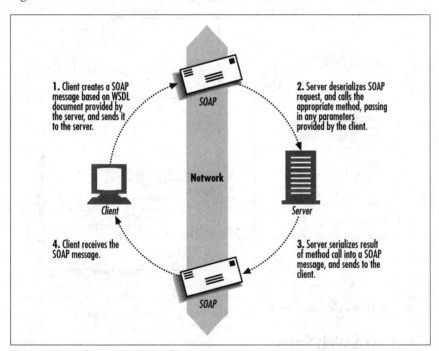

Figure 4-1. Inside an ASP.NET web service

Metadata Attributes

Metadata attributes are somewhat similar in concept to attributes on HTML tags or XML elements. Metadata attributes provide additional information about assemblies, classes, and class members to the CLR. Attributes tell the CLR to treat a particular member a certain way or to automatically provide certain functionality (such as the automatic packaging/unpackaging of SOAP requests for web services).

In terms of file structure, web services in ASP.NET are implemented by *.asmx* pages. An *.asmx* page begins with the @ WebService directive, which contains attributes instructing the CLR how to run the web service. The *.asmx* page can either directly contain the code necessary for the web service to operate or can contain a Class attribute in its @ WebService directive that points to a compiled class containing the implementation code. In this latter case, the file containing the source code for the compiled class is called a code-behind file, as introduced in Chapter 3 and illustrated in Figure 4-2.

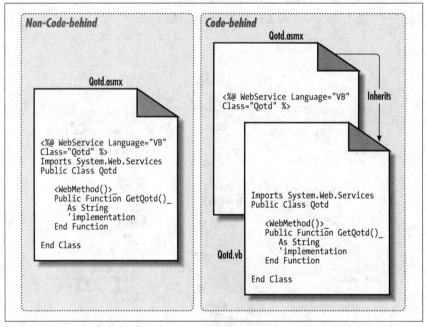

Figure 4-2. How code-behind works

Creating a Web Service

There are two different coding techniques with which one can construct a web service: inline code and code-behind.

Web Service with Inline Code

Creating a single-file web service is quite simple. All that's required is to create a new file, add an @ WebService directive and a class containing the implementation for the methods you want to expose, and decorate the methods to be exposed with the WebMethod attribute. The @ WebService directive supports the following attributes:

Class

Specifies the name of the class containing the implementation of the web service. This attribute is necessary to allow the ASP.NET runtime to locate the compiled class at runtime.

CodeBehind

Specifies the name of a code-behind file that contains the class that implements the web service. This attribute is used by Visual Studio .NET when building the project containing the code-behind class.

Debug

Specifies whether the web service should be compiled with debug symbols.

Language

Specifies the language used for code written inline in the *.asmx* file.

To demonstrate the creation of a web service, look at Example 4-1, which implements a simple "Quote of the Day" web service.

Example 4-1. Quote of the day application (Qotd.asmx)

```
<%@ WebService Language="VB" Class="Qotd" %>
Imports System
Imports System.Data
Imports System.Web
Imports System.Web.Services

Public Class Qotd

    <WebMethod( )> _
    Public Function GetQotd( ) As String
        Dim QuoteDS As New DataSet( )
        Dim Context As HttpContext = HttpContext.Current( )
        Dim QuoteXML As String = Context.Server.MapPath("qotd.xml")
        Dim QuoteCount As Integer
        Dim QuoteToReturn As Integer
        Dim Randomizer As New Random( )

        QuoteDS.ReadXml(QuoteXML)
        QuoteCount = QuoteDS.Tables(0).Rows.Count
        QuoteToReturn = Randomizer.Next(0, QuoteCount)
        Return QuoteDS.Tables(0).Rows(QuoteToReturn)(0) & _
            "<br /><br />" & QuoteDS.Tables(0).Rows(QuoteToReturn)(1)
    End Function

End Class
```

The WebService directive in Example 4-1 specifies Visual Basic .NET as the language used in the web service and specifies that the web service's implementation is contained in a class named Qotd. The next four lines import several namespaces to save the effort of typing in the namespace name each time a member is used in the code.

Next comes the class definition for the Qotd class. This class contains a single function, GetQotd, which returns a string containing a quote and the name of its author, separated by two HTML line breaks. Note that this definition assumes that the consumer of the web service will display the results as HTML. In a later example, we'll provide a more flexible implementation.

Within the method, you create an ADO.NET dataset (see Chapter 7 for more information on ADO.NET) and use the ReadXml method of the DataSet class to read in the stored quotes from a simple XML file. The contents of this file are shown in Example 4-2. Once the data is loaded into the dataset, you check the Count property to determine how many records exist and then use an instance of the Random class to return a random number from 0 to the record count. This number is then used to retrieve the first and second values (which also happen to be the only values) of the desired row, as shown in the following snippet, and return it to the caller of the method:

```
Return QuoteDS.Tables(0).Rows(QuoteToReturn)(0) & _
    "<br /><br />" & QuoteDS.Tables(0).Rows(QuoteToReturn)(1)
```

Note that since collections in .NET are zero-based, Tables(0) refers to the first table in the Tables collection of the dataset (in this case, the only table). You can access the value of a particular field in a particular row in a specific table by using the syntax:

```
My Variable = MyDataset.Tables(tableindex).Rows(rowindex)(fieldindex)
```

Example 4-2. Qotd.xml

```
<Quotes>
  <Quote>
    <QuoteText>Never give in--never, never, never, never, in nothing great or
small, large or petty, never give in except to convictions of honour and good
sense. Never yield to force; never yield to the apparently overwhelming might of
the enemy.</QuoteText>
    <QuoteAuthor>Winston Churchill</QuoteAuthor>
  </Quote>
  <Quote>
    <QuoteText>We shall fight on the beaches. We shall fight on the landing
grounds. We shall fight in the fields, and in the streets, we shall fight in the
hills. We shall never surrender!</QuoteText>
    <QuoteAuthor>Winston Churchill</QuoteAuthor>
  </Quote>
  <Quote>
    <QuoteText>An appeaser is one who feeds a crocodile-hoping it will eat him
last.</QuoteText>
    <QuoteAuthor>Winston Churchill</QuoteAuthor>
  </Quote>
  <Quote>
    <QuoteText>We shape our buildings: thereafter they shape us.</ QuoteText>
```

Example 4-2. Qotd.xml (continued)

```
      <QuoteAuthor>Winston Churchill</QuoteAuthor>
   </Quote>
   <Quote>
      <QuoteText>Science without religion is lame, religion without science is
blind.</QuoteText>
      <QuoteAuthor>Albert Einstein</QuoteAuthor>
   </Quote>
   <Quote>
      <QuoteText>As far as the laws of mathematics refer to reality, they are not
certain, and as far as they are certain, they do not refer to reality.</
QuoteText>
      <QuoteAuthor>Albert Einstein</QuoteAuthor>
   </Quote>
   <Quote>
      <QuoteText>If A equals success, then the formula is A equals X plus Y plus
Z. X is work. Y is play. Z is keep your mouth shut.</QuoteText>
      <QuoteAuthor>Albert Einstein</QuoteAuthor>
   </Quote>
   <Quote>
      <QuoteText>When a man sits with a pretty girl for an hour, it seems like a
minute. But let him sit on a hot stove for a minute-and it's longer than any
hour. That's relativity.</QuoteText>
      <QuoteAuthor>Albert Einstein</QuoteAuthor>
   </Quote>
</Quotes>
```

Once you've added the code in Example 4-1 to a file, saved it with the *.asmx* extension, and created a file called *Qotd.xml* with the text in Example 4-2 in the same virtual directory, you can open the *.asmx* file in a browser to test the implementation. The result should be similar to Figure 4-3.

The main documentation page displayed in Figure 4-3 is generated automatically by the ASP.NET runtime whenever a web service (*.asmx* file) is called from a browser rather than by a SOAP request. You should note three things about the page in Figure 4-3:

- The link to the service description. Accessing this link displays the WSDL contract (see Figure 4-4), which describes the methods exposed by the web service (in much the same way as an IDL file describes a COM object). This contract is also used by .NET clients to generate proxy classes for consuming the web service. This topic is discussed in more detail later in the chapter.

- The link that provides access to a documentation page for the GetQotd method, which is shown in Figure 4-5. If the web service exposed multiple methods, the main documentation page would provide a link for each.

- The main documentation page also displays a recommendation about the default namespace for the web service. This recommendation refers to the XML namespace, which, if not specified, defaults to *http://tempuri.org* and should not be confused with the .NET namespaces. A later example demonstrates how to set the default namespace to a unique URL.

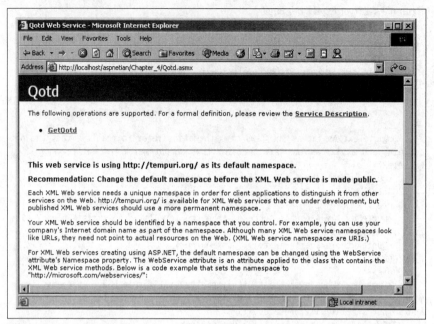

Figure 4-3. Browsing a web service

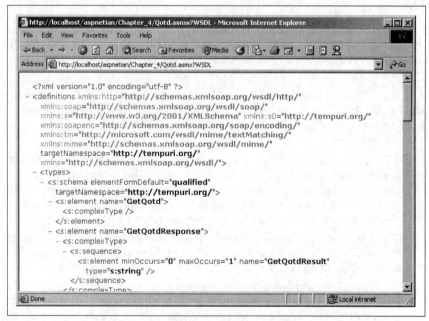

Figure 4-4. Service description for Qotd.asmx

As shown in Figure 4-5, the documentation page for the GetQotd method provides an Invoke button that allows you to test the web service method and that provides documentation on creating SOAP, HTTP GET, and HTTP POST requests for the selected method. In this case, HTTP GET and POST are not shown.

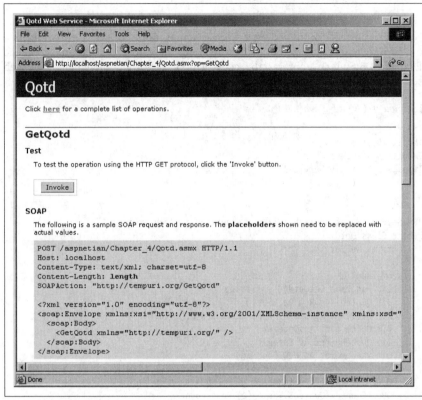

Figure 4-5. GetQotd documentation

If you click the Invoke button, a new browser window should open, displaying XML text similar to the following snippet. (Note that the quotation and author may vary, since they are selected randomly.)

```
<?xml version="1.0" encoding="utf-8" ?>
<string xmlns="http://tempuri.org/">We shape our buildings: thereafter
    they shape us.<br><br>Winston Churchill</string>
```

Because the GetQotd method returns a string containing HTML formatting (the <br/> tags), it will automatically display the quote and author on separate lines if shown in a browser. But what if a consumer of the web service wants to apply a different format to the quote than the author?

With this implementation, they're out of luck, unless they are willing to parse out the two parts and apply the formatting individually that way. To address this issue, look at a modified version of the Qotd web service that uses a code-behind class for its implementation.

Web Service Using Code-Behind

The following snippet is all that's required for the *.asmx* file for our code-behind version of the Qotd web service (*Qotd_cb.asmx*):

```
<%@ WebService Language="VB" Class="aspnetian.Qotd_cb" %>
```

Note that instead of providing the class name, Qotd_cb, we've also added a namespace name, "aspnetian," to reduce the likelihood of naming conflicts. Example 4-3, which contains the code-behind class that implements the web service, defines this namespace.

Example 4-3. Qotd_cb.vb

```
Imports System
Imports System.Data
Imports System.Web
Imports System.Web.Services

Namespace aspnetian

<WebService(Namespace:="http://www.aspnetian.com/webservices/")> _
Public Class Qotd_cb
   Inherits WebService

   <WebMethod( )> _
   Public Function GetQotd( ) As String
      Dim QuoteDS As New DataSet( )
      Dim QuoteXML As String = Server.MapPath("qotd.xml")
      Dim QuoteCount As Integer
      Dim QuoteNumber As Integer
      Dim Randomizer As New Random( )

      QuoteDS.ReadXml(QuoteXML)
      QuoteCount = QuoteDS.Tables(0).Rows.Count
      QuoteNumber = Randomizer.Next(0, QuoteCount)
      Return QuoteDS.Tables(0).Rows(QuoteNumber)(0) & "<br /><br />" _
         & QuoteDS.Tables(0).Rows(QuoteNumber)(1)
   End Function

   <WebMethod( )> _
   Public Function GetQuoteNumber( ) As Integer
      Dim QuoteDS As New DataSet( )
      Dim QuoteXML As String = Server.MapPath("qotd.xml")
      Dim QuoteCount As Integer
      Dim Randomizer As New Random( )

      QuoteDS.ReadXml(QuoteXML)
      QuoteCount = QuoteDS.Tables(0).Rows.Count
      Return Randomizer.Next(0, QuoteCount)
   End Function

   <WebMethod( )> _
   Public Function GetQuote(QuoteNumber As Integer) As String
```

Example 4-3. Qotd_cb.vb (continued)

```
    Dim QuoteDS As New DataSet( )
    Dim QuoteXML As String = Server.MapPath("qotd.xml")
    Dim QuoteCount As Integer
    Dim QuoteToReturn As String

    QuoteDS.ReadXml(QuoteXML)
    QuoteToReturn = QuoteDS.Tables(0).Rows(QuoteNumber)(0)
    Return QuoteToReturn
  End Function

  <WebMethod( )> _
  Public Function GetAuthor(QuoteNumber As Integer) As String
    Dim QuoteDS As New DataSet( )
    Dim QuoteXML As String = Server.MapPath("qotd.xml")
    Dim QuoteCount As Integer
    Dim AuthorToReturn As String

    QuoteDS.ReadXml(QuoteXML)
    AuthorToReturn = QuoteDS.Tables(0).Rows(QuoteNumber)(1)
    Return AuthorToReturn
  End Function

End Class

End Namespace
```

In addition to wrapping the class declaration in a namespace declaration, this example adds a new attribute, WebService, and several new methods. The WebService attribute is added at the class level so we can specify the default namespace (XML namespace) for the web service. This namespace needs to be a value unique to your web service. In the example, the namespace is *http://www.aspnetian.com/webservices/*; for your own web services, you should use your own unique value. You may want to substitute a URL that you control, as doing so will assure you that web services created by others will not use the same value. If you are developing your web service with Visual Basic .NET in Visual Studio .NET 2003, the Namespace attribute will automatically be set to a URL consisting of the value http://tempuri.org/, plus the project name, plus the name of the .asmx file (e.g., *http://tempuri.org/myproject/mywebservice*).

The added methods are GetQuoteNumber, GetQuote, and GetAuthor. These methods demonstrate that even though web service requests are sent as XML text, the input and output parameters of web service methods are still strongly typed. These methods address the potential formatting issue discussed previously by allowing clients to retrieve a quote and its author separately in order to accommodate different formatting for each. To ensure that the matching author for the quote is retrieved, the client would first call GetQuoteNumber to retrieve a randomly generated quote number, and then call GetQuote and/or GetAuthor, passing in the received quote number. This provides the client more flexibility, but does not require the web service to keep track of which quote number was sent to a given client.

An important difference between the single-file web service and the code-behind implementation is that for the code-behind version, you must compile the code-behind class into an assembly manually and place it in the *bin* directory before the web service will work. Note that this step is automatic when you build a web service project in Visual Studio .NET. If you're writing code by hand, this step can be accomplished by using a DOS batch file containing the commands shown in the following snippet:

```
vbc /t:library /r:System.Web.dll /r:System.dll /r:System.Web.Services.dll /
r:System.Xml.dll /r:System.Data.dll /out:bin\qotd_cb.dll qotd_cb.vb

pause
```

Note that all command-line options for the *vbc.exe* compiler should be part of a single command. The pause command allows you to see any warnings or errors generated during compilation before the command window is closed.

Inheriting from WebService

In Example 4-1, the Current property of the HttpContext class is used to get a reference to the Context object for the current request. Getting this reference is necessary to access to the Server intrinsic object so that we can call its MapPath method to get the local path to the XML file used to store the quotes. However, as you add more methods that use the XML file, you end up with redundant calls to HttpContext.Current.

For better readability and maintainability, you can eliminate these calls by having the web service class inherit from System.Web.Services.WebService. Inheriting from WebService automatically provides access to the Server, Session, and Application intrinsic objects, as well as to the HttpContext instance for the current request and the User object representing the authenticated user. In the case of Example 4-3, inheriting from WebService eliminates the calls to HttpContext. Current entirely.

Web services that inherit from the WebService class have access to the ASP.NET Session object. However, you should carefully consider whether your application will benefit from storing state information in the Session collection before using it—particularly if your application may need to scale to more than one web server. ASP.NET now provides out-of-process Session state options that can be used in web farm situations. Unfortunately, because these solutions require, at best, an out-of-process call (and at worst, a cross-machine call), using them results in a significant performance penalty. Regardless of your decision, you should always load-test your application to ensure that it will meet your performance and scalability needs.

Figure 4-6 shows the main documentation page for the code-behind version of the Qotd web service. Note that the main documentation page contains links for each new method exposed by the web service. Also note that the page no longer displays the namespace warning/recommendation, since we set the default namespace in this version.

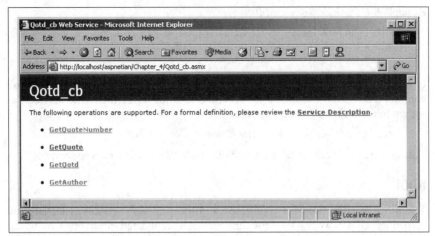

Figure 4-6. Browsing Qotd_cb.asmx

You've written a web service and you tested it by opening the *.asmx* file in a browser and invoking the methods. What's next? Unless your web service will be consumed only by yourself or by someone with whom you have regular communication, you need to publish or advertise your web service in some way. Potential clients also need to locate your web service to use it.

Publishing a web service can be accomplished in either of two ways: through a discovery document or by registering the web service with a UDDI directory.

Discovery Documents

A discovery document is a file with the extension *.disco* that contains references to the WDSL contracts for web services you want to publish, references to documentation for your web services, and/or references to other discovery documents.

Publishing and Locating Web Services

You can publish a discovery document on your web server and provide clients with a link to or a URL for the discovery document. Clients can then use the *disco.exe* .NET command-line utility to generate WSDL contracts locally for creating proxy classes to communicate with the web service. Example 4-4 shows the format of a discovery document for the Qotd web service.

Example 4-4. Qotd.disco

```
<?xml version="1.0"?>
<discovery xmlns="http://schemas.xmlsoap.org/disco/">
   <contractRef
      ref="http://localhost/aspnetian/Chapter_4/Qotd.asmx?wsdl"
      docRef="http://localhost/aspnetian/Chapter_4/Qotd.asmx"
      xmlns="http://schemas.xmlsoap.org/disco/scl/" />
   <contractRef
      ref="http://localhost/aspnetian/Chapter_4/Qotd_cb.asmx?wsdl"
```

Example 4-4. Qotd.disco (continued)

```
         docRef="http://localhost/aspnetian/Chapter_4/Qotd_cb.asmx"
         xmlns="http://schemas.xmlsoap.org/disco/scl/" />
</discovery>
```

Once clients know the location of the discovery file, they can use the *disco.exe* command-line utility to create local WSDL files for all of their web services, as shown in the following code snippet:

```
    disco http://localhost/aspnetian/Chapter_4/Qotd.disco
```

This line creates local WSDL files for both the Qotd and Qotd_cb web services.

UDDI

The other method used for publishing and locating web services is UDDI. Still maturing, UDDI works by providing multiple replicated directories in which public web services can be registered. The UDDI web site (*http://www.uddi.com*) contains a list of the participating directory sites from which clients or providers of web services can choose. Providers of web services give relevant information, such as the type of web service, an appropriate category (such as Construction or Financial and Insurance), and most importantly, the URL for the application's WSDL file. Potential clients can search the UDDI directory for web services that match their needs and then locate and consume them via their WSDL contract.

Consuming a Web Service

In ASP.NET, consuming a web service is nearly as easy as creating one. ASP.NET provides a utility called *wsdl.exe* that can create a proxy class, which is a class that knows all of the necessary details of communicating with the web service via SOAP, as shown in Figure 4-1, and which can be called from a client application the same way as any other managed class. In this way, the proxy class abstracts away the complexities of communication with the web service.

Consuming a web service in ASP.NET requires four steps:

1. Locate the WSDL contract for the desired web service.
2. Create a proxy class by using the *wsdl.exe* command-line utility.
3. Compile the proxy class.
4. Create a new instance of the proxy class in the client application (WinForms, Console, or ASP.NET) and call the desired methods.

In the case of our Qotd_cb web service, you would execute the following command (again, conveniently saved as a DOS batch file) to generate a proxy class based on the web service:

```
    wsdl /l:vb /out:Qotd_cb_proxy.vb http://localhost/ASPdotNET_iaN/Chapter_ 4/
    Qotd_cb.asmx?WSDL

    pause
```

The /1 parameter specifies that the proxy class should be generated in Visual Basic .NET (the default is C#). The /out parameter specifies the name and, optionally, the path of the output file. This is important if you are compiling your proxy class in the same directory as the code-behind class that implements the web service. In this case, if you do not specify the output filename, the file *Qotd_cb.vb* will be overwritten. Once the proxy class has been generated, it should be compiled, and the resulting assembly should be placed in the *bin* directory. This can be accomplished using a command such as the one in the following snippet:

```
vbc /t:library /r:System.Web.dll,System.dll,System.Web.Services.dll, System.
Xml.dll,System.Data.dll /out:bin\qotd_cb_proxy.dll
qotd_cb_proxy.vb

pause
```

Remember that all parameters for the *vbc.exe* compiler should be part of the same command; therefore, there should not be any line breaks if you choose to save the command to a batch file.

Once you've generated and compiled your proxy class, using the web service is exactly like using any other .NET class. You simply create an instance and call the desired methods. Example 4-5 shows the code for a simple ASP.NET page that consumes the Qotd_cb web service.

Example 4-5. Qotd_cb.aspx

```
<%@ Page Language="VB" %>
<%@ Import Namespace="aspnetian" %>
<html>
<head>
<title>Quote of the Day Web service example</title>
<script runat="server">
    Sub Page_Load(Sender As Object , e As EventArgs )
        Dim Quote As New Qotd_cb( )
        Dim QuoteNumber As Integer
        QuoteNumber = Quote.GetQuoteNumber
        Message1.Text = Quote.GetQuote(QuoteNumber)
        Message2.Text = Quote.GetAuthor(QuoteNumber)
    End Sub
</script>
</head>
<body>
    <h1>Demonstration of Quote of the Day Web service</h1>
    <form runat="server">
        <h4><i>"<asp:Literal id="Message1" runat="server" />"</i></h4>
        <h3>--<asp:Literal id="Message2" runat="server" /></h3>
    </form>
</body>
</html>
```

The page imports the aspnetian namespace defined in the Qotd_cb web service class, creates an instance of the proxy class, and then calls the GetQuoteNumber method to retrieve a random quote number. The page then calls the GetQuote and GetAuthor methods, passing in the quote number each time, and returns the result to the Text property of two ASP. NET literal controls. The output of this page is shown in Figure 4-7.

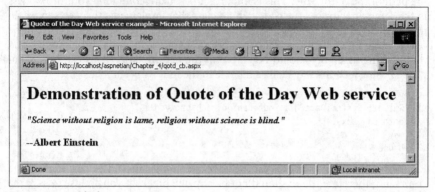

Figure 4-7. Qotd_cb.aspx output

Additional Resources

The following sites provide additional information on the topics discussed in this chapter:

http://www.gotdotnet.com/QuickStart/aspplus/
> The ASP.NET QuickStart samples, which can also be installed locally, provide a wide range of examples and sample code and explanations that can be very useful when starting out. The GotDotNet.com site has sample code available from other users and many other features.

http://www.asp.net/forums/
> Created by the Microsoft ASP.NET team, and moderated by community leaders, the ASP.NET forums includes a forum dedicates specifically to XML Web Services, as well as to other related topics.

5

ASP.NET Server Controls

Controls provide the familiar elements of a graphical user interface (GUI): buttons, drop-down boxes, checkboxes, etc. Server controls are controls that enable server-side processing. They provide a range of functionality, from simple data entry to complex data validation.

ASP.NET ships with a suite of ready-to-run server controls you can use to develop powerful Web Forms pages. A key component of the ASP.NET development model, these server controls abstract significant amounts of programming logic into simple-to-use tags. Server controls make it easy to separate programmatic logic from UI elements using code-behind, because you typically instantiate the controls using a tag-based syntax while keeping your UI-related logic in a separate code-behind file. In practical terms, this means that programmers can hand over a *.aspx* page to UI designers without having to worry about their programming logic getting completely ruined in the process.

In ASP.NET, it's easy for developers to create their own controls from scratch or to build on the functionality of existing controls by creating user controls that combine HTML, server controls, and other page elements, or by creating their own custom server controls. We'll discuss both techniques in Chapter 6.

ASP.NET Server Controls are classified as either *HTML controls* or *web controls*. This chapter summarizes the standard controls and the various methods for creating and modifying them.

HTML Controls

The HTML controls have a one-to-one mapping with HTML tags. You can create HTML controls and change their appearance by modifying their properties. HTML controls have an object model that closely resembles the HTML syntax of the elements, as well as the Dynamic HTML (DHTML) object model.

The attributes of an HTML tag correspond to the properties of the HTML control. The HTML controls are declared by using the standard HTML tags with the attribute runat="server". For example:

```
<input type="text" id="txtName" runat="server">
```

 The id attribute is very important for all server controls if you plan to access your control programmatically, since it defines the name by which the object will be referenced in code.

In ASP.NET, the following HTML tags are supported as HTML controls:

```
<a>
<img>
<form>
<table>
<tr>
<th>
<td>
<select>
<textarea>
<button>
```
All <input> tags

You can declare other HTML tags as server-side controls by using the runat="server" attribute/value pair. However, these controls are not supported; instead, unsupported HTML elements are handled by a generic super HTML server control called HtmlGenericControl. The HTML elements you might typically handle in this way include <div>, <span>, <body>, and <font>.

Web Controls

One of the challenges in developing web applications is that of providing support for different browsers that have different capabilities, proprietary extensions to HTML, and support for different scripting languages, while maintaining the desired level of functionality and consistency. The only way to render content consistently is to detect the browser type and send the appropriate version of the page to that browser. ASP.NET web controls relieve us of this burden by sniffing the browser type and sending the appropriate content based on the capabilities of the browser. ASP.NET server controls use HTML 3.2 for the down-level clients (older browsers that do not support DHTML and CSS) and can generate Dynamic HTML for the up-level clients (such as Internet Explorer 5.5 or later). In the current release of ASP.NET, the only controls that make extensive use of DHTML in up-level browsers are the validation controls (which are discussed in more detail in the "Validation Controls" section later in this chapter). Other controls, such as the Button server control, use client-side JavaScript for initiating postbacks. These postback scripts are designed to work with any Javascript-compatible browser.

Web controls provide an abstract, consistent, and strongly typed object model. They are abstract because their object model does not necessarily reflect HTML syntax. These controls include standard controls like text boxes and radio buttons, as well as rich controls like calendars and data grids. Web controls are always declared with the ASP namespace prefix, sometimes using self-closing tags as follows:

```
<asp:textbox id="txtName" text="Hello, World!" runat="server" />
```

You can alternatively declare a web control by using an opening and closing tag pair. For certain controls, such as the Label and TextBox controls, any text contained between the opening and closing tags will be assigned to the Text property of the control. Thus, the following code fragment is equivalent to the previous one:

```
<asp:textbox id="txtName" runat="server">
    Hello, World!
</asp:textbox>
```

Like element and attribute names in page declarations, the tag and attribute names used to create server controls declaratively are not case-sensitive. However, because the HTML 4.0 standard specifies that tags and attributes should be in lowercase, it's good coding practice to follow this guideline, even though server control tags are not sent to the browser.

 When creating controls programmatically (as discussed later in this chapter), if the language you're using is case-sensitive (such as C#), you'll need to use the correct case when creating controls (e.g., "TextBox" versus "textbox"). Likewise, when you assign an ID to a control using the id attribute of a server control tag, case matters with a case-sensitive language. That is, given the following tag in a *.aspx* page written in C#:

```
<asp:Label id="myLabel" runat="server"/>
```

this code will cause a compiler error:

```
MyLabel.Text = "Hello, World!";
```

while this code will work correctly:

```
myLabel.Text = "Hello, World!";
```

The attributes of web controls declared using the ASP.NET syntax become the properties of the control, and you can access them programmatically. Unlike the HTML controls, the object model of the web controls does not necessarily reflect HTML syntax. The main reason for this behavior is that, depending on the attributes applied to a web control, it may render one of many HTML elements to the browser. For example, <asp:textbox> can render <input type="text">, <input type="password">, or <textarea>, based on the value of the TextBoxMode attribute supplied by the developer at design time.

Using Controls

Server controls have two distinct techniques for using a control in a Web Forms page that can be both useful and confusing: declarative and programmatic techniques. Each has its own purpose, and in some situations (such as when using code-behind), both techniques must be used.

Typically, when you write your pages without code-behind files, you use the declarative technique for using controls in your page. If you need to access those controls programmatically, you would do so by referring to the value of the control's id attribute. For example, if you have an ASP.NET Label control declared as follows:

```
<asp:label id="Message" runat="server"/>
```

you would refer to this control in server-side code as follows:

```
<script runat="server">
    Sub Page_Load()
        Message.Text = "Hello, World!"
    End Sub
</script>
```

If you use code-behind with your pages, or if you wish to create a control dynamically at runtime, you may wish to declare and use a control programmatically, as shown here:

```
Dim Message As New Label()
Message.Text = "Hello, World!"
Page.Controls.Add(Message)
```

Declarative Control Use

Declarative control use is the simpler of the two control techniques. Declarative control utilizes HTML-like tags to declare a server control instance and uses attributes to set control properties. The location of the output of the server control is determined by the location of the tag in the page. This technique also allows HTML visual designers to move tags around, if necessary, without impacting the programmatic logic of the page, which would be contained in either a server-side <script> block or in a code- behind class.

Because this technique is so similar to writing plain vanilla HTML (albeit with different tags), it's frequently used by those familiar with classic ASP programming, once they start using server controls. Example 5-1 shows this technique in action, performing an action that in classic ASP would normally be accomplished using Response.Write. The example uses a Literal control which, unlike using Response.Write from a <script> block, allows more precise control of where the rendered output will appear. Instead of writing output to the browser with Response.Write, the code in the Page_Load event handling procedure sets the Text property of the control to the desired output. When the page is rendered, this output is then sent to the browser.

Example 5-1. SimpleWrite.aspx

```
<%@ Page Language="vb" %>
<html>
<head>
    <title>Declarative Control Example</title>
    <script runat="server">
```

Example 5-1. SimpleWrite.aspx (continued)

```
      Sub Page_Load( )
         'Instead of using Response.Write, we set
         '   the Text property of a literal control.
         '   The placement of the literal control
         '   determines where output appears
         Message.Text = "This text set from Page_Load!"
      End Sub
   </script>
</head>
<body>
   <form runat="server">
      <asp:literal id="Message" runat="server"/>
   </form>
</body>
</html>
```

In addition to the precise control of output, another advantage of this technique is better control over the appearance of the rendered output. Developers can use attributes or CSS Styles to modify the appearance of the control, as described later in this chapter in the section "Modifying Control Appearance."

Programmatic Control Use

While the declarative technique for control creation is generally simpler and more straightforward, at times you may want or need to create controls dynamically (e.g., in response to some user action). In such cases, developers can create controls programmatically—either in a server-side <script> block within the Web Forms page or in its accompanying code-behind class. You can use either HTML server controls or web controls with this technique.

You define controls programmatically by declaring a variable of the control's type, as shown in the following code snippet (Example 5-2 shows a complete page using this technique):

```
' Visual Basic .NET
Dim myText As New TextBox( )

// C#
TextBox myText = new TextBox( );
```

The New keyword (new in C#) creates a new instance of the desired control. Note that some controls will accept arguments passed into the constructor for the control. A Literal control, for example, can accept the desired text for the control as an argument passed to the control's constructor, as shown in the following code snippet:

```
Dim Hello As New Literal("Hello, World!")
```

Once the desired control instance has been created, the control must then be added to the Controls collection of either the page itself or of a container control on the page that will be rendered (allowing its child controls to be rendered as well). The following snippet shows adding a control named Hello to the Controls collection exposed by the Page object:

```
Page.Controls.Add(Hello)          ' VB
```

or:

```
Page.Controls.Add(Hello);         // C#
```

It's important to understand that the previous code snippet will add the control named Hello at the end of the Controls collection. This means that the output of the control can actually appear after any static HTML tags because, unless the page contains <% %> render blocks, ASP.NET treats static HTML in the page as Literal controls at runtime. To place a control at a specific point in the page's (or another control's) Controls collection, use the AddAt method instead of Add:

```
Page.Controls.AddAt(3, Hello)
```

The first argument to the AddAt method is the position (starting from 0) at which you'd like to add the control, while the second is a variable representing the control itself.

> To better understand how ASP.NET renders static HTML, <% %> render blocks, and server controls, turn on tracing for a page (as discussed in Chapter 10) and look at the control tree generated for pages with various combinations of static HTML, server controls, and render blocks. You will find that for pages containing just static HTML, ASP.NET creates a single LiteralControl to represent this HTML on the server. When you add server controls, any static HTML before, after, or between server controls will be represented on the server as a separate LiteralControl. If you add <% %> render blocks, however, controls will not be created on the server for *any* static HTML. This means that if you wish to manipulate the HTML content of the page on the server, you should avoid using render blocks.

Using the AddAt method, however, may not always allow you to place your control as precisely as you might like. A more precise technique for positioning dynamically created controls on the page is to add a Placeholder control to the page using the declarative technique and then add the dynamically created control(s) to its Controls collection. Because the Placeholder control has no UI of its own, if no controls are added to its Controls collection, nothing is rendered to the browser.

> Adding controls dynamically in the middle of a control collection can have unpredictable results when used with pages that post back to the server and maintain their state in ViewState (the default). On postback, the ViewState for controls declared in the Web Forms page is loaded before that of any dynamically created controls. If a control is added to the middle of a control collection, then the page is posted back; you may get errors because the dynamic control for which the ViewState was saved does not exist at the time that View-State is repopulated.

Example 5-2 shows the use of this technique to create the same output as Example 5-1.

Example 5-2. ProgControl.aspx

```
<%@ Page Language="vb" %>
<html>
<head>
    <title>Programmatic Control Example</title>
    <script runat="server">
        Sub Page_Init( )
            'The placement of the Placeholder control
            '    determines where output appears
            Dim Message As New Literal( )
            Message.Text = "This text set from Page_Load!"
            PH.Controls.Add(Message)
        End Sub
    </script>
</head>
<body>
    <form runat="server">
        <asp:placeholder id="PH" runat="server"/>
    </form>
</body>
</html>
```

Finally, because of the inheritance model used in code-behind pages, if you wish to create controls declaratively in your Web Forms page and manipulate those controls from within a code-behind class, you must programmatically create instances of your controls in the code-behind class with IDs that match those declared in the Web Forms page. For developers using Visual Studio .NET, this is done automatically when you drop a control onto the page from the Visual Studio toolbox (or when switching views in the designer). Example 5-3 shows a Web Forms page that specifies a code-behind page containing its programmatic logic.

Example 5-3. ProgControl_cb.aspx

```
<%@ Page Language="c#" src="ProgControl_cb.cs" Inherits="aspnetian.ProgControl"
%>
<html>
<head>
    <title>Programmatic Control Example using Code-behind</title>
</head>
<body>
    <form runat="server">
        <asp:placeholder id="PH" runat="server"/>
    </form>
</body>
</html>
```

Example 5-4 shows the code-behind class (written in C#) for the web page in Example 5-3. It creates the control dynamically and adds it to the Controls collection of the PH Placeholder control. Note that the code-behind class declares an instance of the Placeholder class and gives it the same name (ID) as the control declared in the Web Forms page. This allows the code in the code-behind page to manipulate the control at runtime. Also note that this control instance is declared as a protected member, which means that only code within the code-behind class (or classes that inherit from it, including the Web Forms page in Example 5-3) can access it.

Example 5-4. ProgControl_cb.cs

```
using System;
using System.Web;
using System.Web.UI;
using System.Web.UI.WebControls;

namespace aspnetian
{
    public class ProgControl:Page
    {
        protected PlaceHolder PH = new PlaceHolder();

        void Page_Load()
        {
            // The placement of the Placeholder control
            //    determines where output appears
            Literal Message = new Literal();
            Message.Text = "This text set from Page_Load!";
            PH.Controls.Add(Message);
        }
    }
}
```

Types of Web Controls

Web controls fall into eight categories: input, display, action, selection, databound, rich, validation, and mobile.

Input Controls

Input controls let the user enter text data into the application. ASP.NET supports only one input web control: the TextBox. The TextBox behaves like a single-line or multiline edit control, depending on the value of its TextMode property. Its simplified syntax is as follows:

```
<asp:textbox id="SingleText"
    text="Single Line TextBox"
    runat="server" />

<asp:textbox id="PasswordText"
    text="Password"
    textmode="Password"
    runat="server" />
```

```
<asp:textbox id="MultiText"
    text="Multiline TextBox"
    textmode="Multiline"
    runat="server" />
```

The TextBox control can then be accessed programmatically with a code fragment like:

```
SingleText.Text = "Hello ASP.NET"
PasswordText.Attributes("Value") = "New Password"
MultiText.Text = "Multiline TextBox can hold many lines of text"
```

Note that the text of a TextBox control using the Password text mode cannot be set directly using the Text property, but can be set using the attributes collection as shown in the preceding code snippet (though this is not recommended, since it results in the password being rendered to the client in plain text).

The appearance of input controls when rendered to the browser is shown in Figure 5-1. The code used to generate this figure is shown in Example 5-5.

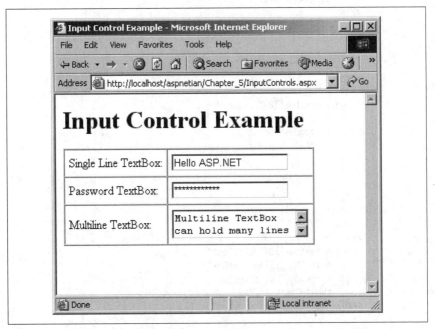

Figure 5-1. Rendering of input controls

Example 5-5. InputControls.aspx

```
<%@ Page Language="vb" %>
<html>
<head>
    <title>Input Control Example</title>
    <script runat="server">
        Sub Page_Load( )
            SingleText.Text = "Hello ASP.NET"
```

Example 5-5. InputControls.aspx (continued)

```
            PasswordText.Attributes("Value") = "New Password"
            MultiText.Text = "Multiline TextBox can hold many lines of text"
        End Sub
    </script>
</head>
<body>
    <h1>Input Control Example</h1>
    <form runat="server">
        <table border="1" cellpadding="5" cellspacing="0">
            <tr>
                <td>
                    Single Line TextBox:
                </td>
                <td>
                    <asp:textbox id="SingleText"
                        text="Single Line TextBox"
                        runat="server" />
                </td>
            </tr>
            <tr>
                <td>
                    Password TextBox:
                </td>
                <td>
                    <asp:textbox id="PasswordText"
                        text="Password"
                        textmode="Password"
                        runat="server" />
                </td>
            </tr>
            <tr>
                <td>
                    Multiline TextBox:
                </td>
                <td>
                    <asp:textbox id="MultiText"
                        text="Multiline TextBox"
                        textmode="Multiline"
                        runat="server" />
                </td>
            </tr>
        </table>
    </form>
</body>
</html>
```

Display Controls

Display controls simply render text or images to the browser. Table 5-1 lists the display controls ASP.NET supports.

Table 5-1. Display controls

Control	Purpose
Image	Displays the image specified in the control's ImageUrl property.
Label	Displays the text specified in the control's Text property.
Panel	Groups a set of controls (like a Frame control in Windows).
Table	Displays a table of information. This control has two collections: TableRows, which contains the rows, and TableCells, which contains the columns in a row.
TableCell	Represents a cell in a row of a Table control.
TableRow	Represents a row inside a Table control.

The syntax of these web controls is as follows:

```
<asp:label id="MyLabel"
    text="This is a Label Control"
    borderstyle="solid"
    bordercolor="Green"
    runat="Server" />

<asp:image id="MyImage"
    imageurl="aspnet.gif"
    runat="Server" />

<asp:panel id="MyPanel"
    backcolor="lightblue"
    bordercolor="Green"
    borderwidth="1" >
    <asp:label id="MyLabel2"
        text="Static Text within the Panel"
        runat="Server"/>
    <br>
    <asp:textbox id="PanelTB" text="TextBox inside Panel" runat="Server"/>
</asp:Panel>
```

They can then be accessed programmatically with a code fragment like the following:

```
MyLabel.Text = "New Label"
MyImage.ImageUrl = "NewImage.gif"
MyPanel.BackImageUrl = "NewImage.gif"
```

The appearance of display controls when rendered to the browser is shown in Figure 5-2. The code used to generate this figure is shown in Example 5-6.

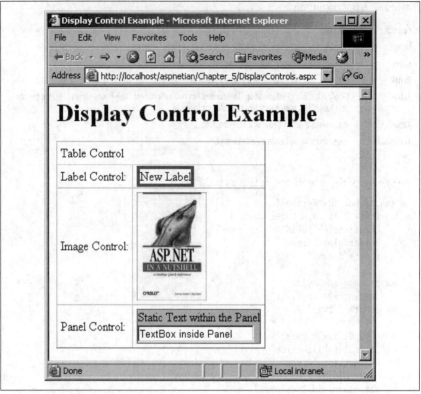

Figure 5-2. Rendering of display controls

Example 5-6. DisplayControls.aspx

```
<%@ Page Language="vb" %>
<html>
<head>
   <title>Display Control Example</title>
   <script runat="server">
      Sub Page_Load( )
         MyLabel.Text = "New Label"
         MyImage.ImageUrl = "aspnetian.jpg"
      End Sub
   </script>
</head>
<body>
   <h1>Display Control Example</h1>
   <form runat="server">
      <asp:table id="MyTable"
         border="1"
         cellpadding="5"
         cellspacing="0"
         runat="server">
         <asp:tablerow runat="server">
```

Example 5-6. DisplayControls.aspx (continued)

```
                <asp:tablecell colspan="2" runat="server">
                    Table Control
                </asp:tablecell>
            </asp:tablerow>
            <asp:tablerow runat="server">
                <asp:tablecell runat="server">
                    Label Control:
                </asp:tablecell>
                <asp:tablecell runat="server">
                    <asp:label id="MyLabel"
                        text="This is a Label Control"
                        borderstyle="solid"
                        bordercolor="Green"
                        runat="Server" />
                </asp:tablecell>
            </asp:tablerow>
            <asp:tablerow runat="server">
                <asp:tablecell runat="server">
                    Image Control:
                </asp:tablecell>
                <asp:tablecell runat="server">
                    <asp:image id="MyImage"
                        imageurl="image.jpg"
                        runat="Server" />
                </asp:tablecell>
            </asp:tablerow>
            <asp:tablerow runat="server">
                <asp:tablecell runat="server">
                    Panel Control:
                </asp:tablecell>
                <asp:tablecell runat="server">
                    <asp:panel id="MyPanel"
                        backcolor="lightblue"
                        bordercolor="Green"
                        borderwidth="1"
                        runat="server">
                        <asp:label id="MyLabel2"
                            text="Static Text within the Panel"
                            runat="Server"/>
                        <br>
                        <asp:textbox id="PanelTB"
                            text="TextBox inside Panel" runat="Server"/>
                    </asp:panel>
                </asp:tablecell>
            </asp:tablerow>
        </asp:table>
    </form>
</body>
</html>
```

Action Controls

Action controls allow users to perform some action on that page, such as navigating to a different URL, submitting a form, resetting a form's values, or executing a client script. Table 5-2 lists the action controls.

Table 5-2. Action controls

Control	Purpose
Button	Displays a command button that posts a form to the server when clicked.
ImageButton	Displays an image that posts a form to the server when clicked.
LinkButton	Displays a hyperlink text that posts a form to the server when clicked.
Hyperlink	Displays a hyperlink text that navigates from one page to another when clicked.

The simplified syntax of these controls is as follows:

```
<asp:button id="MyButton" text="Click Me!!" runat="server"/>

<asp:imagebutton id="MyImageButton"
    imageurl="aspnetian.jpg" runat="Server"/>

<asp:linkbutton id="MyLinkButton" text="Click Me" runat="server"/>

<asp:hyperlink id="MyHyperLink"
    text="Click Me"
    navigateurl="ActionControls.aspx"
    target="_blank"
    runat="server"/>
```

The controls can then be accessed programmatically with code fragments like the following:

```
MyButton.CommandName = "Sort"
MyImageButton.CommandArgument = "Ascending"
MyLinkButton.CommandName = "Filter"
MyHyperLink.NavigateUrl = "http://dotnet.oreilly.com/"
```

In the preceding code snippet, the CommandName property is used on postback to determine which action control was clicked by the user, so as to determine which code should run. For example, you can have multiple button controls on a page, each with its own CommandName, but which all share a single Click event handler. The event handler can then check the CommandEventArgs argument passed into the handler to determine which button was clicked.

The appearance of action controls when rendered to the browser is shown in Figure 5-3. The code used to generate this figure is shown in Example 5-7.

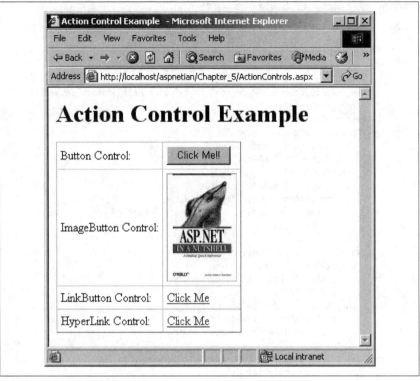

Figure 5-3. Rendering of action controls

Example 5-7. ActionControls.aspx

```
<%@ Page Language="vb" %>
<html>
<head>
  <title>Action Control Example</title>
  <script runat="server">
    Sub Page_Load( )
        MyButton.CommandName = "Sort"
        MyImageButton.CommandArgument = "Ascending"
        MyLinkButton.CommandName = "Filter"
        MyHyperLink.NavigateUrl = " http://dotnet.oreilly.com/"
    End Sub
  </script>
</head>
<body>
  <h1>Action Control Example</h1>
  <form runat="server">
    <asp:table id="MyTable"
        border="1"
        cellpadding="5"
        cellspacing="0"
        runat="server">
```

Example 5-7. ActionControls.aspx (continued)

```
        <asp:tablerow runat="server">
            <asp:tablecell runat="server">
                Button Control:
            </asp:tablecell>
            <asp:tablecell runat="server">
                <asp:button id="MyButton" text="Click Me!!" runat="server"/>
            </asp:tablecell>
        </asp:tablerow>
        <asp:tablerow runat="server">
            <asp:tablecell runat="server">
                ImageButton Control:
            </asp:tablecell>
            <asp:tablecell runat="server">
                <asp:imagebutton id="MyImageButton"
                    imageurl="aspnetian.jpg" runat="Server"/>
            </asp:tablecell>
        </asp:tablerow>
        <asp:tablerow runat="server">
            <asp:tablecell runat="server">
                LinkButton Control:
            </asp:tablecell>
            <asp:tablecell runat="server">
                <asp:linkbutton id="MyLinkButton"
                    text="Click Me" runat="server"/>
            </asp:tablecell>
        </asp:tablerow>
        <asp:tablerow runat="server">
            <asp:tablecell runat="server">
                HyperLink Control:
            </asp:tablecell>
            <asp:tablecell runat="server">
                <asp:hyperlink id="MyHyperLink"
                    text="Click Me"
                    navigateurl="ActionControls.aspx"
                    target="_blank"
                    runat="server"/>
            </asp:tablecell>
        </asp:tablerow>
    </asp:table>
  </form>
</body>
</html>
```

Selection Controls

Selection controls allow the user to select one or more values from a list. They include both the CheckBox and RadioButton controls, which are designed to work in a group. The RadioButton control allows you to select only one option out of the group, whereas the CheckBox control allows you to select zero or more options. Table 5-3 lists the selection controls.

Table 5-3. Selection controls

Control	Purpose
CheckBox	Selects or unselects an option. You can toggle the selection.
RadioButton	Selects only one option out of a group. You can unselect an option only by selecting another RadioButton control in the group.
ListBox	Allows the user to select one or more options from a list represented by ListItem controls. This control always occupies a fixed space in the form.
DropDownList	Allows the user to select only one option out of a list represented by ListItem controls. This control is used where the space in the form is limited.
RadioButtonList	Presents a list of radio buttons represented by ListItem controls and allows selection of only one option.
CheckBoxList	Presents a list of checkboxes represented by ListItem controls and allows you to select zero or more of the options.

The simplified syntax of the selection controls is as follows:

```
<asp:checkbox id="MyCheckBox1"
    text="Vanilla" runat="server"/>

<asp:checkbox id="MyCheckBox2"
    text="Chocolate" runat="server"/>

<asp:radiobutton id="MyRadioButton1" groupname="Group1"
    checked="True" text="Yes" runat="Server"/>

<asp:radiobutton id="MyRadioButton2" groupname="Group1"
    text="No" runat="Server"/>

<asp:listbox id="MyListBox" runat="server">
    <asp:listitem value="Vanilla" selected="true">Vanilla</asp:listitem>
    <asp:listitem value="Chocolate">Chocolate</asp:listitem>
    <asp:listitem value="Strawberry">Strawberry</asp:listitem>
</asp:listbox>

<asp:dropdownlist id="MyDropDownList" runat="server">
    <asp:listitem value="Single" selected="true">Single</asp:listitem>
    <asp:listitem value="Multiline">Multiline</asp:listitem>
    <asp:listitem value="Password">Password</asp:listitem>
</asp:dropdownlist>

<asp:checkboxlist id="MyCheckBoxList"
    repeatdirection="vertical" runat="server">
    <asp:listitem value="Vanilla" text="Vanilla"/>
    <asp:listitem value="Chocolate" text="Chocolate"/>
    <asp:listitem value="Strawberry" text="Strawberry"/>
</asp:checkboxlist>

<asp:radiobuttonlist id="MyRadioButtonList"
    repeatdirection="Horizontal" runat="server">
    <asp:listitem value="Female" text="Female" selected="true"/>
    <asp:listitem value="Male" text="Male"/>
</asp:radiobuttonlist>
```

The controls can then be referenced programmatically with code fragments like the following:

```
MyCheckBox1.Checked = True
MyRadioButton1.Checked = False
MyListBox.SelectionMode = ListSelectionMode.Multiple
MyDropDownList.SelectedIndex = 1
MyCheckBoxList.RepeatDirection = RepeatDirection.Horizontal
MyRadioButtonList.RepeatLayout = RepeatLayout.Table
```

The appearance of the selection controls when rendered to the browser is shown in Figure 5-4. The code used to generate this figure is shown in Example 5-8.

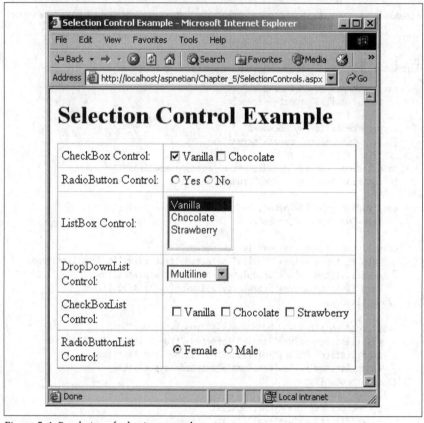

Figure 5-4. Rendering of selection controls

Example 5-8. SelectionControls.aspx

```
<%@ Page Language="vb" %>
<html>
<head>
   <title>Selection Control Example</title>
   <script runat="server">
     Sub Page_Load()
```

Example 5-8. SelectionControls.aspx (continued)

```
            MyCheckBox1.Checked = True
            MyRadioButton1.Checked = False
            MyListBox.SelectionMode = ListSelectionMode.Multiple
            MyDropDownList.SelectedIndex = 1
            MyCheckBoxList.RepeatDirection = RepeatDirection.Horizontal
            MyRadioButtonList.RepeatLayout = RepeatLayout.Table
        End Sub
    </script>
</head>
<body>
    <h1>Selection Control Example</h1>
    <form runat="server">
        <asp:table id="MyTable"
            border="1"
            cellpadding="5"
            cellspacing="0"
            runat="server">
            <asp:tablerow runat="server">
                <asp:tablecell runat="server">
                    CheckBox Control:
                </asp:tablecell>
                <asp:tablecell runat="server">
                    <asp:checkbox id="MyCheckBox1"
                        text="Vanilla" runat="server" />
                    <asp:checkbox id="MyCheckBox2"
                        text="Chocolate" runat="server" />
                </asp:tablecell>
            </asp:tablerow>
            <asp:tablerow runat="server">
                <asp:tablecell runat="server">
                    RadioButton Control:
                </asp:tablecell>
                <asp:tablecell runat="server">
                    <asp:radiobutton id="MyRadioButton1" groupname="Group1"
                        checked="True" text="Yes" runat="Server"/>
                    <asp:radiobutton id="MyRadioButton2" groupname="Group1"
                        text="No" runat="Server"/>
                </asp:tablecell>
            </asp:tablerow>
            <asp:tablerow runat="server">
                <asp:tablecell runat="server">
                    ListBox Control:
                </asp:tablecell>
                <asp:tablecell runat="server">
                    <asp:listbox id="MyListBox" runat="server">
                        <asp:listitem value="Vanilla"
                            selected="true">Vanilla</asp:listitem>
                        <asp:listitem value="Chocolate">Chocolate
                        </asp:listitem>
                        <asp:listitem value="Strawberry">Strawberry
                        </asp:listitem>
                    </asp:listbox>
```

Example 5-8. SelectionControls.aspx (continued)

```
            </asp:tablecell>
        </asp:tablerow>
        <asp:tablerow runat="server">
            <asp:tablecell runat="server">
                DropDownList Control:
            </asp:tablecell>
            <asp:tablecell runat="server">
                <asp:dropdownlist id="MyDropDownList" runat="server">
                    <asp:listitem value="Single"
                        selected="true">Single</asp:listitem>
                    <asp:listitem value="Multiline">Multiline
                    </ asp:listitem>
                    <asp:listitem value="Password">Password</asp:listitem>
                </asp:dropdownlist>
            </asp:tablecell>
        </asp:tablerow>
        <asp:tablerow runat="server">
            <asp:tablecell runat="server">
                CheckBoxList Control:
            </asp:tablecell>
            <asp:tablecell runat="server">
                <asp:checkboxlist id="MyCheckBoxList"
                    repeatdirection="vertical" runat="server">
                    <asp:listitem value="Vanilla" text="Vanilla"/>
                    <asp:listitem value="Chocolate" text="Chocolate"/>
                    <asp:listitem value="Strawberry" text="Strawberry"/>
                </asp:checkboxlist>
            </asp:tablecell>
        </asp:tablerow>
        <asp:tablerow runat="server">
            <asp:tablecell runat="server">
                RadioButtonList Control:
            </asp:tablecell>
            <asp:tablecell runat="server">
                <asp:radiobuttonlist id="MyRadioButtonList"
                    repeatdirection="Horizontal" runat="server">
                    <asp:listitem value="Female"
                        text="Female" selected="true"/>
                    <asp:listitem value="Male" text="Male"/>
                </asp:radiobuttonlist>
            </asp:tablecell>
        </asp:tablerow>
    </asp:table>
  </form>
</body>
</html>
```

Databound Controls

Databound controls render repetitive data and use templates for the customized rendering of data (the so-called *lookless UI*). For example, you can define separate templates for the header, body, and footer of a table of data.

We'll discuss data binding in more detail in Chapter 7. Table 5-4 shows the databound controls.

Table 5-4. Databound controls and their purpose

Control	Purpose
DataGrid	Displays tabular data and can function as an editable grid that supports selecting, editing, sorting, and paging of data.
DataList	Displays a list of items that the user can select and edit.
Repeater	Displays a repeating list of data items. Their control and layout can be specified using templates.

Remember that DataGrid and DataList controls can be used with or without templates, but Repeater controls must have at least one ItemTemplate defined. You can also modify the appearance of DataGrids and DataLists by using a series of style properties, each of which ends with Style. These properties include HeaderStyle, ItemStyle, and FooterStyle. For more information on templates and styles, see the section "Modifying Control Appearance" later in this chapter.

The simplified syntax of the databound controls is as follows:

```
<asp:datagrid id="MyDataGrid"
    allowpaging="true"
    allowsorting="true"
    alternatingitemstyle-backcolor="LightSkyBlue"
    backcolor="Blue"
    forecolor="White"
    cellpadding="2"
    cellspacing="0"
    headerstyle-backcolor="DarkBlue"
    headerstyle-forecolor="Yellow"
    pagerstyle-mode="NumericPages"
    pagesize="5"
        runat="server"/>

<asp:datalist id="MyDataList"
    alternatingitemstyle-backcolor="LightSkyBlue"
    backcolor="Blue"
    bordercolor="Black"
    cellpadding="2"
    cellspacing="0"
    forecolor="White"
    headerstyle-backcolor="DarkBlue"
    headerstyle-forecolor="Yellow"
    repeatcolumns="1"
    repeatdirection="vertical"
    repeatlayout="table"
    runat="server">
    <template name="headertemplate">
        Composers
    </template>
    <template name="itemtemplate">
        <%# databinder.eval(container.dataitem, "name") %>
    </template>
```

```
</asp:datalist>

<asp:repeater id="MyRepeater" runat="server">
    <template name="headertemplate">
        <table cellpadding="5" cellspacing="0">
            <tr>
                <td>Name<hr/></td>
                <td>City<hr/></td>
            </tr>
    </template>
    <template name="itemtemplate">
            <tr>
                <td><%# DataBinder.Eval(Container.DataItem, "name") %></td>
                <td><%# DataBinder.Eval(Container.DataItem, "city") %></td>
            </tr>
    </template>
    <template name="footertemplate">
        </table>
    </template>
</asp:repeater>
```

The controls can then be referenced programmatically with code fragments like:

```
MyDataGrid.DataSource = CreateData( )
MyDataGrid.DataBind( )
MyDataList.DataSource = CreateData( )
MyDataList.DataBind( )
MyRepeater.DataSource = CreateData( )
MyRepeater.DataBind( )
```

The appearance of databound controls when rendered to the browser is shown in Figure 5-5. The code used to generate this figure is shown in Example 5-9.

Example 5-9. DataboundControls.aspx

```
<%@ Page Language="vb" %>
<%@ Import Namespace="System.Data" %>
<html>
<head>
    <title>Databound Control Example</title>
    <script runat="server">
        Sub Page_Load( )
            MyDataGrid.DataSource = CreateData( )
            MyDataGrid.DataBind( )
            MyDataList.DataSource = CreateData( )
            MyDataList.DataBind( )
            MyRepeater.DataSource = CreateData( )
            MyRepeater.DataBind( )
        End Sub
        Function CreateData( ) As DataTable
            Dim DT As New DataTable( )
            Dim Row1, Row2, Row3, Row4 As DataRow
            DT.Columns.Add(New DataColumn("name", _
                System.Type.GetType("System.String")))
            DT.Columns.Add(New DataColumn("city", _
                System.Type.GetType("System.String")))
```

Example 5-9. DataboundControls.aspx (continued)

```
            Row1 = DT.NewRow( )
            Row1("name") = "W.A. Mozart"
            Row1("city") = "Salzburg"
            DT.Rows.Add(Row1)
            Row2 = DT.NewRow( )
            Row2("name") = "Nikolai Rimsky-Korsakov"
            Row2("city") = "Tikhvin"
            DT.Rows.Add(Row2)
            Row3 = DT.NewRow( )
            Row3("name") = "George Frideric Handel"
            Row3("city") = "Halle"
            DT.Rows.Add(Row3)
            Row4 = DT.NewRow( )
            Row4("name") = "J.S. Bach"
            Row4("city") = "Eisenach"
            DT.Rows.Add(Row4)
            Return DT
        End Function
    </script>
</head>
<body>
    <h1>Databound Control Example</h1>
    <form runat="server">
        <asp:table id="MyTable"
            border="1"
            cellpadding="5"
            cellspacing="0"
            runat="server">
            <asp:tablerow runat="server">
                <asp:tablecell runat="server">
                    DataGrid Control:
                </asp:tablecell>
                <asp:tablecell runat="server">
                    <asp:datagrid id="MyDataGrid"
                        allowpaging="true"
                        allowsorting="true"
                        alternatingitemstyle-backcolor="LightSkyBlue"
                        backcolor="Blue"
                        forecolor="White"
                        cellpadding="2"
                        cellspacing="0"
                        headerstyle-backcolor="DarkBlue"
                        headerstyle-forecolor="Yellow"
                        pagerstyle-mode="NumericPages"
                        pagesize="5"
                        runat="server"/>
                </asp:tablecell>
            </asp:tablerow>
            <asp:tablerow runat="server">
                <asp:tablecell runat="server">
                    DataList Control:
                </asp:tablecell>
                <asp:tablecell runat="server">
```

Example 5-9. DataboundControls.aspx (continued)

```
                <asp:datalist id="MyDataList"
                    alternatingitemstyle-backcolor="LightSkyBlue"
                    backcolor="Blue"
                    bordercolor="Black"
                    cellpadding="2"
                    cellspacing="0"
                    forecolor="White"
                    headerstyle-backcolor="DarkBlue"
                    headerstyle-forecolor="Yellow"
                    repeatcolumns="1"
                    repeatdirection="vertical"
                    repeatlayout="table"
                    runat="server">
                    <headertemplate>
                        Composers
                    </headertemplate>
                    <itemtemplate>
                        <%# databinder.eval(container.dataitem, "name") %>
                    </itemtemplate>
                </asp:datalist>
            </asp:tablecell>
        </asp:tablerow>
        <asp:tablerow runat="server">
            <asp:tablecell runat="server">
                Repeater Control:
            </asp:tablecell>
            <asp:tablecell runat="server">
                <asp:repeater id="MyRepeater" runat="server">
                    <headertemplate>
                        <table cellpadding="5" cellspacing="0">
                            <tr>
                                <td>Name<hr/></td>
                                <td>City<hr/></td>
                            </tr>
                    </headertemplate>
                    <itemtemplate>
                            <tr>
                                <td><%# DataBinder.Eval(Container.DataItem, _
                                    "name") %></td>
                                <td><%# DataBinder.Eval(Container.DataItem, _
                                    "city") %></td>
                            </tr>
                    </itemtemplate>
                    <footertemplate>
                        </table>
                    </footertemplate>
                </asp:repeater>
            </asp:tablecell>
        </asp:tablerow>
    </asp:table>
  </form>
</body>
</html>
```

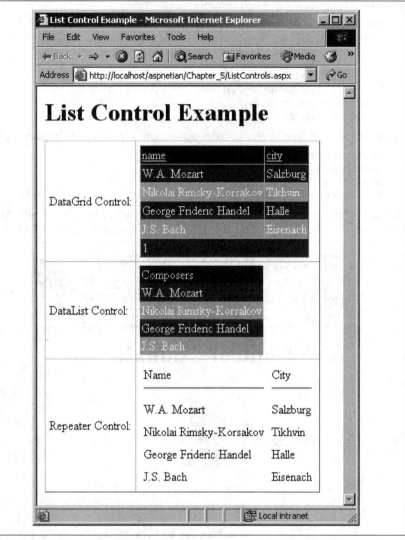

Figure 5-5. Rendering of databound controls

Rich Controls

These high-level custom controls provide rich user interface and functionality. This release of ASP.NET includes two rich controls: the Calendar control and the AdRotator control. Table 5-5 lists the rich controls.

Table 5-5. Rich controls and their purposes

Control	Purpose
AdRotator	Displays different ad images and, when clicked, will navigate to the URL associated with that image. You can define the rotation schedule in an XML file.
Calendar	Displays a monthly calendar and lets the user select a date.

The simplified syntax of the rich controls is as follows:

```
<asp:adrotator id="MyAdRotator" advertisementfile="ads.xml"
    runat="server" />

<asp:calendar id="MyCalendar"
    showdayheader="true"
    todaydaystyle-backcolor="yellow"
    todaydaystyle-forecolor="blue"
    runat="server"/>
```

These controls can then be referenced programmatically with code fragments like:

```
MyAdRotator.KeywordFilter = "Nutshell"
Dim ShortDate As String
ShortDate = MyCalendar.TodaysDate.ToString("D")
MyLabel.Text = "Today is " & ShortDate
```

The appearance of rich controls when rendered to the browser is shown in Figure 5-6. The code used to generate this figure is shown in Example 5-10.

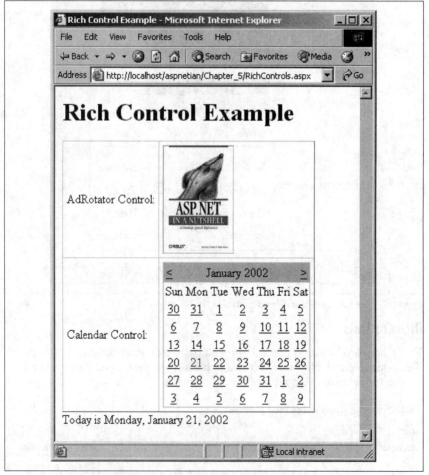

Figure 5-6. Rendering of rich controls

Example 5-10. RichControls.aspx

```
<%@ Page Language="vb" %>
<html>
<head>
    <title>Rich Control Example</title>
    <script runat="server">
        Sub Page_Load( )
            MyAdRotator.KeywordFilter = "Nutshell"
            Dim ShortDate As String
            ShortDate = MyCalendar.TodaysDate.ToString("D")
            MyLabel.Text = "Today is " & ShortDate
        End Sub
    </script>
</head>
<body>
    <h1>Rich Control Example</h1>
    <form runat="server">
        <asp:table id="MyTable"
            border="1"
            cellpadding="5"
            cellspacing="0"
            runat="server">
            <asp:tablerow runat="server">
                <asp:tablecell runat="server">
                    AdRotator Control:
                </asp:tablecell>
                <asp:tablecell runat="server">
                    <asp:adrotator id="MyAdRotator"
                        advertisementfile="ads.xml"
                        runat="server" />
                </asp:tablecell>
            </asp:tablerow>
            <asp:tablerow runat="server">
                <asp:tablecell runat="server">
                    Calendar Control:
                </asp:tablecell>
                <asp:tablecell runat="server">
                    <asp:calendar id="MyCalendar"
                        showdayheader="true"
                        todaydaystyle-backcolor="yellow"
                        todaydaystyle-forecolor="blue"
                        runat="server"/>
                </asp:tablecell>
            </asp:tablerow>
        </asp:table>
        <asp:label id="MyLabel" runat="server"/>
    </form>
</body>
</html>
```

Validation Controls

ASP.NET removes the hassle of duplicating validation code, a common problem of performing data validation using classic ASP, by neatly encapsulating the standard validations into server controls. You can declaratively relate the validation control to the control whose value needs to be validated, using the ControlToValidate attribute. You can also attach multiple validation controls to a single control. The ASP.NET validation server controls provide server-side validation for all browsers and supply client-side validation via JavaScript for browsers that support JavaScript and DHTML. You can also write your own custom client and/or server-side validation functions, as you'll see in the code example for this section.

One feature that most web programmers would like to have is a summary of the validation errors for the values entered into a page's controls. The ValidationSummary control provides this much-desired feature. Table 5-6 lists the validation controls.

Table 5-6. Validation controls

Control	Purpose
CompareValidator	Compares the input in the attached control with a constant value or the property value of another control.
CustomValidator	Invokes custom validation code that you have written.
RangeValidator	Checks if the value is between specified upper and lower limits.
RegularExpressionValidator	Checks if the input matches a pattern defined by a regular expression.
RequiredFieldValidator	Ensures that the user can't skip the required value.
ValidationSummary	Shows a summary of errors emitted by all validators in that form.

The simplified syntax of the validation controls is as follows:

```
<asp:comparevalidator id="cvCompare"
    controltovalidate="value1"
    controltocompare="value2"
    operator="equal"
    type="integer"
    errormessage="Fields are not equal!"
    display="dynamic"
    runat="server"/>

<asp:customvalidator id="cvDate"
    controltovalidate="year"
    errormessage="Not a valid year!"
    onservervalidate="servervalidation"
    clientvalidationfunction="ClientValidate"
    display="dynamic"
    runat="server"/>

<asp:rangevalidator id="rvCompare"
    controltovalidate="value"
```

```
      minimumvalue="0"
      maximumvalue="100"
      type="integer"
      errormessage="Value not in valid range!"
      runat="server"/>

   <asp:regularexpressionvalidator id="reZipCode"
      controltovalidate="zipcode"
      validationexpression="^\d{5}$|^\d{5}-\d{4}$"
      errormessage="Not a valid Zip code!"
      display="static"
      runat="server"/>

   <asp:requiredfieldvalidator id="rfvLogin"
      controltovalidate="login"
      display="static"
      errormessage="Login cannot be blank!"
      runat="server"/>

   <asp:validationsummary id="vsSummary"
      displaymode="bulletlist"
      headertext="Page has the following errors: "
      showsummary="true"
      showmessagebox="false"
      runat="server"/>
```

The controls can then be referenced programmatically with code fragments like:

```
cvCompare.ControlToCompare = "Value3"
cvDate.ClientValidationFunction="ClientValidateLeapYear"
reZipCode.ValidationExpression="^\d{5}$|^\d{5}$"
rfvLogin.InitialValue = "SomeUser"
vsSummary.DisplayMode = ValidationSummaryDisplayMode.List
```

The appearance of validation controls that have detected invalid input when rendered to the browser is shown in Figure 5-7.

The code used to generate this figure is shown in Example 5-11.

Example 5-11. ValidationControls.aspx

```
<%@ Page Language="vb" %>
<html>
<head>
   <title>Validation Control Example</title>
   <script language="javascript">
   <!--
      function ClientValidate(source, arguments)
      {
         //Declare variables.
         var r, re;
         //Create regular expression object.
         re = new RegExp(/^[1-9][0-9][0-9][0-9]$/);
         //Test for match.
```

Example 5-11. ValidationControls.aspx (continued)

```
        r = re.test(arguments.Value);
        //Return results.
        arguments.IsValid = r;
    }
-->
</script>
<script runat="server">
    Sub Page_Load( )
        vsSummary.DisplayMode = ValidationSummaryDisplayMode.List
    End Sub
    Sub ServerValidation (source As object, args _
        As ServerValidateEventArgs)
        Dim RegExVal As New _
            System.Text.RegularExpressions.Regex("^\ d{4}$")
        If RegExVal.IsMatch(args.Value) Then
            args.IsValid = True
        Else
            args.IsValid = False
        End If
    End Sub
</script>
</head>
<body>
    <h1>Validation Control Example</h1>
    <form runat="server">
        <asp:table id="MyTable"
            border="1"
            cellpadding="5"
            cellspacing="0"
            runat="server">
            <asp:tablerow runat="server">
                <asp:tablecell runat="server">
                    Compare Validator Control:
                    <br><br>
                    Enter two numbers to compare
                </asp:tablecell>
                <asp:tablecell runat="server">
                    <asp:textbox id="value1" runat="server"/><br>
                    <asp:textbox id="value2" runat="server"/><br>
                    <asp:comparevalidator id="cvCompare"
                        controltovalidate="value1"
                        controltocompare="value2"
                        operator="equal"
                        type="integer"
                        errormessage="Fields are not equal!"
                        display="dynamic"
                        runat="server"/>
                </asp:tablecell>
            </asp:tablerow>
            <asp:tablerow runat="server">
```

Example 5-11. ValidationControls.aspx (continued)

```
                <asp:tablecell runat="server">
                   CustomValidator Control:
                   <br><br>
                   Enter a 4-digit year
                </asp:tablecell>
                <asp:tablecell runat="server">
                   <asp:textbox id="year" runat="server"/><br>
                   <asp:customvalidator id="cvDate"
                      controltovalidate="year"
                      errormessage="Not a valid year!"
                      onservervalidate="servervalidation"
                      clientvalidationfunction="ClientValidate"
                      display="dynamic"
                      runat="server"/>
                </asp:tablecell>
             </asp:tablerow>
             <asp:tablerow runat="server">
                <asp:tablecell runat="server">
                   RangeValidator Control:
                   <br><br>
                   Enter an integer between 0 and 100
                </asp:tablecell>
                <asp:tablecell runat="server">
                   <asp:textbox id="value" runat="server"/><br>
                   <asp:rangevalidator id="rvCompare"
                      controltovalidate="value"
                      minimumvalue="0"
                      maximumvalue="100"
                      type="integer"
                      errormessage="Value not in valid range!"
                      runat="server"/>
                </asp:tablecell>
             </asp:tablerow>
             <asp:tablerow runat="server">
                <asp:tablecell runat="server">
                   RegularExpressionValidator Control:
                   <br><br>
                   Enter a valid 5 or 9-digit zip code
                </asp:tablecell>
                <asp:tablecell runat="server">
                   <asp:textbox id="zipcode" runat="server"/><br>
                   <asp:regularexpressionvalidator id="reZipCode"
                      controltovalidate="zipcode"
                      validationexpression="^\d{5}$|^\d{5}-\d{4}$"
                      errormessage="Not a valid Zip code!"
                      display="static"
                      runat="server"/>
                </asp:tablecell>
             </asp:tablerow>
             <asp:tablerow runat="server">
```

Example 5-11. ValidationControls.aspx (continued)

```
            <asp:tablecell runat="server">
                RequiredFieldValidator Control:
                <br><br>
                Enter a login name
            </asp:tablecell>
            <asp:tablecell runat="server">
                <asp:textbox id="login" runat="server"/><br>
                <asp:requiredfieldvalidator id="rfvLogin"
                    controltovalidate="login"
                    display="static"
                    errormessage="Login cannot be blank!"
                    runat="server"/>
            </asp:tablecell>
        </asp:tablerow>
        <asp:tablerow runat="server">
            <asp:tablecell runat="server">
                ValidationSummary Control:
            </asp:tablecell>
            <asp:tablecell runat="server">
                <asp:validationsummary id="vsSummary"
                    displaymode="bulletlist"
                    headertext="Page has the following errors: "
                    showsummary="true"
                    showmessagebox="false"
                    runat="server"/>
            </asp:tablecell>
        </asp:tablerow>
        <asp:tablerow runat="server">
            <asp:tablecell colspan="2" runat="server">
                <asp:button text="submit" runat="server"/>
            </asp:tablecell>
        </asp:tablerow>
    </asp:table>
    <asp:label id="MyLabel" runat="server"/>
  </form>
</body>
</html>
```

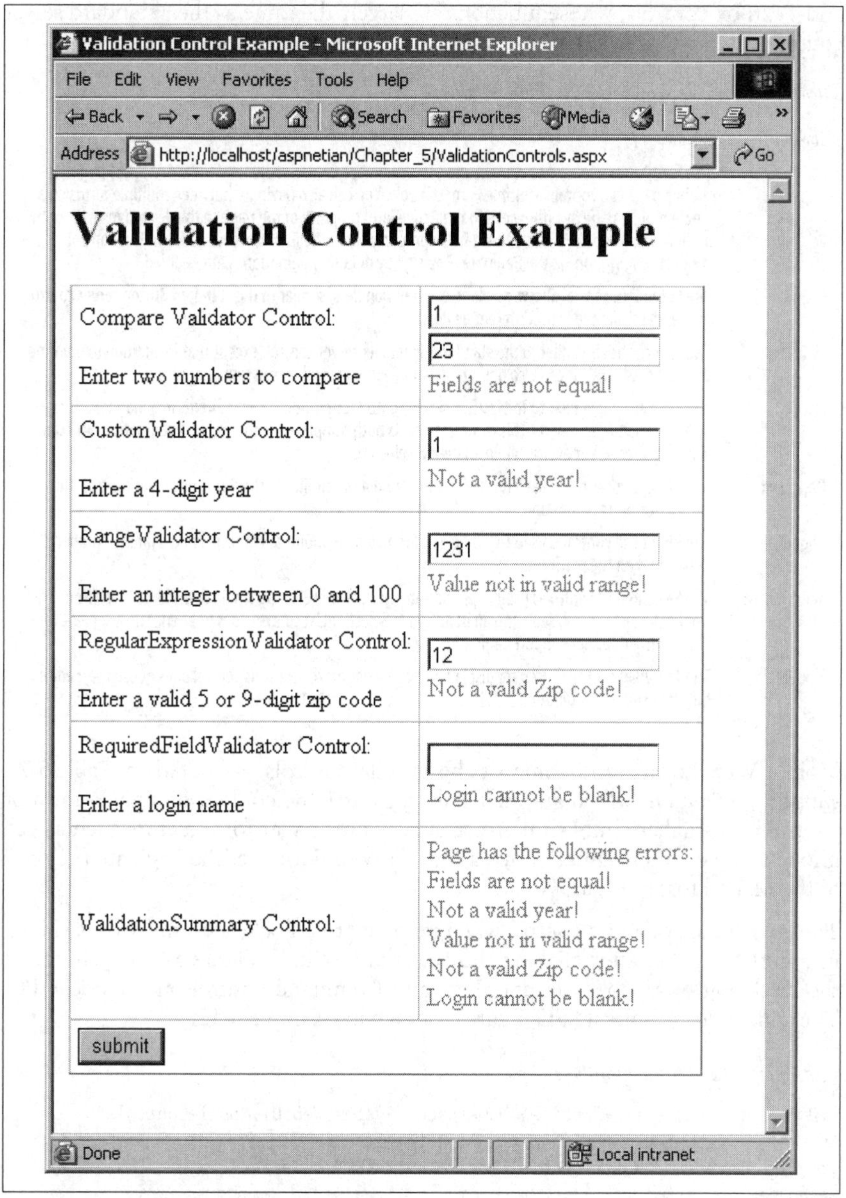

Figure 5-7. Rendering of validation controls

Mobile Controls

The mobile controls, which were available as a separate download as the Microsoft Mobile Internet Toolkit in ASP.NET 1.0, but are integrated into the .NET Framework Version 1.1, provide specialized functionality for building ASP.NET applications that target mobile devices such as PDAs and cell phones. Table 5-7 lists the mobile controls. Some controls, such as the AdRotator, Calendar, Label, Panel, and TextBox controls, whose functions are largely the same as their standard server control counterparts (with the exception of rendering), are omitted for brevity.

Table 5-7. Mobile controls and their purposes

Control	Purpose
Form	The Form control is used to contain one or more mobile controls. Unlike standard ASP.NET pages, a mobile page can contain multiple Form controls. You can also navigate between multiple forms on a single mobile page by either setting the ActiveForm property of the page to the desired form ID, or by adding a Link control with its NavigateUrl property set to the ID of the desired form. This control supports pagination via the Paginate property. By default, pagination is not enabled.
Command	The Command control allows invoking of event handlers, similar to the standard Button server control, but renders adaptively for different devices.
Link	The Link control is similar to the standard HyperLink server control, except that in addition to pointing to a navigable URL, it can also point to a mobile Form control on the same page.
List	The list control is similar to the ListBox server control, but renders a list of items in a manner appropriate to the target device. This control supports both templated rendering and pagination, and can also generate server events when an item is selected.
ObjectList	The ObjectList control is used for displaying bound data, similar to the DataGrid server control. This control supports pagination.
PhoneCall	The PhoneCall control is used to create a UI for making a phone call or displaying a phone number, depending on the platform.
SelectionList	The SelectionList control is used to provide an interface for selecting single or multiple items from a list. Unlike the List control, selecting an item from a SelectionList control does not generate a server event. This control does not support pagination.
TextView	The TextView control is used for displaying large amounts of text. This control does not support editing, but does support pagination.

Mobile Web Forms, and some of the mobile controls (as noted in Table 5-7), support *pagination*, which automatically separates the content of a given form or control into smaller chunks for easier display on smaller form factors such as cell phones. To activate pagination for a Mobile Web Form, set the Paginate property of the desired form to true.

The appearance of a List control when rendered to a PocketPC emulator is shown in Figure 5-8, and, after clicking the SelectionList link, Figure 5-9, which shows the rendering of a Label, SelectionList, and Command control on the PocketPC. The code used to generate this figure is shown in Example 5-12.

Example 5-12. MobileControls.aspx

```
<%@ Register TagPrefix="mobile" Namespace="System.Web.UI.MobileControls"
Assembly="System.Web.Mobile" %>
<%@ Page Inherits="System.Web.UI.MobileControls.MobilePage"
Language="vb" %>
<HEAD>
    <title>Mobile Control Example</title>
    <script runat="server">
        Protected Sub List1_Click(source As Object, _
            e As ListCommandEventArgs)
            Select Case e.ListItem.Value
                Case 2
                    ActiveForm = Form2
                Case 3
```

Example 5-12. MobileControls.aspx (continued)

```
                    ActiveForm = Form3
                Case 4
                    ActiveForm = Form4
            End Select
        End Sub
        Protected Sub Command1_Click(source As Object, e As EventArgs)
            If Not SelectionList1.Selection.Value = "4" Then
                Label1.Text = "You run as Admin too often!"
            Else
                Label1.Text = "Excellent!"
            End If
        End Sub
</script>
</HEAD>
<body xmlns:mobile="http://schemas.microsoft.com/Mobile/WebForm">
    <h1>Mobile Control Example</h1>
    <mobile:Form id="Form1" Runat="server">
        <mobile:Label id="Label2" runat="server">Choose a sample:</mobile:Label>
        <mobile:List id="List1" OnItemCommand="List1_Click" runat="server"
Decoration="Numbered">
            <Item Value="2" Text="SelectionList Sample"></Item>
            <Item Value="3" Text="PhoneCall Sample"></Item>
            <Item Value="4" Text="TextView Sample"></Item>
        </mobile:List>
    </mobile:Form>
    <mobile:Form id="Form2" runat="server">
        <mobile:Label id="Label1" runat="server">How often do you run Windows as
Admin?</mobile:Label>
        <mobile:SelectionList id="SelectionList1" runat="server">
            <Item Value="0" Text="Always"></Item>
            <Item Value="1" Text="Often"></Item>
            <Item Value="2" Text="Sometimes"></Item>
            <Item Value="3" Text="Rarely"></Item>
            <Item Value="4" Text="Never"></Item>
        </mobile:SelectionList>
        <mobile:Command id="Command1" OnClick="Command1_Click" runat="server">
Submit</mobile:Command>
    </mobile:Form>
    <mobile:Form id="Form3" runat="server">
        <mobile:PhoneCall id="PhoneCall1" runat="server" PhoneNumber="(000)555-
1234" AlternateUrl="http://www.aspnetian.com">Call Mom</mobile:PhoneCall>
    </mobile:Form>
    <mobile:Form id="Form4" runat="server">
        <mobile:TextView id="TextView1" runat="server" Wrapping="Wrap">When, in
the course of human events, it becomes necessary for one people to dissolve the
political bonds which have connected them with another, and to assume among the
powers of the earth, the separate and equal station to which the laws of nature
and of nature's God entitle them, a decent respect to the opinions of mankind
requires that they should declare the causes which impel them to the separation.
<br><br>We hold these truths to be self-evident, that all men are created equal,
that they are endowed by their Creator with certain unalienable rights, that
among these are life, liberty and the pursuit of happiness. That to secure these
rights, governments are instituted among men, deriving their just powers from the
```

Example 5-12. MobileControls.aspx (continued)

consent of the governed. That whenever any form of government becomes destructive
to these ends, it is the right of the people to alter or to abolish it, and to
institute new government, laying its foundation on such principles and organizing
its powers in such form, as to them shall seem most likely to effect their safety
and happiness.</mobile:TextView>
    </mobile:Form>
</body>

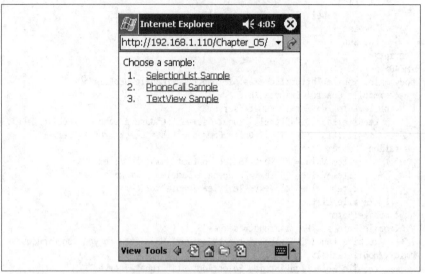

Figure 5-8. Initial rendering of mobile controls on PocketPC

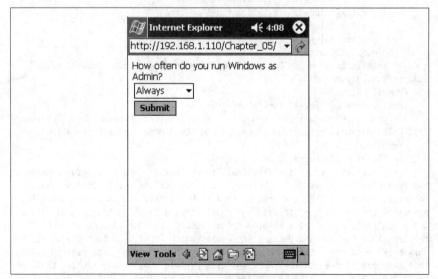

Figure 5-9. Rendering of mobile controls on PocketPC after clicking link

Figure 5-10 shows the rendered output of the PhoneCall control on the Openwave Phone Simulator (available at *http://www.openwave.com/*). Figure 5-11 shows the result of activating the PhoneCall control. The code used to generate these figures is shown in Example 5-13.

Figure 5-10. Initial rendering of PhoneCall control on Openwave Phone Simulator (image courtesy Openwave Systems Inc.)

Example 5-13. PhoneCall.aspx

```
<%@ Register TagPrefix="mobile" Namespace="System.Web.UI.MobileControls"
Assembly="System.Web.Mobile" %>
<%@ Page Inherits="System.Web.UI.MobileControls.MobilePage"
Language="vb" %>
<HEAD>
    <title>PhoneCall Control Example</title>
</HEAD>
<body xmlns:mobile="http://schemas.microsoft.com/Mobile/WebForm">
    <mobile:Form id="Form1" Runat="server">
        <mobile:PhoneCall id="PhoneCall1" runat="server" PhoneNumber="(000)555-
1234" AlternateUrl="http://www.aspnetian.com">Call Mom</mobile:PhoneCall>
    </mobile:Form>
</body>
```

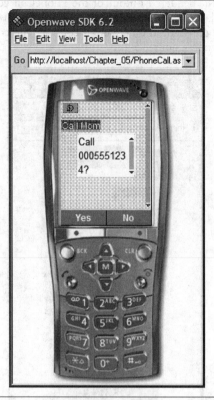

Figure 5-11. Rendering of activated PhoneCall control on Openwave Phone Simulator (image courtesy Openwave Systems Inc.)

In addition to having the mobile controls built into Version 1.1 of the .NET Framework, Visual Studio .NET 2003 provides a new Mobile Web Application project template, which simplifies mobile development by automating helpful settings in *web.config*, and allowing drag-and-drop development of ASP.NET applications for mobile devices.

Handling Control Events

One of the most convenient aspects of the new ASP.NET Web Forms model is that it brings event-driven programming, popularized by Visual Basic, to the web world without all the kludginess of the late unlamented Visual Basic WebClasses. As explained in Chapter 3, ASP.NET has a number of built-in events at the page level for which you can write event handlers to execute code.

Moreover, most server controls expose one or more events for which you can write handlers. Table 5-8 shows a list of common events and the controls that support them. These events and controls are in addition to the standard events, such as Init, Load, PreRender, and UnLoad, that are inherited from the base Control class.

For example, the Button server control exposes the Click and Command events. These events are both raised when the button is clicked, but while the Click event is usually used simply to handle the event for a single button, the Command event can be used to handle clicking on several buttons (so long as the buttons' Command-Name property is set). The CommandName property, along with an optional CommandArgument property, become properties of the CommandEventArgs object, which is passed as a parameter of the Command event handler. You can then examine the CommandName and CommandArgument properties within the event handler code to determine what action(s) to take.

Table 5-8. Common control events

Event	Event type	Description	Controls
OnAdCreated	Change	Raised after creation of the control and immediately before the page is rendered. If an Advertisement file is provided, OnAdCreated is raised after an ad has been selected from the file. Passes an AdCreated-EventArgs argument.	AdRotator
OnClick	Action	Raised when the user clicks the control. Passes an EventArgs argument.	Button ImageButton LinkButton
OnCommand	Action	Raised when a button containing OnCommand, CommandName, and CommandArgument attributes is clicked. Passes a CommandEventArgs argument containing the CommandName and CommandArgument attribute values.	Button ImageButton LinkButton
OnSelectedIndexChanged	Change	Raised when the user changes the selection. Passes an EventArgs argument.	CheckBoxList DropDownList ListBox RadioButtonList
OnCheckedChanged	Change	Raised when the user clicks the control. Passes an EventArgs argument.	CheckBox RadioButton
OnPageIndexChanged	Change	Raised when the user clicks a page selection element. Passes a DataGridPageChangedEventArgs argument.	DataGrid

The basic format of an event handler is as follows:

```
' VB.NET
Sub MyButton_Click(Sender As Object, E As EventArgs)
    'Event handling code
End Sub

// C#
void MyButton_Click(object Sender, EventArgs e)
{
    // Event handling code
}
```

While you can name your event handling procedures whatever you like, it's common to use the *ObjectName_EventName* convention, which makes it very easy to immediately see which procedures are event handlers. All event handlers are passed an Object argument that is a reference to the control from which the event was fired. They are also passed an instance of the EventArgs class or of a class that derives from EventArgs. For example, the OnCommand event of a Button control passes an argument of type CommandEventArgs, which contains information about the command represented by the button:

```
Sub MyButton_Command(Sender As Object, E As CommandEventArgs)
    Message.Text = "Command " & E.CommandName & _
        "was sent."
End Sub
```

As with creating controls, two techniques are available for creating and wiring up event handlers in ASP.NET: declarative and programmatic.

Wiring Up Events in Declarative Tags

The technique typically used to wire up events that are handled in a server-side <script> block, which is probably the simplest way to wire an event handler, is to add the appropriate attribute to the declarative tag used to create the control. The following code snippet sets the OnClick event handler to SubmitBtn_Click:

```
<asp:button id="MyBtn" text="Submit" onclick="MyBtn_Click" runat="server"/>
```

To handle this event, you would then add the following code to your page in a server-side <script> block:

```
' Visual Basic .NET
Sub MyBtn_Click(sender As Object, e As EventArgs)
    'event handling code
End Sub

//C#
void MyBtn_Click(Object sender, EventArgs e)
{
    // event handling code
}
```

The event handler for the Command event of the Button control is wired up in much the same fashion:

```
<asp:button id="Sort"
    text="Sort"
    commandname="Sort"
    commandargument="Descending"
    oncommand="Button_Command"
    runat="server"/>

<asp:button id="Filter"
    text="Filter"
    commandname="Filter"
    commandargument="B"
    oncommand="Button_Command"
    runat="server"/>
```

Note that the event handler changes slightly (EventArgs is replaced by the CommandEventArgs subclass, which contains information about the clicked command button):

```vbnet
' Visual Basic .NET
Sub Button_Command(sender As Object, ce As CommandEventArgs)
    Select ce.CommandName
        Case "Sort"
            ' Sort logic
        Case "Filter"
            ' Filter logic
    End Select
End Sub
```

```csharp
//C#
void Button_Command(Object sender, CommandEventArgs ce)
{
    switch(cs.CommandName)
    {
        case "Sort":
            // Sort logic
        case "Filter":
            // Filter logic
    }
}
```

It's a good habit to name your event handlers based on the name of the control whose event they handle and the name of the event, separated by an underscore (e.g., MyBtn_Click). However, as you can see from the OnCommand event example, you may want to make an exception sometimes.

Wiring Up Events Programmatically

Programmatic wiring of control events is typically used with code-behind classes; it's a little more complicated than the declarative technique, but still pretty straightforward. Note that programmatic event wiring is language dependent. Two techniques wire up events programmatically in Visual Basic .NET and one wires up events in C#.

The preferred approach for programmatically wiring events in Visual Basic .NET uses the WithEvents and Handles keywords to associate event handlers with events. As the following snippet illustrates, you first declare an instance of the desired control using the WithEvents keyword to indicate that you want event support for the instance.

Then you add the Handles clause to the procedure declaration for the event handler, specifying the object and event that it will handle:

```vbnet
Sub Page_Load( )
    Protected WithEvents MyButton As New Button( )
End Sub

Sub MyButton_Click(sender As Object, e As EventArgs) _
Handles MyButton.Click
    'Event handling code
End Sub
```

When declaring control instances in a code-behind class, it's a good idea to use the Protected keyword to ensure that the instance is available only to the class itself and to any class (such as the *.aspx* page) that inherits from it.

An alternate technique in Visual Basic .NET uses the AddHandler statement to specify a control event along with the address of the procedure that should be invoked when that event occurs:

```
Sub Page_Load( )
    Protected MyButton As New Button( )
    AddHandler MyButton.Click, AddressOf MyButton_Click
End Sub

Sub MyButton_Click(sender As Object, e As EventArgs)
    'Event handling code
End Sub
```

A corresponding RemoveHandler statement also allows you to stop handling a particular event. The advantage of this technique is that you can stop and start handling a particular event dynamically. In C#, the += operator is used to assign an event handler to an event:

```
void Page_Load( )
{
    Button MyButton = new Button( );
    MyButton.Click += new EventHandler(this.MyButton_Click);
}

void MyButton_Click(Object sender, EventArgs e)
{
    // Event handling code
}
```

As with Visual Basic's AddHandler keyword, the += operator has a corresponding -= operator that allows you to unwire an event from its handler dynamically.

Modifying Control Appearance

One of the great things about ASP.NET Server Controls is that they are incredibly flexible in allowing developers to define how they should appear on the page. Most server controls expose properties that allow simple formatting, such as fonts and background colors. All server controls also expose properties that allow for setting cascading style sheets (CSS) styles to modify the appearance of a control. Finally, some controls allow the use of templates to further define how the output of the control should appear. Together or individually, these techniques allow ASP.NET developers extensive control over the appearance of their controls.

Properties

Using control properties is the simplest technique for modifying the appearance of a control. Example 5-14 shows a page with two Label controls, one of which uses its default settings. The second Label control has one attribute used to set the Font-Name property. Font is a property that is represented by the FontInfo class. Setting the font-name attribute sets the value of the FontInfo class' Name member. Note that this second Label control also has the BackColor property set (in this case, to blue) in the Page_Load event handler. The output from Example 5-14 is shown in Figure 5-12.

Example 5-14. ControlProps.aspx

```
<%@ Page Language="vb" %>
<html>
<head>
   <title>Control Properties Example</title>
   <script runat="server">
      Sub Page_Load( )
         Label2.BackColor = System.Drawing.Color.LightBlue
      End Sub
   </script>
</head>
<body>
   <h1>Control Properties Example</h1>
   <form runat="server">
      <asp:table id="MyTable" border="1" cellpadding="5"
         cellspacing="0" runat="server">
         <asp:tablerow runat="server">
            <asp:tablecell runat="server">
               Default Label:
            </asp:tablecell>
            <asp:tablecell runat="server">
               <asp:label id="Label1" runat="server">
                  Hello, World!
               </asp:label>
            </asp:tablecell>
         </asp:tablerow>
         <asp:tablerow runat="server">
            <asp:tablecell runat="server">
               Label with Properties:
            </asp:tablecell>
            <asp:tablecell runat="server">
               <asp:label id="Label2" font-name="arial"
                  runat="server">
                  Hello, World!
               </asp:label>
            </asp:tablecell>
         </asp:tablerow>
      </asp:table>
   </form>
</body>
</html>
```

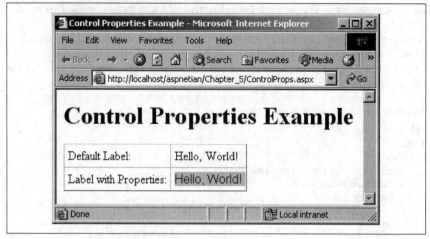

Figure 5-12. Control properties

CSS Styles

A more extensive technique for modifying control appearance involves the use of CSS styles. The base HtmlControl class (from which all HTML controls inherit) exposes a Style property, which contains a collection of CSS styles that are rendered at runtime as attributes on the tag generated by the control. The base WebControl class (from which all web controls inherit) also exposes a Style property and adds a CssClass property, which renders the value of the property as a class attribute on the control. This property allows you to set the style of a control using a CSS class defined in a stylesheet, rather than by setting individual styles. Like many other properties of web and HTML controls, the Style and CssClass properties can be set either declaratively (using attributes) or programmatically. Example 5-15 illustrates the use of both properties. Example 5-16 shows the HTML that would be rendered to the browser by Example 5-15. Note that the ViewState hidden field has been removed for clarity.

Example 5-15. ControlStyles.aspx

```
<%@ Page Language="vb" %>
<html>
<head>
   <title>Control Properties Example</title>
   <script runat="server">
      Sub Page_Load( )
         Label2.Style("background-color") = "silver"
      End Sub
   </script>
   <style>
      .Hello
      {
         font: 14pt arial;
         color:blue;
      }
```

Example 5-15. ControlStyles.aspx (continued)

```
    </style>
</head>
<body>
    <h1>Control Properties Example</h1>
    <form runat="server">
        <asp:table id="MyTable" border="1" cellpadding="5" cellspacing="0"
            runat="server">
            <asp:tablerow runat="server">
                <asp:tablecell runat="server">
                    HtmlInputText Control:
                </asp:tablecell>
                <asp:tablecell runat="server">
                    <input id="Text1" type="text"
                    style="font: 12pt arial;background-color:silver;color:red;"
                    runat="server"/>
                </asp:tablecell>
            </asp:tablerow>
            <asp:tablerow runat="server">
                <asp:tablecell runat="server">
                    Label with Style:
                </asp:tablecell>
                <asp:tablecell runat="server">
                    <asp:label id="Label2" cssclass="Hello" runat="server">
                        Hello, World!
                    </asp:label>
                </asp:tablecell>
            </asp:tablerow>
        </asp:table>
    </form>
</body>
</html>
```

Example 5-16. Rendered HTML from ControlStyles.aspx

```
<html>
<head>
    <title>Control Properties Example</title>
    <style>
        .Hello
        {
            font: 14pt arial;
            color:blue;
        }
    </style>
</head>
<body>
    <h1>Control Properties Example</h1>
    <form name="_ctl0" method="post" action="ControlStyles.aspx"
        id="_ctl0">
        <table id="MyTable" cellspacing="0" cellpadding="5" border="1"
            border="0" style="border-collapse:collapse;">
            <tr>
            <td>
```

Example 5-16. Rendered HTML from ControlStyles.aspx (continued)

```
            HtmlInputText Control:
        </td>
        <td>
            <input name="Text1" id="Text1" type="text"
            style="font: 12pt arial;background-color:silver;color:red;"
            />
        </td>
    </tr>
    <tr>
        <td>
            Label with Style:
        </td>
        <td>
            <span id="Label2" class="Hello"
                style="background-color:silver;">
                Hello, World!
            </span>
        </td>
    </tr>
    </table>
  </form>
</body>
</html>
```

Templates

Certain controls, most notably the Repeater data-bound control, can also use templates to specify the appearance of the control output. In fact, the Repeater control requires at least one template (the ItemTemplate) to display anything at all.

The Repeater works by rendering anything contained in the HeaderTemplate (if defined) and then rendering the contents of its data source based on the ItemTemplate, AlternatingItemTemplate (if defined), and SeparatorTemplate (if defined).

Once all rows of the data source have been rendered, the Repeater then renders the contents of the FooterTemplate (if defined). Figure 5-13 shows the output of *ControlTemplates.aspx*.

Additional Resources

The following site provides additional information on the topics discussed in this chapter:

http://www.asp.net/forums/
    The ASP.NET Forums has several forums dedicated specifically to server control questions, including a forum for the DataGrid, DataList, and Repeater controls, as well as one for the mobile controls.

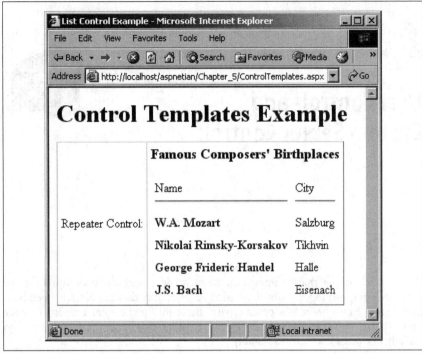

Figure 5-13. Template output

6

User Controls and Custom Server Controls

Reuse, a technique that is important to most developers, allows you to avoid constantly reinventing the wheel by using functionality that has already been built and tested. Reuse increases productivity, by reducing the total amount of code you need to write, and reliability, since by using tested code, you (presumably) already know the code works reliably.

ASP.NET provides a range of options for reuse. The first is the wide variety of built-in server controls that ship with ASP.NET. These server controls alone can eliminate hundreds, or even thousands, of lines of code that needed to be written to achieve the same effect in classic ASP. In addition, the .NET Framework Class Library (FCL) provides hundreds of classes to perform actions (such as sending SMTP email or making network calls) that in classic ASP would have required purchasing a third-party component or making calls into the Win32 API. Of course, the framework classes provide built-in functionality more than reuse. Fortunately, the framework also provides robust support for developing your own classes, user controls, and custom server controls, allowing you to reuse your own code as well.

Going hand-in-hand with reuse is the concept of *extensibility*, the ability to take the existing functionality provided by the .NET Framework and ASP.NET and extend it to perform actions that are more tailored to your particular applications and problem domains. ASP.NET provides a significant number of avenues for extensibility:

Custom server controls
> Allow you to create entirely new controls for use with ASP.NET or to derive from existing controls and extend or modify their functionality.

Components
> As in classic ASP, components are the primary means for extending an ASP.NET application by encapsulating the application's business logic into an easily reusable form. With the .NET Framework, it's easier than ever to

build components, and components are more interoperable across languages than in the COM world. .NET components can also communicate with COM components through an interoperability layer.

HttpHandlers and HttpModules

HttpHandlers are components that are called to perform the processing of specific types of requests made to IIS. HttpModules are components that participate in the processing pipeline of all requests for a given ASP.NET application. These extensibility techniques are beyond the scope of this book, but you can get answers to questions on these topics in the HttpHandlers and HttpModules forum at *http://www.asp.net/forums*.

The rest of this chapter discusses employing ASP.NET user controls and custom server controls for reuse and employing custom server controls for extensibility. The chapter also explains how custom server controls can easily be shared across multiple applications, making reuse simpler than ever.

User Controls

The simplest form of reuse in classic ASP is the include file. By adding the following directive:

```
<!-- #include file = "filename.inc" -->
```

classic ASP developers can place the contents of the specified file inline with the page in which the directive appeared. Unfortunately, this reuse technique is a bit crude and sometimes makes applications harder to debug.

While ASP.NET still supports include files, a better way to provide the same kinds of reuse is through a new feature called *user controls*. User controls can consist of any of the following:

- HTML
- Server-side script
- Controls

all in a file with the *.ascx* file extension. When added to a Web Forms page, ASP.NET treats user controls as objects; these user controls can expose properties and methods like any other object. The rendered output of user controls can also be cached to improve application performance.

Example 6-1 shows a simple user control that provides navigational links to other examples in this chapter. The user control appears in each example to demonstrate how the use of a user control can provide a single point for modifying such frequently used elements as headers, footers, and navigation bars.

Example 6-1. Nav.ascx

```
<%@ Control Language="vb" %>
<table cellpadding="0" cellspacing="0">
    <tr>
        <td valign="top">
            <strong>Navigation Bar</strong><br/>
            <hr width='80%'>
```

Example 6-1. Nav.ascx (continued)

```
        <a href="NavBarClient.aspx"
          onmouseover="img1.src='node_rev.jpg';"
          onmouseout="img1.src='node.jpg';">
          <img border='0' align='absMiddle' alt='NavBar Client'
            src='node.jpg' id='img1' name='img1'></a>
        <a href="NavBarClient.aspx"
          onmouseover="img1.src='node_rev.jpg';"
          onmouseout="img1.src='node.jpg';">NavBar Client</a>
        <hr width='80%'>
        <a href="UCClient.aspx"
          onmouseover="img2.src='alt_node_rev.jpg';"
          onmouseout="img2.src='alt_node.jpg';">
          <img border='0' align='absMiddle' alt='User Control Client'
            src='alt_node.jpg' id='img2' name='img2'></a>
        <a href="UCClient.aspx"
          onmouseover="img2.src='alt_node_rev.jpg';"
          onmouseout="img2.src='alt_node.jpg';">User Control Client</a>
        <hr width='80%'>
        <a href="BlogClient.aspx"
          onmouseover="img3.src='node_rev.jpg';"
          onmouseout="img3.src='node.jpg';">
          <img border='0' align='absMiddle' alt='Blog Client'
            src='node.jpg' id='img3' name='img3'></a>
        <a href="BlogClient.aspx"
          onmouseover="img3.src='node_rev.jpg';"
          onmouseout="img3.src='node.jpg';">Blog Client</a>
        <hr width='80%'>
        <a href="BlogAdd.aspx"
          onmouseover="img3.src='alt_node_rev.jpg';"
          onmouseout="img3.src='alt_node.jpg';">
          <img border='0' align='absMiddle' alt='Add New Blog'
            src='alt_node.jpg' id='img3' name='img3'></a>
        <a href="BlogAdd.aspx"
          onmouseover="img3.src='node_rev.jpg';"
          onmouseout="img3.src='node.jpg';">Add New Blog</a>
        <hr width='80%'>
      </td>
  </tr>
</table>
```

With the exception of the @ Control directive, which is not strictly required, the code in Example 6-1 consists exclusively of HTML and client-side script (for performing a simple mouseover graphics switch). However, the user control could just as easily contain server controls and/or server-side script to perform more complicated tasks.

The @ Control directive performs essentially the same task as the @ Page directive, only for user controls. Chapter 3 lists the attributes of the @ Page and @ Control directives and the purpose of each.

The advantage of using a user control for this type of functionality is that it places all of our navigation logic in a single location. This placement makes it considerably easier to maintain the navigation links for a site. If you used ASP.NET's built-in server controls instead of raw HTML in your navigation user control, you could manipulate those server controls programmatically from the page on which the control is used. For example, you could hide the link to the page that's currently displayed or highlight it in some fashion.

The disadvantage of a user control is that it is not reusable across multiple sites ("site," here, refers to an IIS virtual directory defined as an application). It's also not usually a good idea to tightly couple user interface elements and data, as this control does, because doing so tends to reduce the reusability of a control. Later in this chapter, you'll see how to improve this user control by turning it into a custom server control.

User controls are made available to a page through the use of either the @ Register directive, which prepares a user control on a page declaratively (i.e., using a tag-based syntax like server controls), or, programmatically, using the LoadControl method of the TemplateControl class (from which both the Page class and the UserControl class derive).

Example 6-2 shows a page that uses the @ Register directive and a declarative tag to create the user control shown in Example 6-1. The @ Register directive in Example 6-2 tells ASP.NET to look for any <aspnetian:nav> tags with the runat="server" attribute, and when it finds one, create an instance of the user control and place its output where the tag is located. This allows us to place our control very precisely.

Example 6-2. UCClient.aspx

```
<%@ Page Language="vb" %>
<%@ Register TagPrefix="aspnetian" TagName="nav" Src="Nav.ascx" %>
<html>
<head>
</head>
<body>
    <table border="1" width="100%" cellpadding="20" cellspacing="0">
        <tr>
            <td align="center" width="150">
                <img src="aspnetian.jpg"/>
            </td>
            <td align="center">
                <h1>User Control Client Page<h1>
            </td>
        </tr>
        <tr>
            <td width="150">
                <aspnetian:nav runat="server"/>
            </td>
            <td>
                This is where page content might be placed
                <br/><br/><br/><br/><br/><br/><br/><br/><br/>
            </td>
        </tr>
    </table>
</body>
</html>
```

You can instead create the control dynamically using the LoadControl method and add the control to either the Controls collection of the page, or, better yet, to the Controls collection of a PlaceHolder control. The latter allows you to control the location of the user control based on the location of the placeholder. You might choose to use this technique if you know where you want the control to reside on the page, but don't necessarily want the control loaded and displayed on every request. This technique is shown in Example 6-3.

Example 6-3. UCClient_Prog.aspx

```
<%@ Page Language="vb" %>
<html>
<head>
   <script runat="server">
      Sub Page_Init()
         PH.Controls.Add(LoadControl("Nav.ascx"))
      End Sub
   </script>
</head>
<body>
   <table border="1" width="100%" cellpadding="20" cellspacing="0">
      <tr>
         <td align="center" width="150">
            <img src="aspnetian.jpg"/>
         </td>
         <td align="center">
            <h1>User Control Client Page<h1>
         </td>
      </tr>
      <tr>
         <td width="150">
            <asp:placeholder id="PH" runat="server"/>
         </td>
         <td>
            This is where page content might be placed
            <br/><br/><br/><br/><br/><br/><br/><br/><br/>
         </td>
      </tr>
   </table>
</body>
</html>
```

 If you want to work with the control after loading it using Load-Control, you need to cast the control to the correct type using the *CType* function in Visual Basic .NET or by preceding the control with (*typename*) in C#. Note that this requires that the user control be defined in a class that inherits from UserControl, so this technique would not work with the user control in Example 6-1.

Custom Server Controls

For the reasons cited earlier in the chapter, user controls are not always the ideal choice for reuse. User controls tend to be very good for quickly reusing existing user interface elements and code, but custom server controls are much better for developing reusable building blocks for multiple web applications.

A custom server control is, in its essence, a class that derives from either the Control or WebControl class of the System.Web.UI namespace, or from one of the classes that derive from these controls. Custom server controls can be used in your ASP.NET Web Forms pages in very much the same way you use the built-in server controls that come with ASP.NET. There are two primary categories of custom server controls:

Rendered controls

> Rendered controls consist largely of custom rendering of the text, tags, and any other output you desire, which may be combined with the rendered output of any base class from which your control is derived. Rendered controls override the Render method of the control from which they derive. This method is called automatically by the page containing the control when it's time for the control output to be displayed.

Compositional controls

> Compositional controls get their name from the fact that they are composed of existing controls whose rendered output forms the UI of the custom control. Compositional controls create their constituent controls by overriding the CreateChildControls method of the control from which they derive. This method, like the Render method, is automatically called by ASP.NET at the appropriate time.

When designing a new custom server control, you need to consider some issues to decide which type of control to create:

* Does one existing control provide most, but not all, of the functionality you desire? A rendered control that derives from that control may be the right choice.

* Could the desired functionality be provided by a group of existing controls? A compositional control may be a great way to reuse those controls as a group.

* Do you want to do something that is completely beyond any existing control? You may want to derive your control from the Control class and override the Render method to create your custom output.

Note that by default, custom server controls expose all public members of the class from which they are derived. This exposure is important to consider when designing a control for use by other developers if you want to limit the customizations they can make. For instance, you might not want developers to change the font size of your control. In such a case, you should avoid deriving from a control that exposes that property.

Rendered Controls

Perhaps the best way to understand the process of creating a rendered custom server control is to see one. Example 6-4 shows a class written in Visual Basic .NET that implements a custom navigation control with the same functionality as the *Nav.ascx* user control discussed earlier in this chapter. Unlike the user control, which has the linked pages and images hardcoded into the control itself, the custom control in Example 6-4 gets this information from an XML file.

Example 6-4. NavBar.vb

```vb
Imports Microsoft.VisualBasic
Imports System
Imports System.Data
Imports System.Drawing
Imports System.IO
Imports System.Text
Imports System.Web
Imports System.Web.UI
Imports System.Web.UI.WebControls


Namespace aspnetian

Public Class NavBar
   Inherits Panel

   Private NavDS As DataSet
   Private _showDividers As Boolean = True

   Public Property ShowDividers() As Boolean
     Get
        Return _showDividers
     End Get
     Set
        _showDividers = value
     End Set
   End Property

   Sub NavBar_Load(sender As Object, e As EventArgs) Handles MyBase.Load

     LoadData()

   End Sub

   Protected Overrides Sub Render(Writer As HtmlTextWriter)

     Dim NavDR As DataRow
     Dim RowNum As Integer = 1
     Dim SB As StringBuilder

     MyBase.RenderBeginTag(Writer)
     MyBase.RenderContents(Writer)

     Writer.Write("<hr width='80%'>" & vbCrLf)

     For Each NavDR In NavDS.Tables(0).Rows

        SB = new StringBuilder()
        SB.Append(vbTab)
```

Example 6-4. NavBar.vb (continued)

```
SB.Append("<a href=""")
SB.Append(NavDR("url"))
SB.Append(""" onmouseover=""")
SB.Append("img")
SB.Append(RowNum.ToString())
SB.Append(".src='")
SB.Append(NavDR("moimageUrl"))
SB.Append("';""")
SB.Append(" onmouseout=""")
SB.Append("img")
SB.Append(RowNum.ToString())
SB.Append(".src='")
SB.Append(NavDR("imageUrl"))
SB.Append("';""")
SB.Append(" target='")
SB.Append(NavDR("targetFrame"))
SB.Append("'>")
SB.Append(vbCrLf)
SB.Append(vbTab)
SB.Append(vbTab)
SB.Append("<img border='0' align='absMiddle' alt='")
SB.Append(NavDR("text"))
SB.Append("' src='")
SB.Append(NavDR("imageUrl"))
SB.Append("' id='")
SB.Append("img")
SB.Append(RowNum.ToString())
SB.Append("' name='")
SB.Append("img")
SB.Append(RowNum.ToString())
SB.Append("'></a>")
SB.Append(vbTab)
SB.Append("<a href=""")
SB.Append(NavDR("url"))
SB.Append(""" onmouseover=""")
SB.Append("img")
SB.Append(RowNum.ToString())
SB.Append(".src='")
SB.Append(NavDR("moimageUrl"))
SB.Append("';""")
SB.Append(" onmouseout=""")
SB.Append("img")
SB.Append(RowNum.ToString())
SB.Append(".src='")
SB.Append(NavDR("imageUrl"))
SB.Append("';""")
SB.Append(" target='")
SB.Append(NavDR("targetFrame"))
SB.Append("'>")
SB.Append(NavDR("text"))
SB.Append("</a>")
SB.Append(vbCrLf)
```

Example 6-4. NavBar.vb (continued)

```vb
            If _showDividers = True Then
                SB.Append("<hr width='80%'>")
            Else
                SB.Append("<br/><br/>")
            End If
            SB.Append(vbCrLf)
            Writer.Write(SB.ToString())

            RowNum += 1

        Next

        MyBase.RenderEndTag(Writer)

    End Sub

    Protected Sub LoadData()

        NavDS = New DataSet()

        Try
            NavDS.ReadXml(Page.Server.MapPath("NavBar.xml"))
        Catch fnfEx As FileNotFoundException
            CreateBlankFile()
            Dim Html As String
            Html = "<br>No NavBar.xml file was found, so one was " & _
                "created for you. Follow the directions in the file " & _
                "to populate the required fields and, if desired, " & _
                "the optional fields."
            Me.Controls.Add(New LiteralControl(Html))
        End Try

    End Sub

    Public Sub CreateBlankFile()
        'Code to create a blank XML file with the fields used by
        '   the control. This code is included as a part of the file
        '   NavBar.vb, included with the sample files for the book.
    End Sub

End Class

End Namespace
```

The real meat of the NavBar control begins with the class declaration, which uses the Inherits keyword to declare that the control derives from the Panel control. This gives the control the ability to show a background color, to be hidden or shown as a unit, and to display the contents of its begin and end tags as part of the control.

Next, a couple of local member variables are declared. The location of the declaration is important, since these members need to be accessible to any procedure in the control. A property procedure is then added for the ShowDividers property, which will determine whether the control renders a horizontal line between each node of the control.

In the NavBar_Load method, which handles the Load event for the control (fired automatically by ASP.NET), the LoadData method is called to load the NavBar data from the XML file associated with the control.

Skipping over the Render method temporarily, the LoadData method creates a new instance of the ADO.NET DataSet class and calls its ReadXml method to read the data from the XML file. If no file exists, the LoadData method calls another method (CreateBlankFile) to create a blank XML file with the correct format for use by the developer consuming the control. This technique not only deals gracefully with an error condition; it provides an easier starting point for the developer using the control. Note that the CreateBlankFile method is declared as public, which means it can be called deliberately to create a blank file, if desired.

Last, but certainly not least, the overridden Render method, which is called automatically at runtime when the control is created, iterates through the first (and only) table in the dataset and uses an instance of the StringBuilder class to build the HTML output to render. Once the desired output has been built, the method uses the HtmlTextWriter passed to it by ASP.NET to write the output to the client browser. Note that prior to looping through the rows in the dataset, the render method calls the RenderBeginTag and RenderContents methods of the base Panel control. This renders the opening <div> tag that is the client-side representation of the Panel control, plus anything contained within the opening and closing tags of the NavBar control. Once all the rows have been iterated and their output sent to the browser, the RenderEndTag method is called to send the closing </div> tag to the browser.

This example uses a couple of helper classes that are fairly common in ASP.NET development. The first, the StringBuilder class, is a helper class that is used for constructing strings. Because strings are immutable in the .NET Framework (strings cannot be changed), each time you use string concatenation (i.e., use the VB & operator or the C# + operator), the original string is destroyed and a new string containing the result of the concatenation is created. This can get fairly expensive when you're doing a lot of concatenation, so the StringBuilder class provides a way of constructing strings without the expense of concatenation.

The HtmlTextWriter class, an instance of which is automatically created and passed to the Render method by the ASP.NET runtime, allows you to write text output to the client browser, and includes useful methods (such as WriteBeginTag, WriteEndTag, and WriteAttribute) and shared/static fields for correctly formatting HTML output.

You can compile the code in Example 6-4 by using the following single-line command (which can alternatively be placed in a batch file):

```
vbc /t:library /out:bin\NavBar.dll /r:System.dll,System.Data.dll,
System.Drawing.dll,System.Web.dll,System.Xml.dll NavBar.vb
```

The preceding command requires that you create a *bin* subdirectory under the directory from which the command is launched and that you register the path to the Visual Basic compiler in your PATH environment variable. If you have not registered this path, you will need to provide the full path to the Visual Basic .NET compiler (by default, this path is *%windir%\Microsoft.NET\Framework\ %version%* where *%windir%* is the path to your Windows directory, and *%version%* is the version number of the framework version you have installed).

Example 6-5 shows the XML file used to populate the control, Example 6-6 shows the code necessary to use the NavBar control in a Web Forms page, and Figure 6-1 shows the output of this page.

Example 6-5. NavBar.xml

```
<navBar>
    <!-- node field describes a single node of the control -->
    <node>
        <!-- Required Fields -->
        <!-- url field should contain the absolute or relative
            URL to link to -->
        <url>NavBarClient.aspx</url>
        <!-- text field should contain the descriptive text for
            this node -->
        <text>NavBar Client</text>
        <!-- End Required Fields -->
        <!-- Optional Fields -->
        <!-- imageUrl field should contain the absolute or relative
            URL for an image to be displayed in front of the link -->
        <imageUrl>node.jpg</imageUrl>
        <!-- moimageUrl field should contain the absolute or
            relative URL for an image to be displayed in front of
            the link on mouseover -->
        <moImageUrl>node_rev.jpg</moImageUrl>
        <!-- targetFrame field should contain one of the following:
            _blank, _parent, _self, _top -->
        <targetFrame>_self</targetFrame>
        <!-- End Optional Fields -->
    </node>
    <node>
        <url>UCClient.aspx</url>
        <text>User Control Client</text>
        <imageUrl>alt_node.jpg</imageUrl>
        <moImageUrl>alt_node_rev.jpg</moImageUrl>
        <targetFrame>_self</targetFrame>
    </node>
    <node>
        <url>BlogClient.aspx</url>
        <text>Blog Client</text>
        <imageUrl>node.jpg</imageUrl>
        <moImageUrl>node_rev.jpg</moImageUrl>
        <targetFrame>
        </targetFrame>
    </node>
    <node>
```

Example 6-5. NavBar.xml (continued)

```
        <url>BlogAdd.aspx</url>
        <text>Add New Blog</text>
        <imageUrl>alt_node.jpg</imageUrl>
        <moImageUrl>alt_node_rev.jpg</moImageUrl>
        <targetFrame>
        </targetFrame>
    </node>
</navBar>
```

Example 6-6. NavBarClient.aspx

```
<%@ Page Language="vb" %>
<%@ Register TagPrefix="aspnetian" Namespace="aspnetian"
  Assembly="NavBar" %>
<html>
<head>
   <script runat="server">
      Sub Page_Load( )
         'NB1.CreateBlankFile( )
      End Sub
   </script>
</head>
<body>
   <table border="1" width="100%" cellpadding="20" cellspacing="0">
      <tr>
         <td align="center" width="150">
            <img src="aspnetian.jpg"/>
         </td>
         <td align="center">
            <h1>NavBar Control Client Page<h1>
         </td>
      </tr>
      <tr>
         <td width="150">
            <form runat="server">
               <aspnetian:NavBar id="NB1"
                  showdividers="False" runat="server">
                  <strong>Navigation Bar</strong>
                  <br/>
               </aspnetian:NavBar>
            </form>
         </td>
         <td>
            This is where page content might be placed
            <br/><br/><br/><br/><br/><br/><br/><br/><br/>
         </td>
      </tr>
   </table>
</body>
</html>
```

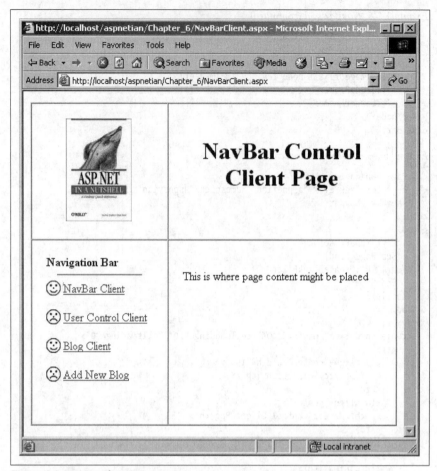

Figure 6-1. NavBarClient.aspx output

Compositional Controls

As mentioned earlier in the chapter, compositional controls render their output by combining appropriate controls within the CreateChildControls method, which is overridden in the custom control.

Example 6-7 shows the C# code for a compositional control that provides simple functionality for a *blog* (which is short for web log). The control has two modes: Add and Display. The mode is determined by the internal member_mode, which can be accessed by the public Mode property.

Like the NavBar control created in the previous example, the class definition for the Blog control specifies that the class derives from the Panel control (using C#'s : syntax), and also implements the INamingContainer interface. The INaming-Container interface contains no members, so there's nothing to actually implement. It's simply used to tell the ASP.NET runtime to provide a separate naming scope for controls contained within the custom control. This helps avoid the possibility of naming conflicts at runtime, and also allows ASP.NET to properly manage the ViewState of child controls.

Also like the NavBar control, the Blog control uses an XML file to store the individual Blog entries. The example uses the same method of retrieving the data, namely creating a dataset and calling its ReadXml method, passing in the name of the XML file.

In addition to declaring the _mode member variable and the BlogDS dataset, the example declares two Textbox controls (which will be used when adding a new blog entry) and two more string member variables (_ addRedirect and _email).

The code in Example 6-7 then creates public property accessors for all three string variables. The Mode property determines whether the control displays existing blogs or displays fields for creating a new blog. The AddRedirect property takes the URL for a page to redirect to when a new blog is added. The Email property takes an email address to link to in each new blog field.

Next, the program overrides the OnInit method of the derived control to handle the Init event when it is called by the runtime. In this event handler, you call the LoadData method, which, like the same method in the NavBar control, loads the data from the XML file or, if no file exists, creates a blank file. It then calls the OnInit method of the base class to ensure that necessary initialization work is done.

Next is the overridden CreateChildControls method. Like the Render method, this method is called automatically by the ASP.NET runtime when the page is instantiated on the server. The timing of when CreateChildControls is called, however, is not predictable, since it may be called at different times during the lifecycle of the page, depending on how the control is coded, and other factors. Since the ASP.NET runtime will deliberately wait as long as possible to create the child controls, you may want to call the EnsureChildControls method (inherited from the Control class) to make sure that controls are created before you attempt to access them. A good example of this is when you expose a public property on your control that gets its value from a child control. If a client of your control attempts to access this property, and the child control has not yet been created, an exception will occur. To avoid this, you would add a call to EnsureChildControls to the property procedure:

```
Public Property MyTextValue( ) As String
    Get
        Me.EnsureChildControls( )
        Return CType(Controls(1), TextBox).Text
    End Get
    Set
        Me.EnsureChildControls( )
        CType(Controls(1), TextBox).Text = value.ToString( )
    End Set
End Property
```

Also unlike the Render method, you don't want to call the CreateChildControls method of the base class, or you'll create a loop in which this method calls itself recursively (and the ASP.NET process will hang). In the CreateChildControls method, you check the value of the _mode member variable and call either the

DisplayBlogs method or the NewBlog method, depending on the value of _mode. Note that this value is set by default to display, so if the property is not set, the control will be in display mode. Also note that the example uses the ToLower method of the String class to ensure that either uppercase or lowercase attribute values work properly.

The DisplayBlogs method iterates through the data returned in the dataset and instantiates controls to display this data. We use an if statement to determine whether more than one entry in a row has the same date. If so, we display only a single date header for the group of entries with the same date. We add an Html-Anchor control to each entry to facilitate the readers' ability to bookmark the URL for a given entry. Then we write out the entry itself and add a contact email address and a link to the specific entry at the end of each entry.

Example 6-7. Blog.cs

```csharp
using System;
using System.Data;
using System.Drawing;
using System.IO;
using System.Web;
using System.Web.UI;
using System.Web.UI.HtmlControls;
using System.Web.UI.WebControls;

namespace aspnetian
{

public class Blog:Panel, INamingContainer
{

    protected DataSet BlogDS;
    protected TextBox TitleTB;
    protected TextBox BlogText;

    private string _addRedirect;
    private string _email;
    private string _mode = "display";

    public string AddRedirect
    {
        get
        {
            return this._addRedirect;
        }
        set
        {
            this._addRedirect = value;
        }
    }

    public string Email
    {
```

Example 6-7. Blog.cs (continued)

```
      get
      {
         return this._email;
      }
      set
      {
         this._email = value;
      }
   }

   public string Mode
   {
      get
      {
         return this._mode;
      }
      set
      {
         this._mode = value;
      }
   }

   protected override void OnInit(EventArgs e)
   {
      LoadData( );
      base.OnInit(e);
   }

   protected override void CreateChildControls( )
   {
      this.Controls.Clear( );
      if (this._mode.ToLower( ) != "add")
      {
         DisplayBlogs( );
      }
      else
      {
         NewBlog( );
      }
   }

   protected void LoadData( )
   {
      BlogDS = new DataSet( );

      try
      {
         BlogDS.ReadXml(Page.Server.MapPath("Blog.xml"));
      }
      catch (FileNotFoundException fnfEx)
      {
         CreateBlankFile( );
```

Example 6-7. Blog.cs (continued)

```
        LoadData( );
    }
}

protected void DisplayBlogs( )
{
    DateTime BlogDate;
    DateTime CurrentDate = new DateTime( );

    DataRowCollection BlogRows = BlogDS.Tables[0].Rows;
    foreach (DataRow BlogDR in BlogRows)
    {
        string BDate = BlogDR["date"].ToString( );
        BlogDate = new DateTime(Convert.ToInt32(BDate.Substring(4, 4)),
            Convert.ToInt32(BDate.Substring(0, 2)),
            Convert.ToInt32(BDate.Substring(2, 2)));

        if (CurrentDate != BlogDate)
        {
            Label Date = new Label( );
            Date.Text = BlogDate.ToLongDateString( );
            Date.Font.Size = FontUnit.Large;
            Date.Font.Bold = true;
            this.Controls.Add(Date);
            this.Controls.Add(new LiteralControl("<br/><br/>"));
            CurrentDate = BlogDate;
        }

        HtmlAnchor Anchor = new HtmlAnchor( );
        Anchor.Name = "#" + BlogDR["anchorID"].ToString( );
        this.Controls.Add(Anchor);

        Label Title = new Label( );
        Title.Text = BlogDR["title"].ToString( );
        Title.Font.Size = FontUnit.Larger;
        Title.Font.Bold = true;
        this.Controls.Add(Title);

        this.Controls.Add(new LiteralControl("<p>"));
        LiteralControl BlogText = new LiteralControl("<div>" +
            BlogDR["text"].ToString( ) + "</div>");
        this.Controls.Add(BlogText);
        this.Controls.Add(new LiteralControl("</p>"));

        HyperLink Email = new HyperLink( );
        Email.NavigateUrl = "mailto:" + BlogDR["email"].ToString( );
        Email.Text = "E-mail me";
        this.Controls.Add(Email);

        this.Controls.Add(new LiteralControl(" | "));

        HyperLink AnchorLink = new HyperLink( );
```

Example 6-7. Blog.cs (continued)

```
        AnchorLink.NavigateUrl = Page.Request.Url.ToString( ) + "#" +
            BlogDR["anchorID"].ToString( );
        AnchorLink.Text = "Link";
        this.Controls.Add(AnchorLink);

        this.Controls.Add(new LiteralControl("<hr width='100%'/><br/>"));
    }
}

protected void NewBlog( )
{
    Label Title = new Label( );
    Title.Text = "Create New Blog";
    Title.Font.Size = FontUnit.Larger;
    Title.Font.Bold = true;
    this.Controls.Add(Title);

    this.Controls.Add(new LiteralControl("<br/><br/>"));

    Label TitleLabel = new Label( );
    TitleLabel.Text = "Title: ";
    TitleLabel.Font.Bold = true;
    this.Controls.Add(TitleLabel);
    TitleTB = new TextBox( );
    this.Controls.Add(TitleTB);

    this.Controls.Add(new LiteralControl("<br/>"));

    Label BlogTextLabel = new Label( );
    BlogTextLabel.Text = "Text: ";
    BlogTextLabel.Font.Bold = true;
    this.Controls.Add(BlogTextLabel);
    BlogText = new TextBox( );
    BlogText.TextMode = TextBoxMode.MultiLine;
    BlogText.Rows = 10;
    BlogText.Columns = 40;
    this.Controls.Add(BlogText);

    this.Controls.Add(new LiteralControl("<br/>"));

    Button Submit = new Button( );
    Submit.Text = "Submit";
    Submit.Click += new EventHandler(this.Submit_Click);
    this.Controls.Add(Submit);
}

protected void Submit_Click(object sender, EventArgs e)
{
    EnsureChildControls( );
    AddBlog( );
}
```

Example 6-7. Blog.cs (continued)

```
protected void AddBlog( )
{
    DataRow NewBlogDR;
    NewBlogDR = BlogDS.Tables[0].NewRow( );
    NewBlogDR["date"] = FormatDate(DateTime.Today);
    NewBlogDR["title"] = TitleTB.Text;
    NewBlogDR["text"] = BlogText.Text;
    NewBlogDR["anchorID"] = Guid.NewGuid().ToString( );
    NewBlogDR["email"] = _email;
    BlogDS.Tables[0].Rows.InsertAt(NewBlogDR, 0);
    BlogDS.WriteXml(Page.Server.MapPath("Blog.xml"));
    Page.Response.Redirect(_addRedirect);
}

protected string FormatDate(DateTime dt)
{
    string retString;

    retString = String.Format("{0:D2}", dt.Month);
    retString += String.Format("{0:D2}", dt.Day);
    retString += String.Format("{0:D2}", dt.Year);
    return retString;
}

protected void CreateBlankFile( )
{
    // code to create new file...omitted to conserve space
}

} // closing bracket for class declaration

} // closing bracket for namespace declaration
```

Displaying the blog entries is only half the battle. While it would certainly be possible to edit the XML file directly in order to add a new blog entry, it makes much more sense to make this a feature of the control. This is what the NewBlog method does. In the NewBlog method, we instantiate Label and TextBox controls for data entry and a Button control to submit the new blog entry. When the Button is clicked, the Submit_Click event handler method is called when the control is re-created on the server. The Submit_Click event handler, in turn, calls the AddBlog method to insert a new row into the BlogDS dataset and then writes the contents of the dataset back to the underlying XML file. Before using the control, of course, we'll need to compile it and place it in the application's *bin* directory. The following snippet can be used to compile the control:

```
csc /t:library /out:bin\blog.dll /r:system.dll,system.data.dll,
system.xml.dll,system.web.dll blog.cs
```

Example 6-8 shows the ASP.NET code necessary to instantiate the Blog control programmatically. Note the use of the PlaceHolder control to precisely locate the Blog control output. For this code to work correctly, the compiled assembly containing the Blog control must reside in the application's *bin* subdirectory.

Figure 6-2 shows the output of the control when used in the client page shown in Example 6-8.

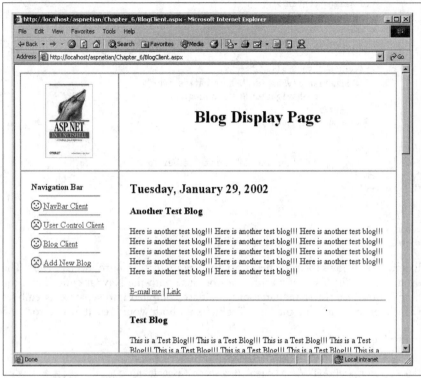

Figure 6-2. Output of BlogClient.aspx

Example 6-8. BlogClient.aspx

```
<%@ Page Language="vb" debug="true" %>
<%@ Register TagPrefix="aspnetian" Namespace="aspnetian"
   Assembly="NavBar" %>
<html>
<head>
   <script runat="server">
      Sub Page_Init()
         Dim Blog1 As New Blog()
         Blog1.SeparatorColor = System.Drawing.Color.Red
         PH.Controls.Add(Blog1)
      End Sub
   </script>
</head>
<body>
   <form runat="server">
   <table border="1" width="100%" cellpadding="20" cellspacing="0">
      <tr>
         <td align="center" width="150">
            <img src="aspnetian.jpg"/>
```

Example 6-8. BlogClient.aspx (continued)

```
            </td>
            <td align="center">
               <h1>Blog Display Page<h1>
            </td>
        </tr>
        <tr>
            <td width="150" valign="top">
               <aspnetian:NavBar id="NB1" runat="server">
                  <strong>Navigation Bar</strong>
                  <br/>
               </aspnetian:NavBar>
            </td>
            <td>
               <asp:placeholder id="PH" runat="server"/>
            </td>
        </tr>
    </table>
    </form>
</body>
</html>
```

Example 6-9 shows the code necessary to instantiate the control declaratively. The example uses the TagPrefix aspnetian2 because both the NavBar control and the Blog control use the same namespace, but are compiled into separate assemblies (which means that using the same TagPrefix for both would result in an error).

Example 6-9. BlogAdd.aspx

```
<%@ Page Language="vb" debug="true" %>
<%@ Register TagPrefix="aspnetian" Namespace="aspnetian"
    Assembly="NavBar" %>
<%@ Register TagPrefix="aspnetian2" Namespace="aspnetian"
    Assembly="Blog" %>
<html>
<head>
   <script runat="server">
      Sub Page_Load( )
         'Uncomment the line below to explicitly create a blank
         '   XML file, then comment the line out again to run the control
         'NB1.CreateBlankFile( )
      End Sub
   </script>
</head>
<body>
   <form runat="server">
   <table border="1" width="100%" cellpadding="20" cellspacing="0">
      <tr>
         <td align="center" width="150">
            <img src="aspnetian.jpg"/>
         </td>
         <td align="center">
            <h1>Blog Add Page<h1>
         </td>
```

Example 6-9. BlogAdd.aspx (continued)

```
      </tr>
      <tr>
        <td width="150" valign="top">
          <aspnetian:NavBar id="NB1" runat="server">
            <strong>Navigation Bar</strong>
            <br/>
          </aspnetian:NavBar>
        </td>
        <td>
          <aspnetian2:Blog id="Blog1"
            mode="Add"
            addredirect="BlogClient.aspx"
            email="blogs@aspnetian.com"
            runat="server"/>
        </td>
      </tr>
    </table>
  </form>
</body>
</html>
```

As you can see, whether the control is used programmatically or declaratively, the amount of code necessary to provide simple blogging functionality is made trivial by the use of a custom server control. Note that you can also have the same page use the Blog control in either Display or Add mode, depending on the user's actions, as explained in the following section.

Adding Design-Time Support

While using the Blog control in a Web Forms page is fairly simple, it's still not 100% intuitive. For example, without documentation, there's no way for someone using the Blog control to know what the appropriate values for the Mode property are. Without explicitly telling developers using the control about the Add mode, it would be difficult for them to discover and use this mode on their own.

For developers using Visual Studio .NET (or another IDE that supports IntelliSense), you can solve this problem by adding design-time support to the control. This is done by using a combination of special metadata attributes added to the control and custom XSD schemas to support IntelliSense statement completion for Web Forms pages. IntelliSense support in code-behind modules is automatic and requires no additional coding.

Part of the challenge of providing design-time support for custom server controls is that different editors in the Visual Studio IDE require different techniques to support design-time functionality. Custom controls automatically support IntelliSense statement completion when working with code-behind modules in Visual Basic .NET or C#. Figure 6-3 shows this statement completion in action for the Blog control.

Unfortunately, when editing Web Forms pages, automatic support for statement completion does not extend to the Design or HTML views (nor does Visual Studio provide built-in support for viewing and editing properties in the Property

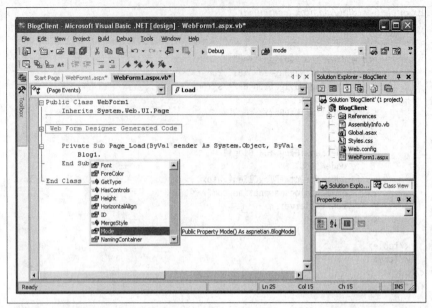

Figure 6-3. IntelliSense in code-behind

browser without additional work in your control). To complicate things further, one technique is necessary for supporting IntelliSense in the Property browser and Design view of the Web Forms editor, while another is necessary for supporting it in the HTML view of the Web Forms editor.

The technique required for supporting property browsing in Design view uses metadata attributes to inform Visual Studio .NET about how to handle the properties. Supporting statement completion and property browsing in HTML view requires creating a custom XSD schema that describes the types in your control. We'll discuss both techniques in the next sections.

Metadata attributes

Visual Studio .NET provides rich support for designing and modifying controls visually by using drag-and-drop techniques and tools, such as the Property browser, and related designers, such as the color picker. Support for these tools is provided by a series of metadata attributes that you can add to your control. These attributes tell the Visual Studio IDE whether to display any properties that your control exposes in the Properties browser, what type the properties are, and which designer should be used to set the properties' values.

To support editing of the AddRedirect property in the Property browser, we would add the following attributes before the Property procedure, as shown in the following code snippet:

```
[
Browsable(true),
Category("Behavior"),
Description("URL to which the page should redirect after
```

```
        successful submission of a new Blog entry."),
    Editor(typeof(System.Web.UI.Design.UrlEditor), typeof(UITypeEditor))
    ]
    public string AddRedirect
    { // property procedure code }
```

These attribute declarations allow the property to be displayed in the Property browser, set the desired category for the property (when properties are sorted by category), provide a description of the property, and tell Visual Studio .NET to use the UrlEditor designer to edit the property's value.

Additional Uses for Metadata

Metadata attributes aren't just for use by the Visual Studio .NET designer. In fact, metadata attributes are used throughout the .NET Framework to allow developers (both the framework developers, and those who use the framework) to add descriptive, configuration, and other types of information to assemblies, classes, and/or class members.

You can also create your own custom attributes in your applications, though the specifics of doing so is beyond the scope of this book.

The attribute syntax shown in this section is for C#. In C#, attributes take the form:

> [*AttributeName*(*AttributeParams*)]

In Visual Basic .NET, attributes are declared with the following syntax:

> <*AttributeName*(*AttributeParams*)>

Visual Basic .NET requires that the attribute declaration appear on the same line as the member it's modifying, so it's usually a good idea to follow the attribute with a VB line continuation character to improve readability:

> ```
> <AttributeName(AttributeParams)> _
> Public Membername()
> ```

In both C# and VB, you can declare multiple attributes within a single set of [ ] or <> brackets by separating multiple attributes with commas.

In addition to setting attributes at the property level, you can set certain attributes at the class and assembly levels. For example, you can use the assembly-level attribute TagPrefix to specify the tag prefix to use for any controls contained in the assembly. Visual Studio .NET then inserts this tag prefix automatically when you add an instance of the control to a Web Forms page from the Visual Studio toolbox. The following code snippet shows the syntax for the TagPrefix attribute. This attribute should be placed within the class module that defines the control, but outside the class and namespace declarations.

```
    [
    assembly: TagPrefix("aspnetian", "aspnetian")
    ]
```

```
namespace aspnetian
{ // control classes, etc. }
```

To complete the integration of a control in the Visual Studio .NET environment, add the ToolBoxData attribute (which tells Visual Studio .NET your preferred tag name for controls inserted from the toolbox) to the class that implements the control:

```
[
ToolboxData("<{0}:Blog runat=server></{0}:Blog>")
]
public class Blog:Panel, INamingContainer
{ // control implementation }
```

Once compiled, the control will support automatic insertion of the @ Register directive, tag prefix, and tag name for the Blog control. To add the control to the Visual Studio .NET toolbox, follow these simple steps:

1. In Design view, select the Web Forms tab of the Visual Studio .NET toolbox.

2. Right-click anywhere in the tab and select Add/Remove Items....

3. With the .NET Framework Components tab selected, click Browse.

4. Browse to the location of the compiled control assembly, select it, and click Open.

5. Click OK.

Once the control has been added to the toolbox, you can add it to a Web Forms page by either double-clicking the control or dragging and dropping it from the toolbox onto the Web Forms page. In either case, Visual Studio .NET will automatically insert the correct @ Register directive, including setting the TagPrefix based on the assembly-level attribute, and will also create a set of tags for the control with the tag name specified in the ToolBoxData attribute.

Adding a control designer

As written, the Blog control will not have any visible interface in the Design view of the Web Forms editor. This can make it more difficult to select the control on the page, and also may make it more difficult to understand what the control will look like at runtime. To correct this problem, we can add support for a designer that will render HTML at design time that approximates the look of the Blog control at runtime. Note that you can also create designers that completely reproduce the runtime output of a control, but doing so is more involved and beyond the scope of this book.

All server control designers derive from the class System.Web.UI.Design. ControlDesigner, which exposes a number of methods you can override to provide design-time rendering for your control. Example 6-10 overrides the GetDesign-TimeHtml method to return simple HTML. Note that the example shows the entire designer class for the Blog control, which you can add to the existing *Blog.cs* class file (making sure that the class declaration is within the namespace curly braces).

Example 6-10. BlogDesigner class

```
public class BlogDesigner:ControlDesigner
{
    public override string GetDesignTimeHtml()
    {
        return "<h1>Blog</h1><hr/><hr/>";
    }
}
```

To tie this designer into the Blog class, we use the `Designer` attribute, as shown in the following snippet. Note that this code also adds a `Description` attribute that describes what the control does.

```
[
Description("Simple Blog control. Supports display of Web log / news
    items from an XML file."),
Designer(typeof(aspnetian.BlogDesigner)),
ToolboxData("<{0}:Blog runat=server></{0}:Blog>")
]
public class Blog:Panel, INamingContainer
{ // class implementation }
```

As you can see, the `BlogDesigner` class is extremely simple, but it adds a lot to the control's design-time appearance on a web page, as shown in Figure 6-4.

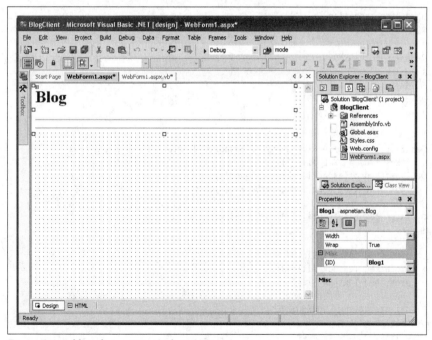

Figure 6-4. Adding design-time rendering

Example 6-11 shows the code for the Blog control, updated with attributes to enable design-time support for the control in Design view and the Property browser. Note that the example adds several using directives to import the namespaces needed to support the attributes and designer classes we've used. The example also adds an enumeration to be used for the value of the Mode property and a new property, SeparatorColor.

Example 6-11. Updated Blog.cs

```
using System;
using System.ComponentModel;
using System.Data;
using System.Drawing;
using System.Drawing.Design;
using System.IO;
using System.Web;
using System.Web.UI;
using System.Web.UI.Design;
using System.Web.UI.HtmlControls;
using System.Web.UI.WebControls;

[
assembly: TagPrefix("aspnetian", "aspnetian")
]

namespace aspnetian
{

public enum BlogMode
{
   Add,
   Display
}

[
Description(@"Simple Blog control. Supports display of Web log / news
   items from an XML file."),
Designer(typeof(aspnetian.BlogDesigner)),
ToolboxData("<{0}:Blog runat=server></{0}:Blog>")
]
public class Blog:Panel, INamingContainer
{

   protected DataSet BlogDS;
   protected TextBox TitleTB;
   protected TextBox BlogText;

   private string _addRedirect;
   private string _email;
   private BlogMode _mode;
   private Color _separatorColor = Color.Black;

   [
```

Example 6-11. Updated Blog.cs (continued)

```
Browsable(true),
Category("Behavior"),
Description("URL to which the page should redirect after
    successful submission of a new Blog entry."),
Editor(typeof(System.Web.UI.Design.UrlEditor), typeof(UITypeEditor))
]
public string AddRedirect
{
    get
    {
        return this._addRedirect;
    }
    set
    {
        this._addRedirect = value;
    }
}

[
Browsable(true),
Category("Behavior"),
Description("Email address the control will use for listing in new
    Blog entries.")
]
public string Email
{
    get
    {
        return this._email;
    }
    set
    {
        this._email = value;
    }
}

[
Browsable(true),
Category("Behavior"),
Description("Controls whether existing Blogs are displayed, or
    fields for creating a new Blog entry.")
]
public BlogMode Mode
{
    get
    {
        return this._mode;
    }
    set
    {
        this._mode = value;
```

Example 6-11. Updated Blog.cs (continued)

```
    }
}

[
Browsable(true),
Category("Appearance"),
Description("Controls the color of the line that separates Blog
   entries when in display mode.")
]
public Color SeparatorColor
{
    get
    {
        return this._separatorColor;
    }
    set
    {
        this._separatorColor = value;
    }
}

protected override void OnInit(EventArgs e)
{
    LoadData();
    base.OnInit(e);
}

protected override void CreateChildControls()
{
    if (this._mode != BlogMode.Add)
    {
        DisplayBlogs();
    }
    else
    {
        NewBlog();
    }
}

protected void LoadData()
{
    BlogDS = new DataSet();

    try
    {
        BlogDS.ReadXml(Page.Server.MapPath("Blog.xml"));
    }
    catch (FileNotFoundException fnfEx)
    {
        CreateBlankFile();
        LoadData();
```

Example 6-11. Updated Blog.cs (continued)

```
        }
    }

    protected void DisplayBlogs( )
    {
        DateTime BlogDate;
        DateTime CurrentDate = new DateTime( );

        DataRowCollection BlogRows = BlogDS.Tables[0].Rows;
        foreach (DataRow BlogDR in BlogRows)
        {
            string BDate = BlogDR["date"].ToString( );
            BlogDate = new DateTime(Convert.ToInt32(BDate.Substring(4, 4)),
                Convert.ToInt32(BDate.Substring(0, 2)),
                Convert.ToInt32(BDate.Substring(2, 2)));

            if (CurrentDate != BlogDate)
            {
                Label Date = new Label( );
                Date.Text = BlogDate.ToLongDateString( );
                Date.Font.Size = FontUnit.Large;
                Date.Font.Bold = true;
                this.Controls.Add(Date);
                this.Controls.Add(new LiteralControl("<br/><br/>"));
                CurrentDate = BlogDate;
            }

            HtmlAnchor Anchor = new HtmlAnchor( );
            Anchor.Name = "#" + BlogDR["anchorID"].ToString( );
            this.Controls.Add(Anchor);

            Label Title = new Label( );
            Title.Text = BlogDR["title"].ToString( );
            Title.Font.Size = FontUnit.Larger;
            Title.Font.Bold = true;
            this.Controls.Add(Title);

            this.Controls.Add(new LiteralControl("<p>"));
            LiteralControl BlogText = new LiteralControl("<div>" +
                BlogDR["text"].ToString( ) + "</div>");
            this.Controls.Add(BlogText);
            this.Controls.Add(new LiteralControl("</p>"));

            HyperLink Email = new HyperLink( );
            Email.NavigateUrl = "mailto:" + BlogDR["email"].ToString( );
            Email.Text = "E-mail me";
            this.Controls.Add(Email);

            this.Controls.Add(new LiteralControl(" | "));
            HyperLink AnchorLink = new HyperLink( );
            AnchorLink.NavigateUrl = Page.Request.Url.ToString( ) + "#" +
                BlogDR["anchorID"].ToString( );
```

Example 6-11. Updated Blog.cs (continued)

```
        AnchorLink.Text = "Link";
        this.Controls.Add(AnchorLink);

        this.Controls.Add(new LiteralControl("<hr color='" +
            _separatorColor.ToKnownColor() + "' width='100%'/><br/>"));
    }
}

protected void NewBlog()
{
    Label Title = new Label();
    Title.Text = "Create New Blog";
    Title.Font.Size = FontUnit.Larger;
    Title.Font.Bold = true;
    this.Controls.Add(Title);

    this.Controls.Add(new LiteralControl("<br/><br/>"));

    Label TitleLabel = new Label();
    TitleLabel.Text = "Title: ";
    TitleLabel.Font.Bold = true;
    this.Controls.Add(TitleLabel);
    TitleTB = new TextBox();
    this.Controls.Add(TitleTB);

    this.Controls.Add(new LiteralControl("<br/>"));

    Label BlogTextLabel = new Label();
    BlogTextLabel.Text = "Text: ";
    BlogTextLabel.Font.Bold = true;
    this.Controls.Add(BlogTextLabel);
    BlogText = new TextBox();
    BlogText.TextMode = TextBoxMode.MultiLine;
    BlogText.Rows = 10;
    BlogText.Columns = 40;
    this.Controls.Add(BlogText);

    this.Controls.Add(new LiteralControl("<br/>"));

    Button Submit = new Button();
    Submit.Text = "Submit";
    Submit.Click += new EventHandler(this.Submit_Click);
    this.Controls.Add(Submit);
}

protected void Submit_Click(object sender, EventArgs e)
{
    EnsureChildControls();
    AddBlog();
}

protected void AddBlog()
{
```

Example 6-11. Updated Blog.cs (continued)

```
    DataRow NewBlogDR;
    NewBlogDR = BlogDS.Tables[0].NewRow( );
    NewBlogDR["date"] = FormatDate(DateTime.Today);
    NewBlogDR["title"] = TitleTB.Text;
    NewBlogDR["text"] = BlogText.Text;
    NewBlogDR["anchorID"] = Guid.NewGuid().ToString( );
    NewBlogDR["email"] = _email;
    BlogDS.Tables[0].Rows.InsertAt(NewBlogDR, 0);
    BlogDS.WriteXml(Page.Server.MapPath("Blog.xml"));
    Page.Response.Redirect(_addRedirect);
  }

  protected string FormatDate(DateTime dt)
  {
    string retString;
    retString = String.Format("{0:D2}", dt.Month);
    retString += String.Format("{0:D2}", dt.Day);
    retString += String.Format("{0:D2}", dt.Year);
    return retString;
  }

  public void CreateBlankFile( )
  {
    // code to create new file...omitted to conserve space
  }

}

public class BlogDesigner:ControlDesigner
{
  public override string GetDesignTimeHtml( )
  {
    return "<h1>Blog</h1><hr/><hr/>";
  }
}

}
```

Custom schemas and Visual Studio annotations

As much as the metadata attributes described in the previous section help provide support for the Blog control at design time, they're missing one important piece: IntelliSense support for adding tags and attributes in the HTML view of the Web Forms editor. For developers who are more comfortable working in HTML than in WYSIWYG style, this oversight is significant.

Since the HTML view of the Web Forms editor uses XSD schemas to determine which elements and attributes to make available in a Web Forms page, to correct the oversight, we need to implement an XSD schema that describes the Blog control and the attributes that it supports. Optionally, we can add annotations to the schema that tell Visual Studio .NET about the various elements and how we'd like them to behave.

Example 6-12 contains the portion of the XSD schema specific to the Blog control. The actual schema file (contained in the sample code for the book, which may be obtained from the book's page at the O'Reilly web site: *http://www.oreilly.com/ catalog/aspdotnetnut2*) also contains type definitions for the Panel control from which the Blog control is derived, as well as other necessary attribute and type definitions. These definitions were copied from the *asp.xsd* schema file created for the built-in ASP.NET Server Controls.

You should never modify the *asp.xsd* schema file directly, but should copy any necessary type or attribute definitions to your custom schema file. While this may seem redundant, if you edit *asp.xsd* directly and a later installation or service pack for the .NET Framework overwrites this file, your custom schema entries will be lost.

Example 6-12. Blog.xsd

```xml
<?xml version="1.0" encoding="utf-8" ?>
<xsd:schema targetNamespace="urn:http://www.aspnetian.com/schemas"
    elementFormDefault="qualified"
    xmlns="urn:http://www.aspnetian.com/schemas"
    xmlns:xsd="http://www.w3.org/2001/XMLSchema"
    xmlns:vs="http://schemas.microsoft.com/Visual-Studio-Intellisense"
    vs:friendlyname="Blog Control Schema"
    vs:ishtmlschema="false"
    vs:iscasesensitive="false"
    vs:requireattributequotes="true" >
  <xsd:annotation>
    <xsd:documentation>
        Blog Control schema.
    </xsd:documentation>
  </xsd:annotation>

  <xsd:element name="Blog" type="BlogDef" />

  <!-- <aspnetian:Blog> -->
  <xsd:complexType name="BlogDef">
    <!-- <aspnetian:Blog>-specific attributes -->
    <xsd:attribute name="AddRedirect" type="xsd:string"
        vs:builder="url"/>
    <xsd:attribute name="Email" type="xsd:string"/>
    <xsd:attribute name="Mode" type="BlogMode"/>
    <xsd:attribute name="SeparatorColor" type="xsd:string"
        vs:builder="color"/>
    <!-- <asp:Panel>-specific attributes -->
    <xsd:attribute name="BackImageUrl" type="xsd:anyURI" />
    <xsd:attribute name="HorizontalAlign" type="HorizontalAlign" />
    <xsd:attribute name="Wrap" type="xsd:boolean" />
    <xsd:attribute name="Enabled" type="xsd:boolean" />
    <xsd:attribute name="BorderWidth" type="ui4" />
    <xsd:attribute name="BorderColor" type="xsd:string"
        vs:builder="color" />
    <xsd:attribute name="BorderStyle" type="BorderStyle" />
```

Example 6-12. Blog.xsd (continued)

```
        <xsd:attributeGroup ref="WebControlAttributes" />
    </xsd:complexType>

    <!-- DataTypes -->
    <xsd:simpleType name="BlogMode">
        <xsd:restriction base="xsd:string">
            <xsd:enumeration value="Add" />
            <xsd:enumeration value="Display" />
        </xsd:restriction>
    </xsd:simpleType>
</xsd:schema>
```

In Example 6-12, note the targetNamespace and xmlns attributes on the root schema element, which define the XML namespace for the control's schema. The value of the targetNamespace and xmlns attributes will also be used as an attribute in your Web Forms page to "wire up" the schema. The <xsd:element> tag defines the root Blog element. The <xsd:complexType> tag defines the attributes for the Blog element, which includes the web control attributes referenced by the <xsd:attributeGroup> tag. Finally, the <xsd:simpleType> tag defines the enumeration for the BlogMode type used as one of the attributes for the Blog element.

Note that Example 6-12 uses the vs:builder annotation to tell Visual Studio .NET to use the Url builder for the AddRedirect attribute and the Color builder for the SeparatorColor attribute. The vs:builder annotation is one of many annotations available to modify schemas. The most commonly used are listed in Table 6-1.

Table 6-1. Common Visual Studio .NET annotations

Annotation	Purpose	Valid values
vs:absolutepositioning	Used at the root <schema> element to determine whether Visual Studio may insert style attributes for positioning.	true/false
vs:blockformatted	Indicates whether leading whitespace may be added to the element during automatic formatting.	true/false
vs:builder	Specifies the builder to be used for editing the related property's value.	color, style, or url
vs:deprecated	Allows a related property to be marked as "deprecated", which prevents it from showing up in the Properties browser and in statement completion.	true/false
vs:empty	Used at the element level to indicate that Visual Studio .NET should use single tag syntax for the related tag (no end tag).	true/false
vs:friendlyname	Used at the root level to provide a display name for the schema.	
vs:iscasesensitive	Used at the root level and specifies whether Visual Studio .NET will treat the related tags in a case-sensitive manner.	true/false
vs:ishtmlschema	Used at the root level and specifies whether the schema is an HTML document schema.	true/false
vs:nonbrowseable	Used at the attribute level and specifies that the attribute should not appear in statement completion.	true/false
vs:readonly	Used at the attribute level and specifies that the attribute may not be modified in the Properties window.	true/false
vs:requireattributequotes	Used at the root level and specifies that the attribute values must have quotes.	true/false

Once you've built your XSD schema, save it to the same location as the *asp.xsd* file (which defaults to *C:\ProgramFiles\Microsoft Visual Studio .NET 2003\ Common7\Packages\schemas\xml*).

To allow Visual Studio .NET to read your custom schema, you'll need to add an xmlns attribute to the <body> tag of the page in which you wish to use the schema, as shown in the following snippet:

```
<body xmlns:aspnetian="urn:http://www.aspnetian.com/schemas">
```

Notice that this code uses the aspnetian prefix with the xmlns attribute to specify that the schema is for controls prefixed with the aspnetian tag prefix. This recall is set up by the TagPrefix attribute (described earlier in "Metadata attributes"). The value of the xmlns attribute should be the same as the targetNamespace attribute defined at the root of the schema.

Once you've wired up your schema via the xmlns attribute, you should be able to type an opening < character and the first few letters of the aspnetian namespace and have the Blog control appear as one of the options for statement completion, as shown in Figure 6-5.

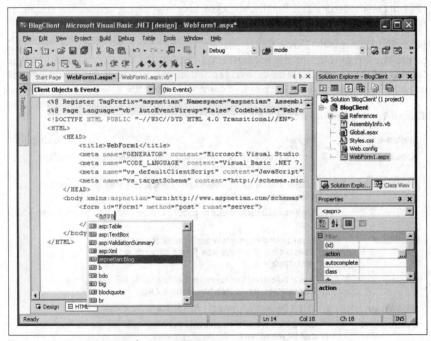

Figure 6-5. Statement completion in HTML view

Example 6-13 shows the code for a page that uses the Blog control from Visual Studio .NET, including the xmlns attribute added to the <body> element.

Example 6-13. BlogClient_VS.aspx

```
<%@ Register TagPrefix="aspnetian" Namespace="aspnetian"
    Assembly="Blog" %>
<%@ Page Language="vb" AutoEventWireup="True" Debug="True"%>
<!DOCTYPE HTML PUBLIC "-//W3C//DTD HTML 4.0 Transitional//EN">
<html>
    <head>
        <title>Blog Client</title>
        <meta content="Microsoft Visual Studio.NET 7.0" name="GENERATOR">
        <meta content="Visual Basic 7.0" name="CODE_LANGUAGE">
        <meta content="JavaScript" name="vs_defaultClientScript">
        <meta content="http://schemas.microsoft.com/intellisense/ie5"
          name="vs_targetSchema">
        <script runat="server">
            Sub Page_Load()
                If Request.QueryString("mode") = "add" Then
                    Blog1.Mode = BlogMode.Add
                    Link1.Visible = False
                    Link2.Visible = False
                Else
                    Blog1.Mode = BlogMode.Display
                    Link1.Visible = True
                    Link2.Visible = True
                End If
            End Sub
        </script>
    </head>
    <body xmlns:aspnetian="urn:http://www.aspnetian.com/schemas">
        <form id="Form1" method="post" runat="server">
            <p><asp:hyperlink id="Link1" runat="server"
                    navigateurl="WebForm1.aspx?mode=add">
                    Add Blog
                </asp:hyperlink></p>
            <p><aspnetian:blog id="Blog1" addredirect="WebForm1.aspx"
                    email="andrew@aspnetian.com" runat="server" >
                </aspnetian:blog></p>
            <p><asp:hyperlink id="Link2" runat="server"
                    navigateurl="WebForm1.aspx?mode=add">
                    Add Blog
                </asp:hyperlink></p>
        </form>
    </body>
</html>
```

Notice that Example 6-13 provides support for both displaying and adding blog entries from within the same page; this is done by omitting the Mode property in the tag that defines the control and setting the Mode programmatically (based on whether or not the page request was the result of the user clicking one of the "Add Blog" Hyperlink controls added to the page).

When the page is loaded for the first time, it will be in Display mode. Clicking one of the hyperlinks will request the page with the mode QueryString element set to add, which will cause the page to render in Add mode.

Adding Client Script

Sometimes you may want to use client-side script in your ASP.NET pages, either with controls or independent of them. In classic ASP, it was possible to write client script to the browser using Response.Write. However, this could get very messy—particularly if you needed to write the same set of code for use with more than one form element.

The ASP.NET Page class provides several methods for sending client script to the browser that make this process simpler and more reliable.

These methods include:

RegisterClientScriptBlock
Renders a string containing the specified client script to the browser.

RegisterHiddenField
Adds an <input> element whose type is set to hidden.

IsClientScriptBlockRegistered
Allows you to test whether a given named script block has been already registered by another control to avoid redundancy.

You might use these methods to pop up a message box on the client with the number of Blogs that currently exist in the XML file. To accomplish this, add the following snippet to the DisplayBlogs method of the Blog control:

```
Page.RegisterClientScriptBlock("Blog", "<script>alert('There are now " +
    BlogRows.Count + " Blogs!');</script>");
```

Then, if any other controls need to use the same script, call IsClientScript-BlockRegistered, passing it the name of the script shown above, Blog, to determine whether to call RegisterClientScriptBlock again. In this way, a single client-side script block may be shared among multiple controls.

 When using any of the methods discussed in this section, you should always check the built-in browser capabilities class to ensure that the client supports script (Request.Browser.JavaScript or Request.Browser.VBScript). Additionally, you should ensure that you call the method(s) either prior to or in the PreRender event handler, to ensure that the script is written to the client properly.

Sharing Controls Across Applications

The architecture of the .NET Framework makes using a custom server control or other assembly as simple as copying that assembly to the *bin* subdirectory of your application and adding the appropriate directives and tags to your page. However, there may be times when you would like multiple applications on the same machine to be able to use the same control, without having multiple local copies of the control's assembly floating around.

Fortunately, .NET addresses this need with the Global Assembly Cache (GAC), a repository of shared assemblies that are accessible to all .NET applications on a

---

given machine. Adding your own control assemblies to the GAC is a relatively straightforward process that requires four steps:

1. Use the *sn.exe* command-line utility to create a public key pair for use in signing your control:

   ```
   sn.exe -k Blog.snk
   ```

2. Add the `AssemblyKeyFileAttribute` to the file containing the control code, passing the path to the keyfile created in Step 1 as an argument. (This is an assembly-level attribute, so it should be placed outside of any namespace or class definitions.) When compiled, this attribute will result in a strongly named assembly that can be placed in the GAC:

   ```
   [assembly: AssemblyKeyFileAttribute("Blog.snk")]
   ```

3. Recompile the control.

4. Add the control to the GAC, either by dragging and dropping the assembly in Windows Explorer or by using the *gacutil.exe* utility, as follows:

   ```
   gacutil -i Blog.dll
   ```

 Note that as with the *csc.exe* and *vbc.exe* command-line compilers, using the *sn.exe* and *gacutil.exe* utilities without a fully qualified path requires that you have the path to these utilities registered as part of your PATH environment variable. The *sn.exe* and *gacutil.exe* utilities are typically located in the *FrameworkSDK\\bin* directory, which is installed either under *ProgramFiles\\Microsoft.NET* or *ProgramFiles\\Microsoft Visual Studio .NET 2003\\SDK\\v1.1\\Bin*, depending on whether you've installed just the .NET Framework SDK or Visual Studio .NET.

Once you've added the control assembly to the GAC, you can use it from any application on the machine. One caveat: to use custom controls that are installed in the GAC, you must supply the version, culture, and public key information for the assembly when adding the @ `Register` directive for the control, as shown in the following snippet (which should appear on a single line):

```
<%@ Register TagPrefix="aspnetian" Namespace="aspnetian" Assembly="Blog,
    Version=0.0.0.0, Culture=neutral, PublicKeyToken=6bd31f35fc9a113b" %>
```

If you've added your control to the Visual Studio .NET toolbox, when you use the control from the toolbox, the correct @ `Register` directive will be generated for you automatically.

Additional Resources

The following site provides additional information on the topics discussed in this chapter:

http://www.aspnextgen.com/
   The DotNetJunkies site, run by Microsoft MVP Award winners Donny Mack and Doug Seven, contains many ASP.NET tutorials, including some on building custom server controls and user controls.

7

Data Access and Data Binding

While writing simple applications without ever accessing data from a backend data store is certainly possible, most applications will, at some point, need to do so. Fortunately, the .NET Framework provides a rich set of classes designed to simplify the process of reading and writing data to both SQL Server and other backend data stores. These classes are collectively referred to as ADO.NET.

This chapter provides an overview of ADO.NET and the various tasks it facilitates—from reading data with the SqlDataReader class to updating data with the DataSet and SqlDataAdapter classes. The chapter also discusses reading from and writing to XML files and provides examples of binding retrieved data to ASP.NET Server Controls.

Data Access and Architecture

Almost everyone agrees that in all but the smallest applications, it is important to avoid performing data access directly from the ASP.NET Web Forms themselves. Accessing data directly from within a Web Form inherently ties the user interface code to the database and table schema that currently exist, making it more difficult to reuse data-access code and maintain the user interface code and backend data.

To keep the code as simple and straightforward as possible, the examples in this chapter perform data access directly from the pages. In a production application, this code should generally reside in either data-tier or business-tier components, which should return XML, a dataset, or some other database-independent structure to the presentation tier for data binding. Remember that you should always perform data calculations and modifications on a tier other than the presentation tier.

ADO.NET: An Overview

The combination of ASP.NET and ADO.NET provides great flexibility in terms of data sources. Unlike classic ADO, in which support for XML was bolted on after the basic interfaces were written, ADO.NET was written from the ground up to deal with XML and does so quite handily. For example, the DataSet class provides built-in support for reading from and writing to XML files and streams, and also provides support for reading, writing, and inferring (from the structure of a table retrieved from a DBMS) XSD schemas. This makes working with XML data quite easy, as demonstrated in the custom control examples in Chapter 6.

ADO.NET also provides excellent support for reading data from a DBMS, including a set of classes for fast, efficient access to data in SQL Server databases and another set of classes to support OLE DB data sources. Most importantly, in the DataSet class, ADO.NET provides an abstract, in-memory representation of data. By design, once the DataSet class is populated, it knows nothing about the backend source from which its data was retrieved; it only knows about the structure of the tables and data it contains and the relationships between them. This allows a great deal of flexibility when manipulating data, passing data between application tiers, or translating data between different DBMS systems.

The .NET Framework Version 1.1 ships with four .NET Data Providers. These data providers are represented by the System.Data.SqlClient namespace, which contains classes for accessing SQL Server data, the System.Data.OleDb namespace, which contains classes for accessing data sources using an OLE DB provider, the System.Data.Odbc namespace, which contains classes for accessing ODBC data sources, and the System.Data.OracleClient namespace, which contains classes for accessing Oracle data. Each provider has a class that derives from the DbDataAdapter base class, which acts as a translator between a data source and the DataSet class, as explained in the next section. For the SqlClient namespace, this class is SqlDataAdapter. For OleDB, it is OleDbDataAdapter, and so on.

 The .NET Framework Data Provider for Oracle requires Version 8.1.7 or later of the Oracle client software (available for download from *http://www.oracle.com/*—you may need to register to access the downloads) to be installed, and also requires MDAC 2.6 or later (available for download from *http://msdn.microsoft.com/downloads/ list/dataaccess.asp*).

Reading Data

There are two basic techniques for reading data in ADO.NET: using data readers and datasets. Additionally, data may be read from either a backend DBMS, such as SQL Server, or from a simple (or complex) XML file. In the next several sections, we'll discuss these techniques and data sources.

Reading from a Database

The following sections describe the use of data readers and datasets, provide an example, and discuss why one would use one technique over the other.

Authentication and Security

When accessing data from a backend database, one of the decisions you'll need to make is how to authenticate the user or application against the database's login credentials. It is fairly common for applications to pass a user ID and password as part of the connection string when opening a connection to the database. However, this is generally not the most secure method, since it requires storing this information in a place where the application can retrieve it when needed.

An even more serious mistake is to have an application log into the database using a privileged account, such as the SQL Server *sa* account. This mode of access allows all queries to run with *sa* privileges. If a malicious user were able to insert a query, they could delete data, modify security settings, or worse, possibly run the xp_cmdshell stored procedure, which would allow them to do just about anything on the database server.

Application code should *never* be run with a system administrator-level account. In fact, if you're going to run application code using a specific user ID and password to log into the database, you should create separate accounts for each application, including distinct accounts for reading and updating. If a particular part of an application requires only read access to the data, then it should use account credentials that are restricted to read-only access. This can help prevent the database or data from being compromised.

When using SQL Server, however, database access should be performed using a trusted connection wherever possible. All examples in this chapter use trusted connections because they do not require storing sensitive information (user IDs and passwords) where someone might be able to get at them.

Because of the security context in which the ASP.NET worker process is run, using trusted connections requires you to take one of two actions:

- Set up the desired database to allow access to the ASPNET account used to run the ASP.NET worker process.
- Turn on Windows Authentication and Impersonation and provide the individual user accounts of those who will access the application with required access to the database. See Chapters 9 and 20 for more information on changing the authentication mode.

Using a data reader

The data reader technique consists of using an instance of either the SqlDataReader, OleDbDataReader, or other data reader class to retrieve the data in a similar fashion to a forward-only, read-only database cursor. Data readers provide lightweight access to data that is recommended when retrieving data for display in a Web Forms page or for other circumstances in which the overhead of a dataset is not desirable.

About the Examples

For the sake of simplicity and consistency, all examples in this chapter that access data from a DBMS use the Pubs sample database in the NetSDK named instance of the Microsoft Data Engine (MSDE). MSDE is a slimmed-down version of SQL Server that fills a role that is similar to Microsoft Access for desktop applications. The NetSDK instance may be installed along with the .NET Framework SDK samples, after installing either the .NET Framework SDK or Visual Studio .NET.

All examples in this chapter use trusted connections rather than pass a user ID and password as part of the connection string. As explained later in the chapter, this requires either adding the ASPNET account under which ASP.NET is run to the desired database or enabling Windows authentication and impersonation in the *web.config* file for the application. The examples in this chapter use the former technique.

Among the sample files included with the book is a batch file named *Add_ ASPNET.bat* that adds the ASPNET account to the NetSDK MSDE instance and assigns it the required permissions in the Pubs sample database. This batch file uses the *Add_ASPNET.sql* file for its commands. Before running *Add_ASPNET.bat*, you will need to open *Add_ASPNET.sql* in a text editor and change all instances of <machine or domain> to the name of the machine or domain containing the ASPNET account. If you modify the *machine.config* file to have the ASP.NET worker process run under a different account than ASPNET, you should modify *Add_ASPNET.sql* to use that account name— including the machine or domain name of the account.

Add_ASPNET.bat itself uses a trusted connection to access MSDE, so you must run this batch file while logged in using an account that has administrative access to the NetSDK instance of MSDE (by default, this will include any members of the Administrators group on the machine on which MSDE is installed). Running *Add_ASPNET.bat* should result in output that looks like that shown in Figure 7-1.

Once you've run *Add_ASPNET.bat*, you're ready to run the samples included with this chapter, which are downloadable from the O'Reilly web site at *http:// examples.oreilly.com/aspnut2/*.

Figure 7-1. Output of Add_ASPNET.bat

The MSDE installation included with Version 1.0 of the .NET Framework SDK is vulnerable to the SQL Slammer worm described in the Microsoft Knowledge Base article Q813440 (*http://support.microsoft.com/?kbid=813440*) and in article Q813850 (*http://support.microsoft.com/?kbid=813850*). If you have installed the NetSDK MSDE instance from the .NET Framework SDK Version 1.0, you should download and install the patch immediately to protect your systems.

Example 7-1 shows the implementation of a SqlDataReader object, which retrieves two columns from the Titles table of the Pubs sample database from the NetSDK instance of MSDE. The output from Example 7-1 should look similar to Figure 7-2.

Example 7-1. ReadTitles.aspx

```
<%@ Page Language="VB" %>
<%@ Import Namespace="System.Data.SqlClient" %>
<html>
   <title>SqlDataReader Example</title>
   <head>
      <script runat="server">
         Sub Page_Load()
            Dim ConnStr As String = "Data Source=(local)\NetSDK;" & _
               "Initial Catalog=Pubs;Trusted_Connection=True;"
            Dim SQL As String = "SELECT title, price FROM titles " & _
               "WHERE PRICE IS NOT NULL"
            Dim PubsConn As New SqlConnection(ConnStr)
            Dim TitlesCmd As New SqlCommand(SQL, PubsConn)
            Dim Titles As SqlDataReader
            PubsConn.Open()
            Titles = TitlesCmd.ExecuteReader()
            Output.Text = "<table>"
            While Titles.Read()
               Output.Text &= "<tr>"
               Output.Text &= "<td>" & Titles.GetString(0) & "</td>"
               Output.Text &= "<td>$" & _
                  Format(Titles.GetDecimal(1), "##0.00") & "</td>"
               Output.Text &= "</tr>"
            End While
            Output.Text &= "</table>"
            Titles.Close()
            PubsConn.Close()
         End Sub
      </script>
   </head>
<body>
   <h1>SqlDataReader Example</h1>
   <asp:label id="Output" runat="server"/>
</body>
</html>
```

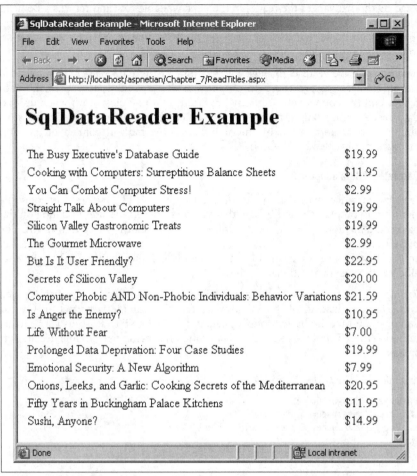

Within the image:

SqlDataReader Example - Microsoft Internet Explorer

File   Edit   View   Favorites   Tools   Help

Back   Search   Favorites   Media

Address http://localhost/aspnetian/Chapter_7/ReadTitles.aspx   Go

SqlDataReader Example

The Busy Executive's Database Guide	$19.99
Cooking with Computers: Surreptitious Balance Sheets	$11.95
You Can Combat Computer Stress!	$2.99
Straight Talk About Computers	$19.99
Silicon Valley Gastronomic Treats	$19.99
The Gourmet Microwave	$2.99
But Is It User Friendly?	$22.95
Secrets of Silicon Valley	$20.00
Computer Phobic AND Non-Phobic Individuals: Behavior Variations	$21.59
Is Anger the Enemy?	$10.95
Life Without Fear	$7.00
Prolonged Data Deprivation: Four Case Studies	$19.99
Emotional Security: A New Algorithm	$7.99
Onions, Leeks, and Garlic: Cooking Secrets of the Mediterranean	$20.95
Fifty Years in Buckingham Palace Kitchens	$11.95
Sushi, Anyone?	$14.99

Done   Local intranet

Figure 7-2. Output of ReadTitles.aspx

Example 7-1 begins by adding an @ `Import` directive to import the System.Data. SqlClient namespace. The example uses an ASP.NET Label control called Output for the display of the retrieved data. To get the data, we create string variables for the connection string and the desired SQL statement and then create a new SqlConnection instance, passing the variable containing the desired connection string to its constructor, which initializes the appropriate properties on the connection. We then create a new SqlCommand instance, passing the SQL string and the new connection object to its constructor. Then we create a SqlData-Reader object variable, open the connection to the database, and set the SqlDataReader object variable to the instance returned by the ExecuteReader method of the `SqlCommand` class.

To display the data, we begin by sending an HTML `<table>` tag to the Text property of the Label control and then loop through the contents of the data reader, adding a row with two cells for each row in the data reader. The SqlDataReaders'

Read method advances the reader to the next available row and returns a Boolean indicating whether there is more data to read. This makes it ideal for looping through data. Note that the example uses the Visual Basic .NET *Format* function to format the price data with trailing zeros.

Finally, once we've read through all the rows in the data reader, we append a closing </table> tag to the Text property of the label and close both the data reader and the connection. It is very important that you close both when using a data reader, since failing to close either object can negatively impact the scalability of your application by interfering with the built-in connection pooling mechanism provided by ADO.NET.

Dataset and data adapter

For circumstances when simply reading through a set of rows once is not sufficient, or if you plan to modify data that you've retrieved for later updating on the backend data store, the data reader will not be sufficient to meet your needs. For these occasions, the DataSet class (part of the System.Data namespace) and the SqlDataAdapter provide more functionality and flexibility than the SqlDataReader, albeit at the cost of additional overhead.

Example 7-2 retrieves the same data as Example 7-1, but uses a SqlDataAdapter and a DataSet instead of the SqlDataReader. This example is written in C#, to demonstrate that the basic syntax of calling the ADO.NET classes is very similar in both VB.NET and C#, with the major difference being the variable declaration syntax.

Example 7-2. ReadTitles_DataSet.aspx

```
<%@ Page Language="C#" %>
<%@ Import Namespace="System.Data" %>
<%@ Import Namespace="System.Data.SqlClient" %>
<html>
   <title>DataSet Example</title>
   <head>
      <script runat="server">
         void Page_Load( )
         {
             String ConnStr = "Data Source=(local)\\NetSDK;"
                + "Initial Catalog=Pubs;Trusted_Connection=True;";
             String SQL = "SELECT title, price FROM titles "
                + "WHERE PRICE IS NOT NULL";
             SqlDataAdapter TitlesAdpt = new SqlDataAdapter(SQL, ConnStr);
             DataSet Titles = new DataSet( );
             // No need to open or close the connection
             //    since the SqlDataAdapter will do this automatically.
             TitlesAdpt.Fill(Titles);
             Output.Text = "<table>";
             foreach (DataRow Title in Titles.Tables[0].Rows)
             {
                 Output.Text += "<tr>";
                 Output.Text += "<td>" + Title[0] + "</td>";
                 Output.Text += "<td>" + String.Format("{0:c}", Title[1])
```

Example 7-2. ReadTitles_DataSet.aspx (continued)

```
                + "</td>";
              Output.Text += "</tr>";
            }
          Output.Text += "</table>";
        }
    </script>
  </head>
<body>
  <h1>DataSet Example</h1>
  <asp:label id="Output" runat="server"/>
</body>
</html>
```

In addition to the @ Import statement for the System.Data.SqlClient namespace, we add another @ Import statement to import the System.Data namespace, which allows us to call the DataSet and DataRow classes without fully qualifying their namespace name.

As in Example 7-1, we begin by creating a connection string and a SQL statement, but unlike Example 7-1, we do not need to create instances of the SqlConnection and SqlCommand objects; by passing the SQL statement and connection string to the constructor of the SqlDataAdapter class, the data adapter instance creates the connection and command objects internally.

Now, instead of creating a SqlDataReader, we create a new SqlDataAdapter, passing in the SQL statement and connection string created earlier, and then create a new dataset. We then call the SqlDataAdapter's Fill method to retrieve the data and store it in the dataset. When the Fill method is called, the SqlDataAdapter creates a connection based on the provided connection string, opens it, executes the query, and then closes the connection. This feature results in simpler and cleaner code and reduces the likelihood of forgetting to close a connection.

If you open a connection associated with a SqlDataAdapter object (or other data adapter object) before calling Fill or Update, the data adapter will not close the connection automatically. If you open the connection explicitly, always be sure to close it, or you may find your scalability suffering.

A good practice is to open the connection in a Try block, and use a Finally block to ensure that the connection is closed, even if an exception is thrown. For more information on Try and Finally, see the discussion of error handling in Chapter 10.

Once the dataset has been filled, we loop through the rows in the first (and only) table of the dataset by using the C# foreach statement, sending output to the Text property of the Label control, as in Example 7-1. Note that the example actually declares the DataRow instance Title within the foreach statement. In Visual Basic .NET, you would declare the instance outside of the loop and then refer to it by name in the For Each statement.

Also note that in C#, when referring by index to items such as the tables in the DataSet object or the items in a DataRow object, you must use square brackets (rather than the parentheses you would use in Visual Basic .NET). This is consistently one of the biggest gotchas in moving from VB.NET to C# and vice-versa. One final difference in the looping code between Examples 7-1 and 7-2 is that since the VB.NET Format function is not available for formatting the price data, we use the static Format method exposed by the String class instead; it formats the data as currency and includes the appropriate regional currency symbol for the current system.

 Another important point to observe about the code in Example 7-2 is that because we're not keeping a database connection open while looping through the data, we can take as much time as we'd like in displaying the data without affecting the ability of others to obtain connections to the database. We can also use the ASP.NET cache engine to cache the entire dataset for later use, if desired, so that we don't have to retrieve the data again. For data that is updated infrequently, this can result in a significant performance improvement, since it is far faster to retrieve a dataset from memory than to requery the data from the database.

The output of Example 7-2 should look much like Figure 7-2 (with the exception of the heading, which will read "DataSet Example").

Reading from XML

One of the neat things about the DataSet class is that it doesn't require a data adapter or a backend DBMS. Instead, you can populate a dataset from an XML file or stream by using the DataSet's ReadXml method. The ReadXml method is overloaded and can read from a Stream, a TextReader, an XmlReader, or from a file by passing the filename as a string. This last technique is illustrated in the custom control examples in Chapter 6, both of which use the ReadXml method to populate a dataset with data from an XML file.

Data Binding

Although Examples 7-1 and 7-2 are written in different languages and use different techniques for retrieving data, they both write out the rendering code for formatting the data manually. In simple examples like these, this does not seem too burdensome. When doing more complex rendering, though, it can become quite involved and produce code that is difficult to maintain.

When working with data in a rich client application, the solution has been to use data-bound controls to display data, allowing the controls to take care of the rendering of each row of data based on control properties set by the developer. Microsoft introduced a similar idea for web development by adding client-side data-binding features to Internet Explorer. However, these features were only useful when you could be certain that all of your clients were using Internet Explorer, and in some cases, their use entailed expensive marshalling of data to the client.

ASP.NET introduces a new server-side data-binding feature that addresses these issues. Data binding to server controls in ASP.NET can significantly reduce the amount of code that needs to be written and maintained for displaying data. In addition, since all data binding occurs on the server side and only HTML is returned to the client, server-side data binding provides great cross-browser compatibility.

You can perform data binding against properties for single-value binding or against data sources that contain multiple rows, such as collections, data tables, and data views, allowing rich formatting of data with a minimum of code. Data binding can be performed explicitly by using the <%# %> syntax, or implicitly by setting the data source of a bindable control to an appropriate object (objects to be bound to must implement the IEnumerable interface). In both cases, the data binding occurs when the Databind method of the page or control is called. Note that when Databind is called at the page level, the Page class will, in turn, call Databind on all of its constituent controls. Therefore, if you have a large number of controls on a page, only a few of which are databound, it may be more efficient to call the Databind method of these controls directly.

Binding to Properties

Example 7-3, one of the simplest possible implementations of data binding, binds to a property exposed at the page level. In this example, we create a public member variable called FontColor, and in the Page_ Load event handler, we set its value to "Red". In the body of the page, we use the <%# %> syntax to tell ASP.NET to evaluate the contents of these brackets when the DataBind method of the page is called. Back in Page_ Load, we call DataBind, which substitutes the value of the FontColor property for the two data binding expressions in the body. The output of Example 7-3 is shown in Figure 7-3. Example 7-4 shows the HTML produced by Example 7-3.

Example 7-3. BindProperty.aspx

```
<%@ Page Language="VB" %>
<html>
<head>
    <title>Simple DataBinding Example</title>
    <script runat="server">
        Dim FontColor As String
        Sub Page_Load( )
            FontColor = "Red"
            DataBind( )
        End Sub
    </script>
</head>
<body>
    <h1>Simple DataBinding Example</h1>
    The value for FontColor is
        <font color="<%# FontColor %>"><%# FontColor %></font>.
</body>
</html>
```

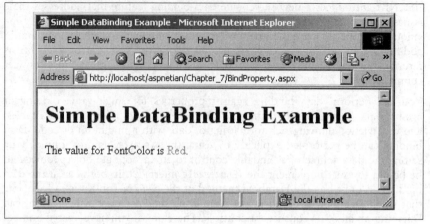

Figure 7-3. Output of BindProperty.aspx

Example 7-4. HTML Output of BindProperty.aspx

```
<html>
<head>
  <title>Simple DataBinding Example</title>
</head>
<body>
  <h1>Simple DataBinding Example</h1>
  The value for FontColor is
    <font color="Red">Red</font>.
</body>
</html>
```

Binding to Collections

While more involved than binding to a property, binding to a collection is still quite simple. Example 7-5 uses an ArrayList to store values that will be bound to an ASP.NET DropDownList control. The DropDownList control and a Label control for output are declared in the body of the page. Setting the autopostback attribute of the DropDownList control to True results in the page being posted back to the server any time the selection in the dropdown is changed. In the Page_ Load event handler, if the page request is not the result of a postback, we declare a new ArrayList and add three items to it. Next, we set the DataSource property of the DropDownList control to be the ArrayList, call the page's DataBind method (which calls DataBind on its children), and then set the initial selection of the DropDownList to the first item.

Whether or not the request is the result of a postback, we then set the output text via the Label's Text property and set the foreground color of the Label control based on the value of the selected item in the dropdown. Note that because the ForeColor property is of type System.Drawing.Color, the example uses the From-Name method exposed by the Color class to translate the string containing the color name to an appropriate instance of the Color class. The output of Example 7-5 is shown in Figure 7-4.

Example 7-5. BindCollection.aspx

```
<%@ Page Language="VB" %>
<html>
<head>
    <title>Collection DataBinding Example</title>
    <script runat="server">
        Dim FontColor As String
        Sub Page_Load( )
            If Not IsPostBack Then
                Dim Colors As New ArrayList( )
                Colors.Add("Red")
                Colors.Add("Green")
                Colors.Add("Blue")
                Color.DataSource = Colors
                DataBind( )
                Color.SelectedIndex = 0
            End If
            Output.Text = "The value for FontColor is " & _
                Color.SelectedItem.Value & "."
            Output.ForeColor = _
                System.Drawing.Color.FromName(Color.SelectedItem.Value)
        End Sub
    </script>
</head>
<body>
    <h1>Collection DataBinding Example</h1>
    <form runat="server">
        Choose a color from the list for the font color:
        <asp:dropdownlist id="Color" autopostback="True" runat="server"/>
        <br/>
        <asp:label id="Output" runat="server"/>
    </form>
</body>
</html>
```

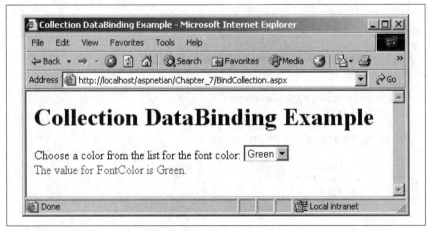

Figure 7-4. Output of BindCollection.aspx

Binding to DataViews

Binding to richer data sources, such as DataTables and DataViews, is even more powerful than binding to collections, though still relatively simple. The DataView class provides a representation of the data in a DataTable that can be sorted and filtered, and also implements the necessary interfaces that allow it to be databound. These data sources can be used by:

- Retrieving data in a dataset and binding to the constituent DataTables
- Building DataViews, based on the data in the data table, or retrieving the table's DefaultView property, which returns an unsorted, unfiltered DataView
- Creating DataTables and/or DataViews programmatically

Binding a DataTable or DataView to controls such as DataGrid, DataList, and Repeater provides an extremely powerful technique for displaying and editing data with a minimum of code. It also provides substantial flexibility in how the data is formatted and displayed.

The examples in the sections "Inserting and Updating Data" and "Deleting Data" demonstrate how to bind the default DataView of a table to a DataGrid for display.

Inserting and Updating Data

Reading and binding data is all very well, but for most applications, it's only part of what the application needs to do. Another important feature is the ability to insert new rows and/or update existing rows of data. As with reading data, the DataSet and SqlDataAdapter (or OleDbDataAdapter) classes come in handy. Another class that is extremely useful is the SqlCommandBuilder (or OleDbCommandBuilder) class, which is discussed later in this section.

Example 7-6, while more complicated than previous examples, adds a relatively small amount of code to support adding and updating rows to the Pubs Titles table.

Example 7-6. InsertUpdateTitles.aspx

```
<%@ Page Language="VB" %>
<%@ Import Namespace="System.Data" %>
<%@ Import Namespace="System.Data.SqlClient" %>
<html>
<head>
    <title>Insert/Update Example</title>
    <script runat="server">
        Dim Titles As New DataSet( )
        Dim TitlesAdpt As New SqlDataAdapter( )

        Sub Page_Load(Sender As Object, e As EventArgs)
            If Not IsPostBack Then
                GetTitleData("")
                BindGrid( )
            End If
        End Sub
```

Example 7-6. InsertUpdateTitles.aspx (continued)

```
    Sub Add_Click(Sender As Object, e As EventArgs)
        Page.RegisterHiddenField("EditMode", "Add")
        title_id.ReadOnly = False
        Display.Visible = False
        InsertUpdate.Visible = True
    End Sub

    Sub Cancel_Click(Sender As Object, e As EventArgs)
        Response.Redirect("InsertUpdateTitles.aspx")
    End Sub

    Sub Edit_Click(sender As Object, e As DataGridCommandEventArgs)
        GetTitleData("WHERE title_id = '" & e.Item.Cells(1).Text & "'")
        title_id.Text = Titles.Tables(0).Rows(0)(0)
        title.Text = Titles.Tables(0).Rows(0)(1)
        type.Text = Titles.Tables(0).Rows(0)(2)
        pub_id.Text = Titles.Tables(0).Rows(0)(3)
        price.Text = String.Format("{0:c}", Titles.Tables(0).Rows(0)(4))
        advance.Text = Titles.Tables(0).Rows(0)(5)
        royalty.Text = Titles.Tables(0).Rows(0)(6)
        ytd_sales.Text = Titles.Tables(0).Rows(0)(7)
        notes.Text = Titles.Tables(0).Rows(0)(8)
        pubdate.Text = Titles.Tables(0).Rows(0)(9)
        Page.RegisterHiddenField("EditMode", "Update")
        Display.Visible = False
        InsertUpdate.Visible = True
    End Sub

    Sub BindGrid()
        TitleGrid.DataSource = Titles.Tables(0).DefaultView
        TitleGrid.DataBind()
    End Sub

    Sub GetTitleData(WhereClause As String)
        Dim ConnStr As String = "Data Source=(local)\NetSDK;" & _
            "Initial Catalog=Pubs;Trusted_Connection=True;"
        Dim SQL As String = "SELECT * FROM titles " & WhereClause
        Dim PubsConn As New SqlConnection(ConnStr)
        Dim TitlesCmd As New SqlCommand(SQL, PubsConn)
        TitlesAdpt.SelectCommand = TitlesCmd
        Dim TitlesCB As New SqlCommandBuilder(TitlesAdpt)
        ' No need to open or close connection,
        '   since the SqlDataAdapter will do this automatically.
        TitlesAdpt.Fill(Titles)
    End Sub

    Sub Submit_Click(Sender As Object, e As EventArgs)
        Select Case Request.Form("EditMode")
            Case "Add"
                GetTitleData("")
                Dim NewRow As DataRow = Titles.Tables(0).NewRow
                NewRow(0) = title_id.Text
                NewRow(1) = title.Text
```

Inserting and Updating Data | **169**

Example 7-6. InsertUpdateTitles.aspx (continued)

```
                NewRow(2) = type.Text
                NewRow(3) = pub_id.Text
                NewRow(4) = Convert.ToDecimal(price.Text.Replace("$", ""))
                NewRow(5) = advance.Text
                NewRow(6) = royalty.Text
                NewRow(7) = ytd_sales.Text
                NewRow(8) = notes.Text
                NewRow(9) = pubdate.Text
                Titles.Tables(0).Rows.Add(NewRow)
                TitlesAdpt.Update(Titles)
            Case "Update"
                GetTitleData("WHERE title_id = '" & title_id.Text & "'")
                Titles.Tables(0).Rows(0)(0) = title_id.Text
                Titles.Tables(0).Rows(0)(1) = title.Text
                Titles.Tables(0).Rows(0)(2) = type.Text
                Titles.Tables(0).Rows(0)(3) = pub_id.Text
                Titles.Tables(0).Rows(0)(4) = _
                    Convert.ToDecimal(price.Text.Replace("$", ""))
                Titles.Tables(0).Rows(0)(5) = advance.Text
                Titles.Tables(0).Rows(0)(6) = royalty.Text
                Titles.Tables(0).Rows(0)(7) = ytd_sales.Text
                Titles.Tables(0).Rows(0)(8) = notes.Text
                Titles.Tables(0).Rows(0)(9) = pubdate.Text
                TitlesAdpt.Update(Titles)
        End Select
        Response.Redirect("InsertUpdateTitles.aspx")
      End Sub
   </script>
</head>
<body>
   <h1>Insert/Update Example</h1>
   <form runat="server">
      <asp:panel id="Display" runat="server">
         <asp:datagrid id="TitleGrid"
            oneditcommand="Edit_Click"
            runat="server">
            <columns>
               <asp:editcommandcolumn
                  buttontype="PushButton" edittext="Edit"/>
            </columns>
         </asp:datagrid>
         <asp:button id="Add"
            text="Add New Title" onclick="Add_Click" runat="server"/>
      </asp:panel>
      <asp:panel id="InsertUpdate" visible="False" runat="server">
         <table border="0">
            <tr>
               <td>Title ID</td>
               <td>
                  <asp:textbox id="title_id"
                     readonly="True" runat="server"/>
               </td>
            </tr>
```

Example 7-6. InsertUpdateTitles.aspx (continued)

```
<tr>
   <td>Title</td>
   <td>
      <asp:textbox id="title" runat="server"/>
   </td>
</tr>
<tr>
   <td>Type</td>
   <td>
      <asp:textbox id="type" runat="server"/>
   </td>
</tr>
<tr>
   <td>Publisher ID</td>
   <td>
      <asp:textbox id="pub_id" runat="server"/>
   </td>
</tr>
<tr>
   <td>Price</td>
   <td>
      <asp:textbox id="price" runat="server"/>
   </td>
</tr>
<tr>
   <td>Advance</td>
   <td>
      <asp:textbox id="advance" runat="server"/>
   </td>
</tr>
<tr>
   <td>Royalty</td>
   <td>
      <asp:textbox id="royalty" runat="server"/>
   </td>
</tr>
<tr>
   <td>Year-to-date Sales</td>
   <td>
      <asp:textbox id="ytd_sales" runat="server"/>
   </td>
</tr>
<tr>
   <td>Notes</td>
   <td>
      <asp:textbox id="notes"
         textmode="MultiLine"
         rows="5"
         columns="20"
         runat="server"/>
   </td>
</tr>
<tr>
```

Example 7-6. InsertUpdateTitles.aspx (continued)

```
            <td>Publishing Date</td>
            <td>
                <asp:textbox id="pubdate" runat="server"/>
            </td>
        </tr>
        <tr>
            <td>
                <asp:button id="Submit"
                  text="Submit" onclick="Submit_Click" runat="server"/ >
            </td>
            <td>
                <asp:button id="Cancel"
                  text="Cancel" onclick="Cancel_Click" runat="server"/ >
            </td>
        </tr>
      </table>
    </asp:panel>
  </form>
</body>
</html>
```

The discussion of the code begins with the <body> section of the page. This section contains a server-side <form> element, which provides support for page postbacks and adds automatic support for such things as control state management. Contained within the form are two Panel controls, which render as <div> elements on the client. Panel controls are very useful when you want to provide more than one set of user interface elements on a page, but only want to display one at a given time.

Inside the first Panel control, which will display items from the Titles table, we declare a DataGrid control, to which we add a ButtonColumn control to provide access to the edit mode of the page and a Button control that will allow us to add a new item. To enable handling of the Edit button in the DataGrid, we set the DataGrid's onEditCommand attribute to the name of the event handler for the Edit button.

The second Panel control contains the form fields that will be used to edit or add a new item, as well as Submit and Cancel buttons. It makes sense for the default mode for the page to be displayed, so we set the Visible property of the second panel control to False. Note that we also set the ReadOnly property of the title_id textbox to True to prevent this field from being edited for existing data, since the Title ID field is what uniquely identifies a title in the table.

Turning to the code, note that the example declares both the DataSet and SqlDataAdapter classes at the page level so that they will be available to all procedures.

In the Page_Load event handler, we check to see if the current request is the result of a postback. If not, we call the GetTitleData method (passing an empty string). The GetTitleData method, which allows us to pass a Where clause argument to be appended to the SQL string, uses the techniques demonstrated previously to retrieve the desired set of rows from the Titles table in the Pubs database.

The main difference between Example 7-5 and the previous examples is that the code in Example 7-5 declares a new SqlCommandBuilder instance, passing it a SqlDataAdapter instance whose SelectCommand property is already set. Here's where ADO.NET magic really happens. The SqlCommandBuilder will automatically generate appropriate Insert, Update, and Delete commands for the Select statement set on the data adapter and populate the InsertCommand, UpdateCommand, and DeleteCommand properties of the SqlDataAdapter with these values. This step saves us the trouble of having to create these statements manually.

If you want to construct Insert, Update, and Delete statements yourself or use stored procedures for these commands, you are free to do so. You can do so by creating separate SqlCommand objects with the desired properties and then setting the InsertCommand, UpdateCommand, or DeleteCommand property of the SqlDataAdapter to the newly created SqlCommand instance.

Once we've filled the dataset with data from the Titles table, we call BindGrid from Page_Load. Calling BindGrid sets the DataSource property of the DataGrid control to the DefaultView property of the first table in the dataset, which returns a DataView containing all the data in the table. At this point, the output of the page should look like Figure 7-5.

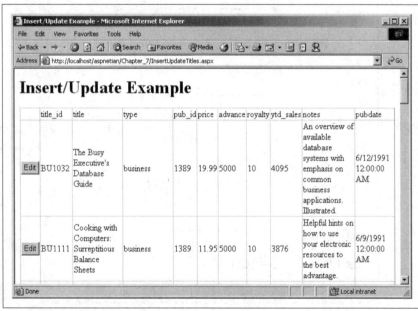

Figure 7-5. Display mode output of InsertUpdateTitles.aspx

The user viewing the page has two options: click the Edit button for one of the rows or scroll down to the bottom of the page and click the Add New Title button (not shown in Figure 7-5).

Clicking the Edit button invokes the Edit_Click event handler, which calls GetTitleData, passing a WHERE clause that causes it to retrieve only the selected row. Next, it sets the form fields in the second panel control to the values returned from GetTitleData, and then registers a hidden form field that indicates that we're updating a row (as opposed to adding a new row). This will become important later, when we submit our changes. Finally, we set the Visible property of the first panel to False and the second to True, which displays the form fields for editing.

If the Add New Title button is clicked, we register a hidden form field (indicating that the Add mode is enabled), set the ReadOnly property of the title_id textbox to False (since we'll need a title ID for the new row), and then reverse the visibility properties of the panel controls again to display the blank form fields. At this point, the output of the page should look like Figure 7-6.

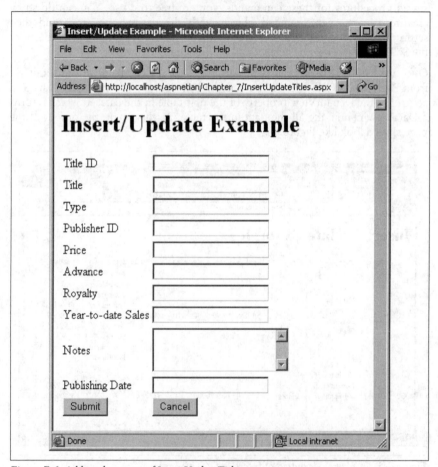

Figure 7-6. Add mode output of InsertUpdateTitles.aspx

In Edit or Add mode, if the user clicks the Cancel button, we simply call Response.Redirect and redirect back to the original page, essentially starting the whole process over again.

If the user clicks Submit, we use a Select Case statement to evaluate whether we're adding a new row or updating an existing one. If we're adding a new row, we call GetTitleData, call the NewRow method of the first table object to create a new DataRow instance, and then set the item values of the new row to the values in the form fields. Once all values have been set, we add the row to the DataTable and (outside of the Select Case statement) call the SqlDataAdapter's Update method, which updates the backend database with the new row.

If we're updating an existing row, we call GetTitleData with a WHERE clause for that specific row, set its items to the values in the form fields, and call Update again to save the changes to the backend database. Once we've called Update, we call Response.Redirect to redirect the user back to the original page, which again clears the decks and starts from scratch (with the new data, of course).

Example 7-5 demonstrates "last-in-wins" data concurrency. Be aware that using this type of concurrency control can result in over-writing changes made by another user between the time data was queried and when it was updated. In a multi-user environment, you should always carefully consider the potential costs and effects of multiple users attempting to update the same data simultaneously and design your applications accordingly. Strategies can include locking data from the time it is read until the update is complete, or using a timestamp before updating to ensure that the data was not modified from its last known state.

Deleting Data

Example 7-7 shows how you can use the DataSet and SqlDataAdapter classes to delete data from the Titles table. This example shows the implementation of an ASP.NET page that displays data from the Titles table and allows users to delete a row from the table by clicking a button.

Unless you don't care about the state of the Pubs sample database, it would probably be a good idea to back up the database before deleting any of the rows in the Titles table (just in case you want to restore the database to its original state later).

As with the previous example, we use a DataGrid control to display the items in the dataset. However, in this case, we set the AutoGenerateColumns property of the DataGrid to False and supply BoundColumn controls for each displayed column. This provides greater flexibility in displaying the data, including the ability to determine which columns are displayed, the header to use for each column, and in the case of the price data, the ability to specify a format string for the data. This example also adds an <alternatingitemstyle> tag to specify that every other row should have a background color of silver. To enable handling of the Delete button, we set the DataGrid's onDeleteCommand method to the name of the event handler for the Delete button.

As with the previous example, Example 7-7 declares both the DataSet and SqlDataAdapter instances at the page level to make them available to all procedures; in the Page_Load event handler, we call GetTitleData and BindGrid, which perform the same operations as in the previous example (although this version of GetTitleData does not allow a WHERE clause).

Once the data is displayed, the user can click the Delete button for a row, which invokes the Delete_Click event handler. In Delete_Click, we call GetTitleData to fill the dataset, and then call the Delete method of the selected row (using the Item.ItemIndex property of the DataGridCommandEventArgs parameter passed to the event handler to determine the correct row to delete). Once the row is deleted from the dataset, we call the Update method of the SqlDataAdapter, passing it the modified dataset, and then call Response.Redirect to redirect the user to the original page.

Example 7-7. DeleteTitles.aspx

```
<%@ Page Language="VB" %>
<%@ Import Namespace="System.Data" %>
<%@ Import Namespace="System.Data.SqlClient" %>
<html>
<head>
   <title>Delete Example</title>
   <script runat="server">
      Dim Titles As New DataSet( )
      Dim TitlesAdpt As New SqlDataAdapter( )

      Sub Page_Load(Sender As Object, e As EventArgs)
         If Not IsPostBack Then
            GetTitleData( )
            BindGrid( )
         End If
      End Sub

      Sub BindGrid( )
         TitleGrid.DataSource = Titles.Tables(0).DefaultView
         TitleGrid.DataBind( )
      End Sub

      Sub GetTitleData( )
         Dim ConnStr As String = "Data Source=(local)\NetSDK;" & _
            "Initial Catalog=Pubs;Trusted_Connection=True;"
         Dim SQL As String = "SELECT * FROM titles"
         Dim PubsConn As New SqlConnection(ConnStr)
         Dim TitlesCmd As New SqlCommand(SQL, PubsConn)
         TitlesAdpt.SelectCommand = TitlesCmd
         Dim TitlesCB As New SqlCommandBuilder(TitlesAdpt)
         ' No need to open or close connection,
         '    since the SqlDataAdapter will do this automatically.
         TitlesAdpt.Fill(Titles)
      End Sub

      Sub Delete_Click(Sender As Object, e As DataGridCommandEventArgs)
         GetTitleData( )
         Titles.Tables(0).Rows(e.Item.ItemIndex).Delete
         TitlesAdpt.Update(Titles)
         Response.Redirect("DeleteTitles.aspx")
      End Sub
   </script>
</head>
<body>
```

Example 7-7. DeleteTitles.aspx (continued)

```
<h1>Delete Example</h1>
<form runat="server">
    <asp:datagrid id="TitleGrid"
        ondeletecommand="Delete_Click"
        cellpadding="3"
        autogeneratecolumns="false"
        runat="server">
        <alternatingitemstyle backcolor="silver"/>
        <columns>
            <asp:buttoncolumn buttontype="PushButton"
                text="Delete" commandname="Delete" />
            <asp:boundcolumn headertext="Title ID"
                datafield="title_id"/>
            <asp:boundcolumn headertext="Title"
                datafield="title"/>
            <asp:boundcolumn headertext="Type"
                datafield="type"/>
            <asp:boundcolumn headertext="Publisher ID"
                datafield="pub_id"/>
            <asp:boundcolumn headertext="Price"
                datafield="price" dataformatstring="{0:c}"/>
        </columns>
    </asp:datagrid>
</form>
</body>
</html>
```

The output of Example 7-7 is shown in Figure 7-7.

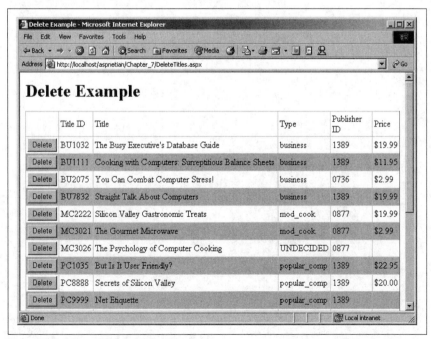

Figure 7-7. Output of DeleteTitles.aspx

Additional Resources

The following sites provide additional information on the topics discussed in this chapter:

http://www.asp.net/forums
> The ASP.NET Forums contain forums for a wide range of data access topics, from SQL Server, Oracle, Access, and other databases, to Active Directory/ LDAP and general data access forums.

http://www.aspnextgen.com/
> The DotNetJunkies site, run by Microsoft MVP Award winners Donny Mack and Doug Seven, contains many ASP.NET tutorials, including tutorials on data access and data binding.

8

ASP.NET Configuration

When working with ASP.NET, you'll be called on to configure your ASP.NET applications. One major advantage that ASP.NET has over classic ASP is that most of the important configuration options for ASP.NET applications are stored in configuration files that reside in the web application directory. This makes it considerably easier to deploy an application from one server to another or to replicate an application across a web farm, since the application's configuration information will be copied along with the Web Form Pages, code-behind classes, and assemblies that make up the application.

Understanding Configuration Files

In ASP.NET, configuration information is stored in one of two files: *machine.config* or *web.config*. While an application can have as many *web.config* files as it has directories and subdirectories (subject to scope limitations of some elements), there is only one *machine.config* file per machine; it contains the default configuration information for every web application, as well as other application types, on the machine. This information includes Windows Forms applications, security settings, remoting settings, and other network settings. You should use extreme caution when editing *machine.config* to avoid accidentally making changes that break other applications. It's probably a good idea to back up the *machine.config* file before editing it, in case you need to restore the original settings.

web.config is an optional configuration file that is stored with each web application. If an application contains a *web.config* file, the file takes precedence over *machine.config* (i.e., the settings in *web.config* override those in *machine.config*). If a web application does not contain a *web.config* file, it inherits its settings from *machine.config*. An application may have multiple *web.config* files, but each must reside in its own directory or subdirectory.

The *web.config* files in an application are hierarchical. Just as the settings in a *web.config* file in the application root will override the settings in *machine.config*, the settings in a *web.config* file in a subdirectory will override those in a *web. config* file in the parent directory.

 ASP.NET provides a facility for locking down configuration settings so they cannot be overridden by child configuration files. If a configuration setting has been locked down in *machine.config*, an exception will be thrown if you attempt to override that setting in *web.config*. In addition, certain settings are limited to machine or application scope. Attempting to override these settings at application or subdirectory scope will also result in an exception being thrown.

The syntax of the *machine.config* and *web.config* files is based on XML. Each configuration section consists of a parent element that may in turn contain attributes or child elements. In the following snippet, the <configuration> and <system.web> elements are standard elements that are required in each *web.config* file. The <authentication> and <authorization> elements are parent configuration elements, while the <deny> element is a child element of the <authorization> element:

```
<configuration>
   <system.web>
      <authentication mode="Windows"/>
      <authorization>
         <deny users="?"/>
      </authorization>
   </system.web>
<configuration>
```

The configuration of an ASP.NET application depends on which elements you include in your *web.config* file and on the values of their attributes (and any attributes of their child elements), as well as the defaults established in the *machine.config* file for that machine. Chapter 20 documents the configuration elements in detail. Most of this chapter looks at practical examples of how to set common configuration settings.

Modifying Configuration Settings

The most important part of configuration for the web developer is, of course, understanding how to modify the configuration files to achieve the desired ends. Unfortunately, in the 1.0 and 1.1 releases of the Framework, there aren't any rich GUI tools for editing configuration files (which sounds like a great third-party opportunity). As a result, editing configuration files is not terribly straightforward. The next several examples illustrate the basic techniques for editing *web.config* files.

Remember that ASP.NET configuration files follow XML syntax rules, including case-sensitivity of element and attribute names. Element and attribute names in ASP.NET configuration files typically use camel casing, in which the first letter of the initial word is lowercase and the first letter of each subsequent word is uppercase.

Related IIS Settings

It is very important to understand that ASP.NET configuration is distinct from IIS configuration. In most cases, configuring an ASP.NET application requires no changes to the configuration of IIS. One exception is that the settings for IIS may still need to be configured to make certain authentication modes, such as Windows authentication, work (although in many cases, the defaults will work fine).

The reason why most configuration settings do not require changes to IIS configuration is that when a request is made for a resource that is handled by ASP.NET, IIS is only involved long enough to hand that request over to the ASP.NET worker process, which is completely separate from IIS. In fact, you can host ASP.NET applications without even using IIS with the classes in the System.Web.Hosting namespace. The operation of the ASP.NET worker process is configured by *machine.config* and *web.config*, while IIS configuration settings remain in the IIS metabase.

Also note that some (but not all) attribute *values* are case-sensitive. While this case-sensitivity is specific to the ASP.NET implementation rather than to XML, it's still a good idea to follow the case used in the examples when modifying configuration files.

Modifying Trace Settings

Tracing is a nifty feature of ASP.NET that allows recording and viewing of a host of valuable information about page requests. Like the other configuration elements considered in this chapter, the <trace> element appears in *machine.config* to set machine-wide default values:

```
<!--
    trace Attributes:
        enabled="[true|false]" - Enable application tracing
        localOnly="[true|false]" - View trace results from localhost only
        pageOutput="[true|false]" - Display trace ouput on individual pages
        requestLimit="[number]" - Number of trace results available in
            trace.axd
        traceMode="[SortByTime|SortByCategory]" - Sorts trace result
            displays based on Time or Category
-->
<trace enabled="false"
    localOnly="true"
    pageOutput="false"
    requestLimit="10"
    traceMode="SortByTime"/>
```

The settings in *machine.config* turn tracing off by default, which is a good thing. Since tracing carries performance overhead, you should enable it only when you are actually using it—usually during development or troubleshooting of an ASP.NET application. You should rarely enable tracing on a deployed production application, both for performance reasons and also to avoid the possibility of trace information being viewed by site visitors. See Chapter 10 for a more detailed discussion of application tracing. Example 8-1 shows the <trace> element modified to enable tracing for an application, with trace output being displayed on each page.

Example 8-1. Enabling tracing

```
<configuration>
   <system.web>
      <trace enabled="true"
         pageOutput="true"/>
   </system.web>
</configuration>
```

You can enable tracing by setting the enabled attribute to True and direct the trace output to the page by setting the pageOutput attribute to True. The attributes shown in Example 8-1 override the settings in *machine.config* (and any parent *web.config* file that contains a <trace> element), while the remaining attributes should retain their default values as set in *machine.config*.

Changing the Authentication Mode

Modifying the <authentication> element of *web.config* should give you a deeper look at how configuration files work. The <authentication> element is included in the *machine.config* file with the following default settings:

```
<!--
    authentication Attributes:
        mode="[Windows|Forms|Passport|None]"
-->
<authentication mode="Windows">

    <!--
        forms Attributes:
            name="[cookie name]" - Name of the cookie used for Forms
                Authentication
            loginUrl="[url]" - Url to redirect client to for Authentication
            protection="[All|None|Encryption|Validation]" - Protection mode
                for data in cookie
            timeout="[seconds]" - Duration of time for cookie to be valid
                (reset on each request)
            path="/" - Sets the path for the cookie
    -->
    <forms name=".ASPXAUTH" loginUrl="login.aspx" protection="All"
        timeout="30" path="/">

        <!--
            credentials Attributes:
                passwordFormat="[Clear|SHA1|MD5]" - format of user password
                    value stored in <user>
        -->
        <credentials passwordFormat="SHA1">
            <!-- <user name="UserName" password="password"/> -->
        </credentials>
```

```
        </forms>

        <!--
            passport Attributes:
                redirectUrl=["url"] - Specifies the page to redirect to, if the
                    page requires authentication, and the user has not signed on
                    with passport
        -->
        <passport redirectUrl="internal"/>

    </authentication>
```

These configuration settings give the machine-wide defaults for authentication in ASP.NET applications. Windows authentication is enabled by default. Note that for Windows authentication to function properly, some form of IIS authentication other than Anonymous must be enabled. The *machine.config* settings also specify defaults for the attributes of the <forms> element, which is used in Forms authentication, and for the <passport> element.

Notice that the formatting of the configuration settings denotes the parent/child relationships of the elements. Both the <forms> and <passport> elements are children of the <authentication> element, while the <credentials> element is the child of the <forms> element. The <user> element (commented out in the preceding code) is in turn the child of the <credentials> element.

You would see the <forms> element specified only in *machine.config* when the mode attribute of the <authentication> element is set to Windows, a setting that does not require any child elements. The reason for this is that these settings are used as defaults for various authentication methods. Supplying values for the attributes of the <forms> element at the machine level provides defaults that are inherited by any application using Forms authentication automatically, while any attribute values for the <forms> element contained in *web.config* files for specific applications override these settings.

Example 8-2 shows an <authentication> element for an application that uses Windows authentication. The <authorization> element is also shown. In this case, this element denies access to anonymous users, which forces authentication, if it has not already occurred.

Example 8-2. Windows authentication settings

```
<configuration>
    <system.web>
        <authentication mode="Windows"/>
        <authorization>
            <deny users="?"/>
        </authorization>
    </system.web>
<configuration>
```

Consider an application in which you want to use Forms authentication (discussed further in Chapter 9) to enable authentication against your own custom credential store. In this case, you would use an authentication element, such as that shown in Example 8-3, along with its child <forms> element, and the

<authorization> element shown in Example 8-2. Note that the <forms> element is required only if you want to override the settings specified in *machine.config*. Example 8-3 specifies a different login page (*myLogin.aspx*) to which unauthenticated users are redirected.

Example 8-3. Forms authentication settings

```
<configuration>
  <system.web>
    <authentication mode="Forms">
      <forms loginUrl="myLogin.aspx"/>
    </authentication>
    <authorization>
      <deny users="?"/>
    </authorization>
  </system.web>
<configuration>
```

Configuring Out-of-Process Session State

The <sessionState> configuration element in *machine.config* sets the following machine-wide defaults:

```
<!-- sessionState Attributes:
    mode="[Off|InProc|StateServer|SQLServer]"
    stateConnectionString="tcpip=server:port"
    stateNetworkTimeout="timeout for network operations with State Server,
        in seconds"
    sqlConnectionString="valid System.Data.SqlClient.SqlConnection string,
        minus Initial Catalog"
    cookieless="[true|false]"
    timeout="timeout in minutes"
-->
<sessionState mode="InProc"
    stateConnectionString="tcpip=127.0.0.1:42424"
    stateNetworkTimeout="10"
    sqlConnectionString="data source=127.0.0.1;user id=sa;password="
    cookieless="false"
    timeout="20"/>
```

Unlike the <authentication> element, the <sessionState> element has no children, only attributes. Like the <authentication> element, the usage of the <sessionState> element in *machine.config* contains a combination of attributes not normally seen in practice, since the purpose of the attributes is to set machine-wide defaults. For example, the default mode of in-process session state (InProc) requires no additional attributes to function. In fact, if you want to use InProc, you do not need to add a <sessionState> element to your *web.config* file at all. Examples 8-4 and 8-5 show the appropriate settings for the <sessionState> element for out-of-process session state using the ASP.NET state service and SQL Server session state, respectively.

Example 8-4. Out-of-process state with state service

```
<configuration>
  <system.web>
    <sessionState mode="StateServer"
        stateConnectionString="tcpip=StateServerName:42424"
        stateNetworkTimeout="30" />
  </system.web>
<configuration>
```

Example 8-4 sets the mode attribute to StateServer, which uses the ASP.NET state NT service installed with ASP.NET to store session state settings for multiple machines. This setting requires the stateConnectionString attribute; since the default setting of 127.0.0.1 (the local machine loopback address) is not terribly useful for sharing state information across multiple machines, you need to replace it with the name of the machine that is responsible for maintaining this information (*StateServerName* in the example).

In out-of-process session state scenarios, a single machine is designated to maintain session values for multiple ASP.NET servers. Therefore, each server using the shared session information should be configured to point to the same state server. To compensate for potential network latency issues, the example changes the default stateNetworkTimeout value of 10 seconds to 30 seconds. Note that inherent in this decision is a tradeoff between avoiding timeouts and potentially poorer application performance.

> Inherent in either type of out-of-process session state is a substantial performance hit due to the need to cross process and/or machine boundaries to retrieve session state information. You should use out-of-process session state only when your need for scalability outweighs your need for absolute performance. You should also test the performance of your chosen session state mode with a tool such as the Microsoft Web Stress tool to ensure that it meets your performance and scalability needs.

Example 8-5. Out-of-process state with SQL Server

```
<configuration>
  <system.web>
    <sessionState mode="SQLServer"
        sqlConnectionString="data source=ServerName;user id=name;password=pwd"
        cookieless="true"/>
  </system.web>
</configuration>
```

Example 8-5 sets the mode attribute to SQLServer, which uses an SQL Server database called ASPState to store session state values to be shared across multiple machines. This database is set up using the *InstallSqlState. sql* batch file installed by default in the directory *%windir%\Microsoft.NET\Framework\%version%*, where *%windir%* is the Windows directory and *%version%* is the version number of the installed framework (the version number is prefixed with a "v" in the actual path).

The SQLServer mode requires the use of the sqlConnectionString attribute. You should always override this attribute, since its default uses the local 127.0.0.1 loopback address and uses the SQL Server *sa* account to connect to the ASPState database. Neither is a good practice in a production application. In Example 8-5 set the data source portion of the connection string to the name of the designated SQL Server state machine and set the user ID and password to an account set up to read and write state data.

Example 8-5 also sets the cookieless attribute to True, anticipating that some users may have disabled cookies. Setting this attribute to True places the session identifier within the URL of all requests, allowing session use without cookies. Note that applications designed for cookieless sessions should use relative rather than absolute URLs for internal links.

A word on security: as noted previously, the default settings for sqlConnectionString use the SQL Server *sa*, or system administrator, account to connect to the ASPState database. This is not a good security practice. Instead, you should always set up a separate account that is purpose-specific (in this case, to read and write session state data) and use that account for connecting to the state database. You may even want to consider setting up a separate account for each ASP.NET application for this purpose; this allows you to track and audit access to the ASPState database on a per application basis more easily. These steps can help minimize the possibility of database security being compromised through over-permissive security settings.

Locking Down Configuration Settings

All of the previous examples rely on the ability to override settings in *machine. config* with settings in the *web.config* file for an individual application. As mentioned earlier, you can also use a *web.config* file located in a child folder of an application to override settings in a parent *web.config* file. However, what if the application developer or the server administrator doesn't want certain settings to be overridden? No problem. The configuration system provides a special element, <location>, that serves this purpose handily.

The basic structure of the <location> element consists of the opening element tag with two attributes, path and allowOverride, followed by the elements to be locked down, and the closing element tag. For example:

```
<location path="pathtocontrol" allowOverride="True|False">
    <!-- Settings to lock down -->
</location>
```

The path attribute, which is optional when locking down configuration settings, is used to specify the application or filename to be controlled by the <location> element. If omitted, the <location> element's settings apply to all children of the configuration file in which it appears. Example 8-6 shows a <location> element which, when added to *machine.config*, requires all ASP.NET applications on the machine to use Windows authentication.

Example 8-6. Locking down configuration settings

```
<configuration>
  <system.web>
    <location allowOverride="False">
      <authentication mode="Windows"/>
    </location>
  </system.web>
<configuration>
```

Note that the <location> element can also be used to configure settings for a child application, directory, or file from a parent configuration file. When used in this manner, the path attribute is required and the allowOverride attribute is optional.

Targeting a Specific Runtime Version

A new feature in Version 1.1 of the .NET Framework is the ability to target a specific version of the .NET runtime with your Web application. This means that if you have a Web application built with the 1.0 version of the framework that will not run on the Version 1.1 framework (for example, if it uses an API that has changed), you can configure your application such that it continues to run under Version 1.0 of the framework (note that the version of the framework you wish to run under must be installed on the target machine).

To configure your application to run under ASP.NET 1.0, open the Internet Information Services administrative applet and navigate to the application or web site you want to configure, as shown in Figure 8-1 (Windows Server 2003 version is shown). Right-click the desired application folder, and select Properties. In the Properties dialog, click the Home Directory tab (shown in Figure 8-2), and then click the Configuration button.

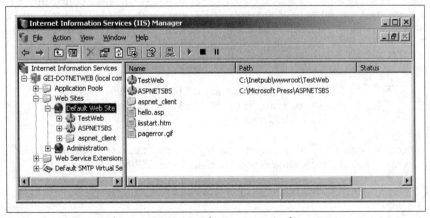

Figure 8-1. Internet Information Services Administration Applet

ASP.NET Configuration

Figure 8-2. Home Directory tab

In the Application Configuration dialog, shown in Figure 8-3, in turn select each of the extensions handled by ASP.NET (you can tell which ones because they will be mapped to *%windir%\Microsoft.NET\Framework\v1.1.4322\aspnet_isapi.dll*, where *%windir%* represents the path to your Windows directory), and click the Edit button. Browse to the *aspnet_isapi.dll* file located in the *%windir%\Microsoft.NET\Framework\v1.1.3705* folder.

 The *v1.1.3705* folder contains the files for Version 1.0 of the .NET Framework, while the *v1.1.4322* folder contains the files for Version 1.1 of the .NET Framework.

Once you've mapped all the extensions to the correct version of *aspnet_isapi.dll*, you're done. Your application is now running under ASP.NET Version 1.0.

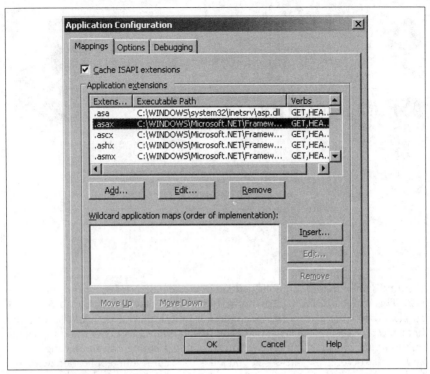

Figure 8-3. Application Configuration dialog

Additional Resources

The following sites provide additional information on the topics discussed in this chapter:

http://www.asp.net/forums/
> The ASP.NET Forums has a forum dedicated to configuration and deployment issues, where you can find answers to all your configuration questions.

http://msdn.microsoft.com/library/en-us/cpgenref/html/
gngrfaspnetconfigurationsectionschema.asp
> The MSDN online reference for the ASP.NET configuration file schema.

9

ASP.NET Security

Security is an extremely complicated subject, and ASP.NET security is no exception. This chapter discusses the approaches you can take to secure your ASP.NET applications. Absent from the discussion are the topics of network, server, and infrastructure security. This should not be interpreted to mean these topics are unimportant. On the contrary, without properly securing any supporting servers and infrastructure, the measures you take to secure your application with the tools made available by the .NET Framework will be for naught. A discussion of these topics, however, is beyond the scope of this book. The security section of the Microsoft TechNet web site, referenced at the end of this chapter, contains a wealth of information on how to secure your servers and network properly, including tools to assist you in this important task.

The importance of securing your applications cannot be stressed enough. Failure to devote the time and resources to get security right can result in data loss, application failure or hijacking, as well as loss of revenue and/or reputation. And it's important that security be considered from the very beginning. Application security added as an afterthought is little better than no security at all.

Securing access to an application or to the resources belonging to an application involves two processes: authentication and authorization. This chapter explains how these processes relate to ASP.NET and how each fits into the overall scheme of allowing or preventing access to ASP.NET application resources. The discussion focuses on the three authentication methods the ASP.NET runtime provides: *Windows*, *Forms*, and *Passport*. The chapter also discusses ACL-based and URL authorization, as well as strategies for obtaining secure access to data and securing web services. The discussion also touches briefly on *code access security*, which underlies the ASP.NET security model.

Authentication Methods

Authentication is the process of positively identifying the person or program making a request. Authentication does not inherently grant access to resources (a function performed by authorization), but provides developers (or the runtime) with a known identity on which to base the decision of whether the request should be granted.

In a classic ASP application, you had essentially two options for authenticating users: rely on IIS to authenticate users based on Windows accounts and later authorize these users based on NT Access Control Lists (ACLs); or roll your own authentication from the ground up to authenticate users against a back-end credentials data store (or potentially against Microsoft Active Directory). Each option had disadvantages. Windows authentication's most secure mode, Integrated Security, required all users to use Internet Explorer (and would not work over many proxy servers), while the roll-your-own option required an extraordinary amount of work to build and test.

ASP.NET provides three built-in options for authentication:

Windows authentication
> Provides similar functionality to IIS authentication in classic ASP, though with some important differences, described in the next section. Windows Authentication works in conjunction with the authentication built into IIS, and uses the identity provided by IIS authentication to perform authorization.

Forms authentication
> Provides a rich infrastructure for "roll-your-own" security scenarios, including support for a common login page, and support for a variety of credential storage options, from databases, to XML, to configuration files, as well as helper methods to manage authentication tasks. This authentication provider will be used most often in Internet scenarios.

Passport authentication
> Allows ASP.NET developers to take advantage of Microsoft's Passport single sign-in solution.

All authentication options for ASP.NET are configured either at the machine-level using the *machine.config* file or at the application level using the *web.config* file. Appropriately, you configure the authentication settings using the <authentication> element, along with its associated attributes and children.

> Authentication settings cannot be configured below the application level. If you need to set different authentication settings on a child directory of an application, you will need to configure that directory as an application in IIS. Authorization settings do not share this limitation.

Windows Authentication

As mentioned earlier, Windows authentication provides much the same functionality in ASP.NET as IIS authentication did in classic ASP. IIS authenticates users based on Windows accounts stored either on the local server or on an associated domain controller, and then passes the identity of the authenticated user to the ASP.NET runtime, which can then use it for authorization. The main reason for choosing the Windows authentication provider is that it requires the least code to implement. Of the three modes of built-in authentication in ASP.NET, Windows authentication is the only one that requires you to configure IIS in addition to configuring the authentication settings in *machine.config* or *web.config*.

As with IIS authentication in classic ASP, Windows authentication is primarily useful in situations in which one of the following conditions exists:

- All clients are using Internet Explorer 4.x or higher, and there are no proxy servers for authentication requests to cross. This is most commonly the case in an intranet scenario and is rare for Internet applications.

- The security requirements of the application make it acceptable to use Basic or Digest IIS authentication (which both have limitations that make them somewhat less secure than integrated authentication).

- The security requirements for the application make it unacceptable to allow anonymous users access to the entire application.

Typically, Windows authentication is used in conjunction with impersonation (see the upcoming section "Impersonation" for more information) to allow the ASP.NET process to make requests using the security context of the authenticated user. You can then restrict access to resources using NTFS Access Control Lists (ACLs) or grant database access by setting up the Windows account of the desired user as a login for the database in question. For more information about this technique, see the section "Code Access Security" later in this chapter.

ASP.NET Windows authentication works by obtaining the security context of the user from IIS (see Figure 9-1). The first step in configuring an application to use Windows authentication is to modify the IIS configuration settings to require one of the nonanonymous authentication methods. To do so, follow these directions:

1. Open the Internet Services Manager.

2. In the lefthand pane, drill down to the web site or virtual root of the application you want to configure.

3. Right-click the application's folder and select Properties to display the <application name> Properties dialog.

4. Click the Directory Security tab, and then click the Edit... button in the Anonymous access and authentication control section.

5. Deselect the Anonymous access checkbox and select one or more of the authentication checkboxes (Basic, Digest, or Integrated Windows).

6. Click OK to dismiss the Authentication methods dialog; then click OK again to dismiss the Properties dialog. Now you're ready to configure your ASP.NET application.

While Basic authentication enables the use of Windows accounts for authentication in a wider array of scenarios, remember that Basic authentication sends the username and password in clear text. This can be an unacceptable risk, particularly if the application does not use Secure Sockets Layer (SSL) encryption to protect the communications. Before selecting Basic authentication as an option, make sure you understand the security ramifications of this choice and that you've taken the necessary steps to mitigate risks associated with this approach.

Similarly, Digest authentication requires that passwords be stored in clear text on the domain controller where the accounts exist. If you decide to use Digest authentication, make sure that the domain controller is secured from network attacks and is physically secured to prevent unauthorized parties from accessing the passwords.

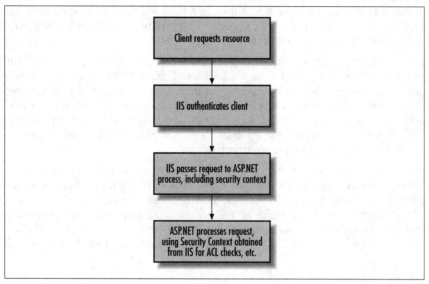

Figure 9-1. Windows authentication process

As shown in Figure 9-1, once a client making a request is authenticated by IIS, the request, along with the security context/identity of the authenticated user, is handed off to the ASP.NET worker process. From this point on, ASP.NET alone is in control.

For ASP.NET to use the security context provided by IIS, the ASP.NET application must be configured for Windows authentication. This configuration is done by adding an <authentication> element to the *web.config* file for the application and setting its mode attribute to Windows, as shown in the following code snippet:

```
<?xml version="1.0" encoding="utf-8" ?>
<configuration>
  <system.web>
    <authentication mode="Windows"/>
    <!--
        Other configuration elements
    -->
  </system.web>
</configuration>
```

Note that because the <authentication> element does not require any child elements for Windows mode, you can use a single tag with a closing / character rather than using a full closing tag.

Impersonation

Impersonation is the practice of having code run in the security context of a particular account. In ASP.NET, impersonation is used to allow code in an ASP.NET
application to be executed in the security context of the authenticated user.

By default, the ASP.NET worker process runs in the context of a special account
called ASPNET. This account has very few privileges, so requests made for ACL-
protected resources (such as files in the filesystem) will fail unless permissions are
explicitly granted to the ASPNET account. This mechanism helps make ASP.NET
applications more secure out of the box.

One alternative to granting explicit permissions to the ASPNET account is to run
the ASP.NET worker process in the context of the SYSTEM account, a highly
privileged account that allows many types of requests to succeed without a need
for impersonation. For example, since SQL Server, by default, allows access to
anyone in the local administrators group, running the ASP.NET worker process as
SYSTEM makes it possible to connect to a local SQL Server database using a
trusted connection without using impersonation.

While this may solve some permissions problems, in practice, running as
SYSTEM is not a good idea, since it provides more privileges than are necessary
for running most ASP.NET applications. One consequence of this is that any
vulnerabilities that occur in IIS or the ASP.NET runtime may then potentially
provide system-level access to those who exploit them. Running the ASP.NET
worker process using the ASPNET account significantly reduces the risk of such
an exploit.

 This setting is controlled by the username attribute of the
`<processModel>` element in *machine.config*.

In most Windows authentication situations, you should enable impersonation to
allow the ASP.NET worker process to make requests using the security context of
the authenticated user. In classic ASP, impersonation is enabled by default. You
can enable impersonation in ASP.NET by adding the `<identity>` element to the
web.config file for the application, with its `impersonate` attribute set to `True`, as
shown in the following code snippet:

```
<?xml version="1.0" encoding="utf-8" ?>
<configuration>
    <system.web>
        <authentication mode="Windows"/>
        <identity impersonate="true"/>
        <!--
            Other configuration elements
        -->
    </system.web>
</configuration>
```

Once impersonation is enabled, you can use NTFS ACLs to authorize accounts
for access to resources. For more information on this technique, see the section
"Authorization" later in this chapter.

Forms Authentication

Forms authentication is probably the most useful built-in ASP.NET authentication module because it provides a very flexible infrastructure for roll-your-own security scenarios. When an application is configured to use Forms authentication, requests for protected resources are redirected to a specified login page, unless the request is accompanied by an authentication token contained in a cookie. For more information on protecting resources when using Forms authentication, see "Authorization," later in this chapter.

Logging in

In the login page, the site developer writes code to check the credentials entered by the user against a backend credentials store. This store can be a relational database such as SQL Server, an XML file, Microsoft Active Directory, or any other storage location of your choice. If the credentials match those stored in the backend credential store, the developer calls the RedirectFromLoginPage method of the FormsAuthentication helper class to send the user back to the page that they originally requested and to set either a session cookie or a persistent cookie containing the authentication token on the user's machine. Once the user is authenticated, he or she can access other resources in the same application without logging in again.

To better illustrate the process by which Forms authentication operates, let's look at an example. In this example, which is based on live code I use to protect downloads on my company site, files in a specific subdirectory of an application are protected using Forms authentication.

The example uses the following files:

web.config
> Configuration file used to enable Forms authentication and to specify the desired access restrictions. See Chapters 8 and 20 for more information on *web.config*.

Login.aspx
> Login page for the application. Accepts login credentials from the user and, if they are valid, redirects the user to the requested URL.

Register.aspx
> Registration page for the application. Allows unregistered users to select login credentials for accessing the application.

Logout.aspx
> Clears the Forms authentication cookie, effectively logging the user out of the secure portion of the application.

Users.xml
> XML file containing the credentials of registered users. Passwords are stored as SHA1-hashed text strings.

To set up Forms authentication, the application is configured with the *web.config* file shown in Example 9-1, which is placed in the root of the application.

Example 9-1. web.config file for Forms authentication

```xml
<?xml version="1.0" encoding="utf-8" ?>
<configuration>
  <location path="files">
    <system.web>
      <authorization>
        <deny users="?"/>
      </authorization>
    </system.web>
  </location>
  <system.web>
    <authentication mode="Forms">
      <forms name=".ASPNETIAN"
        loginUrl="Login.aspx"
        protection="All"
        timeout="60" />
    </authentication>
  </system.web>
</configuration>
```

The `<authentication>` element in Example 9-1 configures the application to use Forms authentication. Its child element, `<forms>`, provides a number of key security elements: a name for the Forms authentication cookie (.ASPNETIAN), the type of protection (encryption, validation, all, or none) for the authentication cookie, the timeout for the cookie (60 minutes in this case, the default being 30), and a login page to which to send unauthenticated users. Note that since the example uses *Login.aspx*, the default, we could omit this attribute.

 In addition to the attributes of the `<forms>` element shown in Example 9-1, there are two new attributes that have been added in Version 1.1 of the .NET Framework, `RequireSsl` and `SlidingExpiration`. These additional attributes are documented in the section on the `<forms>` element, in Chapter 20.

The `<authorization>` element, which is tied to the *files* subdirectory through the use of the `<location>` tag, denies access to any nonauthenticated user. For a more complete discussion of the `<authorization>` element, see "Authorization," later in this chapter.

With this configuration in place, if a user does not already have an authentication cookie, a request for any files in the *files* subdirectory (presuming the file type is handled by ASP.NET) results in the user being redirected to the login page. What if the file type that you want to protect isn't handled by ASP.NET by default? In that case, you can follow these steps to add that type in the IIS configuration for the application:

1. Open the Internet Services Manager applet and locate the application you want to configure.

2. Right-click the application's icon and select Properties.

3. In the Properties dialog, select the Directory (or Home Directory) tab, and click the Configuration... button.

4. On the App Mappings tab, click the Add button.

5. In the Add/Edit Application Extension Mapping dialog, click the Browse... button and browse to the location of *aspnet_isapi.dll*. Typically, this location will be the directory *%windir%\Microsoft.NET\Framework\%version%*, where *%version%* is the version number of the installed .NET Framework. You may need to change the Files of type: drop-down to *.dll to locate this file. Once you've located it, select it and click Open.

6. Now enter the file extension you want to protect (such as *.zip*) or enter .* to associate all file types with ASP.NET.

7. Click OK to accept changes and close each open dialog.

8. Repeat for additional desired file types.

 Using .* to map all file types to ASP.NET is a quick and easy way to protect all types of files for an application configured to use Forms authentication. You should not, however, use this technique if your application contains files, such as classic ASP pages, that are handled by a different ISAPI application because the .* mapping will take precedence and will prevent these file types from working properly.

Once all desired file types are mapped to the ASP.NET ISAPI handler,[*] any request made for one of those file types in the *files* subdirectory results in the user being redirected to *Login.aspx* if they do not already have a Forms authentication cookie for this application. The code for *Login.aspx* is shown in Example 9-2.

Example 9-2. Login.aspx

```
<%@ Page Language="VB" %>
<%@ Import Namespace="System.Data" %>
<%@ Import Namespace="System.Web.Security" %>
<html>
<head>
<title>Login Page</title>
<script runat="server">
    Sub Login_Click(Sender As Object, e As EventArgs)
        Dim LoginDS as DataSet
        If Cache("LoginDS") Is Nothing Then
            LoginDS = New DataSet( )
            LoginDS.ReadXml(Server.MapPath("Users.xml"))
            Cache.Insert("LoginDS", LoginDS, _
                New CacheDependency(Server.MapPath("Users.xml")))
        Else
            LoginDS = Cache("LoginDS")
        End If
        If LoginDS.Tables(0).Select("Email='" & _
            Email.text & "'").Length > 0 Then
```

---

[*] The ISAPI handler takes requests from IIS and hands them off to the ASP.NET worker process, which runs as a separate executable.

Example 9-2. Login.aspx (continued)

```
        Dim LoginRow( ) As DataRow = LoginDS.Tables(0).Select("Email='" _
            & Email.text & "'")
        If LoginRow(0).Item("Password").ToString = _
            FormsAuthentication.HashPasswordForStoringInConfigFile( _
            Password.Text, "SHA1") Then
            FormsAuthentication.RedirectFromLoginPage( _
            Email.Text, Persist.Checked)
        Else
            Message.Text = "Incorrect Password!"
        End If
    Else
        Message.Text = "Email not found. Have you " & _
            "<a href='register.aspx?page=" & _
            Server.UrlEncode(Request.RawUrl) & "'>registered</a>?"
    End If
  End Sub
</script>
</head>
<body>
  <form runat="server">
    <table border="0">
      <tr>
        <td>Email: </td>
        <td><asp:textbox id="Email" runat="server"/></td>
      </tr>
      <tr>
        <td>Password: </td>
        <td><asp:textbox id="Password"
              textmode="Password" runat="server"/></td>
      </tr>
      <tr>
        <td>Persist Authentication Cookie?</td>
        <td><asp:checkbox id="Persist"
              checked="False" runat="server"/></td>
      </tr>
      <tr>
        <td><asp:button text="Submit"
              onclick="Login_Click" runat="server"/></td>
        <td><input type="reset" value="Cancel" runat="server"/></td>
      </tr>
    </table>
    <asp:label id="Message" forecolor="Red" runat="server"/>
  </form>
</body>
</html>
```

The tag-based section of *Login.aspx* is fairly straightforward and presents the user
with textboxes in which to input an email address (used for a login ID) and password. The tag-based section also specifies a checkbox that allows users to persist
the authentication cookie (so they won't need to login again from their machine).

To make coding a little easier, the example adds @ Import directives for both the System.Data and System.Web.Security namespaces. Thus, you can access their members without explicitly using the namespace prefix.

In the Login_Click event handler, the example declares a local DataSet variable and populates it either from the ASP.NET cache or the *Users.xml* file (see Example 9-5), which contains the credentials of registered users. If the dataset is populated from the XML file, we then insert the dataset into the cache for later retrieval (which eliminates the need to read the file, if it has not changed).

The call to Cache.Insert sets up a file dependency on the *Users.xml* file. If that file changes, the cached dataset will be ejected from the cache and the new data will be loaded from the file on the next login request. This allows us to take advantage of the performance advantages of caching, but still ensure that we're always dealing with fresh data.

Once we have a dataset containing all current users, we ensure that the email entered by the user is contained in the table, using the DataTable's Select method:

```
If LoginDS.Tables(0).Select("Email='" & _
        Email.text & "'").Length > 0 Then
```

If the email exists, we get a DataRow containing the credentials associated with that user. We can then compare this hashed password in the dataset with a hashed version of the password entered by the user, which is returned by the HashPasswordForStoringInConfigFile method of the FormsAuthentication class (using the HashPasswordForStoringInConfigFile method means we don't ever store the actual password, making it less likely that our application can be compromised). If the two versions of the password match, we redirect the user back to the page she requested by calling the RedirectFromLoginPage method of the FormsAuthentication class. RedirectFromLoginPage automatically redirects the user to the page specified by the ReturnUrl query string argument. This argument is automatically appended when the user is initially redirected to *Login.aspx*. RedirectFromLoginPage also sets the .ASPNETIAN cookie containing the Forms authentication token. The following code snippet illustrates this process:

```
Dim LoginRow( ) As DataRow = LoginDS.Tables(0).Select("Email='" _
    & Email.text & "'")
If LoginRow(0).Item("Password").ToString = _
    FormsAuthentication.HashPasswordForStoringInConfigFile( _
    Password.Text, "SHA1") Then
    FormsAuthentication.RedirectFromLoginPage(Email.Text, _
    Persist.Checked)
Else
    Message.Text = "Incorrect Password!"
End If
```

If the email address exists, but the password is incorrect, we set the Text property of the Message Label control to inform the user. If the entered email address does not exist, we set the label text to a message that includes a link to a registration page so that the user can self-register. Note that the link includes a query string argument named page, which *Register.aspx* uses to redirect the user back to *Login.aspx* with the original ReturnUrl query string argument intact. Registration is handled by the *Register.aspx* page, shown in Example 9-3.

Example 9-3. Register.aspx

```
<%@ Page Language="VB" %>
<%@ Import Namespace="System.Data" %>
<%@ Import Namespace="System.Web.Security" %>
<html>
<head>
<title>Registration Page</title>
<script runat="server">
   Sub Register_Click(Sender As Object, e As EventArgs)
      If Page.IsValid Then
         Dim LoginDS as New DataSet()
         LoginDS.ReadXml(Server.MapPath("Users.xml"))
         If LoginDS.Tables(0).Select("Email='" & _
            Email.text & "'").Length = 0 Then
            Dim NewUser As DataRow
            NewUser = LoginDS.Tables(0).NewRow()
            NewUser("Email") = Email.Text
            NewUser("Password") = _
               FormsAuthentication.HashPasswordForStoringInConfigFile( _
               Password.Text, "SHA1")
            LoginDS.Tables(0).Rows.Add(NewUser)
            LoginDS.WriteXml(Server.MapPath("Users.xml"))
            Response.Redirect(Request.QueryString("Page"))
         Else
            Message.Text = "User with email: <i>" & Email.Text & _
               "</i> already exists. Please choose another email address. "
         End If
      End If
   End Sub
</script>
</head>
<body>
   <form runat="server">
      <table border="0" cellspacing="10">
         <tr>
            <td>Email: </td>
            <td><asp:textbox id="Email" runat="server"/></td>
         </tr>
         <tr>
            <td>Desired Password: </td>
            <td><asp:textbox id="Password"
                  textmode="Password" runat="server"/></td>
         </tr>
         <tr>
            <td>Confirm Password: </td>
            <td><asp:textbox id="PasswordConfirm"
                  textmode="Password" runat="server"/></td>
         </tr>
         <tr>
            <td><asp:button text="Submit"
                  onclick="Register_Click" runat="server"/></td>
            <td><input type="reset" value="Cancel" runat="server"/></td>
         </tr>
```

Example 9-3. Register.aspx (continued)

```
        </table>
        <asp:comparevalidator id="comparePasswords"
            controltovalidate="Password"
            controltocompare="PasswordConfirm"
            display="dynamic"
            text="Passwords must match!"
            operator="Equal"
            runat="server"/>
        <asp:requiredfieldvalidator id="requireEmail"
            controltovalidate="Email"
            display="dynamic"
            text="Email address required!"
            runat="server"/>
        <asp:requiredfieldvalidator id="requirePassword"
            controltovalidate="Password"
            display="dynamic"
            text="Password required!"
            runat="server"/>
        <asp:label id="Message" runat="server"/>
    </form>
</body>
</html>
```

The tag-based portion of *Register.aspx* is similar to *Login.aspx*, except that the
example adds a textbox (for confirmation of the desired password) and the
following three validation controls:

- A CompareValidator control to validate that the Password and PasswordCon-
  firm textbox values match.

- A RequiredFieldValidator to ensure that the user enters an email address so
  we don't have entries in the XML file with null email values.

- A RequiredFieldValidator to ensure that the user enters a password so we
  don't have entries in the XML file with null password values.

If we want to provide even more validation measures, we could also add a
RegularExpressionValidator to ensure that the provided email address is valid (or
at least in the correct format for a valid email address). However, the previously
mentioned validators are sufficient at least to ensure that the user enters
something.

In the Register_Click event handler, we first test to ensure that the page is valid
(i.e., that all validation controls on the page report are valid). This test avoids
wasting processor time to perform work on invalid data. If the user's browser
supports DHTML, the page will not even be submitted until the validation
control's requirements have been met, thanks to the ability of these controls to
perform client-side validation (in addition to the server-side validation that is
always performed).

If the page is valid, we declare a local DataSet variable and populate it from the
Users.xml file. Then we check to make sure that the email address the user
entered does not already exist in the file. If it does, we use the Text property of an
ASP.NET Label control to ask the user to choose another email address.

If the email address does not exist in the file, we create a new DataRow, populate it with the user's chosen email address and a hashed version of the password,* add the new row to the dataset, and save the dataset back to the XML file, as shown in the following code snippet. Note that this technique does not control concurrency, so if someone modified the contents of the XML file between the time this code read from the file and when it writes to the file, those changes would be overwritten:

```
Dim NewUser As DataRow
NewUser = LoginDS.Tables(0).NewRow( )
NewUser("Email") = Email.Text
NewUser("Password") = _
    FormsAuthentication.HashPasswordForStoringInConfigFile( _
    Password.Text, "SHA1")
LoginDS.Tables(0).Rows.Add(NewUser)
LoginDS.WriteXml(Server.MapPath("Users.xml"))
```

 In order to write to the file *Users.xml* successfully, the account under which the ASP.NET runtime is running must have write access to the file.

Once we've written the new user's information to *Users.xml*, we redirect the user to the page specified by the page's query string argument, as shown in the following line of code:

```
Response.Redirect(Request.QueryString("Page"))
```

Once the user is registered, they should be able to log in successfully. But what about logging out? Although the need for such a mechanism might not be immediately obvious, it is valuable in some instances.

Logging out

Consider an application that deals with sensitive information or is likely to be used from public computers. In such cases, you might want to provide the user with some way to log out to prevent others from accessing private information or accessing application resources using the user's account. In Forms authentication, this is quite simple. You call the static SignOut method of the FormsAuthentication class, as Example 9-4 illustrates. You would redirect users to *Logout.aspx* to accomplish the logout. You could also create a user control containing a button that, when clicked, calls the SignOut method and add that user control to all secured pages of your application.

Example 9-4. Logout.aspx

```
<%@ Page Language="VB" %>
<%@ Import Namespace="System.Web.Security" %>
<html>
<head>
```

---

* Again, you use the FormsAuthentication.HashPasswordForStoringInConfigFile method to hash the password.

Example 9-4. Logout.aspx (continued)

```
<title>Logout Page</title>
<script runat="server">
    Sub Page_Load(Sender As Object, e As EventArgs)
        FormsAuthentication.SignOut( )
        Message.Text = "You have been logged out."
    End Sub
</script>
</head>
<body>
    <asp:label id="Message" runat="server"/>
</body>
</html>
```

Example 9-5 shows the contents of the *Users.xml* file. This example shows how simple an XML file for this purpose can be.

Example 9-5. Users.xml

```
<?xml version="1.0" standalone="yes"?>
<Users>
  <User>
    <Email>andrew@aspnetian.com</Email>
    <Password>816010E041FA485C6E2383C649343D3A0CAD4D25</Password>
  </User>
</Users>
```

Passport Authentication

The Passport authentication module enables ASP.NET applications to take advantage of Microsoft's Passport universal sign-in infrastructure to authenticate users. The Passport system allows each user to have a single password and login (the email address associated with their Passport account) for multiple web sites or applications. This can greatly simplify the login process from the user's perspective, as well as reduce the administrative overhead associated with maintaining user accounts (such as having to send forgetful users their password via email).

To enable Passport authentication in ASP.NET, you need to download and install the Passport SDK. See *http://www.passport.com/business* for instructions on where and how to obtain the SDK.

While you can obtain the Passport SDK and set up a test site for free, you have to pay a license fee to use Passport in a production application. Make sure that you understand all the costs involved before implementing Passport authentication.

Once you've installed the SDK, you need to configure Passport according to the accompanying instructions. Finally, you need to configure the ASP.NET application to use Passport authentication, as shown in the following code snippet:

```
<?xml version="1.0" encoding="utf-8" ?>
<configuration>
  <system.web>
```

```
<authentication mode="Passport">
    <passport redirectUrl="someLocalpage.aspx"/>
</authentication>
<!--
    Other configuration elements
-->
</system.web>
</configuration>
```

Note that the <passport> element and the redirectUrl attribute are optional and are used to specify an internal URL to redirect to if the users making the request have not signed in using their Passport accounts. If the <passport> element is omitted, users who have not logged in using their Passport account will be redirected to a login page on a Passport login server.

Authorization

Authorization is the process of determining whether the user identified by the authentication process is allowed to access the resource that they're requesting or whether to take the action that they're attempting to take (such as updating data in a database). While authentication asks the question "Who are you?", authorization asks the question "Are you allowed to do that?" The answer to that question determines whether the user's action is allowed.

Authorization in ASP.NET takes three forms, which are all discussed in this section: ACL-based authorization, URL authorization, and programmatic authorization.

ACL-Based Authorization

Access Control Lists (ACLs) are used in Windows NT, Windows 2000, Windows XP, and Windows Server 2003 to control access to system resources, such as files and folders in the NTFS filesystem. You can assign Windows user accounts or groups to the ACL for a given resource to allow that user or group access to the resource, or determine what type of access (read, write, change, etc.) is authorized.

ACL-based authorization is useful primarily when using Windows authentication in ASP.NET. IIS uses the authenticated user identity to perform ACL checks and can also make requests for ACL-protected resources by using the user's security context, if impersonation has been enabled.

To protect a file using ACL authorization, right-click the desired file in Windows Explorer and select Properties. Next, click the Security tab to view the current users, groups, and permissions on the file (as shown in Figure 9-2). Use the Add and Remove buttons to add or remove user or group accounts and the checkboxes in the Permissions section to modify permissions for the selected user.

In Windows XP, the Security tab may not appear in the Properties dialog for a file or folder if Simple File Sharing is enabled. To see if this feature is enabled (and to disable it and make the Security tab available), select Tools → Folder Options in Windows Explorer. Then select the View tab, and then in the Advanced Settings section, clear the "Use simple file sharing (recommended)" checkbox.

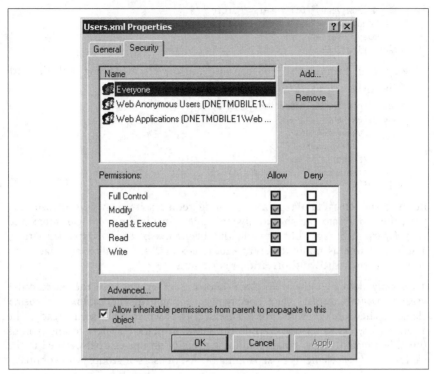

Figure 9-2. File properties dialog

One of the first things you might do in this example is remove the Everyone group from the folder, since this group (as the name suggests) allows anyone who can access the computer to access this file.

 Use caution when removing special accounts (such as the SYSTEM account) from the ACLs for a given resource. Some operating system files require the SYSTEM account to have access to them for the OS to function, so removing those permissions can cause major problems, up to and including not being able to start the OS.

URL Authorization

URL authorization uses the `<allow>` or `<deny>` elements of the `<authorization>` configuration element to control access to folders and files within the application, as we saw in the example on Forms authentication. Access can be allowed or denied based on username, role, and/or HTTP verb used to request the resource. Thus, to allow user Marcie to access any resource in the application with any HTTP verb, but to prevent user Charles from making POST requests, we'd add the following `<authentication>` section to the *web.config* file at the root of the application (you can also add an `<authentication>` section to a *web.config* file in a child directory to override or add to these settings):

```
<authorization>
    <allow verb="GET" users="*" />
```

```
            <allow verb="POST" users="Marcie" />
            <deny verb="POST" users="Charles" />
            <deny users="?" />
    </authorization>
```

As we saw in Example 9-1, you can also use the <location> tag with the path attribute to control access to a specific folder or file:

```
<location path="filetoprotect.aspx">
    <system.web>
        <authorization>
            <deny users="?"/>
        </authorization>
    </system.web>
</location>
```

Because the <location> tag in *web.config* requires its own <system.web> tag pair, the <location> tag should always appear inside the <configuration> and </configuration> tags, but outside the <system.web> and </system.web> tags. You can define as many different <location> tags as you like, and each can contain its own URL authorization restrictions.

To specify domain rather than local accounts or groups, use the *domainname\ userorgroupname* format when specifying the name in the <allow> or <deny> element. There are two wildcards for users, both of which we've seen already. The asterisk (*) refers to all users, while the question mark (?) refers to anonymous (unauthenticated) users. Finally, multiple users or groups can be specified in the <allow> or <deny> elements by separating the list of users or groups with commas.

Programmatic Authorization

You can also perform programmatic checks at runtime to determine whether a user should be allowed to perform certain actions. The primary means of doing this is the IsInRole method, which is defined by the IPrincipal interface and accessible from the User property of the Page class. As with ACL-based authorization, this method is most useful when you're using Windows authentication and want to check whether the authenticated user belongs to a particular Windows group, such as a managers' group. The use of IsInRole is shown in the following code snippet:

```
If Page.User.IsInRole("Managers") Then
    'perform some action restricted to managers
Else
    Message.Text = "You must be a manager to perform this action"
End If
```

Ensuring Input Safety

One of most important rules regarding the acceptance of user input is that all user input should be considered dangerous until proven otherwise. Why is this? For one thing, in a web-based application, it is easy for a malicious user to enter script commands into a textbox (commonly known as a cross-site scripting attack),

---

since it is likely this input will later be displayed by the application such that the script will be executed.

Request Validation

To solve the majority of problems with input safety, the ASP.NET team added a new feature to Version 1.1 of the .NET Framework called *request validation*. Request validation, which is enabled by default in ASP.NET 1.1, automatically checks all forms of input in the Request object for HTML characters, or content, and raises an exception if such content is found.

You should never turn off request validation unless you need to allow users to provide HTML input, and you have provided your own filtering or input checking logic. It is also important to always filter out anything other than the expected input. If you attempt only to filter out known dangerous content, you will most certainly miss something.

Request validation is enabled at the machine level through the validateRequest attribute of the <pages> element in *machine.config*. You can disable request validation at the application level by adding a <pages> element to the application's *web.config* file with the validateRequest attribute set to False. You can disable request validation at the page level by adding the validateRequest attribute to the @ Page directive, with the value set to False.

Other Filtering/Prevention Techniques

If you want to allow HTML input in some parts of your application (or parts of a page), but still want to protect against script attacks, here are a couple of techniques you can use.

Regular expressions

The RegularExpressionValidator control allows specific input based on a given regular expression, while preventing everything else. In the following code snippet, only <i> and <b> tags, spaces, any text (A-Za-z0-9), and the following punctuation: ?!,.'" will be allowed as input.

```
<asp:TextBox id="TextBox1" runat="server"/>
<asp:RegularExpressionValidator runat="server"
    ErrorMessage="Invalid Input Found!"
    ValidationExpression="^([\s\w\?\!\,\.\'\&quot;]*|(</?(i|I|b|B)>))*$"
    ControlToValidate="TextBox1"/>
```

All other input will cause validation to fail.

A good source of useful regular expressions for validating various types of input is *http://www.regexlib.com/*.

HTML encoding

Another technique for filtering input is to HTML encode all input (and/or all output), and use the String.Replace function to allow specific HTML content by replacing the encoded value with an unencoded version. This snippet shows how:

```
Dim InputString As String = Server.HtmlEncode(TextBox1.Text)
InputString = InputString.Replace("&lt;b&gt;", "<b>")
InputString = InputString.Replace("&lt;B&gt;", "<B>")
InputString = InputString.Replace("&lt;/b&gt;", "</b>")
InputString = InputString.Replace("&lt;/B&gt;", "</B>")
InputString = InputString.Replace("&lt;i&gt;", "<i>")
InputString = InputString.Replace("&lt;I&gt;", "<I>")
InputString = InputString.Replace("&lt;/i&gt;", "</i>")
InputString = InputString.Replace("&lt;/I&gt;", "</I>")
```

Like the RegularExpressionValidator code snippet, HTML encoding will allow the use of the <b> and <i> tags. In this case, all other tags will remain encoded. Note that extensive string manipulation can be expensive from a performance standpoint so, where possible, using regular expressions may be more efficient.

 Certain HTML tags, such as the <img> tag, allow script in their attributes. If you allow these tags, you will need to perform additional filtering to ensure that script is not passed in with these tags.

SQL Injection

Another potential input problem occurs when developers use input from users to create SQL queries dynamically. In this case, if the developer does not check the input before concatenating the SQL string, attackers may add a *second* full query to their input, potentially allowing them to access other databases, grant themselves privileges, etc., depending on the account on which the SQL query is run.

Fortunately, it is very easy to prevent SQL injection attacks. All you need to do is avoid creating SQL queries using string concatenation. Rather, you should use stored procedures and/or parameterized queries, which allows you to limit both the type and the length of data provided for a given parameter.

Patching

The best use of the preceding techniques will not protect your application if you miss the important practice of patching. Patching is the practice of applying vendor-provided fixes to the software you use to run your web application. Whether it's your web server, your database software, your operating system, or any other software used in your application, running without security patches installed is an invitation to hackers everywhere.

Fortunately, Microsoft is working to make the patching process easier, with tools such as Windows Update, and a relatively new tool, the Microsoft Baseline Security Analyzer (MBSA). MBSA Version 1.1, available at *http://www.microsoft.com/technet/security/tools/Tools/MBSAhome.asp*, provides both GUI and command-line interfaces for scanning local and remote machines for patch status and common misconfigurations of the following products:

- Windows NT 4.0
- Windows 2000
- Windows XP
- IIS 4.0 and 5.0
- SQL Server 7.0 and 2000
- Internet Explorer 5.01 and later
- Office 2000 and 2002
- Exchange 5.5 and 2000 (patch scanning only)
- Windows Media Player 6.4 and later (patch scanning only)

In addition to tools like Windows Update and MBSA, you can also sign up for notifications of security bulletins at *http://www.microsoft.com/technet/security/bulletin/notify.asp*.

Regardless of how you find out about patches, it is imperative that you keep all software associated with your web application patched and up-to-date.

Code Access Security

Code access security is a new .NET runtime feature that can dramatically reduce the likelihood of applications performing damaging actions by putting significant restrictions in place on untrusted or partially trusted code. While using code access security programmatically in an application is well beyond the scope of this book, even if you never call a single method related to code access security, your ASP.NET applications still use it through settings configured in the *machine.config* configuration file.

The `<trustLevel>` element in *machine.config* defines the mapping of named trust levels to policy files that define the code access security policies associated with a given named trust level. The `<trust>` element in *machine.config* sets the default trust level to `Full`.

If you want to restrict the actions that a given application can take, you can do so by adding a `<location>` tag to *machine.config* that specifies the path to that application and contains a `<trust>` element specifying the desired trust level, as shown in the following code snippet. Setting the `allowOverride` attribute to `False` will prevent the trust level from being overridden in the application's *web.config* file:

```
<location path="Application1" allowOverride="False">
    <system.web>
        <trust level="Low"/>
    </system.web>
</location>
```

As with *web.config*, the `<location>` tag in *machine.config* must be placed outside of the `<system.web>` tags, but must also appear after the `<configSections>` section, or an exception will be thrown.

Additional Resources

The following sites provide additional information on the topics discussed in this chapter:

http://www.gotdotnet.com/team/upgrade/v1/aspnet_account_readme.doc
The GotDotNet reference on changes to the ASP.NET worker process security identity and the effects these changes have had on performing tasks in ASP. NET that require elevated security permissions.

http://msdn.microsoft.com/nhp/Default.asp?contentid=28001369
The MSDN reference for .NET security.

http://www.microsoft.com/technet/security/
The Microsoft TechNet Security home page. The TechNet security site contains articles, patches, and tools that can help you properly configure and secure Windows 2000, IIS, and other Microsoft products to ensure that your applications are not compromised through incorrect server configuration or unpatched vulnerabilities.

10

Error Handling, Debugging, and Tracing

Most code samples in this book don't include code intended to handle errors. It's not that error handling isn't important, but error handling can add complexity, and for the most part we've tried to keep the sample code as simple and clear as possible. Since you'll need to deal with errors in the real world of application programming, the first part of this chapter discusses the variety of techniques available in ASP.NET for handling errors, including custom error pages and structured exception handling—a new feature of Visual Basic .NET.

In addition to handling errors in ASP.NET applications, most developers want to figure out what's causing those errors. To that end, the latter part of this chapter discusses debugging using either the .NET Framework SDK debugger or Visual Studio .NET. The chapter also covers use of the ASP.NET trace feature to troubleshoot application problems.

Error Handling

The goal of error handling (also known as exception handling) is quite simple: to prevent exceptions or errors thrown during the execution of an application request from reaching users. Ideally, users should not know that an exception occurred, or they should at least be provided with an informative message that tells them what they can do to resolve the problem. ASP.NET provides three techniques for achieving this goal:

Custom error pages
    Allow you to assign one or more error pages to be displayed when an exception occurs.

Page_Error and Application_Error events
    Writing event handlers for either or both of these events allows you to catch and handle exceptions at the page or application level.

Structured exception handling

New to Visual Basic .NET, and also available in C#, this type of exception handling allows exceptions to be caught and handled in particular blocks of code.

These three techniques provide broadest (custom error pages, which can handle exceptions from any page in the application) to narrowest (structured exception handling, which handles exceptions for a specific block of code) coverage for handling application exceptions. Figure 10-1 illustrates the relationship of these exception handling techniques to both the exception (shown at the center) and the user, who you're trying to prevent from encountering the exception.

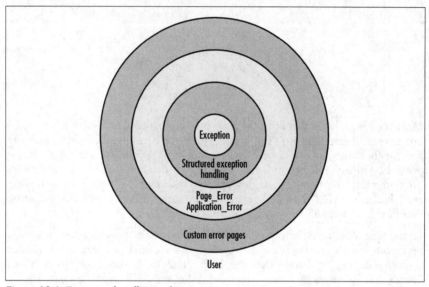

Figure 10-1. Exception handling techniques

The following sections describe these techniques and explain how they fit into an ASP.NET application. Note that you can use all three techniques together, individually, or in whatever combination you like. Using all three techniques in combination would provide broad coverage for most exceptions and more robust specific exceptions handling, but at the cost of maintaining your exception-handling logic in more places.

Custom Error Pages

The most general, but arguably the simplest, technique for handling exceptions in ASP.NET applications is to implement one or more custom error pages. You can do this by creating a web page to display an error message to the user. Then you specify that page as the default error page (or to handle a specific class of error) in *web.config*, using the <customError> configuration element. Example 10-1 shows a *web.config* file that defines a default custom error page called *Error.aspx*. Example 10-2 shows the custom error page itself, which simply displays the path of the page on which the error occurred. Example 10-3 shows the code for a page that will generate a NullReferenceException (which has an HTTP status code of 500).

Error Handling

Example 10-1. Enabling custom errors in web.config

```
<?xml version="1.0" encoding="utf-8" ?>
<configuration>
   <system.web>
      <customErrors defaultRedirect="Error.aspx" mode="On" />
   </system.web>
</configuration>
```

Example 10-2. Error.aspx

```
<%@ Page Language="VB" %>
<html>
<head>
   <title>Error page</title>
</head>
<body>
<h1>Error page</h1>
Error originated on: <%=Request.QueryString("aspxerrorpath") %>
</body>
</html>
```

Example 10-3. Throw500.aspx

```
<%@ Page Language="VB" Debug="True" %>
<html>
<head>
   <title>Throw an Error</title>
   <script runat="server">
      Sub Page_Load( )
         Dim NullText As String = Nothing
         Message.Text = NullText.ToString( )
      End Sub
   </script>
</head>
<body>
   <asp:label id="Message" runat="server"/>
</body>
</html>
```

Instead of the On mode setting for the <customErrors> element, you can set the mode to RemoteOnly or Off (note that these values are case-sensitive). Off will cause detailed error messages containing information about an unhandled exception to be returned to the client, regardless of whether the request is local or remote. Since you don't want users to see error messages if you can avoid it, it's best not to use this value in a production application. RemoteOnly (the default) displays detailed error messages for requests originating from the local host, but displays custom errors (based on the <customErrors> section) to remote clients. On displays the custom error page(s) you specify to any client, regardless of whether the request is local or remote. Using RemoteOnly is a good practice for production applications, since it prevents potentially sensitive information or source code from being displayed to clients, while allowing administrators or developers to view the page locally to read this information.

In addition to providing a default error page, the <customErrors> element also supports the use of child <error> elements to specify custom error pages for specific classes of errors, such as authentication (HTTP 403) or Not Found (HTTP 404) errors, as shown in the following code snippet:

```
<customErrors defaultRedirect="Error.aspx" mode="On">
   <error statusCode="403" redirect="ErrorAccessDenied.aspx"/>
   <error statusCode="404" redirect="ErrorNotFound.aspx"/>
</customErrors>
```

Any errors for which there is not a specific <error> element defined are handled by the page specified by the defaultRedirect attribute. Having different error pages for specific errors allows you to provide more informative messages to users, and perhaps offer some instructions on how the errors can be remedied, while still providing a generic handler for errors outside the scope of the specified handlers.

Another important thing you can do in a custom error page, whether specific or generic, is provide logging or notification of the error so that the site developer or administrator knows that there is a problem and can take action to fix it. In ASP.NET, this process is fairly simple and can be accomplished through the use of the MailMessage and SmtpMail classes, which reside in the System.Web.Mail namespace. Example 10-4 shows a custom error page that uses these classes to notify a site administrator of the error and the page on which it occurred.

Example 10-4. Error_SendMail.aspx

```
<%@ Page Language="VB" %>
<%@ Import Namespace="System.Web.Mail" %>
<html>
<head>
   <title>Error page</title>
   <script runat="server">
      Sub Page_Load( )
         Dim Mail as New MailMessage( )
         'Change the values below to valid email addresses
         Mail.To = "<valid email address>"
         Mail.From = "<valid email address>"
         Mail.Subject = "aspnetian.com error"
         Mail.Body = "An Exception occurred in page " & _
            Request.QueryString("aspxerrorpath")
         'If your SMTP server is not local, change the property below
         '   to a valid server or domain name for the SMTP server
         SmtpMail.SmtpServer = "localhost"
         SmtpMail.Send(Mail)
      End Sub
   </script>
</head>
<body>
<h1>Error page</h1>
```

Example 10-4. Error_SendMail.aspx (continued)

```
Error originated on: <%=Request.QueryString("aspxerrorpath") %>
<br/>
An email has been sent to the administrator of this site notifying them of the
error.
</body>
</html>
```

For the code in Example 10-4 to work, you need to provide valid email addresses for the To and From properties of the MailMessage object instance.

If an unhandled exception occurs in a custom error page, no further redirect will occur, so the user will see a blank page. This situation makes it extremely important for you to ensure that no unhandled exceptions occur in custom error pages. For example, it might be a good idea to wrap the call to *SmtpMail.Send* in Example 10-4 in a Try...Catch block) to handle potential problems with connecting to the specified SMTP server. For more information about using the Try...Catch block, see "Structured Exception Handling," later in this chapter.

The advantage of using custom error pages is that it allows you to handle a lot of errors from a single location (or a small number of locations). The disadvantage is that there's not much you can do to handle the error, other than display a helpful message and notify someone that an error occurred. The reason for this is that you don't have access to the actual exception object in a custom error page, which means you can neither display information about the specific exception nor take steps to handle it.

Page_Error and Application_Error

Another technique for error handling that provides the ability to handle a broad range of application errors is the use of the Error event defined by the Page and HttpApplication classes. Unless AutoEventWireup has been set to False (the default in Web Forms pages created with Visual Studio .NET), ASP.NET automatically calls page or application-level handlers with the name Page_Error or Application_Error if an unhandled exception occurs at the page or application level, respectively. The handler for Page_Error should be defined at the page level, as shown in Example 10-5, while the handler for Application_Error should be defined in the application's *global.asax* file, as shown in Example 10-6.

Example 10-5. Throw500_Page_Error.aspx

```
<%@ Page Language="VB" %>
<%@ Import Namespace="System.Web.Mail" %>
<html>
<head>
    <title>Throw an Error</title>
    <script runat="server">
    Sub Page_Load( )
        Dim NullText As String = Nothing
        Message.Text = NullText.ToString( )
    End Sub
    Sub Page_Error(Source As Object, E As EventArgs)
```

Example 10-5. Throw500_Page_Error.aspx (continued)

```
        Dim ex As Exception = Server.GetLastError()
        If Not ex Is Nothing Then
            Dim Mail as New MailMessage()
            'Change the values below to valid email addresses
            Mail.To = "<valid email address>"
            Mail.From = "<valid email address>"
            Mail.Subject = "aspnetian.com error"
            Mail.Body = "An Exception occurred in page " & _
                Request.RawUrl & ":" & vbCrLf
            Mail.Body &= ex.ToString() & vbCrLf & vbCrLf
            Mail.Body &= "was handled from Page_Error."
            'If your SMTP server is not local, change the property below
            '   to a valid server or domain name for the SMTP server
            SmtpMail.SmtpServer = "localhost"
            SmtpMail.Send(Mail)
            Server.ClearError()
        End If
        Response.Write("An error has occurred. " & _
            "The site administrator has been notified.<br/>" & _
            "Please try your request again later.")
    End Sub
  </script>
</head>
<body>
  <asp:label id="Message" runat="server"/>
</body>
</html>
```

Example 10-5 deliberately causes a NullReferenceException exception by calling ToString on an object that is set to Nothing. In Page_Error, we retrieve this exception by calling Server.GetLastError. The example then creates and sends an email that includes the exception details (calling ToString on an exception object returns the error message and the call stack as a string).

Finally, the code clears the exception by calling Server.ClearError. This last step is important because neither the Page_Error nor the Application_Error handler clears the exception by default. If you don't call ClearError, the exception will bubble up to the next level of handling. For example, if you define both a Page_ Error handler at the page level and an Application_Error handler in *global.asax*, and you do not call ClearError in Page_Error, the Application_Error handler is invoked in addition to Page_ Error. This can be a useful behavior if expected—for example, if you wish to use Page_Error to generate useful messages, while using Application_ Error to log all errors or send notifications. If you're not expecting it, though, this behavior can be confusing, to say the least.

Example 10-6 does essentially the same thing as Example 10-5, but handles errors at the application level, rather than at the page level. You can still access the Server object to get the exception that was thrown. Since Application_Error may handle exceptions for web services as well as for Web Forms pages, Example 10-6 does not attempt to use Response.Write to send a message to the user.

Example 10-6. global.asax

```
<%@ Import Namespace="System.Web.Mail" %>
<script language="VB" runat="server">
    Sub Application_Error(sender As Object, e As EventArgs)
        Dim ex As Exception = Server.GetLastError()
        If Not ex Is Nothing Then
            Dim Mail as New MailMessage()
            'Change the values below to valid email addresses
            Mail.To = <valid email address>
            Mail.From = <valid email address>
            Mail.Subject = "aspnetian.com error"
            Mail.Body = "An Exception occurred in page " & _
                Request.RawUrl & ":" & vbCrLf
            Mail.Body &= ex.ToString() & vbCrlf & vbCrlf
            Mail.Body &= "was handled from Application_Error."
            'If your SMTP server is not local, change the property below
            '   to a valid server or domain name for the SMTP server
            SmtpMail.SmtpServer = "localhost"
            SmtpMail.Send(Mail)
            Server.ClearError()
        End If
    End Sub
</script>
```

Structured Exception Handling

The most specific technique for exception handling, and the most useful in terms of gracefully recovering from the exception, is structured exception handling. Structured exception handling should be familiar to developers of Java and C++, for which it is standard practice, but it is new to the Visual Basic .NET language. Microsoft's new language, C#, also provides built-in support for structured exception handling.

In structured exception handling, you wrap code that may throw an exception in a Try...Catch block, as shown in the following code snippet:

```
'VB.NET
Try
    ' Code that may cause an exception
Catch ex As Exception
    ' Exception handling code
Finally
    ' Code executes whether or not an exception occurs
End Try

//C#
try
{
    // Code that may cause an exception
}
catch (Exception ex)
{
    // Exception handling code
```

```
}
finally
{
    // Code executes whether or not an exception occurs
```

The Try statement (lowercase try in C#) warns the runtime that the code contained within the Try block may cause an exception; the Catch statement (catch in C#) provides code to handle the exception. You can provide more than one Catch statement, with each handling a specific exception, as shown in the following code snippet. Note that each exception to be handled must be of a type derived from the base Exception class:

```
'VB.NET
Try
    ' Code that may cause an exception
Catch nullRefEx As NullReferenceException
    ' Code to handle null reference exception
Catch ex As Exception
    ' Generic exception handling code
End Try

//C#
try
{
    // Code that may cause an exception
}
catch (NullReferenceException nullRefEx)
{
    // Code to handle null reference exception
}
catch (Exception ex)
{
    // Generic exception handling code
}
```

 When using multiple Catch blocks, the blocks for specific exceptions should always appear before any Catch block for generic exceptions, or the specific exceptions will be caught by the generic exception handler.

The Finally statement (finally in C#) is also useful in structured exception handling. When used in conjunction with a Try...Catch block, the Finally statement allows you to specify code that will always be run regardless of whether an exception is thrown. This can be especially useful if you need to run clean-up code that might not otherwise run if an exception occurred, such as code that closes a database connection and/or rolls back a database transaction to avoid leaving data in an inconsistent state. Example 10-7 shows a page that attempts to connect to the Pubs SQL Server database and execute a command that returns a SqlDataReader. If either the connection attempt or the command results in an exception, the code in the Catch block will be executed. The code in the Finally block tests to see if the data reader and/or connection are open. If they are, it closes them.

Example 10-7. ReadTitles.aspx

```vb
<%@ Page Language="VB" %>
<%@ Import Namespace="System.Data" %>
<%@ Import Namespace="System.Data.SqlClient" %>
<html>
   <title>Try-Catch-Finally Example</title>
   <head>
      <script runat="server">
         Sub Page_Load()
            Dim ConnStr As String = "Data Source=(local)\NetSDK;" & _
               "Initial Catalog=Pubs;Trusted_Connection=True;"
            Dim SQL As String = "SELECT title, price FROM title " & _
               "WHERE PRICE IS NOT NULL"
            Dim PubsConn As New SqlConnection(ConnStr)
            Dim TitlesCmd As New SqlCommand(SQL, PubsConn)
            Dim Titles As SqlDataReader
            Try
               PubsConn.Open()
               Titles = TitlesCmd.ExecuteReader()
               Output.Text = "<table>"
               While Titles.Read()
                  Output.Text &= "<tr>"
                  Output.Text &= "<td>" & Titles.GetString(0) & "</td>"
                  Output.Text &= "<td>$" & _
                     Format(Titles.GetDecimal(1), "##0.00") & "</td>"
                  Output.Text &= "</tr>"
               End While
               Output.Text &= "</table>"
            Catch sqlEx As SqlException
               Response.Write("A SqlException has occurred.")
            Catch ex As Exception
               Response.Write("An Exception has occurred.")
            Finally
               If Not Titles Is Nothing Then
                  If Not Titles.IsClosed Then
                     Titles.Close()
                  End If
               End If
               If PubsConn.State = ConnectionState.Open Then
                  PubsConn.Close()
               End If
            End Try
            Response.Write("<br/>The current connection state is: " & _
               PubsConn.State.ToString() & ".")
         End Sub
      </script>
   </head>
<body>
   <h1>SqlDataReader Example</h1>
   <asp:label id="Output" runat="server"/>
</body>
</html>
```

As you can see from the examples in this section, of the available exception-handling techniques, structured exception handling is likely to require the most code to implement. However, it also provides you with the ability to handle the exception transparently to the user in cases when it is possible to recover from the exception. For example, you could modify the code in Example 10-6 to test whether the exception was related to the attempt to open the connection and, if so, retry the connection a predefined number of times. This way, if the exception is the result of a temporary network problem, the exception handling code can potentially handle this problem without the user ever being aware that a problem exists (apart from the slight delay in connecting).

Debugging

Debugging is the process of locating and eliminating errors in an application. Each error falls into one of three categories:

Syntax errors

These errors result from writing code that violates the rules of the language. A good example of a syntax error is failing to end a statement in C# with a semicolon. Syntax errors are typically caught and reported by the compiler, and thus are the easiest to debug.

Crashing semantic errors

These errors result when code that is syntactically correct results in a condition that causes the program to terminate unexpectedly or to hang (for example, looping code whose loop counter is never incremented). Depending on the condition that causes the program to terminate, you may get an error message indicating the cause and (if debugging is enabled for the page) the line number on which the error occurred.

Noncrashing semantic errors

These errors result when code that is syntactically correct and does not cause the application to crash or hang nonetheless results in variables containing data outside of the range expected by the developer, or program code executing in an unexpected order. This type of error is the most difficult to debug.

Both types of semantic errors are most typically the target of debugging efforts, since syntax errors are fairly easy to fix once they are identified by the compiler.

Two main tools are useful for debugging ASP.NET applications: the ASP.NET trace feature (discussed later in this chapter) and debuggers.

Two debuggers are of primary interest to ASP.NET developers: the .NET Framework SDK debugger, which has the substantial advantage of being free, and the Visual Studio .NET debugger, which provides additional debugging features such as remote debugging and the ability to debug native Win32 applications. An important limitation of the SDK debugger is that you cannot use it to edit source files, so you need to use another editor to make changes as you debug. The debugger in Visual Studio .NET allows you to edit your source files (although you need to stop debugging before editing and rebuild the application before restarting the debugger).

To start a debugging session with either debugger, follow these basic steps:

1. Open the debugger (or the Visual Studio .NET IDE).

2. Open the project or files you wish to debug.

3. Ensure that debugging is enabled for all pages and classes that you wish to debug.

4. Set breakpoints in the source code that will halt execution at a chosen point and allow you to step through subsequent code.

5. Start the debugger, either by attaching to running processes for your application (the key process being the *aspnet_wp.exe* process) or by running the Debug Start command in the Visual Studio .NET IDE. Note that you may need to set the desired start page as described in "Using the Visual Studio .NET Debugger," later in this chapter.

The key to debugging in either debugger is ensuring that all code to be debugged is compiled in debug mode. This mode inserts symbols into the compiled assemblies that allow the debuggers to attach to the running code and allows you to step through this code line by line.

In the next two sections we'll look at the specific steps taken to enable debug mode, start debugging sessions, and step through code in both debuggers.

Using the SDK Debugger

Debugging in the SDK debugger, *DbgCLR.exe*, is fairly straightforward. The program is located by default in the *\FrameworkSDK\GuiDebug* folder of either the Visual Studio .NET or .NET Framework install folder. Start by opening the debugger by double-clicking on its executable. The resulting window should look similar to Figure 10-2.

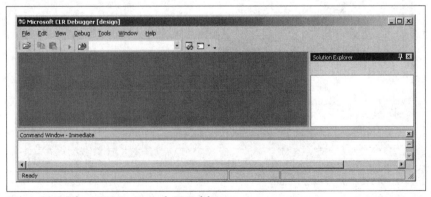

Figure 10-2. The .NET Framework SDK debugger

Now open the ASP.NET pages, code-behind files, and associated class files (for custom server controls, for example) that you wish to debug, using either the File Open File... menu command, or by clicking the Open File button on the toolbar.

Before you go any further, you should ensure that debugging is enabled for all of the pages and class files you've opened. For code contained in ASP.NET pages, enabling it is simple: just add the Debug attribute to the @ Page directive and set its value to True:

```
<%@ Page Language="VB" Debug="True" %>
```

This step will also enable debugging of code contained within a code-behind file that is referenced by the Src attribute of the @ Page directive, which is compiled dynamically the first time the page is requested.

> You can also enable debug mode using the Debug attribute of the <compiler> configuration element in *web.config*.

For code contained within precompiled code-behind files or other precompiled assemblies, you must compile the assembly with the compiler's debug flag set to enable debugging.

Once you've ensured that all your code is ready for debugging, it's time to set a breakpoint. The easiest way to do this is to click in the lefthand margin next to the line of code at which you want the debugger to halt execution. Note that you can set breakpoints only on executable lines of code or procedure declarations. The result will look similar to Figure 10-3.

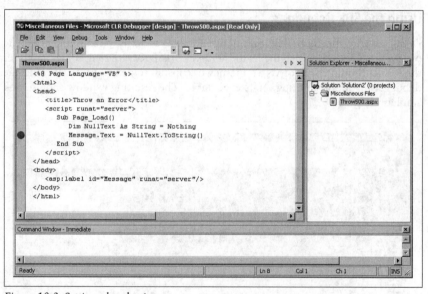

Figure 10-3. Setting a breakpoint

Once you've set your breakpoint, you'll need to open the desired page in Internet Explorer to start the processes to which the debugger will be attached. Once that's done, you can attach the debugger to the necessary processes by selecting Processes... from the Debug menu. This will open the Processes dialog. Select the *aspnet_wp.exe* process, and then click Attach... Next, locate the Internet Explorer process that corresponds to the page you loaded earlier, and attach that as well. At this point, the Processes dialog should look similar to Figure 10-4.

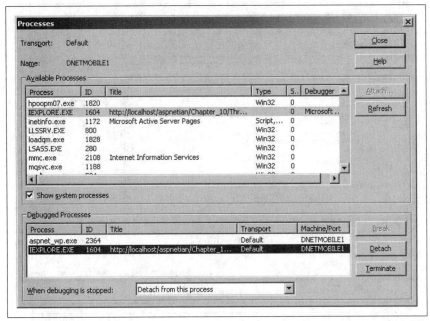

Figure 10-4. Processes dialog

Now simply refresh the page in the browser, and assuming that the line on which you set the breakpoint is in the current flow of the application, the debugger should halt execution at the breakpoint, as shown in Figure 10-5. Then you can view the value of local variables using the Locals window (shown in Figure 10-5) or take advantage of other debugger features to examine your code.

Once program execution has halted at a breakpoint, you can also step through your code line by line using the Step Into, Step Over, and Step Out commands in the Debug menu (or their keyboard shortcuts). This allows you to examine the value of variables as you walk through your code, as well as better determine exactly where a given error is occurring.

 Step Into, Step Over, and Step Out are commands for stepping through your code in debug mode. The only difference between Step Into and Step Over, both of which tell the debugger to execute the next line of code, is how they handle function calls. If the next line of code to be executed is a function call, Step Into will execute the function call, then halt on the first line of code in the function. Step Over instructs the debugger to execute the entire function, and halt execution at the next line of code after the function call.

Step Out, used from within a function call, instructs the debugger to execute every line of code remaining until control is returned to the calling function, and then halt execution on the next line of code after the function call.

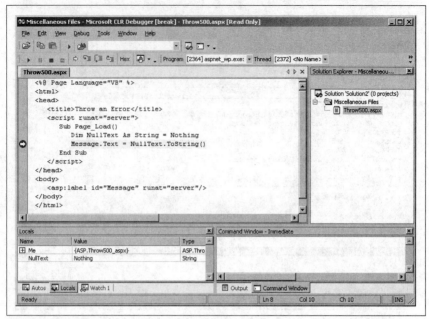

Figure 10-5. Halting on a breakpoint

In addition to setting breakpoints by clicking in the left margin, you can use the New Breakpoint dialog to set *conditional breakpoints* (i.e., breakpoints that only halt execution every *x* number of times they're hit). To open the New Breakpoint dialog, select New Breakpoint... from the Debug menu. The dialog appears in Figure 10-6.

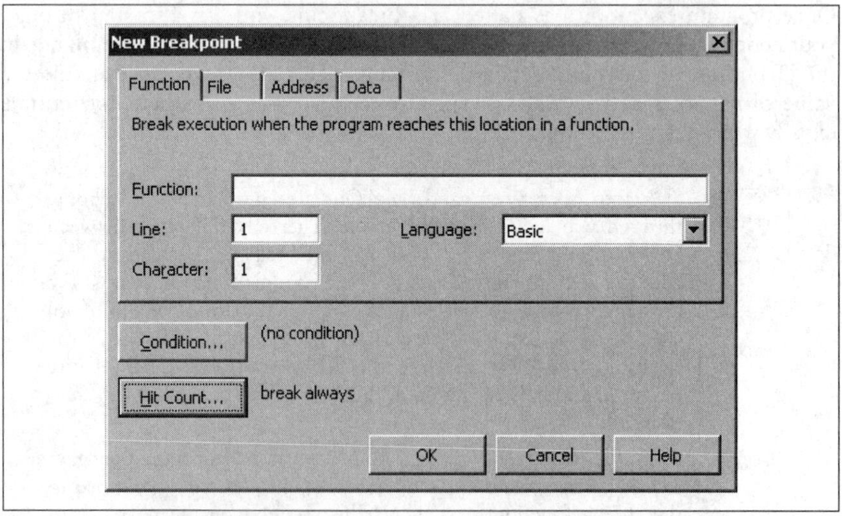

Figure 10-6. New Breakpoint dialog

Using the Visual Studio .NET Debugger

Getting started with debugging in the Visual Studio .NET environment is simpler than with the SDK debugger, even though more debugging options and features are available, because projects are set up by default to support debugging. Assemblies generated for code-behind files in Visual Studio will be compiled in debug mode unless you explicitly tell the IDE to compile them in Release mode. Thus, as long as all of your code is in code-behind, you don't need to do anything further to enable debugging.

If you have a mix of code within server-side <script> blocks in your *.aspx* files and code-behind pages, you'll still need to add the Debug attribute to your *.aspx* files as described in the previous section.

To start debugging in Visual Studio .NET, open the project you want to debug, and then open the page (or pages), code-behind file(s), and/or class file(s) you want to debug. Because the Visual Studio .NET debugger can automatically attach itself to the correct processes when you want to start debugging, you don't need to explicitly attach the processes as described in the previous section (although you can still do it that way if you want to). However, in order to automatically attach the processes, you need to provide a starting point, which should be the first page you want to debug. Simply right-click that page in the Solution Explorer window and select Set As Start Page.

Next, set breakpoints as desired in your code-behind or class files. Setting breakpoints is done the same way in the Visual Studio .NET debugger and the SDK debugger (which is discussed in the previous section).

Once all your breakpoints are set, start debugging by selecting Start from the Debug menu. This should result in a new browser window being opened to the page that you set as the start page and the first breakpoint being hit. At this point, the IDE should look similar to Figure 10-7.

Now you can walk through your code or examine local variables the way you can in the SDK debugger.

Tracing

The other useful tool provided by ASP.NET for debugging is the trace feature. Tracing allows you, through a simple configuration setting or page-level attribute, to have ASP.NET write a whole host of information about the currently executing request to the page or to a trace log. This information includes the SessionID; the time, type, and status code of the request; timing information for events such as Init, PreRender, SaveViewState, and Render; a Control Tree of all controls in the page; and the contents of the Cookies collection, the HTTP Headers, the QueryString collection (if any QueryString values were passed), the Form collection (if any form fields were passed), and the ServerVariables collection.

Essentially, tracing allows you to automatically write out the contents of all collections exposed by the classic ASP Request object, plus some really useful additional information. This allows you to examine a great deal of information about a request on a single page, which can assist greatly in debugging.

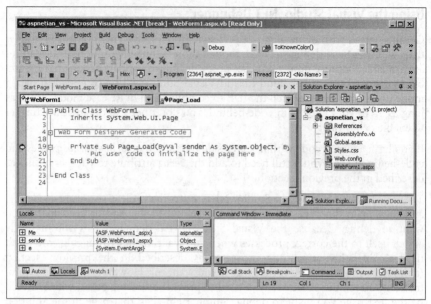

Figure 10-7. Debugging in Visual Studio .NET

More importantly, you can also write to the trace output using the Trace.Write and Trace.Warn methods, which are exposed by the Trace property of the Page class. These methods can now be used in place of Response.Write when you determine the value of a variable on a page at a certain point in page execution or write out a notification that a certain point in the page has been hit. With Trace.Write or Trace.Warn, once you've disabled tracing, you can leave the statements in your code and you don't have to worry about anyone seeing the output. If you've ever deployed a page to production without removing or commenting out your Response.Write statements used for debugging, you'll be grateful for this feature.

Page-Level Tracing

Enabling tracing at the page level is very simple. Simply add the Trace attribute to the @ Page directive and set its value to True, as shown in the following code snippet:

```
<%@ Page Language="VB" Trace="True" %>
```

This provides a quick and easy way to get an overview of what's going on for a given page. The output from a page with tracing enabled looks similar to Figure 10-8.

One downside to enabling tracing at the page level is that if you use it with many pages, it's more work to add and remove the Trace attribute for each page (or to set the attributes to False). This can also make it more likely that you'll forget one and end up with trace information being written out in a production application. Not what you want.

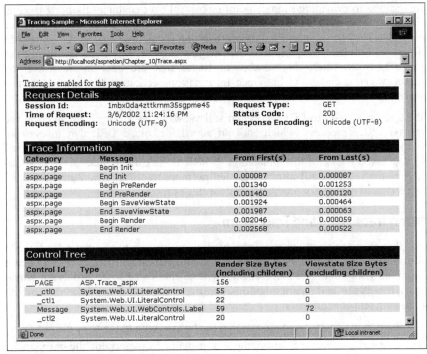

Figure 10-8. Page-level tracing

Application-Level Tracing

ASP.NET provides the ability to enable tracing at the application level through the `<trace>` element in *web.config*. Application-level tracing makes it possible to disable tracing in a single location in your application and makes it easier to enable tracing for multiple pages. Example 10-8 shows a *web.config* file with tracing enabled at the application level.

While the `<trace>` element allows you to enable or disable tracing at the application level, the page-level `Trace` attribute overrides the setting in *web.config*. Thus, if any pages have the `Trace` attribute set to `True`, disabling tracing at the application level will not disable tracing for these pages.

Example 10-8. The `<trace>` element

```
<configuration>
    <system.web>
        <trace enabled="true"
            localOnly="true"
            pageOutput="true"
            requestLimit="15"
            traceMode="SortByCategory" />
    <system.web>
</configuration>
```

In addition to providing a single point of control over enabling/disabling tracing, the <trace> element allows you to control several other factors: whether trace output is visible to machines other than the local host (using the localOnly attribute); whether the output is sent to the page or to a trace log (using the pageOutput attribute); the number of traces that are kept in the trace log (requestLimit); and how the Trace Information section of the trace output is sorted (traceMode).

If pageOutput is set to False, you can still view the trace output by entering the special URL *Trace.axd* (which isn't an actual file, but a URL that invokes an HttpHandler for the trace functionality) from the root of the application. *Trace.axd* lists all saved traces for the application. Note that once the number of traces specified by the requestLimit attribute is met, no more traces are saved until the trace log is cleared. *Trace.axd* provides a link for this purpose.

Using Trace.Write and Trace.Warn

Finally, as mentioned in the introduction to this section, instead of using Response.Write (as done in classic ASP) to write out variable values or flag certain points in your code, ASP.NET enables you to use *Trace.Write* and *Trace.Warn*. Both the Write and Warn methods are overloaded and can take one of the following sets of arguments:

- A single string argument containing the text to write to the trace output.
- One string argument containing a user-defined category for the entry and a second string argument containing the text to write to the trace output.
- One string argument containing a user-defined category for the entry, a second string argument containing the text to write to the trace output, and an Exception argument.

The only difference between Write and Warn is that entries written with the Warn method appear in red text, making them ideal for conditions that require special attention. Example 10-9 shows an ASP.NET page with tracing enabled that uses Trace.Write and Trace.Warn to write to the trace output. Figure 10-9 shows the output of this page.

Example 10-9. Trace.aspx

```
<%@ Page Language="VB" Trace="True" %>
<html>
<head>
   <title>Tracing Sample</title>
   <script runat="server">
      Sub Page_Load( )
         If Page.Trace.IsEnabled = True Then
            Trace.Write("MyCategory", "Hello, Trace!")
            Trace.Warn("MyCategory", "This text will be red!")
            Message.Text = "Tracing is enabled for this page."
         Else
            Message.Text = "Tracing is not enabled for this page."
         End If
      End Sub
```

Example 10-9. Trace.aspx (continued)

```
    </script>
</head>
<body>
    <asp:label id="Message" runat="server"/>
</body>
</html>
```

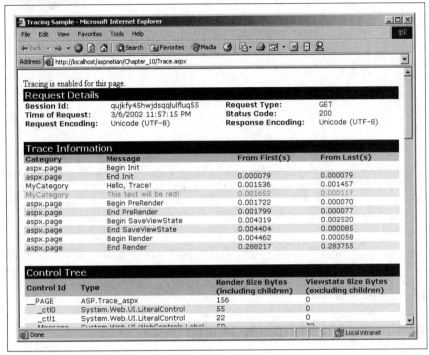

Figure 10-9. Output of Trace.aspx

Additional Resources

The following site provides additional information on the topics discussed in this chapter:

http://samples.gotdotnet.com/quickstart/aspplus/doc/debugcomsdk.aspx
    The ASP.NET QuickStart reference to the .NET Framework SDK Debugger.

11

ASP.NET Deployment

To end Part I of the book, we've saved the best for last. Why do we call it the best? Because compared to classic ASP, deploying an ASP.NET application is extremely simple. In fact, in many cases, you can deploy an application by copying the entire application structure to a new IIS application folder on the target server.

This chapter discusses both simple deployment scenarios, for which the DOS XCOPY command or Windows Explorer are all you'll need. It also discusses more involved scenarios, such as using the Visual Studio Web Setup project type to deploy your application.

Deploying ASP.NET Applications

For most common applications, all you need to do to deploy the application is set up an IIS virtual directory on the target machine and copy the application's files to it. Assuming that the .NET Framework is installed on the target machine, the application should then run without further configuration or setup.

This type of scenario includes both ASP.NET applications written with their code inline in *.aspx* files and those that use code-behind files. Note, however, that deploying the code-behind files themselves is not necessary, as long as you deploy the assembly or assemblies compiled from them.

To deploy an ASP.NET application:

1. Create and configure a new IIS virtual directory (or web site) on the target machine using Internet Services Manager.

2. Use Windows Explorer, XCOPY, FTP, or another transfer mechanism to copy the files and folders contained in the application's root directory to the new directory on the target machine. If you have Visual Studio .NET, you can also use the Copy Project command from the Project menu to deploy the files to a

new location, as described later in this chapter (this does not require step 1, as the Copy Project command will take care of that as well).

As long as any assemblies you're using are in the *bin* subdirectory of your application and you're not using COM components through COM Interop, it's really that simple. Because all application-specific configuration information is contained in your *web.config* file(s), this information is automatically copied with the application. In situations when you use shared assemblies, a little more work is necessary, as we'll discuss in the next section.

Deploying Assemblies

Assemblies are the basic unit of deployment for managed applications, including ASP.NET applications. Assemblies are used in ASP.NET in several ways, each of which has different implications for deployment. The three categories of assembly are described below. The steps required to deploy application-specific and global assemblies appear in subsequent sections.

Automatically generated assemblies
> Includes assemblies that are dynamically generated by the ASP.NET runtime for each *.aspx* page in your application, as well as for code-behind files identified by the src attribute of the @ Page directive, and for global.asax and *.ascx* user control files. Because these assemblies are generated at runtime automatically, no action is required on the part of the developer at deployment time.

Application-specific assemblies
> Includes assemblies resulting from the compilation of code-behind files, whether through building an application in Visual Studio .NET or using the command-line compilers. This category also includes compiled assemblies containing business logic code, and/or assemblies containing custom server controls. All application-specific assemblies should reside in the application's *bin* subdirectory (also known as the local assembly cache), which allows your application to locate and use the assembly's members. There they are automatically loaded into memory by the ASP.NET runtime. Because these assemblies reside within the folder tree of the application, when you deploy the application using XCOPY, FTP, or Windows Explorer, they are copied with the rest of the files in your application and available to the deployed application automatically. Additionally, the ASP.NET runtime automatically modifies the IIS permissions on the local assembly cache directory to deny all HTTP access to the directory, which prevents anyone from reading or accessing assemblies directly.

Global assemblies
> Includes any assemblies that are shared across all applications on a machine by installing them in the global assembly cache (GAC). Assemblies must be strongly named in order to be installed in the GAC and can be versioned to support side-by-side installation of multiple versions of the same assembly.

Deploying Application-Specific Assemblies

As noted in the preceding section, deploying application-specific assemblies is as simple as deploying other application files. As long as the assemblies reside in the *bin* subdirectory of the application, no further action is required on the part of the developer apart from copying the application's files to the target server.

The magic of the *bin* directory is enabled by the `<assemblies>` configuration element in *machine.config*, which contains the following `<add>` element by default:

```
<add assembly="*" />
```

This element tells the ASP.NET runtime to load any assemblies residing in the *bin* subdirectory for use by the application.

Another important point is that when assemblies are loaded by the ASP.NET runtime, the actual physical DLL containing the assembly is never loaded into memory. Instead, the ASP.NET runtime makes a shadow copy of the DLL and loads and locks it on the disk instead (while setting up a file monitor on the original DLL file). This means that you can update the .NET assemblies associated with your application at any time, without the need to shut down IIS or restart the server. The ASP.NET runtime automatically detects when an assembly is updated and serves all new requests using the new version of the assembly. This makes it significantly easier to maintain and update applications with a minimum of downtime.

If you use code-behind for your page-specific logic, you can deploy only the *.aspx* pages and the precompiled assembly (or assemblies) for your code-behind files, without deploying the code-behind files. This allows you to run your application while protecting the source code contained in the actual code-behind files.

Some have argued that, as with Java bytecode, the Intermediate Language (IL) contained in .NET managed assemblies is readily decompiled into a managed language such as C#. Thus, even if you do not deploy the code-behind files for an application, it may still be possible for someone to derive this code from the assemblies by using an IL decompiler, assuming that they could get access to the assemblies, which would require either physical access to the machine, or would require the attacker to exploit a vulnerability that allowed access to the filesystem.

 Application developers should consider the relative value represented by their code versus the effort required to decompile that code, and determine whether additional means for protecting the code are warranted. One such measure is a code obfuscator, which renders most member names meaningless to make understanding of decompiled code more difficult.

Deploying Global Assemblies

The global assembly cache (GAC) provides a centralized location for the storage of assemblies that are to be shared across applications on a given machine. As noted previously, to be stored in the GAC, an assembly must be named strongly. This process is outlined in this section. Because of this requirement, the extra deployment effort entailed, and the fact that global assemblies are available to all applications on a machine by default, you should only use the GAC for assemblies that fit the following profile:

- They need to be shared by many applications.
- The effort of maintaining and/or updating individual local copies of the assembly for each application outweighs the effort of strongly naming and deploying the assembly to the GAC.

The first step in deploying an assembly to the GAC is to provide the assembly with a strong name. This is a three-step process:

1. Generate a cryptographic key pair using the *sn.exe* command line tool:

   ```
   sn -k keyPair.snk
   ```

   To see all the options for the *sn.exe* tool, run sn /? at a command prompt.

2. Add an assembly-level `AssemblyKeyFile` attribute. You can also optionally add an `AssemblyVersion` attribute to provide a version number for the assembly. The * in the following version number example auto-increments the last two of the four version number parts with each compilation:

   ```
   ' VB.NET
   <Assembly: AssemblyKeyFile("keyfile.snk")>
   <Assembly: AssemblyVersion("0.1.*")>

   // C#
   [assembly: AssemblyKeyFile(@"..\..\sgKey.snk")]
   [Assembly: AssemblyVersion("0.1.*")]
   ```

3. Compile the assembly using the appropriate command-line compiler. Note that the key pair should be copied to the location of the code files to be compiled, since this location is where the compiler will look for the file based on the `AssemblyKeyFile` attribute shown previously.

 Assemblies placed in the GAC are given full trust by the code access security system. If an application configured for a lower trust level attempts to call the assembly, an exception of type `SecurityException` will be thrown.

Once the assembly has been strongly named, you can install it into the GAC in any one of three ways:

- Use the *gacutil.exe* command-line tool to install (or uninstall) an assembly into the GAC, as follows:

  ```
  gacutil -i myAssembly.dll
  ```

  Note that this syntax assumes that *gacutil.exe* is called from the directory containing the assembly's physical file. The *gacutil.exe* utility is recommended only for development systems.

- Use Windows Explorer to drag and drop a copy of the assembly to the GAC. Access to the GAC is provided via a Windows Explorer shell extension, which displays the contents of the GAC as the folder *%windir%\Assembly*.

- Use Microsoft Windows Installer 2.0 to create an installation package that will install the assembly or assemblies to the GAC. This installation ensures easier rollback of assemblies and other benefits. See the Windows Installer 2.0 documentation for information on creating Installer packages.

What About COM Components?

If you're using only managed assemblies in your application, the deployment picture is pretty rosy. It's considerably easier to deploy, update, and maintain managed assemblies than it was to maintain COM components in classic ASP. But what if your application requires you to use COM components through the .NET COM interoperability layer?

The good news is that if the version of the COM component you are using is already installed on the target machine, you should need to deploy only the runtime-callable wrapper (RCW) assembly for the component, since that assembly contains the information necessary to locate the component based on information in the registry.

However, if the COM component is a custom component or is not installed on the target system, you need to deploy the COM component to the target system and register it using *regsvr32.exe* as follows:

```
regsvr32 <dllname>
```

Note that you would replace *<dllname>* with the name of the component to register.

Deploying Through Visual Studio .NET

If you are using Visual Studio .NET to create your web applications, you have some additional deployment options at your disposal. These options include simply using Visual Studio's Copy Project command to copy some or all project files to a new location and using a Web Setup project to create a Windows Installer package to install the web application, including creating the necessary IIS directories. These techniques are discussed in the following sections.

In addition to these options, Visual Studio .NET allows you to open a project directly from the Web, so you could theoretically create the project directly on the target server and edit it there. This is only recommended for development systems, since incorrect edits made using this technique on production systems could result in application errors or downtime. To open a project from the Web, simply open Visual Studio .NET and select File → Open → Project From Web....

Deploying Using Copy Project

The simplest option for deploying a project from Visual Studio is to use the Copy Project command. You can access Copy Project by either selecting Copy Project...

from the Project menu or clicking the Copy Project button in the Solution Explorer toolbar, as shown in Figure 11-1.

Figure 11-1. Copy Project button in Solution Explorer

Either method will open the Copy Project dialog, shown in Figure 11-2.

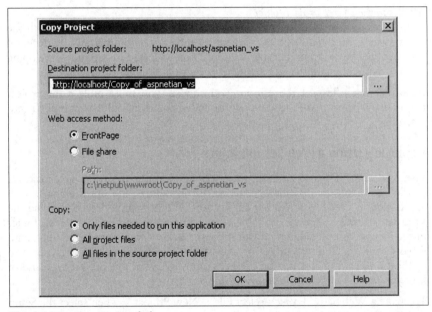

Figure 11-2. Copy Project dialog

The Copy Project dialog gives you a number of options. The first is the destination folder for the project, which is expressed as a URL. You can either enter this URL manually or browse to the desired URL by clicking the ellipsis (...) button.

If you use the browse feature, however, you must select a resource that resolves to a valid URL, such as a web folder in My Network Places.

To copy the project files, you can use either file share access (for copying locally or to a network share) or FrontPage access. FrontPage access requires author permission on the destination web server. If you use FrontPage as the web access method, the destination project folder will be created automatically in IIS, while the File share method requires that you set up this folder manually.

Finally, you have three choices of which files to copy:

Only files needed to run this application
> Copies only the Web Forms, web services, and associated assemblies, without copying any code-behind files to the destination server. This allows you to copy and run your project on another machine without exposing the source code. This option also copies images, style sheets, and other static content as well.

All project files
> Copies all files associated with the project to the destination machine, including code-behind files. This option will not copy files contained in the project folder that are not associated with the project. To keep a file from being copied, you can right-click the file in the Solution Explorer window and select Exclude From Project.

All files in the source project folder
> Copies all files from the project folder, whether they are associated with the project or not. This option is useful for moving a project from one development machine to another, particularly if you will need to continue developing the application on the target machine.

Note that regardless of the options you choose, you must build your project before deploying it, so that any code in code-behind modules is compiled into assemblies.

Deploying Using a Web Setup Project

Visual Studio .NET also adds a completely new project type that now makes it possible to create an installation package for installing (and uninstalling) a web application as easily as any other application. The new project type is called the Web Setup Project, and it is available in the Setup and Deployment Projects folder in the New Project dialog, as shown in Figure 11-3. You can create a Web Setup Project in a standalone solution or as part of the solution containing your web application project. This section provides an overview of this project type and of how you can use it to deploy your web application.

To create a Web Setup Project, select File → New Project.... Then select the Setup and Deployment Projects folder in the lefthand pane of the New Project dialog. Next, select Web Setup Project in the righthand pane. Then fill in the Name and Location boxes and click OK. If you want to add the new project to an existing solution, you should open that solution first and then click the Add to Solution radio button in the New Project dialog.

Once the project is created, you'll be presented with the File System window (see Figure 11-4), which allows you to add files to be deployed to the target system. In addition to the File System window, the Web Setup Project type offers windows

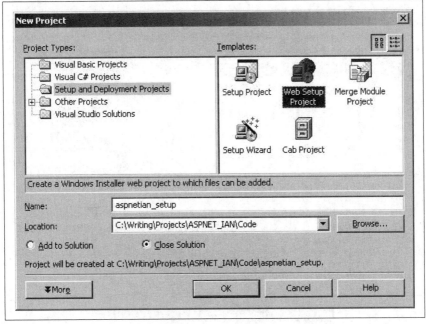

Figure 11-3. New Project dialog

for adding Registry entries and File Type associations, as well as for modifying the user interface that will be displayed by the installer. These windows can be viewed by right-clicking the project name in the Solution Explorer and selecting View <windowname>.

If you created your web setup project as part of the solution containing your web application, you can add all of the necessary files from the application to the setup project simply by right-clicking the Web Application Folder, selecting Add Project Output..., and then selecting both Primary Output and Content Files, as shown in Figure 11-5.

Now, if you build the setup project (note that you should create a fresh build of the web application project first), all necessary files for the web application will be included in the generated setup files.

These files will be located in either the Debug or Release subfolder of the project, depending on whether the Debug or Release configuration is selected in the solution's Configuration Manager.

If you created the web setup project in its own standalone solution, you'll need to add the files manually. Perhaps the easiest way to do this is to highlight the desired files in Windows Explorer and then drag and drop them from Windows Explorer onto the Web Application folder. This will add all selected files and folders to the web application. This step should work fine unless you need to mark any of the subfolders of the application as IIS applications.

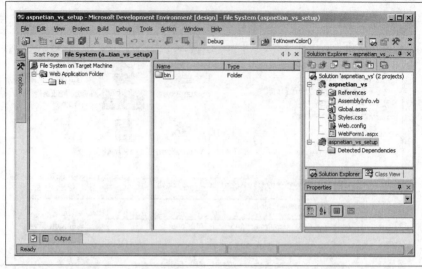

Figure 11-4. File System window

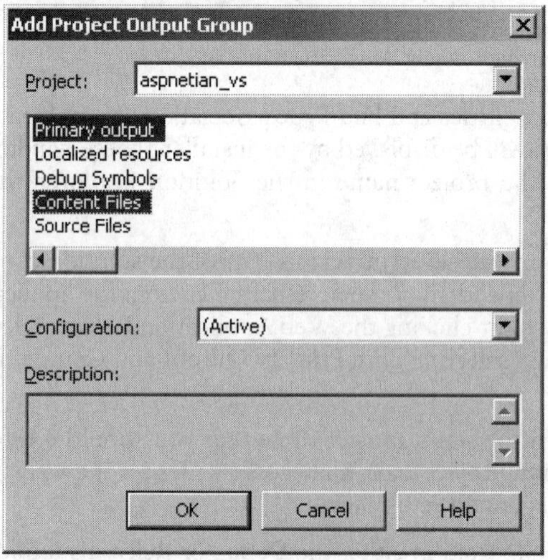

Figure 11-5. Add Project Output dialog

In this case, you'll need to create separate folders for them by right-clicking the File System on Target Machine entry in the File System window, and then selecting Add Special Folder Web Custom Folder. By default, the folder's IsApplication property, which determines whether the folder will be configured as an IIS Application, is set to True. You can use the Property Browser to modify this setting, if desired.

In addition to setting the IsApplication property for Web Custom Folders, you can use the property browser to set a variety of other IIS-specific configuration options for the folders in your setup project. For example, you can specify whether a given folder will allow read or write access or directory browsing, as well as whether the folder should be indexed. This way, you can provide all of the application configuration automatically, allowing the person installing the application to simply double-click the setup file generated by the project and follow a few brief wizard steps to install the application.

Once you've configured the application folders, you will need to build the project to create the setup files. Then you can copy or transfer those files to another machine, run *Setup.exe*, and the application should install and run normally.

Additional Resources

The following site provides additional information on the topics discussed in this chapter:

http://www.gotdotnet.com/quickstart/aspplus/doc/deployment.aspx
   The ASP.NET QuickStart reference for application deployment.

Intrinsic Class Reference

This section devotes a chapter to each of the following major classes that are available as part of the ASP.NET object model:

Page
HttpApplication and HttpApplicatonState
HttpContext
HttpException
HttpRequest
HttpResponse
HttpServerUtility
HttpSessionState

Each chapter adheres to a standardized format that includes the following elements:

- An introduction, which provides a background on the class and how it is used in an ASP.NET application.

- A list of the class members (properties, collections, methods, and events) documented in the chapter.

- A Comments/Troubleshooting section that provides helpful tips on using the class or discusses pitfalls commonly encountered when working with the class.

- Detailed documentation on class properties, with a separate entry devoted to each property.

- Detailed documentation on collections returned by properties of the class, if the class has any, with a separate entry devoted to each collection.

- Detailed documentation on class methods, with a separate entry devoted to each method

- Detailed documentation on events raised by the class, if the class exposes any, with a separate entry devoted to each event.

In addition, Chapter 20 documents configuration settings that can be found in either *machine.config* or *web.config*.

12

The Page Class

In contrast to classic ASP, ASP.NET features a far richer object model that allows virtually every part of an ASP.NET application to be generated and modified dynamically. Central to this ability to generate—and particularly, to modify—content programmatically is the Page class, which is new to ASP.NET.

The Page class (or a class derived from the Page class) represents a request to an *.aspx* page that is processed by the ASP.NET extension to the Internet Information Server or to another web server supporting the .NET Framework. The web page may contain simple HTML and text, .NET code, or a combination of both; in other words, the Page class represents a single instance of a Web Forms page. The requests for that page are served by the compiled object that sends HTML or other content back to the client.

The Page object is recompiled if any source files that form this page, such as a user control, a code-behind file, the *.aspx* page itself, or the application configuration file, are changed.

In the case of single-file ASP.NET pages (i.e., *.aspx* files that combine user interface elements with script), the *.aspx* page is compiled into an instance of a class that derives directly from the Page class. This is evident from the following code:

```
Public Sub Page_Load(o AS Object, e AS EventArgs)
    Dim oType As Type
    oType = Me.GetType
    Do
        Response.Write(oType.Name & "<BR />")
        oType = oType.BaseType
    Loop While Not oType Is Nothing
End Sub
```

The output produced by this code appears as follows:

```
Page1_aspx
Page
TemplateControl
Control
Object
```

Web Forms pages produced by Visual Studio, in contrast, consist of separate *.aspx* and code-behind files. In this case, the *.aspx* page is compiled into an instance of a class that derives from the class in the code-behind file, which in turn derives from the Page class. This is illustrated by the following code-behind file:

```
Option Strict On

Imports Microsoft.VisualBasic
Imports System
Imports System.ComponentModel
Imports System.Web
Imports System.Web.UI

Namespace AspNetPages
    Public Class Page2Class : Inherits Page
        Public Sub Page_Load(o AS Object, e AS EventArgs) _
                Handles MyBase.Load
            Dim oType As Type
            oType = Me.GetType
            Do
                Response.Write(oType.Name & "<BR />")
                oType = oType.BaseType
            Loop While Not oType Is Nothing
        End Sub
    End Class
End Namespace
```

The page produces the following output:

```
Page2_aspx
Page2Class
Page
TemplateControl
Control
Object
```

As the output from these two code examples shows, the Page class derives from the System.Web.UI.TemplateControl class, which defines the functionality common to both the Page class and the UserControl class. Such Page class members as the LoadControl method (which dynamically loads a control at runtime), the AbortTransaction and CommitTransaction events, and the Error event are all inherited from TemplateControl. The TemplateControl class derives from the System.Web.UI.Control class, which defines the members common to all ASP.NET Server Controls. The Control class derives from the Object class, the class from which all .NET reference types are derived directly or indirectly.

Because an object derived from the Page class is globally available whenever ASP.NET is processing a Web Forms page, you do not have to reference the

Page object specifically to access its members. For example, to access the Session property of the Page class, you can use either:

```
Dim oSess As HttpSessionState = Page.Session
```

or:

```
Dim oSess As HttpSessionState = Session
```

In addition to representing the Web Form, the Page object is the container for all controls hosted by the page. All child controls on the page can be accessed through the Page object's Controls collection, which returns a ControlCollection object. For example, the following code iterates the ControlCollection collection and lists the name of each control:

```
Private Sub Page_Load(o As Object, e AS EventArgs)
    Dim ctl As Control
    For each ctl in Controls
        Response.Write(TypeName(ctl) & ": " & ctl.ID & "<BR />")
    Next
End Sub
```

Table 12-1 lists the properties, collections, and methods exposed by the Page class that are documented in this chapter.

Table 12-1. Page class summary

Properties	Collections	Methods	Events
Application	Controls	DataBind	Error
Cache	Validators	FindControl	Init
ClientTarget		HasControls	Load
Context		LoadControl	Unload
EnableViewState		MapPath	
ErrorPage		ResolveUrl	
IsPostBack		Validate	
IsValid			
Request			
Response			
Server			
Session			
SmartNavigation			
Trace			
User			
ViewState			
ViewStateUserKey			

Comments/Troubleshooting

The ASP.NET equivalents of most classic ASP intrinsic objects are returned by properties of the ASP.NET Page class. These properties are shown in Table 12-2.

Table 12-2. ASP.NET equivalents of ASP intrinsic objects

ASP object	Equivalent ASP.NET class	Returned by
Application	HttpApplication and HttpApplicationState	Page.Application property
ASPError	None (ASP.NET uses Structured Exception Handling)	
ObjectContext	HttpContext	Page.Context property
Request	HttpRequest	Page.Request property
Response	HttpResponse	Page.Response property
Server	HttpServerUtility	Page.Server property
Session	HttpSessionState	Page.Session property

In this chapter, we'll use the following code listing as the basis for most examples. Unless otherwise noted, each example will consist of just the Page_Load event handler for that particular example. Any displayed output messages or return values will be shown as the Text property of the ASP.NET Label control named Message or displayed by calling Response.Write:

```
<%@ Page Language="vb" %>
<html>
    <head>
        <script runat="server">
            Sub Page_Load( )
                'Example code will go here
            End Sub
        </script>
    </head>
<body>
    <asp:label id="Message" runat="server"/>
</body>
</html>
```

Properties Reference

Application

HttpApplicationState = Page.Application

Returns an instance of the HttpApplicationState class, which is the equivalent of the ASP intrinsic Application object. An instance of the HttpApplicationState class contains global information that can be shared across multiple sessions and requests within an ASP.NET application. For more information on the HttpApplicationState class and its members, see Chapter 13.

Parameter

HttpApplicationState

A variable of type HttpApplicationState that receives the instance of the HttpApplicationState class.

Example

The following code example uses Page object's Application property to add a name/value pair to the Application object and display the value in a label control. Since all of the properties of the Page object are exposed directly to any code associated with the page, it is not necessary to name the Page class explicitly (i.e., Page.Application) to access the Application property.

```
Sub Page_Load()
    Application("Name") = "John Doe"
    Message.Text = "The value <em>" & CStr(Application("Name")) & _
        "</em> has been added to the Application collection."
End Sub
```

Notes

Although you can retrieve a local object reference to the HttpApplicationState instance for the application, the more common use of this property is to access it directly through the Application property, as shown in the example.

Cache

Cache = Page.Cache

Returns an instance of the Cache class, which represents the cache for an application domain. Using the Cache property, data can be added to and retrieved from the cache.

Parameter

Cache
    A variable of type Cache that will receive the Cache instance.

Example

The following code example adds two name/value pairs to the Cache object using the Cache property of the Page class and displays the values in a label control using the Page object's Cache property:

```
Sub Page_Load(o As Object, e As EventArgs)
    Cache("Name") = "John Doe"
    Cache("Age") = 42
    Message.Text = CStr(Cache.Item("Name")) & " is " & _
        CStr(Cache("Age")) & " years old."
End Sub
```

Notes

Like the Application object, the Cache object is more commonly accessed directly through the Cache property, rather than by obtaining a local object reference to the Cache instance for the application.

Chapter 13 discusses when you might use the ASP.NET Cache rather than the Application state collection, and vice-versa.

The Cache class includes the members shown in Table 12-3.

Table 12-3. Cache class members

Cache member	Description
Add method	Adds an item to the cache
Count property	Indicates the number of items contained in the cache
Get method	Returns an object representing data in the cache with a particular key value
Insert method	Inserts an item into the cache and assigns it a key
Item property	Returns an object representing a cache item based on its key value or sets an item of data in the cache while assigning it a key value
Remove method	Removes an item with a particular key value from the cache

ClientTarget

String = Page.ClientTarget

Gets or sets a string value that allows you to override automatic browser detection in ASP.NET, force the page to be rendered for a browser type configured in *machine.config* or *web.config*, and specified by this property. The available preconfigured values for this property are as follows:

downlevel

The page will be rendered based on the browser capabilities defined for unknown browsers in the <browserCaps> element of *machine.config*.

ie4

The page will be rendered based on the values for Internet Explorer 4.0 configured in the <browserCaps> element of *machine.config*.

ie5

The page will be rendered based on the values for Internet Explorer 5.0 configured in the <browserCaps> element of *machine.config*.

Parameter

String

A string that specifies the alias for the browser capabilities that the page will target.

Example

The following code example initializes the ClientTarget property of the Page class to downlevel, indicating that ASP.NET must render the page for an unknown browser type, which will result in HTML 3.2–compliant output. The example then displays a message indicating whether a set of features is supported. In the case of downlevel, none of the listed features is supported.

```
Sub Page_Load( )
    Page.ClientTarget = "downlevel"
        Message.Text = "Page is set to render for the " & _
    Page.ClientTarget & " alias.<br/>"
    Message.Text &= "Supported features:<br/>"
    Message.Text &= " - JavaScript: " & _
        Request.Browser.JavaScript & "<br/>"
```

```
Message.Text &= " - ActiveX Controls: " & _
    Request.Browser.ActiveXControls & "<br/>"
Message.Text &= " - Frames: " & _
    Request.Browser.Frames & "<br/>"
End Sub
```

Notes

The ClientTarget can also be specified by using the `ClientTarget` attribute of the @ Page directive.

Changing the value of the ClientTarget property in the example to `ie4` will result in output indicating that all of the listed features are supported.

While most server controls render HTML 3.2 for all browsers, the validation controls are an example of controls that render differently, depending on the value of ClientTarget. If the ClientTarget property is set to `downlevel`, then validation is performed on the server side, meaning that if we view the source, no client-side script will perform the validation.

If the ClientTarget is set to `uplevel`, then the validation controls emit client-side JavaScript to perform client-side validation.

Context

```
HttpContext = Page.Context
```

Returns an HttpContext instance containing context information for the current HTTP request.

Parameter

HttpContext
> A variable of type HttpContext that will receive the reference to the current HttpContext instance.

Example

The following code example uses the Context property to return the name of the currently logged in user. This information is also available from the User property of the `Page` class, which is derived from the HttpContext associated with the current request.

```
Sub Page_Load( )
    Message.Text = "Currently logged in as: " & _
        Context.User.Identity.Name
End Sub
```

Notes

A common use of this property is to pass a reference to the HttpContext for the current request to a business object that needs access to the ASP.NET intrinsic objects (Request, Response, etc.). In addition to providing access to the Application, Request, Response, Server, and Session intrinsics, the `HttpContext` class provides access to the Trace and User information for the current HTTP request.

EnableViewState

```
Boolean = Page.EnableViewState
Page.EnableViewState = Boolean
```

Returns or sets a Boolean value that indicates whether the Page maintains its view state and that of server controls it contains. The default value of this property is True, which means that the page maintains its view state.

Parameter

Boolean

A Boolean value that indicates whether the page maintains its view state.

Example

The following code example sets EnableViewState to False using the Enable-ViewState attribute of the @ Page directive and displays its value on the page:

```
<%@ Page Language="vb" EnableViewState="True" %>
<html>
    <head>
        <title></title>
        <script runat="server">
            Sub Page_Load( )
                If Page.EnableViewState = True Then
                    Message.Text = "ViewState is enabled."
                Else
                    Message.Text = "ViewState is disabled."
                End If
            End Sub
        </script>
    </head>
<body>
    <form runat="server">
        <asp:label id="Message" runat="server"/>
    </form>
</body>
</html>
```

Notes

The EnableViewState property can also be specified using the EnableViewState attribute of the @ Page directive, as shown in the example.

Examining a page's HTML source using a browser's View Source feature shows the effect of the EnableViewState property. If the EnableViewState property is set to False, the source will look similar to:

```
<input type="hidden" name="__VIEWSTATE"
       value="dDwxMDA3MzE2MzEyOzs+" />
```

If the EnableViewState property is set to True, the source will look similar to:

```
<input type="hidden" name="__VIEWSTATE"
value="dDwxMDA3MzE2MzEyO3Q8O280O2w8aTwxPjs+O2w8dDw7bDxpPDM+Oz47bDxOPHA8cDxsPF
RleHQ7PjtsPFZhbHVilIG9mIHRoZSBFbmFibGVWaWV3U3RhdGUgcHJvcGVydHkgaXMgVHJ1ZTs
+Pjs+Ozs+Oz4+Oz4=" />
```

The extra characters in the value of the __VIEWSTATE hidden field indicate the view state of the current page. The view state of a page includes the transient properties of server controls, such as BackColor or ForeColor.

Note that pages that do not contain a <form> element with the runat="server" attribute will not save view state, regardless of the value of the EnableViewState property.

ErrorPage

```
String = Page.ErrorPage
Page.ErrorPage = String
```

Returns or sets the name of the page to redirect to in the event of an unhandled page exception.

Parameter

String

A String value that indicates the name of the page to redirect to in the event of an unhandled page exception.

Example

The next example changes the ErrorPage property and shows the executed page when an unhandled exception occurs in the page:

```
Sub Page_Load( )
    Page.ErrorPage = "ErrorPage_Handler.aspx"
    Dim x, y, overflow As Integer
    x = 1
    y = 0
    overflow = x/y
    'This code will not be executed
    Message.Text = "Error Page is " & Page.ErrorPage & "."
End Sub
```

The Page_Load for *ErrorPage_Handler.aspx* follows:

```
Sub Page_Load( )
    Message.Text = "We're sorry. An error occurred during the" & _
        " processing of your request. Please try again later."
End Sub
```

Notes

The ErrorPage property can also be specified using the ErrorPage attribute of the @ Page directive.

IsPostBack

```
Boolean = Page.IsPostBack
```

Returns a Boolean value that indicates if the page is loaded for the first time (False) or is loaded as a result of the client postback (True). This property comes in handy for the logic that needs to be executed the first time the page is executed or every time the page is posted back to itself, depending on how you structure your If statement.

Parameter

Boolean

A Boolean value that indicates if the page is loaded for the first time or is loaded as a result of the client postback.

Example

The next code example uses the IsPostBack property to display different messages in the Label control, depending on whether the page is loaded for the first time or is loaded as a result of the client postback. The first time the page is loaded, the IsPostBack property returns False, causing the string "Non-PostBack" to be displayed. Clicking the button posts the page back to itself, causing IsPostBack to return True and the string "PostBack" to be displayed.

```
<%@ Page Language="vb" %>
<html>
    <head>
        <title></title>
        <script runat="server">
            Sub Page_Load()
                If Page.IsPostBack Then
                    Message.Text = "PostBack"
                Else
                    Message.Text = "Non-PostBack"
                End If
            End Sub
        </script>
    </head>
<body>
    <form runat="server">
        <asp:button id="post" Text="Post page" runat="server"/>
        <asp:label id="Message" runat="server"/>
    </form>
</body>
</html>
```

Notes

The IsPostBack property will return True only for pages that contain a <form> element with the runat="server" attribute and at least one control that causes a postback. This can be a Button control, as shown in the example, or another control, such as a DropDownList control, whose AutoPostBack property is set to True.

IsValid

Boolean = Page.IsValid

Returns a Boolean value, indicating whether any validation controls on the page were unable to successfully validate user input.

Parameter

Boolean

A Boolean indicating whether the validation succeeded.

Example

The example uses the IsValid property to determine whether validation on the current page succeeded, and displays a message:

```vb
<%@ Page Language="vb" %>
<html>
    <head>
        <title></title>
        <script runat="server">
            Sub Page_Load()
                If IsPostBack Then
                    Page.Validate()
                    If Page.IsValid Then
                        Message.Text = "Page is valid."
                    Else
                        Message.Text = "Page is not valid."
                    End If
                End If
            End Sub
        </script>
    </head>
<body>
    <form runat="server">
        Enter your name:
        <asp:textbox id="name" runat="server"/>
        <asp:requiredfieldvalidator
            id="rfvName"
            controltovalidate="name"
            enableclientscript="false"
            errormessage="Required!"
            runat="server"/>
        <br/>
        <asp:button id="submit" Text="Submit" runat="server"/>
        <br/>
        <asp:label id="Message" runat="server"/>
    </form>
</body>
</html>
```

Notes

The IsValid property determines whether the overall validation performed by a form's validator controls has succeeded. If the page has no validator controls, the property's value is always True. Before checking the value of IsValid, you must either call the Page.Validate method, as shown in the example, or have submitted the page with a control (such as a Button, ImageButton, or LinkButton control) whose CausesValidation property is set to True. Otherwise, an exception will occur.

In the example, the EnableClientScript property of the RequiredFieldValidator control is set to False, which disables client-side validation. By default, client-side validation is enabled and the page is never submitted to the server if the validation fails. Uplevel browsers perform validation on the client using client-side scripts, and only when validation succeeds is the page submitted. Only when the page is submitted is the server-side event handler code executed and the message displayed based on the value of the IsValid property.

Checking the IsValid property is important whether client-side validation is enabled, since a malicious client could bypass client-side validation

Request

```
HttpRequest = Page.Request
```

Returns an instance of the HttpRequest class that allows us to access data from the incoming HTTP requests. It's the equivalent of the ASP intrinsic Request object. For more information on the HttpRequest class, see Chapter 16.

Parameter

HttpRequest
> An object of type HttpRequest that contains the data from the incoming HTTP requests.

Example

The following code example uses the ServerVariables collection of the HttpRequest object to display the IP address of the client making the request:

```
Sub Page_Load( )
    Message.Text = "The current request is from: " & _
        CStr(Request.ServerVariables.Item("REMOTE_ADDRESS"))
End Sub
```

Notes

As with the Application and Cache properties, while you can retrieve a local reference to the HttpRequest instance associated with the request, it is more common to access this instance directly through the Request property, as shown in this example.

Response

```
HttpResponse = Page.Response
```

Returns an instance of the HttpResponse class that stores information about the response and allows us to send HTTP response data to a browser. It's the equivalent of the ASP intrinsic Response object. For information on the HttpResponse class, see Chapter 17.

Parameter

HttpResponse
> An object of type HttpResponse that receives the instance of the HttpResponse class.

Example

The following example uses the Response property of the page object to set the ContentType property of the HttpResponse class to text/xml. Setting this property will result in the output of the page being displayed as XML markup in Internet Explorer 5.0 or above.

```
Sub Page_Load( )
    Response.ContentType = "text/xml"
    Message.Text = "This page will be displayed as XML in " & _
        "Internet Explorer 5.0 or above."
End Sub
```

Notes

As with the Application and Cache properties, while you can retrieve a local reference to the HttpResponse instance associated with the request, it is more common to access this instance directly through the Request property, as shown in this example.

Server

HttpServerUtility = Page.Server

Returns an instance of the HttpServerUtility class, which exposes useful methods for working with ASP.NET requests. For more information on the HttpServerUtility class, see Chapter 18.

Parameter

HttpServerUtility
> An object of type HttpServerUtility that may be used to access useful properties and methods exposed by this class.

Example

The following code example uses the Server property to access the HtmlEncode method of the HttpServerUtility class, which allows you to encode HTML tags and characters so that they will be displayed to the user, rather than interpreted and rendered by the browser:

```
Sub Page_Load( )
    Message.Text = Server.HtmlEncode("<em>Hello, World!</em>")
End Sub
```

The HTML rendered from this page would look like the following:

```
<html>
    <head>
        <title>Server property example</title>
    </head>
<body>
    <span id="Message">&lt;em&gt;Hello, World!&lt;/em&gt;</span>
</body>
</html>
```

Notes

As with the Request and Response properties, while you can retrieve a local reference to the HttpServerUtility instance associated with the application, it is more common to access this instance directly through the Server property, as shown in this example.

Session

```
HttpSessionState = Page.Session
```

Returns an object that represents the current user session. A Session object is maintained for each user that requests a page from an ASP.NET application. You can store session-specific data in the Session object and then access it across multiple pages in an ASP.NET application. For more information on the HttpSessionState class, see Chapter 19.

Parameter

HttpSessionState
    An HttpSessionState object that represents the current user session.

Example

The example uses the Session object to display the value of the Mode property, which indicates where session state information is stored:

```
Sub Page_Load( )
    Message.Text = "Current Session State Mode: " &_
            Session.Mode.ToString( )
End Sub
```

Notes

As with the Request and Response properties, while you can retrieve a local reference to the HttpSessionState instance associated with the request, it is more common to access this instance directly through the Session property, as shown in this example.

SmartNavigation

```
Boolean = Page.SmartNavigation
Page.SmartNavigation = Boolean
```

Returns or sets a Boolean indicating whether the SmartNavigation feature is turned on. The SmartNavigation feature, which is compatible only with Internet Explorer, uses <iframe> elements to allow only portions of the page to be refreshed when the page is posted back. This can help eliminate the annoying visual flicker associated with postbacks.

Parameter

Boolean
    A Boolean value that indicates whether or not SmartNavigation is enabled.

Example

The following code example sets the SmartNavigation property to True using the SmartNavigation attribute of the @ Page directive. When the page is posted back, only the current page will be stored in the browser's history, so the Back button will be disabled.

```
<%@ Page Language="vb" SmartNavigation="True" %>
<html>
   <head>
      <title>SmartNavigation property example</title>
      <script runat="server">
         Sub Page_Load( )
            Message.Text = "This Label will change."
            Message2.Text = "This Label will not change."
         End Sub
         Sub UpdateLabel(Sender As Object, e As EventArgs)
            Message.Text = "This Label has changed."
         End Sub
      </script>
   </head>
<body>
   <form runat="server">
      <asp:label id="Message" runat="server"/>
      <asp:button id="update"
         onClick="UpdateLabel"
         text="Click to update label text"
         runat="server"/>
   </form>
   <asp:label id="Message2" runat="server"/>
</body>
</html>
```

Notes

In addition to eliminating flicker when navigating or posting back, Smart-Navigation maintains the current scroll position when a page is posted back and maintains only a single page in the browser's history, which prevents users from clicking the browser's Back button to go to a previous state of the page.

While you can set this property from code, it is recommended that this property be set using the SmartNavigation attribute of the @ Page directive, as shown in this example.

Trace

TraceContext = Page.Trace

Returns the TraceContext object for the current web request. Tracing provides the details about the execution of the web request. The TraceContext class includes the members shown in Table 12-4.

Table 12-4. TraceContext class members

Member	Description
IsEnabled	Indicates whether tracing is enabled for the current page.
TraceMode	A member of the TraceMode enumeration that indicates how items should be sorted. Possible values are SortByCategory and SortByTime. The latter is the default value defined in *machine.config*.
Warn method	Writes a message to the trace log using red text.
Write method	Writes a message to the trace log.

Parameter

TraceContext
   An instance of the TraceContext class.

Example

The example turns tracing on programmatically by using the Trace property of the Page class:

```
Sub Page_Load( )
    If Trace.IsEnabled = True Then
        Message.Text = "Tracing is enabled."
    Else
        Message.Text = "Tracing is not enabled."
    End If
End Sub
```

Notes

As with the Request and Response properties, while you can retrieve a local reference to the TraceContext instance associated with the request, it is more common to access this instance directly through the Trace property, as shown in the preceding example. For more information on application tracing, see Chapter 10.

User

IPrincipal = Page.User

Returns an instance of an object implementing the IPrincipal interface containing security information about the user making the page request. The IPrincipal interface implements the members shown in Table 12-5.

Table 12-5. Iprincipal interface members

Member	Description
Identity property	Returns the Identity object representing the user requesting the page
IsInRole property	Indicates whether the user requesting the page is in a particular role

Parameter

IPrincipal
   An object variable that implements IPrincipal.

Example

The example obtains the user's authentication status and name using the User property and displays it in the browser:

```
Sub Page_Load( )
    Message.Text = "Authenticated: " & _
        User.Identity.IsAuthenticated & "<br/>"
    Message.Text &= "User Name: " & User.Identity.Name
End Sub
```

Notes

For the IPrincipal object returned by the User property to be populated, some form of authentication must be configured in either *machine.config* or *web.config*, and, at a minimum, an authorization rule must be configured that excludes anonymous users. If these conditions are not met, the IsAuthenticated property of the IIdentity object will return False and the Name property will return an empty string.

ViewState

StateBag = Page.ViewState

The ViewState property returns an instance of the StateBag class containing state information for server controls on the page. This StateBag instance can also store arbitrary data that needs to be preserved across multiple requests for the same page.

Parameter

StateBag
> An object of type StateBag that contains the property values for server controls on the page. This StateBag instance can also store arbitrary data that needs to be preserved across multiple requests for the same page.

Example

The following code example sets the ForeColor property of the Message control, and then stores the value of that color in the ViewState StateBag instance. If the page is posted back, the code retrieves the color that was stored, and depending on the name of the color, changes the color from Red to Black, or vice-versa.

```
<%@ Page Language="vb" %>
<html>
    <head>
        <title>ViewState property example</title>
        <script runat="server">
            Sub Page_Load( )
                Dim LocalColor As System.Drawing.Color
                If IsPostBack Then
                    LocalColor = CType(ViewState("LabelColor"), _
                        System.Drawing.Color)
                    If LocalColor.Name = "Black" Then
                        LocalColor = System.Drawing.Color.Red
                    Else
```

```
                    LocalColor = System.Drawing.Color.Black
                End If
                Message.ForeColor = LocalColor
                Message.Text = "Label color is " & LocalColor.Name
                ViewState("LabelColor") = LocalColor
            Else
                Message.ForeColor = System.Drawing.Color.Black
                LocalColor = Message.ForeColor
                Message.Text = "Label color is " & LocalColor.Name
                ViewState("LabelColor") = LocalColor
            End If
        End Sub
    </script>
  </head>
<body>
  <form runat="server">
    <asp:button id="button"
      text="Click to change label color"
      runat="server"/>
    <asp:label id="Message" runat="server"/>
  </form>
</body>
</html>
```

Notes

ViewState, in addition to managing state for server controls automatically, is a convenient place for ambient page state that needs to be maintained from request to request. In addition to storing primitive data types such as integers and strings, the StateBag class can be used to store objects, as long as those objects support serialization, as does the Color structure in the example. When you store an object that supports serialization in ViewState, the object's state is automatically serialized into a form that can be stored in ViewState and deserialized into an object instance when you reference the object again.

Because ViewState does not store type information with the object, you must cast the object retrieved from ViewState to the correct type. In the case of the example, this type is System.Drawing.Color.

Finally, think carefully before storing large objects (such as datasets) in ViewState. Because ViewState is stored as a hidden form field, it is sent to the browser with each request. Storing large objects in ViewState will result in slower page load times.

ViewStateUserKey

```
String = Page.ViewStateUserKey
Page.ViewStateUserKey = String
```

The ViewStateUserKey property sets or returns a string representing a unique identifier for the ViewState for a given request. This property, which must be set in the Page_Init event handler, prevents 1-click attacks (in which a user is induced to click on a link or to take some other action while logged into a site, which would result in their account being used to purchase goods for another person or account) by assigning a unique identifier, such as the user's Session ID to the property. When the request is processed, this value is included in the machine authentication check performed on the ViewState, so if a different value is found during the machine authentication check on postback, an exception is thrown.

Parameter

String

A String containing a unique identifier for the current user.

Example

The following code example sets the ViewStateUserKey property of the Message control to the SessionID of the current user's session. This value is then integrated into the ViewState machine authentication check. If the page is posted back from a user or page with a different SessionID, the machine authentication check will fail, and an exception will be raised.

```
<%@ Page Language="vb" %>
<html>
    <head>
        <title>ViewStateUserKey property example</title>
        <script runat="server">
            Sub Page_Init( )
                Page.ViewStateUserKey = Session.SessionID( )
            End Sub
        </script>
    </head>
<body>
    <form id="Form1" method="post" runat="server">
        <table id="Table1" cellSpacing="1" cellPadding="1" width="100%"
border="1" runat="server">
            <tr>
                <td>
                    <asp:Label id="Label1"
                        runat="server">First Name:</asp:Label></td>
                <td>
                    <asp:TextBox id="FirstName"
                        runat="server"></asp:TextBox></td>
            </tr>
            <tr>
                <td>
                    <asp:Label id="Label2"
                        runat="server">Last Name:</asp:Label></td>
                <td>
                    <asp:TextBox id="LastName"
                        runat="server"></asp:TextBox></td>
            </tr>
            <tr>
                <td>
                    <asp:Button id="Submit"
                        runat="server" Text="Submit"></asp:Button></td>
                <td><input type="reset" value="Reset" runat="server"></td>
            </tr>
        </table>
```

```
        </form>
    </body>
</html>
```

Notes

For the ViewStateUserKey field to be effective, the EnableViewStateMac property for the page must be set to True, which is the default.

Collections Reference

Controls

ControlCollection = Page.Controls

Provides access to the ControlCollection instance associated with the page, with which you can add or manipulate controls at runtime.

Parameter

ControlCollection
    An object of type ControlCollection containing the controls associated with the page.

Example

The code example uses the Controls property to display the Count property of the ControlCollection class instance associated with the page. It then adds a new Label control to the collection and displays the updated Count property by using the new label.

```
Sub Page_Load( )
    Message.Text = "There are currently " & Controls.Count & _
        " controls on the page.<br/>"
    Dim Message2 As New Label
    Controls.AddAt(Controls.Count - 1, Message2)
    Message2.Text = "There are now " & Controls.Count & _
        " controls on the page."
End Sub
```

Notes

As with the Session and Trace properties, while you can retrieve a local reference to the Controls collection associated with the page, it is more common to access this instance directly through the Controls property, as shown in the example.

Note that when adding a control to a page that already contains controls, using the AddAt method of the ControlCollection class allows more precise placement of the control when compared to the Add method, which simply places the control at the end of the collection. In the example, using the Add method would result in the output from the added Label control appearing after the page's closing </html> tag, which is not well-formed HTML and could cause the page to render incorrectly in some browsers.

Validators

ValidatorCollection = `Page.Validators`

Returns an instance of the `ValidatorCollection` class containing all the validator controls contained on the requested page. We can access each validator control by iterating the ValidatorCollection collection.

Parameter

ValidatorCollection
    An object variable of type ValidatorCollection.

Example

The code example displays a Textbox control with a RequiredFieldValidator and RegularExpressionValidator control assigned to it. In Page_Load, the code iterates through the ValidatorCollection returned by the Validators property and displays the ID and ErrorMessage property of each validator in the collection:

```
<%@ Page Language="vb" %>
<html>
   <head>
      <title></title>
      <script runat="server">
         Sub Page_Load( )
            Dim Validator as BaseValidator
            For Each Validator in Validators
               Message.Text &= Validator.ID & " error message: "
               Message.Text &= Validator.ErrorMessage & "<br/>"
            Next
         End Sub
      </script>
   </head>
<body>
   <form runat="server">
      Phone: <asp:textbox id="phone" runat="server"/>
      <asp:requiredfieldvalidator
         id="rfvPhone"
         controltovalidate="phone"
         display="dynamic"
         errormessage="Required!"
         runat="server"/>
      <asp:regularexpressionvalidator
         id="revPhone"
         controltovalidate="phone"
         display="dynamic"
         validationexpression="^[2-9]\d{2}-\d{3}-\d{4}$"
         errormessage="Enter a phone number in the form xxx-xxx-xxxx"
            runat="server"/>
      <br/>
      <asp:button id="submit" text="Submit" runat="server"/>
   </form>
   <br/>
```

```
<asp:label id="Message" runat="server"/>
</body>
</html>
```

Notes

Because we are displaying only properties from the validator controls that are inherited from the BaseValidator control (from which all validation controls are derived), we don't need to cast the validator to its specific type before accessing the properties. If, however, we wanted to display a property that was specific to the type of validator used (such as the ValidationExpression property of the RegularExpressionValidator class), we would need to cast the control to the correct type. In Visual Basic .NET, this is done using the CType keyword.

Methods Reference

DataBind

```
Page.DataBind()
```

Evaluates and resolves any data-binding expressions in the page. It also calls DataBind on all child controls.

Parameters

None.

Example

The following code example uses a data-binding expression to set the ForeColor attribute of a label control tag to the value of local variable named color. When the DataBind method is called in Page_Load, the value of the Color variable is assigned to the ForeColor attribute (which is effectively the same as setting the ForeColor property in code):

```
<%@ Page Language="vb" %>
<html>
   <head>
      <title></title>
      <script runat="server">
         Dim Color As System.Drawing.Color = System.Drawing.Color.Red
         Sub Page_Load()
            Message.Text = "ForeColor is: " & Color.Name
            DataBind()
         End Sub
      </script>
   </head>
<body>
   <asp:label id="Message" ForeColor="<%# Color %>" runat="server"/>
</body>
</html>
```

Notes

If you want to perform data binding on a specific control on the page, such as a DataGrid or DataList control, it may be more efficient to call DataBind on that control rather than on the page, since calling it on the control will avoid any overhead in calling DataBind on controls for which data binding is not needed.

FindControl

```
Control = Page.FinderControl(String)
```

Returns a reference to the control object whose name corresponds to a search string. The FindControl method is a member of the base Control class.

Parameters

Control
> An instance of the Control class that represents the control that is found using the FindControl method. This control must be cast to the correct control type to access members that are specific to the control type.

String
> A string containing the programmatic identifier of the control. This value is the same as the ID attribute of a declarative control or, in the case of controls created at runtime, is the same as the object name defined for the control.

Example

The example finds a control using its ID and changes its background color:

```
Sub Page_Load( )
    Dim TheControl As Control = FindControl("Message")
    If Not TheControl Is Nothing Then
        Dim TheLabel As Label = CType(TheControl, Label)
        TheLabel.Text = "Found the label named Message!"
        TheLabel.BackColor = System.Drawing.Color.Blue
    End If
End Sub
```

Notes

The FindControl method, which is inherited from the Control class (from which the Page class is derived), is useful when dealing with nested controls or user controls that need to manipulate a control in their parent page. For example, code in a user control could call FindControl on the page containing the user control to locate and manipulate a control contained within the page (but outside the user control).

HasControls

```
Boolean = Page.HasControls()
```

Returns a Boolean value that indicates whether the page contains child controls.

Parameter

Boolean

A Boolean value that indicates whether the page contains child controls.

Example

The code example displays a message indicating whether the page has controls in its Controls collection, based on the value returned by HasControls:

```
Sub Page_Load( )
    If Page.HasControls = True Then
        Message.Text = "The page contains controls."
    Else
        Message.Text = "The page does not contain controls."
    End If
End Sub
```

LoadControl

ObjControl = Page.LoadControl(*StrPath*)

Returns an instance of the user control defined in the *strPath* user control file. This allows dynamic loading of user controls instead of using the @ Register directive.

Parameters

objControl

An object of type Control that represents the user control specified in the given path.

strPath

The virtual path to a user control file.

Example

The example uses the LoadControl to load a user control at runtime and adds it to the page's Controls collection:

```
Sub Page_Load( )
    Dim Hello As UserControl = LoadControl("hello.ascx")
    Page.Controls.Add(Hello)
End Sub
```

The user control *hello.ascx* is as follows:

```
<h1>Hello, World!</h1>
```

MapPath

String = Page.MapPath(*virtualPath*)

Returns the physical path that corresponds to a given virtual path.

Parameters

String

A String containing the physical path that corresponds to *virtualPath*.

virtualPath
>A string containing an absolute or relative virtual path.

Example

The example maps the virtual path of the named page to its physical path:

```
Sub Page_Load( )
    Message.Text = MapPath("MapPath.aspx")
End Sub
```

Notes

The Page.MapPath method duplicates the functionality of the Server.MapPath method.

ResolveUrl

```
String = Path.ResolveUrl(strRelativeUrl)
```

Returns an absolute URL corresponding to a relative URL.

Parameters

String
>A string containing the absolute URL.

strRelativeUrl
>A relative URL.

Example

The example maps the current relative URL to an absolute URL:

```
Sub Page_Load( )
    Message.Text = Page.ResolveUrl("ResolveUrl.aspx")
End Sub
```

Validate

```
Page.Validate()
```

Invokes the validation logic for each validator control on the page. When this method is invoked, it iterates the Page object's ValidatorCollection collection and executes the validation logic associated with each validator control.

Example

See the example for the IsValid property.

Notes

The Validate method is called automatically when the user clicks any HTML or ASP button control whose CausesValidation property is True.

Events Reference

Error

```
Sub Page_Error(Sender As Object, e As Event Args)
  'error handling code
End Sub
```

The Error event is fired when an unhandled exception occurs on the page. If no event handler is defined for this event, the Application_Error event is fired. If the exception is still not handled, control is passed to the page (or pages) defined in the <customErrors> element in *web.config*.

Parameters

Sender
> An argument containing information about the object that raised the event.

e
> An object of type EventArgs containing additional information about the event.

Example

The following code example deliberately causes an overflow exception and then handles that exception in the Page_Error handler, displaying the text of the exception and then clearing it:

```
Sub Page_Load( )
    Dim x, y, overflow As Integer
    x = 1
    y = 0
    overflow = x / y
End Sub

Sub Page_Error( )
    Response.Write(Server.GetLastError.ToString( ))
    Server.ClearError
End Sub
```

Notes

The current exception is obtained using the GetLastError method of the Server class. Once you've finished with your error handling, you can either clear the exception by calling Server.ClearError, as shown in the example, or allow the exception to bubble up to the next level of error handling.

Note that the *Sender* and *e* arguments are optional for this event, as shown in the example.

When the AutoEventWireup attribute of the @ Page directive is set to True (the default), ASP.NET will automatically call the event handler for this event, as long as it has the correct Page_Error signature.

Init

```
Sub Page_Init(Sender As Object, e As EventArgs)
  'initialization code
End Sub
```

Parameters

Sender

An argument containing information about the object that raised the event.

e

An object of type EventArgs containing additional information about the event.

Example

The code example initializes a variable for setting the ForeColor property of a label in Page_Init, and then modifies that value to set the ForeColor property of another label in Page_Load:

```
<%@ Page Language="vb" %>
<html>
  <head>
    <title>Init event example</title>
    <script runat="server">
      Dim TheColor As System.Drawing.Color
      Sub Page_Init()
        TheColor = System.Drawing.Color.Red
      End Sub
      Sub Page_Load()
        Message.ForeColor = TheColor
        Message.Text = "The color of the text was set in Page_Init."
        TheColor = System.Drawing.Color.Blue
        Message2.ForeColor = TheColor
        Message2.Text = "The color of the text was set in Page_Load."
      End Sub
    </script>
  </head>
<body>
  <asp:label id="Message" runat="server"/>
  <br/>
  <asp:label id="Message2" runat="server"/>
</body>
</html>
```

Notes

The *Sender* and *e* arguments are optional for this event, as shown in the example.

When the AutoEventWireup attribute of the @ Page directive is set to True (the default), ASP.NET will automatically call the event handler for this event, as long as it has the signature Page_Init.

Load

```
Sub Page_Load(Sender As Object, e As EventArgs)
  'code
End Sub
```

Fired when the page is loaded. Since this event is fired on every page request, we can add any initialization code that needs to be executed at the page level, including the initialization of the page's child controls. When the Load event fires, the page's view state information is also accessible.

The Load event is passed the following arguments by ASP.NET:

Sender
> An argument containing information about the object that raised the event.

e
> An object of type EventArgs containing additional information about the event.

Example

See the example for Init.

Notes

Note that the *Sender* and *e* arguments are optional for this event, as shown in the example.

When the AutoEventWireup attribute of the @ Page directive is set to True (the default), ASP.NET will automatically call the event handler for this event, as long as it has the correct Page_Load event signature.

Unload

```
Sub Page_Unload(Sender As Object, e As EventArgs)
  'cleanup code
End Sub
```

Fired when the page is unloaded from memory. Since this event is fired before the page is unloaded, we can perform cleanup operations, such as closing open files and database connections.

The Unload event is passed the following arguments by ASP.NET:

Sender
> An argument containing information about the object that raised the event.

e
> An object of type EventArgs containing additional information about the event.

Example

The example demonstrates the Unload event by closing a file that was opened for display in the Page_Load event handler:

```
Dim TheFile As System.IO.StreamReader
Sub Page_Load( )
```

```
    TheFile = System.IO.File.OpenText(MapPath("Init.aspx"))
    Message.Text = "<pre>" & _
        Server.HtmlEncode(TheFile.ReadToEnd( )) & "</pre>"
End Sub

Sub Page_Unload( )
    TheFile.Close( )
End Sub
```

Notes

While the Unload event is useful for performing page-level cleanup tasks, for resources such as databases, for which it is possible that an exception will interrupt the normal flow of page processing, it may be better to place the cleanup code for that resource in the Finally block of a Try...Catch...Finally statement, which will ensure that the cleanup code is always executed. For more information on Try...Catch...Finally, see Chapter 10.

Note that the *Sender* and *e* arguments are optional for this event, as shown in the example.

When the AutoEventWireup attribute of the @ Page directive is set to True (the default), ASP.NET will automatically call the event handler for this event, as long as it has the signature Page_Unload.

13

The HttpApplicationState
Class

Developers who are new to web-based development encounter several challenges. Among the most serious is the realization that rather than a single monolithic application, web-based applications are just a series of pages. A web server is like an unusually inattentive waiter. Imagine sitting down for dinner and placing your order for drinks. When you next see the waiter, he asks you again what you would like to drink, as if he has never seen you before. Each request to the web browser is seen as a completely new request, totally unrelated to any previous request.

Several problems with the way web-based applications are structured need to be resolved:

- Session data (data specific to a single user across all pages) needs to be available. While it is always a good idea to minimize session state, it is generally not possible to completely eliminate session state.

- Global data (data required across all pages and to all users) needs to be exposed. Traditional rich-client applications use global variables to store needed data application-wide. Classes instantiated on one page are not available to other pages, so creating global classes is not a solution.

Session data in ASP.NET can be managed in the HttpSessionState class, which will be covered in Chapter 19. Global data can be stored in the HttpApplicationState class, which is covered in this chapter.

ASP.NET creates the illusion that pages are grouped into an application. An instance of the HttpApplicationState class is created the first time any client requests a URL resource from within the virtual directory of a particular application. The HttpContext class (covered in Chapter 14) exposes a property named Application that provides access to the HttpApplicationState class for the application. The Application property and the HttpApplicationState object it returns are also available from the Page class. Since each ASP.NET page inherits from the Page class, the Application property is available to code on every page.

While this chapter covers the `HttpApplicationState` class, ASP.NET offers an alternative way to store information with an application global scope. The `Cache` class allows a developer to store data with an application scope. In addition to caching page output (a topic covered in Chapter 3), ASP.NET allows the developer to store other information within the Cache—in some ways similar to the way information can be stored in the `HttpApplicationState` class. There are, however, significant differences:

- Information stored in the HttpApplicationState object is stored for the life of the application. Information stored in the Cache may be stored for the life of the application (and in any event, may survive at most for the lifetime of the application), but might be purged sooner. The ASP.NET runtime can purge any cached item at any time if system memory becomes scarce. Cached items that are seldom used or unimportant (as the ASP.NET runtime defines these terms) are discarded using a technique called scavenging.

- Information stored in the Cache can be invalidated based upon a specific date and time or a time span. HttpApplicationState has no such ability.

- The developer can supply dependency rules to force the Cache to be refreshed. For instance, you can use a Rube Goldberg-like setup, for which you cache a dataset and use a trigger in SQL Server to modify a file in the filesystem on the web server whenever the underlying table is modified. The cache for a given item can be invalidated based upon that file changing. Thus, you can cache a dataset and have the cached dataset refreshed whenever the underlying SQL Server table is changed. This is not possible with information stored in the HttpApplicationState object.

One significant limitation of both the Cache and the HttpApplicationState objects is that they are not shared across servers in a web farm. While classic ASP programmers will not be surprised by this, ASP.NET programmers who are familiar with the HttpSessionState object might be surprised, since in ASP.NET, session state *can* be shared across a server farm—either in a state server or a special SQL Server database. While having cached items available across all servers on a web farm would be convenient, the nature of what is stored in the HttpApplicationState object makes the lack of a shared data store less critical.

The implications of the difference between HttpApplicationState and the Cache are clear:

- Large chunks of information that might be important should be stored in the Cache. There is little harm in caching something because if it is not used and the memory is needed, the item will be scavenged and the memory used by it freed for the more pressing need.

- Information that can change frequently throughout the life of the application should be stored in the Cache rather than the HttpApplicationState object.

- Information that is stable during the life of the application is best stored in the HttpApplicationState object.

- Information that must always be available and must not be purged should be stored in the HttpApplicationState object rather than the Cache.

- The Cache class is safe for multithreaded operations and does not require separate synchronization, unlike the Application collection (see the method references for the Lock and UnLock methods later in this chapter).

Classic ASP developers often used the Application object to store things like database connection strings. In ASP.NET, there is another alternative for storing small, possibly sensitive bits of information like connection strings. Inside the configuration files for the machine or applications, you can place values called appSettings within the <configuration> tag. For instance:

```
<appSettings>
   <add key="TestKey" value="TestValue" />
</appSettings>
```

Multiple add tags can be placed in the configuration file. To retrieve the value within code, you the System.Configuration.ConfigurationSettings class. Specifically, to retrieve the value saved in the TestKey key above, use the following code:

```
localVar = ConfigurationSettings.AppSettings("TestKey")
```

While you can place the appSettings section in *web.config* or *machine.config*, sensitive values are better stored in the *machine.config* file. *machine.config* is not located in a folder that is in any way mapped within the web-accessible space. Of course, this solution for storing application-level information is really only suitable for static information that does not need to change under program control as the application is running. Often, you can use AppSettings and Application state together, caching the value from AppSettings within the Application object. If a setting with the same key is contained in both the *machine.config* and *web.config* file, the value in *web.config* will be the value returned for the setting.

Much of HttpApplicationState will be familiar to classic ASP developers. The visible additions and changes from classic ASP are not dramatic. Most importantly, virtually all existing classic ASP code dealing with the Application object will work in ASP.NET.

When the first client requests a URL from the application, the Application object's start event is fired. This event can be handled by creating an event handler in the *global.asax* file (the ASP.NET equivalent of *global.asa*) with the following signature:

```
Sub Application_OnStart( )
   'Application initialization code
End Sub
```

The Application start event is called only once within the lifetime of an application. This is where you would usually set Application variables. When the Application ends, a similar event is called with the following signature:

```
Sub Application_OnEnd( )
   'Application cleanup code
End Sub
```

In the Application end event, you would dispose of any resources created in the Application start event. There are a few limitations to what you can do in the Application-level events, since the Response, Session, and Request objects are all unavailable.

The fact that the Application start event is called once within the lifetime of an application was mentioned above. However, what exactly is the lifetime of an application? Whenever the web server starts up, the first client to request a URL from an application marks the beginning of the application's lifetime. Similarly, as the web server stops, either because the underlying service is stopped or the server itself is restarted, the application's lifetime ends. Thus, can you presume that unless the web service restarts or the server itself restarts, the application will continue running? The short answer is "No."

The longer answer is that to ensure that the Application start and Application end events called are coherent (i.e., that code has not been added to Application_End that would require changes to Application_Start after it had already fired, or vice-versa), any time the *global.asax* is changed, the ASP.NET framework detects that the file has changed. Upon sensing the file change, the framework completes any current requests and fires the Application end event (as it existed before the change to *global.asax*). Once the Application end event has fired, the application restarts, flushing all application information and client state information. When the next incoming client request is received, the ASP.NET framework reparses and recompiles the *global.asax* file and raises the Application start event as it appears in the newly saved version of *global.asax*. The moral of this story is that changes to the *global.asax* file should be infrequent, presuming the application must be available 24/7.

One question that sometimes arises is, "Can the Application state of one application be accessed from within another application?" The short answer is "No." The longer answer is that if the other application cooperates, you can create a page in one application that can be called by making an HTTP Request from the other application. There is no support within the ASP.NET Framework to do this explicitly.

Items can be stored in the Application collection in one of four ways:

- By calling the Add method, passing in the name (or key) to assign to the item, and the item's value. This value can be of any type supported by the CLR, including object instances, which are serialized automatically before being stored.
- By calling the Set method, passing in the name (or key) to assign to the item, and the item's value. This value can be any type supported by the CLR, including object instances, which are automatically serialized before being stored.
- By explicitly referring to the Item property, passing a name or index to assign to the new item.
- By implicitly referring to the Item property, passing a name to assign to the new item. This was the most common technique used in classic ASP.

Items can be accessed in one of four ways:

- By retrieving and iterating over the collection of keys in the Application collection (see the Keys collection description for an example).
- By calling the Get method, passing the name of the item to retrieve.

- By explicitly referring to the Item property, passing the name of the item to retrieve.
- By implicitly referring to the Item property, passing the name of the item to retrieve. This was the most common technique used in classic ASP.

Items can be removed from the Application collection in one of several ways:

- By calling the Clear method (clears all items).
- By calling the RemoveAll method (removes all items).
- By calling the Remove method, passing the name of the item to remove.
- By calling the RemoveAt method, passing the index of the item to remove.

Table 13-1 lists the properties, collections, and methods exposed by the HttpApplicationState class.

Table 13-1. HttpApplicationState class summary

Properties	Collections	Methods	Events[a]
Count	AllKeys	Add	Start
Item	Contents	Clear	End
	Keys	Get	
	StaticObjects	GetKey	
		Lock	
		Remove	
		RemoveAll	
		RemoveAt	
		Set	
		Unlock	
		Events	
		Start	
		End	

[a]Events are exposed by the HttpApplication class rather than the HttpApplicationState class.

Comments/Troubleshooting

Understanding the scope of the Application collection for a given application is important. As mentioned above, the Application object is created the first time a client requests a URL within the application. The boundary of that ASP.NET application is defined by the boundary of an IIS application; the boundary of the ASP.NET application includes all of the ASP.NET pages within a single IIS Application and all of its subfolders and virtual directories. It does not, however, include any subfolders that are defined as IIS Applications. Figure 13-1 illustrates the different folder types in IIS. In Figure 13-1, the *SubApp* subfolder is a child folder of the *Chapter_13* application and shares Application state with it. If, however, the *SubApp* folder is configured as an IIS Application (by accessing the Virtual Directory tab of the Properties dialog for the folder and clicking the Create button in the Application Settings section), it will then define its own application boundaries, which will not be shared with the parent *Chapter_ 13* application.

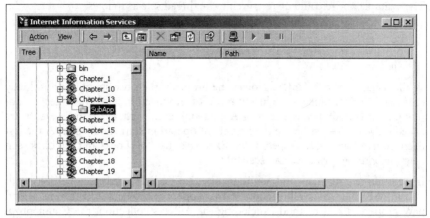

Figure 13-1. IIS folder types

Application
Class

In classic ASP, a big no-no was storing non-thread–safe COM objects (which meant any COM object written in Visual Basic) in the Application collection. This was because such components would force IIS to process requests to the Application that stored the COM object only from the same thread that created the object, which substantially limited scalability. In ASP.NET, this is less of an issue, since all managed .NET components can be stored safely in the Application collection without having an impact on scalability due to threading model considerations.

When accessing any resource potentially shared by many clients, one concern is the synchronization of access to that resource. For instance, imagine that you declare a variable in the application collection to track the number of users currently logged into your application. To do so, in your Session start event handler (also defined in the *global.asax* file and covered completely in Chapter 19), you can place code such as this:

```
LocalVal = Application("Counter")
Application("Counter") = localVal + 1
```

This contrived example (don't use it in your application) shows a problem that can occur with global variables shared by multiple threads. Imagine that two sessions are created simultaneously. Each session gets its local copy of the Application variable, which will be the same since they were requested simultaneously. Then each thread sets the Application variable to its own local value plus one. In the end, though two clients incremented the value of our counter, the value will increase by only one.

Fortunately, a solution is provided within the HttpApplicationState class. The Lock and UnLock methods allow a developer to synchronize access to shared resources. Lock and UnLock must be called in matched pairs. The Lock method is entered only when no other client executes code between calls to Lock and

UnLock. Win32 programmers may recognize the similarity between the use of Lock and Unlock in the HttpApplicationState class and Win32 critical sections.

The example above could be rewritten to be thread safe as follows:

```
Application.Lock( )
LocalVal = Application("Counter")
Application("Counter") = LocalVal + 1
Application.UnLock( )
```

While using Lock and UnLock solves the problem, their use should be absolutely essential. For instance, synchronization of Application-level variables is not required in the Application start or Application end event, since these events are called only once—just before the first client operation starts and just after the last client operation ends, respectively. Excessive use of Lock and UnLock can degrade both performance and scalability.

In addition to properties and methods provided for backwards compatibility with classic ASP, the ASP.NET version of the Application object adds several useful new properties and methods, including the AllKeys collection, the Count property, and the Clear, Get, GetKey, RemoveAll, RemoveAt, and Set methods.

In this chapter, we'll use the following code listing as the basis for most examples in the chapter. Unless otherwise noted, each example consists of just the Page_Load event handler for that particular example. Any output messages or return values displayed are shown as the Text property of the ASP.NET Label control named Message or displayed by calling Response.Write.

```
<%@ Page Language="vb" %>
<html>
    <head>
        <script runat="server">
            Sub Page_Load( )
                'Example code will go here
            End Sub
        </script>
    </head>
<body>
    <asp:label id="Message" runat="server"/>
</body>
</html>
```

Properties Reference

Count

Integer = Application.Count

Returns an integer containing the number of items currently in the Application collection. The Count member is derived from the ICollection interface, which is implemented by the HttpApplicationState class.

Parameter

Integer

An Integer variable that will receive the Count property value.

Example

The example adds two values to the Application collection, displays the count of items in the Application collection, and then uses the Count property as a looping control value to display each item:

```
Sub Page_Load( )
    Application.Clear( )
    Application("foo") = "Hello, "
    Application("bar") = "World!"
    Message.Text = "The Application collection contains " & _
        Application.Count & " items: "
        Dim I as Integer
        For I = 0 To Application.Count - 1
            Message.Text &= Application(I)
        Next
End Sub
```

Notes

The Count property is new for ASP.NET. In addition to using the Count property for looping through the Application collection, you can use the property to keep track of how many items the Application stores at any given time. For example, you could write this information to a log for later review.

Item

```
Object = Application.Item(ByVal name As String)
Application.Item(ByVal name As String) = Object
Object = Application.Item(ByVal index As Integer)
Application.Item(ByVal index As Integer) = Object
```

Returns or sets an Object associated with a particular name or index.

Parameters

Object

A variable of any type (since all .NET types are ultimately derived from object) that will receive or set the item's value.

name

A string argument containing the text key to apply to the item (or by which to retrieve the item).

index

An integer argument containing the index of the item whose value will be retrieved or modified.

Example

The example sets the values of two items in the Application collection. If these items do not already exist in the collection, they will be added. The example then displays the two values.

```
Sub Page_Load( )
    Application.Clear( )
    Application.Item("foo") = "foo"
    Application.Item("foo2") = "foo2"
    Message.Text = Application.Item("foo") & "<br/>"
    Message.Text &= Application.Item(1)
End Sub
```

Notes

The Item property is accessed implicitly when using the syntax:

```
Application("foo") = "foo"
```

This syntax is often seen in classic ASP code. Explicitly referencing the Item property is not required, but listing it may make your code more readable and understandable than accessing it implicitly.

Note that an index may be used as an argument only when modifying a value, not when creating a new item, and the index must be less than the number of items in the Application collection, or an exception will be thrown.

Collections Reference

AllKeys

```
Dim StateVars(Application.Count) As String
StateVars = Application.AllKeys
```

Returns a string array of key names stored in the HttpApplicationState object.

Parameter

StateVars
    A variable of type String array that will receive the array of key names.

Example

The example displays all keys of data stored to the Application object:

```
Sub Page_Load( )
    Dim I as Integer
    Dim StateVars(Application.Count - 1) As String
    StateVars = Application.AllKeys
    For I = 0 to StateVars.Length - 1
        Message.Text = Message.Text + StateVars(I) + "<br/>"
    Next I
End Sub
```

Notes

This property provides a list of key names assigned to all current Application variables.

Contents

```
HttpApplicationState = Application.Contents
```

Returns a reference to the current HttpApplicationState instance.

Parameter

HttpApplicationState
> A variable of type HttpApplicaitonState that will receive the Contents reference.

Example

The example below calls the RemoveAll method through the Contents collection reference and then writes a message:

```
Sub Page_Load( )
Application.Contents.RemoveAll( )
Message.Text = "Removed all items from current Application."
End Sub
```

Application
Class

Notes

This property is provided for backward compatibility with classic ASP. Properties such as the Item property and methods such as Remove and RemoveAll were accessed via the Contents property in classic ASP. In new ASP.NET development, you should access these members directly. For example, instead of calling the RemoveAll method through the Contents property, you can call RemoveAll method directly:

```
Application.RemoveAll( )
```

Keys

```
KeysCollection = Application.Keys
```

Returns a NameObjectCollectionBase.KeysCollection containing the string keys associated with all values stored in the Application collection.

Parameter

KeysCollection
> A variable of type NameObjectCollectionBase.KeysCollection that will receive the Keys property value.

Example

The example loops through the collection of keys in the Application collection, and then displays the key name and the value associated with it by using the Text property of the Message control:

```
Sub Page_Load( )
    Dim Key As String
```

```
      Message.Text = "Application Keys:"
      For Each Key in Application.Keys
         Message.Text &= "<br/>Key:   " & Key
         Message.Text &= "<br/>Value:   " & Application(Key)
      Next
   End Sub
```

Notes

The Keys property provides one of many ways to iterate over the contents of the Application collection.

StaticObjects

HttpStaticObjectsCollection = Application.StaticObjects

Returns an HttpStaticObjectsCollection containing all objects instantiated in *global.asax* using the <object runat="server"> syntax whose scope attribute is set to Application.

Parameter

HttpStaticObjectsCollection
   A variable of type HttpStaticObjectsCollection that will receive the StaticObjects property value.

Example

The example uses the Count property of the HttpStaticObjectsCollection class to display the number of objects in the current application declared with the <object scope="Application" runat="server"/> syntax in *global.asax*. It then checks the type of each object, and if it is a Web TextBox control, adds it to the Controls collection of the current page.

```
   Sub Page_Load()
      Message.Text = "There are " & Application.StaticObjects.Count & _
         " objects declared with the " & _
         "&lt;object runat=&quot;server&quot;&gt; syntax " & _
         "in Application scope."
      Dim myobj As Object
      For Each myObj in Application.StaticObjects
         If myObj.Value.GetType.ToString() = _
            "System.Web.UI.WebControls.TextBox" Then
            Page.Controls.Add(myObj.Value)
         End If
      Next
   End Sub
```

Notes

This property is provided for backward compatibility with classic ASP. You should think carefully before instantiating objects with Session or Application scope because of the impact such objects have on resource usage and application scalability. In most cases, it is advisable to limit objects to page scope.

Note that each object in the collection is represented by the DictionaryEntry structure, so its key and value are not directly accessible. To access the key and/or value, use the Key and/or Value members of the DictionaryEntry structure.

Methods Reference

Add

```
Application.Add(ByVal name As String, ByVal value As Object)
```

Adds a value to the Application collection.

Parameter

name

> A variable of type String that specifies the name of the item to be added to the Application collection.

value

> A variable of type Object that contains the value for the item to be added to the Application collection.

Example

The example adds an item to the Application collection and then displays it:

```
Sub Page_Load( )
    Application.Add("Added", "AddedValue")
    Message.Text = Application("Added")
End Sub
```

Notes

The Add method, which is new in ASP.NET, provides a technique for adding items to the Application collection that is consistent with the technique used for adding items to other .NET collections. Of course, the classic ASP syntax of directly indexing the Application object by using the key name of index works correctly as well.

Clear

```
Application.Clear( )
```

Clears the contents of the Application collection.

Parameters

None.

Example

The example clears the contents of the Application collection and writes a message to the Text property of the Message control that includes the current count of the collection, which should be 0:

```
Sub Page_Load( )
    Application.Clear( )
```

```
    Message.Text = "There are " & Application.Count & _
        " items in the Application collection."
End Sub
```

Notes

The Clear method, which is new for ASP.NET, clears only the contents of the Application collection itself. It does not clear the contents of the StaticObjects collection.

Get

```
Application.Get(ByVal name As String)
Application.Get(ByVal Index As Integer)
```

Gets an element of the Application collection either by name or ordinal position (index) within the Application collection. Generally, the name is used in calls to Get unless you need to get members of the collection inside a loop.

Parameters

name
> A variable of type String that specifies the name of the item to be retrieved from the Application collection.

Index
> A variable of type Integer that specifies the index of the item to be retrieved from the Application collection.

Example

The example below sets and gets a value from the Application collection. It also uses the Get method to write a message to the Text property of the Message control that includes the current value of the newly added element of the Application collection.

```
Sub Page_Load( )
    Application("GetTest") = "Got it!"
    Message.Text = "GetTest = " & Application.Get("GetTest")
End Sub
```

Notes

You can see whether a named value is saved in the Application collection by checking to ensure that its value is not null, as shown in the following code:

```
If Not Application("Foo") is Nothing then
    Message.Text = "Foo is set to " & Application.Get("Foo")
End If
```

GetKey

```
Application.GetKey(ByVal Index As Integer)
```

Retrieves the key name corresponding to the index of a data item stored to the Application object.

Parameter

Index

A variable of type Integer that specifies the index of the key to be retrieved from the Application collection.

Example

The example removes all values from the Application collection in order to start from a known state. Next, it writes a single value to the Application collection. Finally, it saves the key from the first element (index 0) retrieved by a call to GetKey into the Message control.

```
Sub Page_Load( )
    Application.RemoveAll( )
    Application("GetKeyTest") = "Got it!"
    Message.Text = "Key of Application(0) = " & _
                    Application.GetKey(0) & _
                    "<br/>(Should be GetKeyTest)"
End Sub
```

Notes

If *Index* is less than 0 or greater than Application.Count − 1, an ArgumentOutOfRangeException exception will be thrown.

Lock

```
Application.Lock
```

Locks access to an Application collection to facilitate access synchronization.

Parameters

None.

Example

The example locks the application, sets an application page load counter variable, unlocks the application, and displays the value:

```
Sub Page_Load( )
    Application.Lock( )
    Application("Counter") = Application("Counter") + 1
    Application.UnLock( )
    Message.Text = "Counter = " & Application("Counter")
End Sub
```

Notes

In the example, note that we Lock the application, perform any operations that modify values within the Application collection, and UnLock the application as quickly as possible. Any read access to the Application collection can safely take place outside the Lock/UnLock method calls.

Remove

```
Application.Remove(ByVal name As String)
```

Removes an item by name from the Application collection.

Parameter

name

A String argument containing the name (key) of the item to remove.

Example

The example determines whether the item with the key "foo" exists in the Application collection and, if it does, removes the item and displays an appropriate message:

```
Sub Page_Load( )
    If Not Application("foo") Is Nothing Then
        Application.Remove("foo")
        Message.Text = "Item 'foo' was removed."
    Else
        Message.Text = "Item 'foo' does not exist."
    End If
End Sub
```

Notes

The Remove method is provided for backwards compatibility with classic ASP. In classic ASP, this method was accessed through the Contents collection. In ASP.NET, this method can be accessed either directly, as shown above, or through the Contents collection.

RemoveAll

```
Application.RemoveAll( )
```

Removes all items from the Application collection.

Parameters

None.

Example

The example checks to ensure that at least one item is in the Application collection, and if it is, it clears the collection by calling the RemoveAll method.

```
Sub Page_Load( )
    If Application.Count > 0 Then
        Application.RemoveAll( )
        Message.Text = "Application collection cleared."
    Else
        Message.Text = "Application collection is already empty."
    End If
End Sub
```

Notes

The RemoveAll method is provided for backwards compatibility with classic ASP. In classic ASP, this method was accessed through the Contents collection. In ASP.NET, this method can be accessed either directly, as shown above, or through the Contents collection.

RemoveAt

```
Application.RemoveAt(ByVal index As Integer)
```

Removes an item from the Application collection by index. This is a new companion to the Remove method, which removes an item by key.

Parameter

index

> An Integer argument containing the index location of the item to remove from the Application collection.

Example

```
Sub Page_Load( )
    If Application.Count > 0 Then
        Application.RemoveAt(0)
        Message.Text = "The item at index 0 was removed."
    Else
        Message.Text = "The item at index 0 does not exist."
    End If
End Sub
```

Notes

The RemoveAt method allows items to be removed from the Application collection by index rather than by key. As in the example above, the items that follow the removed item will shift one position in the collection when the item is removed. If you remove an item by index and then call RemoveAt again with the same index, you will remove the item that immediately followed the original removed item. If a single item is in the Application collection and you call RemoveAt a second time, an ArgumentOutOfRangeException exception will be thrown.

Set

```
Application.Set(ByVal name As String, ByVal value As Object)
```

Updates the value of an object in the Application collection. This new method allows you to set objects in the Application collection.

Parameters

Name

> A String argument containing the name of the object in the Application collection to be updated.

Value

An Object argument containing the new value of the Application collection object to be updated.

Example

The example uses Set twice—once to set a new item in the Application collection and again to change that value.

```
Sub Page_Load( )
    Application.RemoveAll( )
    Application.Set("TotallyNewVariable","Test!")
    Message.Text = "First: " + Application("TotallyNewVariable") + "<br/>"
    Application.Set("TotallyNewVariable","Test again!")
    Message.Text = Message.Text & "First after Set: " +
    Application("TotallyNewVariable") + "<br/>"
End Sub
```

Notes

Set can be used to add values to the Application collection, but you will normally just use the simple syntax you are used to from classic ASP:

```
Application("TotallyNewVariable") = "Test!"
```

UnLock

```
Application.UnLock
```

Unlocks access to an Application collection to facilitate access synchronization.

Parameters

None.

Example

The example locks the application, sets an application page load counter variable, unlocks the application, and displays the value:

```
Sub Page_Load( )
    Application.Lock( )
    Application("Counter") = Application("Counter") + 1
    Application.UnLock( )
    Message.Text = "Counter = " & Application("Counter")
End Sub
```

Notes

In the example, note that we Lock the application, perform any operations that modify values within the Application collection, and UnLock the application as quickly as possible. Any read access to the Application collection can safely take place outside the Lock/UnLock method calls.

Events Reference

Start

```
Sub Application_OnStart( )
 'Event handler logic
End Sub
```

Fired when the Application is created. The event handler for this event should be defined in the *global.asax* application file.

Parameters

None.

Example

The example writes an entry to both the Application Event log and the IIS log for the application to indicate that the Start event has fired:

```
<Script language="VB" runat="server">
   Sub Application_OnStart( )
      Dim EventLog1 As New System.Diagnostics.EventLog ("Application", _
         ".", "mySource")
      EventLog1.WriteEntry("Application_OnStart fired!")
      Context.Response.AppendToLog("Application_OnStart fired!")
   End Sub
</script>
```

There is one issue with the code above. Security in the released version of the .NET framework has been tightened, so writing to the event log will not work by default in an ASP.NET application.

Notes

The Start event is useful for performing initialization tasks when the application is initialized. You can initialize Application variables that are mostly static.

End

```
Sub Application_OnEnd( )
 'Event handler logic
End Sub
```

Fired when the application is torn down, either when the web server is stopped or when the *global.asax* file is modified. The event handler for this event should be defined in the *global.asax* application file.

Parameters

None.

Example

The example below writes an entry to the Application Event log to indicate that the End event has fired:

```
<Script language="VB" runat="server">
   Sub Application_OnEnd( )
      Dim EventLog1 As New System.Diagnostics.EventLog ("Application", _
         ".", "mySource")
      EventLog1.WriteEntry("Application_OnEnd fired!")
   End Sub
</script>
```

Notes

The End event is useful for performing cleanup tasks when the Application ends, either because the web service stops or the *global.asax* file is changed.

14

The HttpContext Class

With all the knowledge gained about the HttpApplicationState class covered in the last chapter, the next question is, "How you gain access to a copy of the HttpApplicationState within your application?" The good news is that within an ASP.NET page, the Application instance of the HttpApplicationState class is available exactly as it appears in a classic ASP page. The Response, Request, and other objects familiar to classic ASP are also available. These and other objects are available by using the HttpContext class.

Unlike many classes within ASP.NET, the HttpContext class adds new methods and properties but does not contain any significant methods or properties carried over from classic ASP that are deprecated in ASP.NET. New properties include IsCustomErrorEnabled, IsDebuggingEnabled, SkipAuthorization, and Trace.

The HttpContext class encapsulates all the HTTP-specific information about a given HTTP request. The HttpContext class contains an Items collection that allows the developer to store information for the duration of the current request. In some ways, this class is similar to HttpSessionState (discussed in Chapter 19). However, information stored in the HttpContext collection is held only for the duration of the current request. While this might not initially seem useful, it is often helpful.

For instance, suppose an application is structured so that the user enters information into a form and clicks a button with a server-side event handler. When the button's Click handler is called, a different page must get the information. After placing the information gathered from the form in the HttpContext class, the click handler can use the server-side Server.Transfer method to go to the second page without requiring another round trip from the server to the client. In addition to other pages, HttpHandlers and HttpModules that might participate in a given request have access to the context.

The HttpContext object will seem a bit redundant for developers who only write traditional ASP.NET pages. Most of the properties and methods are duplicated in the Page object, so they might not seem important. However, if you are creating other types of ASP.NET code, such as HttpModules and HttpHandlers, the HttpContext class can be a lifesaver. Even developers creating only standard ASP.NET pages might need to use the HttpContext object if they are creating event handlers in the *global.asax* file. In some contexts, the traditional objects used within ASP.NET pages are not available within these *global.asax* event handlers.

Table 14-1 lists the properties, collections, and methods exposed by the HttpContext class.

Table 14-1. HttpContext class summary

Properties	Collections	Methods (instance)	Methods (static/shared)
Application	AllErrors	AddError	GetAppConfig
ApplicationInstance	Items	ClearError	
Cache		GetConfig	
Current		RewritePath	
Error			
Handler			
IsCustomErrorEnabled			
IsDebuggingEnabled			
Request			
Response			
Server			
Session			
SkipAuthorization			
Timestamp			
Trace			
User			

Comments/Troubleshooting

Many HttpContext class properties are topics in their own right. For instance, the Application, Response, Request, and Session properties are accessible here, but covered in detail elsewhere in this book. A couple of methods within HttpContext, however, might require further explanation.

GetConfig sounds like it might be a way to get the appSettings configuration information mentioned in the previous chapter. While it is possible to use GetConfig("appSettings") for that purpose, it requires some casting. GetConfig returns an instance of System.Configuration.ReadOnlyNameValueCollection, which is a private class. To actually use the returned value, you need to cast it to a System.Collections.Specialized.NameValueCollection. Instead of doing this, using ConfigurationSettings.AppSettings is safer and easier. Why is GetConfig there, then? In addition to the appSettings section, a developer can place custom sections within the configuration files, which is what GetConfig is designed for.

The other somewhat unusual (although much more useful) method in HttpContext is RewritePath. The MSDN documentation on this method is, shall we say, sparse. The real use for this method is to silently redirect the user to a different URL.

In this chapter, as in others in the book, we'll use the following code listing as the basis for most examples in the chapter. Unless otherwise noted, each example will consist of the Page_Load event handler for just that particular example. Any output messages or return values displayed will be shown as the Text property of the ASP.NET Label control named Message or displayed by calling Response. Write.

```
<%@ Page Language="vb" %>
<html>
    <head>
        <script runat="server">
            Sub Page_Load( )
                'Example code will go here
            End Sub
        </script>
    </head>
<body>
    <asp:label id="Message" runat="server"/>
</body>
</html>
```

Some examples will show Application handlers within *global.asax* rather than the Page_Load method of a page.

Properties Reference

Application

HttpApplicationState = Context.Application

Returns the current Application state object.

Parameter

HttpApplicationState
    An HttpApplicationState object that will receive the value of the property.

Example

The example sets an application value using the Application instance exposed by the Page class and gets the instance from Context. Finally, it displays the newly set value by using the HttpApplicationState instance retrieved from the Context object (proving they are the same object):

```
Sub Page_Load( )
    Dim App as HttpApplicationState
    Page.Application("Test")="Value"
    App = Context.Application
    Message.Text = App("Test")
End Sub
```

Notes

Often, you will use the copy of Application from the Page class. However, for objects not derived from Page (for instance, HttpHandlers and HttpModules) this is a convenient way to access the Application state.

Do not confuse this property, which returns an instance of type HttpApplicationState, with the ApplicationInstance property, which returns an instance of type HttpApplication.

ApplicationInstance

```
Context.ApplicationInstance = HttpApplication
HttpApplication = Context.ApplicationInstance
```

Returns or sets the current HttpApplication object.

Parameter

HttpApplication
> An HttpApplication object that will receive or set the value of the ApplicationInstance property.

Notes

Generally, you do not need to use the HttpApplication object, since the properties it exposes are usually available through other objects. One exception is when accessing all the methods that allow you to add event handlers for this request.

Cache

```
HttpCache = Context.Cache
```

Returns an instance of the Cache class.

Parameter

HttpCache
> An Object variable of type Cache.

Example

The example retrieves an instance of the Cache class into a local variable and then adds a value to the cache:

```
Sub Application_BeginRequest()
   Dim myCache As Cache
   myCache = Context.Cache
   myCache.Add("Test", "Test", Nothing, _
      System.DateTime.Now.AddHours(1), Nothing, _
      CacheItemPriority.High, Nothing)
End Sub
```

Notes

Note that rather than using the Page_Load event, the example above shows the Application_BeginRequest event handler in *global.asax*; a common use of the

Cache property is to access the cache at points during request processing when the Cache property of the Page object is not available, such as before the Page object is instantiated.

Current

HttpContext = HttpContext.Current

Retrieves the current HttpContext instance.

Parameter

HttpContext
    The current context.

Example

This example uses the IsDebuggingEnabled property, described later in this chapter, to show whether debugging is enabled:

```
Sub Page_Load( )
    Message.Text = HttpContext.Current.IsDebuggingEnabled.ToString( )
End Sub
```

Notes

Current is a shared (static) property, indicating that you can access it without creating an instance of the HttpContext class.

Error

Exception = Context.Error

Returns the first error, if any, associated with the current request.

Parameter

Exception
    An Exception variable to receive the value of the property.

Example

The example checks to see if the Error property on the current context object is null (Nothing in VB.NET). If it is not null, it displays the error; otherwise, it displays a message indicating there is no error.

```
Sub Page_Load( )
    If Not HttpContext.Current.Error Is Nothing then
        Message.Text = HttpContext.Current.Error.ToString( )
    Else
        Message.Text = "No error detected"
    End If
End Sub
```

Handler

```
IHttpHandler = Context.Handler
Context.Handler = IHttpHandler
```

Sets or returns an instance of the IHttpHandler for the current request.

Parameter

IHttpHandler
    An Object variable of a type that implements the IHttpHandler interface.

Notes

The Handler property can be used to specify special handling for this request. To understand this idea, you need to understand how requests are processed in IIS. When a request comes in, unless the item requested is a simple HTML file, the request is generally handled by an Internet Server API (ISAPI) extension. For instance, classic ASP and ASP.NET pages are directed to ISAPI applications that process the request. ISAPI applications are reasonably easy to write in principal, but are very difficult to create in practice. The IHttpHandler interface is the .NET way of allowing the developer to write code for requests to be handled in a way similar to ISAPI applications in IIS, without all of the problems of ISAPI.

IsCustomErrorEnabled

```
Boolean = Context.IsCustomErrorEnabled
```

Returns a Boolean value specifying whether custom errors are enabled for the current request.

Parameter

Boolean
    A Boolean variable to receive the value of this property.

Example

The following example displays True if custom errors are enabled; otherwise, it displays False.

```
Sub Page_Load( )
    Message.Text = "Custom Error Enabled?" & _
        Context.IsCustomErrorEnabled
End Sub
```

Notes

This flag is controlled by the customErrors section in *web.config*. If the customErrors element's mode attribute is set to On, IsCustomErrorEnabled returns True. If the customErrors element's mode attribute is set to False or RemoteOnly, this flag is False.

IsDebuggingEnabled

Boolean = Context.IsDebuggingEnabled

Returns a Boolean value specifying whether debugging is enabled for the current request.

Parameter

Boolean
    A Boolean variable to receive value of this flag.

Example

The example displays True if debugging is enabled; otherwise, it displays False:

```
Sub Page_Load( )
    Message.Text = "Debugging Enabled?" & _
        Context.IsDebuggingEnabled
End Sub
```

Notes

This flag is controlled by the compilation section in *web.config*. If the compilation section's debug attribute is set to True, IsDebuggingEnabled returns True. If the debug attribute in the compilation section is set to False, this property is False.

Request

HttpRequest = Context.Request

Returns the HttpRequest object for the current request.

Parameter

HttpRequest
    An HttpRequest variable to receive the current HttpRequest object.

Notes

This property is provided for applications other than ASP.NET pages (where the Page.Request property is normally used to retrieve the HttpRequest object). Code that does not have access to the properties of the Page class includes HttpHandlers and HttpModules, as well as event handlers in *global.asax*.

Response

HttpResponse = Context.Response

Returns the HttpResponse object for the current request.

Parameter

HttpResponse
    An HttpResponse variable to receive the current HttpResponse object.

Notes

This property is provided for applications other than ASP.NET pages (where the Page.Response property is normally used to retrieve the HttpResponse object).

Code that does not have access to the properties of the Page class includes HttpHandlers and HttpModules, as well as *global.asax*. One common reason for using Context.Response is to write cookies in an HttpModule.

Session

```
HttpSessionState = Context.Session
```

Returns the HttpSession object for the current request.

Parameters

HttpSessionState
    An HttpSessionState object to receive the current session.

Notes

This property is provided for applications other than ASP.NET pages (where the Page.Session property is normally used to retrieve the HttpSessionState object). Code that does not have access to the properties of the Page class includes HttpHandlers and HttpModules, as well as *global.asax*. When using Context.Session in the Application event handlers of *global.asax*, Session is not available in the Application BeginRequest event, but can be used in, for instance, the Application_PreRequestHandlerExecute event.

SkipAuthorization

```
Boolean = Context.SkipAuthorization
Context.SkipAuthentication = Boolean
```

Sets or returns a flag indicating whether the URLAuthorization module will skip the authorization check. The default is False.

Parameter

Boolean
    A Boolean variable returning or setting the flag regarding authorization checks.

Example

The following example retrieves the status of the SkipAuthorization property and displays it in the Message label control:

```
Sub Page_Load( )
    Message.Text = "SkipAuthorization? " _
        & Context.SkipAuthorization
End Sub
```

Notes

To set this value, the ControlPrincipal Flag must be set in the Flags property of the SecurityPermission object. This property is used internally by the Forms and Passport authentication modules.

Timestamp

```
timestamp = Context.Timestamp
```

Returns a DateTime object containing the date and time of the request on the server.

Parameter

timestamp
> An Object variable of type DateTime.

Example

The following example retrieves the date and time of the request and displays it in the Message label control:

```
Sub Page_Load( )
    Message.Text = "Date/Time of Request: " _
    & Context.Timestamp
End Sub
```

Trace

```
TraceContext = Context.Trace
```

Returns the TraceContext for the current request. The members of the TraceContext class are listed in the entry for the Trace property in Chapter 12.

Parameter

TraceContext
> A TraceContext variable to receive the TraceContext object for the current request.

Example

The example retrieves the date and time of the request and displays it in the Message label control.

```
Sub Page_Load( )
    Message.Text = "Trace Enabled? " _
        & Context.Trace.IsEnabled
End Sub
```

Notes

Trace can be enabled by setting the Trace attribute of the @ Page directive to True.

User

```
IPrincipal = Context.User
Context.User = IPrincipal
```

Returns or sets the IPrincipal object for the current request.

Parameter

IPrincipal

> An object that implements the IPrincipal interface. The IPrincipal interface is implemented by the `GenericPrincipal` and the `WindowsPrincipal` classes. IPrincipal defines one property and one method:
>
> *Identity*
>
> > A property that returns a class that implements the IIdentity interface.
>
> *IsInRole(Role as String)*
>
> > A method that returns a Boolean indicating whether the current principal belongs to the specified Role.
>
> The IIdentity interface provides several useful properties:
>
> *AuthenticationType*
>
> > A property that returns the type of authentication used, if the request is authenticated.
>
> *IsAuthenticated*
>
> > A property that returns a Boolean indicating if the user has been authenticated. This property should be checked (to ensure it is True) before checking for AuthenticationType or Name. IsAuthenticated returns False if anonymous authentication is enabled in Internet Information Server and neither Forms nor another authentication method is in use by ASP.NET.
>
> *Name*
>
> > A property that returns the Name of the current user. The user name format depends upon the type of authentication used. For Windows authentication, the name is in the format of `DOMAIN\UserName`.

Example

The example checks to see if the user is authenticated and if so, returns the name of the user:

```
Sub Page_Load( )
    Message.Text = "User.Identity.IsAuthenticated?  " _
        & Context.User.Identity.IsAuthenticated & "<br/>"
    If Context.User.Identity.IsAuthenticated Then
        Message.Text = Message.Text & "User.Identity.Name?  " _
            & Context.User.Identity.Name & "<br/>"
    End If
End Sub
```

Notes

Understanding the values you receive back when checking the User property requires an understanding of ASP.NET and Internet Information Server, since the returned values depend on settings in both.

Collections Reference

The Context object in ASP.NET supports one collection, Items, and an array called AllErrors.

AllErrors

ExceptionArray = Context.AllErrors

Returns an array of Exception objects representing all accumulated errors that occurred in the current request.

As in classic ASP, the Server.GetLastError method returns an ASPError object. This mechanism is still available, though the returned value is now of type Exception rather than ASPError.

Parameters

None.

Example

The example checks to see if the AllErrors array contains any elements and if so, displays them:

```
Sub Page_Load( )
    Dim i as Integer
    Dim e As New Exception("A generalized error.")
    Context.AddError(e)
    If Not Context.AllErrors Is Nothing Then
        For i = 0 to Context.AllErrors.Length - 1
            Message.Text = Message.Text & _
                "Exception: " & _
                Context.AllErrors(i).ToString( ) & "<br/>"
        Next
    Else
        Message.Text = "No Errors to report."
    End if
End Sub
```

Notes

Unlike classic ASP, arrays in ASP.NET are zero-based, so the first element in any collection or array will be 0, not 1. Thus, in the example above, the array is indexed from 0 to Length - 1, not from 1 to Length.

Items

Context.Items(*Name* as String) = *Value*
Value = Context.Items(*Index* as Integer)
Value = Context.Items(*Name* as String)

The Items collection is a key-value collection that can contain any object the developer wishes to save for, at most, the duration of the request. Unlike Session- or Application-level collections that can be used to store values, this collection does not survive past the current request. This collection is the ideal place to store values that need not survive past the current request, especially if the items need to be stored or retrieved in places where the Session or Application objects are not available.

Parameters

Name
> The key name for the value to be stored.

Value
> The object to be stored in the Items collection, or the value to be retrieved.

Index
> The index of the value to be retrieved.

Example

The example adds two values to the Context.Items collection. The first is added traditionally, referring to the key in the Items collection directly. The second is added using the Item's collection's Add method. Finally, the Message label control displays whether the "Foo" value has been set. To display the string key used, you need to use two double quotes, which displays as the literal quote character. In C#, the quote character would need to be escaped by placing a backslash (\) in front of it.

```
Sub Page_Load( )
    Context.Items("Foo")="Bar"
    Context.Items.Add("Bar","Foo")
    Message.Text = "Context.Items.Contains(""Foo"") is " & _
                    Context.Items.Contains("Foo")
End Sub
```

Notes

Unlike classic ASP, collections in ASP.NET are zero-based, so the first element in any collection or array is 0, not 1. While you can, as in the example above, use the Add method to add values to the Items collection, this is virtually never done. Values are almost always retrieved by referring to the Items collection directly, either by using a numeric index or indexing using a key string.

Methods Reference

AddError

`Context.AddError(ByVal ErrorInfo As Exception)`

Adds an Exception object to the array of exceptions returned by the AllErrors property.

Parameter

ErrorInfo
> An Exception object to be added to the array.

Example

The example shows how you can use AddError to add an error to the current request context. The exception is created within a Try block. In the Finally block, the ToString method is used to display the error and the ClearError method is used to clear the error so that the page will display properly.

```
Sub Page_Load( )
    Try
        Context.AddError(New Exception("Test"))
    Finally
        Message.Text = "Context.Error.ToString( ) is " & _
            Context.Error.ToString( )
        Context.ClearError( )
    End Try
End Sub
```

Notes

Adding an exception by using AddError should not be confused with throwing an exception. Using AddError only adds the exception to the array returned by the AllErrors property and does not invoke any of the error handling mechanisms in the application.

ClearError

```
Context.ClearError( )
```

Clears all errors for the current request. Note that even though ClearError is singular, it clears all errors for the current request.

Parameters

None.

Example

The example checks whether there are any errors and then clears them. Finally, it reports if it has cleared any errors.

```
Sub Page_Load( )
    If Not Context.AllErrors Is Nothing Then
        Context.ClearError( )
        Message.Text = "Errors cleared."
    Else
        Message.Text = "No Errors to clear."
    End If
End Sub
```

GetAppConfig

```
Object = HttpContext.GetAppConfig(ByVal name As String)
```

Returns the collection of key/value pairs that are contained in the configuration specified by the *name* argument.

Parameters

Object
> An object containing the keys and values in the configuration sections speci-fied by *name*. This object is often of a type derived from NameValueCollection.

name
> The name of the section to retrieve.

Example

The example shows how you can use the GetAppConfig method to retrieve all items in a configuration by setting from the *web.config* or *machine.config* XML configuration file. While GetAppConfig returns an Object, you must cast the returned object to the NameValueCollection-derived type defined in the configuration section to actually access the information. This method is static, so an instance of the HttpContext class is not required.

```
Sub Page_Load( )
    Dim i As Integer
    Dim nv As NameValueCollection
    nv = CType(HttpContext.GetAppConfig("appSettings"), _
            NameValueCollection)
    For i = 0 To nv.Count - 1
        Response.Write(nv.GetKey(i) & " = " & nv(i) & "<br/>")
    Next
End Sub
```

Notes

Generally you will not use GetAppConfig to get the appSettings section from the configuration file. It is much easier and safer to use ConfigurationSettings.AppSet-tings to get at these values. This method, however, can be used to get information from custom configuration sections.

GetConfig

`Object = Context.GetConfig(ByVal name As String)`

Returns the collection of key/value pairs that are contained in the configuration specified by the *name* argument.

Parameters

Object
> An object containing the keys and values in the configuration sections speci-fied by *name*. This object is often of a type derived from NameValueCollection.

name
> The name of the section to retrieve.

Example

The example shows how you can use the GetConfig method to retrieve all items in a configuration setting from the *web.config* or *machine.config* XML configura-

---

tion file. While GetAppConfig returns an object, you must cast the returned object to the NameValueCollection-derived type defined in the configuration section to actually access the information.

```
Sub Page_Load( )
    Dim i As Integer
    Dim nv As NameValueCollection
    nv = CType(Context.GetConfig("appSettings"), _
            NameValueCollection)
    For i = 0 To nv.Count - 1
        Response.Write(nv.GetKey(i) & " = " & nv(i) & "<br/>")
    Next
End Sub
```

Notes

Generally, you will not use GetConfig to get the appSettings section from the configuration file. It is much easier and safer to use ConfigurationSettings.AppSettings to get these values. This method, however, can be used to get information from custom configuration sections.

RewritePath

```
Context.RewritePath(ByVal newURL As String)
```

Assigns an internal rewrite path.

Parameter

newURL
A String containing a local path to redirect the user silently.

Example

The example below shows how to change the path in a way that is completely transparent to the user. The URL shown in the address bar remains the original URL, and the redirection to the new page does not require a round trip to and from the server. RewritePath is almost always called from *global.asax* rather than an actual page. That is what this example shows.

```
Sub Application_BeginRequest(ByVal sender As Object, _
    ByVal e As EventArgs)
    ' No matter the URL, redirect to this URL...
    Context.RewritePath("/aspnetian/ShowGetConfig.aspx")
End Sub
```

Notes

This method seems to be redundant when compared with methods like Server. Transfer, which allow the developer to change the page being displayed. In fact, RewritePath serves a very unique purpose.

Perhaps you have seen or registered at Web sites that give registered users a unique URL. For instance, you might be given a URL like this:

```
http://www.SomeDomain.com/YourName/default.aspx
```

Implementing such a system that gives a virtual directory to each user is not practical unless you have very few registered users. Using RewritePath, the developer can essentially remove a level of directory hierarchy. This removal occurs without a redirect that would require a round trip to the server, and without changing the URL as it appears in the browser. Some information will be extracted and saved in the Context Items collection for use by pages that will be displayed while translating from the URL entered by the user to the URL used for RewritePath.

In the example above, RewritePath might be sent a URL like this:

```
http://www.SomeDomain.com/default.aspx
```

The "YourName" folder name was removed from the URL, and the application can then be customized for the user identified as "YourName."

15

The HttpException Class

The HttpException class provides a container for communicating error information from various classes used in ASP.NET. The Page, HttpRequest, HttpResponse, HttpServerUtility, and other classes all use the HttpException class to communicate information about errors that occur when calling their methods or properties.

The HttpException class is derived from the Exception class, the base class for all exceptions in the .NET Framework. HttpException adds two methods, GetHtmlErrorMessage and GetHttpCode, as well as other constructor overloads that create HttpException instances based on HTTP error codes.

In addition to its role in communicating error information from the Request, Response, and other ASP.NET intrinsic objects, the HttpException class can be useful in communicating error information from custom components or controls that communicate via HTTP. When an HTTP error occurs in such a component, you can use one of the constructor overloads for the HttpException class to create an instance of HttpException that contains the HTTP status code associated with the result, along with a custom error message, if desired, to the client of the component. This allows you to provide clients with rich, specific error information that they can handle as they choose. Table 15-1 lists the properties, collections, and methods exposed by the HttpException class.

Table 15-1. HttpException class summary

Properties	Methods (public instance)
ErrorCode (inherited from Exception)	GetBaseException (inherited from Exception)
HelpLink (inherited from Exception)	GetHtmlErrorMessage
InnerException (inherited from Exception)	GetHttpCode
Message (inherited from Exception)	ToString (inherited from Exception)
Source (inherited from Exception)	
StackTrace (inherited from Exception)	
TargetSite (inherited from Exception)	

Comments/Troubleshooting

We'll use the following code listing as the basis for most examples in the chapter. Unless otherwise noted, each example will consist of just the Page_Load event handler for that particular example. Any displayed output messages or return values will be shown as the Text property of the ASP.NET Label control named Message or displayed by calling Response.Write:

```
<%@ Page Language="vb" %>
<html>
    <head>
        <script runat="server">
            Sub Page_Load( )
                'Example code will go here
            End Sub
        </script>
    </head>
<body>
    <asp:label id="Message" forecolor="red" runat="server"/>
</body>
</html>
```

Constructor Reference

The HttpException provides several overloaded constructors for communicating custom HTTP error information:

Dim MyHttpEx As New HttpException( )
> Creates an empty instance of HttpException.

Throw New HttpException(string)
> Throws an HttpException whose Message property is set to the value of the string passed into the constructor.

Throw New HttpException(integer, string)
> Throws an HttpException whose GetHttpCode method will return the integer value passed into the constructor, and whose Message property is set to the value of the string passed into the constructor.

Throw New HttpException(string, Exception)
> Throws an HttpException whose Message property is set to the value of the string passed into the constructor, and whose InnerException property is set to the Exception object passed into the constructor.

Throw New HttpException(string, integer)
> Throws an HttpException whose Message property is set to the value of the string passed into the constructor, and whose ErrorCode property is set to the value of the integer passed into the constructor.

Throw New HttpException(integer, string, Exception)
> Throws an HttpException whose GetHttpCode method returns the integer value passed into the constructor, whose Message property is set to the value of the string passed into the constructor, and whose InnerException property is set to the Exception object passed into the constructor.

Throw New HttpException(integer, string, integer)

Throws an HttpException whose GetHttpCode method returns the first integer value passed into the constructor, whose Message property is set to the value of the string passed into the constructor, and whose ErrorCode property is set to the value of the second integer passed into the constructor.

Properties Reference

ErrorCode

`integer = HttpException.ErrorCode`

Returns an integer representing the Win32 error code or HRESULT of the exception. This property is especially useful in situations when you are working with COM objects through COM Interop and need to return or evaluate the HRESULT returned from a COM object failure. When creating HttpException instances in your own code, you can use one of two overloaded constructors (shown earlier in the "Comments/Troubleshooting" section) to set this property for HttpExceptions that you throw.

Parameter

integer

An integer that will receive the HRESULT or Win32 error code from the property.

Example

The code example uses the Page_Load event handler to throw an HttpException with a custom error message and error code, and then uses structured exception handling to catch the exception and display the error message and error code as the text of an ASP.NET Label control:

```
Sub Page_Load( )
    Try
        Throw New HttpException("Threw an error from Page_Load", 100)
    Catch HttpEx As HttpException
        Message.Text = "ERROR:<br/>"
        Message.Text &= "Message: " & HttpEx.Message & "<br/>"
        Message.Text &= "Error Code: " & HttpEx.ErrorCode & "<br/>"
    End Try
End Sub
```

Notes

While the ErrorCode property is primarily useful when working with COM objects, this property is also set by the ASP.NET intrinsic objects when an exception is thrown.

HelpLink

string = HttpException.HelpLink

HttpException.HelpLink = *string*

Sets or returns a string containing the URN or URL to a help file containing information about the exception.

Parameter

string

A string that will set the HelpLink property or receive the help link from the property.

Example

The code example will display the help link associated with a custom HttpException:

```
Sub Page_Load( )
    Try
        Dim myHttpEx As _
            New HttpException("Threw an exception from Page_Load")
        myHttpEx.HelpLink = "file://C:/myHelpDir/myHelpFile.htm"
        Throw myHttpEx
    Catch HttpEx As HttpException
        Message.ForeColor = System.Drawing.Color.Red
        Message.Text = "ERROR:<br/>"
        Message.Text &= "Message: " & HttpEx.Message & "<br/>"
        Message.Text &= "Error Code: " & HttpEx.ErrorCode & "<br/>"
        Message.Text &= "Help Link: " & HttpEx.HelpLink & "<br/>"
    End Try
End Sub
```

Notes

The HelpLink is not always set by exceptions thrown from the ASP.NET intrinsic objects. For example, if you attempt to access the Session intrinsic object when Session state is disabled, an HttpException will be thrown, but its HelpLink property will return an empty string.

InnerException

Exception = HttpException.InnerException

Returns an Exception object containing the inner exception of the HttpException object.

Parameter

Exception

An Exception instance that will be populated by the property.

Example

The code example creates two exceptions, the second of which is created with an overloaded constructor that sets the InnerException property to the first exception. The code throws the second exception, which is caught by the Catch statement. The Catch block then displays the error messages of both the outer and inner exceptions:

```
Sub Page_Load( )
    Try
        Dim myHttpEx As _
            New HttpException("This is a nested exception")
        Throw New HttpException("Threw an exception from Page_Load", _
            myHttpEx)
    Catch HttpEx As HttpException
        Dim InnerHttpEx As HttpException
        InnerHttpEx = CType(HttpEx.InnerException, HttpException)
        Message.Text = "ERROR:<br/>"
        Message.Text &= "Message: " & HttpEx.Message & "<br/>"
        Message.Text &= "Inner Exception Message: " & _
            InnerHttpEx.Message & "<br/>"
    End Try
End Sub
```

Notes

The InnerException property allows exceptions to be nested, which can allow developers to track down the root cause of an exception, even when multiple exceptions are thrown. Because the InnerException property is inherited from the Exception class, other types of exceptions can be nested within an HttpException, and HttpExceptions can be nested within other exception types. The InnerException property can only be set manually through one of the overloaded constructors of the HttpException class.

Message

string = HttpException.Message

Returns a string representing the error message associated with the exception. The error message is the human-readable text description of the error.

Parameter

string
    A string that will receive the error message value from the property.

Example

The code example creates and throws an exception, passing the desired error message into the HttpException constructor, and then displays the Message property of the exception as the Text property of an ASP.NET Label control:

```
Sub Page_Load( )
    Try
        Throw New HttpException("Threw an error from Page_Load")
    Catch HttpEx As HttpException
```

```
            Message.Text = "ERROR:<br/>"
            Message.Text &= "Message: " & HttpEx.Message & "<br/>"
        End Try
    End Sub
```

Notes

The ease with which the Message property can be accessed makes it tempting to simply display this property when an error occurs. A better approach to error handling, however, is to log this information either in the NT Event Log or in your own private application log and handle the error to the user transparently. This provides you with better information to troubleshoot your applications and gives your users a more satisfying (and less frustrating) experience.

Source

```
string = HttpException.Source
HttpException.Source = string
```

Sets or returns a string representing the source of the exception. For custom exceptions that you create and throw, this code may be set to the name of the method and/or class from which the exception is thrown.

Parameter

string
> A string that will receive the value from the property.

Example

The code example causes an exception by attempting to set a Session value on a page for which the enableSessionState attribute of the @ Page directive has been set to False. The example code then displays the resulting error message and source:

```
<%@ Page Language="vb" EnableSessionState="false" %>

...

Sub Page_Load( )
    Try
        Session("foo") = "Foo"
    Catch HttpEx As HttpException
        Message.Text = "ERROR:<br/>"
        Message.Text &= "Message: " & HttpEx.Message & "<br/>"
        Message.Text &= "Source: " & HttpEx.Source & "<br/>"
    End Try
End Sub
```

Notes

In the example, the Source property returns the value System.Web as the source of the Exception, which is not very specific. When creating and throwing your own custom exceptions, be as specific as possible with error messages and source descriptions. Just remember that providing specific information about an exception you're throwing is no substitute for handling the exception condition

---

within your code instead of throwing an exception. If you have sufficient information about what went wrong to correct the problem, doing so is almost always preferable to throwing an exception that will interrupt the flow of the application from your users' standpoint.

StackTrace

string = HttpException.StackTrace

Returns a string containing a list of the methods in the current call stack in which the exception occurred. The method in which the exception occurred is listed first, followed by any additional methods in the call stack (methods that called the method in which the exception occurred), up to the point at which the exception was handled.

Parameter

string
> A string that will receive the stack trace value from the property.

Example

In the code example, the Page_Load event handler calls the ThrowMeAnException method, which throws an HttpException. The exception handler in Page_Load then displays the error message and stack trace:

```
Sub Page_Load( )
    Try
        ThrowMeAnException
    Catch HttpEx As HttpException
        Message.Text = "ERROR:<br/>"
        Message.Text &= "Message: " & HttpEx.Message & "<br/>"
        Message.Text &= "Stack Trace: " & HttpEx.StackTrace & "<br/>"
    End Try
End Sub
Sub ThrowMeAnException( )
    Throw New HttpException("Threw an error from ThrowMeAnException")
End Sub
```

Notes

The stack trace for the example first lists the ThrowMeAnException method, including the local path to the *.aspx* file containing the method and the line number at which the exception was thrown, and then lists the Page_Load method, including the path and line number where the exception originated.

TargetSite

MethodBase = HttpException.TargetSite

Returns a MethodBase instance (the MethodBase class resides in the System.Reflection namespace) representing the method from which the exception was thrown. You can query the properties of MethodBase, such as the Name property, which returns the name of the method. You can also call ToString on the instance to return information about the method in a usable format.

Parameter

MethodBase

An instance of the MethodBase class representing the method from which the exception was thrown.

Example

The code example causes an exception by attempting to set a Session value on a page for which the EnableSessionState attribute of the @ Page directive has been set to False. The example code then displays the resulting error message and uses the Name property of the MethodBase instance returned by the TargetSite property to display the name of the method from which the exception was thrown:

```
<%@ Page Language="vb" EnableSessionState="false" %>

...

Sub Page_Load( )
    Try
        Session("foo") = "Foo"
    Catch HttpEx As HttpException
        Message.Text = "ERROR:<br/>"
        Message.Text &= "Message: " & HttpEx.Message & "<br/>"
        Message.Text &= "Target Site: " & HttpEx.TargetSite.Name & "<br/>"
    End Try
End Sub
```

Notes

In the example, we access the Name property of the MethodBase instance directly, without creating a separate local variable of type MethodBase. This direct access saves us the trouble of either adding an @ Import statement to import the System.Reflection namespace or explicitly declaring the local variable using syntax such as:

```
Dim myMethodBase As System.Reflection.MethodBase
myMethodBase = HttpEx.TargetSite
```

Accessing the Name property of MethodBase directly reduces the amount of code we need to write, but it does so at the expense of being less explicit about what we are actually doing. You should always keep such tradeoffs in mind when writing your code. Writing less code usually seems like a good idea, but if someone other than the original programmer needs to maintain the code, using such shortcuts can make it more difficult for the maintainer to understand what's going on in the code.

Methods Reference

GetBaseException

```
Exception = HttpException.GetBaseException( )
```

Returns an Exception object representing the original exception in a set of nested exceptions. This property provides a shortcut to the innermost exception accessible via the InnerException property.

Parameter

Exception
    An Exception instance that will be populated by the method.

Example

The following code example creates a set of three nested exceptions, the second and third of which are created with an overloaded constructor that sets the Inner-Exception property to the prior exception. The code throws the third exception, which is caught by the Catch statement. The Catch block displays the error message of both the immediate inner exception by using the InnerException property and the original exception by using the Message property of the exception returned by the GetBaseException method:

```
Sub Page_Load( )
    Try
        Dim myHttpEx As _
            New HttpException("This is the original exception")
        Dim myHttpEx2 As _
            New HttpException("This is a nested exception", myHttpEx)
        Throw New HttpException("Threw an exception from Page_Load", _
            myHttpEx2)
    Catch HttpEx As HttpException
        Dim InnerHttpEx As HttpException
        InnerHttpEx = CType(HttpEx.InnerException, HttpException)
        Message.Text = "ERROR:<br/>"
        Message.Text &= "Message: " & HttpEx.Message & "<br/>"
        Message.Text &= "Inner Exception Message: " & _
            InnerHttpEx.Message & "<br/>"
        Message.Text &= "Base Exception Message: " & _
            InnerHttpEx.GetBaseException.Message & "<br/>"
    End Try
End Sub
```

Notes

Like the TargetSite property example, this example accesses a property of the instance returned by the GetBaseException method directly, rather than creating a local instance variable first. The same caveats about reduction in code versus readability apply here.

GetHtmlErrorMessage

string = HttpException.GetHtmlErrorMessage( )

Returns a string containing the HTTP error message (if any) set by the originator of the exception.

Parameter

string
    A string variable that will receive the value from the method.

Notes

This method will return a value only if the HttpException contains an HTTP error message.

GetHttpCode

integer = HttpException.GetHttpCode( )

Returns an integer containing the HTTP status code contained within the exception. For most exceptions thrown by the ASP.NET intrinsic objects, this integer will be 500, indicating an HTTP server error.

Parameter

integer
    An integer variable to receive the HTTP code from the method.

Example

The code example causes an exception by calling Server.Execute on a page that does not exist. The exception is then caught and the HTTP status code is displayed by calling GetHttpCode:

```
Sub Page_Load( )
    Try
        Server.Execute("Foo.aspx")
    Catch HttpEx As HttpException
        Message.Text = "ERROR:<br/>"
        Message.Text &= "Http Status Code: " & _
            HttpEx.GetHttpCode( ) & "<br/>"
    End Try
End Sub
```

Notes

This method is most useful for custom exceptions raised in methods that make HTTP calls, since it allows you to pass back the HTTP result code (404 for not found, 403 for access denied, etc.) to the calling client.

ToString

string = HttpException.ToString( )

Returns a string containing the fully qualified name of the exception, the error message (if available), the name of the inner exception, and the stack trace.

Parameter

string
    A string variable to receive the value from the method.

Example

The code example causes an exception by attempting to set a Session value on a page for which the EnableSessionState attribute of the @ Page directive has been set to False. The example code then displays the string representation of the resulting exception:

```
<%@ Page Language="vb" EnableSessionState="false" %>

Sub Page_Load( )
```

```
    Try
        Session("foo") = "Foo"
    Catch HttpEx As HttpException
        Message.Text = "ERROR:<br/>"
        Message.Text &= "String Representation of Exception: " & _
            HttpEx.ToString( ) & "<br/>"
    End Try
End Sub
```

Notes

This method provides a quick and easy shortcut for displaying the available information about a given exception without having to call the individual methods and
properties of the HttpException object.

16

The HttpRequest Class

The HttpRequest class is ASP.NET's replacement for ASP's Request intrinsic object. Because the HttpRequest class instance for a given ASP.NET page is exposed as the Request property of the Page class (from which all pages are derived), you can code to the HttpRequest class just as you did in ASP. Thus, your existing ASP code will be that much easier to migrate.

The HttpRequest class is used to access information related to a particular HTTP request made by a web client. The HttpRequest class provides access to this information through its properties, collections, and methods.

Each HTTP request from a client consists of an HTTP header and, optionally, a body. The header and body are separated by a blank line. The code following shows a typical HTTP request (without a body):

```
GET /ASPdotNET_iaN/Chapter_16/showHTTP.aspx HTTP/1.0
Connection: Keep-Alive
Accept: image/gif, image/x-xbitmap, image/jpeg, image/pjpeg, image/png, */*
Accept-Charset: iso-8859-1,*,utf-8
Accept-Encoding: gzip
Accept-Language: en
Host: localhost
User-Agent: Mozilla/4.08 [en] (WinNT; U ;Nav)
```

The first line of the HTTP header contains the request type, followed by a space, followed by the requested URL (URI), another space, and the HTTP version number. In the previous example, the request type is GET, the URL is */ASPdotNET_iaN/Chapter_16/showHTTP.aspx* (this URL is relative to the server or domain name), and the HTTP version is 1.0.

While we can gain much information from the text of an HTTP request header (which can be accessed either as a URL-encoded string in the Headers collection or by saving the request to disk by using the SaveAs method), having to parse the text each time we wanted to find a particular piece of information would be a pain.

HTTP Request Types

The current HTTP 1.1 standard (which can be found at *http://www.w3.org/Protocols/rfc2616/rfc2616.html*) defines the valid request types for an HTTP request. These types are:

- OPTIONS
- GET
- HEAD
- POST
- PUT
- DELETE
- TRACE
- CONNECT

While this list shows the valid request types, only the GET and HEAD are required to be supported by general-purpose servers. In practice, most, if not all, requests you'll deal with will be GET and POST type requests.

GET requests simply ask the server to return a resource (such as an HTML or ASP.NET page) specified by the URL passed with the request. GET requests can also pass data to the server by appending it to the URL in the following format:

```
GET /Chapter_16/showHTTP.aspx?name=andrew HTTP/1.0
```

This GET request fragment passes a key/value pair with the value "andrew" represented by the key "name." When more than one key/value pair is passed, each pair is separated by the ampersand (&) character. When using GET requests for passing data, in most cases, data passed with a GET request is limited to around 2K, which is limiting for complex or lengthy data. Pages using data passed by a GET request may be subject to alteration by a user before the request is made. Any data received via a GET request should be validated to ensure that processing or storing it will not cause an undesirable result.

POST requests are used to post data to the server. Like GET requests, this data is passed as one or more key/value pairs, separated by ampersands. Unlike GET requests, the key/value pairs in a POST request are passed in the request body:

```
POST /Chapter_16/showHTTP.aspx HTTP/1.0
name=andrew
```

The HttpRequest class does this work for us, allowing us to deal only with the specific piece(s) of information that we're interested in. Table 16-1 lists the properties, collections, and methods exposed by the HttpRequest class.

Table 16-1. HttpRequest class summary

Properties	Collections	Methods (public instance)
AcceptTypes	Cookies	BinaryRead
ApplicationPath	Files	MapPath

Table 16-1. HttpRequest class summary (continued)

Properties	Collections	Methods (public instance)
Browser	Form	SaveAs
ClientCertificate	Headers	
ContentEncoding	Params	
ContentLength	QueryString	
ContentType	ServerVariables	
FilePath		
HttpMethod		
InputStream		
IsAuthenticated		
IsSecureConnection		
Path		
PathInfo		
PhysicalApplicationPath		
PhysicalPath		
RawUrl		
RequestType		
TotalBytes		
Url		
UrlReferrer		
UserAgent		
UserHostAddress		
UserHostName		
UserLanguages		
Collections		

Comments/Troubleshooting

In ASP, the Request object provided relatively few properties and methods (one each, in fact), supplying most of the information from requests through its collections: ClientCertificate, Cookies, Form, QueryString, and in particular, the ServerVariables collection. With the exception of ClientCertificate (which now returns an instance of the HttpClientCertificate class representing the client's security certificate settings), all of these collections also exist in ASP.NET. A big difference is that the HttpRequest class exposes a substantial number of new properties (many of which are derived from information that was previously available only through the ServerVariables collection), as well as several new methods.

As was the case with ASP, you can request particular GET or POST values (or ServerVariable or Cookie values, for that matter) by passing the key for the value to the Request object (the current instance of the HttpRequest class):

```
Message.Text = Request("myKey")
```

If the key "myKey" exists in any of the collections that the HttpRequest class exposed, the previous code will return it.

Although accessing values as shown in the previous example may seem easy, there are two very good reasons not to use this method.

First, accessing values without specifying the collection in which the value should be found requires ASP.NET to search through each collection until it finds the key (if it finds it). While ASP.NET generally performs significantly faster than ASP, there is still no reason to suffer the unnecessary overhead of this method of accessing values.

Second, using the method shown previously makes your code more difficult to understand, debug, and maintain. Someone attempting to understand how your page operates would not be able to figure out from this code whether the page was expected to be accessed via a GET request or a POST request. Explicitly specifying the desired collection clarifies your intent and makes it easier to track down a problem if your code doesn't work.

In this chapter, we'll use the following code listing as the basis for most examples in the chapter. Unless otherwise noted, each example will consist of only the Page_Load event handler for that particular example. Any displayed output messages or return values will be shown as the Text property of the ASP.NET Label control named Message or displayed by calling Response.Write:

```
<%@ Page Language="vb" %>
<html>
    <head>
        <script runat="server">
            Sub Page_Load( )
                'Example code will go here
            End Sub
        </script>
    </head>
<body>
    <asp:label id="Message" runat="server"/>
</body>
</html>
```

Properties Reference

AcceptTypes

stringArray = Request.AcceptTypes

Returns a string array containing the Multipurpose Internet Mail Extension (MIME) types accepted by the client. You can use this property to determine whether a client can accept certain response types, including application types such as Word or Excel, which are supported only by Internet Explorer.

The following table lists some common MIME types:

MIME type	Description
text/html	HTML text content
text/xml	XML text content
image/gif	GIF-encoded image data
image/jpg	JPEG-encoded image data
application/msword	Binary data for Microsoft Word

Parameter

stringArray
> A string array that receives the array of accept types from the property.

Example

The code example declares a string array and an integer counter variable and assigns the AcceptTypes property value to the array variable. It then iterates the array members using the counter variable, writing each value to the browser by using the Message label control:

```
Sub Page_Load( )
    'Display Accept Types
    Dim MyArray( ) As String
    Dim I As Integer
    MyArray = Request.AcceptTypes
    For I = 0 To MyArray.GetUpperBound(0)
        Message.Text &= "Type " & CStr(I) & ": " & CStr(MyArray(I)) & _
                "<br/>"
    Next I
End Sub
```

The output of the code would look something like this:

Type 0: image/gif
Type 1: image/x-xbitmap
Type 2: image/jpeg
Type 3: image/pjpeg
Type 4: application/vnd.ms-powerpoint
Type 5: application/vnd.ms-excel
Type 6: application/msword
Type 7: */*

Notes

This property can prevent the server from wasting time sending responses to the client that the client cannot handle. For example, a request that would normally be fulfilled by returning an Excel spreadsheet could be fulfilled with an alternate response type for clients that do not support the Excel MIME type, application/vnd.ms-excel.

ApplicationPath

```
stringvar = Request.ApplicationPath
```

Returns a string containing the path to the virtual root of the current application.

Parameter

stringvar
    A string variable to receive the value of the ApplicationPath property.

Example

The code example retrieves the ApplicationPath and writes it to the client using the Message label control:

```
Sub Page_Load( )
    Message.Text = Request.ApplicationPath
End Sub
```

The output of the code should be the name of the virtual root of the application to which the request was sent.

Browser

```
bc = Request.Browser
```

Returns an instance of the HttpBrowserCapabilities class that describes the capabilities of the client browser. You can then use the class instance to determine what capabilities the client browser supports. The HttpBrowserCapabilities class exposes the capabilities of the client browser as a set of Boolean and String properties. Properties of the HttpBrowserCapabilities class include:

ActiveXControls
    A Boolean indicating whether the browser supports ActiveX controls.

AOL
    A Boolean indicating whether the browser is an AOL browser.

BackgroundSounds
    A Boolean indicating whether the browser supports background sounds.

Beta
    A Boolean indicating whether the browser is beta software.

Browser
    A String containing the User-Agent header value.

CDF
    A Boolean indicating whether the browser supports the Channel Definition Format for pushing content.

ClrVersion
    Returns a System.Version object containing version information about the CLR (if any) installed on the client machine (from the User-Agent header). If ClrVersion is not Nothing, you can retrieve version information from four of its Integer properties: Major, Minor, Revision, and Build.

Cookies

A Boolean indicating whether the browser supports cookies.

Crawler

A Boolean indicating whether the browser is a search engine web crawler.

EcmaScriptVersion

Returns an instance of the Version class containing information about the version of ECMAScript supported by the client browser. If EcmaScriptVersion is not Nothing, you can retrieve version information from four of its Integer properties: Major, Minor, Revision, and Build.

Frames

A Boolean indicating whether the browser supports frames.

Item

A Dictionary interface to values (i.e., Request.Browser.Item(*keyname*)).

JavaApplets

A Boolean indicating whether the browser supports Java applets.

JavaScript

A Boolean indicating whether the browser supports JavaScript.

MajorVersion

An Integer representing the browser major version number (for example, for IE 3.01, the MajorVersion property would return 3).

MinorVersion

A Double representing the browser minor version number (for example, for IE 3.01, the MinorVersion property would return .01).

MSDomVersion

Returns an instance of the Version class containing information about the version of the Microsoft XML Document Object Model (DOM) supported by the client browser. If MSDomVersion is not Nothing, you can retrieve version information from four of its Integer properties: Major, Minor, Revision, and Build.

Platform

A String containing the platform name (if any) included in the User-Agent header.

Tables

A Boolean indicating whether the browser supports HTML tables.

Type

A String containing the name and major version of the client browser.

VBScript

A Boolean indicating whether the browser supports VBScript.

Version

A String containing both the major and minor version numbers of the client browser.

W3CDomVersion

Returns an instance of the Version class containing information about the version of the World Wide Web Consortium (W3C) XML DOM supported by the client browser. If W3CDomVersion is not Nothing, you can retrieve version information from four of its Integer properties: Major, Minor, Revision, and Build.

Win16

A Boolean indicating whether the client is a Win16 machine.

Win32

A Boolean indicating whether the client is a Win32 machine.

Parameter

bc

An Object variable of type HttpBrowserCapabilities.

Example

```
Sub Page_Load( )
    Dim bc As HttpBrowserCapabilities
    bc = Request.Browser
    If bc.Cookies Then
        Message.Text = "Cookies are available with this browser"
    Else
        Message.Text = "Cookies are not available with this browser"
    End If
End Sub
```

Notes

You will probably use this property a lot if you plan to support multiple browsers and must provide the highest level of functionality on uplevel browsers such as Internet Explorer 5 or 6 or Netscape 6. For some properties, such as Cookies and JavaScript, the returned Boolean indicates only whether the browser version sending the request supports these features, not whether they are currently enabled in the current user's browser.

This property is especially important when developing custom server controls, since it allows you to have your custom controls automatically tailor their output to a specific browser (or class of browsers). See Chapter 6 for more information on custom control development.

ClientCertificate

```
cs = Request.ClientCertificate
```

Returns an instance of the HttpClientCertificate class, which exposes information about the client security certificate settings. These properties include issuer information, key size, and certificate validity dates.

Parameter

cs

An Object variable of type HttpClientCertificate.

Example

```
Sub Page_Load( )
    Dim cs As HttpClientCertificate
    cs = Request.ClientCertificate
```

```
    Message.Text = "Certificate Issuer is: " & cs.Issuer & "."
End Sub
```

Notes

You will probably use this property in intranet settings, where you have provided
a limited set of clients with certificates (issued from your own Certificate Server)
for accessing your application, rather than requiring them to authenticate by using
a set of credentials entered via the browser. In this case, client certificates are
mapped to NT user accounts to provide secure access. Client certificates can also
be issued by trusted third parties, but this method is rarely used. If no client certificate is installed on the requesting client, this property returns an
HttpClientCertificate instance with no valid property values.

ContentEncoding

```
ce = Request.ContentEncoding
```

Returns an instance of the Encoding class (located in the System.Text namespace),
which represents the character encoding of the body of the current request.

Parameter

ce
> An Object variable of type Encoding.

Example

The example demonstrates how to display the current ContentEncoding to the
user:

```
Sub Page_Load( )
    Dim ce As System.Text.Encoding
    ce = Request.ContentEncoding
    Message.Text = "Current encoding is: " & ce.EncodingName & "."
End Sub
```

For a request using UTF-8 content encoding, the output of this example would
be:

```
Current encoding is: Unicode (UTF-8).
```

ContentLength

```
intvar = Request.ContentLength
```

Returns an integer containing the length, in bytes, of the request sent from the
client. This property includes only the content sent in the body of the HTTP
request and does not include the length of the HTTP headers or of any data sent
as part of an HTTP GET request (which would appear in the headers). If the
HTTP request contains no body, its value is 0.

Parameter

intvar
> An Integer variable to receive the length, in bytes, of the content.

Example

This example demonstrates how to display the length of the current request in the browser:

```
Sub Page_Load( )
    Dim length As Integer
    length = Request.ContentLength
    Message.Text = "Length of request was: " & length & " bytes."
End Sub
```

The following code can be used to post to the example page:

```
<html>
    <head>
        <title>Submit a named parameter via POST</title>
    </head>
<body>
    <form id="form1" action="ContentLength.aspx" method="POST">
        <h3>Name:</h3>
        <input type="text" name="name">
        <input type="submit">
    </form>
</body>
</html>
```

Notes

You can use this property to test the length of content posted via a POST request before acting on that content. For example, if your page receives files from a file input field, you could check the ContentLength property before saving or processing the uploaded file to prevent users from uploading files greater than a specific size. Note that in cases when you receive multiple form fields, you can get more specific data on the size of an uploaded file by referring to the Posted-File.ContentLength property of an HtmlInputFile control used for submitting files.

ContentType

```
stringvar = Request.ContentType
```

Returns a string containing the MIME type of the current client request. On GET requests, this property may return an empty string.

Parameter

stringvar
    A string variable to receive the content type.

Example

The example shows how you can take different actions in your page, depending on the ContentType of the request:

```
Sub Page_Load( )
    Dim ct As String
    ct = Request.ContentType
```

```
      If ct = "application/x-www-form-urlencoded" Then
         'Process form input
         Message.Text = "Form data was submitted."
      Else
         Message.Text = "Content Type of request is: " & ct
      End If
   End Sub
```

The following code can be used to post to the example page:

```
<html>
   <head>
      <title>Submit a named parameter via POST</title>
   </head>
<body>
      <form id="form1" action="ContentType.aspx" method="POST">
         <h3>Name:</h3>
         <input type="text" name="name">
         <input type="submit">
      </form>
</body>
</html>
```

Notes

One potential use for this property is to ensure that the content type of the request is what you expect it to be. This can help avoid wasting processor time with invalid requests and prevent malicious users from attempting to forge requests to your application that send unexpected content.

FilePath

stringvar = Request.FilePath

Returns a string containing the virtual path of the current client request. The virtual path includes the name of the application root folder, any subfolders in the request path, and the requested filename.

Parameter

stringvar
   A string variable to receive the file path.

Example

The example displays the FilePath property to the user:

```
Sub Page_Load( )
   Dim fp As String
   fp = Request.FilePath
   Message.Text = "The virtual path of the current request is: _
         & "<strong>" & fp & "</strong>"
End Sub
```

Notes

This property is identical to the Path property listed later in this chapter.

HttpMethod

stringvar = Request.HttpMethod

Returns a string containing the method (i.e., GET, POST, or HEAD) of the current request.

Parameter

stringvar

    A string variable to receive the HTTP method of the current request.

Example

The example uses the HttpMethod property to determine what action to take for a given request:

```
Sub Page_Load( )
    Select Case Request.HttpMethod
        Case "POST"
            Response.Write("POST requests not allowed!<br/>")
            Response.End
        Case "HEAD"
            Response.Write("HEAD requests not allowed!<br/>")
            Response.End
        Case "GET"
            'Process request
            Message.Text = "GET requests are allowed!<br/>"
        Case Else
            Response.Write("Unknown request: not allowed!<br/>")
            Response.End
    End Select
End Sub
```

Note that we use Response.Write to send the message before calling Response.End. Calling Response.End will immediately terminate processing of the page, which will also prevent rendering of any server control output. The code for a page that makes a POST request to the example page is shown here:

```
<html>
    <head>
        <title>Submit a named parameter via POST</title>
    </head>
<body>
    <form id="form1" action="HttpMethod.aspx" method="POST">
        <h3>Name:</h3>
        <input type="text" name="name">
        <input type="submit">
    </form>
</body>
</html>
```

Notes

In classic ASP, the request method was typically retrieved using the REQUEST_ METHOD key of the ServerVariables collection. Often, this key was used to create self-submitting form pages by displaying a set of form fields when the GET method was detected and processing the input received from the form fields when the POST method was detected. ASP.NET Web Forms provide built-in plumbing for self submitting forms. By adding a form with the runat="server" attribute and adding one or more input type server controls to the form, the developer only needs to check the page's IsPostBack property to determine whether a POST or GET request has been received, and execute the desired code based on that property.

InputStream

inputstream = Request.InputStream

Returns a stream object containing the body of the incoming HTTP request.

Parameter

inputstream
> An Object variable of type stream.

Example

The example uses a byte array to search for a specified character and then copies that character and the remaining contents of the stream to a string. The @ Import directive shown in the example should be placed at the top of the page:

```
<% @ Import Namespace="System.IO" %>

Sub Page_Load( )
    Dim InStream As Stream
    Dim iCounter, StreamLength, iRead As Integer
    Dim OutString As String
    Dim Found As Boolean

    InStream = Request.InputStream
    StreamLength = CInt(InStream.Length)
    Dim ByteArray(StreamLength) As Byte
    iRead = InStream.Read(ByteArray, 0, StreamLength)
    InStream.Close( )

    For iCounter = 0 to StreamLength - 1
        If Found = True Then
            OutString &= Chr(ByteArray(iCounter))
        End If
        If Chr(ByteArray(iCounter)) = "A" Then
            Found = True
            OutString &= Chr(ByteArray(iCounter))
        End If
    Next iCounter

    Message.Text = "Output: " & OutString
End Sub
```

The following code can be used to post to the example page:

```html
<html>
    <head>
    </head>
<body>
    <form id="form1" action="InputStream.aspx" method="POST">
        <h3>Name:</h3>
        <input type="text" name="name">
        <input type="submit">
    </form>
</body>
</html>
```

The code returns as output the first capital A appearing in the request body. Any characters after it are returned to the end of the stream.

Notes

This property is useful if you wish to perform byte-level filtering of the request body. It works only with POST requests, since these requests are the only commonly used HTTP requests that provide a request body.

IsAuthenticated

```
boolvar = Request.IsAuthenticated
```

Returns a Boolean indicating whether the current request is coming from a user who is authenticated. This property refers to authentication against the NTLM account database.

Parameter

boolvar
    A Boolean variable to receive the authentication status of the user.

Example

The example checks to see if the current user is authenticated and it outputs one of two messages, depending on the authentication status of the user. Note that the message delivered to authenticated users utilizes the User property of the page to output the current user's name and domain.

```
Sub Page_Load( )
    Dim boolAuth As Boolean

    boolAuth = Request.IsAuthenticated

    If boolAuth Then
        Message.Text = "User " & Page.User.Identity.Name & " is authenticated."
    Else
        Message.Text = "Current user is not authenticated."
    End If
End Sub
```

Notes

In addition to the IsAuthenticated property that the HttpRequest class exposes, the FormsIdentity, WindowsIdentity, and PassportIdentity classes expose an IsAuthenticated property for much the same purpose as the HttpRequest class. Note that the IsAuthenticated property of the HttpRequest class returns the authentication status of the user regardless of the authentication method used.

IsSecureConnection

`boolvar = Request.IsSecureConnection`

Returns a Boolean indicating whether the current connection uses secure sockets (SSL) for communication.

Parameter

boolvar
    A Boolean variable to receive the SSL status of the current request.

Example

The example shows how you can take different actions depending on whether or not the current request was made via SSL:

```
Sub Page_Load( )
    Dim boolvar As Boolean
    boolvar = Request.IsSecureConnection
    If boolvar = True Then
        Message.Text = "Connection is HTTPS."
    Else
        Message.Text = "Connection is HTTP."
    End If
End Sub
```

Notes

You would typically use this property to determine whether or not to fulfill a request that requires an SSL connection in order to encrypt sensitive data (such as credit card numbers) that might be submitted via the requested page. Additionally, you could use this property on a page that may or may not use SSL to determine how to render output to the page depending on the SSL status. Since encrypting and decrypting content for SSL communication exacts a performance penalty, reducing the number and/or size of graphics used on SSL-enabled pages is generally considered good practice. With this property, you could render more and/or higher-resolution graphics when SSL is not enabled for the request, and render fewer and/or lower-resolution graphics for SSL requests.

Path

`stringvar = Request.Path`

Returns a string containing the virtual path of the current client request. The virtual path includes the name of the application root folder, subfolders in the request path, and the requested filename.

Parameter

stringvar
> A string variable to receive the file path.

Example

The example displays the Path property to the user:

```
Sub Page_Load( )
    Dim path As String
    path = Request.FilePath
    Message.Text = "The virtual path of the current request is: " & path
End Sub
```

Notes

This property is identical to the FilePath property listed earlier in this chapter.

PathInfo

stringvar = Request.PathInfo

Returns a string containing any additional path information (including path information appended to a URL after the filename of the requested resource) passed with the current request.

Parameter

stringvar
> A string variable to receive the additional path information.

Example

The example writes both the Path and PathInfo properties to the client browser:

```
Sub Page_Load( )
    Message.Text = "Path = " & Request.Path & "<br/>"
    Message.Text &= "Additional Path Info = " & Request.PathInfo & "<br/>"
End Sub
```

Notes

PathInfo does not return information such as query string values. PathInfo returns any characters following a forward-slash (/) after the resource (file) name, including the forward-slash itself.

PhysicalApplicationPath

stringvar = Request.PhysicalApplicationPath

Returns a string containing the physical path to the root of the current application.

Parameter

stringvar
> A string variable to receive the application path.

Example

The example writes the PhysicalApplicationPath property to the browser:

```
Sub Page_Load( )
    Dim physAppPath As String
    physAppPath = Request.PhysicalApplicationPath
    Message.Text = "Physical Application Path = " & physAppPath
End Sub
```

Notes

This property is useful when you need to create or write to a file within your web application. Rather than hardcoding a filesystem path in your page, you can use this property in combination with a filename to create or edit a file in the same folder as the page containing the code, regardless of the page's location.

PhysicalPath

stringvar = Request.PhysicalPath

Returns a string containing the physical path to the requested file.

Parameter

stringvar
    A string variable to receive the physical path.

Example

The example writes the PhysicalPath property to the browser:

```
Sub Page_Load( )
    Dim physicalPath As String
    physicalPath = Request.PhysicalPath
    Message.Text = "Physical Path = " & physicalPath
End Sub
```

Notes

Unlike the PhysicalApplicationPath, which returns only the path to the root of the application, the PhysicalPath property returns the full physical path of the requested resource, including any intervening folders and the resource's filename. This property may be useful in combination with ASP.NET's Trace functionality in troubleshooting situations when files you are attempting to write to or read from are not found, or when created files aren't located where you expect them to be. Adding Trace.Write statements to your page to write the Path, PhysicalApplicationPath, and PhysicalPath properties to the trace log (which you can enable by adding the Trace="true" attribute to the @ Page directive) may help you track down such bugs.

RawUrl

stringvar = Request.RawUrl

Returns a string containing the raw URL of the current request. The raw URL consists of the portion of the URL following the domain information. Thus, for the URL *http://search.support.microsoft.com/kb/c.asp*, the raw URL is */kb/c.asp*. The raw URL includes the query string, if one is present.

Parameter

stringvar
  A string variable to receive the raw URL.

Example

The example writes the RawUrl property to the browser:

```
Sub Page_Load( )
   Dim stringvar As String
   stringvar = Request.RawUrl
   Message.Text = "The raw URL is: " & stringvar
End Sub
```

RequestType

stringvar = Request.RequestType

The RequestType property returns a String containing the request type (i.e., GET or POST) of the current request.

Parameter

stringvar
  A string variable to receive the request type.

Example

The example writes the RequestType property to the browser:

```
Sub Page_Load( )
   Dim stringvar As String
   stringvar = Request.RequestType
   Message.Text = "The request type is: " & stringvar
End Sub
```

Notes

This property is listed as read/write; however, there really aren't any situations where it would be useful to change its value. From the read standpoint, this property returns the same information as the read-only HttpMethod property listed earlier in this chapter. If you attempt to change its value, no corresponding change occurs in the value of HttpMethod.

TotalBytes

intvar = Request.TotalBytes

Returns an Integer representing the size of the HTTP request body. The Total-Bytes property does not include the size of the HTTP request headers, or the size of query string values passed with a GET request.

Parameter

intvar
> An Integer variable to receive the size, in bytes, of the current request body.

Example

The example writes the TotalBytes property to the browser:

```
Sub Page_Load( )
    Dim intvar As Integer
    intvar = Request.TotalBytes
    Message.Text = "The size of the current request body is: <br/>"
    Message.Text &= intvar & " bytes."
End Sub
```

The following code can be used to post to the example page:

```
<html>
    <head>
        <title>Submit a named parameter via POST</title>
    </head>
<body>
    <form id="form1" action="TotalBytes.aspx" method="POST">
        <h3>Name:</h3>
        <input type="text" name="name">
        <input type="submit">
    </form>
</body>
</html>
```

Notes

This property's behavior is identical to that of the ContentLength property described earlier in this chapter.

Url

uriObj = Request.Url

Returns an instance of the Uri class containing properties that describe the current URL requested by the user. Properties exposed by the Uri class include Scheme (protocol), Port, and Host.

Parameter

uriObj
> An Object variable of type Uri.

Example

The example uses the Uri object that the Url property returns to write information about the URL for the current request to the browser:

```
Sub Page_Load( )
    Dim myUri As Uri
    myUri = Request.Url

    Message.Text = "Current request URL info - <br/><br/>"
```

```
        Message.Text &= "Protocol: " & myUri.Scheme & "<br/>"
        Message.Text &= "Port: " & myUri.Port & "<br/>"
        Message.Text &= "Host Name: " & myUri.Host & "<br/>"
    End Sub
```

Notes

While the Uri class this property returns has methods as well as properties, you're more likely to use these methods (particularly the CheckHostName and Check-SchemeName methods) when creating your own Uri resource from scratch, rather than when receiving the Uri instance from the Url property.

A note on URIs: Uniform Resource Identifier (URI) (compare to Uniform Resource Locator, or URL) is a more general version of URLs and URNs. In most cases today, URI and URL are identical, although this may change as URNs are used more frequently. For the purposes of the Url property, the terms carry the same meaning.

UrlReferrer

uriObj = Request.UrlReferrer

Returns an instance of the Uri class containing properties that describe the URL for the resource from which the user navigated to the current requested resource. If the user did not navigate to the current resource (i.e., if the current resource is accessed directly), the UrlReferrer property returns Nothing.

Parameter

uriObj
> An Object variable of type Uri.

Example

The example uses the Uri object that the UrlReferrer property returned in order to write information about the URL for the referring resource to the browser:

```
Sub Page_Load( )
    Dim myUri As Uri
    myUri = Request.UrlReferrer

    If Not (myUri Is Nothing) Then
        Message.Text = "Referral URL info - <br/><br/>"
        Message.Text &= "Protocol: " & myUri.Scheme & "<br/>"
        Message.Text &= "Port: " & myUri.Port & "<br/>"
        Message.Text &= "Host Name: " & myUri.Host & "<br/>"
        Message.Text &= "App Path: " & myUri.AbsolutePath & "<br/>"
    Else
        Message.Text = "No referral URL info available."
    End If
End Sub
```

The following code can link to the example page:

```
<html>
    <head>
```

```
        <title>Link to UrlReferrer</title>
    </head>
<body>
    <a href="UrlReferrer.aspx">Go to UrlReferrer.aspx</a>
</body>
</html>
```

Notes

The example code makes sure that the UrlReferrer property returns a valid instance of the Uri class. The UrlReferrer property returns Nothing if the page is accessed directly rather than from a link on another page.

UserAgent

stringvar = Request.UserAgent

Returns a string containing the User-Agent header. The User-Agent string identifies the browser (or other HTTP-capable client software, such as that used on mobile phones, etc.) that the client uses to make the request. Depending on the browser and platform, this string may also identify the operating system the client uses, as well as the version of the installed . NET Framework (IE only).

Parameter

stringvar
   A string variable to receive the User-Agent string.

Example

The example writes the UserAgent property to the browser:

```
Sub Page_Load( )
    Dim stringvar As String
    stringvar = Request.UserAgent
    Message.Text = "User Agent: " & stringvar
End Sub
```

Notes

When you attempt to discern the capabilities of the client browser, using the properties of the HttpBrowserCapabilities object returned by the Request.Browser property is generally easier. However, there may be cases in which the User-Agent for a given client returns information that is not checked for by the HttpBrowserCapabilities class. In this case, you could add the desired information to the <browserCaps> configuration section handler in *machine.config* (see Chapters 8 and 20 for more information on ASP.NET configuration) and then create your own version of the HttpBrowserCapabilities class by inheriting from the built-in class and adding your own property or properties for the User-Agent attribute you're looking for. Or, if you don't want to make that effort, you could simply parse the User-Agent string for the desired attribute by using the User-Agent property.

UserHostAddress

stringvar = Request.UserHostAddress

Returns the IP address of the client making the request.

Parameter

stringvar
> A string variable to receive the client IP address.

Example

The example writes the UserHostAddress, UserHostName, and UserLanguages properties to the browser:

```
Sub Page_Load( )
    Dim HostAddress, HostName, Languages( ) As String
    Dim iCounter As Integer

    HostAddress = Request.UserHostAddress
    HostName = Request.UserHostName
    Languages = Request.UserLanguages

    Message.Text = "Client IP Address: " & HostAddress & "<br/>"
    Message.Text &= "Client Machine Name: " & HostName & "<br/>"
    For iCounter = 0 To Languages.GetUpperBound(0)
        Message.Text &= "Client Language " & iCounter & ": " & _
            CStr(Languages(iCounter)) & "<br/>"
    Next iCounter
End Sub
```

UserHostName

stringvar = Request.UserHostName

Returns a string that contains the DNS hostname of the client making the request.

Parameter

stringvar
> A string variable to receive the hostname.

Example

See the example for the UserHostAddress property.

Notes

If no DNS server is available that can resolve the client IP address to a DNS name, the UserHostName property returns the IP address of the client (just like the UserHostAddress property).

UserLanguages

stringArray = Request.UserLanguages

Returns a sorted string array containing the list of languages supported by the client.

Parameter

stringArray

A string array variable to receive the list of client-supported languages.

Example

See the example for the UserHostAddress property.

Notes

To test this property, you can set support for additional languages in your browser as follows:

- In Internet Explorer 6, select Internet Options... from the Tools menu. On the General tab of the Internet Options dialog, click the Languages... button. Use the Language Preference dialog to add, remove, or move languages up or down on the list of preferred languages.

- In Netscape Navigator 6, select Preferences... from the Edit menu and then select the Languages node in the lefthand tree view. Use the options on the right to add, remove, or move languages up or down on the list.

Now if you browse a page containing the code in the UserHostAddress example, all languages you select will be listed in the order you chose.

Collections Reference

The Request object in ASP.NET supports seven collections, four of which were supported in ASP (Cookies, Forms, QueryString, and ServerVariables), and three of which are new (Files, Headers, and Params).

The collections of the Request class support the following common set of properties:

AllKeys

Returns a string array of all keys in the collection.

Count

Returns an integer count of name/value pairs in the collection.

Item(Index|Key)

Returns an instance of the collection class based on the index or passed-in key. This is the default property, which is why, for example, calling:

```
Response.Cookies (KeyVal)
```

returns the HttpCookie instance corresponding to *KeyVal*.

Keys

Returns a collection of the keys for the collection.

In addition, each collection class exposes the following methods:

CopyTo(Array, Index)

Copies the contents of the collection object to the provided *Array* argument, starting at the provided *Index* argument. Note that the array must be dimensioned to a sufficient size to contain the collection before calling CopyTo.

GetKey(Index)

Returns a string containing the key corresponding to the provided *Index* argument.

With the exception of the Cookies collection, the code used to access keys and values in the collections the Request class exposes is nearly identical in every case. This similarity makes it simple to create your own reusable classes or methods for manipulating the values from these collections, regardless of which collection you are working with.

Cookies

`HttpCookieCollection = Request.Cookies`

The Cookies collection returns an instance of the `HttpCookieCollection` class containing all cookies sent as a part of the current request. The `HttpCookieCollection` class contains an instance of the `HttpCookie` class for each cookie passed as part of the client request. The properties of these HttpCookie instances can be used to access information about the cookie(s).

As in classic ASP, the Cookies collection is still implemented as a collection (in fact, the HttpCookieCollection inherits from the .NET `NameObjectCollectionBase` class), but rather than a collection of string keys and string values, the ASP.NET implementation is a collection of string keys and objects (instances of the `HttpCookie` class). Individual cookies are retrieved into variables of type Http-Cookie, providing access to the cookies' values through class properties.

Dictionary-style cookies (cookies with more than one value) are accessible through the Values property of the `HttpCookie` class, which returns a NameValue-Collection containing the cookie subkeys and values. You can also retrieve individual values by their key with the following syntax:

`HttpCookie.Values("keyname")`

Parameter

HttpCookieCollection

An Object variable of type HttpCookieCollection.

Example

The example retrieves the collection of cookies from the Cookies property and writes out the key and value of each, along with any subkeys of dictionary cookies:

```
Sub Page_Load( )
    Dim Counter1, Counter2 As Integer
    Dim Keys(), SubKeys( ) As String
    Dim CookieColl As HttpCookieCollection
    Dim Cookie As HttpCookie

    ' Get Cookie collection
    CookieColl = Request.Cookies

    ' Get Cookie keys
    Keys = CookieColl.AllKeys
```

```
        ' Get cookies by index
      For Counter1 = 0 To Keys.GetUpperBound(0)
         Cookie = CookieColl(Keys(Counter1))
         Message.Text = "Cookie: " & Cookie.Name & "<br/>"
         Message.Text &= "Expires: " & Cookie.Expires & "<br/>"

         ' Get keys for dictionary cookie into an array
         SubKeys = Cookie.Values.AllKeys
         ' Write dictionary cookie values to the browser
         For Counter2 = 0 To SubKeys.GetUpperBound(0)
            Message.Text &= "Key " & CStr(Counter2) + ": " & _
               SubKeys(Counter2) & "<br/>"
            Message.Text &= "Value " & CStr(Counter2) + ": " & _
               Cookie.Values(Counter2) & "<br/>"
         Next Counter2
         Message.Text &= "<br/>"
      Next Counter1
   End Sub
```

Notes

The ASP implementation of the Cookies collection and the HttpCookieCollection
class returned by the Cookies property expose a common set of properties; these
properties are described in the "Collections Reference" section.

While it is still possible in ASP.NET to retrieve an individual cookie by its text key
as well as its numerical index, the differences in the operation make wholesale
migration of ASP cookie-handling code to ASP.NET impractical without significant changes. For example, the following code will raise exceptions:

```
For Each strKey In Request.Cookies
   Response.Write strKey & " = " & Request.Cookies(strKey) & _
               "<br/>"
   If Request.Cookies(strKey).HasKeys Then
      For Each strSubKey In Request.Cookies(strKey)
         Response.Write "->" & strKey & "(" & strSubKey & _
            ") = " & Request.Cookies(strKey)(strSubKey) & "<br/>"
      Next
   End If
Next
```

Apart from the fact that this code does not explicitly declare its variables or their
types (both of which are required by default in ASP.NET), the previous code fails
because the Request.Cookies(*key*) property returns an instance of HttpCookie,
rather than a string, and the HttpCookie instance cannot be implicitly converted
to a string for the Response.Write statement, which expects a string. Additionally, the call to Request.Cookies(*key*) does not get the subkeys for a dictionary
cookie. Fortunately, the modifications necessary to make the previous code work
are fairly simple and are shown here:

```
For Each strKey In Request.Cookies
   Message.Text = strKey & " = " & _
      Request.Cookies(strKey).ToString( ) & "<br/>"
   If Request.Cookies(strKey).HasKeys Then
      For Each strSubKey In Request.Cookies(strKey).Values
```

```
          Message.Text = "->" & strKey & "(" & strSubKey & _
              ") = " & Request.Cookies(strKey)(strSubKey).ToString() _
              & "<br/>"
        Next
      End If
    Next
```

To solve the first issue, we use the HttpCookie's Value method to get the value of the cookie as a string. The solution to the second issue is to call the Values property of the HttpCookie instance, which allows us to retrieve the subkeys of a dictionary cookie.

Another quirk of the change from the mostly text-based manipulation of cookie keys and values in ASP to class-based manipulation in ASP.NET is that the Expires property of the HttpCookie class is available whether you read or write to a cookie. In ASP, however, attempting to read the Expires property of a cookie would result in an error. Unfortunately, at the time of this writing, the Expires property of HttpCookie does not actually return the expiration of the cookie. Instead, it returns the value 12:00:00 AM, which suggests that despite its readability, the property is not designed to be read from.

Finally, unlike classic ASP, the collections in ASP.NET are zero-based, so the first element in any collection or array is 0, not 1. This is especially important to remember when retrieving values by their index.

Files

HttpFileCollection = `Request.Files`

The Files collection, which is new to ASP.NET, returns a collection of type Http-FileCollection that contains any files uploaded by the user's current request. This collection is especially useful in combination with the HtmlInputFile Server Control, which provides the basic plumbing necessary to upload files via an HTTP POST request. When a user submits one or more files (one per HtmlInput-File control on the submitting page), you can retrieve the files by using the Files collection.

Parameter

HttpFileCollection
> An Object variable of type HttpFileCollection.

Example

The example uses two HtmlInputFile server controls and a server-side <script> block to upload files and process them. The example shows both the <form> section of the page and its controls and the <script> block containing the UploadBtn_OnClick method called by the onServerClick event of the HtmlInput-Button control:

```
<!--Place between the <head> and </head> tags -->
<script runat="server">
  Sub UploadBtn_Click(Sender as Object, e as EventArgs)
    UploadForm.Visible = False
    If InStr(Request.ContentType, "multipart/form-data") Then
```

```
                Dim Counter1 As Integer
                Dim Keys() As String
                Dim Files As HttpFileCollection

                ' Load File collection
                Files = Request.Files
                ' Get names of all files into an array
                Keys = Files.AllKeys
                For Counter1 = 0 To Keys.GetUpperBound(0)
                    Message.Text &= "File ID: " & Keys(Counter1) & "<br/>"
                    Message.Text &= "File Name/Path: " & _
                        Files(Counter1).FileName & "<br/>"
                Next Counter1
            Else
                Message.Text = "Wrong content type!"
            End If
        End Sub
    </script>

    <!-- This section resides between the <body> and </body> tags -->
    <form id="UploadForm" enctype="multipart/form-data" runat="server">
        Select File To Upload to Server:
        <br/>
        <%-- MyFile and MyFile2 are HtmlInputFile controls --%>
        <%-- note the runat attribute --%>
        <input id="MyFile" type="file" runat="server">
        <br/>
        <input id="MyFile2" type="file" runat="server">
        <br/>
        <input id="Submit1" type="submit" value="Upload!"
            onserverclick="UploadBtn_Click" runat="server" >
    </form>
    <asp:label id="Message" runat="server"/>
```

Notes

In classic ASP, file uploading was a painful process that usually involved finding and purchasing a third-party upload control to use on the receiving ASP page to parse and save uploaded files. Thanks to the Files collection, you no longer need to locate and learn how to use third-party controls to upload files. This is bad for the control developers (although we suspect they'll more than make up for the loss by writing new Server Controls), but great for ASP.NET developers.

Two important points to remember about the Files collection to successfully upload files:

- If using a client-side HTML form (no runat="server" attribute), set the method attribute of the form to POST.
- Set the enctype attribute of the form to multipart/form-data.

The upload will succeed only if you take both steps. Note that the code example checks to see if the incoming request is multipart/form-data before attempting to retrieve the files.

It is not necessary to use the HtmlInputFile control to upload files that can be retrieved via the Files collection. As long as the submitting page uses the POST method and the `multipart/form-data` enctype attribute, you can use the standard HTML file input tags:

```
<input type="file" id="myFile" name="myFile">
```

Note the use of the `name` attribute, without which the files collection will not contain the uploaded file for the control.

Form

NameValueCollection = `Request.Form`

The Form collection returns an instance of the `NameValueCollection` class containing all form fields passed along with an HTTP POST request. This collection will contain data only when the Content-Type of the HTTP request is either `application/x-www-form-urlencoded` or `multipart/form-data`.

The Form collection is one of two ways to retrieve data, depending on the HTTP method used to submit the data. The Form collection retrieves data submitted by an HTML form whose `method` attribute is set to `POST`, while the QueryString collection (covered later in this section) retrieves values submitted by HTML forms whose `method` attribute is set to `GET`.

Parameter

NameValueCollection
    An Object variable of type NameValueCollection.

Example

The example demonstrates how ASP.NET allows a single page to be used to submit values via HTTP POST and retrieve and display the values to the user. The example uses the IsPostBack property of the `Page` class to determine whether the request is a result of the form being submitted. If the request is not a postback, the form fields are displayed to allow the user to enter values. If the request is a postback, the page retrieves the Form collection and displays the name and value of each field in the browser.

```
Sub Page_Load( )
    If IsPostBack Then
        Form1.Visible = False
        If Request.HttpMethod = "POST" Then
            Dim Counter1 As Integer
            Dim Keys( ) As String
            Dim FormElements As NameValueCollection

            ' Get Form keys/elements
            FormElements=Request.Form
            ' Get names of form fields into array
            Keys = FormElements.AllKeys
            For Counter1 = 0 To Keys.GetUpperBound(0)
                Message.Text &= "Form " & Counter1 & " name: " & _
                    Keys(Counter1) & "<br/>"
                Message.Text &= "Form " & Counter1 & " value: " & _
```

```
                        FormElements(Counter1) & "<br/>"
            Next Counter1
        End If
    Else
        Form1.Visible = True
    End If
End Sub

<!-- This section resides between the <body> and </body> tags -->
<form id="Form1" runat="server">
    First Name:
    <br/>
    <asp:Textbox id="txtFName" runat="server"/>
    <br/>
    Last Name:
    <br/>
    <asp:Textbox id="txtLName" runat="server"/>
    <br/>
    <asp:Button id="Submit" Text="Submit" runat="server"/>
</form>
<asp:label id="Message" runat="server"/>
```

Notes

The Form collection exposes the same properties and methods described in the "Collections Reference" section and adds the following methods:

Get(Index|Key)
> Returns the contents of the specified item in the NameValueCollection as a comma-delimited String.

GetValues(Index|Key)
> Returns the contents of the specified item in the NameValueCollection as a String array.

Headers

```
NameValueCollection = Request.Headers
```

The Headers collection returns an instance of the `NameValueCollection` class containing all HTTP headers sent with the current request. This collection provides the same information that is returned by calling the Request.ServerVariables collection with the `ALL_HTTP` key.

Parameter

NameValueCollection
> An Object variable of type NameValueCollection.

Example

The example writes the HTTP headers passed with the request to the browser, first by using the ServerVariables("ALL_HTTP") method and then by using the Headers collection:

```
Sub Page_Load( )
    Dim AllHttp As String
```

```
' Get a String with all the HTTP headers
AllHttp = Request.ServerVariables("ALL_HTTP")
' Use Replace to format the String
AllHttp = Replace(AllHttp, "HTTP", "<br/>HTTP"
Message.Text &= AllHttp & "<br/><br/>"

Dim Counter1, Counter2 As Integer
Dim Keys(), subKeys( ) As String
Dim HeaderColl As NameValueCollection

' Load Headers into NameValueCollection
HeaderColl=Request.Headers
' Get keys into an array
Keys = HeaderColl.AllKeys
For Counter1 = 0 To Keys.GetUpperBound(0)
    Message.Text &= "Key: " & Keys(Counter1) & "<br/>"
    ' Get all values under this key
    subKeys = HeaderColl.GetValues(Counter1)
    For Counter2 = 0 To subKeys.GetUpperBound(0)
        Message.Text &= "Value " & CStr(Counter2) & ": " & _
            subKeys(Counter2) & "<br/>"
    Next Counter2
Next Counter1
End Sub
```

Notes

The Headers collection returns only the HTTP headers that were sent as a part of the current request, as opposed to the ServerVariables collection (described later in this section), which contains keys for every HTTP header, regardless of whether a value was passed.

If all you need to do is write the HTTP headers to a file or display them in the browser, it may be simpler to use the ServerVariables collection. In cases when you need to access a specific HTTP header by name or loop through the collection, the Headers collection is the way to go.

Params

NameValueCollection = Request.Params

The Params collection returns an instance of the NameValueCollection class containing key/value pairs for the QueryString, Form, ServerVariables, and Cookies collections. You can use the Params collection to dump all of these collections to a file or to the browser and to troubleshoot an application or track the form values your application receives, regardless of whether they come via GET (QueryString collection) or POST (Form collection).

Parameter

NameValueCollection
    An Object variable of type NameValueCollection.

Example

The example writes the keys and values contained in the Params collection to the browser:

```
Sub Page_Load( )
    Dim Counter1, Counter2 As Integer
    Dim Keys(), subKeys( ) As String
    Dim ParamColl As NameValueCollection

    ' Load Params into NameValueCollection
    ParamColl=Request.Params
    ' Get keys into an array
    Keys = ParamColl.AllKeys
    For Counter1 = 0 To Keys.GetUpperBound(0)
        Message.Text &= "Key: " & Keys(Counter1) & "<br/>"
        ' Get all values under this key
        subKeys = ParamColl.GetValues(Counter1)
        For Counter2 = 0 To subKeys.GetUpperBound(0)
            Message.Text &= "Value " & CStr(Counter2) & ": " & _
                subKeys(Counter2) & "<br/>"
        Next Counter2
        Message.Text &= "<br/>"
    Next Counter1
End Sub
```

The following code can be used to post to the example page:

```
<html>
    <head>
        <title>Submit a named parameter via POST</title>
    </head>
<body>
    <form id="form1" action="Params.aspx" method="POST">
        <h3>Name:</h3>
        <input type="text" name="name">
        <input type="submit">
    </form>
</body>
</html>
```

Notes

The collections are listed in the following order:

- QueryString
- Form
- Cookies
- ServerVariables

While it is possible to have both the Form and QueryString collections populated (for example, if a query string name/value pair is added to the URL for the action attribute of a form by using the POST method), you will normally see one or the other, not both.

QueryString

NameValueCollection = Request.QueryString

The QueryString collection returns an instance of the NameValueCollection class containing all the keys and values passed as a part of the query string (typically by submitting an HTML form that uses the GET method instead of POST).

Parameters

NameValueCollection
An Object variable of type NameValueCollection.

Example

The example writes the contents of the QueryString collection to the browser:

```
Sub Page_Load( )
    Dim Counter1, Counter2 As Integer
    Dim Keys(), subKeys( ) As String
    Dim QSColl As NameValueCollection

    ' Load QS into NameValueCollection
    QSColl=Request.QueryString
    ' Get keys into an array
    Keys = QSColl.AllKeys
    For Counter1 = 0 To Keys.GetUpperBound(0)
      Message.Text &= "Key: " & Keys(Counter1) & "<br/>"
      subKeys = QSColl.GetValues(Counter1) 'Get all values under this key
      For Counter2 = 0 To subKeys.GetUpperBound(0)
        Message.Text &= "Value " & CStr(Counter2) & ": " & _
            subKeys(Counter2) & "<br/>"
      Next Counter2
      Message.Text &= "<br/>"
    Next Counter1
End Sub
```

The following code can be used to post to the example page (note that the form method attribute has been set to GET, which is required for the form value to be sent as part of the query string):

```
<html>
    <head>
        <title>Submit a named parameter via POST</title>
    </head>
<body>
    <form id="form1" action="QueryString.aspx" method="GET">
        <h3>Name:</h3>
        <input type="text" name="name">
        <input type="submit">
    </form>
</body>
</html>
```

Notes

One advantage that the QueryString collection has over the Form collection is that you do not always need to have the user submit a form to use it. Because the query string values are appended to the URL, it is relatively simple to statically add query strings to links within pages or dynamically create anchor tags with query string values appended. In fact, many online stores use this method to drive their catalog pages (by passing a product ID appended onto a link to the page designed to display the product). That page can then retrieve the ID by using the QueryString collection.

Because query string values are passed as plain text appended to the URL, they are more vulnerable to tampering than values passed as a result of a POST operation. If you need to pass important data or data that, if tampered with, could create problems for your application, you should consider encrypting values before adding them to the query string or using another method to pass the values.

Certain characters used in query string processing, including &, ?, %, and +, must be encoded to avoid confusion between their use in your key/ value pair and their role as special characters in a query string. The following table lists the encoding for each of these special characters:

Character	Encoding
&	%26
?	%3f
%	%25
+	%2b
Space	%20

Rather than memorizing these values, you could make your life easier by simply using the UrlEncode method provided by the HttpServerUtility class (covered in Chapter 18), which automatically substitutes the appropriate encoding for any special characters in a string passed to it.

ServerVariables

NameValueCollection = Request.ServerVariables

Parameter
NameValueCollection
    An Object variable of type NameValueCollection.

Example
The example, as in the previous collection-related examples, writes the contents of the ServerVariables collection to the browser:

```
Sub Page_Load( )
    Dim Counter1, Counter2 As Integer
    Dim Keys(), subKeys( ) As String
    Dim SVarsColl As NameValueCollection

    ' Load ServerVariables into NameValueCollection
    SVarsColl=Request.ServerVariables
    ' Get keys into an array
    Keys = SVarsColl.AllKeys
    For Counter1 = 0 To Keys.GetUpperBound(0)
```

```
        Message.Text &= "Key: " & Keys(Counter1) & "<br/>"
        subKeys = SVarsColl.GetValues(Counter1)
        ' Get all values under this key
        For Counter2 = 0 To subKeys.GetUpperBound(0)
            Message.Text &= "Value " & CStr(Counter2) & ": " & _
                subKeys(Counter2) & "<br/>"
        Next Counter2
        Message.Text &= "<br/>"
    Next Counter1
End Sub
```

Notes

In addition to retrieving all the values by looping through the keys, you can access individual values if you know their key. The following list shows the available keys for the ServerVariable collection:

ALL_HTTP
> Returns a string containing all HTTP headers with each header name taking the form HTTP_*headername*, for which *headername* is the name of an HTTP header in all capital letters.

ALL_RAW
> Provides the same information as ALL_HTTP, but header names are not all capital letters and are not prefixed with HTTP_.

APPL_MD_PATH
> Returns the path of the application in the IIS metabase.

APPL_PHYSICAL_PATH
> Returns the physical path that corresponds to APPL_MD_PATH.

AUTH_TYPE
> Returns the authentication method used to validate access to protected content.

AUTH_USER
> Returns the username of the authenticated user in raw form.

AUTH_PASSWORD
> Returns the password entered in the browser's authentication dialog, assuming Basic authentication was used.

LOGON_USER
> Returns the name of the Windows account the current user is logged in to.

REMOTE_USER
> Returns the username string sent by the browser before any authentication filtering has taken place.

CERT_COOKIE
> Returns a unique string identifier for the client certificate.

CERT_FLAGS
> Returns bit flags that represent whether a certificate is present (bit0) and whether the certificate authority for the client certificate is in the list of recognized certificate authorities on the server (bit1).

CERT_ISSUER
> Returns the issuer of the client certificate.

CERT_KEYSIZE

Returns the number of bits for the SSL key (e.g., 40 or 128).

CERT_SECRETKEYSIZE

Returns the number of bits in the server's private key.

CERT_SERIALNUMBER

Returns the serial number of the client certificate.

CERT_SERVER_ISSUER

Returns the issuer of the server certificate.

CERT_SERVER_SUBJECT

Returns the subject field of the server certificate.

CERT_SUBJECT

Returns the subject field of the client certificate.

CONTENT_LENGTH

Returns the length of the content in the body of the HTTP request.

CONTENT_TYPE

Returns the MIME type of the content in the HTTP request.

GATEWAY_INTERFACE

Returns the revision number of the CGI specification used by the server.

HTTPS

Returns either on or off, depending on whether the request came through a secure socket (HTTPS) connection.

HTTPS_KEYSIZE

Returns the size, in bits, of the SSL key.

HTTPS_SECRETKEYSIZE

Returns the number of bits in the server's private key.

HTTPS_SERVER_ISSUER

Returns the issuer of the server certificate.

HTTPS_SERVER_SUBJECT

Returns the subject field of the server certificate.

INSTANCE_ID

Returns the ID for the IIS instance associated with the request. Unless more than one instance of IIS is running, this value is always 1.

INSTANCE_META_PATH

Returns the metabase path to the instance of IIS that responds to the current request.

LOCAL_ADDR

Returns the server address on which the request was received. Useful for servers with multiple NICs and IP addresses to determine which address received the request.

PATH_INFO

Returns any extra path information passed with the request. See the PathInfo property earlier in the chapter for more information.

PATH_TRANSLATED

Returns the physical path corresponding to the virtual path for the request.

QUERY_STRING
>   Returns the raw query string (if any) passed with the request.

REMOTE_ADDR
>   Returns the IP address of the machine making the request.

REMOTE_HOST
>   Returns the DNS name of the machine making the request, if available. Otherwise, returns the IP address.

REQUEST_METHOD
>   Returns the HTTP request method (GET, POST, etc.) used in the request.

SCRIPT_NAME
>   Returns a virtual path to the page being executed.

SERVER_NAME
>   Returns the server name, DNS name, or IP address of the server.

SERVER_PORT
>   Returns the port number on which the request was received.

SERVER_PORT_SECURE
>   Returns a string containing either 0 or 1, depending on whether the request was received on a secure port (1) or not (0).

SERVER_PROTOCOL
>   Returns the name and version of the protocol used to handle the client request. For IE 5.5 and IIS 5, this name and version would be "HTTP/1.1".

SERVER_SOFTWARE
>   Returns the name and version of the web server software.

URL
>   Returns the base URL of the request (i.e., everything after the domain name).

HTTP_CONNECTION
>   Returns the type of connection established.

HTTP_ACCEPT
>   Returns the value of the HTTP Accept header.

HTTP_ACCEPT_ENCODING
>   Returns the value of the HTTP Accept-Encoding header.

HTTP_ACCEPT_LANGUAGE
>   Returns the value of the HTTP Accept-Language header.

HTTP_HOST
>   Returns the value of the HTTP Host header.

HTTP_USER_AGENT
>   Returns the value of the HTTP User-Agent header.

Methods Reference

BinaryRead

`byteArray = Request.BinaryRead(byteCount)`

Returns a byte array containing the number of bytes specified by the *byteCount* argument.

Parameters

byteArray
>An Array variable of type Byte to receive the specified number of bytes from the method.

byteCount
>An integer specifying the number of bytes to return.

Notes

This method provides backward compatibility with classic ASP applications. For new development, using other means (such as the Files collection, etc.) is preferable to achieve the results that this method was used for.

MapPath

```
stringvar = Request.MapPath(virtualPath)
stringvar = Request.MapPath(virtualPath, _
 baseVirtualDirectory, allowCrossMapping)
```

The MapPath method, which the Server object exposed in classic ASP, allows you to retrieve a physical path on the server for a provided virtual path. In ASP.NET, this method is overloaded, meaning that it can be called with two different sets of arguments, as shown in the previous code. The first style, which is the same as in classic ASP, simply passes in a String containing the virtual path to be mapped. The second adds the *baseVirtualDirectory* argument, which specifies a base from which to resolve relative paths, and the *allowCrossMapping* argument, which allows you to map virtual paths that belong to other applications.

Parameters

stringvar
>A String variable to receive the mapped physical path.

virtualPath
>A String argument containing the virtual path to map.

baseVirtualDirectory
>A String argument containing a base path to be used for resolving relative paths.

allowCrossMapping
>A Boolean argument specifying whether paths can be mapped across applications.

Example

The example maps the path of the .NET Framework SDK samples' */QuickStart* directory and writes the result to the browser:

```
Sub Page_Load( )
    Dim VirPath, PhysPath, BasePath As String
    Dim BoolCross As Boolean = True

    VirPath = "/QuickStart"
    BasePath = ""
```

```
    Message.Text = Request.MapPath(VirPath, BasePath, BoolCross)
End Sub
```

Notes

In the previous example, if we had set the *BoolCross* variable to False and called the example code from outside the QuickStart application, an HttpException would be thrown, since this argument must be set to True to map paths across applications.

SaveAs

Request.SaveAs(*filename, includeHeaders*)

Saves the current HTTP request to disk, using the *filename* argument as the path and filename under which to save the request.

Parameters

filename
> A String argument containing the path and filename under which the request should be saved.

includeHeaders
> A Boolean argument indicating whether to save the HTTP header information as part of the request. Note that unless this is a POST request (or other request type with a request body), no information is saved if this argument is set to False.

Example

The example writes the HTTP request headers to the browser (for comparison purposes) and then saves the current request both with and without header information:

```
Sub Page_Load( )
    Message.Text = Request.Headers

    ' Save HTTP Request and Headers to a file
    Request.SaveAs((Request.PhysicalApplicationPath & _
        "HTTPRequest.txt"), True)
    ' Save HTTP Request to a file
    Request.SaveAs((Request.PhysicalApplicationPath & _
        "HTTPRequest_NoHeaders.txt"), False)
End Sub
```

Notes

This method can be very useful when debugging because it allows you to look at all the information sent in a given request (which is particularly useful in POST requests).

17

The HttpResponse Class

Just as the HttpRequest class covered in Chapter 16 is the replacement for the classic ASP intrinsic Request object, the HttpResponse class is ASP.NET's replacement for ASP's intrinsic Response object. Like the HttpRequest class, the HttpResponse class instance for a given ASP.NET page is exposed as a property (the Response property) of the Page class (from which all pages are derived), so code for the HttpResponse class is the same as in classic ASP. For those of you with classic ASP applications that migrate to ASP.NET, this class will save you a lot of work.

The HttpResponse class controls a variety of factors related to ASP.NET's response to a given HTTP request and provides access to the output stream of the response, allowing the writing of text or binary content to the client browser programmatically. The HttpResponse class provides access to this functionality through its properties, collections, and methods, which are shown in Table 17-1.

The control over page output that the HttpResponse class provides includes the character set used and encoding of the response, as well as whether the response is buffered and sent all at once (the default) or sent as output is processed. Methods of the HttpResponse class provide granular control over output sent to the browser, including sending binary or text content and sending HTTP headers and cookies to the client.

Note that several properties and methods exposed by the Response object in classic ASP have been deprecated in ASP.NET in favor of new properties and methods exposed by the HttpResponse class (or, in some cases, by other functionality available in ASP.NET). For properties and methods that have been deprecated and/or replaced by new members in ASP.NET, that fact will be notated in the "Notes" section of the reference for that property or method.

Table 17-1. HttpResponse class summary

Properties	Collections	Methods (instance)
Buffer	Cookies	AddCacheItemDependencies
BufferOutput		AddCacheItemDependency

Table 17-1. HttpResponse class summary (continued)

Properties	Collections	Methods (instance)
Cache		AddFileDependencies
CacheControl		AddFileDependency
Charset		AddHeader
ContentEncoding		AppendHeader
ContentType		AppendToLog
Expires		ApplyAppPathModifier
ExpiresAbsolute		BinaryWrite
IsClientConnected		Clear
Output		ClearContent
OutputStream		ClearHeaders
Status		Close
StatusCode		End
StatusDescription		Flush
SuppressContent		Pics
		Redirect
		Write
		WriteFile

Comments/Troubleshooting

The Response object provides control over both the format of the output sent to the browser and the content. In fact, an ASP.NET page can be written with no static HTML content whatsoever, and can generate that content exclusively through calls to the properties and methods of the response object, if desired. This provides the ability to programmatically generate not just HTML output dynamically, but any output the browser is capable of displaying, including image content and XML. This generation allows ASP.NET to be incredibly flexible in its response to user actions.

In classic ASP, the Response object's Write method was often used for quick and dirty debugging, such as to display a message indicating that a certain point in a page was reached or to display the value of variables used within the page. This simple and effective debugging technique had one major flaw: frequently, these calls to Response.Write left in a page that was moved from a development server to a production server, resulting in end users seeing the debugging message—hardly a desirable outcome. In ASP.NET, the new Trace object (a property of the Page class) provides the ability to write messages to a central trace log rather than to the page itself (although trace output can optionally be directed to the page). This feature allows developers to use the same simple debugging techniques while significantly reducing the likelihood of end users inadvertently seeing debug messages. Tracing in ASP.NET is discussed in Chapter 10.

In this chapter, we'll use the following code listing as the basis for most examples in the chapter. Unless otherwise noted, each example will consist of only the

Page_Load event handler for that particular example. Any output messages or return values displayed will be shown as the Text property of the ASP.NET Label control named Message or displayed by calling Response.Write:

```
<%@ Page Language="vb" %>
<html>
    <head>
        <script runat="server">
            Sub Page_Load()
                'Example code will go here
            End Sub
        </script>
    </head>
<body>
    <asp:label id="Message" runat="server"/>
</body>
</html>
```

Properties Reference

Buffer

```
Boolean = Response.Buffer
Response.Buffer = Boolean
```

Returns or sets a Boolean value that represents whether output is buffered on the server and sent when the request has completely finished processing, or when either the Response.Flush or Response.End methods are called. The default value is True.

Parameter

Boolean
   A Boolean that will receive or set the value of the property.

Notes

This property is supplied for backward compatibility with classic ASP and has been deprecated in favor of the BufferOutput property. New ASP.NET code should use BufferOutput in place of Buffer.

One important difference between the Response.Buffer property in classic ASP and the Buffer and BufferOutput properties in ASP.NET is that in classic ASP, you could not modify the Buffer property beyond the point at which output had been sent to the browser without causing an error. In ASP.NET, because of its compiled (rather than interpreted) nature, you can modify the Buffer or Buffer-Output property at any time, and the change only affects how buffering occurs. This gives developers much more flexibility over how and when their output is buffered. See the BufferOutput example for a demonstration.

BufferOutput

```
Boolean = Response.BufferOutput
Response.BufferOutput = Boolean
```

Returns or sets a Boolean value that represents whether output is buffered on the server and sent when the request has completely finished processing, or when either the Response.Flush or Response.End methods are called. The default value is True.

Parameter

Boolean
A Boolean that will receive or set the value of the property.

Example

The example sets the BufferOutput property to False and then loops 50 times, writing a period to the HTTP output with each loop iteration. It also writes the same output to the Text property of the Message Label control. For the first 10 and the last 21 iterations, BufferOutput is set to False; for iterations 11 through 29, it is set to True.

```
Sub Page_Load( )
    Response.BufferOutput = False
    Dim i As Integer
    For i = 1 To 50
        If (i > 10 And i < 30) Then
            Response.BufferOutput = True
        Else
            Response.BufferOutput = False
        End If
        System.Threading.Thread.Sleep(500)
        Response.Write(".")
        Message.Text &= "."
        'Response.Flush
    Next
    Response.Write("<br/>Done!<br/>")
    Message.Text &= "<br/>Done!<br/>"
End Sub
```

The output of the code would look something like this:

```
.................................................. Done! ................
.................................. Done!
```

The first line of periods should appear one by one until 10 have appeared, then pause, and then 20 more should appear, followed one by one by the rest and finally by the "Done!" statement. The identical output produced by the ASP.NET Label control (as an HTML <span>) will appear at once, since the output of controls on the server is not sent to the client until the control is rendered. This means that for each loop in the example, the code simply adds to a property of the control that will be rendered at a later time, while the text sent by the call to Response.Write is sent to the browser immediately after buffering is turned off.

You can see similar behavior by commenting out the Response.BufferOutput lines in the example (by prepending a single-quote (') character to the line), and uncommenting the Response.Flush line. This commenting and uncommenting will eliminate the pause in the output described previously.

The call to the Shared (static) Thread.Sleep method allows us to pause processing of an ASP.NET request for a given number of milliseconds. This can be useful when you need to wait during processing for whatever reason. However, using this method can impact the total time each request takes to process. In applications requiring high scalability, this may result in an unacceptable impact on the overall throughput of the application, since only a limited number of threads are available to process requests.

To avoid explicitly providing the namespace name when calling Thread.Sleep, add the following line to the page, immediately following the @ Page declaration:

```
<%@ Import Namespace="System.Threading" %>
```

Notes

This property is the ASP.NET equivalent of classic ASP's Buffer property and is preferred over Buffer for new development.

Cache

HttpCachePolicy = Response.Cache

Returns an instance of the HttpCachePolicy class that contains the cache policy of the page. You can use the methods exposed by the HttpCachePolicy class with this class instance to examine which headers or parameters (if any) have been set to vary the output cache, or to modify the current cache settings. The HttpCachePolicy class includes the following members:

HttpCachePolicy member	Description
SetCacheability method	Controls caching by setting the HTTP Cache-Control header.
SetExpires method	Sets the HTTP Expires header. This method takes a DateTime argument that represents the absolute expiration time for the header.
SetLastModified method	Sets the HTTP Last-Modified header. This method takes a DateTime argument that represents the absolute expiration time for the header.
Insert method	Inserts an item into the cache and assigns it a key.
Item property	Returns an Object representing a cache item based on its key value or sets an item of data in the cache while assigning it a key value.
Remove method	Removes an item with a particular key value from the cache.

Parameter

HttpCachePolicy
    An Object variable of type HttpCachePolicy.

Example

The example retrieves an instance of the HttpCachePolicy class into a local variable, sets the expiration time to two minutes after the page is processed, and then sets the cacheability of the of the page to Public. Finally, the Text property of the Message label control is set to the current time.

```
Sub Page_Load( )
    Dim myCachePol As HttpCachePolicy
    myCachePol = Response.Cache
    myCachePol.SetExpires(DateTime.Now.AddSeconds(120))
    myCachePol.SetCacheability(HttpCacheability.Public)
    Message.Text = Now.ToString( )
End Sub
```

The output of the page should be the current date and time. If refreshed, the output should not change until two minutes have elapsed.

Notes

The HttpCachePolicy object returned by this property is the preferred method in ASP.NET for modifying the cache policy for a given page. HttpCachePolicy provides the functionality provided by the classic ASP CacheControl, Expires, and ExpiresAbsolute properties. For example, the HttpCachePolicy class allows you to explicitly prevent the server from caching the response in question, but still allows downstream caching of the response.

You can also set the output caching policies for a page through the @ OutputCache directive and its attributes, although this provides less granular control than that provided by the methods of the HttpCachePolicy class. Caching through the @ OutputCache directive is discussed in Chapter 3.

CacheControl

Response.CacheControl = *String*

Sets the cacheability of the current page.

Parameter

String
    A string variable containing the value to set for the CacheControl property. Valid values include "Public" and "Private".

Example

```
Sub Page_Load( )
    Response.CacheControl = "Public"
    Response.Expires = 2
    Message.Text = Now.ToString( )
End Sub
```

The output of the code above should be identical to the previous example.

Notes

This property has been deprecated in favor of the HttpCacheability class methods.

Charset

```
String = Response.Charset
Response.Charset = String
```

Returns or sets a string representing the character set of the current response. When explicitly set, the value assigned to the Charset property is added to the HTTP Content-Type response header.

Parameter

String
> A string variable to receive or set the value of the property. The default is UTF-8.

Example

The example below sets the character set for the HTTP response to Windows-1255 (note that as the name suggests, this character set is only available on Internet Explorer on Windows clients and may cause other browsers or browsers on other operating systems to display the page incorrectly). It then writes the value of the character set to the Text property of the Message label control. To see the difference between this character set and the default UTF-8 character set, load the page into Internet Explorer, and comment out the line that sets the Charset property, save the page, and reload it in the browser.

```
Sub Page_Load( )
    Response.Charset = "Windows-1255"
    Message.Text = "Current character set is " & Response.Charset
End Sub
```

Notes

Attempting to modify this property after the HTTP headers are sent to the browser results in an HttpException being thrown. This would most likely occur if you disabled output buffering by using the BufferOutput property and then wrote content to the browser by using Response.Write.

If the character set specified by the Charset property is not valid for the browser used by the client, it will be ignored and the default character set for that browser will be used instead. As mentioned above, using the default character set may cause the page to be displayed differently than intended.

ContentEncoding

```
Encoding = Response.ContentEncoding
Response.ContentEncoding = Encoding
```

Returns an instance of the Encoding class representing the encoding of the current response. The Encoding class exposes properties and methods that allow you to examine and modify the system's character encoding—i.e., the way in which characters are stored internally in the system. For example, you can convert a Unicode string to ASCII, UTF-7, or UTF-8.

Parameter

Encoding

An Object variable of type Encoding. Its EncodingName property provides the human-readable name of the encoding type.

Example

The example uses the properties of the Encoding class instance returned from the ContentEncoding property to display the human-readable name and the registered (IANA) name of the current encoding:

```
Sub Page_Load( )
    Message.Text = "Current encoding is " & _
        Response.ContentEncoding.EncodingName & "<br/>"
    Message.Text &= "Current encoding IANA name is " & _
        Response.ContentEncoding.WebName & "<br/>"
End Sub
```

Notes

The ContentEncoding property is new in ASP.NET and provides a richer interface for examining and modifying character set and code page information for the current response. It also provides the only way to convert one character-encoded string to another character encoding (i.e., Unicode to ANSI).

ContentType

```
String = Response.ContentType
Response.ContentType = String
```

Returns or sets a string containing the MIME type of the current response. This allows you to retrieve or set the value of the HTTP Content-Type response header.

Parameter

String

A string variable to receive or set the content type. The default is "text/html".

Example

The following example displays the current MIME content type in the client browser:

```
Sub Page_Load( )
    Message.Text = "Current content type is " & _
        Response.ContentType & "<br/>"
End Sub
```

Notes

The ContentType property is very important, since it enables you to send content to the client browser other than the default HTML. For example, if you want to use the Response.BinaryWrite method to send binary image data to the client browser, you must also set the ContentType property to the appropriate MIME type ("image/jpg" or "image/gif", for example). See the BinaryWrite example for an example of how this is done.

Expires

```
Integer = Response.Expires
Response.Expires = Integer
```

Returns or sets an integer representing the number of minutes before a cached page expires. This property is used in concert with the CacheControl property to control caching of responses.

Parameter

Integer
    An Integer variable to receive or set the expiration in minutes.

Notes

This property is provided for backward compatibility with classic ASP. It has been deprecated in favor of the methods of the HttpCachePolicy instance returned by the Cache property.

ExpiresAbsolute

```
DateTime = Response.Expires
Response.Expires = DateTime
```

Returns or sets a DateTime value representing the date and time at which a cached response should expire.

Parameter

DateTime
    A DateTime variable to receive or set the absolute expiration.

Example

The following example makes the current response cacheable by using the Cache-Control property and then sets the absolute expiration to 30 seconds from the current time:

```
Sub Page_Load( )
    Response.CacheControl = "Public"
    Response.ExpiresAbsolute = DateTime.Now.AddSeconds(30)
    Message.Text = Now.ToString( )
End Sub
```

Notes

This property is provided for backward compatibility with classic ASP. It has been deprecated in favor of the methods of the HttpCachePolicy instance returned by the Cache property.

IsClientConnected

```
Boolean = Response.IsClientConnected
```

Returns a Boolean indicating whether the client is still connected. Returns False if the client is no longer connected.

Parameter

Boolean

A Boolean variable to receive the value of the property.

Example

The example checks the IsClientConnected property before starting a long-running processing task in order to avoid the expense of running the task if the client is no longer connected. If the property returns False, the code calls the Response.End method. Even though the client has disconnected and can no longer receive the buffered output (which is sent when the End method is called), calling the End method is still a good idea, since it will halt further processing of the page and fire the Application_EndRequest event. If you have written cleanup code for the page that is run by the event handler for Application_EndRequest, calling Response.End will ensure that the cleanup code is executed, even if the client disconnects.

```
Sub Page_Load( )
    'Check client connection status
    If Response.IsClientConnected = False Then
        Response.End
    Else
        'Start long-running processing task
    End If
End Sub
```

Notes

The IsClientConnected property is especially useful for long-running processes that require a significant amount of processing resources on the server. By querying the IsClientConnected property before starting an expensive processing task, or by querying the property periodically during processing, you can bypass further processing if the client has disconnected for some reason.

Output

TextWriter = Response.Output

Returns a write-only TextWriter object that can be used to write text directly to the output stream of the current response.

Parameter

TextWriter

An Object variable of type TextWriter. The TextWriter class includes the following members:

Member	Description
Close method	Closes the text writer and releases its resources.
Flush method	Clears the text writer's buffer and writes output to its underlying device.
NewLine property	Gets or sets the new line character(s) used by the TextWriter object.
Write method	Writes data to the text stream.
WriteLine method	Writes data followed by a newline character to the text stream. The NewLine property defines the newline character.

Example

The example declares a local variable of type TextWriter, retrieves an instance of TextWriter from the Output property, and then uses the WriteLine method to write the text "Hello, World!" to the output stream. The WriteLine method writes the specified text (or text representation of nonstring data types), along with a line terminator, specified by setting the NewLine property of the TextWriter. Without setting the NewLine property, the line terminator would affect the formatting of the text sent to the browser. However, it would not alter the formatting of the output as rendered by the browser, since browsers typically ignore whitespace such as non-HTML line terminators when rendering HTML.

```
Sub Page_Load( )
    Dim myWriter As System.IO.TextWriter
    myWriter = Response.Output
    myWriter.NewLine = "<br/>"
    myWriter.WriteLine("Hello, World!")
    myWriter.WriteLine("Hello, World, once again!")
End Sub
```

Notes

The Output property provides an alternative to the Response.Write method when outputting text to the output stream. You could also pass the TextWriter instance retrieved from the Output property to a method of a custom component to allow that component to write text directly to the output stream for the current response.

Like the Response.Write method, the result of writing text to the output stream by using the TextWriter returned from the Output property depends on the location of the code that writes the text. For example, in the code above, the text "Hello, World!" will appear before any static HTML in the page output. This is because the output of the TextWriter and the Response.Write method in this case is processed before the controls on the page are rendered. To make the output of the TextWriter instance or Response.Write appear inline, you could put the code above in a <% %> render block where you want the output to appear. A better approach for locating output in ASP.NET precisely is to add an ASP.NET Literal Server Control at the point in the file where you wish the output to appear and pass the desired output text to the Text property of the Literal control.

To use the TextWriter class without explicitly adding the System.IO namespace to the variable declaration, you can add the @ Import directive directly below the @ Page directive with the namespace attribute set to System.IO, as shown here:

```
<% @ Import Namespace="System.IO" %>
```

OutputStream

Stream = Response.OutputStream

Returns a write-only Stream object that can be used to write binary content directly to the output stream of the current request.

Parameter

Stream

An Object variable of type Stream. The Stream class includes the following members:

Member	Description
BeginWrite method	Begins an asynchronous write operation.
Close method	Closes the stream and releases its resources.
EndWrite method	Ends an asynchronous write operation.
Write method	Writes data to the stream.
WriteByte method	Writes a single byte to the stream and advances the position within the stream one byte.

Notes

The OutputStream property provides an alternative to the Response.BinaryWrite method when outputting binary content to the output stream is desired. You could also pass the Stream instance retrieved from the OutputStream property to a method of a custom component to allow that component to write binary content directly to the output stream for the current response.

Status

```
String = Response.Status
Response.Status = String
```

Returns or sets a String that contains the HTTP status line that will be sent to the client browser.

Parameter

String

A String variable to set or receive the status code of the current request. The default is "200 OK".

Notes

This property is provided for backward compatibility with classic ASP and has been deprecated in ASP.NET in favor of the StatusDescription property. Unlike the Status property, the StatusCode and StatusDescription properties allow you to control the numeric status code portion of the status line and the text description individually.

StatusCode

```
Integer = Response.StatusCode
Response.StatusCode = Integer
```

Returns or sets an integer that represents the HTTP status code that will be returned to the browser.

Parameter

Integer

An integer variable to set or receive the status code. The default is 200. The possible status codes fall into the following ranges:

1xx

The 100 range is for informational messages.

2xx

The 200 range is for success messages.

3xx

The 300 range is for redirection messages. The specific status code indicates whether a page has been moved temporarily or permanently.

4xx

The 400 range is for client error messages. The best-known message is the 404 Not Found message, which indicates that the client has asked for a resource that does not exist on the server. This range also includes status error messages related to client authentication.

5xx

The 500 range is for server error messages. For example, if more requests are received by IIS then can be processed or queued for later processing, clients will receive a 500-series status code with the "Server Too Busy" message.

Example

The example uses the StatusCode and StatusDescription properties to send an HTTP status message to the client. The Response.End method halts further processing and sends the currently buffered output to the client.

```
Sub Page_Load( )
    Response.StatusCode = 542
    Response.StatusDescription = "Server Error - The code is the answer."
    Response.End( )
End Sub
```

Notes

As with other properties that set HTTP response headers, this property cannot be set once HTTP body output is sent to the client using Response.Write or similar methods when buffering has been turned off.

StatusDescription

```
String = Response.StatusDescription
Response.StatusDescription = String
```

Returns or sets a string containing the text HTTP status message that will be sent to the browser along with the status code contained in the StatusCode property.

Parameter

String

A string variable to set or receive the additional path information. The default is OK.

Example

See the example for the StatusCode property.

Notes

As with other properties that set HTTP response headers, this property cannot be set once HTTP body output has been sent to the client (using Response.Write or similar methods) when buffering has been turned off.

SuppressContent

```
Boolean = Response.SuppressContent
Response.SuppressContent = Boolean
```

Returns or sets a Boolean indicating whether HTTP output should be sent to the client.

Parameter

Boolean
> A Boolean variable to receive or set the value of the property. The default is False; content is sent to the client.

Example

The following example writes the text "Hello, World!" to the output (which is buffered by default) and sets SuppressContent to True so that no output is sent to the client.

```
Sub Page_Load( )
    Response.Write("Hello, World!")
    Response.SuppressContent = True
    If Response.SuppressContent Then Response.Close( )
End Sub
```

Notes

Since SuppressContent prevents any output from being returned to the client (including any error messages), the Response.Close method (which closes the network connection to the client) must be called to prevent the client browser from hanging indefinitely.

Collections Reference

The Response object in ASP.NET supports only a single collection, the Cookies collection.

Cookies

```
HttpCookieCollection = Response.Cookies
```

The Cookies collection returns an instance of the HttpCookieCollection class containing all cookies sent as a part of the current request. The HttpCookieCollection class contains an instance of the HttpCookie class for each cookie passed as part of the client request. The properties of these HttpCookie instances can be used to access information about the cookie(s). The Cookies collection of the Response class supports the following set of properties:

AllKeys
Returns a string array of all keys in the collection.

Count
Returns an integer count of the number of name/value pairs in the collection.

Item(Index|Key)
Returns an instance of the collection class based on the index or passed-in key. This is the default property, which is why calling:

```
Response.Cookies (KeyVal)
```
returns the HttpCookie instance corresponding to *KeyVal*.

Keys
Returns a collection of the keys for the collection.

In addition, the HttpCookieCollection class exposes the following methods:

CopyTo(Array, Index)
Copies the contents of the collection object to the provided *Array* argument, starting at the provided *Index* argument. Note that the array must be dimensioned to a sufficient size to contain the collection before calling CopyTo.

GetKey(Index)
Returns a string containing the key corresponding to the provided *Index* argument.

As in classic ASP, the Cookies collection is still implemented as a collection (in fact, the HttpCookieCollection class inherits from the .NET NameObjectCollectionBase class), but rather than a collection of string keys and string values, the ASP.NET implementation is a collection of string keys and objects (instances of the HttpCookie class). Individual cookies are retrieved into variables of type HttpCookie, providing access to the cookies values through class properties.

Dictionary-style cookies (cookies with more than one value) are accessible through the Values property of the HttpCookie class, which returns a NameValueCollection containing the cookie subkeys and values. You can also set individual values by their key with the following syntax:

```
HttpCookie.Values("keyname") = "value"
```

Parameters

HttpCookieCollection
An Object variable of type HttpCookieCollection.

Example

The example creates a login cookie, sets the expiration of the cookie for 30 minutes from the current time, and adds the cookie to the Cookies collection.

```
Sub Page_Load( )
    Dim myCookie As New HttpCookie("LoggedIn")
    myCookie.Value = "True"
    myCookie.Expires = DateTime.Now.AddMinutes(30)
```

```
        Response.Cookies.Add(myCookie)
    End Sub
```

Notes

Unlike classic ASP, the collections in ASP.NET are zero-based, so the first element in any collection or array will be 0, not 1. This is especially important to remember when retrieving values by their index.

Methods Reference

AddCacheItemDependencies

```
Response.AddCacheItemDependencies(ByVal cacheKeys As ArrayList)
```

Adds a list of cache keys contained in an ArrayList to the list of cache item keys upon which the output cache of the current response depends. If one of the cache items identified by the keys is modified, the output cache of the current response will be invalidated and a fresh response will be generated.

Parameter

cacheKeys
    An ArrayList containing one or more cache item key names.

Example

The example shows how you can use the AddCacheItemDependencies method to set a number of cache keys as dependencies for the output cache of the current response. If any of the cache items represented by these keys is modified, the output cache is invalidated and the page is refreshed by using Response.Redirect.

```
<%@ Page Language="vb" %>
<%@ OutputCache Duration="300" VaryByParam="None" %>
<html>
    <head>
        <title>Adding cache dependencies in ASP.NET</title>
        <script runat="server">
            Sub Page_Load( )
                Dim myArrayList As New ArrayList
                myArrayList.Add("Key1")
                myArrayList.Add("Key2")
                Response.AddCacheItemDependencies(myArrayList)
                Message.Text = DateTime.Now.ToString( )
            End Sub
            Sub Button1_Click(sender As Object, e As EventArgs)
                Cache("Key1") = "foo" & DateTime.Now.ToString( )
                Response.Redirect("AddCacheItemDependencies.aspx")
            End Sub
            Sub Button2_Click(sender As Object, e As EventArgs)
                Cache("Key2") = "bar" & DateTime.Now.ToString( )
                Response.Redirect("AddCacheItemDependencies.aspx")
            End Sub
        </script>
```

```
        </head>
    <body>
        <form runat="server">
            <asp:label id="Message" runat="server"/>
            <asp:button id="Button1" text="Change Key 1"
                onClick="Button1_Click" runat="server"/>
            <asp:button id="Button2" text="Change Key 2"
                onClick="Button2_Click" runat="server"/>
        </form>
    </body>
</html>
```

Notes

The AddCacheItemDependencies method is useful when you want to output cache a page, but the page depends on the value of several items stored in the ASP.NET cache. Rather than caching the page with a very short duration to avoid stale data, you can use AddCacheItemDependencies to automatically invalidate the output cache when the dependencies change.

AddCacheItemDependency

```
Response.AddCacheItemDependency(ByVal cacheKey As String)
```

Adds a cache item key to the list of cache keys upon which the output cache of the current response depends. If the cache item identified by the key is modified, the output cache of the current response will be invalidated and a fresh response will be generated.

Parameter

cacheKey
    A String containing the cache item key to add.

Example

The example shows how you can use the AddCacheItemDependency method to set a cache key as a dependency for the output cache of the current response. If the cache item represented by this key is modified, the output cache is invalidated and the page is refreshed by using Response.Redirect.

```
<%@ Page Language="vb" %>
<%@ OutputCache Duration="300" VaryByParam="None" %>
<html>
    <head>
        <title>Adding a cache dependency in ASP.NET</title>
        <script runat="server">
            Sub Page_Load( )
                Response.AddCacheItemDependency("Key1")
                Message.Text = DateTime.Now.ToString( )
            End Sub
            Sub Button1_Click(sender As Object, e As EventArgs)
                Cache("Key1") = "foo" & DateTime.Now.ToString( )
                Response.Redirect("AddCacheItemDependency.aspx")
            End Sub
```

```
        </script>
      </head>
    <body>
      <form runat="server">
        <asp:label id="Message" runat="server"/>
       <asp:button id="Button1" text="Change Key 1" onClick="Button1_Click"
runat="server"/>
      </form>
    </body>
    </html>
```

Notes

The AddCacheItemDependency method provides the same functionality as the AddCacheItemDependencies method, but for a single cache item rather than multiple items.

AddFileDependencies

```
Response.AddFileDependencies(ByVal filenames As ArrayList)
```

Adds a list of files contained in an ArrayList to the list of files upon which the output cache of the current request depends. If any of these files is modified, the output cache is invalidated.

Parameter

filenames
    An ArrayList containing one or more path/filenames.

Example

The example shows how you can use the AddFileDependencies method to set a number of files as dependencies for the output cache of the current response. If any of these files is modified, the output cache is invalidated.

```
<%@ Page Language="vb" %>
<%@ OutputCache Duration="300" VaryByParam="None" %>
<html>
    <head>
        <title>Adding file dependencies in ASP.NET</title>
        <script runat="server">
          Sub Page_Load()
              Dim myArrayList As New ArrayList
              myArrayList.Add(Server.MapPath("dep.txt"))
              myArrayList.Add(Server.MapPath("dep1.txt"))
              Response.AddFileDependencies(myArrayList)
              Message.Text = DateTime.Now.ToString()
          End Sub
        </script>
    </head>
<body>
    <asp:label id="Message" runat="server"/>
</body>
</html>
```

Notes

The AddFileDependencies method is useful when you want to output cache a page, but the page depends on the value of several files on the web server (which can be accessed by a file path from the web server). Rather than caching the page with a very short duration to avoid stale data, you can use AddFileDependencies to automatically invalidate the output cache when the dependencies change.

AddFileDependency

```
Response.AddFileDependency(ByVal filename As String)
```

Adds a file to the list of files upon which the output cache of the current request depends. If the named by the filename argument is modified, the output cache is invalidated.

Parameter

filename
> A String containing the path and filename to add.

Example

The example below shows how you can use the AddFileDependency method to set a file as a dependency for the output cache of the current response. If the file is modified, the output cache is invalidated.

```
<%@ Page Language="vb" %>
<%@ OutputCache Duration="300" VaryByParam="None" %>
<html>
    <head>
        <title>Adding a file dependency in ASP.NET</title>
        <script runat="server">
            Sub Page_Load( )
                Response.AddFileDependency(Server.MapPath("dep.txt"))
                Message.Text = DateTime.Now.ToString( )
            End Sub
        </script>
    </head>
<body>
    <asp:label id="Message" runat="server"/>
</body>
</html>
```

The *dep.txt* file named in the code above should reside in the same directory as the page. The contents of the page can be whatever you choose. If the file content is changed, the cache will be invalidated.

Notes

The AddFileDependency method provides the same functionality as the AddFile-Dependencies method, but for a single file rather than multiple files.

AddHeader

```
Response.AddHeader(ByVal name As String, ByVal value As String)
```

Adds an HTTP header with the specified name and value to the output stream.

Parameters

name
> A String argument containing the name for the header.

value
> A String argument containing the value for the header.

Notes

The AddHeader property provides for backward compatibility with classic ASP. This property has been deprecated in favor of the new AppendHeader method.

AppendHeader

```
Response.AppendHeader(ByVal name As String, _
 ByVal value As String)
```

Adds an HTTP header with the specified name and value to the output stream. This method can be used to add custom HTTP headers or to modify the value of standard HTTP headers.

Parameters

name
> A String argument containing the name for the header.

value
> A String argument containing the value for the header.

Example

The example sets the HTTP Content-Type header to "text/xml" and then displays the new value by setting the Text property of the Message Label control to the value of the ContentType property. This causes the page output to be treated as XML.

```
Sub Page_Load( )
    Response.AppendHeader("Content-Type", "text/xml")
    Message.Text = Response.ContentType
End Sub
```

Notes

When using this method with HTTP headers related to caching policy, if more restrictive settings are applied through the use of the ASP.NET cache APIs, the more restrictive settings will take priority over the settings applied using AppendHeader.

AppendToLog

```
Response.AppendToLog(ByVal param As String)
```

Appends the text specified by the *param* argument to the IIS log file for the current IIS application.

Parameter

param
    A String argument containing the text to be appended to the IIS log.

Example

The following example writes a message to the IIS log for the application the page is a part of, and then writes a message to the ASP.NET Message label control indicating that the message was written:

```
Sub Page_Load( )
    Response.AppendToLog("Hello from Page_Load!")
    Message.Text = "Message written to IIS Log!"
End Sub
```

The IIS log entry generated by the example above looks similar to the following:

```
2001-10-14 00:13:14 127.0.0.1 - 127.0.0.1 80 GET
/ASPdotNET_iaN/Chapter_17/AppendToLog.aspx
Hello+from+Page_Load! 200 BrowserString
```

Notes

Unlike the AppendToLog method in classic ASP, which had a limit of 80 characters per call, you can write as much text as you wish to the log by using AppendToLog in ASP.NET. The IIS Log files are located by default in *%windir%\System32\LogFiles\W3SVCx\exdate.log*, where *%windir%* is the name of the Windows directory, *x* is the number of the Web site for the log (this is the IIS Metabase name for the desired application), and *date* is the creation date of the log file.

ApplyAppPathModifier

```
String = Response.ApplyAppPathModifier(ByVal virtualPath _
                    As String)
```

Given a virtual path to a resource, returns a string containing a new virtual path containing the SessionID. This new virtual path can be used to create absolute URLs for use in applications that use cookieless Sessions.

Parameters

String
    A String argument that will receive the modified virtual path.

virtualPath
    A String argument containing the virtual path to be modified.

Example

The following example retrieves a virtual path including the SessionID and displays the path by using the Text property of the Message label control:

```
Sub Page_Load( )
    Dim NewPath As String
    NewPath = Response.ApplyAppPathModifier(Request.Path)
    Message.Text = "Modified virtual path = " & NewPath
End Sub
```

The *web.config* file to set the Session state handler to use cookieless Sessions is shown below:

```
<configuration>
    <system.web>
        <sessionState mode="InProc" cookieless="true"/>
    </system.web>
</configuration>
```

Notes

This method is very useful when making use of the cookieless Session state functionality introduced by ASP.NET. If the cookieless attribute of the sessionState config section in *web.config* is not set to True, this method will simply return the virtual path passed in without modification.

BinaryWrite

```
Response.BinaryWrite(ByVal buffer( ) As Byte)
```

Allows writing of binary content to the output stream. No modification of the output is performed before sending the binary content to the client.

Parameter

buffer()
   A Byte array containing the binary data to be written to the output stream.

Example

Here is an example of BinaryWrite:

```
Sub Page_Load( )
    Dim ImageStream As New FileStream(MapPath("aspnetian.jpg"), _
        FileMode.Open, FileAccess.Read)
    Dim ImageBytes(ImageStream.Length) As Byte
    ImageStream.Read(ImageBytes, 0, ImageStream.Length)
    ImageStream.Close( )
    Response.ContentType = "image/bmp"
    Response.BinaryWrite(ImageBytes)
    Response.End( )
End Sub
```

Notes

This method is especially useful for writing binary content retrieved from a database to the browser. When writing image or other nontext data to the browser, you should set the Response.ContentType property to the appropriate MIME type for the image type being sent (such as "image/jpg").

Clear

```
Response.Clear( )
```

Clears the content of the current output stream.

Parameters

None

Notes

The Clear method clears all currently buffered output, but does not clear the HTTP response headers. If buffering of output is disabled by setting the Buffer-Output property to False, this method will not have any effect, since it only clears buffered content. This behavior is different from classic ASP, in which calling Clear when buffering is disabled results in an error.

ClearContent

```
Response.ClearContent( )
```

Clears the content of the current output stream.

Parameters

None

Example

The example writes a text message using Response.Write and then clears the buffered output by calling Response.Clear. If buffering is on, the text message will never be sent to the browser.

```
Sub Page_Load( )
    Response.Write("This content will not be seen.")
    Response.Clear( )
    Message.Text = _
        "Content written with <i>Response.Write</i> was cleared."
End Sub
```

Notes

The ClearContent method clears all currently buffered output, but does not clear the HTTP response headers. HTTP headers can be cleared by calling the Clear-Headers method. If buffering of output has been disabled by setting the BufferOutput property to False, the ClearContent method will not have any effect, since it only clears buffered content.

ClearHeaders

```
Response.ClearHeaders( )
```

Clears the HTTP headers from the current output stream.

Parameters

None

Example

The example sets the HTTP Content-Type header to "text/xml", clears the HTTP headers by calling the ClearHeaders method, and then writes the value of the Response.ContentType property to the Text property of the Message ASP.NET Label control. The displayed Content-Type is the default of "text/html".

```
Sub Page_Load( )
    Response.AppendHeader("Content-Type", "text/xml")
    Response.ClearHeaders( )
    Message.Text = Response.ContentType
End Sub
```

Notes

The ClearHeaders method clears only the HTTP response headers, not the buffered content.

Close

```
Response.Close( )
```

Closes the network socket for the current response.

Parameters

None

Example

See the example for the SuppressContent property.

Notes

The Close method can be used to immediately close the network socket for the current response. This closure will typically result in a browser error (such as "Cannot find server") being displayed to the client.

End

```
Response.End( )
```

Stops processing the current request and sends all buffered content to the client immediately.

Parameters

None

Example

The example below writes the text "Hello, World!" to the browser, calls Response. End, and then attempts to set the Text property of the Message ASP.NET Label control to "Hello, World!" However, that code will not be executed, as the End method immediately halts execution of page processing.

```
Sub Page_Load( )
    Response.Write("Hello, World!")
    Response.End( )
    Message.Text = "Hello, World!"
End Sub
```

In fact, the code above will result in only the "Hello, World!" text being output to the browser, as even the rendering of the static HTML and controls in the page will not occur.

Notes

When the End method is called, in addition to sending buffered output to the client and terminating processing, the Application_EndRequest event is fired.

Flush

`Response.Flush( )`

Immediately sends all buffered output to the client.

Parameters

None

Example

See the example for the BufferOutput property. If you comment out the lines that set BufferOutput to False and then uncomment the line that calls Response.Flush, you will see that the Flush method allows you to explicitly send buffered content to the browser.

Notes

Since buffering is on by default in ASP.NET, the Flush method becomes especially useful. Rather than turning off buffering, which results in any content sent from a Response.Write call being sent immediately to the browser, you can use Response.Flush to send content in discrete chunks or to ensure that an entire operation completes before sending the currently buffered content.

You can also combine calls to Response.Flush with calls to Response.Clear to allow you to perform preverification on content before it is sent to the browser. If a given set of calculations or output encounters an error, you can call Response.Clear to clear the problematic output and then replace it with an error message or with other replacement content. If there are no problems with the output, you can call Response.Flush to send the buffered output to the browser and then continue processing.

Pics

```
Response.Pics(ByVal value As String)
```

Adds a PICS-Label header to the output stream for the current response. The Platform for Internet Content Selection (PICS) is used to rate Internet content based on violence, sexual content, language, and nudity.

Parameter

value
   A String argument containing the text for the PICS-Label header.

Example

The following example sets a PICS header that specifies RSAC as the rating organization, sets the rating effective period from 8/1/2001 to 2/28/2002, and sets the ratings as follows:

- Violence - 1
- Sexual content - 2
- Adult Language - 3
- Nudity - 4

```
Sub Page_Load( )
    Dim PICSLabel As String
    PICSLabel &= "(PICS-1.1 <http://www.rsac.org/ratingsv01.html> "
    PICSLabel &= "labels on " & Chr(34)
    PICSLabel &= "2001.08.01T06:00-0000" & Chr(34)
    PICSLabel &= " until " & Chr(34)
    PICSLabel &= "2002.02.28T23:59-0000" & Chr(34)
    PICSLabel &= " ratings (V 1 S 2 L 3 N 4))"
    Response.PICS(PICSLabel)
    Message.Text = PICSLabel
End Sub
```

Notes

The PICS-Label header is used for rating the content of a site. Users can configure their browsers to disallow viewing of sites that send PICS-Label headers, and whose ratings state that the site contains a higher level of content in one of the rated categories than the browser is configured to allow. Additional information on the PICS standard for content ratings is available at the World Wide Web Consortium web site at *http://www.w3c. org*.

Redirect

```
Response.Redirect(ByVal url As String)
Response.Redirect(ByVal url As String, _)
 ByVal endResponse As Boolean)
```

Redirects the currently executing page to another page specified by the URL argument, optionally terminating the processing of the current page.

Parameters

url

A String argument containing the URL for the page to redirect to.

endResponse

A Boolean argument indicating whether to terminate processing of the current page. If the argument is omitted, the method call causes processing of the current page to be discontinued.

Example

The example redirects the current request to *BufferOutput.aspx* and directs ASP.NET to discontinue processing of the current page:

```
Sub Page_Load( )
    Response.Redirect("BufferOutput.aspx", True)
End Sub
```

Notes

Unless additional processing needs to be done in the page from which you call Response.Redirect, you should always pass True as the second argument to Response.Redirect to prevent server resources from being wasted by continuing to process the current page. This feature is new for ASP.NET. When calling Response.Redirect with only the *url* argument, processing of the current page is discontinued automatically.

Note that when redirecting to a page such as *BufferOutput.aspx* in which buffering is turned off, or to a page that calls Response.Flush, the redirect will not complete until the target page has completed processing. This means that all content on the target page will be seen at once, rather than as it is rendered or flushed from the buffer.

Write

```
Response.Write(ByVal ch As Char)
Response.Write(ByVal obj As Object)
Response.Write(ByVal s As String)
Response.Write(ByVal buffer( ) As Char, ByVal index As Integer, _
 ByVal count As Integer)
```

Allows writing of arbitrary content to the output stream. Content may be character data, an Object (using the object's ToString( ) method), or String data.

Parameters

ch

A Char argument containing a character to write to the output stream.

obj

An Object argument containing an object whose string representation will be written to the output stream.

s

A String argument containing text to write to the output stream.

buffer()

A Char array argument containing the characters to write to the output stream.

index

An Integer argument containing the starting point in the Char array from which to begin writing.

count

An Integer argument containing the number of characters to write.

Example

The example creates an array of Chars, sets the values of the Chars, and then loops through the array and displays its contents by calling Response.Write:

```
Sub Page_Load( )
    Dim MyChars(2) As Char
    Dim MyChar As Char
    MyChars(0) = CChar("A")
    MyChars(1) = CChar("B")
    MyChars(2) = CChar("C")
    For Each MyChar in MyChars
        Response.Write(MyChar)
    Next
End Sub
```

Notes

As shown above, the Write method in ASP.NET gains a number of new over-loaded implementations. The above code could also be written by using another overloaded implementation that accepts an array of Chars, a starting index, and the count of Chars to write, as follows:

```
Response.Write(MyChars, 0, 3)
```

The implementation of the Write method that takes an Object as an argument takes advantage of the built-in ToString method of the object class to display the string representation of the object. ToString is inherited by every .NET class and, by default, returns the namespace and class name of the object's class. Classes that wish to send other information about themselves can override the inherited implementation of ToString to send this information.

WriteFile

```
Response.WriteFile(ByVal fileName As String)
Response.WriteFile(ByVal fileName As String, _
 ByVal includeHeaders As Boolean)
Response.WriteFile(ByVal fileHandle As IntPtr, _
 ByVal offset As Long, ByVal size As Long)
Response.WriteFile(ByVal fileName As String, _
 ByVal offset As Long, ByVal size As Long)
```

Writes a file specified in one of the overloaded arguments to the output stream.

Parameters

fileName

A string argument containing the path and filename of the file whose content should be written to the output stream.

includeHeaders

A Boolean argument indicating whether the contents of the file should be written to a memory block.

fileHandle

An argument of type IntPtr containing a handle to a file. You can get the handle by creating a new FileStream object from the file and then querying the FileStream's Handle property.

offset

An argument of type Long containing the byte position in the file from which writing should start.

size

An argument of type Long containing the number of bytes that should be written to the output stream.

Example

The example writes the contents of the file *dep.txt* to the output stream of the current response:

```
Sub Page_Load( )
    Response.WriteFile("dep.txt")
End Sub
```

Notes

The WriteFile method can be used in a variety of ways to output text content directly from a file. Attempts to write other content types (such as image data) will fail.

18

The HttpServerUtility Class

The HttpServerUtility class is ASP.NET's replacement for ASP's intrinsic Server object. Because the Server property of the Page class (from which all pages are derived) exposes the HttpServerUtility class instance for a given ASP.NET page, you can code to the HttpServerUtility class as you did in the Server object in classic ASP, meaning that your existing ASP code is much easier to migrate.

The HttpServerUtility class performs utility functions such as encoding and decoding strings for use in URLs or for plain-text display of content that may contain HTML markup tags. The HttpServerUtility class also provides access to limited error information and provides methods (Execute, Transfer) for modifying the execution of the current request. Table 18-1 lists the properties and methods exposed by the HttpServerUtility class.

Table 18-1. HttpServerUtility class summary

Properties	Collections	Methods (public instance)
MachineName	None	ClearError
ScriptTimeout		CreateObject
		CreateObjectFromClsid
		Execute
		GetLastError
		HtmlDecode
		HtmlEncode
		MapPath
		Transfer
		UrlDecode
		UrlEncode
		UrlPathEncode

Comments/Troubleshooting

In classic ASP, the Server object was used to create COM component instances by using the Server.CreateObject method. CreateObject still exists in ASP.NET, along with a new method, CreateObjectFromClsid, which uses a COM class ID (CLSID) instead of a ProgID to locate the object to create. You should use both methods only when necessary, since even though the details are handled for you, using these methods incurs the cost of interoperating between COM and .NET (unmanaged and managed) code. If there is a .NET alternative to using a COM object, you will get better performance by sticking with the .NET solution.

The ASP.NET version of the Server object also adds a number of useful new utility functions, including HtmlDecode, UrlDecode, and UrlPathEncode. HtmlDecode and UrlDecode are particularly welcome, given that classic ASP developers were stuck either manually implementing functionality to remove URL or HTML encoding from strings that they'd encoded on another page or relying on third party components or scripts to do so. Now this functionality is built in.

In this chapter, we'll use the following code listing as the basis for most examples in the chapter. Unless otherwise noted, each example will consist of the Page_Load event handler for that particular example. Any output messages or return values displayed are shown as the Text property of the ASP.NET Label named Message, or displayed by calling Response.Write.

```
<%@ Page Language="vb" %>
<html>
    <head>
        <script runat="server">
            Sub Page_Load( )
                'Example code will go here
            End Sub
        </script>
    </head>
<body>
    <asp:label id="Message" runat="server"/>
</body>
</html>
```

Properties Reference

MachineName

stringvar = Server.MachineName

Returns a string containing the name of the server on which the code is executing.

Parameter

stringvar
    A string variable that receives the machine name from the property.

Example

This code example declares a string variable, assigns the MachineName property value to the string variable, and then sets the text property of the Message label to the value of ServerName:

```
Sub Page_Load( )
   Dim ServerName As String
   ServerName = Server.MachineName
   Message.Text = "The name of the server is " & ServerName & ".<br/>"
End Sub
```

Notes

This property can be useful for code that needs to be easily portable, but needs to access resources that require the server name.

ScriptTimeout

intvar = Server.ScriptTimeout

Returns an integer containing the length, in milliseconds, a request is allowed to run before timing out.

Parameters

intvar
> An integer variable that receives the script timeout value.

Example

This code example declares an integer variable, sets the ScriptTimeout value to 120 milliseconds, assigns the ScriptTimeout property value to the variable, and then sets the text property of the Message label to the value of the variable:

```
Sub Page_Load( )
   Dim Timeout As String
   Server.ScriptTimeout = 120
   Timeout = CStr(Server.ScriptTimeout)
   Message.Text = "The current ScriptTimeout value is  " & _
       Timeout & ".<br/>"
End Sub
```

Notes

You can use this property to extend or reduce the timeout value in order to allow longer-running processes time to complete, or you can use ScriptTimeout to reduce the overhead associated with inefficient processes by terminating them before completion. The default for this value is set to an extremely high number so that a script will not time out by default. This is for backward compatibility with classic ASP.

Methods Reference

ClearError

```
Server.ClearError( )
```

Clears the last exception thrown.

Parameters

None

Notes

The ClearError method is new to ASP.NET. You can use this method at the beginning of page processing to clear the last exception so that the information provided by the GetLastError method is specific to an exception occurring on the current page.

CreateObject

```
objvar = Server.CreateObject(ProgID)
objvar = Server.CreateObject(Type)
```

Returns a reference to a COM object created based on the supplied ProgID.

Parameters

objvar
> A variable of type Object to receive the reference to the newly created object.

ProgID
> A String variable or literal containing the COM programmatic ID of the desired object.

Type
> The type name of a runtime callable wrapper (RCW) class that the *tlbimp.exe* utility generated to expose a COM object to managed code.

Example

The code example declares an object variable, uses Server.CreateObject to assign a reference to a newly created ADO Recordset object to the variable, and then opens the recordset and returns the RecordCount property to the browser by using the Message label control:

```
Sub Page_Load( )
    Dim rs1
    Dim ConnString As String
    ConnString = "driver={SQL Server};server=(local)\NetSDK;"
    ConnString =  ConnString & "database=Pubs;Trusted_Connection=yes"
    rs1 = Server.CreateObject("ADODB.Recordset")
    ' 1 and 3 are the values for adOpenKeyset and adLockOptimistic
    rs1.Open("SELECT * FROM Authors", ConnString, 1, 3)
    Message.Text = "There are " & rs1.RecordCount & _
        " records in the Authors table.<br/>"
End Sub
```

Figure 18-1 shows the output of a page that combines the example for the CreateObject method with the example for the CreateObjectFromClsid method.

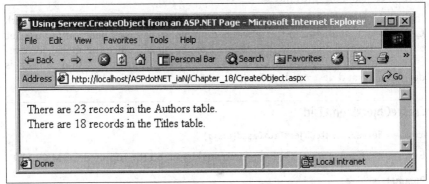

Figure 18-1. Output of CreateObject and CreateObjectFromClsid examples

Notes

This method enables backward compatibility with classic ASP applications and allows the late-bound use of COM components in ASP.NET applications. For new development, it is preferable to use other means to achieve the results that this method was used for in classic ASP. These means include:

- Using the *TlbImp.exe* utility to create a RCW for the component, which enables early binding and optimizes the performance of calls between managed and unmanaged code. If you add a reference to a COM component in the Visual Studio .NET IDE, the RCW is created for you automatically.

- Rewriting custom COM components to run in the managed environment. This method is preferable, as it entirely eliminates the marshalling cost of switching between managed and unmanaged code.

It is important for you to consider the second alternative for COM components that are called frequently and perform a little work each time they're called (as opposed to components that are called once and perform larger amounts of work per call). The distinction between these models is often referred to as "chatty" versus "chunky" communications. The cost of chatty components in marshalling between managed and unmanaged code tends to be significantly higher compared to the amount of work being done in each call. When upgrading COM components to run in the managed environment, you should convert chatty components first and then look at chunky components.

If you want ASP.NET to fire the OnStartPage and OnEndPage events used in some COM components to access the ASP intrinsics, you must add the ASPCompat attribute to the page's @ Page directive:

```
<%@ Page ASPCompat="true" %>
```

When ASPCompat is set to True, ASP.NET creates unmanaged intrinsic objects to pass to the component's OnStartPage method. ASP.NET also switches from executing in multithreaded apartment (MTA) to single-threaded apartment (STA) mode to ensure compatibility with COM components created in Visual Basic 5 or

6. This can have a significant negative impact on performance, so be sure to test your application carefully to determine whether the performance will be acceptable when using this attribute.

In ASP.NET, unlike in ASP, it isn't necessary to use the Set keyword with CreateObject, as shown in the previous example. It also isn't necessary to use Set objName = Nothing to release the reference to the object, since the managed reference is eventually garbage collected, at which point the COM object is dereferenced and destroyed.

CreateObjectFromClsid

objvar = Server.CreateObjectFromClsid(*Clsid*)

Returns a reference to a COM object created based on the supplied COM CLSID.

Parameters

objvar
> A variable of type Object to receive the reference to the newly created object.

Clsid
> A String variable or literal containing the COM CLSID (a type of globally unique identifier (GUID) for the component that is found in the Registry) of the desired object.

Example

The code example declares an object variable, uses Server.CreateObject-FromClsid to assign a reference to a newly created ADO Recordset object to the variable, and then opens the recordset and returns the RecordCount property to the browser using the Message label control.

```
Sub Page_Load( )
    Dim rs1
    Dim ConnString As String
    ConnString = "driver={SQL Server};server=(local)\NetSDK;"
    ConnString =  ConnString & "database=Pubs;Trusted_Connection=yes"
    rs1 = Server.CreateObjectFromClsid( _
        "00000535-0000-0010-8000-00AA006D2EA4")
    ' 1 and 3 are the values for adOpenKeyset and adLockOptimistic
    rs1.Open("SELECT * FROM Titles", ConnString, 1, 3)
    Message.Text &= "There are " & rs1.RecordCount & _
        " records in the Titles table.<br/>"
End Sub
```

Notes

This method is new to ASP.NET and, like the CreateObject method, it allows the late-bound use of COM components in ASP.NET applications.

The other notes relating to the CreateObject method also apply equally to the CreateObjectFromClsid method.

Execute

```
Server.Execute(Path)
Server.Execute(Path, Writer)
```

Executes a request on the URL passed by the *Path* argument and optionally captures the output of the requested page by using an instance of the TextWriter class supplied by the *Writer* argument.

Parameters

Path

A String variable or literal specifying the URL to execute. The URL passed to the Execute method may be absolute (containing all the information needed to locate the resource, including the protocol type and server name) or relative (containing only the relative path of the resource).

Writer

An instance of any class derived from the TextWriter class (found in the System.IO namespace); used to capture the output of the execution of the requested URL.

Example

The code example declares a string variable, creates a new TextWriter, and then calls Server.Execute to execute a page based on the CreateObject example code and capture its results. Figure 18-2 shows the output of the example.

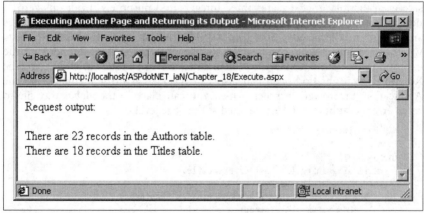

Figure 18-2. Output of CreateObject and CreateObjectFromClsid examples

```
Sub Page_Load( )
    Dim Url As String = "CreateObject.aspx"
    Dim sw As New System.IO.StringWriter( )
    Server.Execute(Url, sw)
    Message.Text = "Request output:<br/><br/>" & sw.ToString( )
End Sub
```

Notes

The Execute method is a useful feature that first appeared in the IIS 5.0 version of Active Server Pages. ASP.NET includes an overloaded version of the method, adding the *Writer* argument for capturing, manipulating, and/or saving the output of the request being executed.

When called passing only the URL, the Execute method automatically inserts the output of the request into the HTML output stream of the calling page.

When called passing both the URL and an object reference derived from the Text-Writer class (such as StringWriter, StreamWriter, or HtmlTextWriter), the output is not automatically added to the HTML output stream, but may be obtained, as in the previous example, by calling the ToString method of the writer class.

GetLastError

```
LastException = Server.GetLastError( )
```

Returns the last exception thrown.

Parameter

LastException
    An object of type Exception to receive the application's last exception.

Example

The code in *GetLastError.aspx* displays a button that, when clicked, calls a server-side event handler that declares three Integers and purposely divides by zero (a no-no) to cause an exception. The code in the Page_Error event handler declares an Exception object and a String, gets the Exception using GetLastError, tests whether the object reference is valid and assigns the Message property of the exception to the string variable, and then writes the value to the browser using the Response.Write method. You can also call the GetLastError method from the Application_Error event handler, which you can place in the *global.asax* file to catch errors that have not been handled at the page level.

```
<%@ Page Language="VB" %>
<html>
<head>
    <title>Examining the Last Error</title>
    <script runat="server">
        Sub CauseError(sender As Object, e As EventArgs)
            Dim x, y, z As Integer

            y = 1
            z = 0
            x = y / z
        End Sub
        Sub Page_Error(Source As Object, E As EventArgs)
            Dim LastError As Exception
            Dim ErrMessage As String
            LastError = Server.GetLastError( )
            If Not LastError Is Nothing Then
```

```
                ErrMessage = LastError.Message
            Else
                ErrMessage = "No Errors"
            End If
            Response.Write("Last Error = " & ErrMessage & "<br/><br/>")
            Server.ClearError()
        End Sub
    </script>
</head>
<body>
    <form runat="server">
        <h4><font face="verdana">Cause an Error to Occur...</font></h4>
        <asp:button text="CauseError" OnClick="CauseError" runat="server"/>
    </form>
</body>
</html>
```

Notes

You'll find this method useful for getting information about an error from a custom error-handling page. GetLastError returns information only when called in the Page_Error or Application_Error event handlers because once these events have been fired, the exception is cleared automatically.

HtmlDecode

```
returnstring = Server.HtmlDecode(s)
Server.HtmlDecode(s,output)
```

Returns a string in which any HTML information encoded by the HtmlEncode method (described later in this chapter) is decoded back into its standard HTML format.

Parameters

returnstring

A String variable to receive the decoded string from the method.

s

A string variable containing the encoded HTML that the method will decode.

output

An instance of any class derived from the TextWriter class (found in the System.IO namespace) used to capture the decoded string.

Example

The code example declares two string variables, sets the value of StrToDecode to the encoded equivalent of <p>Hello, World!</p>, assigns the return value of the Server.HtmlDecode call to StrToReturn, and then writes the value to the browser using the Message label control:

```
Sub Page_Load()
    Dim StrToDecode As String
    Dim StrToReturn As String
    StrToDecode = "&lt;p&gt;Hello, World!&lt;/p&gt;"
```

```
    StrToReturn = Server.HtmlDecode(StrToDecode)
    Message.Text = StrToReturn
End Sub
```

Notes

This method provides a simple way to undo the effects of calling HtmlEncode on a given string. You can also use it as an educational tool to demonstrate the relationship between various characters used in HTML and ASP (such as the greater-than (>) and less-than (<) symbols) and their encoded equivalents.

When called with only the *s* argument, this method returns a string. When called with both an *s* argument and an *output* argument (such as a StringWriter or HtmlTextWriter class instance), the method does not return a value; instead, you can obtain the decoded string by calling the ToString method of the writer object.

While this method is useful, you probably won't use it as frequently as its cousin, UrlDecode, which is described later in this chapter.

HtmlEncode

returnstring = Server.HtmlEncode(*s*)
Server.HtmlEncode(*s*, *output*)

Returns a string in which any HTML tags found are encoded by using the HTML literal equivalents of symbols such as > (>), < (<), and even quotes ("). This allows developers to display HTML and ASP source code on the page, rather than treating it as rendered output or code to execute.

Parameters

returnstring
  A String variable to receive the encoded string from the method.

s
  A string variable containing the HTML that the method will encode.

output
  An instance of any class derived from the TextWriter class, such as a StringWriter class instance (found in the System.IO namespace), used to capture the encoded string.

Example

The code example declares two string variables, sets the value of StrToEncode, assigns the return value of the Server.HtmlEncode call to StrToReturn, and then writes the value to the browser using the Message label control. Note that you have to view the HTML source to see the actual string returned by the method call.

```
Sub Page_Load( )
    Dim StrToEncode As String
    Dim StrToReturn As String
    StrToEncode = "<%@ Page Language=""VB"" %>"
    StrToReturn = Server.HtmlEncode(StrToEncode)
    Message.Text = StrToReturn
End Sub
```

Notes

This method is great for displaying the source of a page for educational purposes. It is also particularly useful for encoding text entered by users that may or may not be displayed or written to the browser. Without this encoding (or some form of filtering or validation of the input), it might be possible for the user to enter script or other code that the browser or server could execute. This possibility could pose a very large security risk.

Whether with HtmlEncode or with some form of filtering or validation, you should always ensure that text entered by your users that will be used or displayed by your application does not contain unexpected characters or content.

Like the HtmlDecode method, HtmlEncode is overloaded. It returns a string when called with the s argument alone, and it does not return a value when called with both an s and an *output* argument. Instead, it sends the encoded HTML to the *output* class instance.

MapPath

PhysicalPath = Server.MapPath(*Path*)

Returns a string containing the physical path in the server's filesystem that corresponds to the virtual or relative path specified by the *Path* argument.

Parameters

PhysicalPath
> A String variable to receive the physical path from the method.

Path
> A String variable containing the virtual or relative path to be mapped.

Example

The code example declares two string variables, sets the value of RelativePath, assigns the return value of the Server.MapPath call to PhysicalPath, and then writes the value to the browser by using the Message label control:

```
Sub Page_Load( )
    Dim RelativePath As String
    Dim PhysicalPath As String
    RelativePath = "HtmlEncode.aspx"
    PhysicalPath = Server.MapPath(RelativePath)
    Message.Text = PhysicalPath
End Sub
```

Notes

You can use this method to determine the physical location for creating a new file in response to a user action or code event.

In classic ASP, attempting to use this method with the MS-DOS (.) and (..) relative directory syntax would result in an error. In ASP.NET, no error occurs. In the previous example, using "../HtmlEncode.aspx" for the *Path* returns a physical path mapping the file *HtmlEncode.aspx* to the parent folder of its physical location.

Using "./HtmlEncode.aspx" for the *Path* returns the same physical path mapping as in the original example.

The MapPath method dynamically determines whether the provided path is a relative or virtual path based on whether the leading character is a slash (/) or backslash (\). If the leading character is either one, the path is assumed to be a complete virtual path. If not, the path is assumed to be relative to the physical path of the currently executing page.

If the last component in *Path* is a filename, the MapPath method does not verify its existence. In other words, the code example returns the same absolute path whether or not *HtmlEncode.aspx* exists.

A more flexible version of the MapPath method has been added to the Request object that enables you to specify a base directory for resolving mappings and lets you allow mapping of paths across different applications. You can read more about the Request.MapPath method in Chapter 16.

Transfer

```
Server.Transfer(Path)
Server.Transfer(Path, preserveForm)
```

Discontinues execution of the current page and transfers execution to the page specified by the *Path* argument. This allows control of an application to be redirected to the page specified by the *Path* argument without any response being sent to the client.

In contrast to the Execute method, which returns control to the page in which it is called once the page specified in the Execute method finishes processing, the Transfer method does not return control to the calling page.

Parameters

Path
> A String variable containing the path to the page to which execution will be transferred.

preserveForm
> A Boolean variable that indicates whether the Form and QueryString collections should be cleared before transferring control to the page that the *Path* argument specifies.

Example

The code example declares a string variable containing the name of the page to transfer control to, and then calls Server.Transfer. Note that the call that sets the Message.Text property will never be executed.

```
Sub Page_Load( )
    Dim Url As String = "CreateObject.aspx"
    Server.Transfer(Url)
    Message.Text = "This code will never be executed!"
End Sub
```

Notes

The ability to clear the Form and QueryString collections prior to passing control to the page that the *Path* argument specifies is new in ASP.NET. This is convenient for passing control to pages that you did not create and that might break if they encounter unexpected values, or if you want to keep the Form or QueryString contents private. If you do not pass a *preserveForm* argument, the default behavior is for the Form and QueryString collections to be preserved.

Make sure that no code in your page must execute after a Server.Transfer. If you have such code, you may want to consider using Server.Execute instead.

UrlDecode

```
returnstring = Server.UrlDecode(s)
Server.UrlDecode(s,output)
```

Returns a string in which any special character sequences resulting from encoding by the UrlEncode method (described later in this chapter) are decoded back into the original format. For example, a URL with a query string such as:

```
http://localhost/ASPdotNET_iaN/Chapter_18/UrlDecode.
aspx?strtodecode=This%20is%20a%20good%20string.
```

would return the following string from the UrlDecode method:

```
This is a good string.
```

Parameters

returnstring
> A string variable to receive the decoded string from the method.

s
> A string variable containing the encoded URL to be decoded by the method.

output
> An instance of any class derived from the TextWriter class (found in the System.IO namespace) used to capture the decoded string. Examples are the StringWriter and HtmlTextWriter classes.

Example

The code example declares two string variables, sets the value of StrToDecode to the encoded equivalent of the QueryString's StrToDecode value, assigns the return value of the Server.UrlDecode call to StrToReturn, and then writes the value to the browser using the Message label control:

```
Sub Page_Load( )
    Dim StrToDecode As String
    Dim StrToReturn As String
    StrToDecode = Request.QueryString("StrToDecode")
    StrToReturn = Server.UrlDecode(StrToDecode)
    Message.Text = StrToReturn
End Sub
```

Notes

New in ASP.NET, this method provides a simple way to undo the effects of calling UrlEncode on a given string. It is especially useful for retrieving values passed in the query string, since these values commonly contain characters, such as spaces and commas, that are not allowed in URLs.

When called with only the *s* argument, this method returns a string. When called with both the *s* argument and *output* argument, the method does not return a value; instead, the decoded string is sent to the *output* writer.

UrlEncode

```
returnstring = Server.UrlEncode(s)
Server.UrlEncode(s, output)
```

Returns a string in which any characters not allowed in URLs are encoded by using the URL literal equivalents, such as %2c for comma and + for space. This makes it very simple to pass any string as a query string value and, thanks to the new UrlDecode method, just as simple to retrieve the unencoded value.

Parameters

returnstring
> A String variable to receive the encoded string from the method.

s
> A String variable containing the value to be encoded by the method.

output
> An instance of any class derived from the TextWriter class (found in the System.IO namespace); used to capture the encoded string. Classes derived from TextWriter include StringWriter and HtmlTextWriter.

Example

The code example declares two string variables, sets the value of StrToEncode, assigns the return value of the Server.UrlEncode call to StrToReturn, and then writes the HTML anchor tag containing a query string with the encoded value to the browser using the Message label control:

```
Sub Page_Load( )
    Dim StrToEncode As String
    Dim StrToReturn As String
    StrToEncode = "Hello, World!"
    StrToReturn = Server.UrlEncode(StrToEncode)
    Message.Text = "<a href=""UrlDecode.aspx?StrToDecode=" & StrToReturn
    Message.Text &= """>" & StrToReturn & " - Click to Decode!</a>"
End Sub
```

Notes

This method replaces non-URL–allowable characters in strings that need to be passed as part of a URL. For example, one of the most difficult things to pass as part of a URL is another URL. The UrlEncode method replaces all slash (/), dot (.), and colon (:) characters for you. Figure 18-3 shows the output of the previous example.

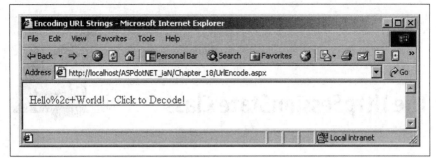

Figure 18-3. Output of server UrlEncode

Like the UrlDecode method, UrlEncode is overloaded. It returns a string when called with the *s* argument alone and does not return a value when called with both the *s* and *output* arguments. Instead, the encoded URL is sent to the writer object.

UrlPathEncode

returnstring = Server.UrlPathEncode(*s*)

Returns a string containing a URL whose path portion is encoded using the URL literal equivalents of symbols such as slash (/), colon (:), and dot (.). The method also encodes any spaces in the remaining portion of the URL, since spaces in the query string may be unexpectedly truncated by some browsers.

Parameters

returnstring

A String variable to receive the encoded string from the method.

s

A String variable containing the URL to be encoded by the method.

Example

The code example declares two string variables, sets the value of StrToEncode, assigns the return value of the Server.UrlPathEncode call to StrToReturn, and then writes the value to the browser as part of a hyperlink:

```
Sub Page_Load( )
    Dim StrToEncode As String
    Dim StrToReturn As String
    StrToEncode = "http://www.aspnetian.com/Chapter18/UrlPathEncode.aspx"
    StrToReturn = Server.UrlPathEncode(StrToEncode)
    Message.Text = "<a href=""UrlPathEncode.aspx?target=" & _
        StrToReturn & """>" & StrToReturn & "</a><br/>"
    Message.Text &= "Target = " & Request("Target")
End Sub
```

Notes

This method existed in classic ASP, but was undocumented.

19

The HttpSessionState Class

A significant challenge for any Web-based application is managing user state. Unlike rich client applications, in which user state can be stored in persistent variables local to the client application, web browsers do not have a comparable built-in facility for persistently storing user state locally. This is because HTTP, the basic communication protocol used in web applications, is essentially a connectionless protocol (the HTTP specification allows persistent connections, but problems with persistent HTTP connections prevent this specification from being widely used). Each HTTP request/response is treated as completely separate from every other request/response. As such, any local variable storage cannot be reliably mapped from the request/response in which they were created to any subsequent request/response.

An early solution to this challenge was the creation of cookies, which are bits of text that are stored either in memory (per-session cookies) or on disk (persistent cookies) and are associated with the domain name from which they originated. This solves the problem of being able to associate a bit of data with more than one request/response, but it has limitations that made it a less than ideal solution:

- Cookies can only store text (or a textual representation of other data), which means that cookie data cannot be made typesafe.

- Cookies are limited in size (the size limit depends on the browser, but is often 4k).

- Cookies can be manipulated on the client. If an application relying on cookies for user state does not take this into account, it is possible that a malicious user could use a manipulated cookie to breach the security of the application.

- Most browsers allow users to turn off or refuse cookies. If users do so, an application that relies on cookies for storing user state may not function correctly.

- Cookies present a potential performance and scalability problem, since all cookies for a given domain are sent with each request/response cycle. This means that sites making substantial use of cookies for state management will send a lot of information over the wire with each request/response cycle, whether that information is needed for that request/response or not.

For these reasons, classic ASP implemented state management through the Session intrinsic object, which provided a collection of key/value pairs for each user for storing user-specific state in memory on the web server. In classic ASP, each user session was identified by a unique identifier called the SessionID, which was sent as a per-session cookie. This alleviated several concerns of using cookies alone for storing user state, including the performance/scalability issue and cookie size limits. However, it still failed to address some issues, including the problem of users who disable cookies. ASP.NET addresses this issue by allowing both cookie-based and cookieless sessions, which are configurable at the application level.

The HttpSessionState class is ASP.NET's replacement for classic ASP's Session intrinsic object. Like the other classes that replace ASP intrinsics, HttpSession-State is exposed as a property of the Page class—in this case, the Session property. Since each ASP.NET page inherits from the Page class, these properties are available to any code in the page. This means that migrating classic ASP code that uses the Session object should be relatively painless.

The HttpSessionState class is used primarily for storing and accessing data that is shared across all the pages accessed by a particular user during a given session of interacting with the application. The HttpSessionState class provides properties and methods that map to the properties, methods, and collections of the classic ASP Session object for backward compatibility. It also adds a number of new properties and methods that increase the convenience of dealing with session state.

As in classic ASP, each user session in ASP.NET is identified by a unique SessionID, which is created at the same time as the user's session, is exposed as a property of the HttpSessionState class. In most cases, developers do not need to concern themselves with this SessionID, since ASP.NET handles it transparently.

A new SessionID is created the first time a user who does not have a current session accesses a page within an ASP.NET application whose session state has not been disabled by setting the enableSessionState attribute of the @ Page directive to False. If the page stores information in the Session collection, or if an event handler is defined for the Session.Start event in the *global.asax* file, then a new session is created and the newly created SessionID is assigned to that session. This delayed creation of the session until it is actually used helps conserve the limited resources of the web server and can help improve the scalability of ASP.NET applications.

When the session is created, the Session.Start event is fired. This event can be handled by creating an event handler in the *global.asax* file (the ASP.NET equivalent of *global.asa*) with the following signature:

```
Sub Session_OnStart( )
    'Session initialization code
End Sub
```

By default, the lifetime of the session for a given user is 20 minutes from the time of the user's last request. This setting is configurable at the application level via the ASP.NET *web.config* configuration file or at the machine level via the *machine.config* configuration file. Refer to Chapter 20 for more information on configuring the session timeout value. When a session ends, either by exceeding the timeout value or by code that calls the Session.Abandon method, the Session.End event is fired. Like the Start event, you can handle this event by adding an event handler to *global.asax* with the following signature:

```
Sub Session_OnEnd()
    'Session cleanup code
End Sub
```

Note that the session does not end automatically when the user closes their browser, so if you want to explicitly end the session when a user is finished, you should implement some kind of logout feature that calls the Session.Abandon method.

In ASP.NET, session state is managed through the SessionStateModule class, which is an HttpModule. HttpModules are classes that derive from IHttpModule and that participate in each HTTP request in an ASP.NET application. The SessionStateModule class is responsible for generating and/or retrieving SessionIDs, firing the Start and End events of the Session object, and abstracting the underlying Session store from the HttpSessionState class.

Session state configuration is handled through the sessionState configuration section of the *machine.config* and *web.config* configuration files. (The session-State configuration section of the *web.config* configuration file will be discussed in detail in Chapter 20.) The *machine.config* file contains the default settings for all applications on the machine, and may be overridden by adding a sessionState section to the *web.config* file for an application. If no sessionState section appears in the application-level configuration file, the defaults in *machine.config* are inherited by the application. As installed, *machine.config* enables in-process session state by using cookies to track the SessionID by default.

ASP.NET adds two new configuration options in addition to the timeout value and enabling/disabling of sessions that were configurable in classic ASP. The first provides built-in support for cookieless sessions. Cookieless sessions are configured in the *web.config* (or *machine.config*) file and implemented through the SessionStateModule class, which automatically modifies all relative URLs in the application and embeds the SessionID, allowing the application to maintain user state without using cookies. ASP.NET also provides the Response.ApplyAppPath-Modifier method, which can create absolute URLs containing the embedded SessionID given a virtual path to a resource. This allows even applications to take advantage of cookieless sessions by using absolute URLs.

The second new configuration option allows session state in ASP.NET to span multiple servers through new out-of-process storage options. ASP.NET state can now be stored in-process (the same as classic ASP), in a special ASP.NET state NT service, or in a SQL Server database. The latter two options allow multiple machines to use the same state storage facility, albeit at the expense of making out-of-process calls to set and retrieve state information. More importantly, all storage options are transparent to the developer. Information is added to and retrieved from the session state store in exactly the same fashion, regardless of which underlying session state store is used. This allows applications to be developed by initially using in-process state storage for the best performance, and later moved to out-of process storage to facilitate scaling out by adding more web servers—all without changing a single line of code in the application.

Items can be stored in the Session collection in one of three ways:

- By calling the Add method, passing in the name to assign to the item and the item's value. This value can be of any type supported by the CLR, including object instances, which are automatically serialized before being stored. The Add method takes the form:

      Session.Add(itemName, itemValue)

- By explicitly referring to the Item property, passing a name or index to assign to the new item:

      Session.Item(*itemName*) = *itemValue*

- By implicitly referring to the Item property, passing a name to assign to the new item. This was the most common technique used in classic ASP.

      Session(itemName) = itemValue

Items in the Session collection can be accessed in one of three ways:

- By retrieving and iterating over the collection of keys in the Session collection (see the Keys collection description for an example).

- By explicitly referring to the Item property, passing the name of the item to retrieve:

      localVar = Session.Item(*itemName*)

- By implicitly referring to the Item property, passing the name of the item to retrieve. This was the most common technique used in classic ASP:

      localVar = Session(itemName)

Items can be removed from the Session collection in one of several ways:

- By calling the Clear method (clears all items).
- By calling the RemoveAll method (removes all items, which is effectively the same as calling the Clear method).
- By calling the Remove method, passing the name of the item to remove.
- By calling the RemoveAt method, passing the index of the item to remove.

Table 19-1 lists the properties, collections, methods, and events exposed by the HttpSessionState class.

Table 19-1. HttpSessionState class summary

Properties	Collections	Methods (public instance)	Events[a]
CodePage	Contents	Abandon	Start
Count	Keys	Add	End
IsCookieless	StaticObjects	Clear	
IsNewSession		CopyTo	

Table 19-1. HttpSessionState class summary (continued)

Properties	Collections	Methods (public instance)	Events[a]
IsReadOnly		Remove	
Item		RemoveAll	
LCID		RemoveAt	
Mode			
SessionID			
Timeout			

[a]These events are exposed by the SessionStateModule class, rather than the HttpSessionState class.

Comments/Troubleshooting

Understanding both the scope and the lifetime of the Session collection for a given user is important when using the Session object. As mentioned above, a new session is created when a user first requests a page within an ASP.NET application for which session state is enabled (session state is enabled by default in in-process mode) and that stores a value in the Session collection. The boundary of that ASP.NET application is defined by the boundary of an IIS application. That is, the boundary of the ASP.NET session includes all ASP.NET pages within a single IIS application and all of its subfolders and virtual directories. It does not, however, include subfolders that are defined as IIS applications. Figure 19-1 illustrates the different folder types in IIS. In Figure 19-1, the *SessionWrite.aspx* file writes a value to the Session collection. Because the folder containing *SessionWrite.aspx* is a virtual directory that is a part of the *Chapter_19* application folder and is not defined as its own folder, the session value written by *SessionWrite.aspx* will be available to any page in either the *Chapter_19* folder or the *SubApp* subfolder. If, however, the *SubApp* folder is configured as an IIS Application (by accessing the Virtual Directory tab of the Properties dialog for the folder and clicking the Create button in the Application Settings section), it will then define its own session boundaries, which will not be shared with the parent *Chapter_19* application.

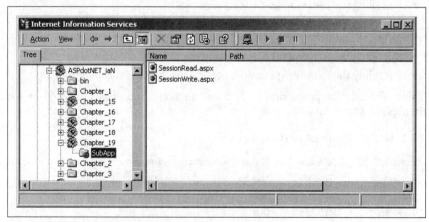

Figure 19-1. IIS folder types

The lifetime of an ASP.NET session is set by default to 20 minutes from the time of the last request to the application that created the session, or until the Session.Abandon method is called.

Keep this lifetime in mind for two reasons:

- Any information that you store at the session level will continue to consume resources (memory, in the case of in-process or state service storage; memory and/or disk space, in the case of SQL Server state storage) for a minimum of 20 minutes (or whatever length you've set for the timeout value), and possibly longer depending on the user's activity in the application. For this reason, you should always carefully consider the potential costs associated with storing an item (particularly object instances) in the Session collection.

- If code in your page relies on an item being in the Session collection, your code could break if and when the session timeout value is exceeded. For this reason, you should always check to make sure that the item exists by testing whether the item evaluates to Nothing (or null in C#) before attempting to access the item's value.

In classic ASP, a big no-no was storing non-thread–safe COM objects (i.e., *any* COM object written in Visual Basic) in the Session collection. This was because such components would force IIS to process requests only to the Session that stored the COM object from the same thread that created the object, which could limit scalability substantially. In ASP.NET, this is less of an issue, since all managed .NET components can be stored safely in the Session collection without the threading model impacting scalability. The concerns about resource usage and scalability still apply, however, so before storing objects in the Session collection, carefully consider just how much memory will probably be consumed by multiple serialized instances of the object being stored by multiple sessions.

The difference between objects added to the Session collection and objects created with Session scope using the <object> tag in *global.asax* is also important. While objects added to the Session collection can be removed by using the Remove, RemoveAll, or Clear methods, objects in the StaticObjects collection (those created in *global.asax*) are not affected by any of these methods.

In addition to properties and methods provided for backward compatibility with classic ASP, the ASP.NET version of the Session object also adds useful new properties and methods, including the Count, IsCookieless, IsNewSession, and IsReadOnly properties, and the Clear, CopyTo, and RemoveAt methods. The Count and CopyTo members are derived from the ICollection interface, which is implemented by the HttpSessionState class.

In this chapter, we'll use the following code listing as the basis for most examples in the chapter. Unless otherwise noted, each example will consist of the Page_ Load event handler for that particular example. Any displayed output messages or return values will be shown as the Text property of the ASP.NET Label named Message or by calling Response.Write.

```
<%@ Page Language="vb" %>
<html>
    <head>
        <script runat="server">
```

```
            Sub Page_Load()
                'Example code will go here
            End Sub
        </script>
    </head>
<body>
    <asp:label id="Message" runat="server"/>
</body>
</html>
```

Properties Reference

CodePage

```
Integer = Session.CodePage
Session.CodePage = Integer
```

Returns or sets an integer indicating the code page to be used in generating the page output. The code page is the character set that contains all characters and punctuation for a given locale setting.

Parameter

Integer
    An Integer variable that will receive or set the code page property value.

Example

The example writes the current code page value to the Text property of the Message label control:

```
Sub Page_Load()
    Message.Text = "Current Code Page is: " & Session.CodePage
End Sub
```

Notes

The CodePage property is provided for compatibility with classic ASP. For new ASP.NET development, you should use the ContentEncoding property of the Response class for formatting output to a given code page, or configure globalization settings in *web.config* (see Chapters 8 and 20 for more information on globalization settings).

In the example above, although the property value is an Integer, ASP.NET automatically casts the Integer value to a String, which is then assigned to the Text property. This works because any .NET object or data type can be represented as a String.

Count

```
Integer = Session.Count
```

Returns an integer containing the number of items currently in the Session collection.

Parameter

Integer
> An Integer variable that will receive the count property value.

Example

The example adds two values to the Session collection, displays the count of the items in the Session collection, and then displays each item, using the Count property as a looping control value:

```
Sub Page_Load( )
    Session("foo") = "Hello, "
    Session("bar") = "World!"
    Message.Text = "The Session collection contains " & _
        Session.Count & " items.</br>"
        Dim I as Integer
        For I = 0 To Session.Count - 1
            Message.Text &= CStr(Session(I)) & "</br>"
        Next
End Sub
```

Notes

The Count property is new for ASP.NET. In addition to using the Count property for looping through the Session collection, you can use the property to keep track of how many items a given Session stores at any given time. For example, you could write this information to a log for later review.

IsCookieless

```
Boolean = Session.IsCookieless
```

Returns a Boolean indicating whether the application is configured for cookieless Session operation.

Parameter

Boolean
> A Boolean variable that will receive the IsCookieless property value.

Example

The example displays a message indicating whether cookieless sessions have been enabled for the current session:

```
Sub Page_Load( )
    If Session.IsCookieless Then
        Message.Text = "The current Session does not use cookies."
    Else
        Message.Text = "The current Session uses cookies."
    End If
End Sub
```

Notes

The IsCookieless property is new for ASP.NET, and is especially useful in combination with the Response.ApplyAppPathModifier method, which allows you to create absolute URLs containing the current SessionID for use with cookieless sessions.

IsNewSession

`Boolean = Session.IsNewSession`

Returns a Boolean indicating whether the current session was created as a result of the current request.

Parameter

Boolean
> A Boolean variable that will receive the IsNewSession property value. Returns True on the request that creates a Session and False for each subsequent request from the same client.

Example

The example tests to see if the current request created a new session and if so, adds a value to the Session collection and then displays a message containing the SessionID of the current session:

```
Sub Page_Load( )
    If Session.IsNewSession Then
        Session("foo") = "foo"
        Message.Text = "The current Session (SessionID: " & _
            Session.SessionID & ") was created with this request."
    Else
        Message.Text = "The current Session (SessionID: " & _
            Session.SessionID & ") existed prior to this request."
    End If
End Sub
```

Notes

The IsNewSession property is very useful when you want to initialize Session collection items for only certain pages. Unlike the Session_OnStart event handler in *global.asax*, which is called when a session is created, regardless of which page creates the session, this property gives you finer-grained control over initialization and session behavior.

As mentioned in the introduction to this chapter, while a new SessionID is generated for each request that does not already have a session, a new session is not created for a given request unless the requested page stores a value in the Session collection or an event handler exists in *global.asax* for the Session Start event.

Thus, if you commented out the line:

```
Session("foo") = "foo"
```

in the example above, and no Session_OnStart event handler was defined in *global.asax*, each request to the page would result in a new SessionID being generated, but no session would actually be created by the request.

IsReadOnly

Boolean = Session.IsReadOnly

Returns a Boolean indicating whether the current session can be written to from the current page. This property is set to True when the EnableSessionState attribute of the @ Page directive is set to ReadOnly.

Parameter

Boolean
>   A Boolean variable that will receive the IsReadOnly property value. The default is False.

Example

The example tests whether the session is set to ReadOnly for the page and if so, displays an appropriate message. If not, it writes a value to the Session collection and then displays a different message:

```
Sub Page_Load( )
    If Session.IsReadOnly Then
        Message.Text = "The current Session (SessionID: " & _
            Session.SessionID & ") is read-only for this page."
    Else
        Session("foo") = "foo"
        Message.Text = "The current Session (SessionID: " & _
            Session.SessionID & ") can be written to from this page."
    End If
End Sub
```

To test this page, add the EnableSessionState attribute to the @ Page directive for the page, setting its value to ReadOnly, as shown here:

```
<%@ Page Language="vb" EnableSessionState="ReadOnly" %>
```

Notes

Read-only session state is new in ASP.NET and is designed to improve the efficiency of pages that require only read access to the Session collection. Attempting to write to the Session collection from a page with the EnableSessionState attribute set to ReadOnly will result in an exception being thrown.

Item

Object = Session.Item(ByVal *name* As String)
Session.Item(ByVal *name* As String) = *Object*
Object = Session.Item(ByVal *index* As Integer)
Session.Item(ByVal *index* As Integer) = *Object*

Returns or sets an object associated with a particular name or index.

Parameters

Object
>   A variable of any type (since all .NET types are ultimately derived from Object) that will receive or set the item's value.

name
> A string argument containing the text key to apply to the item or by which to retrieve the item.

index
> An integer argument containing the index of the item whose value will be retrieved or modified.

Example

The example sets the values of two items in the Session collection. If these items do not already exist in the collection, they will be added. The example then displays the two values:

```
Sub Page_Load( )
    Session.Item("foo") = "foo"
    Session.Item("foo2") = "foo2"
    Message.Text = CStr(Session.Item("foo")) & "</br>"
    Message.Text &= CStr(Session.Item(1))
End Sub
```

Notes

The Item property is accessed implicitly when using the syntax:

```
Session("foo") = "foo"
```

which is commonly seen in classic ASP code. Using the Item property is not required, but it may make your code more readable and understandable than accessing it implicitly.

Note that an index may be used only as an argument when modifying a value, not to create a new item. The index must also be smaller than the number of items in the Session collection or an exception will be thrown.

LCID

```
Integer = Session.LCID
Session.LCID = Integer
```

Returns or sets an integer containing the locale identifier for the session. The locale identifier determines how information such as date/time values is formatted.

Parameter

Integer
> An integer variable that will receive or set the LCID property value.

Example

The example displays the current LCID value and displays the current date and time formatted based on the current LCID. It then changes the LCID to the value for French, displays the LCID value, and displays the current date and time again, this time formatted based on the new LCID:

```
Sub Page_Load( )
    Message.Text = "Current locale ID is: " & Session.LCID & "</br>"
```

```
     Message.Text &= "Current date and time is: " & DateTime.Now() & "</br>"
     Session.LCID = 1036 'France
     Message.Text &= "Current locale ID is: " & Session.LCID & "</br>"
     Message.Text &= "Current date and time is: " & DateTime.Now() & "</br>"
  End Sub
```

Notes

The LCID property is provided for backward compatibility with classic ASP. For new ASP.NET development, you should use the System.Threading.Current-Thread.CurrentCulture.LCID property instead. ASP.NET stores and retrieves the Session.LCID property in System.Threading.CurrentThread.CurrentCulture.LCID.

Mode

SessionStateMode = Session.Mode

Returns one of the values of the SessionStateMode enumeration that describes the mode for which session state for the application has been configured.

Parameter

SessionStateMode
> One of the following members of the SessionStateMode enumeration:

> *InProc*
>> Indicates that session state is stored in-process. This setting provides the best performance when using session state storage, but cannot be shared across multiple servers.

> *Off*
>> Indicates that session state is disabled. This setting provides the best performance overall, but at the expense of not using session state storage.

> *SQLServer*
>> Indicates that session state is stored out-of-process in a SQL Server database. This setting allows state sharing across machines at the expense of some performance.

> *StateServer*
>> Indicates that session state is stored out of process in a special NT service. This setting also allows state sharing across machines at the expense of some performance.

Example

The example writes a message containing the current Session state mode to the Text property of the Message ASP.NET Label control. To get the string representation of the enumeration value, call ToString on the Mode property value as shown:

```
Sub Page_Load()
   Message.Text = "The current Session state mode is: " & _
       Session.Mode.ToString() & ".</br>"
End Sub
```

Notes

The Mode property allows you to test the current mode of session state storage. One use for this property is to determine whether to store information in the Session collection, depending on the mode. Because both the StateServer and SQLServer modes require cross-process communication (which can be very expensive relative to in-process communication), you may wish to provide alternative means for storing certain information if one of these modes is used. Using the Mode property, you can write conditional statements that will decide at runtime whether or not to store a particular value based on the current session state mode. That way, if the session state mode is changed administratively, no change to your code is required.

SessionID

`String = Session.SessionID`

Returns a string containing the unique identifier for the current session.

Parameters

String
> A string variable that will receive the session ID property value.

Example

See the example for the IsReadOnly property.

Notes

The SessionID property value is generated the first time a page for which session state has not been disabled is requested. As noted earlier, the actual session is not created unless either an event handler is provided in *global.asax* for the Session. Start event or a value is stored in the Session collection. The SessionID is stored on the client in a nonpersistent cookie, or if cookieless sessions are enabled, is passed as part of each URL request.

Note that if the client's browser is closed, the client will be unable to access their session (since the nonpersistent cookie will be destroyed when the browser is closed), but the session will continue to exist on the server until the configured timeout period has elapsed. If you want to explicitly expire a session, you can check the IsClientConnected property of the HttpResponse class, which returns a Boolean indicating whether the client has disconnected. If it returns False, you can then call Session.Abandon to expire the session.

While the SessionID value, which is a 120-bit ASCII string in ASP.NET, is unique to a given IIS application instance, it is not guaranteed to be universally unique and therefore should not be used for database identity values or for other purposes requiring universally unique values.

Timeout

```
Integer = Session.Timeout
Session. Timeout = Integer
```

Returns or sets an integer containing the amount of time, in minutes, that can elapse between requests without the session being destroyed. If the timeout value is exceeded, the current session is destroyed and the Session.End event is fired.

Parameter

Integer
    An integer variable that will receive or set the Timeout property value.

Example

The example writes the current value of the Timeout property to the Text property of the Message ASP.NET Label control:

```
Sub Page_Load( )
    Message.Text = "Current Session timeout value is " & _
        Session.Timeout & " minutes."
End Sub
```

Notes

You can use the Timeout property to temporarily override the timeout setting configured in *web.config* or *machine.config*, if you wish to make the value more restrictive for some reason.

Collections Reference

Contents

```
HttpSessionState = Session.Contents
```

Returns a reference to the current HttpSessionState instance.

Parameter

HttpSessionState
    A variable of type HttpSessionState that will receive the Contents reference.

Example

The example below calls the RemoveAll method through the Contents collection reference and then writes a message:

```
Sub Page_Load( )
    Session.Contents.RemoveAll( )
    Message.Text = "Removed all items from current Session."
End Sub
```

Notes

This property is provided for backward compatibility with classic ASP. Properties such as the Item property and methods such as Remove and RemoveAll were accessed via the Contents property in classic ASP. In new ASP.NET development, you should access these members directly.

Keys

KeysCollection = Session.Keys

Returns a NameObjectCollectionBase.KeysCollection containing the string keys associated with all of the values stored in the Session collection.

Parameter

KeysCollection
> A variable of type NameObjectCollectionBase.KeysCollection that will receive the Keys property value.

Example

The example loops through the collection of keys in the Session collection and then displays the key name and the value associated with it by using the Text property of the Message label control:

```
Sub Page_Load( )
    Dim Key As String
    Message.Text = "Session Keys:"
    For Each Key in Session.Keys
        Message.Text &= "<br/>Key:   " & Key
        Message.Text &= "<br/>Value:   " & _
                        CStr(Session(Key))
    Next
End Sub
```

Notes

The Keys property provides one of many ways to iterate over the contents of the Session collection.

StaticObjects

HttpStaticObjectsCollection = Session.StaticObjects

Returns an HttpStaticObjectsCollection containing all objects instantiated in *global.asax* by using the <object runat="server"> syntax whose scope is set to Session.

Parameter

HttpStaticObjectsCollection
> A variable of type HttpStaticObjectsCollection that will receive the StaticObjects property value.

Example

The example uses the Count property of the HttpStaticObjectsCollection class to display the number of objects in the current application declared with the <object scope="session" runat="server"/> syntax in *global.asax*. It then checks the type of

each object and, if it is a TextBox web control, adds it to the Controls collection
of the form:

```
Sub Page_Load( )
    Message.Text = "There are " & Session.StaticObjects.Count & _
        " objects declared with the " & _
        "&lt;object runat=&quot;server&quot;&gt; syntax in Session scope."
    Dim myobj As Object
    For Each myObj in Session.StaticObjects
        If myObj.Value.GetType.ToString( ) = _
            "System.Web.UI.WebControls.TextBox" Then
            myForm.Controls.Add(myObj.Value)
        End If
    Next
End Sub
```

You also need to modify the <body> section of the document as follows:

```
<body>
    <form id="myForm" runat="server">
        <asp:label id="Message" runat="server"/>
    </form>
</body>
```

Notes

This property is provided for backward compatibility with classic ASP. You
should think carefully before instantiating objects with Session or Application
scope because of the impact such objects have on resource usage and application
scalability. In most cases, it is advisable to limit objects to page scope.

Each object in the collection is represented by the DictionaryEntry structure, so its
key and value are not directly accessible. To access the key and/or value, use the
Key and/or Value members of the DictionaryEntry structure, as shown in the
example.

Methods Reference

Abandon

`Session.Abandon( )`

Immediately terminates the current user's session and causes the Session.End
event to be fired.

Parameters

None

Example

The example examines the IsNewSession property to determine if the current
request has resulted in a new session. If so, it adds a value to the Session collection and then displays a message indicating that a new session was created. If a
session already exists, the example displays a button that, when clicked, causes a

postback. This postback results in the Session.Abandon method being called and the session terminated:

```
If Not IsPostBack
    If Session.IsNewSession Then
        Session("foo") = "foo"
        Message.Text = "The current Session (SessionID: " & _
        Session.SessionID & ") was created with this request."
    Else
        Message.Text = "Click the button to abandon the current session."
        Dim AbandonButton As New Button
        AbandonButton.Text = "Abandon Session"
        myForm.Controls.Add(AbandonButton)
    End If
Else
    Session.Abandon()
    Message.Text = "Session abandoned."
End If
```

In order for the postback to work correctly, a server-side form needs to be added within the <body> tags, as shown below:

```
<form id="myForm" runat="server">
    <asp:label id="Message" runat="server"/>
</form>
```

Notes

The Abandon method is very important for controlling resource usage in ASP.NET applications that use session state. If you use session state for storing application data, you should implement a logout method that calls Session.Abandon and make it as easy as possible for your users to access this method (via a button or link on each page). Implementing this method will help prevent resources from being consumed for longer than necessary when a user has already quit using the application.

Note that the End event will be fired only when session state has been configured for in-process operation.

Add

Session.Add(ByVal *name* As String, ByVal *value* As Object)

Adds an item to the Session collection.

Parameters

name
    A string argument containing the name that will be used to refer to the new item.

value
    An object argument containing the value of the new item.

Example

The example declares a local variable, sets its value, and adds an item to the Session collection with the value of the local variable:

```
Sub Page_Load( )
    Dim myBaz As String = "baz"
    Session.Add("baz", myBaz)
    Dim I as Integer
    For I = 0 To Session.Count - 1
        Message.Text &= CStr(Session(I)) & "<br/>"
    Next
End Sub
```

Notes

The Add method, which is new in ASP.NET, provides a technique for adding items to the Session collection, which is consistent with the technique used for adding items to other .NET collections.

Clear

```
Session.Clear( )
```

Clears the contents of the Session collection for the current user.

Parameters

None

Example

The example clears the contents of the Session collection and writes a message to the Text property of the Message label control that includes the current count of the collection, which should be 0:

```
Sub Page_Load( )
    Session.Clear( )
    Message.Text = "There are " & Session.Count & _
        " items in the Session collection."
End Sub
```

Notes

The Clear method, which is new for ASP.NET, clears only the contents of the Session collection itself. It does not clear the contents of the StaticObjects collection.

CopyTo

```
Session.CopyTo(ByVal array As Array, ByVal index As Integer)
```

Copies the contents of the Session collection to a one-dimensional array.

Parameters

array
    An array argument that will receive the session collection values.

index

An integer argument specifying the point in the array at which to begin copying.

Example

The example checks to ensure that at least one item is in the Session collection, and if there is, it creates a local object array, copies the contents of the Session collection to it, and displays the value of the first item:

```
Sub Page_Load()
    If Session.Count > 0 Then
        Dim myArray As Array = Array.CreateInstance(GetType(Object), _
            Session.Count)
        Session.CopyTo(myArray, 0)
        Message.Text = "The first item in the array is: " & _
            CStr(myArray(0))
    End If
End Sub
```

Notes

The CopyTo method is useful if you have a large number of items stored in the Session collection. In such cases, accessing values from a local array variable may be faster and more efficient than accessing the values from the Session collection, particularly when session state is configured to run out of process. The improved efficiency and performance comes at the cost of ease of use, since arrays do not provide the same feature richness as the Session collection.

Remove

```
Session.Remove(ByVal name As String)
```

Removes an item from the Session collection by name.

Parameter

name

A string argument containing the name (key) of the item to remove.

Example

The example determines whether the item with the key "foo" exists in the Session collection and if it does, removes the item and displays an appropriate message:

```
Sub Page_Load()
    If Not Session("foo") Is Nothing Then
        Session.Remove("foo")
        Message.Text = "Item 'foo' was removed."
    Else
        Message.Text = "Item 'foo' does not exist."
    End If
End Sub
```

Notes

The Remove method is provided for backward compatibility with classic ASP. In classic ASP, this method was accessed through the Contents collection. In ASP.NET, this method can be accessed either directly, as shown above, or through the Contents collection.

RemoveAll

```
Session.RemoveAll( )
```

Removes all items from the Session collection.

Parameters

None

Example

The example checks to ensure that at least one item is in the Session collection (although if RemoveAll is called on an empty Session collection, no error will occur), and if it is, it clears the collection by calling the RemoveAll method:

```
Sub Page_Load( )
    If Session.Count > 0 Then
        Session.RemoveAll( )
        Message.Text = "Session collection cleared."
    Else
        Message.Text = "Session collection is already empty."
    End If
End Sub
```

Notes

The RemoveAll method is provided for backward compatibility with classic ASP. In classic ASP, this method was accessed through the Contents collection. In ASP.NET, this method can be accessed either directly, as shown above, or through the Contents collection.

RemoveAll has the same effect as calling the Clear method and like Clear, it clears the contents of the Session collection, but does not remove Session-scoped objects from the StaticObjects collection.

RemoveAt

```
Session.RemoveAt(ByVal index As Integer)
```

Removes an item from the Session collection by index. This is a new companion to the Remove method, which removes an item by key.

Parameter

index
> An integer argument containing the index location of the item to remove from the Session collection.

Example

```
Sub Page_Load( )
    If Session.Count > 0 Then
        Session.RemoveAt(0)
        Message.Text = "The item at index 0 was removed."
    Else
        Message.Text = "The item at index 0 does not exist."
    End If
End Sub
```

Notes

The RemoveAt method allows items to be removed from the Session collection by index rather than by key. As in the example above, the items that follow the removed item will shift one position in the collection when the item is removed. If you remove an item by index and call RemoveAt again with the same index, you will remove the item that immediately followed the original removed item.

Events Reference

Start

```
Sub Session_OnStart( )
 'Event handler logic
End Sub
```

Fired when the session is created. The event handler for this event should be defined in the *global.asax* application file.

Parameters

None

Example

The example writes an entry to both the Application Event log and the IIS log for the application to indicate that the Start event has fired:

```
<Script language="VB" runat="server">
    Sub Session_OnStart( )
        Dim EventLog1 As New System.Diagnostics.EventLog ("Application", _
            ".", "mySource")
        EventLog1.WriteEntry("Session_OnStart fired!")
        Context.Response.AppendToLog("Session_OnStart fired!")
    End Sub
</script>
```

Notes

The Start event is useful for performing initialization tasks for a new session. One limitation of classic ASP, the inability to access the Server. MapPath method in the Session_OnStart event handler, is eliminated in ASP.NET. You can now successfully call Server.MapPath from within this event handler.

End

```
Sub Session_OnEnd( )
  'Event handler logic
End Sub
```

Fired when the session is torn down—either by calling the Abandon method or when the Session.Timeout value expires. The event handler for this event should be defined in the *global.asax* application file.

Parameters

None

Example

The example below writes an entry to the Application Event log to indicate that the End event has fired:

```
<Script language="VB" runat="server">
  Sub Session_OnEnd( )
    Dim EventLog1 As New System.Diagnostics.EventLog ("Application", _
      ".", "mySource")
    EventLog1.WriteEntry("Session_OnEnd fired!")
    ' Response is not available in this event handler
    ' Context.Response.AppendToLog("Session_OnEnd fired!")
  End Sub
</script>
```

Notes

The End event is useful for performing cleanup tasks when the user's session ends—either when the Abandon method is called or when the session times out. Note that the Response object is not available in the context of the Session_OnEnd event handler. Unlike Session_OnStart, the Server.MapPath method is not available. Attempts to access the Response object or the Server.MapPath method from within this event handler will result in an exception being thrown. Since there is no context for displaying exception information, you will not see an error message. You can handle an exception thrown in the Session_OnEnd event handler by creating a handler for the Application.Error event, as shown below:

```
Sub Application_OnError( )
  Dim EventLog1 As New System.Diagnostics.EventLog ("Application", _
    ".", "mySource")
  EventLog1.WriteEntry("Error Occurred. Error info:" &     Server.
GetLastError( ).ToString( ))
  End Sub
```

Note that the End event will be fired only when session state has been configured for in-process operation.

20

web.config Reference

ASP.NET provides a completely new model for configuring web applications. This greatly simplified process makes it considerably easier to deploy application configuration settings, the application's content, and its components. Central to this new configuration model is *web.config*, an XML-based file that contains the configuration settings for your application. Because the file is written in XML, it is both human- and machine-readable.

web.config files configure applications hierarchically—i.e., an application can contain more than one *web.config* file, with each file residing in a separate folder of the application. Settings in a *web.config* file in a child folder of the application root override the settings of the *web.config* file in the parent folder. Settings not defined in the child *web.config* file inherit the settings from the parent *web.config* file. Figure 20-1 demonstrates these rules of precedence.

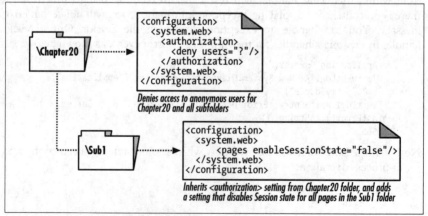

Figure 20-1. Inheriting and overriding web.config settings

In addition to inheriting settings from a *web.config* file defined in a parent folder, all applications on a given machine inherit settings from a file called *machine.config*. The *machine.config* file contains default ASP.NET configuration settings, as well as settings for other .NET application types. Thus, in Figure 20-1, the *Chapter20* folder inherits the *machine.config* setting for the enableSessionState attribute of the <pages> element, which is True by default. The *web.config* file in the *Chapter20* folder overrides the *machine.config* default settings for the <authorization> element, denying access to any anonymous user (any user who has not logged in). The *Sub1* subfolder inherits this setting (as well as all settings defined in *machine.config*) and adds a setting to override the *machine.config* setting for the <pages> element, disabling session state for all pages contained in the *Sub1* folder.

web.config is made up of one or more of the elements listed in the "web.config Elements" section later in this section. The <configuration> element is required, as is its child, <system.web>. All child elements of <system.web> (i.e., the elements that actually provide the configuration information) are optional; however, the use of certain elements may require you to include other elements or child elements. Each element may also contain one or more attributes that affect the behavior of that element.

Certain elements are limited in the scope at which they can be used. Some elements can be used only at the Application level (in the *web.config* file at the root of the application), some only at the machine level (in *machine.config*), and some can be used at any scope (in *machine.config* or in any *web.config* file, whether at application root or subfolder level).

The elements in Table 20-1 are organized both functionally and hierarchically. That is, elements with related functions, such as <authentication> and <authorization>, are grouped together, and child elements immediately follow their parent elements. Thus, the <credentials> element immediately follows the <forms> element, which is its parent, and is immediately followed by <user>, which is a child of <credentials>. Table 20-1 summarizes the *web.config* elements covered in this chapter.

Table 20-1. web.config element summary

<configuration>	<case>	<clear>
<appSettings>	<clientTarget>	<httpModules>
<add>	<add>	<add>
<remove>	<remove>	<remove>
<clear>	<clear>	<clear>
<system.web>	<compilation>	<httpRuntime>
<authentication>	<compilers>	<identity>
<forms>	<compiler>	<machineKey>
<credentials>	<assemblies>	<pages>
<user>	<add>	<processModel>
<passport>	<remove>	<securityPolicy>
<authorization>	<clear>	<trustLevel>
<allow>	<customErrors>	<sessionState>
<deny>	<error>	<trace>
<browserCaps>	<globalization>	<trust>

Table 20-1. web.config element summary (continued)

\<result>	\<httpHandlers>	\<location>
\<use>	\<add>	
\<filter>	\<remove>	

Comments/Troubleshooting

Probably the most common error that is encountered with *web.config* and *machine.config* relates to capitalization. Tags and elements within both these files are *case-sensitive*. Tags and elements follow the naming convention referred to as camel-casing, in which the first letter of the first word of the element or attribute is lowercase, and the first letter of each subsequent word is uppercase. Attribute values are also case-sensitive, but do not follow any particular naming convention.

While the ability of applications and folders to inherit settings from parent *web.config* files is very convenient, it presents security implications. For example, the \<appSettings> element can be used to store key/value pairs for runtime retrieval from your application. If this element is used to store values in the *machine.config* file, these values are available to any application on that machine. In a shared server environment, this could potentially expose information to others in undesirable ways.

Another security issue with both *machine.config* and *web.config* is how to prevent modification of inherited settings. For example, a server administrator might want to configure authentication settings globally in the *machine.config* file and prevent application developers from overriding these settings in their applications. This can be accomplished by using the \<location> element, setting its allowOverride attribute to False and, optionally, setting the path attribute to an application path (if the locked-down settings are to apply only to a specific file or folder).

It is important to exercise caution when working with the *machine.config* file to avoid making changes if you are uncertain of their impact (particularly on other applications). Remember that *machine.config* contains configuration settings not only for all ASP.NET web applications for a given machine, but also for all .NET applications on that machine. Thus, changes to *machine.config* can have a broad impact. It's a good idea to back up the *machine.config* file before editing it, so that if your changes result in problems, you can always restore the previous copy. Another alternative is to place the *machine.config* file under a source code control system, such as Visual Source Safe, and require checkout of the file to make modifications. This provides the ability to roll back changes, as well as the additional ability to track who has made changes to the file.

Finally, your application is required to have a *web.config* file. If the default settings from *machine.config* (or a parent *web.config*) file serve your needs, then omitting this file will simplify your deployment and maintenance tasks. Use *web.config* only when you need to make changes to the default configuration provided by *machine.config*.

web.config Elements

`<configuration>`

```
<configuration>
</configuration>
```

The root element for all configuration files; it is required.

Scope

All

Attributes

None

`<appSettings>`

```
<appSettings>
</appSettings>
```

The `<appSettings>` element can be used to configure custom application settings as key/value pairs. These settings can later be retrieved at runtime using the AppSettings property of the ConfigurationSettings class, as shown in the example. This property is shared (static) and does not require the ConfigurationSettings class to be instantiated before accessing the property.

Scope

Any

Attributes

None

Child Elements

<add>
> The key/value pair to add.

<remove>
> The key to remove.

<clear>
> Clears all previously added key/value pairs.

Example

The following *web.config* section sets an application level key/value pair:

```
<configuration>
   <appSettings>
      <add key="applicationConfigKey" value="bar"/>
   </appSettings>
</configuration>
```

The following ASP.NET page retrieves the value set by the preceding code and also retrieves a value set at the *machine.config* level:

```
<%@ Page Language="VB" %>
<html>
<head>
   <script runat="server">
      Sub Page_Load( )
         Message1.Text &= _
            ConfigurationSettings.AppSettings("machineConfigKey")
         Message2.Text &= _
            ConfigurationSettings.AppSettings("applicationConfigKey")
      End Sub
   </script>
</head>
<body>
   <asp:label id="Message1" runat="server">Machine.Config setting: </
asp:label>
   <br/>
   <asp:label id="Message2" runat="server">Web.Config setting: </ asp:label>
</body>
</html>
```

Notes

As shown in the example, the <appSettings> element can be used separately from the <system.web> element and its children.

For security reasons, use caution when deciding what kinds of data to store using the <appSettings> element. Remember that while the ASP.NET runtime is set up to prevent an application's *web.config* file from being requested or read, this file could still be vulnerable if the security of the web server were breached in some other way. Thus, you should generally avoid storing sensitive information such as usernames and passwords, or connection strings containing usernames and passwords, in the *web.config* file. A better, although still moderately vulnerable, alternative is to store this information at the *machine.config* level, since this file is not within the web space of the application and is not as vulnerable to compromise through attacks on IIS. However, remember that this information will be available to any application on the machine.

<system.web>

```
<system.web>
</system.web>
```

Container element for all elements used in *web.config* files.

Scope

All

Attributes

None

Child Elements

<authentication>, <authorization>, <browserCaps>, <clientTarget>, <compilation>, <customErrors>, <globalization>, <httpHandlers>, <httpModules>, <httpRuntime>, <identity>, <iisFilter>, <machineKey>, <pages>, <processModel>, <securityPolicy>, <sessionState>, <trace>, <trust>, <webServices>

Notes

This element is required in order to use any of its child elements.

<authentication>

```
<authentication>
</authentication>
```

Provides attributes and contains child elements used to configure authentication options in ASP.NET.

Scope

Machine, Application

Attribute

Mode

> Determines the type of authentication that will be used by ASP.NET. Valid values are as follows:

> *Windows (default)*

>> Uses credentials provided by IIS authentication methods (Basic, Digest, Integrated Windows Authentication, or Certificates) to authenticate user requests. Requests can then be permitted or denied based on settings contained within the <authorization> element, using the authenticated username (or an associated group/role name) to allow or deny the request. This is the default authentication mode defined in *machine.config*.

> *Forms*

>> Provides an infrastructure for performing custom authentication in situations when Windows authentication is not possible. When Forms authentication is enabled, users who have not logged in are automatically redirected to a login URL provided as an attribute of the <forms> element. Once logged in, a cookie is sent as an authentication token. Users can be authenticated against any credentials database the developer chooses—from Active Directory to a custom credentials database. This mode requires the inclusion of the <forms> child element.

> *Passport*

>> Takes advantage of Microsoft's Passport authentication service. This mode requires inclusion of the <passport> child element.

> *None*

>> Specifies that no authentication be performed at the ASP.NET level. Requests can still be authenticated at the IIS level using one of the IIS authentication modes in combination with NTFS access control lists (ACLs).

Child Elements

<forms>, <passport>

Example

The example configures the pages within the scope of the configuration file to use ASP.NET forms-based authentication:

```
<configuration>
    <system.web>
        <authentication mode="Forms">
            <forms name="myAuthCookie"
                loginUrl="login.aspx"
                protection="All"
                timeout="30"
                path="/" />
        </authentication>
    </system.web>
</configuration>
```

Notes

The <location> element can be used to configure authentication at the machine level, if desired, and its allowOverride attribute can be used to prevent overriding these settings in individual applications.

Authentication can be a fairly involved topic. For more information on the various ASP.NET authentication methods and how they relate to IIS authentication, please see Chapter 9.

<forms>

```
<forms
 loginUrl=String
 name=String
 path=String

 protection="All|None|Encryption|Validation"
 requireSsl=boolean
 slidingExpiration=boolean
 timeout=Integer>
</forms>
```

Provides attributes and one child element (<credentials>) to configure ASP.NET to use forms-based authentication.

Scope

Machine, Application

Attributes

name

Specifies the name of the authentication cookie. If this attribute is omitted, the value defaults to .ASPXAUTH. When running multiple applications that use forms-based authentication on the same server, it's usually a good idea to give each application its own authentication cookie name—to minimize the risk of authenticated users from one application being treated as authenticated in others.

loginUrl

Specifies the redirect URL for users who do not have a valid authentication cookie. If a user with no authentication cookie requests a page in the application, they will be redirected to this URL to log in. The login page can then redirect the user back to the originally requested page. If this attribute is omitted, the value defaults to `login.aspx`.

protection

Specifies the type of protection used to prevent the authentication cookie from being modified during transit. Valid values are as follows:

All

Cookies are both encrypted (using triple DES encryption, if available) and subjected to data validation. Data validation is performed based on the settings of the `<machineKey>` element. `All` is the default value and is the recommended setting for securing the authentication cookie.

Encryption

Cookies are only encrypted. This reduces overhead associated with cookie protection, but may leave cookies vulnerable to plain-text attacks.

None

Neither encryption nor validation is enabled for cookie protection. This reduces overhead when using forms-based authentication, but provides no protection of the authentication cookie. This attribute is not recommended.

Validation

A validation key is concatenated with cookie data. This key is checked to ensure that cookie data has not been altered in transit.

requireSsl

When set to `True`, prevents compliant browsers from sending the authentication cookie unless the connection is using SSL encryption. The default value is `False`. This attribute is only supported in Version 1.1 of ASP.NET.

slidingExpiration

When set to `True`, each request within the same session will reset the timeout value for the authentication cookie. The default value is `True`. This attribute is supported only in Version 1.1 of ASP.NET.

timeout

Specifies the amount of time, in minutes, before the authentication cookie expires. This is a sliding value, which is reset when a request is received after more than half of the timeout period has elapsed. Note that this attribute does not apply to persistent cookies. The default value is 30.

path

Specifies the path for the authentication cookie. Because many browsers treat the path in a case-sensitive manner, the default is set to the backslash (\) character.

Child Elements

<credentials>

Example

See the example for the <authentication> element.

Notes

Forms-based authentication is only effective when used in conjunction with the <authorization> element to deny anonymous users access to pages within the application.

It's a good idea to use SSL encryption to protect the forms authentication credentials and cookie to prevent the possibility of these credentials being hijacked. If you can't (or don't want to) use SSL, you should at least reduce the default timeout value to lessen the likelihood of someone capturing and impersonating the authentication cookie.

<credentials>

```
<credentials
 passwordFormat="Clear|SHA1|MD5">
</credentials>
```

Allows you to store one or more sets of credentials in the application (or machine) configuration file for later use in authenticating requests. The child <user> element is used to store the actual credentials.

Scope

Machine, Application

Attribute

passwordFormat
    Specifies the format in which passwords will be stored (and compared). Valid options are Clear, SHA1, and MD5.

Child Elements

<user>

Example

The example shows the <credentials> element, which is used to store two user accounts to authenticate against:

```
<credentials passwordFormat = "SHA1">
    <user name="foo" password="794ED3D18464BAFF93F8DED1CFD00D9A2D9FE316"/>
    <user name="bar" password="B7CDD2A2B0F05E6948E5CEED22FA9A38EB28DEC8"/>
</credentials>
```

Notes

Once you've stored the credentials, you can authenticate against them by calling the static (shared) Authenticate method of the FormsAuthentication helper class.

You can use the static (shared) HashPasswordForStoringInConfigFile method of FormsAuthentication to create an MD5 or SHA1 hash of the password for storing in the <user> element. When using the <credentials> element to store credentials, you should always hash passwords, since storing them in readable text presents a potential security risk. Although theoretically, no one should be able to read the configuration file, a server misconfiguration or security vulnerability could conceivably expose this file.

<user>

Stores the username and password for each user defined in the <credentials> element.

Scope

Machine, Application

Attributes

name
    The username to be authenticated against.

password
    The password to be authenticated against.

Child Elements

None

Example

See the example for the <credentials> element.

Notes

You should always use the HashPasswordForStoringInConfigFile method to hash passwords stored in the password attribute. A utility page that creates SHA1 or MD5 hashes of plain text passwords is provided in the examples for Chapter 9.

<passport>

<passport redirectUrl=*Url* />

This optional element configures an internal URL to which unauthenticated requests will be redirected when using Microsoft's Passport authentication provider. This element should be used only when the <authentication> element's mode attribute is set to Passport.

Scope

Machine, Application

Attributes

redirectUrl
    A URL in the application to which requests lacking a Passport authentication token are redirected.

Child Elements

None

Example

This example shows a *web.config* file that configures an application for Passport authentication:

```
<configuration>
  <system.web>
    <authentication mode="Passport">
      <passport redirectUrl="Login.aspx"/>
    </authentication>
  </system.web>
</configuration>
```

Notes

For more information on configuring Passport authentication, see the Passport SDK documentation, which is available from *http://www.passport.com*.

<authorization>

Provides two child elements, <allow> and <deny>, that allow you to configure the users, roles, or HTTP verbs that can be used to access application resources.

Scope

Any

Attributes

None

Child Elements

<allow>, <deny>

Example

The example allows users Mary and John to access application resources using any HTTP verb, while denying POST access to nonauthenticated users:

```
<configuration>
  <system.web>
    <authorization>
      <allow users="Mary, John" />
      <deny users="?" verbs="POST" />
    </authorization>
  </system.web>
</configuration>
```

Notes

The type of authorization implemented by the <authorization> element is referred to as *URL authorization*. You can read more about URL authorization in Chapter 9.

You can specify authorization settings for a specific file or directory in your application that differs from the defaults configured in the root *web.config* file for the application in either of two ways:

- By adding an <authorization> element to the *web.config* file of the desired child directory, as shown in the example.

- By using a <location> tag in the root *web.config* file and setting its path attribute to the desired path, as follows:

```
<configuration>
    <location path="files">
        <system.web>
            <authorization>
                <deny users="?" />
            </authorization>
        </system.web>
    </location>
    <system.web>
        <!--other configuration settings -->
    </system.web>
</configuration>
```

<allow>

Specifies users, roles, and/or HTTP verbs to be authorized for the application.

Scope

Any

Attributes

users
> A comma-delimited list of authorized usernames.

roles
> A comma-delimited list of authorized roles (NT groups).

verbs
> A comma-delimited list of authorized HTTP verbs (GET, HEAD, POST, or DEBUG).

Child Elements

None

Example

See the example for the <authorization> element.

Notes

You can use two wildcards to specify special groups of users:

* When used for the value of the user attribute, allows access for all users. This is the default configuration setting, as defined in *machine.config*.

? When used for the value of the user attribute, allows access to anonymous users. This wildcard is more commonly used with the <deny> element.

\<deny>

Specifies users, roles, and/or HTTP verbs to be denied authorization for the application.

Scope

Any

Attributes

users
> A comma-delimited list of authorized usernames.

roles
> A comma-delimited list of authorized roles (NT groups).

verbs
> A comma-delimited list of authorized HTTP verbs (GET, HEAD, POST, or DEBUG).

Child Elements

None

Example

See the example for the \<authorization> element.

Notes

The same wildcards used by the \<allow> element also apply to the deny element. To deny access to anonymous (non-authenticated) users, set the value of the users attribute of the \<deny> element to ?.

\<browserCaps>

```
<browserCaps>
<result type=className />
<use var=serverVarName />
property1=value
property2=value
propertyN=value
<filter match=string>
property1=value
property2=value
propertyN=value
</filter>
<filter match=string>
<filter match=string with=expressionToSearch>
property1=value
property2=value
propertyN=value
</filter>
</filter>
<filter>
```

```
<case match=string>
property1=value
property2=value
propertyN=value
</case>
<case match=string>
property1=value
property2=value
propertyN=value
</case>
</filter>
</browserCaps>
```

Controls the configuration of the browser capabilities component returned by the Response.Browser property. The property/value pairs under the <use> element configure the default values of the browser capabilities component properties; the property/value pairs in the <filter> elements update these properties based on a match between the string value specified for the match attribute of the <case> element and the value of the var attribute of the <use> element (which is typically set to HTTP_USER_AGENT).

Scope

Any

Attributes

None

Child Elements

<result>, <use>, <filter>

Example

The *machine.config* configuration file contains the default settings for the <browserCaps> element. The default settings provide the best example for modifying or updating this element.

Notes

The primary purpose of this configuration element and its children is to allow the addition of new browser types and to update the capabilities of these browsers. Thus, when a page calls the browser capabilities component, it will receive accurate information about the capabilities of the browser used for the current request.

<result>

```
<result type=className />
```

Specifies the class.

Scope

Any

Attribute

type

> The class name, and optionally, version, culture, and key information that specifies the class that will contain the results of the browser capabilities analysis. This class must derive from HttpCapabilitiesBase. The default (set in *machine.config*) is System.Web.HttpBrowserCapabilities.

Child Elements

None

Notes

The default type of System.Web.HttpBrowserCapabilities is fine in most cases. If you want to add additional properties beyond those defined by the HttpBrowserCapabilities class, you can create your own class (derived from HttpCapabilitiesBase or HttpBrowserCapabilities) and use the <result> element to substitute it.

<use>

```
<use var=serverVariableName as=aliasName />
```

Sets the name of the server variable to use when evaluating browser capabilities.

Scope

Any

Attributes

var

> The name of the server variable to use. The default is HTTP_USER_AGENT.

as

> The string containing a name by which the server variable can be referenced in <case> elements and regular expressions.

Child Elements

None

Notes

The <use> element is followed by property/value pairs that specify the default properties for the browser capabilities component if no match is found with a <filter> element's match attribute (or that of its child <case> element). This usage is demonstrated in the entry for the <browserCaps> element.

<filter>

```
<filter match=string>
 property1=value
 property2=value
 propertyN=value
</filter>
```

```
<filter match=string>
 <filter match=string with=expressionToSearch>
 property1=value
 property2=value
 propertyN=value
 </filter>
</filter>
<filter>
 <case match=string>
 property1=value
 property2=value
 propertyN=value
 </case>
 <case match=string>
 property1=value
 property2=value
 propertyN=value
 </case>
</filter>
```

Specifies a regular expression pattern to search for in the server variable given in the <use> element (or optionally, another expression). Multiple <filter> elements can be contained in the <browserCaps> element; likewise, each <filter> element can contain <case> elements or other <filter> elements. All property assignments for matching <filter> elements will be executed, regardless of their order.

Scope

Any

Attributes

match

> The pattern to match. Uses .NET Framework regular expression syntax. This attribute is optional. If omitted, all requests will be assumed to match and any property/value assignments contained within the <filter> element will be executed.

with

> The regular expression or string to find. This attribute is optional. If omitted, the server variable specified in the <use> element will be searched.

Child Elements

<case>

Notes

The fact that <filter> elements can be nested makes them very flexible in terms of locating subsets of information. For example, the default <browserCaps> element in *machine.config* uses nested <filter> elements to locate both the major and minor browser versions contained in the HTTP_USER_AGENT server variable so that it can assign specific properties that vary among minor versions (i.e., the x in 4.x) of a browser.

<case>

```
<case match=string>
 property1=value
 property2=value
 propertyN=value
</case>
```

Specifies one of a group of exclusive matching cases for which property assignments will be executed. Only the first matching <case> element within a given <filter> element will be executed. The rest will be ignored.

Scope

Any

Attributes

match

> The pattern to match. Uses the .NET Framework regular expression syntax. This attribute is optional. If omitted, all requests will be assumed to match, and any property/value assignments contained within the <filter> element will be executed.

with

> The regular expression or string to find. This attribute is optional. If omitted, the server variable specified in the <use> element will be searched.

Child Elements

None

Notes

This element is useful in situations when you only want a single match. For example, the default <browserCaps> configuration in *machine.config* uses the <case> element to assign the platform, win16, and win32 attributes.

<clientTarget>

```
<clientTarget>
 <add alias=aliasName
 userAgent=userAgentString />
 <remove alias=aliasName />
 <clear />
</clientTarget>
```

Assigns aliases for specified browser user agent strings to be used by ASP.NET Server Controls in deciding what type of content to render.

Scope

Any

Attributes

None

Child Elements

<add>

Adds an alias with the name specified by the alias attribute for the User Agent string specified by the userAgent attribute.

<remove>

Removes a previously configured alias with the name specified by the alias attribute.

<clear>

Clears all previously configured aliases.

Example

This example comes from the default <clientTarget> element:

```
<clientTarget>
    <add alias="ie5"
        userAgent="Mozilla/4.0 (compatible; MSIE 5.5; Windows NT 4.0)" />
    <add alias="ie4"
        userAgent="Mozilla/4.0 (compatible; MSIE 4.0; Windows NT 4.0)" />
    <add alias="uplevel"
        userAgent="Mozilla/4.0 (compatible; MSIE 4.0; Windows NT 4.0)" />
    <add alias="downlevel"
        userAgent="Unknown" />
</clientTarget>
```

Notes

This element is used primarily by the built-in ASP.NET Server Controls. Thus, you should avoid making changes to the existing aliases to avoid preventing these controls from rendering uplevel content.

<compilation>

```
<compilation
 batch=boolean
 batchTimeout=numSeconds
 debug=boolean
 defaultLanguage=languageAlias
 explicit=boolean
 maxBatchSize=maxPages
 maxBatchGeneratedFileSize=maxSize
 numRecompilesBeforeAppRestart=numRecompiles
 strict=boolean
 tempDirectory=dirName >
 <compilers>
 <compiler language=languageAlias
 extension=fileExt
 type=typeName
 warningLevel=number
 compilerOptions=optionString />
 </compilers>
 <assemblies>
 <add assembly=assemblyName />
```

```
<remove assembly=assemblyName />
<clear />
</assemblies>
</compilation>
```

Provides attributes and child elements for configuring the compilation options of ASP.NET applications. All attributes are optional.

Scope

Any

Attributes

batch
> Specifies whether ASP.NET should attempt to batch compile all pages in the application when the first request for a page is made. The default is True.

batchTimeout
> Specifies the amount of time, in seconds, that the compiler will spend attempting to batch compile pages in the application. If the timeout is exceeded, pages will be compiled as they are requested for the first time. The default is 15.

debug
> Specifies whether pages will be compiled with debug symbols. The default is False.

defaultLanguage
> Specifies the language compiler that will be used to compile inline code in ASP.NET pages for which no language is specified. The default is VB (Visual Basic .NET).

explicit
> Specifies whether the Visual Basic .NET Option Explicit compiler option is enabled. The default is True.

maxBatchSize
> Specifies the maximum number of classes generated during batch compilation. The default is 1000.

maxBatchGeneratedFileSize
> Specifies the maximum combined size in KB of generated source files created during batch compilation. The default is 3000.

numRecompilesBeforeAppRestart
> Specifies the number of recompiles before the appDomain containing the application is cycled (a new appDomain is created and the old one is torn down). The default is 15.

strict
> Specifies whether the Visual Basic .NET Option Strict compiler option (which disallows implicit narrowing conversions) is enabled. The default is False.

tempDirectory
> Specifies the directory in which temporary files from dynamically compiled code for the application will be stored. The default is *%windir%\Microsoft.NET\ Framework\%version%\Temporary ASP.NET Files*.

Child Elements

<assemblies>, <compilers>

Example

The example enables the Visual Basic .NET Option Strict compiler option and disables batch compilation:

```
<configuration>
  <system.web>
    <compilation
        batch="false"
        strict="true">
    </compilation>
  </system.web>
</configuration>
```

Notes

Make sure you understand the impact of changes to this element before making modifications. For example, setting the debug attribute to True will have a significant negative impact on performance. While setting the strict attribute to True will reduce the likelihood of bugs from implicit data type conversion, it could also increase the number of compiler errors you get while developing your code.

<assemblies>

```
<assemblies>
 <add assembly=assemblyInfo />
 <remove assembly=assemblyInfo />
 <clear />
</assemblies>
```

Adds or removes assemblies to be referenced and linked during dynamic compilation of ASP.NET pages. By default, the mscorlib, System, System.Drawing, System.EnterpriseServices, System.Web, System.Data, System.Web.Services, and System.Xml assemblies are referenced during dynamic compilation, as are any assemblies located in the application directory's *bin* subdirectory.

Scope

Any

Attributes

None

Child Elements

<add>
    Adds an assembly specified by the assembly attribute to the list of assemblies to be linked during dynamic resource compilation.

<remove>
    Removes a previously configured assembly specified by the assembly attribute from the list of assemblies to be linked during dynamic resource compilation.

<clear>

Clears all previously configured assemblies.

Example

This example shows the <add> element used by the Mobile Internet Toolkit to add the assembly System.Web.Mobile to the list of assemblies for dynamic compilation:

```
<assemblies>
    <add assembly="System.Web.Mobile,
        Version=1.0.3300.0,
        Culture=neutral,
        PublicKeyToken=b03f5f7f11d50a3a" />
</assemblies>
```

Notes

The asterisk (*) wildcard is used with the <add> element to indicate that all assemblies in the application's private assembly cache (by default, the *bin* subdirectory of the application) should be added to the list of assemblies linked during dynamic compilation. This ensures that all members of these assemblies will be available to all the pages in your application automatically.

<compilers>

```
<compilers>
 <compiler language=languageAlias
 extension=fileExt
 type=typeName
 warningLevel=number
 compilerOptions=optionString />
</compilers>
```

Contains one or more <compiler> elements, each of which defines configuration options for a particular compiler to be used with ASP.NET.

Scope

Any

Attributes

None

Child Elements

<compiler>

Notes

Thanks to the <compilers> and <compiler> elements, adding support for a new .NET language in ASP.NET is as simple as adding a new <compiler> element specifying the language aliases, the file extension for class files for the language, and the type information for the language compiler.

\<compiler\>

```
<compiler language=languageAlias
 extension=fileExt
 type=typeName
 warningLevel=number
 compilerOptions=optionString />
```

Specifies configuration options for a given language.

Scope

Any

Attributes

language
> Specifies the name or names by which the language will be specified in the language attribute of the @ Page directive. Multiple names should be separated by semicolons. This attribute is required.

extension
> Specifies the extension(s) used by code-behind files for the specified language. Multiple entries should be separated by semicolons. This attribute is required.

type
> Specifies the .NET type information for the class to be used to compile resources for the specified language. This attribute is required.

warningLevel
> Specifies the compiler warning level for the language. This attribute is optional and may not be supported for all compilers.

compilerOptions
> Specifies a string containing valid compiler options to be passed to the compiler.

Child Elements

None

Notes

The \<compilers\> element in *machine.config* provides a good example of the use of this element. Review that configuration section to see how the Visual Basic .NET, C#, and JScript .NET compilers are configured.

\<customErrors\>

```
<customErrors
 defaultRedirect=Url
 mode=mode >
 <error statusCode=httpStatusCode
 redirect=Url />
</customErrors>
```

Specifies one or more pages to which users should be redirected if an unhandled exception is detected in an ASP.NET application. A default error page can be specified, as well as one or more error pages for specific HTTP error codes.

Scope

Any

Attributes

defaultRedirect

Specifies the URL of the page to which all errors should be redirected when no specific error page is configured for the HTTP status code of the error. This attribute is optional.

mode

Specifies the custom errors mode. Valid values are `Off`, `On`, and `RemoteOnly`. `Off` disables custom error handling, `On` enables custom error pages for both local and remote requests. `RemoteOnly` enables custom error pages for remote requests, while sending detailed error messages for local requests. This attribute is required.

Child Elements

<error>

Example

The example configures a default page to be displayed to remote clients when an unhandled exception is encountered:

```
<configuration>
    <system.web>
        <customErrors
            defaultRedirect="Error.aspx" />
    </system.web>
</configuration>
```

Notes

If you set the `mode` attribute to `RemoteOnly`, you will only be able to see detailed error information from the local machine on which the pages are running. Remote requests will return the custom error page (if any) configured for the status code of the error that occurred.

If you want to see the debug information provided by ASP.NET when an error occurs, the `mode` attribute should be set to `Off`.

<error>

```
<error statusCode=httpStatusCode
 redirect=Url />
```

Specifies a custom error page to handle redirections for a specific HTTP status code.

Scope

Any

Attributes

statusCode
> Specifies the HTTP status code (such as 404 for a "Not Found" error) for the specified custom error page. This attribute is optional.

redirect
> Specifies the URL of the page to which requests with a matching HTTP status code should be redirected. This attribute is optional.

Child Elements

None

Example

The example configures a custom error page for 404 errors, and the default error page configured in the previous example:

```
<configuration>
  <system.web>
    <customErrors
        defaultRedirect="Error.aspx">
      <error statusCode="404" redirect="My404ErrorPage.aspx"/>
    </customErrors>
  </system.web>
</configuration>
```

Notes

While custom error pages provide a convenient way to prevent users from seeing raw error messages (and perhaps provide more helpful messages), they are not a substitute for proper exception handling. By the time an error reaches a custom error page, recovering from the error gracefully will be much more difficult, which can degrade the experience of your users.

<globalization>

```
<globalization
 requestEncoding=encodingString
 responseEncoding=encodingString
 fileEncoding=encodingString
 culture=cultureString
 uiCulture=cultureString />
```

Provides attributes for configuring encoding and culture settings. These attributes are used as the basis for the expected encoding of requests, responses, and files for internationalization.

Scope

Any

Attributes

requestEncoding

Specifies the assumed encoding of incoming requests. This can be any valid encoding string and should match the responseEncoding attribute. The default is UTF-8. This attribute is optional.

responseEncoding

Specifies the content encoding of responses. This can be any valid encoding string and should match the requestEncoding attribute. The default is UTF-8. This attribute is optional.

fileEncoding

Specifies the encoding used to parse *.aspx*, *.asmx*, and *.asax* files. This attribute is optional.

culture

Specifies the assumed culture for incoming requests. The value can be any valid culture string. This attribute is optional.

uiCulture

Specifies the culture for locale-specific resource searches. The value can be any valid culture string. This attribute is optional.

Child Elements

None

Example

This example shows how the default <globalization> settings are configured in *web.config*:

```
<configuration>
   <system.web>
      <globalization
          requestEncoding="utf-8"
          responseEncoding="utf-8" />
   </system.web>
</configuration>
```

Notes

A list of valid culture strings can be found in the .NET Framework documentation for the System.Globalization.CultureInfo class.

<httpHandlers>

```
<httpHandlers>
 <add verb=httpVerbs
 path=pathInfo
 type=typeInfo
 validate=boolean />
 <remove verb=httpVerbs
 path=pathInfo />
 <clear />
</httpHandlers>
```

Adds or removes HttpHandlers, which are used to provide request processing for a specified HTTP verb and/or file type or path. ASP.NET itself is set up as an HttpHandler for *.aspx* and *.asmx* files, and HttpHandlers are used to prevent downloading of source code for other ASP.NET file types, such as *global.asax*.

Scope

Any

Attributes

None

Child Elements

<add>

Adds an HttpHandler. The HTTP verbs (GET, POST, etc.) handled by the HttpHandler are specified by the verb attribute; the asterisk (*) wildcard is used to specify all verbs. The path or file extension to be handled by the HttpHandler is specified by the path attribute. The class used to process the request is specified by the type attribute. This class must implement the IHttpHandler interface. Finally, the validate attribute tells ASP.NET whether or not to attempt to load the class specified by the type attribute before a matching request comes in.

<remove>

Removes a previously configured HttpHandler, based on the specified verb and path attributes. The attributes must match a previously configured <add> element.

<clear>

Clears all previously configured HttpHandlers.

Example

The example configures a custom HttpHandler for the file extension *.aspnetian*:

```
<configuration>
  <system.web>
    <httpHandlers>
      <add verb="*"
          path="*.aspnetian"
          type="aspnetian.aspnetianHandler" />
    </httpHandlers>
  </system.web>
</configuration>
```

Notes

To make the example work properly, you need to map the file extension *.aspnetian* to the ASP.NET ISAPI handler, Otherwise, the request would never be handed to the custom HttpHandler. Chapter 9 has a step-by-step walkthrough of the process for mapping additional file types to the ASP.NET ISAPI handler.

\<httpModules\>

```
<httpModules>
<add
name=moduleName
type=typeInfo />
<remove name=moduleName />
<clear />
</httpModules>
```

Adds or removes HttpModules. HttpModules are special classes that participate in the processing of all application requests. Both ASP.NET caching and session state are implemented as HttpModules, as are the authentication and authorization features of ASP.NET.

Scope

Any

Attributes

None

Child Elements

\<add\>

> Adds an HttpModule. The class that implements the HttpModule is specified by the type attribute. This class must implement the IHttpModule interface. The name attribute provides an alias by which the HttpModule can be referenced—for example, in a later \<remove\> element.

\<remove\>

> Removes a previously configured HttpModule, based on the specified name attribute. The attribute must match a previously configured \<add\> element.

\<clear\>

> Clears all previously configured HttpModules.

Example

The example removes the HttpModule for the Session state provider, which can be useful if you're not using it:

```
<configuration>
    <system.web>
        <httpModules>
            <remove name="Session" />
        </httpModules>
    </system.web>
</configuration>
```

Notes

If you're not using a particular HttpModule, such as the Session state module or authentication modules, you may be able to save overhead by removing these HttpModules from an application's *web.config* file by using the \<remove\> element.

<httpRuntime>

```
<httpRuntime
 appRequestQueueLimit=numRequests
 enableVersionHeader=boolean
 executionTimeout=numSeconds
 maxRequestLength=numKBytes
 minFreeLocalRequestFreeThreads=numThreads
 minFreeThreads=numThreads
 useFullyQualifiedRedirectUrl=boolean />
```

Contains attributes used to configure the settings for the ASP.NET HTTP runtime.

Scope

Any

Attributes

appRequestQueueLimit
> Specifies the upper limit for request queuing. Once this limit has been reached, additional requests will receive a response of "503 - Server Too Busy." The default is 100.

enableVersionHeader
> Specifies whether a special X-AspNet-Version header is sent with each request. The default is True. This attribute is only supported in Version 1.1 of ASP.NET.

executionTimeout
> Specifies the amount of time, in seconds, that a request can execute before being terminated by the runtime. The default is 90.

maxRequestLength
> Specifies the maximum file size, in KB, that can be uploaded by a client to an ASP.NET application. This attribute is used primarily to prevent denial of launched service attacks by attempting to upload very large files to the server. The default is 4096.

minLocalRequestFreeThreads
> Specifies the minimum number of threads that will be reserved for requests from the local host that require additional threads. The default is 4.

minFreeThreads
> Specifies the minimum number of threads that will be reserved for requests that require additional threads. The default is 8.

useFullyQualifiedRedirectUrl
> Specifies whether URLs sent to the client for redirects are fully qualified or relative. The default is False, which specifies that the URL is relative.

Child Elements

None

Example

This example forces client-side redirect URLs to be fully qualified, which is required for some of the mobile controls supplied in the Microsoft Mobile Internet Toolkit:

```
<configuration>
   <system.web>
      <httpRuntime
         useFullyQualifiedRedirectUrl="true" />
   </system.web>
</configuration>
```

Notes

One of the most commonly customized attributes is maxRequestLength, since for sites that need to upload files, 4MB can be fairly limiting. Use caution when increasing this value, however; only increase it as much as necessary for the maximum file size you expect. Making this value too large can make your site vulnerable to denial-of-service attacks.

<identity>

```
<identity
 impersonate=boolean
 userName=string
 password=string />
```

Specifies whether request impersonation is enabled, as well as the identity to be used for requests made from the ASP.NET worker process and the password for that identity.

Scope

Any

Attributes

impersonate

Specifies whether impersonation is enabled for the application. If True, requests made by the ASP.NET worker process will be made with the security context of the account specified by the userName attribute; if that attribute is blank, the context of the account of the logged-in user. The default is False.

userName

Specifies the username of the Windows account to use for impersonation. If the value is left blank or is omitted, requests will be made in the context of the logged-in user.

password

Specifies the password for the account named in the userName attribute. This password is stored in clear text.

Child Elements

None

Example

The example turns on impersonation for the logged-in user authenticated by IIS:

```
<configuration>
  <system.web>
    <identity
        impersonate="true"
        userName="" />
  </system.web>
</configuration>
```

Notes

Because the password attribute stores passwords in readable text, you should carefully consider whether it makes sense to use this functionality. Storing sensitive information, such as passwords, in text files presents a potential security risk.

Recently, Microsoft has made a fix available for ASP.NET that will allow encrypted credentials for this element to be stored in the system registry for a higher level of security. You can find out more about this fix, as well as a utility for encrypting credentials, at the following URLs:

http://support.microsoft.com/default.aspx?scid=kb;EN-US;329250
http://support.microsoft.com/default.aspx?scid=kb;en-us;329290

<machineKey>

```
<machineKey
  validationKey="autogenerate|value"
  decryptionKey="autogenerate|value"
  validation="SHA1|MD5|3DES" />
```

Specifies the settings for cryptographic keys used for validation and decryption of Forms Authentication cookies.

Scope

All

Attributes

validationKey
> The key used for validation of forms authentication cookie data, MAC checking of ViewState, and session state cookies. The default is autogenerate, which generates and stores a random key. For web farm implementations, you can set this value to the same 40- to 128-character key value on each server to ensure that all servers can validate successfully.

decryptionKey
> The key used for decryption of forms authentication cookie data. The default is autogenerate, which generates and stores a random key. For web farm implementations, you can set this value to the same 40- to 128-character key value on each server to ensure that all servers can validate successfully.

validation
> Specifies the type of encryption used for data validation.

Child Elements

None

Notes

For web farms, ensuring that the validationKey and decryptionKey values are synchronized across all servers in the farm is important. If they are not synchronized, you may get errors in Forms Authentication, ViewState errors, or problems with session state.

<pages>

```
<pages
 buffer=boolean
 enableSessionState="true|false|ReadOnly"
 enableViewState=boolean
 enableViewStateMac=boolean
 autoEventWireup=boolean
 smartNavigation=boolean
 pageBaseType=typeInfo
 userControlBaseType=typeInfo
 validateRequest=boolean />
```

Contains attributes used to configure the default settings for ASP.NET pages and user controls. These settings can be overridden by attributes on the @ Page or @ Control directive.

Scope

Any

Attributes

buffer
> Specifies whether buffering of page output is on or off. The default is True.

enableSessionState
> Specifies whether a page has access to the Session state module. Acceptable values include True, False, and ReadOnly. The default is True.

enableViewState
> Specifies whether ViewState is enabled at the page level. The default is True.

enableViewStateMac
> Specifies at the page level whether a machine authentication check (MAC) is performed on the ViewState hidden field. This specification can help identify client-side tampering with the ViewState. The default is True.

autoEventWireup
> Specifies whether ASP.NET will automatically support specific page events, such as Page_Load. The default is True.

smartNavigation
> Specifies whether the Smart Navigation feature, for which IE 5 or above provides support for posting back and refreshing only portions of a page, is turned on at the page level. The default is False.

---

pageBaseType

Specifies the base class from which all pages are derived. The default is System.Web.UI.Page.

userControlBaseType

Specifies the base class from which all user controls are derived. The default is System.Web.UI.UserControl.

validateRequest

Specifies whether ASP.NET will automatically check the Request object for potentially dangerous input. If dangerous input, such as HTML or script, is found, an exception of type HttpRequestValidationException is thrown. The default is True. This attribute is only supported in Version 1.1 of ASP.NET.

Child Elements

None

Example

The example disables both Session state and ViewState at the page level:

```
<configuration>
    <system.web>
        <pages
            enableSessionState="false"
            enableViewState="false" />
    </system.web>
</configuration>
```

Notes

The <pages> element is very useful for setting application-level (or folder-level) defaults for pages in your application. One possible use is to place pages that do not require access to session state in a separate folder and use the <pages> element to disable session state for that folder. In this case, a session will not be created for a user until the user requests a page in your application for which EnableSessionState is True.

The default setting of EnableViewStateMac is True. It's important to remember this because the MAC check uses the settings in the <machineKey> element to create an encrypted version of the ViewState hidden field. In a web farm scenario, the <machineKey> settings for each server in the farm must match. Otherwise, the MAC check will fail when a user's initial request is handled by one server, while a subsequent postback is handled by another server with different settings for <machineKey>.

<processModel>

```
<processModel
 enable=boolean
 timeout="Infinite"|HH:MM:SS
 idleTimeout="Infinite"|HH:MM:SS
 shutdownTimeout="Infinite"|HH:MM:SS
 requestLimit=numRequests
```

```
requestQueueLimit="Infinite"|numRequests
restartQueueLimit="Infinite"|numRequests
memoryLimit=percentMemory

cpuMask=cpuNumBitMask
webGarden=boolean
userName=username
password=password

logLevel="All|None|Errors"
clientConnectedCheck=HH:MM:SS
comAuthenticationLevel="Default|None|Connect|Call|Pkt|
PktIntegrity|PktPrivacy"
comImpersonationLevel="Default|Anonymous|Identify|Impersonate|
Delegate"
responseRestartDeadlockInterval="Infinite"|HH:MM:SS
responseDeadlockInterval="Infinite"|HH:MM:SS
maxWorkerThreads=numThreads
maxIoThreads=numThreads
serverErrorMessageFile=fileName />
```

Contains attributes used to configure the ASP.NET worker process in IIS 5.

Scope

Machine only

Attributes

enable

> Specifies whether the <processModel> settings are enabled. The default is True.

timeout

> Specifies the life span, in the format hh:mm:ss, of the process. When this value expires, a new process is started and the current process is shut down. To disable the timeout, use the value Infinite. The default is Infinite.

idleTimeout

> Specifies the life span of the process, when idle, in the format hh:mm:ss. When this value expires, the current process is shut down. To disable the timeout, use the value Infinite. The default is Infinite.

shutdownTimeout

> Specifies the amount of time, in the format hh:mm:ss, that the process is given to shut down gracefully. When this value expires, the process will be killed. To disable the timeout, use the value Infinite. The default is 0:00:05.

requestLimit

> Specifies the number of requests that can be served by the ASP.NET process before it is shut down and restarted. This attribute can be used to proactively restart the ASP.NET process to compensate for memory leaks or other problems that may be associated with legacy resources (such as COM components) that you need to use in your applications. The default is Infinite, which disables this feature.

requestQueueLimit

> Specifies the number of requests that can be queued by ASP.NET before it is shut down and restarted. This attribute can be used proactively to remedy

situations in which resource contention causes requests to be queued. The default is 5000.

restartQueueLimit

Specifies the number of requests that will remain in the request queue while a process restart based on the requestQueueLimit setting occurs. The default is 10.

memoryLimit

Specifies the upper limit, as a percentage, of the server's physical memory that the ASP.NET process will be allowed to use. If this value is exceeded, a new process will be started up and the current process will be shut down. The default is 60.

cpuMask

Used in web garden scenarios to specify the CPU or CPUs in a multiprocessor server that will run the ASP.NET process. This value is a bitmask. The default is 0xffffffff, which specifies that a worker process should be created for every CPU.

webGarden

Specifies whether web gardening, in which worker processes are tied to specific processors within a multiprocessor server, is enabled. The default is False.

userName

Specifies the identity under which the ASP.NET worker process will be run. This can be a valid NT account or one of two special values:

SYSTEM

Runs the ASP.NET process as the SYSTEM account, which is a highly privileged administrative account.

machine

Runs the ASP.NET process as the ASPNET account (installed with the .NET Framework), which is a special account with few privileges. This process is the default and provides superior out-of-the box security for web applications written with ASP.NET. Note that the documentation for the <processModel> element incorrectly states that SYSTEM is the default.

password

Specifies the password of the account specified by the userName attribute. Use the value AutoGenerate (the default) when using the SYSTEM or machine accounts.

logLevel

Specifies the type of process events that are logged to the NT event log. Valid values are as follows:

All

All process events will be logged.

Errors

Only errors will be logged; this is the default.

None

No process events will be logged.

clientConnectedCheck
> Specifies the amount of time, in the format hh:mm:ss, that a request remains in the queue before the ASP.NET process checks to ensure that the client is still connected. The default is 0:00:05.

comAuthenticationLevel
> Specifies the authentication level used for DCOM security. The default is Connect.

comImpersonationLevel
> Specifies the authentication level used for COM security. The default is Impersonate.

responseRestartDeadlockInterval
> Specifies the amount of time, in the format hh:mm:ss, that will be allowed to elapse between process restarts due to the responseDeadlockInterval attribute value. This specification prevents constant process cycling due to deadlocks. To disable this feature, use the value Infinite. The default is 0:09:00.

responseDeadlockInterval
> Specifies the amount of time, in the format hh:mm:ss, that may elapse without a response when requests are queued. When this value expires, the process will be shut down and restarted. To disable this feature, use the value Infinite. The default is 0:03:00.

maxWorkerThreads
> Specifies the upper limit for worker threads per CPU in the thread pool. The default is 25.

maxIoThreads
> Specifies the upper limit for IO threads per CPU in the thread pool. The default is 25.

serverErrorMessageFile
> Specifies the filename of a file to be displayed when a "Server Unavailable" error occurs.

Child Elements

None

Notes

In IIS 6 native mode, the settings in the <processModel> element will be ignored.

Because the settings in the <processModel> element are read by and applied to the unmanaged *aspnet_isapi.dll* handler that passes requests to the managed *aspnet_wp.exe* worker process (rather than by managed code), changes to the <processModel> element will not be applied until IIS is restarted.

Recently, Microsoft has made a fix available for ASP.NET that will allow encrypted credentials for the userName and password attributes of this element to be stored in the system registry for a higher level of security. You can find out more about this fix, as well as a utility for encrypting credentials at the following URLs:

> *http://support.microsoft.com/default.aspx?scid=kb;EN-US;329250*
> *http://support.microsoft.com/default.aspx?scid=kb;en-us;329290*

\<securityPolicy\>

```
<securityPolicy>
 <trustLevel
 name=trustLevelName
 policyFile=fileName />
</securityPolicy>
```

Configures mappings of trust names (used by the \<trust\> element) to security policy files. The security policy files contain elements that configure the code access security permissions that are specific to that trust level. \<securityPolicy\> can contain one or more \<trustLevel\> elements.

Scope

Machine, Application

Attributes

None

Child Element

\<trustLevel\>

Each \<trustLevel\> element maps a trust-level name to a specific policy file that implements the code access security permissions for that trust level. The name attribute specifies the name by which the trust level will be referred in the \<trust\> element, while the policyFile attribute specifies the name of the policy file to map to the name.

Example

This example comes from the default \<securityPolicy\> element in *machine.config*:

```
<securityPolicy>
    <trustLevel
        name="Full"
        policyFile="internal" />
    <trustLevel
        name="High"
        policyFile="web_hightrust.config" />
    <trustLevel
        name="Low"
        policyFile="web_lowtrust.config" />
    <trustLevel
        name="None"
        policyFile="web_notrust.config" />
</securityPolicy>
```

Notes

For a specific application, if you want to modify the code access security permissions applied, you could create a new CAS policy file and map that file to a custom trust level by using the \<trustLevel\> element. To implement the new security policy, you would add a \<trust\> element to the *web.config* file of the desired application and use it to specify the mapped policy file by name.

<sessionState>

```
<sessionState
mode="Off|Inproc|StateServer|SQLServer"
cookieless=boolean
timeout=numMinutes
stateNetworkTimeout=numSeconds
stateConnectionString="tcpip=server:port"
sqlConnectionString=connString />
```

Scope

Machine, Application

Attributes

mode

Specifies whether session state is enabled, and if so, how the state data will be stored. Valid values are as follows:

Off

The session state is disabled.

InProc

The session state data will be stored in memory on the local server. This is the same model as session state in classic ASP. This session state mode does not allow session state to be shared across servers in a web farm.

StateServer

The session state data will be stored in memory in a special NT state service on a designated state server. This session state mode allows session state to be shared across servers in a web farm.

SQLServer

The session state data will be stored in a special SQL Server database on a designated SQL Server. This session state mode allows session state to be shared across servers in a web farm. This mode also requires running a SQL query (which is included with the .NET Framework SDK) to set up the SQL Server database.

The default is InProc.

cookieless

Specifies whether or not cookies will be used to associate users with specific sessions. If set to True, the session identifier will be automatically munged into the URL for each request. This requires that your application use relative URLs to work correctly. The default is False.

timeout

Specifies the amount of time, in minutes, before the session will time out when inactive (no requests are received with that SessionID). The default is 20.

stateNetworkTimeout

Specifies the amount of time, in seconds, that network operations will time out when working with the StateServer session state mode. The default is 10.

stateConnectionString

Specifies the server name or IP address and TCP port number for the session state server when using StateServer mode. This attribute is required when the mode attribute is StateServer. The default is tcpip=127.0.0.1:42424.

sqlConnectionString

Specifies the SQL Server name and authentication credentials when using SQLServer session mode. This attribute is required when the mode attribute is SQLServer. The default is data source=127.0.0.1;user id=sa;password=. Where possible, this value should use trusted connections to avoid storing a SQL userID and password in the *web.config* or *machine.config* file. To support SQL Server state mode, you need to run the *InstallSqlState.sql* batch file on the target SQL server to create the ASPState database and its associated tables and stored procedures. This file is installed by default in the *%windir%\Microsoft.NET\Framework\%version%* folder.

Child Elements

None

Example

The example configures session state to run in SQL Server mode without cookies:

```
<configuration>
   <system.web>
      <sessionState
         mode="SQLServer"
         cookieless="true"
         sqlConnectionString="data source=myServer;trusted_ connection=true"
/>
   </system.web>
</configuration>
```

Notes

To use SQL Server mode with a trusted connection, the account identity of the ASP.NET worker process must have a login to the SQL Server database and must have permission to access the ASPState and TempDB databases. If you cannot use a trusted connection, you should create a special account specifically to access the state database, and use that account for the sqlConnectionString attribute.

Note that when using either of the out-of-process session state modes, it's wise to use the EnableSessionState attribute of the @ Page directive to disable session state for pages in your application that do not use it. Otherwise, these pages will make unnecessary cross-machine calls to retrieve unused session state information. If you have a page that reads session data but does not alter it, you can also set the EnableSessionState attribute to ReadOnly to avoid the cross-machine call to store updated session data.

\<trace>

```
<trace
  enabled=boolean
  localOnly=boolean
  pageOutput=boolean
  requestLimit=numRequests
  traceMode="SortByTime|SortByCategory" />
```

Scope

Any

Attributes

enabled
> Specifies whether tracing is enabled. The default is False.

localOnly
> Specifies whether or not trace output can be viewed by machines other than the local host. The default is True.

pageOutput
> Specifies whether trace output is rendered to the page or stored in memory and made accessible by the special *Trace.axd* URL. *Trace.axd* maps to an HttpHandler that displays all currently stored traces for a given application. The default is False.

requestLimit
> Specifies the number of requests that can be stored in the trace buffer read by *Trace.axd*. Once the total number of request traces specified by this attribute has been stored, no more traces will be stored until the trace log has been cleared. The page displayed by *Trace.axd* includes a link for clearing the trace log. The default is 10.

traceMode
> Specifies the sort order of items in the Trace Information section of the trace. Valid values are SortByTime and SortByCategory. SortByCategory is useful when you are using Trace.Write and Trace.Warn with your own category names passed as parameters. The default is SortByTime.

Child Elements

None

Example

This example turns tracing on at the application level:

```
<configuration>
  <system.web>
    <trace enabled="true" />
  </system.web>
</configuration>
```

Notes

Chapter 10 provides an overview of how to use the trace functionality of ASP.NET.

<trust>

```
<trust
level="Full|High|Medium|Low|Minimal"
originUrl=URL />
```

Assigns a named trust level created with the <trustLevel> child element of the <securityPolicy> element to a machine, a site, or an application.

Scope

Machine, Application

Attributes

level
> Specifies the trust level to be applied. This attribute can be any value defined by the <securityPolicy> element. The default is Full. This attribute is required.

originUrl
> Specifies URL of origin of an application. This attribute allows classes such as WebRequest, which may need the origin host information for certain security permissions, to work properly. This attribute is optional.

Child Elements

None

Example

This example sets the application CAS permissions, based on a custom trust level:

```
<configuration>
   <system.web>
      <trust level="myTrustLevel" />
   </system.web>
</configuration>
```

Notes

Make sure that you understand the security implications of using custom security policy mappings before using this element. Incorrect permissions can cause major problems for your application.

The syntax shown at the beginning of this section is for Version 1.1 of the .NET Framework.

<location>

```
<location
 path=pathToConfigure
 allowOverride=boolean >
<system.web>
<!-- Configuration settings -->
</system.web>
</location>
```

Allows you to prevent settings in *machine.config* or *web.config* from being overridden in child configuration files. You can also use it to configure settings for specific files or folders from a configuration file in a parent folder.

Scope

Any

Attributes

path

Specifies the path to the file or folder to which the configuration settings contained in the <location> tag pair should be applied.

allowOverride

Specifies whether child configuration files can override values configured within the <location> tag pair. This attribute locks down configuration settings (i.e., at the *machine.config* level) for which you want to enforce uniformity.

Child Element

<system.web>

Example

The example, if used in *machine.config*, would force all applications on the machine to use Windows authentication:

```
<configuration>
    <location
        allowOverride="false">
        <system.web>
            <authentication mode="Windows">
        </system.web>
    </location>
    <system.web>
        <!-- Other configuration settings -->
    </system.web>
</configuration>
```

Notes

This tag provides powerful control over configuration. In addition to the scenario of enforcing an authentication method across all applications, you can also use the path attribute to configure multiple child folders or files from the *web.config* file in the root of the application. Using this configuration can avoid having a large number of child *web.config* files to manage for a larger application.

Namespace Reference

The quick-reference section that follows packs a lot of information into a small space. The introductory section explains how to get the most out of that information: it describes how the quick reference is organized and how to read the individual quick reference entries.

21

Namespace Reference

The quick reference is organized into chapters—one per namespace. Each chapter begins with an overview of the namespace and includes a hierarchy diagram for the types (classes, interfaces, enumerations, delegates, and structs) in the namespace. Quick-reference entries for all the types in the namespace follow the overview.

Figure 21-1 is a sample diagram showing the notation used in this book. This notation is similar to that used in O'Reilly's *Java in a Nutshell*, but it borrows some features from UML.

Classes marked as abstract are shown as a slanted rectangle; classes marked as sealed are shown as an octagonal rectangle. Inheritance is shown as a solid line from the subtype, ending with a hollow triangle that points to the base class. Two notations indicate interface implementation. The lollipop notation is used most of the time, since it is easier to read. In some cases, especially when many types implement a given interface, the shaded box notation with the dashed line is used.

Important relationships between types (associations) are shown with a dashed line ending with an arrow. The figures don't show every possible association. Some types have strong containing relationships with one another. For example, a System.Net.WebException object instance includes a System.Net.WebResponse object instance that represents the HTTP response containing the error details (HTTP status code and error message). To show this relationship, a filled diamond is attached to the containing type with a solid line that points to the contained type.

Entries are organized alphabetically by type and namespace so that related types are grouped near one another. Thus, in order to look up a quick-reference entry for a particular type, you must also know the name of the namespace that contains that type. Usually, the namespace is obvious from the context, and you should have no trouble looking up the quick-reference entry you want. Use the

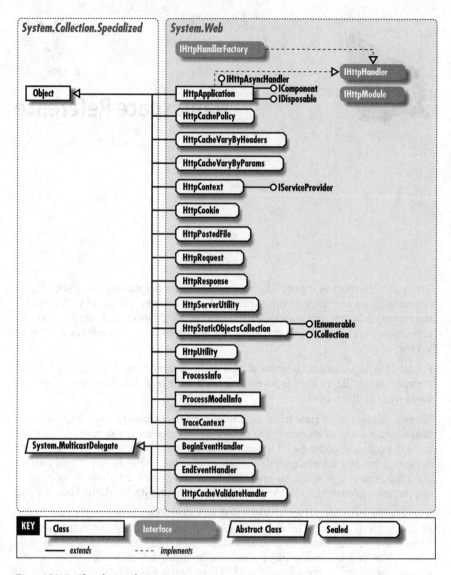

Figure 21-1. Class hierarchy notation

tabs on the outside edge of the book and the dictionary-style headers on the upper corner of each page to help you find the namespace and type you are looking for.

Occasionally, you may need to look up a type for which you do not already know the namespace. In this case, refer to the *Type, Method, Property, and Field Index*, which allows you to look up a type by its name and identify what namespace it is part of, at the end of this book.

Reading a Quick-Reference Entry

Each quick-reference entry contains quite a bit of information. The sections that follow describe the structure of a quick-reference entry, explaining what information is available, where it is found, and what it means. While reading the descriptions that follow, you will find it helpful to flip through the reference section itself to find examples of the described features.

Type Name, Namespace, Assembly, Type Category, and Flags

Each quick-reference entry begins with a four-part title that specifies the name, namespace (followed by the assembly in parentheses), and type category of the type, and may also specify various additional flags that describe the type. The type name appears in bold at the upper-left side of the title. The namespace and assembly appear in smaller print in the lower-left side, below the type name.

The upper-right portion of the title indicates the type category of the type (class, delegate, enum, interface, or struct). The "class" category may include modifiers such as sealed or abstract.

In the lower-right corner of the title, you may find a list of flags that describe the type. The possible flags and their meanings are as follows:

ECMA
> Specifies that the type is part of the ECMA CLI specification.

serializable
> Specifies that the type, or a base class, implements System.Runtime.Serialization.ISerializable or has been flagged with the System.Serializable attribute.

marshal by reference
> This class, or a superclass, derives from System.MarshalByRefObject.

context bound
> This class, or a superclass, derives from System.ContextBoundObject.

disposable
> Specifies that the type implements the System.IDisposable interface.

flag
> Specifies that the enumeration be marked with the System.FlagsAttribute attribute.

Description

The title of each quick-reference entry is followed by a short description of the most important features of the type. This description may be anywhere from a couple of sentences to several paragraphs long.

Synopsis

The most important part of every quick-reference entry is the synopsis, which follows the title and description. The synopsis for a type looks much like its source code, except that the member bodies are omitted and some additional annotations are added. If you know C# syntax, you know how to read the type synopsis.

The first line of the synopsis contains information about the type itself. It begins with a list of type modifiers, such as abstract and sealed. These modifiers are followed by the class, delegate, enum, interface, or struct keyword and then by the name of the type. The type name may be followed by a colon (:) and a base class or interfaces that the type implements.

The type definition line is followed by a list of the members that the type defines. This list includes only members that are explicitly declared in the type, are over-ridden from a base class, or are implementations of an interface member. Members that are simply inherited from a base class are not shown; you will need to look up the base class definition to find those members.

Once again, if you understand basic C# syntax, you should have no trouble making sense of these lines. The listing for each member includes the modifiers, type, and name of the member. For methods, the synopsis also includes the type and name of each method parameter. The member names are in boldface, so it is easy to scan the list of members looking for the one you want. The names of method parameters are in italics to indicate that they should not be used literally. The member listings are printed on alternating gray and white backgrounds to keep them visually separate.

Member availability and flags

Each member listing is a single line that defines the syntax for that member. These listings use C# syntax, so their meaning is immediately clear to any C# programmer. Some auxiliary information associated with each member synopsis, however, requires explanation.

The area to the right of the member synopsis displays a variety of flags that provide additional information about the member. Some flags indicate additional specification details that do not appear in the member syntax itself.

The following flags may be displayed to the right of a member synopsis:

overrides
> Indicates that a method overrides a method in one of its base classes. The flag is followed by the name of the base class that the method overrides.

implements
> Indicates that a method implements a method in an interface. The flag is followed by the name of the implemented interface.

=
> For enumeration fields and constant fields, this flag is followed by the constant value of the field. Only constants of primitive and String types and constants with the value null are displayed. Some constant values are specification details, while others are implementation details. Some constants, such as System.BitConverter.IsLittleEndian, are platform dependent. Platform-dependent values shown in this book conform to the System.PlatformID. Win32NT platform (32-bit Windows NT, 2000, or XP). The reason why symbolic constants are defined, however, is so you can write code that does

---

not rely directly upon the constant value. Use this flag to help you understand the type, but do not rely upon the constant values in your own programs.

Functional grouping of members

Within a type synopsis, the members are not listed in strict alphabetical order. Instead, they are broken down into functional groups and listed alphabetically within each group. Constructors, events, fields, methods, and properties are all listed separately. Instance methods are kept separate from shared (class) methods. Public members are listed separately from protected members. Grouping members by category breaks a type down into smaller, more comprehensible segments, making the type easier to understand. This grouping also makes it easier for you to find a desired member.

Functional groups are separated from one another in a type synopsis with comments, such as:

```
Public Constructors
```

or:

```
// Protected Instance Properties
```

or:

```
// Events
```

The various functional categories follow below (in the order in which they appear in a type synopsis):

Constructors
Displays the constructors for the type. Public and protected constructors are displayed separately in subgroupings. If a type defines no constructor at all, the compiler adds a default parameterless constructor that is displayed here. If a type defines only private constructors, it cannot be instantiated, so no constructor appears. Constructors are listed first because the first thing you do with most types is instantiate them by calling a constructor.

Fields
Displays all fields defined by the type, including constants. Public and protected fields are displayed in separate subgroups. Fields are listed here, near the top of the synopsis, because constant values are often used throughout the type as legal values for method parameters and return values.

Properties
Lists all the properties of the type, breaking them down into subgroups for public and protected shared properties and public and protected instance properties. After the property name, its accessors (get or set) are shown.

Static methods
Lists the static methods (class methods) of the type, broken down into subgroups for public shared methods and protected shared methods.

Public instance methods
Contains all public instance methods.

Protected instance methods
Contains all protected instance methods.

Class Hierarchy

For any type that has a nontrivial inheritance hierarchy, the synopsis is followed by a "Hierarchy" section. This section lists all of the base classes of the type, as well as any interfaces implemented by those base classes. It also lists any interfaces implemented by an interface. In the hierarchy listing, arrows indicate base class to derived class relationships, while the interfaces implemented by a type follow the type name in parentheses. For example, the following hierarchy indicates that System.IO.Stream implements IDisposable and extends MarshalByRefObject, which itself extends Object:

```
System.Object → System.MarshalByRefObject → System.IO.Stream(System.
IDisposable)
```

If a type has subtypes, the "Hierarchy" section is followed by a "Subtypes" section that lists those subtypes. If an interface has implementations, the "Hierarchy" section is followed by an "Implementations" section that lists those implementations. While the "Hierarchy" section shows ancestors of the type, the "Subtypes" or "Implementations" section shows descendants.

Cross References

The hierarchy section of a quick-reference entry is followed by optional cross-reference sections that indicate other related types and methods that may be of interest. These sections include:

Passed to
> This section lists all members (from other types) that are passed an object of this type as an argument, including properties whose values can be set to this type. It is useful when you have an object of a given type and want to know where it can be used.

Returned by
> This section lists all members that return an object of this type, including properties whose values can take on this type. It is useful when you know that you want to work with an object of this type, but don't know how to obtain one.

Valid on
> For attributes, this section lists the attribute targets that the attribute can be applied to.

Associated events
> For delegates, this section lists the events it can handle.

A Note About Type Names

Throughout the quick reference, you'll notice that types are sometimes referred to by type name alone, and at other times are referred to by type name and namespace. If namespaces were always used, the type synopses would become long and hard to read. On the other hand, if namespaces were never used, it would sometimes be difficult to know what type was being referred to. The rules for including or omitting the namespace name are complex. However, they can be summarized as follows:

- If the type name alone is ambiguous, the namespace name is always used.
- If the type is part of the System namespace or is a commonly used type like System.Collection.ICollection, the namespace is omitted.
- If the type being referred to is part of the current namespace (and has a quick-reference entry in the current chapter), the namespace is omitted. The namespace is also omitted if the type being referred to is part of a namespace that contains the current namespace.

22

Converting from C# to VB Syntax

Although information on all types and their members is shown using C# syntax, it is easy to mentally convert to Visual Basic syntax. This chapter will provide the information you need to convert the documentation for each type into the syntax used by Visual Basic.

> This chapter does not aim at providing complete coverage of the syntax for each language element it discusses. Instead, it focuses on direct translation of the syntax of the types used in ASP.NET programming from C# to VB.

General Considerations

The most evident difference between C# and VB syntax is that C# uses the semicolon (;) as a statement terminator, whereas VB uses a line break. Hence, while a statement in C# can occupy multiple lines as long as it is terminated with a semicolon, a VB statement must occupy a single line. Multiline statements in VB must appear with the VB line continuation character (a space followed by an underscore) on all but the last line.

A second, and not quite so evident, difference is that C# is case-sensitive, whereas VB is not. (Uniform casing for VB code is enforced by the Visual Studio environment, but it is by no means required.)

Finally, all types and their members have access modifiers that determine the type or member's accessibility. The keywords for these access modifiers are nearly identical in VB and C#, as Table 22-1 shows.

Table 22-1. Access modifiers in C# and VB

C# keyword	VB keyword
public	Public
private	Private
protected	Protected
internal	Friend
protected internal	Protected Friend

Classes

C# uses the class statement along with opening and closing braces to indicate the beginning and end of a class definition. For example:

```
public class Form : ContainerControl {
    // member definitions
}
```

In VB, a class definition is indicated by the Class... End Class construct:

```
Public Class Form
    ' member definitions
End Class
```

In addition, C# classes can be marked as abstract or sealed; these correspond to the VB MustInherit and NonInheritable keywords, as shown in Table 22-2.

Table 22-2. C# and equivalent VB class modifiers

C# keyword	VB keyword
abstract	MustInherit
sealed	NonInheritable

C# uses the colon to indicate either inheritance or interface implementation. Both the base class and the implemented interfaces are part of the class statement. For example:

```
public class Control : Component, ISynchronizeInvoke, IWin32Window
```

In VB, a base class and any implemented interfaces are specified on separate lines immediately following the Class statement. A class's base class is indicated by preceding its name with the Inherits keyword; any implemented interfaces are indicated by the Implements keyword. Hence, the previous definition of the Control class in C# would appear as follows in VB:

```
Public Class Control
    Inherits Component
    Implements ISynchronizeInvoke, IWin32Window
```

Structures

C# uses the struct statement along with opening and closing braces to indicate the beginning and end of a structure definition. For example:

```
public struct DataGridCell {
    // member definitions
}
```

In VB, a structure definition is indicated by the Structure... End Structure construct:

```
Public Structure DataGridCell
    ' member definitions
End Structure
```

C# uses the colon with structures to indicate interface implementation. Any implemented interfaces are part of the class statement. In VB, any implemented interfaces are specified by an Implements statement on the line immediately following the Structure statement. However, none of the structures documented in the reference section of this book use interface inheritance.

Interfaces

C# uses the interface statement along with opening and closing braces to indicate the beginning and end of an interface definition. For example:

```
public interface IUIService {
    // member definitions
}
```

In VB, an interface definition is indicated by the Interface... End Structure construct:

```
Public Interface IUIService
    ' member definitions
End Interface
```

C# uses the colon with interfaces to specify any implemented interfaces. For example:

```
public interface ISite : IServiceProvider
```

In VB, any implemented interfaces are specified by an Implements statement on the line immediately following the Interface statement. Hence, the previous definition of ISite in C# would appear as follows in VB:

```
Public Interface ISite
    Implements IServiceProvider
```

Class, Structure, and Interface Members

Classes, structures, and interfaces can contain one or more fields, methods, properties, and events. This section will discuss converting the C# syntax for each of these constructs to VB.

Note that .NET supports both static (or shared) members (which apply to the type as a whole, and typically do not require that an object of that type be instantiated) and instance members (which apply only to an instance of that type). Shared or static members are indicated by using the static keyword in C#. For example:

```
public static bool IsMnemonic(char charCode, string text);
```

The corresponding VB keyword is Shared. Hence, the FromResource method, when converted to VB, has the following syntax:

```
Public Shared Function IsMnemonic(charCode As Char, text As String) _
    As Boolean
```

Fields

A field is simply a constant or a variable that is exposed as a publicly accessible member of a type. In C#, for example, the Nowhere field of the DataGrid. HitTestInfo class has the syntax:

```
public static readonly DataGrid.HitTestInfo Nowhere;
```

Note that C# indicates the data type of a field before the name of the field. (For C# data types and their VB equivalents, see Table 22-3.) Also note that fields are most often read-only. Constant fields, in fact, are always read-only. As a result, the use of the C# readonly keyword and the VB ReadOnly keyword with fields is quite common.

The syntax for the Nowhere field in Visual Basic then becomes:

```
Public Shared ReadOnly Nowhere As DataGrid.HitTestInfo
```

Methods

In C#, all methods have a return value, which appears before the name of the function; in contrast, VB differentiates between function and subprocedures. C# functions without an explicit return value return void. For example, one of the overloads of the Bitmap class's MakeTransparent method has the following syntax in C#:

```
public void MakeTransparent();
```

C# methods that return void are expressed as subprocedures in VB. So the corresponding syntax of the MakeTransparent method is:

```
Public Sub MakeTransparent()
```

All C# methods other than those returning void are functions in VB. The function's return value follows appears in an As clause at the end of the function declaration. C# data types and their VB equivalents are shown in Table 22-3. Methods that return arrays are indicated by adding braces ([]) to the return data type in C# and parentheses (())to the return data type in VB.

For example, the Focus method of the Control class has the C# syntax:

```
public bool Focus();
```

The VB equivalent is:

```
Public Function Focus() As Boolean
```

Table 22-3. C# data types and their VB equivalents

C# data type	VB data type
bool	Boolean
byte	Byte
char	Char
decimal	Decimal
double	Double
float	Single
int	Integer
long	Long
object	Object
sbyte	System.SByte
short	Short
string	String
System.Currency	Currency
System.DateTime	Date
uint	System.UInt32
ulong	System.UInt64
ushort	System.UInt16
<class_name>	*<class_name>*
<delegate_name>	*<delegate_name>*
<interface_name>	*<interface_name>*
<structure_name>	*<structure_name>*

Method parameters in C# take the general form:

<data_type> <parameter_name>

In VB, method parameters take the form:

<parameter_name> As <data_type>

where *<data_type>* is any of the data types listed in Table 22-3. If a parameter is an array, its data type is followed by braces in C# (e.g., string[ ] Name), while the parameter name is followed by parentheses in VB (e.g., Name( ) As String).

For example, one of the versions of the Color class's FromArgb method has the following syntax in C#:

```
public static Color FromArgb(int red, int green, int blue);
```

Its VB equivalent is:

```
Public Shared Function FromArgb(red As Integer, _
                        green As Integer, _
                        blue As Integer) As Color
```

VB allows methods to be called using either named or positional parameters. If named parameters are used, the parameter name must correspond to that shown in the documentation. For instance, Color.FromArgb can be called as follows using named parameters:

```
NewColor = Color.FromArgb(blue:=125, _
                          red:=125,
                          green:=125)
```

C# also uses a number of object-oriented qualifiers with methods. These, and their VB equivalents, are shown in Table 22-4.

Table 22-4. C# keywords used with methods and their VB equivalents

C# keyword	VB keyword
abstract	MustOverride
override	Overrides
sealed	NotOverridable
virtual	Overridable

In both C# and VB, constructors have a special syntax. In C#, constructors have the same name as the classes whose objects they instantiate and do not indicate a return value. For example, the constructor for the Button class is:

```
public Button();
```

In VB, the constructor is represented by a call to a class's New subprocedure. The equivalent call to the Button class constructor in VB is:

```
Public Sub New()
```

Properties

The FileDialog.Title property provides a more or less typical example of a property definition using C# syntax:

```
public string Title {get; set;}
```

Like all C# type definitions, the property's data type precedes the property name. The **get**; and **set**; property accessors indicate that this is a read-write property. Read-only properties are indicated with a get; only, while write-only properties are indicated with a set; only.

The equivalent VB property definition is:

```
Public Property Title As String
```

Note that read-write properties are not decorated with additional keywords in VB. Read-only properties, on the other hand, are indicated with the ReadOnly keyword in front of the Property keyword, while write-only properties have the WriteOnly keyword before the Property keyword.

The shared ProductName property of the Application class is read-only. Its C# syntax appears as follows:

```
public static string ProductName {get;}
```

The corresponding VB syntax is:

```
Public Shared ReadOnly Property ProductName As String
```

Note that properties, like methods, can use the object-oriented modifiers listed in Table 22-4.

Events

Events are declared in C# using the event keyword, which is followed by the delegate type returned by the event and the name of the event. For example, the Parse event of the Binding class has the following syntax:

```
public event ConvertEventHandler Parse;
```

The equivalent VB syntax is:

```
Public Event Parse As ConvertEventHandler
```

In addition, the C# event and the VB Event keywords can be preceded by the object modifiers listed in Table 22-4.

Delegates

The syntax for a delegate in C# closely follows the syntax for a method. The delegate statement is followed by the delegate's return type (or void, if there is none) and the delegate name. This in turn is followed by the delegate's parameter list, in which each parameter takes the form:

```
<parameter_type> <parameter_name>
```

For example:

```
public delegate void DragEventHandler(
    object sender,
    DragEventArgs e);
```

In a VB Delegate statement, the Delegate keyword is followed by the Sub keyword (if the delegate returns a void in C#) or the Function keyword (if the delegate returns some other value). For example, in VB, the DragEventHandler delegate has the following syntax:

```
Public Delegate Sub DragEventHandler( _
    sender As Object, _
    e As DragEventArgs)
```

Enumerations

C# uses the enum statement along with opening and closing braces to indicate the beginning and end of an enumeration definition. For example:

```
public enum CheckedState {
    // enumeration members
}
```

In VB, an enumeration is defined by the Enum... End Enum construct. For example, the VB version of the CheckedState enum declaration is:

```
Public Enum CheckedState
    ' enumeration members
End Enum
```

In both C# and VB, the member listing consists of the name of the enumerated member and its value. These are identical in C# and VB, except that C# adds a comma to separate one member of the enumeration from another, whereas VB requires that they be on separate lines. For example, the full declaration of the CheckedState enumeration in C# is:

```
public enum CheckedState {
    Unchecked = 0,
    Checked = 1,
    Indeterminate = 2
}
```

The VB equivalent is:

```
Public Enum CheckedState
    Unchecked = 0
    Checked = 1
    Indeterminate = 2
End Enum
```

23

The System.Web Namespace

The System.Web namespace contains some of the fundamental ingredients for ASP. NET applications. These ingredients include the classes used for the original built-in ASP objects (Request, Response, Application, and Server), as well as classes for managing cookies, configuring page caching, implementing tracing, and retrieving information about the web server and client browser. Aside from the classes required for web services and the Web Forms user interface, the System.Web namespace contains the heart of ASP.NET's functionality. Figures 23-1 and 23-2 show the types in this namespace.

One confusing aspect about the System.Web namespace is Microsoft's "all roads lead to Rome" approach to backward compatibility. For example, the HttpRequest class can be accessed on a Web Form through the Page class (Page.Request), the HttpContext class (Page.Context.Request), and the HttpApplication class (Page.Context.ApplicationInstance. Request). In all cases, the reference is pointing to the same object. Essentially, the HttpContext class encapsulates the fundamental types that relate to an HTTP request. The HttpContext object is made available to all IHttpModule and IHttpHandler instances (which includes HttpApplication, System.Web.UI.Page, and System.Web.UI.UserControl), and some of its properties are "magically" copied into these classes for convenience and backward compatibility. When you use the built-in Request object on a Web Forms page, for example, you use the Request property from the Page class. Generally, using the Page properties is the easiest and least expensive way to access the built-in objects.

Due to backward compatibility, some class names don't match the name of the corresponding built-in object. For example, the Application object is an instance of the HttpApplicationState class, not the HttpApplication class. Similarly, the built-in Response.Cache object references an instance of the HttpCachePolicy class, while the built-in Cache object references the System.Web.Caching.Cache class.

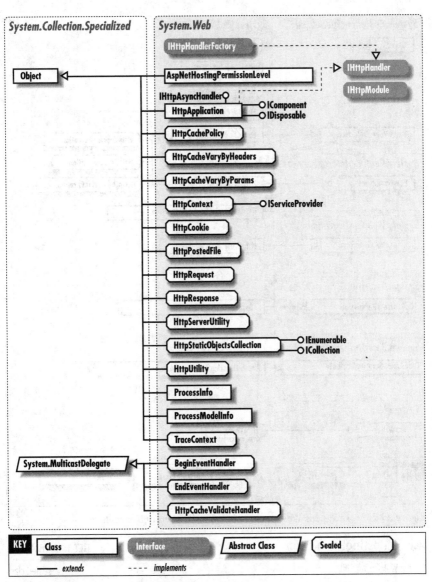

Figure 23-1. Fundamental types from System.Web

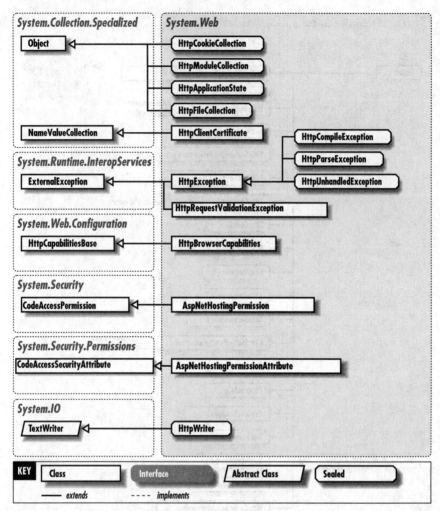

KEY

Class	Interface	Abstract Class	Sealed

—— extends   - - - - implements

Figure 23-2. More System.Web types, including collections and exceptions

AspNetHostingPermission

.NET 1.1, serializable

System.Web (system.dll)   sealed class

With this class, you can ensure that the current assembly has the required code access security permission to host the ASP.NET engine. If you call Demand() and the assembly does not have the required permission, a System.Security.SecurityException will be thrown immediately (which prevents the problem of an unexpected security-related failure later on). You can also use the Deny() method to programmatically revoke this permission.

Note that this class only pertains to code access security (the policy of allowed and disallowed actions configured using the .NET Framework Configuration Tool or the caspol.exe command-line utility). It has nothing to do with ASP.NET or IIS authentication. It will also not be of any interest if you are using IIS the host the ASP.NET engine.

This type was added in .NET 1.1.

```
public sealed class AspNetHostingPermission : System.Security.CodeAccessPermission,
    System.Security.Permissions.IUnrestrictedPermission {
// Public Constructors
  public AspNetHostingPermission(AspNetHostingPermissionLevel level);
  public AspNetHostingPermission(System.Security.Permissions.PermissionState state);
// Public Instance Properties
  public AspNetHostingPermissionLevel Level{set; get; }
// Public Instance Methods
  public override IPermission Copy( );                                          // overrides CodeAccessPermission
  public override void FromXml(System.Security.SecurityElement securityElement);    // overrides CodeAccessPermission
  public override IPermission Intersect(System.Security.IPermissiontarget);      // overrides CodeAccessPermission
  public override bool IsSubsetOf(System.Security.IPermission target);          // overrides CodeAccessPermission
  public bool IsUnrestricted( );                                        // implements IUnrestrictedPermission
  public override SecurityElement ToXml( );                             // overrides CodeAccessPermission
  public override IPermission Union(System.Security.IPermission target);         // overrides CodeAccessPermission
}
```

Hierarchy   System.Object → System.Security.CodeAccessPermission(System.Security.IPermission,
System.Security.ISecurityEncodable, System.Security.IStackWalk) → AspNetHostingPermis-
sion(System.Security.Permissions.IUnrestrictedPermission)

AspNetHostingPermissionAttribute

.NET 1.1, serializable

System.Web (system.dll)   sealed class

With this attribute, you can ensure that the current assembly has the required code
access security permission to host the ASP.NET engine. If it does not, a System.Security.
SecurityException will be thrown immediately (which prevents the problem of an unexpected security-related failure later on). This attribute serves the same purpose as the
AspNetHostingPermission class. The difference is that while AspNetHostingPermission must be used
programmatically (by creating an instance and invoking the corresponding method),
AspNetHostingPermissionAttribute is used declaratively, by adding the attribute to an assembly
or code construct like a class or method declaration.

Note that this type only pertains to code access security (the policy of allowed and
disallowed actions configured using the .NET Framework Configuration Tool or the
caspol.exe command-line utility). It has nothing to do with ASP.NET or IIS authentication. It will also not be of any interest if you are using IIS to host the ASP.NET engine.

```
public sealed class AspNetHostingPermissionAttribute : System.Security.Permissions.CodeAccessSecurityAttribute {
// Public Constructors
  public AspNetHostingPermissionAttribute(System.Security.Permissions.SecurityAction action);
// Public Instance Properties
  public AspNetHostingPermissionLevel Level{set; get; }
// Public Instance Methods
  public override IPermission CreatePermission( );       // overrides System.Security.Permissions.SecurityAttribute
}
```

Hierarchy   System.Object → System.Attribute → System.Security.Permissions.SecurityAttribute →
System.Security.Permissions.CodeAccessSecurityAttribute →
AspNetHostingPermissionAttribute

Valid On   All

AspNetHostingPermissionLevel

System.Web (system.dll)   enum

This enumeration is used in conjunction with the AspNetHostingPermission and AspNetHosting-PermissionAttribute types. It indicates the level of peermissions assigned to an assembly for hosting the ASP.NET engine.

This type was added in .NET 1.1.

```
public enum AspNetHostingPermissionLevel {
  None = 100,
  Minimal = 200,
  Low = 300,
  Medium = 400,
  High = 500,
  Unrestricted = 600
}
```

Hierarchy	System.Object → System.ValueType → System.Enum(System.IComparable, System.IFormattable, System.IConvertible) → AspNetHostingPermissionLevel
Returned By	AspNetHostingPermission.Level, AspNetHostingPermissionAttribute.Level
Passed To	AspNetHostingPermission.{AspNetHostingPermission( ), Level}, AspNetHostingPermissionAttribute.Level

BeginEventHandler

serializable

System.Web (system.web.dll)   delegate

This class is used to connect an event handler to an HttpApplication event. It is used transparently by the ASP.NET framework.

```
public delegate IAsyncResult BeginEventHandler(object sender, EventArgs e, AsyncCallback cb, object extraData);
```

Passed To	HttpApplication.{AddOnAcquireRequestStateAsync( ), AddOnAuthenticateRequestAsync( ), AddOnAuthorizeRequestAsync( ), AddOnBeginRequestAsync( ), AddOnEndRequestAsync( ), AddOnPostRequestHandlerExecuteAsync( ), AddOnPreRequestHandlerExecuteAsync( ), AddOnReleaseRequestStateAsync( ), AddOnResolveRequestCacheAsync( ), AddOnUpdateRequestCacheAsync( )}

EndEventHandler

serializable

System.Web (system.web.dll)   delegate

This class is used to connect an event handler to an HttpApplication event. It is used transparently by the ASP.NET framework.

```
public delegate void EndEventHandler( IAsyncResult ar);
```

Passed To	HttpApplication.{AddOnAcquireRequestStateAsync( ), AddOnAuthenticateRequestAsync( ), AddOnAuthorizeRequestAsync( ), AddOnBeginRequestAsync( ), AddOnEndRequestAsync( ), AddOnPostRequestHandlerExecuteAsync( ), AddOnPreRequestHandlerExecuteAsync( ), AddOnReleaseRequestStateAsync( ), AddOnResolveRequestCacheAsync( ), AddOnUpdateRequestCacheAsync( )}

System.Web (system.web.dll) class

HttpApplication is the default base class from which your web application derives. This class is most notable for the application-level events it provides. You can code event handlers that react to global application events in the *global.asax* file. If you use Visual Studio .NET to create a code-behind class (like *global.asax.vb*), the event handler code will be created in a class called **Global**, which inherits from **HttpApplication**.

The first time a user navigates to a page in your application, the ASP.NET engine creates a pool of **HttpApplication** objects. Whenever your application receives a request, the ASP.NET engine automatically assigns one of these **HttpApplication** instances to serve the request. This **HttpApplication** instance will be reused, but only once the request is complete.

```
public class HttpApplication : IHttpAsyncHandler, IHttpHandler, System.ComponentModel.IComponent, IDisposable {
// Public Constructors
   public HttpApplication( );
// Public Instance Properties
   public HttpApplicationState Application{get; }
   public HttpContext Context{get; }
   public HttpModuleCollection Modules{get; }
   public HttpRequest Request{get; }
   public HttpResponse Response{get; }
   public HttpServerUtility Server{get; }
   public HttpSessionState Session{get; }
   public ISite Site{set; get; }                                    // implements System.ComponentModel.IComponent
   public IPrincipal User{get; }
// Protected Instance Properties
   protected EventHandlerList Events{get; }
// Public Instance Methods
   public void AddOnAcquireRequestStateAsync(BeginEventHandler bh, EndEventHandler eh);
   public void AddOnAuthenticateRequestAsync(BeginEventHandler bh, EndEventHandler eh);
   public void AddOnAuthorizeRequestAsync(BeginEventHandler bh, EndEventHandler eh);
   public void AddOnBeginRequestAsync(BeginEventHandler bh, EndEventHandler eh);
   public void AddOnEndRequestAsync(BeginEventHandler bh, EndEventHandler eh);
   public void AddOnPostRequestHandlerExecuteAsync(BeginEventHandler bh, EndEventHandler eh);
   public void AddOnPreRequestHandlerExecuteAsync(BeginEventHandler bh, EndEventHandler eh);
   public void AddOnReleaseRequestStateAsync(BeginEventHandler bh, EndEventHandler eh);
   public void AddOnResolveRequestCacheAsync(BeginEventHandler bh, EndEventHandler eh);
   public void AddOnUpdateRequestCacheAsync(BeginEventHandler bh, EndEventHandler eh);
   public void CompleteRequest( );
   public virtual void Dispose( );                                  // implements IDisposable
   public virtual string GetVaryByCustomString(HttpContext context, string custom);
   public virtual void Init( );
// Events
   public event EventHandler AcquireRequestState;
   public event EventHandler AuthenticateRequest;
   public event EventHandler AuthorizeRequest;
   public event EventHandler BeginRequest;
   public event EventHandler Disposed;                              // implements System.ComponentModel.IComponent
   public event EventHandler EndRequest;
```

```
    public event EventHandler Error;
    public event EventHandler PostRequestHandlerExecute;
    public event EventHandler PreRequestHandlerExecute;
    public event EventHandler PreSendRequestContent;
    public event EventHandler PreSendRequestHeaders;
    public event EventHandler ReleaseRequestState;
    public event EventHandler ResolveRequestCache;
    public event EventHandler UpdateRequestCache;
}
```

Returned By   HttpContext.ApplicationInstance

Passed To   HttpContext.ApplicationInstance, IHttpModule.Init( ), System.Web.Security.DefaultAuthenti-
                    cationModule.Init( ), System.Web.Security.FileAuthorizationModule.Init( ), System.Web.
                    Security.FormsAuthenticationModule.Init( ), System.Web.Security.PassportAuthentication-
                    Module.Init( ), System.Web.Security.UrlAuthorizationModule.Init( ), System.Web.Security.
                    WindowsAuthenticationModule.Init( ), System.Web.SessionState.SessionStateModule.Init( )

HttpApplicationState

System.Web (system.web.dll)   sealed class

This class provides server-side state management that is available globally across all
client sessions in an ASP.NET application. Application state is not shared across
multiple ASP.NET applications, or across multiple processes or multiple computers in
a single application. (In other words, proxy load balancing in a web farm can thwart
this type of state management.) If you need to store state across multiple web servers,
you may want to use session state instead (see the System.Web.SessionState.HttpSessionState
class for more information).

The HttpApplicationState class exposes a name/value collection of items that can store
simple value types or instances of .NET objects. A single instance of the class is created
automatically the first time a client requests a page in the ASP.NET virtual directory. A
reference is provided through the built-in Application object.

The HttpApplicationState class combines two state collections: Contents and StaticObjects. The
StaticObjects collection contains the application state objects that are defined in the
global.asax file with <object runat=server> tags. This collection is immutable. The Contents
collection contains all the state objects added at runtime.

The Item collection is the default indexer for HttpApplicationState, so you can use the name
of a state object as an index, as in: Application("globalcounter") = 1;. If you assign a value to a
state object that does not exist, it is created automatically. Items are stored as the
generic System.Object type and must be cast to the appropriate types when you retrieve
them.

Multiple clients or threads can access application state values simultaneously. To
avoid synchronization problems, use the Lock( ) method to gain exclusive access to the
application state collection before adding or retrieving an item, followed by the UnLock( )
method. This approach can result in performance degradation, which makes this type
of state management unsuitable for frequently modified values. Using another form of
state management or a relational database is usually a better alternative. HttpApplication-
State objects should also be thread-safe, or you should use synchronization techniques
(like the SyncLock statement).

```
public sealed class HttpApplicationState : System.Collections.Specialized.NameObjectCollectionBase {
// Public Instance Properties
  public string[ ] AllKeys{get; }
  public HttpApplicationState Contents{get; }
  public override int Count{get; }                    // overrides System.Collections.Specialized.NameObjectCollectionBase
  public HttpStaticObjectsCollection StaticObjects{get; }
  public object this[ string name ]{set; get; }
  public object this[ int index ]{get; }
// Public Instance Methods
  public void Add( string name, object value);
  public void Clear( );
  public object Get( int index);
  public object Get( string name);
  public string GetKey( int index);
  public void Lock( );
  public void Remove( string name);
  public void RemoveAll( );
  public void RemoveAt( int index);
  public void Set( string name, object value);
  public void UnLock( );
}
```

Hierarchy   System.Object → System.Collections.Specialized.NameObjectCollectionBase(System.Collections.ICollection, System.Collections.IEnumerable, System.Runtime.Serialization.ISerializable, System.Runtime.Serialization.IDeserializationCallback) → HttpApplicationState

Returned By   HttpApplication.Application, HttpContext.Application, System.Web.Services.WebService. Application, System.Web.UI.Page.Application, System.Web.UI.UserControl.Application

HttpBrowserCapabilities

System.Web (system.web.dll)   class

This class allows you to take advantage of features enabled in the client's browser. It is automatically available through the Browser property of the built-in Request object and corresponds roughly to the MSWC.BrowserCapabilities component that existed in ASP. You can use this class to write browser-specific code for a web page or a custom web page control.

Essentially, the HttpBrowserCapabilities class is a list of properties that describe the client's browser. Many properties return True or False, depending on whether a given capability is enabled in the browser, such as ActiveXControls, BackgroundSounds, CDF (the channel definition format used in webcasting), Cookies, Frames, JavaApplets, JavaScript, and VBScript. Other Boolean values tell you whether or not the browser is AOL-based, a beta, and running on the Win16 or Win32 platform (the AOL, Beta, Win16, and Win32 properties, respectively). Additionally, you can retrieve information such as version number (MajorVersion and MinorVersion), the Platform name (e.g., "Win32"), the browser Type (e.g., "Microsoft Internet Explorer 5"), and the full Version number as a string.

```
public class HttpBrowserCapabilities : System.Web.Configuration.HttpCapabilitiesBase {
// Public Constructors
  public HttpBrowserCapabilities( );
// Public Instance Properties
```

```
public bool ActiveXControls{get; }
public bool AOL{get; }
public bool BackgroundSounds{get; }
public bool Beta{get; }
public string Browser{get; }
public bool CDF{get; }
public Version ClrVersion{get; }
public bool Cookies{get; }
public bool Crawler{get; }
public Version EcmaScriptVersion{get; }
public bool Frames{get; }
public bool JavaApplets{get; }
public bool JavaScript{get; }
public int MajorVersion{get; }
public double MinorVersion{get; }
public Version MSDomVersion{get; }
public string Platform{get; }
public bool Tables{get; }
public Type TagWriter{get; }
public string Type{get; }
public bool VBScript{get; }
public string Version{get; }
public Version W3CDomVersion{get; }
public bool Win16{get; }
public bool Win32{get; }
// Public Instance Methods
public Version[ ] GetClrVersions( );
}
```

Hierarchy	System.Object → System.Web.Configuration.HttpCapabilitiesBase → HttpBrowserCapabilities
Subclasses	System.Web.Mobile.MobileCapabilities
Returned By	HttpRequest.Browser
Passed To	HttpRequest.Browser

HttpCacheability   serializable

System.Web (system.web.dll)   enum

This enumeration is used by the HttpCachePolicy.SetCacheability( ) method of the Http-
CachePolicy class. It allows you to configure how a cached page is shared among users. A
value of Public means that the page can be stored in shared caches on a proxy server, or
ASP.NET's own output cache, and made available to all clients. Private means that the
page can be cached only on the client's computer, will not be stored in the ASP.NET
output cache or on a proxy server, and cannot benefit other users.

```
public enum HttpCacheability {
  NoCache = 1,
  Private = 2,
```

```
    Server = 3,
    ServerAndNoCache = 3,
    Public = 4,
    ServerAndPrivate = 5
}
```

Hierarchy   System.Object → System.ValueType → System.Enum(System.IComparable, System.IFor-
                mattable, System.IConvertible) → HttpCacheability

Passed To   HttpCachePolicy.SetCacheability( )

HttpCachePolicy

System.Web (system.web.dll)   **sealed class**

This class allows you to configure "page" or output caching for an ASP.NET application, which stores a fully rendered page for automatic reuse. A cached page will be
used for GET requests until it expires, as long as the URL request does not have
different query string arguments. A cached page will not be used for POST requests, so
postbacks (such as when a user clicks on button) will bypass the cached page. (This
behavior is slightly and mysteriously different than just using the <OutputCache> page
directive, which always reuses the cached page for any type of request when the VaryBy-
Param attribute is set to None.) To specifically modify this behavior, you can use the
VaryByParams property and the HttpCacheVaryByParams class.

To enable caching for a page, use the SetCacheability( ) method to set the page's visibility
to Public so it can be stored in the shared cache. Then use the SetExpires( ) method to
determine the lifetime of the page in the cache. For example, Response.Cache.SetEx-
pires(DateTime.Now.AddSeconds(60)); will keep a page for 60 seconds, which is enough to make
a substantial performance difference. By default, the cache uses absolute expiration.
You can also invoke the SetSlidingExpiration( ) method, with the parameter True, to enable
sliding expiration. In sliding expiration, the time limit is compared to the time elapsed
since the most recent request, not the time since the first request. You can also use the
AddValidationCallback( ) method to add a callback that decides on a page-by-page basis
whether to allow a cached page to be served. Finally, you can use fragment caching by
developing a Web Form user control for a portion of a page, and caching just that
portion using page directives or the methods of this class.

If your page requires customization based on Session variables or user-specific details
other than a query string, you shouldn't cache the page! In these cases, data caching
will be more useful. With data caching, you manually store specific information, such
as binary data or recordsets. For more information on data caching, refer to the System.
Web.Caching.Cache class.

The HttpCachePolicy class is available through the Cache property of the built-in Response
object. It replaces properties of the Response object that were used to configure caching
in ASP (like CacheControl and Expires). Microsoft uses somewhat confusing nomenclature.
An instance of the HttpCachePolicy class (used to configure page caching) is available
through the built-in Response.Cache object, and the System.Web.Caching.Cache class (used for
data caching) is available through the built-in Cache object. Cache and Response.Cache are
not the same!

```
public sealed class HttpCachePolicy {
// Public Instance Properties
  public HttpCacheVaryByHeaders VaryByHeaders{get; }
```

```
  public HttpCacheVaryByParams VaryByParams{get; }
// Public Instance Methods
  public void AddValidationCallback(HttpCacheValidateHandler handler, object data);
  public void AppendCacheExtension(string extension);
  public void SetAllowResponseInBrowserHistory( bool allow);
  public void SetCacheability(HttpCacheability cacheability);
  public void SetCacheability(HttpCacheability cacheability, string field);
  public void SetETag(string etag);
  public void SetETagFromFileDependencies( );
  public void SetExpires(DateTime date);
  public void SetLastModified(DateTime date);
  public void SetLastModifiedFromFileDependencies( );
  public void SetMaxAge(TimeSpan delta);
  public void SetNoServerCaching( );
  public void SetNoStore( );
  public void SetNoTransforms( );
  public void SetProxyMaxAge(TimeSpan delta);
  public void SetRevalidation(HttpCacheRevalidation revalidation);
  public void SetSlidingExpiration(bool slide);
  public void SetValidUntilExpires(bool validUntilExpires);
  public void SetVaryByCustom(string custom);
}
```

Returned By   HttpResponse.Cache

HttpCacheRevalidation   serializable

System.Web (system.web.dll)   enum

This enumeration is used by the SetRevalidation( ) method of the HttpCachePolicy class, which programmatically forces the revalidation of a page. If you use ProxyCaches with this method, the page will be dropped from all shared caches, but potentially left in the client's local cache. (Technically, this sets the "Cache-Control: proxy-revalidate" HTTP header.) If you use AllCaches, the page will be dropped from all caches. (Technically, this sets the "Cache-Control: must-revalidate" HTTP header.)

```
public enum HttpCacheRevalidation {
  AllCaches = 1,
  ProxyCaches = 2,
  None = 3
}
```

Hierarchy   System.Object → System.ValueType → System.Enum(System.IComparable, System.IFor-
                   mattable, System.IConvertible) → HttpCacheRevalidation

Passed To   HttpCachePolicy.SetRevalidation( )

HttpCacheValidateHandler   serializable

System.Web (system.web.dll)   delegate

A function with this signature can be used for the AddValidationCallback( ) method of the HttpCachePolicy class. Using this method gives you the opportunity to check other dependencies that a cached page may have and either allow the page to be served or invalidate it and require the page to be recompiled. To invalidate a page, set the **validationStatus** parameter to **HttpValidationStatus.Invalid**.

```
public delegate void HttpCacheValidateHandler(HttpContext context, object data,
    ref HttpValidationStatus validationStatus);
```

Passed To   HttpCachePolicy.AddValidationCallback( )

HttpCacheVaryByHeaders

System.Web (system.web.dll)   sealed class

This class is used to set the **VaryByHeaders** property of the **HttpCachePolicy** class. It allows you to specify that separate versions of a page should be cached for different languages or character sets. For example, if you set the **UserCharSet** property of this class to **True**, the "Accept-Charset" field will be included in the HTTP Vary header and a separate version of the page will be cached for each request that has a different character set. The cache page will be reused only among requests that have the same Accept-Charset header.

Alternatively, if type safety is not important, you can set the default Item property to a string that contains the name of a header, or a list of header names separated by semicolons (;). Cached pages will then be reused only among requests that have the same values for the headers you identify.

```
public sealed class HttpCacheVaryByHeaders {
// Public Instance Properties
  public bool AcceptTypes{set; get; }
  public bool this[ string header ]{set; get; }
  public bool UserAgent{set; get; }
  public bool UserCharSet{set; get; }
  public bool UserLanguage{set; get; }
// Public Instance Methods
  public void VaryByUnspecifiedParameters( );
}
```

Returned By   HttpCachePolicy.VaryByHeaders

HttpCacheVaryByParams

System.Web (system.web.dll)   sealed class

This class is used to set the **VaryByParams** property of the **HttpCachePolicy** class. By default, cached pages will be reused only for GET requests with identical query string arguments. However, if you supply an instance of an **HttpCacheVaryByParams** class, the parameters that you specify will be the only criteria that determine whether or not a cached page can be reused. For example, if you specify ProductID, a separate copy of the page's output will be cached every time ASP.NET receives a request for the page with a different ProductID value. You can also use the wildcard asterisk (*) to indicate that all variables will be used to determine whether a page should be cached. This technique is discouraged because it could lead to excesssive copies of the page being stored in the cache, which could cause ASP.NET to clear out other, more useful data.

To specify parameters, set the default item property to a string that contains the name of a variable or to a list of variable names separated by semi-colons (;). Cached pages will be reused among requests that have the same values for these variables (in either the query string or form POST collection). All other variables will be ignored and will not stop a cached page from being reused.

```
public sealed class HttpCacheVaryByParams {
// Public Instance Properties
  public bool IgnoreParams{set; get; }
  public bool this[ string header ]{set; get; }
}
```

Returned By   HttpCachePolicy.VaryByParams

HttpClientCertificate

System.Web (system.web.dll)   class

This class exposes a name/value collection of certification fields specified in the X.509 standard. To get the certification fields for the current request, use the ClientCertificate property of the HttpRequest class. Note that the certification fields are sent only if the client browser is accessing the page through SSL (indicated by a URL starting with *https://* instead of *http://*).

```
public class HttpClientCertificate : System.Collections.Specialized.NameValueCollection {
// Public Instance Properties
  public byte[ ] BinaryIssuer{get; }
  public int CertEncoding{get; }
  public byte[ ] Certificate{get; }
  public string Cookie{get; }
  public int Flags{get; }
  public bool IsPresent{get; }
  public string Issuer{get; }
  public bool IsValid{get; }
  public int KeySize{get; }
  public byte[ ] PublicKey{get; }
  public int SecretKeySize{get; }
  public string SerialNumber{get; }
  public string ServerIssuer{get; }
  public string ServerSubject{get; }
  public string Subject{get; }
  public DateTime ValidFrom{get; }
  public DateTime ValidUntil{get; }
// Public Instance Methods
  public override string Get(string field);                          // overrides NameValueCollection
}
```

Hierarchy   System.Object → System.Collections.Specialized.NameObjectCollectionBase(System.Collections.ICollection, System.Collections.IEnumerable, System.Runtime.Serialization.ISerializable, System.Runtime.Serialization.IDeserializationCallback) → System.Collections.Specialized.NameValueCollection → HttpClientCertificate

Returned By   HttpRequest.ClientCertificate

HttpCompileException

System.Web (system.web.dll)   sealed class

This class represents an HTTP compiler exception.

```
public sealed class HttpCompileException : HttpException {
// Public Instance Properties
  public CompilerResults Results{get; }
  public string SourceCode{get; }
}
```

Hierarchy   System.Object → System.Exception(System.Runtime.Serialization.ISerializable) → System.
                     SystemException → System.Runtime.InteropServices.ExternalException → HttpException
                     → HttpCompileException

HttpContext

System.Web (system.web.dll)   sealed class

The HttpContext class represents the "operating context" of an ASP.NET application. It provides references to instances of fundamental classes like HttpApplicationState and HttpRequest, which are known as intrinsic or "built-in" objects. The HttpContext class is provided to IHttpModule and IHttpHandler instances (like System.Web.UI.Page and HttpApplication), which provide these classes through their own properties. The shared (static) property Current returns the current HttpContext, and is useful if you need to access the built-in ASP.NET objects from another code module like a class (where you won't have access to the System.Web.UI.Page properties). One example is a web service that doesn't inherit from System.Web.Services.WebService. You can also use the shared GetAppConfig() method to retrieve a collection object from the *web.config* file that contains configuration information. Just specify the configuration section you want to examine as a parameter (like "appSettings").

If you are creating your own IHttpHandler class, you will receive the current instance of the HttpContext class as a parameter of the IHttpHandler.ProcessRequest() method. To use the Session property of the HttpContext class, you must also implement either the System.Web. SessionState.IReadOnlySessionState interface or the System.Web.SessionState.IRequiresSessionState interface.

```
public sealed class HttpContext : IServiceProvider {
// Public Constructors
  public HttpContext(HttpRequest request, HttpResponse response);
  public HttpContext(HttpWorkerRequest wr);
// Public Static Properties
  public static HttpContext Current{set; get; }
// Public Instance Properties
  public Exception[ ] AllErrors{get; }
  public HttpApplicationState Application{get; }
  public HttpApplication ApplicationInstance{set; get; }
  public Cache Cache{get; }
  public Exception Error{get; }
  public IHttpHandler Handler{set; get; }
  public bool IsCustomErrorEnabled{get; }
  public bool IsDebuggingEnabled{get; }
```

```
public IDictionary Items{get; }
public HttpRequest Request{get; }
public HttpResponse Response{get; }
public HttpServerUtility Server{get; }
public HttpSessionState Session{get; }
public bool SkipAuthorization{set; get; }
public DateTime Timestamp{get; }
public TraceContext Trace{get; }
public IPrincipal User{set; get; }
// Public Static Methods
public static object GetAppConfig(string name);
// Public Instance Methods
public void AddError(Exception errorInfo);
public void ClearError( );
public object GetConfig(string name);
public void RewritePath(string path);
public void RewritePath(string filePath, string pathInfo, string queryString);
}
```

Returned By   HttpApplication.Context, System.Web.Security.DefaultAuthenticationEventArgs.Context,
System.Web.Security.FormsAuthenticationEventArgs.Context, System.Web.Security.Passpor-
tAuthenticationEventArgs.Context, System.Web.Security.WindowsAuthenticationEventArgs.
Context, System.Web.Services.WebService.Context, System.Web.UI.Control.Context

Passed To   Multiple types

HttpCookie

System.Web (system.web.dll)   sealed class

Use this class to create a client-side cookie. The **HttpCookie** constructor takes a string
representing the name of the cookie. After creating a cookie, you can add information
to it in the form of name/value pairs by using the **HttpCookieCollection.Add( )** method as
follows: objCookies.Values.Add("Name", "John");. Values can be retrieved by using their name
with a syntax like strName = objCookies.Values["Name"];.

To send the cookie to the client browser as part of the HTTP response, use the
AppendCookie( ) method of the **HttpResponse** class. This method stores the cookie on the
client browser. You can then retrieve a cookie from the **HttpResponse** class's cookie
collection on other pages by using the cookie name, as in Response.Cookies["NameList"]. To
ensure compatibility with all browsers, you should not store more than 4096 bytes in a
single cookie.

To make a cookie persist between sessions, set the **Expires** property for the **HttpCookie** to a
date in the future. You can also set the **Secure** property to **True** to restrict the cookie to
Secure Socket Layer (SSL) transmission. A cookie is much less secure than Application
or Session state variables, as information is maintained on the client and transmitted
back and forth continuously.

```
public sealed class HttpCookie {
// Public Constructors
 public HttpCookie( string name);
 public HttpCookie( string name, string value);
```

```
// Public Instance Properties
  public string Domain{set; get; }
  public DateTime Expires{set; get; }
  public bool HasKeys{get; }
  public string Name{set; get; }
  public string Path{set; get; }
  public bool Secure{set; get; }
  public string this[ string key ]{set; get; }
  public string Value{set; get; }
  public NameValueCollection Values{get; }
}
```

Returned By   HttpCookieCollection.{Get( ), this}, System.Web.Security.FormsAuthentication.
                   GetAuthCookie( )

Passed To   HttpCookieCollection.{Add( ), Set( )}, HttpResponse.{AppendCookie( ), SetCookie( )}

HttpCookieCollection

System.Web (system.web.dll)   sealed class

HttpCookieCollection is a name/value collection of HttpCookie objects. The Cookies property of
the HttpResponse class contains the cookies sent from the client with the current request.
The Cookies property of the HttpRequest class contains the cookies sent back from the
server.

These collections contain all the transmitted cookies, including those you have created
automatically in code, and other cookies used by the ASP.NET framework like the
Forms Authentication cookie and the Session state cookie (named ASP.NET_SessionId).

```
public sealed class HttpCookieCollection : System.Collections.Specialized.NameObjectCollectionBase {
// Public Constructors
  public HttpCookieCollection( );
// Public Instance Properties
  public string[ ] AllKeys{get; }
  public HttpCookie this[ int index ]{get; }
  public HttpCookie this[ string name ]{get; }
// Public Instance Methods
  public void Add( HttpCookie cookie);
  public void Clear( );
  public void CopyTo( Array dest, int index);                          // implements ICollection
  public HttpCookie Get( int index);
  public HttpCookie Get( string name);
  public string GetKey( int index);
  public void Remove( string name);
  public void Set( HttpCookie cookie);
}
```

Hierarchy   System.Object → System.Collections.Specialized.NameObjectCollectionBase(System.Collec-
                   tions.ICollection, System.Collections.IEnumerable, System.Runtime.Serialization.ISerializable,
                   System.Runtime.Serialization.IDeserializationCallback) → HttpCookieCollection

Returned By   HttpRequest.Cookies, HttpResponse.Cookies

HttpException

System.Web (system.web.dll) class

This class encapsulates an ASP.NET exception. It is a standard exception object, with the addition of the GetHtmlErrorMessage( ) method and the GetHttpCode( ) method, that returns the HTTP error code representing the error (like 404 for file not found) as an integer. If no HTTP error code exists for the current exception or the InnerException, the status code 500 is returned.

```
public class HttpException : System.Runtime.InteropServices.ExternalException {
// Public Constructors
  public HttpException( );
  public HttpException( int httpCode, string message);
  public HttpException(int httpCode, string message, Exception innerException);
  public HttpException(int httpCode, string message, int hr);
  public HttpException( string message);
  public HttpException(string message, Exception innerException);
  public HttpException( string message, int hr);
// Public Static Methods
  public static HttpException CreateFromLastError(string message);
// Public Instance Methods
  public string GetHtmlErrorMessage( );
  public int GetHttpCode( );
}
```

Hierarchy	System.Object → System.Exception(System.Runtime.Serialization.ISerializable) → System.SystemException → System.Runtime.InteropServices.ExternalException → HttpException
Subclasses	HttpCompileException, HttpParseException, HttpRequestValidationException, HttpUnhandledException

HttpFileCollection

System.Web (system.web.dll) sealed class

This class is a name/value collection of HttpPostedFile instances, which represents incoming files uploaded by a client (using multipart MIME and the HTTP content type of multipart/formdata). The HtmlInputFile class in the System.Web.UI.HtmlControls namespace provides an easier way to allow a user to upload files.

```
public sealed class HttpFileCollection : System.Collections.Specialized.NameObjectCollectionBase {
// Public Instance Properties
  public string[ ] AllKeys{get; }
  public HttpPostedFile this[ int index ]{get; }
  public HttpPostedFile this[ string name ]{get; }
// Public Instance Methods
  public void CopyTo( Array dest, int index);                                  // implements ICollection
  public HttpPostedFile Get( int index);
  public HttpPostedFile Get( string name);
  public string GetKey( int index);
}
```

| **Hierarchy** | System.Object → System.Collections.Specialized.NameObjectCollectionBase(System.Collections.ICollection, System.Collections.IEnumerable, System.Runtime.Serialization.ISerializable, System.Runtime.Serialization.IDeserializationCallback) → HttpFileCollection |

| **Returned By** | HttpRequest.Files |

HttpModuleCollection

System.Web (system.web.dll)   sealed class

This is a name/value collection of IHttpModule instances. It's used by the Modules property of the HttpApplication class to provide a collection of all modules used by your application (as defined in the <httpmodules> section of the application's *web.config* file).

```
public sealed class HttpModuleCollection : System.Collections.Specialized.NameObjectCollectionBase {
// Public Instance Properties
  public string[ ] AllKeys{get; }
  public IHttpModule this[ int index ]{get; }
  public IHttpModule this[ string name ]{get; }
// Public Instance Methods
  public void CopyTo( Array dest, int index);                                              // implements ICollection
  public IHttpModule Get( int index);
  public IHttpModule Get( string name);
  public string GetKey( int index);
}
```

| **Hierarchy** | System.Object → System.Collections.Specialized.NameObjectCollectionBase(System.Collections.ICollection, System.Collections.IEnumerable, System.Runtime.Serialization.ISerializable, System.Runtime.Serialization.IDeserializationCallback) → HttpModuleCollection |

| **Returned By** | HttpApplication.Modules |

HttpParseException

System.Web (system.web.dll)   sealed class

This class represents an exception generated when parsing an ASP.NET file.

```
public sealed class HttpParseException : HttpException {
// Public Instance Properties
  public string FileName{get; }
  public int Line{get; }
}
```

| **Hierarchy** | System.Object → System.Exception(System.Runtime.Serialization.ISerializable) → System.SystemException → System.Runtime.InteropServices.ExternalException → HttpException → HttpParseException |

HttpPostedFile

System.Web (system.web.dll)   sealed class

The HttpPostedFile class allows you to easily manipulate files that are uploaded by the client. An HttpPostedFile instance is provided by the PostedFile property of the System.Web.UI.HtmlControls.HtmlInputFile control.

You can use the SaveAs() method to save a posted file to disk synchronously. The method will return once the file is completely uploaded. Alternatively, you can get a System.IO.Stream object containing the file from the InputStream property and use it to work with the file asynchronously (while it is being uploaded).

```
public sealed class HttpPostedFile {
// Public Instance Properties
   public int ContentLength{get; }
   public string ContentType{get; }
   public string FileName{get; }
   public Stream InputStream{get; }
// Public Instance Methods
   public void SaveAs( string filename);
}
```

Returned By   HttpFileCollection.{Get( ), this}, System.Web.UI.HtmlControls.HtmlInputFile.PostedFile

HttpRequest

System.Web (system.web.dll)   sealed class

The HttpRequest class wraps all information that a client browser passes to the server during an HTTP request. It includes client certificates, cookies, and values submitted through HTML form elements. You can access this information in its entirety as a System.IO.Stream object through the InputStream property, or you can use one of the more useful higher-level properties.

The QueryString property allows you to retrieve values from the URL's query string, which can transfer information from one ASP.NET page to another. This query string takes the form of a series of name/value pairs appended to the URL after a question mark (for example, the client request *http://www.myapp.com/mypage.aspx?var1=hi* will result in a value of "hi" for Request.QueryString["var1"]). The QueryString collection is limited to string data and should not contain sensitive information, as it is clearly visible to the user. To ensure compatibility with all browsers, you should not store more than about 1000 bytes in the query string.

The HttpRequest class also exposes an HttpCookieCollection object in the Cookies property. This is a collection of client-side cookies that your script (or other scripts on your server) have created. They are transmitted to the server with each request in the HTTP Cookie header. This collection is read-only. If you want to modify or add a cookie, use the HttpResponse.Cookies property instead.

The HttpRequest class provides some frequently used, lower-level properties. For example, the Form collection wraps the information returned from the HTML form elements, which you will typically access through the higher-level web control abstraction. Similarly, the Headers and ServerVariables collections allow you to access HTML headers and server variables directly, provided you know their names. Many of these variables now have corresponding read-only properties that you can use more easily, like HttpMethod (the data transfer method like GET or POST), UserHostAddress (the IP address of the client), and UserHostName (the DNS name of remote client). The Browser property is a reference to an HttpBrowserCapabilities object with full information about the user's browser.

Additional information available in the HttpRequest class includes the currently requested URL (Url), the URL from which the request is being made (UrlReferrer), and the root path

for the current ASP.NET application as a virtual path (ApplicationPath) or physical filesystem path (PhysicalApplicationPath).

```
public sealed class HttpRequest {
// Public Constructors
   public HttpRequest(string filename, string url, string queryString);
// Public Instance Properties
   public string[ ] AcceptTypes{get; }
   public string ApplicationPath{get; }
   public HttpBrowserCapabilities Browser{set; get; }
   public HttpClientCertificate ClientCertificate{get; }
   public Encoding ContentEncoding{set; get; }
   public int ContentLength{get; }
   public string ContentType{set; get; }
   public HttpCookieCollection Cookies{get; }
   public string CurrentExecutionFilePath{get; }
   public string FilePath{get; }
   public HttpFileCollection Files{get; }
   public Stream Filter{set; get; }
   public NameValueCollection Form{get; }
   public NameValueCollection Headers{get; }
   public string HttpMethod{get; }
   public Stream InputStream{get; }
   public bool IsAuthenticated{get; }
   public bool IsSecureConnection{get; }
   public NameValueCollection Params{get; }
   public string Path{get; }
   public string PathInfo{get; }
   public string PhysicalApplicationPath{get; }
   public string PhysicalPath{get; }
   public NameValueCollection QueryString{get; }
   public string RawUrl{get; }
   public string RequestType{set; get; }
   public NameValueCollection ServerVariables{get; }
   public string this[ string key ]{get; }
   public int TotalBytes{get; }
   public Uri Url{get; }
   public Uri UrlReferrer{get; }
   public string UserAgent{get; }
   public string UserHostAddress{get; }
   public string UserHostName{get; }
   public string[ ] UserLanguages{get; }
// Public Instance Methods
   public byte[ ] BinaryRead(int count);
   public int[ ] MapImageCoordinates( string imageFieldName);
   public string MapPath(string virtualPath);
   public string MapPath(string virtualPath, string baseVirtualDir, bool allowCrossAppMapping);
   public void SaveAs(string filename, bool includeHeaders);
   public void ValidateInput( );
}
```

HttpRequestValidationException

System.Web (system.web.dll)   sealed class

ASP.NET 1.1 adds a request validation feature designed to prevent some types of
script injection attacks. If request validation is enabled (the default), ASP.NET will
check all posted values, cookies, and the query string for potentially dangerous input.
One example of potentially dangerous input is if the user enters a JavaScript block into
a textbox. This becomes a problem if your code attempts to display the textbox
content by writing it to a web page without first encoding it using the HttpServerUtility.
HtmlEncode( ) method. In this case, your page will not just display the textbox contents--
instead, it will execute the script block. With request validation, however, this
shouldn't occur, as ASP.NET will throw the HttpRequestValidationException when a page with
potentially dangerous content is posted back to the server.

You can disable request validation by setting the validateRequest attribute in the Page
directive to false. In this case, your application should explicitly check or HTML
encode all user input. Note that request validation and the HttpRequestValidationException
class are only found in Version 1.1 of the .NET Framework.

```
public sealed class HttpRequestValidationException : HttpException {
// No public or protected members
}
```

Hierarchy   System.Object → System.Exception(System.Runtime.Serialization.ISerializable) → System.
SystemException → System.Runtime.InteropServices.ExternalException → HttpException
→ HttpRequestValidationException

HttpResponse

System.Web (system.web.dll)   sealed class

The HttpResponse class is used to send information to the client's browser, including
HTML content, HTML headers, and customized cookies. Its name derives from the
fact that it is used to "respond" to an HTTP request.

The Redirect( ) method of the HttpResponse class provides the easiest way to programmatically send the user to another web page. You supply the name of the HTML or ASPX
file as an argument (e.g., Response.Redirect ("newpage.aspx");). As long as the file is in the same
directory as the current page, you don't need to provide a full URL (like *http://www.
mysite/myapplication/newpage.aspx*), although you can use a relative path or fully-
qualified URL. Other ways to transfer a user between pages in an ASP.NET program
include the HttpServerUtility.Transfer( ) method and the System.Web.UI.WebControls.HyperLink web
control.

The Cookies property of the HttpResponse class provides a reference to the application's HttpCookieCollection, which can send custom cookies to the client. The Cache property provides a reference to the application's HttpCachePolicy settings. Both classes are described separately. These properties, along with the Redirect() method, are the most commonly used members of HttpResponse.

In traditional ASP development, the Write() method was often used to append HTML to a web page (e.g., Reponse.Write "<h1>Hello World</h1>";). ASP.NET programs will rarely use this method because it is much easier to handle dynamic content by changing the properties of full-featured web controls on Web Forms. Similarly, the BinaryWrite() method, which allows you to write binary information into the HTTP text stream by supplying a byte array, or the WriteFile() method, which allows you to write the content from a named text file into the output stream, are rarely used.

The BufferOutput property is a Boolean value that determines whether or not the HTTP output is buffered. It is sent to the client only when it is fully rendered and all code has executed. The default is True. The HttpResponse class also provides low-level control over the management of the output buffer, with the Clear(), Flush(), and End() methods. You can also use the AppendToLog() method to write a string of information to the IIS log file on the web server. This method should not be used for debugging, as better options are provided by the TraceContext class.

```
public sealed class HttpResponse {
// Public Constructors
   public HttpResponse(System.IO.TextWriter writer);
// Public Instance Properties
   public bool Buffer{set; get; }
   public bool BufferOutput{set; get; }
   public HttpCachePolicy Cache{get; }
   public string CacheControl{set; get; }
   public string Charset{set; get; }
   public Encoding ContentEncoding{set; get; }
   public string ContentType{set; get; }
   public HttpCookieCollection Cookies{get; }
   public int Expires{set; get; }
   public DateTime ExpiresAbsolute{set; get; }
   public Stream Filter{set; get; }
   public bool IsClientConnected{get; }
   public TextWriter Output{get; }
   public Stream OutputStream{get; }
   public string RedirectLocation{set; get; }
   public string Status{set; get; }
   public int StatusCode{set; get; }
   public string StatusDescription{set; get; }
   public bool SuppressContent{set; get; }
// Public Static Methods
   public static void RemoveOutputCacheItem( string path);
// Public Instance Methods
   public void AddCacheItemDependencies(System.Collections.ArrayList cacheKeys);
   public void AddCacheItemDependency(string cacheKey);
   public void AddFileDependencies(System.Collections.ArrayList filenames);
   public void AddFileDependency(string filename);
   public void AddHeader(string name, string value);
```

```
public void AppendCookie(HttpCookie cookie);
public void AppendHeader(string name, string value);
public void AppendToLog(string param);
public string ApplyAppPathModifier(string virtualPath);
public void BinaryWrite(byte[ ] buffer);
public void Clear( );
public void ClearContent( );
public void ClearHeaders( );
public void Close( );
public void End( );
public void Flush( );
public void Pics(string value);
public void Redirect(string url);
public void Redirect(string url, bool endResponse);
public void SetCookie(HttpCookie cookie);
public void Write(char ch);
public void Write(char[ ] buffer, int index, int count);
public void Write(object obj);
public void Write(string s);
public void WriteFile(IntPtr fileHandle, long offset, long size);
public void WriteFile(string filename);
public void WriteFile(string filename, bool readIntoMemory);
public void WriteFile(string filename, long offset, long size);
}
```

Returned By   HttpApplication.Response, HttpContext.Response, System.Web.UI.Page.Response, System. Web.UI.UserControl.Response

Passed To   HttpContext.HttpContext( )

HttpRuntime

System.Web (system.web.dll)   sealed class

The HttpRuntime class provides ASP.NET runtime services and is used transparently by the ASP.NET framework. In some rare cases, you may want to use it. For example, you can use the ProcessRequest( ) static (shared) method to process an ASP.NET request outside of Internet Information Server and Close( ) to clear the cache and shut down the Common Language Runtime.

```
public sealed class HttpRuntime {
// Public Constructors
 public HttpRuntime( );
// Public Static Properties
 public static string AppDomainAppId{get; }
 public static string AppDomainAppPath{get; }
 public static string AppDomainAppVirtualPath{get; }
 public static string AppDomainId{get; }
 public static string AspInstallDirectory{get; }
 public static string BinDirectory{get; }
 public static Cache Cache{get; }
 public static string ClrInstallDirectory{get; }
```

```
public static string CodegenDir{get; }
public static bool IsOnUNCShare{get; }
public static string MachineConfigurationDirectory{get; }
// Public Static Methods
public static void Close( );
public static void ProcessRequest(HttpWorkerRequest wr);
public static void UnloadAppDomain( );
}
```

HttpServerUtility

System.Web (system.web.dll)   sealed class

This class provides helper methods and is available through the built-in Server object. It provides the useful UrlEncode( ) method, which converts a string into a form suitable for use as a query string variable, and the HtmlEncode( ) method, which converts nonlegal HTML characters in a string into the equivalent HTML entity (i.e., "<" is converted to <) so they can be displayed on a page. Some ASP.NET web controls (like buttons) do not require this conversion, but label controls do. You may need to use the HtmlEncode( ) method manually if you bind a field with URL information from a database. It also always a good idea to use HtmlEncode( ) before displaying user-supplied content to prevent possible script injection attacks.

The HttpServerUtility class provides the MapPath( ) method, which takes a string representing a virtual path and returns the real (physical) path (for example, it could convert "/myapp/index.html" to "E:\Inetpub\wwwroot\myapp\index.html"). It also provides a CreateObject( ) method for instantiating a COM object by using its ProgID (i.e., objInfo=Server.CreateObject ("MSWC.MyInfo");) and the two flow control methods Execute( ) and Transfer( ). The Execute( ) method, which runs the script in a separate ASP.NET page and then returns control to the current page, is rarely used in class-based ASP.NET programming. The Transfer( ) method halts the execution of the current page and transfers execution to the specified page. It is similar to the HttpResponse.Redirect( ) method, but does not require a roundtrip to the client and back and cannot transfer execution to a page on another server (or from an ASP.NET page to an ASP page).

```
public sealed class HttpServerUtility {
// Public Instance Properties
public string MachineName{get; }
public int ScriptTimeout{set; get; }
// Public Instance Methods
public void ClearError( );
public object CreateObject(string progID);
public object CreateObject(Type type);
public object CreateObjectFromClsid(string clsid);
public void Execute(string path);
public void Execute(string path, System.IO.TextWriter writer);
public Exception GetLastError( );
public string HtmlDecode(string s);
public void HtmlDecode(string s, System.IO.TextWriter output);
public string HtmlEncode( string s);
public void HtmlEncode(string s, System.IO.TextWriter output);
public string MapPath(string path);
public void Transfer(string path);
```

```
public void Transfer(string path, bool preserveForm);
public string UrlDecode(string s);
public void UrlDecode(string s, System.IO.TextWriter output);
public string UrlEncode(string s);
public void UrlEncode(string s, System.IO.TextWriter output);
public string UrlPathEncode(string s);
}
```

Returned By   HttpApplication.Server, HttpContext.Server, System.Web.Services.WebService.Server,
                    System.Web.UI.Page.Server, System.Web.UI.UserControl.Server

HttpStaticObjectsCollection

System.Web (system.web.dll)   sealed class

This class provides an immutable name/value collection of objects that is used for the
HttpApplicationState.StaticObjects and System.Web.SessionState.HttpSessionState.StaticObjects collections.

```
public sealed class HttpStaticObjectsCollection : ICollection, IEnumerable {
// Public Constructors
  public HttpStaticObjectsCollection( );
// Public Instance Properties
  public int Count{get; }                                          // implements ICollection
  public bool IsReadOnly{get; }
  public bool IsSynchronized{get; }                                // implements ICollection
  public object SyncRoot{get; }                                    // implements ICollection
  public object this[ string name ]{get; }
// Public Instance Methods
  public void CopyTo(Array array, int index);                      // implements ICollection
  public IEnumerator GetEnumerator( );                             // implements IEnumerable
  public object GetObject(string name);
}
```

Returned By   HttpApplicationState.StaticObjects, System.Web.SessionState.HttpSessionState.StaticObjects

HttpUnhandledException

System.Web (system.web.dll)   sealed class

This class represents a generic HTTP exception.

```
public sealed class HttpUnhandledException : HttpException {
// No public or protected members
}
```

Hierarchy   System.Object → System.Exception(System.Runtime.Serialization.ISerializable) → System.
                   SystemException → System.Runtime.InteropServices.ExternalException → HttpException
                   → HttpUnhandledException

HttpUtility

System.Web (system.web.dll)   sealed class

This class provides static (shared) helper methods. The UrlEncode( ) and UrlDecode( ) methods are the same as those provided by the HttpServerUtility class for encoding a string into a format that's safe for use in a URL. Additionally, a UrlEncodeToBytes( ) method is provided to convert a string into an array of bytes and a UrlEncodeUnicode( ) method to convert a string into a Unicode string.

```
public sealed class HttpUtility {
// Public Constructors
  public HttpUtility( );
// Public Static Methods
  public static string HtmlAttributeEncode(string s);
  public static void HtmlAttributeEncode(string s, System.IO.TextWriter output);
  public static string HtmlDecode(string s);
  public static void HtmlDecode(string s, System.IO.TextWriter output);
  public static string HtmlEncode(string s);
  public static void HtmlEncode(string s, System.IO.TextWriter output);
  public static string UrlDecode(byte[ ] bytes, System.Text.Encoding e);
  public static string UrlDecode(byte[ ] bytes, int offset, int count, System.Text.Encoding e);
  public static string UrlDecode(string str);
  public static string UrlDecode(string str, System.Text.Encoding e);
  public static byte[ ] UrlDecodeToBytes( byte[ ] bytes);
  public static byte[ ] UrlDecodeToBytes(byte[ ] bytes, int offset, int count);
  public static byte[ ] UrlDecodeToBytes( string str);
  public static byte[ ] UrlDecodeToBytes(string str, System.Text.Encoding e);
  public static string UrlEncode( byte[ ] bytes);
  public static string UrlEncode(byte[ ] bytes, int offset, int count);
  public static string UrlEncode(string str);
  public static string UrlEncode(string str, System.Text.Encoding e);
  public static byte[ ] UrlEncodeToBytes(byte[ ] bytes);
  public static byte[ ] UrlEncodeToBytes(byte[ ] bytes, int offset, int count);
  public static byte[ ] UrlEncodeToBytes(string str);
  public static byte[ ] UrlEncodeToBytes(string str, System.Text.Encoding e);
  public static string UrlEncodeUnicode(string str);
  public static byte[ ] UrlEncodeUnicodeToBytes(string str);
  public static string UrlPathEncode(string str);
}
```

HttpValidationStatus   serializable

System.Web (system.web.dll)   enum

This enumeration is used by the HttpCacheValidateHandler delegate. It allows you to specify whether a cached page should remain valid or be invalidated (and then recreated).

```
public enum HttpValidationStatus {
  Invalid = 1,
  IgnoreThisRequest = 2,
  Valid = 3
}
```

Hierarchy	System.Object → System.ValueType → System.Enum(System.IComparable, System.IFormattable, System.IConvertible) → HttpValidationStatus
Passed To	HttpCacheValidateHandler.{BeginInvoke( ), EndInvoke( ), Invoke( )}

HttpWorkerRequest

System.Web (system.web.dll)   abstract class

This abstract class defines the base worker methods and enumerations used for request processing by the ASP.NET engine. It is used by the HttpContext constructor and the ProcessRequest( ) method of the HttpRuntime class. You will not need to use it directly in your code because ASP.NET provides higher-level objects like HttpResponse and HttpRequest. However, you can use the System.Web.Hosting.SimpleWorkerRequest class, which extends HttpWorkerRequest and allows you to host ASP.NET outside of IIS.

```
public abstract class HttpWorkerRequest : IHttpMapPath {
// Public Constructors
  public HttpWorkerRequest( );
// Public Static Fields
  public const int HeaderAccept;                                          // =20
  public const int HeaderAcceptCharset;                                   // =21
  public const int HeaderAcceptEncoding;                                  // =22
  public const int HeaderAcceptLanguage;                                  // =23
  public const int HeaderAcceptRanges;                                    // =20
  public const int HeaderAge;                                             // =21
  public const int HeaderAllow;                                           // =10
  public const int HeaderAuthorization;                                   // =24
  public const int HeaderCacheControl;                                    // =0
  public const int HeaderConnection;                                      // =1
  public const int HeaderContentEncoding;                                 // =13
  public const int HeaderContentLanguage;                                 // =14
  public const int HeaderContentLength;                                   // =11
  public const int HeaderContentLocation;                                 // =15
  public const int HeaderContentMd5;                                      // =16
  public const int HeaderContentRange;                                    // =17
  public const int HeaderContentType;                                     // =12
  public const int HeaderCookie;                                          // =25
  public const int HeaderDate;                                            // =2
  public const int HeaderEtag;                                            // =22
  public const int HeaderExpect;                                          // =26
  public const int HeaderExpires;                                         // =18
  public const int HeaderFrom;                                            // =27
  public const int HeaderHost;                                            // =28
  public const int HeaderIfMatch;                                         // =29
  public const int HeaderIfModifiedSince;                                 // =30
  public const int HeaderIfNoneMatch;                                     // =31
  public const int HeaderIfRange;                                         // =32
  public const int HeaderIfUnmodifiedSince;                               // =33
  public const int HeaderKeepAlive;                                       // =3
  public const int HeaderLastModified;                                    // =19
  public const int HeaderLocation;                                        // =23
  public const int HeaderMaxForwards;                                     // =34
```

```
public const int HeaderPragma;                                           // =4
public const int HeaderProxyAuthenticate;                                // =24
public const int HeaderProxyAuthorization;                               // =35
public const int HeaderRange;                                            // =37
public const int HeaderReferer;                                          // =36
public const int HeaderRetryAfter;                                       // =25
public const int HeaderServer;                                           // =26
public const int HeaderSetCookie;                                        // =27
public const int HeaderTe;                                               // =38
public const int HeaderTrailer;                                          // =5
public const int HeaderTransferEncoding;                                 // =6
public const int HeaderUpgrade;                                          // =7
public const int HeaderUserAgent;                                        // =39
public const int HeaderVary;                                             // =28
public const int HeaderVia;                                              // =8
public const int HeaderWarning;                                          // =9
public const int HeaderWwwAuthenticate;                                  // =29
public const int ReasonCachePolicy;                                      // =2
public const int ReasonCacheSecurity;                                    // =3
public const int ReasonClientDisconnect;                                 // =4
public const int ReasonDefault;                                          // =0
public const int ReasonFileHandleCacheMiss;                              // =1
public const int ReasonResponseCacheMiss;                                // =0
public const int RequestHeaderMaximum;                                   // =40
public const int ResponseHeaderMaximum;                                  // =30
```
// Public Instance Properties
```
public virtual string MachineConfigPath{get; }              // implements IHttpMapPath
public virtual string MachineInstallDirectory{get; }
```
// Public Static Methods
```
public static int GetKnownRequestHeaderIndex(string header);
public static string GetKnownRequestHeaderName(int index);
public static int GetKnownResponseHeaderIndex(string header);
public static string GetKnownResponseHeaderName(int index);
public static string GetStatusDescription(int code);
```
// Public Instance Methods
```
public virtual void CloseConnection( );
public abstract void EndOfRequest( );
public abstract void FlushResponse(bool finalFlush);
public virtual string GetAppPath( );
public virtual string GetAppPathTranslated( );
public virtual string GetAppPoolID( );
public virtual long GetBytesRead( );
public virtual byte[ ] GetClientCertificate( );
public virtual byte[ ] GetClientCertificateBinaryIssuer( );
public virtual int GetClientCertificateEncoding( );
public virtual byte[ ] GetClientCertificatePublicKey( );
public virtual DateTime GetClientCertificateValidFrom( );
public virtual DateTime GetClientCertificateValidUntil( );
public virtual long GetConnectionID( );
public virtual string GetFilePath( );
public virtual string GetFilePathTranslated( );
```

```
    public abstract string GetHttpVerbName( );
    public abstract string GetHttpVersion( );
    public virtual string GetKnownRequestHeader(int index);
    public abstract string GetLocalAddress( );
    public abstract int GetLocalPort( );
    public virtual string GetPathInfo( );
    public virtual byte[ ] GetPreloadedEntityBody( );
    public virtual string GetProtocol( );
    public abstract string GetQueryString( );
    public virtual byte[ ] GetQueryStringRawBytes( );
    public abstract string GetRawUrl( );
    public abstract string GetRemoteAddress( );
    public virtual string GetRemoteName( );
    public abstract int GetRemotePort( );
    public virtual int GetRequestReason( );
    public virtual string GetServerName( );
    public virtual string GetServerVariable(string name);
    public virtual string GetUnknownRequestHeader(string name);
    public virtual string[ ][ ] GetUnknownRequestHeaders( );
    public abstract string GetUriPath( );
    public virtual long GetUrlContextID( );
    public virtual IntPtr GetUserToken( );
    public virtual IntPtr GetVirtualPathToken( );
    public bool HasEntityBody( );
    public virtual bool HeadersSent( );
    public virtual bool IsClientConnected( );
    public virtual bool IsEntireEntityBodyIsPreloaded( );
    public virtual bool IsSecure( );
    public virtual string MapPath(string virtualPath);                          // implements IHttpMapPath
    public virtual int ReadEntityBody(byte[ ] buffer, int size);
    public virtual void SendCalculatedContentLength(int contentLength);
    public abstract void SendKnownResponseHeader(int index, string value);
    public abstract void SendResponseFromFile(IntPtr handle, long offset, long length);
    public abstract void SendResponseFromFile(string filename, long offset, long length);
    public abstract void SendResponseFromMemory(byte[ ] data, int length);
    public virtual void SendResponseFromMemory(IntPtr data, int length);
    public abstract void SendStatus(int statusCode, string statusDescription);
    public abstract void SendUnknownResponseHeader(string name, string value);
    public virtual void SetEndOfSendNotification(EndOfSendNotification callback, object extraData);
}
```

Subclasses   System.Web.Hosting.SimpleWorkerRequest

Passed To   HttpContext.HttpContext( ), HttpRuntime.ProcessRequest( ), EndOfSendNotification.
                    {BeginInvoke( ), Invoke( )}

HttpWorkerRequest.EndOfSendNotification   serializable

System.Web (system.web.dll)   delegate

This delegate is used by the SetEndOfSendNotification( ) method of the HttpWorkerRequest class.

```
public delegate void HttpWorkerRequest.EndOfSendNotification(HttpWorkerRequest wr, object extraData);
```

HttpWriter

marshal by reference, disposable

System.Web (system.web.dll)   sealed class

This is the System.IO.TextWriter object that is used to write directly to an HTTP output stream. It is used internally by the Write() method of the HttpResponse class.

```
public sealed class HttpWriter : System.IO.TextWriter {
// Public Instance Properties
  public override Encoding Encoding{get; }                          // overrides System.IO.TextWriter
  public Stream OutputStream{get; }
// Public Instance Methods
  public override void Close( );                                    // overrides System.IO.TextWriter
  public override void Flush( );                                    // overrides System.IO.TextWriter
  public override void Write(char ch);                             // overrides System.IO.TextWriter
  public override void Write(char[ ] buffer, int index, int count); // overrides System.IO.TextWriter
  public override void Write( object obj);                         // overrides System.IO.TextWriter
  public override void Write( string s);                           // overrides System.IO.TextWriter
  public void WriteBytes(byte[ ] buffer, int index, int count);
  public override void WriteLine( );                               // overrides System.IO.TextWriter
  public void WriteString(string s, int index, int count);
}
```

Hierarchy   System.Object → System.MarshalByRefObject → System.IO.TextWriter(System.IDisposable) → HttpWriter

IHttpAsyncHandler

System.Web (system.web.dll)   interface

This interface is implemented by the HttpApplication class and defines the requirements for asynchronous processing. It is an integral part of the ASP.NET framework and is not used directly by ASP.NET application code.

```
public interface IHttpAsyncHandler : IHttpHandler {
// Public Instance Methods
  public IAsyncResult BeginProcessRequest(HttpContext context, AsyncCallback cb, object extraData);
  public void EndProcessRequest(IAsyncResult result);
}
```

Implemented By HttpApplication

IHttpHandler

System.Web (system.web.dll)   interface

This interface is required to process HTTP requests. It's implemented by the System.Web.UI.Page and HttpApplication classes, but you can use IHttpHandler to create a custom HttpHandler for a lower-level programming model. You can still access the HttpContext object (and, through its properties, built in objects like HttpRequest and HttpResponse), but you cannot use the higher-level Page abstraction. Common uses of handlers include filters and CGI-like applications, especially those returning binary data.

When using the IHttpHandler interface, you must implement the ProcessRequest() method and IsReusable property. The ProcessRequest() method receives an HttpContext object, which

System.Web
Namespace

gives you access to ASP.NET's built-in objects. Use the IsReusable property to declare whether a single instance of your handler can serve multiple requests.

You will also need to modify <httphandlers> section of the *web.config* file to make your custom handler a target for HTTP requests. You can map requests based on the requested page, file type, or HTTP method (GET, PUT, or POST). If you want to create a handler that can process all requests, you should create a custom HttpModule using the IHttpModule interface.

```
public interface IHttpHandler {
// Public Instance Properties
   public bool IsReusable{get; }
// Public Instance Methods
   public void ProcessRequest( HttpContext context);
}
```

Implemented By   HttpApplication, IHttpAsyncHandler, System.Web.Services.Discovery.DiscoveryRequest-Handler, System.Web.UI.Page

Returned By   HttpContext.Handler, IHttpHandlerFactory.GetHandler( ), System.Web.Services.Protocols. WebServiceHandlerFactory.GetHandler( ), System.Web.UI.PageParser. GetCompiledPageInstance( )

Passed To   HttpContext.Handler, IHttpHandlerFactory.ReleaseHandler( ), System.Web.Services.Protocols. WebServiceHandlerFactory.ReleaseHandler( )

IHttpHandlerFactory

System.Web (system.web.dll)   interface

You can implement this interface to create a factory class that can create IHttpHandler instances dynamically. ASP.NET includes standard IHttpHandlerFactory classes like PageHandlerFactory, RestrictedResourceFactory, and WebServiceHandlerFactory (which are not shown in the class library documentation because they are private types).

Using the <httphandlers> section of the *web.config* file, you can map specific requests to directly to an IHttpHandler class or to an IHttpHandlerFactory class, which will dynamically create an appropriate IHttpHandler class by using the GetHandler( ) method.

Note that the standard factory classes used by ASP.NET do not appear in the MSDN help or this reference. These classes are marked Private and are used exclusively by the ASP.NET framework.

```
public interface IHttpHandlerFactory {
// Public Instance Methods
   public IHttpHandler GetHandler(HttpContext context, string requestType, string url, string pathTranslated);
   public void ReleaseHandler( IHttpHandler handler);
}
```

Implemented By   System.Web.Services.Protocols.WebServiceHandlerFactory

IHttpModule

System.Web (system.web.dll)   interface

You can use this interface to create custom HttpModules. HttpModules are added through the <httpmodules> section of the *web.config* file. Some HttpModules that are available to you include FormsAuthenticationModule, PassportAuthenticationModule, and other security modules in the System.Web.Security namespace.

HttpModules are often used for security or logging because they can participate in the processing of every request into an application. HttpModules work by reacting to ASP.NET events. For example, if you want an HttpModule to participate in every web request, you could react to the HttpApplication.BeginRequest event. You can also specify that a HttpModule process other files (for example, JPEG and BMP) rather than just ASP.NET file types by updating the Application Extension Mapping to use *aspnet_ISAPI.dll* to manage the appropriate extension.

```
public interface IHttpModule {
// Public Instance Methods
   public void Dispose( );
   public void Init( HttpApplication context);
}
```

Implemented By   System.Web.Mobile.ErrorHandlerModule, System.Web.Security.{DefaultAuthentication-
                     Module, FileAuthorizationModule, FormsAuthenticationModule,
                     PassportAuthenticationModule, UrlAuthorizationModule, WindowsAuthenticationModule},
                     System.Web.SessionState.SessionStateModule

Returned By   HttpModuleCollection.{Get( ), this}

ProcessInfo

System.Web (system.web.dll)   class

This class encapsulates information about the ASP.NET worker process on the server. It is returned by the ProcessModelInfo class. It includes properties such as the time the process started (StartTime), how long it has been running (Age), and the most memory used so far in bytes (PeakMemoryUsed). The Status property indicates the current state of a process; the ShutdownReason property indicates why the process was terminated, unless it is the current process.

```
public class ProcessInfo {
// Public Constructors
   public ProcessInfo( );
   public ProcessInfo(DateTime startTime, TimeSpan age, int processID, int requestCount, ProcessStatus status,
      ProcessShutdownReason shutdownReason, int peakMemoryUsed);
// Public Instance Properties
   public TimeSpan Age{get; }
   public int PeakMemoryUsed{get; }
   public int ProcessID{get; }
   public int RequestCount{get; }
   public ProcessShutdownReason ShutdownReason{get; }
   public DateTime StartTime{get; }
   public ProcessStatus Status{get; }
```

```
// Public Instance Methods
  public void SetAll(DateTime startTime, TimeSpan age, int processID, int requestCount, ProcessStatus status,
    ProcessShutdownReason shutdownReason, int peakMemoryUsed);
}
```

Returned By   ProcessModelInfo.{GetCurrentProcessInfo( ), GetHistory( )}

ProcessModelInfo

System.Web (system.web.dll)   class

ASP.NET includes automated features for restarting a process when memory leaks or
crashes occur. This class allows you to retrieve information about how the ASP.NET
worker process is performing, along with the history of approximately the last 100
process restarts (a process restart may be in response to an unrecoverble error, blocked
thread, or just automatic maintaince when a certain time or memory threshold is
reached, according to *machine.config* settings). This gives you a basic idea about the
health of your web application and the ASP.NET service.

You can use the static (shared) GetCurrentProcessInfo( ) method to retrieve a ProcessInfo object
representing the current process. You can also use the static GetHistory( ) method and
supply the number of ProcessInfo objects that you want as an argument. The method will
return an array of ProcessInfo objects, starting with the most recent (current) process.

```
public class ProcessModelInfo {
// Public Constructors
  public ProcessModelInfo( );
// Public Static Methods
  public static ProcessInfo GetCurrentProcessInfo( );
  public static ProcessInfo[ ] GetHistory( int numRecords);
}
```

ProcessShutdownReason   serializable

System.Web (system.web.dll)   enum

This enumeration defines constants used by the ProcessInfo class that indicate the reason
a process was ended (or None if it is the current process).

```
public enum ProcessShutdownReason {
  None = 0,
  Unexpected = 1,
  RequestsLimit = 2,
  RequestQueueLimit = 3,
  Timeout = 4,
  IdleTimeout = 5,
  MemoryLimitExceeded = 6,
  PingFailed = 7,
  DeadlockSuspected = 8
}
```

Hierarchy   System.Object → System.ValueType → System.Enum(System.IComparable, System.IFor-
             mattable, System.IConvertible) → ProcessShutdownReason

---

512 | Chapter 23: The System.Web Namespace

ProcessInfo.ShutdownReason

ProcessInfo.{ProcessInfo( ), SetAll( )}

ProcessStatus

serializable

System.Web (system.web.dll)

enum

This enumeration is used by the ProcessInfo class to indicate the status of a process.

```
public enum ProcessStatus {
  Alive = 1,
  ShuttingDown = 2,
  ShutDown = 3,
  Terminated = 4
}
```

Hierarchy   System.Object → System.ValueType → System.Enum(System.IComparable, System.IFormattable, System.IConvertible) → ProcessStatus

Returned By   ProcessInfo.Status

Passed To   ProcessInfo.{ProcessInfo( ), SetAll( )}

TraceContext

System.Web (system.web.dll)

sealed class

The TraceContext class allows you display trace messages that can help you debug ASP.NET applications. To enable tracing for a specific page, insert the page directive Trace="True" in the ASPX file or set the IsEnabled property of the TraceContext class in your code-behind module.

The TraceContext class provides two methods: Write( ) and Warn( ). Both display a message in the current page's trace log, but Warn( ) uses red lettering that is meant to indicate exception information. You can invoke the Write( ) or Warn( ) method with a category string and message string. Often, the category string indicates the position in the code ("In FunctionA"), while the message string indicates specific information ("Exception while opening database"). Additionally, an overloaded version of Write( ) and Warn( ) allows you supply an exception object that ASP.NET will use to extract the appropriate information. Even if you don't use the Write( ) and Warn( ) methods, ASP.NET automatically inserts trace log entries to indicate standard events, and appends a great deal of information after the list of trace message, including performance data, tree-structure information, and state management content.

The TraceContext class is provided as the built-in Trace object. You can use the *web.config* file to set additional tracing options like the default TraceMode, and enable application-wide tracing. Application-wide tracing can be displayed on the page or cached exclusively in memory.

```
public sealed class TraceContext {
// Public Constructors
  public TraceContext( HttpContext context);
// Public Instance Properties
```

```
public bool IsEnabled{set; get; }
public TraceMode TraceMode{set; get; }
// Public Instance Methods
public void Warn(string message);
public void Warn(string category, string message);
public void Warn(string category, string message, Exception errorInfo);
public void Write(string message);
public void Write(string category, string message);
public void Write(string category, string message, Exception errorInfo);
}
```

Returned By   HttpContext.Trace, System.Web.UI.Page.Trace, System.Web.UI.UserControl.Trace

TraceMode   serializable

System.Web (system.web.dll)   enum

This enumeration is used to set the TraceMode property of the TraceContext class. It specifies whether entries in the trace log will be listed alphabetically (SortByCategory) or chronologically (SortByTime).

```
public enum TraceMode {
  SortByTime = 0,
  SortByCategory = 1,
  Default = 2
}
```

Hierarchy   System.Object → System.ValueType → System.Enum(System.IComparable, System.IFormattable, System.IConvertible) → TraceMode

Returned By   TraceContext.TraceMode

Passed To   TraceContext.TraceMode, System.Web.UI.Page.TraceModeValue

24

The System.Web.Caching Namespace

The System.Web.Caching namespace includes types used for ASP.NET data caching. The Cache class is the focal point of this namespace; it contains a collection of cached objects and allows you to set expiration policies and dependencies for each item in the cache. The CacheDependency class encapsulates a cache dependency and allows you to link the validity of a cache item to another item or a file on the web server. The CacheItemRemovedCallback delegate allows you to respond when an object is dropped from the cache. Both types work in conjunction with the Cache class. Together, they allow you to implement sophisticated data caching. Figure 24-1 shows the types in this namespace.

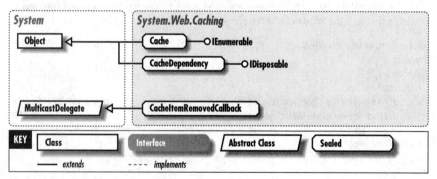

Figure 24-1. The System.Web.Caching namespace

ASP.NET also supports page caching, which stores entire compiled pages for automatic reuse. To configure settings for page caching, you must use the System.Web.HttpCachePolicy class.

Cache

System.Web.Caching (system.web.dll)   sealed class

The Cache class allows your application to use data caching. The Cache class works by exposing a name/value collection where you can store objects that are expensive to create or frequently used. Its use is analogous to the System.Web.HttpApplicationState class, although you use the System.Web.HttpApplicationState to store information that must be retained for long periods of time and the Cache class for volatile objects that may quickly expire and can be dropped automatically when memory declines.

Much like the System.Web.HttpApplicationState class, the Cache class is globally accessible to all clients on a single web server, persists for the lifetime of the ASP.NET application, and has only one instance per application. Unlike the System.Web.HttpApplicationState class, the Cache class is intrinsically thread-safe.

You can add items to the cache as you would with other state collections like System.Web.HttpApplicationState (for example, Cache["myobject"] = dsData;). However, using the overloaded Insert() method allows much more control. For example, you can set an absolute expiration policy in which an item will be removed after a specified time (Cache.Insert("Data", dsData, null, DateTime.Now.AddMinutes(10), NoSlidingExpiration;) or a sliding expiration policy in which an item will be removed after a specified interval of disuse (Cache.Insert("Data", dsData, Nothing, NoAbsoluteExpiration, TimeSpan.FromMinutes(10);). Note that the NoAbsoluteExpiration and NoSlidingExpiration fields from the Cache class allow you to disable the type of caching you don't want to use. Attempts to retrieve a removed cached item will return Nothing (or null).

You can also use a version of the Insert() method with additional parameters for setting cache dependencies (by supplying an instance of a CacheDependency class), priorities (by using the CacheItemPriority enumeration), and a callback (by supplying a CacheItemRemovedCallback delegate).

The Cache class is available through the built-in Cache object and shouldn't be confused with the System.Web.HttpCachePolicy class, which is used to configure page caching and is available through the Response.Cache reference.

```
public sealed class Cache : IEnumerable {
// Public Constructors
  public Cache( );
// Public Static Fields
  public static readonly DateTime NoAbsoluteExpiration;                  // =12/31/9999 11:59:59 PM
  public static readonly TimeSpan NoSlidingExpiration;                   // =00:00:00
// Public Instance Properties
  public int Count{get; }
  public object this[ string key ]{set; get; }
// Public Instance Methods
  public object Add(string key, object value, CacheDependency dependencies, DateTime absoluteExpiration,
    TimeSpan slidingExpiration, CacheItemPriority priority, CacheItemRemovedCallback onRemoveCallback);
  public object Get( string key);
  public IDictionaryEnumerator GetEnumerator( );
  public void Insert( string key, object value);
  public void Insert(string key, object value, CacheDependency dependencies);
  public void Insert(string key, object value, CacheDependency dependencies, DateTime absoluteExpiration,
    TimeSpan slidingExpiration);
```

```
public void Insert(string key, object value, CacheDependency dependencies, DateTime absoluteExpiration, TimeSpan
    slidingExpiration, CacheItemPriority priority, CacheItemRemovedCallback onRemoveCallback);
public object Remove( string key);
}
```

Returned By

System.Web.HttpContext.Cache, System.Web.HttpRuntime.Cache, System.Web.UI.Page.Cache, System.Web.UI.UserControl.Cache

CacheDependency   disposable

System.Web.Caching (system.web.dll)   sealed class

Cache dependencies allow the validity of a cache item to be based on a file or directory on the web server, or on another cache item. When the dependency object changes, the dependent cache item is invalidated and removed automatically. To set up a dependency, you first create a CacheDependency object that references the file, directory, or cache item upon which the dependency will be based. You then use the Cache.Insert( ) method to add the dependent cache item, with the CacheDependency object supplied as a parameter.

The overloaded constructor of the CacheDependency class determines the type of dependency. You can pass a single string argument to set up a dependency on a file or directory (CacheDependency(Server.MapPath("data.xml")) or you can use a second string argument with the key of another cache item (CacheDependency(Nothing, "MyData")). Other versions of the constructor allow you to specify an array of strings specifying files or cache objects. If any one file or object changes, the dependent cache item will be invalidated.

The CacheDependency object begins to monitor for changes as soon as it is created to account for changes that may occur in the brief delay before the dependent cache item is added to the Cache class.

```
public sealed class CacheDependency : IDisposable {
// Public Constructors
  public CacheDependency( string filename);
  public CacheDependency( string[ ] filenames);
  public CacheDependency(string[ ] filenames, DateTime start);
  public CacheDependency(string[ ] filenames, string[ ] cachekeys);
  public CacheDependency(string[ ] filenames, string[ ] cachekeys, CacheDependency dependency);
  public CacheDependency(string[ ] filenames, string[ ] cachekeys, CacheDependency dependency, DateTime start);
  public CacheDependency(string[ ] filenames, string[ ] cachekeys, DateTime start);
  public CacheDependency( string filename, DateTime start);
// Public Instance Properties
  public bool HasChanged{get; }
// Public Instance Methods
  public void Dispose( );                                                          // implements IDisposable
}
```

Returned By   System.Web.UI.BasePartialCachingControl.Dependency

Passed To   Cache.{Add( ), Insert( )}, System.Web.UI.BasePartialCachingControl.Dependency

CacheItemPriority

System.Web.Caching (system.web.dll)

Priorities are hints that can optimize cache scavenging. Essentially, if the ASP.NET engine decides to remove cache items because memory is scarce, it will remove items with a lower priority cost first. The CacheItemPriority enumeration also includes a NotRemovable member that you can use to prevent ASP.NET from removing an object from the cache automatically when memory is low.

```
public enum CacheItemPriority {
    Low = 1,
    BelowNormal = 2,
    Normal = 3,
    Default = 3,
    AboveNormal = 4,
    High = 5,
    NotRemovable = 6
}
```

Hierarchy   System.Object → System.ValueType → System.Enum(System.IComparable, System.IFormattable, System.IConvertible) → CacheItemPriority

Passed To   Cache.{Add( ), Insert( )}

CacheItemRemovedCallback

System.Web.Caching (system.web.dll)

Functions with the CacheItemRemovedCallback signature can be used to respond to the onRemoveCallback when an item is dropped from the cache. For example, this could allow you to perform related cleanup tasks. You are provided with the cache object, its key, and the reason why it was removed (using the CacheItemRemovedReason enumeration).

To specify that a given method should be used for the onRemoveCallback, create a CacheItemRemovedCallback delegate that points to the method, and pass it as an argument to the Cache.Insert( ) method.

```
public delegate void CacheItemRemovedCallback(string key, object value, CacheItemRemovedReason reason);
```

Passed To   Cache.{Add( ), Insert( )}

CacheItemRemovedReason

System.Web.Caching (system.web.dll)

If you have set a callback to occur when a cached item is removed, you will be provided with a CacheItemRemovedReason argument. The CacheItemRemovedReason will be Expired if the sliding or absolute expiration time interval passed, Removed if the object was removed programmatically with the Cache.Remove( ) method or by an Cache.Insert( ) method with the same key, DependencyChanged if the object was invalidated because of a dependency, or Underused if it has been removed to free memory.

```
public enum CacheItemRemovedReason {
    Removed = 1,
```

```
  Expired = 2,
  Underused = 3,
  DependencyChanged = 4
}
```

Hierarchy   System.Object → System.ValueType → System.Enum(System.IComparable, System.IFor-
                 mattable, System.IConvertible) → CacheItemRemovedReason

Passed To   CacheItemRemovedCallback.{BeginInvoke( ), Invoke( )}

25

The System.Web.
Configuration Namespace

The System.Web.Configuration namespace includes a few miscellaneous types used in ASP.NET configuration with the *web.config* file; AuthenticationMode, FormsAuthPassword-Format, and FormsProtectionEnum are all involved in ASP.NET security services. It also provides a ClientTargetSectionHandler class, which provides the basic functionality for processing tags in the *web.config* file, and HttpCapabilitiesBase, which stores a collection of client browser information used by the System.Web.HttpBrowserCapabilities class. Figure 25-1 shows the types in this namespace.

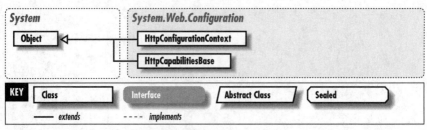

Figure 25-1. The System.Web.Configuration namespace

If you've explored the *machine.config* file, you have probably noticed that there are many other types referenced there that don't appear in this class library reference or the MSDN (including configuration types like HttpCapabilitiesSectionHandler and AuthenticationConfigHandler). These private types aren't available to the client programmer and are part of the low-level ASP.NET infrastructure.

AuthenticationMode   serializable

System.Web.Configuration (system.web.dll)   enum

This enumeration can be used to specify the type of ASP.NET authentication. It is not used in ASP.NET code, but it is used internally by the ASP.NET runtime. You can indicate the AuthenticationMode for an application using the *web.config* file by setting the mode attribute in the authentication tag (for example, <authentication mode="Forms">). The authentication mode you select determines which HttpModule from the System.Web.Security namespace is used to validate a user's credentials.

```
public enum AuthenticationMode {
  None = 0,
  Windows = 1,
  Passport = 2,
  Forms = 3
}
```

Hierarchy   System.Object → System.ValueType → System.Enum(System.IComparable, System.IFormattable, System.IConvertible) → AuthenticationMode

ClientTargetSectionHandler

System.Web.Configuration (system.web.dll)   sealed class

ASP.NET delegates the processing of *web.config* data to configuration section handlers. Section handlers are declared in the *web.config* file using "add" directives inside the <configsections> element. Each element identifies a specific section of configuration data, and the associated System.Configuration.IConfigurationSectionHandler class that is used to process it. By inheriting from this class, you could create your own custom section handler. Note that you do not need to create your own custom section handler just to add application-specific constants to your *web.config* file; these constants can be added to the <appSettings> section and retrieved through the System.Configuration.ConfigurationSettings class.

```
sealed class ClientTargetSectionHandler : System.Configuration.IConfigurationSectionHandler {
// Public Instance Methods
  public object Create(object parent, object configContextObj,
    System.Xml.XmlNode section);              // implements System.Configuration.IConfigurationSectionHandler
}
```

FormsAuthPasswordFormat   serializable

System.Web.Configuration (system.web.dll)   enum

This enumeration specifies the format that ASP.NET uses for encrypting passwords (if you are using Forms Authentication and the System.Web.Security.FormsAuthenticationModule). It is not used in ASP.NET code, but in the *web.config* file by the passwordFormat attribute in the <credentials> element (for example, <credentials passwordFormat="Clear">). When using any format other than clear, the user's password is hashed with an appropriate algorithm and compared to the value stored in the *web.config* file each time authentication is performed. No matter what encryption you use for the password, usernames will still be transmitted in clear text.

```
public enum FormsAuthPasswordFormat {
  Clear = 0,
  SHA1 = 1,
  MD5 = 2
}
```

Hierarchy   System.Object → System.ValueType → System.Enum(System.IComparable, System.IFormattable, System.IConvertible) → FormsAuthPasswordFormat

Configuration
Namespace

FormsProtectionEnum

serializable

System.Web.Configuration (system.web.dll)

enum

This enumeration specifies how ASP.NET protects the Forms Authentication cookie. It is not used in ASP.NET code, but in the *web.config* file by the protection attribute of the forms element (for example, <forms name="name" loginUrl="url" protection="None ">). Encryption uses Triple-DES or DES to encode the cookie before it is transmitted. Validation verifies the cookie hasn't been altered in transit by appending a validation key and then a Message Authentication Code (MAC) to the cookie.

```
public enum FormsProtectionEnum {
  All = 0,
  None = 1,
  Encryption = 2,
  Validation = 3
}
```

Hierarchy   System.Object → System.ValueType → System.Enum(System.IComparable, System.IFormattable, System.IConvertible) → FormsProtectionEnum

HttpCapabilitiesBase

System.Web.Configuration (system.web.dll)

class

This is the base class for the System.Web.HttpBrowserCapabilities class. HttpCapabilitiesBase is weakly typed with a name/value collection of browser settings. These settings are provided (more usefully) as properties by the System.Web.HttpBrowserCapabilities class.

```
public class HttpCapabilitiesBase {
// Public Constructors
  public HttpCapabilitiesBase( );
// Public Instance Properties
  public virtual string this[ string key ]{get; }
// Public Static Methods
  public static HttpCapabilitiesBase GetConfigCapabilities(string configKey, System.Web.HttpRequest request);
// Protected Instance Methods
  protected virtual void Init( );
}
```

Subclasses   System.Web.HttpBrowserCapabilities

HttpConfigurationContext

System.Web.Configuration (system.web.dll)

class

This class supplies the current context information to configuration section handlers in ASP.NET applications. The single VirtualPath property provides the path to the current *web.config* file that is evaluated, unless it is the root *web.config* for the site or the *machine.config* file is being evaluated instead (in which case it will return an empty string).

You don't need to use this class directly in your code.

```
public class HttpConfigurationContext {
// Public Instance Properties
  public string VirtualPath{get; }
}
```

26

The System.Web.Hosting
Namespace

The System.Web.Hosting namespace is not used in ASP.NET web applications; instead, it provides support for hosting the ASP.NET service outside of Internet Information Services (IIS) in a custom hosting application (which you would write using .NET). The two important classes in this namespace are ApplicationHost and SimpleWorkerRequest. The other classes provide lower-level framework support, and are not used directly in an application. Figure 26-1 shows the types in this namespace.

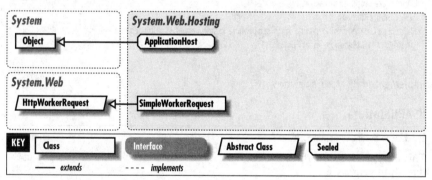

Figure 26-1. The System.Web.Hosting namespace

AppDomainFactory

System.Web.Hosting (system.web.dll)   sealed class

This class supports the .NET Framework infrastructure. You do not need to use it directly in your code.

```
public sealed class AppDomainFactory : IAppDomainFactory {
// Public Constructors
  public AppDomainFactory( );
```

```
// Public Instance Methods
   public object Create(string module, string typeName, string appID, string appPath,
      string strUrlOfAppOrigin, int iZone);                               // implements IAppDomainFactory
}
```

ApplicationHost

System.Web.Hosting (system.web.dll)   sealed class

This class exposes a single shared CreateApplicationHost( ) method, which allows you to
create an application domain that will be used to process ASP.NET requests. This
method accepts three parameters: the hostType (your request-handling class, which will
be created in the new domain), virtualDir (the virtual directory for the application
domain, such as "/MyApp"), and physicalDir (the physical directory for the application
domain where the ASP.NET pages are located, such as "c:\MyApp"). The
CreateApplicationHost( ) method returns the live instance of the hostType class.

```
public sealed class ApplicationHost {
// Public Static Methods
   public static object CreateApplicationHost(Type hostType, string virtualDir, string physicalDir);
}
```

IAppDomainFactory

System.Web.Hosting (system.web.dll)   interface

This interface supports the .NET Framework infrastructure. You do not need to use it
directly in your code.

```
public interface IAppDomainFactory {
// Public Instance Methods
   public object Create(in string module, in string typeName, in string appId, in string appPath,
      in string strUrlOfAppOrigin, in int iZone);
}
```

Implemented By AppDomainFactory

IISAPIRuntime

System.Web.Hosting (system.web.dll)   interface

This interface supports the .NET Framework infrastructure. You do not need to use it
directly in your code.

```
public interface IISAPIRuntime {
// Public Instance Methods
   public void DoGCCollect( );
   public int ProcessRequest(in IntPtr ecb, in int useProcessModel);
   public void StartProcessing( );
   public void StopProcessing( );
}
```

Implemented By ISAPIRuntime

ISAPIRuntime

System.Web.Hosting (system.web.dll)   sealed class

This class supports the .NET Framework infrastructure. You do not need to use it directly in your code.

```
public sealed class ISAPIRuntime : IISAPIRuntime {
// Public Constructors
  public ISAPIRuntime( );
// Public Instance Methods
  public void DoGCCollect( );                                              // implements IISAPIRuntime
  public int ProcessRequest(IntPtr ecb, int iWRType);                      // implements IISAPIRuntime
  public void StartProcessing( );                                          // implements IISAPIRuntime
  public void StopProcessing( );                                           // implements IISAPIRuntime
}
```

SimpleWorkerRequest

System.Web.Hosting (system.web.dll)   class

This class extends the abstract System.Web.HttpWorkerRequest class. It provides features that allow you to read the incoming HTTP request and send an appropriate HTTP response. You can retrieve the URL request with the query string appended (through GetRawUrl()), a server variable by name from a dictionary collection (GetServerVariable()), and the physical file path of the requested URL (GetFilePathTranslated()). You send a response as a series of bytes with the SendResponseFromFile() or SendResponseFromMemory() methods. Use FlushResponse() to send all pending data to the client. If you want to provide higher-level methods or properties, such as those found in the System.Web.HttpResponse and System.Web.HttpRequest classes, you should extend SimpleWorkerRequest.

```
public class SimpleWorkerRequest : System.Web.HttpWorkerRequest {
// Public Constructors
  public SimpleWorkerRequest(string appVirtualDir, string appPhysicalDir, string page, string query,
      System.IO.TextWriter output);
  public SimpleWorkerRequest(string page, string query, System.IO.TextWriter output);
// Public Instance Properties
  public override string MachineConfigPath{get; }              // overrides System.Web.HttpWorkerRequest
  public override string MachineInstallDirectory{get; }        // overrides System.Web.HttpWorkerRequest
// Public Instance Methods
  public override void EndOfRequest( );                        // overrides System.Web.HttpWorkerRequest
  public override void FlushResponse( bool finalFlush);        // overrides System.Web.HttpWorkerRequest
  public override string GetAppPath( );                        // overrides System.Web.HttpWorkerRequest
  public override string GetAppPathTranslated( );              // overrides System.Web.HttpWorkerRequest
  public override string GetFilePath( );                       // overrides System.Web.HttpWorkerRequest
  public override string GetFilePathTranslated( );             // overrides System.Web.HttpWorkerRequest
  public override string GetHttpVerbName( );                   // overrides System.Web.HttpWorkerRequest
  public override string GetHttpVersion( );                    // overrides System.Web.HttpWorkerRequest
  public override string GetLocalAddress( );                   // overrides System.Web.HttpWorkerRequest
  public override int GetLocalPort( );                         // overrides System.Web.HttpWorkerRequest
  public override string GetPathInfo( );                       // overrides System.Web.HttpWorkerRequest
  public override string GetQueryString( );                    // overrides System.Web.HttpWorkerRequest
  public override string GetRawUrl( );                         // overrides System.Web.HttpWorkerRequest
```

```
public override string GetRemoteAddress( );                        // overrides System.Web.HttpWorkerRequest
public override int GetRemotePort( );                              // overrides System.Web.HttpWorkerRequest
public override string GetServerVariable(string name);             // overrides System.Web.HttpWorkerRequest
public override string GetUriPath( );                              // overrides System.Web.HttpWorkerRequest
public override IntPtr GetUserToken( );                            // overrides System.Web.HttpWorkerRequest
public override string MapPath(string path);                       // overrides System.Web.HttpWorkerRequest
public override void SendKnownResponseHeader(int index, string value);  // overrides System.Web.HttpWorkerRequest
public override void SendResponseFromFile(IntPtr handle, long offset,
    long length);                                                  // overrides System.Web.HttpWorkerRequest
public override void SendResponseFromFile(string filename, long offset,
    long length);                                                  // overrides System.Web.HttpWorkerRequest
public override void SendResponseFromMemory(byte[ ] data, int length);  // overrides System.Web.HttpWorkerRequest
public override void SendStatus(int statusCode, string statusDescription);  // overrides System.Web.HttpWorkerRequest
public override void SendUnknownResponseHeader(string name,
    string value);                                                 // overrides System.Web.HttpWorkerRequest
}
```

Hierarchy   System.Object → System.Web.HttpWorkerRequest(System.Web.IHttpMapPath) →
SimpleWorkerRequest

27

The System.Web.Mail Namespace

The System.Web.Mail namespace allows you to send email messages from your ASP.NET application. This capability can use the built-in SMTP service included with IIS or an arbitrary SMTP server, and is similar to the CDO component used in traditional ASP development. The SMTP service in IIS maps its Inbox and Outbox to directories on the server. Message transfer is handled so that the Outbox is always empty and the Inbox never has an incoming queue. Note that in order to use these features, you must correctly configure the default SMTP server in IIS Manager so that it will relay messages to the Internet. If you do not take this step your mail will never be delivered, even though no exceptions will be raised in your code.

Messages and attachments are encapsulated in MailMessage and MailAttachment objects and sent using the SmtpMail helper class, which provides a single Send() method. Figure 27-1 shows the types in this namespace.

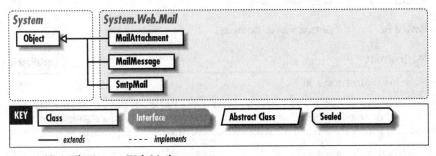

Figure 27-1. The System.Web.Mail namespace

MailAttachment

System.Web.Mail (system.web.dll)   class

This class encapsulates an attachment to an email message. The constructor takes a string argument that identifies the local path to the file, as in MailAttachment(@"c:\temp\ report.pdf"). An optional second argument lets you set the encoding (which will be UUEncode if omitted). Once you create an instance of MailAttachment, you can add it to an instance of the MailMessage class with the MailMessage.Attachments collection. The easiest way to do this is through the Add( ) method of the MailMessage.Attachments class, like this: objMessage.Attachments.Add(objAttachment).

```
public class MailAttachment {
// Public Constructors
  public MailAttachment( string filename);
  public MailAttachment(string filename, MailEncoding encoding);
// Public Instance Properties
  public MailEncoding Encoding{get; }
  public string Filename{get; }
}
```

MailEncoding   serializable

System.Web.Mail (system.web.dll)   enum

This enumeration sets the BodyEncoding property of the MailMessage class and the Encoding property of the MailAttachment class.

```
public enum MailEncoding {
  UUEncode = 0,
  Base64 = 1
}
```

Hierarchy   System.Object → System.ValueType → System.Enum(System.IComparable, System.IFormattable, System.IConvertible) → MailEncoding

Returned By   MailAttachment.Encoding

Passed To   MailAttachment.MailAttachment( )

MailFormat   serializable

System.Web.Mail (system.web.dll)   enum

This enumeration sets the BodyFormat property of the MailMessage class. If you use Html, you can include standard HTML markup tags in the Body property of a MailMessage instance and they will be rendered in the recepient's email program, if supported.

```
public enum MailFormat {
  Text = 0,
  Html = 1
}
```

Hierarchy	System.Object → System.ValueType → System.Enum(System.IComparable, System.IFormattable, System.IConvertible) → MailFormat
Returned By	MailMessage.BodyFormat
Passed To	MailMessage.BodyFormat

MailMessage

System.Web.Mail (system.web.dll)   class

This class encapsulates an email message. To send an email message programmatically, create a MailMessage object, set the appropriate properties, and use the SmtpMail.Send() method.

The properties of the MailMessage class are fairly straightforward and include all the typical details entered in an email program, such as subject, priority, and the email addresses for the sender, recipient, and any carbon-copied recipients (all as strings). You can also use the Attachments collection to add MailAttachment objects to a message.

The actual body of the email message is set as a string through the Body property. You will have to add line return characters as required. If you set the BodyFormat property to MailFormat.Html, you can also insert standard HTML markup tags.

```
public class MailMessage {
// Public Constructors
  public MailMessage( );
// Public Instance Properties
  public IList Attachments{get; }
  public string Bcc{set; get; }
  public string Body{set; get; }
  public Encoding BodyEncoding{set; get; }
  public MailFormat BodyFormat{set; get; }
  public string Cc{set; get; }
  public IDictionary Fields{get; }
  public string From{set; get; }
  public IDictionary Headers{get; }
  public MailPriority Priority{set; get; }
  public string Subject{set; get; }
  public string To{set; get; }
  public string UrlContentBase{set; get; }
  public string UrlContentLocation{set; get; }
}
```

Passed To	SmtpMail.Send( )

MailPriority   serializable

System.Web.Mail (system.web.dll)   enum

This enumeration sets the Priority property of a MailMessage object.

```
public enum MailPriority {
  Normal = 0,
  Low = 1,
```

```
High = 2
}
```

Hierarchy   System.Object → System.ValueType → System.Enum(System.IComparable, System.IFor-
mattable, System.IConvertible) → MailPriority

Returned By   MailMessage.Priority

Passed To   MailMessage.Priority

SmtpMail

System.Web.Mail (system.web.dll)   class

The SmtpMail class represents the SMTP Server. It includes a static **Send( )** method that
you can use to send email programmatically. There are two versions of the **Send( )**
method: one accepts a **MailMessage** object, and the other provides a quick and simple
way to send an email message without creating a **MailMessage** instance (by specifying the
sender's email address, the recipient, the subject, and the body text as string parameters). Before sending a message, set the static **SmtpServer** with the name of IP address of
the mail server (use "localhost" for the current computer).

```
public class SmtpMail {
// Public Static Properties
  public static string SmtpServer{set; get; }
// Public Static Methods
  public static void Send( MailMessage message);
  public static void Send(string from, string to, string subject, string messageText);
}
```

28

The System.Web.Mobile Namespace

Version 1.1 of the .NET Framework incorporates support for mobile devices that have a wide range of abilities, including Pocket PCs, PDAs, and Internet-enabled cellphones. Some devices expect Wireless Markup Language (WML), while others support compact HTML (cHTML) or ordinary HTML content. Fortunately, ASP.NET embraces this diversity with intelligent mobile controls that can render the correct output based on information supplied by the client browser.

The System.Web.Mobile namespace includes the core functionality required for mobile web applications, including classes that process errors, perform forms authentication, and retrieve the capabilities of the client device. Several of these classes are used internally by ASP.NET, while others (namely the MobileCapabilities and MobileFormsAuthentication classes) are accessed directly in your code. Figure 28-1 shows the types in this namespace

The System.Web.Mobile namespace includes two key classes for the mobile ASP.NET developer. The MobileFormsAuthentication class allows you to retrieve fine-grained information about the requirements and abilities of a client device. The MobileFormsAuthentication class provides shared helper methods that allow you to use forms authentication with devices that don't support cookies by embedding encrypted authentication information into the URL.

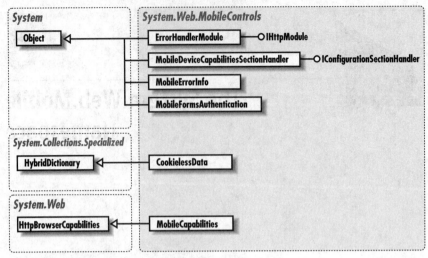

Figure 28-1. The System.Web.Mobile namespace

CookielessData

System.Web.Mobile (system.web.mobile.dll) .NET 1.1

class

Many mobile devices do not support cookies. Fortunately, ASP.NET provides a mobile implementation of forms authentication and session state that does not require cookies, and embeds information into the URL instead. The CookielessData class is used internally to store and retrieve this information. You will not use the CookielessData class directly.

```
public class CookielessData : System.Collections.Specialized.HybridDictionary {
// Public Constructors
  public CookielessData( );
}
```

Hierarchy System.Object → System.Collections.Specialized.HybridDictionary(System.Collections.IDictionary, System.Collections.ICollection, System.Collections.IEnumerable) → CookielessData

ErrorHandlerModule

System.Web.Mobile (system.web.mobile.dll) .NET 1.1

class

This module is used internally by ASP.NET to deal with unhandled exceptions. In the case of an exception, ASP.NET will return a page with a short error message (much as in a standard ASP.NET web page). The error message will be automatically formatted to the target device's expected markup. For WML devices, this will be a card deck. For HTML devices, this will be a page of HTML.

The automatically generated error messages are useful while debugging, but may not be shown to remote clients (depending on your settings in the *web.config* file). A better option is to write custom error pages and specify them using the *web.config* file before deploying a mobile web application.

```
public class ErrorHandlerModule : System.Web.IHttpModule {
// Public Constructors
  public ErrorHandlerModule( );
}
```

MobileCapabilities
.NET 1.1

System.Web.Mobile (system.web.mobile.dll)
class

The MobileCapabilities class extends the System.Web.HttpBrowserCapabilities class with a large number of strongly typed read-only properties that provide information about the capabilities of the client browser. Most of these properties are Boolean (like the various "Supports," "Requires," and "Renders" properties), although some map to simple strings. Examples of the latter include Browser (which might return "Pocket IE," "Microsoft Explorer," "Nokia," "Phone.com," "Ericsson," or "i-mode") and PreferredRenderingMime (which indicates the device's desired MIME type, like "text/html"). ASP.NET automatically examines some of these properties to customize the output it renders.

To access a MobileCapabilities for the current client, examine the System.Web.HttpRequest.Browser property. You will need to cast the object to the MobileCapabilities type.

```
public class MobileCapabilities : System.Web.HttpBrowserCapabilities {
// Public Constructors
  public MobileCapabilities( );
// Public Static Fields
  public static readonly string PreferredRenderingTypeChtml10;              // =chtml10
  public static readonly string PreferredRenderingTypeHtml32;               // =html32
  public static readonly string PreferredRenderingTypeWml11;                // =wml11
  public static readonly string PreferredRenderingTypeWml12;                // =wml12
// Public Instance Properties
  public virtual bool CanCombineFormsInDeck{get; }
  public virtual bool CanInitiateVoiceCall{get; }
  public virtual bool CanRenderAfterInputOrSelectElement{get; }
  public virtual bool CanRenderEmptySelects{get; }
  public virtual bool CanRenderInputAndSelectElementsTogether{get; }
  public virtual bool CanRenderMixedSelects{get; }
  public virtual bool CanRenderOneventAndPrevElementsTogether{get; }
  public virtual bool CanRenderPostBackCards{get; }
  public virtual bool CanRenderSetvarZeroWithMultiSelectionList{get; }
  public virtual bool CanSendMail{get; }
  public virtual int DefaultSubmitButtonLimit{get; }
  public virtual int GatewayMajorVersion{get; }
  public virtual double GatewayMinorVersion{get; }
  public virtual string GatewayVersion{get; }
  public virtual bool HasBackButton{get; }
  public virtual bool HidesRightAlignedMultiselectScrollbars{get; }
  public virtual string InputType{get; }
  public virtual bool IsColor{get; }
  public virtual bool IsMobileDevice{get; }
  public virtual int MaximumRenderedPageSize{get; }
  public virtual int MaximumSoftkeyLabelLength{get; }
  public virtual string MobileDeviceManufacturer{get; }
  public virtual string MobileDeviceModel{get; }
```

```
public virtual int NumberOfSoftkeys{get; }
public virtual string PreferredImageMime{get; }
public virtual string PreferredRenderingMime{get; }
public virtual string PreferredRenderingType{get; }
public virtual bool RendersBreakBeforeWmlSelectAndInput{get; }
public virtual bool RendersBreaksAfterHtmlLists{get; }
public virtual bool RendersBreaksAfterWmlAnchor{get; }
public virtual bool RendersBreaksAfterWmlInput{get; }
public virtual bool RendersWmlDoAcceptsInline{get; }
public virtual bool RendersWmlSelectsAsMenuCards{get; }
public virtual string RequiredMetaTagNameValue{get; }
public virtual bool RequiresAttributeColonSubstitution{get; }
public virtual bool RequiresContentTypeMetaTag{get; }
public virtual bool RequiresDBCSCharacter{get; }
public virtual bool RequiresHtmlAdaptiveErrorReporting{get; }
public virtual bool RequiresLeadingPageBreak{get; }
public virtual bool RequiresNoBreakInFormatting{get; }
public virtual bool RequiresOutputOptimization{get; }
public virtual bool RequiresPhoneNumbersAsPlainText{get; }
public virtual bool RequiresSpecialViewStateEncoding{get; }
public virtual bool RequiresUniqueFilePathSuffix{get; }
public virtual bool RequiresUniqueHtmlCheckboxNames{get; }
public virtual bool RequiresUniqueHtmlInputNames{get; }
public virtual bool RequiresUrlEncodedPostfieldValues{get; }
public virtual int ScreenBitDepth{get; }
public virtual int ScreenCharactersHeight{get; }
public virtual int ScreenCharactersWidth{get; }
public virtual int ScreenPixelsHeight{get; }
public virtual int ScreenPixelsWidth{get; }
public virtual bool SupportsAccesskeyAttribute{get; }
public virtual bool SupportsBodyColor{get; }
public virtual bool SupportsBold{get; }
public virtual bool SupportsCacheControlMetaTag{get; }
public virtual bool SupportsCss{get; }
public virtual bool SupportsDivAlign{get; }
public virtual bool SupportsDivNoWrap{get; }
public virtual bool SupportsEmptyStringInCookieValue{get; }
public virtual bool SupportsFontColor{get; }
public virtual bool SupportsFontName{get; }
public virtual bool SupportsFontSize{get; }
public virtual bool SupportsImageSubmit{get; }
public virtual bool SupportsIModeSymbols{get; }
public virtual bool SupportsInputIStyle{get; }
public virtual bool SupportsInputMode{get; }
public virtual bool SupportsItalic{get; }
public virtual bool SupportsJPhoneMultiMediaAttributes{get; }
public virtual bool SupportsJPhoneSymbols{get; }
public virtual bool SupportsQueryStringInFormAction{get; }
public virtual bool SupportsRedirectWithCookie{get; }
public virtual bool SupportsSelectMultiple{get; }
public virtual bool SupportsUncheck{get; }
```

```
// Public Instance Methods
  public bool HasCapability(string delegateName, string optionalParameter);
}
```

Hierarchy   System.Object → System.Web.Configuration.HttpCapabilitiesBase → System.Web.Http-
              BrowserCapabilities → MobileCapabilities

Returned By System.Web.UI.MobileControls.Adapters.ControlAdapter.Device, System.Web.UI.MobileCon-
              trols.Adapters.MobileTextWriter.Device, System.Web.UI.MobileControls.MobilePage.Device

Passed To   System.Web.UI.MobileControls.Adapters.ChtmlMobileTextWriter.ChtmlMobileTextWriter( ),
              System.Web.UI.MobileControls.Adapters.HtmlMobileTextWriter.HtmlMobileTextWriter( ),
              System.Web.UI.MobileControls.Adapters.MobileTextWriter.MobileTextWriter( ), System.
              Web.UI.MobileControls.Adapters.UpWmlMobileTextWriter.UpWmlMobileTextWriter( ),
              System.Web.UI.MobileControls.Adapters.WmlMobileTextWriter.WmlMobileTextWriter( )

MobileDeviceCapabilitiesSectionHandler   .NET 1.1

System.Web.Mobile (system.web.mobile.dll)   class

This class is used internally by the ASP.NET framework to read information about
supported mobile devices from the *machine.config* file. You will not use this class
directly.

```
public class MobileDeviceCapabilitiesSectionHandler : System.Configuration.IConfigurationSectionHandler {
// Public Constructors
  public MobileDeviceCapabilitiesSectionHandler( );
}
```

MobileErrorInfo   .NET 1.1

System.Web.Mobile (system.web.mobile.dll)   class

This class is used in conjunction with the ErrorHandlerModule to create adaptive error
messages. You do not use it directly.

```
public class MobileErrorInfo {
// Public Static Fields
  public static readonly string ContextKey;                                  // =MobileErrorInfo
// Public Instance Properties
  public string Description{set; get; }
  public string File{set; get; }
  public string LineNumber{set; get; }
  public string MiscText{set; get; }
  public string MiscTitle{set; get; }
  public string this[ string key ]{set; get; }
  public string Type{set; get; }
}
```

Returned By   System.Web.UI.MobileControls.ErrorFormatterPage.ErrorInfo

System.Web.Mobile (system.web.mobile.dll)   class

This helper class supports cookieless ASP.NET forms authentication. When using forms authentication with a mobile device, you can still use the System.Web.Security.Forms-Authentication helper class. However, if your mobile device does not support cookies, you can use the alternate RedirectFromLoginPage( ) and SignOut( ) methods.

The RedirectFromLoginPage( ) method adds encrypted authentication information to the query string, instead of creating a cookie. The SignOut( ) method removes this information. These are the only two methods provided by the MobileFormsAuthentication class. If you need other forms authentication functionality, you can use the shared members of the System.Web.Security.FormsAuthentication. For example, you might use System.Web.Security.Forms-Authentication.Authenticate( ) to validate user-supplied credentials against values in a configuration file.

Remember, information in the URL will be preserved if your application uses relative URL redirects. However, if the user types in a new URL, or you use an absolute URL to redirect the user, any session and authentication information will be lost.

```
public class MobileFormsAuthentication {
// Public Static Methods
   public static void RedirectFromLoginPage(string userName, bool createPersistentCookie);
   public static void RedirectFromLoginPage(string userName, bool createPersistentCookie, string strCookiePath);
   public static void SignOut( );
}
```

29

The System.Web.Security Namespace

The System.Web.Security namespace includes the modules that implement various types of ASP.NET authentication, such as WindowsAuthenticationModule, FormsAuthenticationModule, and PassportAuthenticationModule. You don't interact directly with these modules in an ASP.NET application; instead, the ASP.NET framework uses the appropriate module (based on the options you have set in the *web.config* file) to authenticate the user. After this point, ASP.NET provides identity information in the System.Web.HttpContext.User property and uses this identity to authorize access to resources such as files and URLs (using modules like UrlAuthorizationModule and FileAuthorizationModule, which are also found in this namespace).

One reason you might use the types in this namespace is to handle authentication events. Generic security events, like System.Web.HttpApplication.AuthenticateRequest and System.Web.HttpApplication.AuthorizeRequest, are already available in the *global.asax* file. However, each authentication module also provides its own Authenticate event, which can be used to validate a user programmatically or attach a new System.Security.Principal.IIdentity instance. Event handlers for Authenticate events are coded in the *global.asax* file, but defined in this namespace.

Another important class in this namespace is FormsAuthentication. This class provides the shared methods you need to use in your login page if you use ASP.NET's forms-based security. These methods let you authenticate a user, instruct ASP.NET to issue the authenticated forms cookie, and redirect the user to the original requested page.

Note that many security options are not reflected in these classes. When implementing a custom authorization/authentication scheme, you should first examine all the security options provided in the *web.config* file. Internet Information Server (IIS) also provides an additional layer of security configuration.

Figures 29-1 and 29-2 show the types in this namespace.

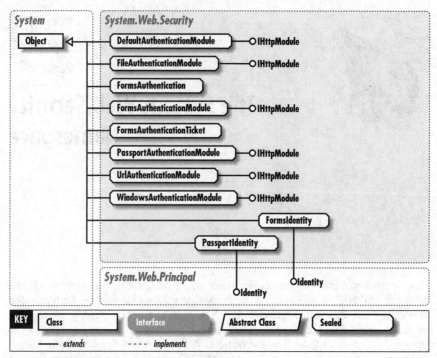

Figure 29-1. Core types from the System.Web.Security namespace

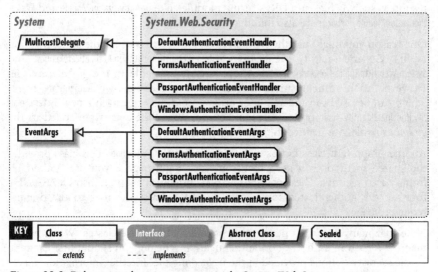

Figure 29-2. Delegates and event arguments in the System.Web.Security namespace

DefaultAuthenticationEventArgs

System.Web.Security (system.web.dll)   sealed class

This class provides a reference to the System.Web.HttpContext object for the DefaultAuthenticationModule.Authenticate event. Unlike all other Authenticate events, this event does not provide objects that allow you to set or examine user identity information; the DefaultAuthenticationModule is used only when the authentication mode is set to "None."

```
public sealed class DefaultAuthenticationEventArgs : EventArgs {
// Public Constructors
  public DefaultAuthenticationEventArgs(System.Web.HttpContext context);
// Public Instance Properties
  public HttpContext Context{get; }
}
```

Hierarchy   System.Object → System.EventArgs → DefaultAuthenticationEventArgs

Passed To   DefaultAuthenticationEventHandler.{BeginInvoke( ), Invoke( )}

DefaultAuthenticationEventHandler   serializable

System.Web.Security (system.web.dll)   delegate

This delegate represents an event handler for the DefaultAuthenticationModule.Authenticate event. It provides a custom DefaultAuthenticationEventArgs object with a reference to the current System.Web.HttpContext. This event handler must be coded in the *global.asax*, using the event name DefaultAuthentication_OnAuthenticate (and it does not need to be connected with a Handles keyword or the AddHandler( ) command).

```
public delegate void DefaultAuthenticationEventHandler(object sender, DefaultAuthenticationEventArgs e);
```

Associated Events DefaultAuthenticationModule.Authenticate( )

DefaultAuthenticationModule

System.Web.Security (system.web.dll)   sealed class

The ASP.NET framework uses this authentication module automatically when no other authentication module is specified in the current context (for example, when you set <authentication mode="None"> in the *web.config* file. This is similar to how many traditional ASP applications work. IIS authentication is still used and access to local system resources is provided in the context of a local system process account (or the IUSR_ MACHINENAME account) according to the IIS settings. However, ASP.NET page requests will not require additional authentication.

```
public sealed class DefaultAuthenticationModule : System.Web.IHttpModule {
// Public Constructors
  public DefaultAuthenticationModule( );
// Public Instance Methods
  public void Dispose( );                                    // implements System.Web.IHttpModule
  public void Init(System.Web.HttpApplication app);          // implements System.Web.IHttpModule
// Events
  public event DefaultAuthenticationEventHandler Authenticate;
}
```

FileAuthorizationModule

System.Web.Security (system.web.dll)   sealed class

This class is used automatically when you use the WindowsAuthenticationModule class. ASP.NET uses FileAuthorizationModule to determine whether a specified file operation should be allowed or denied, based on the currently authenticated NT user account (and using Access Control Lists (ACLs)).

```
public sealed class FileAuthorizationModule : System.Web.IHttpModule {
// Public Constructors
  public FileAuthorizationModule( );
// Public Instance Methods
  public void Dispose( );                                              // implements System.Web.IHttpModule
  public void Init(System.Web.HttpApplication app);                    // implements System.Web.IHttpModule
}
```

FormsAuthentication

System.Web.Security (system.web.dll)   sealed class

This class contains the shared (static) methods that you use in your custom login page to authenticate a user when using the FormsAuthenticationModule class. Typically, the first method your login page uses is the Authenticate( ) method, which compares a supplied user ID and password against the list of allowed logins defined in the *web.config* file. If this method returns True, the information is valid and you can use the RedirectFromLoginPage( ) method to issue the Forms cookie and redirect the user to the previously requested page, all at once. You need to supply the user ID to this method, along with a Boolean createPersistentCookie parameter. If createPersistentCookie is set to True, a "permanent" cookie (with an expiration date of fifty years into the future) will be created so that the user never needs to log in when they return to the site. This cookie is suitable only for applications that use authentication for personalization rather than security.

Other methods you might want to use in this class include SignOut( ), which removes the current Forms cookie, and SetAuthCookie( ), which creates the Forms cookie but does not redirect the user. (You could then retrieve the original requested URL by using the GetRedirectUrl( ) method and make a decision about whether to redirect the user to this page or to a default main page.)

You can also use the GetAuthCookie( ) method, which returns the Forms cookie as a System. Web.HttpCookie object. In this case, the user is not authenticated (and won't be able to access other pages in your application) until the cookie is added to the System.Web.HttpResponse.Cookies collection. You can work with this cookie on a lower level by using methods like Decrypt( ).

```
public sealed class FormsAuthentication {
// Public Constructors
  public FormsAuthentication( );
// Public Static Properties
  public static string FormsCookieName{get; }
  public static string FormsCookiePath{get; }
  public static bool RequireSSL{get; }
  public static bool SlidingExpiration{get; }
// Public Static Methods
```

```
  public static bool Authenticate(string name, string password);
  public static FormsAuthenticationTicket Decrypt(string encryptedTicket);
  public static string Encrypt(FormsAuthenticationTicket ticket);
  public static HttpCookie GetAuthCookie(string userName, bool createPersistentCookie);
  public static HttpCookie GetAuthCookie(string userName, bool createPersistentCookie, string strCookiePath);
  public static string GetRedirectUrl(string userName, bool createPersistentCookie);
  public static string HashPasswordForStoringInConfigFile(string password, string passwordFormat);
  public static void Initialize( );
  public static void RedirectFromLoginPage(string userName, bool createPersistentCookie);
  public static void RedirectFromLoginPage(string userName, bool createPersistentCookie, string strCookiePath);
  public static FormsAuthenticationTicket RenewTicketIfOld(FormsAuthenticationTicket tOld);
  public static void SetAuthCookie(string userName, bool createPersistentCookie);
  public static void SetAuthCookie(string userName, bool createPersistentCookie, string strCookiePath);
  public static void SignOut( );
}
```

FormsAuthenticationEventArgs

System.Web.Security (system.web.dll)   sealed class

This class is a custom System.EventArgs that is used in the event handler for the FormsAuthen-ticationModule.Authenticate event. It provides two properties: Context, which provides a reference to the current System.Web.HttpContext, and User, which will be a null reference because information is not yet retrieved from the Forms authentication cookie. This event is not typically used because Forms authentication already uses the custom code you have created for the login page.

```
public sealed class FormsAuthenticationEventArgs : EventArgs {
// Public Constructors
  public FormsAuthenticationEventArgs(System.Web.HttpContext context);
// Public Instance Properties
  public HttpContext Context{get; }
  public IPrincipal User{set; get; }
}
```

Hierarchy   System.Object → System.EventArgs → FormsAuthenticationEventArgs

Passed To   FormsAuthenticationEventHandler.{BeginInvoke( ), Invoke( )}

FormsAuthenticationEventHandler   serializable

System.Web.Security (system.web.dll)   delegate

This delegate represents the event handler that can be used to handle the FormsAuthentica-tionModule.Authenticate event. This event handler must be coded in *global.asax*, using the event name WindowsAuthentication_OnAuthenticate.

```
public delegate void FormsAuthenticationEventHandler(object sender, FormsAuthenticationEventArgs e);
```

Associated Events FormsAuthenticationModule.Authenticate( )

FormsAuthenticationModule

System.Web.Security (system.web.dll)   sealed class

This module, when loaded through the *web.config* file (<authentication mode="Forms">), provides Forms-based authentication. In this model, the ASP.NET framework uses a special authentication cookie. If it is not present, users are redirected to a custom ASP.NET page where they can acquire the cookie once they log in successfully. If the cookie is present, ASP.NET fires the Authenticate event, places identity information in the System.Web.HttpContext.User property, and allows access. You can react to this event by creating an event handler called FormsAuthentication_OnAuthenticate in the *global.asax* file.

Several additional settings, including the URL for the login page and the length of time before the cookie expires, can be set in the *web.config* file. The actual authentication for the user is performed in the custom code you create for the login page. This code uses the helper methods in the FormsAuthentication class to authenticate the user and assign the Forms authentication cookie.

```
public sealed class FormsAuthenticationModule : System.Web.IHttpModule {
// Public Constructors
  public FormsAuthenticationModule( );
// Public Instance Methods
  public void Dispose( );                                    // implements System.Web.IHttpModule
  public void Init( System.Web.HttpApplication app);         // implements System.Web.IHttpModule
// Events
  public event FormsAuthenticationEventHandler Authenticate;
}
```

FormsAuthenticationTicket   serializable

System.Web.Security (system.web.dll)   sealed class

This class wraps the information in the Forms authentication cookie. This information includes the expiration and issue date (Expiration and IssueDate), the username (Name), and an application-defined string that can be stored in the cookie (UserData). An instance of this class is provided through the FormsIdentity.Ticket property.

```
public sealed class FormsAuthenticationTicket {
// Public Constructors
  public FormsAuthenticationTicket(int version, string name, DateTime issueDate, DateTime expiration, bool isPersistent,
    string userData);
  public FormsAuthenticationTicket(int version, string name, DateTime issueDate, DateTime expiration, bool isPersistent,
    string userData, string cookiePath);
  public FormsAuthenticationTicket(string name, bool isPersistent, int timeout);
// Public Instance Properties
  public string CookiePath{get; }
  public DateTime Expiration{get; }
  public bool Expired{get; }
  public bool IsPersistent{get; }
  public DateTime IssueDate{get; }
  public string Name{get; }
  public string UserData{get; }
  public int Version{get; }
}
```

Returned By	FormsAuthentication.{Decrypt( ), RenewTicketIfOld( )}, FormsIdentity.Ticket

Passed To	FormsAuthentication.{Encrypt( ), RenewTicketIfOld( )}, FormsIdentity.FormsIdentity( )

FormsIdentity   serializable

System.Web.Security (system.web.dll)   sealed class

This System.Security.Principal.IIdentity instance provides information to the FormsAuthentication-Module about the current user identity. This information consists of the username (Name), the type of authentication (AuthenticationType), which will always be "Forms," and the corresponding ticket object (Ticket)

```
public sealed class FormsIdentity : System.Security.Principal.IIdentity {
// Public Constructors
   public FormsIdentity(FormsAuthenticationTicket ticket);
// Public Instance Properties
   public string AuthenticationType{get; }          // implements System.Security.Principal.IIdentity
   public bool IsAuthenticated{get; }               // implements System.Security.Principal.IIdentity
   public string Name{get; }                        // implements System.Security.Principal.IIdentity
   public FormsAuthenticationTicket Ticket{get; }
}
```

PassportAuthenticationEventArgs

System.Web.Security (system.web.dll)   sealed class

This class is a custom System.EventArgs object that is used in the event handler for the PassportAuthenticationModule.Authenticate event. It provides three properties: Context, which provides a reference to the current System.Web.HttpContext; User, which will be a null reference and Identity, which will contain the information received from Passport as a PassportIdentity object.

You can implement a custom authentication scheme and set the User value programmatically to the appropriate user identity. If you do not set it to a non-null value, the PassportAuthenticationModule will create a System.Security.Principal.WindowsPrincipal object based on the information supplied in the PassportIdentity object and assign it to the System.Web.HttpContext.User property.

```
public sealed class PassportAuthenticationEventArgs : EventArgs {
// Public Constructors
   public PassportAuthenticationEventArgs(PassportIdentity identity, System.Web.HttpContext context);
// Public Instance Properties
   public HttpContext Context{get; }
   public PassportIdentity Identity{get; }
   public IPrincipal User{set; get; }
}
```

Hierarchy	System.Object → System.EventArgs → PassportAuthenticationEventArgs

Passed To	PassportAuthenticationEventHandler.{BeginInvoke( ), Invoke( )}

PassportAuthenticationEventHandler

serializable

System.Web.Security (system.web.dll)   delegate

This delegate represents the event handler that can be used to handle the PassportAuthenti-cationModule.Authenticate event. This event handler must be coded in the *global.asax* file, using the event handler name PassportAuthentication_OnAuthenticate.

```
public delegate void PassportAuthenticationEventHandler(object sender, PassportAuthenticationEventArgs e);
```

Associated Events   PassportAuthenticationModule.Authenticate( )

PassportAuthenticationModule

System.Web.Security (system.web.dll)   sealed class

This module, when loaded through the *web.config* file (<authentication mode="Passport">), provides authentication using Microsoft's Passport service. In this model, the ASP.NET framework will check for the Passport "ticket" (an encrypted value in a cookie or the query string) and use it to authenticate the user. If no ticket is present, or if it has expired, the user will be redirected to the Passport service's login page. The user will be redirected automatically to the original ASP.NET page with the correct ticket after logging in. At this point, the Authenticate event will be fired. You can handle this event with an event handler named PassportAuthentication_OnAuthenticate in the *global.asax* file.

The location of the Passport login page is set using the <passport redirectUrl> element in the *web.config* file.

```
public sealed class PassportAuthenticationModule : System.Web.IHttpModule {
// Public Constructors
  public PassportAuthenticationModule( );
// Public Instance Methods
  public void Dispose( );                                          // implements System.Web.IHttpModule
  public void Init(System.Web.HttpApplication app);                // implements System.Web.IHttpModule
// Events
  public event PassportAuthenticationEventHandler Authenticate;
}
```

PassportIdentity

System.Web.Security (system.web.dll)   sealed class

This class wraps information from the Passport user profile. For example, you can retrieve the 64-bit Passport User ID (PUID) from the Name property, along with information about how long the user has been signed in (TimeSinceSignIn), how old the current ticket is (TicketAge), and whether the password is currently saved on the user's Passport login page (HasSavedPassword). Additionally, you can get information about any error associated with the current ticket (Error), although you must compare the number to values in the Passport documentation, as no enumeration is currently supplied. Other information from the Passport profile (including everything from the user's birth date to the user's language preference) is available through the Item name/value collection. For information on valid attribute names, consult the Passport documentation.

The PassportIdentity class also provides several methods, many of which are shared and available without a PassportIdentity instance (such as those used for encryption and compression). You can use LoginUser( ) to redirect a user to the Passport sign-in page or initiate a Passport-aware client authentication exchange. You can also use SignOut( ) to end the user's session.

Note that you can pass -1 to any Passport method in place of an optional integer parameter. This indicates that Passport should use the default value from the registry and is equivalent to omitting optional parameters.

```
public sealed class PassportIdentity : System.Security.Principal.IIdentity {
// Public Constructors
  public PassportIdentity( );
// Public Instance Properties
  public string AuthenticationType{get; }                              // implements System.Security.Principal.IIdentity
  public int Error{get; }
  public bool GetFromNetworkServer{get; }
  public bool HasSavedPassword{get; }
  public bool HasTicket{get; }
  public string HexPUID{get; }
  public bool IsAuthenticated{get; }                                   // implements System.Security.Principal.IIdentity
  public string Name{get; }                                            // implements System.Security.Principal.IIdentity
  public string this[ string strProfileName ]{get; }
  public int TicketAge{get; }
  public int TimeSinceSignIn{get; }
// Public Static Methods
  public static string Compress(string strData);
  public static bool CryptIsValid( );
  public static int CryptPutHost(string strHost);
  public static int CryptPutSite(string strSite);
  public static string Decompress(string strData);
  public static string Decrypt(string strData);
  public static string Encrypt(string strData);
  public static void SignOut(string strSignOutDotGifFileName);
// Public Instance Methods
  public string AuthUrl( );
  public string AuthUrl( string strReturnUrl);
  public string AuthUrl(string strReturnUrl, int iTimeWindow, bool fForceLogin, string strCoBrandedArgs, int iLangID,
      string strNameSpace, int iKPP, bool bUseSecureAuth);
  public string AuthUrl(string strReturnUrl, int iTimeWindow, int iForceLogin, string strCoBrandedArgs, int iLangID,
      string strNameSpace, int iKPP, int iUseSecureAuth);
  public string AuthUrl2( );
  public string AuthUrl2(string strReturnUrl);
  public string AuthUrl2(string strReturnUrl, int iTimeWindow, bool fForceLogin, string strCoBrandedArgs, int iLangID,
      string strNameSpace, int iKPP, bool bUseSecureAuth);
  public string AuthUrl2(string strReturnUrl, int iTimeWindow, int iForceLogin, string strCoBrandedArgs, int iLangID,
      string strNameSpace, int iKPP, int iUseSecureAuth);
  public object GetCurrentConfig(string strAttribute);
  public string GetDomainAttribute(string strAttribute, int iLCID, string strDomain);
  public string GetDomainFromMemberName(string strMemberName);
  public bool GetIsAuthenticated(int iTimeWindow, bool bForceLogin, bool bCheckSecure);
  public bool GetIsAuthenticated(int iTimeWindow, int iForceLogin, int iCheckSecure);
  public string GetLoginChallenge( );
  public string GetLoginChallenge(string strReturnUrl);
```

```
public string GetLoginChallenge(string szRetURL, int iTimeWindow, int fForceLogin, string szCOBrandArgs, int iLangID,
    string strNameSpace, int iKPP, int iUseSecureAuth, object oExtraParams);
public object GetOption(string strOpt);
public object GetProfileObject( string strProfileName);
public bool HasFlag( int iFlagMask);
public bool HasProfile(string strProfile);
public bool HaveConsent(bool bNeedFullConsent, bool bNeedBirthdate);
public int LoginUser( );
public int LoginUser(string strReturnUrl);
public int LoginUser(string szRetURL, int iTimeWindow, bool fForceLogin, string szCOBrandArgs, int iLangID,
    string strNameSpace, int iKPP, bool fUseSecureAuth, object oExtraParams);
public int LoginUser(string szRetURL, int iTimeWindow, int fForceLogin, string szCOBrandArgs, int iLangID,
    string strNameSpace, int iKPP, int iUseSecureAuth, object oExtraParams);
public string LogoTag( );
public string LogoTag(string strReturnUrl);
public string LogoTag(string strReturnUrl, int iTimeWindow, bool fForceLogin, string strCoBrandedArgs, int iLangID,
    bool fSecure, string strNameSpace, int iKPP, bool bUseSecureAuth);
public string LogoTag(string strReturnUrl, int iTimeWindow, int iForceLogin, string strCoBrandedArgs, int iLangID,
    int iSecure, string strNameSpace, int iKPP, int iUseSecureAuth);
public string LogoTag2( );
public string LogoTag2(string strReturnUrl);
public string LogoTag2(string strReturnUrl, int iTimeWindow, bool fForceLogin, string strCoBrandedArgs, int iLangID,
    bool fSecure, string strNameSpace, int iKPP, bool bUseSecureAuth);
public string LogoTag2(string strReturnUrl, int iTimeWindow, int iForceLogin, string strCoBrandedArgs, int iLangID,
    int iSecure, string strNameSpace, int iKPP, int iUseSecureAuth);
public string LogoutURL( );
public string LogoutURL(string szReturnURL, string szCOBrandArgs, int iLangID, string strDomain, int iUseSecureAuth);
public void SetOption(string strOpt, object vOpt);
public object Ticket(string strAttribute);
// Protected Instance Methods
protected override void Finalize( );                                                    // overrides object
}
```

Returned By	PassportAuthenticationEventArgs.Identity
Passed To	PassportAuthenticationEventArgs.PassportAuthenticationEventArgs( )

UrlAuthorizationModule

System.Web.Security (system.web.dll)   sealed class

ASP.NET uses this class automatically to determine whether access to a specified resource (a URL requested by the client) should be allowed or denied, based on the identity of the currently authenticated user. This class is used as needed, but is not directly referenced in the *web.config* file. You can configure URL authorization by adding a list of users or roles in the <allow> or <deny> elements of the <authorization> section of a configuration file.

Both the FormsAuthenticationModule and PassportAuthenticationModule set the System.Web.HttpContext. SkipAuthorization property to True when redirecting the client to a login page so they can bypass the UrlAuthorizationModule checks.

```
public sealed class UrlAuthorizationModule : System.Web.IHttpModule {
// Public Constructors
  public UrlAuthorizationModule( );
// Public Instance Methods
  public void Dispose( );                                    // implements System.Web.IHttpModule
  public void Init(System.Web.HttpApplication app);          // implements System.Web.IHttpModule
}
```

WindowsAuthenticationEventArgs

System.Web.Security (system.web.dll)   sealed class

This class is a custom System.EventArgs that is used in the event handler for the WindowsAuthenticationModule.Authenticate event. It provides three properties: Context, which provides a reference to the current System.Web.HttpContext; User, which will be a null reference and Identity, which will contain the information received from IIS. You can implement a custom authentication scheme and set the User property programmatically to the appropriate user identity. If you don't set it to a non-null value, the WindowsAuthenticationModule creates a System.Security.Principal.WindowsPrincipal object based on the information supplied by IIS and assign it to the System.Web.HttpContext.User property.

The easiest way to set a default identity for impersonation is by using the settings in the *web.config* file. You should use this event only if you need to implement a custom authentication scheme.

```
public sealed class WindowsAuthenticationEventArgs : EventArgs {
// Public Constructors
  public WindowsAuthenticationEventArgs(System.Security.Principal.WindowsIdentity identity,
    System.Web.HttpContext context);
// Public Instance Properties
  public HttpContext Context{get; }
  public WindowsIdentity Identity{get; }
  public IPrincipal User{set; get; }
}
```

Hierarchy   System.Object → System.EventArgs → WindowsAuthenticationEventArgs

Passed To   WindowsAuthenticationEventHandler.{BeginInvoke( ), Invoke( )}

WindowsAuthenticationEventHandler   serializable

System.Web.Security (system.web.dll)   delegate

This delegate represents the event handler that can be used to handle the WindowsAuthenticationModule.Authenticate event. This event handler must be coded in *global.asax*, using an event handler named WindowsAuthentication_OnAuthenticate.

```
public delegate void WindowsAuthenticationEventHandler(object sender, WindowsAuthenticationEventArgs e);
```

Associated Events WindowsAuthenticationModule.Authenticate( )

WindowsAuthenticationModule

System.Web.Security (system.web.dll)   **sealed class**

This module, when loaded through the *web.config* file (<**authentication mode="Windows"**>), provides Windows/IIS authentication. In this model, IIS authenticates the user identity for the current web request using any supported method (including Basic, Digest, or Integrated Windows), and then passes that account to the ASP.NET application, which it uses to access the resources it needs. The WindowsAuthenticationModule uses a System. Security.Principal.WindowsIdentity object to hold user information received from IIS and constructs a System.Security.Principal.WindowsPrincipal object to provide information about group memberships. The System.Security.Principal.WindowsPrincipal object is attached to the application context and provided through the System.Web.HttpContext.User property. This module also provides a single event, Authenticate, which you can access through the WindowsAuthentication_OnAuthenticate event handler in the *global.asax* file.

This type of authentication scheme is particularly useful in corporate intranet scenarios, where IIS can be set to Integrated Windows authentication and all users can access the application under their network accounts.

```
public sealed class WindowsAuthenticationModule : System.Web.IHttpModule {
// Public Constructors
  public WindowsAuthenticationModule( );
// Public Instance Methods
  public void Dispose( );                                           // implements System.Web.IHttpModule
  public void Init(System.Web.HttpApplication app);                 // implements System.Web.IHttpModule
// Events
  public event WindowsAuthenticationEventHandler Authenticate;
}
```

30

The System.Web.Services Namespace

The System.Web.Services namespace contains the types used for creating web services. Web services are "component-like" units of programming logic that exist on a web server as *.asmx* files. Web services can be incorporated seamlessly into Windows or ASP.NET applications. Web services differ from many other methods of remote method invocation (like DCOM) in that they use open XML-based standards, work over normal text HTTP channels, and can be consumed (with a little more programming work) from applications on other platforms and non-Windows operating systems.

The System.Web.Services namespace is the starting point for creating web services. It contains a WebService class that custom web services can inherit from and the WebMethodAttribute and WebServiceAttribute, which are used to mark web service classes and methods and add additional information. Most types in other web service namespaces are used seamlessly by the .NET framework and are not used directly by the .NET programmer. Figure 30-1 shows the types in this namespace.

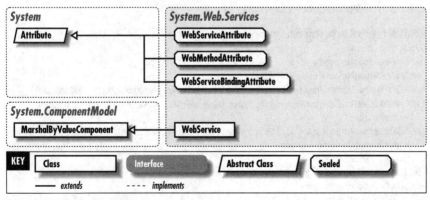

Figure 30-1. The System.Web.Services namespace

WebMethodAttribute

System.Web.Services (system.web.services.dll)   sealed class

Use the WebMethodAttribute to mark all the methods that should be made available to web service clients. All methods marked with this attribute will be accessible automatically and will be included in the WSDL document (and the proxy class) that .NET generates. Methods that are not marked with this attribute will not visible or usable, even if they are public.

You can set various properties when you use this attribute. For example, the Description property contains a string of information about a web method and is used for automatically generated description documents and the Internet Explorer test page. CacheDuration specifies (in seconds) how long a response will be cached and reused for web method requests with identical parameter values. EnableSession allows you to configure whether session support is enabled for your web method. By default, a web service method will not be cached at all, and session support will not be enabled. The BufferResponse property is rarely used, as it only applies to HTTP requests. By default, BufferResponse is True, as responses are serialized to memory and transferred only when complete. This ensures best performance for small amounts of data. Note that if you disable response buffering, you will not be able to use the method in conjunction with a custom SOAP extension.

The MessageName property is used to add an alias to a method. This property is most commonly used with polymorphic (overloaded) methods, which must be given unique names, or "disambiguated," before you can use them as web methods. When adding overloaded methods, the original method should retain its name for compatibility with existing clients.

The TransactionOption property allows a web method to take part in a COM+ transaction. Due to the stateless nature of the HTTP protocol, web service methods can only participate as the root object in a transaction. This means that both System.EnterpriseServices.TransactionOption.RequiresNew and System.EnterpriseServices.TransactionOption.Required will have the same effect, causing the web method to start a new transaction when it is invoked. Other COM objects that require transactions can then be created and used by the web method. A transaction started in this way is committed automatically when the method ends, unless the method explicitly calls System.EnterpriseServices.ContextUtil.SetAbort( ) or an unhandled exception occurs.

To set a property of the WebMethodAttribute, specify it by name in the attribute declaration (as in [WebMethod(EnableSession = True)])

```
public sealed class WebMethodAttribute : Attribute {
// Public Constructors
  public WebMethodAttribute( );
  public WebMethodAttribute( bool enableSession);
  public WebMethodAttribute(bool enableSession, System.EnterpriseServices.TransactionOption transactionOption);
  public WebMethodAttribute(bool enableSession, System.EnterpriseServices.TransactionOption transactionOption,
    int cacheDuration);
  public WebMethodAttribute(bool enableSession, System.EnterpriseServices.TransactionOption transactionOption,
    int cacheDuration, bool bufferResponse);
// Public Instance Properties
  public bool BufferResponse{set; get; }
  public int CacheDuration{set; get; }
  public string Description{set; get; }
  public bool EnableSession{set; get; }
```

```
  public string MessageName{set; get; }
  public TransactionOption TransactionOption{set; get; }
}
```

Hierarchy   System.Object → System.Attribute → WebMethodAttribute

Returned By   System.Web.Services.Description.ProtocolReflector.MethodAttribute

Valid On   Method

WebService   disposable

System.Web.Services (system.web.services.dll)   class

When creating a web service, you can inherit from this class to gain access to the built-in ASP.NET objects Application (the current System.Web.HttpApplicationState collection), Server, Session, User, and Context (which provides access to the built-in Request and Response objects). If you don't need to access these objects (or if you choose to go through the Context property) you don't need to derive your web service from this class.

When creating a web service class, all web methods must be marked with the WebMethodAttribute. To configure additional activities, you should also add the WebServiceAttribute to the class declaration.

```
public class WebService : System.ComponentModel.MarshalByValueComponent {
// Public Constructors
  public WebService( );
// Public Instance Properties
  public HttpApplicationState Application{get; }
  public HttpContext Context{get; }
  public HttpServerUtility Server{get; }
  public HttpSessionState Session{get; }
  public IPrincipal User{get; }
}
```

Hierarchy   System.Object → System.ComponentModel.MarshalByValueComponent(System.Compo-
                   nentModel.IComponent, System.IDisposable, System.IServiceProvider) → WebService

WebServiceAttribute

System.Web.Services (system.web.services.dll)   sealed class

This attribute is not required to create a web service, but it should be used before a web service is deployed to specify a unique XML namespace and allow clients to distinguish your web service from others on the Web. By default, if you do not use this attribute, the default namespace *http://tempuri.org/* is used. Namespaces look like URLs, but they do not actually need to correspond to valid locations on the Web. In a web service, the XML namespace is used to uniquely identify parts of the Service Description (WSDL) file that specifically pertain to the web service. The Name property identifies the local portion of the XML qualified name, which will be the web service class name by default. Elements of the WSDL contract that are specific to WSDL use the *http://schemas.xmlsoap.org/wsdl/* namespace.

Ideally, you should use a namespace that you control, such as your company's web site address. This XML namespace should not be confused with the .NET namespace used programmatically by clients. For more information on XML qualified names, see *http://www.w3.org/TR/REC-xml-names*.

You can also set a Description property, which contains information about your web service that will be displayed in automatically generated description documents and the Internet Explorer test page.

```
public sealed class WebServiceAttribute : Attribute {
// Public Constructors
   public WebServiceAttribute( );
// Public Static Fields
   public const string DefaultNamespace;                                    // =http://tempuri.org/
// Public Instance Properties
   public string Description{set; get; }
   public string Name{set; get; }
   public string Namespace{set; get; }
}
```

Hierarchy　　　　System.Object → System.Attribute → WebServiceAttribute

Valid On　　　　Class

WebServiceBindingAttribute

System.Web.Services (system.web.services.dll)　　　　　　　　　　　　　　　　sealed class

This attribute is used to mark the class declaration of the proxy class that allows communication between a client and a web service. It defines a Web Service Description Language (WSDL) binding. The Name and the Namespace properties must be set to the name and XML namespace of the web service. These properties match the corresponding properties in the WebServiceAttribute.

You must also use a System.Web.Services.Protocols.SoapDocumentMethodAttribute or System.Web. Services.Protocols.SoapRpcMethodAttribute to describe the binding for each individual web service method represented in the proxy class. This code is generated automatically in the proxy class by adding a Visual Studio .NET web reference or using the *WSDL.exe* utility included with ASP.NET.

```
public sealed class WebServiceBindingAttribute : Attribute {
// Public Constructors
   public WebServiceBindingAttribute( );
   public WebServiceBindingAttribute( string name);
   public WebServiceBindingAttribute(string name, string ns);
   public WebServiceBindingAttribute(string name, string ns, string location);
// Public Instance Properties
   public string Location{set; get; }
   public string Name{set; get; }
   public string Namespace{set; get; }
}
```

Hierarchy　　　　System.Object → System.Attribute → WebServiceBindingAttribute

Valid On　　　　Class

The System.Web.Services. Configuration Namespace

The System.Web.Services.Configuration namespace contains three .NET attributes that are useful if you want to add custom format extensions to your web services (in other words, if you want to insert additional XML elements to your web service's WSDL service description). One practical reason to use a format extension is if your web service requires a SOAP extension that runs at both the server and the client end. By default, no information about SOAP extensions is added to the service description, meaning that clients may not be aware that they need to use a given extension (for example, a security or encryption extension) before they can use the web service.

To use a format extension in this way, you need to start by deriving a custom class from System.Web.Services.Description.ServiceDescriptionFormatExtension, which represents the actual format extension. Next, you use the XmlFormatExtensionAttribute in this namespace with the class to define the extension points where the extension should apply. Optionally, you can use the XmlFormatExtensionPointAttribute class with the custom format extension class to specify a member in the class that will act as a new extension point, and the XmlFormatExtensionPrefixAttribute to set an XML namespace for the elements generated by the format extension. Finally, you configure your format extension to run within the <serviceDescriptionFormatExtension-Types> section of the configuration file. Figure 31-1 shows the types in this namespace.

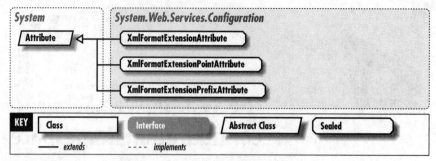

Figure 31-1. The System.Web.Services.Configuration namespace

XmlFormatExtensionAttribute

System.Web.Services.Configuration (system.web.services.dll)   **sealed class**

This attribute is applied to the declaraction of a custom System.Web.Services.Description.Service-DescriptionFormatExtension class. It specifes that the format extension runs at one or more extension points. The constructors specify the name of the XML element that will be added to the WSDL document by the service description format extension (element-Name) and the XML namespace for this element (ns). Depending on the constructor you use, you can supply up to four points where the format extension should run (extensionPoint)

```
public sealed class XmlFormatExtensionAttribute : Attribute {
// Public Constructors
  public XmlFormatExtensionAttribute( );
  public XmlFormatExtensionAttribute(string elementName, string ns, Type extensionPoint1);
  public XmlFormatExtensionAttribute(string elementName, string ns, Type[ ] extensionPoints);
  public XmlFormatExtensionAttribute(string elementName, string ns, Type extensionPoint1, Type extensionPoint2);
  public XmlFormatExtensionAttribute(string elementName, string ns, Type extensionPoint1, Type extensionPoint2,
     Type extensionPoint3);
  public XmlFormatExtensionAttribute(string elementName, string ns, Type extensionPoint1, Type extensionPoint2,
     Type extensionPoint3, Type extensionPoint4);
// Public Instance Properties
  public string ElementName{set; get; }
  public Type[ ] ExtensionPoints{set; get; }
  public string Namespace{set; get; }
}
```

Hierarchy   System.Object → System.Attribute → XmlFormatExtensionAttribute

Valid On   Class

XmlFormatExtensionPointAttribute

System.Web.Services.Configuration (system.web.services.dll)   **sealed class**

Like all the attributes in this namespace, the XmlFormatExtensionPointAttribute is applied to the custom System.Web.Services.Description.ServiceDescriptionFormatExtension class. Use this attribute to specify that a member of the custom format extension class should have its own custom format extension associated with it. MemberName specifies the member of the format extension class (as a string) that has its own format extension. AllowElements is True (the default) if the member of the class implementing the format extension can accept raw XML elements.

```
public sealed class XmlFormatExtensionPointAttribute : Attribute {
// Public Constructors
  public XmlFormatExtensionPointAttribute(string memberName);
// Public Instance Properties
  public bool AllowElements{set; get; }
  public string MemberName{set; get; }
}
```

Hierarchy   System.Object → System.Attribute → XmlFormatExtensionPointAttribute

Valid On   Class

XmlFormatExtensionPrefixAttribute

System.Web.Services.Configuration (system.web.services.dll)   sealed class

This attribute specifies the XML namespace (the constructor's ns parameter) and XML namespace prefix (the constructor's prefix parameter) that will be used for all format extensions generated by a custom format extension class. This attribute is applied to the custom System.Web.Services.Description.ServiceDescriptionFormatExtension class.

```
public sealed class XmlFormatExtensionPrefixAttribute : Attribute {
// Public Constructors
  public XmlFormatExtensionPrefixAttribute( );
  public XmlFormatExtensionPrefixAttribute(string prefix, string ns);
// Public Instance Properties
  public string Namespace{set; get; }
  public string Prefix{set; get; }
}
```

Hierarchy   System.Object → System.Attribute → XmlFormatExtensionPrefixAttribute

Valid On   Class

32

The System.Web.Services. Description Namespace

The System.Web.Services.Description namespace includes types used to represent the elements of Web Service Description Language (WSDL), an XML grammar that describes web services and specifies how to interact with them. Web services created with ASP.NET automatically generate their own WSDL documents, which contain all the information a client needs to interact with them and invoke their methods. You can retrieve this document by requesting the appropriate *.asmx* file with *?WSDL* appended to the end of the URL (as in *http://www.mysite.com/myservice.asmx?WSDL*).

The starting point for understanding this namespace is the ServiceDescription class, which represents the complete WSDL document and provides collections of Binding, Message, Types, and Service objects. The ServiceDescription class also provides Read() and Write() methods, which allow you to convert between actual WSDL documents and their object representation. Finally, you can also use the ServiceDescriptionReflector class to create a ServiceDescription object based on an existing web service by supplying the web service's URL.

Another interesting class in this namespace is ServiceDescriptionImporter, which provides the functionality .NET uses to create proxy classes based on WSDL documents. Most other classes represent a particular portion of a WSDL document, and you do not provide any additional functionality.

All details of WSDL implementation are "abstracted away" from you when creating or consuming a web service with .NET. For that reason, you may have little need to use the types in this namespace. To learn more about the specifics of the WSDL standard on which these types are based, refer to *http://www.w3.org/TR/wsdl*. Figure 32-1 shows ServiceDescriptionFormatExtension-derived types, and Figure 32-2 shows other types. Figure 32-3 contains the collections in this namespace.

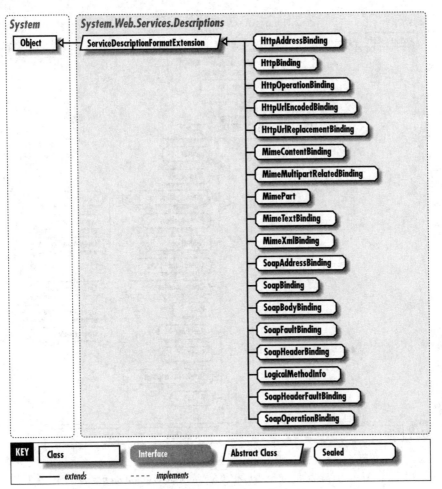

System

Object

System.Web.Services.Descriptions

ServiceDescriptionFormatExtension

HttpAddressBinding

HttpBinding

HttpOperationBinding

HttpUrlEncodedBinding

HttpUrlReplacementBinding

MimeContentBinding

MimeMultipartRelatedBinding

MimePart

MimeTextBinding

MimeXmlBinding

SoapAddressBinding

SoapBinding

SoapBodyBinding

SoapFaultBinding

SoapHeaderBinding

LogicalMethodInfo

SoapHeaderFaultBinding

SoapOperationBinding

KEY Class   Interface   Abstract Class   Sealed

——— extends   - - - - implements

Figure 32-1. ServiceDescriptionFormatExtension-derived types

Description
Namespace

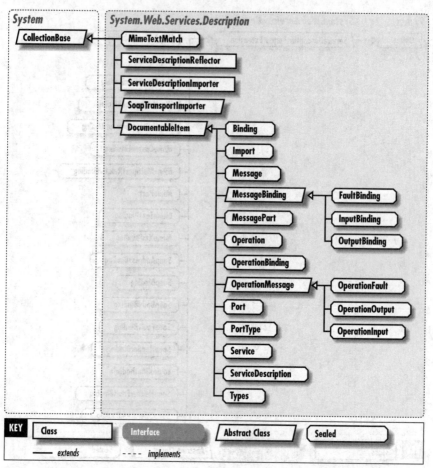

Figure 32-2. More types from the System.Web.Services.Description namespace

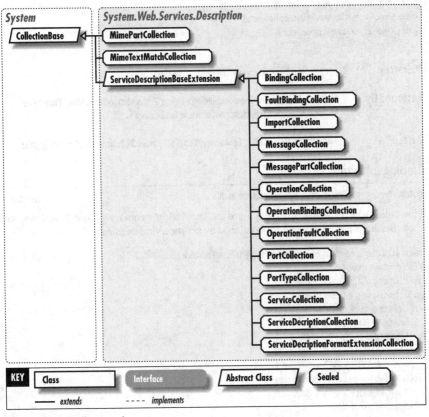

Figure 32-3. Collection classes

Binding

System.Web.Services.Description (system.web.services.dll)   sealed class

A WSDL document defines abstract information for data types, messages, and operations. A binding bridges the gap between abstract, protocol-independent information, and the encoding of that information (the concrete physical representation of messages on the wire). The Binding class represents the WSDL <binding> element, which provides binding information for a single protocol. For example, the WSDL document ASP.NET generates for a web service called StockQuotes would have three bindings: StockQuotesHttpGet, StockQuotesHttpPost, and StockQuotesSoap.

A Binding contains a collection of OperationBinding objects (provided through the Operations property). Bindings must define WSDL ports (represented by the Port class).

```
public sealed class Binding : DocumentableItem {
// Public Constructors
   public Binding( );
// Public Instance Properties
   public ServiceDescriptionFormatExtensionCollection Extensions{get; }
   public string Name{set; get; }
```

```
    public OperationBindingCollection Operations{get; }
    public ServiceDescription ServiceDescription{get; }
    public XmlQualifiedName Type{set; get; }
}
```

Hierarchy   System.Object → DocumentableItem → Binding

Returned By   BindingCollection.this, OperationBinding.Binding, ProtocolImporter.Binding, ProtocolRe-
                   flector.Binding, ServiceDescriptionCollection.GetBinding( )

Passed To   BindingCollection.{Add( ), Contains( ), CopyTo( ), IndexOf( ), Insert( ), Remove( ), this}

BindingCollection

System.Web.Services.Description (system.web.services.dll)   sealed class

This collection of Binding objects is used by the Bindings property of the ServiceDescription
class. Bindings can be accessed by name or by position (index number).

```
public sealed class BindingCollection : ServiceDescriptionBaseCollection {
// Public Instance Properties
   public Binding this[ string name ]{get; }
   public Binding this[ int index ]{set; get; }
// Public Instance Methods
   public int Add( Binding binding);
   public bool Contains( Binding binding);
   public void CopyTo( Binding[ ] array, int index);
   public int IndexOf( Binding binding);
   public void Insert( int index, Binding binding);
   public void Remove( Binding binding);
// Protected Instance Methods
   protected override string GetKey( object value);                    // overrides ServiceDescriptionBaseCollection
   protected override void SetParent(object value,  object parent);    // overrides ServiceDescriptionBaseCollection
}
```

Hierarchy   System.Object → System.Collections.CollectionBase(System.Collections.IList, System.Collec-
                   tions.ICollection, System.Collections.IEnumerable) → ServiceDescriptionBaseCollection →
                   BindingCollection

Returned By   ServiceDescription.Bindings

DocumentableItem

System.Web.Services.Description (system.web.services.dll)   abstract class

This abstract base class is used by several different classes in the System.Web.Services.Descrip-
tion namespace. It provides only one property, Documentation, which represents the
<documentation> element that can be added inside other WSDL language elements to
provide human-readable information (like a descriptive comment). This tag is generated automatically when you use the Description property of the System.Web.Services.
WebMethodAttribute or System.Web.Services.WebServiceAttribute.

```
public abstract class DocumentableItem {
// Protected Constructors
  protected DocumentableItem( );
// Public Instance Properties
  public string Documentation{set; get; }
}
```

Subclasses   Multiple types

FaultBinding

System.Web.Services.Description (system.web.services.dll)   sealed class

This binding specifies the concrete transmission format for any error messages that
occur during an operation. It maps to the WSDL <fault> element in the <binding>
element.

```
public sealed class FaultBinding : MessageBinding {
// Public Constructors
  public FaultBinding( );
// Public Instance Properties
  public override ServiceDescriptionFormatExtensionCollection Extensions{get; }        // overrides MessageBinding
}
```

Hierarchy   System.Object → DocumentableItem → MessageBinding → FaultBinding

Returned By   FaultBindingCollection.this

Passed To   FaultBindingCollection.{Add( ), Contains( ), CopyTo( ), IndexOf( ), Insert( ), Remove( ),
this}

FaultBindingCollection

System.Web.Services.Description (system.web.services.dll)   sealed class

This collection of FaultBinding objects is used by the OperationBinding.Faults property. Each
FaultBinding can be accessed by name or position (index number).

```
public sealed class FaultBindingCollection : ServiceDescriptionBaseCollection {
// Public Instance Properties
  public FaultBinding this[ string name ]{get; }
  public FaultBinding this[ int index ]{set; get; }
// Public Instance Methods
  public int Add( FaultBinding bindingOperationFault);
  public bool Contains( FaultBinding bindingOperationFault);
  public void CopyTo( FaultBinding[ ] array, int index);
  public int IndexOf( FaultBinding bindingOperationFault);
  public void Insert(int index, FaultBinding bindingOperationFault);
  public void Remove( FaultBinding bindingOperationFault);
// Protected Instance Methods
  protected override string GetKey( object value);                        // overrides ServiceDescriptionBaseCollection
  protected override void SetParent(object value, object parent);         // overrides ServiceDescriptionBaseCollection
}
```

Hierarchy System.Object → System.Collections.CollectionBase(System.Collections.IList, System.Collections.ICollection, System.Collections.IEnumerable) → ServiceDescriptionBaseCollection → FaultBindingCollection

Returned By OperationBinding.Faults

HttpAddressBinding

System.Web.Services.Description (system.web.services.dll)   sealed class

Represents an extensibility element added to the WSDL <port> element, which enables HTTP binding to a specific web service address. The Location property specifies the base URL address for the web service.

```
public sealed class HttpAddressBinding : ServiceDescriptionFormatExtension {
// Public Constructors
  public HttpAddressBinding( );
// Public Instance Properties
  public string Location{set; get; }
}
```

Hierarchy   System.Object → ServiceDescriptionFormatExtension → HttpAddressBinding

HttpBinding

System.Web.Services.Description (system.web.services.dll)   sealed class

Represents an extensibility element added to the WSDL <binding> element, which allows information to be transmitted by HTTP. The Verb property is a string that can have three values: an empty string (the default), "POST" (which specifies that requests will use HTTP POST), or "GET" (which specifies that requests will use HTTP GET).

```
public sealed class HttpBinding : ServiceDescriptionFormatExtension {
// Public Constructors
  public HttpBinding( );
// Public Static Fields
  public const string Namespace;                     // =http://schemas.xmlsoap.org/wsdl/http/
// Public Instance Properties
  public string Verb{set; get; }
}
```

Hierarchy   System.Object → ServiceDescriptionFormatExtension → HttpBinding

HttpOperationBinding

System.Web.Services.Description (system.web.services.dll)   sealed class

Represents an extensibility element added to the WSDL <operation> element, which allows a web service method to be invoked over HTTP. The Location property specifes the relative URL of a web service operation (using the base specified by HttpOperationBinding).

```
public sealed class HttpOperationBinding : ServiceDescriptionFormatExtension {
// Public Constructors
```

```
public HttpOperationBinding( );
// Public Instance Properties
public string Location{set; get; }
}
```

Hierarchy   System.Object → ServiceDescriptionFormatExtension → HttpOperationBinding

HttpUrlEncodedBinding

System.Web.Services.Description (system.web.services.dll)   **sealed class**

Represents an extensibility element added to a WSDL InputBinding object. It indicates that the request will send data using the standard URL encoding format ("*name=value&name2=value2*") over HTTP. This class does not provide any properties.

```
public sealed class HttpUrlEncodedBinding : ServiceDescriptionFormatExtension {
// Public Constructors
public HttpUrlEncodedBinding( );
}
```

Hierarchy   System.Object → ServiceDescriptionFormatExtension → HttpUrlEncodedBinding

HttpUrlReplacementBinding

System.Web.Services.Description (system.web.services.dll)   **sealed class**

Represents an extensibility element added to a WSDL InputBinding object. It indicates that the request will send data using a custom format over HTTP.

```
public sealed class HttpUrlReplacementBinding : ServiceDescriptionFormatExtension {
// Public Constructors
public HttpUrlReplacementBinding( );
}
```

Hierarchy   System.Object → ServiceDescriptionFormatExtension → HttpUrlReplacementBinding

Import

System.Web.Services.Description (system.web.services.dll)   **sealed class**

This class represents the WSDL <import> element, which associates an XML namespace with a document location. The familiar XML equivalent is <import namespace="uri" location="uri"/>. This equivalent allows a WSDL document to be split into multiple subdocuments, each with a unique XML namespace, which can then be imported as needed.

```
public sealed class Import : DocumentableItem {
// Public Constructors
public Import( );
// Public Instance Properties
public string Location{set; get; }
public string Namespace{set; get; }
public ServiceDescription ServiceDescription{get; }
}
```

Hierarchy	System.Object → DocumentableItem → Import
Returned By	ImportCollection.this
Passed To	ImportCollection.{Add( ), Contains( ), CopyTo( ), IndexOf( ), Insert( ), Remove( ), this}

ImportCollection

System.Web.Services.Description (system.web.services.dll)   sealed class

This collection of Import objects is used by the Imports property of the ServiceDescription class to specify XML namespaces for a WSDL document. You can retrieve an individual Import object by index number.

```
public sealed class ImportCollection : ServiceDescriptionBaseCollection {
// Public Instance Properties
  public Import this[ int index ]{set; get; }
// Public Instance Methods
  public int Add(Import import);
  public bool Contains(Import import);
  public void CopyTo(Import[ ] array, int index);
  public int IndexOf(Import import);
  public void Insert(int index, Import import);
  public void Remove(Import import);
// Protected Instance Methods
  protected override void SetParent(object value, object parent);              // overrides ServiceDescriptionBaseCollection
}
```

Hierarchy	System.Object → System.Collections.CollectionBase(System.Collections.IList, System.Collections.ICollection, System.Collections.IEnumerable) → ServiceDescriptionBaseCollection → ImportCollection
Returned By	ServiceDescription.Imports

InputBinding

System.Web.Services.Description (system.web.services.dll)   sealed class

This specific binding is used to specify the encoding of an input message. The Input-Binding class provides a Extensions property, which contains a collection consisting of a single binding. This binding varies depending on the type of protocol that this element applies to (HTTP POST, HTTP GET, or SOAP). For example, this collection would contain a HttpUrlEncodedBinding for HTTP GET messages, a MimeContentBinding for HTTP POST messages, or a SoapBodyBinding for SOAP messages.

```
public sealed class InputBinding : MessageBinding {
// Public Constructors
  public InputBinding( );
// Public Instance Properties
  public override ServiceDescriptionFormatExtensionCollection Extensions{get; }              // overrides MessageBinding
}
```

Hierarchy	System.Object → DocumentableItem → MessageBinding → InputBinding

Returned By	OperationBinding.Input
Passed To	OperationBinding.Input

Message

System.Web.Services.Description (system.web.services.dll) sealed class

This class represents the WSDL <message> element, which is used to describe the contents of messages exchanged between a client and the web service. For every method in a web service, a WSDL document contains an input and output message. There are also separate message definitions for every protocol type. For example, for a method called GetInfo, ASP.NET would generate GetInfoHttpPostIn and GetInfoHttpPostOut messages, along with corresponding messages for HTTP GET and SOAP. Messages consist of zero or more MessagePart objects, which specify method parameters and return values.

```
public sealed class Message : DocumentableItem {
// Public Constructors
  public Message( );
// Public Instance Properties
  public string Name{set; get; }
  public MessagePartCollection Parts{get; }
  public ServiceDescription ServiceDescription{get; }
// Public Instance Methods
  public MessagePart FindPartByName( string partName);
  public MessagePart[ ] FindPartsByName( string[ ] partNames);
}
```

Hierarchy	System.Object → DocumentableItem → Message
Returned By	MessageCollection.this, MessagePart.Message, ProtocolImporter.{InputMessage, OutputMessage}, ProtocolReflector.{InputMessage, OutputMessage}, ServiceDescriptionCollection. GetMessage( )
Passed To	MessageCollection.{Add( ), Contains( ), CopyTo( ), IndexOf( ), Insert( ), Remove( ), this}

MessageBinding

System.Web.Services.Description (system.web.services.dll) abstract class

This abstract class is implemented by FaultBinding, InputBinding, and OutputBinding. Binding specifies how abstract data formats are mapped to the concrete protocol used for transmission.

```
public abstract class MessageBinding : DocumentableItem {
// Protected Constructors
  protected MessageBinding( );
// Public Instance Properties
  public abstract ServiceDescriptionFormatExtensionCollection Extensions{get; }
  public string Name{set; get; }
  public OperationBinding OperationBinding{get; }
}
```

Description
Namespace

System.Object → DocumentableItem → MessageBinding

Subclasses FaultBinding, InputBinding, OutputBinding

MessageCollection

System.Web.Services.Description (system.web.services.dll)   sealed class

This collection of Message objects is used by the Messages property of the ServiceDescription class to represent all <message> elements in a WSDL document. You can access an invidual Message by name or position (index number).

```
public sealed class MessageCollection : ServiceDescriptionBaseCollection {
// Public Instance Properties
  public Message this[ string name ]{get; }
  public Message this[ int index ]{set; get; }
// Public Instance Methods
  public int Add( Message message);
  public bool Contains( Message message);
  public void CopyTo( Message[ ] array, int index);
  public int IndexOf( Message message);
  public void Insert( int index, Message message);
  public void Remove( Message message);
// Protected Instance Methods
  protected override string GetKey( object value);              // overrides ServiceDescriptionBaseCollection
  protected override void SetParent(object value, object parent);    // overrides ServiceDescriptionBaseCollection
}
```

Hierarchy System.Object → System.Collections.CollectionBase(System.Collections.IList, System.Collections.ICollection, System.Collections.IEnumerable) → ServiceDescriptionBaseCollection → MessageCollection

Returned By ProtocolReflector.HeaderMessages, ServiceDescription.Messages

MessagePart

System.Web.Services.Description (system.web.services.dll)   sealed class

This class represents a WSDL <part> element, which is contained in a <message> element. Each MessagePart object corresponds to a single parameter or a return value for a function, and specifies the variable's Name and either an XML Type or an XML Element, which refers to an element from the Types collection.

For example, a GetStockQuote method would have several messages, including GetStock-QuoteHttpGetOut, and would have a single MessagePart representing the return value. Return values are given the Name "parameters" for a SOAP request or "Body" for an HTTP request.

```
public sealed class MessagePart : DocumentableItem {
// Public Constructors
  public MessagePart( );
// Public Instance Properties
  public XmlQualifiedName Element{set; get; }
  public Message Message{get; }
```

```
public string Name{set; get; }
public XmlQualifiedName Type{set; get; }
}
```

Hierarchy   System.Object → DocumentableItem → MessagePart

Returned By   Message.{FindPartByName( ), FindPartsByName( )}, MessagePartCollection.this

Passed To   MessagePartCollection.{Add( ), Contains( ), CopyTo( ), IndexOf( ), Insert( ), Remove( ), this}

MessagePartCollection

System.Web.Services.Description (system.web.services.dll)   **sealed class**

This collection of MessagePart objects is used by the Parts property of the Message class to represent the return value and parameters of a message. You can access an invidual MessagePart by name or position (index number).

```
public sealed class MessagePartCollection : ServiceDescriptionBaseCollection {
// Public Instance Properties
  public MessagePart this[ string name ]{get; }
  public MessagePart this[ int index ]{set; get; }
// Public Instance Methods
  public int Add(MessagePart messagePart);
  public bool Contains(MessagePart messagePart);
  public void CopyTo( MessagePart[ ] array, int index);
  public int IndexOf( MessagePart messagePart);
  public void Insert( int index, MessagePart messagePart);
  public void Remove( MessagePart messagePart);
// Protected Instance Methods
  protected override string GetKey( object value);              // overrides ServiceDescriptionBaseCollection
  protected override void SetParent(object value, object parent);    // overrides ServiceDescriptionBaseCollection
}
```

Hierarchy   System.Object → System.Collections.CollectionBase(System.Collections.IList, System.Collections.ICollection, System.Collections.IEnumerable) → ServiceDescriptionBaseCollection → MessagePartCollection

Returned By   Message.Parts

MimeContentBinding

System.Web.Services.Description (system.web.services.dll)   **sealed class**

This binding represents an extensibility element added to an InputBinding or an Output-Binding element.

This binding is generally used for an HTTP POST input message (represented by OperationInput). It includes a Type property, which specifies the MIME encoding type (typically application/x-www-form-urlencoded) used for encoding data for HTTP transmission. The Part property specifes the name of the message part to which the binding applies.

```
public sealed class MimeContentBinding : ServiceDescriptionFormatExtension {
// Public Constructors
```

```
  public MimeContentBinding( );
// Public Static Fields
  public const string Namespace;                                    // =http://schemas.xmlsoap.org/wsdl/mime/
// Public Instance Properties
  public string Part{set; get; }
  public string Type{set; get; }
}
```

Hierarchy   System.Object → ServiceDescriptionFormatExtension → MimeContentBinding

MimeMultipartRelatedBinding

System.Web.Services.Description (system.web.services.dll)   sealed class

Represents an extensibility element added to an InputBinding or an OutputBinding element. This class supports multipart MIME messages that use different MIME types for different portions of the message body.

The Parts property provides a collection of MessagePart objects. Each one represents an extensibility element added to the MimeMultipartRelatedBinding to specify the MIME format for a single portion of the MIME message.

```
public sealed class MimeMultipartRelatedBinding : ServiceDescriptionFormatExtension {
// Public Constructors
  public MimeMultipartRelatedBinding( );
// Public Instance Properties
  public MimePartCollection Parts{get; }
}
```

Hierarchy   System.Object → ServiceDescriptionFormatExtension → MimeMultipartRelatedBinding

MimePart

System.Web.Services.Description (system.web.services.dll)   sealed class

This class represents an extensibility element added to a MimeMultipartRelatedBinding object. The Extensions collection can include MimeContentBinding, MimeXmlBinding, and SoapBodyBinding objects. Each one specifies the concrete MIME type for a portion of the multipart MIME message (these classes all provide a Part property that references the MessagePart object to which the MIME binding applies).

```
public sealed class MimePart : ServiceDescriptionFormatExtension {
// Public Constructors
  public MimePart( );
// Public Instance Properties
  public ServiceDescriptionFormatExtensionCollection Extensions{get; }
}
```

Hierarchy   System.Object → ServiceDescriptionFormatExtension → MimePart

Returned By   MimePartCollection.this

Passed To   MimePartCollection.{Add( ), Contains( ), CopyTo( ), IndexOf( ), Insert( ), Remove( ), this}

MimePartCollection

System.Web.Services.Description (system.web.services.dll)   sealed class

This class provides a collection of MimePart objects used by the MimeMultipartRelatedBinding class. Individual MimePart objects can be retrieved only by index number.

```
public sealed class MimePartCollection : CollectionBase {
// Public Constructors
  public MimePartCollection( );
// Public Instance Properties
  public MimePart this[ int index ]{set; get; }
// Public Instance Methods
  public int Add(MimePart mimePart);
  public bool Contains(MimePart mimePart);
  public void CopyTo(MimePart[ ] array, int index);
  public int IndexOf(MimePart mimePart);
  public void Insert(int index, MimePart mimePart);
  public void Remove(MimePart mimePart);
}
```

Hierarchy   System.Object → System.Collections.CollectionBase(System.Collections.IList, System.Collections.ICollection, System.Collections.IEnumerable) → MimePartCollection

Returned By   MimeMultipartRelatedBinding.Parts

MimeTextBinding

System.Web.Services.Description (system.web.services.dll)   sealed class

This class represents an extensibility element added to an InputBinding, an OutputBinding, or a MimePart object. It includes a single Matches property, which specifies the text patterns for which the HTTP transmission is searched.

```
public sealed class MimeTextBinding : ServiceDescriptionFormatExtension {
// Public Constructors
  public MimeTextBinding( );
// Public Static Fields
  public const string Namespace;                    // =http://microsoft.com/wsdl/mime/textMatching/
// Public Instance Properties
  public MimeTextMatchCollection Matches{get; }
}
```

Hierarchy   System.Object → ServiceDescriptionFormatExtension → MimeTextBinding

MimeTextMatch

System.Web.Services.Description (system.web.services.dll)   sealed class

This class represents a text pattern that will be searched for in the HTTP transmission. Type specifies the MIME type of the message, Pattern specifies the pattern, and Repeats sets the number of times the search will be performed (the default is 1, but you can specify System.Int32.MaxValue to get all matches).

```
public sealed class MimeTextMatch {
// Public Constructors
  public MimeTextMatch( );
// Public Instance Properties
  public int Capture{set; get; }
  public int Group{set; get; }
  public bool IgnoreCase{set; get; }
  public MimeTextMatchCollection Matches{get; }
  public string Name{set; get; }
  public string Pattern{set; get; }
  public int Repeats{set; get; }
  public string RepeatsString{set; get; }
  public string Type{set; get; }
}
```

Returned By   MimeTextMatchCollection.this

Passed To   MimeTextMatchCollection.{Add( ), Contains( ), CopyTo( ), IndexOf( ), Insert( ), Remove( ), this}

MimeTextMatchCollection

System.Web.Services.Description (system.web.services.dll)   **sealed class**

This class provides a collection of MimeTextMatch objects used by the MimeTextBinding class. Individual MimePart objects can be retrieved only by index number.

```
public sealed class MimeTextMatchCollection : CollectionBase {
// Public Constructors
  public MimeTextMatchCollection( );
// Public Instance Properties
  public MimeTextMatch this[ int index ]{set; get; }
// Public Instance Methods
  public int Add( MimeTextMatch match);
  public bool Contains( MimeTextMatch match);
  public void CopyTo( MimeTextMatch[ ] array, int index);
  public int IndexOf( MimeTextMatch match);
  public void Insert( int index, MimeTextMatch match);
  public void Remove( MimeTextMatch match);
}
```

Hierarchy   System.Object → System.Collections.CollectionBase(System.Collections.IList, System.Collections.ICollection, System.Collections.IEnumerable) → MimeTextMatchCollection

Returned By   MimeTextBinding.Matches, MimeTextMatch.Matches

MimeXmlBinding

System.Web.Services.Description (system.web.services.dll)   **sealed class**

This class represents an extensibility element added to an InputBinding, an OutputBinding, or a MimePart object. It specifies an XML schema for messages, but is not SOAP-compliant.

By default, ASP.NET uses this binding for HTTP GET and POST output messages, which are represented by the OperationOutput class.

```
public sealed class MimeXmlBinding : ServiceDescriptionFormatExtension {
// Public Constructors
  public MimeXmlBinding( );
// Public Instance Properties
  public string Part{set; get; }
}
```

Hierarchy   System.Object → ServiceDescriptionFormatExtension → MimeXmlBinding

Operation

System.Web.Services.Description (system.web.services.dll)   sealed class

This class represents the WSDL <operation> element. It describes an operation, which consists of one or more OperationMessage objects. In a WSDL document, an <operation> element exists for every method in your web service. (Actually, there will be three copies of this set of operation elements: one for each different type of transmission, contained in differently named <portType> elements.)

Every operation is associated with exactly one OperationInput and one OperationOutput object.

```
public sealed class Operation : DocumentableItem {
// Public Constructors
  public Operation( );
// Public Instance Properties
  public OperationFaultCollection Faults{get; }
  public OperationMessageCollection Messages{get; }
  public string Name{set; get; }
  public string[ ] ParameterOrder{set; get; }
  public string ParameterOrderString{set; get; }
  public PortType PortType{get; }
// Public Instance Methods
  public bool IsBoundBy( OperationBinding operationBinding);
}
```

Hierarchy   System.Object → DocumentableItem → Operation

Returned By   OperationCollection.this, OperationMessage.Operation, ProtocolImporter.Operation, ProtocolReflector.Operation

Passed To   OperationCollection.{Add( ), Contains( ), CopyTo( ), IndexOf( ), Insert( ), Remove( ), this}

OperationBinding

System.Web.Services.Description (system.web.services.dll)   sealed class

This class represents the <operation> element in the <binding> element of a WSDL document. Each OperationBinding specifies how the abstract data for input and output messages is encoded. The binding thus consists of InputBinding and OutputBinding objects, and optionally, a FaultBinding object.

```
public sealed class OperationBinding : DocumentableItem {
// Public Constructors
  public OperationBinding( );
// Public Instance Properties
  public Binding Binding{get; }
  public ServiceDescriptionFormatExtensionCollection Extensions{get; }
  public FaultBindingCollection Faults{get; }
  public InputBinding Input{set; get; }
  public string Name{set; get; }
  public OutputBinding Output{set; get; }
}
```

Hierarchy   System.Object → DocumentableItem → OperationBinding

Returned By   MessageBinding.OperationBinding, OperationBindingCollection.this, ProtocolImporter.Oper-
                   ationBinding, ProtocolReflector.OperationBinding

Passed To   Operation.IsBoundBy( ), OperationBindingCollection.{Add( ), Contains( ), CopyTo( ),
                   IndexOf( ), Insert( ), Remove( ), this}

OperationBindingCollection

System.Web.Services.Description (system.web.services.dll)   sealed class

This collection of OperationBinding objects is used for the Operations property of the Binding
class. You can access each OperationBinding element by position (index number).

```
public sealed class OperationBindingCollection : ServiceDescriptionBaseCollection {
// Public Instance Properties
  public OperationBinding this[ int index ]{set; get; }
// Public Instance Methods
  public int Add( OperationBinding bindingOperation);
  public bool Contains( OperationBinding bindingOperation);
  public void CopyTo( OperationBinding[ ] array, int index);
  public int IndexOf( OperationBinding bindingOperation);
  public void Insert(int index, OperationBinding bindingOperation);
  public void Remove( OperationBinding bindingOperation);
// Protected Instance Methods
  protected override void SetParent(object value, object parent);     // overrides ServiceDescriptionBaseCollection
}
```

Hierarchy   System.Object → System.Collections.CollectionBase(System.Collections.IList, System.Collec-
                   tions.ICollection, System.Collections.IEnumerable) → ServiceDescriptionBaseCollection →
                   OperationBindingCollection

Returned By   Binding.Operations

OperationCollection

System.Web.Services.Description (system.web.services.dll) sealed class

This collection of Operation objects is used by the Operations property of the PortType class. You can access each Operation element by position (index number).

```
public sealed class OperationCollection : ServiceDescriptionBaseCollection {
// Public Instance Properties
  public Operation this[ int index ]{set; get; }
// Public Instance Methods
  public int Add( Operation operation);
  public bool Contains( Operation operation);
  public void CopyTo( Operation[ ] array, int index);
  public int IndexOf( Operation operation);
  public void Insert( int index, Operation operation);
  public void Remove( Operation operation);
// Protected Instance Methods
  protected override void SetParent(object value, object parent);      // overrides ServiceDescriptionBaseCollection
}
```

Hierarchy   System.Object → System.Collections.CollectionBase(System.Collections.IList, System.Collections.ICollection, System.Collections.IEnumerable) → ServiceDescriptionBaseCollection → OperationCollection

Returned By   PortType.Operations

OperationFault

System.Web.Services.Description (system.web.services.dll) sealed class

This class represents a OperationMessage object that defines the specifications for error messages returned by a web service.

```
public sealed class OperationFault : OperationMessage {
// Public Constructors
  public OperationFault( );
}
```

Hierarchy   System.Object → DocumentableItem → OperationMessage → OperationFault

Returned By   OperationFaultCollection.this

Passed To   OperationFaultCollection.{Add( ), Contains( ), CopyTo( ), IndexOf( ), Insert( ), Remove( ), this}

OperationFaultCollection

System.Web.Services.Description (system.web.services.dll) sealed class

This collection of OperationFault objects is used by the Operation.Faults property. You can access each OperationFault element by name or position (index number).

```
public sealed class OperationFaultCollection : ServiceDescriptionBaseCollection {
// Public Instance Properties
  public OperationFault this[ string name ]{get; }
  public OperationFault this[ int index ]{set; get; }
// Public Instance Methods
  public int Add( OperationFault operationFaultMessage);
  public bool Contains(OperationFault operationFaultMessage);
  public void CopyTo( OperationFault[ ] array, int index);
  public int IndexOf( OperationFault operationFaultMessage);
  public void Insert(int index, OperationFault operationFaultMessage);
  public void Remove( OperationFault operationFaultMessage);
// Protected Instance Methods
  protected override string GetKey( object value);                  // overrides ServiceDescriptionBaseCollection
  protected override void SetParent(object value, object parent);   // overrides ServiceDescriptionBaseCollection
}
```

Hierarchy   System.Object → System.Collections.CollectionBase(System.Collections.IList, System.Collections.ICollection, System.Collections.IEnumerable) → ServiceDescriptionBaseCollection → OperationFaultCollection

Returned By   Operation.Faults

OperationFlow   serializable

System.Web.Services.Description (system.web.services.dll)   enum

This enumeration is used for the OperationMessageCollection.Flow property. It indicates the direction of message transmission. Notification indicates that an endpoint or service sends a message. OneWay indicates that the endpoint or service receives a message. RequestResponse indicates that an endpoint or services receives the message, and then sends a response, while SolicitResponse indicates the reverse.

```
public enum OperationFlow {
  None = 0,
  OneWay = 1,
  Notification = 2,
  RequestResponse = 3,
  SolicitResponse = 4
}
```

Hierarchy   System.Object → System.ValueType → System.Enum(System.IComparable, System.IFormattable, System.IConvertible) → OperationFlow

Returned By   OperationMessageCollection.Flow

Passed To   ProtocolImporter.IsOperationFlowSupported( )

OperationInput

System.Web.Services.Description (system.web.services.dll)   sealed class

This class represents the WSDL <input> element. It defines an abstract message format for sending information to a specific web method by referring to the appropriate Message object.

```
public sealed class OperationInput : OperationMessage {
// Public Constructors
  public OperationInput( );
}
```

Hierarchy   System.Object → DocumentableItem → OperationMessage → OperationInput

Returned By   OperationMessageCollection.Input

OperationMessage

System.Web.Services.Description (system.web.services.dll)   abstract class

This abstract class represents the WSDL <message> element. There are two types of operations recognized in WSDL, input and output. These operations are represented specifically by the classes OperationInput and OperationOutput, both of which derive from this class. OperationFault also derives from this class.

```
public abstract class OperationMessage : DocumentableItem {
// Protected Constructorsprotected OperationMessage( );
// Public Instance Properties
  public XmlQualifiedName Message{set; get; }
  public string Name{set; get; }
  public Operation Operation{get; }
}
```

Hierarchy   System.Object → DocumentableItem → OperationMessage

Subclasses   OperationFault, OperationInput, OperationOutput

Returned By   OperationMessageCollection.this

Passed To   OperationMessageCollection.{Add( ), Contains( ), CopyTo( ), IndexOf( ), Insert( ), Remove( ), this}

OperationMessageCollection

System.Web.Services.Description (system.web.services.dll)   sealed class

This collection of OperationMessage objects is used by the Messages property of the Operation class. You can access each OperationMessage element by position (index number).

```
public sealed class OperationMessageCollection : ServiceDescriptionBaseCollection {
// Public Instance Properties
  public OperationFlow Flow{get; }
  public OperationInput Input{get; }
```

```
    public OperationOutput Output{get; }
    public OperationMessage this[ int index ]{set; get; }
// Public Instance Methods
    public int Add( OperationMessage operationMessage);
    public bool Contains( OperationMessage operationMessage);
    public void CopyTo( OperationMessage[ ] array, int index);
    public int IndexOf( OperationMessage operationMessage);
    public void Insert(int index, OperationMessage operationMessage);
    public void Remove( OperationMessage operationMessage);
// Protected Instance Methods
    protected override void OnInsert(int index, object value);           // overrides System.Collections.CollectionBase
    protected override void OnSet(int index, object oldValue, object newValue);   // overrides ServiceDescriptionBaseCollection

    protected override void OnValidate( object value);                   // overrides System.Collections.CollectionBase
    protected override void SetParent(object value, object parent);      // overrides ServiceDescriptionBaseCollection

}
```

Hierarchy   System.Object → System.Collections.CollectionBase(System.Collections.IList, System.Collections.ICollection, System.Collections.IEnumerable) → ServiceDescriptionBaseCollection → OperationMessageCollection

Returned By   Operation.Messages

OperationOutput

System.Web.Services.Description (system.web.services.dll)   **sealed class**

This class represents the WSDL <output> element. It defines an abstract message format for retrieving information from a specific web method (by referring to the appropriate Message object).

```
public sealed class OperationOutput : OperationMessage {
// Public Constructors
    public OperationOutput( );
}
```

Hierarchy   System.Object → DocumentableItem → OperationMessage → OperationOutput

Returned By   OperationMessageCollection.Output

OutputBinding

System.Web.Services.Description (system.web.services.dll)   **sealed class**

This specific binding is used to specify the encoding of an output message. The OutputBinding class provides a Extensions property, which contains a collection of one binding. This binding varies depending on the type of protocol that this element applies to (HTTP POST, HTTP GET, or SOAP). For example, this collection would contain a MimeXmlBinding for HTTP messages and a SoapBodyBinding for SOAP messages.

```
public sealed class OutputBinding : MessageBinding {
// Public Constructors
```

```
public OutputBinding( );
// Public Instance Properties
  public override ServiceDescriptionFormatExtensionCollection Extensions{get; }          // overrides MessageBinding
}
```

Hierarchy	System.Object → DocumentableItem → MessageBinding → OutputBinding

Returned By	OperationBinding.Output

Passed To	OperationBinding.Output

Port

System.Web.Services.Description (system.web.services.dll)   sealed class

This class represents the WSDL <port> element. It defines a service endpoint, which
is the URL required to access the web service. In a WSDL document generated by
ASP.NET, you will find three <port> elements: one for each type of transmission
(HTTP GET, HTTP POST, and SOAP). Each element will point to the same URL,
which is the fully qualified location of your *.asmx* file (for example, *http://www.
mysite.com/ws/MyService.asmx*).

```
public sealed class Port : DocumentableItem {
// Public Constructors
  public Port( );
// Public Instance Properties
  public XmlQualifiedName Binding{set; get; }
  public ServiceDescriptionFormatExtensionCollection Extensions{get; }
  public string Name{set; get; }
  public Service Service{get; }
}
```

Hierarchy	System.Object → DocumentableItem → Port

Returned By	PortCollection.this, ProtocolImporter.Port, ProtocolReflector.Port

Passed To	PortCollection.{Add( ), Contains( ), CopyTo( ), IndexOf( ), Insert( ), Remove( ), this}

PortCollection

System.Web.Services.Description (system.web.services.dll)   sealed class

This collection of Port objects is used by the Ports property of the Service class to represent all the <port> elements in a WSDL document. You can access each Port element by
name or position (index number).

```
public sealed class PortCollection : ServiceDescriptionBaseCollection {
// Public Instance Properties
  public Port this[ string name ]{get; }
  public Port this[ int index ]{set; get; }
// Public Instance Methods
  public int Add( Port port);
  public bool Contains( Port port);
```

```
public void CopyTo( Port[ ] array, int index);
public int IndexOf( Port port);
public void Insert( int index, Port port);
public void Remove( Port port);
// Protected Instance Methods
protected override string GetKey( object value);                      // overrides ServiceDescriptionBaseCollection
protected override void SetParent(object value,                        // overrides ServiceDescriptionBaseCollection
    object parent);
}
```

Hierarchy   System.Object → System.Collections.CollectionBase(System.Collections.IList, System.Collections.ICollection, System.Collections.IEnumerable) → ServiceDescriptionBaseCollection → PortCollection

Returned By   Service.Ports

PortType

System.Web.Services.Description (system.web.services.dll)   sealed class

This class represents the WSDL <portType> element. It groups a set of related Operation objects, and identifies them with a Name. In a WSDL document generated by ASP.NET, there are three <portType> elements: one relating to HTTP GET, another for HTTP POST, and one for SOAP transmissions. ASP.NET creates these elements using the name of your web service and adding a suffix describing the type of transmission (for example, MyWebServiceHttpGet).

```
public sealed class PortType : DocumentableItem {
// Public Constructors
  public PortType( );
// Public Instance Properties
  public string Name{set; get; }
  public OperationCollection Operations{get; }
  public ServiceDescription ServiceDescription{get; }
}
```

Hierarchy   System.Object → DocumentableItem → PortType

Returned By   Operation.PortType, PortTypeCollection.this, ProtocolImporter.PortType, ProtocolReflector.PortType, ServiceDescriptionCollection.GetPortType( )

Passed To   PortTypeCollection.{Add( ), Contains( ), CopyTo( ), IndexOf( ), Insert( ), Remove( ), this}

PortTypeCollection

System.Web.Services.Description (system.web.services.dll)   sealed class

This collection of PortType objects (which are themselves collections of Operation objects) is used by the PortTypes property of the ServiceDescription class to represent all <portType> elements in a WSDL document. You can access each PortType element by name or position (index number).

```
public sealed class PortTypeCollection : ServiceDescriptionBaseCollection {
// Public Instance Properties
  public PortType this[ string name ]{get; }
  public PortType this[ int index ]{set; get; }
// Public Instance Methods
  public int Add( PortType portType);
  public bool Contains( PortType portType);
  public void CopyTo( PortType[ ] array, int index);
  public int IndexOf( PortType portType);
  public void Insert( int index, PortType portType);
  public void Remove( PortType portType);
// Protected Instance Methods
  protected override string GetKey( object value);                    // overrides ServiceDescriptionBaseCollection
  protected override void SetParent(object value, object parent);      // overrides ServiceDescriptionBaseCollection

}
```

Hierarchy	System.Object → System.Collections.CollectionBase(System.Collections.IList, System.Collections.ICollection, System.Collections.IEnumerable) → ServiceDescriptionBaseCollection → PortTypeCollection

Returned By	ServiceDescription.PortTypes

ProtocolImporter

System.Web.Services.Description (system.web.services.dll)   abstract class

This type supports the .NET Framework infrastructure. You don't need to use it directly in your code.

```
public abstract class ProtocolImporter {
// Protected Constructorsprotected ProtocolImporter( );
// Public Instance Properties
  public XmlSchemas AbstractSchemas{get; }
  public Binding Binding{get; }
  public string ClassName{get; }
  public CodeIdentifiers ClassNames{get; }
  public CodeNamespace CodeNamespace{get; }
  public CodeTypeDeclaration CodeTypeDeclaration{get; }
  public XmlSchemas ConcreteSchemas{get; }
  public Message InputMessage{get; }
  public string MethodName{get; }
  public Operation Operation{get; }
  public OperationBinding OperationBinding{get; }
  public Message OutputMessage{get; }
  public Port Port{get; }
  public PortType PortType{get; }
  public abstract string ProtocolName{get; }
  public XmlSchemas Schemas{get; }
  public Service Service{get; }
  public ServiceDescriptionCollection ServiceDescriptions{get; }
  public ServiceDescriptionImportStyle Style{get; }
```

```
public ServiceDescriptionImportWarnings Warnings{set; get; }
// Public Instance Methods
public void AddExtensionWarningComments(System.CodeDom.CodeCommentStatementCollection comments,
    ServiceDescriptionFormatExtensionCollection extensions);
public Exception OperationBindingSyntaxException(string text);
public Exception OperationSyntaxException( string text);
public void UnsupportedBindingWarning( string text);
public void UnsupportedOperationBindingWarning(string text);
public void UnsupportedOperationWarning( string text);
// Protected Instance Methods
protected abstract CodeTypeDeclaration BeginClass( );
protected virtual void BeginNamespace( );
protected virtual void EndClass( );
protected virtual void EndNamespace( );
protected abstract CodeMemberMethod GenerateMethod( );
protected abstract bool IsBindingSupported( );
protected abstract bool IsOperationFlowSupported(OperationFlow flow);
}
```

Subclasses   SoapProtocolImporter

ProtocolReflector

System.Web.Services.Description (system.web.services.dll)   abstract class

This type supports the .NET Framework infrastructure. You don't need to use it
directly in your code.

```
public abstract class ProtocolReflector {
// Protected Constructors
  protected ProtocolReflector( );
// Public Instance Properties
  public Binding Binding{get; }
  public string DefaultNamespace{get; }
  public MessageCollection HeaderMessages{get; }
  public Message InputMessage{get; }
  public LogicalMethodInfo Method{get; }
  public WebMethodAttribute MethodAttribute{get; }
  public LogicalMethodInfo[ ] Methods{get; }
  public Operation Operation{get; }
  public OperationBinding OperationBinding{get; }
  public Message OutputMessage{get; }
  public Port Port{get; }
  public PortType PortType{get; }
  public abstract string ProtocolName{get; }
  public XmlReflectionImporter ReflectionImporter{get; }
  public XmlSchemaExporter SchemaExporter{get; }
  public XmlSchemas Schemas{get; }
  public Service Service{get; }
  public ServiceDescription ServiceDescription{get; }
  public ServiceDescriptionCollection ServiceDescriptions{get; }
  public Type ServiceType{get; }
```

```
public string ServiceUrl{get; }
// Public Instance Methods
public ServiceDescription GetServiceDescription(string ns);
// Protected Instance Methods
protected virtual void BeginClass( );
protected virtual void EndClass( );
protected abstract bool ReflectMethod( );
protected virtual string ReflectMethodBinding( );
}
```

Returned By	SoapExtensionReflector.ReflectionContext
Passed To	SoapExtensionReflector.ReflectionContext

Service

System.Web.Services.Description (system.web.services.dll)   sealed class

This class represents the WSDL <service> element. It groups multiple related Port objects and identifies them with a Name. To invoke a web service method, a client sends a SOAP request identifying the service, the port in that service, and the operation it wants executed along with the input parameter values.

```
public sealed class Service : DocumentableItem {
// Public Constructors
public Service( );
// Public Instance Properties
public ServiceDescriptionFormatExtensionCollection Extensions{get; }
public string Name{set; get; }
public PortCollection Ports{get; }
public ServiceDescription ServiceDescription{get; }
}
```

Hierarchy	System.Object → DocumentableItem → Service
Returned By	Port.Service, ProtocolImporter.Service, ProtocolReflector.Service, ServiceCollection.this, ServiceDescriptionCollection.GetService( )
Passed To	ServiceCollection.{Add( ), Contains( ), CopyTo( ), IndexOf( ), Insert( ), Remove( ), this}

ServiceCollection

System.Web.Services.Description (system.web.services.dll)   sealed class

This collection of Service objects is used by the Services property of the ServiceDescription class to represent all <service> elements in a WSDL document. You can access each Service element by name or position (index number).

```
public sealed class ServiceCollection : ServiceDescriptionBaseCollection {
// Public Instance Properties
public Service this[ string name ]{get; }
public Service this[ int index ]{set; get; }
// Public Instance Methods
```

```
 public int Add( Service service);
 public bool Contains( Service service);
 public void CopyTo( Service[ ] array, int index);
 public int IndexOf( Service service);
 public void Insert( int index, Service service);
 public void Remove( Service service);
// Protected Instance Methods
 protected override string GetKey( object value);                    // overrides ServiceDescriptionBaseCollection
 protected override void SetParent(object value, object parent);     // overrides ServiceDescriptionBaseCollection
}
```

Hierarchy	System.Object → System.Collections.CollectionBase(System.Collections.IList, System.Collections.ICollection, System.Collections.IEnumerable) → ServiceDescriptionBaseCollection → ServiceCollection
Returned By	ServiceDescription.Services

ServiceDescription

System.Web.Services.Description (system.web.services.dll)   sealed class

The ServiceDescription class represents a valid WSDL document, complete with appropriate namespaces, elements, and attributes. The elements of the WSDL file are all represented by other, distinct classes in the System.Web.Services.Description namespace, and provided through the properties of the ServiceDescription class. At the top level, a WSDL document contains a series of definitions in a <definitions> element. These definitions define Types, Message, PortType, Binding, and Service elements.

The ServiceDescription class also provides a Read() and Write() method. Both methods are overloaded to allow you to serialize information to or from a System.IO.Stream, a System.IO.TextReader, a System.IO.TextWriter, a System.Xml.XmlReader, a System.Xml.XmlWriter, or a string containing a fully qualified path and filename.

There are three ways to create a ServiceDescription object. You can use the New keyword and create one manually, you can use the ServiceDescriptionReflector to create one from a live web service, or you can use the shared Read() method to create one from a WSDL file. For example, you can create a ServiceDescription object, with all its subobjects fully populated by using a syntax like MyServiceDesc = ServiceDescription.Read("MyFile.xml");.

```
public sealed class ServiceDescription : DocumentableItem {
// Public Constructors
 public ServiceDescription( );
// Public Static Fields
 public const string Namespace;                                      // =http://schemas.xmlsoap.org/wsdl/
// Public Static Properties
 public static XmlSerializer Serializer{get; }
// Public Instance Properties
 public BindingCollection Bindings{get; }
 public ServiceDescriptionFormatExtensionCollection Extensions{get; }
 public ImportCollection Imports{get; }
 public MessageCollection Messages{get; }
 public string Name{set; get; }
 public PortTypeCollection PortTypes{get; }
```

```
public string RetrievalUrl{set; get; }
public ServiceDescriptionCollection ServiceDescriptions{get; }
public ServiceCollection Services{get; }
public string TargetNamespace{set; get; }
public Types Types{set; get; }
// Public Static Methods
public static bool CanRead( System.Xml.XmlReader reader);
public static ServiceDescription Read(System.IO.Stream stream);
public static ServiceDescription Read( string fileName);
public static ServiceDescription Read(System.IO.TextReader textReader);
public static ServiceDescription Read(System.Xml.XmlReader reader);
// Public Instance Methods
public void Write( System.IO.Stream stream);
public void Write( string fileName);
public void Write( System.IO.TextWriter writer);
public void Write( System.Xml.XmlWriter writer);
}
```

Hierarchy	System.Object → DocumentableItem → ServiceDescription
Returned By	Binding.ServiceDescription, Import.ServiceDescription, Message.ServiceDescription, PortType. ServiceDescription, ProtocolReflector.{GetServiceDescription( ), ServiceDescription}, Service. ServiceDescription, ServiceDescriptionCollection.this, System.Web.Services.Discovery. ContractReference.Contract
Passed To	ServiceDescriptionCollection.{Add( ), Contains( ), CopyTo( ), IndexOf( ), Insert( ), Remove( ), this}, ServiceDescriptionImporter.AddServiceDescription( )

ServiceDescriptionBaseCollection

System.Web.Services.Description (system.web.services.dll)   abstract class

This is the base class for many of the strongly typed collection classes in this namespace. Classes that derive from ServiceDescriptionBaseCollection end with the word "Collection," as in PortCollection. These classes are strongly typed, but not named. This differs from the classes that represent WSDL language elements. For example, the Port-Type class represents a WSDL language element, contains other elements as Operation objects, and does not inherit from ServiceDescriptionBaseCollection.

```
public abstract class ServiceDescriptionBaseCollection : CollectionBase {
// Protected Instance Properties
  protected virtual IDictionary Table{get; }
// Protected Instance Methods
  protected virtual string GetKey( object value);
  protected override void OnClear( );                                          // overrides System.Collections.CollectionBase
  protected override void OnInsertComplete(int index, object value);           // overrides System.Collections.CollectionBase
  protected override void OnRemove(int index, object value);                   // overrides System.Collections.CollectionBase
  protected override void OnSet(int index, object oldValue, object newValue);  // overrides System.Collections.CollectionBase
  protected virtual void SetParent(object value, object parent);
}
```

Hierarchy	System.Object → System.Collections.CollectionBase(System.Collections.IList, System.Collections.ICollection, System.Collections.IEnumerable) → ServiceDescriptionBaseCollection
Subclasses	Multiple types

ServiceDescriptionCollection

System.Web.Services.Description (system.web.services.dll)   sealed class

This is a collection of ServiceDescription objects. Every ServiceDescription object provides a reference to the ServiceDescriptionCollection that it is a part of in its ServiceDescription.ServiceDescriptions property. You can access each ServiceDescription element by name or position (index number).

```
public sealed class ServiceDescriptionCollection : ServiceDescriptionBaseCollection {
// Public Constructors
  public ServiceDescriptionCollection( );
// Public Instance Properties
  public ServiceDescription this[ string ns ]{get; }
  public ServiceDescription this[ int index ]{set; get; }
// Public Instance Methods
  public int Add( ServiceDescription serviceDescription);
  public bool Contains(ServiceDescription serviceDescription);
  public void CopyTo(ServiceDescription[ ] array, int index);
  public Binding GetBinding(System.Xml.XmlQualifiedName name);
  public Message GetMessage(System.Xml.XmlQualifiedName name);
  public PortType GetPortType(System.Xml.XmlQualifiedName name);
  public Service GetService(System.Xml.XmlQualifiedName name);
  public int IndexOf(ServiceDescription serviceDescription);
  public void Insert(int index, ServiceDescription serviceDescription);
  public void Remove(ServiceDescription serviceDescription);
// Protected Instance Methods
  protected override string GetKey( object value);              // overrides ServiceDescriptionBaseCollection
}
```

Hierarchy	System.Object → System.Collections.CollectionBase(System.Collections.IList, System.Collections.ICollection, System.Collections.IEnumerable) → ServiceDescriptionBaseCollection → ServiceDescriptionCollection
Returned By	ProtocolImporter.ServiceDescriptions, ProtocolReflector.ServiceDescriptions, ServiceDescription.ServiceDescriptions, ServiceDescriptionImporter.ServiceDescriptions, ServiceDescriptionReflector.ServiceDescriptions

ServiceDescriptionFormatExtension

System.Web.Services.Description (system.web.services.dll)   abstract class

This abstract class allows you to create a WSDL extensibility element. Extensibility elements can be added at many levels by adding a ServiceDescriptionFormatExtension object to the Extensions collection of a class in this namespace. Note that you will also need to derive your own SoapExtensionImporter class if you need to extend the import process to use your extensibility element when generating a proxy class.

```
public abstract class ServiceDescriptionFormatExtension {
// Protected Constructors
  protected ServiceDescriptionFormatExtension( );
// Public Instance Properties
  public bool Handled{set; get; }
  public object Parent{get; }
  public bool Required{set; get; }
}
```

Subclasses　　　Multiple types

ServiceDescriptionFormatExtensionCollection

System.Web.Services.Description (system.web.services.dll)　　　　　　　　　　　sealed class

This collection of objects is derived from ServiceDescriptionFormatExtension. It is used in various classes in this namespace, including Types, Port, Service, and Binding, allowing you to implement type extensions at several different levels. For example, the InputBinding. Extensions property provides a ServiceDescriptionFormatExtensionCollection that could contain a HttpUrlEncodedBinding or SoapBodyBinding.

```
public sealed class ServiceDescriptionFormatExtensionCollection : ServiceDescriptionBaseCollection {
// Public Constructors
  public ServiceDescriptionFormatExtensionCollection(object parent);
// Public Instance Properties
  public object this[ int index ]{set; get; }                                 // implements IList
// Public Instance Methods
  public int Add( object extension);                                          // implements IList
  public bool Contains( object extension);                                    // implements IList
  public void CopyTo( object[ ] array, int index);
  public object Find( Type type);
  public XmlElement Find( string name, string ns);
  public object[ ] FindAll( Type type);
  public XmlElement[ ] FindAll( string name, string ns);
  public int IndexOf( object extension);                                      // implements IList
  public void Insert( int index, object extension);                           // implements IList
  public bool IsHandled( object item);
  public bool IsRequired( object item);
  public void Remove( object extension);                                      // implements IList
// Protected Instance Methods
  protected override void OnValidate( object value);         // overrides System.Collections.CollectionBase
  protected override void SetParent(object value, object parent);    // overrides ServiceDescriptionBaseCollection
}
```

Hierarchy　　　System.Object → System.Collections.CollectionBase(System.Collections.IList, System.Collections.ICollection, System.Collections.IEnumerable) → ServiceDescriptionBaseCollection → ServiceDescriptionFormatExtensionCollection

Returned By　　　Binding.Extensions, MessageBinding.Extensions, MimePart.Extensions, OperationBinding. Extensions, Port.Extensions, Service.Extensions, ServiceDescription.Extensions, Types. Extensions

Passed To　　　ProtocolImporter.AddExtensionWarningComments( )

ServiceDescriptionImporter

System.Web.Services.Description (system.web.services.dll)   class

The ServiceDescriptionImporter is used to programmatically create a proxy class for a web service. Clients invoke web service methods by creating an instance of the proxy class and invoking the corresponding method on the proxy class.

To create a proxy class, first use the AddServiceDescription() method to add a ServiceDescription to the ServiceDescriptions collection. Then create the proxy class with the Import() method.

When using the AddServiceDescription() method, use the **appSettingUrlKey** and **appSettingBaseUrl** parameters to specify how the Url property will be generated for the web service proxy class.

```
public class ServiceDescriptionImporter {
// Public Constructors
  public ServiceDescriptionImporter( );
// Public Instance Properties
  public string ProtocolName{set; get; }
  public XmlSchemas Schemas{get; }
  public ServiceDescriptionCollection ServiceDescriptions{get; }
  public ServiceDescriptionImportStyle Style{set; get; }
// Public Instance Methods
  public void AddServiceDescription(ServiceDescription serviceDescription, string appSettingUrlKey,
    string appSettingBaseUrl);
  public ServiceDescriptionImportWarnings Import(System.CodeDom.CodeNamespace codeNamespace,
    System.CodeDom.CodeCompileUnit codeCompileUnit);
}
```

ServiceDescriptionImportStyle   serializable

System.Web.Services.Description (system.web.services.dll)   enum

This enumeration is used for the ServiceDescriptionImporter.Style property; it specifies whether a ServiceDescriptionImporter.Import() method call will be made to the server or client. When you import to the client computer, you will receive a proxy class with synchronous and asynchronous methods for invoking each method within the web service, just as if .NET generated the proxy class for you automatically. A server import, however, will generate an abstract class with abstract members, which you must override to provide the appropriate implementation.

```
public enum ServiceDescriptionImportStyle {
  Client = 0,
  Server = 1
}
```

Hierarchy   System.Object → System.ValueType → System.Enum(System.IComparable, System.IFor-
                     mattable, System.IConvertible) → ServiceDescriptionImportStyle

Returned By   ProtocolImporter.Style, ServiceDescriptionImporter.Style

Passed To   ServiceDescriptionImporter.Style

ServiceDescriptionImportWarnings

serializable

System.Web.Services.Description (system.web.services.dll)   enum

This enumeration is used for the return value from the ServiceDescriptionImporter.Import( ) method. It can indicate common problems creating the proxy class, including the failure to create a required or optional ServiceDescriptionFormatExtension or an unsupported type of Binding or Operation.

```
public enum ServiceDescriptionImportWarnings {
  NoCodeGenerated = 1,
  OptionalExtensionsIgnored = 2,
  RequiredExtensionsIgnored = 4,
  UnsupportedOperationsIgnored = 8,
  UnsupportedBindingsIgnored = 16,
  NoMethodsGenerated = 32
}
```

Hierarchy   System.Object → System.ValueType → System.Enum(System.IComparable, System.IFormattable, System.IConvertible) → ServiceDescriptionImportWarnings

Returned By   ProtocolImporter.Warnings, ServiceDescriptionImporter.Import( )

Passed To   ProtocolImporter.Warnings

ServiceDescriptionReflector

System.Web.Services.Description (system.web.services.dll)   class

This class allows you to dynamically create a ServiceDescription object that represents a "live" web service. To use this class, invoke the Reflect( ) method with the web service URL as a string. The WSDL document for the web service will be added to the ServiceDescriptions collection. You can also retrieve any associated XML schemas from the Schemas collection.

```
public class ServiceDescriptionReflector {
// Public Constructors
  public ServiceDescriptionReflector( );
// Public Instance Properties
  public XmlSchemas Schemas{get; }
  public ServiceDescriptionCollection ServiceDescriptions{get; }
// Public Instance Methods
  public void Reflect( Type type, string url);
}
```

SoapAddressBinding

System.Web.Services.Description (system.web.services.dll)   class

This class represents an extensibility element added to the WSDL <port> element, which enables SOAP binding to a specific web service address. The Location property specifies the base URI for the web service port.

```
public class SoapAddressBinding : ServiceDescriptionFormatExtension {
// Public Constructors
   public SoapAddressBinding( );
// Public Instance Properties
   public string Location{set; get; }
}
```

Hierarchy   System.Object → ServiceDescriptionFormatExtension → SoapAddressBinding

SoapBinding

System.Web.Services.Description (system.web.services.dll)   class

This class represents an extensibility element added to the WSDL <binding> element,
which allows information to be transmitted via SOAP encoding. The Style property
specifies whether Document or RPC encoding is used, and the Transport property specifies a URI (such as "SMTP" or "HTTP").

```
public class SoapBinding : ServiceDescriptionFormatExtension {
// Public Constructors
   public SoapBinding( );
// Public Static Fields
   public const string HttpTransport;                        // =http://schemas.xmlsoap.org/soap/http
   public const string Namespace;                            // =http://schemas.xmlsoap.org/wsdl/soap/
// Public Instance Properties
   public SoapBindingStyle Style{set; get; }
   public string Transport{set; get; }
}
```

Hierarchy   System.Object → ServiceDescriptionFormatExtension → SoapBinding

Returned By   SoapProtocolImporter.SoapBinding

SoapBindingStyle   serializable

System.Web.Services.Description (system.web.services.dll)   enum

This enumeration provides different SOAP transport options. Procedure-oriented
messages use the Rpc value and can contain parameters and return values. Document-
oriented messages, however, use the value Document and typically contain documents.

```
public enum SoapBindingStyle {
   Default = 0,
   Document = 1,
   Rpc = 2
}
```

Hierarchy   System.Object → System.ValueType → System.Enum(System.IComparable, System.IFor-
                       mattable, System.IConvertible) → SoapBindingStyle

Returned By   SoapBinding.Style, SoapOperationBinding.Style

Passed To   SoapBinding.Style, SoapOperationBinding.Style

SoapBindingUse

serializable

System.Web.Services.Description (system.web.services.dll)   enum

This enumeration applies to SOAP extensibility elements and specifies the XML encoding of a message. Encoded specifies that the message parts are encoded using the given encoding rules (which are usually specified in a corresponding Encoding property), while Literal indicates that the message parts represent a concrete schema and Default specifies an empty string for the corresponding XML use attribute. Classes that use this enumeration expose a Use property (as in SoapBodyBinding.Use and SoapFaultBinding.Use).

```
public enum SoapBindingUse {
  Default = 0,
  Encoded = 1,
  Literal = 2
}
```

Hierarchy   System.Object → System.ValueType → System.Enum(System.IComparable, System.IFormattable, System.IConvertible) → SoapBindingUse

Returned By SoapBodyBinding.Use, SoapFaultBinding.Use, SoapHeaderBinding.Use, SoapHeaderFaultBinding.Use, System.Web.Services.Protocols.SoapDocumentMethodAttribute.Use, System.Web.Services.Protocols.SoapDocumentServiceAttribute.Use

Passed To   SoapBodyBinding.Use, SoapFaultBinding.Use, SoapHeaderBinding.Use, SoapHeaderFaultBinding.Use, System.Web.Services.Protocols.SoapDocumentMethodAttribute.Use, System.Web.Services.Protocols.SoapDocumentServiceAttribute.{SoapDocumentServiceAttribute( ), Use}

SoapBodyBinding

System.Web.Services.Description (system.web.services.dll)   class

This class represents an extensibility element added to an InputBinding or an OutputBinding object. This binding is used for SOAP input and output messages (represented by OperationInput and OperationOutput objects). It specifies that data is encoded for SOAP transmission and does not provide any properties.

```
public class SoapBodyBinding : ServiceDescriptionFormatExtension {
// Public Constructors
  public SoapBodyBinding( );
// Public Instance Properties
  public string Encoding{set; get; }
  public string Namespace{set; get; }
  public string[ ] Parts{set; get; }
  public string PartsString{set; get; }
  public SoapBindingUse Use{set; get; }
}
```

Hierarchy   System.Object → ServiceDescriptionFormatExtension → SoapBodyBinding

SoapExtensionImporter

System.Web.Services.Description (system.web.services.dll)   **abstract class**

This class is used by the .NET framework, not directly by your code.

```
public abstract class SoapExtensionImporter {
// Protected Constructors
  protected SoapExtensionImporter( );
// Public Instance Properties
  public SoapProtocolImporter ImportContext{set; get; }
// Public Instance Methods
  public abstract void ImportMethod(System.CodeDom.CodeAttributeDeclarationCollection metadata);
}
```

SoapExtensionReflector

System.Web.Services.Description (system.web.services.dll)   **abstract class**

This class is used by the .NET framework, not directly by your code.

```
public abstract class SoapExtensionReflector {
// Protected Constructors
  protected SoapExtensionReflector( );
// Public Instance Properties
  public ProtocolReflector ReflectionContext{set; get; }
// Public Instance Methods
  public abstract void ReflectMethod( );
}
```

SoapFaultBinding

System.Web.Services.Description (system.web.services.dll)   **class**

This class represents an extensibility element added to the WSDL <fault> element
(enclosed in the <operation> element) that allows information to be transmitted via
SOAP. The encoding is indicated with the Encoding and Use properties and the
namespace with the Namespace property.

```
public class SoapFaultBinding : ServiceDescriptionFormatExtension {
// Public Constructors
  public SoapFaultBinding( );
// Public Instance Properties
  public string Encoding{set; get; }
  public string Namespace{set; get; }
  public SoapBindingUse Use{set; get; }
}
```

Hierarchy   System.Object → ServiceDescriptionFormatExtension → SoapFaultBinding

SoapHeaderBinding

System.Web.Services.Description (system.web.services.dll)   class

This class represents an extensibility element added to the WSDL <input> or <output> element (enclosed in the <operation> element), which allows information to be transmitted via SOAP. The encoding is indicated with the SoapFaultBinding.Encoding and SoapFaultBinding.Use properties, and the namespace is indicated with the SoapFaultBinding. Namespace property.

```
public class SoapHeaderBinding : ServiceDescriptionFormatExtension {
// Public Constructors
  public SoapHeaderBinding( );
// Public Instance Properties
  public string Encoding{set; get; }
  public SoapHeaderFaultBinding Fault{set; get; }
  public bool MapToProperty{set; get; }
  public XmlQualifiedName Message{set; get; }
  public string Namespace{set; get; }
  public string Part{set; get; }
  public SoapBindingUse Use{set; get; }
}
```

Hierarchy   System.Object → ServiceDescriptionFormatExtension → SoapHeaderBinding

SoapHeaderFaultBinding

System.Web.Services.Description (system.web.services.dll)   class

This class represents an extensibility element added to the WSDL <input> or <output> element (enclosed in the <operation> element) that allows information to be transmitted via SOAP. It specifies the SOAP header types used to transmit error information within the SOAP header. The encoding is indicated with the SoapFaultBinding.Encoding and Soap-FaultBinding.Use properties and the namespace with the SoapFaultBinding.Namespace property.

```
public class SoapHeaderFaultBinding : ServiceDescriptionFormatExtension {
// Public Constructors
  public SoapHeaderFaultBinding( );
// Public Instance Properties
  public string Encoding{set; get; }
  public XmlQualifiedName Message{set; get; }
  public string Namespace{set; get; }
  public string Part{set; get; }
  public SoapBindingUse Use{set; get; }
}
```

Hierarchy   System.Object → ServiceDescriptionFormatExtension → SoapHeaderFaultBinding

Returned By   SoapHeaderBinding.Fault

Passed To   SoapHeaderBinding.Fault

SoapOperationBinding

System.Web.Services.Description (system.web.services.dll) class

This class represents an extensibility element added to the WSDL <operation> element, which allows information to be transmitted via SOAP encoding. The Style property specifies whether Document or RPC encoding is used, and the SoapAction property contains a string with the URI for the SOAP header.

```
public class SoapOperationBinding : ServiceDescriptionFormatExtension {
// Public Constructors
  public SoapOperationBinding( );
// Public Instance Properties
  public string SoapAction{set; get; }
  public SoapBindingStyle Style{set; get; }
}
```

Hierarchy System.Object → ServiceDescriptionFormatExtension → SoapOperationBinding

SoapProtocolImporter

System.Web.Services.Description (system.web.services.dll) class

This class is used by the .NET framework, not directly by your code.

```
public class SoapProtocolImporter : ProtocolImporter {
// Public Constructors
  public SoapProtocolImporter( );
// Public Instance Properties
  public override string ProtocolName{get; }                           // overrides ProtocolImporter
  public SoapBinding SoapBinding{get; }
  public SoapCodeExporter SoapExporter{get; }
  public SoapSchemaImporter SoapImporter{get; }
  public XmlCodeExporter XmlExporter{get; }
  public XmlSchemaImporter XmlImporter{get; }
// Protected Instance Methods
  protected override CodeTypeDeclaration BeginClass( );                // overrides ProtocolImporter
  protected override void BeginNamespace( );                           // overrides ProtocolImporter
  protected override void EndClass( );                                 // overrides ProtocolImporter
  protected override void EndNamespace( );                             // overrides ProtocolImporter
  protected override CodeMemberMethod GenerateMethod( );               // overrides ProtocolImporter
  protected override bool IsBindingSupported( );                       // overrides ProtocolImporter
  protected override bool IsOperationFlowSupported(OperationFlow flow); // overrides ProtocolImporter
  protected virtual bool IsSoapEncodingPresent(string uriList);
}
```

Hierarchy System.Object → ProtocolImporter → SoapProtocolImporter

Returned By SoapExtensionImporter.ImportContext, SoapTransportImporter.ImportContext

Passed To SoapExtensionImporter.ImportContext, SoapTransportImporter.ImportContext

SoapTransportImporter

System.Web.Services.Description (system.web.services.dll)   abstract class

This class serves as a base class for custom classes that import SOAP transmission protocols into web services. Note, however, that the current implementation of web services does not support these user-defined classes.

```
public abstract class SoapTransportImporter {
// Protected Constructorsprotected SoapTransportImporter( );
// Public Instance Properties
   public SoapProtocolImporter ImportContext{set; get; }
// Public Instance Methods
   public abstract void ImportClass( );
   public abstract bool IsSupportedTransport(string transport);
}
```

Types

System.Web.Services.Description (system.web.services.dll)   sealed class

This class represents the WSDL <types> element. It provides abstract data type definitions that can be used for the WSDL messages. You can access them through the Schemas property. The preferred (and default) type system used with WSDL is XSD. You can also add type extensibility elements, which are represented in this class by the Extensions property. This property will contain an empty collection in the default implementation of this class.

When ASP.NET generates a WSDL document for your web service, it includes an entry in the <types> element for every method, specifying the input parameter information. It also specifies the return value information, if applicable, in an entry that has your method name with the word "Response" added (for example, GetStockQuoteResponse). Additionally, if your web method accepts or returns a custom class or structure, a separate entry will be added to the <types> element to describe the data members of that class.

```
public sealed class Types : DocumentableItem {
// Public Constructors
   public Types( );
// Public Instance Properties
   public ServiceDescriptionFormatExtensionCollection Extensions{get; }
   public XmlSchemas Schemas{get; }
}
```

Hierarchy   System.Object → DocumentableItem → Types

Returned By   ServiceDescription.Types

Passed To   ServiceDescription.Types

33

The System.Web.Services. Discovery Namespace

The System.Web.Services.Discovery namespace includes the classes that model .NET web service discovery documents (usually seen as *.disco* or *.vsdisco* files). These classes are generally not used directly, as the discovery process is automated in tools such as Visual Studio .NET. However, they could be used to create programs that worked with discovery documents for reasons other than consuming a given web service. For example, you could create a utility that parses multiple discovery documents and retrieves aggregate information.

The discovery process has little to do with Universal Description, Design, Discovery, and Integration (UDDI), the cross-vendor initiative for publishing information about business and their web services in an online repository. (In fact, UDDI repositories can provide links to web services or discovery documents.) Discovery documents are a simple approach—essentially nothing more than a collection of links without any associated documentation or categorization. These "links" can point to WSDL service descriptions, XSD schemas, or other discovery documents. It's also important to note that discovery in Versions 1.0 and 1.1 of the .NET Framework does not use the WS-Inspection standard, which is slated to eventually replace DISCO.

A good starting point to understanding this namespace is the DiscoveryDocument class, which represents a single *.disco* or *.vsdisco* file. The most useful type in this namespace is the DiscoveryClientProtocol class, which allows you to invoke web service discovery programmatically. Figure 33-1 shows the types in this namespace.

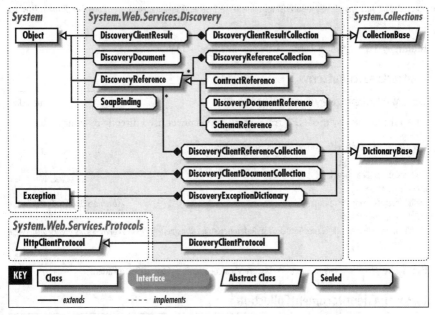

Figure 33-1. The System.Web.Services.Discovery namespace

ContractReference

System.Web.Services.Discovery (system.web.services.dll)   class

This class represents a discovery document reference to a WSDL service description. This is the most common type of reference in a discovery document and the most useful, as it directly corresponds to a web service that the client can consume. The Contract property returns the System.Web.Services.Description.ServiceDescription object that represents the service description. Ref provides the URL to the WSDL document as a string, while DocRef provides the URL to the web service that the WSDL document describes.

```
public class ContractReference : DiscoveryReference {
// Public Constructors
  public ContractReference( );
  public ContractReference(string href);
  public ContractReference(string href, string docRef);
// Public Static Fields
  public const string Namespace;                                         // =http://schemas.xmlsoap.org/disco/scl/
// Public Instance Properties
  public ServiceDescription Contract{get; }
  public override string DefaultFilename{get; }                          // overrides DiscoveryReference
  public string DocRef{set; get; }
  public string Ref{set; get; }
  public override string Url{set; get; }                                 // overrides DiscoveryReference
// Public Instance Methods
  public override object ReadDocument(System.IO.Stream stream);          // overrides DiscoveryReference
  public override void WriteDocument(object document, System.IO.Stream stream);  // overrides DiscoveryReference
// Protected Instance Methods
```

```
    protected internal override void Resolve(string contentType, System.IO.Stream stream);     // overrides DiscoveryReference
}
```

Hierarchy   System.Object → DiscoveryReference → ContractReference

ContractSearchPattern

System.Web.Services.Discovery (system.web.services.dll)   **sealed class**

This type is used by the .NET framework and is never used directly by your code.

```
public sealed class ContractSearchPattern : DiscoverySearchPattern {
// Public Constructors
  public ContractSearchPattern( );
// Public Instance Properties
  public override string Pattern{get; }                                    // overrides DiscoverySearchPattern
// Public Instance Methods
  public override DiscoveryReference GetDiscoveryReference(string filename);     // overrides DiscoverySearchPattern
}
```

Hierarchy   System.Object → DiscoverySearchPattern → ContractSearchPattern

DiscoveryClientDocumentCollection

System.Web.Services.Discovery (system.web.services.dll)   **sealed class**

This class is a collection of DiscoveryDocument instances. It can be used to represent the discovery documents that are downloaded to a client during the discovery process.

```
public sealed class DiscoveryClientDocumentCollection : DictionaryBase {
// Public Constructors
  public DiscoveryClientDocumentCollection( );
// Public Instance Properties
  public ICollection Keys{get; }                                    // implements System.Collections.IDictionary
  public object this[ string url ]{set; get; }
  public ICollection Values{get; }                                  // implements System.Collections.IDictionary
// Public Instance Methods
  public void Add(string url, object value);
  public bool Contains(string url);
  public void Remove(string url);
}
```

Hierarchy   System.Object → System.Collections.DictionaryBase(System.Collections.IDictionary,
                    System.Collections.ICollection, System.Collections.IEnumerable) →
                    DiscoveryClientDocumentCollection

Returned By   DiscoveryClientProtocol.Documents

DiscoveryClientProtocol   **marshal by reference, disposable**

System.Web.Services.Discovery (system.web.services.dll)   **class**

Most types in this namespace are used for modeling discovery documents. This class provides the utility methods that allow you to reflect on URLs and create the appropriate discovery document objects. This class is based on two properties: Documents, which contains a collection of discovery documents, and References, which will contain a collection of disovery document references when the discovery process is complete.

To start the discovery process, you need to know the location of the discovery document you want to process (which could have been retrieved through a service like UDDI). You can then use the Discover() method and supply the appropriate URL as a string. (Alternatively, you can use the DiscoverAny() method if you are not sure whether the URL points to a discovery document, WSDL service description, or XSD file.) If the document is valid, the document will be added to the References and Documents collection. In addition, all references contained in the discovery document are added to the References collection, but they are not validated.

To verify the discovery document's references (the next stage of the discovery process), you should use the ResolveOneLevel() method, which moves through the References collection and ensures that all valid references are added to the Documents collection. Alternatively, you can use the ResolveAll() method, which will examine any nested discovery documents. For example, if you have a discovery document that references another discovery document, which references a third discovery document, the ResolveAll() method will burrow through all the levels. Errors found during the reference resolving process are not thrown and caught in your code, but added to the Errors collection. Additional information found in the discovery document (such as SOAP bindings) will be added to the AdditionalInformation collection.

The DiscoveryClientProtocol class also contains methods that let you download discovery documents to files on the client computer. You can use the Download() method to send the discovery document at a specified URL to a System.IO.Stream, and the WriteAll() method to write all discovery documents, XSD files, and Service Descriptions in the Documents property to the supplied directory. In this case, the file designated by the topLevelFileName argument is used to store a map of saved documents, which you can read to recreate the DiscoveryClientProtocol instance by using the ReadAll() method. The format used in this file is XML.

```
public class DiscoveryClientProtocol : System.Web.Services.Protocols.HttpWebClientProtocol {
// Public Constructors
  public DiscoveryClientProtocol( );
// Public Instance Properties
  public IList AdditionalInformation{get; }
  public DiscoveryClientDocumentCollection Documents{get; }
  public DiscoveryExceptionDictionary Errors{get; }
  public DiscoveryClientReferenceCollection References{get; }
// Public Instance Methods
  public DiscoveryDocument Discover(string url);
  public DiscoveryDocument DiscoverAny(string url);
  public Stream Download(ref string url);
  public Stream Download(ref string url, ref string contentType);
  public DiscoveryClientResultCollection ReadAll(string topLevelFilename);
  public void ResolveAll( );
  public void ResolveOneLevel( );
  public DiscoveryClientResultCollection WriteAll(string directory, string topLevelFilename);
}
```

Hierarchy	System.Object → System.MarshalByRefObject → System.ComponentModel.Compo-nent(System.ComponentModel.IComponent, System.IDisposable) → System.Web.Services. Protocols.WebClientProtocol → System.Web.Services.Protocols.HttpWebClientProtocol → DiscoveryClientProtocol
Returned By	DiscoveryReference.ClientProtocol
Passed To	DiscoveryReference.ClientProtocol

DiscoveryClientProtocol.DiscoveryClientResultsFile

System.Web.Services.Discovery (system.web.services.dll)   sealed class

This class provides the results of the DiscoveryClientProtocol.WriteAll( ) method. The Results property provides a collection of DiscoveryClientResult objects with information about all references that were written to disk.

```
public sealed class DiscoveryClientProtocol.DiscoveryClientResultsFile {
// Public Constructors
  public DiscoveryClientProtocol.DiscoveryClientResultsFile( );
// Public Instance Properties
  public DiscoveryClientResultCollection Results{get; }
}
```

DiscoveryClientReferenceCollection

System.Web.Services.Discovery (system.web.services.dll)   sealed class

This class represents a collection of discovery document references (links to WSDL service descriptions, XSD files, or other discovery documents), much like the DiscoveryCli-entResultCollection class. However, the DiscoveryClientResultCollection class provides the discovery references from a single discovery document, while DiscoveryClientReferenceCollection is usually used to provide the aggregated references from multiple documents. The Discov-eryClientReferenceCollection class is used by the DiscoveryClientProtocol.References property.

```
public sealed class DiscoveryClientReferenceCollection : DictionaryBase {
// Public Constructors
  public DiscoveryClientReferenceCollection( );
// Public Instance Properties
  public ICollection Keys{get; }                                    // implements System.Collections.IDictionary
  public DiscoveryReference this[ string url ]{set; get; }
  public ICollection Values{get; }                                  // implements System.Collections.IDictionary
// Public Instance Methods
  public void Add(DiscoveryReference value);
  public void Add(string url, DiscoveryReference value);
  public bool Contains(string url);
  public void Remove(string url);
}
```

Hierarchy	System.Object → System.Collections.DictionaryBase(System.Collections.IDictionary, System.Collections.ICollection, System.Collections.IEnumerable) → DiscoveryClientReferenceCollection
Returned By	DiscoveryClientProtocol.References

DiscoveryClientResult

System.Web.Services.Discovery (system.web.services.dll)   sealed class

This class represents some of the details in a discovery document reference. It's used in conjunction with the DiscoveryClientProtocol.WriteAll( ) method, which writes the references from multiple discovery documents to disk in one batch operation, and summarizes the results with a collection of DiscoveryClientResult objects. You can use the Filename property to determine the file that the corresponding discovery reference is saved in.

```
public sealed class DiscoveryClientResult {
// Public Constructors
  public DiscoveryClientResult( );
  public DiscoveryClientResult(Type referenceType, string url, string filename);
// Public Instance Properties
  public string Filename{set; get; }
  public string ReferenceTypeName{set; get; }
  public string Url{set; get; }
}
```

Returned By   DiscoveryClientResultCollection.this

Passed To   DiscoveryClientResultCollection.{Add( ), Contains( ), Remove( ), this}

DiscoveryClientResultCollection

System.Web.Services.Discovery (system.web.services.dll)   sealed class

This class contains a collection of DiscoveryClientResult objects. It's used by the the Results property in conjunction with the DiscoveryClientProtocol.WriteAll( ) method, and can contain information about the references from multiple discovery documents.

```
public sealed class DiscoveryClientResultCollection : CollectionBase {
// Public Constructors
  public DiscoveryClientResultCollection( );
// Public Instance Properties
  public DiscoveryClientResult this[ int i ]{set; get; }
// Public Instance Methods
  public int Add(DiscoveryClientResult value);
  public bool Contains(DiscoveryClientResult value);
  public void Remove(DiscoveryClientResult value);
}
```

Hierarchy   System.Object → System.Collections.CollectionBase(System.Collections.IList, System.Collections.ICollection, System.Collections.IEnumerable) → DiscoveryClientResultCollection

Returned By   DiscoveryClientProtocol.{ReadAll( ), WriteAll( )}, DiscoveryClientResultsFile.Results

DiscoveryDocument

System.Web.Services.Discovery (system.web.services.dll)   sealed class

This class represents a discovery document (usually found as a *.disco* or *.vsdisco* file). The discovery document is an XML document that contains references to any number of web services (actually, it points to their WSDL service descriptions), XSD files, or other discovery documents. The References property contains a list of the discover document references. The Read() and Write() methods serialize or deserialize the DiscoveryDocument to or from a System.IO.Stream, System.IO.TextWriter, or System.Xml.XmlWriter.

```
public sealed class DiscoveryDocument {
// Public Constructors
  public DiscoveryDocument( );
// Public Static Fields
  public const string Namespace;                                    // =http://schemas.xmlsoap.org/disco/
// Public Instance Properties
  public IList References{get; }
// Public Static Methods
  public static bool CanRead(System.Xml.XmlReader xmlReader);
  public static DiscoveryDocument Read(System.IO.Stream stream);
  public static DiscoveryDocument Read(System.IO.TextReader reader);
  public static DiscoveryDocument Read(System.Xml.XmlReader xmlReader);
// Public Instance Methods
  public void Write(System.IO.Stream stream);
  public void Write(System.IO.TextWriter writer);
  public void Write(System.Xml.XmlWriter writer);
}
```

Returned By   DiscoveryClientProtocol.{Discover( ), DiscoverAny( )}, DiscoveryDocumentReference. Document

DiscoveryDocumentLinksPattern

System.Web.Services.Discovery (system.web.services.dll)   class

This type is used by the .NET framework and is never used directly by your code.

```
public class DiscoveryDocumentLinksPattern : DiscoverySearchPattern {
// Public Constructors
  public DiscoveryDocumentLinksPattern( );
// Public Instance Properties
  public override string Pattern{get; }                              // overrides DiscoverySearchPattern
// Public Instance Methods
  public override DiscoveryReference GetDiscoveryReference(string filename);   // overrides DiscoverySearchPattern
}
```

Hierarchy   System.Object → DiscoverySearchPattern → DiscoveryDocumentLinksPattern

DiscoveryDocumentReference

System.Web.Services.Discovery (system.web.services.dll)   sealed class

This class represents a discovery document reference to another discovery document. The Ref property provides a string with the discovery document's URL. The Documents property returns another DiscoveryDocument object that represents the discovery document and its references.

```
public sealed class DiscoveryDocumentReference : DiscoveryReference {
// Public Constructors
```

```
  public DiscoveryDocumentReference( );
  public DiscoveryDocumentReference(string href);
// Public Instance Properties
  public override string DefaultFilename{get; }                              // overrides DiscoveryReference
  public DiscoveryDocument Document{get; }
  public string Ref{set; get; }
  public override string Url{set; get; }                                     // overrides DiscoveryReference
// Public Instance Methods
  public override object ReadDocument(System.IO.Stream stream);              // overrides DiscoveryReference
  public void ResolveAll( );
  public override void WriteDocument(object document, System.IO.Stream stream);  // overrides DiscoveryReference
// Protected Instance Methods
  protected internal override void Resolve(string contentType, System.IO.Stream stream);  // overrides DiscoveryReference
}
```

Hierarchy   System.Object → DiscoveryReference → DiscoveryDocumentReference

DiscoveryDocumentSearchPattern

System.Web.Services.Discovery (system.web.services.dll)   sealed class

This type is used by the .NET framework and is never used directly by your code.

```
public sealed class DiscoveryDocumentSearchPattern : DiscoverySearchPattern {
// Public Constructors
  public DiscoveryDocumentSearchPattern( );
// Public Instance Properties
  public override string Pattern{get; }                                      // overrides DiscoverySearchPattern
// Public Instance Methods
  public override DiscoveryReference GetDiscoveryReference(string filename);  // overrides DiscoverySearchPattern
}
```

Hierarchy   System.Object → DiscoverySearchPattern → DiscoveryDocumentSearchPattern

DiscoveryExceptionDictionary

System.Web.Services.Discovery (system.web.services.dll)   sealed class

This class is a collection of exception objects. It is used by the DiscoveryClientProtocol.Errors property to represent all errors that occured during the discovery process.

```
public sealed class DiscoveryExceptionDictionary : DictionaryBase {
// Public Constructors
  public DiscoveryExceptionDictionary( );
// Public Instance Properties
  public ICollection Keys{get; }                                   // implements System.Collections.IDictionary
  public Exception this[ string url ]{set; get; }
  public ICollection Values{get; }                                 // implements System.Collections.IDictionary
// Public Instance Methods
  public void Add(string url, Exception value);
  public bool Contains(string url);
  public void Remove(string url);
}
```

Hierarchy	System.Object → System.Collections.DictionaryBase(System.Collections.IDictionary, System.Collections.ICollection, System.Collections.IEnumerable) → DiscoveryExceptionDictionary
Returned By	DiscoveryClientProtocol.Errors

DiscoveryReference

System.Web.Services.Discovery (system.web.services.dll)   **abstract class**

A discovery document can refer to three things: WSDL service descriptions, XSD documents, or other discovery files. These references are represented by three different classes in this namespace (ContractReference, DiscoveryDocumentReference, and SchemaReference), all of which inherit from this abstract base class.

```
public abstract class DiscoveryReference {
// Protected Constructorsprotected DiscoveryReference( );
// Public Instance Properties
  public DiscoveryClientProtocol ClientProtocol{set; get; }
  public virtual string DefaultFilename{get; }
  public abstract string Url{set; get; }
// Protected Static Methods
  protected static string FilenameFromUrl( string url);
// Public Instance Methods
  public abstract object ReadDocument(System.IO.Stream stream);
  public void Resolve( );
  public abstract void WriteDocument(object document, System.IO.Stream stream);
// Protected Instance Methods
  protected internal abstract void Resolve(string contentType, System.IO.Stream stream);
}
```

Subclasses	ContractReference, DiscoveryDocumentReference, SchemaReference
Returned By	DiscoveryClientReferenceCollection.this, DiscoveryReferenceCollection.this, DiscoverySearch-Pattern.GetDiscoveryReference( )
Passed To	DiscoveryClientReferenceCollection.{Add( ), this}, DiscoveryReferenceCollection.{Add( ), Contains( ), Remove( ), this}

DiscoveryReferenceCollection

System.Web.Services.Discovery (system.web.services.dll)   **sealed class**

This class provides a collection of discovery references (instances of one of the three classes that inherit from DiscoveryReference). It can be used to represent all the references in a given discovery document.

```
public sealed class DiscoveryReferenceCollection : CollectionBase {
// Public Constructors
  public DiscoveryReferenceCollection( );
// Public Instance Properties
  public DiscoveryReference this[ int i ]{set; get; }
// Public Instance Methods
```

```
  public int Add( DiscoveryReference value);
  public bool Contains( DiscoveryReference value);
  public void Remove( DiscoveryReference value);
}
```

Hierarchy   System.Object → System.Collections.CollectionBase(System.Collections.IList, System.Collections.ICollection, System.Collections.IEnumerable) → DiscoveryReferenceCollection

DiscoveryRequestHandler

System.Web.Services.Discovery (system.web.services.dll)   **sealed class**

This type is used by the .NET framework and is never used directly by your code.

```
public sealed class DiscoveryRequestHandler : System.Web.IHttpHandler {
// Public Constructors
  public DiscoveryRequestHandler( );
// Public Instance Properties
  public bool IsReusable{get; }                                          // implements System.Web.IHttpHandler
// Public Instance Methods
  public void ProcessRequest(System.Web.HttpContext context);            // implements System.Web.IHttpHandler
}
```

DiscoverySearchPattern

System.Web.Services.Discovery (system.web.services.dll)   **abstract class**

This type is used by the .NET framework and is never used directly by your code.

```
public abstract class DiscoverySearchPattern {
// Protected Constructors
  protected DiscoverySearchPattern( );
// Public Instance Properties
  public abstract string Pattern{get; }
// Public Instance Methods
  public abstract DiscoveryReference GetDiscoveryReference(string filename);
}
```

Subclasses   ContractSearchPattern, DiscoveryDocumentLinksPattern, DiscoveryDocumentSearchPattern, XmlSchemaSearchPattern

DynamicDiscoveryDocument

System.Web.Services.Discovery (system.web.services.dll)   **sealed class**

This type is used by the .NET framework and is never used directly by your code.

```
public sealed class DynamicDiscoveryDocument {
// Public Constructors
  public DynamicDiscoveryDocument( );
// Public Static Fields
  public const string Namespace;                          // =urn:schemas-dynamicdiscovery:disco.2000-03-17
// Public Instance Properties
  public ExcludePathInfo[ ] ExcludePaths{set; get; }
```

```
// Public Static Methods
  public static DynamicDiscoveryDocument Load(System.IO.Stream stream);
// Public Instance Methods
  public void Write( System.IO.Stream stream);
}
```

ExcludePathInfo

System.Web.Services.Discovery (system.web.services.dll)   sealed class

This type is used by the .NET framework and is never used directly by your code.

```
public sealed class ExcludePathInfo {
// Public Constructors
  public ExcludePathInfo( );
  public ExcludePathInfo( string path);
// Public Instance Properties
  public string Path{set; get; }
}
```

Returned By   DynamicDiscoveryDocument.ExcludePaths

Passed To   DynamicDiscoveryDocument.ExcludePaths

SchemaReference

System.Web.Services.Discovery (system.web.services.dll)   sealed class

This class represents a discovery document reference to an XML Schema Definition
(XSD) document. This is the least common type of reference in a discovery document.
The Ref property provides a string with the XSD file's URL. The Schema property returns
a full System.Xml.Schema.XmlSchema object that represents the XSD document.

```
public sealed class SchemaReference : DiscoveryReference {
// Public Constructors
  public SchemaReference( );
  public SchemaReference( string url);
// Public Static Fields
  public const string Namespace;                          // =http://schemas.xmlsoap.org/disco/schema/
// Public Instance Properties
  public override string DefaultFilename{get; }                              // overrides DiscoveryReference
  public string Ref{set; get; }
  public XmlSchema Schema{get; }
  public string TargetNamespace{set; get; }
  public override string Url{set; get; }                                     // overrides DiscoveryReference
// Public Instance Methods
  public override object ReadDocument(System.IO.Stream stream);              // overrides DiscoveryReference
  public override void WriteDocument(object document, System.IO.Stream stream);   // overrides DiscoveryReference
// Protected Instance Methods
  protected internal override void Resolve(string contentType, System.IO.Stream stream);  // overrides DiscoveryReference
}
```

Hierarchy   System.Object → DiscoveryReference → SchemaReference

SoapBinding

System.Web.Services.Discovery (system.web.services.dll) sealed class

This class represents a SOAP binding in a discovery document. You could add a SOAP binding for versioning (or to indicate additional information about a group of web services). SOAP bindings are specified in the discovery document by adding a SOAP XML element with an XML namespace equal to the Namespace constant.

```
public sealed class SoapBinding {
// Public Constructors
  public SoapBinding( );
// Public Static Fields
  public const string Namespace;                              // =http://schemas.xmlsoap.org/disco/soap/
// Public Instance Properties
  public string Address{set; get; }
  public XmlQualifiedName Binding{set; get; }
}
```

XmlSchemaSearchPattern

System.Web.Services.Discovery (system.web.services.dll) sealed class

This type is used by the .NET framework and is never used directly by your code.

```
public sealed class XmlSchemaSearchPattern : DiscoverySearchPattern {
// Public Constructors
  public XmlSchemaSearchPattern( );
// Public Instance Properties
  public override string Pattern{get; }                                    // overrides DiscoverySearchPattern
// Public Instance Methods
  public override DiscoveryReference GetDiscoveryReference(string filename);   // overrides DiscoverySearchPattern
}
```

Hierarchy   System.Object → DiscoverySearchPattern → XmlSchemaSearchPattern

Discovery Namespace

34

The System.Web.Services. Protocols Namespace

The System.Web.Services.Protocols namespace contains types that support communication between a client and a web service. The types define protocols that encode and transmit data across an Internet connection, including HTTP GET, HTTP POST, and SOAP.

The primary use of these types is to support the proxy class that manages the communication between web service and client. You can create this proxy class automatically by using the Visual Studio .NET IDE or the *WSDL.exe* command-line utility, or you can code it by hand. This class will inherit from HttpGetClientProtocol, HttpPostClientProtocol, or SoapHttpClientProtocol (which is the most common choice and the default for automatically generated proxy classes). Other important types in this namespace include the attributes that you use to set the encoding for SOAP request and response messages, such as SoapDocumentMethodAttribute.

This class also provides types you can use to create SOAP extensions. Typically, SOAP extensions are used to directly access the SOAP messages exchanged between web services and clients before they are sent or deserialized into objects. The SoapExtension class and SoapExtensionAttribute are the basic building blocks for SOAP extensions. You can also use SoapHeader and SoapHeaderAttribute classes to create custom SOAP headers for your message. You can then create web service methods that require specific custom SOAP headers. Figures 34-1 and 34-2 show the types in this namespace.

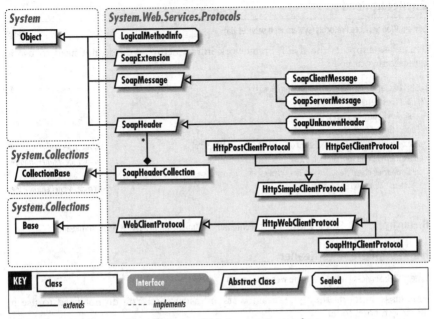

Figure 34-1. Some types from the System.Web.Services.Protocols namespace

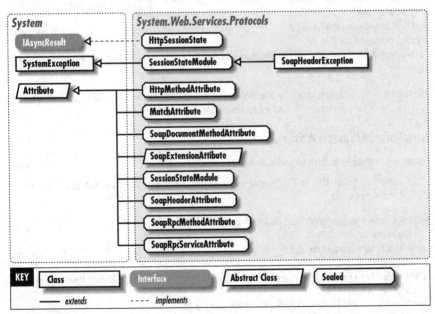

Figure 34-2. More types from the System.Web.Services.Protocols namespace

AnyReturnReader

System.Web.Services.Protocols (system.web.services.dll)   **class**

This class supports the .NET Framework infrastructure. You do not need to use it directly in your code.

```
public class AnyReturnReader : MimeReturnReader {
// Public Constructors
  public AnyReturnReader( );
// Public Instance Methods
  public override object GetInitializer(LogicalMethodInfo methodInfo);          // overrides MimeFormatter
  public override void Initialize(object o);                                    // overrides MimeFormatter
  public override object Read(System.Net.WebResponse response,
    System.IO.Stream responseStream);                                          // overrides MimeReturnReader
}
```

Hierarchy   System.Object → MimeFormatter → MimeReturnReader → AnyReturnReader

HtmlFormParameterReader

System.Web.Services.Protocols (system.web.services.dll)   **class**

This class supports the .NET Framework infrastructure. You do not need to use it directly in your code.

```
public class HtmlFormParameterReader : ValueCollectionParameterReader {
// Public Constructors
  public HtmlFormParameterReader( );
// Public Instance Methods
  public override object[ ] Read(System.Web.HttpRequest request);              // overrides MimeParameterReader
}
```

Hierarchy   System.Object → MimeFormatter → MimeParameterReader → ValueCollectionParame-
                       terReader → HtmlFormParameterReader

HtmlFormParameterWriter

System.Web.Services.Protocols (system.web.services.dll)   **class**

This class supports the .NET Framework infrastructure. You do not need to use it directly in your code.

```
public class HtmlFormParameterWriter : UrlEncodedParameterWriter {
// Public Constructors
  public HtmlFormParameterWriter( );
// Public Instance Properties
  public override bool UsesWriteRequest{get; }                                 // overrides MimeParameterWriter
// Public Instance Methods
  public override void InitializeRequest(System.Net.WebRequest request,
    object[ ] values);                                                         // overrides MimeParameterWriter
  public override void WriteRequest(System.IO.Stream requestStream,
    object[ ] values);                                                         // overrides MimeParameterWriter
}
```

System.Object → MimeFormatter → MimeParameterWriter → UrlEncodedParameter-
Writer → HtmlFormParameterWriter

HttpGetClientProtocol

marshal by reference, disposable

System.Web.Services.Protocols (system.web.services.dll)   class

You can inherit from this class to create a proxy class that communicates by using the
HTTP GET protocol, which sends parameters in the query string portion of the URL.
When using this class, you must use the corresponding HttpMethodAttribute to bind proxy
class methods to web service methods.

```
public class HttpGetClientProtocol : HttpSimpleClientProtocol {
// Public Constructors
  public HttpGetClientProtocol( );
// Protected Instance Methods
  protected override WebRequest GetWebRequest(Uri uri);              // overrides HttpWebClientProtocol
}
```

Hierarchy   System.Object → System.MarshalByRefObject → System.ComponentModel.Compo-
nent(System.ComponentModel.IComponent, System.IDisposable) → WebClientProtocol →
HttpWebClientProtocol → HttpSimpleClientProtocol → HttpGetClientProtocol

HttpMethodAttribute

System.Web.Services.Protocols (system.web.services.dll)   sealed class

This attribute is used to bind methods in an HttpGetClientProtocol or HttpPostClientProtocol
proxy class to web service methods.

The ParameterFormatter property specifies how the proxy encodes parameters before
sending them to a web service method. The ReturnFormatter property specifies how the
proxy class decodes the web method's return value. Both values must be set, as there is
no default value. Set ReturnFormatter to the UrlParameterWriter type if you are using HTTP
GET or the HtmlFormParameterWriter type if you are using HTTP POST. Always set ParameterFormatter to the XmlReturnReader type. An example attribute declaration for HTTP GET is
<HttpMethodAttribute(GetType(XmlReturnReader), GetType(UrlParameterWriter))>.

```
public sealed class HttpMethodAttribute : Attribute {
// Public Constructors
  public HttpMethodAttribute( );
  public HttpMethodAttribute(Type returnFormatter, Type parameterFormatter);
// Public Instance Properties
  public Type ParameterFormatter{set; get; }
  public Type ReturnFormatter{set; get; }
}
```

Hierarchy   System.Object → System.Attribute → HttpMethodAttribute

Valid On   Method

HttpPostClientProtocol

System.Web.Services.Protocols (system.web.services.dll)   class

You can inherit from this class to create a proxy class that communicates by using the HTTP POST protocol, which encodes parameters in the body of the HTTP request. When using this class, you must use the corresponding HttpMethodAttribute to bind proxy class methods to web service methods.

```
public class HttpPostClientProtocol : HttpSimpleClientProtocol {
// Public Constructors
    public HttpPostClientProtocol( );
// Protected Instance Methods
    protected override WebRequest GetWebRequest(Uri uri);                    // overrides HttpWebClientProtocol
}
```

Hierarchy   System.Object → System.MarshalByRefObject → System.ComponentModel.Compo-
                       nent(System.ComponentModel.IComponent, System.IDisposable) → WebClientProtocol →
                       HttpWebClientProtocol → HttpSimpleClientProtocol → HttpPostClientProtocol

HttpSimpleClientProtocol

System.Web.Services.Protocols (system.web.services.dll)   abstract class

This abstract class provides basic functionality for communicating with a web service over HTTP. This class is inherited by HttpGetClientProtocol and HttpPostClientProtocol, both of which your proxy classes can derive from directly. Parameters for an HTTP proxy are encoded by using application/x-www-form-urlencoded content type.

```
public abstract class HttpSimpleClientProtocol : HttpWebClientProtocol {
// Protected Constructors
    protected HttpSimpleClientProtocol( );
// Protected Instance Methods
    protected IAsyncResult BeginInvoke(string methodName, string requestUrl, object[ ] parameters,
        AsyncCallback callback, object asyncState);
    protected object EndInvoke( IAsyncResult asyncResult);
    protected object Invoke(string methodName, string requestUrl, object[ ] parameters);
}
```

Hierarchy   System.Object → System.MarshalByRefObject → System.ComponentModel.Compo-
                       nent(System.ComponentModel.IComponent, System.IDisposable) → WebClientProtocol →
                       HttpWebClientProtocol → HttpSimpleClientProtocol

Subclasses   HttpGetClientProtocol, HttpPostClientProtocol

HttpWebClientProtocol

System.Web.Services.Protocols (system.web.services.dll)   abstract class

This abstract base class provides basic functionality for communication between a web service and proxy class. The System.Web.Services.Discovery.DiscoveryClientProtocol, HttpSimpleClientPro-tocol, and SoapHttpClientProtocol classes all inherit from HttpWebClientProtocol. The proxy class inherits from one of these derived classes, depending on which transmission protocol it uses.

You can use the Proxy property to connect to a web service through a firewall, as in WS.Proxy = New WebProxy("http://proxyserver:80", True). This property will override the computer's default Internet settings. You can also set the AllowAutoRedirect property to allow a client to follow server redirects. This is False by default for security reasons. The UserAgent property is automatically set to something like "MS Web Services Client Protocol 1.0.2509.0," where 1.0.2509.0 is the Common Language Runtime version.

The CookieContainer property is important when connecting to a web service that uses ASP.NET's session state facility. To allow a proxy class to reuse the same session on subsequent calls, you must explicitly create a new (empty) System.Net.CookieContainer object and assign it to the CookieContainer property. This allows the proxy class to store the session cookie with each call. If you want multiple proxy class instances to access the same session, or if you want to recreate a proxy class and use a previous session that has not yet timed out, you must take extra steps to transfer or store the System.Net.Cookie-Container object.

```
public abstract class HttpWebClientProtocol : WebClientProtocol {
// Protected Constructors
  protected HttpWebClientProtocol( );
// Public Instance Properties
  public bool AllowAutoRedirect{set; get; }
  public X509CertificateCollection ClientCertificates{get; }
  public CookieContainer CookieContainer{set; get; }
  public IWebProxy Proxy{set; get; }
  public bool UnsafeAuthenticatedConnectionSharing{set; get; }
  public string UserAgent{set; get; }
// Protected Instance Methods
  protected override WebRequest GetWebRequest( Uri uri);                          // overrides WebClientProtocol
  protected override WebResponse GetWebResponse(System.Net.WebRequest request);   // overrides WebClientProtocol
  protected override WebResponse GetWebResponse(System.Net.WebRequest request,
     IAsyncResult result);                                                        // overrides WebClientProtocol
}
```

Hierarchy	System.Object → System.MarshalByRefObject → System.ComponentModel.Compo-nent(System.ComponentModel.IComponent, System.IDisposable) → WebClientProtocol → HttpWebClientProtocol
Subclasses	HttpSimpleClientProtocol, SoapHttpClientProtocol, System.Web.Services.Discovery. DiscoveryClientProtocol

LogicalMethodInfo

System.Web.Services.Protocols (system.web.services.dll)   sealed class

A LogicalMethodInfo object is provided to the SoapExtension.GetInitializer( ) method. This object contains information about the web service or proxy class method where the custom SoapExtensionAttribute is applied.

```
public sealed class LogicalMethodInfo {
// Public Constructors
  public LogicalMethodInfo(System.Reflection.MethodInfo methodInfo);
// Public Instance Properties
  public ParameterInfo AsyncCallbackParameter{get; }
```

```
public ParameterInfo AsyncResultParameter{get; }
public ParameterInfo AsyncStateParameter{get; }
public MethodInfo BeginMethodInfo{get; }
public ICustomAttributeProvider CustomAttributeProvider{get; }
public Type DeclaringType{get; }
public MethodInfo EndMethodInfo{get; }
public ParameterInfo[ ] InParameters{get; }
public bool IsAsync{get; }
public bool IsVoid{get; }
public MethodInfo MethodInfo{get; }
public string Name{get; }
public ParameterInfo[ ] OutParameters{get; }
public ParameterInfo[ ] Parameters{get; }
public Type ReturnType{get; }
public ICustomAttributeProvider ReturnTypeCustomAttributeProvider{get; }
// Public Static Methods
public static LogicalMethodInfo[ ] Create(System.Reflection.MethodInfo[ ] methodInfos);
public static LogicalMethodInfo[ ] Create(System.Reflection.MethodInfo[ ] methodInfos, LogicalMethodTypes types);
public static bool IsBeginMethod(System.Reflection.MethodInfo methodInfo);
public static bool IsEndMethod(System.Reflection.MethodInfo methodInfo);
// Public Instance Methods
public IAsyncResult BeginInvoke(object target, object[ ] values, AsyncCallback callback, object asyncState);
public object[ ] EndInvoke(object target, IAsyncResult asyncResult);
public object GetCustomAttribute(Type type);
public object[ ] GetCustomAttributes(Type type);
public object[ ] Invoke(object target, object[ ] values);
public override string ToString( );                                          // overrides object
}
```

Returned By   System.Web.Services.Description.ProtocolReflector.{Method, Methods}, SoapMessage.
                   MethodInfo

Passed To   MimeFormatter.{GetInitializer( ), GetInitializers( )}, SoapExtension.GetInitializer( ), ValueCol-
                   lectionParameterReader.IsSupported( )

LogicalMethodTypes   serializable

System.Web.Services.Protocols (system.web.services.dll)   enum

This enumeration specifies whether a web service method was invoked synchronously
or asynchronously with the corresponding "Begin" method.

```
public enum LogicalMethodTypes {
  Sync = 1,
  Async = 2
}
```

Hierarchy   System.Object → System.ValueType → System.Enum(System.IComparable, System.IFor-
                  mattable, System.IConvertible) → LogicalMethodTypes

Passed To   LogicalMethodInfo.Create( )

MatchAttribute

System.Web.Services.Protocols (system.web.services.dll)   sealed class

.NET allows you to create screen-scraping web services that search the HTML content on a web page by using a regular expression. To create a pattern matching web service, you need to create a WSDL document with <match> elements. These match elements specify the regular expression to use when parsing the contents of the page and how many matches should be returned. When the client builds the proxy class for a pattern-matching web service, it will include a MatchAttribute that describes the match elements you added to the WSDL document.

The Pattern property specfies the regular expression pattern to use when searching the web page. IgnoreCase specifies whether the regular expression should be run in case-sensitive mode (the default). MaxRepeats specifies the maximum number of matches that will be returned (-1, the default, indicates all). Finally, Group specifies a grouping of related matches, while Capture specifies the index of a match within a group.

```
public sealed class MatchAttribute : Attribute {
// Public Constructors
  public MatchAttribute(string pattern);
// Public Instance Properties
  public int Capture{set; get; }
  public int Group{set; get; }
  public bool IgnoreCase{set; get; }
  public int MaxRepeats{set; get; }
  public string Pattern{set; get; }
}
```

Hierarchy   System.Object → System.Attribute → MatchAttribute

Valid On   All

MimeFormatter

System.Web.Services.Protocols (system.web.services.dll)   abstract class

This class supports the .NET Framework infrastructure. You do not need to use it directly in your code.

```
public abstract class MimeFormatter {
// Protected Constructors
  protected MimeFormatter( );
// Public Static Methods
  public static MimeFormatter CreateInstance(Type type, object initializer);
  public static object GetInitializer(Type type, LogicalMethodInfo methodInfo);
  public static object[ ] GetInitializers(Type type, LogicalMethodInfo[ ] methodInfos);
// Public Instance Methods
  public abstract object GetInitializer(LogicalMethodInfo methodInfo);
  public virtual object[ ] GetInitializers(LogicalMethodInfo[ ] methodInfos);
  public abstract void Initialize(object initializer);
}
```

Subclasses   MimeParameterReader, MimeParameterWriter, MimeReturnReader

MimeParameterReader

System.Web.Services.Protocols (system.web.services.dll)   abstract class

This class supports the .NET Framework infrastructure. You do not need to use it directly in your code.

```
public abstract class MimeParameterReader : MimeFormatter {
// Protected Constructors
  protected MimeParameterReader( );
// Public Instance Methods
  public abstract object[ ] Read(System.Web.HttpRequest request);
}
```

Hierarchy   System.Object → MimeFormatter → MimeParameterReader

Subclasses   ValueCollectionParameterReader

MimeParameterWriter

System.Web.Services.Protocols (system.web.services.dll)   abstract class

This class supports the .NET Framework infrastructure. You do not need to use it directly in your code.

```
public abstract class MimeParameterWriter : MimeFormatter {
// Protected Constructors
  protected MimeParameterWriter( );
// Public Instance Properties
  public virtual Encoding RequestEncoding{set; get; }
  public virtual bool UsesWriteRequest{get; }
// Public Instance Methods
  public virtual string GetRequestUrl(string url, object[ ] parameters);
  public virtual void InitializeRequest(System.Net.WebRequest request, object[ ] values);
  public virtual void WriteRequest(System.IO.Stream requestStream, object[ ] values);
}
```

Hierarchy   System.Object → MimeFormatter → MimeParameterWriter

Subclasses   UrlEncodedParameterWriter

MimeReturnReader

System.Web.Services.Protocols (system.web.services.dll)   abstract class

This class supports the .NET Framework infrastructure. You do not need to use it directly in your code.

```
public abstract class MimeReturnReader : MimeFormatter {
// Protected Constructors
  protected MimeReturnReader( );
// Public Instance Methods
  public abstract object Read(System.Net.WebResponse response, System.IO.Stream responseStream);
}
```

Hierarchy	System.Object → MimeFormatter → MimeReturnReader
Subclasses	AnyReturnReader, NopReturnReader, TextReturnReader, XmlReturnReader

NopReturnReader

System.Web.Services.Protocols (system.web.services.dll)   class

This class supports the .NET Framework infrastructure. You do not need to use it directly in your code.

```
public class NopReturnReader : MimeReturnReader {
// Public Constructors
  public NopReturnReader( );
// Public Instance Methods
  public override object GetInitializer(LogicalMethodInfo methodInfo);        // overrides MimeFormatter
  public override void Initialize( object initializer);                        // overrides MimeFormatter
  public override object Read(System.Net.WebResponse response,
    System.IO.Stream responseStream);                                          // overrides MimeReturnReader
}
```

Hierarchy	System.Object → MimeFormatter → MimeReturnReader → NopReturnReader

PatternMatcher

System.Web.Services.Protocols (system.web.services.dll)   sealed class

This class supports the .NET Framework infrastructure. You do not need to use it directly in your code.

```
public sealed class PatternMatcher {
// Public Constructors
  public PatternMatcher( Type type);
// Public Instance Methods
  public object Match( string text);
}
```

SoapClientMessage

System.Web.Services.Protocols (system.web.services.dll)   sealed class

This class represents a SOAP request sent by a proxy client or SOAP response received by a proxy client. It inherits from SoapMessage, which defines most of the functionality used for SOAP messages.

```
public sealed class SoapClientMessage : SoapMessage {
// Public Instance Properties
  public override string Action{get; }                                         // overrides SoapMessage
  public SoapHttpClientProtocol Client{get; }
  public override LogicalMethodInfo MethodInfo{get; }                          // overrides SoapMessage
  public override bool OneWay{get; }                                           // overrides SoapMessage
  public override string Url{get; }                                            // overrides SoapMessage
// Protected Instance Methods
  protected override void EnsureInStage( );                                    // overrides SoapMessage
```

```
protected override void EnsureOutStage( );                          // overrides SoapMessage
}
```

Hierarchy   System.Object → SoapMessage → SoapClientMessage

SoapDocumentMethodAttribute

System.Web.Services.Protocols (system.web.services.dll)   sealed class

This attribute is used to specify the encoding for SOAP request and response messages.
You can apply this attribute to methods in a web service or in methods in a proxy class
that derives from SoapHttpClientProtocol (where it's required to bind the messages to the
appropriate web method). You use this attribute, instead of SoapRpcMethodAttribute, when
you want to use the Document encoding standard.

There are two options for encoding XML information in a SOAP message: RPC and
Document. ASP.NET's default is Document. The Document style specifies that
messages are encoded as described in an XSD schema. When Document style is used,
the WSDL document defines the XSD schemas for SOAP requests and SOAP
responses. For more information on the SOAP specification, see *http://www.w3.org/
TR/SOAP/*.

One reason you might want to apply this attribute to a web method is to explicitly set
the OneWay property. For example, by adding [SoapDocumentMethod(OneWay = true)] before a
web method, you ensure that the method will return immediately and can finish
processing asynchronously. This ensures that the client doesn't need to wait for the
method to return or call it asynchronously. However, this web method will not be able
to access the System.Web.HttpContext for the client and will not be able to set a return value.
If the client needs to know about the success or result of such a web method, you will
have to implement a second method and use some type of ticket-issuing system to
keep track of the outstanding request.

```
public sealed class SoapDocumentMethodAttribute : Attribute {
// Public Constructors
  public SoapDocumentMethodAttribute( );
  public SoapDocumentMethodAttribute( string action);
// Public Instance Properties
  public string Action{set; get; }
  public string Binding{set; get; }
  public bool OneWay{set; get; }
  public SoapParameterStyle ParameterStyle{set; get; }
  public string RequestElementName{set; get; }
  public string RequestNamespace{set; get; }
  public string ResponseElementName{set; get; }
  public string ResponseNamespace{set; get; }
  public SoapBindingUse Use{set; get; }
}
```

Hierarchy   System.Object → System.Attribute → SoapDocumentMethodAttribute

Valid On   Method

SoapDocumentServiceAttribute

System.Web.Services.Protocols (system.web.services.dll) sealed class

This attribute can be applied to a web service's class declaration. It specifies that the default encoding for SOAP request and response messages will be Document. The client can override this default by using the SoapRpcMethodAttribute. This attribute is rarely used because the default in ASP.NET proxy classes is already Document encoding.

```
public sealed class SoapDocumentServiceAttribute : Attribute {
// Public Constructors
  public SoapDocumentServiceAttribute( );
  public SoapDocumentServiceAttribute(System.Web.Services.Description.SoapBindingUse use);
  public SoapDocumentServiceAttribute(System.Web.Services.Description.SoapBindingUse use,
    SoapParameterStyle paramStyle);
// Public Instance Properties
  public SoapParameterStyle ParameterStyle{set; get; }
  public SoapServiceRoutingStyle RoutingStyle{set; get; }
  public SoapBindingUse Use{set; get; }
}
```

Hierarchy   System.Object → System.Attribute → SoapDocumentServiceAttribute

Valid On   Class

SoapException

System.Web.Services.Protocols (system.web.services.dll) class

This class is a generic exception for SOAP-related problems. The Common Language Runtime can throw a SoapException when it encounters an incorrectly formatted SOAP message. Also, any error that occurs inside a web service method is caught on the server and returned to the client as a SoapException. ASP.NET will then set the SoapException property (which identifies the web service URL) and the Code property (using one of the fault code fields) automatically.

When you are creating your own web methods, you may need to provide more information about exceptions. To do so, catch any server errors and create and throw a corresponding SoapException object. You can specify application-specific details about the error by adding custom XML content to the Detail property.

```
public class SoapException : SystemException {
// Public Constructors
  public SoapException(string message, System.Xml.XmlQualifiedName code);
  public SoapException(string message, System.Xml.XmlQualifiedName code, Exception innerException);
  public SoapException(string message, System.Xml.XmlQualifiedName code, string actor);
  public SoapException(string message, System.Xml.XmlQualifiedName code, string actor, Exception innerException);
  public SoapException(string message, System.Xml.XmlQualifiedName code, string actor, System.Xml.XmlNode detail);
  public SoapException(string message, System.Xml.XmlQualifiedName code, string actor, System.Xml.XmlNode detail,
    Exception innerException);
// Public Static Fields
  public static readonly XmlQualifiedName ClientFaultCode;     // =http://schemas.xmlsoap.org/soap/envelope/:Client
  public static readonly XmlQualifiedName DetailElementName;                                          // =detail
```

```
public static readonly XmlQualifiedName MustUnderstandFaultCode;
                                // =http://schemas.xmlsoap.org/soap/envelope/:MustUnderstand
public static readonly XmlQualifiedName ServerFaultCode;        // =http://schemas.xmlsoap.org/soap/envelope/:Server
public static readonly XmlQualifiedName VersionMismatchFaultCode;
                                // =http://schemas.xmlsoap.org/soap/envelope/:VersionMismatch
// Public Instance Properties
 public string Actor{get; }
 public XmlQualifiedName Code{get; }
 public XmlNode Detail{get; }
}
```

Hierarchy	System.Object → System.Exception(System.Runtime.Serialization.ISerializable) → System.SystemException → SoapException
Subclasses	SoapHeaderException
Returned By	SoapMessage.Exception

SoapExtension

System.Web.Services.Protocols (system.web.services.dll)   **abstract class**

You can inherit from this class to create a custom SOAP extension, which allows you to access and manipulate SOAP messages before they are sent or converted into objects. SOAP extensions can be used to implement additional encryption, compression, or tracing. They can also be applied to web services or web service clients.

The key to using a derived SoapExtension class is overriding the ProcessMessage( ) method. This method is called automatically by the ASP.NET framework at several different SoapMessageStages and provides you with the current SoapMessage object. You also connect your SoapExtension to a proxy class or web service method by using a custom SoapExtensionAttribute.

You can initialize a SoapExtension with a constructor method and the Initialize( ) and GetInitializer( ) methods. The GetInitializer( ) method is called only once (the first time a SOAP request is made). It gives you the opportunity to retrieve information about the web service or proxy method (in the methodInfo parameter) and custom SoapExtensionAttribute and return an appropriate initialization object. This object will be cached and provided to the Initialize( ) method, which is called every time a SOAP request is made.

```
public abstract class SoapExtension {
// Protected Constructors
 protected SoapExtension( );
// Public Instance Methods
 public virtual Stream ChainStream(System.IO.Stream stream);
 public abstract object GetInitializer(LogicalMethodInfo methodInfo, SoapExtensionAttribute attribute);
 public abstract object GetInitializer(Type serviceType);
 public abstract void Initialize(object initializer);
 public abstract void ProcessMessage( SoapMessage message);
}
```

SoapExtensionAttribute

System.Web.Services.Protocols (system.web.services.dll)   abstract class

When using a SoapExtension, you must also derive a custom SoapExtensionAttribute. This attribute is used to "connect" methods in your web service or proxy class to the corresponding extension.

When creating a custom SoapExtensionAttribute, you need to override the ExtensionType property so that it returns the type of your custom SoapExtension class. You can then use your custom attribute to mark methods in your web service or proxy class. ASP.NET will automatically use the specified SoapExtension when the associated method is invoked.

```
public abstract class SoapExtensionAttribute : Attribute {
// Protected Constructors
  protected SoapExtensionAttribute( );
// Public Instance Properties
  public abstract Type ExtensionType{get; }
  public abstract int Priority{set; get; }
}
```

Hierarchy	System.Object → System.Attribute → SoapExtensionAttribute
Passed To	SoapExtension.GetInitializer( )
Valid On	All

SoapHeader

System.Web.Services.Protocols (system.web.services.dll)   abstract class

This class allows you to create custom SOAP headers, which are used to send additional information to or from a web service. For example, rather than require an extra security parameter to authenticate every web service method, you could use a custom SoapHeader. The client could then set a simple property of the proxy class, and the header would be sent automatically with every web method request.

To use a custom SoapHeader, create a class that inherits from SoapHeader, and add the member variables you need to contain additional information (in this case, some sort of security credentials). When invoking a method, instantiate your custom SoapHeader, set its properties accordingly, and send it to the web service or proxy class. The web service must provide a member variable to receive the SoapHeader and must indicate which methods will process the custom header. It marks these methods with a SoapHeaderAttribute.

The Actor property is specified by the SOAP standard and should be set to the URL of the web service. If you set the MustUnderstand property to True, the method in the class receiving the message must set the DidUnderstand property to True, or a SoapHeaderException will be thrown. Note that ASP.NET automatically defaults MustUnderstand to True and automatically defaults DidUnderstand to True as long as the recipient (for example, the web service) contains the custom header class definition. The only time DidUnderstand will not be automatically set to True is when you explicitly retrieve unknown SOAP headers.

```
public abstract class SoapHeader {
// Protected Constructors
```

```
  protected SoapHeader( );
// Public Instance Properties
  public string Actor{set; get; }
  public bool DidUnderstand{set; get; }
  public string EncodedMustUnderstand{set; get; }
  public bool MustUnderstand{set; get; }
}
```

Subclasses	SoapUnknownHeader
Returned By	SoapHeaderCollection.this
Passed To	SoapHeaderCollection.{Add( ), Contains( ), CopyTo( ), IndexOf( ), Insert( ), Remove( ), this}

SoapHeaderAttribute

System.Web.Services.Protocols (system.web.services.dll)   sealed class

This attribute is used to receive a custom SoapHeader. Before you can use this attribute, you need to add a member variable of the appropriate SoapHeader type to your web service or proxy class (for example, Public ReceivedHeader As MyCustomHeader). Before invoking a method, the client will set this member to the appropriate header object. You must also add a SoapHeaderAttribute to each method that wants to process the custom header. This declaration specifies the class member that received the custom header object, as in [SoapHeader(MemberName = "ReceivedHeader"].

If a method will process more than one SoapHeader, just add multiple SoapHeaderAttribute declarations. You can also receive all headers that are not defined in the web service by creating a member array of SoapUnknownHeader objects and using it in the SoapHeaderAttribute declaration.

```
public sealed class SoapHeaderAttribute : Attribute {
// Public Constructors
  public SoapHeaderAttribute( string memberName);
// Public Instance Properties
  public SoapHeaderDirection Direction{set; get; }
  public string MemberName{set; get; }
  public bool Required{set; get; }                                                    // obsolete
}
```

Hierarchy	System.Object → System.Attribute → SoapHeaderAttribute
Valid On	Method

SoapHeaderCollection

System.Web.Services.Protocols (system.web.services.dll)   class

This class contains a collection of SoapHeader objects. It is used for the SoapMessage.Headers property, which contains all the headers in a single SOAP request or response message.

```
public class SoapHeaderCollection : CollectionBase {
// Public Constructors
  public SoapHeaderCollection( );
```

```
// Public Instance Properties
  public SoapHeader this[ int index ]{set; get; }
// Public Instance Methods
  public int Add(SoapHeader header);
  public bool Contains(SoapHeader header);
  public void CopyTo(SoapHeader[ ] array, int index);
  public int IndexOf(SoapHeader header);
  public void Insert(int index, SoapHeader header);
  public void Remove(SoapHeader header);
}
```

Hierarchy   System.Object → System.Collections.CollectionBase(System.Collections.IList, System.Collec-
                     tions.ICollection, System.Collections.IEnumerable) → SoapHeaderCollection

Returned By   SoapMessage.Headers

SoapHeaderDirection   serializable, flag

System.Web.Services.Protocols (system.web.services.dll)   enum

This enumeration is used to set the SoapHeaderAttribute.Direction property. The direction is
relative to the receiving method where the attribute is placed. A value of InOut on a web
method specifies that the SoapHeader is sent to the method and back to the client with
possible modifications.

```
public enum SoapHeaderDirection {
  In = 0x00000001,
  Out = 0x00000002,
  InOut = 0x00000003,
  Fault = 0x00000004
}
```

Hierarchy   System.Object → System.ValueType → System.Enum(System.IComparable, System.IFor-
                     mattable, System.IConvertible) → SoapHeaderDirection

Returned By   SoapHeaderAttribute.Direction

Passed To   SoapHeaderAttribute.Direction

SoapHeaderException

System.Web.Services.Protocols (system.web.services.dll)   class

This class represents an error processing a SoapHeader. Typically, it results when a header
with a SoapHeader.MustUnderstand property of True is processed by the receiving method, but
the corresponding SoapHeader.DidUnderstand property is not set to True.

```
public class SoapHeaderException : SoapException {
// Public Constructors
  public SoapHeaderException(string message, System.Xml.XmlQualifiedName code);
  public SoapHeaderException(string message, System.Xml.XmlQualifiedName code, Exception innerException);
  public SoapHeaderException(string message, System.Xml.XmlQualifiedName code, string actor);
  public SoapHeaderException(string message, System.Xml.XmlQualifiedName code, string actor, Exception innerException);
}
```

SoapHttpClientProtocol

marshal by reference, disposable

System.Web.Services.Protocols (system.web.services.dll)   class

You can inherit from this class to create a proxy class that communicates by using the
SOAP protocol over HTTP. This is the most commonly used class for creating proxies
and the default in proxy classes that .NET generates automatically. When using this
class, you must also use the corresponding SoapDocumentMethodAttribute or SoapRpcMethodAttribute to bind a proxy class method to a web service method.

```
public class SoapHttpClientProtocol : HttpWebClientProtocol {
// Public Constructors
  public SoapHttpClientProtocol( );
// Public Instance Methods
  public void Discover( );
// Protected Instance Methods
  protected IAsyncResult BeginInvoke(string methodName, object[ ] parameters, AsyncCallback callback, object asyncState);
  protected object[ ] EndInvoke( IAsyncResult asyncResult);
  protected override WebRequest GetWebRequest( Uri uri);                        // overrides HttpWebClientProtocol
  protected object[ ] Invoke(string methodName, object[ ] parameters);
}
```

Hierarchy   System.Object → System.MarshalByRefObject → System.ComponentModel.Compo-
                   nent(System.ComponentModel.IComponent, System.IDisposable) → WebClientProtocol →
                   HttpWebClientProtocol → SoapHttpClientProtocol

Returned By   SoapClientMessage.Client

SoapMessage

System.Web.Services.Protocols (system.web.services.dll)   abstract class

This class represents a SOAP request or SOAP response used to communicate between
a web service and proxy class. The SoapMessage class is used primarily for SOAP extensions. SOAP extensions, which derive from SoapExtension, receive a SoapMessage object at
each SoapMessageStage as an argument to SoapExtension.ProcessMessage() method, which is
called automatically by the ASP.NET framework.

The SoapMessage class provides methods that allow you to retrieve the web service
method parameters and the return value encoded in the SOAP message. For a SoapClient-
Message, you should use the GetInParameterValue() method if the SOAP message is in the
SoapMessageStage.BeforeSerialize stage, or the GetOutParameterValue() method if it's in the SoapMes-
sageStage.AfterSerialize stage. For a SoapServerMessage, the reverse is true.

To verify that the parameters are available, you can use the EnsureInStage() or
EnsureOutStage() method (a System.InvalidOperationException will be thrown if the message is not
in a compatible stage). Alternatively, you can use the Stage property to determine the
state when the SoapMessage was generated.

```
public abstract class SoapMessage {
// Public Instance Properties
  public abstract string Action{get; }
```

```
public string ContentEncoding{set; get; }
public string ContentType{set; get; }
public SoapException Exception{get; }
public SoapHeaderCollection Headers{get; }
public abstract LogicalMethodInfo MethodInfo{get; }
public abstract bool OneWay{get; }
public SoapMessageStage Stage{get; }
public Stream Stream{get; }
public abstract string Url{get; }
// Public Instance Methods
public object GetInParameterValue( int index);
public object GetOutParameterValue( int index);
public object GetReturnValue( );
// Protected Instance Methods
protected abstract void EnsureInStage( );
protected abstract void EnsureOutStage( );
protected void EnsureStage( SoapMessageStage stage);
}
```

Subclasses	SoapClientMessage, SoapServerMessage
Passed To	SoapExtension.ProcessMessage( )

SoapMessageStage   serializable

System.Web.Services.Protocols (system.web.services.dll)   enum

This enumeration indicates the stage that a **SoapMessage** is in. Messages are serialized into SOAP before they are transmitted over the Internet and deserialized when they are received. Both the web service and the proxy client send and receive messages, so both participate in the serialization and deserialization process.

```
public enum SoapMessageStage {
  BeforeSerialize = 1,
  AfterSerialize = 2,
  BeforeDeserialize = 4,
  AfterDeserialize = 8
}
```

Hierarchy	System.Object → System.ValueType → System.Enum(System.IComparable, System.IFormattable, System.IConvertible) → SoapMessageStage
Returned By	SoapMessage.Stage
Passed To	SoapMessage.EnsureStage( )

SoapParameterStyle   serializable

System.Web.Services.Protocols (system.web.services.dll)   enum

This enumeration is used when applying a **SoapDocumentMethodAttribute** or **SoapDocumentServiceAttribute**. It specifies how web service parameter information is encoded in a SOAP message. If you use **Bare**, parameter information will be placed in multiple elements under the Body element. If you specify **Wrapped**, all parameters will be wrapped in a single element beneath the Body element. **Default** uses the default web service parameter style, which will be **Wrapped** unless the web service includes a SoapDocumentServiceAttribute in its class declaration that specifies differently.

```
public enum SoapParameterStyle {
    Default = 0,
    Bare = 1,
    Wrapped = 2
}
```

Hierarchy   System.Object → System.ValueType → System.Enum(System.IComparable, System.IFormattable, System.IConvertible) → SoapParameterStyle

Returned By   SoapDocumentMethodAttribute.ParameterStyle, SoapDocumentServiceAttribute. ParameterStyle

Passed To   SoapDocumentMethodAttribute.ParameterStyle, SoapDocumentServiceAttribute.{ParameterStyle, SoapDocumentServiceAttribute( )}

SoapRpcMethodAttribute

System.Web.Services.Protocols (system.web.services.dll)   **sealed class**

This attribute is used to specify the encoding for SOAP request and response messages. You can apply this attribute to methods in a web service or in methods in a proxy class that derives from SoapHttpClientProtocol (where it's required to bind the messages to the appropriate web method). You use this attribute, instead of SoapDocumentMethodAttribute, when you want to use the RPC encoding standard.

There are two options for encoding XML information in a SOAP message: RPC and Document. ASP.NET's default is Document. RPC (found in section 7 of the SOAP specification) specifies that all method parameters be wrapped in a single element named after the web service method and that each element be named after their respective parameter name. If you apply this attribute to a web method, it will not be able to return objects because no XSD schema will be generated.

```
public sealed class SoapRpcMethodAttribute : Attribute {
// Public Constructors
    public SoapRpcMethodAttribute( );
    public SoapRpcMethodAttribute( string action);
// Public Instance Properties
    public string Action{set; get; }
    public string Binding{set; get; }
    public bool OneWay{set; get; }
    public string RequestElementName{set; get; }
    public string RequestNamespace{set; get; }
    public string ResponseElementName{set; get; }
    public string ResponseNamespace{set; get; }
}
```

Hierarchy   System.Object → System.Attribute → SoapRpcMethodAttribute

Valid On   Method

SoapRpcServiceAttribute

System.Web.Services.Protocols (system.web.services.dll)   sealed class

This attribute can be applied to a web service's class declaration. It specifies that the default encoding for SOAP request and response messages will be RPC. The client can override this default by using the SoapDocumentMethodAttribute. If you apply this attribute, the web service will not be able to return objects because no XSD schema will be generated.

```
public sealed class SoapRpcServiceAttribute : Attribute {
// Public Constructors
   public SoapRpcServiceAttribute( );
// Public Instance Properties
   public SoapServiceRoutingStyle RoutingStyle{set; get; }
}
```

Hierarchy   System.Object → System.Attribute → SoapRpcServiceAttribute

Valid On   Class

SoapServerMessage

System.Web.Services.Protocols (system.web.services.dll)   sealed class

This class represents a SOAP request sent by a web service or SOAP response received by a web service. It inherits from the SoapMessage class, which contains most of the functionality for SOAP messages.

```
public sealed class SoapServerMessage : SoapMessage {
// Public Instance Properties
   public override string Action{get; }                          // overrides SoapMessage
   public override LogicalMethodInfo MethodInfo{get; }           // overrides SoapMessage
   public override bool OneWay{get; }                            // overrides SoapMessage
   public object Server{get; }
   public override string Url{get; }                            // overrides SoapMessage
// Protected Instance Methods
   protected override void EnsureInStage( );                     // overrides SoapMessage
   protected override void EnsureOutStage( );                    // overrides SoapMessage
}
```

Hierarchy   System.Object → SoapMessage → SoapServerMessage

SoapServiceRoutingStyle   serializable

System.Web.Services.Protocols (system.web.services.dll)   enum

This enumeration is used to specify the SoapDocumentServiceAttribute.RoutingStyle and the SoapRpcServiceAttribute.RoutingStyle properties. Allowed values are RequestElement (the message is routed based on the first child element in the body of the SOAP message) and SoapAction (the SOAP message is routed based on the SOAPAction HTTP header).

```
public enum SoapServiceRoutingStyle {
   SoapAction = 0,
```

```
    RequestElement = 1
}
```

Hierarchy   System.Object → System.ValueType → System.Enum(System.IComparable, System.IFor-
                  mattable, System.IConvertible) → SoapServiceRoutingStyle

Returned By   SoapDocumentServiceAttribute.RoutingStyle, SoapRpcServiceAttribute.RoutingStyle

Passed To   SoapDocumentServiceAttribute.RoutingStyle, SoapRpcServiceAttribute.RoutingStyle

SoapUnknownHeader

System.Web.Services.Protocols (system.web.services.dll)   sealed class

This class represents a **SoapHeader** that was not understood by the receiving method in
the web service or proxy class. You can receive all unknown headers by creating an
array of SoapUnknownHeader objects and using it with the **SoapHeaderAttribute**.

```
public sealed class SoapUnknownHeader : SoapHeader {
// Public Constructors
  public SoapUnknownHeader( );
// Public Instance Properties
  public XmlElement Element{set; get; }
}
```

Hierarchy   System.Object → SoapHeader → SoapUnknownHeader

TextReturnReader

System.Web.Services.Protocols (system.web.services.dll)   class

This class supports the .NET Framework infrastructure. You do not need to use it
directly in your code.

```
public class TextReturnReader : MimeReturnReader {
// Public Constructors
  public TextReturnReader( );
// Public Instance Methods
  public override object GetInitializer(LogicalMethodInfo methodInfo);        // overrides MimeFormatter
  public override void Initialize(object o);                                  // overrides MimeFormatter
  public override object Read(System.Net.WebResponse response,
    System.IO.Stream responseStream);                                  // overrides MimeReturnReader
}
```

Hierarchy   System.Object → MimeFormatter → MimeReturnReader → TextReturnReader

UrlEncodedParameterWriter

System.Web.Services.Protocols (system.web.services.dll)   abstract class

This class supports the .NET Framework infrastructure. You do not need to use it
directly in your code.

```
public abstract class UrlEncodedParameterWriter : MimeParameterWriter {
// Protected Constructorsprotected UrlEncodedParameterWriter( );
// Public Instance Properties
   public override Encoding RequestEncoding{set; get; }                              // overrides MimeParameterWriter
// Public Instance Methods
   public override object GetInitializer(LogicalMethodInfo methodInfo);              // overrides MimeFormatter
   public override void Initialize(object initializer);                             // overrides MimeFormatter
// Protected Instance Methods
   protected void Encode(System.IO.TextWriter writer, object[ ] values);
   protected void Encode(System.IO.TextWriter writer, string name, object value);
}
```

Hierarchy   System.Object → MimeFormatter → MimeParameterWriter →
UrlEncodedParameterWriter

Subclasses   HtmlFormParameterWriter, UrlParameterWriter

UrlParameterReader

System.Web.Services.Protocols (system.web.services.dll)   class

This class supports the .NET Framework infrastructure. You do not need to use it
directly in your code.

```
public class UrlParameterReader : ValueCollectionParameterReader {
// Public Constructors
   public UrlParameterReader( );
// Public Instance Methods
   public override object[ ] Read(System.Web.HttpRequest request);                  // overrides MimeParameterReader
}
```

Hierarchy   System.Object → MimeFormatter → MimeParameterReader → ValueCollectionParameterReader → UrlParameterReader

UrlParameterWriter

System.Web.Services.Protocols (system.web.services.dll)   class

This class supports the .NET Framework infrastructure. You do not need to use it
directly in your code.

```
public class UrlParameterWriter : UrlEncodedParameterWriter {
// Public Constructors
   public UrlParameterWriter( );
// Public Instance Methods
   public override string GetRequestUrl(string url, object[ ] parameters);          // overrides MimeParameterWriter
}
```

Hierarchy   System.Object → MimeFormatter → MimeParameterWriter → UrlEncodedParameter-
Writer → UrlParameterWriter

ValueCollectionParameterReader

System.Web.Services.Protocols (system.web.services.dll)   abstract class

This class supports the .NET Framework infrastructure. You do not need to use it directly in your code.

```
public abstract class ValueCollectionParameterReader : MimeParameterReader {
// Protected Constructors
  protected ValueCollectionParameterReader( );
// Public Static Methods
  public static bool IsSupported(LogicalMethodInfo methodInfo);
  public static bool IsSupported(System.Reflection.ParameterInfo paramInfo);
// Public Instance Methods
  public override object GetInitializer(LogicalMethodInfo methodInfo);        // overrides MimeFormatter
  public override void Initialize(object o);                                  // overrides MimeFormatter
// Protected Instance Methods
  protected object[ ] Read(System.Collections.Specialized.NameValueCollection collection);
}
```

Hierarchy   System.Object → MimeFormatter → MimeParameterReader → ValueCollectionParameterReader

Subclasses   HtmlFormParameterReader, UrlParameterReader

WebClientAsyncResult

System.Web.Services.Protocols (system.web.services.dll)   class

This class is used to return a result when invoking a web service method asynchronously, through the corresponding "Begin" and "End" methods. These method variants are created for you when you generate a proxy automatically by using Visual Studio.NET or *wsdl.exe*.

```
public class WebClientAsyncResult : IAsyncResult {
// Public Instance Properties
  public object AsyncState{get; }                    // implements IAsyncResult
  public WaitHandle AsyncWaitHandle{get; }           // implements IAsyncResult
  public bool CompletedSynchronously{get; }          // implements IAsyncResult
  public bool IsCompleted{get; }                     // implements IAsyncResult
// Public Instance Methods
  public void Abort( );
}
```

WebClientProtocol   marshal by reference, disposable

System.Web.Services.Protocols (system.web.services.dll)   abstract class

This is the base class for all web server proxy classes. It includes basic properties like Url, which is usually set to the appropriate web service address in the proxy class's constructor, and Timeout, which specifies a value in milliseconds. By default, the proxy class uses a Timeout of -1, which represents infinity, although the web server can still time out the request on the server side. The RequestEncoding property is overridden by derived classes to provide the appropriate character encoding.

To set Credentials, you must use a System.Net.ICredentials object like System.Net.NetworkCredential and set the credentials that are specific to the type of authentication you are using. You can also set the PreAuthenticate property to True, which will cause the proxy class to automatically send authentication information with every request.

```
public abstract class WebClientProtocol : System.ComponentModel.Component {
// Protected Constructors
  protected WebClientProtocol( );
// Public Instance Properties
  public string ConnectionGroupName{set; get; }
  public ICredentials Credentials{set; get; }
  public bool PreAuthenticate{set; get; }
  public Encoding RequestEncoding{set; get; }
  public int Timeout{set; get; }
  public string Url{set; get; }
// Protected Static Methods
  protected static void AddToCache(Type type, object value);
  protected static object GetFromCache( Type type);
// Public Instance Methods
  public virtual void Abort( );
// Protected Instance Methods
  protected virtual WebRequest GetWebRequest( Uri uri);
  protected virtual WebResponse GetWebResponse(System.Net.WebRequest request);
  protected virtual WebResponse GetWebResponse(System.Net.WebRequest request, IAsyncResult result);
}
```

Hierarchy System.Object → System.MarshalByRefObject → System.ComponentModel.Component(System.ComponentModel.IComponent, System.IDisposable) → WebClientProtocol

Subclasses HttpWebClientProtocol

WebServiceHandlerFactory

System.Web.Services.Protocols (system.web.services.dll)   class

This class is used by ASP.NET to instantiate an appropriate HttpHandler for handling web service requests. You do not need to use this class directly in your code.

```
public class WebServiceHandlerFactory : System.Web.IHttpHandlerFactory {
// Public Constructors
  public WebServiceHandlerFactory( );
// Public Instance Methods
  public IHttpHandler GetHandler(                              // implements System.Web.IHttpHandlerFactory
    System.Web.HttpContext context, string verb, string url, string filePath);
  public void ReleaseHandler(                                  // implements System.Web.IHttpHandlerFactory
    System.Web.IHttpHandler handler);
}
```

XmlReturnReader

System.Web.Services.Protocols (system.web.services.dll)   class

This class supports the .NET Framework infrastructure. You do not need to use it directly in your code.

Hierarchy   System.Object → MimeFormatter → MimeReturnReader → XmlReturnReader

```
public class XmlReturnReader : MimeReturnReader {
// Public Constructors
  public XmlReturnReader( );
// Public Instance Methods
  public override object GetInitializer(LogicalMethodInfo methodInfo);          // overrides MimeFormatter
  public override object[ ] GetInitializers(MethodInfo[ ] methodInfos);       // overrides MimeFormatterLogical
  public override void Initialize(object o);                                    // overrides MimeFormatter
  public override object Read(System.Net.WebResponse response,
    System.IO.Stream responseStream);                                         // overrides MimeReturnReader
}
```

35

The System.Web.SessionState Namespace

The System.Web.SessionState namespace provides the types used for session state management, which stores information that is specific to one session or client. Each user accessing an ASP.NET application has a separate session state collection. Session state is ideal for sensitive data (like credit card numbers and mailing addresses) because it is stored exclusively on the server. It is also well suited for complex data or custom .NET objects that cannot be easily serialized to a client-side cookie.

To support session state, each active ASP.NET session is identified and tracked with a unique 120-bit session ID string. Session ID values are created and managed automatically by the ASP.NET framework by using an algorithm that guarantees uniqueness and randomness so that they can't be regenerated by a malicious user. When a client requests an ASP.NET page, the appropriate ID is transmitted from the client by a cookie or a modified ("munged") URL. ASP.NET worker processes then retrieve the serialized data from the state server as a binary stream, convert it into live objects, and place these objects into the HttpSessionState class's key/value collection. This class is the core of the System.Web.SessionState namespace. Most other classes in this namespace are used transparently by the ASP.NET framework, except the IReadOnlySessionState and IRequiresSessionState interfaces, which allow custom System.Web.IHttpHandler instances to access session data.

Session state is typically removed if no requests are received within a specified timeframe (typically about 20 minutes). This is the main trade-off of session state storage: you must choose a timeframe short enough to allow valuable memory to be reclaimed on the server, but long enough to allow a user to continue a session after a short delay.

Note that most session state settings, including the method session ID transmission, the type of storage, and the timeout, are all configured through the <sessionstate> section of the *web.config* file. Figure 35-1 shows the types in this namespace.

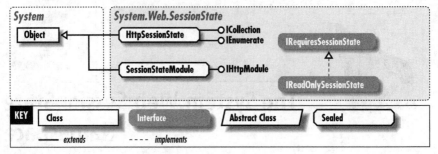

Figure 35-1. The System.Web.SessionState namespace

HttpSessionState

System.Web.SessionState (system.web.dll)   sealed class

The HttpSessionState class provides server-side state management that is stored on a per-client basis. The HttpSessionState class exposes a key/value collection of items that can store simple value types or instances of any serializable .NET class. You can also store instances of your own custom objects in session state, provided you make them serializable by adding the SerializableAttribute to the class declaration. You can add and access items in the HttpSessionState collection as you would with other ASP.NET collections, including System.Web.HttpApplicationState and System.Web.Caching.Cache. Unlike these classes, session state can be stored outside of the main ASP.NET process. This allows it to be shared across multiple computers in a web farm and persist after server restarts.

The HttpSessionState class combines two state collections: Contents and StaticObjects. The Static-Objects collection contains the application state objects that are defined in the *global.asax* file with <object runat="server"> tags. This collection is immutable. The Contents collection contains all the state objects added at runtime.

The Item collection is the default indexer for HttpSessionState, so you can use the name of a state object as an index, as in: Session["userName"] = "Lucy";. If you assign a value to a state object that does not exist, it is created automatically. Items are stored as the generic System.Object type and must be cast to the appropriate types when you retrieve them.

Other properties allow you to get information about whether or not the session has just been created with the current request (IsNewSession) and what type of session ID transmission (IsCookieless) and session storage (Mode) is being used. You can use the SessionID property to retrieve the session ID string, but you will not need to, as it is created and managed automatically by the ASP.NET framework. A reference is provided to the HttpSessionState class through the built-in Session object. Use Abandon() to end a session immediately and release memory occupied by session state objects without waiting for the session to time out.

```
public sealed class HttpSessionState : ICollection, IEnumerable {
// Public Instance Properties
  public int CodePage{set; get; }
  public HttpSessionState Contents{get; }
  public int Count{get; }                                            // implements ICollection
  public bool IsCookieless{get; }
  public bool IsNewSession{get; }
  public bool IsReadOnly{get; }
```

```
public bool IsSynchronized{get; }                                            // implements ICollection
public KeysCollection Keys{get; }
public int LCID{set; get; }
public SessionStateMode Mode{get; }
public string SessionID{get; }
public HttpStaticObjectsCollection StaticObjects{get; }
public object SyncRoot{get; }                                                 // implements ICollection
public object this[ int index ]{set; get; }
public object this[ string name ]{set; get; }
public int Timeout{set; get; }
// Public Instance Methods
public void Abandon( );
public void Add(string name, object value);
public void Clear( );
public void CopyTo(Array array, int index);                                  // implements ICollection
public IEnumerator GetEnumerator( );                                         // implements IEnumerable
public void Remove(string name);
public void RemoveAll( );
public void RemoveAt( int index);
}
```

Returned By   System.Web.HttpApplication.Session, System.Web.HttpContext.Session, System.Web.
                     Services.WebService.Session, System.Web.UI.Page.Session, System.Web.UI.UserControl.
                     Session

IReadOnlySessionState

System.Web.SessionState (system.web.dll)   interface

This interface should be implemented by a custom HttpHandler (any class that inter-
prets web requests and implements System.Web.IHttpHandler). The IReadOnlySessionState
interface contains no members and is used only as a marker. When present, it tells
ASP.NET that the HttpHandler should be given readonly access to the HttpSessionState
collection.

Every HttpHandler should implement either IReadOnlySessionState or IRequiresSessionState, or
session state variables will not be accessible.

```
public interface IReadOnlySessionState : IRequiresSessionState {
// No public or protected members
}
```

IRequiresSessionState

System.Web.SessionState (system.web.dll)   interface

This interface should be implemented by a custom HttpHandler. This interface
contains no members and is used only as a marker. When present, it tells ASP.NET
that the HttpHandler should be given read and write access to the HttpSessionState
collection.

Every HttpHandler should implement either IReadOnlySessionState or IRequiresSessionState, or
session state variables will not be accessible.

```
public interface IRequiresSessionState {
// No public or protected members
}
```

Implemented By   IReadOnlySessionState

IStateRuntime

System.Web.SessionState (system.web.dll)   interface

This interface defines a contract for the **StateRuntime** class.

```
public interface IStateRuntime {
// Public Instance Methods
    public void ProcessRequest(in IntPtr tracker, in int verb, in string uri, in int exclusive, in int timeout,
        in int lockCookieExists, in int lockCookie, in int contentLength, in IntPtr content);
    public void StopProcessing( );
}
```

Implemented By   StateRuntime

SessionStateMode   serializable

System.Web.SessionState (system.web.dll)   enum

This enumeration allows you to identify the type of ASP.NET session storage by using
the **HttpSessionState.Mode** property. It also allows you to specify it by using the **mode**
attribute of the <sessionState> tag in the *web.config* file (for example, <sessionState
mode="SQLServer">).

Session state can be stored locally in the ASP.NET process (**InProc**, the method used in
traditional ASP applications), in a separate server (**StateServer**), or serialized to a temporary table in an SQL Server database (**SQLServer**), which the ASP.NET worker processes
access and manage automatically. Note that both **StateServer** and **SQLServer** methods allow
state to be shared across servers in web farm/web garden scenarios and retained in the
case of a server restart.

```
public enum SessionStateMode {
    Off = 0,
    InProc = 1,
    StateServer = 2,
    SQLServer = 3
}
```

Hierarchy   System.Object → System.ValueType → System.Enum(System.IComparable, System.IFor-
                     mattable, System.IConvertible) → SessionStateMode

Returned By   HttpSessionState.Mode

SessionStateModule

System.Web.SessionState (system.web.dll)   sealed class

This class implements session state storage, taking care of tasks like the generation of
unique session IDs and the storage and retrieval of state information from an external

state provider, as directed by the ASP.NET framework. It is not used directly in your code, but is specified in the *machine.config* file.

```
public sealed class SessionStateModule : System.Web.IHttpModule {
// Public Constructors
    public SessionStateModule( );
// Public Instance Methods
    public void Dispose( );                                          // implements System.Web.IHttpModule
    public void Init( System.Web.HttpApplication app);               // implements System.Web.IHttpModule
// Events
    public event EventHandler End;
    public event EventHandler Start;
}
```

SessionStateSectionHandler

System.Web.SessionState (system.web.dll)   class

The SessionStateSectionHandler class, like all section handlers, is responsible for parsing a portion of the *web.config* file and applying ASP.NET settings accordingly. The SessionStateSectionHandler considers the data in the <sessionstate> sections. This class is used transparently by the ASP.NET framework and is not used directly in your code.

```
class SessionStateSectionHandler : System.Configuration.IConfigurationSectionHandler {
// Public Instance Methods
    public object Create(object parent, SectionHandlerobject configContextObj, System.Xml.XmlNode section);
                                                                   // implements System.Configuration.IConfiguration
}
```

StateRuntime

System.Web.SessionState (system.web.dll)   sealed class

This class is used by the ASP.NET framework to provide session state support. It is not used directly in your code.

```
public sealed class StateRuntime : IStateRuntime {
// Public Constructors
    public StateRuntime( );
// Public Instance Methods
    public void ProcessRequest(IntPtr tracker, int verb, string uri, int exclusive, int timeout,
        int lockCookieExists, int lockCookie, int contentLength, IntPtr content);   // implements IStateRuntime
    public void StopProcessing( );                                                  // implements IStateRuntime
}
```

36

The System.Web.UI Namespace

The System.Web.UI namespace provides types that allow you to create controls and Web Forms (*.aspx* pages). Many of these types provide support for controls in the System.Web.UI.HtmlControls and System.Web.UI.WebControls namespaces and are not used directly in your code. Some of these types provide parsing, data binding, and template functionality. The System.Web.UI namespace also includes a number of fundamental classes like Control (the base class for all HTML, web, and user controls), Page (the base class for every *.aspx* Web Forms page you create), and UserControl (the class representing all *.ascx* user controls).

Many of the types in this namespace are useful if you want to create your own custom controls. These types include the IPostBackDataHandler and IPostBackEventHandler interfaces (used to access postback data and raise control events), the HtmlTextWriter class (used to create a control's HTML user interface), the INamingContainer interface (used to create composite controls), and the ITemplate interface (used to create templated controls with configurable HTML). Additionally, the System.Web.UI namespace also contains types used for control styles (AttributeCollection and CssStyleCollection) and view state management (StateBag and StateItem).

Figure 36-1 shows the controls and control builders for this namespace. Figure 36-2 shows attributes as well as a delegate and its related event arguments. Figure 36-3 shows the remaining types.

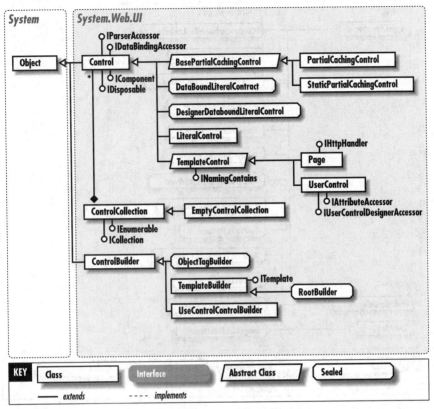

Figure 36-1. Controls and control builders

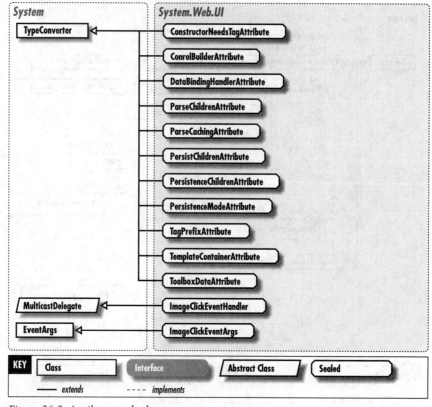

Figure 36-2. Attributes and other types

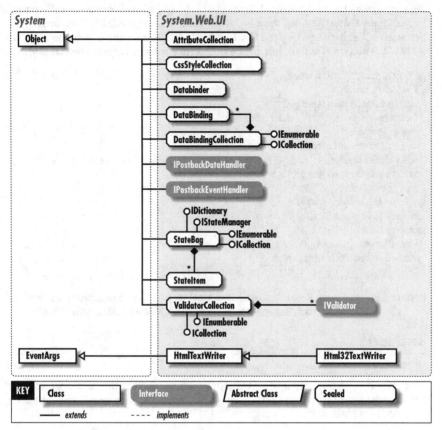

Figure 36-3. More types from System.Web.UI

AttributeCollection

System.Web.UI (system.web.dll)   sealed class

AttributeCollection is a name/value collection of all attributes declared in the opening tag of an ASP.NET server control (which should not be confused with .NET metadata attributes). For example, an HTML text area element has rows and cols attributes that specify its size. You can access and modify the collection of control attributes for any HTML server control through the System.Web.UI.HtmlControls.HtmlControl.Attributes collection. You can also access most important attributes as control properties. Note that you cannot iterate through the AttributeCollection class because it does not directly implement the System.Collections.IEnumerable interface. Use the read-only Keys collection instead.

Web Controls also provide an attribute collection through the System.Web.UI.WebControls. WebControl.Attributes property. However, because web controls are "abstracted away" from the underlying HTML interface code, you cannot directly access the underlying attributes for the composite HTML elements of a control. Instead, this collection will typically contain a single style attribute. You can still add your own attributes to the collection (for example, TextBox1.Attributes("key") = strKey). These attributes will be rendered to the client by most web controls.

One useful way to use the AttributeCollection class is to add a JavaScript event to a control. For example, TextBox1.Attributes["onblur"] = "javascript:alert('Focus lost!');"; adds a "lost focus" Java-Script event. This will work for HTML controls and some simple web controls (like System.Web.UI.WebControls.TextBox), but not for others (like System.Web.UI.WebControls.Calendar).

```
public sealed class AttributeCollection {
// Public Constructors
   public AttributeCollection( StateBag bag);
// Public Instance Properties
   public int Count{get; }
   public CssStyleCollection CssStyle{get; }
   public ICollection Keys{get; }
   public string this[ string key ]{set; get; }
// Public Instance Methods
   public void Add( string key, string value);
   public void AddAttributes( HtmlTextWriter writer);
   public void Clear( );
   public void Remove( string key);
   public void Render( HtmlTextWriter writer);
}
```

Returned By   System.Web.UI.HtmlControls.HtmlControl.Attributes, UserControl.Attributes, System.Web.UI.WebControls.ListItem.Attributes, System.Web.UI.WebControls.WebControl.Attributes

BaseParser

System.Web.UI (system.web.dll)   class

This class is used transparently by the .NET framework. It is the base class used for parsing, the process by which code in an *.aspx* file is interpreted and ultimately rendered as HTML.

```
public class BaseParser {
// Public Constructors
   public BaseParser( );
}
```

Subclasses   TemplateParser

BasePartialCachingControl   disposable

System.Web.UI (system.web.dll)   abstract class

This base class supports fragment caching, which allows portions of an ASP.NET page to be cached. This class is inherited by the PartialCachingControl and StaticPartialCachingControl classes.

```
public abstract class BasePartialCachingControl : Control {
// Protected Constructors
   protected BasePartialCachingControl( );
// Public Instance Properties
   public CacheDependency Dependency{set; get; }
// Public Instance Methods
   public override void Dispose( );                                                           // overrides Control
```

```
// Protected Instance Methods
   protected override void OnInit(EventArgs e);                              // overrides Control
   protected override void Render(HtmlTextWriter output);                    // overrides Control
}
```

Hierarchy System.Object → Control(System.ComponentModel.IComponent, System.IDisposable, IParserAccessor, IDataBindingsAccessor) → BasePartialCachingControl

Subclasses PartialCachingControl, StaticPartialCachingControl

BuildMethod   serializable

System.Web.UI (system.web.dll)   delegate

This delegate is used exclusively by the ASP.NET framework. It specifies the signature for a method used to build a control and is used in the StaticPartialCachingControl. BuildCachedControl() method. It is not used in your code.

```
public delegate Control BuildMethod();
```

Passed To StaticPartialCachingControl.{BuildCachedControl(), StaticPartialCachingControl()}

BuildTemplateMethod   serializable

System.Web.UI (system.web.dll)   delegate

This delegate is used exclusively by the ASP.NET framework. It specifies the signature for a method used to build a template-based control like a **Page** and is used by the CompiledTemplateBuilder class. It is not used in your code.

```
public delegate void BuildTemplateMethod(Control control);
```

Passed To CompiledTemplateBuilder.CompiledTemplateBuilder()

CompiledTemplateBuilder

System.Web.UI (system.web.dll)   sealed class

This utility class is used exclusively by the ASP.NET framework when generating controls. It is not used in your code.

```
public sealed class CompiledTemplateBuilder : ITemplate {
// Public Constructors
   public CompiledTemplateBuilder(BuildTemplateMethod buildTemplateMethod);
// Public Instance Methods
   public void InstantiateIn( Control container);                          // implements ITemplate
}
```

ConstructorNeedsTagAttribute

System.Web.UI (system.web.dll)   sealed class

This attribute is used in the class declaration for a control. You add it, with the parameter set to **True**, to indicate that a control's constructor requires an HTML tag. This tag is used for the System.Web.UI.HtmlControls.HtmlTableCell and System.Web.UI.HtmlControls.HtmlGenericControl classes, which can represent different HTML elements. For example, a System.Web.UI.

HtmlControls.HtmlTableCell could represent a <td> or <th> tag, depending on what tag is provided in the constructor.

```
public sealed class ConstructorNeedsTagAttribute : Attribute {
// Public Constructors
  public ConstructorNeedsTagAttribute( );
  public ConstructorNeedsTagAttribute( bool needsTag);
// Public Instance Properties
  public bool NeedsTag{get; }
}
```

Hierarchy   System.Object → System.Attribute → ConstructorNeedsTagAttribute

Valid On   Class

Control   disposable

System.Web.UI (system.web.dll)   class

The Control class defines properties, methods, and events that all server controls in ASP.NET require. ASP.NET controls do not inherit directly from this class; instead, they inherit from either the System.Web.UI.HtmlControls.HtmlControl or the System.Web.UI.WebControls.WebControl class, both of which inherit from the Control class. Similarly, the Page and UserControl classes inherit from TemplateControl, which inherits from this class.

The Control class contains many of the typical members you would expect in a control, including properties that reference the root of the control tree (Page) and a collection of contained controls (Controls). The EnableViewState property determines whether ASP.NET maintains the control's state automatically by using a hidden field. The ViewState property provides the StateBag collection of state information.

Most Control methods are used transparently by the ASP.NET framework, such as Render( ), which generates the HTML output of a control, and LoadViewState( ) and SaveViewState( ), which manage view state automatically. One interesting method is DataBind( ), which binds controls to arrays or data tables. Third party controls can also extend these methods.

You can inherit from the Control class to create a simple ASP.NET control. Override the Render( ) method so that the control can generate its own output by using the supplied HtmlTextWriter. If you are creating a composite control, you must also override the CreateChildControls( ) method. Use this method to instantiate new server-based ASP.NET controls or LiteralControl objects and add them to the collection of child controls by using the Add( ) method. If you need to access child controls from another procedure, and you are not sure if they have been created yet, you can use the EnsureChildControls( ) method, which automatically calls CreateChildControls( ), if needed. You should also implement the INamingContainer interface to ensure that child controls are created in a distinct namespace.

Usually, it is easier to derive from System.Web.UI.WebControls.WebControl when creating a custom control, as this class provides basic style and color options and manages the state for these properties automatically. If your control does not provide user interface, you may want to derive from the more basic Control class.

```
public class Control : System.ComponentModel.IComponent, IDisposable, IParserAccessor, IDataBindingsAccessor {
// Public Constructors
```

```
public Control( );
// Public Instance Properties
    public Control BindingContainer{get; }
    public virtual string ClientID{get; }
    public virtual ControlCollection Controls{get; }
    public virtual bool EnableViewState{set; get; }
    public virtual string ID{set; get; }
    public virtual Control NamingContainer{get; }
    public virtual Page Page{set; get; }
    public virtual Control Parent{get; }
    public ISite Site{set; get; }                                        // implements System.ComponentModel.IComponent
    public virtual string TemplateSourceDirectory{get; }
    public virtual string UniqueID{get; }
    public virtual bool Visible{set; get; }
// Protected Instance Properties
    protected bool ChildControlsCreated{set; get; }
    protected virtual HttpContext Context{get; }
    protected EventHandlerList Events{get; }
    protected bool HasChildViewState{get; }
    protected bool IsTrackingViewState{get; }
    protected virtual StateBag ViewState{get; }
    protected virtual bool ViewStateIgnoresCase{get; }
// Public Instance Methods
    public virtual void DataBind( );
    public virtual void Dispose( );                                      // implements IDisposable
    public virtual Control FindControl( string id);
    public virtual bool HasControls( );
    public void RenderControl( HtmlTextWriter writer);
    public string ResolveUrl( string relativeUrl);
    public void SetRenderMethodDelegate(RenderMethod renderMethod);
// Protected Instance Methods
    protected internal virtual void AddedControl(Control control, int index);
    protected virtual void AddParsedSubObject( object obj);              // implements IParserAccessor
    protected void BuildProfileTree(string parentId, bool calcViewState);
    protected void ClearChildViewState( );
    protected virtual void CreateChildControls( );
    protected virtual ControlCollection CreateControlCollection( );
    protected virtual void EnsureChildControls( );
    protected virtual Control FindControl(string id, int pathOffset);
    protected bool IsLiteralContent( );
    protected virtual void LoadViewState( object savedState);
    protected string MapPathSecure( string virtualPath);
    protected virtual bool OnBubbleEvent(object source, EventArgs args);
    protected virtual void OnDataBinding( EventArgs e);
    protected virtual void OnInit( EventArgs e);
    protected virtual void OnLoad( EventArgs e);
    protected virtual void OnPreRender( EventArgs e);
    protected virtual void OnUnload( EventArgs e);
    protected void RaiseBubbleEvent(object source, EventArgs args);
    protected internal virtual void RemovedControl(Control control);
    protected virtual void Render( HtmlTextWriter writer);
```

```
protected virtual void RenderChildren(HtmlTextWriter writer);
protected virtual object SaveViewState( );
protected virtual void TrackViewState( );
// Events
public event EventHandler DataBinding;
public event EventHandler Disposed;                    // implements System.ComponentModel.IComponent
public event EventHandler Init;
public event EventHandler Load;
public event EventHandler PreRender;
public event EventHandler Unload;
}
```

Subclasses   Multiple types

Returned By   BuildMethod.{EndInvoke( ), Invoke( )}, ControlCollection.{Owner, this}, System.Web.UI.
                    Design.ControlParser.ParseControl( ), DesignTimeTemplateParser.ParseControl( ), System.
                    Web.UI.MobileControls.Form.ControlToPaginate, PartialCachingControl.CachedControl,
                    TemplateControl.{LoadControl( ), ParseControl( )}, System.Web.UI.WebControls.CheckBox-
                    List.FindControl( )

Passed To   Multiple types

ControlBuilder

System.Web.UI (system.web.dll)   class

This class is used transparently by the ASP.NET network when generating a Page
object. It works with the appropriate parser object to build the relevant controls. You
can derive from this class to create your custom control builders for your custom
controls. Just override the appropriate methods and apply the ControlBuilderAttribute to
your control class to instruct ASP.NET to use your custom ControlBuilder. For example,
you could override the AllowWhitespaceLiterals( ) method to return False. This override
instructs ASP.NET to refrain from creating LiteralControl objects for any whitespace it
finds inside a control. Note, however, that it is easiest and most common to use the
standard ControlBuilder for your custom controls.

```
public class ControlBuilder {
// Public Constructors
  public ControlBuilder( );
// Public Instance Properties
  public Type ControlType{get; }
  public bool HasAspCode{get; }
  public string ID{set; get; }
  public Type NamingContainerType{get; }
  public string TagName{get; }
// Protected Instance Properties
  protected bool FChildrenAsProperties{get; }
  protected bool FIsNonParserAccessor{get; }
  protected bool InDesigner{get; }
  protected TemplateParser Parser{get; }
// Public Static Methods
  public static ControlBuilder CreateBuilderFromType(TemplateParser parser, ControlBuilder parentBuilder,
    Type type, string tagName, string id, System.Collections.IDictionary attribs, int line, string sourceFileName);
```

```
// Public Instance Methods
  public virtual bool AllowWhitespaceLiterals( );
  public virtual void AppendLiteralString( string s);
  public virtual void AppendSubBuilder(ControlBuilder subBuilder);
  public virtual void CloseControl( );
  public virtual Type GetChildControlType(string tagName, System.Collections.IDictionary attribs);
  public virtual bool HasBody( );
  public virtual bool HtmlDecodeLiterals( );
  public virtual void Init(TemplateParser parser, ControlBuilder parentBuilder, Type type, string tagName, string id,
      System.Collections.IDictionary attribs);
  public virtual bool NeedsTagInnerText( );
  public virtual void OnAppendToParentBuilder(ControlBuilder parentBuilder);
  public virtual void SetTagInnerText( string text);
}
```

Subclasses	Multiple types
Passed To	ObjectTagBuilder.{AppendSubBuilder( ), Init( )}

ControlBuilderAttribute

System.Web.UI (system.web.dll)   sealed class

This attribute specifies the control builder that a custom control should use. If you want your control to use the standard control builder, you do not need to use this attribute. If you have created a custom ControlBuilder class, you can instruct ASP.NET to use it to create a control by adding this attribute to the control's class declaration, as in [ControlBuilder(typeOf(MyControlBuilder))].

```
public sealed class ControlBuilderAttribute : Attribute {
// Public Constructors
  public ControlBuilderAttribute( Type builderType);
// Public Static Fields
  public static readonly ControlBuilderAttribute Default;            // =System.Web.UI.ControlBuilderAttribute
// Public Instance Properties
  public Type BuilderType{get; }
// Public Instance Methods
  public override bool Equals( object obj);                          // overrides Attribute
  public override int GetHashCode( );                               // overrides Attribute
  public override bool IsDefaultAttribute( );                       // overrides Attribute
}
```

Hierarchy	System.Object → System.Attribute → ControlBuilderAttribute
Valid On	Class

ControlCollection

System.Web.UI (system.web.dll)   class

This class represents a collection of controls. It allows pages and other controls to specify their child controls (as with the Page.Controls Property).

```
public class ControlCollection : ICollection, IEnumerable {
// Public Constructors
  public ControlCollection(Control owner);
// Public Instance Properties
  public int Count{get; }                                               // implements ICollection
  public bool IsReadOnly{get; }
  public bool IsSynchronized{get; }                                     // implements ICollection
  public object SyncRoot{get; }                                         // implements ICollection
  public virtual Control this[ int index ]{get; }
// Protected Instance Properties
  protected Control Owner{get; }
// Public Instance Methods
  public virtual void Add(Control child);
  public virtual void AddAt(int index, Control child);
  public virtual void Clear( );
  public virtual bool Contains( Control c);
  public void CopyTo(Array array, int index);                           // implements ICollection
  public IEnumerator GetEnumerator( );                                  // implements IEnumerable
  public virtual int IndexOf(Control value);
  public virtual void Remove(Control value);
  public virtual void RemoveAt(int index);
}
```

Subclasses   EmptyControlCollection

Returned By   Control.{Controls, CreateControlCollection( )}

CssStyleCollection

System.Web.UI (system.web.dll)   sealed class

This class contains a name-value collection of cascading style sheet (CSS) attributes for
a specific control. CSS styles are used to configure many aspects of a control's appearance (such as font and color) and are supported for both web controls and HTML
controls. A CssStyleCollection is provided through the System.Web.UI.HtmlControls.HtmlControl.Style
and System.Web.UI.WebControls.WebControl.Style properties. This collection is similar to the
AttributeCollection class, and you can retrieve values by using the specific attribute name or
enumerating through the read-only Keys collection.

```
public sealed class CssStyleCollection {
// Public Instance Properties
  public int Count{get; }
  public ICollection Keys{get; }
  public string this[ string key ]{set; get; }
// Public Instance Methods
  public void Add(string key, string value);
  public void Clear( );
  public void Remove(string key);
}
```

Returned By   AttributeCollection.CssStyle, System.Web.UI.HtmlControls.HtmlControl.Style, System.Web.UI.
WebControls.WebControl.Style

DataBinder

System.Web.UI (system.web.dll)   sealed class

This class contains a single shared utility method, Eval( ), which allows you to specify data binding for controls like System.Web.UI.WebControls.DataList and System.Web.UI.WebControls. Repeater. The Eval( ) method accepts a string that identifies a field in the control's data source and uses it to retrieve the corresponding information. For example, the statement <%# DataBinder.Eval(Container.DataItem, "Name") %> in a template for a data control would retrieve data from the Name field of the control's bound data table. Note that you don't need to use this method to create a data binding expression (you can just use the <%# Container.DataItem("Name") %> syntax, which is faster). However, using the DataBinder method gives you the chance to supply a format string to configure date or numeric values.

```
public sealed class DataBinder {
// Public Constructors
  public DataBinder( );
// Public Static Methods
  public static object Eval(object container, string expression);
  public static string Eval(object container, string expression, string format);
  public static object GetIndexedPropertyValue(object container, string expr);
  public static string GetIndexedPropertyValue(object container, string propName, string format);
  public static object GetPropertyValue(object container, string propName);
  public static string GetPropertyValue(object container, string propName, string format);
}
```

DataBinding

System.Web.UI (system.web.dll)   sealed class

This class represents a design-time data binding, which is contained in the DataBindingCollection. Generally, most developers will create data bindings at runtime instead, which allows increased flexibility and more transparent code.

You can configure data binding expressions by clicking the ellipsis (...) next to the (DataBindings) option in the Visual Studio .NET Properties window. Every data binding consists of an expression identifying the source (Expression), the bound property (PropertyName), and the data type (PropertyType).

```
public sealed class DataBinding {
// Public Constructors
  public DataBinding(string propertyName, Type propertyType, string expression);
// Public Instance Properties
  public string Expression{set; get; }
  public string PropertyName{get; }
  public Type PropertyType{get; }
// Public Instance Methods
  public override bool Equals(object obj);                                            // overrides object
  public override int GetHashCode( );                                                 // overrides object
}
```

Returned By   DataBindingCollection.this

Passed To   DataBindingCollection.{Add( ), Remove( )}

DataBindingCollection

System.Web.UI (system.web.dll)   sealed class

This collection of DataBinding objects represents data binding expressions configured at design time.

```
public sealed class DataBindingCollection : ICollection, IEnumerable {
// Public Constructors
  public DataBindingCollection( );
// Public Instance Properties
  public int Count{get; }                                                                     // implements ICollection
  public bool IsReadOnly{get; }
  public bool IsSynchronized{get; }                                                           // implements ICollection
  public string[ ] RemovedBindings{get; }
  public object SyncRoot{get; }                                                               // implements ICollection
  public DataBinding this[ string propertyName ]{get; }
// Public Instance Methods
  public void Add(DataBinding binding);
  public void Clear( );
  public void CopyTo( Array array, int index);                                                // implements ICollection
  public IEnumerator GetEnumerator( );                                                        // implements IEnumerable
  public void Remove(DataBinding binding);
  public void Remove(string propertyName);
  public void Remove(string propertyName, bool addToRemovedList);
}
```

Returned By   System.Web.UI.Design.HtmlControlDesigner.DataBindings, IDataBindingsAccessor.
DataBindings

DataBindingHandlerAttribute

System.Web.UI (system.web.dll)   sealed class

This class is used for controls requiring special data binding handlers. For example, the System.Web.UI.WebControls.Calendar control uses a System.Web.UI.Design.CalendarDataBindingHandler class that derives from System.Web.UI.Design.DataBindingHandler. This custom data binding handler is specified by using the DataBindingHandlerAttribute in the control's class declaration.

```
public sealed class DataBindingHandlerAttribute : Attribute {
// Public Constructors
  public DataBindingHandlerAttribute( );
  public DataBindingHandlerAttribute(string typeName);
  public DataBindingHandlerAttribute(Type type);
// Public Static Fields
  public static readonly DataBindingHandlerAttribute Default;                   // =System.Web.UI.DataBindingHandlerAttribute
// Public Instance Properties
  public string HandlerTypeName{get; }
}
```

Hierarchy   System.Object → System.Attribute → DataBindingHandlerAttribute

Valid On   Class

DataBoundLiteralControl

disposable

System.Web.UI (system.web.dll)   sealed class

ASP.NET creates a DataBoundLiteralControl for each data binding expression it finds on a page (such as <%# Container.DataItem("Name") %>). You do not need to create this control directly.

```
public sealed class DataBoundLiteralControl : Control {
// Public Constructors
  public DataBoundLiteralControl(int staticLiteralsCount, int dataBoundLiteralCount);
// Public Instance Properties
  public string Text{get; }
// Public Instance Methods
  public void SetDataBoundString( int index, string s);
  public void SetStaticString( int index, string s);
// Protected Instance Methods
  protected override ControlCollection CreateControlCollection( );          // overrides Control
  protected override void LoadViewState( object savedState);                // overrides Control
  protected override void Render( HtmlTextWriter output);                   // overrides Control
  protected override object SaveViewState( );                               // overrides Control
}
```

Hierarchy   System.Object → Control(System.ComponentModel.IComponent, System.IDisposable, IParserAccessor, IDataBindingsAccessor) → DataBoundLiteralControl

DesignerDataBoundLiteralControl

disposable

System.Web.UI (system.web.dll)   sealed class

This class is used for data-binding expressions configured at design time. You do not need to create this control directly.

```
public sealed class DesignerDataBoundLiteralControl : Control {
// Public Constructors
  public DesignerDataBoundLiteralControl( );
// Public Instance Properties
  public string Text{set; get; }
// Protected Instance Methods
  protected override ControlCollection CreateControlCollection( );          // overrides Control
  protected override void LoadViewState( object savedState);                // overrides Control
  protected override void Render( HtmlTextWriter output);                   // overrides Control
  protected override object SaveViewState( );                               // overrides Control
}
```

Hierarchy   System.Object → Control(System.ComponentModel.IComponent, System.IDisposable, IParserAccessor, IDataBindingsAccessor) → DesignerDataBoundLiteralControl

DesignTimeParseData

System.Web.UI (system.web.dll)   sealed class

This class is used by the ASP.NET framework to parse .aspx files at design time. You do not use it in your code.

```
public sealed class DesignTimeParseData {
// Public Constructors
  public DesignTimeParseData(System.ComponentModel.Design.IDesignerHost designerHost, string parseText);
// Public Instance Properties
  public EventHandler DataBindingHandler{set; get; }
  public IDesignerHost DesignerHost{get; }
  public string DocumentUrl{set; get; }
  public string ParseText{get; }
}
```

Passed To   DesignTimeTemplateParser.{ParseControl( ), ParseTemplate( )}

DesignTimeTemplateParser

System.Web.UI (system.web.dll)   sealed class

This control is used by the ASP.NET framework to parse templated controls in *.aspx* files at design time. You do not use it in your code.

```
public sealed class DesignTimeTemplateParser {
// Public Static Methods
  public static Control ParseControl(DesignTimeParseData data);
  public static ITemplate ParseTemplate(DesignTimeParseData data);
}
```

EmptyControlCollection

System.Web.UI (system.web.dll)   class

This class represents a collection of controls that is always empty. Using the Add( ) method will trigger an exception.

```
public class EmptyControlCollection : ControlCollection {
// Public Constructors
  public EmptyControlCollection( Control owner);
// Public Instance Methods
  public override void Add( Control child);                        // overrides ControlCollection
  public override void AddAt( int index, Control child);           // overrides ControlCollection
}
```

Hierarchy   System.Object → ControlCollection(System.Collections.ICollection, System.Collections.IEnumerable) → EmptyControlCollection

Html32TextWriter   marshal by reference, disposable

System.Web.UI (system.web.dll)   class

This class derives from HtmlTextWriter and is used by the ASP.NET framework to generate HTML output for ASP.NET controls.

```
public class Html32TextWriter : HtmlTextWriter {
// Public Constructors
  public Html32TextWriter( System.IO.TextWriter writer);
  public Html32TextWriter(System.IO.TextWriter writer, string tabString);
```

```
// Protected Instance Properties
  protected Stack FontStack{get;}
// Public Instance Methods
  public override void RenderBeginTag(HtmlTextWriterTag tagKey);          // overrides HtmlTextWriter
  public override void RenderEndTag();                                    // overrides HtmlTextWriter
// Protected Instance Methods
  protected override string GetTagName(HtmlTextWriterTag tagKey);         // overrides HtmlTextWriter
  protected override bool OnStyleAttributeRender(string name, string value,
    HtmlTextWriterStyle key);                                            // overrides HtmlTextWriter
  protected override bool OnTagRender(string name, HtmlTextWriterTag key); // overrides HtmlTextWriter
  protected override string RenderAfterContent();                        // overrides HtmlTextWriter
  protected override string RenderAfterTag();                            // overrides HtmlTextWriter
  protected override string RenderBeforeContent();                       // overrides HtmlTextWriter
  protected override string RenderBeforeTag();                           // overrides HtmlTextWriter
}
```

Hierarchy   System.Object → System.MarshalByRefObject → System.IO.TextWriter(System.IDisposable) → HtmlTextWriter → Html32TextWriter

HtmlTextWriter   marshal by reference, disposable

System.Web.UI (system.web.dll)   class

The ASP.NET framework uses this class when writing the client-side HTML for a Web Forms page. It contains a wealth of methods for rendering the appropriate content, and derives from the more generic System.IO.TextWriter. Typically, you will not use this class directly in your code, unless you are a control developer.

When deriving custom controls from Control or System.Web.UI.WebControls.WebControl, you can override the Render() or RenderContents() method and create the control's output by using the supplied HtmlTextWriter. Commonly used methods include Write(), which can output text or HTML tags, AddStyleAttribute(), which specifies a CSS style attribute for the next tag, and RenderBeginTag() and RenderEndTag(), which make it easy to insert open and closing HTML tags while keeping the code readable. The HtmlTextWriter also performs automatic indentation of the HTML output.

```
public class HtmlTextWriter : System.IO.TextWriter {
// Public Constructors
  public HtmlTextWriter( System.IO.TextWriter writer);
  public HtmlTextWriter(System.IO.TextWriter writer, string tabString);
// Public Static Fields
  public const string DefaultTabString;                                  // =
  public const char DoubleQuoteChar;                                     // =0x00000022
  public const string EndTagLeftChars;                                   // =</
  public const char EqualsChar;                                          // =0x0000003D
  public const string EqualsDoubleQuoteString;                           // =="
  public const string SelfClosingChars;                                  // =/
  public const string SelfClosingTagEnd;                                 // =/>
  public const char SemicolonChar;                                       // =0x0000003B
  public const char SingleQuoteChar;                                     // =0x00000027
  public const char SlashChar;                                           // =0x0000002F
  public const char SpaceChar;                                           // =0x00000020
  public const char StyleEqualsChar;                                     // =0x0000003A
```

```
public const char TagLeftChar;                                                      // =0x0000003C
public const char TagRightChar;                                                     // =0x0000003E
// Public Instance Properties
public override Encoding Encoding{get; }                                            // overrides System.IO.TextWriter
public int Indent{set; get; }
public TextWriter InnerWriter{set; get; }
public override string NewLine{set; get; }                                          // overrides System.IO.TextWriter
// Protected Instance Properties
protected HtmlTextWriterTag TagKey{set; get; }
protected string TagName{set; get; }
// Protected Static Methods
protected static void RegisterAttribute(string name, HtmlTextWriterAttribute key);
protected static void RegisterStyle(string name, HtmlTextWriterStyle key);
protected static void RegisterTag(string name, HtmlTextWriterTag key);
// Public Instance Methods
public virtual void AddAttribute(HtmlTextWriterAttribute key, string value);
public virtual void AddAttribute(HtmlTextWriterAttribute key, string value, bool fEncode);
public virtual void AddAttribute(string name, string value);
public virtual void AddAttribute(string name, string value, bool fEndode);
public virtual void AddStyleAttribute(HtmlTextWriterStyle key, string value);
public virtual void AddStyleAttribute(string name, string value);
public override void Close( );                                                       // overrides System.IO.TextWriter
public override void Flush( );                                                       // overrides System.IO.TextWriter
public virtual void RenderBeginTag(HtmlTextWriterTag tagKey);
public virtual void RenderBeginTag(string tagName);
public virtual void RenderEndTag( );
public override void Write(bool value);                                             // overrides System.IO.TextWriter
public override void Write(char value);                                            // overrides System.IO.TextWriter
public override void Write(char[ ] buffer);                                        // overrides System.IO.TextWriter
public override void Write(char[ ] buffer, int index,                             // overrides System.IO.TextWriterint count);
public override void Write( double value);                                         // overrides System.IO.TextWriter
public override void Write(int value);                                             // overrides System.IO.TextWriter
public override void Write(long value);                                            // overrides System.IO.TextWriter
public override void Write(object value);                                          // overrides System.IO.TextWriter
public override void Write( float value);                                          // overrides System.IO.TextWriter
public override void Write(string s);                                              // overrides System.IO.TextWriter
public override void Write(string format, object arg0);                           // overrides System.IO.TextWriter
public override void Write(string format, params object[ ] arg);                  // overrides System.IO.TextWriter
public override void Write(string format, object arg0, object arg1);              // overrides System.IO.TextWriter
public virtual void WriteAttribute(string name, string value);
public virtual void WriteAttribute(string name, string value, bool fEncode);
public virtual void WriteBeginTag(string tagName);
public virtual void WriteEndTag(string tagName);
public virtual void WriteFullBeginTag(string tagName);
public override void WriteLine( );                                                  // overrides System.IO.TextWriter
public override void WriteLine(bool value);                                         // overrides System.IO.TextWriter
public override void WriteLine(char value);                                         // overrides System.IO.TextWriter
public override void WriteLine(char[ ] buffer);                                     // overrides System.IO.TextWriter
public override void WriteLine(char[ ] buffer, int index, int count);               // overrides System.IO.TextWriter
public override void WriteLine(double value);                                       // overrides System.IO.TextWriter
public override void WriteLine(int value);                                          // overrides System.IO.TextWriter
```

```
public override void WriteLine(long value);                                              // overrides System.IO.TextWriter
public override void WriteLine(object value);                                            // overrides System.IO.TextWriter
public override void WriteLine(float value);                                             // overrides System.IO.TextWriter
public override void WriteLine(string s);                                                // overrides System.IO.TextWriter
public override void WriteLine(string format, object arg0);                              // overrides System.IO.TextWriter
public override void WriteLine(string format, params object[ ] arg);                     // overrides System.IO.TextWriter
public override void WriteLine(string format, object arg0, object arg1);                 // overrides System.IO.TextWriter
public override void WriteLine(uint value);                                              // overrides System.IO.TextWriter
public void WriteLineNoTabs(string s);
public virtual void WriteStyleAttribute(string name, string value);
public virtual void WriteStyleAttribute(string name, string value, bool fEncode);
// Protected Instance Methods
protected virtual void AddAttribute(string name, string value, HtmlTextWriterAttribute key);
protected virtual void AddStyleAttribute(string name, string value, HtmlTextWriterStyle key);
protected virtual string EncodeAttributeValue(HtmlTextWriterAttribute attrKey, string value);
protected string EncodeAttributeValue(string value, bool fEncode);
protected string EncodeUrl( string url);
protected virtual void FilterAttributes( );
protected HtmlTextWriterAttribute GetAttributeKey(string attrName);
protected string GetAttributeName(HtmlTextWriterAttribute attrKey);
protected HtmlTextWriterStyle GetStyleKey(string styleName);
protected string GetStyleName(HtmlTextWriterStyle styleKey);
protected virtual HtmlTextWriterTag GetTagKey(string tagName);
protected virtual string GetTagName(HtmlTextWriterTag tagKey);
protected bool IsAttributeDefined(HtmlTextWriterAttribute key);
protected bool IsAttributeDefined(HtmlTextWriterAttribute key, out string value);
protected bool IsStyleAttributeDefined(HtmlTextWriterStyle key);
protected bool IsStyleAttributeDefined(HtmlTextWriterStyle key, out string value);
protected virtual bool OnAttributeRender(string name, string value, HtmlTextWriterAttribute key);
protected virtual bool OnStyleAttributeRender(string name, string value, HtmlTextWriterStyle key);
protected virtual bool OnTagRender(string name, HtmlTextWriterTag key);
protected virtual void OutputTabs( );
protected string PopEndTag( );
protected void PushEndTag( string endTag);
protected virtual string RenderAfterContent( );
protected virtual string RenderAfterTag( );
protected virtual string RenderBeforeContent( );
protected virtual string RenderBeforeTag( );
}
```

Hierarchy	System.Object → System.MarshalByRefObject → System.IO.TextWriter(System.IDisposable) → HtmlTextWriter
Subclasses	Html32TextWriter, System.Web.UI.MobileControls.Adapters.MultiPartWriter
Returned By	System.Web.UI.MobileControls.Adapters.HtmlPageAdapter.CreateTextWriter( ), System.Web.UI.MobileControls.Adapters.WmlPageAdapter.CreateTextWriter( ), System.Web.UI.MobileControls.IPageAdapter.CreateTextWriter( ), Page.CreateHtmlTextWriter( )
Passed To	Multiple types

HtmlTextWriterAttribute

serializable

System.Web.UI (system.web.dll)   enum

This enumeration specifies the HTML attributes that should be written to the opening tag of an HTML element when a client request is processed. It is used by several methods in the HtmlTextWriter class.

```
public enum HtmlTextWriterAttribute {
  Accesskey = 0,
  Align = 1,
  Alt = 2,
  Background = 3,
  Bgcolor = 4,
  Border = 5,
  Bordercolor = 6,
  Cellpadding = 7,
  Cellspacing = 8,
  Checked = 9,
  Class = 10,
  Cols = 11,
  Colspan = 12,
  Disabled = 13,
  For = 14,
  Height = 15,
  Href = 16,
  Id = 17,
  Maxlength = 18,
  Multiple = 19,
  Name = 20,
  Nowrap = 21,
  Onchange = 22,
  Onclick = 23,
  ReadOnly = 24,
  Rows = 25,
  Rowspan = 26,
  Rules = 27,
  Selected = 28,
  Size = 29,
  Src = 30,
  Style = 31,
  Tabindex = 32,
  Target = 33,
  Title = 34,
  Type = 35,
  Valign = 36,
  Value = 37,
  Width = 38,
  Wrap = 39
}
```

Hierarchy	System.Object → System.ValueType → System.Enum(System.IComparable, System.IFor-mattable, System.IConvertible) → HtmlTextWriterAttribute
Returned By	HtmlTextWriter.GetAttributeKey( )
Passed To	HtmlTextWriter.{AddAttribute( ), EncodeAttributeValue( ), GetAttributeName( ), IsAttributeDefined( ), OnAttributeRender( ), RegisterAttribute( )}

HtmlTextWriterStyle

serializable

System.Web.UI (system.web.dll)

enum

This enumeration specifies HTML styles that the methods in the HtmlTextWriter class can use to create output.

```
public enum HtmlTextWriterStyle {
    BackgroundColor = 0,
    BackgroundImage = 1,
    BorderCollapse = 2,
    BorderColor = 3,
    BorderStyle = 4,
    BorderWidth = 5,
    Color = 6,
    FontFamily = 7,
    FontSize = 8,
    FontStyle = 9,
    FontWeight = 10,
    Height = 11,
    TextDecoration = 12,
    Width = 13
}
```

Hierarchy	System.Object → System.ValueType → System.Enum(System.IComparable, System.IFor-mattable, System.IConvertible) → HtmlTextWriterStyle
Returned By	HtmlTextWriter.GetStyleKey( )
Passed To	HtmlTextWriter.{AddStyleAttribute( ), GetStyleName( ), IsStyleAttributeDefined( ), OnStyleAttributeRender( ), RegisterStyle( )}

HtmlTextWriterTag

serializable

System.Web.UI (system.web.dll)

enum

This enumeration represents different HTML tags for the HtmlTextWriter class. For example, you can use a value from this enumeration as a parameter for the HtmlText-Writer.RenderBeginTag( ) method to specify what tag should be written to the output stream.

```
public enum HtmlTextWriterTag {
    Unknown = 0,
    A = 1,
    Acronym = 2,
    Address = 3,
```

```
Area = 4,
B = 5,
Base = 6,
Basefont = 7,
Bdo = 8,
Bgsound = 9,
Big = 10,
Blockquote = 11,
Body = 12,
Br = 13,
Button = 14,
Caption = 15,
Center = 16,
Cite = 17,
Code = 18,
Col = 19,
Colgroup = 20,
Dd = 21,
Del = 22,
Dfn = 23,
Dir = 24,
Div = 25,
Dl = 26,
Dt = 27,
Em = 28,
Embed = 29,
Fieldset = 30,
Font = 31,
Form = 32,
Frame = 33,
Frameset = 34,
H1 = 35,
H2 = 36,
H3 = 37,
H4 = 38,
H5 = 39,
H6 = 40,
Head = 41,
Hr = 42,
Html = 43,
I = 44,
Iframe = 45,
Img = 46,
Input = 47,
Ins = 48,
Isindex = 49,
Kbd = 50,
Label = 51,
Legend = 52,
Li = 53,
Link = 54,
```

```
Map = 55,
Marquee = 56,
Menu = 57,
Meta = 58,
Nobr = 59,
Noframes = 60,
Noscript = 61,
Object = 62,
Ol = 63,
Option = 64,
P = 65,
Param = 66,
Pre = 67,
Q = 68,
Rt = 69,
Ruby = 70,
S = 71,
Samp = 72,
Script = 73,
Select = 74,
Small = 75,
Span = 76,
Strike = 77,
Strong = 78,
Style = 79,
Sub = 80,
Sup = 81,
Table = 82,
Tbody = 83,
Td = 84,
Textarea = 85,
Tfoot = 86,
Th = 87,
Thead = 88,
Title = 89,
Tr = 90,
Tt = 91,
U = 92,
Ul = 93,
Var = 94,
Wbr = 95,
Xml = 96
}
```

Hierarchy   System.Object → System.ValueType → System.Enum(System.IComparable, System.IFor-
                  mattable, System.IConvertible) → HtmlTextWriterTag

Returned By   HtmlTextWriter.{GetTagKey( ), TagKey}, System.Web.UI.WebControls.WebControl.TagKey

Passed To   HtmlTextWriter.{GetTagName( ), OnTagRender( ), RegisterTag( ), RenderBeginTag( ),
                  TagKey}, System.Web.UI.WebControls.WebControl.WebControl( )

IAttributeAccessor

System.Web.UI (system.web.dll)   interface

This interface is implemented by the System.Web.UI.WebControls.WebControl and System.Web.UI.
HtmlControls.HtmlControl base control classes. It allows you to programmatically access and
modify any of the attributes that are defined in the opening tag of a server control. For
example, you can use GetAttribute( ) to access an attribute by name and retrieve its string
vlaue, and you can use SetAttribute( ) to access an attribute by name and supply a new
string value that should be applied. This interface is primarily of interest if you want to
provide this functionality in a custom control that does not derive from System.Web.UI.
WebControls.WebControl or System.Web.UI.HtmlControls.HtmlControl.

```
public interface IAttributeAccessor {
// Public Instance Methods
  public string GetAttribute(string key);
  public void SetAttribute(string key, string value);
}
```

Implemented By   UserControl, System.Web.UI.HtmlControls.HtmlControl, System.Web.UI.MobileControls.
{DeviceSpecificChoice, MobileControl}, System.Web.UI.WebControls.{ListItem, WebControl}

IDataBindingsAccessor

System.Web.UI (system.web.dll)   interface

This interface is implemented by all controls that derive from Control. It allows access to
the corresponding DataBindingCollection through the DataBindings property. As the DataBinding-
Collection represents data bindings created in the IDE, the properties in this interface are
only valid at design time.

```
public interface IDataBindingsAccessor {
// Public Instance Properties
  public DataBindingCollection DataBindings{get; }
  public bool HasDataBindings{get; }
}
```

Implemented By   Control

ImageClickEventArgs

System.Web.UI (system.web.dll)   sealed class

This custom System.EventArgs object provides extra information for some image-click
events. These include the System.Web.UI.WebControls.ImageButton.Click and System.Web.UI.HtmlCon-
trols.HtmlInputImage.ServerClick events. Note that the System.Web.UI.WebControls.Image and System.
Web.UI.HtmlControls.HtmlImage controls do not use this class.

The extra information consists of two coordinates indicating the exact position where
the image was clicked: X and Y. These coordinates are measured from the top-left
corner, which has the coordinates (0, 0) by convention.

```
public sealed class ImageClickEventArgs : EventArgs {
// Public Constructors
  public ImageClickEventArgs(int x, int y);
```

```
// Public Instance Fields
  public int X;
  public int Y;
}
```

Hierarchy	System.Object → System.EventArgs → ImageClickEventArgs
Passed To	System.Web.UI.HtmlControls.HtmlInputImage.OnServerClick( ), ImageClickEventHandler. {BeginInvoke( ), Invoke( )}, System.Web.UI.WebControls.ImageButton.OnClick( )

ImageClickEventHandler   serializable

System.Web.UI (system.web.dll)   delegate

This delegate specifies the signature for the event handler that handles the System.Web.UI. WebControls.ImageButton.Click and System.Web.UI.HtmlControls.HtmlInputImage.ServerClick events. This event handler receives extra information about the exact coordinates where the image was clicked.

```
public delegate void ImageClickEventHandler(object sender, ImageClickEventArgs e);
```

Associated Events	System.Web.UI.HtmlControls.HtmlInputImage.ServerClick( ), System.Web.UI.WebControls. ImageButton.Click( )

INamingContainer

System.Web.UI (system.web.dll)   interface

This is a marker interface. When ASP.NET renders a control that implements INaming-Container, it creates a new namespace and uses it for any child controls. This guarantees that the child control IDs will be unique on the page. This interface is used for controls that dynamically generate a series of similar controls, such as System.Web.UI.WebControls. Repeater and System.Web.UI.WebControls.RadioButtonList. If you are developing your own composite control, you will also need to implement this interface.

```
public interface INamingContainer {
// No public or protected members
}
```

Implemented By	TemplateControl, System.Web.UI.MobileControls.{List, ObjectList, TemplateContainer}, System.Web.UI.WebControls.{CheckBoxList, DataGrid, DataGridItem, DataList, DataListItem, RadioButtonList, Repeater, RepeaterItem}

IParserAccessor

System.Web.UI (system.web.dll)   interface

This interface is implemented by the Control class. It allows the ASP.NET framework to access the parser for the control.

```
public interface IParserAccessor {
// Public Instance Methods
  public void AddParsedSubObject( object obj);
}
```

IPostBackDataHandler

System.Web.UI (system.web.dll)   interface

This interface, which is implemented by many ASP.NET Server Controls, allows a
control to receive and process postback data. It consists of two methods. The first,
LoadPostData(), allows a control to receive the form data and update its properties as
required. ASP.NET calls this method automatically on postback. It provides form data
as a collection in the postCollection argument and a postDataKey argument identifying the
control's key (i.e., postCollection(postDataKey) will contain the posted information for the
control). The control returns True from this method to indicate that its state has
changed, or False if it hasn't. ASP.NET calls the second method, RaisePostDataChangedEvent(),
automatically after LoadPostData() if the control's state is changed. The control can use
this method to raise any required events. Events should never be raised from the
LoadPostData() method because other controls may not have loaded their state information yet.

```
public interface IPostBackDataHandler {
// Public Instance Methods
    public bool LoadPostData(string postDataKey, System.Collections.Specialized.NameValueCollection postCollection);
    public void RaisePostDataChangedEvent( );
}
```

Implemented By   Multiple types

IPostBackEventHandler

System.Web.UI (system.web.dll)   interface

This interface allows a control to raise events in response to a postback operation. This
interface is commonly used for button controls like System.Web.UI.WebControls.Button and
System.Web.UI.WebControls.ImageButton. It can be used instead of, or in conjunction with, the
IPostBackDataHandler interface. The distinction is that the RaisePostBackEvent() method is
always called when a postback event occurs. The IPostBackDataHandler.
RaisePostDataChangedEvent() method is called only if the control's state has changed, and is
thus more suited for a "Change" event than a "Click" event.

```
public interface IPostBackEventHandler {
// Public Instance Methods
    public void RaisePostBackEvent( string eventArgument);
}
```

Implemented By   Multiple types

Passed To   Page.{RaisePostBackEvent( ), RegisterRequiresRaiseEvent( )}

IStateManager

System.Web.UI (system.web.dll)   interface

This interface provides methods that are used to manage view state, which is the set of
information that describes a control's current state. View state is stored in a hidden

---

field on a Web Forms page, so it can be maintained across postbacks. State management is built into the Control class, and you can write values into the Control.ViewState collection to store any information you need without using IStateManager. However, you can also create a custom control that implements this interface to customize how state management works. The IStateManager consists of three methods: SaveViewState(), which stores changes to an object, LoadViewState(), which retrieves and applies previously stored values, and TrackViewState(), which sets the IsTrackingViewState property to True and instructs ASP.NET to track changes to the control's view state.

```
public interface IStateManager {
// Public Instance Properties
  public bool IsTrackingViewState{get; }
// Public Instance Methods
  public void LoadViewState(object state);
  public object SaveViewState( );
  public void TrackViewState( );
}
```

Implemented By Multiple types

ITagNameToTypeMapper

System.Web.UI (system.web.dll)   interface

This interface consists of a single method GetControlType(), which accepts a string containing a control tag and returns a System.Type object identifying the corresponding control class.

```
interface ITagNameToTypeMapper {
// Public Instance Methods
  public Type GetControlType(string tagName, System.Collections.IDictionary attribs);
}
```

ITemplate

System.Web.UI (system.web.dll)   interface

Templates allow controls to make portions of their user interface configurable. Templates are used in classes like System.Web.UI.WebControls.DataList and can be added in your own custom controls by declaring properties of type ITemplate (for example, an ItemStyle or HeaderStyle property). This allows the user to specify a template for a portion of your control.

Your custom control code uses a supplied template by invoking the InstantiateIn() method. This method accepts a control reference and populates its Control.Controls collection with one or more server controls that represent the user interface defined in the template. The control you supply to the InstantiateIn() method could be the current control, or one of the current control's children. Note that you do not need to write the implementation code for this method, as the .NET framework provides it intrinsically.

```
public interface ITemplate {
// Public Instance Methods
  public void InstantiateIn(Control container);
}
```

Implemented By   CompiledTemplateBuilder, TemplateBuilder

Returned By   Multiple types

Passed To   Multiple types

IUserControlDesignerAccessor

System.Web.UI (system.web.dll)   interface

This interface defines the properties the IDE should be able to access to retrieve information about a user control at design time. This includes two properties, InnerText (the complete content inside the user control tag) and TagName (the tag name used by the control). The UserControl class implements the IUserControlDesignerAccessor interface.

```
public interface IUserControlDesignerAccessor {
// Public Instance Properties
  public string InnerText{set; get; }
  public string TagName{set; get; }
}
```

Implemented By   UserControl

IValidator

System.Web.UI (system.web.dll)   interface

This interface defines members used for validation controls. The Validate() method is used to examine supplied information, compare it with the valid parameters, and update IsValid property appropriately. The ErrorMessage contains the message that should be generated for the user when the supplied information is not valid.

When creating a custom validation control, you do not need to implement this interface. Instead, you should inherit from one of the validation classes in the System.Web.UI. WebControls namespace. The base class, System.Web.UI.WebControls.BaseValidator, implements this interface.

```
public interface IValidator {
// Public Instance Properties
  public string ErrorMessage{set; get; }
  public bool IsValid{set; get; }
// Public Instance Methods
  public void Validate( );
}
```

Implemented By   System.Web.UI.MobileControls.BaseValidator, System.Web.UI.WebControls.BaseValidator

Returned By   ValidatorCollection.this

Passed To   ValidatorCollection.{Add( ), Contains( ), Remove( )}

LiteralControl

System.Web.UI (system.web.dll)

The ASP.NET parser automatically creates LiteralControl instances for any text or HTML it finds in a page that does not correspond to a server control, and then adds them to the containing control's Control.Controls collection. You should not confuse this class with the System.Web.UI.WebControls.Literal control class, which can be used to add simple text to a web page (much like an unformatted Label control).

```
public class LiteralControl : Control {
// Public Constructors
  public LiteralControl( );
  public LiteralControl( string text);
// Public Instance Properties
  public virtual string Text{set; get; }
// Protected Instance Methods
  protected override ControlCollection CreateControlCollection( );          // overrides Control
  protected override void Render( HtmlTextWriter output);                   // overrides Control
}
```

Hierarchy   System.Object → Control(System.ComponentModel.IComponent, System.IDisposable, IParserAccessor, IDataBindingsAccessor) → LiteralControl

Returned By   TemplateControl.CreateResourceBasedLiteralControl( )

LosFormatter

System.Web.UI (system.web.dll)

This class is used by ASP.NET to implement Limited Object Serialization (LOS) for view state. It converts the data stored in every control's StateBag into a lightly encrypted, condensed ASCII field that is added to the page as a hidden input control. While you can store complex information in the StateBag, the LosFormatter is optimized for strings, arrays, hashtables, and other primitive .NET types defined in the System namespace. This class provides functionality through the methods Serialize( ) and Deserialize( ).

```
public sealed class LosFormatter {
// Public Constructors
  public LosFormatter( );
  public LosFormatter(bool enableMac, string macKeyModifier);
// Public Instance Methods
  public object Deserialize( System.IO.Stream stream);
  public object Deserialize( string input);
  public object Deserialize( System.IO.TextReader input);
  public void Serialize(System.IO.Stream stream, object value);
  public void Serialize(System.IO.TextWriter output, object value);
}
```

ObjectConverter

obsolete

System.Web.UI (system.web.dll)

sealed class

This class is used automatically by the ASP.NET framework and never used directly in your code.

```
public sealed class ObjectConverter {
// Public Constructors
  public ObjectConverter( );
// Public Static Methods
  public static object ConvertValue(object value, Type toType, string formatString);
}
```

ObjectTagBuilder

System.Web.UI (system.web.dll)

sealed class

This class is used automatically by the ASP.NET framework and never used directly in your code.

```
public sealed class ObjectTagBuilder : ControlBuilder {
// Public Constructors
  public ObjectTagBuilder( );
// Public Instance Methods
  public override void AppendLiteralString( string s);                          // overrides ControlBuilder
  public override void AppendSubBuilder(ControlBuilder subBuilder);             // overrides ControlBuilder
  public override void Init(TemplateParser parser, ControlBuilder parentBuilder, Type type,
    string tagName, string id, System.Collections.IDictionary attribs);          // overrides ControlBuilder
}
```

Hierarchy   System.Object → ControlBuilder → ObjectTagBuilder

OutputCacheLocation

serializable

System.Web.UI (system.web.dll)

enum

You can enable output caching for an ASP.NET page by using the System.Web.Http-CachePolicy class or adding a page directive. This enumeration is used by ASP.NET when it calls the Page.InitOutputCache( ) method. It specifies whether the page is cached locally on the client (Client), on the web server (Server), or on another server between the client and the web server (Downstream).

```
public enum OutputCacheLocation {
  Any = 0,
  Client = 1,
  Downstream = 2,
  Server = 3,
  None = 4,
  ServerAndClient = 5
}
```

Hierarchy   System.Object → System.ValueType → System.Enum(System.IComparable, System.IFormattable, System.IConvertible) → OutputCacheLocation

Passed To   Page.InitOutputCache( )

System.Web.UI (system.web.dll)   class

All Web Forms you create for an ASP.NET application derive implicitly or explicitly from **Page**. This class, which is a special subclass of **Control**, adds additional page-specific functionality. For example, rather than simply providing the **Control.Context** property, the **Page** class provides the traditional built-in objects through references like **Response**, **Request**, and **Application**. The **Page** class also provides properties that allow you to use tracing (**Trace** and **TraceEnabled**) and access all the validation controls and information about whether their validation was successful (**Validators** and **IsValid**).

Another useful property is **IsPostBack**, which you can test in the **Load** event. Typically, you will skip control initialization if this property returns **True**, indicating that the page has already been displayed and the control values will be persisted in view state. You can also set **AspCompatMode** to **True** so the **Page** will be executed on a single-threaded apartment (STA) thread. This setting allows the page to call other STA components, such as those you may have developed with Visual Basic 6 (although it can hamper performance significantly).

Most **Page** methods are used by the ASP.NET framework and will never be used in your code. One exception is **MapPath()**, which returns the physical path on the server that corresponds to a specified virtual path (URL).

```
public class Page : TemplateControl, System.Web.IHttpHandler {
// Public Constructors
  public Page( );
// Protected Static Fields
  protected const string postEventArgumentID;                      // =___EVENTARGUMENT
  protected const string postEventSourceID;                        // =___EVENTTARGET
// Public Instance Properties
  public HttpApplicationState Application{get; }
  public Cache Cache{get; }
  public string ClientTarget{set; get; }
  public override bool EnableViewState{set; get; }                      // overrides Control
  public string ErrorPage{set; get; }
  public override string ID{set; get; }                                 // overrides Control
  public bool IsPostBack{get; }
  public bool IsReusable{get; }                            // implements System.Web.IHttpHandler
  public bool IsValid{get; }
  public HttpRequest Request{get; }
  public HttpResponse Response{get; }
  public HttpServerUtility Server{get; }
  public virtual HttpSessionState Session{get; }
  public bool SmartNavigation{set; get; }
  public TraceContext Trace{get; }
  public IPrincipal User{get; }
  public ValidatorCollection Validators{get; }
  public string ViewStateUserKey{set; get; }
  public override bool Visible{set; get; }                              // overrides Control
// Protected Instance Properties
  protected bool AspCompatMode{set; }
  protected bool Buffer{set; }
  protected int CodePage{set; }
```

```
protected string ContentType{set; }
protected override HttpContext Context{get; }                              // overrides Control
protected string Culture{set; }
protected bool EnableViewStateMac{set; get; }
protected ArrayList FileDependencies{set; }
protected int LCID{set; }
protected string ResponseEncoding{set; }
protected bool TraceEnabled{set; }
protected TraceMode TraceModeValue{set; }
protected int TransactionMode{set; }
protected string UICulture{set; }
// Public Instance Methods
public void DesignerInitialize( );
public string GetPostBackClientEvent(Control control, string argument);
public string GetPostBackClientHyperlink(Control control, string argument);
public string GetPostBackEventReference(Control control);
public string GetPostBackEventReference(Control control, string argument);
public virtual int GetTypeHashCode( );
public bool IsClientScriptBlockRegistered( string key);
public bool IsStartupScriptRegistered(string key);
public string MapPath(string virtualPath);
public void ProcessRequest(System.Web.HttpContext context);               // implements System.Web.IHttpHandler
public void RegisterArrayDeclaration(string arrayName, string arrayValue);
public virtual void RegisterClientScriptBlock(string key, string script);
public virtual void RegisterHiddenField(string hiddenFieldName, string hiddenFieldInitialValue);
public void RegisterOnSubmitStatement(string key, string script);
public void RegisterRequiresPostBack(Control control);
public virtual void RegisterRequiresRaiseEvent(IPostBackEventHandler control);
public virtual void RegisterStartupScript(string key, string script);
public void RegisterViewStateHandler( );
public virtual void Validate( );
public virtual void VerifyRenderingInServerForm(Control control);
// Protected Instance Methods
protected IAsyncResult AspCompatBeginProcessRequest(System.Web.HttpContext context,
    AsyncCallback cb, object extraData);
protected void AspCompatEndProcessRequest(IAsyncResult result);
protected virtual HtmlTextWriter CreateHtmlTextWriter(System.IO.TextWriter tw);
protected virtual NameValueCollection DeterminePostBackMode( );
protected virtual void InitOutputCache(int duration, string varyByHeader, string varyByCustom,
    OutputCacheLocation location, string varyByParam);
protected virtual object LoadPageStateFromPersistenceMedium( );
protected virtual void RaisePostBackEvent(IPostBackEventHandler sourceControl, string eventArgument);
protected virtual void SavePageStateToPersistenceMedium(object viewState);
}
```

Hierarchy	System.Object → Control(System.ComponentModel.IComponent, System.IDisposable, IParserAccessor, IDataBindingsAccessor) → TemplateControl(INamingContainer) → Page(System.Web.IHttpHandler)
Subclasses	System.Web.UI.MobileControls.MobilePage

Returned By	Control.Page
Passed To	Control.Page, UserControl.InitializeAsUserControl( )

PageParser

System.Web.UI (system.web.dll)   sealed class

This class provides a page parser that compiles an *.aspx* file into a custom Page object.

```
public sealed class PageParser : TemplateControlParser {
// Public Constructors
  public PageParser( );
// Public Static Methods
  public static IHttpHandler GetCompiledPageInstance(string virtualPath, string inputFile,
    System.Web.HttpContext context);
// Protected Instance Methods
  protected override Type CompileIntoType( );                              // overrides TemplateParser
}
```

Hierarchy	System.Object → BaseParser → TemplateParser → TemplateControlParser → PageParser

Pair

System.Web.UI (system.web.dll)   class

This class is used internally for the LosFormatter. It contains two types that can be serialized into view state.

```
public class Pair {
// Public Constructors
  public Pair( );
  public Pair( object x, object y);
// Public Instance Fields
  public object First;
  public object Second;
}
```

ParseChildrenAttribute

System.Web.UI (system.web.dll)   sealed class

You can use this attribute to mark the class declaration for any custom controls that you create. If you specify True for the ChildrenAsProperties property, the ASP.NET parser will treat any sub-elements inside your control tag as object properties. If you do not use this attribute or you specify False, ASP.NET will assume that nested elements should be added as child controls. In this case, you can still set object properties by using the "object walker" syntax, where properties are split by using a dash (as in <MyControls MyObject-MyProperty="Value" />).

```
public sealed class ParseChildrenAttribute : Attribute {
// Public Constructors
  public ParseChildrenAttribute( );
  public ParseChildrenAttribute(bool childrenAsProperties);
```

UI Namespace

```
    public ParseChildrenAttribute(bool childrenAsProperties, string defaultProperty);
// Public Static Fields
    public static readonly ParseChildrenAttribute Default;                    // = System.Web.UI.ParseChildrenAttribute
// Public Instance Properties
    public bool ChildrenAsProperties{set; get; }
    public string DefaultProperty{set; get; }
// Public Instance Methods
    public override bool Equals( object obj);                                           // overrides Attribute
    public override int GetHashCode( );                                                  // overrides Attribute
    public override bool IsDefaultAttribute( );                                          // overrides Attribute
}
```

Hierarchy   System.Object → System.Attribute → ParseChildrenAttribute

Valid On   Class

PartialCachingAttribute

System.Web.UI (system.web.dll)   **sealed class**

This class specifies the attributes that can be set on user controls for fragment caching. To enable fragment caching, use the <OutputCache> directive at the beginning of the appropriate *.ascx* file. ASP.NET will automatically generate this attribute when the user control is requested. Alternatively, you can leave out the directive and use this attribute in the code-behind class for the user control.

```
public sealed class PartialCachingAttribute : Attribute {
// Public Constructors
    public PartialCachingAttribute( int duration);
    public PartialCachingAttribute(int duration, string varyByParams, string varyByControls, string varyByCustom);
    public PartialCachingAttribute(int duration, string varyByParams, string varyByControls, string varyByCustom,
        bool shared);
// Public Instance Properties
    public int Duration{get; }
    public bool Shared{get; }
    public string VaryByControls{get; }
    public string VaryByCustom{get; }
    public string VaryByParams{get; }
}
```

Hierarchy   System.Object → System.Attribute → PartialCachingAttribute

Valid On   Class

PartialCachingControl   **disposable**

System.Web.UI (system.web.dll)   **class**

This class is utilized by the ASP.NET framework to use fragment caching with user controls. You can enable fragment caching by using the OutputCache directive at the beginning of the appropriate *.ascx* file.

```
public class PartialCachingControl : BasePartialCachingControl {
// Public Instance Properties
  public Control CachedControl{get; }
}
```

Hierarchy System.Object → Control(System.ComponentModel.IComponent, System.IDisposable,
IParserAccessor, IDataBindingsAccessor) → BasePartialCachingControl →
PartialCachingControl

PersistChildrenAttribute

System.Web.UI (system.web.dll)   sealed class

This attribute indicates how the child controls of an ASP.NET Server Control should
be persisted at design time. If set to True, the child controls are persisted as nested inner
server control tags. If False, the properties of the control may be persisted as inner tags.

```
public sealed class PersistChildrenAttribute : Attribute {
// Public Constructors
  public PersistChildrenAttribute( bool persist);
// Public Static Fields
  public static readonly PersistChildrenAttribute Default;          // =System.Web.UI.PersistChildrenAttribute
  public static readonly PersistChildrenAttribute No;               // =System.Web.UI.PersistChildrenAttribute
  public static readonly PersistChildrenAttribute Yes;              // =System.Web.UI.PersistChildrenAttribute
// Public Instance Properties
  public bool Persist{get; }
// Public Instance Methods
  public override bool Equals( object obj);                          // overrides Attribute
  public override int GetHashCode( );                                // overrides Attribute
  public override bool IsDefaultAttribute( );                        // overrides Attribute
}
```

Hierarchy   System.Object → System.Attribute → PersistChildrenAttribute

Valid On   Class

PersistenceMode   serializable

System.Web.UI (system.web.dll)   enum

This enumeration provides values for the PersistenceModeAttribute. PersistenceModeAttribute.
Attribute instructs ASP.NET to persist a property in a control's HTML tag as an
attribute. This is the default and does not require the use of the PersistenceModeAttribute.
You can also use PersistenceModeAttribute.InnerDefaultProperty or PersistenceModeAttribute.EncodedInner-
DefaultProperty to designate a property as the inner content of control tag. Only one
property can be used in this way, and the only difference between these two options is
whether the ASP.NET framework will automatically perform HTML encoding before
persisting the value. Finally, PersistenceModeAttribute.InnerProperty persists the property as a
nested tag inside the control tag.

```
public enum PersistenceMode {
  Attribute = 0,
  InnerProperty = 1,
```

```
    InnerDefaultProperty = 2,
    EncodedInnerDefaultProperty = 3
}
```

Hierarchy   System.Object → System.ValueType → System.Enum(System.IComparable, System.IFor-
                   mattable, System.IConvertible) → PersistenceMode

Returned By   PersistenceModeAttribute.Mode

Passed To   PersistenceModeAttribute.PersistenceModeAttribute( )

PersistenceModeAttribute

System.Web.UI (system.web.dll)   sealed class

This attribute specifies how a control property should be persisted in the opening tag
in the *.aspx* file, using one of the PersistenceMode values. You can use this attribute for the
properties in any custom controls that you make.

```
public sealed class PersistenceModeAttribute : Attribute {
// Public Constructors
  public PersistenceModeAttribute( PersistenceMode mode);
// Public Static Fields
  public static readonly PersistenceModeAttribute Attribute;          // =System.Web.UI.PersistenceModeAttribute
  public static readonly PersistenceModeAttribute Default;            // =System.Web.UI.PersistenceModeAttribute
  public static readonly PersistenceModeAttribute EncodedInnerDefaultProperty;
                                                                      // =System.Web.UI.PersistenceModeAttribute
  public static readonly PersistenceModeAttribute InnerDefaultProperty;  // =System.Web.UI.PersistenceModeAttribute
  public static readonly PersistenceModeAttribute InnerProperty;      // =System.Web.UI.PersistenceModeAttribute
// Public Instance Properties
  public PersistenceMode Mode{get; }
// Public Instance Methods
  public override bool Equals( object obj);                           // overrides Attribute
  public override int GetHashCode( );                                // overrides Attribute
  public override bool IsDefaultAttribute( );                        // overrides Attribute
}
```

Hierarchy   System.Object → System.Attribute → PersistenceModeAttribute

Valid On   All

PropertyConverter

System.Web.UI (system.web.dll)   sealed class

This class is used by the .NET framework, not directly by your own code.

```
public sealed class PropertyConverter {
// Public Static Methods
  public static object EnumFromString(Type enumType, string value);
  public static string EnumToString(Type enumType, object enumValue);
  public static object ObjectFromString(Type objType, System.Reflection.MemberInfo propertyInfo, string value);
}
```

RenderMethod

System.Web.UI (system.web.dll)   delegate

This delegate is used exclusively by the ASP.NET framework. It specifies the signature for a method used to render a control.

```
public delegate void RenderMethod(HtmlTextWriter output, Control container);
```

Passed To   Control.SetRenderMethodDelegate( )

RootBuilder

System.Web.UI (system.web.dll)   sealed class

This class is used by the .NET framework, not directly by your own code.

```
public sealed class RootBuilder : TemplateBuilder {
// Public Constructors
  public RootBuilder( TemplateParser parser);
// Public Instance Methods
  public override Type GetChildControlType(string tagName,
    System.Collections.IDictionary attribs);                                              // overrides ControlBuilder
}
```

Hierarchy   System.Object → ControlBuilder → TemplateBuilder(ITemplate) → RootBuilder

SimpleWebHandlerParser

System.Web.UI (system.web.dll)   abstract class

This class provides basic functionality used to parse web handler files. It is used by the .NET framework, not directly by your own code.

```
public abstract class SimpleWebHandlerParser {
// Protected Constructors
  protected SimpleWebHandlerParser(System.Web.HttpContext context, string virtualPath, string physicalPath);
// Protected Instance Properties
  protected abstract string DefaultDirectiveName{get; }
// Protected Instance Methods
  protected Type GetCompiledTypeFromCache( );
}
```

Subclasses   WebServiceParser

StateBag

System.Web.UI (system.web.dll)   sealed class

Every control stores view state information in a StateBag provided in the Control.ViewState property, if you enabled the Control.EnableViewState property. View state includes information representing all properties of a control or page and any custom items you added. Information is provided in a key/value collection and is accessed much like the System.Web.SessionState.HttpSessionState or System.Web.Caching.Cache class. You can add a value to the StateBag collection like this: ViewState["NewObject"] = ds;.

The StateBag can contain primitive types or full-fledged serializable objects. When retrieving an object, you will have to cast it to the correct type. Also note that you can enumerate through the StateBag collection by using the StateItem enumerator.

```
public sealed class StateBag : IStateManager, IDictionary, ICollection, IEnumerable {
// Public Constructors
  public StateBag( );
  public StateBag(bool ignoreCase);
// Public Instance Properties
  public int Count{get; }                                             // implements ICollection
  public ICollection Keys{get; }                          // implements System.Collections.IDictionary
  public object this[ string key ]{set; get; }
  public ICollection Values{get; }                        // implements System.Collections.IDictionary
// Public Instance Methods
  public StateItem Add(string key, object value);
  public void Clear( );                                   // implements System.Collections.IDictionary
  public IDictionaryEnumerator GetEnumerator( );          // implements System.Collections.IDictionary
  public bool IsItemDirty(string key);
  public void Remove(string key);
  public void SetItemDirty(string key, bool dirty);
}
```

Returned By Control.ViewState, System.Web.UI.MobileControls.MobileControl.CustomAttributes, System. Web.UI.WebControls.DataGridColumn.ViewState

Passed To AttributeCollection.AttributeCollection( ), System.Web.UI.WebControls.Style.Style( ), System. Web.UI.WebControls.TableItemStyle.TableItemStyle( ), System.Web.UI.WebControls.Table-Style.TableStyle( )

StateItem

System.Web.UI (system.web.dll)   sealed class

This class represents an item in the StateBag collection and is used to track changes to that item. The actual stored object is contained in the Value property. An additional piece of information is provided in the IsDirty property, which is True if the item has been changed since being saved into the StateBag collection. Changes to an item in the StateBag are saved when the ASP.NET framework calls the Control.SaveViewState( ) method.

When you retrieve an option from the StateBag collection using the default indexer StateBag.Item, you will receive the actual object. If, however, you want to enumerate through the StateBag collection using for each syntax, you should create a StateItem enumerator. You can also retrieve a StateItem object from the StateBag.Add( ) method.

```
public sealed class StateItem {
// Public Instance Properties
  public bool IsDirty{set; get; }
  public object Value{set; get; }
}
```

Returned By StateBag.Add( )

StaticPartialCachingControl

System.Web.UI (system.web.dll)   class

When you include a user control on your page, and specify that it should be cached (either by using the standard OutputCache directive in the *.ascx* file, or the PartialCachingAttribute in the the user control's code-behind file), an instance of the StaticPartialCachingControl class will be placed in the control hierarchy of the page as a parent to the cached user control.

```
public class StaticPartialCachingControl : BasePartialCachingControl {
// Public Constructors
  public StaticPartialCachingControl(string ctrlID, string guid, int duration, string varyByParams, string varyByControls,
    string varyByCustom, BuildMethod buildMethod);
// Public Static Methods
  public static void BuildCachedControl(Control parent, string ctrlID, string guid, int duration, string varyByParams,
    string varyByControls, string varyByCustom, BuildMethod buildMethod);
}
```

Hierarchy   System.Object → Control(System.ComponentModel.IComponent, System.IDisposable,
                     IParserAccessor, IDataBindingsAccessor) → BasePartialCachingControl →
                     StaticPartialCachingControl

TagPrefixAttribute

System.Web.UI (system.web.dll)   sealed class

Tag prefixes are used to identify control elements in an *.aspx* file. For example, all pre-built ASP.NET controls have a tag prefix of asp:, as in <asp:Label />. You can use the TagPrefixAttribute for your custom controls to define a different tag, which can help you distinguish your controls easily. The portion of the tag after the tag prefix is the control class name. Alternatively, you can use the <Register> directive in the *.aspx* file (not the code-behind file).

```
public sealed class TagPrefixAttribute : Attribute {
// Public Constructors
  public TagPrefixAttribute(string namespaceName, string tagPrefix);
// Public Instance Properties
  public string NamespaceName{get; }
  public string TagPrefix{get; }
}
```

Hierarchy   System.Object → System.Attribute → TagPrefixAttribute

Valid On   Assembly

TemplateBuilder

System.Web.UI (system.web.dll)   class

This class works with the ASP.NET framework to parse and build a templated control when a request is made for a Web Forms page. It is not used in your code.

```
public class TemplateBuilder : ControlBuilder, ITemplate {
// Public Constructors
  public TemplateBuilder( );
// Public Instance Properties
  public virtual string Text{set; get; }
// Public Instance Methods
  public override void Init(TemplateParser parser, ControlBuilder parentBuilder, Type type,
      string tagName, string ID, System.Collections.IDictionary attribs);     // overrides ControlBuilder
  public virtual void InstantiateIn( Control container);                      // implements ITemplate
  public override bool NeedsTagInnerText( );                                  // overrides ControlBuilder
  public override void SetTagInnerText( string text);                         // overrides ControlBuilder
}
```

Hierarchy   System.Object → ControlBuilder → TemplateBuilder(ITemplate)

Subclasses   RootBuilder, System.Web.UI.MobileControls.DeviceSpecificChoiceTemplateBuilder

TemplateContainerAttribute

System.Web.UI (system.web.dll)   sealed class

This attribute is used when creating templated controls, which allow the control user
to specify a portion of the control's user interface. This functionality is implemented in
controls like System.Web.UI.WebControls.Repeater and System.Web.UI.WebControls.DataList, which
format bound data according to specified templates. In these controls, and in any
custom templated controls you make, the TemplateContainerAttribute is applied to every ITemplate property. The attribute specifies the type of the container control the template will
be instantiated in, so that casting is not required to evaluate data binding expressions.
For example, the System.Web.UI.WebControls.DataList.ItemTemplate property is a ITemplate property that allows you to set or retrieve the template for items in the list. This particular
property has the attribute [TemplateContainer(typeof(System.Web.UI.WebControls.DataListItem))].

```
public sealed class TemplateContainerAttribute : Attribute {
// Public Constructors
  public TemplateContainerAttribute( Type containerType);
// Public Instance Properties
  public Type ContainerType{get; }
}
```

Hierarchy   System.Object → System.Attribute → TemplateContainerAttribute

Valid On   Property

TemplateControl   disposable

System.Web.UI (system.web.dll)   abstract class

This abstract class provides basic functionality for template controls, which include
Page and UserControl. This functionality includes transaction support and various properties, methods, and events that are used and managed transparently by the ASP.NET
framework.

```
public abstract class TemplateControl : Control, INamingContainer {
// Protected Constructors
    protected TemplateControl( );
// Protected Instance Properties
    protected virtual int AutoHandlers{set; get; }
    protected virtual bool SupportAutoEvents{get; }
// Public Static Methods
    public static object ReadStringResource( Type t);
// Public Instance Methods
    public Control LoadControl( string virtualPath);
    public ITemplate LoadTemplate( string virtualPath);
    public Control ParseControl( string content);
// Protected Instance Methods
    protected virtual void Construct( );
    protected LiteralControl CreateResourceBasedLiteralControl(int offset, int size, bool fAsciiOnly);
    protected virtual void FrameworkInitialize( );
    protected virtual void OnAbortTransaction( EventArgs e);
    protected virtual void OnCommitTransaction( EventArgs e);
    protected virtual void OnError( EventArgs e);
    protected void SetStringResourcePointer(object stringResourcePointer, int maxResourceOffset);
    protected void WriteUTF8ResourceString(HtmlTextWriter output, int offset, int size, bool fAsciiOnly);
// Events
    public event EventHandler AbortTransaction;
    public event EventHandler CommitTransaction;
    public event EventHandler Error;
}
```

Hierarchy System.Object → Control(System.ComponentModel.IComponent, System.IDisposable, IParserAccessor, IDataBindingsAccessor) → TemplateControl(INamingContainer)

Subclasses Page, UserControl

TemplateControlParser

System.Web.UI (system.web.dll) abstract class

This abstract class includes some of the functionality for parsing ASP.NET files and interpreting tags as controls. PageParser derives from this class. It is not used in your code.

```
public abstract class TemplateControlParser : TemplateParser {
// Protected Constructors
    protected TemplateControlParser( );
}
```

Hierarchy System.Object → BaseParser → TemplateParser → TemplateControlParser

Subclasses PageParser

TemplateParser

System.Web.UI (system.web.dll)   abstract class

This abstract class includes some of the functionality for parsing ASP.NET files.
TemplateControlParser derives directly from this class. It is not used in your code.

```
public abstract class TemplateParser : BaseParser {
// Protected Instance Methods
  protected abstract Type CompileIntoType( );
}
```

Hierarchy   System.Object → BaseParser → TemplateParser

Subclasses   TemplateControlParser

Returned By   ControlBuilder.Parser

Passed To   ControlBuilder.{CreateBuilderFromType( ), Init( )}, RootBuilder.RootBuilder( )

ToolboxDataAttribute

System.Web.UI (system.web.dll)   sealed class

This attribute is used when you are creating your own custom controls (typically by
inheriting from System.Web.UI.WebControls.WebControl or Control). By default, designers like
Visual Studio .NET will create an empty tag when you drag a control from the toolbox
onto the design surface. This empty tag represents a control in its default state. Rather
than using the empty tag, you can specify initial values and default HTML will be
placed inside the control tag by using this attribute. For example, the attribute <Toolbox-
Data("<{0}:MyLabel Text='MyLabel' BackColor='Yellow' runat='server'></{0}:MyLabel>")> configures the
initial tag for a custom label control with a yellow background. Note that all occur-
rences of {0} in the supplied Data string will be replaced, by the designer, with the tag
prefix associated with the MyLabel class.

```
public sealed class ToolboxDataAttribute : Attribute {
// Public Constructors
  public ToolboxDataAttribute(string data);
// Public Static Fields
  public static readonly ToolboxDataAttribute Default;              // =System.Web.UI.ToolboxDataAttribute
// Public Instance Properties
  public string Data{get; }
// Public Instance Methods
  public override bool Equals(object obj);                          // overrides Attribute
  public override int GetHashCode( );                              // overrides Attribute
  public override bool IsDefaultAttribute( );                      // overrides Attribute
}
```

Hierarchy   System.Object → System.Attribute → ToolboxDataAttribute

Valid On   Class

Triplet

System.Web.UI (system.web.dll)   class

This class is used internally for the LosFormatter. It contains three types that can be combined and serialized into view state.

```
public class Triplet {
// Public Constructors
  public Triplet( );
  public Triplet(object x, object y);
  public Triplet(object x, object y, object z);
// Public Instance Fields
  public object First;
  public object Second;
  public object Third;
}
```

UserControl   disposable

System.Web.UI (system.web.dll)   class

This class represents a user control, or *.ascx* file, inside a Web Form. A user control allows you to share commonly used portions of user interface. User controls are similar to *.aspx* pages and can contain HTML, server controls, and event handling logic. They are instantiated and cached in much the same way as Page objects and contain many of the same properties. The difference is that user controls must be situated inside a Web Forms page. User controls should not be confused with custom web controls, which you can create by inheriting from System.Web.UI.WebControls.WebControl.

When using fragment caching with user controls, remember that you will not be able to modify any of the properties of the UserControl; the cached control will be loaded as straight HTML rather than a UserControl object.

```
public class UserControl : TemplateControl, IAttributeAccessor, IUserControlDesignerAccessor {
// Public Constructors
  public UserControl( );
// Public Instance Properties
  public HttpApplicationState Application{get; }
  public AttributeCollection Attributes{get; }
  public Cache Cache{get; }
  public bool IsPostBack{get; }
  public HttpRequest Request{get; }
  public HttpResponse Response{get; }
  public HttpServerUtility Server{get; }
  public HttpSessionState Session{get; }
  public TraceContext Trace{get; }
// Public Instance Methods
  public void DesignerInitialize( );
  public void InitializeAsUserControl( Page page);
  public string MapPath(string virtualPath);
// Protected Instance Methods
  protected override void LoadViewState(object savedState);                                   // overrides Control
```

```
    protected override void OnInit(EventArgs e);                                    // overrides Control
    protected override object SaveViewState( );                                     // overrides Control
}
```

Hierarchy　　　System.Object → Control(System.ComponentModel.IComponent, System.IDisposable,
　　　　　　　　　　IParserAccessor, IDataBindingsAccessor) → TemplateControl(INamingContainer) → User-
　　　　　　　　　　Control(IAttributeAccessor, IUserControlDesignerAccessor)

Subclasses　　　System.Web.UI.MobileControls.MobileUserControl

UserControlControlBuilder

System.Web.UI (system.web.dll)   class

This class provides a control designer for all user controls, which is used implicitly. It
provides the following basic functionality: it adds a child control to the UserControl.Controls
collection for every nested control that it encounters within the user control tag, and it
creates literal controls to represent any text between nested control tags. You can
create a custom control builder for your user controls by deriving from this class.

```
public class UserControlControlBuilder : ControlBuilder {
// Public Constructors
    public UserControlControlBuilder( );
// Public Instance Methods
    public override bool NeedsTagInnerText( );                                       // overrides ControlBuilder
    public override void SetTagInnerText(string text);                               // overrides ControlBuilder
}
```

Hierarchy　　　System.Object → ControlBuilder → UserControlControlBuilder

ValidationPropertyAttribute

System.Web.UI (system.web.dll)   sealed class

This attribute specifies which property of a server control should be used for validation. Typically, this is a property like Text, Value, or SelectedItem. The ValidationPropertyAttribute
is used only when you create custom controls; existing ASP.NET controls use it
intrinsically.

This attribute is applied to the class declaration, not a specific property. You can
specify the property to validate through the attribute's **Name** property, as in:
[ValidationProperty("Text")].

```
public sealed class ValidationPropertyAttribute : Attribute {
// Public Constructors
    public ValidationPropertyAttribute(string name);
// Public Instance Properties
    public string Name{get; }
}
```

Hierarchy　　　System.Object → System.Attribute → ValidationPropertyAttribute

Valid On　　　Class

ValidatorCollection

System.Web.UI (system.web.dll)   sealed class

This class contains a collection of validation controls (controls that implement IVali-dator, usually by deriving from System.Web.UI.WebControls.BaseValidator). It is used for the Page.Validators property, which provides a collection of all validation controls on a Web Forms page. For more information about validation controls, refer to the System.Web.UI.WebControls namespace.

```
public sealed class ValidatorCollection : ICollection, IEnumerable {
// Public Constructors
  public ValidatorCollection( );
// Public Instance Properties
  public int Count{get; }                                    // implements ICollection
  public bool IsReadOnly{get; }
  public bool IsSynchronized{get; }                          // implements ICollection
  public object SyncRoot{get; }                              // implements ICollection
  public IValidator this[ int index ]{get; }
// Public Instance Methods
  public void Add(IValidator validator);
  public bool Contains(IValidator validator);
  public void CopyTo(Array array, int index);                // implements ICollection
  public IEnumerator GetEnumerator( );                       // implements IEnumerable
  public void Remove(IValidator validator);
}
```

Returned By   Page.Validators

WebServiceParser

System.Web.UI (system.web.dll)   class

This class is used by the ASP.NET framework when handling web service requests. It is not used directly in your code.

```
public class WebServiceParser : SimpleWebHandlerParser {
// Protected Instance Properties
  protected override string DefaultDirectiveName{get; }      // overrides SimpleWebHandlerParser
// Public Static Methods
  public static Type GetCompiledType(string inputFile, System.Web.HttpContext context);
}
```

Hierarchy   System.Object → SimpleWebHandlerParser → WebServiceParser

UI Namespace

37

The System.Web.UI.Design Namespace

The System.Web.UI.Design namespace contains types used for providing design-time support for the Web Forms user interface. These types fall into four basic categories: type converters, UI type editors, designers, and other helper classes (such as classes that provide ASP.NET data binding support). Type converters allow control properties to be converted to and from base data types, which allows them to be displayed and edited in the Properties Window. Type converters also extend runtime support, but they are only used implicitly and never instantiated directly. Type converter classes derive from System.ComponentModel.TypeConverter and end with the word "Converter" by convention. Unlike type converters, UI type editors are used exclusively in the design environment. They provide the custom user interface that is used to select special property values from the Properties window (like a control's color). UI type editors derive from System.Drawing.Design.UITypeEditor and end with the word "Editor."

Designers help provide the design-time representation of a control. They derive from System.ComponentModel.Design.ComponentDesigner and end with the word "Designer." The System.Web.UI.Design namespace contains the base designers used for ASP.NET controls. ASP.NET controls use different designers than Windows Form controls because they are rendered by using HTML rather than Windows-specific GDI+ functions. For custom designers that extend specific controls, refer to the System.Web.UI.Design.WebControls namespace.

Generally, the types in the System.Web.UI.Design namespace are never used directly in the runtime logic of an application. However, they are useful for ASP.NET control designers. For example, if you are creating a custom Web Forms control from scratch, you may want to derive from ControlDesigner to create a custom designer. However, you may find it more convenient to extend an existing web control—in which case, you would continue using the default designers, type converters, and UI type editors, or derive custom versions from the corresponding control-specific class in the System.Web.UI.Design.WebControls namespace, if it exists.

Figure 37-1 shows the fundamental types in this namespace, and Figure 37-2 shows the remaining types.

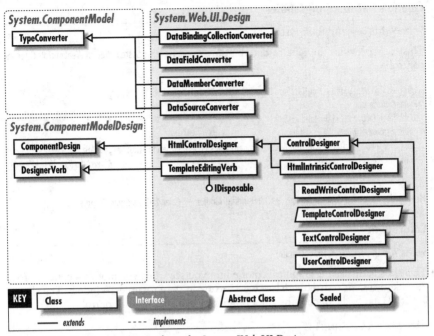

Figure 37-1. Fundamental types from the System.Web.UI.Design namespace

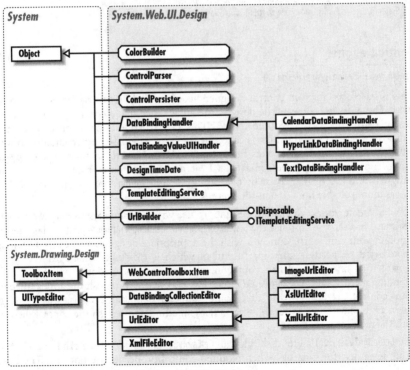

Figure 37-2. More types from the System.Web.UI.Design namespace

CalendarDataBindingHandler

System.Web.UI.Design (system.design.dll)   class

This class provides the type of data binding used by the System.Web.UI.WebControls.Calendar control.

```
public class CalendarDataBindingHandler : DataBindingHandler {
// Public Constructors
  public CalendarDataBindingHandler( );
// Public Instance Methods
  public override void DataBindControl(System.ComponentModel.Design.IDesignerHost designerHost,
      System.Web.UI.Control control);                                    // overrides DataBindingHandler
}
```

Hierarchy   System.Object → DataBindingHandler → CalendarDataBindingHandler

ColorBuilder

System.Web.UI.Design (system.design.dll)   sealed class

This class launches the graphical color editor you see when you modify a control property like System.Web.UI.WebControls.WebControl.ForeColor in the Properties Window. The shared BuildColor( ) method launches the color builder for the appropriate control.

```
public sealed class ColorBuilder {
// Public Static Methods
  public static string BuildColor(System.ComponentModel.IComponent component,
      System.Windows.Forms.Control owner, string initialColor);
}
```

ControlDesigner   disposable

System.Web.UI.Design (system.design.dll)   class

This is base class for web control designers like System.Web.UI.Design.WebControls.AdRotatorDesigner. These designers create the design-time appearance that a control provides to the design editor (like Visual Studio .NET). This HTML code is provided through the GetDesignTimeHtml( ) method, which is called by the host. The base implementation of the GetDesignTimeHtml( ) method invokes the System.Web.UI.Control.Render( ) method of the appropriate control to create the same HTML at design time as at runtime. A custom designer modifies this behavior by overriding the GetDesignTimeHtml( ) to provide HTML that is more suitable for a design-time representation.

You can create your own custom designer to use with a custom System.Web.UI.WebControls. WebControl. In this case, you use the System.ComponentModel.DesignerAttribute on the class declaration of your control to connect it with the appropriate designer. You can set various ControlDesigner properties—the most useful of which is AllowResize, which restricts your control to a fixed size. When your control is resized, the designer will call corresponding methods like OnControlResize( ) to give you a chance to refresh the appearance of your control accordingly. At this point you can call UpdateDesignTimeHtml( ), which instructs the host to call your GetDesignTimeHtml( ) method and refresh the control display with the new content.

The GetDesignTimeHtml( ) method should call GetEmptyDesignTimeHtml( ) if the rendered HTML string is empty (for example, when required control properties are not set). The base implementation of GetEmptyDesignTimeHtml( ) returns the fully qualified name of the control. Alternatively, you may want to override this property to supply a place holder using the CreatePlaceHolderDesignTimeHtml( ). You may also want to override GetErrorDesignTimeHtml( ) method with specific information based on the exception object that is provided.

```
public class ControlDesigner : HtmlControlDesigner {
// Public Constructors
  public ControlDesigner( );
// Public Instance Properties
  public virtual bool AllowResize{get; }
  public virtual bool DesignTimeHtmlRequiresLoadComplete{get; }
  public virtual string ID{set; get; }
  public bool IsDirty{set; get; }
  public bool ReadOnly{set; get; }
// Protected Instance Properties
  protected object DesignTimeElementView{get; }
// Public Instance Methods
  public virtual string GetDesignTimeHtml( );
  public virtual string GetPersistInnerHtml( );
  public override void Initialize(System.ComponentModel.IComponent component);
                              // overrides System.ComponentModel.Design.ComponentDesigner
  public bool IsPropertyBound( string propName);
  public virtual void OnComponentChanged(object sender,
    System.ComponentModel.Design.ComponentChangedEventArgs ce);
  public void RaiseResizeEvent( );
  public virtual void UpdateDesignTimeHtml( );
// Protected Instance Methods
  protected string CreatePlaceHolderDesignTimeHtml( );
  protected string CreatePlaceHolderDesignTimeHtml(string instruction);
  protected virtual string GetEmptyDesignTimeHtml( );
  protected virtual string GetErrorDesignTimeHtml(Exception e);
  protected override void OnBehaviorAttached( );                // overrides HtmlControlDesigner
  protected override void OnBindingsCollectionChanged(string propName);  // overrides HtmlControlDesigner
  protected virtual void OnControlResize( );
  protected override void PreFilterProperties(System.Collections.IDictionary properties);  // overrides HtmlControlDesigner
}
```

Hierarchy   System.Object → System.ComponentModel.Design.ComponentDesigner(System.ComponentModel.Design.IDesigner, System.IDisposable, System.ComponentModel.Design.IDesignerFilter) → HtmlControlDesigner → ControlDesigner

Subclasses   Multiple types

ControlParser

System.Web.UI.Design (system.design.dll)   sealed class

This class is used predominantly by the ASP.NET framework. It allows you to generate a System.Web.UI.Control object from a string that represents the persisted control. You can perform this operating using the ParseControl( ) method, and you can cast the Control to the appropriate type to interact with it.

```
public sealed class ControlParser {
// Public Static Methods
  public static Control ParseControl(System.ComponentModel.Design.IDesignerHost designerHost, string controlText);
  public static Control ParseControl(System.ComponentModel.Design.IDesignerHost designerHost, string controlText,
     string directives);
  public static ITemplate ParseTemplate(System.ComponentModel.Design.IDesignerHost designerHost,
     string templateText);
  public static ITemplate ParseTemplate(System.ComponentModel.Design.IDesignerHost designerHost,
     string templateText, string directives);
}
```

ControlPersister

System.Web.UI.Design (system.design.dll)   sealed class

This class provides shared (static) helper methods that retrieve the information used to
persist a control and its state. For example, the PersistControl() method returns a string
that looks very similar to the control tag used in the *.aspx* file, with the named class
used instead of the "asp:" prefix. Typically, this class is used only by the IDE.

```
public sealed class ControlPersister {
// Public Static Methods
  public static string PersistControl(System.Web.UI.Control control);
  public static string PersistControl(System.Web.UI.Control control, System.ComponentModel.Design.IDesignerHost host);
  public static void PersistControl(System.IO.TextWriter sw, System.Web.UI.Control control);
  public static void PersistControl(System.IO.TextWriter sw, System.Web.UI.Control control,
     System.ComponentModel.Design.IDesignerHost host);
  public static string PersistInnerProperties(object component, System.ComponentModel.Design.IDesignerHost host);
  public static void PersistInnerProperties(System.IO.TextWriter sw, object component,
     System.ComponentModel.Design.IDesignerHost host);
}
```

DataBindingCollectionConverter

System.Web.UI.Design (system.design.dll)   class

This custom System.ComponentModel.TypeConverter class provides a single method, ConvertTo(),
which is used to convert System.Web.UI.DataBindingCollection objects.

```
public class DataBindingCollectionConverter : System.ComponentModel.TypeConverter {
// Public Constructors
  public DataBindingCollectionConverter();
// Public Instance Methods
  public override object ConvertTo(System.ComponentModel.ITypeDescriptorContext context,
     System.Globalization.CultureInfo culture,
     object value, Type destinationType);                         // overrides System.ComponentModel.TypeConverter
}
```

Hierarchy   System.Object → System.ComponentModel.TypeConverter →
                     DataBindingCollectionConverter

DataBindingCollectionEditor

System.Web.UI.Design (system.design.dll)   class

This class is a custom System.Drawing.Design.UITypeEditor used for editing data-binding collections.

```
public class DataBindingCollectionEditor : System.Drawing.Design.UITypeEditor {
// Public Constructors
  public DataBindingCollectionEditor( );
// Public Instance Methods
  public override object EditValue(System.ComponentModel.ITypeDescriptorContext context,
    IServiceProvider provider, object value);                // overrides System.Drawing.Design.UITypeEditor
  public override UITypeEditorEditStyle GetEditStyle(System.ComponentModel.ITypeDescriptorContext context);
                                                            // overrides System.Drawing.Design.UITypeEditor
}
```

Hierarchy   System.Object → System.Drawing.Design.UITypeEditor → DataBindingCollectionEditor

DataBindingHandler

System.Web.UI.Design (system.design.dll)   abstract class

This a base class for all design-time data-binding handlers. In provides a single method, DataBindControl( ), which binds the specified control.

```
public abstract class DataBindingHandler {
// Protected Constructors
  protected DataBindingHandler( );
// Public Instance Methods
  public abstract void DataBindControl(System.ComponentModel.Design.IDesignerHost designerHost,
    System.Web.UI.Control control);
}
```

Subclasses   CalendarDataBindingHandler, HyperLinkDataBindingHandler, TextDataBindingHandler,
System.Web.UI.Design.WebControls.ListControlDataBindingHandler

DataBindingValueUIHandler

System.Web.UI.Design (system.design.dll)   class

This class helps create a user interface for editing control data binding. The OnGetUIValueItem( ) method adds the actual binding.

```
public class DataBindingValueUIHandler {
// Public Constructors
  public DataBindingValueUIHandler( );
// Public Instance Methods
  public void OnGetUIValueItem(System.ComponentModel.ITypeDescriptorContext context,
    System.ComponentModel.PropertyDescriptor propDesc, System.Collections.ArrayList valueUIItemList);
}
```

DataFieldConverter

System.Web.UI.Design (system.design.dll)   **class**

This class provides a System.ComponentModel.TypeConverter that can be used to convert a string to and from a data field. You will not need to access this class directly, unless you want to use it for a custom ASP.NET control—in which case, you can bind it to the appropriate property by using the System.ComponentModel.TypeConverterAttribute.

```
public class DataFieldConverter : System.ComponentModel.TypeConverter {
// Public Constructors
  public DataFieldConverter( );
// Public Instance Methods
  public override bool CanConvertFrom(System.ComponentModel.ITypeDescriptorContext context,
    Type sourceType);                                // overrides System.ComponentModel.TypeConverter
  public override object ConvertFrom(System.ComponentModel.ITypeDescriptorContext context,
    System.Globalization.CultureInfo culture, object value);      // overrides System.ComponentModel.TypeConverter
  public override StandardValuesCollection GetStandardValues(System.ComponentModel.ITypeDescriptorContext context);
                                                   // overrides System.ComponentModel.TypeConverter
  public override bool GetStandardValuesExclusive(System.ComponentModel.ITypeDescriptorContext context);
                                                   // overrides System.ComponentModel.TypeConverter
  public override bool GetStandardValuesSupported(System.ComponentModel.ITypeDescriptorContext context);
                                                   // overrides System.ComponentModel.TypeConverter
}
```

Hierarchy   System.Object → System.ComponentModel.TypeConverter → DataFieldConverter

DataMemberConverter

System.Web.UI.Design (system.design.dll)   **class**

This class provides a System.ComponentModel.TypeConverter that can be used to convert a string to a database table name, and vice versa. You will not need to access this class directly, unless you want to use it for a custom ASP.NET control—in which case you can bind it to the DataMember property by using the System.ComponentModel. TypeConverterAttribute.

```
public class DataMemberConverter : System.ComponentModel.TypeConverter {
// Public Constructors
  public DataMemberConverter( );
// Public Instance Methods
  public override bool CanConvertFrom(System.ComponentModel.ITypeDescriptorContext context, Type sourceType);
                                                   // overrides System.ComponentModel.TypeConverter
  public override object ConvertFrom(System.ComponentModel.ITypeDescriptorContext context,
    System.Globalization.CultureInfo culture, object value);      // overrides System.ComponentModel.TypeConverter
  public override StandardValuesCollection GetStandardValues(System.ComponentModel.ITypeDescriptorContext context);
                                                   // overrides System.ComponentModel.TypeConverter
  public override bool GetStandardValuesExclusive(System.ComponentModel.ITypeDescriptorContext context);
                                                   // overrides System.ComponentModel.TypeConverter
  public override bool GetStandardValuesSupported(System.ComponentModel.ITypeDescriptorContext context);
                                                   // overrides System.ComponentModel.TypeConverter
}
```

Hierarchy   System.Object → System.ComponentModel.TypeConverter → DataMemberConverter

DataSourceConverter

System.Web.UI.Design (system.design.dll)   class

This class provides a System.ComponentModel.TypeConverter that can be used to convert a string to a data source object and vice versa. You will not need to access this class directly, unless you want to use it for a custom ASP.NET control—in which case you can bind it to the DataSource property by using the System.ComponentModel.TypeConverterAttribute.

```
public class DataSourceConverter : System.ComponentModel.TypeConverter {
// Public Constructors
  public DataSourceConverter( );
// Public Instance Methods
  public override bool CanConvertFrom(System.ComponentModel.ITypeDescriptorContext context, Type sourceType);
                                                          // overrides System.ComponentModel.TypeConverter
  public override object ConvertFrom(System.ComponentModel.ITypeDescriptorContext context,
    System.Globalization.CultureInfo culture, object value);     // overrides System.ComponentModel.TypeConverter
  public override StandardValuesCollection GetStandardValues(System.ComponentModel.ITypeDescriptorContext context);
                                                          // overrides System.ComponentModel.TypeConverter
  public override bool GetStandardValuesExclusive(System.ComponentModel.ITypeDescriptorContext context);
                                                          // overrides System.ComponentModel.TypeConverter
  public override bool GetStandardValuesSupported(System.ComponentModel.ITypeDescriptorContext context);
                                                          // overrides System.ComponentModel.TypeConverter
}
```

Hierarchy   System.Object → System.ComponentModel.TypeConverter → DataSourceConverter

DesignTimeData

System.Web.UI.Design (system.design.dll)   sealed class

This class provides shared helper methods that the design-time host (IDE) can use to generate "dummy" information for a sample rendering of a complex control. Typically, this class is used with table controls, as maintaining a database connection in design mode would be too resource-intensive, and the data source provider may not even be available. Using the CreateDummyDataTable( ) method, a default table is created that uses no information from the actual data source. This table could be used before a control's DataSource property is set.

Visual Studio .NET can also use a minimum amount of information to help present a design-time rendering of data tables. The GetDataFields( ) and GetDataMembers( ) methods retrieve a basic amount of information about the structure of the data source, which is then used when a dummy table is created with CreateSampleDataTable( ). The GetDesignTimeDataSource( ) method adds sample rows into the specified data table control.

```
public sealed class DesignTimeData {
// Public Static Fields
  public static readonly EventHandler DataBindingHandler;                          // =System.EventHandler
// Public Static Methods
  public static DataTable CreateDummyDataTable( );
  public static DataTable CreateSampleDataTable(System.Collections.IEnumerable referenceData);
  public static PropertyDescriptorCollection GetDataFields(System.Collections.IEnumerable dataSource);
  public static IEnumerable GetDataMember(System.ComponentModel.IListSource dataSource, string dataMember);
  public static string[ ] GetDataMembers( object dataSource);
```

```
    public static IEnumerable GetDesignTimeDataSource(System.Data.DataTable dataTable, int minimumRows);
    public static IEnumerable GetSelectedDataSource(System.ComponentModel.IComponent component,
        string dataSource, string dataMember);
    public static object GetSelectedDataSource(System.ComponentModel.IComponent component, string dataSource);
}
```

HtmlControlDesigner   disposable

System.Web.UI.Design (system.design.dll)   class

This class provides basic functionality for all ASP.NET control designers. If you want
to create your own control designer, inherit instead from ControlDesigner, which derives
from HtmlControlDesigner.

```
public class HtmlControlDesigner : System.ComponentModel.Design.ComponentDesigner {
// Public Constructors
    public HtmlControlDesigner( );
// Public Instance Properties
    public IHtmlControlDesignerBehavior Behavior{set; get; }
    public DataBindingCollection DataBindings{get; }
    public virtual bool ShouldCodeSerialize{set; get; }
// Protected Instance Properties
    protected object DesignTimeElement{get; }
// Public Instance Methods
    public virtual void OnSetParent( );
// Protected Instance Methods
    protected override void Dispose(bool disposing);          // overrides System.ComponentModel.Design.ComponentDesigner
    protected virtual void OnBehaviorAttached( );
    protected virtual void OnBehaviorDetaching( );
    protected virtual void OnBindingsCollectionChanged(string propName);
    protected override void PreFilterEvents(System.Collections.IDictionary events);
                                                       // overrides System.ComponentModel.Design.ComponentDesigner
    protected override void PreFilterProperties(System.Collections.IDictionary properties);
                                                       // overrides System.ComponentModel.Design.ComponentDesigner
}
```

Hierarchy	System.Object → System.ComponentModel.Design.ComponentDesigner(System.Compo-nentModel.Design.IDesigner, System.IDisposable, System.ComponentModel.Design.IDesignerFilter) → HtmlControlDesigner
Subclasses	ControlDesigner, HtmlIntrinsicControlDesigner
Returned By	IHtmlControlDesignerBehavior.Designer
Passed To	IHtmlControlDesignerBehavior.Designer

HtmlIntrinsicControlDesigner   disposable

System.Web.UI.Design (system.design.dll)   class

This base class provides a basic designer for HTML controls (the controls contained in
the System.Web.UI.HtmlControls namespace).

```
public class HtmlIntrinsicControlDesigner : HtmlControlDesigner {
// Public Constructors
  public HtmlIntrinsicControlDesigner( );
}
```

Hierarchy   System.Object → System.ComponentModel.Design.ComponentDesigner(System.Compo-
                  nentModel.Design.IDesigner, System.IDisposable, System.ComponentModel.Design.
                  IDesignerFilter) → HtmlControlDesigner → HtmlIntrinsicControlDesigner

HyperLinkDataBindingHandler

System.Web.UI.Design (system.design.dll)   class

This class provides a data-binding handler for the hyperlink property used in some
ASP.NET controls.

```
public class HyperLinkDataBindingHandler : DataBindingHandler {
// Public Constructors
  public HyperLinkDataBindingHandler( );
// Public Instance Methods
  public override void DataBindControl( System.ComponentModel.Design.IDesignerHost designerHost,
    System.Web.UI.Control control);                                    // overrides DataBindingHandler
}
```

Hierarchy   System.Object → DataBindingHandler → HyperLinkDataBindingHandler

IControlDesignerBehavior

System.Web.UI.Design (system.design.dll)   interface

This class Defines an interface that enables the extension of specific behaviors of a
control designer.

```
public interface IControlDesignerBehavior {
// Public Instance Properties
  public object DesignTimeElementView{get; }
  public string DesignTimeHtml{set; get; }
// Public Instance Methods
  public void OnTemplateModeChanged( );
}
```

IDataSourceProvider

System.Web.UI.Design (system.design.dll)   interface

This interface specifies the behavior required for designers that interact with a data
source, such as System.Web.UI.Design.WebControls.ListControlDesigner and System.Web.UI.Design.WebCon-
trols.DataGridDesigner. The interface provides two methods designed to convert a data
source to a more useful object. GetSelectedDataSource( ) retrieves the selected data source
object as a loosely typed System.Object. GetResolvedSelectedDataSource( ) retrieves the resolved
data source as a System.Collections.IEnumerable object, like a System.Array or a System.Data.DataView
instance.

```
public interface IDataSourceProvider {
// Public Instance Methods
```

```
    public IEnumerable GetResolvedSelectedDataSource( );
    public object GetSelectedDataSource( );
}
```

Implemented By   System.Web.UI.Design.WebControls.{BaseDataListDesigner, ListControlDesigner,
                     RepeaterDesigner}

IHtmlControlDesignerBehavior

System.Web.UI.Design (system.design.dll)   interface

This class defines an interface that enables the extension of specific behaviors of an
HTML control designer.

```
public interface IHtmlControlDesignerBehavior {
// Public Instance Properties
    public HtmlControlDesigner Designer{set; get; }
    public object DesignTimeElement{get; }
// Public Instance Methods
    public object GetAttribute(string attribute, bool ignoreCase);
    public object GetStyleAttribute(string attribute, bool designTimeOnly, bool ignoreCase);
    public void RemoveAttribute(string attribute, bool ignoreCase);
    public void RemoveStyleAttribute(string attribute, bool designTimeOnly, bool ignoreCase);
    public void SetAttribute(string attribute, object value, bool ignoreCase);
    public void SetStyleAttribute(string attribute, bool designTimeOnly, object value, bool ignoreCase);
}
```

Returned By   HtmlControlDesigner.Behavior

Passed To   HtmlControlDesigner.Behavior

ImageUrlEditor

System.Web.UI.Design (system.design.dll)   class

This class provides a System.Drawing.Design.UITypeEditor that can be used when modifying
properties that correspond to Internet URLs. This class extends on the basic UrlEditor
class and is customized for creating URLs that point to image files. The differences are
minor: the Filter property is overridden to provide the "*.gif; *.jpg; *.jpeg; *.bmp; *.wmf;
*.png" file filter, and the Caption of the designer window is modified to "Select Image
File." This class is used, for example, by the ImageUrl property of the System.Web.UI.WebCon-
trols.HyperLink control.

```
public class ImageUrlEditor : UrlEditor {
// Public Constructors
    public ImageUrlEditor( );
// Protected Instance Properties
    protected override string Caption{get; }                                          // overrides UrlEditor
    protected override string Filter{get; }                                           // overrides UrlEditor
}
```

Hierarchy   System.Object → System.Drawing.Design.UITypeEditor → UrlEditor → ImageUrlEditor

ITemplateEditingFrame

System.Web.UI.Design (system.design.dll)   interface

This interface is implemented by System.Web.UI.Design.WebControls.DataListDesigner and System. Web.UI.Design.WebControls.DataGridDesigner. It allows them to support in-place editing of a control template at design time. The properties of this interface represent the characteristics of the template editing area (like InitialHeight, InitialWidth, and ControlStyle). The methods are used to manage the template editing area (like Save( ) and Resize( )).

Note that a System.Web.UI.WebControls.DataGrid control uses templates (and hence template editing) only if you have added a System.Web.UI.WebControls.TemplateColumn.

```
public interface ITemplateEditingFrame : IDisposable {
// Public Instance Properties
  public Style ControlStyle{get; }
  public int InitialHeight{set; get; }
  public int InitialWidth{set; get; }
  public string Name{get; }
  public string[ ] TemplateNames{get; }
  public Style[ ] TemplateStyles{get; }
  public TemplateEditingVerb Verb{set; get; }
// Public Instance Methods
  public void Close( bool saveChanges);
  public void Open( );
  public void Resize( int width, int height);
  public void Save( );
  public void UpdateControlName( string newName);
}
```

Returned By   ITemplateEditingService.CreateFrame( ), TemplatedControlDesigner.{ActiveTemplateEditing-
                  Frame, CreateTemplateEditingFrame( )}, TemplateEditingService.CreateFrame( )

Passed To   TemplatedControlDesigner.{EnterTemplateMode( ), GetTemplateContent( ),
                  SetTemplateContent( )}

ITemplateEditingService

System.Web.UI.Design (system.design.dll)   interface

This class supports design-time control template editing.

```
public interface ITemplateEditingService {
// Public Instance Properties
  public bool SupportsNestedTemplateEditing{get; }
// Public Instance Methods
  public ITemplateEditingFrame CreateFrame(TemplatedControlDesigner designer, string frameName,
    string[ ] templateNames);
  public ITemplateEditingFrame CreateFrame(TemplatedControlDesigner designer, string frameName,
    string[ ] templateNames, System.Web.UI.WebControls.Style controlStyle,
    System.Web.UI.WebControls.Style[ ] templateStyles);
  public string GetContainingTemplateName(System.Web.UI.Control control);
}
```

Implemented By TemplateEditingService

IWebFormReferenceManager

System.Web.UI.Design (system.design.dll)   interface

This interface allows the IDE to look up and manage references (to .NET types) used in a web form.

```
public interface IWebFormReferenceManager {
// Public Instance Methods
  public Type GetObjectType(string tagPrefix, string typeName);
  public string GetRegisterDirectives( );
  public string GetTagPrefix(Type objectType);
}
```

IWebFormsBuilderUIService

System.Web.UI.Design (system.design.dll)   interface

This interface defines methods that can be used to launch a custom System.Drawing.Design. UITypeEditor object for assigning URLs (BuildUrl( )) or colors (BuildColor( )).

```
public interface IWebFormsBuilderUIService {
// Public Instance Methods
  public string BuildColor(System.Windows.Forms.Control owner, string initialColor);
  public string BuildUrl(System.Windows.Forms.Control owner, string initialUrl, string baseUrl, string caption,
    string filter, UrlBuilderOptions options);
}
```

IWebFormsDocumentService

System.Web.UI.Design (system.design.dll)   interface

This interface provides methods for tracking the state of a Web Forms document, handling load-time events, determining a document's location, setting a document selection, and managing a document's "Undo" service.

```
public interface IWebFormsDocumentService {
// Public Instance Properties
  public string DocumentUrl{get; }
  public bool IsLoading{get; }
// Public Instance Methods
  public object CreateDiscardableUndoUnit( );
  public void DiscardUndoUnit( object discardableUndoUnit);
  public void EnableUndo( bool enable);
  public void UpdateSelection( );
// Events
  public event EventHandler LoadComplete;
}
```

ReadWriteControlDesigner   disposable

System.Web.UI.Design (system.design.dll)   class

This class provides functionality for designers. In the .NET framework, only the System. Web.UI.Design.WebControls.PanelDesigner derives from this class. It uses read/write functionality to provide a design-time surface where you can directly type static inner text for the Panel control. Note that this class bypasses the ControlDesigner.GetDesignTimeHtml( ) method, because the design surface will be drawn using the ControlDesigner. GetDesignTimeHtml( ) method of the designers for the child controls.

```
public class ReadWriteControlDesigner : ControlDesigner {
// Public Constructors
  public ReadWriteControlDesigner( );
// Public Instance Methods
  public override void OnComponentChanged(object sender,
    System.ComponentModel.Design.ComponentChangedEventArgs ce);      // overrides ControlDesigner
// Protected Instance Methods
  protected virtual void MapPropertyToStyle(string propName, object varPropValue);
  protected override void OnBehaviorAttached( );                      // overrides ControlDesigner
}
```

Hierarchy   System.Object → System.ComponentModel.Design.ComponentDesigner(System.Compo-
nentModel.Design.IDesigner, System.IDisposable, System.ComponentModel.Design.
IDesignerFilter) → HtmlControlDesigner → ControlDesigner → ReadWriteControlDesigner

Subclasses   System.Web.UI.Design.WebControls.PanelDesigner

TemplatedControlDesigner   disposable

System.Web.UI.Design (system.design.dll)   abstract class

This designer supports the template editing features that allow you to enter template information into a control at design-time. These features include a slew of methods for creating a template-editing frame, updating the control properties and design-time HTML accordingly, and providing context menu verbs. System.Web.UI.Design.WebControls. BaseDataListDesigner inherits from this class.

```
public abstract class TemplatedControlDesigner : ControlDesigner {
// Public Constructors
  public TemplatedControlDesigner( );
// Public Instance Properties
  public ITemplateEditingFrame ActiveTemplateEditingFrame{get; }
  public bool CanEnterTemplateMode{get; }
  public bool InTemplateMode{get; }
// Protected Instance Properties
  protected virtual bool HidePropertiesInTemplateMode{get; }
// Public Instance Methods
  public void EnterTemplateMode(ITemplateEditingFrame newTemplateEditingFrame);
  public void ExitTemplateMode(bool fSwitchingTemplates, bool fNested, bool fSave);
  public override string GetPersistInnerHtml( );                     // overrides ControlDesigner
  public virtual string GetTemplateContainerDataItemProperty(string templateName);
  public virtual IEnumerable GetTemplateContainerDataSource(string templateName);
  public abstract string GetTemplateContent(ITemplateEditingFrame editingFrame, string templateName,
    out bool allowEditing);
  public TemplateEditingVerb[ ] GetTemplateEditingVerbs( );
  public virtual Type GetTemplatePropertyParentType(string templateName);
  public override void OnComponentChanged(object sender,
    System.ComponentModel.Design.ComponentChangedEventArgs ce);      // overrides ControlDesigner
  public override void OnSetParent( );                               // overrides HtmlControlDesigner
```

```
public abstract void SetTemplateContent(ITemplateEditingFrame editingFrame, string templateName,
    string templateContent);
public override void UpdateDesignTimeHtml( );                                    // overrides ControlDesigner
// Protected Instance Methods
protected abstract ITemplateEditingFrame CreateTemplateEditingFrame(TemplateEditingVerb verb);
protected abstract TemplateEditingVerb[ ] GetCachedTemplateEditingVerbs( );
protected ITemplate GetTemplateFromText( string text);
protected string GetTextFromTemplate(System.Web.UI.ITemplate template);
protected override void OnBehaviorAttached( );                                   // overrides ControlDesigner
protected virtual void OnTemplateModeChanged( );
protected override void PreFilterProperties(System.Collections.IDictionary properties);   // overrides ControlDesigner
protected void SaveActiveTemplateEditingFrame( );
}
```

Hierarchy System.Object → System.ComponentModel.Design.ComponentDesigner(System.Compo-
nentModel.Design.IDesigner, System.IDisposable, System.ComponentModel.Design.
IDesignerFilter) → HtmlControlDesigner → ControlDesigner → TemplatedControlDesigner

Subclasses System.Web.UI.Design.WebControls.BaseDataListDesigner

Passed To ITemplateEditingService.CreateFrame( ), TemplateEditingService.CreateFrame( ), Template-
EditingVerb.TemplateEditingVerb( )

TemplateEditingService   disposable

System.Web.UI.Design (system.design.dll)   sealed class

This class implements the ITemplateEditingService interface and provides IDE functionality
for editing the templates for controls like System.Web.UI.WebControls.DataList and System.Web.UI.
WebControls.DataGrid. This class offers a CreateFrame( ) method, which takes a reference to a
TemplatedControlDesigner and returns an ITemplateEditingFrame instance for it.

```
public sealed class TemplateEditingService : ITemplateEditingService, IDisposable {
// Public Constructors
public TemplateEditingService(System.ComponentModel.Design.IDesignerHost designerHost);
// Public Instance Properties
public bool SupportsNestedTemplateEditing{get; }                                 // implements ITemplateEditingService
// Public Instance Methods
public ITemplateEditingFrame CreateFrame(TemplatedControlDesigner designer, string frameName,
    string[ ] templateNames);                                                    // implements ITemplateEditingService
public ITemplateEditingFrame CreateFrame(TemplatedControlDesigner designer, string frameName,
    string[ ] templateNames, System.Web.UI.WebControls.Style controlStyle,
    System.Web.UI.WebControls.Style[ ] templateStyles);                          // implements ITemplateEditingService
public void Dispose( );                                                          // implements IDisposable
public string GetContainingTemplateName(System.Web.UI.Control control);          // implements ITemplateEditingService
// Protected Instance Methods
protected override void Finalize( );                                             // overrides object
}
```

TemplateEditingVerb

System.Web.UI.Design (system.design.dll)   class

This class represents a type of verb that can be invoked only by a template editor (like TemplatedControlDesigner, System.Web.UI.Design.WebControls.DataListDesigner, and System.Web.UI.Design. WebControls.DataGridDesigner). A verb is a menu command that appears in the context menu when you right-click a control.

```
public class TemplateEditingVerb : System.ComponentModel.Design.DesignerVerb, IDisposable {
// Public Constructors
  public TemplateEditingVerb(string text, int index, TemplatedControlDesigner designer);
// Public Instance Properties
  public int Index{get; }
// Public Instance Methods
  public void Dispose( );                                                    // implements IDisposable
// Protected Instance Methods
  protected virtual void Dispose( bool disposing);
  protected override void Finalize( );                                          // overrides object
}
```

Hierarchy	System.Object → System.ComponentModel.Design.MenuCommand → System.Compo-nentModel.Design.DesignerVerb → TemplateEditingVerb(System.IDisposable)
Returned By	ITemplateEditingFrame.Verb, TemplatedControlDesigner.{GetCachedTemplateEditingVerbs( ), GetTemplateEditingVerbs( )}
Passed To	ITemplateEditingFrame.Verb, TemplatedControlDesigner.CreateTemplateEditingFrame( )

TextControlDesigner

System.Web.UI.Design (system.design.dll)   class

The TextControlDesigner can be used as a base class for all controls that provide a Text property. The HyperLinkDesigner, LabelDesigner, and LinkButtonDesigner all derive from this class.

```
public class TextControlDesigner : ControlDesigner {
// Public Constructors
  public TextControlDesigner( );
// Public Instance Methods
  public override string GetDesignTimeHtml( );                                  // overrides ControlDesigner
  public override string GetPersistInnerHtml( );                                // overrides ControlDesigner
  public override void Initialize(System.ComponentModel.IComponent component);  // overrides ControlDesigner
}
```

Hierarchy	System.Object → System.ComponentModel.Design.ComponentDesigner(System.Compo-nentModel.Design.IDesigner, System.IDisposable, System.ComponentModel.Design. IDesignerFilter) → HtmlControlDesigner → ControlDesigner → TextControlDesigner
Subclasses	System.Web.UI.Design.WebControls.{HyperLinkDesigner, LabelDesigner, LinkButtonDesigner}

TextDataBindingHandler

System.Web.UI.Design (system.design.dll)   class

This DataBindingHandler class provides data binding for the Text property of a control, using an overridden DataBindingHandler.DataBindControl( ) method.

```
public class TextDataBindingHandler : DataBindingHandler {
// Public Constructors
  public TextDataBindingHandler( );
// Public Instance Methods
  public override void DataBindControl(System.ComponentModel.Design.IDesignerHost designerHost,
    System.Web.UI.Control control);                                    // overrides DataBindingHandler
}
```

Hierarchy   System.Object → DataBindingHandler → TextDataBindingHandler

UrlBuilder

System.Web.UI.Design (system.design.dll)   sealed class

This class contains shared (static) helper methods that support the various UrlEditor classes. Essentially, the UrlEditor class provides the user interface used for choosing a URL for a property at design time, and the BuildUrl( ) method is invoked to create a string representing the selected URL.

```
public sealed class UrlBuilder {
// Public Static Methods
  public static string BuildUrl(System.ComponentModel.IComponent component, System.Windows.Forms.Control owner,
    string initialUrl, string caption, string filter);
  public static string BuildUrl(System.ComponentModel.IComponent component, System.Windows.Forms.Control owner,
    string initialUrl, string caption, string filter, UrlBuilderOptions options);
}
```

UrlBuilderOptions   serializable, flag

System.Web.UI.Design (system.design.dll)   enum

This enumeration specifies whether a URL is fully qualified (None) or relative to the current document (NoAbsolute). This enumeration is set by the various UrlEditor classes and ultimately used by UrlBuilder.BuildUrl( ) to create a string representing the specified URL.

```
public enum UrlBuilderOptions {
  None = 0x00000000,
  NoAbsolute = 0x00000001
}
```

Hierarchy   System.Object → System.ValueType → System.Enum(System.IComparable, System.IFor-
                     mattable, System.IConvertible) → UrlBuilderOptions

Returned By   UrlEditor.Options

Passed To   IWebFormsBuilderUIService.BuildUrl( ), UrlBuilder.BuildUrl( )

UrlEditor

System.Web.UI.Design (system.design.dll)   class

This class provides a System.Drawing.Design.UITypeEditor that can be used when modifying properties that correspond to Internet URLs. An example is the System.Web.UI.WebControls.HyperLink.NavigateUrl property of the System.Web.UI.WebControls.HyperLink control. Note that this class, like all type editors, implements the user interface linked to the appropriate property in the Properties Window. The actual construction of the URL is supported by the methods in the UrlBuilder class.

```
public class UrlEditor : System.Drawing.Design.UITypeEditor {
// Public Constructors
  public UrlEditor( );
// Protected Instance Properties
  protected virtual string Caption{get; }
  protected virtual string Filter{get; }
  protected virtual UrlBuilderOptions Options{get; }
// Public Instance Methods
  public override object EditValue(System.ComponentModel.ITypeDescriptorContext context,
    IServiceProvider provider, object value);                                // overrides System.Drawing.Design.UITypeEditor
  public override UITypeEditorEditStyle GetEditStyle(System.ComponentModel.ITypeDescriptorContext context);
                                                                             // overrides System.Drawing.Design.UITypeEditor
}
```

Hierarchy   System.Object → System.Drawing.Design.UITypeEditor → UrlEditor

Subclasses   ImageUrlEditor, XmlUrlEditor, XslUrlEditor

UserControlDesigner   disposable

System.Web.UI.Design (system.design.dll)   class

This class provides a custom designer for user controls (page-like groups of text, controls, and scripting contained in *.ascx* files). This designer provides the design-time HTML used when you insert a user control onto a Web Forms page. This design-time HTML consists of a generic, labeled gray box that does not render any of the actual content.

```
public class UserControlDesigner : ControlDesigner {
// Public Constructors
  public UserControlDesigner( );
// Public Instance Properties
  public override bool AllowResize{get; }                                              // overrides ControlDesigner
  public override bool ShouldCodeSerialize{set; get; }                                 // overrides HtmlControlDesigner
// Public Instance Methods
  public override string GetDesignTimeHtml( );                                         // overrides ControlDesigner
  public override string GetPersistInnerHtml( );                                       // overrides ControlDesigner
}
```

Hierarchy   System.Object → System.ComponentModel.Design.ComponentDesigner(System.Compo-
                       nentModel.Design.IDesigner, System.IDisposable, System.ComponentModel.Design.
                       IDesignerFilter) → HtmlControlDesigner → ControlDesigner → UserControlDesigner

This class represents a toolbox item for a web control. Toolbox items are the icons you use to insert controls when designing a Web Forms page.

```
public class WebControlToolboxItem : System.Drawing.Design.ToolboxItem {
// Public Constructors
  public WebControlToolboxItem( );
  public WebControlToolboxItem( Type type);
// Public Instance Methods
  public object GetToolAttributeValue(System.ComponentModel.Design.IDesignerHost host, Type attributeType);
  public string GetToolHtml(System.ComponentModel.Design.IDesignerHost host);
  public Type GetToolType(System.ComponentModel.Design.IDesignerHost host);
  public override void Initialize(Type type);                              // overrides System.Drawing.Design.ToolboxItem
// Protected Instance Methods
  protected override IComponent[ ] CreateComponentsCore(System.ComponentModel.Design.IDesignerHost host);
                                                                // overrides System.Drawing.Design.ToolboxItem
  protected override void Deserialize(System.Runtime.Serialization.SerializationInfo info,
    System.Runtime.Serialization.StreamingContext context);     // overrides System.Drawing.Design.ToolboxItem
  protected override void Serialize(System.Runtime.Serialization.SerializationInfo info,
    System.Runtime.Serialization.StreamingContext context);     // overrides System.Drawing.Design.ToolboxItem
}
```

Hierarchy System.Object → System.Drawing.Design.ToolboxItem(System.Runtime.Serialization.ISerializable) → WebControlToolboxItem

XmlFileEditor

System.Web.UI.Design (system.design.dll) class

This class provides the interface used for selecting an XML file from the standard open file dialog. It works in conjunction with XmlUrlEditor.

```
public class XmlFileEditor : System.Drawing.Design.UITypeEditor {
// Public Constructors
  public XmlFileEditor( );
// Public Instance Methods
  public override object EditValue(System.ComponentModel.ITypeDescriptorContext context,
    IServiceProvider provider, object value);                   // overrides System.Drawing.Design.UITypeEditor
  public override UITypeEditorEditStyle GetEditStyle(System.ComponentModel.ITypeDescriptorContext context);
                                                                // overrides System.Drawing.Design.UITypeEditor
}
```

Hierarchy System.Object → System.Drawing.Design.UITypeEditor → XmlFileEditor

XmlUrlEditor

System.Web.UI.Design (system.design.dll) class

This class provides a System.Drawing.Design.UITypeEditor that can be used when modifying properties that correspond to Internet URLs. This class extends on the basic UrlEditor and is customized for creating URLs that point to XML files. The differences are minor: the ImageUrlEditor.Filter property is overridden to provide the "*.xml" file filter and the ImageUrlEditor.Caption of the designer window is modified to "Select XML File." This class is used, for example, by the DocumentSource property of the System.Web.UI.WebControls.Xml control.

```
public class XmlUrlEditor : UrlEditor {
// Public Constructors
   public XmlUrlEditor( );
// Protected Instance Properties
   protected override string Caption{get; }                          // overrides UrlEditor
   protected override string Filter{get; }                           // overrides UrlEditor
   protected override UrlBuilderOptions Options{get; }               // overrides UrlEditor
}
```

Hierarchy   System.Object → System.Drawing.Design.UITypeEditor → UrlEditor → XmlUrlEditor

XslUrlEditor

System.Web.UI.Design (system.design.dll)   class

This class provides a System.Drawing.Design.UITypeEditor that can be used when modifying properties that correspond to Internet URLs. This class extends on the basic UrlEditor and is customized for creating URLs that point to XSL transform files. The differences are minor: the ImageUrlEditor.Filter property is overridden to provide the "*.xsl; *.xslt" file filter and the ImageUrlEditor.Caption of the designer window is modified to "Select XSL Transform File." This class is used, for example, by the TransformSource property of the System.Web.UI.WebControls.Xml control.

```
public class XslUrlEditor : UrlEditor {
// Public Constructors
   public XslUrlEditor( );
// Protected Instance Properties
   protected override string Caption{get; }                          // overrides UrlEditor
   protected override string Filter{get; }                           // overrides UrlEditor
   protected override UrlBuilderOptions Options{get; }               // overrides UrlEditor
}
```

Hierarchy   System.Object → System.Drawing.Design.UITypeEditor → UrlEditor → XslUrlEditor

38

The System.Web.UI.Design. WebControls Namespace

The types in the System.Web.UI.Design.WebControls namespace extend Visual Studio's design-time support for creating web controls. Most types in this namespace are designers that provide special design-time–specific HTML (which may be only slightly different than runtime HTML) and custom System.Drawing.Design.UITypeEditor classes that provide the graphic interface for modifying some special properties. The most detailed implementations of these features can be found in the types used for the System.Web.UI.WebControls.DataGrid and System.Web.UI.WebControls.DataList controls, such as DataGridComponentEditor and DataGridDesigner. These classes provide sophisticated property builders that offer complete design-time customization in a multipage "applet."

These designers, UI type editors, and component editors have no effect on the runtime capabilities of a control. They are also not used directly in code. That means that the System.Web.UI.Design.WebControls namespace is probably of most interest to developers who are interested in creating controls and add-ins of their own and want to review Microsoft's examples. Unfortunately, while you can review the interfaces these types have and extend them in your own code, the implementation details are not provided. Usually, it makes most sense to create control designers that inherit from the base System.Web.UI.Design.ControlDesigner class.

Figures 38-1 and 38-2 show the types in this namespace.

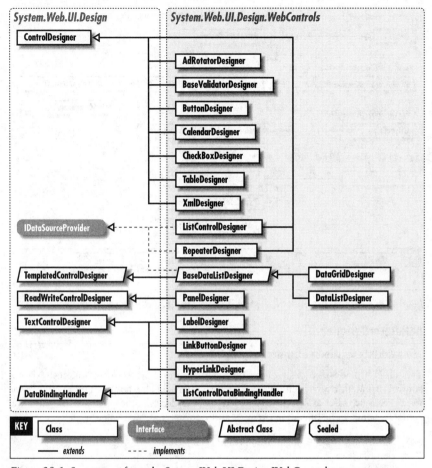

Figure 38-1. Some types from the System.Web.UI.Design.WebControls namespace

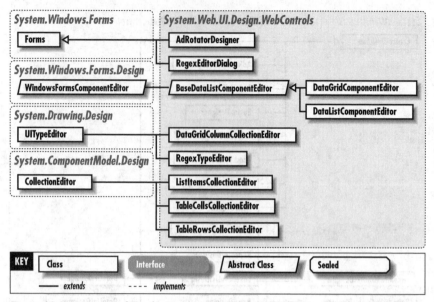

Figure 38-2. More types from the System.Web.UI.Design.WebControls namespace

AdRotatorDesigner

disposable

System.Web.UI.Design.WebControls (system.design.dll)   class

This class provides the design-time representation of a System.Web.UI.WebControls.AdRotator control, using an overridden GetDesignTimeHtml( ) method. This control ignores the System.Web.UI.WebControls.AdRotator.AdvertisementFile property at design time and just displays the control's name and a blank picture icon in the corner.

```
public class AdRotatorDesigner : System.Web.UI.Design.ControlDesigner {
// Public Constructors
  public AdRotatorDesigner( );
// Public Instance Methods
  public override string GetDesignTimeHtml( );              // overrides System.Web.UI.Design.ControlDesigner
}
```

Hierarchy   System.Object → System.ComponentModel.Design.ComponentDesigner(System.ComponentModel.Design.IDesigner, System.IDisposable, System.ComponentModel.Design.IDesignerFilter) → System.Web.UI.Design.HtmlControlDesigner → System.Web.UI.Design.ControlDesigner → AdRotatorDesigner

BaseDataListComponentEditor

System.Web.UI.Design.WebControls (system.design.dll)   abstract class

This abstract class provides basic functionality for the DataListComponentEditor and DataGridComponentEditor classes, which provide the Property Builder user interface for editing complex properties for these controls.

```
public abstract class BaseDataListComponentEditor : System.Windows.Forms.Design.WindowsFormsComponentEditor {
// Public Constructors
   public BaseDataListComponentEditor(int initialPage);
// Public Instance Methods
   public override bool EditComponent(System.ComponentModel.ITypeDescriptorContext context,
      object obj, System.Windows.Forms.IWin32Window parent);
                              // overrides System.Windows.Forms.Design.WindowsFormsComponentEditor

// Protected Instance Methods
   protected override int GetInitialComponentEditorPageIndex( );
                              // overrides System.Windows.Forms.Design.WindowsFormsComponentEditor
}
```

Hierarchy	System.Object → System.ComponentModel.ComponentEditor → System.Windows.Forms. Design.WindowsFormsComponentEditor → BaseDataListComponentEditor
Subclasses	DataGridComponentEditor, DataListComponentEditor

BaseDataListDesigner
disposable

System.Web.UI.Design.WebControls (system.design.dll)   *abstract class*

This abstract class provides basic functionality for the DataListDesigner and DataGridDesigner classes. This includes functionality for styles, additional verbs for the context menu, and other helper methods for data binding.

```
public abstract class BaseDataListDesigner : System.Web.UI.Design.TemplatedControlDesigner, System.Web.UI.Design.
IDataSourceProvider {
// Public Constructors
   public BaseDataListDesigner( );
// Public Instance Properties
   public string DataKeyField{set; get; }
   public string DataMember{set; get; }
   public string DataSource{set; get; }
   public override bool DesignTimeHtmlRequiresLoadComplete{get; }    // overrides System.Web.UI.Design.ControlDesigner
   public override DesignerVerbCollection Verbs{get; }    // overrides System.ComponentModel.Design.ComponentDesigner
// Public Instance Methods
   public IEnumerable GetResolvedSelectedDataSource( );    // implements System.Web.UI.Design.IDataSourceProvider
   public object GetSelectedDataSource( );    // implements System.Web.UI.Design.IDataSourceProvider
   public override IEnumerable GetTemplateContainerDataSource(string templateName);
                              // overrides System.Web.UI.DesignTemplatedControlDesigner
   public override void Initialize(System.ComponentModel.IComponent component);
                              // overrides System.Web.UI.Design.ControlDesigner

   public override void OnComponentChanged(object sender,
      System.ComponentModel.Design.ComponentChangedEventArgs e);
                              // overrides System.Web.UI.Design.TemplatedControlDesigner

// Protected Instance Methods
   protected override void Dispose( bool disposing);    // overrides System.Web.UI.Design.HtmlControlDesigner
   protected IEnumerable GetDesignTimeDataSource(System.Collections.IEnumerable selectedDataSource,
      int minimumRows, out bool dummyDataSource);
   protected IEnumerable GetDesignTimeDataSource(int minimumRows, out bool dummyDataSource);
   protected internal void InvokePropertyBuilder(int initialPage);
   protected void OnAutoFormat( object sender, EventArgs e);
```

```
    protected internal virtual void OnDataSourceChanged( );
    protected void OnPropertyBuilder(object sender, EventArgs e);
    protected internal void OnStylesChanged( );
    protected abstract void OnTemplateEditingVerbsChanged( );
    protected override void PreFilterProperties(System.Collections.IDictionary properties);
                                      // overrides System.Web.UI.Design.TemplatedControlDesigner
}
```

Hierarchy   System.Object → System.ComponentModel.Design.ComponentDesigner(System.Compo-
                   nentModel.Design.IDesigner, System.IDisposable, System.ComponentModel.Design.
                   IDesignerFilter) → System.Web.UI.Design.HtmlControlDesigner → System.Web.UI.Design.
                   ControlDesigner → System.Web.UI.Design.TemplatedControlDesigner → BaseDataListDe-
                   signer(System.Web.UI.Design.IDataSourceProvider)

Subclasses   DataGridDesigner, DataListDesigner

BaseValidatorDesigner   disposable

System.Web.UI.Design.WebControls (system.design.dll)   class

This class provides the design-time representation of controls that inherit from the
System.Web.UI.WebControls.BaseValidator control, including System.Web.UI.WebControls.CompareVali-
dator, System.Web.UI.WebControls.CustomValidator, System.Web.UI.WebControls.RangeValidator, System.Web.UI.
WebControls.RegularExpressionValidator, and System.Web.UI.WebControls.RequiredFieldValidator. It uses an
overridden GetDesignTimeHtml( ) method. Validation controls display the control class
name in red lettering at design time (or the Text property, if set).

```
public class BaseValidatorDesigner : System.Web.UI.Design.ControlDesigner {
// Public Constructors
    public BaseValidatorDesigner( );
// Public Instance Methods
    public override string GetDesignTimeHtml( );           // overrides System.Web.UI.Design.ControlDesigner
}
```

Hierarchy   System.Object → System.ComponentModel.Design.ComponentDesigner(System.Compo-
                   nentModel.Design.IDesigner, System.IDisposable, System.ComponentModel.Design.
                   IDesignerFilter) → System.Web.UI.Design.HtmlControlDesigner → System.Web.UI.Design.
                   ControlDesigner → BaseValidatorDesigner

ButtonDesigner   disposable

System.Web.UI.Design.WebControls (system.design.dll)   class

This class provides the design-time representation of a System.Web.UI.WebControls.Button
control, using an overridden GetDesignTimeHtml( ) method. If the System.Web.UI.WebControls.
Button.Text property is empty, you will see the control's name displayed in square
brackets.

```
public class ButtonDesigner : System.Web.UI.Design.ControlDesigner {
// Public Constructors
    public ButtonDesigner( );
// Public Instance Methods
    public override string GetDesignTimeHtml( );           // overrides System.Web.UI.Design.ControlDesigner
}
```

Hierarchy   System.Object → System.ComponentModel.Design.ComponentDesigner(System.ComponentModel.Design.IDesigner, System.IDisposable, System.ComponentModel.Design.IDesignerFilter) → System.Web.UI.Design.HtmlControlDesigner → System.Web.UI.Design.ControlDesigner → ButtonDesigner

CalendarAutoFormatDialog

marshal by reference, disposable

System.Web.UI.Design.WebControls (system.design.dll)   class

This class works in conjunction with the CalendarDesigner class. It displays an "auto format" window that allows the user to change several formatting-related properties at once by choosing one of the presets it provides.

```
public class CalendarAutoFormatDialog : System.Windows.Forms.Form {
// Public Constructors
  public CalendarAutoFormatDialog(System.Web.UI.WebControls.Calendar calendar);
// Protected Instance Methods
  protected void DoDelayLoadActions( );
  protected void OnActivated( object source, EventArgs e);
  protected void OnOKClicked( object source, EventArgs e);
  protected void OnSelChangedScheme(object source, EventArgs e);
  protected void SaveComponent( );
}
```

Hierarchy   System.Object → System.MarshalByRefObject → System.ComponentModel.Component(System.ComponentModel.IComponent, System.IDisposable) → System.Windows.Forms.Control(System.Windows.Forms.IOleControl, System.Windows.Forms.IOleObject, System.Windows.Forms.IOleInPlaceObject, System.Windows.Forms.IOleInPlaceActiveObject, System.Windows.Forms.IOleWindow, System.Windows.Forms.IViewObject, System.Windows.Forms.IViewObject2, System.Windows.Forms.IPersist, System.Windows.Forms.IPersistStreamInit, System.Windows.Forms.IPersistPropertyBag, System.Windows.Forms.IPersistStorage, System.Windows.Forms.IQuickActivate, System.ComponentModel.ISynchronizeInvoke, System.Windows.Forms.IWin32Window) → System.Windows.Forms.ScrollableControl → System.Windows.Forms.ContainerControl(System.Windows.Forms.IContainerControl) → System.Windows.Forms.Form → CalendarAutoFormatDialog

CalendarDesigner

disposable

System.Web.UI.Design.WebControls (system.design.dll)   class

This class provides the design-time representation for the System.Web.UI.WebControls.Calendar control. It works in conjunction with the CalendarAutoFormatDialog class to provide an "auto format" window, adding a special verb to the context menu and responding to format changes by updating the corresponding properties.

```
public class CalendarDesigner : System.Web.UI.Design.ControlDesigner {
// Public Constructors
  public CalendarDesigner( );
// Public Instance Properties
  public override DesignerVerbCollection Verbs{get; }          // overrides System.ComponentModel.Design.ComponentDesigner
// Public Instance Methods
  public override void Initialize(System.ComponentModel.IComponent component);
                                                              // overrides System.Web.UI.Design.ControlDesigner
```

```
// Protected Instance Methods
  protected void OnAutoFormat( object sender, EventArgs e);
}
```

Hierarchy   System.Object → System.ComponentModel.Design.ComponentDesigner(System.Compo-
                  nentModel.Design.IDesigner, System.IDisposable, System.ComponentModel.Design.
                  IDesignerFilter) → System.Web.UI.Design.HtmlControlDesigner → System.Web.UI.Design.
                  ControlDesigner → CalendarDesigner

CheckBoxDesigner   disposable

System.Web.UI.Design.WebControls (system.design.dll)   class

This class provides the design-time representation of a System.Web.UI.WebControls.CheckBox
control, using an overridden GetDesignTimeHtml( ) method. If the System.Web.UI.WebControls.
CheckBox.Text property is empty, the control's name will be displayed in square brackets.

```
public class CheckBoxDesigner : System.Web.UI.Design.ControlDesigner {
// Public Constructors
  public CheckBoxDesigner( );
// Public Instance Methods
  public override string GetDesignTimeHtml( );                 // overrides System.Web.UI.Design.ControlDesigner
}
```

Hierarchy   System.Object → System.ComponentModel.Design.ComponentDesigner(System.Compo-
                  nentModel.Design.IDesigner, System.IDisposable, System.ComponentModel.Design.
                  IDesignerFilter) → System.Web.UI.Design.HtmlControlDesigner → System.Web.UI.Design.
                  ControlDesigner → CheckBoxDesigner

DataGridColumnCollectionEditor

System.Web.UI.Design.WebControls (system.design.dll)   class

This class is a System.Drawing.Design.UITypeEditor that provides a graphical interface for
configuring the column collection provided in the System.Web.UI.WebControls.DataGrid.Columns
property.

```
public class DataGridColumnCollectionEditor : System.Drawing.Design.UITypeEditor {
// Public Constructors
  public DataGridColumnCollectionEditor( );
// Public Instance Methods
  public override object EditValue(ComponentModel.ITypeDescriptorContext context,
    IServiceProvider provider, object value);              // overrides System.Drawing.Design.UITypeEditorSystem.
  public override UITypeEditorEditStyle GetEditStyle(System.ComponentModel.ITypeDescriptorContext context);
                                                          // overrides System.Drawing.Design.UITypeEditor
}
```

Hierarchy   System.Object → System.Drawing.Design.UITypeEditor → DataGridColumnCollectionEditor

DataGridComponentEditor

System.Web.UI.Design.WebControls (system.design.dll)   class

This class provides a custom System.ComponentModel.ComponentEditor used to edit complex
property information for the System.Web.UI.WebControls.DataGrid control in a special graphical

---

window with multiple pages. This window, which includes information for configuring columns, paging, format, and borders, can be displayed by choosing "Property Builder" from the context menu.

```
public class DataGridComponentEditor : BaseDataListComponentEditor {
// Public Constructors
  public DataGridComponentEditor( );
  public DataGridComponentEditor( int initialPage);
// Protected Instance Methods
  protected override Type[ ] GetComponentEditorPages( );
                              // overrides System.Windows.Forms.Design.WindowsFormsComponentEditor
}
```

Hierarchy   System.Object → System.ComponentModel.ComponentEditor → System.Windows.Forms.
Design.WindowsFormsComponentEditor → BaseDataListComponentEditor →
DataGridComponentEditor

DataGridDesigner   disposable

System.Web.UI.Design.WebControls (system.design.dll)   class

This class provides the design-time representation of a System.Web.UI.WebControls.DataGrid control. A sample table is displayed if no connection is made. If you bind to a data source at design time, the schema is used to create column headings, and the formatting options you have selected are also shown. However, the actual data rows use dummy values (like "abc") generated by the System.Web.UI.Design.DesignTimeData class.

```
public class DataGridDesigner : BaseDataListDesigner {
// Public Constructors
  public DataGridDesigner( );
// Public Instance Methods
  public override string GetDesignTimeHtml( );                  // overrides System.Web.UI.Design.ControlDesigner
  public override string GetTemplateContainerDataItemProperty(string templateName);
                                                      // overrides System.Web.UI.Design.TemplatedControlDesigner
  public override string GetTemplateContent(System.Web.UI.Design.ITemplateEditingFrame editingFrame,
      string templateName, out bool allowEditing);    // overrides System.Web.UI.Design.TemplatedControlDesigner
  public override Type GetTemplatePropertyParentType(string templateName);
                                                      // overrides System.Web.UI.Design.TemplatedControlDesigner
  public override void Initialize(System.ComponentModel.IComponent component);    // overrides BaseDataListDesigner
  public virtual void OnColumnsChanged( );
  public override void SetTemplateContent(System.Web.UI.Design.ITemplateEditingFrame editingFrame,
      string templateName, string templateContent);   // overrides System.Web.UI.Design.TemplatedControlDesigner
// Protected Instance Methods
  protected override ITemplateEditingFrame CreateTemplateEditingFrame(System.Web.UI.Design.TemplateEditingVerb verb);
                                                      // overrides System.Web.UI.Design.TemplatedControlDesigner
  protected override void Dispose( bool disposing);                            // overrides BaseDataListDesigner
  protected override TemplateEditingVerb[ ] GetCachedTemplateEditingVerbs( );
                                                      // overrides System.Web.UI.Design.TemplatedControlDesigner
  protected override string GetEmptyDesignTimeHtml( );          // overrides System.Web.UI.Design.ControlDesigner
  protected override string GetErrorDesignTimeHtml(Exception e);  // overrides System.Web.UI.Design.ControlDesigner
  protected override void OnTemplateEditingVerbsChanged( );                    // overrides BaseDataListDesigner
}
```

Hierarchy   System.Object → System.ComponentModel.Design.ComponentDesigner(System.Compo-
nentModel.Design.IDesigner, System.IDisposable, System.ComponentModel.Design.
IDesignerFilter) → System.Web.UI.Design.HtmlControlDesigner → System.Web.UI.Design.
ControlDesigner → System.Web.UI.Design.TemplatedControlDesigner → BaseDataListDe-
signer(System.Web.UI.Design.IDataSourceProvider) → DataGridDesigner

DataListComponentEditor

System.Web.UI.Design.WebControls (system.design.dll)   class

This class provides a custom System.ComponentModel.ComponentEditor used to edit complex
property information for the System.Web.UI.WebControls.DataList in a special graphical
window with multiple pages. This window can be displayed by choosing "Property
Builder" from the context menu.

```
public class DataListComponentEditor : BaseDataListComponentEditor {
// Public Constructors
  public DataListComponentEditor( );
  public DataListComponentEditor( int initialPage);
// Protected Instance Methods
  protected override Type[ ] GetComponentEditorPages( );
                               // overrides System.Windows.Forms.Design.WindowsFormsComponentEditor
}
```

Hierarchy   System.Object → System.ComponentModel.ComponentEditor → System.Windows.Forms.
Design.WindowsFormsComponentEditor → BaseDataListComponentEditor →
DataListComponentEditor

DataListDesigner   disposable

System.Web.UI.Design.WebControls (system.design.dll)   class

This class provides the design-time representation of a System.Web.UI.WebControls.DataList
control. A message indicating how to configure template options is displayed if no
template information is entered.

```
public class DataListDesigner : BaseDataListDesigner {
// Public Constructors
  public DataListDesigner( );
// Public Instance Properties
  public override bool AllowResize{get; }                      // overrides System.Web.UI.Design.ControlDesigner
// Protected Instance Properties
  protected bool TemplatesExist{get; }
// Public Instance Methods
  public override string GetDesignTimeHtml( );                 // overrides System.Web.UI.Design.ControlDesigner
  public override string GetTemplateContainerDataItemProperty(string templateName);
                               // overrides System.Web.UI.Design.TemplatedControlDesigner
  public override string GetTemplateContent(System.Web.UI.Design.ITemplateEditingFrame editingFrame,
    string templateName, out bool allowEditing);              // overrides System.Web.UI.Design.TemplatedControlDesigner
  public override void Initialize(System.ComponentModel.IComponent component);   // overrides BaseDataListDesigner
  public override void SetTemplateContent(System.Web.UI.Design.ITemplateEditingFrame editingFrame,
    string templateName, string templateContent);            // overrides System.Web.UI.Design.TemplatedControlDesigner
// Protected Instance Methods
```

```
    protected override ITemplateEditingFrame CreateTemplateEditingFrame(System.Web.UI.Design.TemplateEditingVerb verb);
                                                    // overrides System.Web.UI.Design.TemplatedControlDesigner
    protected override void Dispose( bool disposing);        // overrides BaseDataListDesigner
    protected override TemplateEditingVerb[ ] GetCachedTemplateEditingVerbs( );
                                                    // overrides System.Web.UI.Design.TemplatedControlDesigner
    protected override string GetEmptyDesignTimeHtml( );         // overrides System.Web.UI.Design.ControlDesigner
    protected override string GetErrorDesignTimeHtml(Exception e);    // overrides System.Web.UI.Design.ControlDesigner
    protected override void OnTemplateEditingVerbsChanged( );              // overrides BaseDataListDesigner
}
```

Hierarchy   System.Object → System.ComponentModel.Design.ComponentDesigner(System.Compo-
nentModel.Design.IDesigner, System.IDisposable, System.ComponentModel.Design.
IDesignerFilter) → System.Web.UI.Design.HtmlControlDesigner → System.Web.UI.Design.
ControlDesigner → System.Web.UI.Design.TemplatedControlDesigner → BaseDataListDe-
signer(System.Web.UI.Design.IDataSourceProvider) → DataListDesigner

HyperLinkDesigner   disposable

System.Web.UI.Design.WebControls (system.design.dll)   class

This class provides the design-time representation of a System.Web.UI.WebControls.HyperLink
control, using an overridden GetDesignTimeHtml( ) method. If the System.Web.UI.WebControls.
HyperLink.Text property is empty, the control's name will be displayed in square brackets.

```
public class HyperLinkDesigner : System.Web.UI.Design.TextControlDesigner {
// Public Constructors
  public HyperLinkDesigner( );
// Public Instance Methods
  public override string GetDesignTimeHtml( );                    // overrides System.Web.UI.Design.TextControlDesigner
}
```

Hierarchy   System.Object → System.ComponentModel.Design.ComponentDesigner(System.Compo-
nentModel.Design.IDesigner, System.IDisposable, System.ComponentModel.Design.
IDesignerFilter) → System.Web.UI.Design.HtmlControlDesigner → System.Web.UI.Design.
ControlDesigner → System.Web.UI.Design.TextControlDesigner → HyperLinkDesigner

LabelDesigner   disposable

System.Web.UI.Design.WebControls (system.design.dll)   class

This class provides the design-time representation of a System.Web.UI.WebControls.Label
control, using an overridden GetDesignTimeHtml( ) method. If the System.Web.UI.WebControls.
Label.Text property is empty, the control's name will be displayed in square brackets.

```
public class LabelDesigner : System.Web.UI.Design.TextControlDesigner {
// Public Constructors
  public LabelDesigner( );
}
```

Hierarchy   System.Object → System.ComponentModel.Design.ComponentDesigner(System.Compo-
nentModel.Design.IDesigner, System.IDisposable, System.ComponentModel.Design.
IDesignerFilter) → System.Web.UI.Design.HtmlControlDesigner → System.Web.UI.Design.
ControlDesigner → System.Web.UI.Design.TextControlDesigner → LabelDesigner

LinkButtonDesigner

disposable

System.Web.UI.Design.WebControls (system.design.dll)   class

This class provides the design-time representation of a System.Web.UI.WebControls.LinkButton control, using an overridden GetDesignTimeHtml( ) method. If the System.Web.UI.WebControls.Link-Button.Text property is empty, the control's name will be displayed in square brackets.

```
public class LinkButtonDesigner : System.Web.UI.Design.TextControlDesigner {
// Public Constructors
  public LinkButtonDesigner( );
}
```

Hierarchy   System.Object → System.ComponentModel.Design.ComponentDesigner(System.Compo-
                   nentModel.Design.IDesigner, System.IDisposable, System.ComponentModel.Design.
                   IDesignerFilter) → System.Web.UI.Design.HtmlControlDesigner → System.Web.UI.Design.
                   ControlDesigner → System.Web.UI.Design.TextControlDesigner → LinkButtonDesigner

ListControlDataBindingHandler

System.Web.UI.Design.WebControls (system.design.dll)   class

This class provides a data-binding handler that lets you connect controls derived from System.Web.UI.WebControls.ListControl to a data source.

```
public class ListControlDataBindingHandler : System.Web.UI.Design.DataBindingHandler {
// Public Constructors
  public ListControlDataBindingHandler( );
// Public Instance Methods
  public override void DataBindControl(System.ComponentModel.Design.IDesignerHost designerHost,
     System.Web.UI.Control control);                        // overrides System.Web.UI.Design.DataBindingHandler
}
```

Hierarchy   System.Object → System.Web.UI.Design.DataBindingHandler →
                   ListControlDataBindingHandler

ListControlDesigner

disposable

System.Web.UI.Design.WebControls (system.design.dll)   class

This class provides the design-time representation for several list controls derived from System.Web.UI.WebControls.ListControl. The design-time view displays any items you have added through the ListItemsCollectionEditor, or it may show the text "Unbound" if no data is entered or "Databound" if it is linked to a data source.

```
public class ListControlDesigner : System.Web.UI.Design.ControlDesigner, System.Web.UI.Design.IDataSourceProvider {
// Public Constructors
  public ListControlDesigner( );
// Public Instance Properties
  public string DataMember{set; get; }
  public string DataSource{set; get; }
  public string DataTextField{set; get; }
  public string DataValueField{set; get; }
// Public Instance Methods
```

```
public override string GetDesignTimeHtml();                          // overrides System.Web.UI.Design.ControlDesigner
public IEnumerable GetResolvedSelectedDataSource();           // implements System.Web.UI.Design.IDataSourceProvider
public object GetSelectedDataSource();                        // implements System.Web.UI.Design.IDataSourceProvider
public override void Initialize(System.ComponentModel.IComponent component);
                                                                     // overrides System.Web.UI.Design.ControlDesigner
public override void OnComponentChanged(object source,
    System.ComponentModel.Design.ComponentChangedEventArgs ce);  // overrides System.Web.UI.Design.ControlDesigner
public virtual void OnDataSourceChanged();
// Protected Instance Methods
protected override void PreFilterProperties(System.Collections.IDictionary properties);
                                                                     // overrides System.Web.UI.Design.ControlDesigner
}
```

Hierarchy   System.Object → System.ComponentModel.Design.ComponentDesigner(System.Compo-
                 nentModel.Design.IDesigner, System.IDisposable, System.ComponentModel.Design.
                 IDesignerFilter) → System.Web.UI.Design.HtmlControlDesigner → System.Web.UI.Design.
                 ControlDesigner → ListControlDesigner(System.Web.UI.Design.IDataSourceProvider)

ListItemsCollectionEditor

System.Web.UI.Design.WebControls (system.design.dll)   class

This class is a System.Drawing.Design.UITypeEditor that provides a graphical interface for
adding list items and configuring their properties at design time. It's used to configure
the Items property for controls such as System.Web.UI.WebControls.CheckBoxList, System.Web.UI.
WebControls.RadioButtonList, and System.Web.UI.WebControls.ListBox.

```
public class ListItemsCollectionEditor : System.ComponentModel.Design.CollectionEditor {
// Public Constructors
public ListItemsCollectionEditor(Type type);
// Protected Instance Methods
protected override bool CanSelectMultipleInstances();    // overrides System.ComponentModel.Design.CollectionEditor
}
```

Hierarchy   System.Object → System.Drawing.Design.UITypeEditor → System.ComponentModel.
                 Design.CollectionEditor → ListItemsCollectionEditor

PanelDesigner   disposable

System.Web.UI.Design.WebControls (system.design.dll)   class

This class provides the design-time representation for the System.Web.UI.WebControls.Panel
control. The design-time view corresponds closely with the runtime view, except it
adds a thin border to make the panel control's size and position clearly visible.

```
public class PanelDesigner : System.Web.UI.Design.ReadWriteControlDesigner {
// Public Constructors
public PanelDesigner();
// Protected Instance Methods
protected override void MapPropertyToStyle(string propName, object varPropValue);
                                                                     // overrides System.Web.UI.Design.ReadWriteControlDesigner
protected override void OnBehaviorAttached();                 // overrides System.Web.UI.Design.ReadWriteControlDesigner
}
```

Hierarchy   System.Object → System.ComponentModel.Design.ComponentDesigner(System.Compo-
nentModel.Design.IDesigner, System.IDisposable, System.ComponentModel.Design.
IDesignerFilter) → System.Web.UI.Design.HtmlControlDesigner → System.Web.UI.Design.
ControlDesigner → System.Web.UI.Design.ReadWriteControlDesigner → PanelDesigner

RegexEditorDialog   marshal by reference, disposable

System.Web.UI.Design.WebControls (system.design.dll)   class

This class works in conjunction with the RegexTypeEditor to provide a dialog box for
editing regular expressions at design time.

```
public class RegexEditorDialog : System.Windows.Forms.Form {
// Public Constructors
  public RegexEditorDialog(System.ComponentModel.ISite site);
// Public Instance Properties
  public string RegularExpression{set; get; }
// Protected Instance Methods
  protected void cmdHelp_Click(object sender, EventArgs e);
  protected void cmdOK_Click(object sender, EventArgs e);
  protected void cmdTestValidate_Click(object sender, EventArgs args);
  protected override void Dispose(bool disposing);                    // overrides System.Windows.Forms.Form
  protected void lstStandardExpressions_SelectedIndexChanged(object sender, EventArgs e);
  protected void RegexTypeEditor_Activated(object sender, EventArgs e);
  protected void txtExpression_TextChanged(object sender, EventArgs e);
}
```

Hierarchy   System.Object → System.MarshalByRefObject → System.ComponentModel.Compo-
nent(System.ComponentModel.IComponent, System.IDisposable) → System.Windows.
Forms.Control(System.Windows.Forms.IOleControl, System.Windows.Forms.IOleObject,
System.Windows.Forms.IOleInPlaceObject, System.Windows.Forms.IOleInPlaceActiveObject,
System.Windows.Forms.IOleWindow, System.Windows.Forms.IViewObject, System.
Windows.Forms.IViewObject2, System.Windows.Forms.IPersist, System.Windows.Forms.
IPersistStreamInit, System.Windows.Forms.IPersistPropertyBag, System.Windows.Forms.
IPersistStorage, System.Windows.Forms.IQuickActivate, System.ComponentModel.ISynchro-
nizeInvoke, System.Windows.Forms.IWin32Window) → System.Windows.Forms.
ScrollableControl → System.Windows.Forms.ContainerControl(System.Windows.Forms.
IContainerControl) → System.Windows.Forms.Form → RegexEditorDialog

RegexTypeEditor

System.Web.UI.Design.WebControls (system.design.dll)   class

This class is a System.Drawing.Design.UITypeEditor that provides a graphical interface for
configuring the ValidationExpression for the System.Web.UI.WebControls.RegularExpressionValidator
control. It works in conjunction with the RegexEditorDialog to provide a window that
allows you to enter new regular expressions or choose from a list of common options.

```
public class RegexTypeEditor : System.Drawing.Design.UITypeEditor {
// Public Constructors
  public RegexTypeEditor( );
// Public Instance Methods
```

```
public override object EditValue(System.ComponentModel.ITypeDescriptorContext context,
    IServiceProvider provider, object value);            // overrides System.Drawing.Design.UITypeEditor
public override UITypeEditorEditStyle GetEditStyle(System.ComponentModel.ITypeDescriptorContext context);
                                                          // overrides System.Drawing.Design.UITypeEditor
}
```

Hierarchy   System.Object → System.Drawing.Design.UITypeEditor → RegexTypeEditor

RepeaterDesigner   disposable

System.Web.UI.Design.WebControls (system.design.dll)   class

This class provides the design-time representation for the System.Web.UI.WebControls.Repeater control. The design-time view shows headings and other static content, but not data-bound items. If no templates are entered, the control displays the message "Switch to HTML view to edit the control's templates."

```
public class RepeaterDesigner : System.Web.UI.Design.ControlDesigner, System.Web.UI.Design.IDataSourceProvider {
// Public Constructors
  public RepeaterDesigner( );
// Public Instance Properties
  public string DataMember{set; get; }
  public string DataSource{set; get; }
// Protected Instance Properties
  protected bool TemplatesExist{get; }
// Public Instance Methods
  public override string GetDesignTimeHtml( );                     // overrides System.Web.UI.Design.ControlDesigner
  public IEnumerable GetResolvedSelectedDataSource( );          // implements System.Web.UI.Design.IDataSourceProvider
  public object GetSelectedDataSource( );                       // implements System.Web.UI.Design.IDataSourceProvider
  public override void Initialize(System.ComponentModel.IComponent component);
                                                                // overrides System.Web.UI.Design.ControlDesigner
  public override void OnComponentChanged(object source,
    System.ComponentModel.Design.ComponentChangedEventArgs ce);  // overrides System.Web.UI.Design.ControlDesigner
  public virtual void OnDataSourceChanged( );
// Protected Instance Methods
  protected override void Dispose( bool disposing);             // overrides System.Web.UI.Design.HtmlControlDesigner
  protected IEnumerable GetDesignTimeDataSource(System.Collections.IEnumerable selectedDataSource,
    int minimumRows);
  protected IEnumerable GetDesignTimeDataSource(int minimumRows);
  protected override string GetEmptyDesignTimeHtml( );          // overrides System.Web.UI.Design.ControlDesigner
  protected override string GetErrorDesignTimeHtml(Exception e);  // overrides System.Web.UI.Design.ControlDesigner
  protected override void PreFilterProperties(System.Collections.IDictionary properties);
                                                                // overrides System.Web.UI.Design.ControlDesigner
}
```

Hierarchy   System.Object → System.ComponentModel.Design.ComponentDesigner(System.Compo-
                     nentModel.Design.IDesigner, System.IDisposable, System.ComponentModel.Design.
                     IDesignerFilter) → System.Web.UI.Design.HtmlControlDesigner → System.Web.UI.Design.
                     ControlDesigner → RepeaterDesigner(System.Web.UI.Design.IDataSourceProvider)

TableCellsCollectionEditor

System.Web.UI.Design.WebControls (system.design.dll)   class

This class is a System.Drawing.Design.UITypeEditor that provides a graphical interface for adding System.Web.UI.WebControls.TableCell objects to a System.Web.UI.WebControls.TableRow at design time. The same window also allows you to configure System.Web.UI.WebControls.Table-Cell properties. This designer is accessed through the TableRowsCollectionEditor.

```
public class TableCellsCollectionEditor : System.ComponentModel.Design.CollectionEditor {
// Public Constructors
  public TableCellsCollectionEditor( Type type);
// Protected Instance Methods
  protected override bool CanSelectMultipleInstances( );        // overrides System.ComponentModel.Design.CollectionEditor
  protected override object CreateInstance( Type itemType);     // overrides System.ComponentModel.Design.CollectionEditor
}
```

Hierarchy   System.Object → System.Drawing.Design.UITypeEditor → System.ComponentModel.
                      Design.CollectionEditor → TableCellsCollectionEditor

TableDesigner   disposable

System.Web.UI.Design.WebControls (system.design.dll)   class

This class provides the design-time representation of the System.Web.UI.WebControls.Table control. This closely resembles the runtime representation, except when the table is empty (in which case dummy data is used) or if you use code to modify the table programmatically before it is displayed.

```
public class TableDesigner : System.Web.UI.Design.ControlDesigner {
// Public Constructors
  public TableDesigner( );
// Public Instance Methods
  public override string GetDesignTimeHtml( );         // overrides System.Web.UI.Design.ControlDesigner
  public override string GetPersistInnerHtml( );       // overrides System.Web.UI.Design.ControlDesigner
}
```

Hierarchy   System.Object → System.ComponentModel.Design.ComponentDesigner(System.Compo-
                      nentModel.Design.IDesigner, System.IDisposable, System.ComponentModel.Design.
                      IDesignerFilter) → System.Web.UI.Design.HtmlControlDesigner → System.Web.UI.Design.
                      ControlDesigner → TableDesigner

TableRowsCollectionEditor

System.Web.UI.Design.WebControls (system.design.dll)   class

This class is a System.Drawing.Design.UITypeEditor that provides a graphical interface for adding System.Web.UI.WebControls.TableRow objects to a System.Web.UI.WebControls.Table at design time. The same window also allows you to configure System.Web.UI.WebControls.TableRow properties.

```
public class TableRowsCollectionEditor : System.ComponentModel.Design.CollectionEditor {
// Public Constructors
  public TableRowsCollectionEditor( Type type);
```

```
// Protected Instance Methods
    protected override bool CanSelectMultipleInstances( );     // overrides System.ComponentModel.Design.CollectionEditor
    protected override object CreateInstance( Type itemType);     // overrides System.ComponentModel.Design.CollectionEditor
}
```

Hierarchy System.Object → System.Drawing.Design.UITypeEditor → System.ComponentModel.
Design.CollectionEditor → TableRowsCollectionEditor

XmlDesigner   disposable

System.Web.UI.Design.WebControls (system.design.dll)   class

This class provides the design-time representation for the System.Web.UI.WebControls.Xml
control. The design-time view shows the default message "Use this control to perform
XSL transforms" rather than the actual XML content.

```
public class XmlDesigner : System.Web.UI.Design.ControlDesigner {
// Public Constructors
    public XmlDesigner( );
// Public Instance Methods
    public override string GetDesignTimeHtml( );                    // overrides System.Web.UI.Design.ControlDesigner
    public override void Initialize(System.ComponentModel.IComponent component);
                                                                    // overrides System.Web.UI.Design.ControlDesigner
// Protected Instance Methods
    protected override void Dispose( bool disposing);               // overrides System.Web.UI.Design.
HtmlControlDesigner
    protected override string GetEmptyDesignTimeHtml( );            // overrides System.Web.UI.Design.ControlDesigner
}
```

Hierarchy System.Object → System.ComponentModel.Design.ComponentDesigner(System.Compo-
nentModel.Design.IDesigner, System.IDisposable, System.ComponentModel.Design.
IDesignerFilter) → System.Web.UI.Design.HtmlControlDesigner → System.Web.UI.Design.
ControlDesigner → XmlDesigner

39

The System.Web.UI. HtmlControls Namespace

The System.Web.UI.HtmlControls namespace includes classes for HTML server controls. HTML server controls are ASP.NET controls that raise events on the server and provide a simple object model that allows you to set some basic properties. Unlike web controls, which are found in the System.Web.UI.WebControls namespace, each HTML server control corresponds directly to an HTML element like <textarea> or <input>. Web controls are generally preferred in ASP.NET development because they are abstracted away from the low-level HTML details and they provide a richer object model with many more events, sophisticated data binding, automatic state management, and validation controls. HTML server controls are most often used when upgrading existing ASP pages. A standard HTML element can be converted into an HTML server control by adding the attribute runat="server" in the tag. This makes it extremely simple to convert a static HTML page into a dynamic page that allows controls to be manipulated as objects during postbacks.

All controls in this namespace derive from HtmlControl. This class provides basic functionality, including a name/value collection of attributes and CSS style properties. In addition, controls that require both an opening and closing tag inherit from HtmlContainerControl. This class adds a HtmlContainerControl.InnerText and HtmlContainer-Control.InnerHtml property which allow you to access the text contained inside the tag. HTML elements that don't have corresponding classes can be represented by the HtmlGenericControl class. Note that only button and hyperlink controls trigger server postbacks. Many controls provide a ServerChanged event, which won't fire after a control is modified until a postback occurs.

To understand all the available attributes and CSS properties, you may want to refer to an HTML reference. There are many excellent HTML references on the web, or you can refer to O'Reilly's *HTML & XHTML: The Definitive Guide* by Chuck Musciano and Bill Kennedy.

Figure 39-1 shows the types in this namespace.

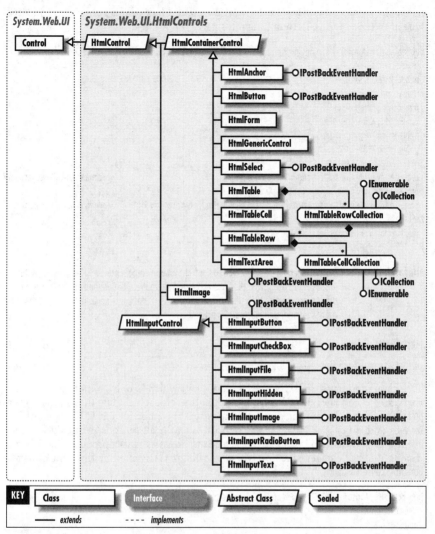

Figure 39-1. The System.Web.UI.HtmlControls namespace

HtmlAnchor

disposable

System.Web.UI.HtmlControls (system.web.dll)   class

This class represents the <A> anchor tag in HTML, which provides a hyperlink. The linked text is contained inside the tag and can be accessed through the InnerHtml property. You can also programmatically change the linked page (HRef), the target frame (Target), and the window title for the target (Title). Even if the HRef property is not set, you can handle the ServerClick event and use a Response.Redirect statement to load a different page. The HtmlAnchor control also supports data binding to the HRef and InnerHtml properties.

You can use an anchor tag to mark a bookmark in a page, in which case you set the Name property but not the HRef property. In this case, you don't need to include any text

inside the tag, as in <a Name="TopicName"/>. To make a link to this bookmark, add #Topic-
Name at the end of the URL requesting this page.

```
public class HtmlAnchor : HtmlContainerControl, System.Web.UI.IPostBackEventHandler {
// Public Constructors
  public HtmlAnchor( );
// Public Instance Properties
  public string HRef{set; get; }
  public string Name{set; get; }
  public string Target{set; get; }
  public string Title{set; get; }
// Protected Instance Methods
  protected override void OnPreRender(EventArgs e);                      // overrides System.Web.UI.Control
  protected virtual void OnServerClick(EventArgs e);
  protected override void RenderAttributes(System.Web.UI.HtmlTextWriter writer);      // overrides HtmlContainerControl
// Events
  public event EventHandler ServerClick;
}
```

Hierarchy   System.Object → System.Web.UI.Control(System.ComponentModel.IComponent, System.
                    IDisposable, System.Web.UI.IParserAccessor, System.Web.UI.IDataBindingsAccessor) →
                    HtmlControl(System.Web.UI.IAttributeAccessor) → HtmlContainerControl → HtmlAn-
                    chor(System.Web.UI.IPostBackEventHandler)

HtmlButton   disposable

System.Web.UI.HtmlControls (system.web.dll)   class

This class represents the HTML 4.0 <button> tag, which is only supported in Internet
Explorer 4.0 and later. It differs from other button types, including the standard HtmlInputButton control, because it can be composed from embedded HTML elements like
images and other ASP.NET server controls. As with all buttons, it provides a click
event that you can handle directly (HtmlInputButton.ServerClick) and a property that lets you
disable automatic page validation when a postback is triggered by this control (HtmlIn-
putButton.CausesValidation).

```
public class HtmlButton : HtmlContainerControl, System.Web.UI.IPostBackEventHandler {
// Public Constructors
  public HtmlButton( );
// Public Instance Properties
  public bool CausesValidation{set; get; }
// Protected Instance Methods
  protected override void OnPreRender( EventArgs e);                      // overrides System.Web.UI.Control
  protected virtual void OnServerClick( EventArgs e);
  protected override void RenderAttributes(System.Web.UI.HtmlTextWriter writer);      // overrides HtmlContainerControl
// Events
  public event EventHandler ServerClick;
}
```

Hierarchy   System.Object → System.Web.UI.Control(System.ComponentModel.IComponent, System.
                    IDisposable, System.Web.UI.IParserAccessor, System.Web.UI.IDataBindingsAccessor) →
                    HtmlControl(System.Web.UI.IAttributeAccessor) → HtmlContainerControl → Html-
                    Button(System.Web.UI.IPostBackEventHandler)

HtmlContainerControl

System.Web.UI.HtmlControls (system.web.dll)   abstract class

This abstract class provides functionality for all HTML server controls that require closing tags. For example, an HtmlAnchor control must always be closed (<a>Text</a> and <a/> are valid anchor tags, but <a> alone is not). An HtmlImage control, on the other hand, does not need a closing tag.

Every control that requires a closing tag has the ability to contain text. This information is provided through the InnerText and InnerHtml properties. Both properties retrieve all the content between the opening and closing control tag. The difference is that InnerText automatically encodes and decodes special characters into their corresponding HTML entities. For example, if you set the InnerText property to Hello, the < and > symbols are converted to the HTML equivalents < and >. This instructs the browser to display Hello as plain text. However, if you set the InnerHtml property to Hello, the < and > symbols will be interpreted as HTML markup tags and the word "Hello" will be displayed in bold.

```
public abstract class HtmlContainerControl : HtmlControl {
// Public Constructors
   public HtmlContainerControl( );
   public HtmlContainerControl( string tag);
// Public Instance Properties
   public virtual string InnerHtml{set; get; }
   public virtual string InnerText{set; get; }
// Protected Instance Methods
   protected override ControlCollection CreateControlCollection( );            // overrides HtmlControl
   protected override void LoadViewState( object savedState);          // overrides System.Web.UI.Control
   protected override void Render(System.Web.UI.HtmlTextWriter writer);        // overrides HtmlControl
   protected override void RenderAttributes(System.Web.UI.HtmlTextWriter writer);   // overrides HtmlControl
   protected virtual void RenderEndTag( System.Web.UI.HtmlTextWriter writer);
}
```

Hierarchy   System.Object → System.Web.UI.Control(System.ComponentModel.IComponent, System.
                IDisposable, System.Web.UI.IParserAccessor, System.Web.UI.IDataBindingsAccessor) →
                HtmlControl(System.Web.UI.IAttributeAccessor) → HtmlContainerControl

Subclasses   HtmlAnchor, HtmlButton, HtmlForm, HtmlGenericControl, HtmlSelect, HtmlTable, HtmlTable-
                Cell, HtmlTableRow, HtmlTextArea

HtmlControl

System.Web.UI.HtmlControls (system.web.dll)   abstract class

This is the base class for all HTML server controls. It includes basic functionality—like the Disabled property, which you can use to make a control read-only, and the TagName property, which identifies the HTML tag that underlies this control (for example, "div" or "a").

Additionally, you can set and retrieve various other properties through the weakly typed Attributes collection, which contains a name/value collection of all the attributes applied to a tag. You can add a new attribute by assigning to it, as in MyText. Attributes["onblur"]="javascript:alert('Focus lost!');";. This statement, which adds a client-side

JavaScript event through an attribute, is the equivalent of using the tag <input type="text" id="MyText" onblur="javascript:alert('Focus lost!');" runat="server"/>. Some attributes may be provided as properties in the derived class. Another dictionary collection, Style, allows you to specify CSS properties for a tag (as in MyText.Style["width"] = "120px").

(Refer to *Cascading Style Sheets: The Definitive Guide* (O'Reilly) for more information on different HTML and CSS tag elements.)

```
public abstract class HtmlControl : System.Web.UI.Control, System.Web.UI.IAttributeAccessor {
// Public Constructors
  public HtmlControl( );
  public HtmlControl( string tag);
// Public Instance Properties
  public AttributeCollection Attributes{get; }
  public bool Disabled{set; get; }
  public CssStyleCollection Style{get; }
  public virtual string TagName{get; }
// Protected Instance Properties
  protected override bool ViewStateIgnoresCase{get; }                    // overrides System.Web.UI.Control
// Protected Instance Methods
  protected override ControlCollection CreateControlCollection( );       // overrides System.Web.UI.Control
  protected override void Render(System.Web.UI.HtmlTextWriter writer);   // overrides System.Web.UI.Control
  protected virtual void RenderAttributes(System.Web.UI.HtmlTextWriter writer);
  protected virtual void RenderBeginTag(System.Web.UI.HtmlTextWriter writer);
}
```

Hierarchy   System.Object → System.Web.UI.Control(System.ComponentModel.IComponent, System. IDisposable, System.Web.UI.IParserAccessor, System.Web.UI.IDataBindingsAccessor) → HtmlControl(System.Web.UI.IAttributeAccessor)

Subclasses   HtmlContainerControl, HtmlImage, HtmlInputControl

HtmlForm   disposable

System.Web.UI.HtmlControls (system.web.dll)   class

This class represents the HTML <form> tag, which is used as a container for other input controls. All ASP.NET Server Controls that post back to the server must be contained in an HtmlForm tag. The properties of this control shouldn't be changed. The Method property (set to "post") is particularly important. If modified, you may not be able to use the built-in postback and control state management services provided by ASP.NET.

```
public class HtmlForm : HtmlContainerControl {
// Public Constructors
  public HtmlForm( );
// Public Instance Properties
  public string Enctype{set; get; }
  public string Method{set; get; }
  public virtual string Name{set; get; }
  public string Target{set; get; }
// Protected Instance Methods
  protected override void OnInit( EventArgs e);                          // overrides System.Web.UI.Control
```

```
protected override void Render(System.Web.UI.HtmlTextWriter output);              // overrides HtmlContainerControl
protected override void RenderAttributes(System.Web.UI.HtmlTextWriter writer);      // overrides HtmlContainerControl
protected override void RenderChildren(System.Web.UI.HtmlTextWriter writer);        // overrides System.Web.UI.Control
}
```

Hierarchy   System.Object → System.Web.UI.Control(System.ComponentModel.IComponent, System.
              IDisposable, System.Web.UI.IParserAccessor, System.Web.UI.IDataBindingsAccessor) →
              HtmlControl(System.Web.UI.IAttributeAccessor) → HtmlContainerControl → HtmlForm

HtmlGenericControl   disposable

System.Web.UI.HtmlControls (system.web.dll)   class

This class is used for HTML elements that are not directly represented by other
controls in this namespace (including <span>, <div>, and <body>). The primary use of
the HtmlGenericControl is usually to set or modify attributes and styles, using the Attributes
and Style properties inherited from HtmlControl. Note that the TagName property can be
modified, allowing you to change the tag programmatically before the page is rendered
as HTML and sent to the client browser.

```
public class HtmlGenericControl : HtmlContainerControl {
// Public Constructors
  public HtmlGenericControl( );
  public HtmlGenericControl( string tag);
// Public Instance Properties
  public string TagName{set; get; }                                              // overrides HtmlControl
}
```

Hierarchy   System.Object → System.Web.UI.Control(System.ComponentModel.IComponent, System.
              IDisposable, System.Web.UI.IParserAccessor, System.Web.UI.IDataBindingsAccessor) →
              HtmlControl(System.Web.UI.IAttributeAccessor) → HtmlContainerControl →
              HtmlGenericControl

HtmlImage   disposable

System.Web.UI.HtmlControls (system.web.dll)   class

This class represents the HTML <img> tag, which is used to display a picture file specified by a URL. You can set various properties for this control, including the image file
(Src), and the alignment and size of the picture. The Alt property specifies the alternate
text, which will appear in place of the image if it cannot be downloaded, and may be
displayed as a tooltip over a successfully downloaded image in uplevel browsers.

```
public class HtmlImage : HtmlControl {
// Public Constructors
  public HtmlImage( );
// Public Instance Properties
  public string Align{set; get; }
  public string Alt{set; get; }
  public int Border{set; get; }
  public int Height{set; get; }
  public string Src{set; get; }
  public int Width{set; get; }
```

```
    protected override void RenderAttributes(System.Web.UI.HtmlTextWriter writer);          // overrides HtmlControl
}
```

Hierarchy System.Object → System.Web.UI.Control(System.ComponentModel.IComponent, System.
IDisposable, System.Web.UI.IParserAccessor, System.Web.UI.IDataBindingsAccessor) →
HtmlControl(System.Web.UI.IAttributeAccessor) → HtmlImage

HtmlInputButton   disposable

System.Web.UI.HtmlControls (system.web.dll)   class

This class can represent the HTML <input type=button> tag, the <input type=submit> tag,
and the <input type=reset> tag. Reset buttons are used to clear input fields on the current
form and do not trigger a postback. Submit and input buttons in ASP.NET trigger a
postback and provide a ServerClick event that you can use to perform other tasks. Additionally, you can use the CausesValidation property to skip postback page validation when
this button is clicked.

```
public class HtmlInputButton : HtmlInputControl, System.Web.UI.IPostBackEventHandler {
// Public Constructors
    public HtmlInputButton( );
    public HtmlInputButton( string type);
// Public Instance Properties
    public bool CausesValidation{set; get; }
// Protected Instance Methods
    protected override void OnPreRender( EventArgs e);                            // overrides System.Web.UI.Control
    protected virtual void OnServerClick( EventArgs e);
    protected override void RenderAttributes(System.Web.UI.HtmlTextWriter writer);          // overrides HtmlInputControl
// Events
    public event EventHandler ServerClick;
}
```

Hierarchy System.Object → System.Web.UI.Control(System.ComponentModel.IComponent, System.
IDisposable, System.Web.UI.IParserAccessor, System.Web.UI.IDataBindingsAccessor) →
HtmlControl(System.Web.UI.IAttributeAccessor) → HtmlInputControl → HtmlInput-
Button(System.Web.UI.IPostBackEventHandler)

HtmlInputCheckBox   disposable

System.Web.UI.HtmlControls (system.web.dll)   class

This class represents the HTML <input type=checkbox> tag and indicates the user's selection through its Checked property. You can also react to the ServerChange event, which will
fire only after a postback is triggered (for example, by clicking a submit button). Note
that this control does not have an associated text label.

```
public class HtmlInputCheckBox : HtmlInputControl, System.Web.UI.IPostBackDataHandler {
// Public Constructors
    public HtmlInputCheckBox( );
// Public Instance Properties
    public bool Checked{set; get; }
// Protected Instance Methods
```

```
protected override void OnPreRender( EventArgs e);                    // overrides System.Web.UI.Control
protected virtual void OnServerChange( EventArgs e);
// Events
public event EventHandler ServerChange;
}
```

Hierarchy   System.Object → System.Web.UI.Control(System.ComponentModel.IComponent, System.
IDisposable, System.Web.UI.IParserAccessor, System.Web.UI.IDataBindingsAccessor) →
HtmlControl(System.Web.UI.IAttributeAccessor) → HtmlInputControl → HtmlInputCh-
eckBox(System.Web.UI.IPostBackDataHandler)

HtmlInputControl   disposable

System.Web.UI.HtmlControls (system.web.dll)   abstract class

This abstract class provides basic functionality for all controls based on the HTML
<input> tag. The Value property represents the information entered in the control, and
the Type property is a string that identifies the value of the input element's type
attribute (for example, "checkbox" or "text"). By default, the Name property is identical to System.Web.UI.Control.UniqueID, although it can be used to group together related
HtmlInputRadioButton controls with different identifiers.

```
public abstract class HtmlInputControl : HtmlControl {
// Public Constructors
    public HtmlInputControl(string type);
// Public Instance Properties
    public virtual string Name{set; get; }
    public string Type{get; }
    public virtual string Value{set; get; }
// Protected Instance Methods
    protected override void RenderAttributes(System.Web.UI.HtmlTextWriter writer);    // overrides HtmlControl
}
```

Hierarchy   System.Object → System.Web.UI.Control(System.ComponentModel.IComponent, System.
IDisposable, System.Web.UI.IParserAccessor, System.Web.UI.IDataBindingsAccessor) →
HtmlControl(System.Web.UI.IAttributeAccessor) → HtmlInputControl

Subclasses   HtmlInputButton, HtmlInputCheckBox, HtmlInputFile, HtmlInputHidden, HtmlInputImage,
HtmlInputRadioButton, HtmlInputText

HtmlInputFile   disposable

System.Web.UI.HtmlControls (system.web.dll)   class

This class represents the HTML <input type=file> tag, which allows the user to upload a
binary or text file. This control is rendered as a text box with a paired Browse button.
The Browse button opens a standard file selection dialog box. The chosen file is not
transmitted until the form is posted to the server (usually through a submit button).
You can then add code in the event handler of this button to save or otherwise manipulate the file using the PostedFile property, which provides a System.Web.HttpPostedFile object.

You can use the HtmlInputFile property to specify a comma-separated list of MIME file
types that your control will accept. You can also change the maximum path length for
the filename (MaxLength) and the width of the file path text box (Size). The HtmlForm.Enctype

property of the containing form must be set to **multipart/form-data** to allow file uploads. You can limit the maximum size of file uploads using the **maxRequestLength** setting in the *web.config* file. By default, file uploads larger than 4096 KB will not be allowed.

```
public class HtmlInputFile : HtmlInputControl, System.Web.UI.IPostBackDataHandler {
// Public Constructors
  public HtmlInputFile( );
// Public Instance Properties
  public string Accept{set; get; }
  public int MaxLength{set; get; }
  public HttpPostedFile PostedFile{get; }
  public int Size{set; get; }
  public override string Value{set; get; }                              // overrides HtmlInputControl
// Protected Instance Methods
  protected override void OnPreRender( EventArgs e);                    // overrides System.Web.UI.Control
}
```

Hierarchy   System.Object → System.Web.UI.Control(System.ComponentModel.IComponent, System. IDisposable, System.Web.UI.IParserAccessor, System.Web.UI.IDataBindingsAccessor) → HtmlControl(System.Web.UI.IAttributeAccessor) → HtmlInputControl → HtmlInput-File(System.Web.UI.IPostBackDataHandler)

HtmlInputHidden   disposable

System.Web.UI.HtmlControls (system.web.dll)   class

This class represents the HTML <input type=hidden> tag, which allows you to store hidden information that will be sent with all postbacks. This technique is commonly used to store information without using cookies or session state. ASP.NET automatically uses a hidden input field to preserve the contents of server controls that have the System.Web.UI.Control.EnableViewState property set to True.

You can also react to the ServerChange event. Because the hidden input field will be changed only through code on the server, this event will fire immediately in response to changes implemented by your code.

```
public class HtmlInputHidden : HtmlInputControl, System.Web.UI.IPostBackDataHandler {
// Public Constructors
  public HtmlInputHidden( );
// Protected Instance Methods
  protected override void OnPreRender( EventArgs e);                    // overrides System.Web.UI.Control
  protected virtual void OnServerChange( EventArgs e);
// Events
  public event EventHandler ServerChange;
}
```

Hierarchy   System.Object → System.Web.UI.Control(System.ComponentModel.IComponent, System. IDisposable, System.Web.UI.IParserAccessor, System.Web.UI.IDataBindingsAccessor) → HtmlControl(System.Web.UI.IAttributeAccessor) → HtmlInputControl → HtmlIn-putHidden(System.Web.UI.IPostBackDataHandler)

HtmlInputImage

System.Web.UI.HtmlControls (system.web.dll)   class

This class represents the HTML <input type=image> element, which creates a graphical button. Unlike HtmlButton controls, HtmlInputImage controls are supported on all standard browsers. This class includes many of the same properties as HtmlImage, such as settings for alignment. It also includes the alternate text and Src, which specifies the file used for the button image. As with all button controls, it provides a click event you can handle directly (ServerClick) and a property that lets you disable automatic page validation when a postback is triggered by this control (CausesValidation).

```
public class HtmlInputImage : HtmlInputControl, System.Web.UI.IPostBackDataHandler, System.Web.UI.
IPostBackEventHandler {
// Public Constructors
  public HtmlInputImage( );
// Public Instance Properties
  public string Align{set; get; }
  public string Alt{set; get; }
  public int Border{set; get; }
  public bool CausesValidation{set; get; }
  public string Src{set; get; }
// Protected Instance Methods
  protected override void OnPreRender( EventArgs e);              // overrides System.Web.UI.Control
  protected virtual void OnServerClick(
    System.Web.UI.ImageClickEventArgs e);
  protected override void RenderAttributes(                       // overrides HtmlInputControl
    System.Web.UI.HtmlTextWriter writer);
// Events
  public event ImageClickEventHandler ServerClick;
}
```

Hierarchy   System.Object → System.Web.UI.Control(System.ComponentModel.IComponent, System.
                       IDisposable, System.Web.UI.IParserAccessor, System.Web.UI.IDataBindingsAccessor) →
                       HtmlControl(System.Web.UI.IAttributeAccessor) → HtmlInputControl → HtmlInputI-
                       mage(System.Web.UI.IPostBackDataHandler, System.Web.UI.IPostBackEventHandler)

HtmlInputRadioButton

System.Web.UI.HtmlControls (system.web.dll)   class

This class represents the HTML <input type=radio> tag. The Checked property indicates whether the radio button is selected. If you set the Name property of more than one radio button to the same value, you form a group that allows only one option to be selected at a time. Note that this control does not have any associated text.

```
public class HtmlInputRadioButton : HtmlInputControl, System.Web.UI.IPostBackDataHandler {
// Public Constructors
  public HtmlInputRadioButton( );
// Public Instance Properties
  public bool Checked{set; get; }
  public override string Name{set; get; }                         // overrides HtmlInputControl
  public override string Value{set; get; }                        // overrides HtmlInputControl
```

```
// Protected Instance Methods
  protected override void OnPreRender( EventArgs e);                              // overrides System.Web.UI.Control
  protected virtual void OnServerChange( EventArgs e);
  protected override void RenderAttributes(System.Web.UI.HtmlTextWriter writer);  // overrides HtmlInputControl
// Events
  public event EventHandler ServerChange;
}
```

Hierarchy   System.Object → System.Web.UI.Control(System.ComponentModel.IComponent, System.
IDisposable, System.Web.UI.IParserAccessor, System.Web.UI.IDataBindingsAccessor) →
HtmlControl(System.Web.UI.IAttributeAccessor) → HtmlInputControl → HtmlInputRa-
dioButton(System.Web.UI.IPostBackDataHandler)

HtmlInputText   disposable

System.Web.UI.HtmlControls (system.web.dll)   class

This class represents the HTML <input type=text> or <input type=password> tag, which allow
the user to enter a single line of text. If you use the password type, the user's input will
be masked with the "*" character for display purposes.

Text entered in this control is provided in the Value property. You can specify the width
of the textbox by using the Size property and the maximum number of allowed characters by using MaxLength. You can also react to the ServerChange event, which will fire only
after a postback is triggered (for example, when the user clicks a submit button).

```
public class HtmlInputText : HtmlInputControl, System.Web.UI.IPostBackDataHandler {
// Public Constructors
  public HtmlInputText( );
  public HtmlInputText( string type);
// Public Instance Properties
  public int MaxLength{set; get; }
  public int Size{set; get; }
  public override string Value{set; get; }                                        // overrides HtmlInputControl
// Protected Instance Methods
  protected override void OnPreRender(EventArgs e);                               // overrides System.Web.UI.Control
  protected virtual void OnServerChange(EventArgs e);
  protected override void RenderAttributes(System.Web.UI.HtmlTextWriter writer);  // overrides HtmlInputControl
// Events
  public event EventHandler ServerChange;
}
```

Hierarchy   System.Object → System.Web.UI.Control(System.ComponentModel.IComponent, System.
IDisposable, System.Web.UI.IParserAccessor, System.Web.UI.IDataBindingsAccessor) →
HtmlControl(System.Web.UI.IAttributeAccessor) → HtmlInputControl → HtmlInput-
Text(System.Web.UI.IPostBackDataHandler)

HtmlSelect   disposable

System.Web.UI.HtmlControls (system.web.dll)   class

This class represents the HTML <select> tag, which allows the user to choose an option
from a drop-down list box. To add an item to the list, use the Add() method of the Items
property. The HtmlSelect control also supports data binding to its Items property.

To retrieve the currently selected item, you can use SelectedIndex property to find the ordinal number of the chosen item (-1 if no selection has been made), or the Value property to retrieve the text of the selected item. If you have set Multiple to True, more than one item may be selected and only the first item will be returned by the SelectedIndex and Value properties. Instead, you will have to iterate through the Items collection and check the System.Web.UI.WebControls.ListItem.Selected property for each one.

You can also react to the ServerChange event, which will fire only after a postback is triggered (for example, when the user clicks a submit button).

```
public class HtmlSelect : HtmlContainerControl, System.Web.UI.IPostBackDataHandler {
// Public Constructors
  public HtmlSelect( );
// Public Instance Properties
  public virtual string DataMember{set; get; }
  public virtual object DataSource{set; get; }
  public virtual string DataTextField{set; get; }
  public virtual string DataValueField{set; get; }
  public override string InnerHtml{set; get; }                                   // overrides HtmlContainerControl
  public override string InnerText{set; get; }                                   // overrides HtmlContainerControl
  public ListItemCollection Items{get; }
  public bool Multiple{set; get; }
  public string Name{set; get; }
  public virtual int SelectedIndex{set; get; }
  public int Size{set; get; }
  public string Value{set; get; }
// Protected Instance Properties
  protected virtual int[ ] SelectedIndices{get; }
// Protected Instance Methods
  protected override void AddParsedSubObject( object obj);                       // overrides System.Web.UI.Control
  protected virtual void ClearSelection( );
  protected override ControlCollection CreateControlCollection( );               // overrides HtmlContainerControl
  protected override void LoadViewState( object savedState);                     // overrides HtmlContainerControl
  protected override void OnDataBinding(EventArgs e);                            // overrides System.Web.UI.Control
  protected override void OnPreRender(EventArgs e);                             // overrides System.Web.UI.Control
  protected virtual void OnServerChange(EventArgs e);
  protected override void RenderAttributes(System.Web.UI.HtmlTextWriter writer); // overrides HtmlContainerControl
  protected override void RenderChildren(System.Web.UI.HtmlTextWriter writer);   // overrides System.Web.UI.Control
  protected override object SaveViewState( );                                    // overrides System.Web.UI.Control
  protected virtual void Select( int[ ] selectedIndices);
  protected override void TrackViewState( );                                     // overrides System.Web.UI.Control
// Events
  public event EventHandler ServerChange;
}
```

Hierarchy   System.Object → System.Web.UI.Control(System.ComponentModel.IComponent, System. IDisposable, System.Web.UI.IParserAccessor, System.Web.UI.IDataBindingsAccessor) → HtmlControl(System.Web.UI.IAttributeAccessor) → HtmlContainerControl → HtmlSelect(System.Web.UI.IPostBackDataHandler)

HtmlTable

System.Web.UI.HtmlControls (system.web.dll)   class

This class provides a powerful way to access the HTML <table> element. You can also use it to dynamically generate an HTML table by adding HtmlTableRow objects to the Rows collection and adding HtmlTableCell objects to each row. Programmatically created tables must be recreated with every postback.

Most other properties for the HtmlTable class correspond to formatting options, including the background color (BgColor), alignment (Align), and dimensions (Height and Width). You can also set values in pixels for the width of the border around the table (Border), the spacing between cells (CellSpacing), and the spacing between cell borders and content (CellPadding).

```
public class HtmlTable : HtmlContainerControl {
// Public Constructors
    public HtmlTable( );
// Public Instance Properties
    public string Align{set; get; }
    public string BgColor{set; get; }
    public int Border{set; get; }
    public string BorderColor{set; get; }
    public int CellPadding{set; get; }
    public int CellSpacing{set; get; }
    public string Height{set; get; }
    public override string InnerHtml{set; get; }              // overrides HtmlContainerControl
    public override string InnerText{set; get; }              // overrides HtmlContainerControl
    public virtual HtmlTableRowCollection Rows{get; }
    public string Width{set; get; }
// Protected Instance Methods
    protected override ControlCollection CreateControlCollection( );    // overrides HtmlContainerControl
    protected override void RenderChildren(System.Web.UI.HtmlTextWriter writer);    // overrides System.Web.UI.Control
    protected override void RenderEndTag(System.Web.UI.HtmlTextWriter writer);    // overrides HtmlContainerControl
}
```

Hierarchy   System.Object → System.Web.UI.Control(System.ComponentModel.IComponent, System. IDisposable, System.Web.UI.IParserAccessor, System.Web.UI.IDataBindingsAccessor) → HtmlControl(System.Web.UI.IAttributeAccessor) → HtmlContainerControl → HtmlTable

HtmlTableCell

System.Web.UI.HtmlControls (system.web.dll)   class

This class represents individual <td> (table data) and <th> (table header) elements contained in an HTML table row. The InnerHtml and InnerText properties allow you to access the content stored in an individual cell. Most other properties are used to fine-tune the appearance of a particular cell. You can set NoWrap to configure whether or not the contents in a cell will wrap and RowSpan and ColSpan to specify that a cell should span the specified number of columns or rows.

```
public class HtmlTableCell : HtmlContainerControl {
// Public Constructors
    public HtmlTableCell( );
```

```
  public HtmlTableCell( string tagName);
// Public Instance Properties
  public string Align{set; get; }
  public string BgColor{set; get; }
  public string BorderColor{set; get; }
  public int ColSpan{set; get; }
  public string Height{set; get; }
  public bool NoWrap{set; get; }
  public int RowSpan{set; get; }
  public string VAlign{set; get; }
  public string Width{set; get; }
// Protected Instance Methods
  protected override void RenderEndTag(System.Web.UI.HtmlTextWriter writer);        // overrides HtmlContainerControl
}
```

Hierarchy   System.Object → System.Web.UI.Control(System.ComponentModel.IComponent, System.
                 IDisposable, System.Web.UI.IParserAccessor, System.Web.UI.IDataBindingsAccessor) →
                 HtmlControl(System.Web.UI.IAttributeAccessor) → HtmlContainerControl → HtmlTableCell

Returned By   HtmlTableCellCollection.this

Passed To   HtmlTableCellCollection.{Add( ), Insert( ), Remove( )}

HtmlTableCellCollection

System.Web.UI.HtmlControls (system.web.dll)   sealed class

This collection of HtmlTableCell objects is used by the Cells property of the HtmlTableRow
class.

```
public sealed class HtmlTableCellCollection : ICollection, IEnumerable {
// Public Instance Properties
  public int Count{get; }                                                         // implements ICollection
  public bool IsReadOnly{get; }
  public bool IsSynchronized{get; }                                               // implements ICollection
  public object SyncRoot{get; }                                                   // implements ICollection
  public HtmlTableCell this[ int index ]{get; }
// Public Instance Methods
  public void Add(HtmlTableCell cell);
  public void Clear( );
  public void CopyTo( Array array, int index);                                    // implements ICollection
  public IEnumerator GetEnumerator( );                                            // implements IEnumerable
  public void Insert(int index, HtmlTableCell cell);
  public void Remove(HtmlTableCell cell);
  public void RemoveAt (int index);
}
```

Returned By   HtmlTableRow.Cells

HtmlTableRow

System.Web.UI.HtmlControls (system.web.dll)   class

This class represents an individual `<tr>` table row element in an HTML table. Each table row contains a group of HtmlTableCell objects, which is provided through the Cells property. Most other properties are used for fine-tuning the appearance of a row.

```
public class HtmlTableRow : HtmlContainerControl {
// Public Constructors
  public HtmlTableRow( );
// Public Instance Properties
  public string Align{set; get; }
  public string BgColor{set; get; }
  public string BorderColor{set; get; }
  public virtual HtmlTableCellCollection Cells{get; }
  public string Height{set; get; }
  public override string InnerHtml{set; get; }                    // overrides HtmlContainerControl
  public override string InnerText{set; get; }                    // overrides HtmlContainerControl
  public string VAlign{set; get; }
// Protected Instance Methods
  protected override ControlCollection CreateControlCollection( );    // overrides HtmlContainerControl
  protected override void RenderChildren(System.Web.UI.HtmlTextWriter writer);  // overrides System.Web.UI.Control
  protected override void RenderEndTag(System.Web.UI.HtmlTextWriter writer);    // overrides HtmlContainerControl
}
```

Hierarchy   System.Object → System.Web.UI.Control(System.ComponentModel.IComponent, System. IDisposable, System.Web.UI.IParserAccessor, System.Web.UI.IDataBindingsAccessor) → HtmlControl(System.Web.UI.IAttributeAccessor) → HtmlContainerControl → HtmlTableRow

Returned By   HtmlTableRowCollection.this

Passed To   HtmlTableRowCollection.{Add( ), Insert( ), Remove( )}

HtmlTableRowCollection

System.Web.UI.HtmlControls (system.web.dll)   sealed class

This collection of HtmlTableRow objects is used by the Rows property of the HtmlTable class.

```
public sealed class HtmlTableRowCollection : ICollection, IEnumerable {
// Public Instance Properties
  public int Count{get; }                                         // implements ICollection
  public bool IsReadOnly{get; }
  public bool IsSynchronized{get; }                               // implements ICollection
  public object SyncRoot{get; }                                   // implements ICollection
  public HtmlTableRow this[ int index ]{get; }
// Public Instance Methods
  public void Add( HtmlTableRow row);
  public void Clear( );
  public void CopyTo(Array array, int index);                     // implements ICollection
  public IEnumerator GetEnumerator( );                            // implements IEnumerable
  public void Insert(int index, HtmlTableRow row);
```

```
    public void Remove(HtmlTableRow row);
    public void RemoveAt(int index);
}
```

Returned By   HtmlTable.Rows

HtmlTextArea   disposable

System.Web.UI.HtmlControls (system.web.dll)   class

This class represents the HTML <textarea> tag, which allows the user to enter multiple lines of text. Text entered in this control is provided in the Value property. You can specify the size of the text box by using the Rows property and the Cols property (the character width). Both default to -1 to indicate that a standard size will be used. You can also react to the ServerChange event, which will fire only after a postback is triggered (for example, when a user clicks a submit button).

```
public class HtmlTextArea : HtmlContainerControl, System.Web.UI.IPostBackDataHandler {
// Public Constructors
    public HtmlTextArea( );
// Public Instance Properties
    public int Cols{set; get; }
    public virtual string Name{set; get; }
    public int Rows{set; get; }
    public string Value{set; get; }
// Protected Instance Methods
    protected override void AddParsedSubObject( object obj);                    // overrides System.Web.UI.Control
    protected override void OnPreRender( EventArgs e);                          // overrides System.Web.UI.Control
    protected virtual void OnServerChange( EventArgs e);
    protected override void RenderAttributes(System.Web.UI.HtmlTextWriter writer);   // overrides HtmlContainerControl
// Events
    public event EventHandler ServerChange;
}
```

Hierarchy   System.Object → System.Web.UI.Control(System.ComponentModel.IComponent, System. IDisposable, System.Web.UI.IParserAccessor, System.Web.UI.IDataBindingsAccessor) → HtmlControl(System.Web.UI.IAttributeAccessor) → HtmlContainerControl → HtmlTextArea(System.Web.UI.IPostBackDataHandler)

40

The System.Web.UI. MobileControls Namespace

The System.Web.UI.MobileControls namespace includes the ASP.NET mobile controls. Many of these classes closely resemble the web form controls in the System.Web.UI. WebControls namespace. However, there are two key differences. First of all, because mobile devices typically use lighter-weight browsers that don't offer rich client features like JavaScript and Dynamic HTML, the mobile controls can only offer a subset of the web control functionality. Also, because mobile controls need to render to different types of markup (like cHTML, HTML, and WML), each mobile control needs the support of a set of control adapters. You'll find the control adapters for each control in the System.Web.UI.MobileControls.Adapters namespace. Figures 40-1 through 40-5 show the types in this namespace.

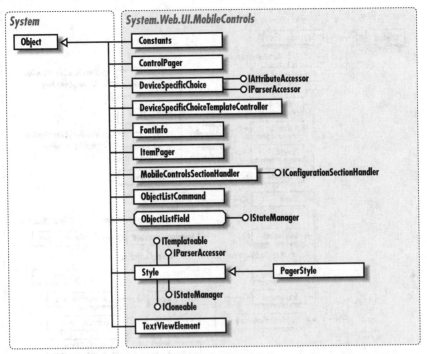

Figure 40-1. Some types from the System.Web.UI.MobileControls namespace

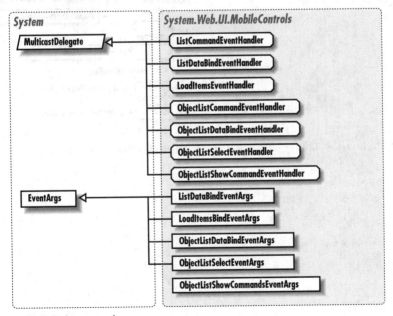

Figure 40-2. Delegates and event arguments

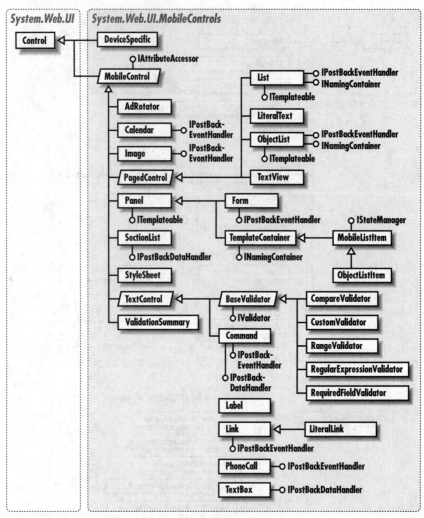

Figure 40-3. Controls from the System.Web.UI.MobileControls namespace

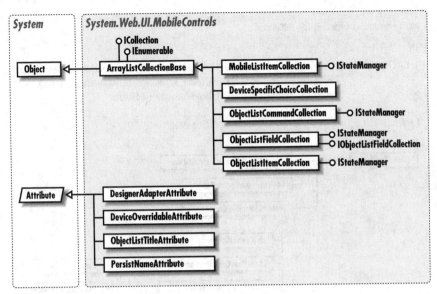

Figure 40-4. Attributes and collections

AdRotator

.NET 1.1, disposable

System.Web.UI.MobileControls (system.web.mobile.dll)   class

The AdRotator control allows you display a randomly selected image on a mobile page. Every time the page is refreshed, a new image will be selected from the list specified in the associated XML configuration file (referenced by the AdvertisementFile property). The AdRotator works in almost exactly the same manner as the full-scale ASP.NET System.Web. UI.WebControls.AdRotator web control, using the same XML configuration file format, and raising the same AdCreated event (which allows you to update other parts of the mobile page to correspond with the dynamically selected advertisement). The only significant difference is the addition of the ImageKey property, which allows you to specify an alternate image URL. For example, if you set ImageKey to ImageUrl1, ASP.NET will render the image specified by the <ImageUrl1> element in the randomly selected advertisement, instead of the image specified by the default <ImageUrl> element. This gives you the flexibility to create mobile pages that support multiple different devices, each of which may require a different image format, by adding multiple custom image URLs.

```
public class AdRotator : MobileControl {
// Public Constructors
  public AdRotator( );
// Public Instance Properties
  public string AdvertisementFile{set; get; }
  public string ImageKey{set; get; }
  public string KeywordFilter{set; get; }
  public string NavigateUrlKey{set; get; }
// Protected Instance Methods
  protected virtual AdRotator CreateWebAdRotator( );
  protected virtual void OnAdCreated(System.Web.UI.WebControls.AdCreatedEventArgs e);
  protected override void Render(System.Web.UI.HtmlTextWriter writer);                // overrides MobileControl
```

```
// Events
    public event AdCreatedEventHandler AdCreated;
}
```

Hierarchy   System.Object → System.Web.UI.Control(System.ComponentModel.IComponent, System.
                 IDisposable, System.Web.UI.IParserAccessor, System.Web.UI.IDataBindingsAccessor) →
                 MobileControl(System.Web.UI.IAttributeAccessor) → AdRotator

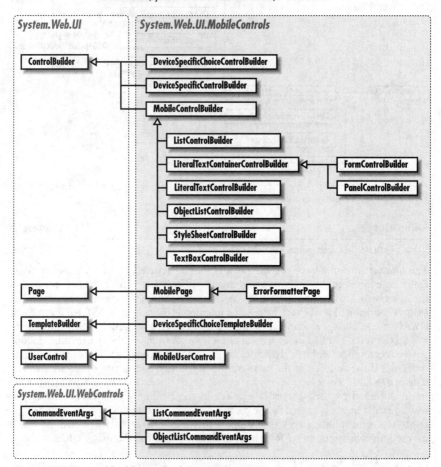

Figure 40-5. Control builders and other types

Alignment   serializable

System.Web.UI.MobileControls (system.web.mobile.dll)   enum

The Alignment enumeration is used to set the horizontal positioning of an item on its
parent container, such as a panel or form. Every mobile control supports this option
through the base MobileControl.Alignment property. For example, you can use this property
to set an image so it aligns to the right side of a form. If you use the value NotSet the
alignment is inherited from the control's style or, if the style is not defined, from the
control's parent control.

```
public enum Alignment {
  NotSet = 0,
  Left = 1,
  Center = 2,
  Right = 3
}
```

Hierarchy	System.Object → System.ValueType → System.Enum(System.IComparable, System.IFormattable, System.IConvertible) → Alignment
Returned By	MobileControl.Alignment, Style.Alignment
Passed To	MobileControl.Alignment, Style.Alignment

ArrayListCollectionBase .NET 1.1

System.Web.UI.MobileControls (system.web.mobile.dll)   class

Defines a basic collection that is extended by classes like ObjectListCommandCollection and DeviceSpecificChoiceCollection. It is not intended for direct use in ASP.NET applications.

```
public class ArrayListCollectionBase : ICollection, IEnumerable {
// Public Instance Properties
  public int Count{get; }                                              // implements ICollection
  public bool IsReadOnly{get; }
  public bool IsSynchronized{get; }                                    // implements ICollection
  public object SyncRoot{get; }                                        // implements ICollection
// Protected Instance Properties
  protected ArrayList Items{set; get; }
// Public Instance Methods
  public void CopyTo( Array array, int index);                         // implements ICollection
  public IEnumerator GetEnumerator( );                                 // implements IEnumerable
}
```

Subclasses	DeviceSpecificChoiceCollection, MobileListItemCollection, ObjectListCommandCollection, ObjectListFieldCollection, ObjectListItemCollection

BaseValidator .NET 1.1, disposable

System.Web.UI.MobileControls (system.web.mobile.dll)   abstract class

This abstract class is the basis for all mobile validation controls, and it plays the same role as the System.Web.UI.WebControls.BaseValidator class in a full-blown ASP.NET web form, with some minor limitations and the ability for device-specific support. The BaseValidator class includes a Validate() method, which does not return a value, but updates the IsValid property. When using validation controls on a mobile page, you should check the MobilePage.IsValid property. This value will only be True if all validation controls on the page have successfully validated their input.

The ControlToValidate property specifies the control that a validator will verify. The ASP.NET mobile controls that support validation include the TextBox (in which case the TextBox.Text property is validated) and the SelectionList control (in which case the SelectionList.SelectedIndex property is validated). You can create custom controls that can participate in validation using the System.Web.UI.ValidationPropertyAttribute attribute.

The ErrorMessage property specifies the message that will be displayed in the validation control if validation fails, although this text can be overridden by changing the validation control's Text property. The ErrorMessage will also appear in a page's ValidationSummary control, if present on the page. By default, ASP.NET will not render any output for a control if it is not visible. This means that space will not be allocated for a validation control unless validation fails. The Display property allows you to allocate space for a validation control by specifying System.Web.UI.WebControls.ValidatorDisplay.Static, which may be required if your validation control is in a table. You can also set this property to System. Web.UI.WebControls.ValidatorDisplay.None to specify that no validation message will be displayed in the control, although one will still be shown in the ValidationSummary control, if used.

```
public abstract class BaseValidator : TextControl, System.Web.UI.IValidator {
// Protected Constructorsprotected BaseValidator( );
// Public Instance Properties
   public string ControlToValidate{set; get; }
   public ValidatorDisplay Display{set; get; }
   public string ErrorMessage{set; get; }                          // implements System.Web.UI.IValidator
   public bool IsValid{set; get; }                                 // implements System.Web.UI.IValidator
   public override string StyleReference{set; get; }               // overrides MobileControl
   public override int VisibleWeight{get; }                        // overrides MobileControl
// Public Instance Methods
   public void Validate( );                                        // implements System.Web.UI.IValidator
// Protected Instance Methods
   protected void CheckControlValidationProperty(string name, string propertyName);
   protected virtual bool ControlPropertiesValid( );
   protected virtual BaseValidator CreateWebValidator( );
   protected abstract bool EvaluateIsValid( );
   protected override void OnInit(EventArgs e);                    // overrides MobileControl
   protected override void OnPreRender(EventArgs e);               // overrides MobileControl
}
```

Hierarchy   System.Object → System.Web.UI.Control(System.ComponentModel.IComponent, System. IDisposable, System.Web.UI.IParserAccessor, System.Web.UI.IDataBindingsAccessor) → MobileControl(System.Web.UI.IAttributeAccessor) → TextControl → BaseValidator(System. Web.UI.IValidator)

Subclasses   CompareValidator, CustomValidator, RangeValidator, RegularExpressionValidator, RequiredFieldValidator

Returned By   System.Web.UI.MobileControls.Adapters.HtmlValidatorAdapter.Control, System.Web.UI. MobileControls.Adapters.WmlValidatorAdapter.Control

BooleanOption   serializable

System.Web.UI.MobileControls (system.web.mobile.dll)   enum

The BooleanOption values are used to set style options (predominantly, the FontInfo.Bold and FontInfo.Italic properties used with mobile controls). If you use the value NotSet, the font attributes are inherited from the control's style or, if the style is not defined, from the control's parent control.

```
public enum BooleanOption {
  False = 0,
  True = 1,
  NotSet = -1
}
```

Hierarchy   System.Object → System.ValueType → System.Enum(System.IComparable, System.IFor-
mattable, System.IConvertible) → BooleanOption

Returned By   FontInfo.{Bold, Italic}

Passed To   FontInfo.{Bold, Italic}

Calendar

.NET 1.1, disposable

System.Web.UI.MobileControls (system.web.mobile.dll)   class

The Calendar mobile control wraps a full-blown System.Web.UI.WebControls.Calendar web
control instance, and provides a subset of its functionality (depending on the capabilities of the mobile device). The mobile Calendar class provides most of the same
properties, including the SelectionChanged event, the SelectedDate and SelectedDates properties,
and numerous other display-related properties. The SelectionMode property determines
what type of selections are allowed for the calendar (day, week, or month). The Calendar
does not expose other properties specific to HTML rendering, but you can access the
underlying System.Web.UI.WebControls.Calendar web control through the WebCalendar property
and modify these settings directly. Keep in mind, however, that these settings will not
apply when the calendar is rendered to cHTML or WML. In this case, the full calendar
cannot be shown, and a multiple-screen "wizard-like" calendar control will be used
instead.

```
public class Calendar : MobileControl, System.Web.UI.IPostBackEventHandler {
// Public Constructors
  public Calendar( );
// Public Instance Properties
  public string CalendarEntryText{set; get; }
  public FirstDayOfWeek FirstDayOfWeek{set; get; }
  public DateTime SelectedDate{set; get; }
  public SelectedDatesCollection SelectedDates{get; }
  public CalendarSelectionMode SelectionMode{set; get; }
  public bool ShowDayHeader{set; get; }
  public DateTime VisibleDate{set; get; }
  public Calendar WebCalendar{get; }
// Public Instance Methods
  public void RaiseSelectionChangedEvent( );
// Protected Instance Methods
  protected virtual Calendar CreateWebCalendar( );
  protected virtual void OnSelectionChanged( );
// Events
  public event EventHandler SelectionChanged;
}
```

Hierarchy	System.Object → System.Web.UI.Control(System.ComponentModel.IComponent, System. IDisposable, System.Web.UI.IParserAccessor, System.Web.UI.IDataBindingsAccessor) → MobileControl(System.Web.UI.IAttributeAccessor) → Calendar(System.Web.UI. IPostBackEventHandler)
Returned By	System.Web.UI.MobileControls.Adapters.ChtmlCalendarAdapter.Control, System.Web.UI. MobileControls.Adapters.HtmlCalendarAdapter.Control, System.Web.UI.MobileControls. Adapters.WmlCalendarAdapter.Control

Command   .NET 1.1, disposable

System.Web.UI.MobileControls (system.web.mobile.dll)   class

The Command control renders as a command button or a link, depending on the device. Though the style differs depending on the device, the Text will always appear. The Command control plays the same role as the System.Web.UI.WebControls.Button on a full-blown web page, triggering a postback when selected and raising a server-side Click event. In addition, the ItemCommand will fire with additional information about the command in a System.Web.UI.WebControls.CommandEventArgs object. This information includes the System.Web.UI. WebControls.Button.CommandName and System.Web.UI.WebControls.Button.CommandArgument properties of the System.Web.UI.WebControls.Button. The ItemCommand event is useful when you are creating composite or data-bound controls that include buttons, because the event will is bubbled up to parent controls. If you do not need this functionality, you can simply handle the Click event. If the mobile device supports softkeys, you can set the label that will be used for the corresponding softkey through the SoftkeyLabel property. Otherwise, the Text property will be used for the label if it less than nine characters (or the label "Go" will be displayed if it is not).

You can set the CausesValidation property to determine whether page validation will be performed when the command is selected, before the Click or ItemCommand events fire.

```
public class Command : TextControl, System.Web.UI.IPostBackEventHandler, System.Web.UI.IPostBackDataHandler {
// Public Constructors
  public Command( );
// Public Instance Properties
  public bool CausesValidation{set; get; }
  public string CommandArgument{set; get; }
  public string CommandName{set; get; }
  public CommandFormat Format{set; get; }
  public string ImageUrl{set; get; }
  public string SoftkeyLabel{set; get; }
// Protected Instance Methods
  protected override bool IsFormSubmitControl( );                           // overrides MobileControl
  protected virtual void OnClick( EventArgs e);
  protected virtual void OnItemCommand( System.Web.UI.WebControls.CommandEventArgs e)
  protected override void OnPreRender( EventArgs e);                        // overrides MobileControl
// Events
  public event EventHandler Click;
  public event CommandEventHandler ItemCommand;
}
```

Hierarchy	System.Object → System.Web.UI.Control(System.ComponentModel.IComponent, System. IDisposable, System.Web.UI.IParserAccessor, System.Web.UI.IDataBindingsAccessor) →

MobileControl(System.Web.UI.IAttributeAccessor) → TextControl → Command(System.
Web.UI.IPostBackEventHandler, System.Web.UI.IPostBackDataHandler)

Returned By   System.Web.UI.MobileControls.Adapters.HtmlCommandAdapter.Control, System.Web.UI.
MobileControls.Adapters.WmlCommandAdapter.Control

CommandFormat   serializable

System.Web.UI.MobileControls (system.web.mobile.dll)   enum

You can set the Command.Format property to a value from this enumeration, to indicate
whether the command should be rendered as a hyperlink (Link) or button (Button).

```
public enum CommandFormat {
  Button = 0,
  Link = 1
}
```

Hierarchy   System.Object → System.ValueType → System.Enum(System.IComparable, System.IFor-
mattable, System.IConvertible) → CommandFormat

Returned By   Command.Format

Passed To   Command.Format

CompareValidator   .NET 1.1, disposable

System.Web.UI.MobileControls (system.web.mobile.dll)   class

This CompareValidator compares the input control (ControlToValidate) to a specified value
(ValueToCompare) or a value in another control (ControlToCompare). Both values will be
converted to the data type specified by Type before they are compared. Note that if you
set both ValueToCompare and ControlToCompare, the latter will take precedence.

The Operator property specifies the expression that must be met in order for validation
to succeed. In other words, ControlToValidate <Operator> ControlToCompare must be true. The
compare validator works the same as the System.Web.UI.WebControls.CompareValidator used with
full-fledged Web Forms.

```
public class CompareValidator : BaseValidator {
// Public Constructors
  public CompareValidator( );
// Public Instance Properties
  public string ControlToCompare{set; get; }
  public ValidationCompareOperator Operator{set; get; }
  public ValidationDataType Type{set; get; }
  public string ValueToCompare{set; get; }
// Protected Instance Methods
  protected override bool ControlPropertiesValid( );              // overrides BaseValidator
  protected override BaseValidator CreateWebValidator( );         // overrides BaseValidator
  protected override bool EvaluateIsValid( );                     // overrides BaseValidator
}
```

Hierarchy   System.Object → System.Web.UI.Control(System.ComponentModel.IComponent, System. IDisposable, System.Web.UI.IParserAccessor, System.Web.UI.IDataBindingsAccessor) → MobileControl(System.Web.UI.IAttributeAccessor) → TextControl → BaseValidator(System. Web.UI.IValidator) → CompareValidator

Constants   .NET 1.1

System.Web.UI.MobileControls (system.web.mobile.dll)   class

This class is entirely made up of read-only constants for the mobile page. Controls can make use of these constants when rendering markup.

```
public class Constants {
// Public Constructors
  public Constants( );
// Public Static Fields
  public static readonly string AlternatingItemTemplateTag;              // =AlternatingItemTemplate
  public static readonly string ContentTemplateTag;                      // =ContentTemplate
  public static readonly int DefaultSessionsStateHistorySize;            // =5
  public static readonly string EventArgumentID;                         // =__EA
  public static readonly string EventSourceID;                           // =__ET
  public static readonly string FooterTemplateTag;                       // =FooterTemplate
  public static readonly string FormIDPrefix;                            // =#
  public static readonly string HeaderTemplateTag;                       // =HeaderTemplate
  public static readonly string ItemDetailsTemplateTag;                  // =ItemDetailsTemplate
  public static readonly string ItemTemplateTag;                         // =ItemTemplate
  public static readonly string LabelTemplateTag;                        // =LabelTemplate
  public static readonly string OptimumPageWeightParameter;              // =optimumPageWeight
  public static readonly string PagePrefix;                              // =__PG_
  public static readonly string ScreenCharactersHeightParameter;         // =screenCharactersHeight
  public static readonly string ScriptTemplateTag;                       // =ScriptTemplate
  public static readonly char SelectionListSpecialCharacter;             // =0x0000002A
  public static readonly string SeparatorTemplateTag;                    // =SeparatorTemplate
  public static readonly string SymbolProtocol;                          // =symbol:
  public static readonly string UniqueFilePathSuffixVariable;            // =__ufps=
  public static readonly string UniqueFilePathSuffixVariableWithoutEqual; // =__ufps
}
```

ControlPager   .NET 1.1

System.Web.UI.MobileControls (system.web.mobile.dll)   class

The ControlPager is used by a Form to paginate its contained controls according to the screen dimensions of the client device, provided Form.Paginate is set to True. During the pagination process, the ControlPager is submitted to the PagedControl.PaginateRecursive( ) method of the Form. The ControlPager provides the desired "weight" for the page (Page-Weight) and the remaining space on the page (RemainingWeight). As a rule of thumb, each display line corresponds to 100 units.

```
public class ControlPager {
// Public Constructors
  public ControlPager(Form form, int pageWeight);
// Public Static Fields
```

```
public static readonly int DefaultWeight;                                                    // =100
public static readonly int UseDefaultWeight;                                                 // =-1
// Public Instance Properties
  public int PageCount{set; get; }
  public int PageWeight{get; }
  public int RemainingWeight{set; get; }
// Public Instance Methods
  public ItemPager GetItemPager(MobileControl control, int itemCount, int itemsPerPage, int itemWeight);
  public int GetPage( int weight);
}
```

Passed To   ItemPager.ItemPager( ), MobileControl.PaginateRecursive( )

CustomValidator
.NET 1.1, disposable

System.Web.UI.MobileControls (system.web.mobile.dll)   class

The CustomValidator control allows you to define your own validation routines. A similar task could be performed by writing manual validation code in the click event for a submit button, but using a CustomValidator allows you to create validation code that will run any time the page is validated, and can provide a "vote" used for the MobilePage. IsValid property along with all other validation controls. A CustomValidator can also be easily reused to validate multiple controls.

To provide server-side validation, create an event handler for the ServerValidate event. The string from the input control and the result of the validation is stored in the provided System.Web.UI.WebControls.ServerValidateEventArgs object. In this way, the CompareValidator works exactly the same as the System.Web.UI.WebControls.CustomValidator control, although it doesn't include the ability to define client-side validation logic using a JavaScript function, because few mobile devices would support it.

```
public class CustomValidator : BaseValidator {
// Public Constructors
  public CustomValidator( );
// Protected Instance Methods
  protected override bool ControlPropertiesValid( );                            // overrides BaseValidator
  protected override BaseValidator CreateWebValidator( );                       // overrides BaseValidator
  protected override bool EvaluateIsValid( );                                   // overrides BaseValidator
  protected virtual bool OnServerValidate(string value);
// Events
  public event ServerValidateEventHandler ServerValidate;
}
```

Hierarchy   System.Object → System.Web.UI.Control(System.ComponentModel.IComponent, System. IDisposable, System.Web.UI.IParserAccessor, System.Web.UI.IDataBindingsAccessor) → MobileControl(System.Web.UI.IAttributeAccessor) → TextControl → BaseValidator(System. Web.UI.IValidator) → CustomValidator

DesignerAdapterAttribute .NET 1.1

System.Web.UI.MobileControls (system.web.mobile.dll) class

This attribute is used to associate a control with a specific adapter. You apply this adapter to the control class declaration, and specify the fully-qualified name of the adapter class in the TypeName property.

```
public class DesignerAdapterAttribute : Attribute {
// Public Constructors
  public DesignerAdapterAttribute(string adapterTypeName);
  public DesignerAdapterAttribute(Type adapterType);
// Public Instance Properties
  public virtual string TypeName{get; }
}
```

Hierarchy   System.Object → System.Attribute → DesignerAdapterAttribute

Valid On   Class

DeviceOverridableAttribute obsolete, .NET 1.1

System.Web.UI.MobileControls (system.web.mobile.dll) class

This attribute indicates whether you can override a device adapter.

```
public class DeviceOverridableAttribute : Attribute {
// Public Constructors
  public DeviceOverridableAttribute( );
  public DeviceOverridableAttribute(bool overridable);
// Public Instance Properties
  public bool Overridable{get; }
}
```

Hierarchy   System.Object → System.Attribute → DeviceOverridableAttribute

Valid On   All

DeviceSpecific .NET 1.1, disposable

System.Web.UI.MobileControls (system.web.mobile.dll) class

This class represents the <DeviceSpecific> element in a *.aspx* file, which provides a way to specify conditional control information depending on the target device. A <DeviceSpecific> element contains one or more <Choice> elements, each of which contains attributes that specify how to evaluate the choice against the capabilities of the client device. When the page is loaded at run time, the first matching choice is used.

```
public class DeviceSpecific : System.Web.UI.Control {
// Public Constructors
  public DeviceSpecific( );
// Public Instance Properties
  public DeviceSpecificChoiceCollection Choices{get; }
  public override bool EnableViewState{set; get; }                    // overrides System.Web.UI.Control
```

```
    public bool HasTemplates{get; }
    public MobilePage MobilePage{get; }
    public object Owner{get; }
    public DeviceSpecificChoice SelectedChoice{get; }
    public override bool Visible{set; get; }                              // overrides System.Web.UI.Control
// Public Instance Methods
    public ITemplate GetTemplate(string templateName);
// Protected Instance Methods
    protected override void AddParsedSubObject(object obj);               // overrides System.Web.UI.Control
// Events
    public event EventHandler DataBinding;                                // overrides System.Web.UI.Control
    public event EventHandler Disposed;                                   // overrides System.Web.UI.Control
    public event EventHandler Init;                                       // overrides System.Web.UI.Control
    public event EventHandler Load;                                       // overrides System.Web.UI.Control
    public event EventHandler PreRender;                                  // overrides System.Web.UI.Control
    public event EventHandler Unload;                                     // overrides System.Web.UI.Control
}
```

Hierarchy   System.Object → System.Web.UI.Control(System.ComponentModel.IComponent, System.
              IDisposable, System.Web.UI.IParserAccessor, System.Web.UI.IDataBindingsAccessor) →
              DeviceSpecific

Returned By   MobileControl.DeviceSpecific, Style.DeviceSpecific

Passed To   MobileControl.DeviceSpecific, Style.DeviceSpecific

DeviceSpecificChoice   .NET 1.1

System.Web.UI.MobileControls (system.web.mobile.dll)   class

This class represents the <Choice> element in a *.aspx* file. Each <Choice> element represents a distinct condition (typically corresponding to a different type of client device or
set of client device abilities). When the page is loaded at run time, the first matching
choice is used. For example, you might create a <Choice> element that specifies a Filter
string "WML", which matches an entry in the <deviceFilters> section of the *machine.config*
file. The settings in this choice will only be used if the target device supports WML (and
hasn't matched any previous choice conditions).

```
public class DeviceSpecificChoice : System.Web.UI.IParserAccessor, System.Web.UI.IAttributeAccessor {
// Public Constructors
    public DeviceSpecificChoice( );
// Public Instance Properties
    public string Argument{set; get; }
    public IDictionary Contents{get; }
    public string Filter{set; get; }
    public bool HasTemplates{get; }
    public IDictionary Templates{get; }
    public string Xmlns{set; get; }
}
```

Returned By   DeviceSpecific.SelectedChoice, DeviceSpecificChoiceCollection.this

Passed To   DeviceSpecificChoiceCollection.{Add( ), AddAt( ), Remove( )}

DeviceSpecificChoiceCollection

.NET 1.1

System.Web.UI.MobileControls (system.web.mobile.dll)   class

This class represents a collection of <Choice> elements nested in a <DeviceSpecific> in a *.aspx* file.

```
public class DeviceSpecificChoiceCollection : ArrayListCollectionBase {
// Public Instance Properties
  public ArrayList All{get; }
  public DeviceSpecificChoice this[ int index ]{get; }
// Public Instance Methods
  public void Add(DeviceSpecificChoice choice);
  public void AddAt(int index, DeviceSpecificChoice choice);
  public void Clear( );
  public void Remove( DeviceSpecificChoice choice);
  public void RemoveAt( int index);
}
```

Hierarchy   System.Object → ArrayListCollectionBase(System.Collections.ICollection, System.Collections.IEnumerable) → DeviceSpecificChoiceCollection

Returned By   DeviceSpecific.Choices

DeviceSpecificChoiceControlBuilder

.NET 1.1

System.Web.UI.MobileControls (system.web.mobile.dll)   class

This class is used by ASP.NET to parse the <Choice> element in a *.aspx* file class. You do not need to use this class in your own code.

```
public class DeviceSpecificChoiceControlBuilder : System.Web.UI.ControlBuilder {
// Public Constructors
  public DeviceSpecificChoiceControlBuilder( );
// Public Instance Methods
  public override void AppendLiteralString(string text);               // overrides System.Web.UI.ControlBuilder
  public override void AppendSubBuilder(System.Web.UI.ControlBuilder subBuilder);
                                                                       // overrides System.Web.UI.ControlBuilder
  public override Type GetChildControlType(string tagName, System.Collections.IDictionary attributes);
                                                                       // overrides System.Web.UI.ControlBuilder
  public override void Init(System.Web.UI.TemplateParser parser, System.Web.UI.ControlBuilder parentBuilder,
    Type type, string tagName, string id, System.Collections.IDictionary attributes); // overrides System.Web.UI.ControlBuilder
}
```

Hierarchy   System.Object → System.Web.UI.ControlBuilder → DeviceSpecificChoiceControlBuilder

DeviceSpecificChoiceTemplateBuilder

.NET 1.1

System.Web.UI.MobileControls (system.web.mobile.dll)   class

This class is used internally by ASP.NET. You do not need to use this class in your own code.

```
public class DeviceSpecificChoiceTemplateBuilder : System.Web.UI.TemplateBuilder {
// Public Constructors
   public DeviceSpecificChoiceTemplateBuilder( );
// Public Instance Methods
   public override void AppendLiteralString(string text);                    // overrides System.Web.UI.ControlBuilder
   public override void AppendSubBuilder(System.Web.UI.ControlBuilder subBuilder);
                                                                             // overrides System.Web.UI.ControlBuilder
   public override void Init(System.Web.UI.TemplateParser parser, System.Web.UI.ControlBuilder parentBuilder, Type type,
      string tagName, string id, System.Collections.IDictionary attributes);      // overrides System.Web.UI.TemplateBuilder
}
```

Hierarchy   System.Object → System.Web.UI.ControlBuilder → System.Web.UI.Template-
                     Builder(System.Web.UI.ITemplate) → DeviceSpecificChoiceTemplateBuilder

DeviceSpecificChoiceTemplateContainer   .NET 1.1

System.Web.UI.MobileControls (system.web.mobile.dll)   class

This class is used internally by ASP.NET. You do not need to use this class in your
own code.

```
public class DeviceSpecificChoiceTemplateContainer {
// Public Constructors
   public DeviceSpecificChoiceTemplateContainer( );
// Public Instance Properties
   public string Name{set; get; }
   public ITemplate Template{set; get; }
}
```

DeviceSpecificControlBuilder   .NET 1.1

System.Web.UI.MobileControls (system.web.mobile.dll)   class

This class is used by ASP.NET to parse the <DeviceSpecific> element in a .aspx file class.
You do not need to use this class in your own code.

```
public class DeviceSpecificControlBuilder : System.Web.UI.ControlBuilder {
// Public Constructors
   public DeviceSpecificControlBuilder( );
// Public Instance Methods
   public override void AppendLiteralString( string text);                   // overrides System.Web.UI.ControlBuilder
   public override Type GetChildControlType(string tagName,
      System.Collections.IDictionary attributes);                            // overrides System.Web.UI.ControlBuilder
}
```

Hierarchy   System.Object → System.Web.UI.ControlBuilder → DeviceSpecificControlBuilder

ErrorFormatterPage   .NET 1.1, disposable

System.Web.UI.MobileControls (system.web.mobile.dll)   class

This class is used to support the error handling with mobile pages. If an unhandled
exception is thrown from a mobile page, and no custom error page is defined in the
web.config file, and the client is not an HTML browser capable of rendering a rich

error page, a terse device-specific message will be returned. To create this message, ASP.NET automatically instantiates an ErrorFormatterPage instance, applies the appropriate data, and renders the result.

```
public class ErrorFormatterPage : MobilePage {
// Public Constructors
  public ErrorFormatterPage( );
// Protected Instance Properties
  protected MobileErrorInfo ErrorInfo{get; }
// Protected Instance Methods
  protected virtual void InitContent( );
  protected override object LoadPageStateFromPersistenceMedium( );      // overrides MobilePage
  protected override void OnInit(EventArgs e);                          // overrides MobilePage
  protected override void SavePageStateToPersistenceMedium(object viewState);  // overrides MobilePage
}
```

Hierarchy   System.Object → System.Web.UI.Control(System.ComponentModel.IComponent, System.
IDisposable, System.Web.UI.IParserAccessor, System.Web.UI.IDataBindingsAccessor) →
System.Web.UI.TemplateControl(System.Web.UI.INamingContainer) → System.Web.UI.
Page(System.Web.IHttpHandler) → MobilePage → ErrorFormatterPage

FontInfo   .NET 1.1

System.Web.UI.MobileControls (system.web.mobile.dll)   class

The FontInfo class provides a subset of the functionality of the System.Web.UI.WebControls.
FontInfo, which represents the font specifications supported by mobile devices. These include the ability to specify font family, italic and bold styles, and the font size (which only supports the limited set of values provided by the FontSize enumeration).

```
public class FontInfo {
// Public Instance Properties
  public BooleanOption Bold{set; get; }
  public BooleanOption Italic{set; get; }
  public string Name{set; get; }
  public FontSize Size{set; get; }
// Public Instance Methods
  public override string ToString( );                                   // overrides object
}
```

Returned By   MobileControl.Font, Style.Font

FontSize   serializable

System.Web.UI.MobileControls (system.web.mobile.dll)   enum

This enumeration defines the supported size options for mobile control fonts. Note that an exact point size cannot be used. If you use the value NotSet for a control, the size will be inherited from the control's style or, if that style is not defined, from the control's parent control.

```
public enum FontSize {
  NotSet = 0,
  Normal = 1,
```

```
    Small = 2,
    Large = 3
}
```

Hierarchy	System.Object → System.ValueType → System.Enum(System.IComparable, System.IFor-mattable, System.IConvertible) → FontSize
Returned By	FontInfo.Size
Passed To	FontInfo.Size

Form
.NET 1.1, disposable

System.Web.UI.MobileControls (system.web.mobile.dll)   class

A Form is the outermost grouping of controls in a mobile page. All mobile controls must be placed inside a form. You can add multiple forms to a page, although only one will be visible at a time. To change the currently displayed form, you can set the ActiveForm property, or you can create a Link control with a Link.NavigateUrl set to the name of the desired form (preceded by the # symbol). Forms cannot be nested (although you can nest one or more Panel controls).

The Form control supports literal text. You can also insert markup tags directly into the literal text of a Form. Supported tags include <a> (anchor), <b> (bold), <i> (italic),
 (line break), and <p> (paragraph). These tags will be rendered in a device-independent manner, which means that a <p> could conceivably be translated into a <br> tag if required by the client device. In order to ensure compatibility across a broad range of devices, all other tags are ignored, and will never affect the control's output.

```
public class Form : Panel, System.Web.UI.IPostBackEventHandler {
// Public Constructors
  public Form( );
// Public Instance Properties
  public string Action{set; get; }
  public override bool BreakAfter{set; get; }                              // overrides Panel
  public Control ControlToPaginate{set; get; }
  public int CurrentPage{set; get; }
  public Panel Footer{get; }
  public Panel Header{get; }
  public FormMethod Method{set; get; }
  public int PageCount{get; }
  public PagerStyle PagerStyle{get; }
  public Panel Script{get; }
  public string Title{set; get; }
// Protected Instance Properties
  protected override bool PaginateChildren{get; }                          // overrides Panel
// Public Instance Methods
  public override void CreateDefaultTemplatedUI(                           // overrides Panelbool doDataBind);
  public IList GetLinkedForms(int optimumPageWeight);
  public virtual bool HasActivateHandler( );
  public virtual bool HasDeactivateHandler( );
  public override void PaginateRecursive( );                               // overrides PanelControlPager pager
// Protected Instance Methods
```

```
protected override void LoadPrivateViewState(object state);              // overrides MobileControl
protected virtual void OnActivate(EventArgs e);
protected override void OnDataBinding(EventArgs e);                       // overrides MobileControl
protected virtual void OnDeactivate(EventArgs e);
protected override void OnInit( EventArgs e);                             // overrides Panel
protected virtual void OnPaginated( EventArgs e);
protected override void OnPreRender( EventArgs e);                        // overrides MobileControl
protected override void Render(System.Web.UI.HtmlTextWriter writer);      // overrides MobileControl
protected override object SavePrivateViewState( );                       // overrides MobileControl
// Events
public event EventHandler Activate;
public event EventHandler Deactivate;
public event EventHandler Paginated;
}
```

Hierarchy   System.Object → System.Web.UI.Control(System.ComponentModel.IComponent, System.
IDisposable, System.Web.UI.IParserAccessor, System.Web.UI.IDataBindingsAccessor) →
MobileControl(System.Web.UI.IAttributeAccessor) → Panel(ITemplateable) →
Form(System.Web.UI.IPostBackEventHandler)

Returned By   System.Web.UI.MobileControls.Adapters.HtmlFormAdapter.Control, System.Web.UI.Mobile-
Controls.Adapters.WmlFormAdapter.Control, System.Web.UI.MobileControls.Adapters.
WmlMobileTextWriter.CurrentForm, MobileControl.{Form, ResolveFormReference( )},
MobilePage.{ActiveForm, GetForm( )}

Passed To   System.Web.UI.MobileControls.Adapters.HtmlPageAdapter.{GetFormUrl( ), IsFormRendered(
), RenderForm( ), RenderPostBackHeader( )}, System.Web.UI.MobileControls.Adapters.
WmlMobileTextWriter.{BeginForm( ), RenderBeginForm( )}, System.Web.UI.MobileControls.
Adapters.WmlPageAdapter.{IsFormRendered( ), RenderForm( )}, ControlPager.ControlPager(
), MobilePage.ActiveForm

FormControlBuilder
                                                                                    .NET 1.1

System.Web.UI.MobileControls (system.web.mobile.dll)   class

The FormControlBuilder class is used internally by ASP.NET. It is created by the page parser
when it encounters a <mobile:Form> tag, and used to process the literal text it contains.

```
public class FormControlBuilder : LiteralTextContainerControlBuilder {
// Public Constructors
  public FormControlBuilder( );
// Public Instance Methods
  public override void AppendSubBuilder(System.Web.UI.ControlBuilder subBuilder);
                                                  // overrides LiteralTextContainerControlBuilder
}
```

Hierarchy   System.Object → System.Web.UI.ControlBuilder → MobileControlBuilder → LiteralText-
ContainerControlBuilder → FormControlBuilder

FormMethod

System.Web.UI.MobileControls (system.web.mobile.dll)   enum

This enumeration is used in conjunction with the Form.Method property to specify how data will be submitted with a form. If supported, you will almost always use Post, which submits information in the body of a request. A Get request, on the other hand, submits data as query string arguments in the URL. This approach may not work with all types of data, and may be subject to length requirements.

```
public enum FormMethod {
  Get = 0,
  Post = 1
}
```

Hierarchy	System.Object → System.ValueType → System.Enum(System.IComparable, System.IFormattable, System.IConvertible) → FormMethod
Returned By	Form.Method
Passed To	Form.Method

IControlAdapter

System.Web.UI.MobileControls (system.web.mobile.dll)   interface

This interface defines the key members that are required for all device-specific control adapters. The System.Web.UI.MobileControls.Adapters namespace includes a set of control adapters for every control in this namespace. For example, the TextBox has a corresponding System.Web.UI.MobileControls.Adapters.ChtmlTextBoxAdapter for rendering cHTML output, a System.Web.UI.MobileControls.Adapters.HtmlTextBoxAdapter for rendering HTML, and a System.Web.UI.MobileControls.Adapters.WmlTextBoxAdapter for rendering WML.

```
public interface IControlAdapter {
// Public Instance Properties
  public MobileControl Control{set; get; }
  public int ItemWeight{get; }
  public MobilePage Page{get; }
  public int VisibleWeight{get; }
// Public Instance Methods
  public void CreateTemplatedUI( bool doDataBind);
  public bool HandlePostBackEvent( string eventArgument);
  public void LoadAdapterState( object state);
  public bool LoadPostData(string postDataKey, System.Collections.Specialized.NameValueCollection postCollection,
      object controlPrivateData, out bool dataChanged);
  public void OnInit( EventArgs e);
  public void OnLoad( EventArgs e);
  public void OnPreRender( EventArgs e);
  public void OnUnload( EventArgs e);
  public void Render( System.Web.UI.HtmlTextWriter writer);
  public object SaveAdapterState( );
}
```

Implemented By IPageAdapter, System.Web.UI.MobileControls.Adapters.ControlAdapter

Returned By MobileControl.Adapter, MobilePage.GetControlAdapter( )

Image .NET 1.1, disposable

System.Web.UI.MobileControls (system.web.mobile.dll) class

The Image control displays the image specified by the ImageUrl property. Because
different mobile devices support different image formats, you will almost always use
device-specific <Choice> elements to ensure that each type of device receives a different
ImageUrl (which will point to a different image format). For example, an image
formatted as a *.gif* file will be displayed on HTML-capable browsers, but will not be
displayed on WML-capable browsers. For WML-capable browsers, you need an image
formatted as a *.wbmp* file. The Image control itself does not provide any ability to
convert images from one format to another, or modify any image characteristics. (For
example, if a client supports only monochrome images, the Image control will not automatically convert a color image to monochrome.)

In some cases, the ImageUrl will not contain the URL for an image, but a scheme that
indicates device-specific information. For example, WML 1.1 phones that support
glyphs recognize the symbol: scheme. On an i-more phone, the ImageUrl "symbol:63726"
maps to a heart icon.

```
public class Image : MobileControl, System.Web.UI.IPostBackEventHandler {
// Public Constructors
  public Image( );
// Public Instance Properties
  public string AlternateText{set; get; }
  public string ImageUrl{set; get; }
  public string NavigateUrl{set; get; }
  public string SoftkeyLabel{set; get; }
}
```

Hierarchy System.Object → System.Web.UI.Control(System.ComponentModel.IComponent, System.
IDisposable, System.Web.UI.IParserAccessor, System.Web.UI.IDataBindingsAccessor) →
MobileControl(System.Web.UI.IAttributeAccessor) → Image(System.Web.UI.
IPostBackEventHandler)

Returned By System.Web.UI.MobileControls.Adapters.HtmlImageAdapter.Control, System.Web.UI.Mobile-
Controls.Adapters.WmlImageAdapter.Control

IObjectListFieldCollection .NET 1.1

System.Web.UI.MobileControls (system.web.mobile.dll) interface

This interface defines the basic members for the ObjectListFieldCollection. It extends the
System.Collections.ICollection interface with the ability to retrieve all fields (both explicitly
defined fields and automatically generated fields).

```
public interface IObjectListFieldCollection : ICollection, IEnumerable {
// Public Instance Properties
  public ObjectListField this[ int index ]{get; }
// Public Instance Methods
```

```
   public ObjectListField[ ] GetAll( );
   public int IndexOf( ObjectListField field);
   public int IndexOf( string fieldIDOrTitle);
}
```

Implemented By   ObjectListFieldCollection

Returned By   ObjectList.AllFields

System.Web.UI.MobileControls (system.web.mobile.dll)   interface

This interface defines the key members that are required for all device-specific page
adapters. Classes like System.Web.UI.MobileControls.Adapters.ChtmlPageAdapter, System.Web.UI.Mobile-
Controls.Adapters.HtmlPageAdapter,   and   System.Web.UI.MobileControls.Adapters.WmlPageAdapter
implement this interface, and render ASP.NET mobile pages into device specific
markup like cHTML, HTML, or WML.

```
public interface IPageAdapter : IControlAdapter {
// Public Instance Properties
   public IList CacheVaryByHeaders{get; }
   public IDictionary CookielessDataDictionary{set; get; }
   public int OptimumPageWeight{get; }
   public MobilePage Page{set; get; }                                    // implements IControlAdapter
   public bool PersistCookielessData{set; get; }
// Public Instance Methods
   public HtmlTextWriter CreateTextWriter(System.IO.TextWriter writer);
   public NameValueCollection DeterminePostBackMode(System.Web.HttpRequest request, string postEventSourceID,
      string postEventArgumentID, System.Collections.Specialized.NameValueCollection baseCollection);
   public bool HandleError(Exception e, System.Web.UI.HtmlTextWriter writer);
   public bool HandlePagePostBackEvent(string eventSource, string eventArgument);
}
```

Implemented By   System.Web.UI.MobileControls.Adapters.{HtmlPageAdapter, WmlPageAdapter}

Returned By   MobilePage.Adapter

ItemPager   .NET 1.1

System.Web.UI.MobileControls (system.web.mobile.dll)   class

The ItemPager is used by controls that have long text length and support internal pagination, such as the List, LiteralText, and ObjectList controls. The ASP.NET rendering ending
creates the ItemPager while paginating a page, using the corresponding ControlPager of the
containing Form.

```
public class ItemPager {
// Public Constructors
   public ItemPager( );
   public ItemPager(ControlPager pager, MobileControl control, int itemCount, int itemsPerPage, int itemWeight);
```

```
// Public Instance Properties
  public int ItemCount{get; }
  public int ItemIndex{get; }
}
```

Returned By   ControlPager.GetItemPager( )

ITemplateable   .NET 1.1

System.Web.UI.MobileControls (system.web.mobile.dll)   interface

This is a marker interface. It includes no members, but it identifies control classes that support templating. Classes that support templating include the List, ObjectList, and Panel.

```
public interface ITemplateable {
// No public or protected members
}
```

Implemented By   List, ObjectList, Panel, Style

Label   .NET 1.1, disposable

System.Web.UI.MobileControls (system.web.mobile.dll)   class

This class represents a label control, which allows you to place text on a page and modify it later using the Text property. The Label control does not support internal paging, and thus must be contained on a single page. If you need to use a text control that supports a large amount of text and provides paging, use the TextView control instead.

```
public class Label : TextControl {
// Public Constructors
  public Label( );
}
```

Hierarchy   System.Object → System.Web.UI.Control(System.ComponentModel.IComponent, System.
IDisposable, System.Web.UI.IParserAccessor, System.Web.UI.IDataBindingsAccessor) →
MobileControl(System.Web.UI.IAttributeAccessor) → TextControl → Label

Link   .NET 1.1, disposable

System.Web.UI.MobileControls (system.web.mobile.dll)   class

The Link control represents a hyperlink to another URL (or another Form on the current page). You specify the URL using the NavigateUrl property. If the URL begins with a number symbol (#), it is interpreted as a pointer to a form on the current page. You can set the display text through the Text property or, if this property is left blank, the NavigateUrl will be used for the display text.

```
public class Link : TextControl, System.Web.UI.IPostBackEventHandler {
// Public Constructors
  public Link( );
// Public Instance Properties
  public string NavigateUrl{set; get; }
```

```
public string SoftkeyLabel{set; get; }
```
// Public Instance Methods
```
public override void AddLinkedForms(System.Collections.IList linkedForms);                    // overrides MobileControl
}
```

Hierarchy	System.Object → System.Web.UI.Control(System.ComponentModel.IComponent, System. IDisposable, System.Web.UI.IParserAccessor, System.Web.UI.IDataBindingsAccessor) → MobileControl(System.Web.UI.IAttributeAccessor) → TextControl → Link(System.Web.UI. IPostBackEventHandler)
Subclasses	LiteralLink
Returned By	System.Web.UI.MobileControls.Adapters.HtmlLinkAdapter.Control, System.Web.UI.Mobile-Controls.Adapters.WmlLinkAdapter.Control

List   .NET 1.1, disposable

System.Web.UI.MobileControls (system.web.mobile.dll)   class

The List control allows you to display a list of static strings or text links. These items can be added declaratively (through the *.aspx* file or configured with the property designer in Visual Studio .NET), or they can be added and examined programmatically through the Items property. This property provides a collection of MobileListItem instances, each of which can define visible text (MobileListItem.Text) and a non-visible value (MobileListItem.Value). In addition, the List control supports data binding. You simply need to set the DataSource property to a valid data source (like an System.Collections.ArrayList, System.Data.DataTable, or System.Data.DataView), and then specify the properties or fields to bind using the DataTextField and DataValueField properties.

You can apply bullets or automatic numbering to the list items using the Decoration property, and you can use the properties inherited from the base PagedControl class to split the list over multiple mobile pages. To specify that the items should be rendered as hyperlinks, set the ItemsAsLinks to True. When the user clicks an item, the ItemCommand event will be fired with information about the source item.

```
public class List : PagedControl, System.Web.UI.INamingContainer, IListControl, ITemplateable,
    System.Web.UI.IPostBackEventHandler {
// Public Constructors
  public List( );
// Public Instance Properties
  public virtual string DataMember{set; get; }
  public virtual object DataSource{set; get; }
  public string DataTextField{set; get; }
  public string DataValueField{set; get; }
  public ListDecoration Decoration{set; get; }
  public bool HasItemCommandHandler{get; }
  public MobileListItemCollection Items{get; }
  public bool ItemsAsLinks{set; get; }
// Protected Instance Properties
  protected override int InternalItemCount{get; }                                             // overrides PagedControl
// Public Instance Methods
  public override void CreateDefaultTemplatedUI(bool doDataBind);                             // overrides MobileControl
  public override void EnsureTemplatedUI( );                                                  // overrides MobileControl
```

```
// Protected Instance Methods
  protected override void AddParsedSubObject( object obj);                          // overrides MobileControl
  protected override void CreateChildControls( );                                   // overrides System.Web.UI.Control
  protected virtual void CreateItems(System.Collections.IEnumerable dataSource);
  protected override void EnsureChildControls( );                                   // overrides System.Web.UI.Control
  protected override void LoadViewState( object savedState);                        // overrides MobileControl
  protected override bool OnBubbleEvent(object sender, EventArgs e);                 // overrides System.Web.UI.Control
  protected override void OnDataBinding( EventArgs e);                              // overrides MobileControl
  protected virtual void OnItemCommand(ListCommandEventArgs e);
  protected virtual void OnItemDataBind(ListDataBindEventArgs e);                   // implements IListControl
  protected override void OnLoadItems(LoadItemsEventArgs e);                        // overrides PagedControl
  protected override void OnPageChange(int oldPageIndex, int newPageIndex);         // overrides PagedControl
  protected override void OnPreRender( EventArgs e);                                // overrides PagedControl
  protected override object SaveViewState( );                                       // overrides MobileControl
  protected override void TrackViewState( );                                        // overrides MobileControl
// Events
  public event ListCommandEventHandler ItemCommand;
  public event ListDataBindEventHandler ItemDataBind;
}
```

Hierarchy   System.Object → System.Web.UI.Control(System.ComponentModel.IComponent, System.
IDisposable, System.Web.UI.IParserAccessor, System.Web.UI.IDataBindingsAccessor) →
MobileControl(System.Web.UI.IAttributeAccessor) → PagedControl → List(System.Web.UI.
INamingContainer, IListControl, ITemplateable, System.Web.UI.IPostBackEventHandler)

Returned By   System.Web.UI.MobileControls.Adapters.HtmlListAdapter.Control, System.Web.UI.Mobile-
Controls.Adapters.WmlListAdapter.Control

ListCommandEventArgs   .NET 1.1

System.Web.UI.MobileControls (system.web.mobile.dll)   class

This custom EventArgs object contains information about the item the user clicked when
the List.ItemCommand event fires. The CommandName property will contain a null reference
(Nothing), while the ListItem identifies the MobileListItem that was clicked.

```
public class ListCommandEventArgs : System.Web.UI.WebControls.CommandEventArgs {
// Public Constructors
  public ListCommandEventArgs(MobileListItem item, object commandSource);
  public ListCommandEventArgs(MobileListItem item, object commandSource,
    System.Web.UI.WebControls.CommandEventArgs originalArgs);
// Protected Static Fields
  protected static readonly string DefaultCommand;                                 // =Default
// Public Instance Properties
  public object CommandSource{get; }
  public MobileListItem ListItem{get; }
}
```

Hierarchy   System.Object → System.EventArgs → System.Web.UI.WebControls.CommandEventArgs
→ ListCommandEventArgs

Passed To   List.OnItemCommand( ), ListCommandEventHandler.{BeginInvoke( ), Invoke( )}

ListCommandEventHandler

.NET 1.1, serializable

System.Web.UI.MobileControls (system.web.mobile.dll)   delegate

This delegate defines the signature required for an event handler of the List.ItemCommand event. This event will fire when any list item is clicked, provided the List.ItemsAsLinks property is True.

```
public delegate void ListCommandEventHandler(object sender, ListCommandEventArgs e);
```

Associated Events List.ItemCommand( )

ListControlBuilder

.NET 1.1

System.Web.UI.MobileControls (system.web.mobile.dll)   class

The ListControlBuilder class is used internally by ASP.NET. It is created by the page parser when it encounters a <mobile:List> or <mobile:SelectionList> tag. It is used to process any contained <mobile:Item> tags that define the initial set of items that will be added to the List or SelectionList.

```
public class ListControlBuilder : MobileControlBuilder {
// Public Constructors
  public ListControlBuilder( );
// Public Instance Methods
  public override Type GetChildControlType(string tagName,
    System.Collections.IDictionary attributes);                    // overrides MobileControlBuilder
}
```

Hierarchy   System.Object → System.Web.UI.ControlBuilder → MobileControlBuilder →
                 ListControlBuilder

ListDataBindEventArgs

.NET 1.1

System.Web.UI.MobileControls (system.web.mobile.dll)   class

This custom EventArgs object contains information provided to methods that handle the List.ItemDataBind event. This information includes the MobileListItem that is being bound (List-Item) and the data item that is being bound to it (DataItem). For example, if you are binding a list to a System.Data.DataTable, the DataItem will return the corresponding System.Data.DataRow object.

```
public class ListDataBindEventArgs : EventArgs {
// Public Constructors
  public ListDataBindEventArgs(MobileListItem item, object dataItem);
// Public Instance Properties
  public object DataItem{get; }
  public MobileListItem ListItem{get; }
}
```

Hierarchy   System.Object → System.EventArgs → ListDataBindEventArgs

Passed To   List.OnItemDataBind( ), ListDataBindEventHandler.{BeginInvoke( ), Invoke( )}, SelectionList.
                 OnItemDataBind( )

ListDataBindEventHandler

.NET 1.1, serializable

System.Web.UI.MobileControls (system.web.mobile.dll)   delegate

This delegate defines the signature required for an event handler of the List.ItemDataBind event. This event will fire every time an item is added from a bound data source, giving you the chance to apply any required formatting to the bound data.

```
public delegate void ListDataBindEventHandler(object sender, ListDataBindEventArgs e);
```

Associated Events List.ItemDataBind( ), SelectionList.ItemDataBind( )

ListDecoration

serializable

System.Web.UI.MobileControls (system.web.mobile.dll)   enum

This enumeration is used in conjunction with the List.Decoration property. It identifies additional formatting that will be applied to the list items, like bullets or automatic numbering.

```
public enum ListDecoration {
  None = 0,
  Bulleted = 1,
  Numbered = 2
}
```

Hierarchy   System.Object → System.ValueType → System.Enum(System.IComparable, System.IFormattable, System.IConvertible) → ListDecoration

Returned By   List.Decoration

Passed To   List.Decoration

ListSelectType

serializable

System.Web.UI.MobileControls (system.web.mobile.dll)   enum

This enumeration is used in conjunction with the SelectionList.IsMultiSelect property. It allows you to define how the list should be rendered. Several styles are supported, depending on the device. If you need multi-select capability, you can use the CheckBox or MultipleSelectionListBox style. If you want a single-select list, you can use DropDown, ListBox, or Radio.

```
public enum ListSelectType {
  DropDown = 0,
  ListBox = 1,
  Radio = 2,
  MultiSelectListBox = 3,
  CheckBox = 4
}
```

Hierarchy   System.Object → System.ValueType → System.Enum(System.IComparable, System.IFormattable, System.IConvertible) → ListSelectType

Returned By	SelectionList.SelectType
Passed To	SelectionList.SelectType

LiteralLink
.NET 1.1, disposable

System.Web.UI.MobileControls (system.web.mobile.dll)   class

This control is created to represent hyperlinks found in the literal text inside a container control (like a Form or Panel). These links will be marked using the anchor tag (<a>). If you want to programmatically interact with a hyperlink on a mobile page, you will use the Link mobile control class instead.

```
public class LiteralLink : Link {
// Public Constructors
  public LiteralLink( );
}
```

Hierarchy	System.Object → System.Web.UI.Control(System.ComponentModel.IComponent, System. IDisposable, System.Web.UI.IParserAccessor, System.Web.UI.IDataBindingsAccessor) → MobileControl(System.Web.UI.IAttributeAccessor) → TextControl → Link(System.Web.UI. IPostBackEventHandler) → LiteralLink

LiteralText
.NET 1.1, disposable

System.Web.UI.MobileControls (system.web.mobile.dll)   class

This control is created to represent literal text found inside a container control (like a Form or Panel). You can use a LiteralText control to programmatically add content to a form, although it is generally more common to use a Label control.

```
public class LiteralText : PagedControl {
// Public Constructors
  public LiteralText( );
// Public Instance Properties
  public string PagedText{get; }
  public string Text{set; get; }
// Protected Instance Properties
  protected override int InternalItemCount{get; }            // overrides PagedControl
  protected override int ItemWeight{get; }                   // overrides PagedControl
}
```

Hierarchy	System.Object → System.Web.UI.Control(System.ComponentModel.IComponent, System. IDisposable, System.Web.UI.IParserAccessor, System.Web.UI.IDataBindingsAccessor) → MobileControl(System.Web.UI.IAttributeAccessor) → PagedControl → LiteralText
Returned By	System.Web.UI.MobileControls.Adapters.HtmlLiteralTextAdapter.Control, System.Web.UI. MobileControls.Adapters.WmlLiteralTextAdapter.Control

LiteralTextContainerControlBuilder

.NET 1.1

System.Web.UI.MobileControls (system.web.mobile.dll)

class

The LiteralTextContainerControlBuilder class is used internally by ASP.NET. It defines basic functionality for parsing controls that can contain literal text, like the Form or Panel. The FormControlBuilder and PanelControlBuilder classes derive from LiteralTextContainerControlBuilder.

```
public class LiteralTextContainerControlBuilder : MobileControlBuilder {
// Public Instance Methods
   public override void AppendLiteralString(string text);                    // overrides System.Web.UI.ControlBuilder
   public override void AppendSubBuilder(System.Web.UI.ControlBuilder subBuilder);
                                                                             // overrides System.Web.UI.ControlBuilder
}
```

Hierarchy	System.Object → System.Web.UI.ControlBuilder → MobileControlBuilder → LiteralTextContainerControlBuilder

Subclasses	FormControlBuilder, PanelControlBuilder

LiteralTextControlBuilder

.NET 1.1

System.Web.UI.MobileControls (system.web.mobile.dll)

class

The LiteralTextControlBuilder class is used internally by ASP.NET. It is created by the page parser to process the literal text in a mobile page that is contained by a container like a Form or Panel.

```
public class LiteralTextControlBuilder : MobileControlBuilder {
// Public Constructors
   public LiteralTextControlBuilder( );
// Public Instance Methods
   public override bool AllowWhitespaceLiterals( );                          // overrides MobileControlBuilder
}
```

Hierarchy	System.Object → System.Web.UI.ControlBuilder → MobileControlBuilder → LiteralTextControlBuilder

LoadItemsEventArgs

.NET 1.1

System.Web.UI.MobileControls (system.web.mobile.dll)

class

This custom EventArgs class provides additional information to methods that handle the PagedControl.LoadItems event (whcih fires when a custom-paginated control requires data). This information includes the ItemIndex (which indicates the first required item), and the ItemCount (which indicates the number of required items). Your code must then prepare this subset of the data, submit it to the control by setting the DataSource property, and call the MobileControl.DataBind( ) to bind the data.

```
public class LoadItemsEventArgs : EventArgs {
// Public Constructors
   public LoadItemsEventArgs( int index, int count);
// Public Instance Properties
   public int ItemCount{get; }
```

```
public int ItemIndex{get; }
}
```

LoadItemsEventHandler   .NET 1.1, serializable

System.Web.UI.MobileControls (system.web.mobile.dll)   delegate

This delegate represents the method that will handle the PagedControl.LoadItems event. This event fires when a control that uses internal pagination requires more data. You can examine the range of data that is being requested by inspecting the LoadItemsEventArgs. ItemIndex and LoadItemsEventArgs.ItemCount properties. You can then prepare this subset of the data, and bind it to the appropriate control.

```
public delegate void LoadItemsEventHandler(object sender, LoadItemsEventArgs e);
```

Associated Events List.LoadItems( ), LiteralText.LoadItems( ), ObjectList.LoadItems( ), PagedControl. LoadItems( ), TextView.LoadItems( )

MobileControl   .NET 1.1, disposable

System.Web.UI.MobileControls (system.web.mobile.dll)   abstract class

All mobile controls derive from the base MobileControl class (which in turn derives from the even more basic System.Web.UI.Control class). When creating your own mobile controls, you can derive from MobileControl or a specific mobile control class. Some of the functionality added by the MobileControl class includes pagination support, basic style settings, and support for device-specific control adapters (specified by the Adapter property).

```
public abstract class MobileControl : System.Web.UI.Control, System.Web.UI.IAttributeAccessor {
// Protected Constructors
  protected MobileControl( );
// Public Instance Properties
  public IControlAdapter Adapter{get; }
  public virtual Alignment Alignment{set; get; }
  public virtual Color BackColor{set; get; }
  public virtual bool BreakAfter{set; get; }
  public StateBag CustomAttributes{get; }
  public DeviceSpecific DeviceSpecific{set; get; }
  public int FirstPage{set; get; }
  public virtual FontInfo Font{get; }
  public virtual Color ForeColor{set; get; }
  public Form Form{get; }
  public virtual bool IsTemplated{get; }
  public int LastPage{set; get; }
  public MobilePage MobilePage{get; }
  public virtual string StyleReference{set; get; }
  public virtual int VisibleWeight{get; }
  public virtual Wrapping Wrapping{set; get; }
```

```
   protected string InnerText{set; get; }
   protected virtual bool PaginateChildren{get; }
   protected internal virtual Style Style{get; }
```
```
   public virtual void AddLinkedForms(System.Collections.IList linkedForms);
   public virtual void CreateDefaultTemplatedUI(bool doDataBind);
   public virtual void EnsureTemplatedUI( );
   public virtual ITemplate GetTemplate(string templateName);
   public bool IsVisibleOnPage(int pageNumber);
   public virtual void PaginateRecursive(ControlPager pager);
   public void RenderChildren(System.Web.UI.HtmlTextWriter writer);          // overrides System.Web.UI.Control
   public Form ResolveFormReference(string formID);
   public string ResolveUrl(string relativeUrl);                             // overrides System.Web.UI.Control
```
```
   protected override void AddedControl(System.Web.UI.Control control, int index);   // overrides System.Web.UI.Control
   protected override void AddParsedSubObject( object obj);                   // overrides System.Web.UI.Control
   protected virtual Style CreateStyle( );
   protected virtual void CreateTemplatedUI(bool doDataBind);
   protected virtual bool IsFormSubmitControl( );
   protected virtual void LoadPrivateViewState(object state);
   protected override void LoadViewState( object savedState);                 // overrides System.Web.UI.Control
   protected override void OnDataBinding( EventArgs e);                       // overrides System.Web.UI.Control
   protected override void OnInit( EventArgs e);                             // overrides System.Web.UI.Control
   protected override void OnLoad( EventArgs e);                             // overrides System.Web.UI.Control
   protected virtual void OnPageChange(int oldPageIndex, int newPageIndex);
   protected override void OnPreRender( EventArgs e);                        // overrides System.Web.UI.Control
   protected virtual void OnRender(System.Web.UI.HtmlTextWriter writer);
   protected override void OnUnload( EventArgs e);                           // overrides System.Web.UI.Control
   protected override void RemovedControl(System.Web.UI.Control control);     // overrides System.Web.UI.Control
   protected override void Render(System.Web.UI.HtmlTextWriter writer);       // overrides System.Web.UI.Control
   protected virtual object SavePrivateViewState( );
   protected override object SaveViewState( );                               // overrides System.Web.UI.Control
   protected override void TrackViewState( );                               // overrides System.Web.UI.Control
}
```

Hierarchy   System.Object → System.Web.UI.Control(System.ComponentModel.IComponent, System.
                   IDisposable, System.Web.UI.IParserAccessor, System.Web.UI.IDataBindingsAccessor) →
                   MobileControl(System.Web.UI.IAttributeAccessor)

Subclasses   AdRotator, Calendar, Image, PagedControl, Panel, SelectionList, StyleSheet, TextControl,
                   ValidationSummary

Returned By   System.Web.UI.MobileControls.Adapters.ControlAdapter.Control, IControlAdapter.Control,
                   Style.Control

Passed To   System.Web.UI.MobileControls.Adapters.ControlAdapter.Control, ControlPager.
                   GetItemPager( ), IControlAdapter.Control, ItemPager.ItemPager( ), MobilePage.
                   {GetControlAdapter( ), GetPrivateViewState( )}

MobileControlBuilder

System.Web.UI.MobileControls (system.web.mobile.dll)   class

The MobileControlBuilder class is used internally by ASP.NET. It defines basic functionality for parsing mobile controls (in other words, reading the markup defined in the *.aspx* file, and using it to generate the appropriate control objects). All the mobile control builders derive from MobileControlBuilder. If you create a control that has it's own custom persistence format, you will have to provide a control builder that can parse your control tags.

The MobileControlBuilder includes basic functionality, like ignoring white space and recognizing <DeviceSpecific> tags. It also applies some rules, enforcing the requirement that forms and style sheets are top-level controls, and that styles can only be defined in style sheets.

```
public class MobileControlBuilder : System.Web.UI.ControlBuilder {
// Public Constructors
   public MobileControlBuilder( );
// Public Instance Methods
   public override bool AllowWhitespaceLiterals( );                    // overrides System.Web.UI.ControlBuilder
   public override Type GetChildControlType(string tagName, System.Collections.IDictionary attributes);
                                                                       // overrides System.Web.UI.ControlBuilder
}
```

Hierarchy   System.Object → System.Web.UI.ControlBuilder → MobileControlBuilder

Subclasses   ListControlBuilder, LiteralTextContainerControlBuilder, LiteralTextControlBuilder, ObjectList-
                    ControlBuilder, StyleSheetControlBuilder, TextBoxControlBuilder

MobileControlsSectionHandler

System.Web.UI.MobileControls (system.web.mobile.dll)   class

This class is used internally by ASP.NET. It reads mobile control information from the <mobileControls> tag, which defines adapter sets that map ASP.NET mobile controls to control adapters. The <mobileControls> tag is place in the <system.web> section of the *web.config* and *machine.config* configuration files.

```
public class MobileControlsSectionHandler : System.Configuration.IConfigurationSectionHandler {
// Public Constructors
   public MobileControlsSectionHandler( );
}
```

MobileListItem

System.Web.UI.MobileControls (system.web.mobile.dll)   class

The MobileListItem pepresents an individual item in a List or SelectionList control. You can iterate through a collection of all the MobileListItem instances in the list using the control's Items collection. In addition, some events (like List.ItemCommand and List.ItemDataBind) provide a MobileListItem instance that identifies the appropriate item in the list.

You can determine whether or not an item is selected using the Selected property. In addition, you can retrieve the text for the list item (Text and Value), and if the item is data-bound, you can retrieve the corresponding data object (DataItem).

```
public class MobileListItem : TemplateContainer, System.Web.UI.IStateManager {
// Public Constructors
  public MobileListItem( );
  public MobileListItem( MobileListItemType itemType);
  public MobileListItem(object dataItem, string text, string value);
  public MobileListItem( string text);
  public MobileListItem( string text, string value);
// Public Instance Properties
  public object DataItem{set; get; }
  public int Index{get; }
  public bool Selected{set; get; }
  public string Text{set; get; }
  public string Value{set; get; }
// Public Static Methods
  public static MobileListItem FromString(string s);
  public static implicit operator MobileListItem(string s);
// Public Instance Methods
  public override bool Equals(object o);                                    // overrides object
  public override int GetHashCode( );                                       // overrides object
  public override string ToString( );                                       // overrides object
// Protected Instance Methods
  protected override bool OnBubbleEvent(object source, EventArgs e);        // overrides System.Web.UI.Control
}
```

Hierarchy   System.Object → System.Web.UI.Control(System.ComponentModel.IComponent, System.
                   IDisposable, System.Web.UI.IParserAccessor, System.Web.UI.IDataBindingsAccessor) →
                   MobileControl(System.Web.UI.IAttributeAccessor) → Panel(ITemplateable) → Template-
                   Container(System.Web.UI.INamingContainer) → MobileListItem(System.Web.UI.
                   IStateManager)

Subclasses   ObjectListItem

Returned By   ListCommandEventArgs.ListItem, ListDataBindEventArgs.ListItem, MobileListItemCollection.
                   {GetAll( ), this}, SelectionList.Selection

Passed To   ListCommandEventArgs.ListCommandEventArgs( ), ListDataBindEventArgs.
                   ListDataBindEventArgs( ), MobileListItemCollection.{Add( ), Contains( ), IndexOf( ), Insert( ),
                   Remove( ), SetAll( )}

MobileListItemCollection   .NET 1.1

System.Web.UI.MobileControls (system.web.mobile.dll)   class

This is a strongly typed collection of MobileListItem instances. It's used to represent the
current list of items in a List or SelectionList control (through the Items property).

```
public class MobileListItemCollection : ArrayListCollectionBase, System.Web.UI.IStateManager {
// Public Constructors
  public MobileListItemCollection( );
  public MobileListItemCollection(System.Collections.ArrayList items);
// Public Instance Properties
  public MobileListItem this[ int index ]{get; }
```

```
// Public Instance Methods
   public void Add(MobileListItem item);
   public virtual void Add( string item);
   public void Clear( );
   public bool Contains(MobileListItem item);
   public MobileListItem[ ] GetAll( );
   public int IndexOf(MobileListItem item);
   public void Insert(int index, MobileListItem item);
   public virtual void Insert( int index, string item);
   public void Remove(MobileListItem item);
   public virtual void Remove(string item);
   public void RemoveAt( int index);
   public void SetAll( MobileListItem[ ] value);
}
```

Hierarchy   System.Object → ArrayListCollectionBase(System.Collections.ICollection, System.Collec-
               tions.IEnumerable) → MobileListItemCollection(System.Web.UI.IStateManager)

Returned By   List.Items, SelectionList.Items

MobileListItemType   serializable

System.Web.UI.MobileControls (system.web.mobile.dll)   enum

When a List or ObjectList control is rendered in templated mode, empty list items are
created for headers, footers, and separators. You can identify these items by their
MobileListItemType.

```
public enum MobileListItemType {
   HeaderItem = 0,
   ListItem = 1,
   FooterItem = 2,
   SeparatorItem = 3
}
```

Hierarchy   System.Object → System.ValueType → System.Enum(System.IComparable, System.IFor-
               mattable, System.IConvertible) → MobileListItemType

Passed To   MobileListItem.MobileListItem( )

MobilePage   .NET 1.1, disposable

System.Web.UI.MobileControls (system.web.mobile.dll)   class

The MobilePage class is the base class for all the mobile pages you create. It derives from
the base ASP.NET web form page System.Web.UI.Page class. Some of most important properties include those that deal with the Form controls on the page. These include the
ActiveForm property, which provides the ability to determine (or set) the active Form, and
Forms, which returns a collection with all the Form instances on a page.

When you create a new mobile page in Visual Studio .NET, a new class will be derived
from MobilePage. Any code you add to handle control events will be placed inside this
class.

```
public class MobilePage : System.Web.UI.Page {
// Public Constructors
  public MobilePage( );
// Public Static Fields
  public static readonly string HiddenPostEventArgumentId;                      // = __EVENTARGUMENT
  public static readonly string HiddenPostEventSourceId;                        // = __EVENTTARGET
  public static readonly string HiddenVariablePrefix;                           // = __V_
  public static readonly string PageClientViewStateKey;                         // = __P
  public static readonly string ViewStateID;                                    // = __VIEWSTATE
// Public Instance Properties
  public string AbsoluteFilePath{get; }
  public Form ActiveForm{set; get; }
  public IPageAdapter Adapter{get; }
  public bool AllowCustomAttributes{set; get; }
  public string ClientViewState{get; }
  public bool DesignMode{get; }
  public virtual MobileCapabilities Device{get; }
  public IList Forms{get; }
  public IDictionary HiddenVariables{get; }
  public string QueryStringText{get; }
  public string RelativeFilePath{get; }
  public StyleSheet StyleSheet{set; get; }
  public string UniqueFilePathSuffix{get; }
// Public Instance Methods
  public virtual IControlAdapter GetControlAdapter(MobileControl control);
  public Form GetForm(string id);
  public object GetPrivateViewState(MobileControl ctl);
  public bool HasHiddenVariables( );
  public string MakePathAbsolute(string virtualPath);
  public void RedirectToMobilePage(string url);
  public void RedirectToMobilePage(string url, bool endResponse);
  public override void Validate( );                                             // overrides System.Web.UI.Page
  public override void VerifyRenderingInServerForm(System.Web.UI.Control control);  // overrides System.Web.UI.Page
// Protected Instance Methods
  protected override void AddedControl(System.Web.UI.Control control, int index);   // overrides System.Web.UI.Control
  protected override void AddParsedSubObject(object o);                             // overrides System.Web.UI.Control
  protected override HtmlTextWriter CreateHtmlTextWriter(System.IO.TextWriter writer);  // overrides System.Web.UI.Page
  protected override NameValueCollection DeterminePostBackMode( );                 // overrides System.Web.UI.Page
  protected override void InitOutputCache(int duration, string varyByHeader, string varyByCustom,
    System.Web.UI.OutputCacheLocation location, string varyByParam);              // overrides System.Web.UI.Page
  protected override object LoadPageStateFromPersistenceMedium( );                // overrides System.Web.UI.Page
  protected override void LoadViewState(object savedState);                       // overrides System.Web.UI.Control
  protected virtual void OnDeviceCustomize( EventArgs e);
  protected override void OnError(EventArgs e);                                   // overrides System.Web.UI.TemplateControl
  protected override void OnInit(EventArgs e);                                    // overrides System.Web.UI.Control
  protected override void OnLoad(EventArgs e);                                    // overrides System.Web.UI.Control
  protected override void OnPreRender(EventArgs e);                               // overrides System.Web.UI.Control
  protected override void OnUnload(EventArgs e);                                  // overrides System.Web.UI.Control
  protected virtual void OnViewStateExpire(EventArgs e);
  protected override void RaisePostBackEvent(System.Web.UI.IPostBackEventHandler sourceControl,
    string eventArgument);                                                        // overrides System.Web.UI.Page
```

```
protected override void RemovedControl(System.Web.UI.Control control);              // overrides System.Web.UI.Control
protected override void Render(System.Web.UI.HtmlTextWriter writer);                 // overrides System.Web.UI.Control
protected override void SavePageStateToPersistenceMedium(object view);               // overrides System.Web.UI.Page
protected override object SaveViewState( );                                          // overrides System.Web.UI.Control
}
```

Hierarchy	System.Object → System.Web.UI.Control(System.ComponentModel.IComponent, System. IDisposable, System.Web.UI.IParserAccessor, System.Web.UI.IDataBindingsAccessor) → System.Web.UI.TemplateControl(System.Web.UI.INamingContainer) → System.Web.UI. Page(System.Web.IHttpHandler) → MobilePage
Subclasses	ErrorFormatterPage
Returned By	System.Web.UI.MobileControls.Adapters.ControlAdapter.Page, System.Web.UI.MobileControls.Adapters.WmlMobileTextWriter.Page, DeviceSpecific.MobilePage, IControlAdapter. Page, IPageAdapter.Page, MobileControl.MobilePage
Passed To	System.Web.UI.MobileControls.Adapters.ControlAdapter.Page, System.Web.UI.MobileControls.Adapters.UpWmlMobileTextWriter.UpWmlMobileTextWriter( ), System.Web.UI. MobileControls.Adapters.WmlMobileTextWriter.WmlMobileTextWriter( ), IPageAdapter.Page

MobileUserControl

System.Web.UI.MobileControls (system.web.mobile.dll)   class

This class represents a mobile user control, or *.ascx* file. Mobile user controls play the exact same role as web form user controls (as represented by the System.Web.UI.UserControl class), allowing you to share commonly used portions of the user interface. Mobile user controls are similar to mobile pages, and can contain mobile controls and event handling logic. They are instantiated and cached in much the same was as MobilePage objects, and contain many of the same properties. The difference is that user controls must be situated inside a page.

```
public class MobileUserControl : System.Web.UI.UserControl {
// Public Constructors
  public MobileUserControl( );
// Protected Instance Methods
  protected override void AddParsedSubObject(object o);               // overrides System.Web.UI.Control
}
```

Hierarchy	System.Object → System.Web.UI.Control(System.ComponentModel.IComponent, System. IDisposable, System.Web.UI.IParserAccessor, System.Web.UI.IDataBindingsAccessor) → System.Web.UI.TemplateControl(System.Web.UI.INamingContainer) → System.Web.UI. UserControl(System.Web.UI.IAttributeAccessor, System.Web.UI.IUserControlDesignerAccessor) → MobileUserControl

ObjectList

System.Web.UI.MobileControls (system.web.mobile.dll)   class

The ObjectList control is a data-bound list that allows you to display multiple pieces of information from System.Data.DataRow objects in a System.Data.DataTable, or any other type of object in a collection. Unlike the simpler List control, you cannot directly add items to or remove items from an ObjectList. Instead, you must set the DataSource property and call the DataBind( ) method.

The appearance of the ObjectList depends on the type of mobile device and the control property settings. Usually, the ObjectList appears as a single list of values drawn from the data-bound object. For example, if you are binding a table of customers, you might configure the ObjectList to display a list of customer IDs by setting the LabelField property to "ID". The user can then select the ID (on a WML browser) or click the "More" link (on an HTML browser) to show the full item information and any item-specific commands you have defined. You can specify the fields that will be shown in the detailed view in one of two ways. If you set AutoGenerateFields to True, all the fields (or public properties) will be shown for the bound objects. Alternatively, set AutoGenerateFields to False and add a collection of ObjectListField instances (one for each field or property you want to bind) to the Fields collection. In addition, you can configure the rendering of the control so that it creates a table that shows multiple fields for each item. This is only supported for HTML devices. To enable this behavior, set the TableFields to a list of property or field names separated by semicolons (as in "ID;FirstName;LastName").

The ObjectList also allows you to define commands that can be invoked for any item in the list. You can define these commands by adding ObjectListCommand instances to the Commands collection. Visual Studio .NET provides rich designer support for the ObjectList control, including a property builder that allows you to specify bound columns and define list commands.

```
public class ObjectList : PagedControl, System.Web.UI.INamingContainer, ITemplateable,
    System.Web.UI.IPostBackEventHandler {
// Public Constructors
    public ObjectList( );
// Public Static Properties
    public static string SelectMoreCommand{get; }
// Public Instance Properties
    public IObjectListFieldCollection AllFields{get; }
    public bool AutoGenerateFields{set; get; }
    public string BackCommandText{set; get; }
    public virtual ObjectListCommandCollection Commands{get; }
    public Style CommandStyle{set; get; }
    public virtual string DataMember{set; get; }
    public virtual object DataSource{set; get; }
    public string DefaultCommand{set; get; }
    public Panel Details{get; }
    public string DetailsCommandText{set; get; }
    public virtual ObjectListFieldCollection Fields{get; }
    public bool HasItemCommandHandler{get; }
    public virtual ObjectListItemCollection Items{get; }
    public string LabelField{set; get; }
    public int LabelFieldIndex{get; }
    public Style LabelStyle{set; get; }
    public string MoreText{set; get; }
    public int SelectedIndex{set; get; }
    public ObjectListItem Selection{get; }
    public int[ ] TableFieldIndices{get; }
    public string TableFields{set; get; }
    public ObjectListViewMode ViewMode{set; get; }
```

```
// Protected Instance Properties
  protected override int InternalItemCount{get; }                                    // overrides PagedControl
// Public Instance Methods
  public void CreateTemplatedItemDetails(bool doDataBind);
  public void CreateTemplatedItemsList(bool doDataBind);
  public override void DataBind( );                                                  // overrides System.Web.UI.Control
  public override void EnsureTemplatedUI( );                                         // overrides MobileControl
  public void PreShowItemCommands(int itemIndex);
  public void RaiseDefaultItemEvent(int itemIndex);
  public bool SelectListItem(int itemIndex, bool selectMore);
// Protected Instance Methods
  protected override void AddParsedSubObject(object obj);                            // overrides MobileControl
  protected void CreateAutoGeneratedFields(System.Collections.IEnumerable dataSource);
  protected override void CreateChildControls( );                                    // overrides System.Web.UI.Control
  protected virtual ObjectListItem CreateItem(object dataItem);
  protected virtual void CreateItems(System.Collections.IEnumerable dataSource);
  protected override void EnsureChildControls( );                                    // overrides System.Web.UI.Control
  protected override void LoadPrivateViewState(object state);                        // overrides PagedControl
  protected override void LoadViewState( object savedState);                         // overrides MobileControl
  protected override bool OnBubbleEvent(object sender, EventArgs e);                 // overrides System.Web.UI.Control
  protected override void OnDataBinding( EventArgs e);                               // overrides MobileControl
  protected virtual void OnItemCommand(ObjectListCommandEventArgs e);
  protected virtual void OnItemDataBind(ObjectListDataBindEventArgs e);
  protected virtual void OnItemSelect(ObjectListSelectEventArgs e);
  protected override void OnLoadItems(LoadItemsEventArgs e);                         // overrides PagedControl
  protected override void OnPreRender(EventArgs e);                                  // overrides PagedControl
  protected virtual void OnShowItemCommands(ObjectListShowCommandsEventArgs e);
  protected override object SavePrivateViewState( );                                 // overrides PagedControl
  protected override object SaveViewState( );                                        // overrides MobileControl
  protected override void TrackViewState( );                                         // overrides MobileControl
// Events
  public event ObjectListCommandEventHandler ItemCommand;
  public event ObjectListDataBindEventHandler ItemDataBind;
  public event ObjectListSelectEventHandler ItemSelect;
  public event ObjectListShowCommandsEventHandler ShowItemCommands;
}
```

Hierarchy   System.Object → System.Web.UI.Control(System.ComponentModel.IComponent, System.
                     IDisposable, System.Web.UI.IParserAccessor, System.Web.UI.IDataBindingsAccessor) →
                     MobileControl(System.Web.UI.IAttributeAccessor) → PagedControl → ObjectList(System.
                     Web.UI.INamingContainer, ITemplateable, System.Web.UI.IPostBackEventHandler)

Returned By   System.Web.UI.MobileControls.Adapters.HtmlObjectListAdapter.Control, System.Web.UI.
                     MobileControls.Adapters.WmlObjectListAdapter.Control

ObjectListCommand   .NET 1.1

System.Web.UI.MobileControls (system.web.mobile.dll)   class

This class represents a command that can be invoked on an item in an ObjectList control.
Each command has descriptive text (**Text**) and a string name (**Name**) that will be

provided when the ObjectList.ItemCommand event fires. You assign commands to an ObjectList by adding ObjectListCommand instances to the ObjectList.Commands collection.

```
public class ObjectListCommand {
// Public Constructors
  public ObjectListCommand( );
  public ObjectListCommand(string name, string text);
// Public Instance Properties
  public string Name{set; get; }
  public string Text{set; get; }
}
```

Returned By   ObjectListCommandCollection.this

Passed To   ObjectListCommandCollection.{Add( ), AddAt( )}

ObjectListCommandCollection   .NET 1.1

System.Web.UI.MobileControls (system.web.mobile.dll)   class

The ObjectListCommandCollection contains a collection of commands that can be invoked on items in an ObjectList. The ObjectList.Commands property is an ObjectListCommandCollection.

```
public class ObjectListCommandCollection : ArrayListCollectionBase, System.Web.UI.IStateManager {
// Public Instance Properties
  public ObjectListCommand this[ int index ]{get; }
// Public Instance Methods
  public void Add( ObjectListCommand command);
  public void AddAt( int index, ObjectListCommand command);
  public void Clear( );
  public int IndexOf( string s);
  public void Remove( string s);
  public void RemoveAt( int index);
}
```

Hierarchy   System.Object → ArrayListCollectionBase(System.Collections.ICollection, System.Collections.IEnumerable) → ObjectListCommandCollection(System.Web.UI.IStateManager)

Returned By   ObjectList.Commands, ObjectListShowCommandsEventArgs.Commands

Passed To   ObjectListShowCommandsEventArgs.ObjectListShowCommandsEventArgs( )

ObjectListCommandEventArgs   .NET 1.1

System.Web.UI.MobileControls (system.web.mobile.dll)   class

This custom EventArgs class defines the additional information that will be sent to methods that handle the ObjectList.ItemCommand event. This information includes the string name that identifies the ObjectListCommand (CommandName), and an ObjectListItem that represents the item on which the command was invoked (ListItem).

```
public class ObjectListCommandEventArgs : System.Web.UI.WebControls.CommandEventArgs {
// Public Constructors
```

```
public ObjectListCommandEventArgs(ObjectListItem item, object commandSource,
    System.Web.UI.WebControls.CommandEventArgs originalArgs);
public ObjectListCommandEventArgs(ObjectListItem item, string commandName);
// Protected Static Fields
protected static readonly string DefaultCommand;                              // =Default
// Public Instance Properties
public object CommandSource{get; }
public ObjectListItem ListItem{get; }
}
```

Hierarchy   System.Object → System.EventArgs → System.Web.UI.WebControls.CommandEventArgs
                → ObjectListCommandEventArgs

Passed To   ObjectList.OnItemCommand( ), ObjectListCommandEventHandler.{BeginInvoke( ), Invoke( )}

ObjectListCommandEventHandler   .NET 1.1, serializable

System.Web.UI.MobileControls (system.web.mobile.dll)   delegate

This delegate defines the signature for methods that handle the ObjectList.ItemCommand
event (which fires when a custom ObjectListCommand is selected for a given item).

```
public delegate void ObjectListCommandEventHandler(object sender, ObjectListCommandEventArgs e);
```

Associated Events ObjectList.ItemCommand( )

ObjectListControlBuilder   .NET 1.1

System.Web.UI.MobileControls (system.web.mobile.dll)   class

The FormControlBuilder class is used internally by ASP.NET. It is created by the page parser
when it encounters a <mobile:ObjectList> tag, and used to process the contained <Field>
and <Command> elements that define list items.

```
public class ObjectListControlBuilder : MobileControlBuilder {
// Public Constructors
public ObjectListControlBuilder( );
// Public Instance Methods
public override Type GetChildControlType(string tagName, System.Collections.IDictionary attributes);
                                                          // overrides MobileControlBuilder
}
```

Hierarchy   System.Object → System.Web.UI.ControlBuilder → MobileControlBuilder →
                ObjectListControlBuilder

ObjectListDataBindEventArgs   .NET 1.1

System.Web.UI.MobileControls (system.web.mobile.dll)   class

This custom EventArgs class defines the additional information that will be sent to
methods that handle the ObjectList.ItemDataBind event. This information includes the
ObjectListItem that is being bound bound in the list (ListItem), and the System.Data.DataRow or
other object that is supplying the data (DataItem).

```
public class ObjectListDataBindEventArgs : EventArgs {
// Public Constructors
  public ObjectListDataBindEventArgs(ObjectListItem item, object dataItem);
// Public Instance Properties
  public object DataItem{get; }
  public ObjectListItem ListItem{get; }
}
```

Hierarchy   System.Object → System.EventArgs → ObjectListDataBindEventArgs

Passed To   ObjectList.OnItemDataBind( ), ObjectListDataBindEventHandler.{BeginInvoke( ), Invoke( )}

ObjectListDataBindEventHandler   .NET 1.1, serializable

System.Web.UI.MobileControls (system.web.mobile.dll)   delegate

This delegate defines the signature for methods that handle the ObjectList.ItemDataBind
event (which fires once for each item, as it is is bound to the ObjectList).

```
public delegate void ObjectListDataBindEventHandler(object sender, ObjectListDataBindEventArgs e);
```

Associated Events ObjectList.ItemDataBind( )

ObjectListField   .NET 1.1

System.Web.UI.MobileControls (system.web.mobile.dll)   sealed class

The ObjectListField represents a single field or property in an object that is bound to the
ObjectList control. You can choose the fields you want to display in one of two ways. If
you set ObjectList.AutoGenerateFields to True, all the fields (or public properties) will be shown
for bound objects. If you set ObjectList.AutoGenerateFields to False, you can define the fields
that should be shown by adding ObjectListField instances (one for each field or property
you want to bind) to the ObjectList.Fields collection.

```
public sealed class ObjectListField : System.Web.UI.IStateManager {
// Public Constructors
  public ObjectListField( );
// Public Instance Properties
  public string DataField{set; get; }
  public string DataFormatString{set; get; }
  public string Name{set; get; }
  public string Title{set; get; }
  public bool Visible{set; get; }
// Public Instance Methods
  public void DataBindItem(int fieldIndex, ObjectListItem item);
}
```

Returned By   IObjectListFieldCollection.{GetAll( ), this}, ObjectListFieldCollection.{GetAll( ), this}

Passed To   IObjectListFieldCollection.IndexOf( ), ObjectListFieldCollection.{Add( ), AddAt( ), IndexOf( ), Remove( ), SetAll( )}

ObjectListFieldCollection

System.Web.UI.MobileControls (system.web.mobile.dll) class

This is a strongly typed collection of ObjectListField instances. It's used to define the fields that should be shown in an ObjectList (through the ObjectList.Fields property).

```
public class ObjectListFieldCollection : ArrayListCollectionBase, IObjectListFieldCollection, System.Web.UI.IStateManager {
// Public Instance Properties
  public ObjectListField this[ int index ]{get; }                   // implements IObjectListFieldCollection
// Public Instance Methods
  public void Add(ObjectListField field);
  public void AddAt(int index, ObjectListField field);
  public void Clear( );
  public ObjectListField[ ] GetAll( );                              // implements IObjectListFieldCollection
  public int IndexOf(ObjectListField field);                       // implements IObjectListFieldCollection
  public int IndexOf(string fieldIDOrName);                        // implements IObjectListFieldCollection
  public void Remove(ObjectListField field);
  public void RemoveAt(int index);
  public void SetAll(ObjectListField[ ] value);
}
```

Hierarchy   System.Object → ArrayListCollectionBase(System.Collections.ICollection, System.Collections.IEnumerable) → ObjectListFieldCollection(IObjectListFieldCollection, System.Web.UI.IStateManager)

Returned By   ObjectList.Fields

ObjectListItem

System.Web.UI.MobileControls (system.web.mobile.dll) class

The ObjectListItem represents an individual item in an ObjectList. You do not create ObjectListItem instances manually; instead, they are created automatically as the list is bound. You can iterate through a collection of all the ObjectListItem instances in the list using the ObjectList.Items collection. In addition, some events (like ObjectList.ItemCommand, ObjectList.ItemSelect, and ObjectList.ItemDataBind) provide an ObjectListItem instance that identifies the appropriate item in the list.

You can determine whether or not an item is selected using the Selected property. In addition, you can use the Item property (which is the default indexer) to examine the properties or fields of the bound object. For example, if the bound object has a property named ID, you can use the syntax ObjectListItem["ID"] to retrieve its value. If you try to retrieve a property that doesn't exist, you will receive a null reference, but no error will occur.

```
public class ObjectListItem : MobileListItem {
// Public Instance Properties
  public string this[ int index ]{set; get; }
  public string this[ string key ]{set; get; }
// Public Instance Methods
  public override bool Equals( object obj);                        // overrides MobileListItem
  public override int GetHashCode( );                             // overrides MobileListItem
// Protected Instance Methods
  protected override bool OnBubbleEvent(object source, EventArgs e);  // overrides MobileListItem
}
```

Hierarchy	System.Object → System.Web.UI.Control(System.ComponentModel.IComponent, System. IDisposable, System.Web.UI.IParserAccessor, System.Web.UI.IDataBindingsAccessor) → MobileControl(System.Web.UI.IAttributeAccessor) → Panel(ITemplateable) → Template-Container(System.Web.UI.INamingContainer) → MobileListItem(System.Web.UI. IStateManager) → ObjectListItem
Returned By	ObjectList.{CreateItem( ), Selection}, ObjectListCommandEventArgs.ListItem, ObjectListDat-aBindEventArgs.ListItem, ObjectListItemCollection.{GetAll( ), this}, ObjectListSelectEventArgs. ListItem, ObjectListShowCommandsEventArgs.ListItem
Passed To	System.Web.UI.MobileControls.Adapters.HtmlObjectListAdapter.RenderItemDetails( ), System.Web.UI.MobileControls.Adapters.WmlObjectListAdapter.{RenderItemDetails( ), RenderItemMenu( )}, ObjectListCommandEventArgs.ObjectListCommandEventArgs( ), ObjectListDataBindEventArgs.ObjectListDataBindEventArgs( ), ObjectListField.DataBindItem( ), ObjectListItemCollection.{Contains( ), IndexOf( )}, ObjectListSelectEventArgs. ObjectListSelectEventArgs( ), ObjectListShowCommandsEventArgs. ObjectListShowCommandsEventArgs( )

ObjectListItemCollection   .NET 1.1

System.Web.UI.MobileControls (system.web.mobile.dll)   class

This is a strongly typed collection of ObjectListItem instances. It's used to represent the current list of items in an ObjectList (through the ObjectList.Items property). You can use this collection to view the items in an ObjectList, but you cannot directly add or remove items from the collection list, because the ObjectList is always bound to a data source.

```
public class ObjectListItemCollection : ArrayListCollectionBase, System.Web.UI.IStateManager {
// Public Instance Properties
  public ObjectListItem this[ int index ]{get; }
// Public Instance Methods
  public void Clear( );
  public bool Contains(ObjectListItem item);
  public ObjectListItem[ ] GetAll( );
  public int IndexOf(ObjectListItem item);
}
```

Hierarchy	System.Object → ArrayListCollectionBase(System.Collections.ICollection, System.Collec-tions.IEnumerable) → ObjectListItemCollection(System.Web.UI.IStateManager)
Returned By	ObjectList.Items

ObjectListSelectEventArgs   .NET 1.1

System.Web.UI.MobileControls (system.web.mobile.dll)   class

This custom EventArgs class defines the additional information that will be sent to methods that handle the ObjectList.ItemSelect event. This information includes the ObjectList-Item that is being bound bound in the list (ListItem), and a Boolean variable that indicates whether there is more information to be shown for the item (SelectMore). You do not need to handle this event. By default, the control will show a new page that contains the full list of fields or proeprties for the item when it is selected.

```
public class ObjectListSelectEventArgs : EventArgs {
// Public Constructors
  public ObjectListSelectEventArgs(ObjectListItem item, bool selectMore);
// Public Instance Properties
  public ObjectListItem ListItem{get; }
  public bool SelectMore{get; }
  public bool UseDefaultHandling{set; get; }
}
```

Hierarchy   System.Object → System.EventArgs → ObjectListSelectEventArgs

Passed To   ObjectList.OnItemSelect( ), ObjectListSelectEventHandler.{BeginInvoke( ), Invoke( )}

ObjectListSelectEventHandler   .NET 1.1, serializable

System.Web.UI.MobileControls (system.web.mobile.dll)   delegate

```
public delegate void ObjectListSelectEventHandler(object sender, ObjectListSelectEventArgs e);
```

This delegate defines the signature for methods that handle the ObjectList.ItemSelect event
(which fires when the user selects an item from an ObjectList).

Associated Events ObjectList.ItemSelect( )

ObjectListShowCommandsEventArgs   .NET 1.1

System.Web.UI.MobileControls (system.web.mobile.dll)   class

This custom EventArgs class defines the additional information that will be sent to
methods that handle the ObjectList.ShowItemCommands event. This information includes the
ObjectListItem that is being bound in the list (ListItem), and a the collection of commands
that will be shown (Commands). You can programmatically add or remove ObjectListCommand instances to this collection to create an item-specific set of commands.

```
public class ObjectListShowCommandsEventArgs : EventArgs {
// Public Constructors
  public ObjectListShowCommandsEventArgs(ObjectListItem item, ObjectListCommandCollection commands);
// Public Instance Properties
  public ObjectListCommandCollection Commands{get; }
  public ObjectListItem ListItem{get; }
}
```

Hierarchy   System.Object → System.EventArgs → ObjectListShowCommandsEventArgs

Passed To   ObjectList.OnShowItemCommands( ), ObjectListShowCommandsEventHandler.
                   {BeginInvoke( ), Invoke( )}

ObjectListShowCommandsEventHandler   .NET 1.1, serializable

System.Web.UI.MobileControls (system.web.mobile.dll)   delegate

This delegate defines the signature for methods that handle the ObjectList.ShowItemCom-
mands event (which occurs just before the commands are shown for a selected item in

the ObjectList). Your event handler can then customize the collection of ObjectListCommand objects depending on the item that has been selected.

```
public delegate void ObjectListShowCommandsEventHandler(object sender, ObjectListShowCommandsEventArgs e);
```

Associated Events ObjectList.ShowItemCommands( )

ObjectListTitleAttribute   .NET 1.1

System.Web.UI.MobileControls (system.web.mobile.dll)   class

This class is used internally by the ObjectList to automatically generated a collection of ObjectListField instances when ObjectList.AutoGenerateFields is True.

```
public class ObjectListTitleAttribute : Attribute {
// Public Constructors
  public ObjectListTitleAttribute(string title);
// Public Instance Properties
  public virtual string Title{get; }
}
```

Hierarchy   System.Object → System.Attribute → ObjectListTitleAttribute

Valid On   Property

ObjectListViewMode   serializable

System.Web.UI.MobileControls (system.web.mobile.dll)   enum

This enumeration is used in conjunction with the ObjectList.ViewMode property. The ObjectList supports three different view states. Initially, when an ObjectList is first shown, it will use the List mode, which shows all items. You can programmatically change the view mode to show the details or commands for a specific item. First, set the ObjectList. SelectedIndex property so that an item is selected. Next, set ObjectList.ViewMode to Details or Commands. Note that in HTML, these settings are equivalent, because the details view is combined with the commands view, with the commands appearing as hyperlinks below the details.

```
public enum ObjectListViewMode {
  List = 0,
  Commands = 1,
  Details = 2
}
```

Hierarchy   System.Object → System.ValueType → System.Enum(System.IComparable, System.IFor-
                   mattable, System.IConvertible) → ObjectListViewMode

Returned By   ObjectList.ViewMode

Passed To   ObjectList.ViewMode

PagedControl

System.Web.UI.MobileControls (system.web.mobile.dll)　　　　　　　　　　　　abstract class

The PagedControl class defines the basic functionality for controls that use internal pagination, and can divide their content over multiple pages. These includes the List, LiteralText, ObjectList, and TextView controls, all of which derive from this class. To create a custom control that supports internal pagination, derive it from PagedControl. Override the ItemWeight property so that it returns the approximate weight of an individual item in the control. (The default weight is 100, which corresponds to a single line on the device using the default unit system.) Then, when rendering the control's output, call the FirstVisibleItemIndex( ) method, which will tell you the first item to render, and the VisibleItemCount( ) method to determine how many items to render. Your paged control will automatically fire the LoadItems event as needed.

```
public abstract class PagedControl : MobileControl {
// Protected Constructors
  protected PagedControl( );
// Public Instance Properties
  public int FirstVisibleItemIndex{get; }
  public int ItemCount{set; get; }
  public int ItemsPerPage{set; get; }
  public int VisibleItemCount{get; }
  public override int VisibleWeight{get; }                      // overrides MobileControl
// Protected Instance Properties
  protected abstract int InternalItemCount{get; }
  protected virtual int ItemWeight{get; }
// Public Instance Methods
  public override void PaginateRecursive(ControlPager pager);   // overrides MobileControl
// Protected Instance Methods
  protected override void LoadPrivateViewState(object state);   // overrides MobileControl
  protected virtual void OnLoadItems(LoadItemsEventArgs e);
  protected override void OnPageChange(int oldPageIndex, int newPageIndex);  // overrides MobileControl
  protected override void OnPreRender(EventArgs e);             // overrides MobileControl
  protected override object SavePrivateViewState( );           // overrides MobileControl
// Events
  public event LoadItemsEventHandler LoadItems;
}
```

Hierarchy　　　System.Object → System.Web.UI.Control(System.ComponentModel.IComponent, System. IDisposable, System.Web.UI.IParserAccessor, System.Web.UI.IDataBindingsAccessor) → MobileControl(System.Web.UI.IAttributeAccessor) → PagedControl

Subclasses　　　List, LiteralText, ObjectList, TextView

PagerStyle

System.Web.UI.MobileControls (system.web.mobile.dll)　　　　　　　　　　　　class

The PagerStyle is a custom Style object with additional properties specific to the pagination user interface of a form, most of which consits of static text strings. You can access these properties for a Form by using the Form.PagerStyle property. The properties you might want to customize include NextPageText, PreviousPageText, and PageLabel

```
public class PagerStyle : Style {
// Public Constructors
  public PagerStyle( );
// Public Static Fields
  public static readonly object NextPageTextKey;              // =System.Web.UI.MobileControls.Style+Property
  public static readonly object PageLabelKey;                 // =System.Web.UI.MobileControls.Style+Property
  public static readonly object PreviousPageTextKey;          // =System.Web.UI.MobileControls.Style+Property
// Public Instance Properties
  public string NextPageText{set; get; }
  public string PageLabel{set; get; }
  public string PreviousPageText{set; get; }
// Public Instance Methods
  public string GetNextPageText( int currentPageIndex);
  public string GetPageLabelText(int currentPageIndex, int pageCount);
  public string GetPreviousPageText( int currentPageIndex);
}
```

Hierarchy   System.Object → Style(System.Web.UI.IParserAccessor, ITemplateable, System.Web.UI. IStateManager, System.ICloneable) → PagerStyle

Returned By   Form.PagerStyle

Panel   .NET 1.1, disposable

System.Web.UI.MobileControls (system.web.mobile.dll)   class

The Panel is a flexible container for mobile controls. The Panel control is commonly used to hide or show groups of controls (by setting the Visible property), or to keep controls together for the purposes of pagination. The style attributes and pagination settings you apply to a Panel will be applied to all child controls automatically. A Panel does not provide a provide a border or visual appearance beyond its constituent controls and any literal text.

The Panel supports literal text, although once added, you cannot easily modify this text at runtime. You can also insert markup tags directly into the literal text of a Panel. Supported tags include <a> (anchor), <b> (bold), <i> (italic),
 (line break), and <p> (paragraph). These tags will be rendered in a device-independent manner, which means that a <p> could conceivably be translated into a <br> tag if required by the client device. In order to ensure compatibility across a broad range of devices, all other tags are ignored, and will never affect the control's output.

```
public class Panel : MobileControl, ITemplateable {
// Public Constructors
  public Panel( );
// Public Instance Properties
  public override bool BreakAfter{set; get; }                            // overrides MobileControl
  public Panel Content{get; }
  public virtual bool Paginate{set; get; }
// Protected Instance Properties
  protected override bool PaginateChildren{get; }                        // overrides MobileControl
// Public Instance Methods
  public override void AddLinkedForms( System.Collections.IList linkedForms);   // overrides MobileControl
  public override void CreateDefaultTemplatedUI(bool doDataBind);        // overrides MobileControl
```

```
  public override void PaginateRecursive(ControlPager pager);                          // overrides MobileControl
// Protected Instance Methods
  protected override void OnInit( EventArgs e);                                         // overrides MobileControl
}
```

Hierarchy	System.Object → System.Web.UI.Control(System.ComponentModel.IComponent, System. IDisposable, System.Web.UI.IParserAccessor, System.Web.UI.IDataBindingsAccessor) → MobileControl(System.Web.UI.IAttributeAccessor) → Panel(ITemplateable)
Subclasses	Form, TemplateContainer
Returned By	System.Web.UI.MobileControls.Adapters.HtmlPanelAdapter.Control, System.Web.UI.Mobile-Controls.Adapters.WmlPanelAdapter.Control, Form.{Footer, Header, Script}, ObjectList.Details

PanelControlBuilder   .NET 1.1

System.Web.UI.MobileControls (system.web.mobile.dll)   class

The PanelControlBuilder class is used internally by ASP.NET. It is created by the page parser when it encounters a <mobile:Panel> tag, and used to process the literal text it contains.

```
public class PanelControlBuilder : LiteralTextContainerControlBuilder {
// Public Constructors
  public PanelControlBuilder( );
}
```

Hierarchy	System.Object → System.Web.UI.ControlBuilder → MobileControlBuilder → LiteralText-ContainerControlBuilder → PanelControlBuilder

PersistNameAttribute   .NET 1.1

System.Web.UI.MobileControls (system.web.mobile.dll)   class

This attribute is a part of the .NET infrastructure, and is never used directly in your application code.

```
public class PersistNameAttribute : Attribute {
// Public Constructors
  public PersistNameAttribute( string name);
// Public Static Fields
  public static readonly PersistNameAttribute Default;        // =System.Web.UI.MobileControls.PersistNameAttribute
// Public Instance Properties
  public string Name{get; }
// Public Instance Methods
  public override bool Equals(object obj);                                             // overrides Attribute
  public override int GetHashCode( );                                                 // overrides Attribute
  public override bool IsDefaultAttribute( );                                         // overrides Attribute
}
```

Hierarchy	System.Object → System.Attribute → PersistNameAttribute
Valid On	Class

PhoneCall

System.Web.UI.MobileControls (system.web.mobile.dll)   class

The PhoneCall control is used on devices that have telephone ability. On these devices, it will render as a command that the user can select to dial the specified phone number. You can set the Text property to configure the text that will appear, and you must set the PhoneNumber property to specify the nunber that will be dialed when the control is selected. This property accepts a string that can use multiple phone number formats, including brackes, dashes, and periods. A phone number can start with the + sign and an optional country or region code. Examples of valid numbers include 800.522.2920, +1 (425) 885-8080, and +91335303197. i-Mode phones impose their own rules on valid phone numbers, which are described in detail the MSDN reference.

On a device that does not provide telephony capability, the PhoneCall control can render as a link to a URL. You can set this URL using the AlternateUrl property. In addition, you can configure the text that will be displayed using the AlternateFormat string. By default, this property is "{0} {1}". This means that on non-telephony devices, the PhoneCall will display the Text property with the PhoneNumber property concatenated to it (with a space separating them). You can alter the AlternateFormat property to insert your own text.

```
public class PhoneCall : TextControl, System.Web.UI.IPostBackEventHandler {
// Public Constructors
    public PhoneCall( );
// Public Instance Properties
    public string AlternateFormat{set; get; }
    public string AlternateUrl{set; get; }
    public string PhoneNumber{set; get; }
    public string SoftkeyLabel{set; get; }
// Public Instance Methods
    public override void AddLinkedForms(System.Collections.IList linkedForms);      // overrides MobileControl
// Protected Instance Methods
    protected override void OnPreRender( EventArgs e);                              // overrides MobileControl
}
```

Hierarchy	System.Object → System.Web.UI.Control(System.ComponentModel.IComponent, System. IDisposable, System.Web.UI.IParserAccessor, System.Web.UI.IDataBindingsAccessor) → MobileControl(System.Web.UI.IAttributeAccessor) → TextControl → PhoneCall(System. Web.UI.IPostBackEventHandler)
Returned By	System.Web.UI.MobileControls.Adapters.HtmlPhoneCallAdapter.Control, System.Web.UI. MobileControls.Adapters.WmlPhoneCallAdapter.Control

RangeValidator

.NET 1.1, disposable

System.Web.UI.MobileControls (system.web.mobile.dll)   class

This class represents a validation control that tests to make sure the value of the input control (ControlToValidate) is equal to or between the MinimumValue and MaximumValue. All values will be converted to the data type specified by CompareValidator.Type before the validation is performed. Valid data types include integer, double, date, currency, and string (which uses alphabetic character-code based comparison). In this way, the RangeValidator control works identically to the System.Web.UI.WebControls.RangeValidator control for full-fledged web pages.

Validation automatically succeeds if the input control is empty. To require a value, use the RequiredFieldValidator control in addition to the RangeValidator control (although it won't render client-side validation code).

```
public class RangeValidator : BaseValidator {
// Public Constructors
  public RangeValidator( );
// Public Instance Properties
  public string MaximumValue{set; get; }
  public string MinimumValue{set; get; }
  public ValidationDataType Type{set; get; }
// Protected Instance Methods
  protected override bool ControlPropertiesValid( );        // overrides BaseValidator
  protected override BaseValidator CreateWebValidator( );   // overrides BaseValidator
  protected override bool EvaluateIsValid( );               // overrides BaseValidator
}
```

Hierarchy   System.Object → System.Web.UI.Control(System.ComponentModel.IComponent, System. IDisposable, System.Web.UI.IParserAccessor, System.Web.UI.IDataBindingsAccessor) → MobileControl(System.Web.UI.IAttributeAccessor) → TextControl → BaseValidator(System. Web.UI.IValidator) → RangeValidator

RegularExpressionValidator   .NET 1.1, disposable

System.Web.UI.MobileControls (system.web.mobile.dll)   class

The RegularExpressionValidator is a type of validation control that compares an input control against a pattern specified in the ValidationExpression. Regular expression validation is ideally suited for verifying predictable sequences of characters, such as those in social security numbers, email addresses, telephone numbers, and postal codes. Validation will succeed if the input control is empty, unless you also use a RequiredFieldValidator control. In this way, the RegularExpressionValidator control works identically to the System. Web.UI.WebControls.RegularExpressionValidator control for full-fledged web pages (although it won't render client-side validation code).

```
public class RegularExpressionValidator : BaseValidator {
// Public Constructors
  public RegularExpressionValidator( );
// Public Instance Properties
  public string ValidationExpression{set; get; }
// Protected Instance Methods
  protected override BaseValidator CreateWebValidator( );   // overrides BaseValidator
  protected override bool EvaluateIsValid( );               // overrides BaseValidator
}
```

Hierarchy   System.Object → System.Web.UI.Control(System.ComponentModel.IComponent, System. IDisposable, System.Web.UI.IParserAccessor, System.Web.UI.IDataBindingsAccessor) → MobileControl(System.Web.UI.IAttributeAccessor) → TextControl → BaseValidator(System. Web.UI.IValidator) → RegularExpressionValidator

RequiredFieldValidator

.NET 1.1, disposable

System.Web.UI.MobileControls (system.web.mobile.dll)   class

This class represents a validation control that is used to force user entry in a corresponding input control, like a TextBox. Validation fails if the value in the input control does not differ from the InitialValue property. By default, InitialValue is set to System.String. Empty, and validation will succeed as long as some information has been added to the input control. In this way, the RequiredFieldValidator control works identically to the System. Web.UI.WebControls.RequiredFieldValidator control for full-fledged web pages (although it won't render client-side validation code).

You can use a combination of different validation controls for a single control. For example, you could use a RequiredFieldValidator to ensure that a value is entered, and a RangeValidator to ensure that the value is within a specified data range. This is often required, as validators like RangeValidator will automatically validate a control if it is empty, regardless of the properties you have set.

```
public class RequiredFieldValidator : BaseValidator {
// Public Constructors
   public RequiredFieldValidator( );
// Public Instance Properties
   public string InitialValue{set; get; }
// Protected Instance Methods
   protected override BaseValidator CreateWebValidator( );                              // overrides BaseValidator
   protected override bool EvaluateIsValid( );                                          // overrides BaseValidator
}
```

Hierarchy   System.Object → System.Web.UI.Control(System.ComponentModel.IComponent, System. IDisposable, System.Web.UI.IParserAccessor, System.Web.UI.IDataBindingsAccessor) → MobileControl(System.Web.UI.IAttributeAccessor) → TextControl → BaseValidator(System. Web.UI.IValidator) → RequiredFieldValidator

SelectionList

.NET 1.1, disposable

System.Web.UI.MobileControls (system.web.mobile.dll)   class

The SelectionList control presents a list of items from which the user can choose. The SelectionList is different from the List control in several ways, namely, it supports multiple selection, does not raise server-side selection events, and does not support pagination. In addition, it supports drop-down and combo-box styles (through the SelectType property). Typically, you will use the List control as a navigation tool where each item acts as a command, and the SelectionList to display a list of items that will be used in conjunction with another operation.

You can retrieve the currently selected MobileListItem from the Selection property, or its index from the SelectedIndex property. If the list supports multiple selection (is type ListSelectType.MultiSelectListBox) this will only return the first selected item. To find all selected items you will need to iterate over the collection of Items and check the Selected property of each one.

```
public class SelectionList : MobileControl, System.Web.UI.IPostBackDataHandler, IListControl {
// Public Constructors
   public SelectionList( );
// Public Instance Properties
```

```
public virtual string DataMember{set; get; }
public virtual object DataSource{set; get; }
public string DataTextField{set; get; }
public string DataValueField{set; get; }
public bool IsMultiSelect{get; }
public MobileListItemCollection Items{get; }
public int Rows{set; get; }
public int SelectedIndex{set; get; }
public MobileListItem Selection{get; }
public ListSelectType SelectType{set; get; }
public string Title{set; get; }
// Protected Instance Methods
  protected override void AddParsedSubObject( object obj);            // overrides MobileControl
  protected virtual void CreateItems(System.Collections.IEnumerable dataSource);
  protected override void LoadViewState( object savedState);          // overrides MobileControl
  protected override void OnDataBinding( EventArgs e);                // overrides MobileControl
  protected virtual void OnItemDataBind(ListDataBindEventArgs e);     // implements IListControl
  protected override void OnPreRender( EventArgs e);                  // overrides MobileControl
  protected virtual void OnSelectedIndexChanged( EventArgs e);
  protected override object SaveViewState( );                         // overrides MobileControl
  protected override void TrackViewState( );                          // overrides MobileControl
// Events
  public event ListDataBindEventHandler ItemDataBind;
  public event EventHandler SelectedIndexChanged;
}
```

Hierarchy   System.Object → System.Web.UI.Control(System.ComponentModel.IComponent, System.
IDisposable, System.Web.UI.IParserAccessor, System.Web.UI.IDataBindingsAccessor) →
MobileControl(System.Web.UI.IAttributeAccessor) → SelectionList(System.Web.UI.IPost-
BackDataHandler, IListControl)

Returned By   System.Web.UI.MobileControls.Adapters.HtmlSelectionListAdapter.Control, System.Web.UI.
MobileControls.Adapters.WmlSelectionListAdapter.Control

Style   .NET 1.1

System.Web.UI.MobileControls (system.web.mobile.dll)   class

Styles define multiple appearance-related properties that apply to all mobile controls.
These settings configure alignment, foreground and background color, and font. In
addition, specialized controls can use custom Style objects that add additional properties. Style objects are most often used with stylesheets, which allow an easy way to
apply consistent style settings to multiple controls. See the StyleSheet class reference for
more information.

Note that mobile controls support a wide range of devices. Style properties may be
ignored, depending on the capabilities of the client device.

```
public class Style : System.Web.UI.IParserAccessor, ITemplateable, System.Web.UI.IStateManager, ICloneable {
// Public Constructors
  public Style( );
// Public Static Fields
  public static readonly object AlignmentKey;                   // =System.Web.UI.MobileControls.Style+Property
```

```
public static readonly object BackColorKey;              // =System.Web.UI.MobileControls.Style+Property
public static readonly object BoldKey;                   // =System.Web.UI.MobileControls.Style+Property
public static readonly object FontNameKey;               // =System.Web.UI.MobileControls.Style+Property
public static readonly object FontSizeKey;               // =System.Web.UI.MobileControls.Style+Property
public static readonly object ForeColorKey;              // =System.Web.UI.MobileControls.Style+Property
public static readonly object ItalicKey;                 // =System.Web.UI.MobileControls.Style+Property
public static readonly object WrappingKey;               // =System.Web.UI.MobileControls.Style+Property
// Public Instance Properties
   public Alignment Alignment{set; get; }
   public Color BackColor{set; get; }
   public MobileControl Control{get; }
   public DeviceSpecific DeviceSpecific{set; get; }
   public FontInfo Font{get; }
   public Color ForeColor{set; get; }
   public bool IsTemplated{get; }
   public string Name{set; get; }
   public virtual string StyleReference{set; get; }
   public object this[ object key ]{set; get; }
   public object this[ object key, bool inherit ]{get; }
   public Wrapping Wrapping{set; get; }
// Protected Instance Properties
   protected internal StateBag State{get; }
// Public Static Methods
   public static object RegisterStyle(string name, Type type, object defaultValue, bool inherit);
// Public Instance Methods
   public void ApplyTo(System.Web.UI.WebControls.WebControl control);
   public object Clone( );                                  // implements ICloneable
   public ITemplate GetTemplate( string templateName);
}
```

Subclasses	PagerStyle
Returned By	System.Web.UI.MobileControls.Adapters.ControlAdapter.Style, MobileControl.CreateStyle( ), ObjectList.{CommandStyle, LabelStyle}, StyleSheet.this
Passed To	System.Web.UI.MobileControls.Adapters.HtmlMobileTextWriter.{EnterStyle( ), ExitStyle( )}, System.Web.UI.MobileControls.Adapters.MobileTextWriter.{EnterFormat( ), EnterLayout( ), EnterStyle( ), ExitFormat( ), ExitLayout( ), ExitStyle( )}, ObjectList.{CommandStyle, Label-Style}, StyleSheet.this

StyleSheet   .NET 1.1, disposable

System.Web.UI.MobileControls (system.web.mobile.dll)   **class**

Style sheets are used to give mobile controls a consistent appearance. To use a style sheet, first add it to a mobile web page or user control. You can then create one or more Style objects for the control and add them to the Styles collection. (You can do this programmatically, or at design-time using the StyleSheet property builder.) Once you have created at least one style, you can assign it to any controls on the page.

You can also use external style sheets to provide a consistent appearance for multiple pages. An external style sheet is a StyleSheet placed in a separate *.ascx* (user control) file.

To use an external style sheet, you must create a local **StyleSheet** control, and set the **ReferencePath** property to the path name of the *.ascx* file that contains the external style sheet.

```
public class StyleSheet : MobileControl {
// Public Constructors
  public StyleSheet( );
// Public Static Properties
  public static StyleSheet Default{get; }
// Public Instance Properties
  public override Alignment Alignment{set; get; }          // overrides MobileControl
  public override Color BackColor{set; get; }              // overrides MobileControl
  public override bool BreakAfter{set; get; }              // overrides MobileControl
  public override bool EnableViewState{set; get; }         // overrides System.Web.UI.Control
  public override FontInfo Font{get; }                     // overrides MobileControl
  public override Color ForeColor{set; get; }              // overrides MobileControl
  public string ReferencePath{set; get; }
  public override string StyleReference{set; get; }        // overrides MobileControl
  public ICollection Styles{get; }
  public Style this[ string name ]{set; get; }
  public override bool Visible{set; get; }                 // overrides System.Web.UI.Control
  public override Wrapping Wrapping{set; get; }            // overrides MobileControl
// Public Instance Methods
  public void Clear( );
  public void Remove( string name);
// Protected Instance Methods
  protected override void AddParsedSubObject( object o);   // overrides MobileControl
  protected override void LoadViewState( object savedState); // overrides MobileControl
  protected override object SaveViewState( );              // overrides MobileControl
  protected override void TrackViewState( );               // overrides MobileControl
}
```

Hierarchy	System.Object → System.Web.UI.Control(System.ComponentModel.IComponent, System. IDisposable, System.Web.UI.IParserAccessor, System.Web.UI.IDataBindingsAccessor) → MobileControl(System.Web.UI.IAttributeAccessor) → StyleSheet
Returned By	MobilePage.StyleSheet
Passed To	MobilePage.StyleSheet

StyleSheetControlBuilder   .NET 1.1

System.Web.UI.MobileControls (system.web.mobile.dll)   class

The FormControlBuilder class is used internally by ASP.NET. It is created by the page parser when it encounters a <mobile:StyleSheet> tag, and used to process contained styles.

```
public class StyleSheetControlBuilder : MobileControlBuilder {
// Public Constructors
  public StyleSheetControlBuilder( );
// Public Instance Methods
```

```
    public override Type GetChildControlType(string name, System.Collections.IDictionary attributes);
                                                                      // overrides MobileControlBuilder
}
```

Hierarchy   System.Object → System.Web.UI.ControlBuilder → MobileControlBuilder →
                   StyleSheetControlBuilder

TemplateContainer   .NET 1.1, disposable

System.Web.UI.MobileControls (system.web.mobile.dll)   class

The TemplateContainer class is used with controls that support templating. Essentially,
controls that use templates will add child controls inside separate TemplateContainer
instances. The TemplateContainer class inherits from the Panel class, which gives it the
ability to host child controls.

```
public class TemplateContainer : Panel, System.Web.UI.INamingContainer {
// Public Constructors
  public TemplateContainer( );
// Public Instance Properties
  public override bool BreakAfter{set; get; }                                // overrides Panel
}
```

Hierarchy   System.Object → System.Web.UI.Control(System.ComponentModel.IComponent, System.
                   IDisposable, System.Web.UI.IParserAccessor, System.Web.UI.IDataBindingsAccessor) →
                   MobileControl(System.Web.UI.IAttributeAccessor) → Panel(ITemplateable) → Template-
                   Container(System.Web.UI.INamingContainer)

Subclasses   MobileListItem

TextBox   .NET 1.1, disposable

System.Web.UI.MobileControls (system.web.mobile.dll)   class

The TextBox control allows the user to input a single line of text. You can retrieve the
text through the Text property. In addition, you can set the Boolean Password field so that
all input characters are masked (typically using an asterisk) or the Boolean Numeric field
so that only number characters will are allowed. Not all devices support the Numeric
property (for example, it will have no effect in an HTML page), so it is recommended
that you use some type of validation or validation controls if you need to ensure that
input is numeric.

```
public class TextBox : TextControl, System.Web.UI.IPostBackDataHandler {
// Public Constructors
  public TextBox( );
// Public Instance Properties
  public int MaxLength{set; get; }
  public bool Numeric{set; get; }
  public bool Password{set; get; }
  public int Size{set; get; }
  public string Title{set; get; }
// Protected Instance Methods
  protected virtual void OnTextChanged( EventArgs e);
```

```
// Events
  public event EventHandler TextChanged;
}
```

Hierarchy   System.Object → System.Web.UI.Control(System.ComponentModel.IComponent, System.
               IDisposable, System.Web.UI.IParserAccessor, System.Web.UI.IDataBindingsAccessor) →
               MobileControl(System.Web.UI.IAttributeAccessor) → TextControl → TextBox(System.Web.
               UI.IPostBackDataHandler)

Returned By   System.Web.UI.MobileControls.Adapters.HtmlTextBoxAdapter.Control, System.Web.UI.Mobi-
                 leControls.Adapters.WmlTextBoxAdapter.Control

TextBoxControlBuilder   .NET 1.1

System.Web.UI.MobileControls (system.web.mobile.dll)   class

The TextBoxControlBuilder class is used internally by ASP.NET. It is created by the page
parser when it encounters a <mobile:TextBox> element, and used to take the literal text in
the tag and add it to the TextBox.Text property.

```
public class TextBoxControlBuilder : MobileControlBuilder {
// Public Constructors
  public TextBoxControlBuilder( );
// Public Instance Methods
  public override bool AllowWhitespaceLiterals( );                 // overrides MobileControlBuilder
}
```

Hierarchy   System.Object → System.Web.UI.ControlBuilder → MobileControlBuilder →
               TextBoxControlBuilder

TextControl   .NET 1.1, disposable

System.Web.UI.MobileControls (system.web.mobile.dll)   abstract class

This abstract class defines base functionality for several control classes, including the
TextBox, Label, Link, and Command classes. It defines both a Text property and InnerText property (which includes the text of any nested child controls).

```
public abstract class TextControl : MobileControl {
// Protected Constructors
  protected TextControl( );
// Public Instance Properties
  public string Text{set; get; }
}
```

Hierarchy   System.Object → System.Web.UI.Control(System.ComponentModel.IComponent, System.
               IDisposable, System.Web.UI.IParserAccessor, System.Web.UI.IDataBindingsAccessor) →
               MobileControl(System.Web.UI.IAttributeAccessor) → TextControl

Subclasses   BaseValidator, Command, Label, Link, PhoneCall, TextBox

Returned By   System.Web.UI.MobileControls.Adapters.HtmlLabelAdapter.Control, System.Web.UI.Mobile-
                 Controls.Adapters.WmlLabelAdapter.Control

System.Web.UI.MobileControls (system.web.mobile.dll)   class

The TextView control is similar to the Label in that it provides a control that displays text which you can programmatically modify through the Text property. However, the Text-View also has the ability to subdivide its content over multiple pages automatically. If the TextView is on a Panel or Form which has its Paginate property set to True, the text it contains will automatically be divided into distinct TextViewElement objects, one for each page. You can access individual TextViewElement instances using the GetElement( ) method (and supplying an index number), and you can use properties like FirstVisibleElementIndex and LastVisibleElementIndex to examine the pagination that has been applied automatically.

You can use insert markup tags directly into the text of a TextView. Supported tags include <a> (anchor), <b> (bold), <i> (italic),
 (line break), and <p> (paragraph). These tags will be rendered in a device-independent manner, which means that a <p> could conceivably be translated into a <br> tag if required by the client device. In order to ensure compatibility across a broad range of devices, all other tags are ignored, and will never affect the control's output.

```
public class TextView : PagedControl {
// Public Constructors
   public TextView( );
// Public Instance Properties
   public int FirstVisibleElementIndex{get; }
   public int FirstVisibleElementOffset{get; }
   public int ItemCount{set; get; }                                          // overrides PagedControl
   public int ItemsPerPage{set; get; }                                       // overrides PagedControl
   public int LastVisibleElementIndex{get; }
   public int LastVisibleElementOffset{get; }
   public string Text{set; get; }
// Protected Instance Properties
   protected override int InternalItemCount{get; }                           // overrides PagedControl
   protected override int ItemWeight{get; }                                  // overrides PagedControl
// Public Instance Methods
   public TextViewElement GetElement( int index);
   public override void PaginateRecursive(ControlPager pager);               // overrides PagedControl
// Protected Instance Methods
   protected override void OnRender(System.Web.UI.HtmlTextWriter writer);    // overrides MobileControl
// Events
   public event LoadItemsEventHandler LoadItems;                             // overrides PagedControl
}
```

Hierarchy   System.Object → System.Web.UI.Control(System.ComponentModel.IComponent, System. IDisposable, System.Web.UI.IParserAccessor, System.Web.UI.IDataBindingsAccessor) → MobileControl(System.Web.UI.IAttributeAccessor) → PagedControl → TextView

Returned By   System.Web.UI.MobileControls.Adapters.HtmlTextViewAdapter.Control, System.Web.UI. MobileControls.Adapters.WmlTextViewAdapter.Control

TextViewElement

System.Web.UI.MobileControls (system.web.mobile.dll)   class

The TextViewElement represents a portion of the text of a TextView, which is split automatically to accomodate the size of the client's pages. You can access individual TextViewElement instances using the TextView.GetElement( ) method (and supplying an index number), and you can use TextView properties like TextView.FirstVisibleElementIndex and TextView.LastVisibleElementIndex to examine the pagination that has been applied automatically. You can also determine the formatting and text in a given element by examining properties like Text, IsBold, and IsItalic.

```
public class TextViewElement {
// Public Instance Properties
  public bool BreakAfter{get; }
  public bool IsBold{get; }
  public bool IsItalic{get; }
  public string Text{get; }
  public string Url{get; }
}
```

Returned By   TextView.GetElement( )

ValidationSummary

System.Web.UI.MobileControls (system.web.mobile.dll)   class

The ValidationSummary plays the same role as the System.Web.UI.WebControls.ValidationSummary control in a web page. The ValidationSummary receives the error text messages from all the validation controls on the mobile form, and presents them inline or on a separate form. You specify the form that should be validated using the FormToValidate property. The ValidationSummary is populated automatically when the form is validated.

```
public class ValidationSummary : MobileControl {
// Public Constructors
  public ValidationSummary( );
// Public Instance Properties
  public string BackLabel{set; get; }
  public string FormToValidate{set; get; }
  public string HeaderText{set; get; }
  public override string StyleReference{set; get; }        // overrides MobileControl
// Public Instance Methods
  public string[ ] GetErrorMessages( );
// Protected Instance Methods
  protected override void OnLoad( EventArgs e);            // overrides MobileControl
}
```

Hierarchy   System.Object → System.Web.UI.Control(System.ComponentModel.IComponent, System.IDisposable, System.Web.UI.IParserAccessor, System.Web.UI.IDataBindingsAccessor) → MobileControl(System.Web.UI.IAttributeAccessor) → ValidationSummary

Returned By   System.Web.UI.MobileControls.Adapters.HtmlValidationSummaryAdapter.Control, System.Web.UI.MobileControls.Adapters.WmlValidationSummaryAdapter.Control

Wrapping

serializable

System.Web.UI.MobileControls (system.web.mobile.dll) enum

This enumeration is used to set the MobileControl.Wrapping property, which specifies if a control can span multiple lines. To find out if a mobile device supports non-wrappable lines, you can check the System.Web.Mobile.MobileCapabilities.SupportsDivNoWrap. property.

```
public enum Wrapping {
  NotSet = 0,
  Wrap = 1,
  NoWrap = 2
}
```

Hierarchy   System.Object → System.ValueType → System.Enum(System.IComparable, System.IFor-mattable, System.IConvertible) → Wrapping

Returned By   MobileControl.Wrapping, Style.Wrapping

Passed To   MobileControl.Wrapping, Style.Wrapping

41

The System.Web.UI. MobileControls.Adapters Namespace

ASP.NET mobile pages are built on a device adapter model that allows pages to support multiple different devices that have different capabilities or expect different types of markup. This allows developers to create device-independent mobile forms that will render into WML, cHTML (compact HTML), or HTML. The mobile controls are mapped to specific adapters that generate the appropriate output using the <mobileControls> section of the *web.config* and *machine.config* files. Microsoft provides regular updates to support additional devices (available for online download), and you can even develop your own control adapter classes.

The System.Web.UI.MobileControls.Adapters namespace defines three adapter sets. These include WML-specific classes (which render WML 1.1), cHTML-specific classes (which render HTML 3.0 without any client-side scripting), and HTML-specific classes (which render HTML 3.2 without client-side scripting). You can extend these adapters and customize the output by overriding the Render() method they provide, or you can create your own by implementing the System.Web.UI.MobileControls. IControlAdapter and System.Web.UI.MobileControls.IPageAdapter interfaces. Figures 41-1 and 41-2 show the types from this namespace.

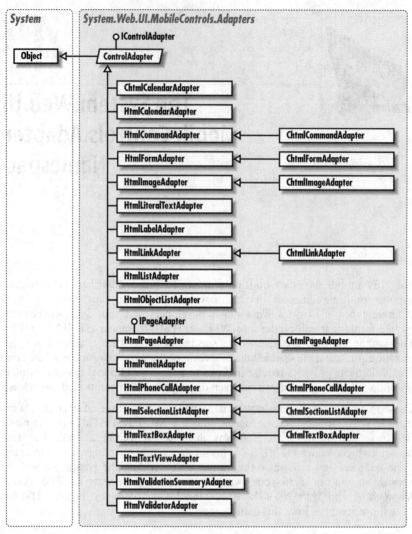

Figure 41-1. Some types from the System.Web.UI.MobileControls.Adapters namespace

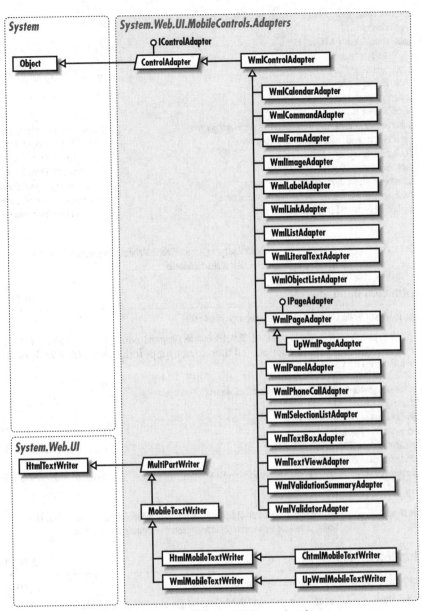

Figure 41-2. More types from System.Web.UI.MobileControls.Adapters

ChtmlCalendarAdapter

.NET 1.1

System.Web.UI.MobileControls.Adapters (system.web.mobile.dll)   class

This adapter renders the System.Web.UI.MobileControls.Calendar control to cHTML. The calendar cannot be displayed on a single page; instead, it will be rendered as a sort of date-picker "wizard" over multiple pages.

```
public class ChtmlCalendarAdapter : HtmlControlAdapter {
// Public Constructors
  public ChtmlCalendarAdapter( );
// Public Instance Properties
  public override bool RequiresFormTag{get; }                              // overrides HtmlControlAdapter
// Protected Instance Properties
  protected Calendar Control{get; }
// Public Instance Methods
  public override bool HandlePostBackEvent(string eventArgument);          // overrides ControlAdapter
  public override void LoadAdapterState( object state);                    // overrides HtmlControlAdapter
  public override void OnInit( EventArgs e);                               // overrides ControlAdapter
  public override void OnLoad( EventArgs e);                               // overrides ControlAdapter
  public override void OnPreRender( EventArgs e);                          // overrides ControlAdapter
  public override void Render( HtmlMobileTextWriter writer);              // overrides HtmlControlAdapter
  public override object SaveAdapterState( );                             // overrides HtmlControlAdapter
}
```

Hierarchy System.Object → ControlAdapter(System.Web.UI.MobileControls.IControlAdapter) → HtmlControlAdapter → ChtmlCalendarAdapter

ChtmlCommandAdapter   .NET 1.1

System.Web.UI.MobileControls.Adapters (system.web.mobile.dll)   class

This adapter renders the System.Web.UI.MobileControls.Command control to cHTML. cHTML devices do not support JavaScript, and thus do not support the System.Web.UI.MobileControls.CommandFormat.Link style.

```
public class ChtmlCommandAdapter : HtmlCommandAdapter {
// Public Constructors
  public ChtmlCommandAdapter( );
// Public Instance Properties
  public override bool RequiresFormTag{get; }                              // overrides HtmlControlAdapter
// Protected Instance Methods
  protected override void AddAttributes(HtmlMobileTextWriter writer);      // overrides HtmlControlAdapter
}
```

Hierarchy System.Object → ControlAdapter(System.Web.UI.MobileControls.IControlAdapter) → HtmlControlAdapter → HtmlCommandAdapter → ChtmlCommandAdapter

ChtmlFormAdapter   .NET 1.1

System.Web.UI.MobileControls.Adapters (system.web.mobile.dll)   class

This adapter renders the System.Web.UI.MobileControls.Form control to cHTML.

```
public class ChtmlFormAdapter : HtmlFormAdapter {
// Public Constructors
  public ChtmlFormAdapter( );
// Protected Instance Methods
  protected override bool RenderExtraHeadElements(HtmlMobileTextWriter writer);   // overrides HtmlFormAdapter
  protected internal override void RenderPagerTag(HtmlMobileTextWriter writer,
    int pageToNavigate, string text);                                            // overrides HtmlFormAdapter
```

```
    protected override bool ShouldRenderFormTag( );                              // overrides HtmlFormAdapter
}
```

Hierarchy   System.Object → ControlAdapter(System.Web.UI.MobileControls.IControlAdapter) →
                      HtmlControlAdapter → HtmlFormAdapter → ChtmlFormAdapter

ChtmlImageAdapter   .NET 1.1

System.Web.UI.MobileControls.Adapters (system.web.mobile.dll)   class

This adapter renders the System.Web.UI.MobileControls.Image control to cHTML. Usually, it
will select the appropriate cHTML-compatible image from the device-specific ImageUrl
you specify.

```
public class ChtmlImageAdapter : HtmlImageAdapter {
// Public Constructors
    public ChtmlImageAdapter( );
// Protected Instance Methods
    protected override void AddAttributes(HtmlMobileTextWriter writer);          // overrides HtmlControlAdapter
    protected internal override void RenderImage(HtmlMobileTextWriter writer);    // overrides HtmlImageAdapter
}
```

Hierarchy   System.Object → ControlAdapter(System.Web.UI.MobileControls.IControlAdapter) →
                      HtmlControlAdapter → HtmlImageAdapter → ChtmlImageAdapter

ChtmlLinkAdapter   .NET 1.1

System.Web.UI.MobileControls.Adapters (system.web.mobile.dll)   class

This adapter renders the System.Web.UI.MobileControls.Link control to cHTML.

```
public class ChtmlLinkAdapter : HtmlLinkAdapter {
// Public Constructors
    public ChtmlLinkAdapter( );
// Protected Instance Methods
    protected override void AddAttributes(HtmlMobileTextWriter writer);          // overrides HtmlControlAdapter
}
```

Hierarchy   System.Object → ControlAdapter(System.Web.UI.MobileControls.IControlAdapter) →
                      HtmlControlAdapter → HtmlLinkAdapter → ChtmlLinkAdapter

ChtmlMobileTextWriter   .NET 1.1, marshal by reference, disposable

System.Web.UI.MobileControls.Adapters (system.web.mobile.dll)   class

Device adapters that render cHTML use the ChtmlMobileTextWriter to write their output.
The ChtmlMobileTextWriter instance is provided in adapter methods like Render( ).

```
public class ChtmlMobileTextWriter : HtmlMobileTextWriter {
// Public Constructors
    public ChtmlMobileTextWriter(System.IO.TextWriter writer, System.Web.Mobile.MobileCapabilities device);
}
```

System.Object → System.MarshalByRefObject → System.IO.TextWriter(System.IDispos-
able) → System.Web.UI.HtmlTextWriter → MultiPartWriter → MobileTextWriter →
HtmlMobileTextWriter → ChtmlMobileTextWriter

ChtmlPageAdapter   .NET 1.1

System.Web.UI.MobileControls.Adapters (system.web.mobile.dll)   class

The ChtmlPageAdapter renders System.Web.UI.MobileControls.MobilePage instances to cHTML. The
process for rendering a device-specific page is much the same as the process for
rendering a device-specific control, although the page adapter has additional responsibilities. These include creating the device-specific text writer for all adapters (using
CreateTextWriter()), retrieving postback data (using DeterminePostBackMode() and
HandlePagePostBackEvent()), and handling errors (using HandleError()).

```
public class ChtmlPageAdapter : HtmlPageAdapter {
// Public Constructors
   public ChtmlPageAdapter( );
// Protected Instance Properties
   protected override string EventArgumentKey{get; }                        // overrides HtmlPageAdapter
   protected override string EventSourceKey{get; }                          // overrides HtmlPageAdapter
// Public Static Methods
   public static bool DeviceQualifies(System.Web.HttpContext context);
// Public Instance Methods
   public override HtmlTextWriter CreateTextWriter(System.IO.TextWriter writer);    // overrides HtmlPageAdapter
   public override NameValueCollection DeterminePostBackMode(System.Web.HttpRequest request,
      string postEventSourceID, string postEventArgumentID,
      System.Collections.Specialized.NameValueCollection baseCollection);          // overrides HtmlPageAdapter
   public override void RenderPostBackEvent(HtmlMobileTextWriter writer, string target,
      string argument);                                                            // overrides HtmlPageAdapter
   public override void RenderPostBackHeader(HtmlMobileTextWriter writer,
      System.Web.UI.MobileControls.Form form);                                     // overrides HtmlPageAdapter
}
```

Hierarchy   System.Object → ControlAdapter(System.Web.UI.MobileControls.IControlAdapter) →
HtmlControlAdapter → HtmlPageAdapter(System.Web.UI.MobileControls.IPageAdapter) →
ChtmlPageAdapter

ChtmlPhoneCallAdapter   .NET 1.1

System.Web.UI.MobileControls.Adapters (system.web.mobile.dll)   class

This adapter renders the System.Web.UI.MobileControls.PhoneCall control to cHTML by using a
"tel:" URL on a device with telephony capability.

```
public class ChtmlPhoneCallAdapter : HtmlPhoneCallAdapter {
// Public Constructors
   public ChtmlPhoneCallAdapter( );
// Protected Instance Methods
   protected override void AddAttributes(HtmlMobileTextWriter writer);             // overrides HtmlControlAdapter
}
```

Hierarchy   System.Object → ControlAdapter(System.Web.UI.MobileControls.IControlAdapter) →
HtmlControlAdapter → HtmlPhoneCallAdapter → ChtmlPhoneCallAdapter

ChtmlSelectionListAdapter

.NET 1.1

System.Web.UI.MobileControls.Adapters (system.web.mobile.dll)   class

This adapter renders the System.Web.UI.MobileControls.SelectionList control to cHTML.

```
public class ChtmlSelectionListAdapter : HtmlSelectionListAdapter {
// Public Constructors
  public ChtmlSelectionListAdapter( );
// Public Instance Properties
  public override bool RequiresFormTag{get; }                               // overrides HtmlControlAdapter
// Public Instance Methods
  public override void Render(HtmlMobileTextWriter writer);              // overrides HtmlSelectionListAdapter
}
```

Hierarchy   System.Object → ControlAdapter(System.Web.UI.MobileControls.IControlAdapter) →
HtmlControlAdapter → HtmlSelectionListAdapter → ChtmlSelectionListAdapter

ChtmlTextBoxAdapter

.NET 1.1

System.Web.UI.MobileControls.Adapters (system.web.mobile.dll)   class

This adapter renders the System.Web.UI.MobileControls.TextBox control to cHTML.

```
public class ChtmlTextBoxAdapter : HtmlTextBoxAdapter {
// Public Constructors
  public ChtmlTextBoxAdapter( );
// Public Instance Properties
  public override bool RequiresFormTag{get; }                               // overrides HtmlControlAdapter
// Protected Instance Methods
  protected override void AddAttributes(HtmlMobileTextWriter writer);    // overrides HtmlControlAdapter
}
```

Hierarchy   System.Object → ControlAdapter(System.Web.UI.MobileControls.IControlAdapter) →
HtmlControlAdapter → HtmlTextBoxAdapter → ChtmlTextBoxAdapter

ControlAdapter

.NET 1.1

System.Web.UI.MobileControls.Adapters (system.web.mobile.dll)   abstract class

The ControlAdapter provides an abstract base class that is used to derive the device-
specific adapter classes in this namespace. The ControlAdapter provides a default implementation of the System.Web.UI.MobileControls.IControlAdapter interface required for all control
adapters. It defines methods for handling postback and viewstate data, and rendering
the actual control content (through the System.Web.UI.MobileControls.IControlAdapter.Render( )
method). Controls that derive from ControlAdapter should use the base implementation of
the Render( ) method for rendering all child controls. This allows the adapter to be used
with composite controls.

Most control adapters will not derive directly from this class. For example, all the
WML-specific adapters derive from WmlControlAdapter, which in turn derives from the

base ControlAdapter class. This is also true of HTML adpters, which derive form HtmlControlAdapter.

```
public abstract class ControlAdapter : System.Web.UI.MobileControls.IControlAdapter {
// Protected Constructorsprotected ControlAdapter( );
// Protected Static Fields
    protected static readonly int BackLabel;                                        // =0
    protected static readonly int CallLabel;                                        // =8
    protected static readonly int GoLabel;                                          // =1
    protected static readonly int LinkLabel;                                        // =7
    protected static readonly int MoreLabel;                                        // =3
    protected static readonly int NextLabel;                                        // =5
    protected static readonly int OKLabel;                                          // =2
    protected static readonly int OptionsLabel;                                     // =4
    protected static readonly int PreviousLabel;                                    // =6
// Public Instance Properties
    public MobileControl Control{set; get; }              // implements System.Web.UI.MobileControls.IControlAdapter
    public virtual MobileCapabilities Device{get; }
    public virtual int ItemWeight{get; }                 // implements System.Web.UI.MobileControls.IControlAdapter
    public virtual MobilePage Page{set; get; }           // implements System.Web.UI.MobileControls.IControlAdapter
    public Style Style{get; }
    public virtual int VisibleWeight{get; }              // implements System.Web.UI.MobileControls.IControlAdapter
// Public Instance Methods
    public virtual void CreateTemplatedUI( bool doDataBind);   // implements System.Web.UI.MobileControls.IControlAdapter
    public virtual bool HandlePostBackEvent(string eventArgument);
                                                         // implements System.Web.UI.MobileControls.IControlAdapter
    public virtual void LoadAdapterState(object state);  // implements System.Web.UI.MobileControls.IControlAdapter
    public virtual bool LoadPostData(string key, System.Collections.Specialized.NameValueCollection data,
        object controlPrivateData, out bool dataChanged);  // implements System.Web.UI.MobileControls.IControlAdapter
    public virtual void OnInit( EventArgs e);            // implements System.Web.UI.MobileControls.IControlAdapter
    public virtual void OnLoad( EventArgs e);            // implements System.Web.UI.MobileControls.IControlAdapter
    public virtual void OnPreRender( EventArgs e);       // implements System.Web.UI.MobileControls.IControlAdapter
    public virtual void OnUnload( EventArgs e);          // implements System.Web.UI.MobileControls.IControlAdapter
    public virtual void Render(System.Web.UI.HtmlTextWriter writer);
                                                         // implements System.Web.UI.MobileControls.IControlAdapter
    public virtual object SaveAdapterState( );           // implements System.Web.UI.MobileControls.IControlAdapter
// Protected Instance Methods
    protected virtual int CalculateOptimumPageWeight( int defaultPageWeight);
    protected string GetDefaultLabel( int labelID);
    protected void RenderChildren(System.Web.UI.HtmlTextWriter writer);
}
```

Subclasses   HtmlControlAdapter, WmlControlAdapter

HtmlCalendarAdapter   .NET 1.1

System.Web.UI.MobileControls.Adapters (system.web.mobile.dll)   class

This adapter renders the System.Web.UI.MobileControls.Calendar control to HTML. In this case, the adatper simply renders the HTML of the underlying System.Web.UI.WebControls.Calendar control, which is provided in the System.Web.UI.MobileControls.Calendar.WebCalendar property.

```
public class HtmlCalendarAdapter : HtmlControlAdapter {
// Public Constructors
  public HtmlCalendarAdapter( );
// Protected Instance Properties
  protected Calendar Control{get; }
// Public Instance Methods
  public override void Render( HtmlMobileTextWriter writer);                    // overrides HtmlControlAdapter
}
```

Hierarchy   System.Object → ControlAdapter(System.Web.UI.MobileControls.IControlAdapter) → HtmlControlAdapter → HtmlCalendarAdapter

HtmlCommandAdapter
.NET 1.1

System.Web.UI.MobileControls.Adapters (system.web.mobile.dll)   class

This adapter renders the System.Web.UI.MobileControls.Command control to HTML.

```
public class HtmlCommandAdapter : HtmlControlAdapter {
// Public Constructors
  public HtmlCommandAdapter( );
// Protected Instance Properties
  protected Command Control{get; }
// Public Instance Methods
  public override bool LoadPostData(string key, System.Collections.Specialized.NameValueCollection data,
    object controlPrivateData, out bool dataChanged);                          // overrides ControlAdapter
  public override void Render( HtmlMobileTextWriter writer);                    // overrides HtmlControlAdapter
}
```

Hierarchy   System.Object → ControlAdapter(System.Web.UI.MobileControls.IControlAdapter) → HtmlControlAdapter → HtmlCommandAdapter

Subclasses   ChtmlCommandAdapter

HtmlControlAdapter
.NET 1.1

System.Web.UI.MobileControls.Adapters (system.web.mobile.dll)   class

All HTML-specific control adapters (which render HTML 3.2 with no client-side script) derive from this base class. It overrides the basic functionality defined in the ControlAdapter class to add HTML-specific support for hyperlinks, and to ensure that the FormAdapter property references a valid HtmlFormAdapter.

```
public class HtmlControlAdapter : ControlAdapter {
// Public Constructors
  public HtmlControlAdapter( );
// Protected Static Fields
  protected static readonly int NotSecondaryUI;                                // =-1
// Public Instance Properties
  public virtual bool RequiresFormTag{get; }
// Protected Instance Properties
  protected HtmlFormAdapter FormAdapter{get; }
  protected HtmlPageAdapter PageAdapter{get; }
```

```
    protected int SecondaryUIMode{set; get; }
// Public Instance Methods
    public override void LoadAdapterState( object state);                           // overrides ControlAdapter
    public virtual void Render( HtmlMobileTextWriter writer);
    public override void Render(System.Web.UI.HtmlTextWriter writer) ;              // overrides ControlAdapter
    public override object SaveAdapterState( );                                     // overrides ControlAdapter
// Protected Instance Methods
    protected virtual void AddAccesskeyAttribute(HtmlMobileTextWriter writer);
    protected virtual void AddAttributes(HtmlMobileTextWriter writer);
    protected virtual void AddJPhoneMultiMediaAttributes(HtmlMobileTextWriter writer);
    protected void ExitSecondaryUIMode( );
    protected virtual void RenderAsHiddenInputField(HtmlMobileTextWriter writer);
    protected void RenderBeginLink(HtmlMobileTextWriter writer, string target);
    protected void RenderEndLink(HtmlMobileTextWriter writer);
    protected void RenderPostBackEventAsAnchor(HtmlMobileTextWriter writer, string argument, string linkText);
    protected void RenderPostBackEventAsAttribute(HtmlMobileTextWriter writer, string attributeName, string argument);
    protected void RenderPostBackEventReference(HtmlMobileTextWriter writer, string argument);
}
```

Hierarchy   System.Object → ControlAdapter(System.Web.UI.MobileControls.IControlAdapter) →
                   HtmlControlAdapter

Subclasses   Multiple types

HtmlFormAdapter   .NET 1.1

System.Web.UI.MobileControls.Adapters (system.web.mobile.dll)   class

This adapter renders the System.Web.UI.MobileControls.Form control to HTML.

```
public class HtmlFormAdapter : HtmlControlAdapter {
// Public Constructors
    public HtmlFormAdapter( );
// Protected Instance Properties
    protected Form Control{get; }
// Public Instance Methods
    public override void Render( HtmlMobileTextWriter writer);                      // overrides HtmlControlAdapter
// Protected Instance Methods
    protected internal void DisablePager( );
    protected virtual void RenderBodyTag(HtmlMobileTextWriter writer, System.Collections.IDictionary attributes);
    protected virtual bool RenderExtraHeadElements(HtmlMobileTextWriter writer);
    protected virtual void RenderPager(HtmlMobileTextWriter writer);
    protected internal virtual void RenderPagerTag(HtmlMobileTextWriter writer, int pageToNavigate, string text);
    protected virtual bool ShouldRenderFormTag( );
}
```

Hierarchy   System.Object → ControlAdapter(System.Web.UI.MobileControls.IControlAdapter) →
                   HtmlControlAdapter → HtmlFormAdapter

Subclasses   ChtmlFormAdapter

Returned By   HtmlControlAdapter.FormAdapter

HtmlImageAdapter

System.Web.UI.MobileControls.Adapters (system.web.mobile.dll)   class

This adapter renders the System.Web.UI.MobileControls.Image control to HTML, which supports most image types.

```
public class HtmlImageAdapter : HtmlControlAdapter {
// Public Constructors
  public HtmlImageAdapter( );
// Protected Instance Properties
  protected Image Control{get; }
// Public Instance Methods
  public override void Render(HtmlMobileTextWriter writer);              // overrides HtmlControlAdapter
// Protected Instance Methods
  protected internal virtual void RenderImage(HtmlMobileTextWriter writer);
}
```

Hierarchy   System.Object → ControlAdapter(System.Web.UI.MobileControls.IControlAdapter) →
                     HtmlControlAdapter → HtmlImageAdapter

Subclasses   ChtmlImageAdapter

HtmlLabelAdapter

System.Web.UI.MobileControls.Adapters (system.web.mobile.dll)   class

This adapter renders the System.Web.UI.MobileControls.Label control to HTML.

```
public class HtmlLabelAdapter : HtmlControlAdapter {
// Public Constructors
  public HtmlLabelAdapter( );
// Protected Instance Properties
  protected TextControl Control{get; }
// Public Instance Methods
  public override void Render(HtmlMobileTextWriter writer);              // overrides HtmlControlAdapter
// Protected Instance Methods
  protected internal bool WhiteSpace(string s);
}
```

Hierarchy   System.Object → ControlAdapter(System.Web.UI.MobileControls.IControlAdapter) →
                     HtmlControlAdapter → HtmlLabelAdapter

HtmlLinkAdapter

System.Web.UI.MobileControls.Adapters (system.web.mobile.dll)   class

This adapter renders the System.Web.UI.MobileControls.Link control to HTML.

```
public class HtmlLinkAdapter : HtmlControlAdapter {
// Public Constructors
  public HtmlLinkAdapter( );
// Protected Instance Properties
  protected Link Control{get; }
```

// Public Instance Methods
```
public override void Render(HtmlMobileTextWriter writer);                    // overrides HtmlControlAdapter
}
```

Hierarchy   System.Object → ControlAdapter(System.Web.UI.MobileControls.IControlAdapter) →
                      HtmlControlAdapter → HtmlLinkAdapter

Subclasses   ChtmlLinkAdapter

HtmlListAdapter   .NET 1.1

System.Web.UI.MobileControls.Adapters (system.web.mobile.dll)   class

This adapter renders the System.Web.UI.MobileControls.List control to HTML.

```
public class HtmlListAdapter : HtmlControlAdapter {
// Public Constructors
  public HtmlListAdapter( );
// Protected Instance Properties
  protected List Control{get; }
// Public Instance Methods
  public override void Render(HtmlMobileTextWriter writer);                    // overrides HtmlControlAdapter
// Protected Instance Methods
  protected virtual void RenderList(HtmlMobileTextWriter writer);
}
```

Hierarchy   System.Object → ControlAdapter(System.Web.UI.MobileControls.IControlAdapter) →
                      HtmlControlAdapter → HtmlListAdapter

HtmlLiteralTextAdapter   .NET 1.1

System.Web.UI.MobileControls.Adapters (system.web.mobile.dll)   class

This adapter renders literal text (represented by the System.Web.UI.MobileControls.LiteralText
control) to cHTML.

```
public class HtmlLiteralTextAdapter : HtmlControlAdapter {
// Public Constructors
  public HtmlLiteralTextAdapter( );
// Protected Instance Properties
  protected LiteralText Control{get; }
// Public Instance Methods
  public override void Render(HtmlMobileTextWriter writer);                    // overrides HtmlControlAdapter
}
```

Hierarchy   System.Object → ControlAdapter(System.Web.UI.MobileControls.IControlAdapter) →
                      HtmlControlAdapter → HtmlLiteralTextAdapter

HtmlMobileTextWriter   .NET 1.1, marshal by reference, disposable

System.Web.UI.MobileControls.Adapters (system.web.mobile.dll)   class

Device adapters that render HTML use the HtmlMobileTextWriter to write their output. The
HtmlMobileTextWriter instance is provided in adapter methods like Render( ).

```
public class HtmlMobileTextWriter : MobileTextWriter {
// Public Constructors
   public HtmlMobileTextWriter(System.IO.TextWriter writer, System.Web.Mobile.MobileCapabilities device);
// Protected Instance Properties
   protected internal bool RenderBodyColor{set; get; }
   protected internal bool RenderBold{set; get; }
   protected internal bool RenderDivAlign{set; get; }
   protected internal bool RenderDivNoWrap{set; get; }
   protected internal bool RenderFontColor{set; get; }
   protected internal bool RenderFontName{set; get; }
   protected internal bool RenderFontSize{set; get; }
   protected internal bool RenderItalic{set; get; }
   protected internal bool RequiresNoBreakInFormatting{set; get; }
// Public Instance Methods
   public void BeginStyleContext( );
   public void EndStyleContext( );
   public override void EnterFormat(System.Web.UI.MobileControls.Style style);          // overrides MobileTextWriter
   public override void EnterLayout(System.Web.UI.MobileControls.Style style);          // overrides MobileTextWriter
   public void EnterStyle(System.Web.UI.MobileControls.Style style);                    // overrides MobileTextWriter
   public override void ExitFormat(System.Web.UI.MobileControls.Style style);           // overrides MobileTextWriter
   public override void ExitFormat(System.Web.UI.MobileControls.Style style, bool breakAfter); // overrides MobileTextWriter
   public override void ExitLayout(System.Web.UI.MobileControls.Style style);           // overrides MobileTextWriter
   public override void ExitLayout(System.Web.UI.MobileControls.Style style, bool breakAfter);  // overrides MobileTextWriter
   public void ExitStyle(System.Web.UI.MobileControls.Style style);                     // overrides MobileTextWriter
   public void ExitStyle(System.Web.UI.MobileControls.Style style, bool breakAfter);
   public override void Write(char c);                                  // overrides System.Web.UI.HtmlTextWriter
   public override void Write(string text);                            // overrides System.Web.UI.HtmlTextWriter
   public override void WriteBeginTag(string tag);                     // overrides System.Web.UI.HtmlTextWriter
   public void WriteBreak( );
   public override void WriteEncodedText(string text);                             // overrides MobileTextWriter
   public override void WriteFullBeginTag(string tag);                 // overrides System.Web.UI.HtmlTextWriter
   public void WriteHiddenField(string name, string value);
   public override void WriteLine(string text);                        // overrides System.Web.UI.HtmlTextWriter
   public void WriteText(string text, bool encodeText);
   public void WriteUrlParameter(string name, string value);
// Protected Instance Methods
   protected internal void MarkStyleContext( );
   protected internal void UnMarkStyleContext( );
}
```

Hierarchy	System.Object → System.MarshalByRefObject → System.IO.TextWriter(System.IDisposable) → System.Web.UI.HtmlTextWriter → MultiPartWriter → MobileTextWriter → HtmlMobileTextWriter
Subclasses	ChtmlMobileTextWriter
Passed To	Multiple types

System.Web.UI.MobileControls.Adapters (system.web.mobile.dll) class

This adapter renders the System.Web.UI.MobileControls.ObjectList control to HTML. The list can be rendered in one of two basic formats. If you have not set any System.Web.UI.MobileControls.ObjectList.TableFields, the list is rendered as a table with the property or field specified by System.Web.UI.MobileControls.ObjectList.LabelItem displayed for each item. The user can view a menu of related commands and a list of additional fields for the item by clicking a "More" link next to the item. Alternatively, if you have set one or more System.Web.UI.MobileControls.ObjectList.TableFields, these will be used to create a table for each item, which will be shown instead of the simple list.

```
public class HtmlObjectListAdapter : HtmlControlAdapter {
// Public Constructors
  public HtmlObjectListAdapter( );
// Protected Instance Properties
  protected ObjectList Control{get; }
// Public Instance Methods
  public override void CreateTemplatedUI( bool doDataBind);              // overrides ControlAdapter
  public override bool HandlePostBackEvent(string eventArgument);        // overrides ControlAdapter
  public override void OnInit( EventArgs e);                             // overrides ControlAdapter
  public override void OnPreRender( EventArgs e);                        // overrides ControlAdapter
  public override void Render( HtmlMobileTextWriter writer);            // overrides HtmlControlAdapter
// Protected Instance Methods
  protected bool HasCommands( );
  protected bool HasDefaultCommand( );
  protected bool HasItemDetails( );
  protected bool OnlyHasDefaultCommand( );
  protected virtual void RenderItemDetails(HtmlMobileTextWriter writer,
    System.Web.UI.MobileControls.ObjectListItem item);
  protected virtual void RenderItemsList( HtmlMobileTextWriter writer);
  protected virtual bool ShouldRenderAsTable( );
}
```

Hierarchy   System.Object → ControlAdapter(System.Web.UI.MobileControls.IControlAdapter) → HtmlControlAdapter → HtmlObjectListAdapter

HtmlPageAdapter .NET 1.1

System.Web.UI.MobileControls.Adapters (system.web.mobile.dll) class

The HtmlPageAdapter renders System.Web.UI.MobileControls.MobilePage instances to HTML. The process for rendering a device-specific page is much the same as the process for rendering a device-specific control, although the page adapter has additional responsibilities. These include creating the device-specific text writer for all adapters (using CreateTextWriter( )), retrieving postback data (using DeterminePostBackMode( ) and HandlePagePostBackEvent( )), and handling errors (using HandleError( )).

```
public class HtmlPageAdapter : HtmlControlAdapter, System.Web.UI.MobileControls.IPageAdapter {
// Public Constructors
  public HtmlPageAdapter( );
// Protected Constructors
```

```
   protected internal HtmlPageAdapter(int defaultPageWeight);
// Public Instance Properties
   public virtual IList CacheVaryByHeaders{get; }              // implements System.Web.UI.MobileControls.IPageAdapter
   public IDictionary CookielessDataDictionary{set; get; }     // implements System.Web.UI.MobileControls.IPageAdapter
   public virtual int OptimumPageWeight{get; }                 // implements System.Web.UI.MobileControls.IPageAdapter
   public override MobilePage Page{set; get; }                                       // overrides ControlAdapter
   public bool PersistCookielessData{set; get; }               // implements System.Web.UI.MobileControls.IPageAdapter
// Protected Instance Properties
   protected virtual string EventArgumentKey{get; }
   protected virtual string EventSourceKey{get; }
// Public Static Methods
   public static bool DeviceQualifies(System.Web.HttpContext context);
// Public Instance Methods
   public virtual HtmlTextWriter CreateTextWriter(System.IO.TextWriter writer);
                                                              // implements System.Web.UI.MobileControls.IPageAdapter
   public virtual NameValueCollection DeterminePostBackMode(System.Web.HttpRequest request,
      string postEventSourceID, string postEventArgumentID,
      System.Collections.Specialized.NameValueCollection baseCollection);
                                                              // implements System.Web.UI.MobileControls.IPageAdapter
   public string GetFormUrl(System.Web.UI.MobileControls.Form form);
   public virtual bool HandleError(Exception e, System.Web.UI.HtmlTextWriter writer);
                                                              // implements System.Web.UI.MobileControls.IPageAdapter
   public virtual bool HandlePagePostBackEvent(string eventSource, string eventArgument);
                                                              // implements System.Web.UI.MobileControls.IPageAdapter
   public virtual bool IsFormRendered(System.Web.UI.MobileControls.Form form);
   public override void Render(HtmlMobileTextWriter writer);                    // overrides HtmlControlAdapter
   public virtual void RenderForm(HtmlMobileTextWriter writer, System.Web.UI.MobileControls.Form form);
   public virtual void RenderPostBackEvent(HtmlMobileTextWriter writer, string target, string argument);
   public virtual void RenderPostBackHeader(HtmlMobileTextWriter writer, System.Web.UI.MobileControls.Form form);
   public virtual void RenderUrlPostBackEvent(HtmlMobileTextWriter writer, string target, string argument);
// Protected Instance Methods
   protected void RenderHiddenVariables(HtmlMobileTextWriter writer);
}
```

Hierarchy System.Object → ControlAdapter(System.Web.UI.MobileControls.IControlAdapter) →
             HtmlControlAdapter → HtmlPageAdapter(System.Web.UI.MobileControls.IPageAdapter)

Subclasses ChtmlPageAdapter

Returned By HtmlControlAdapter.PageAdapter

HtmlPanelAdapter   .NET 1.1

System.Web.UI.MobileControls.Adapters (system.web.mobile.dll)   class

This adapter renders the System.Web.UI.MobileControls.Panel control to HTML.

```
public class HtmlPanelAdapter : HtmlControlAdapter {
// Public Constructors
   public HtmlPanelAdapter( );
// Protected Instance Properties
   protected Panel Control{get; }
```

```
// Public Instance Methods
  public override void OnInit( EventArgs e);                                           // overrides ControlAdapter
  public override void Render( HtmlMobileTextWriter writer);                           // overrides HtmlControlAdapter
}
```

Hierarchy   System.Object → ControlAdapter(System.Web.UI.MobileControls.IControlAdapter) →
                       HtmlControlAdapter → HtmlPanelAdapter

HtmlPhoneCallAdapter   .NET 1.1

System.Web.UI.MobileControls.Adapters (system.web.mobile.dll)   class

This adapter renders the System.Web.UI.MobileControls.PhoneCall control to HTML by using a
"tel:" URL on a device with telephony capability.

```
public class HtmlPhoneCallAdapter : HtmlControlAdapter {
// Public Constructors
  public HtmlPhoneCallAdapter( );
// Protected Instance Properties
  protected PhoneCall Control{get; }
// Public Instance Methods
  public override void Render(HtmlMobileTextWriter writer);                            // overrides HtmlControlAdapter
}
```

Hierarchy   System.Object → ControlAdapter(System.Web.UI.MobileControls.IControlAdapter) →
                       HtmlControlAdapter → HtmlPhoneCallAdapter

Subclasses   ChtmlPhoneCallAdapter

HtmlSelectionListAdapter   .NET 1.1

System.Web.UI.MobileControls.Adapters (system.web.mobile.dll)   class

This adapter renders the System.Web.UI.MobileControls.SelectionList control to HTML.

```
public class HtmlSelectionListAdapter : HtmlControlAdapter {
// Public Constructors
  public HtmlSelectionListAdapter( );
// Protected Instance Properties
  protected SelectionList Control{get; }
// Public Instance Methods
  public override bool LoadPostData(string key, System.Collections.Specialized.NameValueCollection data,
    object controlPrivateData, out bool dataChanged);                                  // overrides ControlAdapter
  public override void OnInit(EventArgs e);                                            // overrides ControlAdapter
  public override void Render(HtmlMobileTextWriter writer);                            // overrides HtmlControlAdapter
// Protected Instance Methods
  protected override void RenderAsHiddenInputField(HtmlMobileTextWriter writer);       // overrides HtmlControlAdapter
}
```

Hierarchy   System.Object → ControlAdapter(System.Web.UI.MobileControls.IControlAdapter) →
                       HtmlControlAdapter → HtmlSelectionListAdapter

Subclasses   ChtmlSelectionListAdapter

HtmlTextBoxAdapter

System.Web.UI.MobileControls.Adapters (system.web.mobile.dll)   class

This adapter renders the System.Web.UI.MobileControls.TextBox control to HTML.

```
public class HtmlTextBoxAdapter : HtmlControlAdapter {
// Public Constructors
  public HtmlTextBoxAdapter( );
// Protected Instance Properties
  protected TextBox Control{get; }
// Public Instance Methods
  public override void OnInit(EventArgs e);                        // overrides ControlAdapter
  public override void Render(HtmlMobileTextWriter writer);        // overrides HtmlControlAdapter
// Protected Instance Methods
  protected override void RenderAsHiddenInputField(HtmlMobileTextWriter writer);    // overrides HtmlControlAdapter
}
```

Hierarchy   System.Object → ControlAdapter(System.Web.UI.MobileControls.IControlAdapter) →
                     HtmlControlAdapter → HtmlTextBoxAdapter

Subclasses   ChtmlTextBoxAdapter

HtmlTextViewAdapter

System.Web.UI.MobileControls.Adapters (system.web.mobile.dll)   class

This adapter renders the System.Web.UI.MobileControls.TextView control to HTML.

```
public class HtmlTextViewAdapter : HtmlControlAdapter {
// Public Constructors
  public HtmlTextViewAdapter( );
// Protected Instance Properties
  protected TextView Control{get; }
// Public Instance Methods
  public override void Render(HtmlMobileTextWriter writer);        // overrides HtmlControlAdapter
}
```

Hierarchy   System.Object → ControlAdapter(System.Web.UI.MobileControls.IControlAdapter) →
                     HtmlControlAdapter → HtmlTextViewAdapter

HtmlValidationSummaryAdapter

System.Web.UI.MobileControls.Adapters (system.web.mobile.dll)   class

This adapter renders the System.Web.UI.MobileControls.ValidationSummary control (which
displays a list of validation errors) to HTML.

```
public class HtmlValidationSummaryAdapter : HtmlControlAdapter {
// Public Constructors
  public HtmlValidationSummaryAdapter( );
// Protected Instance Properties
  protected ValidationSummary Control{get; }
// Public Instance Methods
```

```
public override void OnInit( EventArgs e);                          // overrides ControlAdapter
public override void Render( HtmlMobileTextWriter writer);          // overrides HtmlControlAdapter
}
```

Hierarchy   System.Object → ControlAdapter(System.Web.UI.MobileControls.IControlAdapter) →
                  HtmlControlAdapter → HtmlValidationSummaryAdapter

HtmlValidatorAdapter   .NET 1.1

System.Web.UI.MobileControls.Adapters (system.web.mobile.dll)   class

This adapter renders all the validation controls (which derive from System.Web.UI.Mobile-
Controls.BaseValidator) control to HTML.

```
public class HtmlValidatorAdapter : HtmlControlAdapter {
// Public Constructors
  public HtmlValidatorAdapter( );
// Protected Instance Properties
  protected BaseValidator Control{get; }
// Public Instance Methods
  public override void Render( HtmlMobileTextWriter writer);        // overrides HtmlControlAdapter
}
```

Hierarchy   System.Object → ControlAdapter(System.Web.UI.MobileControls.IControlAdapter) →
                  HtmlControlAdapter → HtmlValidatorAdapter

MobileTextWriter   .NET 1.1, marshal by reference, disposable

System.Web.UI.MobileControls.Adapters (system.web.mobile.dll)   class

All adapters render mobile controls using a special System.Web.UI.HtmlTextWriter that is
customized for the type of markup. For example, device adapters that render cHTML
use the ChtmlMobileTextWriter, and those that use WML use the WmlMobileTextWriter. All these
classes inherit from the base MobileTextWriter, which defines the basic methods for
writing, text, styles, and URL information.

```
public class MobileTextWriter : MultiPartWriter {
// Public Constructors
  public MobileTextWriter(System.IO.TextWriter writer, System.Web.Mobile.MobileCapabilities device);
// Public Instance Properties
  public MobileCapabilities Device{get; }
  public override bool SupportsMultiPart{get; }                     // overrides MultiPartWriter
// Public Instance Methods
  public override void AddResource(string url, string contentType);   // overrides MultiPartWriter
  public override void BeginFile(string url, string contentType, string charset);  // overrides MultiPartWriter
  public override void BeginResponse( );                             // overrides MultiPartWriter
  public override void EndFile( );                                   // overrides MultiPartWriter
  public override void EndResponse( );                               // overrides MultiPartWriter
  public virtual void EnterFormat(System.Web.UI.MobileControls.Style style);
  public virtual void EnterLayout(System.Web.UI.MobileControls.Style style);
  public void EnterStyle(System.Web.UI.MobileControls.Style style);
  public virtual void ExitFormat(System.Web.UI.MobileControls.Style style);
  public virtual void ExitFormat(System.Web.UI.MobileControls.Style style, bool breakAfter);
  public virtual void ExitLayout(System.Web.UI.MobileControls.Style style);
```

```
    public virtual void ExitLayout(System.Web.UI.MobileControls.Style style, bool breakAfter);
    public void ExitStyle(System.Web.UI.MobileControls.Style style);
    public virtual void WriteEncodedText( string text);
    public virtual void WriteEncodedUrl( string url);
    public virtual void WriteEncodedUrlParameter(string urlText);
// Protected Instance Methods
    protected void WriteUrlEncodedString(string s, bool argument);
}
```

Hierarchy   System.Object → System.MarshalByRefObject → System.IO.TextWriter(System.IDispos-
                 able) → System.Web.UI.HtmlTextWriter → MultiPartWriter → MobileTextWriter

Subclasses   HtmlMobileTextWriter, WmlMobileTextWriter

MultiPartWriter   .NET 1.1, marshal by reference, disposable

System.Web.UI.MobileControls.Adapters (system.web.mobile.dll)   abstract class

This class supports the MobileTextWriter, which is used to render mobile control output.

```
public abstract class MultiPartWriter : System.Web.UI.HtmlTextWriter {
// Protected Constructorsprotected MultiPartWriter( System.IO.TextWriter writer);
// Public Instance Properties
    public virtual bool SupportsMultiPart{get; }
// Public Instance Methods
    public void AddResource( string url);
    public abstract void AddResource(string url, string contentType);
    public abstract void BeginFile(string url, string contentType, string charset);
    public abstract void BeginResponse( );
    public abstract void EndFile( );
    public abstract void EndResponse( );
    public virtual string NewUrl( string filetype);
}
```

Hierarchy   System.Object → System.MarshalByRefObject → System.IO.TextWriter(System.IDispos-
                 able) → System.Web.UI.HtmlTextWriter → MultiPartWriter

Subclasses   MobileTextWriter

UpWmlMobileTextWriter   .NET 1.1, marshal by reference, disposable

System.Web.UI.MobileControls.Adapters (system.web.mobile.dll)   class

Provides a customized WmlMobileTextWriter that is optimized for use with Openwave's UP
browser.

```
public class UpWmlMobileTextWriter : WmlMobileTextWriter {
// Public Constructors
    public UpWmlMobileTextWriter(System.IO.TextWriter writer, System.Web.Mobile.MobileCapabilities device,
        System.Web.UI.MobileControls.MobilePage page);
// Public Instance Methods
    public override void BeginCustomMarkup( );                         // overrides WmlMobileTextWriter
    public override void BeginForm(Controls.Form form);        // overrides WmlMobileTextWriterSystem.Web.UI.Mobile
```

public override void **EndForm**( );	*// overrides WmlMobileTextWriter*
public override void **RenderBeginHyperlink**(string *targetUrl*, bool *encodeUrl*,	
string *softkeyLabel*, bool *implicitSoftkeyLabel*, bool *mapToSoftkey*);	*// overrides WmlMobileTextWriter*
public override void **RenderBeginPostBack**(string *softkeyLabel*, bool *implicitSoftkeyLabel*,	
bool *mapToSoftkey*);	*// overrides WmlMobileTextWriter*
public override void **RenderBeginSelect**(string *name*, string *iname*, string *ivalue*,	
string *title*, bool *multiSelect*);	*// overrides WmlMobileTextWriter*
public override void **RenderEndHyperlink**(bool *breakAfter*);	*// overrides WmlMobileTextWriter*
public override void **RenderEndPostBack**(string *target*, string *argument*,	
WmlPostFieldType *postBackType*, bool *includeVariables*, bool *breakAfter*);	*// overrides WmlMobileTextWriter*
public override void **RenderEndSelect**(bool *breakAfter*);	*// overrides WmlMobileTextWriter*
public override void **RenderImage**(string *source*, string *localSource*, string *alternateText*,	
bool *breakAfter*);	*// overrides WmlMobileTextWriter*
public override void **RenderSelectOption**(string *text*);	*// overrides WmlMobileTextWriter*
public override void **RenderSelectOption**(string *text*, string *value*);	*// overrides WmlMobileTextWriter*
public override void **RenderText**(string *text*, bool *breakAfter*, bool *encodeText*);	*// overrides WmlMobileTextWriter*
public override void **RenderTextBox**(string *id*, string *value*, string *format*, string *title*,	
bool *password*, int *size*, int *maxLength*, bool *generateRandomID*, bool *breakAfter*);	*// overrides WmlMobileTextWriter*
// Protected Instance Methods	
protected override void **AnalyzePostBack**(bool *includeVariables*,	
WmlPostFieldType *postBackType*);	*// overrides WmlMobileTextWriter*
protected override string **CalculateFormPostBackUrl**(bool *externalSubmit*,	
ref bool *encode*);	*// overrides WmlMobileTextWriter*
protected override string **CalculateFormQueryString**( );	*// overrides WmlMobileTextWriter*
protected override void **OpenParagraph**(WmlLayout *layout*,bool *writeAlignment*,	
bool *writeWrapping*);	*// overrides WmlMobileTextWriter*
protected override void **PostAnalyzeForm**( );	*// overrides WmlMobileTextWriter*
protected override void **RenderEndForm**( );	*// overrides WmlMobileTextWriter*

}

Hierarchy System.Object → System.MarshalByRefObject → System.IO.TextWriter(System.IDisposable) → System.Web.UI.HtmlTextWriter → MultiPartWriter → MobileTextWriter → WmlMobileTextWriter → UpWmlMobileTextWriter

UpWmlPageAdapter   .NET 1.1

System.Web.UI.MobileControls.Adapters (system.web.mobile.dll)   class

Provides a customized WmlPageAdapter that is optimized for use with Openwave's UP browser.

public class **UpWmlPageAdapter** : WmlPageAdapter {
// Public Constructors
public **UpWmlPageAdapter**( );
// Public Static Methods
public static bool **DeviceQualifies**(System.Web.HttpContext *context*);
// Public Instance Methods
public override HtmlTextWriter **CreateTextWriter**(System.IO.TextWriter *writer*);   *// overrides WmlPageAdapter*

}

Hierarchy System.Object → ControlAdapter(System.Web.UI.MobileControls.IControlAdapter) → WmlControlAdapter → WmlPageAdapter(System.Web.UI.MobileControls.IPageAdapter) → UpWmlPageAdapter

---

WmlCalendarAdapter

System.Web.UI.MobileControls.Adapters (system.web.mobile.dll)   class

This adapter renders the System.Web.UI.MobileControls.Calendar control to WML. The calendar cannot be displayed on a single screen; instead, it will be rendered as a sort of date-picker "wizard" over multiple screens.

```
public class WmlCalendarAdapter : WmlControlAdapter {
// Public Constructors
  public WmlCalendarAdapter( );
// Protected Instance Properties
  protected Calendar Control{get; }
// Public Instance Methods
  public override bool HandlePostBackEvent(string eventArgument);              // overrides ControlAdapter
  public override void LoadAdapterState( object state);                        // overrides WmlControlAdapter
  public override void OnInit( EventArgs e);                                   // overrides ControlAdapter
  public override void OnLoad( EventArgs e);                                   // overrides ControlAdapter
  public override void OnPreRender( EventArgs e);                              // overrides ControlAdapter
  public override void Render( WmlMobileTextWriter writer);                    // overrides WmlControlAdapter
  public override object SaveAdapterState( );                                  // overrides WmlControlAdapter
}
```

Hierarchy   System.Object → ControlAdapter(System.Web.UI.MobileControls.IControlAdapter) →
                     WmlControlAdapter → WmlCalendarAdapter

WmlCommandAdapter

System.Web.UI.MobileControls.Adapters (system.web.mobile.dll)   class

This adapter renders the System.Web.UI.MobileControls.Command control to WML.

```
public class WmlCommandAdapter : WmlControlAdapter {
// Public Constructors
  public WmlCommandAdapter( );
// Protected Instance Properties
  protected Command Control{get; }
// Public Instance Methods
  public override void Render( WmlMobileTextWriter writer);                    // overrides WmlControlAdapter
}
```

Hierarchy   System.Object → ControlAdapter(System.Web.UI.MobileControls.IControlAdapter) →
                     WmlControlAdapter → WmlCommandAdapter

WmlControlAdapter

System.Web.UI.MobileControls.Adapters (system.web.mobile.dll)   class

All WML-specific control adapters derive from this base class. It overrides the basic functionality defined in the ControlAdapter class to add WML-specific support for hyperlinks and postbakcs, and to ensure that the FormAdapter property references a valid WmlFormAdapter.

```
public class WmlControlAdapter : ControlAdapter {
// Public Constructors
  public WmlControlAdapter( );
// Protected Static Fields
  protected static readonly int NotSecondaryUI;                                              // =-1
// Protected Instance Properties
  protected WmlFormAdapter FormAdapter{get; }
  protected WmlPageAdapter PageAdapter{get; }
  protected int SecondaryUIMode{set; get; }
// Public Instance Methods
  public override void LoadAdapterState( object state);                          // overrides ControlAdapter
  public override void Render(System.Web.UI.HtmlTextWriter writer);              // overrides ControlAdapter
  public virtual void Render( WmlMobileTextWriter writer);
  public override object SaveAdapterState( );                                    // overrides ControlAdapter
// Protected Instance Methods
  protected string DeterminePostBack( string target);
  protected void ExitSecondaryUIMode( );
  protected virtual string GetPostBackValue( );
  protected void RenderBeginLink(WmlMobileTextWriter writer, string targetUrl, string softkeyLabel,
    bool implicitSoftkeyLabel, bool mapToSoftkey);
  protected void RenderEndLink(WmlMobileTextWriter writer, string targetUrl, bool breakAfter);
  protected void RenderLink(WmlMobileTextWriter writer, string targetUrl, string softkeyLabel,
    bool implicitSoftkeyLabel, bool mapToSoftkey, string text, bool breakAfter);
  protected void RenderPostBackEvent(WmlMobileTextWriter writer, string argument, string softkeyLabel,
    bool mapToSoftkey, string text, bool breakAfter);
  protected void RenderPostBackEvent(WmlMobileTextWriter writer, string argument, string softkeyLabel,
    bool mapToSoftkey, string text, bool breakAfter, WmlPostFieldType postBackType);
  protected void RenderSubmitEvent(WmlMobileTextWriter writer, string softkeyLabel, string text, bool breakAfter);
}
```

Hierarchy   System.Object → ControlAdapter(System.Web.UI.MobileControls.IControlAdapter) →
                   WmlControlAdapter

Subclasses   Multiple types

WmlFormAdapter   .NET 1.1

System.Web.UI.MobileControls.Adapters (system.web.mobile.dll)   class

This adapter renders the System.Web.UI.MobileControls.Form control to WML.

```
public class WmlFormAdapter : WmlControlAdapter {
// Public Constructors
  public WmlFormAdapter( );
// Protected Instance Properties
  protected Form Control{get; }
// Public Instance Methods
  public virtual IDictionary CalculatePostBackVariables( );
  public override bool HandlePostBackEvent(string eventArgument);               // overrides ControlAdapter
  public override void Render( WmlMobileTextWriter writer);                     // overrides WmlControlAdapter
// Protected Instance Methods
  protected internal virtual void RenderCardTag(WmlMobileTextWriter writer, System.Collections.IDictionary attributes);
```

```
protected internal virtual void RenderExtraCardElements(WmlMobileTextWriter writer);
protected virtual void RenderPager(WmlMobileTextWriter writer);
}
```

| Hierarchy | System.Object → ControlAdapter(System.Web.UI.MobileControls.IControlAdapter) → |
| | WmlControlAdapter → WmlFormAdapter |

| Returned By | WmlControlAdapter.FormAdapter |

WmlImageAdapter

System.Web.UI.MobileControls.Adapters (system.web.mobile.dll)   class

This adapter renders the System.Web.UI.MobileControls.Image control to WML. Usually, it will select the appropriate cHTML-compatible image from the device-specific ImageUrl you specify (which is typically a *.wbmp* file).

```
public class WmlImageAdapter : WmlControlAdapter {
// Public Constructors
  public WmlImageAdapter( );
// Protected Instance Properties
  protected Image Control{get; }
// Public Instance Methods
  public override void Render( WmlMobileTextWriter writer);        // overrides WmlControlAdapter
}
```

| Hierarchy | System.Object → ControlAdapter(System.Web.UI.MobileControls.IControlAdapter) → |
| | WmlControlAdapter → WmlImageAdapter |

WmlLabelAdapter

System.Web.UI.MobileControls.Adapters (system.web.mobile.dll)   class

This adapter renders the System.Web.UI.MobileControls.Label control to WML.

```
public class WmlLabelAdapter : WmlControlAdapter {
// Public Constructors
  public WmlLabelAdapter( );
// Protected Instance Properties
  protected TextControl Control{get; }
// Public Instance Methods
  public override void Render( WmlMobileTextWriter writer);        // overrides WmlControlAdapter
}
```

| Hierarchy | System.Object → ControlAdapter(System.Web.UI.MobileControls.IControlAdapter) → |
| | WmlControlAdapter → WmlLabelAdapter |

WmlLinkAdapter

System.Web.UI.MobileControls.Adapters (system.web.mobile.dll)   class

This adapter renders the System.Web.UI.MobileControls.Link control to WML.

```
public class WmlLinkAdapter : WmlControlAdapter {
// Public Constructors
```

Adapters
Namespace

```
   public WmlLinkAdapter( );
// Protected Instance Properties
   protected Link Control{get; }
// Public Instance Methods
   public override void Render( WmlMobileTextWriter writer);              // overrides WmlControlAdapter
}
```

Hierarchy   System.Object → ControlAdapter(System.Web.UI.MobileControls.IControlAdapter) →
                 WmlControlAdapter → WmlLinkAdapter

WmlListAdapter   .NET 1.1

System.Web.UI.MobileControls.Adapters (system.web.mobile.dll)   class

This adapter renders the System.Web.UI.MobileControls.List control to WML.

```
public class WmlListAdapter : WmlControlAdapter {
// Public Constructors
   public WmlListAdapter( );
// Protected Instance Properties
   protected List Control{get; }
// Public Instance Methods
   public override void OnInit( EventArgs e);                              // overrides ControlAdapter
   public override void Render( WmlMobileTextWriter writer);              // overrides WmlControlAdapter
}
```

Hierarchy   System.Object → ControlAdapter(System.Web.UI.MobileControls.IControlAdapter) →
                 WmlControlAdapter → WmlListAdapter

WmlLiteralTextAdapter   .NET 1.1

System.Web.UI.MobileControls.Adapters (system.web.mobile.dll)   class

This adapter renders literal text (represented by the System.Web.UI.MobileControls.LiteralText
control) to WML.

```
public class WmlLiteralTextAdapter : WmlControlAdapter {
// Public Constructors
   public WmlLiteralTextAdapter( );
// Protected Instance Properties
   protected LiteralText Control{get; }
// Public Instance Methods
   public override void Render( WmlMobileTextWriter writer);              // overrides WmlControlAdapter
}
```

Hierarchy   System.Object → ControlAdapter(System.Web.UI.MobileControls.IControlAdapter) →
                 WmlControlAdapter → WmlLiteralTextAdapter

WmlMobileTextWriter   .NET 1.1, marshal by reference, disposable

System.Web.UI.MobileControls.Adapters (system.web.mobile.dll)   class

Device adapters that render WML use the WmlMobileTextWriter to write their output. The
WmlMobileTextWriter instance is provided in adapter methods like Render( ).

```
public class WmlMobileTextWriter : MobileTextWriter {
// Public Constructors
    public WmlMobileTextWriter(System.IO.TextWriter writer, System.Web.Mobile.MobileCapabilities device,
        System.Web.UI.MobileControls.MobilePage page);
// Public Instance Properties
    public bool AnalyzeMode{set; get; }
// Protected Instance Properties
    protected Form CurrentForm{get; }
    protected virtual WmlFormat DefaultFormat{get; }
    protected virtual WmlLayout DefaultLayout{get; }
    protected int NumberOfSoftkeys{get; }
    protected MobilePage Page{get; }
    protected bool PendingBreak{set; get; }
// Public Instance Methods
    public void AddFormVariable(string clientID, string value, bool generateRandomID);
    public virtual void BeginCustomMarkup( );
    public virtual void BeginForm(System.Web.UI.MobileControls.Form form);
    public virtual void EndCustomMarkup( );
    public virtual void EndForm( );
    public override void EnterFormat(System.Web.UI.MobileControls.Style style);       // overrides MobileTextWriter
    public override void EnterLayout(System.Web.UI.MobileControls.Style style);       // overrides MobileTextWriter
    public override void ExitFormat(System.Web.UI.MobileControls.Style style);        // overrides MobileTextWriter
    public override void ExitLayout(System.Web.UI.MobileControls.Style style, bool breakAfter);   // overrides MobileTextWriter
    public virtual bool IsValidSoftkeyLabel(string label);
    public virtual void RenderBeginHyperlink(string targetUrl, bool encodeUrl, string softkeyLabel,
        bool implicitSoftkeyLabel, bool mapToSoftkey);
    public virtual void RenderBeginPostBack(string softkeyLabel, bool implicitSoftkeyLabel, bool mapToSoftkey);
    public virtual void RenderBeginSelect(string name, string iname, string ivalue, string title, bool multiSelect);
    public virtual void RenderEndHyperlink( bool breakAfter);
    public virtual void RenderEndPostBack(string target, string argument, WmlPostFieldType postBackType,
        bool includeVariables, bool breakAfter);
    public virtual void RenderEndSelect( bool breakAfter);
    public virtual void RenderExtraCards( );
    public virtual void RenderGoAction(string target, string argument, WmlPostFieldType postBackType,
        bool includeVariables);
    public virtual void RenderImage(string source, string localSource, string alternateText, bool breakAfter);
    public virtual void RenderSelectOption( string text);
    public virtual void RenderSelectOption(string text, string value);
    public void RenderText( string text);
    public void RenderText( string text, bool breakAfter);
    public virtual void RenderText(string text, bool breakAfter, bool encodeText);
    public virtual void RenderTextBox(string id, string value, string format, string title, bool password, int size,
        int maxLength, bool generateRandomID, bool breakAfter);
    public virtual void ResetFormattingState( );
    public override void WriteAttribute(string attribute, string value, bool encode);   // overrides System.Web.UI.HtmlTextWriter
    public override void WriteEncodedText(string text);                                  // overrides MobileTextWriter
    public override void WriteEncodedUrl(string url);                                    // overrides MobileTextWriter
    public void WritePostField(string name, string value);
    public void WritePostField(string name, string value, WmlPostFieldType type);
    public void WritePostFieldVariable(string name, string arg);
    public void WriteText( string text, bool encodeText);
```

```
// Protected Instance Methods
  protected virtual void AnalyzePostBack(bool includeVariables, WmlPostFieldType postBackType);
  protected virtual string CalculateFormPostBackUrl(bool externalSubmit, ref bool encode);
  protected virtual string CalculateFormQueryString( );
  protected virtual void CloseCharacterFormat( );
  protected virtual void CloseParagraph( );
  protected virtual void EnsureFormat( );
  protected virtual void EnsureLayout( );
  protected internal string MapClientIDToShortName(string clientID, bool generateRandomID);
  protected virtual void OpenCharacterFormat(WmlFormat format, bool writeBold, bool writeItalic, bool writeSize);
  protected virtual void OpenParagraph(WmlLayout layout, bool writeAlignment, bool writeWrapping);
  protected virtual void PostAnalyzeForm( );
  protected virtual void RenderBeginForm(System.Web.UI.MobileControls.Form form);
  protected void RenderDoEvent(string doType, string target, string arg, WmlPostFieldType postBackType,
    string text, bool includeVariables);
  protected virtual void RenderEndForm( );
  protected void RenderFormDoEvent(string doType, string arg, WmlPostFieldType postBackType, string text);
  protected virtual bool UsePostBackCard(bool includeVariables);
  protected void WriteBreak( );
  protected void WriteTextEncodedAttribute(string attribute, string value);
}
```

Hierarchy	System.Object → System.MarshalByRefObject → System.IO.TextWriter(System.IDisposable) → System.Web.UI.HtmlTextWriter → MultiPartWriter → MobileTextWriter → WmlMobileTextWriter

Subclasses	UpWmlMobileTextWriter

Passed To	WmlControlAdapter.{Render( ), RenderBeginLink( ), RenderEndLink( ), RenderLink( ), RenderPostBackEvent( ), RenderSubmitEvent( )}, WmlFormAdapter.RenderPager( ), WmlObjectListAdapter.{RenderItemDetails( ), RenderItemMenu( ), RenderItemsList( )}, WmlPageAdapter.RenderForm( )

WmlObjectListAdapter   .NET 1.1

System.Web.UI.MobileControls.Adapters (system.web.mobile.dll)   class

This adapter renders the System.Web.UI.MobileControls.ObjectList control to WML over several screens. The list is initially rendered as a select list, and the property or field specified by System.Web.UI.MobileControls.ObjectList.LabelItem is displayed for each item. The user can select the item, and view a menu of related commands or a list of additional fields for the item.

```
public class WmlObjectListAdapter : WmlControlAdapter {
// Public Constructors
  public WmlObjectListAdapter( );
// Protected Instance Properties
  protected ObjectList Control{get; }
// Public Instance Methods
  public override void CreateTemplatedUI(bool doDataBind);              // overrides ControlAdapter
  public override bool HandlePostBackEvent(string eventArgument);       // overrides ControlAdapter
  public override void OnPreRender(EventArgs e);                        // overrides ControlAdapter
```

public override void **Render**(WmlMobileTextWriter *writer*);   *// overrides WmlControlAdapter*
// Protected Instance Methods
protected bool **HasCommands**( );
protected bool **HasDefaultCommand**( );
protected bool **HasItemDetails**( );
protected bool **OnlyHasDefaultCommand**( );
protected virtual void **RenderItemDetails**(WmlMobileTextWriter *writer*,
   System.Web.UI.MobileControls.ObjectListItem *item*);
protected virtual void **RenderItemMenu**(WmlMobileTextWriter *writer*,
   System.Web.UI.MobileControls.ObjectListItem *item*);
protected virtual void **RenderItemsList**(WmlMobileTextWriter *writer*);
protected virtual bool **ShouldRenderAsTable**( );
}

Hierarchy   System.Object → ControlAdapter(System.Web.UI.MobileControls.IControlAdapter) →
                WmlControlAdapter → WmlObjectListAdapter

WmlPageAdapter   .NET 1.1

System.Web.UI.MobileControls.Adapters (system.web.mobile.dll)   class

The WmlPageAdapter renders System.Web.UI.MobileControls.MobilePage instances to WML. The
process for rendering a device-specific page is much the same as the process for
rendering a device-specific control, although the page adapter has additional responsibilities. These include creating the device-specific text writer for all adapters (using
CreateTextWriter( )), retrieving postback data (using DeterminePostBackMode( ) and
HandlePagePostBackEvent( )), and handling errors (using HandleError( )).

public class **WmlPageAdapter** : WmlControlAdapter, System.Web.UI.MobileControls.IPageAdapter {
// Public Constructors
  public **WmlPageAdapter**( );
// Public Instance Properties
  public virtual IList **CacheVaryByHeaders**{get; }   *// implements System.Web.UI.MobileControls.IPageAdapter*
  public IDictionary **CookielessDataDictionary**{set; get; }   *// implements System.Web.UI.MobileControls.IPageAdapter*
  public virtual int **OptimumPageWeight**{get; }   *// implements System.Web.UI.MobileControls.IPageAdapter*
  public override MobilePage **Page**{set; get; }   *// overrides ControlAdapter*
  public bool **PersistCookielessData**{set; get; }   *// implements System.Web.UI.MobileControls.IPageAdapter*
// Public Static Methods
  public static bool **DeviceQualifies**(System.Web.HttpContext *context*);
// Public Instance Methods
  public virtual HtmlTextWriter **CreateTextWriter**(System.IO.TextWriter *writer*);
                                   // implements System.Web.UI.MobileControls.IPageAdapter
  public virtual NameValueCollection **DeterminePostBackMode**(System.Web.HttpRequest *request*,
    string *postEventSourceID*, string *postEventArgumentID*,
    System.Collections.Specialized.NameValueCollection *baseCollection*);
                                   // implements System.Web.UI.MobileControls.IPageAdapter
  public virtual bool **HandleError**(Exception *e*,
    System.Web.UI.HtmlTextWriter *writer*);   *// implements System.Web.UI.MobileControls.IPageAdapter*
  public virtual bool **HandlePagePostBackEvent**(string *eventSource*,
    string *eventArgument*);   *// implements System.Web.UI.MobileControls.IPageAdapter*
  public virtual bool **IsFormRendered**(System.Web.UI.MobileControls.Form *form*);
  public override void **Render**(WmlMobileTextWriter *writer*);   *// overrides WmlControlAdapter*

```
  public virtual bool RendersMultipleForms( );
// Protected Instance Methods
  protected virtual void RenderForm(WmlMobileTextWriter writer, System.Web.UI.MobileControls.Form form);
}
```

Hierarchy   System.Object → ControlAdapter(System.Web.UI.MobileControls.IControlAdapter) →
                   WmlControlAdapter → WmlPageAdapter(System.Web.UI.MobileControls.IPageAdapter)

Subclasses   UpWmlPageAdapter

Returned By   WmlControlAdapter.PageAdapter

WmlPanelAdapter   .NET 1.1

System.Web.UI.MobileControls.Adapters (system.web.mobile.dll)   class

This adapter renders the System.Web.UI.MobileControls.Panel control to WML.

```
public class WmlPanelAdapter : WmlControlAdapter {
// Public Constructors
  public WmlPanelAdapter( );
// Protected Instance Properties
  protected Panel Control{get; }
// Public Instance Methods
  public override void Render(WmlMobileTextWriter writer);                      // overrides WmlControlAdapter
}
```

Hierarchy   System.Object → ControlAdapter(System.Web.UI.MobileControls.IControlAdapter) →
                   WmlControlAdapter → WmlPanelAdapter

WmlPhoneCallAdapter   .NET 1.1

System.Web.UI.MobileControls.Adapters (system.web.mobile.dll)   class

This adapter renders the System.Web.UI.MobileControls.PhoneCall control to WML by using a
"tel:" URL on a device with telephony capability.

```
public class WmlPhoneCallAdapter : WmlControlAdapter {
// Public Constructors
  public WmlPhoneCallAdapter( );
// Protected Instance Properties
  protected PhoneCall Control{get; }
// Public Instance Methods
  public override void Render(WmlMobileTextWriter writer);                      // overrides WmlControlAdapter
}
```

Hierarchy   System.Object → ControlAdapter(System.Web.UI.MobileControls.IControlAdapter) →
                   WmlControlAdapter → WmlPhoneCallAdapter

WmlSelectionListAdapter   .NET 1.1

System.Web.UI.MobileControls.Adapters (system.web.mobile.dll)   class

This adapter renders the System.Web.UI.MobileControls.SelectionList control to WML.

```
public class WmlSelectionListAdapter : WmlControlAdapter {
// Public Constructors
  public WmlSelectionListAdapter( );
// Protected Instance Properties
  protected SelectionList Control{get; }
// Public Instance Methods
  public override bool LoadPostData(string key, System.Collections.Specialized.NameValueCollection data,
      object controlPrivateData, out bool dataChanged);                      // overrides ControlAdapter
  public override void OnInit( EventArgs e);                                 // overrides ControlAdapter
  public override void OnPreRender( EventArgs e);                            // overrides ControlAdapter
  public override void Render( WmlMobileTextWriter writer);                  // overrides WmlControlAdapter
// Protected Instance Methods
  protected override string GetPostBackValue( );                            // overrides WmlControlAdapter
}
```

Hierarchy   System.Object → ControlAdapter(System.Web.UI.MobileControls.IControlAdapter) →
WmlControlAdapter → WmlSelectionListAdapter

WmlTextBoxAdapter   .NET 1.1

System.Web.UI.MobileControls.Adapters (system.web.mobile.dll)   class

This adapter renders the System.Web.UI.MobileControls.TextBox control to WML.

```
public class WmlTextBoxAdapter : WmlControlAdapter {
// Public Constructors
  public WmlTextBoxAdapter( );
// Protected Instance Properties
  protected TextBox Control{get; }
// Public Instance Methods
  public override void OnInit( EventArgs e);                                 // overrides ControlAdapter
  public override void Render( WmlMobileTextWriter writer);                  // overrides WmlControlAdapter
// Protected Instance Methods
  protected override string GetPostBackValue( );                            // overrides WmlControlAdapter
}
```

Hierarchy   System.Object → ControlAdapter(System.Web.UI.MobileControls.IControlAdapter) →
WmlControlAdapter → WmlTextBoxAdapter

WmlTextViewAdapter   .NET 1.1

System.Web.UI.MobileControls.Adapters (system.web.mobile.dll)   class

This adapter renders the System.Web.UI.MobileControls.TextView control to HTML.

```
public class WmlTextViewAdapter : WmlControlAdapter {
// Public Constructors
  public WmlTextViewAdapter( );
// Protected Instance Properties
  protected TextView Control{get; }
// Public Instance Methods
  public override void Render( WmlMobileTextWriter writer);                  // overrides WmlControlAdapter
}
```

System.Object → ControlAdapter(System.Web.UI.MobileControls.IControlAdapter) → WmlControlAdapter → WmlTextViewAdapter

WmlValidationSummaryAdapter .NET 1.1

System.Web.UI.MobileControls.Adapters (system.web.mobile.dll) class

This adapter renders the System.Web.UI.MobileControls.ValidationSummary control (which displays a list of validation errors) to WML.

```
public class WmlValidationSummaryAdapter : WmlControlAdapter {
// Public Constructors
  public WmlValidationSummaryAdapter( );
// Protected Instance Properties
  protected ValidationSummary Control{get; }
// Public Instance Methods
  public override void OnInit( EventArgs e);                      // overrides ControlAdapter
  public override void Render( WmlMobileTextWriter writer);       // overrides WmlControlAdapter
}
```

Hierarchy System.Object → ControlAdapter(System.Web.UI.MobileControls.IControlAdapter) → WmlControlAdapter → WmlValidationSummaryAdapter

WmlValidatorAdapter .NET 1.1

System.Web.UI.MobileControls.Adapters (system.web.mobile.dll) class

This adapter renders all the validation controls (which derive from System.Web.UI.Mobile-Controls.BaseValidator) control to WML.

```
public class WmlValidatorAdapter : WmlControlAdapter {
// Public Constructors
  public WmlValidatorAdapter( );
// Protected Instance Properties
  protected BaseValidator Control{get; }
// Public Instance Methods
  public override void Render( WmlMobileTextWriter writer);       // overrides WmlControlAdapter
}
```

Hierarchy System.Object → ControlAdapter(System.Web.UI.MobileControls.IControlAdapter) → WmlControlAdapter → WmlValidatorAdapter

42

The System.Web.UI. WebControls Namespace

The System.Web.UI.WebControls namespace contains types used for web controls. Web controls are ASP.NET's most full-featured controls and range from straightforward elements like Button to sophisticated controls like Calendar, AdRotator, and DataGrid. Web controls are more abstract than HTML controls. Rather than wrapping specific HTML elements, web controls can consist of a combination of HTML elements and vary their user interface depending on the capabilities of the client browser. They also provide a richer set of formatting properties and events. For example, all input controls provide an AutoPostback property that, when set to True, allows your code to react immediately to a Change event (like a checkbox being checked or a new list selection).

This namespace contains the WebControl class, which is the base class for all web controls. Web controls include traditional standards like TextBox, Button, RadioButton, and CheckBox, and more unusual and advanced controls like Calendar, AdRotator, and the list controls CheckBoxList and RadioButtonList.

Some of the most interesting controls in this namespace include those used for data-bound tables. Typically, DataGrid provides the most powerful options, with features for paging, sorting, and automatic selection and editing. You can also use the DataList class for a templated list or the Repeater class for a simple data-bound repeater that allows completely customized layout but has no built-in formatting or support for higher-level features like selection and editing.

Other useful controls in this namespace include the validation controls that derive from BaseValidator. These controls include CompareValidator (which compares data to an expected value), RangeValidator (which ensures that data falls in a specified range), RegularExpressionValidator (which validates data using a regular expression), RequiredField-Validator (which ensures that data has been entered), and CustomValidator (which allows you to create your own validation routines). Optionally, validation results can be displayed using the ValidationSummary control.

Figure 42-1 shows the controls in this namespace. Figures 42-2 and 42-3 show the remaining types, including delegates and events.

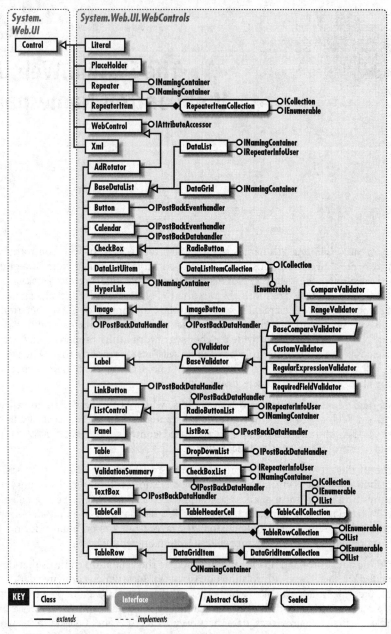

Figure 42-1. Controls in the System.Web.UI.WebControls namespace

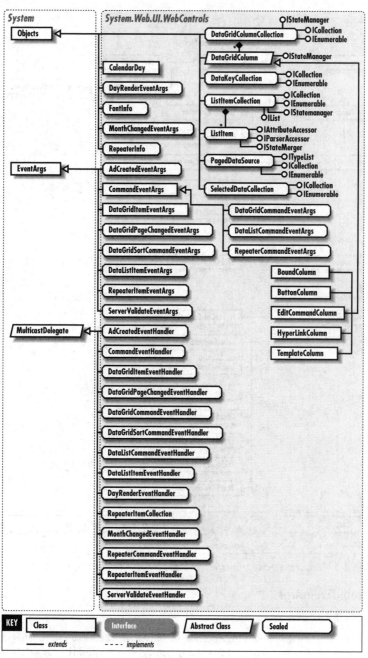

Figure 42-2. Delegates, events, and other types

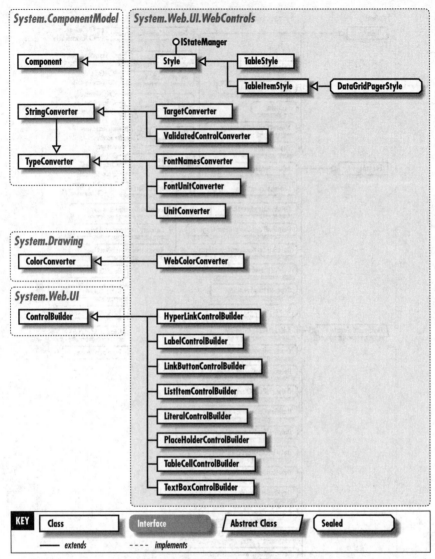

Figure 42-3. Remaining types from the System.Web.UI.WebControls namespace

AdCreatedEventArgs

System.Web.UI.WebControls (system.web.dll)   sealed class

This class supplies additional information to the **AdRotator.AdCreated** event. This information is drawn from the corresponding entry in the XML file defining the advertisements for the **AdRotator** control. In addition, the **AdProperties** property provides a read-only collection that provides all properties of the current advertisement.

One use of the AdCreatedEventArgs class and AdRotator.AdCreated event is to update a Web Forms page to correspond with the current advertisement. For example, you could use code like this: Sponsor.Text = "Visit our sponsor at" & e.NavigateURL;.

```
public sealed class AdCreatedEventArgs : EventArgs {
// Public Constructors
   public AdCreatedEventArgs(System.Collections.IDictionary adProperties);
// Public Instance Properties
   public IDictionary AdProperties{get; }
   public string AlternateText{set; get; }
   public string ImageUrl{set; get; }
   public string NavigateUrl{set; get; }
}
```

Hierarchy   System.Object → System.EventArgs → AdCreatedEventArgs

Passed To   System.Web.UI.MobileControls.AdRotator.OnAdCreated( ), AdCreatedEventHandler.{BeginInvoke( ), Invoke( )}, AdRotator.OnAdCreated( )

AdCreatedEventHandler   serializable

System.Web.UI.WebControls (system.web.dll)   delegate

This delegate defines the signature required for the AdRotator.AdCreated event handler.

```
public delegate void AdCreatedEventHandler(object sender, AdCreatedEventArgs e);
```

Associated Events System.Web.UI.MobileControls.AdRotator.AdCreated( ), AdRotator.AdCreated( )

AdRotator   disposable

System.Web.UI.WebControls (system.web.dll)   class

The AdRotator class allows you to provide one of the hallmarks of the Internet: banner ads. The AdRotator randomly chooses a different graphic to display every time the page is refreshed by reading from a list of entries specified in an XML file (and referenced by the AdvertisementFile property). The XML file specifies details like image URL, the link URL, and an "impressions" value that allows you to weigh an advertisement so that it is displayed more or less frequently than others in the file. If the picture does not fit the size or aspect ratio of the control, it will be stretched, compressed, or otherwise mangled to fit.

The Target property allows you to specify the frame that will be used to display the linked page if the user clicks on a banner ad. You can specify a frame in the current window, or you can use special values like "_blank", "_parent", "_top", or "_self". The KeywordFilter property allows you to specify a subset of advertisements to use for the AdRotator. For example, your site could use a single XML file for all ads, but assign different keywords to different types of ads. Depending on what page the AdRotator is used on, you can decide to use only the group of advertisements that matches the current content.

Clicking on the AdRotator does not fire an event, but automatically transfers the users to the appropriate page. Use the AdCreated event to integrate the current page with the current advertisement. This event provides information in an AdCreatedEventArgs object about the selected ad, which can be modified or used to set corresponding properties on other controls on the current page.

```
public class AdRotator : WebControl {
// Public Constructors
  public AdRotator( );
// Public Instance Properties
  public string AdvertisementFile{set; get; }
  public override FontInfo Font{get; }                                    // overrides WebControl
  public string KeywordFilter{set; get; }
  public string Target{set; get; }
// Protected Instance Methods
  protected override ControlCollection CreateControlCollection( );        // overrides System.Web.UI.Control
  protected virtual void OnAdCreated( AdCreatedEventArgs e);
  protected override void OnPreRender( EventArgs e);                      // overrides System.Web.UI.Control
  protected override void Render(System.Web.UI.HtmlTextWriter writer);    // overrides WebControl
// Events
  public event AdCreatedEventHandler AdCreated;
}
```

Hierarchy   System.Object → System.Web.UI.Control(System.ComponentModel.IComponent, System. IDisposable, System.Web.UI.IParserAccessor, System.Web.UI.IDataBindingsAccessor) → WebControl(System.Web.UI.IAttributeAccessor) → AdRotator

Returned By   System.Web.UI.MobileControls.AdRotator.CreateWebAdRotator( )

BaseCompareValidator   disposable

System.Web.UI.WebControls (system.web.dll)   abstract class

This abstract class provides basic functionality for the CompareValidator and RangeValidator classes, which perform validation through comparisons. The shared (static) GetFullYear( ) method converts a two-digit year (like "98") to a four-digit representation ("1998"), while CutoffYear sets the maximum four-digit year value that it will allow to be represented in two digits. The shared CanConvert( ) method determines whether a string can be converted to a given ValidationDataType, while the Type property sets the ValidationDataType that the current instance of the control is validating text against.

```
public abstract class BaseCompareValidator : BaseValidator {
// Protected Constructors
  protected BaseCompareValidator( );
// Protected Static Properties
  protected static int CutoffYear{get; }
// Public Instance Properties
  public ValidationDataType Type{set; get; }
// Public Static Methods
  public static bool CanConvert(string text, ValidationDataType type);
// Protected Static Methods
  protected static bool Compare(string leftText, string rightText, ValidationCompareOperator op,  ValidationDataType type);
  protected static bool Convert(string text, ValidationDataType type, out object value);
  protected static string GetDateElementOrder( );
  protected static int GetFullYear( int shortYear);
// Protected Instance Methods
```

```
    protected override void AddAttributesToRender(System.Web.UI.HtmlTextWriter writer);      // overrides BaseValidator
    protected override bool DetermineRenderUplevel( );                                         // overrides BaseValidator
}
```

Hierarchy	System.Object → System.Web.UI.Control(System.ComponentModel.IComponent, System. IDisposable, System.Web.UI.IParserAccessor, System.Web.UI.IDataBindingsAccessor) → WebControl(System.Web.UI.IAttributeAccessor) → Label → BaseValidator(System.Web.UI. IValidator) → BaseCompareValidator
Subclasses	CompareValidator, RangeValidator

BaseDataList

disposable

System.Web.UI.WebControls (system.web.dll)   abstract class

This abstract class provides basic functionality for the DataList and DataGrid web controls. These controls include data binding (through the DataBind( ) method and properties like DataSource), and simple formatting through various table-specific properties, including CellPadding (the space between content in a cell and the cell borders), CellSpacing (the space between cells), and HorizontalAlign (the position of the table relative to the page or adjacent content).

```
public abstract class BaseDataList : WebControl {
// Public Constructors
  public BaseDataList( );
// Public Instance Properties
  public virtual int CellPadding{set; get; }
  public virtual int CellSpacing{set; get; }
  public override ControlCollection Controls{get; }                     // overrides System.Web.UI.Control
  public virtual string DataKeyField{set; get; }
  public DataKeyCollection DataKeys{get; }
  public string DataMember{set; get; }
  public virtual object DataSource{set; get; }
  public virtual GridLines GridLines{set; get; }
  public virtual HorizontalAlign HorizontalAlign{set; get; }
// Protected Instance Properties
  protected ArrayList DataKeysArray{get; }
// Public Static Methods
  public static bool IsBindableType( Type type);
// Public Instance Methods
  public override void DataBind( );                                     // overrides System.Web.UI.Control
// Protected Instance Methods
  protected override void AddParsedSubObject( object obj);             // overrides System.Web.UI.Control
  protected override void CreateChildControls( );                       // overrides System.Web.UI.Control
  protected abstract void CreateControlHierarchy( bool useDataSource);
  protected override void OnDataBinding( EventArgs e);                  // overrides System.Web.UI.Control
  protected virtual void OnSelectedIndexChanged( EventArgs e);
  protected abstract void PrepareControlHierarchy( );
  protected override void Render(System.Web.UI.HtmlTextWriter writer);  // overrides WebControl
// Events
  public event EventHandler SelectedIndexChanged;
}
```

Hierarchy   System.Object → System.Web.UI.Control(System.ComponentModel.IComponent, System.IDisposable, System.Web.UI.IParserAccessor, System.Web.UI.IDataBindingsAccessor) → WebControl(System.Web.UI.IAttributeAccessor) → BaseDataList

Subclasses   DataGrid, DataList

BaseValidator   disposable

System.Web.UI.WebControls (system.web.dll)   abstract class

This abstract class is the basis for all validation controls. It supplies a Validate( ) method, which does not return a value, but updates the IsValid property. When using validation controls on a Web Forms page, you should check the System.Web.UI.Page.IsValid property. This value will be True only if all validation controls on the page have successfully validated their input. The BaseValidator class also provides various other methods that are not used directly when creating a Web Forms page.

The ControlToValidate property specifies the control that a validator will verify. The ErrorMessage property specifies the message that will be displayed in the validation control if validation fails, although this text can be overridden by changing the validation control's Text property. The ErrorMessage will also appear in a page's ValidationSummary control, if present.

By default, ASP.NET will not render any HTML for a control if it is not visible. This means that space will not be allocated for a validation control unless validation fails. The Display property allows you to allocate space for a validation control by specifying ValidatorDisplay.Static, which may be required if your validation control is in a table. You can also set this property to ValidatorDisplay.None to specify that no validation message will be displayed in the control, although one will still be shown in the ValidationSummary control, if used.

```
public abstract class BaseValidator : Label, System.Web.UI.IValidator {
// Protected Constructors
  protected BaseValidator( );
// Public Instance Properties
  public string ControlToValidate{set; get; }
  public ValidatorDisplay Display{set; get; }
  public bool EnableClientScript{set; get; }
  public override bool Enabled{set; get; }                              // overrides WebControl
  public string ErrorMessage{set; get; }                     // implements System.Web.UI.IValidator
  public override Color ForeColor{set; get; }                           // overrides WebControl
  public bool IsValid{set; get; }                            // implements System.Web.UI.IValidator
// Protected Instance Properties
  protected bool PropertiesValid{get; }
  protected bool RenderUplevel{get; }
// Public Static Methods
  public static PropertyDescriptor GetValidationProperty(object component);
// Public Instance Methods
  public void Validate( );                                   // implements System.Web.UI.IValidator
// Protected Instance Methods
  protected override void AddAttributesToRender(System.Web.UI.HtmlTextWriter writer);   // overrides WebControl
  protected void CheckControlValidationProperty(string name, string propertyName);
  protected virtual bool ControlPropertiesValid( );
```

```
protected virtual bool DetermineRenderUplevel( );
protected abstract bool EvaluateIsValid( );
protected string GetControlRenderID(string name);
protected string GetControlValidationValue(string name);
protected override void OnInit(EventArgs e);                          // overrides System.Web.UI.Control
protected override void OnPreRender(EventArgs e);                     // overrides System.Web.UI.Control
protected override void OnUnload(EventArgs e);                        // overrides System.Web.UI.Control
protected void RegisterValidatorCommonScript( );
protected virtual void RegisterValidatorDeclaration( );
protected override void Render(System.Web.UI.HtmlTextWriter writer);  // overrides WebControl
}
```

Hierarchy   System.Object → System.Web.UI.Control(System.ComponentModel.IComponent, System.
IDisposable, System.Web.UI.IParserAccessor, System.Web.UI.IDataBindingsAccessor) →
WebControl(System.Web.UI.IAttributeAccessor) → Label → BaseValidator(System.Web.UI.
IValidator)

Subclasses   BaseCompareValidator, CustomValidator, RegularExpressionValidator, RequiredFieldValidator

Returned By   System.Web.UI.MobileControls.BaseValidator.CreateWebValidator( )

BorderStyle   serializable

System.Web.UI.WebControls (system.web.dll)   enum

This enumeration is used to set the border style for most web controls. It is used by the
WebControl.BorderStyle property.

```
public enum BorderStyle {
  NotSet = 0,
  None = 1,
  Dotted = 2,
  Dashed = 3,
  Solid = 4,
  Double = 5,
  Groove = 6,
  Ridge = 7,
  Inset = 8,
  Outset = 9
}
```

Hierarchy   System.Object → System.ValueType → System.Enum(System.IComparable, System.IFor-
mattable, System.IConvertible) → BorderStyle

Returned By   Style.BorderStyle, WebControl.BorderStyle

Passed To   Style.BorderStyle, WebControl.BorderStyle

BoundColumn

System.Web.UI.WebControls (system.web.dll)   **class**

The BoundColumn class represents the default type of column used in a **DataGrid** control. A BoundColumn is "bound," or linked, to a specific field in a data source. It provides a **DataField** property that specifies the field used from the data source for the column's content. As with all ASP.NET data binding, the "bind" is in one direction: from the database to the output control.

```
public class BoundColumn : DataGridColumn {
// Public Constructors
  public BoundColumn( );
// Public Static Fields
  public static readonly string thisExpr;                                            // =!
// Public Instance Properties
  public virtual string DataField{set; get; }
  public virtual string DataFormatString{set; get; }
  public virtual bool ReadOnly{set; get; }
// Public Instance Methods
  public override void Initialize( );                                 // overrides DataGridColumn
  public override void InitializeCell(TableCell cell, int columnIndex, ListItemType itemType);    // overrides DataGridColumn
// Protected Instance Methods
  protected virtual string FormatDataValue( object dataValue);
}
```

Hierarchy   System.Object → DataGridColumn(System.Web.UI.IStateManager) → BoundColumn

Button   **disposable**

System.Web.UI.WebControls (system.web.dll)   **class**

This class represents a simple command button (also known as a push button). **Button** controls always generate a postback when clicked. As with all button-like server controls, you can set the CausesValidation property to determine whether page validation will be performed when the button is clicked, before the button event handling code is executed. Depending on the client browser's support for DHTML, an invalid page may prevent the postback from occurring and the button event handling code from executing if CausesValidation is **True**.

When clicked, a **Button** raises a **Click** event followed by a **Command** event. The **Command** event passes extra information about the button in a **CommandEventArgs** object. This information includes the **CommandName** and **CommandArgument** properties of the **Button**. A typical CommandName identifies the requested action (like "Sort").

```
public class Button : WebControl, System.Web.UI.IPostBackEventHandler {
// Public Constructors
  public Button( );
// Public Instance Properties
  public bool CausesValidation{set; get; }
  public string CommandArgument{set; get; }
  public string CommandName{set; get; }
  public string Text{set; get; }
// Protected Instance Methods
```

```
protected override void AddAttributesToRender(System.Web.UI.HtmlTextWriter writer);        // overrides WebControl
protected virtual void OnClick( EventArgs e);
protected virtual void OnCommand( CommandEventArgs e);
protected override void RenderContents(System.Web.UI.HtmlTextWriter writer);                // overrides WebControl
// Events
public event EventHandler Click;
public event CommandEventHandler Command;
}
```

Hierarchy   System.Object → System.Web.UI.Control(System.ComponentModel.IComponent, System.
IDisposable, System.Web.UI.IParserAccessor, System.Web.UI.IDataBindingsAccessor) →
WebControl(System.Web.UI.IAttributeAccessor) → Button(System.Web.UI.
IPostBackEventHandler)

ButtonColumn

System.Web.UI.WebControls (system.web.dll)   class

The ButtonColumn class represents a type of column that can be used in a DataGrid control.
This column consists of buttons that raise the DataGrid.ItemCommand event. These buttons
can be displayed as graphical push buttons (like Button) or text links, depending on the
ButtonType property.

The Text property determines what text is displayed for the button, while the Command-
Name property specifies a string of additional information that will be sent to the
DataGrid.ItemCommand event through the DataGridCommandEventArgs object.

If you set the Text and CommandName properties, all buttons in the column will share the
same information. Alternatively, you can set the DataTextField property to use data
binding and the DataTextFormatString property to specify formatting rules.

```
public class ButtonColumn : DataGridColumn {
// Public Constructors
  public ButtonColumn( );
// Public Instance Properties
  public virtual ButtonColumnType ButtonType{set; get; }
  public virtual string CommandName{set; get; }
  public virtual string DataTextField{set; get; }
  public virtual string DataTextFormatString{set; get; }
  public virtual string Text{set; get; }
// Public Instance Methods
  public override void Initialize( );                                                    // overrides DataGridColumn
  public override void InitializeCell(TableCell cell, int columnIndex, ListItemType itemType);    // overrides DataGridColumn
// Protected Instance Methods
  protected virtual string FormatDataTextValue( object dataTextValue);
}
```

Hierarchy   System.Object → DataGridColumn(System.Web.UI.IStateManager) → ButtonColumn

ButtonColumnType

System.Web.UI.WebControls (system.web.dll)

serializable

enum

You can use this enumeration to set the **ButtonColumn.ButtonType** property. Use **PushButton** to create graphical buttons that look like individual **Button** controls and **LinkButton** to create hyperlink-style buttons that look like individual **LinkButton** controls.

```
public enum ButtonColumnType {
  LinkButton = 0,
  PushButton = 1
}
```

Hierarchy   System.Object → System.ValueType → System.Enum(System.IComparable, System.IFormattable, System.IConvertible) → ButtonColumnType

Returned By   ButtonColumn.ButtonType, EditCommandColumn.ButtonType

Passed To   ButtonColumn.ButtonType, EditCommandColumn.ButtonType

Calendar

disposable

System.Web.UI.WebControls (system.web.dll)

class

The class is used for the Calendar control, which displays a single month of the year at a time and allows users to move forward and backward from month to month and select one or more dates. The **SelectionMode** property determines what type of selections are allowed (day, week, or month). You can also create an event handler for the **DayRender** event, use it to examine each day in the calendar and decide if you would like to apply special formatting, add additional content in the corresponding table cell, or make the day unselectable.

If only a single day is selected, it will be provided in the **SelectedDate** property. If you use a **SelectionMode** that allows the user to select multiple dates, they will be contained in the **SelectedDates** collection.

The other properties of the calendar are used to customize its appearance, allowing you to hide header and title information, choose styles, and disable month-to-month navigation. Note that if you hide the title portion by setting the **ShowTitle** property to **False**, the month navigation controls will also be hidden. You can also respond to a **SelectionChanged** event that fires when the user chooses a new date and the **VisibleMonthChanged** event that fires when the user navigates to a different month.

```
public class Calendar : WebControl, System.Web.UI.IPostBackEventHandler {
// Public Constructors
  public Calendar( );
// Public Instance Properties
  public int CellPadding{set; get; }
  public int CellSpacing{set; get; }
  public TableItemStyle DayHeaderStyle{get; }
  public DayNameFormat DayNameFormat{set; get; }
  public TableItemStyle DayStyle{get; }
  public FirstDayOfWeek FirstDayOfWeek{set; get; }
  public string NextMonthText{set; get; }
  public NextPrevFormat NextPrevFormat{set; get; }
```

```
public TableItemStyle NextPrevStyle{get; }
public TableItemStyle OtherMonthDayStyle{get; }
public string PrevMonthText{set; get; }
public DateTime SelectedDate{set; get; }
public SelectedDatesCollection SelectedDates{get; }
public TableItemStyle SelectedDayStyle{get; }
public CalendarSelectionMode SelectionMode{set; get; }
public string SelectMonthText{set; get; }
public TableItemStyle SelectorStyle{get; }
public string SelectWeekText{set; get; }
public bool ShowDayHeader{set; get; }
public bool ShowGridLines{set; get; }
public bool ShowNextPrevMonth{set; get; }
public bool ShowTitle{set; get; }
public TitleFormat TitleFormat{set; get; }
public TableItemStyle TitleStyle{get; }
public TableItemStyle TodayDayStyle{get; }
public DateTime TodaysDate{set; get; }
public DateTime VisibleDate{set; get; }
public TableItemStyle WeekendDayStyle{get; }
// Protected Instance Methods
   protected override ControlCollection CreateControlCollection( );          // overrides System.Web.UI.Control
   protected bool HasWeekSelectors(CalendarSelectionMode selectionMode);
   protected override void LoadViewState( object savedState);               // overrides WebControl
   protected virtual void OnDayRender(TableCell cell, CalendarDay day);
   protected override void OnPreRender( EventArgs e);                       // overrides System.Web.UI.Control
   protected virtual void OnSelectionChanged( );
   protected virtual void OnVisibleMonthChanged( DateTime newDate, DateTime previousDate);
   protected override void Render(System.Web.UI.HtmlTextWriter writer);      // overrides WebControl
   protected override object SaveViewState( );                             // overrides WebControl
   protected override void TrackViewState( );                              // overrides WebControl
// Events
   public event DayRenderEventHandler DayRender;
   public event EventHandler SelectionChanged;
   public event MonthChangedEventHandler VisibleMonthChanged;
}
```

Hierarchy   System.Object → System.Web.UI.Control(System.ComponentModel.IComponent, System.
                    IDisposable, System.Web.UI.IParserAccessor, System.Web.UI.IDataBindingsAccessor) →
                    WebControl(System.Web.UI.IAttributeAccessor) → Calendar(System.Web.UI.
                    IPostBackEventHandler)

Returned By   System.Web.UI.MobileControls.Calendar.{CreateWebCalendar( ), WebCalendar}

Passed To   System.Web.UI.Design.WebControls.CalendarAutoFormatDialog.CalendarAutoFormatDialog( )

CalendarDay

System.Web.UI.WebControls (system.web.dll)   class

This class represents a single day in the Calendar control. You can use this class in the
Calendar.DayRender event to programmatically configure specific dates. The Calendar.DayRender

event fires once for each day in the Calendar, and it provides the CalendarDay object for that day. At this point, you can modify its properties.

For example, you can compare dates against valid date ranges stored in a database and set the IsSelectable property to False for all dates that you don't want the user to be able to select. Or you could examine the IsOtherMonth property to verify that the day is in the currently displayed month and the IsWeekend property to confirm that the day is on a weekend, and then change the background color of the containing cell to highlight it. Note, however, that the background color is not a property of the CalendarDay object. Instead, it is a property of the TableCell object that is also provided to you in the event through the DayRenderEventArgs class. For more information, refer to the DayRenderEventArgs object.

```
public class CalendarDay {
// Public Constructors
    public CalendarDay(DateTime date, bool isWeekend, bool isToday, bool isSelected, bool isOtherMonth,
        string dayNumberText);
// Public Instance Properties
    public DateTime Date{get; }
    public string DayNumberText{get; }
    public bool IsOtherMonth{get; }
    public bool IsSelectable{set; get; }
    public bool IsSelected{get; }
    public bool IsToday{get; }
    public bool IsWeekend{get; }
}
```

Returned By   DayRenderEventArgs.Day

Passed To   Calendar.OnDayRender( ), DayRenderEventArgs.DayRenderEventArgs( )

CalendarSelectionMode

serializable

System.Web.UI.WebControls (system.web.dll)

enum

This enumeration specifies the type of selection that a user can perform with a Calendar control. Day allows the user to select a single day, DayWeek allows the user to select a single day or an entire week, DayWeekMonth allows a specific day, week, or month to be chosen, and None does not allow any kind of date selection. The calendar does not support noncontiguous multiple day selections.

```
public enum CalendarSelectionMode {
    None = 0,
    Day = 1,
    DayWeek = 2,
    DayWeekMonth = 3
}
```

Hierarchy   System.Object → System.ValueType → System.Enum(System.IComparable, System.IFormattable, System.IConvertible) → CalendarSelectionMode

Returned By   System.Web.UI.MobileControls.Calendar.SelectionMode, Calendar.SelectionMode

Passed To   System.Web.UI.MobileControls.Calendar.SelectionMode, Calendar.{HasWeekSelectors( ), SelectionMode}

CheckBox
disposable

System.Web.UI.WebControls (system.web.dll) class

This class represents a single checkbox that can be selected (**True**) or left unchecked (**False**). The CheckBox class also provides a **TextAlign** property, which specifies whether text will appear on the right or left side of the checkbox. To determine whether a checkbox is selected, examine the **Checked** property. If you want to use a checkbox with list data, the **CheckBoxList** control may be more convenient.

```
public class CheckBox : WebControl, System.Web.UI.IPostBackDataHandler {
// Public Constructors
   public CheckBox( );
// Public Instance Properties
   public virtual bool AutoPostBack{set; get; }
   public virtual bool Checked{set; get; }
   public virtual string Text{set; get; }
   public virtual TextAlign TextAlign{set; get; }
// Protected Instance Methods
   protected virtual void OnCheckedChanged( EventArgs e);
   protected override void OnPreRender( EventArgs e);              // overrides System.Web.UI.Control
   protected override void Render(System.Web.UI.HtmlTextWriter writer);           // overrides WebControl
// Events
   public event EventHandler CheckedChanged;
}
```

Hierarchy   System.Object → System.Web.UI.Control(System.ComponentModel.IComponent, System. IDisposable, System.Web.UI.IParserAccessor, System.Web.UI.IDataBindingsAccessor) → WebControl(System.Web.UI.IAttributeAccessor) → CheckBox(System.Web.UI. IPostBackDataHandler)

Subclasses   RadioButton

CheckBoxList
disposable

System.Web.UI.WebControls (system.web.dll) class

This class represents a list of checkboxes that can be selected in any combination. Though this class is generated out of individual checkboxes, it acts like an integrated list. For example, ASP.NET will add or remove checkbox items as needed when you bind it to a data source. You can use **RepeatDirection** to specify how checkboxes will be grouped together if **RepeatColumns** is greater than 1. For example, if you set **RepeatDirection** to **RepeatDirection.Vertical**, and **RepeatColumns** to 2, the first two list items will be displayed in the first columns, the next two will be displayed on the second column, and so on. If you set **RepeatDirection** to **RepeatDirection.Horizontal**, your list will still have the same number of rows and columns, but checkbox items will be filled first by column, and then by row.

Individual checkboxes are grouped together automatically in an HTML table, which you can fine-tune with the **CellPadding** and **CellSpacing** properties. Alternatively, you can set **RepeatLayout** to **RepeatLayout.Flow** to specify that an HTML table should not be used.

Most of the list-specific functionality, such as determining the selected item and reacting to a **SelectedIndexChanged** event, is provided by the **ListControl** class, which CheckBox-List inherits from. To determine what items are checked in a checkbox list, iterate through the **Items** collection and test the **ListItem.Selected** property of each item in the list.

```
public class CheckBoxList : ListControl, IRepeatInfoUser, System.Web.UI.INamingContainer,
    System.Web.UI.IPostBackDataHandler {
// Public Constructors
  public CheckBoxList( );
// Public Instance Properties
  public virtual int CellPadding{set; get; }
  public virtual int CellSpacing{set; get; }
  public virtual int RepeatColumns{set; get; }
  public virtual RepeatDirection RepeatDirection{set; get; }
  public virtual RepeatLayout RepeatLayout{set; get; }
  public virtual TextAlign TextAlign{set; get; }
// Protected Instance Methods
  protected override Style CreateControlStyle( );                          // overrides WebControl
  protected override Control FindControl(string id, int pathOffset);       // overrides System.Web.UI.Control
  protected override void OnPreRender( EventArgs e);                       // overrides ListControl
  protected override void Render(System.Web.UI.HtmlTextWriter writer);     // overrides WebControl
}
```

Hierarchy   System.Object → System.Web.UI.Control(System.ComponentModel.IComponent, System.
IDisposable, System.Web.UI.IParserAccessor, System.Web.UI.IDataBindingsAccessor) →
WebControl(System.Web.UI.IAttributeAccessor) → ListControl → CheckBoxList(IRepeatIn-
foUser, System.Web.UI.INamingContainer, System.Web.UI.IPostBackDataHandler)

CommandEventArgs

System.Web.UI.WebControls (system.web.dll)   class

This class is used by the CommandEventHandler to provide extra information to a Command
event handler. This information is stored in two properties: CommandName and CommandArgument, which are both strings. These properties are used only by your code, and can
thus be used to store any information you need. For example, you might set Command-
Name to "Sort" and CommandArgument to "Ascending."

```
public class CommandEventArgs : EventArgs {
// Public Constructors
  public CommandEventArgs( CommandEventArgs e);
  public CommandEventArgs(string commandName, object argument);
// Public Instance Properties
  public object CommandArgument{get; }
  public string CommandName{get; }
}
```

Hierarchy   System.Object → System.EventArgs → CommandEventArgs

Subclasses   DataGridCommandEventArgs, DataListCommandEventArgs, RepeaterCommandEventArgs,
System.Web.UI.MobileControls.{ListCommandEventArgs, ObjectListCommandEventArgs}

Passed To   System.Web.UI.MobileControls.Command.OnItemCommand( ), System.Web.UI.MobileCon-
trols.ListCommandEventArgs.ListCommandEventArgs( ), System.Web.UI.MobileControls.
ObjectListCommandEventArgs.ObjectListCommandEventArgs( ), Button.OnCommand( ),
CommandEventHandler.{BeginInvoke( ), Invoke( )}, DataGridCommandEventArgs.
DataGridCommandEventArgs( ), DataListCommandEventArgs.DataListCommandEventArgs( ),
ImageButton.OnCommand( ), LinkButton.OnCommand( ), RepeaterCommandEventArgs.
RepeaterCommandEventArgs( )

CommandEventHandler

serializable

System.Web.UI.WebControls (system.web.dll)   delegate

Many button controls, such as Button, ImageButton, and LinkButton, provide both a Click and a Command event. The Command event allows you to send extra information identifying a command name and command arguments in an instance of CommandEventArgs.

```
public delegate void CommandEventHandler(object sender, CommandEventArgs e);
```

Associated Events   System.Web.UI.MobileControls.Command.ItemCommand( ), Button.Command( ), Image-
Button.Command( ), LinkButton.Command( )

CompareValidator

disposable

System.Web.UI.WebControls (system.web.dll)   class

This class represents a validation control that compares the input control (ControlToVali-date) to a specified value (ValueToCompare) or a value in another control (ControlToCompare). Both values will be converted to the data type specified by Type before they are compared. Note that if you set both ValueToCompare and ControlToCompare, the latter will take precedence.

The Operator property specifies the expression that must be met in order for validation to succeed. In other words, ControlToValidate <Operator> ControlToCompare must be true.

```
public class CompareValidator : BaseCompareValidator {
// Public Constructors
  public CompareValidator( );
// Public Instance Properties
  public string ControlToCompare{set; get; }
  public ValidationCompareOperator Operator{set; get; }
  public string ValueToCompare{set; get; }
// Protected Instance Methods
  protected override void AddAttributesToRender(System.Web.UI.HtmlTextWriter writer);
                                                          // overrides BaseCompareValidator
  protected override bool ControlPropertiesValid( );                 // overrides BaseValidator
  protected override bool EvaluateIsValid( );                        // overrides BaseValidator
}
```

Hierarchy   System.Object → System.Web.UI.Control(System.ComponentModel.IComponent, System.
IDisposable, System.Web.UI.IParserAccessor, System.Web.UI.IDataBindingsAccessor) →
WebControl(System.Web.UI.IAttributeAccessor) → Label → BaseValidator(System.Web.UI.
IValidator) → BaseCompareValidator → CompareValidator

CustomValidator

disposable

System.Web.UI.WebControls (system.web.dll)   class

The CustomValidator control allows you to define your own validation routines. A similar task could be performed by writing manual validation code in the click event for a submit button, but using a CustomValidator allows you to configure client-side validation, create an error message that will be included in the validation summary, and provide a "vote" used for the combined System.Web.UI.Page.IsValid property along with all other validation controls. A CustomValidator can also be reused easily to validate multiple controls.

To provide server-side validation, create an event handler for the **ServerValidate** event. The string from the input control and the result of the validation is stored in the provided **ServerValidateEventArgs** object. You can also perform client-side validation, which can improve the responsiveness of your application by reducing the need for round trips to the server. However, because client-side validation will not be performed in some browsers and is easy to circumvent, it should never be used in place of server validation. To use client-side validation, set the **ClientValidationFunction** to the name of a JavaScript or VBScript function in the *.aspx* code portion of your page (not the code-behind class). This script function should be in a language that the client browser can understand, which means that JavaScript is the best choice if you are supporting non-Microsoft browsers. The function must be in the form **function ValidationFunctionName(source, value)**, where **value** is the value to be validated. This function should return **True** or **False** to indicate whether the validation succeeded. ASP.NET will take care of the code necessary to display the corresponding error message. Note that this is a very bad idea if your function uses "secret" logic to validate a password or key, as this logic will be easily retrievable by the client!

```
public class CustomValidator : BaseValidator {
// Public Constructors
   public CustomValidator( );
// Public Instance Properties
   public string ClientValidationFunction{set; get; }
// Protected Instance Methods
   protected override void AddAttributesToRender(System.Web.UI.HtmlTextWriter writer);   // overrides BaseValidator
   protected override bool ControlPropertiesValid( );                                     // overrides BaseValidator
   protected override bool EvaluateIsValid( );                                            // overrides BaseValidator
   protected virtual bool OnServerValidate( string value);
// Events
   public event ServerValidateEventHandler ServerValidate;
}
```

Hierarchy System.Object → System.Web.UI.Control(System.ComponentModel.IComponent, System. IDisposable, System.Web.UI.IParserAccessor, System.Web.UI.IDataBindingsAccessor) → WebControl(System.Web.UI.IAttributeAccessor) → Label → BaseValidator(System.Web.UI. IValidator) → CustomValidator

DataGrid   disposable

System.Web.UI.WebControls (system.web.dll)   class

The **DataGrid** control is, at its simplest, a data-bound list displayed in a table grid structure. It provides a rich set of functionality that makes it the most versatile data-bound control, including support for selection, editing, deleting, paging, and sorting.

Columns can be added to a **DataGrid** in two ways. First, if the **AutoGenerateColumns** property is **True**, a **BoundColumn** will be created for every column in the data source specified by **DataSource**. Alternatively, you can define columns by adding nested tags in the *.aspx* file. (If you mix both approaches, the automatically generated columns will always be added last.) Columns can be **BoundColumn**, **ButtonColumn**, **EditCommandColumn**, **HyperLinkColumn**, or **TemplateColumn** controls (each of which are described separately in this namespace). The order that the columns appear is determined by the order the column tags are listed in the *.aspx*, and you can manipulate them programmatically through the **Columns** collection. Note that this collection does not contain automatically generated columns—only ones that have defined templates.

The DataGrid has a number of properties that allow you to control its appearance. You can set TableItemStyle objects for various properties, including footers, headers (used automatically for column titles), and items. (The corresponding DataGrid properties end with the word "Style.") You can also use the ShowHeader and ShowFooter properties to configure whether headers and footers will be displayed.

To allow row selection for DataGrid, set the SelectedItemTemplate to look different than the ItemTemplate. Then add a button column that allows selection (for example, you might use the text "Select") and set the SelectedIndex property to the appropriate row in the ItemCommand event handler. To allow in-place editing, add an EditCommandColumn column and set the EditItemIndex (then rebind to the data source) in the EditCommand event handler. Any properties that are not marked as read-only in the template will be editable through automatically provided text boxes. You can handle the UpdateCommand event to commit the actual change. To disable editing or selection for a DataGrid, set the EditItemIndex or SelectedIndex to -1.

To provide sorting, enable the AllowSorting property and rebind the appropriate sorted data in response to the SortCommand event. Finally, to provide paging, enable the AllowPaging property and set a number of rows in the PageSize property. When the PageIndexChanged event is triggered, set the CurrentPageIndex to the appropriate page. Note that automatic paging causes the complete data table to be retrieved, even though only a few rows are being displayed. To optimize performance, you should enable the AllowCustomPaging property and provide custom data access code in the CurrentPageIndex event handler. When using custom paging, you must also set the VirtualItemCount property to the total number of records to allow the DataGrid to determine the total number of pages needed.

```
public class DataGrid : BaseDataList, System.Web.UI.INamingContainer {
// Public Constructors
    public DataGrid( );
// Public Static Fields
    public const string CancelCommandName;              // =Cancel
    public const string DeleteCommandName;              // =Delete
    public const string EditCommandName;                // =Edit
    public const string NextPageCommandArgument;        // =Next
    public const string PageCommandName;                // =Page
    public const string PrevPageCommandArgument;        // =Prev
    public const string SelectCommandName;              // =Select
    public const string SortCommandName;                // =Sort
    public const string UpdateCommandName;              // =Update
// Public Instance Properties
    public virtual bool AllowCustomPaging{set; get; }
    public virtual bool AllowPaging{set; get; }
    public virtual bool AllowSorting{set; get; }
    public virtual TableItemStyle AlternatingItemStyle{get; }
    public virtual bool AutoGenerateColumns{set; get; }
    public virtual string BackImageUrl{set; get; }
    public virtual DataGridColumnCollection Columns{get; }
    public int CurrentPageIndex{set; get; }
    public virtual int EditItemIndex{set; get; }
```

```
public virtual TableItemStyle EditItemStyle{get; }
public virtual TableItemStyle FooterStyle{get; }
public virtual TableItemStyle HeaderStyle{get; }
public virtual DataGridItemCollection Items{get; }
public virtual TableItemStyle ItemStyle{get; }
public int PageCount{get; }
public virtual DataGridPagerStyle PagerStyle{get; }
public virtual int PageSize{set; get; }
public virtual int SelectedIndex{set; get; }
public virtual DataGridItem SelectedItem{get; }
public virtual TableItemStyle SelectedItemStyle{get; }
public virtual bool ShowFooter{set; get; }
public virtual bool ShowHeader{set; get; }
public virtual int VirtualItemCount{set; get; }
// Protected Instance Methods
protected virtual ArrayList CreateColumnSet( PagedDataSource dataSource, bool useDataSource);
protected override void CreateControlHierarchy(bool useDataSource);                    // overrides BaseDataList
protected override Style CreateControlStyle( );                                        // overrides WebControl
protected virtual DataGridItem CreateItem(int itemIndex, int dataSourceIndex, ListItemType itemType);
protected virtual void InitializeItem(DataGridItem item, DataGridColumn[ ] columns);
protected virtual void InitializePager(DataGridItem item, int columnSpan, PagedDataSource pagedDataSource);
protected override void LoadViewState( object savedState);                             // overrides WebControl
protected override bool OnBubbleEvent(object source, EventArgs e);              // overrides System.Web.UI.Control
protected virtual void OnCancelCommand(DataGridCommandEventArgs e);
protected virtual void OnDeleteCommand(DataGridCommandEventArgs e);
protected virtual void OnEditCommand(DataGridCommandEventArgs e);
protected virtual void OnItemCommand(DataGridCommandEventArgs e);
protected virtual void OnItemCreated(DataGridItemEventArgs e);
protected virtual void OnItemDataBound(DataGridItemEventArgs e);
protected virtual void OnPageIndexChanged(DataGridPageChangedEventArgs e);
protected virtual void OnSortCommand(DataGridSortCommandEventArgs e);
protected virtual void OnUpdateCommand(DataGridCommandEventArgs e);
protected override void PrepareControlHierarchy( );                                    // overrides BaseDataList
protected override object SaveViewState( );                                            // overrides WebControl
protected override void TrackViewState( );                                             // overrides WebControl
// Events
public event DataGridCommandEventHandler CancelCommand;
public event DataGridCommandEventHandler DeleteCommand;
public event DataGridCommandEventHandler EditCommand;
public event DataGridCommandEventHandler ItemCommand;
public event DataGridItemEventHandler ItemCreated;
public event DataGridItemEventHandler ItemDataBound;
public event DataGridPageChangedEventHandler PageIndexChanged;
public event DataGridSortCommandEventHandler SortCommand;
public event DataGridCommandEventHandler UpdateCommand;
}
```

Hierarchy   System.Object → System.Web.UI.Control(System.ComponentModel.IComponent, System. IDisposable, System.Web.UI.IParserAccessor, System.Web.UI.IDataBindingsAccessor) → WebControl(System.Web.UI.IAttributeAccessor) → BaseDataList → DataGrid(System.Web. UI.INamingContainer)

Passed To   DataGridColumnCollection.DataGridColumnCollection( )

DataGridColumn

System.Web.UI.WebControls (system.web.dll)   abstract class

This abstract base class is used for all types of columns that can be added to a DataGrid control, including BoundColumn, ButtonColumn, HyperLinkColumn, EditCommandColumn, and Template-Column. It includes basic formatting-related properties, including TableItemStyle objects for the header, footer, and items, and an image file to be displayed in the header (HeaderIm900ageUrl). The SortExpression property specifies the field that will be used to order the DataGrid when sorting according to this column.

```
public abstract class DataGridColumn : System.Web.UI.IStateManager {
// Public Constructors
  public DataGridColumn( );
// Public Instance Properties
  public virtual TableItemStyle FooterStyle{get; }
  public virtual string FooterText{set; get; }
  public virtual string HeaderImageUrl{set; get; }
  public virtual TableItemStyle HeaderStyle{get; }
  public virtual string HeaderText{set; get; }
  public virtual TableItemStyle ItemStyle{get; }
  public virtual string SortExpression{set; get; }
  public bool Visible{set; get; }
// Protected Instance Properties
  protected bool DesignMode{get; }
  protected bool IsTrackingViewState{get; }                    // implements System.Web.UI.IStateManager
  protected DataGrid Owner{get; }
  protected StateBag ViewState{get; }
// Public Instance Methods
  public virtual void Initialize( );
  public virtual void InitializeCell(TableCell cell, int columnIndex, ListItemType itemType);
  public override string ToString( );                          // overrides object
// Protected Instance Methods
  protected virtual void LoadViewState( object savedState);    // implements System.Web.UI.IStateManager
  protected virtual void OnColumnChanged( );
  protected virtual object SaveViewState( );                   // implements System.Web.UI.IStateManager
  protected virtual void TrackViewState( );                    // implements System.Web.UI.IStateManager
}
```

Subclasses   BoundColumn, ButtonColumn, EditCommandColumn, HyperLinkColumn, TemplateColumn

Returned By   DataGridColumnCollection.this

Passed To   DataGrid.InitializeItem( ), DataGridColumnCollection.{Add( ), AddAt( ), IndexOf( ), Remove( )}

WebControls
Namespace

DataGridColumnCollection

System.Web.UI.WebControls (system.web.dll)   **sealed class**

This is the collection of DataGridColumn objects in a DataGrid control. It is provided through the DataGrid.Columns property. You can use this collection to programmatically add or remove columns, but these changes will not be automatically persisted over postbacks because the DataGrid.Columns property is not stored in view state. This collection will only contain columns that have been added through templates, not automatically generated ones.

```
public sealed class DataGridColumnCollection : ICollection, IEnumerable, System.Web.UI.IStateManager {
// Public Constructors
    public DataGridColumnCollection(DataGrid owner, System.Collections.ArrayList columns);
// Public Instance Properties
    public int Count{get; }                                                  // implements ICollection
    public bool IsReadOnly{get; }
    public bool IsSynchronized{get; }                                        // implements ICollection
    public object SyncRoot{get; }                                            // implements ICollection
    public DataGridColumn this[ int index ]{get; }
// Public Instance Methods
    public void Add( DataGridColumn column);
    public void AddAt( int index, DataGridColumn column);
    public void Clear( );
    public void CopyTo( Array array, int index);                             // implements ICollection
    public IEnumerator GetEnumerator( );                                     // implements IEnumerable
    public int IndexOf( DataGridColumn column);
    public void Remove( DataGridColumn column);
    public void RemoveAt( int index);
}
```

Returned By   DataGrid.Columns

DataGridCommandEventArgs

System.Web.UI.WebControls (system.web.dll)   **sealed class**

The DataGridCommandEventArgs class provides more information for the ItemCommand, Cancel-Command, DeleteCommand, EditCommand, and UpdateCommand events of the DataGrid control. This information consists of an Item property identifying the affected DataGridItem and a CommandSource property that refers to the button or hyperlink that was clicked. You have to cast this object to an appropriate type to read its properties.

```
public sealed class DataGridCommandEventArgs : CommandEventArgs {
// Public Constructors
    public DataGridCommandEventArgs(DataGridItem item, object commandSource, CommandEventArgs originalArgs);
// Public Instance Properties
    public object CommandSource{get; }
    public DataGridItem Item{get; }
}
```

Hierarchy   System.Object → System.EventArgs → CommandEventArgs →
                    DataGridCommandEventArgs

Passed To DataGrid.{OnCancelCommand( ), OnDeleteCommand( ), OnEditCommand( ),
OnItemCommand( ), OnUpdateCommand( )}, DataGridCommandEventHandler.
{BeginInvoke( ), Invoke( )}, DataGridSortCommandEventArgs.
DataGridSortCommandEventArgs( )

DataGridCommandEventHandler

serializable

System.Web.UI.WebControls (system.web.dll)   delegate

This delegate specifies the parameters for the event handler routine that handles the
ItemCommand, CancelCommand, DeleteCommand, EditCommand, and UpdateCommand events of the Data-
Grid control. This event handler receives additional information about the item that was
clicked.

```
public delegate void DataGridCommandEventHandler(object source, DataGridCommandEventArgs e);
```

Associated Events DataGrid.{CancelCommand( ), DeleteCommand( ), EditCommand( ), ItemCommand( ),
UpdateCommand( )}

DataGridItem

disposable

System.Web.UI.WebControls (system.web.dll)   class

This class represents an individual item in the DataGrid control. You can access a DataGrid-
Item through the DataGrid.Items collection or from a DataGrid event handler.

The DataGridItem class inherits most of its properties from System.Web.UI.Control. In addition,
it provides an ItemIndex that gives its index in the DataGrid.Items collection, an ItemType property that identifies what type of item this is (a header, footer, alternating row, etc.), and
a DataItem property that returns the corresponding data item (such as a System.Data.
DataRowView instance).

```
public class DataGridItem : TableRow, System.Web.UI.INamingContainer {
// Public Constructors
    public DataGridItem(int itemIndex, int dataSetIndex, ListItemType itemType);
// Public Instance Properties
    public virtual object DataItem{set; get; }
    public virtual int DataSetIndex{get; }
    public virtual int ItemIndex{get; }
    public virtual ListItemType ItemType{get; }
// Protected Instance Methods
    protected override bool OnBubbleEvent(object source, EventArgs e);          // overrides System.Web.UI.Control
    protected internal virtual void SetItemType(ListItemType itemType);
}
```

Hierarchy System.Object → System.Web.UI.Control(System.ComponentModel.IComponent, System.
IDisposable, System.Web.UI.IParserAccessor, System.Web.UI.IDataBindingsAccessor) →
WebControl(System.Web.UI.IAttributeAccessor) → TableRow → DataGridItem(System.
Web.UI.INamingContainer)

Returned By DataGrid.{CreateItem( ), SelectedItem}, DataGridCommandEventArgs.Item, DataGridItemCol-
lection.this, DataGridItemEventArgs.Item

Passed To DataGrid.{InitializeItem( ), InitializePager( )}, DataGridCommandEventArgs.
DataGridCommandEventArgs( ), DataGridItemEventArgs.DataGridItemEventArgs( )

DataGridItemCollection

System.Web.UI.WebControls (system.web.dll)   class

This custom collection class contains **DataGridItem** objects. It is used for the **DataGrid.Items** property of the DataGrid control.

```
public class DataGridItemCollection : ICollection, IEnumerable {
// Public Constructors
  public DataGridItemCollection(System.Collections.ArrayList items);
// Public Instance Properties
  public int Count{get; }                                              // implements ICollection
  public bool IsReadOnly{get; }
  public bool IsSynchronized{get; }                                    // implements ICollection
  public object SyncRoot{get; }                                        // implements ICollection
  public DataGridItem this[ int index ]{get; }
// Public Instance Methods
  public void CopyTo( Array array, int index);                        // implements ICollection
  public IEnumerator GetEnumerator( );                                // implements IEnumerable
}
```

Returned By   DataGrid.Items

DataGridItemEventArgs

System.Web.UI.WebControls (system.web.dll)   class

This class provides extra information for the **DataGrid.ItemCreated** and **DataGrid.ItemDataBound** events, which consists of an Item property with the current **DataGridItem** object.

```
public class DataGridItemEventArgs : EventArgs {
// Public Constructors
  public DataGridItemEventArgs( DataGridItem item);
// Public Instance Properties
  public DataGridItem Item{get; }
}
```

Hierarchy   System.Object → System.EventArgs → DataGridItemEventArgs

Passed To   DataGrid.{OnItemCreated( ), OnItemDataBound( )}, DataGridItemEventHandler.
                       {BeginInvoke( ), Invoke( )}

DataGridItemEventHandler   serializable

System.Web.UI.WebControls (system.web.dll)   delegate

This delegate defines the parameter list for methods that handle the **DataGrid.ItemCreated** and **DataGrid.ItemDataBound** events. These events provides extra information about the current DataGridItem through the **DataGridItemEventArgs** class.

```
public delegate void DataGridItemEventHandler(object sender, DataGridItemEventArgs e);
```

Associated Events DataGrid.{ItemCreated( ), ItemDataBound( )}

DataGridPageChangedEventArgs

System.Web.UI.WebControls (system.web.dll)   **sealed class**

This class provides extra information for the DataGrid.PageIndexChanged event. This information includes the CommandSource, which will always be the DataGridItem that represents the page selection control, and the NewPageIndex, which indicates the selected page (the first page is 0, although it the corresponding link in the DataGrid will be displayed as "1").

```
public sealed class DataGridPageChangedEventArgs : EventArgs {
// Public Constructors
   public DataGridPageChangedEventArgs(object commandSource, int newPageIndex);
// Public Instance Properties
   public object CommandSource{get; }
   public int NewPageIndex{get; }
}
```

Hierarchy	System.Object → System.EventArgs → DataGridPageChangedEventArgs
Passed To	DataGrid.OnPageIndexChanged( ), DataGridPageChangedEventHandler.{BeginInvoke( ), Invoke( )}

DataGridPageChangedEventHandler   **serializable**

System.Web.UI.WebControls (system.web.dll)   **delegate**

This delegate specifies the parameter list that a method must have to handle the Data-Grid.PageIndexChanged event. If you are using automatic paging (and have set the DataGrid.AllowPaging property to True, but the DataGrid.AllowCustomPaging property to False), your event handler only needs to set the new DataGrid.CurrentPageIndex.

```
public delegate void DataGridPageChangedEventHandler(object source, DataGridPageChangedEventArgs e);
```

Associated Events DataGrid.PageIndexChanged( )

DataGridPagerStyle   **marshal by reference, disposable**

System.Web.UI.WebControls (system.web.dll)   **sealed class**

This class represents a special style class derived from TableItemStyle that allows you to configure the pager controls for the DataGrid control. It is provided through the DataGrid.PagerStyle property. Pager controls (special links that allow you to see one "page" of data at a time) are displayed in a separate row at the bottom of the table, provided you have enabled the DataGrid.AllowPaging property.

Aside from setting the standard style properties, you can also use the Mode property to configure the type of pager buttons used (multiple numeric or previous/next). If you are using previous/next buttons (PagerMode.NextPrev), you can also set the associated text for the links using the NextPageText and PrevPageText properties (which default to the < and > signs). If you use numeric link buttons (PagerMode.NumericPages), you can also set the maximum number of links that will be displayed at a time through the PageButtonCount property. If there are more pages than specified in this property, a link with ellipses (...) is automatically displayed in the pager row, which allows the user to show the next or previous set of numeric links.

```
public sealed class DataGridPagerStyle : TableItemStyle {
// Public Instance Properties
  public PagerMode Mode{set; get; }
  public string NextPageText{set; get; }
  public int PageButtonCount{set; get; }
  public PagerPosition Position{set; get; }
  public string PrevPageText{set; get; }
  public bool Visible{set; get; }
// Public Instance Methods
  public override void CopyFrom( Style s);                          // overrides TableItemStyle
  public override void MergeWith( Style s);                         // overrides TableItemStyle
  public override void Reset( );                                    // overrides TableItemStyle
}
```

Hierarchy   System.Object → System.MarshalByRefObject → System.ComponentModel.Compo-
nent(System.ComponentModel.IComponent, System.IDisposable) → Style(System.Web.UI.
IStateManager) → TableItemStyle → DataGridPagerStyle

Returned By   DataGrid.PagerStyle

DataGridSortCommandEventArgs

System.Web.UI.WebControls (system.web.dll)   sealed class

This class provides extra information for the DataGrid.SortCommand event. This information includes the CommandSource, which will always be the DataGridItem that represents the
header row, and the SortExpression, which indicates the column (field) title. If you use a
System.Data.DataView for your data source, you can assign this expression to the Sort
property.

```
public sealed class DataGridSortCommandEventArgs : EventArgs {
// Public Constructors
  public DataGridSortCommandEventArgs(object commandSource, DataGridCommandEventArgs dce);
// Public Instance Properties
  public object CommandSource{get; }
  public string SortExpression{get; }
}
```

Hierarchy   System.Object → System.EventArgs → DataGridSortCommandEventArgs

Passed To   DataGrid.OnSortCommand( ), DataGridSortCommandEventHandler.{BeginInvoke( ),
Invoke( )}

DataGridSortCommandEventHandler   serializable

System.Web.UI.WebControls (system.web.dll)   delegate

This delegate specifies the parameter list that a subroutine must have to handle the
DataGrid.SortCommand event. This event specifies additional information about the selected
column (DataGridSortCommandEventArgs.SortExpression), which you can use to build a new data
source. This event handler should then rebind the data source to the DataGrid control to
update the display.

public delegate void **DataGridSortCommandEventHandler**(object *source*, DataGridSortCommandEventArgs *e*);

Associated Events   DataGrid.SortCommand( )

DataKeyCollection

System.Web.UI.WebControls (system.web.dll)   sealed class

The DataKeyCollection class contains a read-only collection of primary field key names as strings. This class is used by the BaseDataList.DataKeys property to facillitate editing (for example, you can use a unique ID for your key field and use it to build SQL statements when you need to update a record in response to a user edit operation). You must specify the data key you want to use in the BaseDataList.DataKeyField property before you bind the data list.

```
public sealed class DataKeyCollection : ICollection, IEnumerable {
// Public Constructors
   public DataKeyCollection(System.Collections.ArrayList keys);
// Public Instance Properties
   public int Count{get; }                                               // implements ICollection
   public bool IsReadOnly{get; }
   public bool IsSynchronized{get; }                                     // implements ICollection
   public object SyncRoot{get; }                                         // implements ICollection
   public object this[ int index ]{get; }
// Public Instance Methods
   public void CopyTo( Array array, int index);                         // implements ICollection
   public IEnumerator GetEnumerator( );                                 // implements IEnumerable
}
```

Returned By   BaseDataList.DataKeys

DataList   disposable

System.Web.UI.WebControls (system.web.dll)   class

The DataList control is a data-bound list that is configured through templates in the *.aspx* file. It does not provide quite the extent of features found in the DataGrid control. It does provide support for automatic selection (by setting the SelectedIndex property) and editing (by setting the EditItemIndex property), but not for automatic paging or sorting. Also, there is no support for default column types or automatically generated rows, so you will always need to specify at least an ItemTemplate. Templates for the DataList are bracketed inside the appropriate template tag (like <ItemTemplate>) and may contain a data-binding expression (for example, <%# Container.DataItem("Description") %>). You can also add HTML tags or tags for ASP.NET controls to these templates manually for a customized appearance.

You can use the AlternatingItemTemplate property to allow items to alternate between two styles, the EditItemTemplate to specify how items will appear when they are being edited, and the SelectedItemTemplate to specify how items will appear when they are selected. The HeaderTemplate, FooterTemplate, and SeparatorTemplate allow you specify layout and content for special rows. The DataList has a number of properties that allow you to control its appearance. You can set TableItemStyle objects for various properties, including footers, headers (used automatically for column titles), and items. (The corresponding DataList properties end with the word "Style.") You can also use the ShowHeader and ShowFooter properties to configure whether headers and footers will be displayed.

```
public class DataList : BaseDataList, System.Web.UI.INamingContainer, IRepeatInfoUser {
// Public Constructors
  public DataList( );
// Public Static Fields
  public const string CancelCommandName;                                              // =Cancel
  public const string DeleteCommandName;                                              // =Delete
  public const string EditCommandName;                                                  // =Edit
  public const string SelectCommandName;                                              // =Select
  public const string UpdateCommandName;                                            // =Update
// Public Instance Properties
  public virtual TableItemStyle AlternatingItemStyle{get; }
  public virtual ITemplate AlternatingItemTemplate{set; get; }
  public virtual int EditItemIndex{set; get; }
  public virtual TableItemStyle EditItemStyle{get; }
  public virtual ITemplate EditItemTemplate{set; get; }
  public virtual bool ExtractTemplateRows{set; get; }
  public virtual TableItemStyle FooterStyle{get; }
  public virtual ITemplate FooterTemplate{set; get; }
  public override GridLines GridLines{set; get; }                            // overrides BaseDataList
  public virtual TableItemStyle HeaderStyle{get; }
  public virtual ITemplate HeaderTemplate{set; get; }
  public virtual DataListItemCollection Items{get; }
  public virtual TableItemStyle ItemStyle{get; }
  public virtual ITemplate ItemTemplate{set; get; }
  public virtual int RepeatColumns{set; get; }
  public virtual RepeatDirection RepeatDirection{set; get; }
  public virtual RepeatLayout RepeatLayout{set; get; }
  public virtual int SelectedIndex{set; get; }
  public virtual DataListItem SelectedItem{get; }
  public virtual TableItemStyle SelectedItemStyle{get; }
  public virtual ITemplate SelectedItemTemplate{set; get; }
  public virtual TableItemStyle SeparatorStyle{get; }
  public virtual ITemplate SeparatorTemplate{set; get; }
  public virtual bool ShowFooter{set; get; }
  public virtual bool ShowHeader{set; get; }
// Protected Instance Methods
  protected override void CreateControlHierarchy(bool useDataSource);          // overrides BaseDataList
  protected override Style CreateControlStyle( );                                 // overrides WebControl
  protected virtual DataListItem CreateItem(int itemIndex, ListItemType itemType);
  protected virtual void InitializeItem( DataListItem item);
  protected override void LoadViewState( object savedState);                     // overrides WebControl
  protected override bool OnBubbleEvent(object source, EventArgs e);        // overrides System.Web.UI.Control
  protected virtual void OnCancelCommand( DataListCommandEventArgs e);
  protected virtual void OnDeleteCommand( DataListCommandEventArgs e);
  protected virtual void OnEditCommand( DataListCommandEventArgs e);
  protected virtual void OnItemCommand( DataListCommandEventArgs e);
  protected virtual void OnItemCreated(DataListItemEventArgs e);
  protected virtual void OnItemDataBound( DataListItemEventArgs e);
```

```
    protected virtual void OnUpdateCommand( DataListCommandEventArgs e);
    protected override void PrepareControlHierarchy( );                          // overrides BaseDataList
    protected override void RenderContents(System.Web.UI.HtmlTextWriter writer);  // overrides WebControl
    protected override object SaveViewState( );                                   // overrides WebControl
    protected override void TrackViewState( );                                    // overrides WebControl
 // Events
    public event DataListCommandEventHandler CancelCommand;
    public event DataListCommandEventHandler DeleteCommand;
    public event DataListCommandEventHandler EditCommand;
    public event DataListCommandEventHandler ItemCommand;
    public event DataListItemEventHandler ItemCreated;
    public event DataListItemEventHandler ItemDataBound;
    public event DataListCommandEventHandler UpdateCommand;
 }
```

Hierarchy System.Object → System.Web.UI.Control(System.ComponentModel.IComponent, System.
IDisposable, System.Web.UI.IParserAccessor, System.Web.UI.IDataBindingsAccessor) →
WebControl(System.Web.UI.IAttributeAccessor) → BaseDataList → DataList(System.Web.
UI.INamingContainer, IRepeatInfoUser)

DataListCommandEventArgs

System.Web.UI.WebControls (system.web.dll)   sealed class

The DataListCommandEventArgs class provides more information for the ItemCommand, Cancel-
Command, DeleteCommand, EditCommand, and UpdateCommand events of the DataList control. This
information consists of an Item property identifying the affected DataListItem, and a
CommandSource property that refers to the button or hyperlink that was clicked. You will
have to cast this object to an appropriate type to read its properties.

```
public sealed class DataListCommandEventArgs : CommandEventArgs {
 // Public Constructors
    public DataListCommandEventArgs(DataListItem item, object commandSource, CommandEventArgs originalArgs);
 // Public Instance Properties
    public object CommandSource{get; }
    public DataListItem Item{get; }
 }
```

Hierarchy System.Object → System.EventArgs → CommandEventArgs →
DataListCommandEventArgs

Passed To DataList.{OnCancelCommand( ), OnDeleteCommand( ), OnEditCommand( ),
OnItemCommand( ), OnUpdateCommand( )}, DataListCommandEventHandler.
{BeginInvoke( ), Invoke( )}

DataListCommandEventHandler   serializable

System.Web.UI.WebControls (system.web.dll)   delegate

This delegate specifies the parameters for the event handler routine that handles the
ItemCommand, CancelCommand, DeleteCommand, EditCommand, and UpdateCommand events of the
DataList control. This event handler receives additional information about the item that
was clicked.

```
public delegate void DataListCommandEventHandler(object source, DataListCommandEventArgs e);
```

Associated Events   DataList.{CancelCommand( ), DeleteCommand( ), EditCommand( ), ItemCommand( ), UpdateCommand( )}

DataListItem
disposable

System.Web.UI.WebControls (system.web.dll)   class

This class represents an individual item in the DataList control. You can access it through the DataList.Items collection or from a DataList event.

DataListItem inherits most of its properties from System.Web.UI.Control. In addition, it provides an ItemIndex that gives its index in the DataList.Items collection, an ItemType prop900erty that identifies what type of item this is (a header, footer, alternating row, etc.), and a DataItem property that returns the corresponding data item (such as a System. Data.DataRowView instance).

```
public class DataListItem : WebControl, System.Web.UI.INamingContainer {
// Public Constructors
  public DataListItem(int itemIndex, ListItemType itemType);
// Public Instance Properties
  public virtual object DataItem{set; get; }
  public virtual int ItemIndex{get; }
  public virtual ListItemType ItemType{get; }
// Public Instance Methods
  public virtual void RenderItem(System.Web.UI.HtmlTextWriter writer, bool extractRows, bool tableLayout);
// Protected Instance Methods
  protected override Style CreateControlStyle( );                                        // overrides WebControl
  protected override bool OnBubbleEvent(object source, EventArgs e);              // overrides System.Web.UI.Control
  protected internal virtual void SetItemType(ListItemType itemType);
}
```

Hierarchy   System.Object → System.Web.UI.Control(System.ComponentModel.IComponent, System. IDisposable, System.Web.UI.IParserAccessor, System.Web.UI.IDataBindingsAccessor) → WebControl(System.Web.UI.IAttributeAccessor) → DataListItem(System.Web.UI. INamingContainer)

Returned By   DataList.{CreateItem( ), SelectedItem}, DataListCommandEventArgs.Item, DataListItemCol-lection.this, DataListItemEventArgs.Item

Passed To   DataList.InitializeItem( ), DataListCommandEventArgs.DataListCommandEventArgs( ), Data-ListItemEventArgs.DataListItemEventArgs( )

DataListItemCollection

System.Web.UI.WebControls (system.web.dll)   sealed class

This custom collection class contains DataListItem objects. It is used for the DataList.Items property of the DataList control.

```
public sealed class DataListItemCollection : ICollection, IEnumerable {
// Public Constructors
  public DataListItemCollection(System.Collections.ArrayList items);
```

```
// Public Instance Properties
  public int Count{get; }                                                    // implements ICollection
  public bool IsReadOnly{get; }
  public bool IsSynchronized{get; }                                          // implements ICollection
  public object SyncRoot{get; }                                              // implements ICollection
  public DataListItem this[ int index ]{get; }
// Public Instance Methods
  public void CopyTo( Array array, int index);                               // implements ICollection
  public IEnumerator GetEnumerator( );                                       // implements IEnumerable
}
```

Returned By   DataList.Items

DataListItemEventArgs

System.Web.UI.WebControls (system.web.dll)   sealed class

This class provides extra information for the DataList.ItemCreated and DataList.ItemDataBound events. This information consists of an Item property that contains the current DataList-Item object.

```
public sealed class DataListItemEventArgs : EventArgs {
// Public Constructors
  public DataListItemEventArgs( DataListItem item);
// Public Instance Properties
  public DataListItem Item{get; }
}
```

Hierarchy   System.Object → System.EventArgs → DataListItemEventArgs

Passed To   DataList.{OnItemCreated( ), OnItemDataBound( )}, DataListItemEventHandler.
                 {BeginInvoke( ), Invoke( )}

DataListItemEventHandler   serializable

System.Web.UI.WebControls (system.web.dll)   delegate

This delegate defines the parameter list for methods that handle the DataList.ItemCreated and DataList.ItemDataBound events. These events provide extra information about the current DataListItem through the DataListItemEventArgs class.

```
public delegate void DataListItemEventHandler(object sender, DataListItemEventArgs e);
```

Associated Events   DataList.{ItemCreated( ), ItemDataBound( )}

DayNameFormat   serializable

System.Web.UI.WebControls (system.web.dll)   enum

This enumeration is used to set the Calendar.DayNameFormat property, which configures how days are displayed at the top of the calendar grid. Days can be displayed in Full (e.g., "Tuesday"), in a Short version ("Tues"), or by using the FirstLetter or FirstTwoLetters ("T" or "Tu").

```
public enum DayNameFormat {
  Full = 0,
  Short = 1,
  FirstLetter = 2,
  FirstTwoLetters = 3
}
```

Hierarchy   System.Object → System.ValueType → System.Enum(System.IComparable, System.IFor-
              mattable, System.IConvertible) → DayNameFormat

Returned By   Calendar.DayNameFormat

Passed To   Calendar.DayNameFormat

DayRenderEventArgs

System.Web.UI.WebControls (system.web.dll)   sealed class

This object is provided to the DayRenderEventHandler. It identifies the CalendarDay that is
about to be added and the TableCell that contains the date by means of the Day and Cell
properties. The Calendar.DayRender event is fired for every currently displayed day. This
includes days from the preceding and following month, which are used to fill out the
first and last week on the calendar.

```
public sealed class DayRenderEventArgs {
// Public Constructors
  public DayRenderEventArgs(TableCell cell, CalendarDay day);
// Public Instance Properties
  public TableCell Cell{get; }
  public CalendarDay Day{get; }
}
```

Passed To   DayRenderEventHandler.{BeginInvoke( ), Invoke( )}

DayRenderEventHandler   serializable

System.Web.UI.WebControls (system.web.dll)   delegate

This delegate defines the subroutine used to handle the Calendar.DayRender event. This
event fires as each day is added to the currently displayed calendar month and
provides additional information about the day in a DayRenderEventArgs object. The properties of this object can be modified to programmatically change the display color for a
specific date or to make certain dates unselectable.

```
public delegate void DayRenderEventHandler(object sender, DayRenderEventArgs e);
```

Associated Events Calendar.DayRender( )

DropDownList   disposable

System.Web.UI.WebControls (system.web.dll)   class

This class provides a single-selection drop-down list control. Various properties, such
as BorderColor, BorderStyle, and BorderWidth, allow you to configure its appearance. To add

items programmatically, use the Items collection or use the DataBind() method to bind to a data source (such as a System.Data.DataTable or a System.Array).

Use the SelectedIndex property to determine the selected item or the SelectedItem property, which returns a ListItem object that specifies the associated text.

```
public class DropDownList : ListControl, System.Web.UI.IPostBackDataHandler {
// Public Constructors
   public DropDownList( );
// Public Instance Properties
   public override Color BorderColor{set; get; }                              // overrides WebControl
   public override BorderStyle BorderStyle{set; get; }                        // overrides WebControl
   public override Unit BorderWidth{set; get; }                               // overrides WebControl
   public override int SelectedIndex{set; get; }                             // overrides ListControl
   public override string ToolTip{set; get; }                                 // overrides WebControl
// Protected Instance Methods
   protected override void AddAttributesToRender(System.Web.UI.HtmlTextWriter writer);    // overrides WebControl
   protected override ControlCollection CreateControlCollection( );           // overrides System.Web.UI.Control
   protected override void RenderContents(System.Web.UI.HtmlTextWriter writer);           // overrides WebControl
}
```

Hierarchy   System.Object → System.Web.UI.Control(System.ComponentModel.IComponent, System. IDisposable, System.Web.UI.IParserAccessor, System.Web.UI.IDataBindingsAccessor) → WebControl(System.Web.UI.IAttributeAccessor) → ListControl → DropDownList(System. Web.UI.IPostBackDataHandler)

EditCommandColumn

System.Web.UI.WebControls (system.web.dll)   class

The EditCommandColumn class is a special type of column used with the DataGrid control. It provides an "Edit" button or link (depending on the ButtonType property) that, when clicked, fires the DataGrid.EditCommand event. This event allows you to initiate editing for a row by using the DataGrid.EditItemIndex property (after which you must rebind to the data source).

While editing is in progress, the EditCommandColumn displays "Cancel" and "Update" buttons instead of an "Edit" button. These will trigger the DataGrid.CancelCommand and DataGrid.UpdateCommand events, respectively. In these events, you can add the code required to commit changes to the data source and cancel editing (by setting DataGrid. EditItemIndex to -1). Rebind to the data source before returning the page.

Note that you must provide values for the CancelText, EditText, and UpdateText properties (like "Cancel", "Edit", and "Update"). Otherwise, the associated command buttons will not appear in the column when editing is underway.

```
public class EditCommandColumn : DataGridColumn {
// Public Constructors
   public EditCommandColumn( );
// Public Instance Properties
   public virtual ButtonColumnType ButtonType{set; get; }
   public virtual string CancelText{set; get; }
   public virtual string EditText{set; get; }
   public virtual string UpdateText{set; get; }
// Public Instance Methods
```

```
public override void InitializeCell(TableCell cell, int columnIndex, ListItemType itemType);    // overrides DataGridColumn
}
```

Hierarchy   System.Object → DataGridColumn(System.Web.UI.IStateManager) →
                     EditCommandColumn

FirstDayOfWeek   serializable

System.Web.UI.WebControls (system.web.dll)   enum

This enumeration is used by the Calendar.FirstDayOfWeek property to determine how a
month is broken up into rows of weeks in the display. If you choose the value Sunday,
every row in the calendar display will start on Sunday and end with Saturday. Default
instructs ASP.NET to use the current regional settings defined on the web server.

```
public enum FirstDayOfWeek {
  Sunday = 0,
  Monday = 1,
  Tuesday = 2,
  Wednesday = 3,
  Thursday = 4,
  Friday = 5,
  Saturday = 6,
  Default = 7
}
```

Hierarchy   System.Object → System.ValueType → System.Enum(System.IComparable, System.IFor-
                     mattable, System.IConvertible) → FirstDayOfWeek

Returned By   System.Web.UI.MobileControls.Calendar.FirstDayOfWeek, Calendar.FirstDayOfWeek

Passed To   System.Web.UI.MobileControls.Calendar.FirstDayOfWeek, Calendar.FirstDayOfWeek

FontInfo

System.Web.UI.WebControls (system.web.dll)   sealed class

This class represents font information and is used in many controls through the
WebControl.Font property. This class contains the font properties that are supported in
ASP.NET Web Forms and differs slightly from the System.Drawing.Font object used in
other types of .NET applications.

```
public sealed class FontInfo {
// Public Instance Properties
  public bool Bold{set; get; }
  public bool Italic{set; get; }
  public string Name{set; get; }
  public string[ ] Names{set; get; }
  public bool Overline{set; get; }
  public FontUnit Size{set; get; }
  public bool Strikeout{set; get; }
  public bool Underline{set; get; }
// Public Instance Methods
```

```
public void CopyFrom( FontInfo f);
public void MergeWith( FontInfo f);
public bool ShouldSerializeNames( );
public override string ToString( );                                              // overrides object
}
```

Returned By   Style.Font, WebControl.Font

FontNamesConverter

System.Web.UI.WebControls (system.web.dll)   class

```
public class FontNamesConverter : System.ComponentModel.TypeConverter {
// Public Constructors
   public FontNamesConverter( );
// Public Instance Methods
   public override bool CanConvertFrom(System.ComponentModel.ITypeDescriptorContext context,
      Type sourceType);                             // overridcs System.ComponentModel.TypeConverter
   public override object ConvertFrom(System.ComponentModel.ITypeDescriptorContext context,
      System.Globalization.CultureInfo culture, object value);   // overrides System.ComponentModel.TypeConverter
   public override object ConvertTo(System.ComponentModel.ITypeDescriptorContext context,
      System.Globalization.CultureInfo culture, object value, Type destinationType);
                                                     // overrides System.ComponentModel.TypeConverter
}
```

The FontNamesConverter class is a type converter that can convert between a font name array and a string that contains a list of font names separated by commas (as often appears in an HTML page). This class is never accessed directly. You can access its functionality through the System.ComponentModel.TypeDescriptor helper class.

Hierarchy   System.Object → System.ComponentModel.TypeConverter → FontNamesConverter

FontSize   serializable

System.Web.UI.WebControls (system.web.dll)   enum

This enumeration is used to set the FontUnit.Type property using one of the font size constants defined by the HTML 4.0 standard.

```
public enum FontSize {
   NotSet = 0,
   AsUnit = 1,
   Smaller = 2,
   Larger = 3,
   XXSmall = 4,
   XSmall = 5,
   Small = 6,
   Medium = 7,
   Large = 8,
   XLarge = 9,
   XXLarge = 10
}
```

Hierarchy	System.Object → System.ValueType → System.Enum(System.IComparable, System.IFor-mattable, System.IConvertible) → FontSize
Returned By	FontUnit.Type
Passed To	FontUnit.FontUnit( )

FontUnit

System.Web.UI.WebControls (system.web.dll)   struct

This class represents the size of a font and is used by the FontInfo.Size property. The size of the font can be specified in two ways. You can use the Type property, which uses one of the HTML 4.0 standard font size specifications (which are duplicated as static read-only fields in this class) or the Unit property, which uses a Unit structure that can specify an exact point size.

```
public struct FontUnit {
// Public Constructors
   public FontUnit( FontSize type);
   public FontUnit( int value);
   public FontUnit( string value);
   public FontUnit(string value, System.Globalization.CultureInfo culture);
   public FontUnit( Unit value);
// Public Static Fields
   public static readonly FontUnit Empty;
   public static readonly FontUnit Large;                                              // =Large
   public static readonly FontUnit Larger;                                             // =Larger
   public static readonly FontUnit Medium;                                             // =Medium
   public static readonly FontUnit Small;                                              // =Small
   public static readonly FontUnit Smaller;                                            // =Smaller
   public static readonly FontUnit XLarge;                                             // =X-Large
   public static readonly FontUnit XSmall;                                             // =X-Small
   public static readonly FontUnit XXLarge;                                            // =XX-Large
   public static readonly FontUnit XXSmall;                                            // =XX-Small
// Public Instance Properties
   public bool IsEmpty{get; }
   public FontSize Type{get; }
   public Unit Unit{get; }
// Public Static Methods
   public static FontUnit Parse( string s);
   public static FontUnit Parse(string s, System.Globalization.CultureInfo culture);
   public static FontUnit Point( int n);
   public static bool operator !=(FontUnit left,      FontUnit right);
   public static bool operator = =(FontUnit left,      FontUnit right);
   public static implicit operator FontUnit( int n);
// Public Instance Methods
   public override bool Equals( object obj);                                  // overrides ValueType
   public override int GetHashCode( );                                        // overrides ValueType
   public override string ToString( );                                        // overrides ValueType
   public string ToString(System.Globalization.CultureInfo culture);
}
```

Hierarchy	System.Object → System.ValueType → FontUnit
Returned By	FontInfo.Size
Passed To	FontInfo.Size

FontUnitConverter

System.Web.UI.WebControls (system.web.dll) class

The FontUnitConverter class is a type converter that can convert between a FontUnit and other basic data types. This class is never accessed directly. You can access its functionality through the System.ComponentModel.TypeDescriptor helper class.

```
public class FontUnitConverter : System.ComponentModel.TypeConverter {
// Public Constructors
  public FontUnitConverter( );
// Public Instance Methods
  public override bool CanConvertFrom(System.ComponentModel.ITypeDescriptorContext context,
    Type sourceType);                              // overrides System.ComponentModel.TypeConverter
  public override object ConvertFrom(System.ComponentModel.ITypeDescriptorContext context,
    System.Globalization.CultureInfo culture, object value);    // overrides System.ComponentModel.TypeConverter
  public override object ConvertTo(System.ComponentModel.ITypeDescriptorContext context,
    System.Globalization.CultureInfo culture, object value, Type destinationType);
                                                   // overrides System.ComponentModel.TypeConverter
  public override StandardValuesCollection GetStandardValues(System.ComponentModel.ITypeDescriptorContext context);
                                                   // overrides System.ComponentModel.TypeConverter
  public override bool GetStandardValuesExclusive(System.ComponentModel.ITypeDescriptorContext context);
                                                   // overrides System.ComponentModel.TypeConverter
  public override bool GetStandardValuesSupported(System.ComponentModel.ITypeDescriptorContext context);
                                                   // overrides System.ComponentModel.TypeConverter
}
```

Hierarchy	System.Object → System.ComponentModel.TypeConverter → FontUnitConverter

GridLines serializable

System.Web.UI.WebControls (system.web.dll) enum

This enumeration specifies what grid lines are visible in a table. It is used by the Data-Grid, DataList, and Table classes.

```
public enum GridLines {
  None = 0,
  Horizontal = 1,
  Vertical = 2,
  Both = 3
}
```

Hierarchy	System.Object → System.ValueType → System.Enum(System.IComparable, System.IFormattable, System.IConvertible) → GridLines
Returned By	BaseDataList.GridLines, Table.GridLines, TableStyle.GridLines
Passed To	BaseDataList.GridLines, Table.GridLines, TableStyle.GridLines

HorizontalAlign

serializable

System.Web.UI.WebControls (system.web.dll)

enum

This enumeration specifies how contents will be laid out in a container. The classes that use it include DataGrid, Table, and Panel.

```
public enum HorizontalAlign {
  NotSet = 0,
  Left = 1,
  Center = 2,
  Right = 3,
  Justify = 4
}
```

Hierarchy   System.Object → System.ValueType → System.Enum(System.IComparable, System.IFor-
                    mattable, System.IConvertible) → HorizontalAlign

Returned By   BaseDataList.HorizontalAlign, Panel.HorizontalAlign, Table.HorizontalAlign, TableCell.Hori-
                    zontalAlign, TableItemStyle.HorizontalAlign, TableRow.HorizontalAlign, TableStyle.
                    HorizontalAlign

Passed To   BaseDataList.HorizontalAlign, Panel.HorizontalAlign, Table.HorizontalAlign, TableCell.Hori-
                    zontalAlign, TableItemStyle.HorizontalAlign, TableRow.HorizontalAlign, TableStyle.
                    HorizontalAlign

HyperLink

disposable

System.Web.UI.WebControls (system.web.dll)

class

This class represents a link to another web page, which is specified by the NavigateUrl property. The control can be displayed as text specified by the Text property or as the image located at ImageUrl. If both properties are set, ImageUrl takes precedence, provided the image file is available, and the Text is used for an image tooltip. The Target property specifies the name of the frame that the linked page will be loaded into. Note that you cannot respond to the link click in code. If you want to provide this type of behavior, use the LinkButton control instead.

The HyperLink control also supports databinding to its Text and NavigateUrl properties.

```
public class HyperLink : WebControl {
// Public Constructors
  public HyperLink( );
// Public Instance Properties
  public virtual string ImageUrl{set; get; }
  public string NavigateUrl{set; get; }
  public string Target{set; get; }
  public virtual string Text{set; get; }
// Protected Instance Methods
  protected override void AddAttributesToRender(System.Web.UI.HtmlTextWriter writer);      // overrides WebControl
  protected override void AddParsedSubObject( object obj);            // overrides System.Web.UI.Control
  protected override void LoadViewState( object savedState);                // overrides WebControl
  protected override void RenderContents(System.Web.UI.HtmlTextWriter writer);          // overrides WebControl
}
```

System.Object → System.Web.UI.Control(System.ComponentModel.IComponent, System. IDisposable, System.Web.UI.IParserAccessor, System.Web.UI.IDataBindingsAccessor) → WebControl(System.Web.UI.IAttributeAccessor) → HyperLink

HyperLinkColumn

System.Web.UI.WebControls (system.web.dll)   class

The HyperLinkColumn class represents a column that can be used in a DataGrid control. To have a column with the same hyperlink in every row, you can set Text (the displayed anchor text) and NavigateUrl (the link destination). Alternatively, you can bind a data field to the DataTextField and DataNavigateUrlField properties (which will then take precedence over any set values for the Text and NavigateUrl properties). Typically, this information will be specified by using a data binding expression in a template definition in the *.aspx* file.

Additionally, you can set the Target property to indicate the target window or frame name for the hyperlink. You can also use the DataTextFormatString property to provide a custom format string to use with the DataTextField property.

```
public class HyperLinkColumn : DataGridColumn {
// Public Constructors
  public HyperLinkColumn( );
// Public Instance Properties
  public virtual string DataNavigateUrlField{set; get; }
  public virtual string DataNavigateUrlFormatString{set; get; }
  public virtual string DataTextField{set; get; }
  public virtual string DataTextFormatString{set; get; }
  public virtual string NavigateUrl{set; get; }
  public virtual string Target{set; get; }
  public virtual string Text{set; get; }
// Public Instance Methods
  public override void Initialize( );                                                           // overrides DataGridColumn
  public override void InitializeCell(TableCell cell, int columnIndex, ListItemType itemType);    // overrides DataGridColumn
// Protected Instance Methods
  protected virtual string FormatDataNavigateUrlValue( object dataUrlValue);
  protected virtual string FormatDataTextValue( object dataTextValue);
}
```

Hierarchy   System.Object → DataGridColumn(System.Web.UI.IStateManager) → HyperLinkColumn

HyperLinkControlBuilder

System.Web.UI.WebControls (system.web.dll)   class

The ASP.NET parser uses this class to generate HTML for any HyperLink controls on a requested Web Forms page. The AllowWhitespaceLiterals( ) property is overridden to always return False. You will not need to use this class directly in application code.

```
public class HyperLinkControlBuilder : System.Web.UI.ControlBuilder {
// Public Constructors
  public HyperLinkControlBuilder( );
// Public Instance Methods
```

```
public override bool AllowWhitespaceLiterals( );                                    // overrides System.Web.UI.ControlBuilder
}
```

Hierarchy   System.Object → System.Web.UI.ControlBuilder → HyperLinkControlBuilder

Image   disposable

System.Web.UI.WebControls (system.web.dll)   class

This class represents an Image control on a Web Forms page, which is used to display
any supported graphic (including *.jpg*, *.bmp*, *.gif*, and *.png* files). To specify the picture
that should appear in this control, set a URL to the file by using the ImageUrl property.
You can specify a string of AlternateText, which will be displayed in browsers that do not
support graphics or if the picture file is not available. You can also set a Font for the
alternate text. Many browsers also show this text as a tooltip when the user positions
the mouse over the image.

An Image control cannot capture mouse clicks. To respond to image click events, use
the ImageButton control instead.

```
public class Image : WebControl {
// Public Constructors
   public Image( );
// Public Instance Properties
   public virtual string AlternateText{set; get; }
   public override bool Enabled{set; get; }                                         // overrides WebControl
   public override FontInfo Font{get; }                                             // overrides WebControl
   public virtual ImageAlign ImageAlign{set; get; }
   public virtual string ImageUrl{set; get; }
// Protected Instance Methods
   protected override void AddAttributesToRender(System.Web.UI.HtmlTextWriter writer);  // overrides WebControl
   protected override void RenderContents(System.Web.UI.HtmlTextWriter writer);         // overrides WebControl
}
```

Hierarchy   System.Object → System.Web.UI.Control(System.ComponentModel.IComponent, System.
                    IDisposable, System.Web.UI.IParserAccessor, System.Web.UI.IDataBindingsAccessor) →
                    WebControl(System.Web.UI.IAttributeAccessor) → Image

Subclasses   ImageButton

ImageAlign   serializable

System.Web.UI.WebControls (system.web.dll)   enum

This enumeration specifies the alignment used for an Image control. Left and Right specify
an alignment relative to the web page. Text will wrap around an Image control on the
opposite side. Other values are relative to the current text line. For example, Bottom and
Middle align the bottom or middle of an image with the lower edge of a text line.
AbsBottom, AbsMiddle, and Top, on the other hand, are relative to the bottom, middle, or
top of the largest element in the same line.

```
public enum ImageAlign {
   NotSet = 0,
   Left = 1,
```

```
    Right = 2,
    Baseline = 3,
    Top = 4,
    Middle = 5,
    Bottom = 6,
    AbsBottom = 7,
    AbsMiddle = 8,
    TextTop = 9
}
```

Hierarchy   System.Object → System.ValueType → System.Enum(System.IComparable, System.IFor-
                       mattable, System.IConvertible) → ImageAlign

Returned By   Image.ImageAlign

Passed To   Image.ImageAlign

ImageButton   disposable

System.Web.UI.WebControls (system.web.dll)   class

This class extends the Image class to provide an image control that can respond to
button clicks. The ImageButton class provides both a Click and a Command event, which will
fire when the image is clicked. Use the Command event and the CommandName property to
specify additional information that will be provided to the event handler. This technique is sometimes used to allow the same event handler to respond to clicks from
multiple ImageButton controls and determine what control fired the event.

By default, clicking an ImageButton control will cause page validation to occur. To
change this behavior, set the CausesValidation property to False.

```
public class ImageButton : Image, System.Web.UI.IPostBackDataHandler, System.Web.UI.IPostBackEventHandler {
// Public Constructors
    public ImageButton( );
// Public Instance Properties
    public bool CausesValidation{set; get; }
    public string CommandArgument{set; get; }
    public string CommandName{set; get; }
// Protected Instance Properties
    protected override HtmlTextWriterTag TagKey{get; }                                       // overrides WebControl
// Protected Instance Methods
    protected override void AddAttributesToRender(System.Web.UI.HtmlTextWriter writer);           // overrides Image
    protected virtual void OnClick(System.Web.UI.ImageClickEventArgs e);
    protected virtual void OnCommand( CommandEventArgs e);
    protected override void OnPreRender( EventArgs e);                                    // overrides System.Web.UI.Control
// Events
    public event ImageClickEventHandler Click;
    public event CommandEventHandler Command;
}
```

Hierarchy   System.Object → System.Web.UI.Control(System.ComponentModel.IComponent, System.
                       IDisposable, System.Web.UI.IParserAccessor, System.Web.UI.IDataBindingsAccessor) →
                       WebControl(System.Web.UI.IAttributeAccessor) → Image → ImageButton(System.Web.UI.
                       IPostBackDataHandler, System.Web.UI.IPostBackEventHandler)

IRepeatInfoUser

System.Web.UI.WebControls (system.web.dll)   interface

This interface specifies the contract for the RepeatInfo class. These requirements include properties that identify whether footer or header information is present (HasFooter and HasHeader) and identify the number of times the chosen control will be repeated (RepeatedItemCount). This interface also requires a method for rendering the chosen control (RenderItem()), which will be used for each repetition.

```
public interface IRepeatInfoUser {
// Public Instance Properties
  public bool HasFooter{get; }
  public bool HasHeader{get; }
  public bool HasSeparators{get; }
  public int RepeatedItemCount{get; }
// Public Instance Methods
  public Style GetItemStyle(ListItemType itemType, int repeatIndex);
  public void RenderItem(ListItemType itemType, int repeatIndex, RepeatInfo repeatInfo,
    System.Web.UI.HtmlTextWriter writer);
}
```

Implemented By   CheckBoxList, DataList, RadioButtonList

Passed To   RepeatInfo.RenderRepeater( )

Label
                                                                                               disposable

System.Web.UI.WebControls (system.web.dll)   class

This class represents a Label control, which allows you to place text on a page and modify it later by using the Text property. You can use HTML tags like <br> and <i> in the text string to format portions of the control.

```
public class Label : WebControl {
// Public Constructors
  public Label( );
// Public Instance Properties
  public virtual string Text{set; get; }
// Protected Instance Methods
  protected override void AddParsedSubObject( object obj);                    // overrides System.Web.UI.Control
  protected override void LoadViewState( object savedState);                           // overrides WebControl
  protected override void RenderContents(System.Web.UI.HtmlTextWriter writer);          // overrides WebControl
}
```

Hierarchy   System.Object → System.Web.UI.Control(System.ComponentModel.IComponent, System. IDisposable, System.Web.UI.IParserAccessor, System.Web.UI.IDataBindingsAccessor) → WebControl(System.Web.UI.IAttributeAccessor) → Label

Subclasses   BaseValidator

LabelControlBuilder

System.Web.UI.WebControls (system.web.dll)   class

The ASP.NET parser uses this class to generate HTML for Label controls on a requested Web Forms page. You don't need to use this class directly in application code.

```
public class LabelControlBuilder : System.Web.UI.ControlBuilder {
// Public Constructors
  public LabelControlBuilder( );
// Public Instance Methods
  public override bool AllowWhitespaceLiterals( );                    // overrides System.Web.UI.ControlBuilder
}
```

Hierarchy   System.Object → System.Web.UI.ControlBuilder → LabelControlBuilder

LinkButton   disposable

System.Web.UI.WebControls (system.web.dll)   class

This class represents a control that appears like a HyperLink control, but fires a Click and Command event like a Button control would. A good use of this control is to provide a hyperlink that navigates to another web page but allows you to perform some programmatic cleanup (for example, clearing session variables) before you redirect the user.

Like all button controls, the LinkButton class provides a CausesValidation property you can set to prevent page validation from occurring when the control is clicked. It also provides the standard CommandName and CommandArgument properties that allow you to specify additional information that will be sent to a Command event.

```
public class LinkButton : WebControl, System.Web.UI.IPostBackEventHandler {
// Public Constructors
  public LinkButton( );
// Public Instance Properties
  public bool CausesValidation{set; get; }
  public string CommandArgument{set; get; }
  public string CommandName{set; get; }
  public virtual string Text{set; get; }
// Protected Instance Methods
  protected override void AddAttributesToRender(                          // overrides WebControl
System.Web.UI.HtmlTextWriter writer);
  protected override void AddParsedSubObject( object obj);               // overrides System.Web.UI.Control
  protected override void LoadViewState( object savedState);             // overrides WebControl
  protected virtual void OnClick( EventArgs e);
  protected virtual void OnCommand( CommandEventArgs e);
  protected override void OnPreRender( EventArgs e);                     // overrides System.Web.UI.Control
  protected override void RenderContents(System.Web.UI.HtmlTextWriter writer);   // overrides WebControl
// Events
  public event EventHandler Click;
  public event CommandEventHandler Command;
}
```

LinkButtonControlBuilder

System.Web.UI.WebControls (system.web.dll)   class

The ASP.NET parser uses this class to generate HTML for any LinkButton controls on a
requested Web Forms page. You will not need to use this class directly in application
code.

```
public class LinkButtonControlBuilder : System.Web.UI.ControlBuilder {
// Public Constructors
  public LinkButtonControlBuilder( );
// Public Instance Methods
  public override bool AllowWhitespaceLiterals( );          // overrides System.Web.UI.ControlBuilder
}
```

Hierarchy   System.Object → System.Web.UI.ControlBuilder → LinkButtonControlBuilder

ListBox   disposable

System.Web.UI.WebControls (system.web.dll)   class

This class represents a list box control. Use the Rows property to set how many rows
you want to be displayed in the control at once (and hence, how much space the list
box will occupy). You can also set the SelectionMode property to ListSelectionMode.Multiple if
you want a user to be able to select more than one item from the list box at once.

Most of the list-specific functionality, such as determining the selected item and
reacting to a SelectedIndexChanged event, is provided by the ListControl class, which ListBox
inherits from.

```
public class ListBox : ListControl, System.Web.UI.IPostBackDataHandler {
// Public Constructors
  public ListBox( );
// Public Instance Properties
  public override Color BorderColor{set; get; }                          // overrides WebControl
  public override BorderStyle BorderStyle{set; get; }                    // overrides WebControl
  public override Unit BorderWidth{set; get; }                           // overrides WebControl
  public virtual int Rows{set; get; }
  public virtual ListSelectionMode SelectionMode{set; get; }
  public override string ToolTip{set; get; }                             // overrides WebControl
// Protected Instance Methods
  protected override void AddAttributesToRender(System.Web.UI.HtmlTextWriter writer);   // overrides WebControl
  protected override void OnPreRender( EventArgs e);                     // overrides ListControl
  protected override void RenderContents(System.Web.UI.HtmlTextWriter writer);          // overrides WebControl
}
```

Hierarchy   System.Object → System.Web.UI.Control(System.ComponentModel.IComponent, System.
IDisposable, System.Web.UI.IParserAccessor, System.Web.UI.IDataBindingsAccessor) →
WebControl(System.Web.UI.IAttributeAccessor) → ListControl → ListBox(System.Web.UI.
IPostBackDataHandler)

ListControl

System.Web.UI.WebControls (system.web.dll)   abstract class

This abstract base class for all list controls includes data-binding functionality (such as DataTextFormatString, which specifies the formatting of bound text), an Items collection, and properties for returning the first selected item (SelectedIndex and SelectedItem).

Note that items in the ListControl class do not correspond to the specific derived control type. For example, a CheckBoxList control returns its selected item as a ListItem, as all list controls do, not as an individual checkbox control.

```
public abstract class ListControl : WebControl {
// Public Constructors
  public ListControl( );
// Public Instance Properties
  public virtual bool AutoPostBack{set; get; }
  public virtual string DataMember{set; get; }
  public virtual object DataSource{set; get; }
  public virtual string DataTextField{set; get; }
  public virtual string DataTextFormatString{set; get; }
  public virtual string DataValueField{set; get; }
  public virtual ListItemCollection Items{get; }
  public virtual int SelectedIndex{set; get; }
  public virtual ListItem SelectedItem{get; }
  public virtual string SelectedValue{set; get; }
// Public Instance Methods
  public virtual void ClearSelection( );
// Protected Instance Methods
  protected override void LoadViewState( object savedState);           // overrides WebControl
  protected override void OnDataBinding( EventArgs e);                  // overrides System.Web.UI.Control
  protected override void OnPreRender( EventArgs e);                    // overrides System.Web.UI.Control
  protected virtual void OnSelectedIndexChanged( EventArgs e);
  protected override object SaveViewState( );                           // overrides WebControl
  protected override void TrackViewState( );                           // overrides WebControl
// Events
  public event EventHandler SelectedIndexChanged;
}
```

Hierarchy   System.Object → System.Web.UI.Control(System.ComponentModel.IComponent, System. IDisposable, System.Web.UI.IParserAccessor, System.Web.UI.IDataBindingsAccessor) → WebControl(System.Web.UI.IAttributeAccessor) → ListControl

Subclasses   CheckBoxList, DropDownList, ListBox, RadioButtonList

ListItem

System.Web.UI.WebControls (system.web.dll)   sealed class

This class represents an individual item from the list of a ListControl, such as CheckBoxList, DropDownList, RadioButtonList, and ListBox. The Text property returns the text for the list item, the Value property returns the contents of the "hidden" value attribute, and the Selected property indicates whether or not it is currently selected, which is useful for list controls that allow multiple selections.

WebControls
Namespace

```
public sealed class ListItem : System.Web.UI.IStateManager, System.Web.UI.IParserAccessor,
    System.Web.UI.IAttributeAccessor {
// Public Constructors
  public ListItem( );
  public ListItem( string text);
  public ListItem( string text, string value);
// Public Instance Properties
  public AttributeCollection Attributes{get; }
  public bool Selected{set; get; }
  public string Text{set; get; }
  public string Value{set; get; }
// Public Static Methods
  public static ListItem FromString( string s);
// Public Instance Methods
  public override bool Equals( object o);                                           // overrides object
  public override int GetHashCode( );                                              // overrides object
  public override string ToString( );                                             // overrides object
}
```

Returned By   ListControl.SelectedItem, ListItemCollection.{FindByText( ), FindByValue( ), this}

Passed To   ListItemCollection.{Add( ), AddRange( ), Contains( ), IndexOf( ), Insert( ), Remove( )}

ListItemCollection

System.Web.UI.WebControls (system.web.dll)   **sealed class**

This class contains a collection of ListItem objects, which represents the items in a list control. This collection is used by the ListControl.Items property.

```
public sealed class ListItemCollection : IList, ICollection, IEnumerable, System.Web.UI.IStateManager {
// Public Constructors
  public ListItemCollection( );
// Public Instance Properties
  public int Capacity{set; get; }
  public int Count{get; }                                                         // implements ICollection
  public bool IsReadOnly{get; }                                                   // implements IList
  public bool IsSynchronized{get; }                                               // implements ICollection
  public object SyncRoot{get; }                                                   // implements ICollection
  public ListItem this[ int index ]{get; }
// Public Instance Methods
  public void Add( ListItem item);
  public void Add( string item);
  public void AddRange( ListItem[ ] items);
  public void Clear( );                                                           // implements IList
  public bool Contains( ListItem item);
  public void CopyTo( Array array, int index);                                    // implements ICollection
  public ListItem FindByText( string text);
  public ListItem FindByValue( string value);
  public IEnumerator GetEnumerator( );                                            // implements IEnumerable
  public int IndexOf( ListItem item);
  public void Insert( int index, ListItem item);
```

```
public void Insert( int index, string item);
public void Remove( ListItem item);
public void Remove( string item);
public void RemoveAt( int index);                                        // implements IList
}
```

Returned By   System.Web.UI.HtmlControls.HtmlSelect.Items, ListControl.Items

ListItemControlBuilder

System.Web.UI.WebControls (system.web.dll)   class

The ASP.NET parser uses this class to generate HTML for any ListItem controls on a
requested Web Forms page. You will not need to use this class directly in application
code.

```
public class ListItemControlBuilder : System.Web.UI.ControlBuilder {
// Public Constructors
  public ListItemControlBuilder( );
// Public Instance Methods
  public override bool AllowWhitespaceLiterals( );        // overrides System.Web.UI.ControlBuilder
  public override bool HtmlDecodeLiterals( );             // overrides System.Web.UI.ControlBuilder
}
```

Hierarchy   System.Object → System.Web.UI.ControlBuilder → ListItemControlBuilder

ListItemType   serializable

System.Web.UI.WebControls (system.web.dll)   enum

This enumeration specifies the type of item for a row in a DataList, DataGrid, or Repeater
control. It is not used for other list controls that derive from ListControl.

Item types include headers and footers, separators, and the controls used to move
from one data page to the next (Pager). If an item is currently in edit mode, the value
EditItem is returned; if the item is selected, SelectedItem is used. AlternatingItem indicates an
alternating item, which will be an even-numbered item (counting is zero-based).

```
public enum ListItemType {
  Header = 0,
  Footer = 1,
  Item = 2,
  AlternatingItem = 3,
  SelectedItem = 4,
  EditItem = 5,
  Separator = 6,
  Pager = 7
}
```

Hierarchy   System.Object → System.ValueType → System.Enum(System.IComparable, System.IFor-
                    mattable, System.IConvertible) → ListItemType

Returned By   DataGridItem.ItemType, DataListItem.ItemType, RepeaterItem.ItemType

Passed To DataGrid.CreateItem( ), DataGridColumn.InitializeCell( ), DataGridItem.DataGridItem( ),
DataList.CreateItem( ), DataListItem.DataListItem( ), IRepeatInfoUser.{GetItemStyle( ),
RenderItem( )}, Repeater.CreateItem( ), RepeaterItem.RepeaterItem( )

ListSelectionMode   serializable

System.Web.UI.WebControls (system.web.dll)   enum

This enumeration specifies whether list controls (which derive from ListControl) allow
only one selection at a time or multiple selections.

```
public enum ListSelectionMode {
  Single = 0,
  Multiple = 1
}
```

Hierarchy System.Object → System.ValueType → System.Enum(System.IComparable, System.IFor-
mattable, System.IConvertible) → ListSelectionMode

Returned By ListBox.SelectionMode

Passed To ListBox.SelectionMode

Literal   disposable

System.Web.UI.WebControls (system.web.dll)   class

You can use a Literal control to put plain text on a page (optionally, with embedded
HTML markup tags). In this respect, the Literal control is somewhat like the Label
control, except it cannot use any special formatting, styles, or fonts.

Do not confuse the Literal control with the System.Web.UI.LiteralControl class. The latter is
used by ASP.NET to represent static HTML content found on a web page that will not
be made available to your code as a server-side control.

```
public class Literal : System.Web.UI.Control {
// Public Constructors
  public Literal( );
// Public Instance Properties
  public string Text{set; get; }
// Protected Instance Methods
  protected override void AddParsedSubObject( object obj);           // overrides System.Web.UI.Control
  protected override ControlCollection CreateControlCollection( );   // overrides System.Web.UI.Control
  protected override void Render(System.Web.UI.HtmlTextWriter output);  // overrides System.Web.UI.Control
}
```

Hierarchy System.Object → System.Web.UI.Control(System.ComponentModel.IComponent, System.
IDisposable, System.Web.UI.IParserAccessor, System.Web.UI.IDataBindingsAccessor) →
Literal

LiteralControlBuilder

System.Web.UI.WebControls (system.web.dll)   class

The ASP.NET parser uses this class to generate HTML for any Literal controls on a requested Web Forms page. You will not need to use this class directly in application code.

```
public class LiteralControlBuilder : System.Web.UI.ControlBuilder {
// Public Constructors
  public LiteralControlBuilder( );
// Public Instance Methods
  public override bool AllowWhitespaceLiterals( );                      // overrides System.Web.UI.ControlBuilder
  public override void AppendSubBuilder(System.Web.UI.ControlBuilder subBuilder);
                                                                       // overrides System.Web.UI.ControlBuilder
}
```

Hierarchy   System.Object → System.Web.UI.ControlBuilder → LiteralControlBuilder

MonthChangedEventArgs

System.Web.UI.WebControls (system.web.dll)   sealed class

This custom System.EventArgs class provides additional information for the Calendar.VisibleMonthChanged event. The additional information consists of two properties: PreviousDate and NewDate (which will typically be the first of the newly selected month).

```
public sealed class MonthChangedEventArgs {
// Public Constructors
  public MonthChangedEventArgs(DateTime newDate, DateTime previousDate);
// Public Instance Properties
  public DateTime NewDate{get; }
  public DateTime PreviousDate{get; }
}
```

Passed To   MonthChangedEventHandler.{BeginInvoke( ), Invoke( )}

MonthChangedEventHandler   serializable

System.Web.UI.WebControls (system.web.dll)   delegate

This delegate specifies the parameter list that a subroutine requires to handle the Calendar.VisibleMonthChanged event, which occurs when the user clicks one of the navigation controls to "page" to another month. This event provides additional information about the previous and new selected date.

```
public delegate void MonthChangedEventHandler(object sender, MonthChangedEventArgs e);
```

Associated Events Calendar.VisibleMonthChanged( )

NextPrevFormat

serializable

System.Web.UI.WebControls (system.web.dll)

enum

This enumeration is used to set the Calendar.NextPrevFormat property. It determines the appearance of the navigation controls that allow the user to move from month to month. ShortMonth will display an abbreviated month name on the previous and next month controls (like "Jan"), while FullMonth will display the full name of the month. If you use CustomText, you must set the corresponding Calendar.NextMonthText and Calendar.PrevMonthText programmatically (typically, in the Calendar.VisibleMonthChanged event handler).

```
public enum NextPrevFormat {
  CustomText = 0,
  ShortMonth = 1,
  FullMonth = 2
}
```

Hierarchy	System.Object → System.ValueType → System.Enum(System.IComparable, System.IFormattable, System.IConvertible) → NextPrevFormat
Returned By	Calendar.NextPrevFormat
Passed To	Calendar.NextPrevFormat

PagedDataSource

System.Web.UI.WebControls (system.web.dll)

sealed class

The PagedDataSource class wraps a System.Collections.ICollection data source to implement "paged views" using the best available interface to enumerate over the data. This class uses indexed access if it is available (as in classes derived from System.Array or implementing System.Collections.IList) or the System.Collections.IEnumerable interface if indexed access is not available.

This class is used internally by the DataGrid control to provide its paging abilities. It is not used in your code unless you develop a data-bound control that supports paging.

```
public sealed class PagedDataSource : ICollection, IEnumerable, System.ComponentModel.ITypedList {
// Public Constructors
  public PagedDataSource( );
// Public Instance Properties
  public bool AllowCustomPaging{set; get; }
  public bool AllowPaging{set; get; }
  public int Count{get; }                                          // implements ICollection
  public int CurrentPageIndex{set; get; }
  public IEnumerable DataSource{set; get; }
  public int DataSourceCount{get; }
  public int FirstIndexInPage{get; }
  public bool IsCustomPagingEnabled{get; }
  public bool IsFirstPage{get; }
  public bool IsLastPage{get; }
  public bool IsPagingEnabled{get; }
  public bool IsReadOnly{get; }
  public bool IsSynchronized{get; }                                // implements ICollection
```

```
public int PageCount{get; }
public int PageSize{set; get; }
public object SyncRoot{get; }                                                    // implements ICollection
public int VirtualCount{set; get; }
// Public Instance Methods
public void CopyTo( Array array, int index);                                     // implements ICollection
public IEnumerator GetEnumerator( );                                             // implements IEnumerable
public PropertyDescriptorCollection GetItemProperties(System.ComponentModel.PropertyDescriptor[ ] listAccessors);
                                          // implements System.ComponentModel.ITypedList
public string GetListName(System.ComponentModel.PropertyDescriptor[ ] listAccessors);
                                          // implements System.ComponentModel.ITypedList
}
```

Passed To   DataGrid.{CreateColumnSet( ), InitializePager( )}

PagerMode   serializable

System.Web.UI.WebControls (system.web.dll)   enum

This enumeration allows you to configure the type of pager controls used on the Data-
Grid control to browse from page to page. Each "page" shows a table with a subset of
the data. If you use NextPrev, next/previous buttons will be displayed (which are typically rendered as greater-than and less-than signs). If you use NumericPages, each page
will be given a number and a series of number links (starting at 1) will be displayed
that allow a user to jump to a nonsequential page. Additional pager options, such as
the text for next/previous buttons and the number of numeric pages displayed at a
time, are available through the properties of the DataGridPagerStyle class.

```
public enum PagerMode {
  NextPrev = 0,
  NumericPages = 1
}
```

Hierarchy   System.Object → System.ValueType → System.Enum(System.IComparable, System.IFor-
                  mattable, System.IConvertible) → PagerMode

Returned By   DataGridPagerStyle.Mode

Passed To   DataGridPagerStyle.Mode

PagerPosition   serializable

System.Web.UI.WebControls (system.web.dll)   enum

This enumeration specifies the alignment of the pager controls for a DataGrid within the
appropriate cell. The pager controls are always placed in the last row after the data and
footer.

```
public enum PagerPosition {
  Bottom = 0,
  Top = 1,
  TopAndBottom = 2
}
```

Hierarchy	System.Object → System.ValueType → System.Enum(System.IComparable, System.IFormattable, System.IConvertible) → PagerPosition
Returned By	DataGridPagerStyle.Position
Passed To	DataGridPagerStyle.Position

Panel   disposable

System.Web.UI.WebControls (system.web.dll)   class

This class represents a Panel control, which acts as a simple container for other web controls. A panel is often used to group related controls, such as **RadioButton** controls that share the same **RadioButton.GroupName**. Panels are also used to disable or hide entire groups of controls at once, by setting the **Visible** or **Enabled** property of the containing panel. They are also useful for adding dynamically generated controls, as in **Panel1. Controls.Add(New LiteralControl("<br>"));**.

You can set a background image for your panel by specifying a URL for the **BackImageUrl** property. You can also type text directly into a panel on the design-time surface in Visual Studio .NET. Use the **Wrap** property to set whether this content is wrapped. If it is not, the **Panel** is automatically extended to the required width.

```
public class Panel : WebControl {
// Public Constructors
  public Panel( );
// Public Instance Properties
  public virtual string BackImageUrl{set; get; }
  public virtual HorizontalAlign HorizontalAlign{set; get; }
  public virtual bool Wrap{set; get; }
// Protected Instance Methods
  protected override void AddAttributesToRender(System.Web.UI.HtmlTextWriter writer);        // overrides WebControl
}
```

Hierarchy	System.Object → System.Web.UI.Control(System.ComponentModel.IComponent, System. IDisposable, System.Web.UI.IParserAccessor, System.Web.UI.IDataBindingsAccessor) → WebControl(System.Web.UI.IAttributeAccessor) → Panel

PlaceHolder   disposable

System.Web.UI.WebControls (system.web.dll)   class

This class represents a "placeholder" control, which is a container used to store controls that may be added to a page dynamically at some point in its processing. Placeholders prevent an HTML page from "collapsing." For example, if you create a text box control and set the **TextBox.Visible** property to **False**, no HTML will be rendered for the control. This could cause the layout of the page to change unexpectedly, particularly with tables. Placeholders avert this problem. To add a control to a placeholder, use **Add( )**. Note that placeholders, unlike most web controls, derive directly from **System. Web.UI.Control**, not from **WebControl**.

```
public class PlaceHolder : System.Web.UI.Control {
// Public Constructors
```

```
  public PlaceHolder( );
}
```

Hierarchy   System.Object → System.Web.UI.Control(System.ComponentModel.IComponent, System.
IDisposable, System.Web.UI.IParserAccessor, System.Web.UI.IDataBindingsAccessor) →
PlaceHolder

PlaceHolderControlBuilder

System.Web.UI.WebControls (system.web.dll)   class

The ASP.NET parser uses this class to generate HTML for any PlaceHolder controls on a
requested Web Forms page. You will not need to use this class directly in application
code.

```
public class PlaceHolderControlBuilder : System.Web.UI.ControlBuilder {
// Public Constructors
  public PlaceHolderControlBuilder( );
// Public Instance Methods
  public override bool AllowWhitespaceLiterals( );                // overrides System.Web.UI.ControlBuilder
}
```

Hierarchy   System.Object → System.Web.UI.ControlBuilder → PlaceHolderControlBuilder

RadioButton   disposable

System.Web.UI.WebControls (system.web.dll)   class

This class represents a radio button control that allows a user to select one item from a
selection of options. Each option in a group of radio buttons is a distinct RadioButton
object, but each control shares the same GroupName. To determine whether a radio
button has been selected, examine the Checked property. If you want to use a radio
button with list data, the CheckBoxList control may be more convenient.

```
public class RadioButton : CheckBox {
// Public Constructors
  public RadioButton( );
// Public Instance Properties
  public virtual string GroupName{set; get; }
// Protected Instance Methods
  protected override void OnPreRender( EventArgs e);                             // overrides CheckBox
}
```

Hierarchy   System.Object → System.Web.UI.Control(System.ComponentModel.IComponent, System.
IDisposable, System.Web.UI.IParserAccessor, System.Web.UI.IDataBindingsAccessor) →
WebControl(System.Web.UI.IAttributeAccessor) → CheckBox(System.Web.UI.IPostBackDa-
taHandler) → RadioButton

RadioButtonList   disposable

System.Web.UI.WebControls (system.web.dll)   class

This class represents a list of radio buttons that allow only a single selection. Though
this class is generated out of individual radio buttons, it acts like an integrated list. For

example, ASP.NET will add or remove items as needed when you bind this control to a data source. You can use RepeatDirection to specify how items will be grouped together if RepeatColumns is greater than 1. For example, if you set RepeatDirection to RepeatDirection. Vertical, and RepeatColumns to 2, the first two list items will be displayed in the first columns, the next two will be displayed on the second column, and so on. If you set RepeatDirection to RepeatDirection.Horizontal, your list will still have the same number of rows and columns, but radio button items will be filled first by column, and then by row.

Individual radio buttons are automatically grouped together in an HTML table, which you can fine-tune with the CellPadding and CellSpacing properties. Alternatively, you can set RepeatLayout to RepeatLayout.Flow to specify that an HTML table should not be used.

Most list-specific functionality, such as determining the selected item and reacting to a SelectedIndexChanged event, is provided by the ListControl class, from which RadioButtonList inherits.

```
public class RadioButtonList : ListControl, IRepeatInfoUser, System.Web.UI.INamingContainer, System.Web.UI.
IPostBackDataHandler {
// Public Constructors
  public RadioButtonList( );
// Public Instance Properties
  public virtual int CellPadding{set; get; }
  public virtual int CellSpacing{set; get; }
  public virtual int RepeatColumns{set; get; }
  public virtual RepeatDirection RepeatDirection{set; get; }
  public virtual RepeatLayout RepeatLayout{set; get; }
  public virtual TextAlign TextAlign{set; get; }
// Protected Instance Methods
  protected override Style CreateControlStyle( );                           // overrides WebControl
  protected override void Render(System.Web.UI.HtmlTextWriter writer);      // overrides WebControl
}
```

Hierarchy System.Object → System.Web.UI.Control(System.ComponentModel.IComponent, System. IDisposable, System.Web.UI.IParserAccessor, System.Web.UI.IDataBindingsAccessor) → WebControl(System.Web.UI.IAttributeAccessor) → ListControl → RadioButtonList(IRepeatInfoUser, System.Web.UI.INamingContainer, System.Web.UI.IPostBackDataHandler)

RangeValidator   disposable

System.Web.UI.WebControls (system.web.dll)   class

This class represents a validation control that tests to make sure the value of the input control (ControlToValidate) is equal to or between the MinimumValue and MaximumValue. All values will be converted to the data type specified by CompareValidator.Type before validation is performed. Valid data types include integer, double, date, currency, and string (which uses an alphabetic character-code based comparison).

Validation automatically succeeds if the input control is empty. To require a value, use the RequiredFieldValidator control in addition to the RangeValidator control.

```
public class RangeValidator : BaseCompareValidator {
// Public Constructors
  public RangeValidator( );
// Public Instance Properties
  public string MaximumValue{set; get; }
```

```
    public string MinimumValue{set; get; }
// Protected Instance Methods
    protected override void AddAttributesToRender(System.Web.UI.HtmlTextWriter writer);
                                                                    // overrides BaseCompareValidator
    protected override bool ControlPropertiesValid( );                        // overrides BaseValidator
    protected override bool EvaluateIsValid( );                               // overrides BaseValidator
}
```

Hierarchy   System.Object → System.Web.UI.Control(System.ComponentModel.IComponent, System.
                     IDisposable, System.Web.UI.IParserAccessor, System.Web.UI.IDataBindingsAccessor) →
                     WebControl(System.Web.UI.IAttributeAccessor) → Label → BaseValidator(System.Web.UI.
                     IValidator) → BaseCompareValidator → RangeValidator

RegularExpressionValidator   disposable

System.Web.UI.WebControls (system.web.dll)   class

The RegularExpressionValidator is a type of validation control that compares an input control
against a pattern specified in the ValidationExpression. Regular expression validation is
ideally suited for verifying predictable sequences of characters, such as those in social
security numbers, email addresses, telephone numbers, and postal codes. Validation
will succeed if the input control is empty, unless you also use a RequiredFieldValidator
control.

Validation is always performed on the server. If the client browser supports Java-
Script, validation will be performed there as well, which can save a roundtrip if errors
are present. The regular expression validation performed by the JavaScript code is a
subset of the full System.Text.RegularExpressions.Regex syntax. Support for it is client-
dependent, and the RegularExpressionValidator will not attempt to perform client-side regular
expression validation on any browser other than Internet Explorer.

```
public class RegularExpressionValidator : BaseValidator {
// Public Constructors
    public RegularExpressionValidator( );
// Public Instance Properties
    public string ValidationExpression{set; get; }
// Protected Instance Methods
    protected override void AddAttributesToRender(System.Web.UI.HtmlTextWriter writer);   // overrides BaseValidator
    protected override bool EvaluateIsValid( );                               // overrides BaseValidator
}
```

Hierarchy   System.Object → System.Web.UI.Control(System.ComponentModel.IComponent, System.
                     IDisposable, System.Web.UI.IParserAccessor, System.Web.UI.IDataBindingsAccessor) →
                     WebControl(System.Web.UI.IAttributeAccessor) → Label → BaseValidator(System.Web.UI.
                     IValidator) → RegularExpressionValidator

RepeatDirection   serializable

System.Web.UI.WebControls (system.web.dll)   enum

This enumeration specifies how items are organized in some list controls. It usually
works in conjunction with a RepeatColumns property, which sets the dimensions of the
table. For example, if you have a list with twenty elements and you set RepeatColumns to
five, you automatically have four rows, regardless of what RepeatDirection you choose.

If RepeatDirection is Vertical, items are filled into columns from left to right, and then row-by-row. If you use Horizontal, the items are filled from top to bottom, and then column-by-column to satisfy the required number of columns.

```
public enum RepeatDirection {
  Horizontal = 0,
  Vertical = 1
}
```

Hierarchy	System.Object → System.ValueType → System.Enum(System.IComparable, System.IFormattable, System.IConvertible) → RepeatDirection
Returned By	CheckBoxList.RepeatDirection, DataList.RepeatDirection, RadioButtonList.RepeatDirection, RepeatInfo.RepeatDirection
Passed To	CheckBoxList.RepeatDirection, DataList.RepeatDirection, RadioButtonList.RepeatDirection, RepeatInfo.RepeatDirection

Repeater   disposable

System.Web.UI.WebControls (system.web.dll)   class

This class represents a special kind of data-bound list control that can contain repeating buttons, static text, and other controls. The Repeater control requires more work than a straightforward DataGrid or DataList control because it contains no built-in styles or layout. Instead, you must create templates for the Repeater using HTML and ASP.NET tags in the *.aspx* file. Each template is bracketed inside the appropriate template tag (like <ItemTemplate>). You do not set the corresponding System.Web.UI.ITemplate properties of this class directly.

Every Repeater control requires an ItemTemplate. Additionally, an AlternatingItemTemplate can be used to allow items to alternate between two styles. These two templates will be bound when you use the DataBind() method. The other templates, like HeaderTemplate, FooterTemplate, and SeparatorTemplate, will not. If the DataSource property is set but no data is returned, only the HeaderTemplate and FooterTemplate will be rendered. If the DataSource property is not set (it will be null by default), the control is not rendered at all.

The Repeater control is unique because it allows you to enter any HTML content in a template, and even split HTML tags across more than one template. To use a table in your Repeater control, you should include the begin table tag (<table>) in the HeaderTemplate and the end table tag (</table>) in the FooterTemplate. You can then use a single table row tag (<tr>) in the ItemTemplate and multiple table data tags (<td>).

The Repeater has no built-in support for item selection or editing. You can include a Button control inside an ItemTemplate, although you will have to write its tag manually, rather than using the Visual Studio .NET designer. When the user clicks this button, a ItemCommand event will be fired. This event provides additional information about the selected button and list item.

```
public class Repeater : System.Web.UI.Control, System.Web.UI.INamingContainer {
// Public Constructors
  public Repeater();
// Public Instance Properties
  public virtual ITemplate AlternatingItemTemplate{set; get; }
  public override ControlCollection Controls{get; }                    // overrides System.Web.UI.Control
```

```
    public virtual string DataMember{set; get; }
    public virtual object DataSource{set; get; }
    public virtual ITemplate FooterTemplate{set; get; }
    public virtual ITemplate HeaderTemplate{set; get; }
    public virtual RepeaterItemCollection Items{get; }
    public virtual ITemplate ItemTemplate{set; get; }
    public virtual ITemplate SeparatorTemplate{set; get; }
// Public Instance Methods
    public override void DataBind( );                                    // overrides System.Web.UI.Control
// Protected Instance Methods
    protected override void CreateChildControls( );                     // overrides System.Web.UI.Control
    protected virtual void CreateControlHierarchy(bool useDataSource);
    protected virtual RepeaterItem CreateItem(int itemIndex,      ListItemType itemType);
    protected virtual void InitializeItem( RepeaterItem item);
    protected override bool OnBubbleEvent(object sender, EventArgs e);   // overrides System.Web.UI.Control
    protected override void OnDataBinding( EventArgs e);                // overrides System.Web.UI.Control
    protected virtual void OnItemCommand(RepeaterCommandEventArgs e);
    protected virtual void OnItemCreated( RepeaterItemEventArgs e);
    protected virtual void OnItemDataBound(RepeaterItemEventArgs e);
// Events
    public event RepeaterCommandEventHandler ItemCommand;
    public event RepeaterItemEventHandler ItemCreated;
    public event RepeaterItemEventHandler ItemDataBound;
}
```

Hierarchy   System.Object → System.Web.UI.Control(System.ComponentModel.IComponent, System. IDisposable, System.Web.UI.IParserAccessor, System.Web.UI.IDataBindingsAccessor) → Repeater(System.Web.UI.INamingContainer)

RepeaterCommandEventArgs

System.Web.UI.WebControls (system.web.dll)   sealed class

This class provides additional information for the ItemCommand event of the Repeater control, which occurs when a button in an item is clicked. This additional information consists of a Item property, which represents the repeater item where the button is located, and a CommandSource property, which refers to the button in the item that fired this event. Before using the CommandSource property, you will have to cast it to the appropriate type.

It may seem that the Repeater.ItemCommand event provides more than one way to determine its source. However, these references are not equivalent. The sender parameter indicates the Repeater instance where the event took place, while the Item property specifies the item in the Repeater and the CommandSource property identifies the specific button in the item.

```
public sealed class RepeaterCommandEventArgs : CommandEventArgs {
// Public Constructors
    public RepeaterCommandEventArgs(RepeaterItem item, object commandSource, CommandEventArgs originalArgs);
// Public Instance Properties
    public object CommandSource{get; }
    public RepeaterItem Item{get; }
}
```

Hierarchy	System.Object → System.EventArgs → CommandEventArgs → RepeaterCommandEventArgs
Passed To	Repeater.OnItemCommand( ), RepeaterCommandEventHandler.{BeginInvoke( ), Invoke( )}

RepeaterCommandEventHandler

serializable

System.Web.UI.WebControls (system.web.dll)

delegate

This delegate specifies the parameters for the event handler routine that handles the ItemCommand event of the Repeater control. This event handler receives additional information about the item that was clicked.

```
public delegate void RepeaterCommandEventHandler(object source, RepeaterCommandEventArgs e);
```

Associated Events Repeater.ItemCommand( )

RepeaterItem

disposable

System.Web.UI.WebControls (system.web.dll)

class

This class represents an individual item in the Repeater control. You can access a RepeaterItem through the Repeater.Items collection or from a Repeater event.

RepeaterItem inherits most of its properties from System.Web.UI.Control. In addition, it provides an ItemIndex that gives its index in the Repeater.Items collection, an ItemType property that identifies what type of item this is (a header, footer, alternating row, etc.), and a DataItem property that returns the corresponding data item (such as a System.Data.DataRowView instance).

```
public class RepeaterItem : System.Web.UI.Control, System.Web.UI.INamingContainer {
// Public Constructors
  public RepeaterItem(int itemIndex, ListItemType itemType);
// Public Instance Properties
  public virtual object DataItem{set; get; }
  public virtual int ItemIndex{get; }
  public virtual ListItemType ItemType{get; }
// Protected Instance Methods
  protected override bool OnBubbleEvent(object source, EventArgs e);        // overrides System.Web.UI.Control

}
```

Hierarchy	System.Object → System.Web.UI.Control(System.ComponentModel.IComponent, System.IDisposable, System.Web.UI.IParserAccessor, System.Web.UI.IDataBindingsAccessor) → RepeaterItem(System.Web.UI.INamingContainer)
Returned By	Repeater.CreateItem( ), RepeaterCommandEventArgs.Item, RepeaterItemCollection.this, RepeaterItemEventArgs.Item
Passed To	Repeater.InitializeItem( ), RepeaterCommandEventArgs.RepeaterCommandEventArgs( ), RepeaterItemEventArgs.RepeaterItemEventArgs( )

RepeaterItemCollection

System.Web.UI.WebControls (system.web.dll)   sealed class

This custom collection class contains **RepeaterItem** objects. It is used for the **Repeater.Items** property of the **Repeater** control.

```
public sealed class RepeaterItemCollection : ICollection, IEnumerable {
// Public Constructors
   public RepeaterItemCollection(System.Collections.ArrayList items);
// Public Instance Properties
   public int Count{get; }                                                        // implements ICollection
   public bool IsReadOnly{get; }
   public bool IsSynchronized{get; }                                              // implements ICollection
   public object SyncRoot{get; }                                                  // implements ICollection
   public RepeaterItem this[ int index ]{get; }
// Public Instance Methods
   public void CopyTo( Array array, int index);                                   // implements ICollection
   public IEnumerator GetEnumerator( );                                           // implements IEnumerable
}
```

Returned By   Repeater.Items

RepeaterItemEventArgs

System.Web.UI.WebControls (system.web.dll)   sealed class

This class provides additional information for the **ItemCreated** and **ItemDataBound** events of the **Repeater** control. This additional information consists of an **Item** property, which represents the item that was just added to the **Repeater** control or bound to the data source.

```
public sealed class RepeaterItemEventArgs : EventArgs {
// Public Constructors
   public RepeaterItemEventArgs( RepeaterItem item);
// Public Instance Properties
   public RepeaterItem Item{get; }
}
```

Hierarchy   System.Object → System.EventArgs → RepeaterItemEventArgs

Passed To   Repeater.{OnItemCreated( ), OnItemDataBound( )}, RepeaterItemEventHandler.
                       {BeginInvoke( ), Invoke( )}

RepeaterItemEventHandler   serializable

System.Web.UI.WebControls (system.web.dll)   delegate

This delegate specifies the parameters for the event handler routine that handles the **ItemCreated** and **ItemDataBound** events of the **Repeater** control. This event handler receives additional information about the item that was just created or bound through the **RepeaterItemEventArgs** class.

```
public delegate void RepeaterItemEventHandler(object sender, RepeaterItemEventArgs e);
```

Associated Events Repeater.{ItemCreated( ), ItemDataBound( )}

RepeatInfo

System.Web.UI.WebControls (system.web.dll)   **sealed class**

This class includes information about how various list controls, including **CheckBoxList**, **DataList**, and **RadioButtonList**, should repeat their items in a list. It is used primarily by control developers.

```
public sealed class RepeatInfo {
// Public Constructors
 public RepeatInfo( );
// Public Instance Properties
 public bool OuterTableImplied{set; get; }
 public int RepeatColumns{set; get; }
 public RepeatDirection RepeatDirection{set; get; }
 public RepeatLayout RepeatLayout{set; get; }
// Public Instance Methods
 public void RenderRepeater(System.Web.UI.HtmlTextWriter writer, IRepeatInfoUser user, Style controlStyle,
    WebControl baseControl);
}
```

Passed To   IRepeatInfoUser.RenderItem( )

RepeatLayout   **serializable**

System.Web.UI.WebControls (system.web.dll)   **enum**

This enumeration specifies the layout of items in certain list controls. **Table** specifies that items are held in separate cells in a table structure, while **Flow** specifies that no special formatting is used.

```
public enum RepeatLayout {
 Table = 0,
 Flow = 1
}
```

Hierarchy   System.Object → System.ValueType → System.Enum(System.IComparable, System.IFor-
                     mattable, System.IConvertible) → RepeatLayout

Returned By   CheckBoxList.RepeatLayout, DataList.RepeatLayout, RadioButtonList.RepeatLayout, Repeat-
                     Info.RepeatLayout

Passed To   CheckBoxList.RepeatLayout, DataList.RepeatLayout, RadioButtonList.RepeatLayout, Repeat-
                     Info.RepeatLayout

RequiredFieldValidator   **disposable**

System.Web.UI.WebControls (system.web.dll)   **class**

This class represents a validation control that is used to force user entry in a corresponding input control, like a **TextBox**. Validation fails if the value in the input control does not differ from the **InitialValue** property. By default, **InitialValue** is set to **System.String. Empty** and validation will succeed as long as some information has been added to the input control.

You can use a combination of different validation controls for a single control. For example, you could use a RequiredFieldValidator to ensure that a value is entered and a RangeValidator to ensure that the value is within a specified data range. This is often required, as validators like RangeValidator will automatically validate a control if it is empty, regardless of the properties you have set.

```
public class RequiredFieldValidator : BaseValidator {
// Public Constructors
   public RequiredFieldValidator( );
// Public Instance Properties
   public string InitialValue{set; get; }
// Protected Instance Methods
   protected override void AddAttributesToRender(System.Web.UI.HtmlTextWriter writer);    // overrides BaseValidator
   protected override bool EvaluateIsValid( );                                              // overrides BaseValidator
}
```

Hierarchy System.Object → System.Web.UI.Control(System.ComponentModel.IComponent, System. IDisposable, System.Web.UI.IParserAccessor, System.Web.UI.IDataBindingsAccessor) → WebControl(System.Web.UI.IAttributeAccessor) → Label → BaseValidator(System.Web.UI. IValidator) → RequiredFieldValidator

SelectedDatesCollection

System.Web.UI.WebControls (system.web.dll)   sealed class

This class represents a collection of System.DateTime objects. It is used by the SelectedDates property of the Calendar class to provide all the dates that have been selected.

The Calendar.SelectedDates property is used when the Calendar.SelectionMode property is set to either CalendarSelectionMode.DayWeek or CalendarSelectionMode.DayWeekMonth, both of which allow multiple selections (by week or month). If the Calendar.SelectionMode property is set to CalendarSelectionMode.Day, the Calendar.SelectedDate property should be used to determine the selected date instead.

```
public sealed class SelectedDatesCollection : ICollection, IEnumerable {
// Public Constructors
   public SelectedDatesCollection(System.Collections.ArrayList dateList);
// Public Instance Properties
   public int Count{get; }                                                                  // implements ICollection
   public bool IsReadOnly{get; }
   public bool IsSynchronized{get; }                                                        // implements ICollection
   public object SyncRoot{get; }                                                            // implements ICollection
   public DateTime this[ int index ]{get; }
// Public Instance Methods
   public void Add( DateTime date);
   public void Clear( );
   public bool Contains( DateTime date);
   public void CopyTo( Array array, int index);                                             // implements ICollection
   public IEnumerator GetEnumerator( );                                                     // implements IEnumerable
   public void Remove( DateTime date);
   public void SelectRange(DateTime fromDate, DateTime toDate);
}
```

Returned By System.Web.UI.MobileControls.Calendar.SelectedDates, Calendar.SelectedDates

ServerValidateEventArgs

System.Web.UI.WebControls (system.web.dll)   sealed class

This derived System.EventArgs class is used for the CustomValidator.ServerValidate event. This class provides a Value property, which specifies the value that needs to be examined, and an IsValid property, which the event handling code sets to indicate whether the value is valid (True) or invalid (False).

```
public sealed class ServerValidateEventArgs : EventArgs {
// Public Constructors
  public ServerValidateEventArgs(string value, bool isValid);
// Public Instance Properties
  public bool IsValid{set; get; }
  public string Value{get; }
}
```

Hierarchy   System.Object → System.EventArgs → ServerValidateEventArgs

Passed To   ServerValidateEventHandler.{BeginInvoke( ), Invoke( )}

ServerValidateEventHandler   serializable

System.Web.UI.WebControls (system.web.dll)   delegate

This delegate specifies the signature an event handler method must have in order to receive the ServerValidate event of the CustomValidator control. This delegate uses a special System.EventArgs object, ServerValidateEventArgs, which passes the value that needs to be validated and allows the event handling code to specify whether validation was successful.

```
public delegate void ServerValidateEventHandler(object source, ServerValidateEventArgs args);
```

Associated Events   System.Web.UI.MobileControls.CustomValidator.ServerValidate( ), CustomValidator.
                        ServerValidate( )

Style   marshal by reference, disposable

System.Web.UI.WebControls (system.web.dll)   class

This class represents style attributes that can be applied to a portion of the user interface on a web page. This class is not used by web controls or HTML controls, which allow programmatic access to style attributes through a System.Web.UI.CssStyleCollection object provided through their own Style property. Instead, the Style class is used as a base class for the TableStyle and TableItemStyle classes.

```
public class Style : System.ComponentModel.Component, System.Web.UI.IStateManager {
// Public Constructors
  public Style( );
  public Style( System.Web.UI.StateBag bag);
// Public Instance Properties
  public Color BackColor{set; get; }
  public Color BorderColor{set; get; }
  public BorderStyle BorderStyle{set; get; }
  public Unit BorderWidth{set; get; }
```

```
   public string CssClass{set; get; }
   public FontInfo Font{get; }
   public Color ForeColor{set; get; }
   public Unit Height{set; get; }
   public Unit Width{set; get; }
// Protected Instance Properties
   protected internal virtual bool IsEmpty{get; }
   protected bool IsTrackingViewState{get; }                          // implements System.Web.UI.IStateManager
   protected internal StateBag ViewState{get; }
// Public Instance Methods
   public void AddAttributesToRender(System.Web.UI.HtmlTextWriter writer);
   public virtual void AddAttributesToRender(System.Web.UI.HtmlTextWriter writer, WebControl owner);
   public virtual void CopyFrom( Style s);
   public virtual void MergeWith( Style s);
   public virtual void Reset( );
   public override string ToString( );                               // overrides System.ComponentModel.Component
// Protected Instance Methods
   protected internal void LoadViewState( object state);             // implements System.Web.UI.IStateManager
   protected internal virtual object SaveViewState( );               // implements System.Web.UI.IStateManager
   protected internal virtual void SetBit( int bit);
   protected internal virtual void TrackViewState( );                // implements System.Web.UI.IStateManager
}
```

Hierarchy	System.Object → System.MarshalByRefObject → System.ComponentModel.Component(System.ComponentModel.IComponent, System.IDisposable) → Style(System.Web.UI.IStateManager)
Subclasses	TableItemStyle, TableStyle
Returned By	System.Web.UI.Design.ITemplateEditingFrame.{ControlStyle, TemplateStyles}, IRepeatInfoUser.GetItemStyle( ), WebControl.{ControlStyle, CreateControlStyle( )}
Passed To	System.Web.UI.Design.ITemplateEditingService.CreateFrame( ), System.Web.UI.Design.TemplateEditingService.CreateFrame( ), RepeatInfo.RenderRepeater( ), TableItemStyle.{CopyFrom( ), MergeWith( )}, WebControl.{ApplyStyle( ), MergeStyle( )}

WebControls
Namespace

Table   disposable

System.Web.UI.WebControls (system.web.dll)   class

This class provides a powerful object model for creating HTML tables. It is similar to, but more abstract than, the System.Web.UI.HtmlControls.HtmlTable class. It also allows ASP.NET to optimize rendering for both down-level and up-level browsers. You can use it to dynamically generate an HTML table by adding TableRow objects to the Rows collection and adding TableCell objects to each row. Note that if you create or modify a table's structure programmatically, these changes will not be preserved across postbacks and you will have to reconstruct them manually; table rows and cells are controls of their own, not properties of Table.

Most other properties for the Table class correspond to formatting options, including a background image (BackImageUrl), alignment (HorizontalAlign), gridlines (GridLines), the spacing between cells (CellSpacing), and the spacing between cell borders and content (CellPadding).

Table | 883

This class is often used by control developers, while the **DataGrid** and **DataList** controls are preferred for ASP.NET applications, particularly if data binding is required.

```
public class Table : WebControl {
// Public Constructors
   public Table( );
// Public Instance Properties
   public virtual string BackImageUrl{set; get; }
   public virtual int CellPadding{set; get; }
   public virtual int CellSpacing{set; get; }
   public virtual GridLines GridLines{set; get; }
   public virtual HorizontalAlign HorizontalAlign{set; get; }
   public virtual TableRowCollection Rows{get; }
// Protected Instance Methods
   protected override void AddAttributesToRender(System.Web.UI.HtmlTextWriter writer);        // overrides WebControl
   protected override ControlCollection CreateControlCollection( );               // overrides System.Web.UI.Control
   protected override Style CreateControlStyle( );                                 // overrides WebControl
   protected override void RenderContents(System.Web.UI.HtmlTextWriter writer);    // overrides WebControl
}
```

Hierarchy   System.Object → System.Web.UI.Control(System.ComponentModel.IComponent, System. IDisposable, System.Web.UI.IParserAccessor, System.Web.UI.IDataBindingsAccessor) → WebControl(System.Web.UI.IAttributeAccessor) → Table

TableCell   disposable

System.Web.UI.WebControls (system.web.dll)   class

This class represents individual table cells in a **TableRow**. The **Text** property allows you to access the content stored in the cell. Most other properties are used to fine-tune its appearance. You can set **Wrap** to configure whether or not the contents in a cell will wrap, and **RowSpan** and **ColumnSpan** to specify that a cell should span the specified number of columns or rows.

```
public class TableCell : WebControl {
// Public Constructors
   public TableCell( );
// Public Instance Properties
   public virtual int ColumnSpan{set; get; }
   public virtual HorizontalAlign HorizontalAlign{set; get; }
   public virtual int RowSpan{set; get; }
   public virtual string Text{set; get; }
   public virtual VerticalAlign VerticalAlign{set; get; }
   public virtual bool Wrap{set; get; }
// Protected Instance Methods
   protected override void AddAttributesToRender(System.Web.UI.HtmlTextWriter writer);        // overrides WebControl

   protected override void AddParsedSubObject( object obj);          // overrides System.Web.UI.Control
   protected override Style CreateControlStyle( );                    // overrides WebControl
   protected override void RenderContents(System.Web.UI.HtmlTextWriter writer);    // overrides WebControl
}
```

Hierarchy	System.Object → System.Web.UI.Control(System.ComponentModel.IComponent, System. IDisposable, System.Web.UI.IParserAccessor, System.Web.UI.IDataBindingsAccessor) → WebControl(System.Web.UI.IAttributeAccessor) → TableCell
Subclasses	TableHeaderCell
Returned By	DayRenderEventArgs.Cell, TableCellCollection.this
Passed To	Calendar.OnDayRender( ), DataGridColumn.InitializeCell( ), DayRenderEventArgs. DayRenderEventArgs( ), TableCellCollection.{Add( ), AddAt( ), AddRange( ), GetCellIndex( ), Remove( )}

TableCellCollection

System.Web.UI.WebControls (system.web.dll)   sealed class

This collection of TableCell and TableHeaderCell objects is used by the Cells property of the TableRow class.

```
public sealed class TableCellCollection : IList, ICollection, IEnumerable {
// Public Instance Properties
  public int Count{get; }                                                     // implements ICollection
  public bool IsReadOnly{get; }                                               // implements IList
  public bool IsSynchronized{get; }                                           // implements ICollection
  public object SyncRoot{get; }                                               // implements ICollection
  public TableCell this[ int index ]{get; }
// Public Instance Methods
  public int Add( TableCell cell);
  public void AddAt( int index, TableCell cell);
  public void AddRange( TableCell[ ] cells);
  public void Clear( );                                                       // implements IList
  public void CopyTo( Array array, int index);                               // implements ICollection
  public int GetCellIndex( TableCell cell);
  public IEnumerator GetEnumerator( );                                        // implements IEnumerable
  public void Remove( TableCell cell);
  public void RemoveAt( int index);                                           // implements IList
}
```

Returned By	TableRow.Cells

TableCellControlBuilder

System.Web.UI.WebControls (system.web.dll)   class

The ASP.NET parser uses this class to generate HTML for any TableCell controls on a requested Web Forms page. You will not need to use this class directly in application code.

```
public class TableCellControlBuilder : System.Web.UI.ControlBuilder {
// Public Constructors
  public TableCellControlBuilder( );
// Public Instance Methods
```

```
    public override bool AllowWhitespaceLiterals( );                    // overrides System.Web.UI.ControlBuilder
}
```

Hierarchy   System.Object → System.Web.UI.ControlBuilder → TableCellControlBuilder

TableHeaderCell   disposable

System.Web.UI.WebControls (system.web.dll)   class

This class represents individual table header cells in a **TableRow**. It derives all of its properties from **TableCell**.

```
public class TableHeaderCell : TableCell {
// Public Constructors
  public TableHeaderCell( );
}
```

Hierarchy   System.Object → System.Web.UI.Control(System.ComponentModel.IComponent, System.
IDisposable, System.Web.UI.IParserAccessor, System.Web.UI.IDataBindingsAccessor) →
WebControl(System.Web.UI.IAttributeAccessor) → TableCell → TableHeaderCell

TableItemStyle   marshal by reference, disposable

System.Web.UI.WebControls (system.web.dll)   class

This class encapsulates the formatting for a row in a table-based control. It is used to apply formatting to headers, footers, and other items in the **DataGrid** and **Calendar** controls. It is not used for the **Table** control.

```
public class TableItemStyle : Style {
// Public Constructors
  public TableItemStyle( );
  public TableItemStyle( System.Web.UI.StateBag bag);
// Public Instance Properties
  public virtual HorizontalAlign HorizontalAlign{set; get; }
  public virtual VerticalAlign VerticalAlign{set; get; }
  public virtual bool Wrap{set; get; }
// Public Instance Methods
  public override void AddAttributesToRender(System.Web.UI.HtmlTextWriter writer, WebControl owner); // overrides Style
  public override void CopyFrom( Style s);                                                // overrides Style
  public override void MergeWith( Style s);                                               // overrides Style
  public override void Reset( );                                                          // overrides Style
}
```

Hierarchy   System.Object → System.MarshalByRefObject → System.ComponentModel.Compo-
nent(System.ComponentModel.IComponent, System.IDisposable) → Style(System.Web.UI.
IStateManager) → TableItemStyle

Subclasses   DataGridPagerStyle

Returned By   Multiple types

System.Web.UI.WebControls (system.web.dll)

This class represents an individual row element in a Table control. Each table row contains a group of TableCell objects, which is provided through the Cells property. Most other properties are used for fine-tuning the appearance of a row.

```
public class TableRow : WebControl {
// Public Constructors
  public TableRow( );
// Public Instance Properties
  public virtual TableCellCollection Cells{get; }
  public virtual HorizontalAlign HorizontalAlign{set; get; }
  public virtual VerticalAlign VerticalAlign{set; get; }
// Protected Instance Methods
  protected override ControlCollection CreateControlCollection( );    // overrides System.Web.UI.Control
  protected override Style CreateControlStyle( );                     // overrides WebControl
}
```

Hierarchy	System.Object → System.Web.UI.Control(System.ComponentModel.IComponent, System.IDisposable, System.Web.UI.IParserAccessor, System.Web.UI.IDataBindingsAccessor) → WebControl(System.Web.UI.IAttributeAccessor) → TableRow
Subclasses	DataGridItem
Returned By	TableRowCollection.this
Passed To	TableRowCollection.{Add( ), AddAt( ), AddRange( ), GetRowIndex( ), Remove( )}

TableRowCollection

System.Web.UI.WebControls (system.web.dll)

This collection of TableRow objects is used by the Rows property of the Table class.

```
public sealed class TableRowCollection : IList, ICollection, IEnumerable {
// Public Instance Properties
  public int Count{get; }                                  // implements ICollection
  public bool IsReadOnly{get; }                            // implements IList
  public bool IsSynchronized{get; }                        // implements ICollection
  public object SyncRoot{get; }                            // implements ICollection
  public TableRow this[ int index ]{get; }
// Public Instance Methods
  public int Add( TableRow row);
  public void AddAt( int index, TableRow row);
  public void AddRange( TableRow[ ] rows);
  public void Clear( );                                    // implements IList
  public void CopyTo( Array array, int index);             // implements ICollection
  public IEnumerator GetEnumerator( );                     // implements IEnumerable
  public int GetRowIndex( TableRow row);
  public void Remove( TableRow row);
  public void RemoveAt( int index);                        // implements IList
}
```

Returned By	Table.Rows

TableStyle

System.Web.UI.WebControls (system.web.dll)   class

The TableStyle class is primarily used by control developers. It encapsulates some of the formatting options that can be applied to an HTML table. These options correspond to properties of the Table class.

```
public class TableStyle : Style {
// Public Constructors
  public TableStyle( );
  public TableStyle( System.Web.UI.StateBag bag);
// Public Instance Properties
  public virtual string BackImageUrl{set; get; }
  public virtual int CellPadding{set; get; }
  public virtual int CellSpacing{set; get; }
  public virtual GridLines GridLines{set; get; }
  public virtual HorizontalAlign HorizontalAlign{set; get; }
// Public Instance Methods
  public override void AddAttributesToRender(System.Web.UI.HtmlTextWriter writer, WebControl owner);  // overrides Style
  public override void CopyFrom( Style s);                                                            // overrides Style
  public override void MergeWith( Style s);                                                           // overrides Style
  public override void Reset( );                                                                      // overrides Style
}
```

Hierarchy   System.Object → System.MarshalByRefObject → System.ComponentModel.Compo-
                    nent(System.ComponentModel.IComponent, System.IDisposable) → Style(System.Web.UI.
                    IStateManager) → TableStyle

TargetConverter

System.Web.UI.WebControls (system.web.dll)   class

The TargetConverter class is a type converter that allows conversions between an ordinary string and the "target" string used to specify the target frame or window for a hyperlink, as in AdRotator.Target. This conversion allows the target property to be displayed in the Property window. This class is never accessed directly. You can access its functionality through the System.ComponentModel.TypeDescriptor helper class.

```
public class TargetConverter : System.ComponentModel.StringConverter {
// Public Constructors
  public TargetConverter( );
// Public Instance Methods
  public override StandardValuesCollection GetStandardValues(System.ComponentModel.ITypeDescriptorContext context);
                                                     // overrides System.ComponentModel.TypeConverter
  public override bool GetStandardValuesExclusive(System.ComponentModel.ITypeDescriptorContext context);
                                                     // overrides System.ComponentModel.TypeConverter
  public override bool GetStandardValuesSupported(System.ComponentModel.ITypeDescriptorContext context);
                                                     // overrides System.ComponentModel.TypeConverter
}
```

Hierarchy   System.Object → System.ComponentModel.TypeConverter → System.ComponentModel.
                    StringConverter → TargetConverter

TemplateColumn

System.Web.UI.WebControls (system.web.dll)   **class**

This class represents a type of column that can be added to the **DataGrid** control. A TemplateColumn allows you to create fully customized output in the **DataGrid** by using templates. These templates are defined by using the *.aspx* (not the properties of this class), which is similar to the method used by the **DataList** and **Repeater** controls. Templates allow you to combine several different fields in a single column and add other HTML elements and ASP.NET controls.

In the **TemplateColumn** definition in the *.aspx* file, you can define up to four templates: **HeaderTemplate**, **ItemTemplate**, **EditItemTemplate**, and **FooterTemplate**. Inside these template definitions, you can insert data binding expressions or HTML and ASP.NET elements.

```
public class TemplateColumn : DataGridColumn {
// Public Constructors
   public TemplateColumn( );
// Public Instance Properties
   public virtual ITemplate EditItemTemplate{set; get; }
   public virtual ITemplate FooterTemplate{set; get; }
   public virtual ITemplate HeaderTemplate{set; get; }
   public virtual ITemplate ItemTemplate{set; get; }
// Public Instance Methods
   public override void InitializeCell(TableCell cell, int columnIndex, ListItemType itemType);   // overrides DataGridColumn
}
```

Hierarchy   System.Object → DataGridColumn(System.Web.UI.IStateManager) → TemplateColumn

TextAlign   **serializable**

System.Web.UI.WebControls (system.web.dll)   **enum**

This enumeration is used to set the **CheckBox.TextAlign** and **RadioButton.TextAlign** properties. This value specifies whether text will be placed to the left or right of the control.

```
public enum TextAlign {
   Left = 1,
   Right = 2
}
```

Hierarchy   System.Object → System.ValueType → System.Enum(System.IComparable, System.IFormattable, System.IConvertible) → TextAlign

Returned By   CheckBox.TextAlign, CheckBoxList.TextAlign, RadioButtonList.TextAlign

Passed To   CheckBox.TextAlign, CheckBoxList.TextAlign, RadioButtonList.TextAlign

TextBox   **disposable**

System.Web.UI.WebControls (system.web.dll)   **class**

This class represents the text box web control and provides properties to configure text wrapping, the maximum accepted length, and the size in fixed character widths and row-heights (Columns and Rows). This class also includes a single event, TextChanged, which will fire only when the text box loses focus and a post back is generated.

The text box is abstracted away from any specific HTML element. Depending on your settings, ASP.NET will use the appropriate <input type="text">, <input type="password">, or <textarea> HTML tag.

```
public class TextBox : WebControl, System.Web.UI.IPostBackDataHandler {
// Public Constructors
  public TextBox( );
// Public Instance Properties
  public virtual bool AutoPostBack{set; get; }
  public virtual int Columns{set; get; }
  public virtual int MaxLength{set; get; }
  public virtual bool ReadOnly{set; get; }
  public virtual int Rows{set; get; }
  public virtual string Text{set; get; }
  public virtual TextBoxMode TextMode{set; get; }
  public virtual bool Wrap{set; get; }
// Protected Instance Properties
  protected override HtmlTextWriterTag TagKey{get; }                              // overrides WebControl
// Protected Instance Methods
  protected override void AddAttributesToRender(System.Web.UI.HtmlTextWriter writer);     // overrides WebControl
  protected override void AddParsedSubObject( object obj);                    // overrides System.Web.UI.Control
  protected override void OnPreRender( EventArgs e);                          // overrides System.Web.UI.Control
  protected virtual void OnTextChanged( EventArgs e);
  protected override void Render(System.Web.UI.HtmlTextWriter writer);             // overrides WebControl
// Events
  public event EventHandler TextChanged;
}
```

Hierarchy System.Object → System.Web.UI.Control(System.ComponentModel.IComponent, System. IDisposable, System.Web.UI.IParserAccessor, System.Web.UI.IDataBindingsAccessor) → WebControl(System.Web.UI.IAttributeAccessor) → TextBox(System.Web.UI. IPostBackDataHandler)

TextBoxControlBuilder

System.Web.UI.WebControls (system.web.dll)   class

The ASP.NET parser uses this class to generate HTML for any TextBox controls on a requested Web Forms page. You will not need to use this class directly in application code.

```
public class TextBoxControlBuilder : System.Web.UI.ControlBuilder {
// Public Constructors
  public TextBoxControlBuilder( );
// Public Instance Methods
  public override bool AllowWhitespaceLiterals( );              // overrides System.Web.UI.ControlBuilder
  public override bool HtmlDecodeLiterals( );                   // overrides System.Web.UI.ControlBuilder
}
```

Hierarchy System.Object → System.Web.UI.ControlBuilder → TextBoxControlBuilder

TextBoxMode
serializable

System.Web.UI.WebControls (system.web.dll) enum

This enumeration is used for the **TextBox.TextMode** property. It allows special text box styles, including **Password**, where all characters will be displayed as asterisks (*), and **MultiLine**. **MultiLine** allows text on multiple lines and will automatically wrap text as it is entered (if the **TextBox.Wrap** property is **True**).

```
public enum TextBoxMode {
  SingleLine = 0,
  MultiLine = 1,
  Password = 2
}
```

Hierarchy   System.Object → System.ValueType → System.Enum(System.IComparable, System.IFormattable, System.IConvertible) → TextBoxMode

Returned By   TextBox.TextMode

Passed To   TextBox.TextMode

TitleFormat
serializable

System.Web.UI.WebControls (system.web.dll) enum

This enumeration specifies the format used for the title of the **Calendar** control. **Month** displays the month but not the year (for example, "September"). **MonthYear** displays both the month and year (for example, "September 2001").

```
public enum TitleFormat {
  Month = 0,
  MonthYear = 1
}
```

Hierarchy   System.Object → System.ValueType → System.Enum(System.IComparable, System.IFormattable, System.IConvertible) → TitleFormat

Returned By   Calendar.TitleFormat

Passed To   Calendar.TitleFormat

Unit
struct

System.Web.UI.WebControls (system.web.dll)

This class is a simple value type used to represent a specific increment of a specific unit of measurement. The **Unit** class combines a numeric **Value** property that quantifies the size with a **Type** property that indicates what scale of measurement is being used. Several shared (static) methods are provided to convert a value of a specific scale to a unit. For example, you can use **Percentage( )** to convert a percentage value to a unit that has the corresponding **Type** set to **UnitType.Percentage**.

```
public struct Unit {
// Public Constructors
```

```
public Unit( double value);
public Unit( double value, UnitType type);
public Unit( int value);
public Unit( string value);
public Unit(string value, System.Globalization.CultureInfo culture);
// Public Static Fields
public static readonly Unit Empty;
// Public Instance Properties
public bool IsEmpty{get; }
public UnitType Type{get; }
public double Value{get; }
// Public Static Methods
public static Unit Parse( string s);
public static Unit Parse(string s, System.Globalization.CultureInfo culture);
public static Unit Percentage( double n);
public static Unit Pixel( int n);
public static Unit Point( int n);
public static bool operator !=(Unit left,      Unit right);
public static bool operator = =(Unit left,      Unit right);
public static implicit operator Unit( int n);
// Public Instance Methods
public override bool Equals( object obj);                                      // overrides ValueType
public override int GetHashCode( );                                           // overrides ValueType
public override string ToString( );                                          // overrides ValueType
public string ToString(System.Globalization.CultureInfo culture);
}
```

Hierarchy   System.Object → System.ValueType → Unit

Returned By   FontUnit.Unit, Style.{BorderWidth, Height, Width}, WebControl.{BorderWidth, Height, Width}

Passed To   FontUnit.FontUnit( ), Style.{BorderWidth, Height, Width}, WebControl.{BorderWidth, Height, Width}

UnitConverter

System.Web.UI.WebControls (system.web.dll)   class

This class provides the functionality needed to convert a Unit structure to a System.Int32 value. This class is never accessed directly. You can access its functionality through the System.ComponentModel.TypeDescriptor helper class.

```
public class UnitConverter : System.ComponentModel.TypeConverter {
// Public Constructors
public UnitConverter( );
// Public Instance Methods
public override bool CanConvertFrom(System.ComponentModel.ITypeDescriptorContext context,
    Type sourceType);                                  // overrides System.ComponentModel.TypeConverter
public override object ConvertFrom(System.ComponentModel.ITypeDescriptorContext context,
    System.Globalization.CultureInfo culture, object value);    // overrides System.ComponentModel.TypeConverter
```

```
   public override object ConvertTo(System.ComponentModel.ITypeDescriptorContext context,
      System.Globalization.CultureInfo culture, object value, Type destinationType);
                                             // overrides System.ComponentModel.TypeConverter
}
```

Hierarchy   System.Object → System.ComponentModel.TypeConverter → UnitConverter

UnitType   serializable

System.Web.UI.WebControls (system.web.dll)   enum

This enumeration is used to support different measurement units, which are used for setting various properties in controls, including WebControl.Height, WebControl.Width, and Unit.

A Point is a unit of measurement that represents 1/72 of an inch. A Pica is equivalent to 12 points. The Percentage value is relative to the parent element. An Em is relative to the height of a parent element's font (so 2 em specifies a font size that is twice as large as that of the parent). An Ex is relative to the height of the lowercase letter "x" of the parent element's font.

```
public enum UnitType {
   Pixel = 1,
   Point = 2,
   Pica = 3,
   Inch = 4,
   Mm = 5,
   Cm = 6,
   Percentage = 7,
   Em = 8,
   Ex = 9
}
```

Hierarchy   System.Object → System.ValueType → System.Enum(System.IComparable, System.IFor-
                      mattable, System.IConvertible) → UnitType

Returned By   Unit.Type

Passed To   Unit.Unit( )

ValidatedControlConverter

System.Web.UI.WebControls (system.web.dll)   class

This class is used to provide a list of validatable controls in the property browser. It allows you to set properties like CompareValidator.ControlToValidate at design time.

```
public class ValidatedControlConverter : System.ComponentModel.StringConverter {
// Public Constructors
   public ValidatedControlConverter( );
// Public Instance Methods
   public override StandardValuesCollection GetStandardValues(System.ComponentModel.ITypeDescriptorContext context);
                                             // overrides System.ComponentModel.TypeConverter
   public override bool GetStandardValuesExclusive(System.ComponentModel.ITypeDescriptorContext context);
                                             // overrides System.ComponentModel.TypeConverter
```

```
  public override bool GetStandardValuesSupported(System.ComponentModel.ITypeDescriptorContext context);
                                              // overrides System.ComponentModel.TypeConverter
}
```

Hierarchy   System.Object → System.ComponentModel.TypeConverter → System.ComponentModel.
StringConverter → ValidatedControlConverter

ValidationCompareOperator   serializable

System.Web.UI.WebControls (system.web.dll)   enum

This enumeration specifies the type of comparison that will be performed by a Compare-
Validator control. The CompareValidator control evaluates the expression ControlToValidate
<Operator> ControlToCompare. (You can also substitute CompareValidator.ValueToCompare instead of
CompareValidator.ControlToCompare.) If the expression evaluates True, the validation result is
valid.

```
public enum ValidationCompareOperator {
  Equal = 0,
  NotEqual = 1,
  GreaterThan = 2,
  GreaterThanEqual = 3,
  LessThan = 4,
  LessThanEqual = 5,
  DataTypeCheck = 6
}
```

Hierarchy   System.Object → System.ValueType → System.Enum(System.IComparable, System.IFor-
mattable, System.IConvertible) → ValidationCompareOperator

Returned By   System.Web.UI.MobileControls.CompareValidator.Operator, CompareValidator.Operator

Passed To   System.Web.UI.MobileControls.CompareValidator.Operator, BaseCompareValidator.
Compare( ), CompareValidator.Operator

ValidationDataType   serializable

System.Web.UI.WebControls (system.web.dll)   enum

This enumeration specifies the data type that is used for the CompareValidator and RangeValidator controls.

```
public enum ValidationDataType {
  String = 0,
  Integer = 1,
  Double = 2,
  Date = 3,
  Currency = 4
}
```

Hierarchy   System.Object → System.ValueType → System.Enum(System.IComparable, System.IFor-
mattable, System.IConvertible) → ValidationDataType

Returned By	System.Web.UI.MobileControls.CompareValidator.Type, System.Web.UI.MobileControls. RangeValidator.Type, BaseCompareValidator.Type
Passed To	System.Web.UI.MobileControls.CompareValidator.Type, System.Web.UI.MobileControls. RangeValidator.Type, BaseCompareValidator.{CanConvert( ), Compare( ), Convert( ), Type}

ValidationSummary

System.Web.UI.WebControls (system.web.dll)

disposable

class

The ValidationSummary control receives the error text messages from all validation controls on the Web Forms page and presents them in a single paragraph or list. This occurs automatically on post back, provided that the ShowSummary property is set to True. Alternatively (or in addition), you can set the ShowMessageBox property to True to display a message box with the summary when validation errors occur. This message box uses client-side JavaScript and will be provided only if the browser supports it and the EnableClientScript property is set to True. You can also add a title to the summary by using the HeaderText property.

```
public class ValidationSummary : WebControl {
// Public Constructors
  public ValidationSummary( );
// Public Instance Properties
  public ValidationSummaryDisplayMode DisplayMode{set; get; }
  public bool EnableClientScript{set; get; }
  public override Color ForeColor{set; get; }              // overrides WebControl
  public string HeaderText{set; get; }
  public bool ShowMessageBox{set; get; }
  public bool ShowSummary{set; get; }
// Protected Instance Methods
  protected override void AddAttributesToRender(System.Web.UI.HtmlTextWriter writer);    // overrides WebControl
  protected override void OnPreRender( EventArgs e);         // overrides System.Web.UI.Control
  protected override void Render(System.Web.UI.HtmlTextWriter writer);    // overrides WebControl
}
```

Hierarchy	System.Object → System.Web.UI.Control(System.ComponentModel.IComponent, System. IDisposable, System.Web.UI.IParserAccessor, System.Web.UI.IDataBindingsAccessor) → WebControl(System.Web.UI.IAttributeAccessor) → ValidationSummary

ValidationSummaryDisplayMode

serializable

System.Web.UI.WebControls (system.web.dll)

enum

This enumeration specifies the way that a ValidationSummary control will display error messages—either as a combined SingleParagraph, as a List, or as a BulletList.

```
public enum ValidationSummaryDisplayMode {
  List = 0,
  BulletList = 1,
  SingleParagraph = 2
}
```

Hierarchy	System.Object → System.ValueType → System.Enum(System.IComparable, System.IFormattable, System.IConvertible) → ValidationSummaryDisplayMode

Returned By   ValidationSummary.DisplayMode

Passed To   ValidationSummary.DisplayMode

ValidatorDisplay   serializable

System.Web.UI.WebControls (system.web.dll)   enum

This enumeration is used to specify how a validation control should display error messages. Static instructs ASP.NET to reserve space on your Web Forms page for a validation control so that the page layout won't change when an error message is displayed. Dynamic specifies that you want to dynamically add the error message to the page. It means that several validation controls can share the same place on the page and that the page layout may change when an error message is displayed (unless you have enclosed the validator in an HTML element that is large enough to accommodate its maximum size).

This enumeration does not affect the display of the error message in a ValidationSummary control.

```
public enum ValidatorDisplay {
    None = 0,
    Static = 1,
    Dynamic = 2
}
```

Hierarchy   System.Object → System.ValueType → System.Enum(System.IComparable, System.IFormattable, System.IConvertible) → ValidatorDisplay

Returned By   System.Web.UI.MobileControls.BaseValidator.Display, BaseValidator.Display

Passed To   System.Web.UI.MobileControls.BaseValidator.Display, BaseValidator.Display

VerticalAlign   serializable

System.Web.UI.WebControls (system.web.dll)   enum

This enumeration allows you to align an object or text along the vertical axis. It is used in TableRow and TableCell controls.

```
public enum VerticalAlign {
    NotSet = 0,
    Top = 1,
    Middle = 2,
    Bottom = 3
}
```

Hierarchy   System.Object → System.ValueType → System.Enum(System.IComparable, System.IFormattable, System.IConvertible) → VerticalAlign

Returned By   TableCell.VerticalAlign, TableItemStyle.VerticalAlign, TableRow.VerticalAlign

Passed To   TableCell.VerticalAlign, TableItemStyle.VerticalAlign, TableRow.VerticalAlign

WebColorConverter

System.Web.UI.WebControls (system.web.dll)　　　　　　　　　　　　　　　　　　　　　　class

The WebColorConverter class is a type converter that allows control color properties to be converted from one data type to another. This allows color value to be displayed in the property browser. This class is never accessed directly; you can access its functionality through the System.ComponentModel.TypeDescriptor helper class.

```
public class WebColorConverter : System.Drawing.ColorConverter {
// Public Constructors
   public WebColorConverter( );
// Public Instance Methods
   public override object ConvertFrom(System.ComponentModel.ITypeDescriptorContext context,
      System.Globalization.CultureInfo culture, object value);          // overrides System.Drawing.ColorConverter
   public override object ConvertTo(System.ComponentModel.ITypeDescriptorContext context,
      System.Globalization.CultureInfo culture, object value, Type destinationType); // overrides System.Drawing.ColorConverter
}
```

Hierarchy　　　　System.Object → System.ComponentModel.TypeConverter → System.Drawing.ColorConverter → WebColorConverter

WebControl　　　　　　　　　　　　　　　　　　　　　　　　　　　　disposable

System.Web.UI.WebControls (system.web.dll)　　　　　　　　　　　　　　　　　　　　　　class

This class is the base class for all web controls. The WebControl class derives much of its basic functionality from System.Web.UI.Control, including functionality for data binding and using view state. The WebControl class adds additional user-interface specific members for configuring the control's appearance—including a collection of CSS attributes (Style), color options (BackColor and ForeColor), a shortcut key (AccessKey), and various border style, font, and dimension properties. One interesting property that is specific to web controls is CssClass, which sets the Cascading Style Sheet class applied to the control. This is rendered as the class attribute in HTML (for example, <input type=text class="class1" style="ForeColor:red">). Some properties, such as AccessKey, may not be supported on down-level browsers.

All methods and the TagName, TagKey, Attributes, and Style properties are provided for developers to use or override in custom web controls. If you want to create a server control that renders user interface (HTML), you should extend one of the web control classes or inherit directly from WebControl rather than the more basic System.Web.UI.Control class. You should override the RenderContents( ) method, which provides a System.Web.UI.HtmlText-Writer for generating output. You do not need to manually output style attributes (or the basic HTML tag, if you have supplied it to the base WebControl constructor), as the WebControl class will handle these details automatically. Alternatively, you can override Render( ) for more fine-grained control. You may also want to implement the interfaces System.Web.UI.IPostBackDataHandler and System.Web.UI.IPostBackEventHandler to allow the control to retrieve postback data and fire events on postback.

```
public class WebControl : System.Web.UI.Control, System.Web.UI.IAttributeAccessor {
// Public Constructors
   public WebControl( System.Web.UI.HtmlTextWriterTag tag);
// Protected Constructors
   protected WebControl( );
```

```
    protected WebControl( string tag);
// Public Instance Properties
    public virtual string AccessKey{set; get; }
    public AttributeCollection Attributes{get; }
    public virtual Color BackColor{set; get; }
    public virtual Color BorderColor{set; get; }
    public virtual BorderStyle BorderStyle{set; get; }
    public virtual Unit BorderWidth{set; get; }
    public Style ControlStyle{get; }
    public bool ControlStyleCreated{get; }
    public virtual string CssClass{set; get; }
    public virtual bool Enabled{set; get; }
    public virtual FontInfo Font{get; }
    public virtual Color ForeColor{set; get; }
    public virtual Unit Height{set; get; }
    public CssStyleCollection Style{get; }
    public virtual short TabIndex{set; get; }
    public virtual string ToolTip{set; get; }
    public virtual Unit Width{set; get; }
// Protected Instance Properties
    protected virtual HtmlTextWriterTag TagKey{get; }
    protected virtual string TagName{get; }
// Public Instance Methods
    public void ApplyStyle( Style s);
    public void CopyBaseAttributes( WebControl controlSrc);
    public void MergeStyle( Style s);
    public virtual void RenderBeginTag(System.Web.UI.HtmlTextWriter writer);
    public virtual void RenderEndTag(System.Web.UI.HtmlTextWriter writer);
// Protected Instance Methods
    protected virtual void AddAttributesToRender(System.Web.UI.HtmlTextWriter writer);
    protected virtual Style CreateControlStyle( );
    protected override void LoadViewState( object savedState);                   // overrides System.Web.UI.Control
    protected override void Render(System.Web.UI.HtmlTextWriter writer);          // overrides System.Web.UI.Control
    protected virtual void RenderContents(System.Web.UI.HtmlTextWriter writer);
    protected override object SaveViewState( );                                   // overrides System.Web.UI.Control
    protected override void TrackViewState( );                                    // overrides System.Web.UI.Control
}
```

Hierarchy   System.Object → System.Web.UI.Control(System.ComponentModel.IComponent, System.
                 IDisposable, System.Web.UI.IParserAccessor, System.Web.UI.IDataBindingsAccessor) →
                 WebControl(System.Web.UI.IAttributeAccessor)

Subclasses   Multiple types

Passed To   System.Web.UI.MobileControls.Style.ApplyTo( ), RepeatInfo.RenderRepeater( ), Style.
                 AddAttributesToRender( )

System.Web.UI.WebControls (system.web.dll)   class

The Xml control is used to display an XML document on your Web Forms page. To specify the XML document, set the Document property to a System.Xml.XmlDocument object, set the DocumentContent property to a string containing XML content, or set the Document-Source property with a string specifying a filename. If you set more than one property, the most recent one will take effect.

Optionally, you can specify an XSL Transform document, which will format the XML document before it is displayed. To specify an XSL Transform document, set the Transform property to a System.Xml.Xsl.XslTransform object or set the TransformSource property with a string specifying a filename for the XSL file.

```
public class Xml : System.Web.UI.Control {
// Public Constructors
  public Xml( );
// Public Instance Properties
  public XmlDocument Document{set; get; }
  public string DocumentContent{set; get; }
  public string DocumentSource{set; get; }
  public XslTransform Transform{set; get; }
  public XsltArgumentList TransformArgumentList{set; get; }
  public string TransformSource{set; get; }
// Protected Instance Methods
  protected override void AddParsedSubObject( object obj);            // overrides System.Web.UI.Control
  protected override void Render(System.Web.UI.HtmlTextWriter output);   // overrides System.Web.UI.Control
}
```

Hierarchy   System.Object → System.Web.UI.Control(System.ComponentModel.IComponent, System.
                 IDisposable, System.Web.UI.IParserAccessor, System.Web.UI.IDataBindingsAccessor) → Xml

Type, Method, Property, and Field Index

A

A: HtmlTextWriterTag

Abandon( ): HttpSessionState

Abort( ): WebClientAsyncResult, WebClient-Protocol

AbortTransaction: TemplateControl

AboveNormal: CacheItemPriority

AbsBottom: ImageAlign

AbsMiddle: ImageAlign

AbsoluteFilePath: MobilePage

AbstractSchemas: ProtocolImporter

Accept: HtmlInputFile

AcceptTypes: HttpCacheVaryByHeaders, Http-Request

Accesskey: HtmlTextWriterAttribute

AccessKey: WebControl

AcquireRequestState: HttpApplication

Acronym: HtmlTextWriterTag

Action: Form, SoapClientMessage, Soap-DocumentMethodAttribute, SoapMessage, SoapRpcMethodAttribute, SoapServer-Message

Activate: Form

ActiveForm: MobilePage

ActiveTemplateEditingFrame: Templated-ControlDesigner

ActiveXControls: HttpBrowserCapabilities

Actor: SoapException, SoapHeader

Adapter: MobileControl, MobilePage

AdCreated: AdRotator

AdCreatedEventArgs: System.Web.UI. WebControls

AdCreatedEventHandler: System.Web.UI. WebControls

Add( ): AttributeCollection, BindingCollection, Cache, ControlCollection, CssStyleCollection, DataBindingCollection, DataGridColumn-Collection, DeviceSpecificChoiceCollection, DiscoveryClientDocumentCollection, DiscoveryClientReferenceCollection, DiscoveryClientResultCollection, Discovery-ExceptionDictionary, DiscoveryReference-Collection, EmptyControlCollection, Fault-BindingCollection, HtmlTableCellCollection, HtmlTableRowCollection, HttpApplication-State, HttpCookieCollection, HttpSession-State, ImportCollection, ListItemCollection, MessageCollection, MessagePartCollection, MimePartCollection, MimeTextMatch-Collection, MobileListItemCollection, Object-ListCommandCollection, ObjectListField-Collection, OperationBindingCollection, OperationCollection, OperationFault-Collection, OperationMessageCollection, Port-Collection, PortTypeCollection, SelectedDates-Collection, ServiceCollection, ServiceDescriptionCollection, Service-

DescriptionFormatExtensionCollection, Soap-HeaderCollection, StateBag, TableCell-Collection, TableRowCollection, ValidatorCollection

AddAccesskeyAttribute( ): HtmlControlAdapter

AddAt( ): ControlCollection, DataGridColumn-Collection, DeviceSpecificChoiceCollection, EmptyControlCollection, ObjectList-CommandCollection, ObjectListField-Collection, TableCellCollection, TableRow-Collection

AddAttribute( ): HtmlTextWriter

AddAttributes( ): AttributeCollection, ChtmlCommandAdapter, ChtmlImage-Adapter, ChtmlLinkAdapter, ChtmlPhoneCall-Adapter, ChtmlTextBoxAdapter, HtmlControl-Adapter

AddAttributesToRender( ): BaseCompare-Validator, BaseValidator, Button, Compare-Validator, CustomValidator, DropDownList, HyperLink, Image, ImageButton, LinkButton, ListBox, Panel, RangeValidator, Regular-ExpressionValidator, RequiredFieldValidator, Style, Table, TableCell, TableItemStyle, Table-Style, TextBox, ValidationSummary, WebControl

AddCacheItemDependencies( ): HttpResponse

AddCacheItemDependency( ): HttpResponse

AddedControl( ): MobileControl, MobilePage

AddError( ): HttpContext

AddExtensionWarningComments( ): Protocol-Importer

AddFileDependencies( ): HttpResponse

AddFileDependency( ): HttpResponse

AddFormVariable( ): WmlMobileTextWriter

AddHeader( ): HttpResponse

AdditionalInformation: DiscoveryClientProtocol

AddJPhoneMultiMediaAttributes( ): Html-ControlAdapter

AddLinkedForms( ): Link, MobileControl, Panel, PhoneCall

AddOnAcquireRequestStateAsync( ): Http-Application

AddOnAuthenticateRequestAsync( ): Http-Application

AddOnAuthorizeRequestAsync( ): Http-Application

AddOnBeginRequestAsync( ): HttpApplication

AddOnEndRequestAsync( ): HttpApplication

AddOnPostRequestHandlerExecuteAsync( ): HttpApplication

AddOnPreRequestHandlerExecuteAsync( ): HttpApplication

AddOnReleaseRequestStateAsync( ): Http-Application

AddOnResolveRequestCacheAsync( ): Http-Application

AddOnUpdateRequestCacheAsync( ): Http-Application

AddParsedSubObject( ): BaseDataList, Control, DeviceSpecific, HtmlSelect, HtmlTextArea, HyperLink, IParserAccessor, Label, Link-Button, List, Literal, MobileControl, Mobile-Page, MobileUserControl, ObjectList, SelectionList, StyleSheet, TableCell, TextBox, Xml

AddRange( ): ListItemCollection, TableCell-Collection, TableRowCollection

AddResource( ): MobileTextWriter, MultiPart-Writer

Address: HtmlTextWriterTag, SoapBinding

AddServiceDescription( ): Service-DescriptionImporter

AddStyleAttribute( ): HtmlTextWriter

AddToCache( ): WebClientProtocol

AddValidationCallback( ): HttpCachePolicy

AdProperties: AdCreatedEventArgs

AdRotator: System.Web.UI.MobileControls, System.Web.UI.WebControls

AdRotatorDesigner: System.Web.UI.Design. WebControls

AdvertisementFile: AdRotator

AfterDeserialize: SoapMessageStage

AfterSerialize: SoapMessageStage

Age: ProcessInfo

Align: HtmlImage, HtmlInputImage, HtmlTable, HtmlTableCell, HtmlTableRow, HtmlText-WriterAttribute

Alignment: MobileControl, Style, StyleSheet, System.Web.UI.MobileControls

AlignmentKey: Style

Alive: ProcessStatus

All: DeviceSpecificChoiceCollection, Forms-ProtectionEnum

AllCaches: HttpCacheRevalidation

AllErrors: HttpContext

AllFields: ObjectList

AllKeys: HttpApplicationState, HttpCookie-Collection, HttpFileCollection, HttpModule-Collection

AllowAutoRedirect: HttpWebClientProtocol

AllowCustomAttributes: MobilePage

AllowCustomPaging: DataGrid, PagedData-Source

AllowElements: XmlFormatExtensionPoint-Attribute

AllowPaging: DataGrid, PagedDataSource

AllowResize: ControlDesigner, DataList-Designer, UserControlDesigner

AllowSorting: DataGrid

AllowWhitespaceLiterals( ): ControlBuilder, HyperLinkControlBuilder, Label-ControlBuilder, LinkButtonControlBuilder, ListItemControlBuilder, LiteralControlBuilder, LiteralTextControlBuilder, Mobile-ControlBuilder, PlaceHolderControlBuilder, TableCellControlBuilder, TextBoxControl-Builder

Alt: HtmlImage, HtmlInputImage, HtmlText-WriterAttribute

AlternateFormat: PhoneCall

AlternateText: AdCreatedEventArgs, Image

AlternateUrl: PhoneCall

AlternatingItem: ListItemType

AlternatingItemStyle: DataGrid, DataList

AlternatingItemTemplate: DataList, Repeater

AlternatingItemTemplateTag: Constants

AnalyzeMode: WmlMobileTextWriter

AnalyzePostBack( ): UpWmlMobileTextWriter, WmlMobileTextWriter

Any: OutputCacheLocation

AnyReturnReader: System.Web.Services.Proto-cols

AOL: HttpBrowserCapabilities

AppDomainAppId: HttpRuntime

AppDomainAppPath: HttpRuntime

AppDomainAppVirtualPath: HttpRuntime

AppDomainFactory: System.Web.Hosting

AppDomainId: HttpRuntime

AppendCacheExtension( ): HttpCachePolicy

AppendCookie( ): HttpResponse

AppendHeader( ): HttpResponse

AppendLiteralString( ): ControlBuilder, DeviceSpecificChoiceControlBuilder, Device-SpecificChoiceTemplateBuilder, DeviceSpecificControlBuilder, LiteralText-ContainerControlBuilder, ObjectTagBuilder

AppendSubBuilder( ): ControlBuilder, DeviceSpecificChoiceControlBuilder, Device-SpecificChoiceTemplateBuilder, FormControl-Builder, LiteralControlBuilder, LiteralText-ContainerControlBuilder, ObjectTagBuilder

AppendToLog( ): HttpResponse

Application: HttpApplication, HttpContext, Page, UserControl, WebService

ApplicationHost: System.Web.Hosting

ApplicationInstance: HttpContext

ApplicationPath: HttpRequest

ApplyAppPathModifier( ): HttpResponse

ApplyStyle( ): WebControl

ApplyTo( ): Style

Area: HtmlTextWriterTag

Argument: DeviceSpecificChoice

ArrayListCollectionBase: System.Web.UI.MobileControls

AspCompatBeginProcessRequest( ): Page

AspCompatEndProcessRequest( ): Page

AspInstallDirectory: HttpRuntime

AspNetHostingPermission: System.Web

AspNetHostingPermissionAttribute: System.Web

AspNetHostingPermissionLevel: System.Web

AsUnit: FontSize

Async: LogicalMethodTypes

AsyncCallbackParameter: LogicalMethodInfo

AsyncResultParameter: LogicalMethodInfo

AsyncState: WebClientAsyncResult

AsyncStateParameter: LogicalMethodInfo

AsyncWaitHandle: WebClientAsyncResult

Attachments: MailMessage

Attribute: PersistenceMode, PersistenceMode-Attribute

AttributeCollection: System.Web.UI

Attributes: HtmlControl, ListItem, UserControl, WebControl

Authenticate: DefaultAuthenticationModule, FormsAuthenticationModule, Passport-AuthenticationModule, Windows-AuthenticationModule

Authenticate( ): FormsAuthentication

AuthenticateRequest: HttpApplication

AuthenticationMode: System.Web.Configuration

AuthenticationType: FormsIdentity, PassportIdentity

AuthorizeRequest: HttpApplication

AuthUrl( ): PassportIdentity

AuthUrl2( ): PassportIdentity

AutoGenerateColumns: DataGrid

AutoGenerateFields: ObjectList

AutoPostBack: CheckBox, ListControl, TextBox

B

B: HtmlTextWriterTag

BackColor: MobileControl, Style, StyleSheet, WebControl

BackColorKey: Style

BackCommandText: ObjectList

Background: HtmlTextWriterAttribute

BackgroundColor: HtmlTextWriterStyle

BackgroundImage: HtmlTextWriterStyle

BackgroundSounds: HttpBrowserCapabilities

BackImageUrl: DataGrid, Panel, Table, TableStyle

BackLabel: ControlAdapter, ValidationSummary

Bare: SoapParameterStyle

Base: HtmlTextWriterTag

Base64: MailEncoding

BaseCompareValidator: System.Web.UI.WebControls

BaseDataList: System.Web.UI.WebControls

BaseDataListComponentEditor: System.Web.UI.Design.WebControls

BaseDataListDesigner: System.Web.UI.Design.WebControls

Basefont: HtmlTextWriterTag

Baseline: ImageAlign

BaseParser: System.Web.UI

BasePartialCachingControl: System.Web.UI

BaseValidator: System.Web.UI.MobileControls, System.Web.UI.WebControls

BaseValidatorDesigner: System.Web.UI.Design.WebControls

Bcc: MailMessage

Bdo: HtmlTextWriterTag

BeforeDeserialize: SoapMessageStage

BeforeDoneWithSession: HttpContext

BeforeSerialize: SoapMessageStage

BeginClass( ): ProtocolImporter, Protocol-Reflector, SoapProtocolImporter

BeginCustomMarkup( ): UpWmlMobile-TextWriter, WmlMobileTextWriter

BeginEventHandler: System.Web

BeginFile( ): MobileTextWriter, MultiPartWriter

BeginForm( ): UpWmlMobileTextWriter, WmlMobileTextWriter

BeginInvoke( ): AdCreatedEventHandler, BeginEventHandler, BuildMethod, BuildTemplateMethod, CacheItem-RemovedCallback, CommandEventHandler, DataGridCommandEventHandler, DataGrid-ItemEventHandler, DataGridPageChanged-EventHandler, DataGridSortCommandEvent-Handler, DataListCommandEventHandler, DataListItemEventHandler, DayRenderEvent-Handler, DefaultAuthenticationEventHandler, EndEventHandler, EndOfSendNotification, FormsAuthenticationEventHandler, HttpCacheValidateHandler, HttpSimpleClient-Protocol, ImageClickEventHandler, List-CommandEventHandler, ListDataBindEvent-Handler, LoadItemsEventHandler, LogicalMethodInfo, MonthChangedEvent-Handler, ObjectListCommandEventHandler, ObjectListDataBindEventHandler, Object-ListSelectEventHandler, ObjectListShow-CommandsEventHandler, Passport-AuthenticationEventHandler, RenderMethod, RepeaterCommandEventHandler, Repeater-ItemEventHandler, ServerValidateEvent-Handler, SoapHttpClientProtocol, Windows-AuthenticationEventHandler

BeginMethodInfo: LogicalMethodInfo

BeginNamespace( ): ProtocolImporter, Soap-ProtocolImporter

BeginProcessRequest( ): IHttpAsyncHandler

BeginRequest: HttpApplication

BeginResponse( ): MobileTextWriter, MultiPart-Writer

BeginStyleContext( ): HtmlMobileTextWriter

Behavior: HtmlControlDesigner

BelowNormal: CacheItemPriority

Beta: HttpBrowserCapabilities

Bgcolor: HtmlTextWriterAttribute

BgColor: HtmlTable, HtmlTableCell, Html-TableRow

Bgsound: HtmlTextWriterTag

Big: HtmlTextWriterTag

BinaryIssuer: HttpClientCertificate

BinaryRead( ): HttpRequest

BinaryWrite( ): HttpResponse

Binding: OperationBinding, Port, Protocol-Importer, ProtocolReflector, SoapBinding, SoapDocumentMethodAttribute, Soap-RpcMethodAttribute, System.Web.Services. Description

BindingCollection: System.Web.Services. Description

BindingContainer: Control

Bindings: ServiceDescription

BinDirectory: HttpRuntime

Blockquote: HtmlTextWriterTag

Body: HtmlTextWriterTag, MailMessage

BodyEncoding: MailMessage

BodyFormat: MailMessage

Bold: FontInfo

BoldKey: Style

BooleanOption: System.Web.UI.MobileControls

Border: HtmlImage, HtmlInputImage, Html-Table, HtmlTextWriterAttribute

BorderCollapse: HtmlTextWriterStyle

Bordercolor: HtmlTextWriterAttribute

BorderColor: DropDownList, HtmlTable, HtmlTableCell, HtmlTableRow, HtmlText-WriterStyle, ListBox, Style, WebControl

BorderStyle: DropDownList, HtmlText-WriterStyle, ListBox, Style, System.Web.UI. WebControls, WebControl

BorderWidth: DropDownList, HtmlText-WriterStyle, ListBox, Style, WebControl

Both: GridLines

Bottom: ImageAlign, PagerPosition, Vertical-Align

BoundColumn: System.Web.UI.WebControls

Br: HtmlTextWriterTag

BreakAfter: Form, MobileControl, Panel, Style-Sheet, TemplateContainer, TextViewElement

Browser: HttpBrowserCapabilities, HttpRequest

Buffer: HttpResponse

BufferOutput: HttpResponse

BufferResponse: WebMethodAttribute

BuildCachedControl( ): StaticPartialCaching-Control

BuildColor( ): ColorBuilder, IWebFormsBuilder-UIService

BuilderType: ControlBuilderAttribute

BuildMethod: System.Web.UI

BuildProfileTree( ): Control

BuildTemplateMethod: System.Web.UI

BuildUrl( ): IWebFormsBuilderUIService, UrlBuilder

Bulleted: ListDecoration

BulletList: ValidationSummaryDisplayMode

Button: CommandFormat, HtmlTextWriterTag, System.Web.UI.WebControls

ButtonColumn: System.Web.UI.WebControls

ButtonColumnType: System.Web.UI. WebControls

ButtonDesigner: System.Web.UI.Design. WebControls

ButtonType: ButtonColumn, EditCommand-Column

C

Cache: HttpContext, HttpResponse, Http-Runtime, Page, System.Web.Caching, User-Control

CacheControl: HttpResponse

CachedControl: PartialCachingControl

CacheDependency: System.Web.Caching

CacheDuration: WebMethodAttribute

CacheItemPriority: System.Web.Caching

CacheItemRemovedCallback: System.Web. Caching

CacheItemRemovedReason: System.Web. Caching

CacheVaryByHeaders: HtmlPageAdapter,
IPageAdapter, WmlPageAdapter

CalculateFormPostBackUrl( ): UpWml-
MobileTextWriter, WmlMobileTextWriter

CalculateFormQueryString( ): UpWml-
MobileTextWriter, WmlMobileTextWriter

CalculateOptimumPageWeight( ): Control-
Adapter

CalculatePostBackVariables( ):
WmlFormAdapter

Calendar: System.Web.UI.MobileControls,
System.Web.UI.WebControls

CalendarAdapterFirstPrompt: SR

CalendarAdapterOptionChooseDate: SR

CalendarAdapterOptionChooseMonth: SR

CalendarAdapterOptionChooseWeek: SR

CalendarAdapterOptionEra: SR

CalendarAdapterOptionPrompt: SR

CalendarAdapterOptionType: SR

CalendarAdapterTextBoxErrorMessage: SR

CalendarAutoFormatDialog: System.Web.UI.
Design.WebControls

CalendarDataBindingHandler: System.Web.UI.
Design

CalendarDay: System.Web.UI.WebControls

CalendarDesigner: System.Web.UI.Design.
WebControls

CalendarEntryText: Calendar

CalendarSelectionMode: System.Web.UI.
WebControls

CallLabel: ControlAdapter

CancelCommand: DataGrid, DataList

CancelCommandName: DataGrid, DataList

CancelText: EditCommandColumn

CanCombineFormsInDeck: MobileCapabilities

CanConvert( ): BaseCompareValidator

CanConvertFrom( ): DataFieldConverter,
DataMemberConverter, DataSourceConverter,
FontNamesConverter, FontUnitConverter,
UnitConverter

CanEnterTemplateMode: TemplatedControl-
Designer

CanInitiateVoiceCall: MobileCapabilities

CanRead( ): DiscoveryDocument, Service-
Description

CanRenderAfterInputOrSelectElement:
MobileCapabilities

CanRenderEmptySelects: MobileCapabilities

**CanRenderInputAndSelectElements-
Together:** MobileCapabilities

CanRenderMixedSelects: MobileCapabilities

**CanRenderOneventAndPrevElements-
Together:** MobileCapabilities

CanRenderPostBackCards: MobileCapabilities

**CanRenderSetvarZeroWithMulti-
SelectionList:** MobileCapabilities

CanSelectMultipleInstances( ): ListItems-
CollectionEditor, TableCellsCollectionEditor,
TableRowsCollectionEditor

CanSendMail: MobileCapabilities

Capacity: ListItemCollection

Caption: HtmlTextWriterTag

Capture: MatchAttribute, MimeTextMatch

CausesValidation: Button, Command, Html-
Button, HtmlInputButton, HtmlInputImage,
ImageButton, LinkButton

Cc: MailMessage

CDF: HttpBrowserCapabilities

Cell: DayRenderEventArgs

Cellpadding: HtmlTextWriterAttribute

CellPadding: BaseDataList, Calendar, Check-
BoxList, HtmlTable, RadioButtonList, Table,
TableStyle

Cells: HtmlTableRow, TableRow

Cellspacing: HtmlTextWriterAttribute

CellSpacing: BaseDataList, Calendar, Check-
BoxList, HtmlTable, RadioButtonList, Table,
TableStyle

Center: Alignment, HorizontalAlign, HtmlText-
WriterTag

CertEncoding: HttpClientCertificate

Certificate: HttpClientCertificate

ChainStream( ): SoapExtension

Charset: HttpResponse

CheckBox: ListSelectType, System.Web.UI.
WebControls

CheckBoxDesigner: System.Web.UI.Design.
WebControls

CheckBoxList: System.Web.UI.WebControls

CheckControlValidationProperty( ): Base-
Validator

Checked: CheckBox, HtmlInputCheckBox, Html-
InputRadioButton, HtmlTextWriterAttribute

CheckedChanged: CheckBox

ChildrenAsProperties: ParseChildrenAttribute

Choices: DeviceSpecific

ChtmlCalendarAdapter: System.Web.UI.
MobileControls.Adapters

ChtmlCommandAdapter: System.Web.UI.
MobileControls.Adapters

ChtmlFormAdapter: System.Web.UI.Mobile-
Controls.Adapters

ChtmlImageAdapter: System.Web.UI.Mobile-
Controls.Adapters

**ChtmlImageAdapterDecimalCodeExpected-
AfterGroupChar:** SR

ChtmlLinkAdapter: System.Web.UI.Mobile-
Controls.Adapters

ChtmlMobileTextWriter: System.Web.UI.
MobileControls.Adapters

ChtmlPageAdapter: System.Web.UI.Mobile-
Controls.Adapters

ChtmlPageAdapterRedirectLinkLabel: SR

ChtmlPageAdapterRedirectPageContent: SR

ChtmlPhoneCallAdapter: System.Web.UI.
MobileControls.Adapters

ChtmlSelectionListAdapter: System.Web.UI.
MobileControls.Adapters

ChtmlTextBoxAdapter: System.Web.UI.Mobile-
Controls.Adapters

Cite: HtmlTextWriterTag

Class: HtmlTextWriterAttribute

ClassName: ProtocolImporter

ClassNames: ProtocolImporter

Clear: FormsAuthPasswordFormat

Clear( ): AttributeCollection, ControlCollection,
CssStyleCollection, DataBindingCollection,
DataGridColumnCollection, Device-
SpecificChoiceCollection, HtmlTableCell-
Collection, HtmlTableRowCollection, Http-
ApplicationState, HttpCookieCollection,
HttpResponse, HttpSessionState, ListItem-
Collection, MobileListItemCollection, Object-
ListCommandCollection, ObjectListField-
Collection, ObjectListItemCollection,
SelectedDatesCollection, StateBag, Style-
Sheet, TableCellCollection, TableRow-
Collection

ClearChildViewState( ): Control

ClearContent( ): HttpResponse

ClearError( ): HttpContext, HttpServerUtility

ClearHeaders( ): HttpResponse

ClearSelection( ): HtmlSelect, ListControl

Click: Button, Command, ImageButton, Link-
Button

Client: OutputCacheLocation, Service-
DescriptionImportStyle, SoapClientMessage

ClientCertificate: HttpRequest

ClientCertificates: HttpWebClientProtocol

ClientFaultCode: SoapException

ClientID: Control

ClientProtocol: DiscoveryReference

ClientTarget: Page

ClientValidationFunction: CustomValidator

ClientViewState: MobilePage

Clone( ): Style

Close( ): HtmlTextWriter, HttpResponse, Http-
Runtime, HttpWriter, ITemplateEditingFrame

CloseCharacterFormat( ): WmlMobile-
TextWriter

CloseConnection( ): HttpWorkerRequest

CloseControl( ): ControlBuilder

CloseParagraph( ): WmlMobileTextWriter

ClrInstallDirectory: HttpRuntime

ClrVersion: HttpBrowserCapabilities

Cm: UnitType

cmdHelp_Click( ): RegexEditorDialog

cmdOK_Click( ): RegexEditorDialog

cmdTestValidate_Click( ): RegexEditorDialog

Code: HtmlTextWriterTag, SoapException

CodegenDir: HttpRuntime

CodeNamespace: ProtocolImporter

CodePage: HttpSessionState

CodeTypeDeclaration: ProtocolImporter

Col: HtmlTextWriterTag

Colgroup: HtmlTextWriterTag

Color: HtmlTextWriterStyle

ColorBuilder: System.Web.UI.Design

Cols: HtmlTextArea, HtmlTextWriterAttribute

Colspan: HtmlTextWriterAttribute

ColSpan: HtmlTableCell

Columns: DataGrid, TextBox

ControlPropertiesValid( ): BaseValidator, CompareValidator, CustomValidator, RangeValidator

Controls: BaseDataList, Control, Repeater

ControlStyle: ITemplateEditingFrame, WebControl

ControlStyleCreated: WebControl

ControlToCompare: CompareValidator

ControlToPaginate: Form

ControlToValidate: BaseValidator

ControlType: ControlBuilder

Convert( ): BaseCompareValidator

ConvertFrom( ): DataFieldConverter, DataMemberConverter, DataSourceConverter, FontNamesConverter, FontUnitConverter, UnitConverter, WebColorConverter

ConvertTo( ): DataBindingCollectionConverter, FontNamesConverter, FontUnitConverter, UnitConverter, WebColorConverter

ConvertValue( ): ObjectConverter

Cookie: HttpClientCertificate

CookieContainer: HttpWebClientProtocol

CookielessData: System.Web.Mobile

CookielessDataDictionary: HtmlPageAdapter, IPageAdapter, WmlPageAdapter

CookiePath: FormsAuthenticationTicket

Cookies: HttpBrowserCapabilities, HttpRequest, HttpResponse

Copy( ): AspNetHostingPermission

CopyBaseAttributes( ): WebControl

CopyFrom( ): DataGridPagerStyle, FontInfo, Style, TableItemStyle, TableStyle

CopyTo( ): ArrayListCollectionBase, BindingCollection, ControlCollection, DataBindingCollection, DataGridColumnCollection, DataGridItemCollection, DataKeyCollection, DataListItemCollection, FaultBindingCollection, HtmlTableCellCollection, HtmlTableRowCollection, HttpCookieCollection, HttpFileCollection, HttpModuleCollection, HttpSessionState, HttpStaticObjectsCollection, ImportCollection, ListItemCollection, MessageCollection, MessagePartCollection, MimePartCollection, MimeTextMatchCollection, OperationBindingCollection, OperationCollection, OperationFaultCollection, Operation-

MessageCollection, PagedDataSource, PortCollection, PortTypeCollection, RepeaterItemCollection, SelectedDatesCollection, ServiceCollection, ServiceDescriptionCollection, ServiceDescriptionFormatExtensionCollection, SoapHeaderCollection, TableCellCollection, TableRowCollection, ValidatorCollection

Count: ArrayListCollectionBase, AttributeCollection, Cache, ControlCollection, CssStyleCollection, DataBindingCollection, DataGridColumnCollection, DataGridItemCollection, DataKeyCollection, DataListItemCollection, HtmlTableCellCollection, HtmlTableRowCollection, HttpApplicationState, HttpSessionState, HttpStaticObjectsCollection, ListItemCollection, PagedDataSource, RepeaterItemCollection, SelectedDatesCollection, StateBag, TableCellCollection, TableRowCollection, ValidatorCollection

Crawler: HttpBrowserCapabilities

Create( ): AppDomainFactory, IAppDomainFactory, LogicalMethodInfo

CreateApplicationHost( ): ApplicationHost

CreateAutoGeneratedFields( ): ObjectList

CreateBuilderFromType( ): ControlBuilder

CreateChildControls( ): BaseDataList, Control, List, ObjectList, Repeater

CreateColumnSet( ): DataGrid

CreateComponentsCore( ): WebControlToolboxItem

CreateControlCollection( ): AdRotator, Calendar, Control, DataBoundLiteralControl, DesignerDataBoundLiteralControl, DropDownList, HtmlContainerControl, HtmlControl, HtmlSelect, HtmlTable, HtmlTableRow, Literal, LiteralControl, Table, TableRow

CreateControlHierarchy( ): BaseDataList, DataGrid, DataList, Repeater

CreateControlStyle( ): CheckBoxList, DataGrid, DataList, DataListItem, RadioButtonList, Table, TableCell, TableRow, WebControl

CreateDefaultTemplatedUI( ): Form, List, MobileControl, Panel

CreateDiscardableUndoUnit( ): IWebFormsDocumentService

CreateDummyDataTable( ): DesignTimeData

CreateFrame( ): ITemplateEditingService, TemplateEditingService

CreateFromLastError( ): HttpException

CreateHtmlTextWriter( ): MobilePage, Page

CreateInstance( ): MimeFormatter, TableCells-CollectionEditor, TableRowsCollectionEditor

CreateItem( ): DataGrid, DataList, ObjectList, Repeater

CreateItems( ): List, ObjectList, SelectionList

CreateObject( ): HttpServerUtility

CreateObjectFromClsid( ): HttpServerUtility

CreatePermission( ): AspNetHosting-PermissionAttribute

CreatePlaceHolderDesignTimeHtml( ): ControlDesigner

CreateResourceBasedLiteralControl( ): TemplateControl

CreateSampleDataTable( ): DesignTimeData

CreateStyle( ): MobileControl

CreateTemplatedItemDetails( ): ObjectList

CreateTemplatedItemsList( ): ObjectList

CreateTemplatedUI( ): ControlAdapter, Html-ObjectListAdapter, IControlAdapter, Mobile-Control, WmlObjectListAdapter

CreateTemplateEditingFrame( ): DataGrid-Designer, DataListDesigner, Templated-ControlDesigner

CreateTextWriter( ): ChtmlPageAdapter, Html-PageAdapter, IPageAdapter, UpWmlPage-Adapter, WmlPageAdapter

CreateWebAdRotator( ): AdRotator

CreateWebCalendar( ): Calendar

CreateWebValidator( ): BaseValidator, CompareValidator, CustomValidator, RangeV-alidator, RegularExpressionValidator, RequiredFieldValidator

Credentials: WebClientProtocol

CryptIsValid( ): PassportIdentity

CryptPutHost( ): PassportIdentity

CryptPutSite( ): PassportIdentity

CssClass: Style, WebControl

CssStyle: AttributeCollection

CssStyleCollection: System.Web.UI

Currency: ValidationDataType

Current: HttpContext

CurrentExecutionFilePath: HttpRequest

CurrentPage: Form

CurrentPageIndex: DataGrid, PagedDataSource

CustomAttributeProvider: LogicalMethodInfo

CustomAttributes: MobileControl

CustomText: NextPrevFormat

CustomValidator: System.Web.UI.Mobile-Controls, System.Web.UI.WebControls

D

Dashed: BorderStyle

Data: ToolboxDataAttribute

DataBind( ): BaseDataList, Control, ObjectList, Repeater

DataBindControl( ): CalendarDataBinding-Handler, DataBindingHandler, HyperLinkData-BindingHandler, ListControlDataBinding-Handler, TextDataBindingHandler

DataBinder: System.Web.UI

DataBinding: Control, DeviceSpecific, System.Web.UI

DataBindingCollection: System.Web.UI

DataBindingCollectionConverter: System.Web.UI.Design

DataBindingCollectionEditor: System.Web.UI.Design

DataBindingHandler: DesignTimeData, DesignTimeParseData, System.Web.UI.Design

DataBindingHandlerAttribute: System.Web.UI

DataBindings: HtmlControlDesigner, IData-BindingsAccessor

DataBindingValueUIHandler: System.Web.UI.Design

DataBindItem( ): ObjectListField

DataBoundLiteralControl: System.Web.UI

DataField: BoundColumn, ObjectListField

DataFieldConverter: System.Web.UI.Design

DataFormatString: BoundColumn, ObjectList-Field

DataGrid: System.Web.UI.WebControls

DataGridColumn: System.Web.UI.WebControls

DataGridColumnCollection: System.Web.UI.WebControls

DataGridColumnCollectionEditor: System.Web.UI.Design.WebControls

Decoration: List

Decrypt( ): FormsAuthentication, Passport-
Identity

Default: CacheItemPriority, ControlBuilder-
Attribute, DataBindingHandlerAttribute, First-
DayOfWeek, ParseChildrenAttribute, Persist-
ChildrenAttribute, PersistenceModeAttribute,
PersistNameAttribute, SoapBindingStyle,
SoapBindingUse, SoapParameterStyle, Style-
Sheet, ToolboxDataAttribute, TraceMode

DefaultAuthentication: HttpApplication

DefaultAuthenticationEventArgs: System.
Web.Security

DefaultAuthenticationEventHandler: System.
Web.Security

DefaultAuthenticationModule: System.Web.
Security

DefaultCommand: ListCommandEventArgs,
ObjectList, ObjectListCommandEventArgs

DefaultFilename: ContractReference,
DiscoveryDocumentReference, Discovery-
Reference, SchemaReference

DefaultNamespace: ProtocolReflector,
WebServiceAttribute

DefaultProperty: ParseChildrenAttribute

DefaultSessionsStateHistorySize: Constants

DefaultSubmitButtonLimit: MobileCapabilities

DefaultTabString: HtmlTextWriter

DefaultWeight: ControlPager

Del: HtmlTextWriterTag

DeleteCommand: DataGrid, DataList

DeleteCommandName: DataGrid, DataList

Dependency: BasePartialCachingControl

DependencyChanged: CacheItemRemoved-
Reason

Description: MobileErrorInfo, WebMethod-
Attribute, WebServiceAttribute

Deserialize( ): LosFormatter, WebControl-
ToolboxItem

Designer: IHtmlControlDesignerBehavior

DesignerAdapterAttribute: System.Web.UI.
MobileControls

DesignerDataBoundLiteralControl: System.
Web.UI

DesignerHost: DesignTimeParseData

DesignerInitialize( ): Page, UserControl

DesignMode: MobilePage

DesignTimeData: System.Web.UI.Design

DesignTimeElement: IHtmlControlDesigner-
Behavior

DesignTimeElementView: IControlDesigner-
Behavior

DesignTimeHtml: IControlDesignerBehavior

DesignTimeHtmlRequiresLoadComplete:
BaseDataListDesigner, ControlDesigner

DesignTimeParseData: System.Web.UI

DesignTimeTemplateParser: System.Web.UI

Detail: SoapException

DetailElementName: SoapException

Details: ObjectList, ObjectListViewMode

DetailsCommandText: ObjectList

DeterminePostBack( ): WmlControlAdapter

DeterminePostBackMode( ): Chtml-
PageAdapter, HtmlPageAdapter, IPage-
Adapter, MobilePage, Page, WmlPageAdapter

DetermineRenderUplevel( ): BaseCompare-
Validator, BaseValidator

Device: ControlAdapter, MobilePage, Mobile-
TextWriter

DeviceOverridableAttribute: System.Web.UI.
MobileControls

DeviceQualifies( ): ChtmlPageAdapter, Html-
PageAdapter, UpWmlPageAdapter,
WmlPageAdapter

DeviceSpecific: MobileControl, Style, System.
Web.UI.MobileControls

DeviceSpecificChoice: System.Web.UI.Mobile-
Controls

DeviceSpecificChoiceCollection: System.Web.
UI.MobileControls

DeviceSpecificChoiceControlBuilder: System.
Web.UI.MobileControls

DeviceSpecificChoiceTemplateBuilder: System.
Web.UI.MobileControls

DeviceSpecificChoiceTemplateContainer:
System.Web.UI.MobileControls

DeviceSpecificControlBuilder: System.Web.UI.
MobileControls

Dfn: HtmlTextWriterTag

DidUnderstand: SoapHeader

Dir: HtmlTextWriterTag

Direction: SoapHeaderAttribute

EditItemStyle: DataGrid, DataList

EditItemTemplate: DataList, TemplateColumn

EditText: EditCommandColumn

EditValue( ): DataBindingCollectionEditor, DataGridColumnCollectionEditor, RegexTypeEditor, UrlEditor, XmlFileEditor

Element: MessagePart, SoapUnknownHeader

ElementName: XmlFormatExtensionAttribute

Em: HtmlTextWriterTag, UnitType

Embed: HtmlTextWriterTag

Empty: FontUnit, Unit

EmptyControlCollection: System.Web.UI

EnableClientScript: BaseValidator, ValidationSummary

Enabled: BaseValidator, Image, WebControl

EnableSession: WebMethodAttribute

EnableUndo( ): IWebFormsDocumentService

EnableViewState: Control, DeviceSpecific, Page, StyleSheet

Encode( ): UrlEncodedParameterWriter

EncodeAttributeValue( ): HtmlTextWriter

Encoded: SoapBindingUse

EncodedInnerDefaultProperty: PersistenceMode, PersistenceModeAttribute

EncodedMustUnderstand: SoapHeader

EncodeUrl( ): HtmlTextWriter

Encoding: HtmlTextWriter, HttpWriter, MailAttachment, SoapBodyBinding, SoapFaultBinding, SoapHeaderBinding, SoapHeaderFaultBinding

Encrypt( ): FormsAuthentication, PassportIdentity

Encryption: FormsProtectionEnum

Enctype: HtmlForm

End: SessionStateModule

End( ): HttpResponse

EndClass( ): ProtocolImporter, ProtocolReflector, SoapProtocolImporter

EndCustomMarkup( ): WmlMobileTextWriter

EndEventHandler: System.Web

EndFile( ): MobileTextWriter, MultiPartWriter

EndForm( ): UpWmlMobileTextWriter, WmlMobileTextWriter

EndInvoke( ): AdCreatedEventHandler, BeginEventHandler, BuildMethod, BuildTemplateMethod, CacheItemRemovedCallback, CommandEventHandler, DataGridCommandEventHandler, DataGridItemEventHandler, DataGridPageChangedEventHandler, DataGridSortCommandEventHandler, DataListCommandEventHandler, DataListItemEventHandler, DayRenderEventHandler, DefaultAuthenticationEventHandler, EndEventHandler, EndOfSendNotification, FormsAuthenticationEventHandler, HttpCacheValidateHandler, HttpSimpleClientProtocol, ImageClickEventHandler, ListCommandEventHandler, ListDataBindEventHandler, LoadItemsEventHandler, LogicalMethodInfo, MonthChangedEventHandler, ObjectListCommandEventHandler, ObjectListDataBindEventHandler, ObjectListSelectEventHandler, ObjectListShowCommandsEventHandler, PassportAuthenticationEventHandler, RenderMethod, RepeaterCommandEventHandler, RepeaterItemEventHandler, ServerValidateEventHandler, SoapHttpClientProtocol, WindowsAuthenticationEventHandler

EndMethodInfo: LogicalMethodInfo

EndNamespace( ): ProtocolImporter, SoapProtocolImporter

EndOfRequest( ): HttpWorkerRequest, SimpleWorkerRequest

EndOfSendNotification: System.Web

EndProcessRequest( ): IHttpAsyncHandler

EndRequest: HttpApplication

EndResponse( ): MobileTextWriter, MultiPartWriter

EndStyleContext( ): HtmlMobileTextWriter

EndTagLeftChars: HtmlTextWriter

EnsureChildControls( ): Control, List, ObjectList

EnsureFormat( ): WmlMobileTextWriter

EnsureInStage( ): SoapClientMessage, SoapMessage, SoapServerMessage

EnsureLayout( ): WmlMobileTextWriter

EnsureOutStage( ): SoapClientMessage, SoapMessage, SoapServerMessage

EnsureStage( ): SoapMessage

EnsureTemplatedUI( ): List, MobileControl, ObjectList

EnterFormat( ): HtmlMobileTextWriter, MobileTextWriter, WmlMobileTextWriter

---

FindPartByName( ): Message

FindPartsByName( ): Message

First: Pair, Triplet

FirstDayOfWeek: Calendar, System.Web.UI.
WebControls

FirstIndexInPage: PagedDataSource

FirstLetter: DayNameFormat

FirstPage: MobileControl

FirstTwoLetters: DayNameFormat

FirstVisibleElementIndex: TextView

FirstVisibleElementOffset: TextView

FirstVisibleItemIndex: PagedControl

Flags: HttpClientCertificate

Flow: OperationMessageCollection, Repeat-
Layout

Flush( ): HtmlTextWriter, HttpResponse, Http-
Writer

FlushResponse( ): HttpWorkerRequest, Simple-
WorkerRequest

Font: AdRotator, HtmlTextWriterTag, Image,
MobileControl, Style, StyleSheet, WebControl

FontFamily: HtmlTextWriterStyle

FontInfo: System.Web.UI.MobileControls,
System.Web.UI.WebControls

FontNameKey: Style

FontNamesConverter: System.Web.UI.
WebControls

FontSize: HtmlTextWriterStyle, System.Web.UI.
MobileControls, System.Web.UI.WebControls

FontSizeKey: Style

FontStyle: HtmlTextWriterStyle

FontUnit: System.Web.UI.WebControls

FontUnitConverter: System.Web.UI.
WebControls

FontWeight: HtmlTextWriterStyle

Footer: Form, ListItemType

FooterItem: MobileListItemType

FooterStyle: DataGrid, DataGridColumn, DataList

FooterTemplate: DataList, Repeater, Template-
Column

FooterTemplateTag: Constants

FooterText: DataGridColumn

For: HtmlTextWriterAttribute

ForeColor: BaseValidator, MobileControl, Style,
StyleSheet, ValidationSummary, WebControl

ForeColorKey: Style

Form: HtmlTextWriterTag, HttpRequest, Mobile-
Control, System.Web.UI.MobileControls

FormAdapterMultiControlsAttempt-
SecondaryUI: SR

Format: Command

FormatDataNavigateUrlValue( ): Hyper-
LinkColumn

FormatDataTextValue( ): ButtonColumn,
HyperLinkColumn

FormatDataValue( ): BoundColumn

FormControlBuilder: System.Web.UI.Mobile-
Controls

FormIDPrefix: Constants

FormMethod: System.Web.UI.MobileControls

Forms: AuthenticationMode, MobilePage

FormsAuthentication: System.Web.Security

FormsAuthenticationEventArgs: System.Web.
Security

FormsAuthenticationEventHandler: System.
Web.Security

FormsAuthenticationModule: System.Web.
Security

FormsAuthenticationTicket: System.Web.Secu-
rity

FormsAuthPasswordFormat: System.Web.
Configuration

FormsCookieName: FormsAuthentication

FormsCookiePath: FormsAuthentication

FormsIdentity: System.Web.Security

FormsProtectionEnum: System.Web.Configura-
tion

FormToValidate: ValidationSummary

Frame: HtmlTextWriterTag

Frames: HttpBrowserCapabilities

Frameset: HtmlTextWriterTag

FrameworkInitialize( ): TemplateControl

Friday: FirstDayOfWeek

From: MailMessage

FromString( ): ListItem, MobileListItem

FromXml( ): AspNetHostingPermission

Full: DayNameFormat

FullMonth: NextPrevFormat

GetDomainFromMemberName( ): PassportIdentity

GetDouble( ): SR

GetEditStyle( ): DataBindingCollectionEditor, DataGridColumnCollectionEditor, RegexTypeEditor, UrlEditor, XmlFileEditor

GetElement( ): TextView

GetEmptyDesignTimeHtml( ): ControlDesigner, DataGridDesigner, DataListDesigner, RepeaterDesigner, XmlDesigner

GetEnumerator( ): ArrayListCollectionBase, Cache, ControlCollection, DataBindingCollection, DataGridColumnCollection, DataGridItemCollection, DataKeyCollection, DataListItemCollection, HtmlTableCellCollection, HtmlTableRowCollection, HttpSessionState, HttpStaticObjectsCollection, ListItemCollection, PagedDataSource, RepeaterItemCollection, SelectedDatesCollection, StateBag, TableCellCollection, TableRowCollection, ValidatorCollection

GetErrorDesignTimeHtml( ): ControlDesigner, DataGridDesigner, DataListDesigner, RepeaterDesigner

GetErrorMessages( ): ValidationSummary

GetFilePath( ): HttpWorkerRequest, SimpleWorkerRequest

GetFilePathTranslated( ): HttpWorkerRequest, SimpleWorkerRequest

GetFloat( ): SR

GetForm( ): MobilePage

GetFormUrl( ): HtmlPageAdapter

GetFromCache( ): WebClientProtocol

GetFromNetworkServer: PassportIdentity

GetFullYear( ): BaseCompareValidator

GetHandler( ): IHttpHandlerFactory, WebServiceHandlerFactory

GetHashCode( ): ControlBuilderAttribute, DataBinding, FontUnit, ListItem, MobileListItem, ObjectListItem, ParseChildrenAttribute, PersistChildrenAttribute, PersistenceModeAttribute, PersistNameAttribute, ToolboxDataAttribute, Unit

GetHistory( ): ProcessModelInfo

GetHtmlErrorMessage( ): HttpException

GetHttpCode( ): HttpException

GetHttpVerbName( ): HttpWorkerRequest, SimpleWorkerRequest

GetHttpVersion( ): HttpWorkerRequest, SimpleWorkerRequest

GetIndexedPropertyValue( ): DataBinder

GetInitialComponentEditorPageIndex( ): BaseDataListComponentEditor

GetInitializer( ): AnyReturnReader, MimeFormatter, NopReturnReader, SoapExtension, TextReturnReader, UrlEncodedParameterWriter, ValueCollectionParameterReader, XmlReturnReader

GetInitializers( ): MimeFormatter, XmlReturnReader

GetInParameterValue( ): SoapMessage

GetInt( ): SR

GetIsAuthenticated( ): PassportIdentity

GetItemPager( ): ControlPager

GetItemProperties( ): PagedDataSource

GetItemStyle( ): IRepeatInfoUser

GetKey( ): BindingCollection, FaultBindingCollection, HttpApplicationState, HttpCookieCollection, HttpFileCollection, HttpModuleCollection, MessageCollection, MessagePartCollection, OperationFaultCollection, PortCollection, PortTypeCollection, ServiceCollection, ServiceDescriptionBaseCollection, ServiceDescriptionCollection

GetKnownRequestHeader( ): HttpWorkerRequest

GetKnownRequestHeaderIndex( ): HttpWorkerRequest

GetKnownRequestHeaderName( ): HttpWorkerRequest

GetKnownResponseHeaderIndex( ): HttpWorkerRequest

GetKnownResponseHeaderName( ): HttpWorkerRequest

GetLastError( ): HttpServerUtility

GetLinkedForms( ): Form

GetListName( ): PagedDataSource

GetLocalAddress( ): HttpWorkerRequest, SimpleWorkerRequest

GetLocalPort( ): HttpWorkerRequest, SimpleWorkerRequest

GetLoginChallenge( ): PassportIdentity

GetLong( ): SR

GetTemplateEditingVerbs( ): Templated-
ControlDesigner

GetTemplateFromText( ): TemplatedControl-
Designer

GetTemplatePropertyParentType( ): Data-
GridDesigner, TemplatedControlDesigner

GetTextFromTemplate( ): TemplatedControl-
Designer

GetToolAttributeValue( ): WebControl-
ToolboxItem

GetToolHtml( ): WebControlToolboxItem

GetToolType( ): WebControlToolboxItem

GetTypeHashCode( ): Page

GetUnknownRequestHeader( ): HttpWorker-
Request

GetUnknownRequestHeaders( ): Http-
WorkerRequest

GetUriPath( ): HttpWorkerRequest, Simple-
WorkerRequest

GetUrlContextID( ): HttpWorkerRequest

GetUserToken( ): HttpWorkerRequest, Simple-
WorkerRequest

GetValidationProperty( ): BaseValidator

GetVaryByCustomString( ): HttpApplication

GetVirtualPathToken( ): HttpWorkerRequest

GetWebRequest( ): HttpGetClientProtocol,
HttpPostClientProtocol, HttpWebClient-
Protocol, SoapHttpClientProtocol, WebClient-
Protocol

GetWebResponse( ): HttpWebClientProtocol,
WebClientProtocol

GoLabel: ControlAdapter

GreaterThan: ValidationCompareOperator

GreaterThanEqual: ValidationCompareOperator

GridLines: BaseDataList, DataList, System.Web.
UI.WebControls, Table, TableStyle

Groove: BorderStyle

Group: MatchAttribute, MimeTextMatch

GroupName: RadioButton

H

H1: HtmlTextWriterTag

H2: HtmlTextWriterTag

H3: HtmlTextWriterTag

H4: HtmlTextWriterTag

H5: HtmlTextWriterTag

H6: HtmlTextWriterTag

Handled: ServiceDescriptionFormatExtension

HandleError( ): HtmlPageAdapter, IPage-
Adapter, WmlPageAdapter

HandlePagePostBackEvent( ): Html-
PageAdapter, IPageAdapter, WmlPage-
Adapter

HandlePostBackEvent( ): ChtmlCalendar-
Adapter, ControlAdapter, HtmlObjectList-
Adapter, IControlAdapter, WmlCalendar-
Adapter, WmlFormAdapter,
WmlObjectListAdapter

Handler: HttpContext

HandlerTypeName: DataBindingHandler-
Attribute

HasActivateHandler( ): Form

HasAspCode: ControlBuilder

HasBackButton: MobileCapabilities

HasBody( ): ControlBuilder

HasCapability( ): MobileCapabilities

HasChanged: CacheDependency

HasCommands( ): HtmlObjectListAdapter,
WmlObjectListAdapter

HasControls( ): Control

HasDataBindings: IDataBindingsAccessor

HasDeactivateHandler( ): Form

HasDefaultCommand( ): HtmlObject-
ListAdapter, WmlObjectListAdapter

HasEntityBody( ): HttpWorkerRequest

HasFlag( ): PassportIdentity

HasFooter: IRepeatInfoUser

HasHeader: IRepeatInfoUser

HasHiddenVariables( ): MobilePage

HashPasswordForStoringInConfigFile( ):
FormsAuthentication

HasItemCommandHandler: List, ObjectList

HasItemDetails( ): HtmlObjectListAdapter,
WmlObjectListAdapter

HasKeys: HttpCookie

HasProfile( ): PassportIdentity

HasSavedPassword: PassportIdentity

HasSeparators: IRepeatInfoUser

HasTemplates: DeviceSpecific, DeviceSpecific-
Choice

HttpBrowserCapabilities: System.Web

HttpCacheability: System.Web

HttpCachePolicy: System.Web

HttpCacheRevalidation: System.Web

HttpCacheValidateHandler: System.Web

HttpCacheVaryByHeaders: System.Web

HttpCacheVaryByParams: System.Web

HttpCapabilitiesBase: System.Web.Configuration

HttpClientCertificate: System.Web

HttpCompileException: System.Web

HttpConfigurationContext: System.Web.Configuration

HttpContext: System.Web

HttpCookie: System.Web

HttpCookieCollection: System.Web

HttpException: System.Web

HttpFileCollection: System.Web

HttpGetClientProtocol: System.Web.Services.Protocols

HttpMethod: HttpRequest

HttpMethodAttribute: System.Web.Services.Protocols

HttpModuleCollection: System.Web

HttpOperationBinding: System.Web.Services.Description

HttpParseException: System.Web

HttpPostClientProtocol: System.Web.Services.Protocols

HttpPostedFile: System.Web

HttpRequest: System.Web

HttpRequestValidationException: System.Web

HttpResponse: System.Web

HttpRuntime: System.Web

HttpServerUtility: System.Web

HttpSessionState: System.Web.SessionState

HttpSimpleClientProtocol: System.Web.Services.Protocols

HttpStaticObjectsCollection: System.Web

HttpTransport: SoapBinding

HttpUnhandledException: System.Web

HttpUrlEncodedBinding: System.Web.Services.Description

HttpUrlReplacementBinding: System.Web.Services.Description

HttpUtility: System.Web

HttpValidationStatus: System.Web

HttpWebClientProtocol: System.Web.Services.Protocols

HttpWorkerRequest: System.Web

HttpWriter: System.Web

HyperLink: System.Web.UI.WebControls

HyperLinkColumn: System.Web.UI.WebControls

HyperLinkControlBuilder: System.Web.UI.WebControls

HyperLinkDataBindingHandler: System.Web.UI.Design

HyperLinkDesigner: System.Web.UI.Design.WebControls

I

I: HtmlTextWriterTag

IAppDomainFactory: System.Web.Hosting

IAttributeAccessor: System.Web.UI

IControlAdapter: System.Web.UI.MobileControls

IControlDesignerBehavior: System.Web.UI.Design

Id: HtmlTextWriterAttribute

ID: Control, ControlBuilder, ControlDesigner, Page

IDataBindingsAccessor: System.Web.UI

IDataSourceProvider: System.Web.UI.Design

Identity: PassportAuthenticationEventArgs, WindowsAuthenticationEventArgs

IdleTimeout: ProcessShutdownReason

Iframe: HtmlTextWriterTag

IgnoreCase: MatchAttribute, MimeTextMatch

IgnoreParams: HttpCacheVaryByParams

IgnoreThisRequest: HttpValidationStatus

IHtmlControlDesignerBehavior: System.Web.UI.Design

IHttpAsyncHandler: System.Web

IHttpHandler: System.Web

IHttpHandlerFactory: System.Web

IHttpModule: System.Web

IISAPIRuntime: System.Web.Hosting

Image: System.Web.UI.MobileControls, System.Web.UI.WebControls

ImageAlign: Image, System.Web.UI.WebControls

ImageButton: System.Web.UI.WebControls

ImageClickEventArgs: System.Web.UI

ImageClickEventHandler: System.Web.UI

ImageKey: AdRotator

ImageUrl: AdCreatedEventArgs, Command, HyperLink, Image

ImageUrlEditor: System.Web.UI.Design

Img: HtmlTextWriterTag

Import: System.Web.Services.Description

Import( ): ServiceDescriptionImporter

ImportClass( ): SoapTransportImporter

ImportCollection: System.Web.Services.Description

ImportContext: SoapExtensionImporter, SoapTransportImporter

ImportMethod( ): SoapExtensionImporter

Imports: ServiceDescription

In: SoapHeaderDirection

INamingContainer: System.Web.UI

Inch: UnitType

Indent: HtmlTextWriter

Index: MobileListItem, TemplateEditingVerb

IndexOf( ): BindingCollection, ControlCollection, DataGridColumnCollection, FaultBindingCollection, ImportCollection, IObjectListFieldCollection, ListItemCollection, MessageCollection, MessagePartCollection, MimePartCollection, MimeTextMatchCollection, MobileListItemCollection, ObjectListCommandCollection, ObjectListFieldCollection, ObjectListItemCollection, OperationBindingCollection, OperationCollection, OperationFaultCollection, OperationMessageCollection, PortCollection, PortTypeCollection, ServiceCollection, ServiceDescriptionCollection, ServiceDescriptionFormatExtensionCollection, SoapHeaderCollection

Init: Control, DeviceSpecific

Init( ): ControlBuilder, DefaultAuthenticationModule, DeviceSpecificChoiceControlBuilder, DeviceSpecificChoiceTemplateBuilder, FileAuthorizationModule, FormsAuthenticationModule, HttpApplication, HttpCapabilitiesBase, IHttpModule, ObjectTagBuilder, PassportAuthenticationModule, SessionStateModule, TemplateBuilder, UrlAuthorizationModule, WindowsAuthenticationModule

InitContent( ): ErrorFormatterPage

InitialHeight: ITemplateEditingFrame

Initialize( ): AnyReturnReader, BaseDataListDesigner, BoundColumn, ButtonColumn, CalendarDesigner, ControlDesigner, DataGridColumn, DataGridDesigner, DataListDesigner, FormsAuthentication, HyperLinkColumn, ListControlDesigner, MimeFormatter, NopReturnReader, RepeaterDesigner, SoapExtension, TextControlDesigner, TextReturnReader, UrlEncodedParameterWriter, ValueCollectionParameterReader, WebControlToolboxItem, XmlDesigner, XmlReturnReader

InitializeAsUserControl( ): UserControl

InitializeCell( ): BoundColumn, ButtonColumn, DataGridColumn, EditCommandColumn, HyperLinkColumn, TemplateColumn

InitializeItem( ): DataGrid, DataList, Repeater

InitializePager( ): DataGrid

InitializeRequest( ): HtmlFormParameterWriter, MimeParameterWriter

InitialValue: RequiredFieldValidator

InitialWidth: ITemplateEditingFrame

InitOutputCache( ): MobilePage, Page

InnerDefaultProperty: PersistenceMode, PersistenceModeAttribute

InnerHtml: HtmlContainerControl, HtmlSelect, HtmlTable, HtmlTableRow

InnerProperty: PersistenceMode, PersistenceModeAttribute

InnerText: HtmlContainerControl, HtmlSelect, HtmlTable, HtmlTableRow, IUserControlDesignerAccessor

InnerWriter: HtmlTextWriter

InOut: SoapHeaderDirection

InParameters: LogicalMethodInfo

InProc: SessionStateMode

Input: HtmlTextWriterTag, OperationBinding, OperationMessageCollection

InputBinding: System.Web.Services.Description

InputMessage: ProtocolImporter, Protocol-
Reflector

InputStream: HttpPostedFile, HttpRequest

InputType: MobileCapabilities

Ins: HtmlTextWriterTag

Insert( ): BindingCollection, Cache, Fault-
BindingCollection, HtmlTableCellCollection,
HtmlTableRowCollection, ImportCollection,
ListItemCollection, MessageCollection,
MessagePartCollection, MimePartCollection,
MimeTextMatchCollection, MobileListItem-
Collection, OperationBindingCollection,
OperationCollection, OperationFault-
Collection, OperationMessageCollection, Port-
Collection, PortTypeCollection, Service-
Collection, ServiceDescriptionCollection,
ServiceDescriptionFormatExtensionCollection,
SoapHeaderCollection

Inset: BorderStyle

InstantiateIn( ): CompiledTemplateBuilder,
ITemplate, TemplateBuilder

Integer: ValidationDataType

InTemplateMode: TemplatedControlDesigner

Intersect( ): AspNetHostingPermission

Invalid: HttpValidationStatus

Invoke( ): AdCreatedEventHandler, BeginEvent-
Handler, BuildMethod, BuildTemplate-
Method, CacheItemRemovedCallback,
CommandEventHandler, DataGridCommand-
EventHandler, DataGridItemEventHandler,
DataGridPageChangedEventHandler,
DataGridSortCommandEventHandler, Data-
ListCommandEventHandler, DataListItem-
EventHandler, DayRenderEventHandler,
DefaultAuthenticationEventHandler,
EndEventHandler, EndOfSendNotification,
FormsAuthenticationEventHandler,
HttpCacheValidateHandler, HttpSimpleClient-
Protocol, ImageClickEventHandler, List-
CommandEventHandler, ListDataBindEvent-
Handler, LoadItemsEventHandler,
LogicalMethodInfo, MonthChangedEvent-
Handler, ObjectListCommandEventHandler,
ObjectListDataBindEventHandler, Object-
ListSelectEventHandler, ObjectListShow-
CommandsEventHandler, Passport-
AuthenticationEventHandler, RenderMethod,
RepeaterCommandEventHandler, Repeater-
ItemEventHandler, ServerValidateEvent-

Handler, SoapHttpClientProtocol, Windows-
AuthenticationEventHandler

IObjectListFieldCollection: System.Web.UI.
MobileControls

IPageAdapter: System.Web.UI.MobileControls

IParserAccessor: System.Web.UI

IPostBackDataHandler: System.Web.UI

IPostBackEventHandler: System.Web.UI

IReadOnlySessionState: System.Web.Session-
State

IRepeatInfoUser: System.Web.UI.WebControls

IRequiresSessionState: System.Web.Session-
State

ISAPIRuntime: System.Web.Hosting

IsAsync: LogicalMethodInfo

IsAttributeDefined( ): HtmlTextWriter

IsAuthenticated: FormsIdentity, HttpRequest,
PassportIdentity

IsBeginMethod( ): LogicalMethodInfo

IsBindableType( ): BaseDataList

IsBindingSupported( ): ProtocolImporter, Soap-
ProtocolImporter

IsBold: TextViewElement

IsBoundBy( ): Operation

IsClientConnected: HttpResponse

IsClientConnected( ): HttpWorkerRequest

IsClientScriptBlockRegistered( ): Page

IsColor: MobileCapabilities

IsCompleted: WebClientAsyncResult

IsCookieless: HttpSessionState

IsCustomErrorEnabled: HttpContext

IsCustomPagingEnabled: PagedDataSource

IsDebuggingEnabled: HttpContext

IsDefaultAttribute( ): ControlBuilderAttribute,
ParseChildrenAttribute, PersistChildren-
Attribute, PersistenceModeAttribute, Persist-
NameAttribute, ToolboxDataAttribute

IsDirty: ControlDesigner, StateItem

IsEmpty: FontUnit, Unit

IsEnabled: TraceContext

IsEndMethod( ): LogicalMethodInfo

IsEntireEntityBodyIsPreloaded( ): Http-
WorkerRequest

IsFirstPage: PagedDataSource

IsFormRendered( ): HtmlPageAdapter, WmlPageAdapter

IsFormSubmitControl( ): Command, Mobile-Control

IsHandled( ): ServiceDescriptionFormat-ExtensionCollection

Isindex: HtmlTextWriterTag

IsItalic: TextViewElement

IsItemDirty( ): StateBag

IsLastPage: PagedDataSource

IsLiteralContent( ): Control

IsLoading: IWebFormsDocumentService

IsMobileDevice: MobileCapabilities

IsMultiSelect: SelectionList

IsNewSession: HttpSessionState

IsOnUNCShare: HttpRuntime

IsOperationFlowSupported( ): Protocol-Importer, SoapProtocolImporter

IsOtherMonth: CalendarDay

IsPagingEnabled: PagedDataSource

IsPersistent: FormsAuthenticationTicket

IsPostBack: Page, UserControl

IsPresent: HttpClientCertificate

IsPropertyBound( ): ControlDesigner

IsReadOnly: ArrayListCollectionBase, Control-Collection, DataBindingCollection, DataGrid-ColumnCollection, DataGridItemCollection, DataKeyCollection, DataListItemCollection, HtmlTableCellCollection, HtmlTableRow-Collection, HttpSessionState, HttpStatic-ObjectsCollection, ListItemCollection, Paged-DataSource, RepeaterItemCollection, SelectedDatesCollection, TableCellCollection, TableRowCollection, ValidatorCollection

IsRequired( ): ServiceDescriptionFormat-ExtensionCollection

IsReusable: DiscoveryRequestHandler, IHttp-Handler, Page

IsSecure( ): HttpWorkerRequest

IsSecureConnection: HttpRequest

IsSelectable: CalendarDay

IsSelected: CalendarDay

IsSoapEncodingPresent( ): SoapProtocol-Importer

IsStartupScriptRegistered( ): Page

IsStyleAttributeDefined( ): HtmlTextWriter

IsSubsetOf( ): AspNetHostingPermission

IssueDate: FormsAuthenticationTicket

Issuer: HttpClientCertificate

IsSupported( ): ValueCollection-ParameterReader

IsSupportedTransport( ): SoapTransport-Importer

IsSynchronized: ArrayListCollectionBase, ControlCollection, DataBindingCollection, DataGridColumnCollection, DataGridItem-Collection, DataKeyCollection, DataListItem-Collection, HtmlTableCellCollection, Html-TableRowCollection, HttpSessionState, HttpStaticObjectsCollection, ListItem-Collection, PagedDataSource, RepeaterItem-Collection, SelectedDatesCollection, TableCell-Collection, TableRowCollection, ValidatorCollection

IStateManager: System.Web.UI

IStateRuntime: System.Web.SessionState

IsTemplated: MobileControl, Style

IsToday: CalendarDay

IsTrackingViewState: IStateManager

IsUnrestricted( ): AspNetHostingPermission

IsValid: BaseValidator, HttpClientCertificate, IValidator, Page, ServerValidateEventArgs

IsValidSoftkeyLabel( ): WmlMobileTextWriter

IsVisibleOnPage( ): MobileControl

IsVoid: LogicalMethodInfo

IsWeekend: CalendarDay

Italic: FontInfo

ItalicKey: Style

Item: AttributeCollection, BindingCollection, Cache, ControlCollection, CssStyleCollection, DataBindingCollection, DataGridColumn-Collection, DataGridCommandEventArgs, DataGridItemCollection, DataGridItemEvent-Args, DataKeyCollection, DataListCommand-EventArgs, DataListItemCollection, DataList-ItemEventArgs, DeviceSpecificChoiceCollection, Discovery-ClientDocumentCollection, DiscoveryClient-ReferenceCollection, DiscoveryClientResult-Collection, DiscoveryExceptionDictionary, DiscoveryReferenceCollection, FaultBinding-Collection, HtmlTableCellCollection, Html-TableRowCollection, HttpApplicationState,

LastVisibleElementOffset: TextView

LCID: HttpSessionState

Left: Alignment, HorizontalAlign, ImageAlign, TextAlign

Legend: HtmlTextWriterTag

LessThan: ValidationCompareOperator

LessThanEqual: ValidationCompareOperator

Level: AspNetHostingPermission, AspNetHostingPermissionAttribute

Li: HtmlTextWriterTag

Line: HttpParseException

LineNumber: MobileErrorInfo

Link: CommandFormat, HtmlTextWriterTag, System.Web.UI.MobileControls

LinkButton: ButtonColumnType, System.Web.UI.WebControls

LinkButtonControlBuilder: System.Web.UI.WebControls

LinkButtonDesigner: System.Web.UI.Design.WebControls

LinkLabel: ControlAdapter

List: ObjectListViewMode, System.Web.UI.MobileControls, ValidationSummaryDisplay-Mode

ListBox: ListSelectType, System.Web.UI.WebControls

ListCommandEventArgs: System.Web.UI.MobileControls

ListCommandEventHandler: System.Web.UI.MobileControls

ListControl: System.Web.UI.WebControls

ListControlBuilder: System.Web.UI.Mobile-Controls

ListControlDataBindingHandler: System.Web.UI.Design.WebControls

ListControlDesigner: System.Web.UI.Design.WebControls

ListDataBindEventArgs: System.Web.UI.MobileControls

ListDataBindEventHandler: System.Web.UI.MobileControls

ListDecoration: System.Web.UI.MobileControls

ListItem: ListCommandEventArgs, ListDataBind-EventArgs, MobileListItemType, ObjectList-CommandEventArgs, ObjectListDataBind-EventArgs, ObjectListSelectEventArgs,

ObjectListShowCommandsEventArgs, System.Web.UI.WebControls

ListItemCollection: System.Web.UI.WebControls

ListItemControlBuilder: System.Web.UI.WebControls

ListItemsCollectionEditor: System.Web.UI.Design.WebControls

ListItemType: System.Web.UI.WebControls

ListSelectionMode: System.Web.UI.WebControls

ListSelectType: System.Web.UI.MobileControls

Literal: SoapBindingUse, System.Web.UI.WebControls

LiteralControl: System.Web.UI

LiteralControlBuilder: System.Web.UI.WebControls

LiteralLink: System.Web.UI.MobileControls

LiteralText: System.Web.UI.MobileControls

LiteralTextContainerControlBuilder: System.Web.UI.MobileControls

LiteralTextControlBuilder: System.Web.UI.MobileControls

Load: Control, DeviceSpecific

Load( ): DynamicDiscoveryDocument

LoadAdapterState( ): ChtmlCalendarAdapter, ControlAdapter, HtmlControlAdapter, IControlAdapter, WmlCalendarAdapter, WmlControlAdapter

LoadComplete: IWebFormsDocumentService

LoadControl( ): TemplateControl

LoadItems: PagedControl, TextView

LoadItemsEventArgs: System.Web.UI.Mobile-Controls

LoadItemsEventHandler: System.Web.UI.MobileControls

LoadPageStateFromPersistenceMedium( ): ErrorFormatterPage, MobilePage, Page

LoadPostData( ): ControlAdapter, Html-CommandAdapter, HtmlSelectionListAdapter, IControlAdapter, IPostBackDataHandler, WmlSelectionListAdapter

LoadPrivateViewState( ): Form, MobileControl, ObjectList, PagedControl

LoadTemplate( ): TemplateControl

LoadViewState( ): Calendar, Control, Data-BoundLiteralControl, DataGrid, Data-GridColumn, DataList, DesignerDataBound-LiteralControl, HtmlContainerControl, HtmlSelect, HyperLink, IStateManager, Label, LinkButton, List, ListControl, MobileControl, MobilePage, ObjectList, SelectionList, Style-Sheet, UserControl, WebControl

Location: HttpAddressBinding, Http-OperationBinding, Import, SoapAddress-Binding, WebServiceBindingAttribute

Lock( ): HttpApplicationState

LogicalMethodInfo: System.Web.Services. Protocols

LogicalMethodTypes: System.Web.Services. Protocols

LoginUser( ): PassportIdentity

LogoTag( ): PassportIdentity

LogoTag2( ): PassportIdentity

LogoutURL( ): PassportIdentity

LosFormatter: System.Web.UI

Low: AspNetHostingPermissionLevel, Cache-ItemPriority, MailPriority

lstStandardExpressions_ SelectedIndexChanged( ): Regex-EditorDialog

M

MachineConfigPath: HttpWorkerRequest, SimpleWorkerRequest

MachineConfigurationDirectory: HttpRuntime

MachineInstallDirectory: HttpWorkerRequest, SimpleWorkerRequest

MachineName: HttpServerUtility

MailAttachment: System.Web.Mail

MailEncoding: System.Web.Mail

MailFormat: System.Web.Mail

MailMessage: System.Web.Mail

MailPriority: System.Web.Mail

MajorVersion: HttpBrowserCapabilities

MakePathAbsolute( ): MobilePage

Map: HtmlTextWriterTag

MapImageCoordinates( ): HttpRequest

MapPath( ): HttpRequest, HttpServerUtility, HttpWorkerRequest, Page, SimpleWorker-Request, UserControl

MapPathSecure( ): Control

MapPropertyToStyle( ): PanelDesigner, Read-WriteControlDesigner

MapToProperty: SoapHeaderBinding

Marquee: HtmlTextWriterTag

Match( ): PatternMatcher

MatchAttribute: System.Web.Services.Protocols

Matches: MimeTextBinding, MimeTextMatch

MaximumRenderedPageSize: Mobile-Capabilities

MaximumSoftkeyLabelLength: Mobile-Capabilities

MaximumValue: RangeValidator

Maxlength: HtmlTextWriterAttribute

MaxLength: HtmlInputFile, HtmlInputText, TextBox

MaxRepeats: MatchAttribute

MD5: FormsAuthPasswordFormat

Medium: AspNetHostingPermissionLevel, Font-Size, FontUnit

MemberName: SoapHeaderAttribute, XmlFormatExtensionPointAttribute

MemoryLimitExceeded: Process-ShutdownReason

Menu: HtmlTextWriterTag

MergeStyle( ): WebControl

MergeWith( ): DataGridPagerStyle, FontInfo, Style, TableItemStyle, TableStyle

Message: MessagePart, OperationMessage, SoapHeaderBinding, SoapHeader-FaultBinding, System.Web.Services.Description

MessageBinding: System.Web.Services.Description

MessageCollection: System.Web.Services. Description

MessageName: WebMethodAttribute

MessagePart: System.Web.Services.Description

MessagePartCollection: System.Web.Services. Description

Messages: Operation, ServiceDescription

Meta: HtmlTextWriterTag

Method: Form, HtmlForm, ProtocolReflector

MethodAttribute: ProtocolReflector

MethodInfo: LogicalMethodInfo, Soap-
ClientMessage, SoapMessage, SoapServer-
Message

MethodName: ProtocolImporter

Methods: ProtocolReflector

Middle: ImageAlign, VerticalAlign

MimeContentBinding: System.Web.Services.
Description

MimeFormatter: System.Web.Services.Protocols

MimeMultipartRelatedBinding: System.Web.
Services.Description

MimeParameterReader: System.Web.Services.
Protocols

MimeParameterWriter: System.Web.Services.
Protocols

MimePart: System.Web.Services.Description

MimePartCollection: System.Web.Services.
Description

MimeReturnReader: System.Web.Services.
Protocols

MimeTextBinding: System.Web.Services.
Description

MimeTextMatch: System.Web.Services.Descrip-
tion

MimeTextMatchCollection: System.Web.
Services.Description

MimeXmlBinding: System.Web.Services.
Description

Minimal: AspNetHostingPermissionLevel

MinimumValue: RangeValidator

MinorVersion: HttpBrowserCapabilities

MiscText: MobileErrorInfo

MiscTitle: MobileErrorInfo

Mm: UnitType

MobileCapabilities: System.Web.Mobile

MobileControl: System.Web.UI.MobileControls

MobileControlBuilder: System.Web.UI.Mobile-
Controls

MobileControlsSectionHandler: System.Web.
UI.MobileControls

MobileDeviceCapabilitiesSectionHandler:
System.Web.Mobile

MobileDeviceManufacturer: MobileCapabilities

MobileDeviceModel: MobileCapabilities

MobileErrorInfo: System.Web.Mobile

MobileFormsAuthentication: System.Web.
Mobile

MobileListItem: System.Web.UI.MobileControls

MobileListItemCollection: System.Web.UI.
MobileControls

MobileListItemType: System.Web.UI.Mobile-
Controls

MobilePage: DeviceSpecific, MobileControl,
System.Web.UI.MobileControls

MobileTextWriter: System.Web.UI.Mobile-
Controls.Adapters

MobileTextWriterNotMultiPart: SR

MobileUserControl: System.Web.UI.Mobile-
Controls

Mode: DataGridPagerStyle, HttpSessionState,
PersistenceModeAttribute

Modules: HttpApplication

Monday: FirstDayOfWeek

Month: TitleFormat

MonthChangedEventArgs: System.Web.UI.
WebControls

MonthChangedEventHandler: System.Web.UI.
WebControls

MonthYear: TitleFormat

MoreLabel: ControlAdapter

MoreText: ObjectList

MSDomVersion: HttpBrowserCapabilities

MultiLine: TextBoxMode

MultiPartWriter: System.Web.UI.Mobile-
Controls.Adapters

Multiple: HtmlSelect, HtmlTextWriterAttribute,
ListSelectionMode

MultiSelectListBox: ListSelectType

MustUnderstand: SoapHeader

MustUnderstandFaultCode: SoapException

N

Name: Binding, DeviceSpecificChoice-
TemplateContainer, FontInfo, Forms-
AuthenticationTicket, FormsIdentity, Html-
Anchor, HtmlForm, HtmlInputControl,
HtmlInputRadioButton, HtmlSelect, HtmlText-
Area, HtmlTextWriterAttribute, HttpCookie,
ITemplateEditingFrame, LogicalMethodInfo,
Message, MessageBinding, MessagePart,
MimeTextMatch, ObjectListCommand, Object-

ListField, Operation, OperationBinding, OperationMessage, PassportIdentity, PersistNameAttribute, Port, PortType, Service, ServiceDescription, Style, ValidationPropertyAttribute, WebServiceAttribute, WebServiceBindingAttribute

Names: FontInfo

Namespace: ContractReference, DiscoveryDocument, DynamicDiscoveryDocument, HttpBinding, Import, MimeContentBinding, MimeTextBinding, SchemaReference, ServiceDescription, SoapBinding, SoapBodyBinding, SoapFaultBinding, SoapHeaderBinding, SoapHeaderFaultBinding, WebServiceAttribute, WebServiceBindingAttribute, XmlFormatExtensionAttribute, XmlFormatExtensionPrefixAttribute

NamespaceName: TagPrefixAttribute

NamingContainer: Control

NamingContainerType: ControlBuilder

NavigateUrl: AdCreatedEventArgs, HyperLink, HyperLinkColumn, Image, Link

NavigateUrlKey: AdRotator

NeedsTag: ConstructorNeedsTagAttribute

NeedsTagInnerText( ): ControlBuilder, TemplateBuilder, UserControlControlBuilder

NewDate: MonthChangedEventArgs

NewLine: HtmlTextWriter

NewPageIndex: DataGridPageChangedEventArgs

NewUrl( ): MultiPartWriter

NextLabel: ControlAdapter

NextMonthText: Calendar

NextPageCommandArgument: DataGrid

NextPageText: DataGridPagerStyle, PagerStyle

NextPageTextKey: PagerStyle

NextPrev: PagerMode

NextPrevFormat: Calendar, System.Web.UI. WebControls

NextPrevStyle: Calendar

No: PersistChildrenAttribute

NoAbsolute: UrlBuilderOptions

NoAbsoluteExpiration: Cache

Nobr: HtmlTextWriterTag

NoCache: HttpCacheability

NoCodeGenerated: ServiceDescriptionImportWarnings

Noframes: HtmlTextWriterTag

NoMethodsGenerated: ServiceDescriptionImportWarnings

None: AspNetHostingPermissionLevel, AuthenticationMode, BorderStyle, CalendarSelectionMode, FormsProtectionEnum, GridLines, HttpCacheRevalidation, ListDecoration, OperationFlow, OutputCacheLocation, ProcessShutdownReason, UrlBuilderOptions, ValidatorDisplay

NopReturnReader: System.Web.Services.Protocols

Normal: CacheItemPriority, FontSize, MailPriority, WmlPostFieldType

Noscript: HtmlTextWriterTag

NoSlidingExpiration: Cache

NotEqual: ValidationCompareOperator

Notification: OperationFlow

NotRemovable: CacheItemPriority

NotSecondaryUI: HtmlControlAdapter, WmlControlAdapter

NotSet: Alignment, BooleanOption, BorderStyle, FontSize, HorizontalAlign, ImageAlign, VerticalAlign, Wrapping

Nowrap: HtmlTextWriterAttribute

NoWrap: HtmlTableCell, Wrapping

Numbered: ListDecoration

NumberOfSoftkeys: MobileCapabilities

Numeric: TextBox

NumericPages: PagerMode

O

Object: HtmlTextWriterTag

ObjectConverter: System.Web.UI

ObjectFromString( ): PropertyConverter

ObjectList: System.Web.UI.MobileControls

ObjectListAdapter_InvalidPostedData: SR

ObjectListCommand: System.Web.UI.MobileControls

ObjectListCommandCollection: System.Web. UI.MobileControls

ObjectListCommandEventArgs: System.Web. UI.MobileControls

ObjectListCommandEventHandler: System. Web.UI.MobileControls

ObjectListControlBuilder: System.Web.UI. MobileControls

ObjectListDataBindEventArgs: System.Web.UI. MobileControls

ObjectListDataBindEventHandler: System. Web.UI.MobileControls

ObjectListField: System.Web.UI.MobileControls

ObjectListFieldCollection: System.Web.UI. MobileControls

ObjectListItem: System.Web.UI.MobileControls

ObjectListItemCollection: System.Web.UI. MobileControls

ObjectListSelectEventArgs: System.Web.UI. MobileControls

ObjectListSelectEventHandler: System.Web.UI. MobileControls

ObjectListShowCommandsEventArgs: System. Web.UI.MobileControls

ObjectListShowCommandsEventHandler: System.Web.UI.MobileControls

ObjectListTitleAttribute: System.Web.UI. MobileControls

ObjectListViewMode: System.Web.UI.Mobile-Controls

ObjectTagBuilder: System.Web.UI

Off: SessionStateMode

OKLabel: ControlAdapter

Ol: HtmlTextWriterTag

OnAbortTransaction( ): TemplateControl

OnActivate( ): Form

OnActivated( ): CalendarAutoFormatDialog

OnAdCreated( ): AdRotator

OnAppendToParentBuilder( ): ControlBuilder

OnAttributeRender( ): HtmlTextWriter

OnAutoFormat( ): BaseDataListDesigner, CalendarDesigner

OnBehaviorAttached( ): ControlDesigner, HtmlControlDesigner, PanelDesigner, Read-WriteControlDesigner, TemplatedControl-Designer

OnBehaviorDetaching( ): HtmlControlDesigner

OnBindingsCollectionChanged( ): Control-Designer, HtmlControlDesigner

OnBubbleEvent( ): Control, DataGrid, Data-GridItem, DataList, DataListItem, List, Mobile-ListItem, ObjectList, ObjectListItem, Repeater, RepeaterItem

OnCancelCommand( ): DataGrid, DataList

Onchange: HtmlTextWriterAttribute

OnCheckedChanged( ): CheckBox

OnClear( ): ServiceDescriptionBaseCollection

Onclick: HtmlTextWriterAttribute

OnClick( ): Button, Command, ImageButton, LinkButton

OnColumnChanged( ): DataGridColumn

OnColumnsChanged( ): DataGridDesigner

OnCommand( ): Button, ImageButton, Link-Button

OnCommitTransaction( ): TemplateControl

OnComponentChanged( ): BaseDataList-Designer, ControlDesigner, ListControl-Designer, ReadWriteControlDesigner, RepeaterDesigner, TemplatedControlDesigner

OnControlResize( ): ControlDesigner

OnDataBinding( ): BaseDataList, Control, Form, HtmlSelect, List, ListControl, MobileControl, ObjectList, Repeater, SelectionList

OnDataSourceChanged( ): ListControlDesigner, RepeaterDesigner

OnDayRender( ): Calendar

OnDeactivate( ): Form

OnDeleteCommand( ): DataGrid, DataList

OnDeviceCustomize( ): MobilePage

OnEditCommand( ): DataGrid, DataList

OnError( ): MobilePage, TemplateControl

OneWay: OperationFlow, SoapClientMessage, SoapDocumentMethodAttribute, Soap-Message, SoapRpcMethodAttribute, Soap-ServerMessage

OnGetUIValueItem( ): DataBindingValue-UIHandler

OnInit( ): BasePartialCachingControl, Base-Validator, ChtmlCalendarAdapter, Control, ControlAdapter, ErrorFormatterPage, Form, HtmlForm, HtmlObjectListAdapter, Html-PanelAdapter, HtmlSelectionListAdapter, HtmlTextBoxAdapter, HtmlValidation-SummaryAdapter, IControlAdapter, Mobile-Control, MobilePage, Panel, UserControl, WmlCalendarAdapter, WmlListAdapter,

---

PreferredRenderingTypeHtml32: Mobile-
Capabilities

PreferredRenderingTypeWml11: Mobile-
Capabilities

PreferredRenderingTypeWml12: Mobile-
Capabilities

PreFilterEvents( ): HtmlControlDesigner

PreFilterProperties( ): BaseDataListDesigner,
ControlDesigner, HtmlControlDesigner,
ListControlDesigner, RepeaterDesigner,
TemplatedControlDesigner

Prefix: XmlFormatExtensionPrefixAttribute

PrepareControlHierarchy( ): BaseDataList,
DataGrid, DataList

PreRender: Control, DeviceSpecific

PreRequestHandlerExecute: HttpApplication

PreSendRequestContent: HttpApplication

PreSendRequestHeaders: HttpApplication

PreShowItemCommands( ): ObjectList

PreviousDate: MonthChangedEventArgs

PreviousLabel: ControlAdapter

PreviousPageText: PagerStyle

PreviousPageTextKey: PagerStyle

PrevMonthText: Calendar

PrevPageCommandArgument: DataGrid

PrevPageText: DataGridPagerStyle

Priority: MailMessage, SoapExtensionAttribute

Private: HttpCacheability

ProcessID: ProcessInfo

ProcessInfo: System.Web

ProcessMessage( ): SoapExtension

ProcessModelInfo: System.Web

ProcessRequest( ): DiscoveryRequestHandler,
HttpRuntime, IHttpHandler, IISAPIRuntime,
ISAPIRuntime, IStateRuntime, Page, State-
Runtime

ProcessShutdownReason: System.Web

ProcessStatus: System.Web

PropertyConverter: System.Web.UI

PropertyName: DataBinding

PropertyType: DataBinding

ProtocolImporter: System.Web.Services.
Description

ProtocolName: ProtocolImporter, Protocol-
Reflector, ServiceDescriptionImporter, Soap-
ProtocolImporter

ProtocolReflector: System.Web.Services.
Description

Proxy: HttpWebClientProtocol

ProxyCaches: HttpCacheRevalidation

Public: HttpCacheability

PublicKey: HttpClientCertificate

PushButton: ButtonColumnType

PushEndTag( ): HtmlTextWriter

Q

Q: HtmlTextWriterTag

QueryString: HttpRequest

QueryStringText: MobilePage

R

Radio: ListSelectType

RadioButton: System.Web.UI.WebControls

RadioButtonList: System.Web.UI.WebControls

RaiseBubbleEvent( ): Control

RaiseDefaultItemEvent( ): ObjectList

RaisePostBackEvent( ): IPostBackEventHandler,
MobilePage, Page

RaisePostDataChangedEvent( ): IPostBack-
DataHandler

RaiseResizeEvent( ): ControlDesigner

RaiseSelectionChangedEvent( ): Calendar

RangeValidator: System.Web.UI.Mobile-
Controls, System.Web.UI.WebControls

Raw: WmlPostFieldType

RawUrl: HttpRequest

Read( ): AnyReturnReader, DiscoveryDocument,
HtmlFormParameterReader, Mime-
ParameterReader, MimeReturnReader,
NopReturnReader, ServiceDescription, Text-
ReturnReader, UrlParameterReader, Value-
CollectionParameterReader, XmlReturnReader

ReadAll( ): DiscoveryClientProtocol

ReadDocument( ): ContractReference,
DiscoveryDocumentReference, Discovery-
Reference, SchemaReference

ReadEntityBody( ): HttpWorkerRequest

Collection, ObjectListFieldCollection, Table-CellCollection, TableRowCollection

RemoveAttribute( ): IHtmlControlDesigner-Behavior

Removed: CacheItemRemovedReason

RemovedBindings: DataBindingCollection

RemovedControl( ): MobileControl, MobilePage

RemoveOutputCacheItem( ): HttpResponse

RemoveStyleAttribute( ): IHtmlControl-DesignerBehavior

Render( ): AdRotator, AttributeCollection, BaseDataList, BasePartialCachingControl, BaseValidator, Calendar, CheckBox, Check-BoxList, ChtmlCalendarAdapter, Chtml-SelectionListAdapter, Control, Control-Adapter, DataBoundLiteralControl, DesignerDataBoundLiteralControl, Form, HtmlCalendarAdapter, Html-CommandAdapter, HtmlContainerControl, HtmlControl, HtmlControlAdapter, HtmlForm, HtmlFormAdapter, HtmlImageAdapter, Html-LabelAdapter, HtmlLinkAdapter, HtmlList-Adapter, HtmlLiteralTextAdapter, HtmlObject-ListAdapter, HtmlPageAdapter, HtmlPanelAdapter, HtmlPhoneCallAdapter, HtmlSelectionListAdapter, HtmlText-BoxAdapter, HtmlTextViewAdapter, Html-ValidationSummaryAdapter, HtmlValidator-Adapter, IControlAdapter, Literal, LiteralControl, MobileControl, MobilePage, RadioButtonList, TextBox, Validation-Summary, WebControl, WmlCalendar-Adapter, WmlCommandAdapter, WmlControl-Adapter, WmlFormAdapter, WmlImageAdapter, WmlLabelAdapter, WmlLinkAdapter, WmlListAdapter, WmlLiteralTextAdapter, WmlObjectList-Adapter, WmlPageAdapter, WmlPanel-Adapter, WmlPhoneCallAdapter, WmlSelectionListAdapter, WmlText-BoxAdapter, WmlTextViewAdapter, WmlValidationSummaryAdapter, WmlValidatorAdapter, Xml

RenderAfterContent( ): Html32TextWriter, HtmlTextWriter

RenderAfterTag( ): Html32TextWriter, Html-TextWriter

RenderAsHiddenInputField( ): Html-ControlAdapter, HtmlSelectionListAdapter, HtmlTextBoxAdapter

RenderAttributes( ): HtmlAnchor, HtmlButton, HtmlContainerControl, HtmlControl, Html-Form, HtmlImage, HtmlInputButton, Html-InputControl, HtmlInputImage, HtmlInput-RadioButton, HtmlInputText, HtmlSelect, HtmlTextArea

RenderBeforeContent( ): Html32TextWriter, HtmlTextWriter

RenderBeforeTag( ): Html32TextWriter, Html-TextWriter

RenderBeginForm( ): WmlMobileTextWriter

RenderBeginHyperlink( ): UpWmlMobile-TextWriter, WmlMobileTextWriter

RenderBeginLink( ): HtmlControlAdapter, WmlControlAdapter

RenderBeginPostBack( ): UpWmlMobile-TextWriter, WmlMobileTextWriter

RenderBeginSelect( ): UpWmlMobile-TextWriter, WmlMobileTextWriter

RenderBeginTag( ): Html32TextWriter, Html-Control, HtmlTextWriter, WebControl

RenderBodyTag( ): HtmlFormAdapter

RenderChildren( ): Control, ControlAdapter, HtmlForm, HtmlSelect, HtmlTable, HtmlTableRow, MobileControl

RenderContents( ): Button, DataList, DropDownList, HyperLink, Image, Label, Link-Button, ListBox, Table, TableCell, WebControl

RenderControl( ): Control

RenderDoEvent( ): WmlMobileTextWriter

RenderEndForm( ): UpWmlMobileTextWriter, WmlMobileTextWriter

RenderEndHyperlink( ): UpWmlMobile-TextWriter, WmlMobileTextWriter

RenderEndLink( ): HtmlControlAdapter, WmlControlAdapter

RenderEndPostBack( ): UpWmlMobile-TextWriter, WmlMobileTextWriter

RenderEndSelect( ): UpWmlMobileTextWriter, WmlMobileTextWriter

RenderEndTag( ): Html32TextWriter, Html-ContainerControl, HtmlTable, HtmlTableCell, HtmlTableRow, HtmlTextWriter, WebControl

RenderExtraCards( ): WmlMobileTextWriter

RenderExtraHeadElements( ): Chtml-
FormAdapter, HtmlFormAdapter

RenderForm( ): HtmlPageAdapter, WmlPage-
Adapter

RenderFormDoEvent( ): WmlMobileTextWriter

RenderGoAction( ): WmlMobileTextWriter

RenderHiddenVariables( ): HtmlPageAdapter

RenderImage( ): UpWmlMobileTextWriter,
WmlMobileTextWriter

RenderItem( ): DataListItem, IRepeatInfoUser

RenderItemDetails( ): HtmlObjectListAdapter,
WmlObjectListAdapter

RenderItemMenu( ): WmlObjectListAdapter

RenderItemsList( ): HtmlObjectListAdapter,
WmlObjectListAdapter

RenderLink( ): WmlControlAdapter

RenderList( ): HtmlListAdapter

RenderMethod: System.Web.UI

RenderPager( ): HtmlFormAdapter, WmlForm-
Adapter

RenderPostBackEvent( ): ChtmlPageAdapter,
HtmlPageAdapter, WmlControlAdapter

RenderPostBackEventAsAnchor( ): Html-
ControlAdapter

RenderPostBackEventAsAttribute( ): Html-
ControlAdapter

RenderPostBackEventReference( ): Html-
ControlAdapter

RenderPostBackHeader( ): ChtmlPageAdapter,
HtmlPageAdapter

RenderRepeater( ): RepeatInfo

RendersBreakBeforeWmlSelectAndInput:
MobileCapabilities

RendersBreaksAfterHtmlLists: Mobile-
Capabilities

RendersBreaksAfterWmlAnchor: Mobile-
Capabilities

RendersBreaksAfterWmlInput: Mobile-
Capabilities

RenderSelectOption( ): UpWmlMobile-
TextWriter, WmlMobileTextWriter

RendersMultipleForms( ): WmlPageAdapter

RenderSubmitEvent( ): WmlControlAdapter

RendersWmlDoAcceptsInline: Mobile-
Capabilities

RendersWmlSelectsAsMenuCards: Mobile-
Capabilities

RenderText( ): UpWmlMobileTextWriter,
WmlMobileTextWriter

RenderTextBox( ): UpWmlMobileTextWriter,
WmlMobileTextWriter

RenderUrlPostBackEvent( ): HtmlPageAdapter

RenewTicketIfOld( ): FormsAuthentication

RepeatColumns: CheckBoxList, DataList, Radio-
ButtonList, RepeatInfo

RepeatDirection: CheckBoxList, DataList, Radio-
ButtonList, RepeatInfo, System.Web.UI.
WebControls

RepeatedItemCount: IRepeatInfoUser

Repeater: System.Web.UI.WebControls

RepeaterCommandEventArgs: System.Web.UI.
WebControls

RepeaterCommandEventHandler: System.
Web.UI.WebControls

RepeaterDesigner: System.Web.UI.Design.
WebControls

RepeaterItem: System.Web.UI.WebControls

RepeaterItemCollection: System.Web.UI.
WebControls

RepeaterItemEventArgs: System.Web.UI.
WebControls

RepeaterItemEventHandler: System.Web.UI.
WebControls

RepeatInfo: System.Web.UI.WebControls

RepeatLayout: CheckBoxList, DataList, Radio-
ButtonList, RepeatInfo, System.Web.UI.
WebControls

Repeats: MimeTextMatch

RepeatsString: MimeTextMatch

Request: HttpApplication, HttpContext, Page,
UserControl

RequestCount: ProcessInfo

RequestElement: SoapServiceRoutingStyle

RequestElementName: SoapDocumentMethod-
Attribute, SoapRpcMethodAttribute

RequestEncoding: MimeParameterWriter,
UrlEncodedParameterWriter, WebClient-
Protocol

RequestHeaderMaximum: HttpWorkerRequest

RequestNamespace: SoapDocumentMethod-
Attribute, SoapRpcMethodAttribute

RequestQueueLimit: ProcessShutdownReason

RequestResponse: OperationFlow

RequestsLimit: ProcessShutdownReason

RequestType: HttpRequest

Required: ServiceDescriptionFormatExtension, SoapHeaderAttribute

RequiredExtensionsIgnored: Service-DescriptionImportWarnings

RequiredFieldValidator: System.Web.UI. MobileControls, System.Web.UI.WebControls

RequiredMetaTagNameValue: Mobile-Capabilities

RequiresAttributeColonSubstitution: Mobile-Capabilities

RequiresContentTypeMetaTag: Mobile-Capabilities

RequiresDBCSCharacter: MobileCapabilities

RequiresFormTag: ChtmlCalendarAdapter, ChtmlCommandAdapter, ChtmlSelection-ListAdapter, ChtmlTextBoxAdapter, Html-ControlAdapter

RequiresHtmlAdaptiveErrorReporting: MobileCapabilities

RequiresLeadingPageBreak: MobileCapabilities

RequiresNoBreakInFormatting: Mobile-Capabilities

RequiresOutputOptimization: Mobile-Capabilities

RequiresPhoneNumbersAsPlainText: Mobile-Capabilities

RequireSSL: FormsAuthentication

RequiresSpecialViewStateEncoding: Mobile-Capabilities

RequiresUniqueFilePathSuffix: Mobile-Capabilities

RequiresUniqueHtmlCheckboxNames: Mobile-Capabilities

RequiresUniqueHtmlInputNames: Mobile-Capabilities

RequiresUrlEncodedPostfieldValues: Mobile-Capabilities

Reset( ): DataGridPagerStyle, Style, Table-ItemStyle, TableStyle

ResetFormattingState( ): WmlMobile-TextWriter

Resize( ): ITemplateEditingFrame

Resolve( ): DiscoveryReference

ResolveAll( ): DiscoveryClientProtocol, DiscoveryDocumentReference

ResolveFormReference( ): MobileControl

ResolveOneLevel( ): DiscoveryClientProtocol

ResolveRequestCache: HttpApplication

ResolveUrl( ): Control, MobileControl

Response: HttpApplication, HttpContext, Page, UserControl

ResponseElementName: Soap-DocumentMethodAttribute, SoapRpcMethod-Attribute

ResponseHeaderMaximum: HttpWorker-Request

ResponseNamespace: SoapDocumentMethod-Attribute, SoapRpcMethodAttribute

Results: DiscoveryClientResultsFile, Http-CompileException

RetrievalUrl: ServiceDescription

ReturnFormatter: HttpMethodAttribute

ReturnType: LogicalMethodInfo

ReturnTypeCustomAttributeProvider: LogicalMethodInfo

RewritePath( ): HttpContext

Ridge: BorderStyle

Right: Alignment, HorizontalAlign, ImageAlign, TextAlign

RootBuilder: System.Web.UI

RoutingStyle: SoapDocumentServiceAttribute, SoapRpcServiceAttribute

Rows: HtmlTable, HtmlTextArea, HtmlText-WriterAttribute, ListBox, SelectionList, Table, TextBox

Rowspan: HtmlTextWriterAttribute

RowSpan: HtmlTableCell, TableCell

Rpc: SoapBindingStyle

Rt: HtmlTextWriterTag

Ruby: HtmlTextWriterTag

Rules: HtmlTextWriterAttribute

S

S: HtmlTextWriterTag

Samp: HtmlTextWriterTag

Saturday: FirstDayOfWeek

Save( ): ITemplateEditingFrame

Target: AdRotator, HtmlAnchor, HtmlForm, HtmlTextWriterAttribute, HyperLink, HyperLinkColumn

TargetConverter: System.Web.UI.WebControls

TargetNamespace: SchemaReference, ServiceDescription

Tbody: HtmlTextWriterTag

Td: HtmlTextWriterTag

Template: DeviceSpecificChoiceTemplateContainer

TemplateBuilder: System.Web.UI

TemplateColumn: System.Web.UI.WebControls

TemplateContainer: System.Web.UI.MobileControls

TemplateContainerAttribute: System.Web.UI

TemplateControl: System.Web.UI

TemplateControlParser: System.Web.UI

TemplatedControlDesigner: System.Web.UI.Design

TemplateEditingService: System.Web.UI.Design

TemplateEditingVerb: System.Web.UI.Design

TemplateNames: ITemplateEditingFrame

TemplateParser: System.Web.UI

Templates: DeviceSpecificChoice

TemplateSourceDirectory: Control

TemplateStyles: ITemplateEditingFrame

Terminated: ProcessStatus

Text: Button, ButtonColumn, CheckBox, DataBoundLiteralControl, DesignerDataBoundLiteralControl, HyperLink, HyperLinkColumn, Label, LinkButton, ListItem, Literal, LiteralControl, LiteralText, MailFormat, MobileListItem, ObjectListCommand, TableCell, TemplateBuilder, TextBox, TextControl, TextView, TextViewElement

TextAlign: CheckBox, CheckBoxList, RadioButtonList, System.Web.UI.WebControls

Textarea: HtmlTextWriterTag

TextBox: System.Web.UI.MobileControls, System.Web.UI.WebControls

TextBoxControlBuilder: System.Web.UI.MobileControls, System.Web.UI.WebControls

TextBoxMode: System.Web.UI.WebControls

TextChanged: TextBox

TextControl: System.Web.UI.MobileControls

TextControlDesigner: System.Web.UI.Design

TextDataBindingHandler: System.Web.UI.Design

TextDecoration: HtmlTextWriterStyle

TextMode: TextBox

TextReturnReader: System.Web.Services.Protocols

TextTop: ImageAlign

TextView: System.Web.UI.MobileControls

TextViewElement: System.Web.UI.MobileControls

Tfoot: HtmlTextWriterTag

Th: HtmlTextWriterTag

Thead: HtmlTextWriterTag

Third: Triplet

thisExpr: BoundColumn

Thursday: FirstDayOfWeek

Ticket: FormsIdentity

Ticket( ): PassportIdentity

TicketAge: PassportIdentity

Timeout: HttpSessionState, ProcessShutdownReason, WebClientProtocol

TimeSinceSignIn: PassportIdentity

Timestamp: HttpContext

Title: Form, HtmlAnchor, HtmlTextWriterAttribute, HtmlTextWriterTag, ObjectListField, ObjectListTitleAttribute, SelectionList, TextBox

TitleFormat: Calendar, System.Web.UI.WebControls

TitleStyle: Calendar

To: MailMessage

TodayDayStyle: Calendar

TodaysDate: Calendar

ToolboxDataAttribute: System.Web.UI

ToolTip: DropDownList, ListBox, WebControl

Top: ImageAlign, PagerPosition, VerticalAlign

TopAndBottom: PagerPosition

ToString( ): DataGridColumn, FontInfo, FontUnit, ListItem, LogicalMethodInfo, MobileListItem, Style, Unit

TotalBytes: HttpRequest

ToXml( ): AspNetHostingPermission

Tr: HtmlTextWriterTag

Trace: HttpContext, Page, UserControl

Index

About the Authors

G. Andrew Duthie is the founder and Principal of Graymad Enterprises, Inc., providing training and consulting in Microsoft Web development technologies. In addition to his work on O'Reilly books, Andrew is a frequent speaker at industry conferences, including the DevConnections family of conferences, VSLive!, Software Development, and Microsoft's DeveloperDays. He has also written articles on ASP.NET for *SQL Server Magazine* and *MSDN Magazine*. When not writing, speaking, or consulting, Andrew enjoys relaxing with his wife, Jennifer, reading science fiction and fantasy novels, and smoking his meershaum pipe. You can reach Andrew by email at *andrew@graymad.com*.

Matthew MacDonald is an author, educator, and MCSD developer. He's a regular contributor to programming journals such as *Inside Visual Basic* and *C# Today*. He is the author of several books about .NET programming, including *The Book of VB.NET* (No Starch Press). Matthew is coauthor of O'Reilly's *Programming .NET Web Services* and a contributor to *C# in a Nutshell*.

Colophon

Our look is the result of reader comments, our own experimentation, and feedback from distribution channels. Distinctive covers complement our distinctive approach to technical topics, breathing personality and life into potentially dry subjects.

The animal on the cover of *ASP.NET in a Nutshell*, Second Edition, is a stingray. The stingray is a flat, rectangular fish with no dorsal or anal fins that lives in shallow coastal areas around the world. It hides itself in the sandy or silty sea bottom while feeding on fish, crustaceans, and mollusks. The stingray is best known for its long tail, which holds a serrated spine near the tail base. When threatened, this spine injects a powerful, and often fatal, venom into its victim. The venom contains proteins that can slow an animal's respiration rate to dangerous levels. Humans are often surprised to learn, however, that the stingray is normally gentle and nonaggressive.

Contrary to popular belief, stingrays usually sting humans only when stepped on by unsuspecting swimmers. When threatened in this manner, the animal reflexively whips its tail back to defend itself. This defense is effective against most animals, except for its main predator, the shark.

Communities living near stingrays have valued the animal for centuries—particularly in Polynesia, Malaysia, Central America, and Coastal Africa, where the stingray's spine was used to create spears, knives, and other tools. More recently, the stingray has become a popular tourist attraction; the stingray has been a major source of tourist income over the past decade in some island resorts in the Caribbean. Resorts in the Cayman Islands have taken special measures to educate humans about the stingray. Some resorts in this area even advertise beaches where tourists can swim and play with the animal.

Jane Ellin was the production editor and proofreader for *ASP.NET in a Nutshell*, Second Edition. Derek Di Matteo, Colleen Gorman, and Claire Cloutier provided quality control. Mary Agner and Jamie Peppard provided production support. Julie Hawks wrote the index.

Emma Colby designed the cover of this book, based on a series design by Edie Freedman. The cover image is a 19th-century engraving from the Dover Pictorial Archive. Emma Colby produced the cover layout with QuarkXPress 4.1 using Adobe's ITC Garamond font.

David Futato designed the interior layout. This book was converted by Andrew Savikas and Joe Wizda to FrameMaker 5.5.6 with a format conversion tool created by Erik Ray, Jason McIntosh, Neil Walls, and Mike Sierra that uses Perl and XML technologies. The text font is Linotype Birka; the heading font is Adobe Myriad Condensed; and the code font is LucasFont's TheSans Mono Condensed. The illustrations that appear in the book were produced by Robert Romano and Jessamyn Read using Macromedia FreeHand 9 and Adobe Photoshop 6. The tip and warning icons were drawn by Christopher Bing. This colophon was written by Ann Schirmer.

Other Titles Available from O'Reilly

How to stay in touch with O'Reilly

1. Visit our award-winning web site

http://www.oreilly.com/

★ "Top 100 Sites on the Web"—PC Magazine
★ CIO Magazine's Web Business 50 Awards

Our web site contains a library of comprehensive product information (including book excerpts and tables of contents), downloadable software, background articles, interviews with technology leaders, links to relevant sites, book cover art, and more. File us in your bookmarks or favorites!

2. Join our email mailing lists

Sign up to get email announcements of new books and conferences, special offers, and O'Reilly Network technology newsletters at:

http://elists.oreilly.com

It's easy to customize your free elists subscription so you'll get exactly the O'Reilly news you want.

3. Get examples from our books

To find example files for a book, go to:

http://www.oreilly.com/catalog

select the book, and follow the "Examples" link.

4. Work with us

Check out our web site for current employment opportunites:

http://jobs.oreilly.com/

5. Register your book

Register your book at:
http://register.oreilly.com

6. Contact us

O'Reilly & Associates, Inc.
1005 Gravenstein Hwy North
Sebastopol, CA 95472 USA
TEL: 707-827-7000 or 800-998-9938
     (6am to 5pm PST)
FAX: 707-829-0104

order@oreilly.com
For answers to problems regarding your order or our products. To place a book order online visit:

http://www.oreilly.com/order_new/

catalog@oreilly.com
To request a copy of our latest catalog.

booktech@oreilly.com
For book content technical questions or corrections.

corporate@oreilly.com
For educational, library, government, and corporate sales.

proposals@oreilly.com
To submit new book proposals to our editors and product managers.

international@oreilly.com
For information about our international distributors or translation queries. For a list of our distributors outside of North America check out:

http://international.oreilly.com/distributors.html

adoption@oreilly.com
For information about academic use of O'Reilly books, visit:

http://academic.oreilly.com

O'REILLY®

To order: *800-998-9938* • *order@oreilly.com* • *www.oreilly.com*
Online editions of most O'Reilly titles are available by subscription at *safari.oreilly.com*
Also available at most retail and online bookstores.